VELOCITY

1 ft per second (ft/sec) = 0.3048 m/sec = 18.3 m/min = 1.1 km per hour
    (km/hr) = 0.68 mile/hr (mph).
1 mph = 88 ft/min = 1.47 ft/sec = 0.45 m/sec = 26.8 m/min = 1.61
    km/hr.
1 km/hr = 16.7 m/min = 0.28 m/sec = 0.91 ft/sec = 0.62 mph.

WEIGHTS

1 ounce (oz) = 0.0625 lb = 28.35 grams (g) = 0.028 kg
1 pound (lb) = 16 oz = 454 g = 0.454 kg
1 g = 0.035 oz = 0.0022 lb = 0.001 kg
1 kg = 35.27 oz = 2.2 lb = 1000 g

TEMPERATURE

$0°C = 32°F$
$100°C = 212°F$
$273°K = 0°C = 32°F$
$°C = (°F - 32) \times \frac{5}{9}$
$°F = (\frac{9}{5} °C) + 32$

SI UNITS (*Systéme International*)

PHYSICAL QUANTITY	UNIT	SYMBOL
Mass	kilogram	kg
Distance	meter	m
Time	second	sec
Amount of substance	mole	mol
Force	newton	N
Work	joule	J
Power	watt	W
Velocity	meters per sec	$m \cdot sec^{-1}$
Torque	newton-meter	N-m
Acceleration	meters per second per second	$m \cdot sec^{-2}$
Volume	liter	L

The Physiological Basis of Physical Education and Athletics

FOURTH EDITION

Edward L. Fox
The Ohio State University

Richard W. Bowers
Bowling Green State University

Merle L. Foss
The University of Michigan

wcb
Wm. C. Brown Publishers
Dubuque, Iowa

Dedicated
to
Ann Roberts Fox
and
the memory
of
Edward Lyle Fox

preface

Our involvement with the fourth edition of *The Physiological Basis of Physical Education and Athletics* has carried with it a mix of strong emotion and challenge. One co-author (RWB), in a sense, has been part of the book since its inception. D.K. Mathews was the professor of a graduate seminar in which Ed Fox and he were students. Many of the topics that were discussed in that seminar formed the basis of the first edition of the text. The second author (MLF) had known Ed Fox professionally for many years. Both authors are very familiar with the fine reputation the text has enjoyed.

Our challenge in writing this new edition was to preserve the clarity of presentation, the writing style, and character that have been the hallmarks of previous editions. Time after time we found ourselves in appreciation of the writing style, depth of comprehension, and insightful explanations to the topics. We felt challenged to update the references in a way that would retain the integrity of the previous editions.

The fourth edition has retained the purpose of being written for the physical educator and coach. Additionally, those individuals involved in fitness testing and counseling will find many useful thoughts and concepts. Presenting those essential materials that will help ensure the safe and sensible conduct of not only sport and physical education programs but also physical fitness programs has been a primary purpose for completing this edition.

Major topical additions and updates include material in metabolism, muscle fiber typing, cardiorespiratory control mechanisms, ergogenic aids and drugs in sport, exercise in the cold, the female athlete, exercise and training for fitness and health, and endocrine responses to exercise. New illustrations have been added and all artwork has been re-worked for a uniform appearance.

It is our hope that students will be challenged to learn the scientific or physiological reasons for training and conditioning. Further, it is our hope that students can themselves eventually challenge current concepts and provide new and insightful information for the future.

We would like to thank Edward F. Murphy of Saunders College Publishing for his continued support, encouragement, and direction throughout the preparation of this revision. We also would like to thank E.W. Banister (Simon Fraser University), William Bynum (California State University), Professor Joe Dramise (College of St. Scholastica), Roger Glaser (Wright State), Frederick Roby (University of Arizona), and Robert Serfass (University of Minnesota) for their most helpful and critical review of the manuscript.

A special note of thanks goes to Ann Snyder for her critique of the chapter on the Female Athlete. We want to express our appreciation to all of our colleagues, friends, and students with whom we have interacted over the years. In a very real sense, our thoughts are a product of all of those valued associations.

A very special note of gratitude goes to Ann Fox-Day. We appreciate her trust in us to carry on, in some small way, the work of her late husband, Edward Lyle Fox.

Richard W. Bowers
Merle L. Foss

contents

4 Measurement of Energy, Work, and Power 61

section 2   NEUROMUSCULAR CONCEPTS

5   Skeletal Muscle: Structure and Function   **88**

6   Nervous Control of Muscular Movement   **134**

section **3** CARDIORESPIRATORY CONSIDERATIONS

9 Gas Exchange and Transport **224**

10 Blood Flow and Gas Transport **242**

11 Cardiorespiratory Control **265**

section 4 PHYSICAL TRAINING

12 Methods of Physical Training **286**

13 Physiological Effects of Physical Training 323

14 Exercise and Training in Females 375

15 Exercise and Training for Health and Fitness 416

section 5 ENVIRONMENTAL ASPECTS

16 Diffusion, Osmosis, and Drowning 450

section 6 NUTRITION AND BODY WEIGHT CONTROL

19 Nutrition and Exercise Performance 526

20 Exercise, Body Composition, and Weight Control 553

21 Exercise and Acid-Base Balance 596

22 Exercise and the Endocrine System 604

23 Drugs and Ergogenic Aids 631

chapter 1

Introduction to Sports Medicine and Exercise Physiology

What Are Sports Medicine and Exercise Physiology?
Overview of the Text
  Bioenergetics
  Neuromuscular Concepts

Cardiorespiratory Considerations
Physical Training
Environmental Aspects
Nutrition and Body Weight Control
Special Considerations

The major concepts to be learned from this chapter are as follows:

- Comprehension of exercise physiology is important for physical educators, coaches, trainers, and fitness instructors.
- *Sports medicine* is a term that refers to all aspects of sport and exercise science.
- Because of recent research and an upsurge of interest in physical fitness and wellness, today's young professionals are faced with increased learning challenges and career opportunities.
- Exercise physiology is an aspect of sports medicine that involves the study of how the body, from a functional standpoint, responds, adjusts, and adapts to exercise.

Today more than ever before it is necessary for physical educators, coaches, trainers, and fitness instructors to recognize the vital part *science* plays in the successful conduct of physical education, athletic, and activity programs. Over the past thirty years the number of exercise physiology laboratories has increased tremendously. As a result much new knowledge dealing with how best to train athletic teams and to develop fitness for health has appeared in the scientific literature.

Further evidence of advancement in the scientific area of physical education and athletics was the formation of the American College of Sports Medicine (ACSM) in 1954. The college membership is made up of physical educators, athletic trainers, coaches, exercise physiologists, physicians, nutritionists, and other interested professional groups. Membership in the college

1

rose to 3000 from 1954 to 1975, and then doubled to over 6000 between 1975 and 1978. Now with over 13,000 members, the American College of Sports Medicine is the largest and most influential sports medicine group in the world. In 1984, the ACSM National Center was moved from Madison, Wisconsin to Indianapolis, Indiana. There also are 10 regional chapters located throughout the USA. The national ACSM organization meets once a year, at which time research papers covering all aspects of the science of sports and exercise are presented. *Medicine and Science in Sports and Exercise,* published six times a year by the College, is an international journal containing research articles dealing with all facets of sports medicine. The ACSM also publishes position stands and opinion statements on specific topics and public issues and offers certification programs for Fitness Instructors, Exercise Test Technologists, Exercise Specialists, and Exercise Program Directors.

Another example of the ever-increasing interest in sports medicine was the formation of the Committee on the Medical Aspects of Sports in 1959, an organization of the American Medical Association. This group does an excellent job in disseminating literature concerned with protecting the health of the athlete as well as holding seminars for coaches, trainers, and physicians.

The Association for Fitness in Business (AFB), formerly called the American Association of Fitness Directors in Business and Industry, was organized in 1974 to meet the growing need of a variety of professionals and their support staffs who began to develop worksite fitness and health promotion programs. The AFB holds a national conference each year and also has developed a network of regional chapters to disseminate information regarding promotion and management of programs in corporate, hospital, private, and community settings.

Still other organizations about which the informed student should be aware are the American Alliance for Health, Physical Education, Recreation and Dance (AAHPERD), the United States Olympic Committee (USOC), the President's Council on Physical Fitness and Sports (President's Council), and the Federation Internationale de Medicine Sportive (FIMS). Student membership is available in ACSM, AFB, and AAHPERD, whereas appointment to the other groups is necessary for direct involvement.

For you to contribute to the best of your ability to all aspects of physical education, athletics, and fitness leadership will require a good understanding of the available scientific knowledge. Not only will such understanding result in better teams and better programs of activities but it will also enable you to guard the health of your students, athletes, and clients, which is one of your primary responsibilities. Then too, knowing the reasons *why* you select a particular approach for accomplishing a specific task immediately establishes you as a professional rather than a technician.

It is also apparent that the recent and rapid expansion of knowledge and interest in sports medicine requires that you learn much more factual and technical information than your predecessors. At the same time, you are favored by having a greater number of career opportunities open to you. There are few career tracks today that offer more variety, personal challenge, and opportunity for service than those related to the educational, scientific, and clinical aspects of sports medicine and exercise science.

What Are Sports Medicine and Exercise Physiology?

In the preceding discussion, the terms "sports medicine" and "exercise physiology" were mentioned several times. Since these terms may have different meanings to different people, let's define them here. Sports medicine is an all-encompassing term that refers to all aspects, not just medical, of sport and exercise. Examples of such aspects would be (1) athletic medicine, (2) biomechanics, (3) clinical medicine, (4) growth and development, (5) psychology and sociology, (6) nutrition, (7) motor control, and (8) physiology. This latter aspect is synonymous with exercise physiology or the physiology of exercise. As the term implies, this aspect of sports medicine involves the study of how the body, from a functional standpoint, responds, adjusts, and adapts to exercise. This includes acute exercise, i.e., single bouts of exercise, as well as chronic or prolonged exercise, as is the case with exercise training. In other words, as the title of this book states, exercise physiology provides the physiological basis of physical education, fitness, and athletic programs.

Overview of the Text

This textbook focuses exclusively on exercise physiology. Therefore, to further define and understand what exercise physiology is all about, an overview of the text seems appropriate at this time. In writing the chapters that follow, a concerted effort has been made to eliminate those aspects of physiology which from your standpoint might be considered of academic interest only. Our concern has been to cover materials you will be able to put to immediate use in the school gymnasium, the exercise center, and on the athletic field. In other words, you, the student, have been kept in mind, rather than your professor.

This book is divided into seven sections: Section 1, Bioenergetics; Section 2, Neuromuscular Concepts; Section 3, Cardiorespiratory Considerations; Section 4, Physical Training; Section 5, Environmental Aspects; Section 6, Nutrition and Body Weight Control; and Section 7, Special Considerations.

Bioenergetics

If you were asked to select a term that might be considered a common denominator for all phases of physical education, exercise, and athletics, what would it be? After a little deliberation, it is hoped that you would agree that *energy* is the term most appropriate. It is for this reason that bioenergetics (Chapters 2, 3, and 4) is considered an important concept for you to master; let us see why this may be true.

It is through the release of energy that a muscle becomes able to contract. The way in which energy stores are depleted depends essentially on the fitness of the person and on the kind of physical activity being performed. You can significantly improve performance through training programs by modifying or increasing energy stores. The type of program you design will require knowledge about depletion and replacement of these energy stores for the specific activity to be performed.

Food is our *indirect* source of energy. In the body it goes through a profound series of chemical reactions, collectively referred to as the *metabolic pathways*. In so doing, it leads to the formation of a compound called *adenosine triphosphate (ATP)*, which is the body's direct source of energy. Studying these pathways will allow you to make valid and safe applications to your physical education, fitness, and athletic programs concerning (1) nutrition and performance, (2) the onset and delay of muscular fatigue, (3) body weight control, (4) specificity of training programs, and (5) heat balance.

These are a few of the important reasons for comprehending well the information dealing with energy in Chapter 2. Of passing interest, it might be mentioned that the term *energy* appears in every chapter of this book, for after all this is truly what you deal with throughout the fields of physical education, physical fitness, and athletics.

During activity, energy stores become depleted and fatigue results. Chapter 3 is devoted to the important metabolic considerations following exercise that enable the body to recharge its energy systems.

In Chapter 4, the primary mission will be to tell you how energy is *measured* in the exercise physiology laboratory. Knowing the quantity of energy required to perform an activity enables us to report this in units of work or power (if we wish to express the amount of work done in a given period of time). The information contained in Chapter 4 will also permit you to make accurate judgments regarding the level of intensity of a given activity. It will leave you with a basic understanding of how measurement of oxygen consumption indirectly but accurately reflects the energy required for performing an activity. Of interest to you might be knowing how the energy being expended while an athlete runs a mile is indirectly measured or the manner in which scientists at NASA measure the energy required by an astronaut working in space.

Neuromuscular Concepts

All movement is dependent upon muscular contractions. Performance levels can be enhanced if the teacher and coach more completely comprehend the structure and function of skeletal muscle in terms of different fiber types, the fuels they use, and how quickly they fatigue (Chapter 5), and the nervous control of muscular movement in terms of motor unit recruitment (Chapter 6). It is especially for this reason that Section 2 helps the coach and teacher to better understand what fundamental neuromuscular processes are involved as we improve our motor skills.

What is the best way to develop strength? What equipment is most appropriate for my school or college, e.g., Nautilus, barbells, Mini Gym? Are isometric exercises better than isotonic programs? What is an isokinetic contraction? These and a number of other questions are answered in Chapter 7. Included is a discussion of flexibility and its relationship to performance and suggestions for the formulation of weight training programs using the progressive overload principle.

Cardiorespiratory Considerations

Understanding the functions of the respiratory and circulatory systems is important to the physical educator, coach, and fitness instructor, perhaps more so today than ever before. For example, adult fitness programs for presumably healthy individuals, as well as for patients with chronic lung or heart disease, are centered on increasing the functional capacity of the cardiorespiratory system. Such programs are fast becoming major responsibilities of physical educators and fitness instructors.

Ventilation (moving air in and out of the lungs) may be 5 to 6 liters of air per minute at rest, while at exercise it may reach as high as 170 liters per minute! Chapter 8 helps us understand the physiology and mechanics of pulmonary ventilation during rest and exercise as well as controversial concepts such as the possible existence of an anaerobic threshold.

Moving oxygen into the muscles for the manufacture of ATP and removing CO_2, the by-product of metabolism, constitute the main ingredients of Chapter 9. Exercise and training modify the O_2 and CO_2 exchange systems. Consequently, such knowledge concerning how these modifications take place becomes important to the coach, athlete, and program participant.

Just as the mechanisms for gas exchange are modified through exercise and training, blood flow and gas transport mechanisms are likewise affected. Changes in cardiac output, distribution of blood flow, and hemodynamics are covered in Chapter 10.

Through the combined efforts of the respiratory and circulatory centers located in the brain, regulation of pulmonary ventilation and blood flow is enacted. Changes in heart rate, stroke volume, blood distribution to various organs, and venous return are the important circulatory effects considered in Chapter 11, Cardiorespiratory Control.

Physical Training

It is important for you to be familiar with the principles and effects of physical training, which are presented in Chapters 12 and 13. This knowledge is vital to the training schedule, whether it is track and field, swimming, basketball, or conditioning of the most poorly fit individuals in a hospital cardiac rehabilitation setting. Training programs discussed include interval training, sprint training, continuous slow-running and fast-running training, repetition training, and others. However, one thing must be made clear: without a good comprehension of Section 1, you will not realize the greatest possible profit from Chapters 12 and 13.

Chapter 14 discusses the effects of gender and age on exercise and training. Such factors as body size and composition; energy systems; strength; and performance records of the female, with some comparisons with those of the male, are covered. Gynecological problems are also thoroughly discussed.

The interest in adult fitness programs is greater than ever before. As mentioned earlier, these kinds of exercise programs are to a large part the responsibility of the physical educator. How to safely prescribe proper exercise programs for adults is covered in Chapter 15. In addition, the effects of these programs on the overall health status of the participant are also presented.

Environmental Aspects

Chapter 16 considers osmosis, diffusion, and drowning. Although it appears that these subjects are not directly applicable to our interests, nothing could be further from the truth. Life is maintained at the cellular level and knowledge concerning how particles move into and out of the cell will help us to understand much about the physiology of sport. You will appreciate the sequential events that are likely to occur in a situation of near drowning. As a consequence, you will be better prepared in first-aid procedures. Most important, Chapter 16 lays the foundation for understanding water and electrolyte balance and the hazards involved in severely dehydrating the athlete prior to performance.

Exploring appears to be a very natural part of humanity's heritage. In the fifteenth century, Columbus was "in the headlines"; today we read about the exploits of astronauts probing the mysteries of space and aquanauts exploring the depths of the oceans and seas. Once we move from our habitual environment, physical and physiological considerations must be examined and properly dealt with to ensure safety and peak performance. In Chapter 17 these considerations, which confront humans both under the sea and at altitude, will be studied. As a result, you should be able to counsel the scuba diver as well as recognize problems that will confront the athlete who performs at high altitude.

At one time, not too long ago, lack of knowledge concerning the heat balance of the athlete was responsible for 25 to 30 per cent of the fatalities in football. Mastery of the material covered in Chapter 18 will help to guard against water and salt (electrolyte) imbalance in the athlete. If such imbalances do occur, the ability of teams to operate at peak efficiency will be significantly diminished, and the danger of heat illness will be greatly increased.

You will learn how easy it is to condition or *acclimatize* athletes to work more efficiently in hot environments. The problems associated with the individual's ability to lose heat because of protective clothing as well as how to guard against the cold during prolonged outdoor exposures will also be discussed.

Nutrition and Body Weight Control

To perform at peak efficiency, an athlete (or anyone for that matter) must be well nourished. The material in Chapter 19 not only helps you to teach and apply proper dietary practices, but also includes suggestions for nutrition before, during, and following exercise. You will also find a suggested dietary regimen to increase intramuscular glycogen stores for improving endurance performance.

The subject of obesity—its definition and suggestions for contending with the problem—is contained in Chapter 20. Instructions for determining certain skinfolds and other anthropometric measures are also covered. Methods for estimating percentage body fat and computing lean body mass and for predicting minimal weights for high school and college wrestlers are highlights of this chapter.

Special Considerations

These considerations include exercise and acid-base balance (Chapter 21), exercise and the endocrine system (Chapter 22), and drugs and ergogenic aids (Chapter 23).

The acid-base balance within the body fluids is very carefully regulated. During heavy exercise, lactic acid is formed, upsetting this delicate balance temporarily and allowing body fluids to become acidic. In Chapter 21, you will learn how pulmonary ventilation and the kidney function to maintain a proper acid-base medium.

As just indicated, maintenance of the internal environment of the body (homeostasis) is made more difficult during exercise. Thus adjustments in regulatory mechanisms are required. Some of these adjustments are brought about by the nervous system and others by the endocrine system through the release of chemicals or hormones into the blood stream. How this latter system functions in maintaining the homeostasis required of the body during exercise is covered in Chapter 22. A discussion of how the endocrine and nervous systems work together in obtaining this important goal is also included.

Sometimes a coach or an athlete resorts to measures other than training and practice of skills to improve athletic performance. Such work aids (ergogenic aids) may include music, shouting words of encouragement, and psychological aids such as hypnosis. However, too often drugs are used as "ergogenic aids" with the hope that they will significantly improve exercise performance. In Chapter 23, you will learn what scientific studies have shown concerning such practices as blood doping, the use of amphetamines, breathing pure oxygen, the use of anabolic steroids, and so forth.

Finally, there is a glossary plus eight appendices. Appendix A is a list of common symbols and abbreviations used by most exercise physiologists in this country and elsewhere. Appendix B contains a list of pulmonary symbols along with a number of typical resting values for selected respiratory tests. Appendix C is a comprehensive discussion of gas laws and their application to exercise physiology. Appendix D gives the formulae for the calculation of oxygen consumption and carbon dioxide production. Appendix E provides a nomogram for calculating body surface area and for conversion of body weight in pounds to body weight in kilograms. Appendix F includes examples of and administrative hints for group interval training programs designed for college men and women. Appendix G contains tests of anaerobic and aerobic power. Appendix H contains a partial list of substances viewed as doping compounds by the International Olympic Committee.

SELECTED READINGS

PERIODICALS DEALING PREDOMINANTLY WITH THE SCIENCE OF EXERCISE PHYSIOLOGY, PHYSICAL EDUCATION, AND ATHLETICS

Acta Physiologica Scandinavica (*Acta Physiol Scand.*)
Ergonomics
The European Journal of Applied Physiology (*Europ J Appl Physiol.*, formerly *Arbeitsphysiologie* (*Arbeitsphysiol.*) and *Internationale Zeitschrift fur Angewandte Physiologie Einschlesslich Arbeitsphysiologie* (*Int Z Angew Physiol.*)
International Sport Sciences (*Int Sports Sci.*)
Journal of Applied Physiology (*J Appl Physiol.*) or *Journal of Applied Physiology: Respiratory, Environmental and Exercise Physiology* (*J Appl Physiol: Respirat Environ Exercise Physiol.*)
Journal of Sports Medicine and Physical Fitness (*J Sports Med.*)
Medicine and Science in Sports (*Med Sci Sports.*) or *Medicine and Science in Sports and Exercise* (*Med Sci Sports Exercise.*)
The Physician and Sportsmedicine (*Physician Sportsmed.*)
Research Quarterly (*Res Q.*) or *Research Quarterly for Exercise and Sport* (*Res Q Exer Sport*)

BOOKS DEALING WITH THE PHYSIOLOGY OF EXERCISE AND HUMAN PERFORMANCE

American College of Sports Medicine: *Encyclopedia of Sport Sciences and Medicine.* New York, Macmillan, 1971.

American College of Sports Medicine: *Exercise and Sport Sciences Reviews.* Vols 1-3. Orlando, Academic Press, Inc., 1973-1975. Vols. 4 & 5, Santa Barbara, Calif., Journal Publishing Affiliates, 1976 & 1977. Vols. 6-13, New York, Macmillan, 1978-1985.

Åstrand, P.-O., and Rodahl, K.: *Textbook of Work Physiology*, 3rd ed. New York, McGraw-Hill, 1986.

Brooks, G. and Fahey, T.: *Exercise Physiology: Human Bioenergetics and Its Applications.* New York, John Wiley, 1984.

Brown, R., and Kenyon, G. (eds.): *Classical Studies on Physical Activity.* Englewood Cliffs, N.J., Prentice-Hall, 1968.

deVries, H.: *Physiology of Exercise for Physical Education and Athletics,* 4th ed. Dubuque, Iowa, Wm. C. Brown, 1986.

Edington, D. W., and Edgerton, V. R.: *The Biology of Physical Activity.* Boston, Houghton Mifflin, 1976.

Falls, H. (ed.): *Exercise Physiology.* New York, Academic Press, 1968.

Fox, E. L.: *Sports Physiology.* Philadelphia, W. B. Saunders, 1979.

Fox, E. L., and Mathews, D. K.: *Interval Training.* Philadelphia, W. B. Saunders, 1974.

Horvath, S., and Horvath, E.: *The Harvard Fatigue Laboratory: Its History and Contributions.* Englewood Cliffs, N.J., Prentice-Hall, 1973.

Jensen, C., and Fisher, A.: *Scientific Basis of Athletic Conditioning,* 2nd ed. Philadelphia, Lea and Febiger, 1979.

Johnson, E., and Buskirk, E. (eds.): *Science and Medicine of Exercise and Sports,* 2nd ed. New York, Harper and Row, 1973.

Karpovich, P., and Sinning, W.: *Physiology of Muscular Activity,* 7th ed. Philadelphia, W. B. Saunders, 1971.

Lamb, D. R.: *Physiology of Exercise: Responses and Adaptations,* 2nd ed. New York, Macmillan, 1984.

Larson, L. (ed.): *Fitness, Health, and Work Capacity: International Standards for Assessment.* New York, Macmillan, 1974.

McArdle, W., Katch, F., and Katch, V.: *Exercise Physiology: Energy, Nutrition and Human Performance,* 2 ed. Philadelphia, Lea and Febiger, 1986.

Morehouse, L. E., and Miller, A. T.: *Physiology of Exercise,* 7th ed. St. Louis, C. V. Mosby, 1976.

Noble, B. J.: *Physiology of Exercise and Sport.* St. Louis, Times Mirror/Mosby College, 1986.

Pollock, M., Wilmore, J., and Fox, S. III.: *Health and Fitness Through Physical Activity.* New York, John Wiley, 1978.

Pollock, M., Wilmore, J., and Fox, S. III.: *Exercise in Health and Disease.* Philadelphia, W. B. Saunders, 1984.

Poortmans, J., and Niset, G. (eds.): *Biochemistry of Exercise IV-B.* Baltimore, University Park Press, 1979.

Quigley, T. B. (ed.): *Year Book of Sports Medicine.* Chicago, Year Book Medical, 1979.

Rarick, G. (ed.): *Physical Activity: Human Growth and Development.* New York, Academic Press, 1973.

Ricci, B.: *Physiological Basis of Human Performance.* Philadelphia, Lea and Febiger, 1967.

Robinson, S.: "Physiology of Muscular Exercise." In Mountcastle, V. (ed.): *Medical Physiology*, 13th ed., vol. 2, Chap. 55. St. Louis, C. V. Mosby, 1974.

Ryan, A. J., and Allman, F. L., Jr. (eds.): *Sports Medicine.* New York, Academic Press, 1974.

Shepard, R. J.: *Biochemistry of Physical Activity.* Springfield, Ill., Charles C Thomas, 1984.

Simonson, E.: *Physiology of Work Capacity and Fatigue.* Springfield, Ill., Charles C Thomas, 1971.

Strauss, R. H. (ed.): *Sports Medicine.* Philadelphia, W. B. Saunders, 1984.

Wilmore, J. H.: *Athletic Training and Physical Fitness*, 2nd ed. Boston, Allyn and Bacon, 1982.

T he main theme of this section is energy—what it is, where it comes from, and how it is produced and used by the human body during rest and exercise. The objective is to enable you, as physical educators, or coaches, or sport scientists, to apply in the gymnasia, on the athletic fields, and in the classrooms, the knowledge gained from understanding energy. For example, you will learn in this section the scientific basis for the development of athletic training and conditioning programs. Has the thought ever occurred to you that there is an important physiological reason why the sprinter should be trained differently from the distance runner? Have you ever thought about what enables muscles to contract and what fatigue is and how its onset may be delayed in certain activities? The materials contained in this section will also enable you to understand better the relationship between nutrition and performance and to understand how body weight and body temperature are controlled. Finally, you will learn that the energy concept pervades *all* phases of physical education and athletics.

Our discussion of energy starts with the energy sources available to the human body and how they are used during rest and exercise (Chapter 2). Next, we proceed to the replenishment of these sources during recovery from exercise (Chapter 3) and finally to the measurement of energy production and to the efficiency of the human body during the performance of various kinds of exercise (Chapter 4).

section 1

BIOENERGETICS

chapter 2

Energy Sources

The major concepts to be learned from this chapter are as follows:

- All energy used by the biological world is ultimately derived from the sun.
- The immediate energy source for all activity in humans, as well as in most other biological systems, comes from the breakdown of a single chemical compound—adenosine triphosphate, or ATP.
- The metabolic production of ATP by muscle and other cells comes from the energy released through the breakdown of foods and other compounds and involves both an anaerobic (without oxygen) and aerobic (with oxygen) series of chemical reactions.
- Whether ATP is supplied anaerobically or aerobically to the working muscles depends upon the intensity and duration of the activity performed.

Introduction

We are aware that all human activity centers around the capability to provide energy on a continuous basis. Without a continuous source of energy, cells, including muscle, cease to function and die. Energy is provided through the metabolic degradation of, principally, two foods, carbohydrates and fats. Carbohydrates are metabolized through glycolysis and the Krebs Cycle. Fats are also metabolized through the Krebs Cycle but begin with a process called Beta oxidation.

As indicated, the production of energy is an ongoing activity requiring both aerobic and anaerobic processes. The purpose of this chapter is to study the concept of energy in general and then specifically to study the energy sources available to humans during rest and exercise.

Energy Defined

Before much meaning can be given to a discussion of energy sources, we need to define **energy.** Probably all of us have some idea of the nature of energy. Such common words as force, power, strength, vigor, movement, life, and even spirit more or less suggest the idea of energy. These terms, however, do not give us a satisfactory description of the exact meaning of energy. Furthermore, they do not lend themselves to scientific quantitation. Scientists, therefore, define energy as the *capacity to perform work.* **Work** they define as the application of a force through a distance. As a result, energy and work are inseparable. We will be concerned with the relationships between energy and work in Chapter 4. Right now, let us continue with our discussion of energy.

There are six forms of energy: (1) chemical, (2) mechanical, (3) heat, (4) light, (5) electrical, and (6) nuclear. Each can be converted from one form to another. This "transformation of energy" is a fascinating and exciting story, particularly as applied to the biological world. Specifically, we are interested in the transformation of chemical energy into mechanical energy. Mechanical energy is manifestated in human movement, the source of which comes from converting food to chemical energy within our body.

The Biological Energy Cycle

All energy in our solar system originates in the sun. Where does this energy, called *solar energy,* come from? Solar energy actually arises from nuclear energy. Some of this nuclear energy reaches the earth as sunlight or light energy. The millions of green plants that populate our earth store a portion of this energy from the sunlight in still another form—chemical energy. In turn, this chemical energy is utilized by green plants to build food molecules such as glucose, cellulose, proteins, and lipids from carbon dioxide (CO_2) and water (H_2O). This process, whereby green plants manufacture their own food, is called **photosynthesis.** We, on the other hand, are not capable of doing this; we must eat plants and other animals for our food supplies. We are, therefore, directly dependent on plant life and, ultimately, on the sun for our energy.

Food in the presence of O_2 is broken down to CO_2 and H_2O with the liberation of chemical energy by a metabolic process called **respiration.** The sole purpose of metabolic respiration is to supply the energy we need to carry out such biological processes as the chemical work of growth and the mechanical work of muscular contraction. This entire process is called the biological energy cycle (Fig. 2-1).

Adenosine Triphosphate—ATP

We now know what energy is, where it originates, and that it is supplied to us by the foods we eat. Our next problem is to understand how this energy is used to perform physiological work, particularly the mechanical work of muscular contraction. The

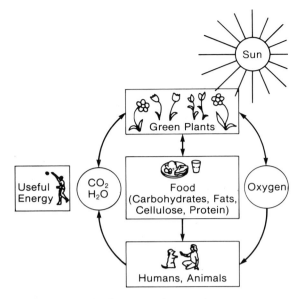

Figure 2-1. The biological energy cycle. Energy from sunlight is used by plants to build food molecules from CO_2 and H_2O, with oxygen being given off. Both plants and animals, including humans, in turn, use oxygen to break down foods for the energy they need to live.

energy liberated during the breakdown of food is *not directly* used to do work. Rather, it is employed to manufacture another chemical compound called **adenosine triphosphate,** or, more simply, **ATP,** which is stored in all muscle cells. Only from the energy released by the breakdown of this compound can the cell perform its specialized work.

The structure of ATP* consists of one very complex component, adenosine, and three less complicated parts called phosphate groups. For our purposes, its chemical importance lies in the phosphate groups. In Figure 2-2A, a simplified structure of ATP is shown. The bonds between the two terminal phosphate groups repre-

*For a detailed discussion of the structure of ATP, refer to McGilvery.

sent so-called high-energy bonds. When one of these phosphate bonds is broken, i.e., removed from the rest of the molecule, 7 to 12 **kilocalories**† of energy are liberated, and adenosine diphosphate (ADP) plus inorganic phosphate (Pi) are formed (Fig. 2-2B). *This energy released during the breakdown of ATP represents the immediate source of energy that can be used by the muscle cell to perform its work.*

Sources of ATP

Since the hydrolysis (breakdown) of ATP releases energy for muscular contraction, the question is raised: "How is this important compound supplied to each muscle cell?" First, it must be realized that at any one moment there is a limited quantity of ATP in a muscle cell and that ATP is constantly being used and regenerated. Regeneration of ATP requires energy. There are three common energy-yielding processes for the production of ATP: (1) the ATP-PC, or phosphogen, system. In this system, the energy for resynthesis of ATP comes from only one compound, phosphocreatine (PC). (2) Anaerobic glycolysis, or the lactic acid system, provides ATP from the partial degradation of glucose or glycogen. (3) The third system, the "oxygen system" really has two parts: part A involves the completion of the oxidation of the carbohydrates and part B involves the oxidation of fatty acids. Both parts of the oxygen system have as their final route of oxidation, the Krebs Cycle. Because some protein can also be oxidized through the Krebs Cycle, it is appropriately called the final common pathway.

All three suppliers of energy for ATP

†A kilocalorie (kcal) is the amount of heat energy required to raise 1 kilogram (kg) of water 1 degree Celsius (°C). A calorie (cal) is the amount of heat required to raise 1 gram (g) of water 1° C. One thousand cal equals 1 kcal. The kcal will be the caloric term used most often in this text.

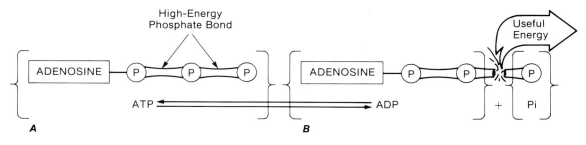

Figure 2-2. *A,* Simplified structure of ATP, showing high-energy phosphate bonds. *B,* Breakdown of ATP to ADP and inorganic phosphate (Pi), with the release of useful energy. The breakdown of 1 mole of ATP yields between 7 and 12 kilocalories (kcal) of energy.

resynthesis operate in the same general manner. The energy liberated from the breakdown of foodstuffs and the energy released when PC is broken down are used to put the ATP molecule back together again; i.e., the energy is used to "drive" the reaction shown in Figure 2-2 from right *(B)* to left *(A)*. In other words, the energy released from the breakdown of foods and PC is functionally linked or coupled to the energy needs of resynthesizing ATP from ADP and Pi (Fig. 2-3). The functional coupling of energy from one series of reactions to another is referred to biochemically as **coupled reactions** and is the fundamental principle involved in the metabolic production of ATP.

Anaerobic Sources of ATP—
Anaerobic Metabolism

Two of the three metabolic systems involved in ATP resynthesis mentioned previously, the ATP-PC (phosphagen) system and anaerobic glycolysis (lactic acid system), are **anaerobic.** Anaerobic means without oxygen, and metabolism refers to the various series of chemical reactions that take place within the body (e.g., within the muscle cell), including those just mentioned. Thus *anaerobic metabolism,* or anaerobic generation of ATP, refers to the resynthesis of ATP through chemical reac-

tions that do not require the presence of the oxygen we breathe.

The ATP-PC (phosphagen) system. Since this anaerobic system is least complicated (but in no way least important), we will discuss it first. Phosphocreatine, like ATP, is stored in muscle cells. Because both ATP and PC contain phosphate groups, they are collectively referred to as phosphagens (hence the name "phosphagen system"). PC is also similar to ATP in that when its phosphate group is removed, a large amount of energy is liberated (Fig. 2-4). The end products of this breakdown are creatine (C) and inorganic phosphate (Pi). As previously discussed, the energy is immediately available and is biochemically coupled to the resynthesis of ATP. For example, as rapidly as ATP is broken down

Figure 2-3. The principle of coupled reactions. The energy released from the breakdown of foods and phosphocreatine (PC) is functionally linked or coupled to the energy needs of resynthesizing ATP from ADP (adenosine diphosphate) and Pi (inorganic phosphate).

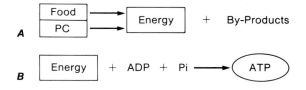

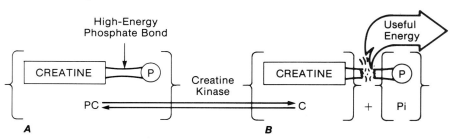

Figure 2-4. *A,* Simplified structure of phosphocreatine (PC) showing high-energy phosphate bond. *B,* Breakdown of PC to creatine (C) and inorganic phosphate (Pi), with the release of energy used to resynthesize ATP.

during muscular contraction, it is continuously re-formed from ADP and Pi by the energy liberated during the breakdown of the stored PC. These coupled reactions can be summarized as follows:

$$PC \rightarrow Pi + C + \textbf{Energy}$$
$$\textbf{Energy} + ADP + Pi \rightarrow ATP$$

It should be mentioned at this time that the preceding equations are overly simplified. In the body, they are more complicated and require the presence of **enzymes,** which are protein compounds that accelerate the speed of the individual reactions. Actually, all metabolic reactions occurring in the body require the presence of enzymes, including the breakdown of ATP.

Ironically, the only means by which PC can be re-formed from Pi and C is from the energy released by the breakdown of ATP! This occurs during recovery from exercise, with the primary source of ATP coming from that obtained through the breakdown of foodstuffs. *Thus, when PC stores are depleted in the ultra high-intensity activities of sprinting, they cannot effectively be replenished until recovery has started.* We will discuss this and other recovery processes in more detail in the next chapter.

How much ATP energy is available from the phosphagen system? The answer to this question is contained in Table 2-1. Several points in the table are worth highlighting. First, notice that storage of PC in the muscle exceeds that of ATP; but this makes sense, because the function of PC is to provide energy for ATP resynthesis. Second, the abbreviation mM refers to **millimoles,** a unit of measure used in quantifying amounts of chemical compounds. A **mole** is a given amount of a chemical compound by weight, the latter being dependent upon the numbers and kinds of atoms making up the compound. Remember that 1000 mM is equal to 1 mole, and that when 1 mole of ATP is broken down, between 7 and 12 kcal of usable energy are released. Third, notice that only between 570 and 690 mM of phosphagen are stored in the total muscle mass of the body. This is equivalent to between 5.7 and 6.9 kcal of ATP energy, which does not represent very much energy for use during exercise. For example, the phosphagen stores in the working muscles would probably be exhausted after only about 10 seconds of all-out exercise, such as sprinting 100 meters. The total amount of ATP energy available from the phosphagen system is very limited.

The importance of the phosphagen system to physical education and athletics is exemplified by the powerful, quick starts of sprinters, football players, high jumpers,

TABLE 2-1			

Estimation of the Energy Available In the Body Through the Phosphagen (ATP-PC) System

	ATP	PC	Total Phosphagen (ATP + PC)
1. Muscular concentration			
a. mM/kg muscle*	4-6	15-17	19-23
b. mM total muscle mass†	120-180	450-510	570-690
2. Useful energy‡			
a. kcal/kg muscle	0.04-0.06	0.15-0.17	0.19-0.23
b. kcal total muscle mass	1.2-1.8	4.5-5.1	5.7-6.9

*Based on data from Hultman[10] and Karlsson.[13]

†Assuming 30 kg of muscle in a 70 kg man.

‡Assuming 10 kcal per mole ATP.

and shot-putters, and by similar activities that require only a few seconds to complete. Without this system, fast, powerful movements could not be performed, because such activities demand a rapidly available supply rather than a large amount of ATP energy. The phosphagen system *represents the most rapidly available source of ATP for use by the muscle.* Some of the reasons for this are that (1) it does not depend on a long series of chemical reactions, (2) it does not depend on transporting the oxygen we breathe to the working muscles, and (3) that both ATP and PC are stored directly within the contractile mechanisms of the muscles.

Anaerobic glycolysis* (lactic acid system). The other anaerobic system in which ATP is resynthesized within the muscle, anaerobic glycolysis, involves an incomplete breakdown of one of the foodstuffs, **carbohydrate** (sugar), to **lactic acid** (hence the name "lactic acid system").

In the body, all carbohydrates are converted to the simple sugar **glucose,** which can either be immediately used in that form or stored in the liver and muscle as **glycogen** for use later. For our purposes, carbohydrates, sugar, glucose, and glycogen have equivalent meanings with respect to metabolism. Lactic acid is a product of anaerobic glycolysis.

Holloszy states that there appears to be an upper limit to the amount of lactic acid that can accumulate before a performer must stop with severe muscular fatigue.[9] One possible explanation for this limitation is that intracellular pH drops as lactic acid accumulates in muscle, resulting in inhibition of the rate-limiting enzyme phosphofructokinase (PFK).[19,22]

From a chemical standpoint, anaerobic glycolysis is more complicated than the phosphagen system in that it requires 12 separate but sequential chemical reactions for completion. This series of reactions was discovered in the 1930s by Gustav Embden and Otto Meyerhof, two German scientists. For this reason, anaerobic glycolysis is sometimes referred to as the Embden-Meyerhof cycle, but more commonly it is referred to simply as glycolysis.

---

*Glycolysis literally means the splitting of glucose (McGilvery, p. 484). Anaerobic glycolysis then refers to the partial breakdown of glucose in the absence of oxygen.

How is glycogen used for resynthesizing ATP? As just indicated, glycogen is chemically broken down into lactic acid by a series of reactions. During this breakdown, energy is released and, through coupled reactions, is used to resynthesize ATP. Several steps in the glycolytic process are shown schematically in Figure 2-5. Again, it should be emphasized that the series of reactions shown is overly simplified, and includes only a few of the 12 individual reactions known to be involved in glycolysis. In addition, each of the reactions requires the presence of a specific enzyme in order for the reactions to occur at a sufficient speed. As previously indicated, one of the most important enzymes in this respect is PFK. Other controlling enzymes include hexokinase, pyruvate kinase, and lactic dehydrogenase.[1]

Only a few moles of ATP can be resynthesized from glycogen during anaerobic glycolysis as compared with the yield possible when oxygen is present. For example, during anaerobic glycolysis only 3 moles of

ATP can be resynthesized from the breakdown of 1 mole, or 180 grams (about 6 ounces), of glycogen. As we will soon see, in the presence of sufficient oxygen, the complete breakdown of the same amount of glycogen yields 39 moles of ATP.

The summary equations of the coupled reactions for ATP resynthesis from anaerobic glycolysis are as follows:

$$(C_6H_{12}O_6)_n \longrightarrow 2C_3H_6O_3 + \textbf{Energy}$$
(glycogen)   (lactic acid)
$$\textbf{Energy} + 3ADP + 3Pi \rightarrow 3ATP$$

During exercise, the useful ATP production from anaerobic glycolysis is actually less than the 3 moles of ATP (3ATP) shown in the preceding equations. The reason for this is that during exhaustive exercise, the muscles and blood can tolerate the accumulation of only about 60 to 70 grams (2 to $2\frac{1}{2}$ ounces) of lactic acid before fatigue sets in. If all 180 grams of glycogen were broken down anaerobically during exercise, 180 grams of lactic acid (represented as $2C_3H_6O_3$ in the above equation) would be formed. Therefore, from a practical viewpoint, only between 1 and 1.2 moles of ATP can be totally resynthesized from anaerobic glycolysis during heavy exercise before lactic acid in blood and muscles reaches exhausting levels.*

Anaerobic glycolysis, like the phosphagen system, is extremely important to us during exercise primarily because it also provides a relatively rapid supply of ATP. For example, exercises that can be performed at maximum rate for between 1 and 3 minutes (such as sprinting 400 and 800 meters) depend heavily upon the phospha-

Figure 2-5. Anaerobic glycolysis. Glycogen is chemically broken down by a series of reactions into lactic acid. During this breakdown, energy is released and, through coupled reactions, is used to resynthesize ATP.

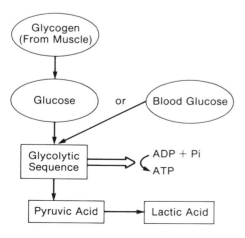

---

*The breakdown of glycogen to 180 grams of lactic acid yields enough energy for the resynthesis of 3 moles of ATP. Therefore, the breakdown of glycogen to only 60 or 70 grams of lactic acid yields enough energy for the resynthesis of $180/3 \times 60/x = 1$ mole of ATP or $180/3 \times 70/x = 1.16$ or 1.2 moles of ATP.

TABLE 2–2

Estimation of the Energy Available in the Body Through Anaerobic Glycolysis (Lactic Acid System)*

	Per kg Muscle	Total Muscle Mass
1. Maximal lactic acid tolerance (grams)†	2.0–2.3	60–70
2. ATP formation (millimoles)	33–38	1000–1200
3. Useful energy (kilocalories)	0.33–0.38	10.0–12.0

*Assumptions same as in Table 2–1.

†Based on data from Karlsson.[13]

gen system and anaerobic glycolysis for ATP formation.

The total ATP energy available in the body through anaerobic glycolysis is estimated in Table 2-2. As mentioned before, if the muscles can tolerate 2.0 to 2.3 grams of lactic acid per kilogram of muscle, or 60 to 70 grams for the total muscle mass, then the maximal amount of ATP manufactured by glycolysis would be between 1.0 and 1.2 moles (1000 to 1200 millimoles). Under these conditions, notice that this is about twice as much ATP as that which is obtainable from the ATP-PC system.

In summary, anaerobic glycolysis (1) results in the formation of lactic acid, which is related to muscular fatigue; (2) does not require the presence of oxygen; (3) uses *only* carbohydrates (glycogen and glucose) as its food fuel; and (4) releases enough energy for the resynthesis of only a few moles of ATP.

Aerobic Sources of ATP— Aerobic Metabolism

Before describing the reactions of the aerobic system, it is important to introduce a number of biochemical terms: acetyl group, NAD^+, NADH, FAD^+, and $FADH_2$. An acetyl group, for our purposes, can be simply defined as a two-carbon molecule. For example, pyruvic acid (a three-carbon molecule) loses CO_2 to become an acetyl group before entering the Krebs Cycle. Likewise, in fatty acid metabolism, two-carbon groups are formed to enter the Krebs Cycle.

NAD^+ (nicotinamide adenine dinucleotide) and FAD^+ (flavo adenine dinucleotide) serve as hydrogen acceptors. H^+ is cleaved from carbohydrates during glycolysis and Krebs Cycle activity. The removal of H^+ ions from a compound is one form of oxidation. When a compound "accepts" an H^+ ion, it is said to be reduced. Thus, NADH and $FADH_2$ are the reduced forms of NAD^+ and FAD^+. The function of both NADH and $FADH_2$ is to carry electrons through the electron transport system (see p. 21).*

In the presence of oxygen, 1 mole of glycogen is completely broken down to carbon dioxide (CO_2) and water (H_2O), releasing sufficient energy to resynthesize 39 moles of ATP. This is by far the largest yield of ATP energy. Such a yield, as you might guess, requires many reactions and enzyme systems, all of which are much more complex than in the two anaerobic systems just discussed. Like the anaerobic systems, the reactions of the oxygen system occur within the muscle cell but, unlike the former, are confined to specialized, sub-

*For further explanation refer to McGilvery (1983) and West (1985).

cellular compartments called **mitochondria** (singular = **mitochondrion**). These compartments, shown in Figure 2-6, contain an elaborate membrane system consisting of a series of inward folds and

Figure 2-6. Mitochondria. *A,* An electron micrograph of a longitudinal section of rat skeletal muscle, showing several mitochondria. *B,* A schematic illustration of a mitochondrion showing its extensive membrane system and cristae, the latter of which contain the enzyme systems for aerobic metabolism. Notice that the cristae are also visible in the mitochondria shown in the electron micrograph. (Electron micrograph courtesy Dr. James Cirrito, The Ohio State University, Columbus, Ohio).

A

B

convolutions called **cristae.** Cristae are thought to contain most, if not all, of the enzyme systems required for aerobic metabolism. Skeletal muscle is proliferated with mitochondria (illustrated in Fig. 2-6).

The many reactions of the aerobic system can be divided into three main series: (1) **aerobic glycolysis,** (2) the **Krebs Cycle,** and (3) the **electron transport system.**

Aerobic glycolysis. The first series of reactions involved in the aerobic breakdown of glycogen to CO_2 and H_2O is glycolysis. This may come as a surprise, since it was just said that glycolysis is an anaerobic pathway. Actually, there is only one difference between the anaerobic glycolysis discussed earlier and the aerobic glycolysis that occurs when there is a sufficient supply of oxygen: *lactic acid does not accumulate in the presence of oxygen.* In other words, the presence of oxygen inhibits the accumulation of lactic acid but *not* the resynthesis of ATP. Oxygen does this by diverting the majority of the lactic acid precursor pyruvic acid, into the aerobic system *after* the ATP is resynthesized (Fig. 2-7). Thus, during aerobic glycolysis, 1 mole of glycogen is broken down into 2 moles of pyruvic acid, releasing enough energy for resynthesizing 3 moles of ATP. These coupled reactions can be summarized as follows:

$$(C_6H_{12}O_6)_n \longrightarrow 2C_3H_4O_3 + \textbf{Energy}$$
(glycogen)   (pyruvic acid)
$$\textbf{Energy} + 3ADP + 3Pi \rightarrow 3ATP$$

Additionally, 2 NAD^+ are reduced to 2 NADH's which are diverted to the electron transport system where 6 more ATP's are generated (3 for each NADH).

The Krebs Cycle. Next, the pyruvic acid formed during aerobic glycolysis passes into the mitochondria and continues to be broken down in a series of reactions

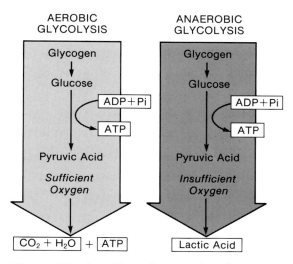

Figure 2-7. Aerobic and anaerobic glycolysis. The breakdown of glycogen to pyruvic acid with ATP resynthesis does not require oxygen. With oxygen present (aerobic glycolysis), pyruvic acid is further broken down to CO_2 and H_2O with more ATP resynthesized. Without oxygen (anaerobic glycolysis), pyruvic acid is converted to lactic acid with no further ATP resynthesized.

called the *Krebs Cycle* after its discoverer, Sir Hans Krebs. For this important discovery, he won the Nobel Prize in Physiology or Medicine in 1953. This cycle is also known as the *tricarboxylic acid (TCA) cycle* and as the *citric acid cycle* after some of the chemical compounds found in the cycle. A number of significant events occur during the Krebs Cycle in which we have an interest: (1) carbon dioxide is produced, (2) oxidation (and reduction) occur, and (3) ATP is produced.

Immediately CO_2 is removed from pyruvic acid transforming it from a 3-carbon compound to a 2-carbon compound (an acetyl group). This acetyl group combines with co-enzyme A to form acetyl co-enzyme A. CO_2 is also formed in the Krebs Cycle. All CO_2 produced diffuses into the blood and is carried to the lungs where it is eliminated from the body.

Remembering that oxidation is the removal of electrons from a chemical compound, electrons are removed in the form of hydrogen atoms (H) from the carbon atoms of what was formerly pyruvic acid and before that, glycogen. The hydrogen atom, you may recall, contains a positively charged particle called a proton (referred to here as a hydrogen ion) and a negatively charged particle called an electron. In other words:

$$\begin{array}{ccccc} H & \longrightarrow & H^+ & + & e^- \\ \text{(hydrogen} & & \text{(hydrogen} & & \text{(electron)} \\ \text{atom)} & & \text{ion)} & & \end{array}$$

Thus when hydrogen atoms are removed from a compound, that compound is said to have been oxidized.

The production of CO_2 and the removal of electrons in the Krebs Cycle are related as follows: pyruvic acid (in its modified form) contains carbon (C), hydrogen (H), and oxygen (O); when H is removed, only C and O, i.e., the chemical components of carbon dioxide, remain. Thus in the Krebs Cycle, pyruvic acid is oxidized resulting in the production of CO_2. The Krebs Cycle is shown schematically in Figure 2-8. In the Krebs Cycle itself, only two ATP units are formed for each unit of glycogen. At four different sites in the Krebs Cycle, H^+ ions are removed and passed through the electron transport system where the end result is the formation of water and ATP units!

The electron transport system (ETS). Continuing in the breakdown of glycogen, the end product, H_2O, is formed from the hydrogen ions and electrons that are removed in the Krebs Cycle and the *oxygen* we breathe. The specific series of reactions in which H_2O is formed is called the *electron transport system* (ETS) or the *respiratory chain*. Essentially what happens is that the hydrogen ions and elec-

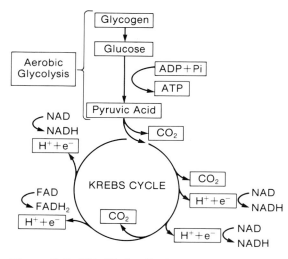

Figure 2-8. The Krebs Cycle. Pyruvic acid, the end product of aerobic glycolysis, enters the Krebs Cycle after a slight chemical alteration. Once in the cycle, two further chemical events take place: (1) the release of CO_2, which eventually is eliminated from the body by the lungs; and (2) oxidation, i.e., the removal of hydrogen ions (H^+) and electrons (e^-), which ultimately enter the electron transport system for further chemical alterations.

trons enter the ETS via $FADH_2$ and NADH and are "transported" to oxygen by "electron carriers" in a series of enzymatic reactions, the end product of which is water. In other words:

$$4H^+ + 4e^- + O_2 \rightarrow 2H_2O$$

that is, 4 hydrogen ions ($4H^+$) plus 4 electrons ($4e^-$) plus 1 mole of oxygen (O_2) yield 2 moles of water ($2H_2O$). As the electrons are carried down the respiratory chain, energy is released, and ATP is resynthesized in coupled reactions. NADH enters the ETS at a slightly higher level than $FADH_2$ and thus "yields" 3 ATP per pass, while $FADH_2$ yields 2 ATP per pass. This is shown in Figure 2-9. Overall, 12 pairs of electrons are removed from 1 mole of glycogen, and thus

36 moles of ATP are generated. Therefore, during aerobic metabolism, most of the total of 39 moles of ATP are resynthesized in the electron transport system at the same time water is formed.

Summary equations for aerobic metabolism. A summary of the coupled reactions involved in the aerobic breakdown of 1 mole of glycogen is as follows:

$$(C_6H_{12}O_6)_n + 6O_2 \rightarrow 6CO_2 + 6H_2O$$
$$\text{(glycogen)} \qquad\qquad + \textbf{Energy}$$
$$\textbf{Energy} + 39ADP + 39Pi \rightarrow 39ATP$$

Note that 39 moles of ATP are resynthesized, 3 ATPs from aerobic glycolysis, 30 ATPs from the passage of NADH into the ETS, 4 ATPs from the passage of $FADH_2$ into the ETS, and 2 ATPs from the Krebs Cycle itself. Also note that when blood glucose is the source of carbohydrate fuel, one additional ATP is "consumed" in converting glucose to glucose-1-phosphate (see Fig. 2-10). It should be further noted that it requires 6 moles of oxygen ($6O_2$) to break down 180 grams (1 mole) of glycogen. Since 1 mole of any gas (in our case, oxygen) occupies 22.4 liters at standard temperature and pressure, 6 moles of O_2= 6×22.4=134.4 liters. Therefore, 134.4 liters of O_2 are required to resynthesize 39 moles of ATP or $134.4 \div 39 = 3.45$ liters of O_2 required per mole of ATP resynthesized. In other words, any time 3.45 liters of O_2 are consumed by the body, 1 mole of ATP is aerobically synthesized. At rest, this would take between 10 and 15 minutes. During maximal exercise, however, it would take most of us only about 1 minute!

The aerobic system and fat metabolism. So far, we have discussed the aerobic breakdown only of glycogen, a carbohydrate. The other two foodstuffs, **fat** and **protein,** can also be aerobically broken down to CO_2 and H_2O, releasing energy for ATP resynthesis. Fats (usually 16- or

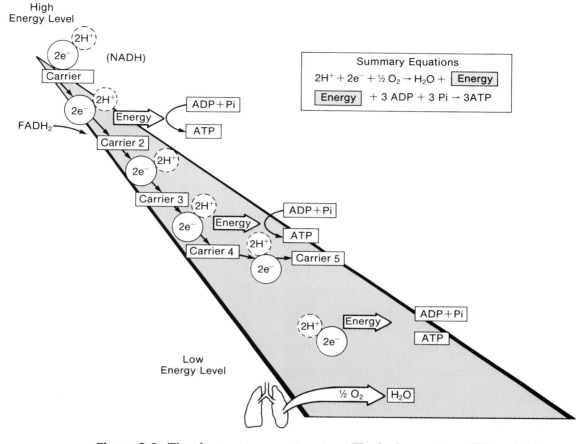

Figure 2-9. The electron transport system. The hydrogen ions (H^+) and electrons (e^-) removed in the Krebs Cycle have a high energy level as they enter the electron transport system. Here two major chemical events take place. First, the hydrogen ions and electrons are "transported" by electron carriers to the oxygen we breathe to form water (H_2O) through a series of enzymatic reactions; and second, at the same time, ATP is resynthesized in coupled reactions from the energy released. For every pair of electrons transported, an average of 3 moles of ATP is resynthesized. (Modified and redrawn from Lehninger.[17])

18-carbon chains) in the form of triglycerides are broken down into two-carbon compounds (acyl groups) by a series of reactions called beta-oxidation for entry into the Krebs Cycle and ETS (see Fig. 2-11).

Fatty acids must be "activated" for beta oxidation (β-oxidation) at the expense of 1 ATP. Then in the process of beta-oxidation, one $FADH_2$ and one NADH are generated, which pass through the ETS. A total of 5 ATPs will be generated in this initial process (3 ATPs from NADH and 2 ATPs from $FADH_2$). Just as with the acyl groups from pyruvic acid, 1 ATP, 3 NADH, and 1 $FADH_2$ are produced in the Krebs Cycle for each acyl group. Remembering that for each NADH 3 ATPs are resynthesized and for each $FADH_2$ 2 ATPs are

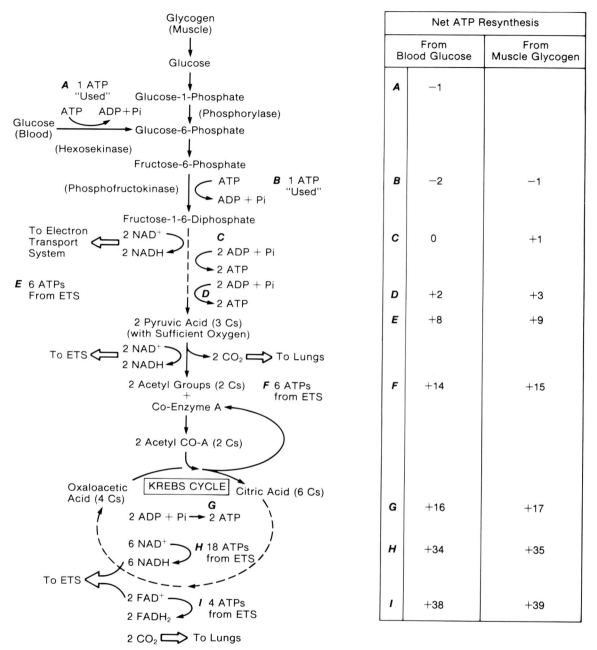

Figure 2-10. Sources of ATP resynthesis from the complete oxidation of carbohydrate in the form of either blood glucose or muscle glycogen. The two columns on the right side of the figure represent the net production of ATP at each level of glycolysis (including the Krebs Cycle). The dashed lines indicate that several reactions have been omitted. The key enzymes hexosekinase, phosphorylase, and phosphofructokinase are in parentheses. These three enzymes are closely related to adaptations to training.

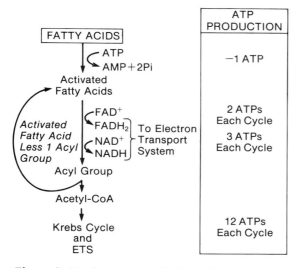

Figure 2-11. Summary of fatty acid metabolism (aerobic). Fatty acids are "activated" for beta-oxidation, then in a series of cyclic events, 2-carbon units (acyl groups) are separated and enter the Krebs Cycle as acetyl-CoA. The total number of moles of ATP produced depends upon the specific fatty acid and the number of carbons in the fatty acid.

resynthesized, a total of 12 ATPs are produced in the Krebs Cycle and ETS. The net production of ATP with activation of fatty acids, β-oxidation, and first passage through the Krebs Cycle is 16 ATPs (17 − 1).

Upon subsequent passes through β-oxidation and the Krebs Cycle, 17 ATPs will be resynthesized. On the last passage,

involving a 4-carbon chain, there will be 17 and 12 ATPs resynthesized (the last acyl group does not go through β-oxidation). Different fatty acids will result in varying amounts of ATP resynthesized. For two typical fatty acids, stearic acid (an 18-carbon molecule) and palmitic acid (a 16-carbon molecule) there would be 147 and 130 ATPs produced, respectively. Table 2-3 summarizes these observations.

Note that 1 mole of palmitic acid (a little over half of a pound) releases enough energy to resynthesize 130 moles of ATP, substantially more than from 1 mole of glycogen. However, 23 moles or $23 \times 22.4 = 515.2$ liters of O_2 are required. Therefore, 3.96 liters of O_2 are required per mole of ATP resynthesized ($515.2 \div 130 = 3.96$).

You will recall from the general equation for the oxidation of 1 mole of glycogen that 6 moles of oxygen are required (or 6×22.4 liters of oxygen per mole = 134.4 liters of oxygen) and 3.45 liters of oxygen to produce 1 mole of ATP. Thus to produce 1 mole of ATP via fatty acid oxidation requires about 15% more oxygen than to produce 1 mole of ATP by the complete degradation of glycogen. In other words, it requires more O_2 to generate 1 mole of ATP from the aerobic breakdown of fat than from glycogen.

Role of protein in aerobic metabolism.   Thus far we have discussed the fate of carbohydrates and fats in the metabolic scheme. What of protein? Protein is indeed

TABLE 2-3

Net Production of ATP From Two Typical Fatty Acids

	Stearic Acid (18-carbon chain)	Palmitic Acid (16-carbon chain)
Activation and first pass (17 − 1):	16 ATP	16 ATP
Next 6 passes (6 × 17)	102 ATP	
Next 5 passes (5 × 17)		85 ATP
Last pass (17) plus (12)	29 ATP	29 ATP
TOTAL ATP PRODUCTION	147 ATP	130 ATP

a source of ATP but plays only a very minor role during rest and, under most conditions of exercise, has almost no role whatsoever. In starvation, conditions of carbohydrate deprivation, and feats of unusual endurance (6 day races), protein catabolism may become significant.[2,15,16]

Total aerobic energy in muscle. It is difficult to estimate the total muscular energy that can be manufactured through the oxygen system, since all three foodstuffs are used. However, as a basis for comparison with the anaerobic systems, the total aerobic energy available in the muscles from glycogen alone is given in Table 2-4. It is easily seen that the oxygen system is by far the most efficient with respect to ATP production (compare with Tables 2-1 and 2-2). For example, the amount of ATP available from the aerobic breakdown of all the glycogen in the muscles is between 87 and 98 moles! This is nearly 50 times more than that made available by the two anaerobic systems combined. Additionally, another 80 to 100 grams of glycogen are stored in the liver,[12] and if all were used for aerobic metabolism, another 17 to 22 moles of ATP would be generated.

We have seen that the aerobic system is capable of utilizing both fats and glycogen for resynthesizing large amounts of ATP without simultaneously generating fatiguing by-products. For this reason, it is the preferred system under resting conditions. With respect to physical education and athletics, it is also easy to see that the aerobic system is particularly suited for manufacturing ATP during prolonged endurance-type exercise. For example, during marathon running (42.2 kilometers, or 26.2 miles), it can be estimated that a total of about 150 moles of ATP (approximately 1 mole of ATP every minute) are required.[4,8] Such a large, sustained output of ATP energy is possible because large amounts of glycogen, fats, and oxygen are readily available to the working skeletal muscles.

A summary of the complete aerobic system is shown in Figure 2-12.

Comparing the Energy Systems

As a final consideration, let us compare the three energy systems, first, in their general characteristics (Table 2-5) and second, in their maximal **capacity** and **power** with respect to ATP production. Capacity refers to an amount independent of time, whereas power refers to a rate, i.e., an amount in a given time. From what has already been said concerning the energy systems, you should be able to rank them with respect to both their relative capacities and powers. To check your answers, consult Table 2-6.

TABLE 2-4

Estimation of the Energy Available From Muscle Glycogen Through the Aerobic (Oxygen) System*

	Muscle Glycogen	
	Per kg Muscle	Total Muscle Mass
1. Muscular concentration (grams)	13–15†	400–450
2. ATP formation (moles)	2.8–3.2	87–98
3. Useful energy (kcal)	28–32	870–980

*Assumptions the same as in Table 2-1.

†Based on data from Hultman.[10]

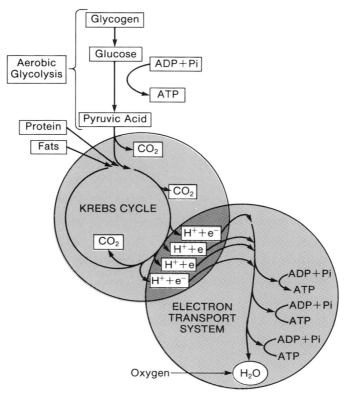

Figure 2-12. Summary of the aerobic (oxygen) system. Glycogen is oxidized in three major series of chemical reactions, aerobic glycolysis in which pyruvic acid is formed and some ATP resynthesized; the Krebs Cycle in which CO_2 is produced, and H^+ and e^- are removed; and the electron transport system in which H_2O is formed from H^+, e^-, and oxygen, and more ATP is resynthesized. Fats and proteins, when used as fuels for ATP resynthesis, also go through the Krebs Cycle and the electron transport system.

TABLE 2-5

General Characteristics of the Three Systems by Which ATP is Formed

System	Food or Chemical Fuel	O_2 Required	Speed	Relative ATP Production
Anaerobic				
ATP-PC system	Phosphocreatine	No	Fastest	Few; limited
Lactic acid system	Glycogen (glucose)	No	Fast	Few; limited
Aerobic				
Oxygen system	Glycogen, fats, proteins	Yes	Slow	Many; unlimited

TABLE 2-6

Maximal Capacity and Power of the Three Energy Systems

System	Maximal Power (Moles of ATP Per Minute)	Maximal Capacity (Total Moles ATP Available)
Phosphagen (ATP-PC)	3.6	0.7
Anaerobic glycolysis (lactic acid)	1.6	1.2
Aerobic or oxygen (from glycogen only)	1.0	90.0

The Aerobic and Anaerobic Systems during Rest and Exercise

There are at least three important features of the anaerobic and aerobic systems under conditions of rest and exercise that need further consideration: (1) the types of food-stuffs being metabolized, (2) the relative roles played by each system, and (3) the presence and accumulation of lactic acid in the blood.

Rest

From Figure 2-13A, we see that under resting conditions about two-thirds of the food fuel is contributed by fats and the other one-third by carbohydrates (glycogen and glucose). Protein is not shown in the diagram because, as pointed out earlier, its contribution as a food fuel is negligible. Also, as is indicated, the aerobic system is the only energy system in operation. This is true because our oxygen transport system (heart and lungs) is capable of supplying each cell with sufficient oxygen and, therefore, with adequate ATP to satisfy all the energy requirements of the resting state (Fig. 2-13B). The molecules of ATP shown coming from the anaerobic system are considered as part of the aerobic yield, since, as we indicated earlier, they are likewise formed in the presence of oxygen.

Although the aerobic system is the only one in operation, perhaps you have noticed (Fig. 2-13B) that there is a small but constant amount of lactic acid present in the blood (about 10 mg for every 100 ml

Figure 2-13. *A,* The aerobic system supplies all the ATP required in the resting state. *B,* During rest, oxygen consumption (0.3 liter/minute) remains constant and is adequate to supply the required ATP; as a consequence, the blood lactic acid level remains within the normal range (10 mg %). The combination of these factors indicates that metabolism is aerobic.

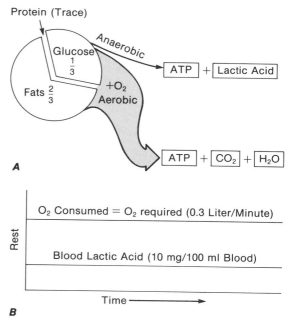

of blood).* The reason for this is rather complicated and a thorough understanding would require considerable knowledge of the chemistry of the individual reactions involved. Suffice it to say that there is an abundance of LDH (lactic dehydrogenase), the enzyme that catalyzes the reaction of pyruvic acid to lactic acid. For our purposes, the fact that the lactic acid level remains constant and does not accumulate tells us that anaerobic glycolysis is *not* operating. We see, then, that at rest the foodstuffs utilized are fats and carbohydrates, and the necessary ATP is supplied solely by the aerobic system.

Exercise

Both anaerobic and aerobic systems contribute ATP during exercise; however, their relative roles are dependent upon (1) the types of exercises performed, (2) the state of training, and (3) the diet of the athlete. To begin our discussion, we can divide the many types of exercises into two categories: (1) exercises that can be performed for only short periods of time but which require maximal effort, and (2) exercises that can be performed for relatively long periods of time but which require submaximal effort. Later we will point out the interaction and significance of the roles played by the three energy systems in exercises that do not easily fit into one or the other of these categories. The understanding of this concept is vitally important to you in planning training programs.

Saltin and Karlsson[21] have described glycogen depletion patterns with activities requiring from 30 to 120% of maximal oxygen consumption (see Fig. 2-14A). Along with other observations to be made in the

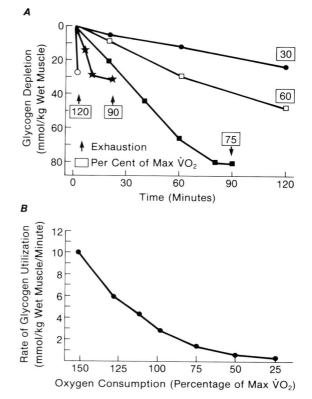

Figure 2-14. Glycogen depletion patterns during exhaustive work on the bicycle. Both absolute (*A*) and relative (*B*) glycogen depletion are related to the intensity of work. Note that in part *A*, exhaustion was not achieved during the 30% and 60% rides. (Modified from Saltin and Karlsson[21].)

following paragraphs, we can begin to comprehend some of the limiting factors in exercise. It is interesting to note that with activities requiring less than 60% or more than 90% of aerobic capacity, glycogen stores are not significantly depleted. In Figure 2-14B the rate of glycogen utilization can be seen to be related to the relative workload. The rate of glycogen utilization increases sharply with increasing workloads. At very high workloads, where exhaustion occurs very rapidly, there is still about 70% of the initial glycogen stores

---

*Ten milligrams (mg) in 100 milliliters (ml) of blood is usually expressed as milligrams per cent (mg %) or mg per deciliter (mg/dl). Another example: 15 gm of hemoglobin in 100 ml of blood would be read as 15 gm %.

remaining. At workloads requiring 65 to 95% of the subjects aerobic capacity, exhaustion was highly related to glycogen levels approaching zero.

Saltin and Karlsson have reported glycogen utilization rates of 0.3, 0.7, 1.4, 3.4, and 10 mmoles glucose units per kg of wet muscle per minute for workloads of 25, 50, 75, 100, and 150% of the aerobic capacity, respectively.[21] Figure 2-14B illustrates these observations.

Exercises of short duration. Exercises in this category include sprinting events such as the 100-, 200-, and 400-meter dashes, the 800-meter run, and other events in which the required rate of work can be maintained for up to only 2 or possibly 3 minutes.

Figure 2-15A shows the relative roles of the energy systems when performing these types of exercises. Here we see that the major food fuel is carbohydrates, with fats minor and proteins—once again—negligible contributors. We also see that the predominant system is anaerobic. This does not mean to imply, however, that it is the *only* system operating. It merely indicates that the energy or ATP required for these types of exercises cannot be supplied via the aerobic system alone. As a consequence, most of the ATP must be supplied anaerobically by the phosphagen system and anaerobic glycolysis. Phosphocreatine (PC) levels, with short, very high-intensity work will drop to very low levels and remain low until the exercise stops. Likewise, PC is rapidly replenished (within minutes) during recovery.

There are two reasons why there is a limitation of the aerobic system in supplying adequate ATP during the performance of any exercise: (1) each of us has a ceiling for his or her **aerobic power** or the maximum rate at which we can consume oxygen; and (2) it takes at least 2 or 3 minutes for oxygen consumption to increase to a new, higher level. For example, trained athletes have maximal aerobic powers of between 3.0 and 5.0 liters of O_2 per minute for females[5] and males,[20] respectively, whereas the maximum for the untrained female[6] is around 2.2 liters per minute and for the untrained male,[7] 3.2 liters per minute. These levels of O_2 consumption are not nearly enough in either case to supply all the ATP needed for such an effort as the 100-meter dash, which may require in excess of 45 liters per minute (about 8 liters of O_2 per 100 meters or per 10 seconds).

Even if it were possible to consume oxygen at a rate that would alone meet the energy or ATP requirement, it would take the first 2 or 3 minutes of exercise to accelerate the oxygen consumption to the required level. The reason for this delayed increase in oxygen consumption deals with the time it takes for adequate biochemical and physiological adjustments to become manifest. This holds true during the transition from rest to an exercise of any intensity and from an exercise of lower intensity to one of higher intensity. The period during which the level of oxygen consumption is below that necessary to supply all the ATP required of any exercise is called the **oxygen deficit** (Fig. 2-15B). It is during this oxygen deficit period that the phosphagen system and anaerobic glycolysis are called upon to supply most of the ATP required for the exercise. This means that during short-term but high-intensity exercises, such as those mentioned before, there will always be an oxygen deficit throughout the duration of the exercise, with the major source of ATP from the two anaerobic systems.

From Figure 2-15C we see that the rapid acceleration in anaerobic glycolysis is accompanied by an equally rapid accumulation of lactic acid. However, accumulated lactic acid assumes a significant role in activities lasting from about 2 minutes to 10 minutes. PC depletion and the rate of ATP resyntheses are very important in

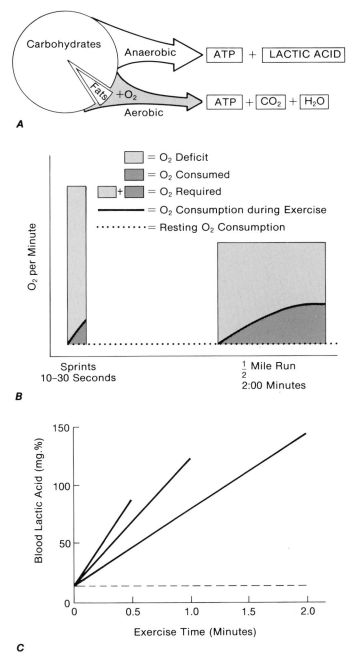

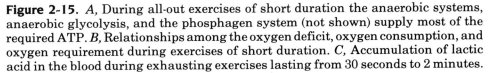

Figure 2-15. *A,* During all-out exercises of short duration the anaerobic systems, anaerobic glycolysis, and the phosphagen system (not shown) supply most of the required ATP. *B,* Relationships among the oxygen deficit, oxygen consumption, and oxygen requirement during exercises of short duration. *C,* Accumulation of lactic acid in the blood during exhausting exercises lasting from 30 seconds to 2 minutes.

activities lasting less than 3 minutes. To give relief to the intense work stress, exercise must either be stopped or continued at a much lower intensity. Blood lactic acid levels as high as 200 mg % have been recorded during competitive sprinting events in track and in swimming.[18] Such high levels are some 20 times greater than those normally found under resting conditions (10 mg %).

The level of blood lactic acid, then, is an excellent indicator of which energy system is predominantly used during exercise. If the level is high, the primary system used must have been anaerobic glycolysis; if the level is low, the aerobic system predominated.

Prolonged exercises. Any exercise that can be maintained for relatively long periods of time should be included under this category. By relatively long periods of time, we mean 10 minutes or longer. In such cases, the major foodstuffs are again carbohydrates and fats (Fig. 2-16A). For activities lasting up to 20 minutes (e.g., continuous running) carbohydrates generally are the dominant fuel source for resynthesis of ATP, while fats play a relatively minor role. High, but not maximal, levels of lactic acid will appear in the blood. As the time of performance proceeds past an hour, glycogen stores begin to show significant decreases in concentration and fats become more important as a source for ATP resynthesis. The "mix" of glycogen and fat utilization will vary with different athletes for a variety of reasons including state of training, proportions of fast-twitch and slow-twitch muscle fibers (see Chapter 5), and initial glycogen stores.

In these types of exercises, the major source of ATP is supplied by the aerobic system. The lactic acid and ATP-PC systems also contribute, but only at the *beginning* of the exercise, before oxygen consumption reaches a new steady-state level; during this time an oxygen deficit is in-

curred. Once oxygen consumption reaches a new steady-state level (in about 2 or 3 minutes) it is sufficient to supply all of the ATP energy required for the exercise (Fig. 2-16B). For this reason, blood lactic acid does not accumulate to very high levels during exercise lasting more than an hour. Anaerobic glycolysis shuts down once steady-state oxygen consumption is reached, and the small amount of lactic acid accumulated prior to this time remains relatively constant until the end of the exercise (Fig. 2-16C). A good example of this is during marathon running.[4,8] These athletes run 42.2 kilometers (26.2 miles) in about 2.5 hours, but at the end of the race their blood lactic acid levels are only about two to three times those found at rest.[4] The fatigue experienced by these runners at the end of a race is, therefore, due to factors other than high blood lactic acid levels. Some of the more important factors leading to this type of fatigue are: (1) low blood glucose levels due to depletion of liver glycogen stores; (2) local muscular fatigue due to depletion of muscle glycogen stores; (3) loss of water (dehydration) and electrolytes, which leads to high body temperature; and (4) boredom and the physical beating in general that the body has sustained.[3]

In prolonged activities of very low intensity such as walking, playing golf, and certain industrial tasks, lactic acid does not accumulate above the normal resting level. This is so because the phosphagen system alone is sufficient to supply the additional ATP energy needed prior to reaching a steady state of oxygen consumption. In these cases, fatigue can be delayed up to 6 hours or more, and the cause is not clear.

The preceding information can be extremely useful to you as a coach. For example, one of the most important aspects of competitive middle distance and distance running is pacing. If an athlete starts an endurance race too fast or begins his or her

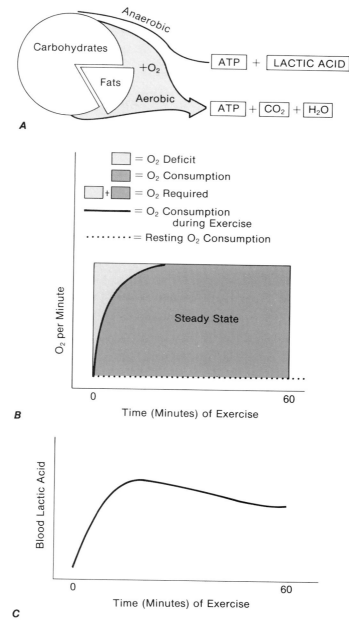

Figure 2-16. *A,* During prolonged submaximal exercises, the major source of ATP is through the aerobic system. *B,* Anaerobic glycolysis and the phosphagen system also contribute ATP but only at the beginning of submaximal exercise (O_2 deficit), before oxygen consumption reaches a constant level (steady state). *C,* Once a steady-state oxygen consumption is reached, the small amount of lactic acid accumulated during the O_2 deficit period remains relatively constant until the end of exercise.

final sprint too soon, lactic acid will accumulate to very high levels and the muscle glycogen stores will be depleted early in the race. As you will recall, this is true because as the intensity of the exercise increases, so does the amount of energy required from the anaerobic systems. Consequently, the race may be lost, owing to this early onset of fatigue. Well-informed coaches, or athletes for that matter, would never let this happen. Instead, from a physiological standpoint, they would advocate that the runner maintain a steady, but sufficient, pace throughout most of the race, then finish with an all-out effort. In other words, the onset of fatigue due to lactic acid accumulation and muscle glycogen depletion should be delayed until the end of the race.

Having made this generalized observation, we must also recognize that in the special case of middle distance runners there are a variety of racing strategies. In one instance a particular runner always seems to come from behind and "out sprint" the field during the last 300 yards while another runner has to "break on top and improve his position." Each elite runner has found a strategy that works best for him or her physiologically. The "sprinter" perhaps has a higher percentage of fast-twitch fibers (fast glycolytic) while the "front runner" may have more slow-twitch fibers (slow oxidative).

Just as an anaerobic capacity is important in the performance of exercises of short duration, the **maximal aerobic power** is a significant factor in the performance of prolonged activities. This stems from the fact that the aerobic system supplies the majority of energy required of these types of exercises. Maximal aerobic power (abbreviated $\mathbf{max\dot{V}O_2}$, or $\mathbf{\dot{V}O_2}$)* is

defined as the maximal rate at which oxygen can be consumed. *The higher an athlete's maximal aerobic power, the more successfully he or she will perform in endurance events, provided all other factors that contribute to a championship performance are present* (Fig. 2-17).

Interaction of Aerobic and Anaerobic Energy Sources during Exercise

Thus far, we have discussed the energy systems during exercises that have either been short-term, high-intensity efforts (anaerobic), or long-term, low-intensity efforts (aerobic). What about those exercise activities that fall in between these categories? Are they anaerobic or aerobic activities? As illustrated in Figure 2-18, it is not possible to classify such activities as strictly either anaerobic or aerobic. Rather, they require a blend of both anaerobic and

Figure 2-17. The higher an athlete's maximal aerobic power, the more successfully he or she will perform in endurance events, provided all other factors contributing to a championship performance are present. (Based on data from Karlsson and Saltin.[14])

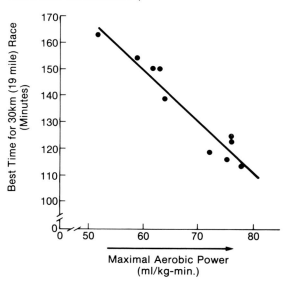

*The V stands for volume, O_2 for oxygen, and the dot over the V ($\dot{V}$) stands for per unit of time, usually 1 minute. Thus max $\dot{V}O_2$, or $\dot{V}O_2$max, = maximal oxygen consumption = maximal aerobic power.

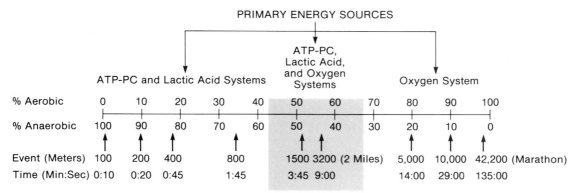

Figure 2-18. The approximate percentage of contribution of aerobic and anaerobic energy sources in selected track events. Nonshaded areas represent predominance of either anaerobic (left) or aerobic (right) metabolism. The shaded area represents events in which anaerobic and aerobic systems are of nearly equal importance.

aerobic metabolism. Take, for example, the 1500-meter and mile runs. In these activities, the anaerobic systems supply the major portion of ATP during the sprint at both the start and finish of the race, with the aerobic system predominating during the middle, or steady-state, period of the run. Overall, these runs demand about half of the required ATP from anaerobic sources and half from aerobic sources.

The illustration in Figure 2-18 represents what we can call an **energy continuum** for track events. In other words, those events to the left, such as the 100-meter dash, are almost 100 per cent anaerobic, whereas those far to the right, such as the marathon, are clearly aerobic. In between these two extremes are the so-called gray zones, in which various mixtures of anaerobic and aerobic metabolism are required during performance. These latter activities are often the most difficult for the athlete to perform because all of the energy systems are involved to a large extent. Also, these activities are often most difficult to prepare an athlete for, because he or she must spend time during training developing both anaerobic and aerobic systems.

The energy continuum concept, of course, applies to all activities, not just track events. It will be useful to us during our discussions of training programs in a later chapter.

Summary

The primary concern of this chapter is energy. The sun is the ultimate source of all energy on earth, for it is through solar radiation that carbohydrates in plants are formed. Humans and animals eat plants and other animals for food. In the human body, food energy is used to manufacture adenosine triphosphate, or ATP—the chemical compound that, when broken down, supplies energy for muscular contraction and other biological processes.

The production of ATP involves both anaerobic (without oxygen) and aerobic (with oxygen) metabolism (chemical reactions). There are two anaerobic systems: (1) the phosphagen, or ATP-PC system; and (2) anaerobic glycolysis, or the lactic acid system.

The phosphagens (ATP + PC, a chemical compound similar to ATP) are stored within the contractile mechanisms of muscle and provide the most rapidly available source of ATP for use by the muscle. This energy system is the major one used for ATP production during high-intensity, short-duration exercises, such as sprinting 100 meters. Anaerobic glycolysis releases energy for ATP synthesis through the partial breakdown of carbohydrates (glycogen and glucose) to lactic acid. Lactic acid causes muscular fatigue when it accumulates in the blood and muscles. Anaerobic glycolysis is also a major supplier of ATP during high-intensity, short-duration activities, such as sprinting 400 and 800 meters. Activities that depend heavily on the phosphagen system and anaerobic glycolysis are called anaerobic activities.

The aerobic, or oxygen, system releases energy for ATP production from the breakdown mainly of carbohydrates and fats, and sometimes of protein, to carbon dioxide and water. Although the oxygen system yields by far the most ATP, it requires several series of complex chemical reactions. With carbohydrates, in the first series of reactions, called aerobic glycolysis, glycogen is broken down to pyruvic acid; then in the Krebs Cycle, carbon dioxide is produced and electrons, in the form of hydrogen atoms, are removed. In the final series of reactions, hydrogen atoms (electrons) are "transported" to the oxygen we breathe; water is formed, and ATP is synthesized. With fats as the fuel, the reactions are the same with the exception of the first series, which in this case is called beta oxidation. The oxygen system is used predominantly during low-intensity, long-duration exercises, such as the marathon. Such activities are called aerobic exercises.

Many exercise activities require a blend of both anaerobic and aerobic metabolism. For example, in the 1500-meter run, the anaerobic systems supply the major portion of ATP during the sprint at both the start and finish of the race, with the oxygen systems predominating during the middle, or steady-state, period of the run. This information is useful when developing training programs.

Questions

1. How is energy defined?
2. Name the six forms of energy.
3. Diagram the biological energy cycle.
4. What is the immediate source of energy for muscular contraction?
5. What are coupled reactions and what biochemical purpose do they serve?
6. Define anaerobic and aerobic metabolism.
7. Describe each of the three ways by which ATP is resynthesized.
8. How is lactic acid formed?
9. Distinguish between aerobic and anaerobic glycolysis.
10. What are the functions of the Krebs Cycle and the electron transport system?
11. How is fat used to synthesize ATP?
12. What are the capacities and powers of the three energy systems?
13. Under conditions of either rest or exercise, what are the three important features of the anaerobic and aerobic pathways that we must consider?
14. Discuss the considerations in question 13 as they would apply during rest and exercise.
15. Identify the predominant energy systems (phosphagen, anaerobic glycolysis, or oxygen system) used during the following activities: (a) 100-meter dash, (b) 400-meter dash, (c) 1500-meter run, and (d) marathon.

References

1. Brooks, G. A., and Fahey, T. D.: *Exercise Physiology: Human Bioenergetics and Its Applications.* New York, John Wiley, 1984, p. 82.
2. Cahill, G. F., Jr.: Metabolic role of muscle. In Pernow, B., and Saltin, B. (eds.): *Muscle Metabolism during Exercise.* New York, Plenum Press, 1971, pp. 103-109.
3. Costill, D. L.: Muscular exhaustion during distance running. *Physician Sportsmed.* 2(10):36-41, 1974.
4. Costill, D. L., and Fox, E. L.: Energetics of marathon running. *Med Sci Sports.* 1: 81-86, 1969.
5. Drinkwater, B. L.: Physiological responses of women to exercise. In Wilmore, J. L., (ed.): *Exercise and Sport Sciences Reviews,* vol. 1. New York, Academic Press, 1973, pp. 125-153.
6. Drinkwater, B. L., Horvath, S. M., and Wells, C. L.: Aerobic power of females, ages 10 to 68. *J Gerontol.* 30(4):385-394, 1975.
7. Fox, E. L., Billings, C. E., Bartels, R. L., Bason, R., and Mathews, D. K.: Fitness standards for male college students. *Int Z Angew Physiol.* 31:231-236, 1973.
8. Fox, E. L., and Costill, D. L.: Estimated cardiorespiratory responses during marathon running. *Arch Environ Health.* 24: 315-324, 1972.
9. Holloszy, J. O.: Muscle metabolism during exercise. *Arch Physical Med Rehab.* 63: 231-234, May, 1982.
10. Hultman, E.: Studies on muscle metabolism of glycogen and active phosphate in man with special reference to exercise and diet. *Scand J Clin Lab Invest* (Suppl 94). 19:1-63, 1967.
11. Hultman, E., Bergstrom, J., and McClennan-Anderson, N.: Breakdown and resynthesis of phosphocreatine and adenosine triphosphate in connection with muscular work in man. *Scand J Clin Invest.* 19:56-66, 1967.
12. Hultman, E., and Nilsson, L. H.: Liver glycogen in man. Effect of different diets and muscular exercise. In Pernow B., and Saltin, B. (eds.): *Muscle Metabolism during Exercise.* New York, Plenum Press, 1971, pp. 143-151.
13. Karlsson, J.: Lactate and phosphagen concentrations in working muscle of man. *Acta Physiol Scand* (Suppl). 358:1-72, 1971.
14. Karlsson, J., and Saltin, B.: Diet, muscle glycogen and endurance performance. *J Appl Physiol.* 31(2):203-206, 1971.
15. Lemon, P. W. R.: Effect of initial muscle glycogen levels on protein catabolism during exercise. *J Appl Physiol.* 48:624-629, 1980.
16. Lemon, P. W. R., and Nagle, F. J.: Effects of exercise on protein and amino acid metabolism. *Med Sci Sports Exercise.* 13:141-149, 1981.
17. Lehninger, A. L.: *Bioenergetics,* 2nd ed. New York, W. A. Benjamin, 1971, p. 100.
18. Robinson, S.: Physiology of muscular exercises. In Mountcastle, V. B. (ed.): *Medical Physiology,* 13th ed., vol. 2. St. Louis, C. V. Mosby, 1974, p. 1279.
19. Sahlin, K.: Intracellular pH and energy metabolism in skeletal muscle in man. *Acta Physiol Scand.* (Suppl 455). 1-56, 1978.
20. Saltin, B., and Astrand, P.-O.: Maximal oxygen uptake in athletes. *J Appl Physiol.* 23:353-358, 1967.
21. Saltin, B., and Karlsson, J.: Muscle glycogen utilization during work of different intensities. In Pernow, B., and Saltin, B. (eds.): *Muscle Metabolism during Exercise.* New York, Plenum Press, 1971, pp. 289-299.
22. Triveldi, B., and Danforth, W. H.: Effect of pH on kinetics of frog muscle phosphofructokinase. *J Biol Chem.* 241:4110-4112, 1966.

SELECTED READINGS

Fox, E. L.: *Sports Physiology.* Philadelphia, W. B. Saunders, 1984, pp. 1-53.
Gollnick, P. D., and Hermansen, L.: Biochemical adaptations to exercise: anaerobic metabolism. In Wilmore, J. H. (ed.): *Exercise and Sport Sciences Reviews,* vol. 1. New York, Academic Press, 1973, pp. 1-43.
Gollnick, P. D., and King, D. W.: Energy release in the muscle cell. *Med Sci Sports.* 1:23-31, 1969.
Hermansen, L.: Anaerobic energy release. *Med Sci Sports.* 1:32-38, 1969.
Holloszy, J. O.: Biochemical adaptations to exercise: aerobic metabolism. In Wilmore, J. H. (ed.): *Exercise and Sport Sciences Reviews,* vol. 1. New York, Academic Press, 1973, pp. 45-71.

Howald, H., and Poortmans, J. R. (eds.): *Metabolic Adaptations to Prolonged Physical Exercise*. Basel, Switzerland, Birkhauser-Verlag, 1975.

Keul, J., Doll, E., and Keppler, D.: *Energy Metabolism of Human Muscle* (Translated by J. S. Skinner). Baltimore, University Park Press, 1972.

Lehninger, A. L.: *Bioenergetics,* 2nd ed. New York, W. A. Benjamin, 1971.

Margaria, R.: *Biomechanics and Energetics of Muscular Exercise*. Oxford, Oxford University Press, 1976, pp. 1–58.

McGilvery, R. W.: The use of fuels for muscular work. In Howald, H., and Poortmans, J. R. (eds.): *Metabolic Adaptations to Prolonged Physical Exercise*. Basel, Switzerland, Birkhauser-Verlag, 1975, pp. 12–30.

McGilvery, R. W.: *Biochemistry: A Functional Approach*. Philadelphia, W. B. Saunders, 1983.

Milvey, P. (ed.): Metabolism in prolonged exercise. *Ann NY Acad Sci.* 301(1):3–97, 1977.

Pernow, B., and Saltin, B. (eds.): *Muscle Metabolism during Exercise*. New York, Plenum Press, 1971.

Poortmans, J. R. (ed.): *Biochemistry of Exercise*. Baltimore, University Park Press, 1968.

Sahlin, K., Palmskog, G., and Hultman, E.: Adenine nucleotide and IMP contents of the quadriceps muscle in man after exercise. *Pflugers Arch.* 374:193–198, 1978.

West, J. B.: *(Best and Taylors) Physiological Basis of Medical Practice*. Baltimore, Williams and Wilkins, 1985.

chapter 3

Recovery From Exercise

The major concepts to be learned from this chapter are as follows:

- The purpose during recovery from exercise is to restore the muscles and the rest of the body to their pre-exercise condition.
- Restoration of the body during recovery includes replenishing the energy stores that were depleted and removing lactic acid that was accumulated during exercise; both processes require ATP energy.
- The oxygen consumed during the recovery period, in part, supplies the immediate ATP energy required during the recovery period.
- Restoration of the muscle phosphagen stores (ATP + PC) requires only a few minutes, whereas full restoration of the muscle and liver glycogen stores requires a day or more.
- The speed of removal of lactic acid from blood and muscle can be greatly increased by performing light exercise rather than by resting during the recovery period.
- Small amounts of oxygen, stored in

muscle in chemical combination with myoglobin, are important during the performance of intermittent exercise, because they are used during the work intervals and are quickly restored during the recovery intervals.

In addition to understanding the different roles played by the metabolic energy systems during rest and exercise, we need to understand how the energy systems respond during the recovery process. Any form of exercise represents an acute disturbance in the homeostasis of the resting athlete. Recovery from exercise, then, represents the sum total of the processes that return the exerciser to the resting state. To address the complex processes of recovery, the following topics will be discussed: recovery oxygen (oxygen debt), replenishment of energy stores, removal of lactic acid from blood and muscle, and restoration of oxygen stores. Additionally, some practical guidelines for recovery will be included.

Terminology

It has been clear for a number of years now that the elevated oxygen consumption during recovery is reflective of more than merely replacing oxygen that was "borrowed" in exercise or to convert lactic acid

to pyruvic acid. For this reason, it has been suggested that the expression "recovery oxygen" be substituted for the classic "oxygen debt" expression. Further, oxygen consumption in recovery has two major components: a rapid-recovery oxygen phase and a slow-recovery oxygen phase. Traditionally, these have been termed the alactacid component and the lactacid component, respectively. Table 3-1 is a summary of the classic and suggested new terminology.

The Recovery Oxygen

We all know that during recovery from exercise our energy demand is considerably less since we are no longer exercising. However, our oxygen consumption continues at a relatively high level for a period of time, the length of which is dependent on the intensity of the preceding exercise. The amount of oxygen consumed during recovery—above that which would have ordinarily been consumed at rest in the same time—has been called the **recovery oxygen.** This is shown schematically in Figure 3-1. The term oxygen debt was first used in 1922 by the eminent British physiologist A. V. Hill.[36] This was the same year that he, jointly with O. Meyerhof, received a Nobel Prize for Physiology or Medicine.

The concept of recovery oxygen, previously called oxygen debt, as originally developed by Hill, meant that the oxygen

TABLE 3-1

New and Traditional Expressions for Components of Oxygen Consumption During Recovery From Exercise.

Traditional	Suggested	Abbreviation
1. Oxygen debt	Recovery oxygen	
2. Alactacid oxygen debt	Rapid-recovery O_2 phase	RRP
3. Lactacid oxygen debt	Slow-recovery O_2 phase	SRP

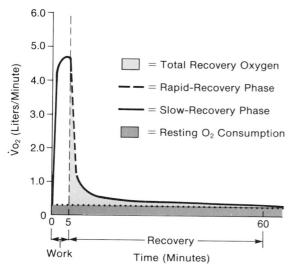

Figure 3-1. Recovery oxygen. The amount of oxygen consumed during recovery, above that which would have been consumed at rest in the same time is called the recovery oxygen. Recovery oxygen consumption consists of a rapid phase and a slow phase. (Based on data from Fox et al.[22])

Rapid-Recovery (Alactacid) and Slow-Recovery (Lactacid) Oxygen Consumption Components

You will notice in Figure 3-1 that the oxygen consumption following exhaustive exercise decreases exponentially with time. That is to say, the rate at which oxygen is consumed is not constant throughout the recovery period. During the first 2 or 3 minutes of recovery, oxygen consumption decreases very rapidly, then more slowly until a constant rate is reached. The initial rapid portion of the oxygen debt had been named the alactacid oxygen debt component but is now called the **rapid-recovery O_2 phase (RRP),** whereas the slower phase had been named the lactacid oxygen debt component, but is now called the **slow-recovery O_2 phase (SRP).**[36,49] The lactacid component was so named because at the time it was thought that the oxygen consumed during this phase of the debt was quantitatively related to the removal of the lactic acid accumulated in the blood and muscles during exercise. The term "alactacid" (the prefix "a" means *not*) was used because the oxygen consumed during the rapid portion of the debt was found to be independent of the removal of lactic acid during recovery. At one time, it was thought that the entire oxygen debt was lactacid in nature, i.e., that it resulted from the removal of the lactic acid accumulated during exercise.[35] When it was first shown in 1933 that an oxygen debt could be incurred in the absence of lactic acid accumulation, the term "alactacid oxygen debt" was used.[49] The elevated oxygen consumption during slow-recovery phase is now known to be associated with a number of physiological events including elevated body temperature, the oxygen cost of ventilation (see Chapter 8), glycogen resynthesis, the calorigenic effect of catecholamines, and the oxygen cost of heart activity. Hagberg, et al. state that the greater part of the slow-

consumed above the resting level during recovery was primarily used to provide energy for restoring the body to its pre-exercise condition, including replenishing the energy stores that were depleted and removing any lactic acid that was accumulated during exercise. Many erroneously interpret the older terminology, oxygen debt, to mean that the extra oxygen consumed during recovery is being used to replace oxygen that was "borrowed" from somewhere within the body during exercise. Actually, during maximal exercise, depletion of the oxygen stored in the muscle itself (in combination with myoglobin) and in the venous blood would amount to only about 0.6 liter. Recovery oxygen levels, on the other hand, have been found to be nearly 30 times larger than this in athletes after maximal exercise.

recovery phase oxygen consumption can be accounted for by the effect of temperature on metabolism.[26]

Replenishment of Energy Stores during Recovery

Two important questions to answer here are (1) What energy stores are depleted during exercise, and (2) how are they replenished during recovery? The first question should be easy for you to answer. You will recall that there are two sources of energy that are depleted to various extents during exercise: (1) the phosphagens ATP and PC stored in the muscle cells, and (2) the glycogen stored in large amounts in muscle as well as in the liver, which serves as an important source of fuel during most exercise activities. If you are wondering why fats have not been included in our list, the reason is that they are not replenished directly during recovery but instead are rebuilt indirectly through the replenishment of carbohydrates (glucose and glycogen). We will not concern ourselves too much with this latter point but will, in answering the second question, concentrate on the replenishment of the other two energy sources: ATP-PC and glycogen.

Restoration of ATP + PC and the Rapid-Recovery Phase

Direct measurement of the phosphagen stores in human skeletal muscle is rather difficult. However, several studies in which this was done have shown that most of the ATP and PC depleted in the muscle during exercise are restored very rapidly, i.e., within a few minutes following exercise.[29,39,42,43,52,53] The results of one of the first studies[39] of this kind are shown in Figure 3-2. In this experiment, the subjects rode a bicycle ergometer (stationary bicycle) for 10 minutes. Muscle tissue samples were taken from the vastus lateralis (one of the quadriceps muscles) by needle biopsy be-

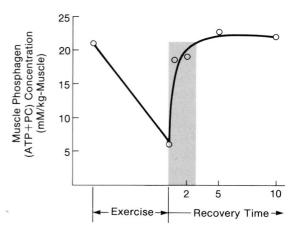

Figure 3-2. The muscular stores of ATP + PC that were depleted during exercise are restored within a few minutes following exercise. Notice that the phosphagen restoration is 70% completed in 30 seconds and essentially 100% completed within about 3 to 5 minutes. (Based on data from Hultman et al.[39])

fore exercise and at various times during recovery. The samples were subsequently analyzed for ATP and PC concentrations. Notice from the figure that the phosphagen restoration is very rapid at first (shaded area), then somewhat slower, being 70% completed within 30 seconds and 100% completed within 3 to 5 minutes.

In a more recent study,[29] the restoration of muscle phosphocreatine (PC) alone was examined, again in the vastus lateralis, during recovery from exhausting bicycle exercise. In these experiments, PC restoration was examined under two different recovery conditions: (1) when the muscles under study had a normal blood flow (intact circulation) and (2) when the blood flow to the muscles was occluded (occluded circulation). The results are shown in Figure 3-3. With an intact circulation, it can be seen that restoration of PC was very rapid at first (shaded area), then much slower. For example, after 2 minutes of recovery, 84% of the PC depleted during exercise was restored, with 89% restored

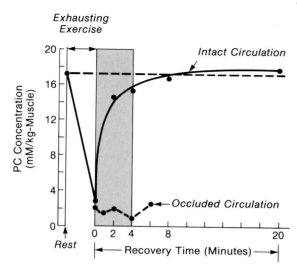

Figure 3-3. Restoration of PC during recovery from exhausting exercise. Two recoveries were used: (1) when the muscles had a normal blood flow (intact circulation) and (2) when the blood flow to the muscles was occluded (occluded circulation). With an intact circulation, the majority (90%) of PC was restored to the muscles within 4 minutes of recovery. No restoration of PC took place when the blood flow was occluded, indicating that oxygen is required for this process. (Based on data from Harris et al.[29])

after 4 minutes. By 8 minutes, 97% of the PC was restored to the muscles. Although the complete restoration of PC was somewhat longer in the last experiment, the findings essentially confirm the earlier studies in that the majority of the muscular stores of ATP and PC depleted during exercise are restored within a few minutes of recovery. In addition, the results from studies in which the muscle phosphagens have been directly measured agree with other studies that have indirectly or theoretically dealt with phosphagen restoration.[15,47,48]

Energetics of Phosphagen Restoration

The ATP energy required for phosphagen restoration is provided mainly by the aerobic system through the oxygen consumed during the RRP (alactacid debt) of the recovery oxygen period (oxygen debt).[17,52,53] The fact that oxygen is required for this process is clearly shown in Figure 3-3. Notice that when the blood flow (circulation), and thus the oxygen supply, to the muscles was occluded during recovery, no resynthesis of PC took place. Nevertheless, it has been recently suggested that a small part of the energy required for phosphagen restoration may also be derived without oxygen through anaerobic glycolysis.[11,18]

At any rate, as shown in Figure 3-4, the aerobic energy made available from phosphagen replenishment comes about from the breakdown of carbohydrate and fats (and perhaps a small amount of lactic acid) to CO_2 and H_2O via the Krebs Cycle and the electron transport system. Some of the ATP thus resynthesized is stored directly in the muscles, whereas some is broken down immediately, with the energy released used to resynthesize PC. Then PC is also stored in the muscle. It is important to emphasize that PC can only by resynthesized in coupled reactions from the energy released when ATP is broken down. In other words, ATP, but not PC, is directly resynthesized from the energy released from the breakdown of foods.

Since most of the energy for phosphagen restoration comes from the rapid-recovery phase, it too is repaid very rapidly and takes at most only about 3 minutes to be completed (Fig. 3-1). Its speed of repayment can be estimated from analysis of the oxygen consumption curve during the first few minutes of recovery. When estimated in this manner, the **half-reaction time** of repayment is about 30 seconds.[47] This means that in 30 seconds, ½ of the total alactacid debt is repaid; in 1 minute, ¾; in 1½ minutes, ⅞; and in 3 minutes, ⁶³/₆₄. However, as just pointed out, the actual rate at which the ATP and PC stores are replenished is somewhat greater, i.e., with 70% rather than 50% restored in 30 seconds.

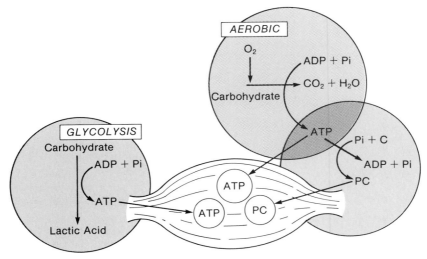

Figure 3-4. The oxygen consumed during the rapid-recovery phase of recovery oxygen provides the majority of energy necessary to replenish ATP and PC stores in muscle that were depleted during exercise. Some of the ATP resynthesized is directly stored in muscle, whereas some is broken down immediately to resynthesize PC (phosphocreatine), which is then stored in the muscle. Note that anaerobic glycolysis may also provide some energy (ATP) for phosphagen restoration. (From Fox, E. L.[21])

The reason for this discrepancy is that the amount of oxygen consumed during recovery includes not only that required to replenish the ATP and PC stores, but also (1) a certain amount of extra oxygen needed to replace the depleted oxygen stores (about 0.6 liter of oxygen in maximal exercise); (2) about 50 ml of extra oxygen required of the still-activated heart and respiratory muscles;[16,59] (3) a certain amount of extra oxygen required by the body in general due to increased tissue temperature;[8-10] and (4) catecholamine (norepinepherine) effects.[25] With these corrections, the half-reaction time is around 20 seconds, which is in close agreement with the actual phosphagen restoration rate as determined from muscle sample analysis.[17,47,49]

The greater the phosphagen depletion during exercise, the greater the oxygen required for the restoration during recovery. Thus these two quantities, phospha-gen restoration and the RRP levels, should be related. While such a relationship has not been experimentally determined, theoretically it should look like that shown in Figure 3-5. The relationship is based on the fact that it requires 3.45 liters of oxygen to manufacture one mole of ATP (p. 22). This idea has been used indirectly to evaluate the maximal phosphagen capacity in men[20] as well as in women[28] (see Fig. 14-5). Typical values for both the phosphagen stores (as given on p. 27) and the RRP are indicated in the figure by the shaded areas.

The maximum size of the rapid-recovery phase ranges between 2.0 and 3.0 liters of oxygen in untrained males;[54] higher values are associated with well-trained athletes. For example, RRP levels of over 6 liters have been recorded in male competitive rowers.[27] As shown by the relationship in Figure 3-5, such a large RRP can be interpreted to mean that a large amount of

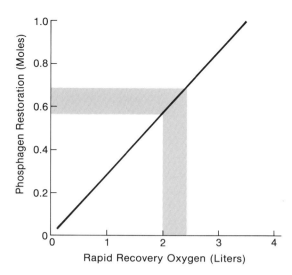

Figure 3-5. The greater the phosphagen depletion during exercise, the greater the amount of oxygen required during recovery for restoration. This relationship between the rapid-recovery phase and phosphagen restoration in muscle is based on the fact that 3.45 liters of oxygen are required to manufacture one mole of ATP. Typical values of phosphagen stores and rapid-recovery oxygen levels are illustrated by the shaded areas.

phosphagen was restored during recovery, and thus a large amount was depleted, or used, during exercise. This has important applications in physical education and athletics because the sprinter who can incur a large RRP level will be more successful, generally speaking, than one who incurs a smaller level. As we learned in the last chapter, the amount of ATP + PC available (capacity) and its rate of utilization (power) are directly related to the athlete's ability to generate and sustain power movements or activities such as sprinting. Through a properly designed training program, you can improve the phosphagen system and hence performance in such activities. On page 673 you will find a practical way in which to indirectly measure the power

capabilities of the phosphagen system of your athletes.

Muscle Glycogen Resynthesis

It was believed for nearly 50 years that the muscular stores of glycogen depleted during exercise were resynthesized from lactic acid during the immediate recovery period (1 to 2 hours) following exercise. It is now known that this is not true.[7,34,38,46,51] The full repletion of the muscle glycogen stores following exercise requires several days and is dependent upon two major factors: (1) the type of exercise performed that caused the glycogen depletion, and (2) the amount of dietary carbohydrate consumed during the recovery period. There are two different types of exercises that have been used to study muscle glycogen depletion and repletion: (1) *continuous endurance-like activities;* i.e., low-intensity, long-duration exercises; and (2) *intermittent, exhaustive activities,* i.e., high-intensity, short-duration exercises. Our discussion will center on these two types of exercises and will include in each a discussion of the influence of the dietary intake of carbohydrates.

1. *Muscle Glycogen Depletion and Repletion—Continuous Endurance Exercise.* The pattern of muscle glycogen depletion–repletion during and following endurance exercise is shown in Figure 3-6. The exercise in these studies consisted of 1 hour of endurance activities (e.g., swimming, running, or bicycling) followed by 1 hour of heavier, exhausting exercise. One can observe from the figure that:

(a) Only an insignificant amount of muscle glycogen is resynthesized within the immediate recovery period (1 to 2 hours) following endurance exercise;

(b) The complete resynthesis of muscle glycogen following endurance exercise requires a high dietary in-

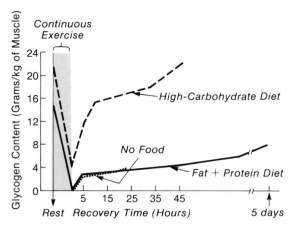

Figure 3-6. Only an insignificant amount of muscle glycogen is resynthesized within the immediate recovery period following continuous, prolonged exercise. The complete resynthesis of muscle glycogen following this kind of exercise requires a high dietary intake of carbohydrate over at least a 2-day (46-hour) period. Without carbohydrate intake, only a small amount of glycogen is resynthesized even over a 5-day period. (Based on data from Hultman and Bergström[38] and Piehl.[51])

take of carbohydrates over a 2-day (≅46-hour) recovery period.

(c) Without a high carbohydrate intake only a small amount of glycogen is resynthesized even over a 5-day period; and

(d) Replenishment of muscle glycogen following a high-carbohydrate diet is most rapid during the first several hours of recovery from endurance exercise, being 60% completed in 10 hours.

(e) There appears to be no difference in glycogen resynthesis whether simple sugars (sucrose, glucose) or complex sugars (starches) are consumed during the first 24 hours following exhaustive work. However, the next 24 hours saw greater glycogen storage with complex carbohydrates as the food source.[13]

From a practical viewpoint, the preceding information is important to coaches and endurance athletes. The reason for this is related to the importance of muscle glycogen as a metabolic fuel during heavy and prolonged exercise activities. As mentioned in Chapter 2, glycogen represents the only metabolic fuel for anaerobic glycolysis and is a major fuel for the aerobic system during various stages of endurance activities. There is also some evidence that when the glycogen stores within a muscle are low or depleted, muscle fatigues, even though fats are still available as fuel.[3,31] Thus, adequate levels of muscle glycogen should be maintained at all times. This is not always easy, given severe endurance training schedules, such as running several miles every day, and given the 2 days required to fully replenish the glycogen stores. An example of this is shown in Figure 3-7. The muscle glycogen stores were progressively depleted over a 3-day period during which 16 kilometers (10 miles) were run each day.[12] This occurred in spite of the fact that the runners consumed normal amounts of carbohydrates during this time.

2. *Muscle Glycogen Depletion and Repletion—Intermittent, Short-Duration*

Figure 3-7. The muscle glycogen stores are progressively depleted over a 3-day period when 16 kilometers (10 miles) are run each day. (Based on data from Costill et al.[12])

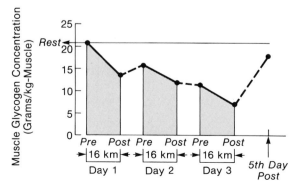

Exercise. Several recent studies[34,46] have been conducted in which muscle glycogen replenishment has been examined following intermittent, short-duration exercise. The results of these studies are shown in Figure 3-8*A* and *B*. In *A*, the exercise consisted of riding a bicycle ergometer at very heavy loads for 1-minute intervals with 3 minutes of rest between bouts. This pattern was continued until the subjects were exhausted and could no longer maintain at least 30 seconds of work during one of the exercise bouts. During the recovery period, either a normal, mixed diet or a high-carbohydrate diet was consumed. In *B*, the subjects performed three exhausting 1-minute exercise bouts, again on a bicycle ergometer, with 4 minutes of rest allowed between bouts. The recovery was followed for only 30 minutes during which time no food was consumed by the subjects. The following conclusions concerning muscle glycogen resynthesis after intermittent exercise were based on the results of these studies (Fig. 3-8):

Figure 3-8. Muscle glycogen resynthesis following intermittent exercise to exhaustion. Notice that significant amounts of glycogen can be resynthesized within, *B*, 30 minutes to, *A*, 2 hours of recovery even in the absence of food intake. Notice also, *A*, that complete resynthesis of muscle glycogen following this kind of exercise requires 24 hours. (Data in *A* from MacDougall et al.;[46] data in *B* from Hermansen and Vaage.[34])

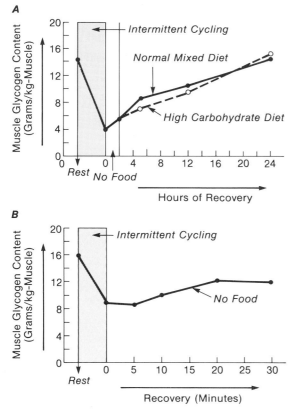

(a) A significant amount of muscle glycogen can be resynthesized within 30 minutes to 2 hours of recovery and in the absence of food (carbohydrate) intake.

(b) The complete resynthesis of muscle glycogen does *not* require a greater-than-normal intake of carbohydrates.

(c) With either a normal or a high-carbohydrate diet, complete resynthesis of muscle glycogen requires a 24-hour recovery period.

(d) Muscle glycogen resynthesis is most rapid during the first several hours of recovery, being 39% completed in 2 hours and 53% completed in 5 hours.

The fact that significant amounts of muscle glycogen can be resynthesized within 2 hours of recovery from intermittent, short-duration exercise without food intake is also important for the coach to know and has application to the nonendurance athlete who often must compete several times in one day (e.g., heats in track and swimming events, and gymnastics, wrestling, and basketball tournaments).

Physiological Factors Related to Differences in Muscle Glycogen Resynthesis

Why is muscle glycogen resynthesis different following continuous versus intermittent exercise? The answer to this question is not entirely known. However, there are several factors that may be involved. One of these may be related to the overall amount of glycogen depleted during exercise. For example, with continuous exercise, about twice the amount of glycogen was depleted than with intermittent exercise (compare Figs. 3-7 and 3-8). Thus with less overall glycogen to resynthesize, less time is needed. This idea is supported by the fact that in the first 24 hours of recovery, about the same total amount of glycogen was resynthesized regardless of whether the preceding exercise was continuous or intermittent.

Another factor that may be important here has to do with the availability of **glycogen precursors.** In order to synthesize glycogen (as well as any compound), adequate amounts of its constituents (precursors) must also be available. Common precursors of glycogen are lactic acid, pyruvic acid, and glucose (to name a few). These must be available to the liver and muscle in which most of the resynthesis begins. Following prolonged continuous exercise, most of these precursors are found in limited amounts, whereas following intermittent exercise, they are usually in normal or even in above-normal amounts. Therefore, following intermittent exercise, glycogen synthesis starts sooner. Also, this idea helps explain why the dietary intake of carbohydrates is required following continuous exercise, but not following intermittent, and why a greater-than-normal intake of carbohydrate does not accelerate glycogen resynthesis following intermittent exercise.

A final factor that may help explain differences in glycogen resynthesis following various kinds of exercise might be related to the different types of fibers found in skeletal muscle. Most human muscles contain two basic fiber types: a **fast, glycolytic fiber (FG),** which is preferentially recruited during the performance of short-duration, high-intensity work (such as the intermittent exercises being discussed here), and a **slow, oxidative fiber (SO),** which is used preferentially during prolonged, continuous exercise. There is some evidence that glycogen resynthesis in FG fibers is faster than in SO fibers.[51] Consequently, glycogen resynthesis would be expected to be faster following intermittent exercise, since FG fibers are used to a greater extent in this kind of activity than in endurance exercise. For more information on fiber types and their characteristics read Chapter 5.

Energetics of Muscle Glycogen Resynthesis

The resynthesis of glycogen involves a series of complicated chemical reactions, each requiring specific enzymes.[45] Whereas for our purposes we will not need to discuss these reactions in detail, it should be made clear that such a process requires energy. For the most part, this energy comes in the form of ATP generated by the aerobic system. Part of this energy requirement might be met through the oxygen consumed during SRP. However, this would be true only for the glycogen resynthesized during the immediate post-exercise recovery period (1 to 2 hours), since the slow-recovery phase is generally completed by this time. Also, it should be mentioned that a quantitative relationship between glycogen resynthesis during recovery and the ATP energy provided by the SRP has not been experimentally determined.

Muscle Glycogen Supercompensation

The amount and rate of glycogen resynthesis in skeletal muscle during recovery from exercise can be increased to values much higher than normal (supercompensated) by following a special exercise–diet procedure. This information has proven to be useful to the coach insofar as the training table is concerned, for such a procedure has been shown to significantly improve endurance performance. More detailed information concerning muscle glycogen supercompensation appears in Chapter 19.

Liver Glycogen Replenishment

As mentioned in the last chapter, liver glycogen represents a sizable energy store. Unfortunately, not many studies in humans have been conducted in which the liver glycogen stores were examined. However, the results of one such study[40] are shown in Figure 3-9. In this study, liver glycogen concentration was determined at rest (by removing a small piece of tissue with a special biopsy needle), following 1 hour of heavy bicycle exercise (Fig. 3-9A) and during several days of carbohydrate starvation followed by a high-carbohydrate diet (Fig. 3-9B). As can be seen from the figure, liver glycogen is considerably reduced following exercise with a further reduction during several days of carbohydrate starvation. Notice also that an overshoot, or supercompensation, takes place within 1 day after carbohydrate refeeding. In rats[7] it has been shown that no resynthesis of liver glycogen occurs during 24 hours of recovery from exercise during which time no food is consumed. Although comparable studies on humans have not been conducted, it is reasonable to assume that similar results would be found. As with muscle glycogen resynthesis, the energy requirement for liver glycogen re-

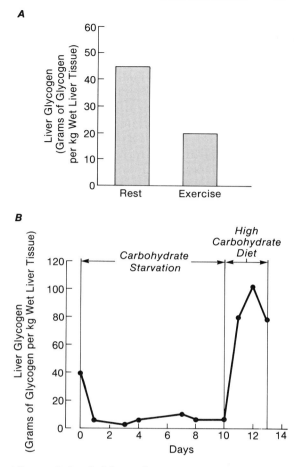

Figure 3-9. *A,* Liver glycogen is considerably reduced following exercise, *B,* with a further reduction during several days of carbohydrate starvation. Note the overshoot, or supercompensation, 1 day after carbohydrate refeeding. (Based on data from Hultman and Nilsson.[40])

synthesis is derived from the aerobic system.

Removal of Lactic Acid from Blood and Muscle

It was mentioned in the last chapter that when lactic acid, the product of anaerobic glycolysis, accumulates in blood and muscle, fatigue sets in. Therefore, full recovery from exercises in which maximal amounts of lactic acid have accumulated involves the removal of lactic acid from both the blood and the skeletal muscles that were active during the preceding exercise period.

Several important questions related to this process that need answering are (1) how long does it take to remove the accumulated lactic acid, (2) what factors influence the speed of lactic acid removal, (3) what happens to the lactic acid, and (4) what is the relationship between the removal of lactic acid during recovery and the slow-recovery phase?

Speed of Lactic Acid Removal

The time course of the removal of lactic acid from blood and muscle is shown in Figure 3-10. The exercise in this case consisted of five 1-minute bouts of pedaling on a bicycle ergometer.[44] Five-minute rest periods were allowed between work bouts. During the recovery period, the subjects (all males) rested while seated on the bi-

Figure 3-10. Lactic acid is removed from the blood and muscles during recovery from exhausting exercise. In general, 25 minutes of rest-recovery are required to remove half of the accumulated lactic acid. (Based on data from Karlsson and Saltin.[44])

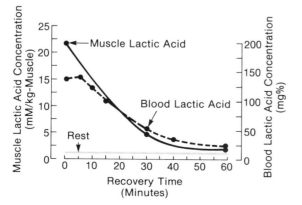

cycle **(rest-recovery).** Notice that it required at least 1 hour of recovery to remove most of the accumulated lactic acid. The same amount of time is also required following running to exhaustion on a treadmill.[22] In general, it can be said that 25 minutes of rest-recovery are required following maximal exercise in order to remove half of the accumulated lactic acid.[32] This means that about 95% of the lactic acid will be removed in 1 hour and 15 minutes of rest-recovery from maximal exercise.

The lactic acid concentrations shown in the figure represent average maximal values for both muscle and blood. During submaximal, but heavy, exercise, in which the accumulation of lactic acid is not as great, less time is required for its removal during recovery.

Effects of Exercise during Recovery on the Speed of Lactic Acid Removal

You probably noticed that the term "rest-recovery" was used in the preceding discussion. This means, as pointed out before, that the subjects rested throughout the duration of the recovery period. It has been demonstrated that lactic acid can be removed from blood and muscle more rapidly following heavy to maximal exercise by performing light exercise rather than by resting throughout the recovery period.[2,4-6, 24,32,33] Such a recovery is referred to as **exercise-recovery** and is similar to the warm-down procedures that most athletes have practiced for many years. An example of the effects of exercise-recovery on lactic acid removal is shown in Figure 3-11. In these experiments,[4] the subjects ran a mile on 3 separate days. Three different recovery periods were used: (1) rest, (2) continuous exercise consisting of jogging at a self-selected pace, and (3) intermittent exercise of the kind normally practiced by athletes. Both exercise-recoveries resulted in substantial increases in the rate of lactic

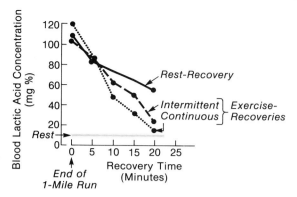

Figure 3-11. Lactic acid can be removed from blood and muscle more rapidly following heavy to maximal exercise by performing light exercise during recovery (exercise-recovery) rather than by resting throughout the recovery period. (Based on data from Bonen and Belcastro.[4])

acid removed from the blood. Note also that the removal rate was fastest during the continuous jogging recovery. From this information, it would be wise to advise athletes to exercise continuously throughout the recovery period rather than intermittently, which is their normal practice.

How much exercise should be performed during recovery in order to promote optimal lactic acid removal? The answer to this question can be found in Figure 3-12. The rate of blood lactic acid removal (vertical axis) is shown plotted against the intensity of the exercise performed during recovery (horizontal axis). The latter is expressed in three different units: (1) the amount of oxygen consumed during exercise ($\dot{V}O_2$) as a percentage of the subject's maximal aerobic power (per cent $\dot{V}O_2$max);* (2) as milli-

liters of oxygen consumed per kilogram of body weight per minute of exercise (ml/kg-min); and (3) as the amount of oxygen consumed during exercise in liters per minute (L/min). The recovery exercise intensity that produces the fastest or optimal rate of removal of blood lactic acid has been calculated to be between 30% and 45% $\dot{V}O_2$max. This corresponds to oxygen consumptions between 1.0 to 1.5 L/min, or between 15 to 20 ml/kg-min (shaded area in figure). However, it should be pointed out that these figures were calculated for exercise-recovery performed on a bicycle ergometer with untrained subjects. With trained subjects performing recovery exercise consisting of running or walking, it has been shown that lactic acid removal is optimal at intensities between 50% and 65% $\dot{V}O_2$max.[24,33] The major reason for this difference is probably more related to the state of training of the subjects than to the difference in exercise

Figure 3-12. For untrained subjects, the recovery exercise that produces the fastest or optimal rate of removal of blood lactic acid is one in which the oxygen consumption ($\dot{V}O_2$) is between 30% and 45% $\dot{V}O_2$max, or 1.0 to 1.5 liters per minute, or 15 to 20 milliliters per kilogram of body weight per minute (shaded area). (Based on data from Belcastro and Bonen.[2])

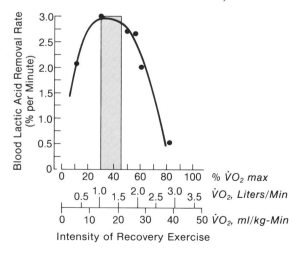

*For example, if a subject's $\dot{V}O_2$max is 50 milliliters of oxygen per kilogram of body weight per minute (ml/kg-min), or 3.5 liters of oxygen per minute (L/min), then an exercise load requiring 25 ml/kg-min, or 1.75 L/min, would represent 50% $\dot{V}O_2$max (25/50, or 1.75/3.5 × 100 = 50%).

modes (running or walking versus bicycling). In other words, the higher the fitness level, the higher the recovery exercise intensity for optimal lactic acid removal.

One more point about Figure 3-12 needs mentioning. When the intensity of the recovery exercise is either below or above the optimal limits (shaded area), lactic acid is removed more slowly. In fact, notice that when the intensity of the recovery exercise is greater than 60% $\dot{V}O_2$max, the removal rate of lactic acid is actually less than that during rest-recovery. The reason for this is that during the recovery exercise itself, more lactic acid is being produced.

One investigator suggested that active recovery should be nearer 70% of $\dot{V}O_2$max for the first several minutes, then about 40% of $\dot{V}O_2$max for the later recovery period.[57] Intuitively, the elite middle distance athlete often appears to follow this procedure after a race—a fairly rapid pace for a few minutes followed by a longer slow pace.

Fate of Lactic Acid—Physiology of Lactic Acid Removal

So far we have learned that lactic acid is removed from blood and muscle during recovery from exercise, and that its removal is faster during exercise-recovery than during rest-recovery. Our next task is to learn what happens to the lactic acid and why its removal is faster during exercise-recovery.

There are four possible fates of lactic acid.

1. *Excretion in Urine and Sweat.* Lactic acid is known to be excreted in the urine[41] and sweat.[1] However, the amount of lactic acid removed in this manner during recovery from exercise is negligible.

2. *Conversion to Glucose and/or Glycogen.* Since lactic acid is a break-down product of carbohydrate (glucose and glycogen), it can be reconverted to either of these compounds in the liver (glycogen and glucose) and in muscle (glycogen) given the required ATP energy. However, as previously mentioned, glycogen resynthesis in muscle and liver is extremely slow compared with lactic acid removal. In addition, the magnitude of the changes in the blood glucose levels during recovery are also minimal. Therefore, conversion of lactic acid to glucose and glycogen accounts for only a minor fraction of the total lactic acid removed.[7,14,23]

3. *Conversion to Protein.* Carbohydrates, including lactic acid, can be chemically converted into protein within the body. However, once again, only a relatively small amount of lactic acid has been shown to be converted to protein during the immediate recovery period following exercise.[23]

4. *Oxidation/Conversion to CO_2 and H_2O.* Lactic acid can be used as a metabolic fuel for the oxygen system, mostly by skeletal muscle,[7,23,32,33,37] but heart muscle,[56] brain,[50] liver,[51] and kidney[60] tissues are also capable of this function. In the presence of oxygen, lactic acid is first converted to pyruvic acid and then to CO_2 and H_2O in the Krebs Cycle and the electron transport system, respectively. Of course, ATP is resynthesized in coupled reactions in the electron transport system.

The use of lactic acid as a metabolic fuel for the aerobic system accounts for the majority of the lactic acid removed during recovery from exercise. While this holds true for both rest- and exercise-recoveries, oxidation accounts for more lactic acid removal in the latter than in the former. As just mentioned, several organs are known to be capable of oxidizing lactic acid. However, it is fairly well agreed that skeletal muscle is the major organ involved in this process.[7,23,32,33,37] In fact, most of the lactic acid oxidized by muscle is thought to occur within slow-twitch rather than fast-twitch fibers.[4-6] These are major reasons why lactic acid removal is faster during exercise-recovery than during rest-recovery. For example, in the former, both the blood flow carrying lactic acid to the muscles and the metabolic rate of the active muscles are greatly increased. In addition, the type of exercise used during most exercise-recoveries preferentially recruits slow-twitch fibers to perform the work.

A summary of the fate of the lactic acid removed from blood and muscle during rest-recovery is shown in Figure 3-13. The percentages given in the figure were determined from experiments performed on rats after 4 hours of recovery.[23]

Lactic Acid Removal and the Slow-Recovery Phase

As mentioned earlier (p. 41), it was once thought that the oxygen consumed during the SRP of the recovery oxygen time was quantitatively related to the removal of lactic acid during the immediate recovery period from exercise. As shown in Figure

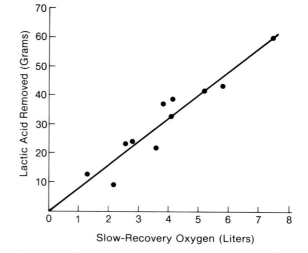

Figure 3-14. A relationship exists between the oxygen consumed during the slow-recovery phase and the removal of lactic acid from the blood; however, the exact amount of oxygen required to remove a given quantity of lactic acid varies considerably. (Based on data from Fox et al.[23])

3-14, a relationship has been experimentally determined between the slow-recovery phase and the removal of lactic acid from the blood. However, the exact amount of oxygen required to remove a given quantity of lactic acid varies considerably.[24,55] Such a poor quantitative relationship is not surprising, for, as we have seen, there are many possible fates of lactic acid, each of which requires varying amounts of energy. Nevertheless, it is reasonable to suspect that at least part of the oxygen and ATP energy requirement associated with lactic acid removal is met by the oxygen consumed during the slow-recovery phase.

The size of the slow-recovery phase is not greatly affected by intensities of work below 65% of $\dot{V}O_2$max. However, in exercise above 65% $\dot{V}O_2$max and longer than 5 minutes, the slow-recovery phase has a greater magnitude.[26] The maximum size of the SRP normally ranges between 5 and 10 liters[22]

Figure 3-13. The fate of lactic acid. The lactic acid removed from blood and muscle during recovery can be converted to glucose, protein, glycogen, or CO_2 and H_2O (oxidized). The last two conversions are the major fates. (Based on data from Gaesser and Brooks.[23])

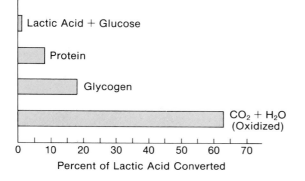

and is usually larger in athletes, particularly in those who train for and participate in sprintlike activities.

As implied by the name, the slow-recovery phase (SRP) of recovery oxygen time is slow compared with that of the rapid-recovery phase (RRP). For example, the SRP has a half-reaction time of 15 minutes, about 30 times slower than that of the RRP.[47] This means that after an hour of rest-recovery, the SRP is generally completed. During exercise-recovery, the SRP is not only smaller by about 1 to 2 liters, but is reduced more quickly.[24]

Restoration of Oxygen Stores

Earlier, it was mentioned that oxygen is stored within the body (p. 41). Although these stores are small, they are of importance during exercise, particularly intermittent exercise, because they are used during the work periods and are then replenished during the rest periods.

O_2-Myoglobin Stores

Oxygen is stored mainly in the muscle in chemical combination with **myoglobin,** a complex protein compound similar to hemoglobin found in the blood. In fact, myoglobin is often referred to as muscle hemoglobin. Although myoglobin acts as a store for oxygen, it also is thought to be involved functionally in the actual transfer (diffusion) of oxygen from the blood (capillaries) to the mitochondria within the muscle cell where it is consumed. Thus myoglobin has a dual role: storage of oxygen and facilitation of the diffusion of oxygen from blood to the mitochondria.

Size and Importance of
O_2-Myoglobin Stores

As just mentioned, the O_2-myoglobin stores are small. For example, it has been estimated that only 11.2 milliliters (ml) of oxygen are stored with myoglobin per kilogram (kg) of muscle mass.[30] Assuming a total of 30 kg (66 pounds) of muscle mass in a person weighing 70 kg (154 pounds), this amounts to around 336 ml of oxygen (30 $\times$ 11.2 = 336 ml O_2). In athletes, who generally have larger muscle masses, the total O_2-myoglobin stores, although larger, may still be only 500 ml.* However, the O_2-myoglobin stores are important during intermittent exercise not because of their size, but because of their rapid restoration during the recovery periods. This allows them to be used over and over during the work periods of the exercise. An example of this effect is shown in Figure 3-15. The intermittent work performed in these experiments consisted of alternating 15 seconds of work on a bicycle ergometer with 15 seconds of rest-recovery for 1 hour. It was calculated that the O_2-myoglobin stores contributed 20% of the total ATP energy required during this time.[19] This was more than from either the stored phosphagens or anaerobic glycolysis.

The importance of the oxygen stores can be further emphasized by the following calculations:

1. Assuming that the total muscle mass involved during the intermittent work performed in the preceding experiments was 15 kg, then the total O_2-myoglobin stores involved was 15 $\times$ 11.2 = 168 ml of oxygen.
2. Alternating 15 seconds of work with 15 seconds of rest-recovery over a period of 1 hour means that there were two rest-recovery periods each minute, or 120 over the hour. Assuming that only half of the stores were replenished during each of the rest-recovery

---

*Assuming that the stored oxygen is used in breaking down carbohydrate, 500 ml of oxygen would resynthesize 145 millimoles, or .145 moles, of ATP, enough to meet the energy requirements for about 2 minutes of rest.

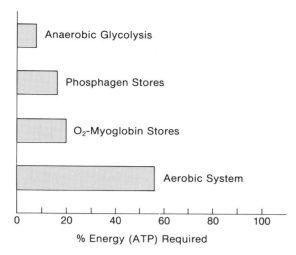

x-axis labels: Anaerobic Glycolysis, Phosphagen Stores, O₂-Myoglobin Stores, Aerobic System

% Energy (ATP) Required

Figure 3-15. The O_2-myoglobin stores are important during intermittent exercise because they are used during the work intervals and are quickly restored during the recovery intervals. As shown here, 20% of the total energy required during 1 hour of work consisting of 15 seconds of work alternated with 15 seconds of recovery was derived from the O_2-myoglobin stores. (Based on data from Essén et al.[19])

periods, then $168/2 = 84$ ml of oxygen were restored per rest period, or $84 \times 120 = 10{,}080$ ml, or 10 liters, of oxygen over the hour. This represents a substantial amount of oxygen for use during the work periods, e.g., enough to generate 3 moles of ATP aerobically.

Mechanism of Replenishment of the O₂-Myoglobin Stores

Since oxygen is bound to myoglobin in chemical combination, the restoration of the O_2-myoglobin stores depends mainly on the availability of oxygen. In turn, the availability of oxygen is dependent upon its *partial pressure.* The concept of partial pressure will be discussed in a later chapter (p. 225). For our present purposes, we need only to remember that during exercise, particularly heavy exercise, the availability of oxygen (partial pressure) is low. Consequently, the oxygen that was combined with myoglobin is released to the muscle and is eventually given up to the mitochondria. Just the opposite is true during recovery from exercise. Here the availability of oxygen is greatly increased, causing a recharging of myoglobin with oxygen, a process that is thought to require only a few seconds to complete.[19] As pointed out earlier (p. 44), the oxygen consumed during the rapid-recovery phase supplies the necessary oxygen for restoration of the O_2-myoglobin stores.

Some Practical Recovery Guidelines

From the previous discussion, you should be able to draw some practical guidelines concerning minimal and maximal times required for adequate recovery from various exhausting exercise performances. To check yourself, see Table 3-2.

Summary

The purpose during recovery from exercise is to restore the muscles and the rest of the body to their pre-exercise condition.

During recovery from exercise, oxygen consumption remains elevated above resting levels. The additional oxygen consumed above rest is termed the recovery oxygen. During the first 2 or 3 minutes of recovery, there is a high rate of oxygen consumption followed by a gradual decline to near resting levels. The initial 2 to 3 minutes of recovery has been named the rapid-recovery phase, whereas the slower phase has been named the slow-recovery phase.

Most of the muscular stores of ATP and PC that were depleted during exercise are rapidly restored during the first 3 to 5 minutes of the recovery period. The ATP energy required for this process is supplied mainly by the aerobic system through the

TABLE 3-2

Suggested Minimum and Maximum Recovery Times Following Exhaustive Exercise

Recovery Process	Suggested Recovery Time	
	Minimum	Maximum
Restoration of muscle phosphagen stores (ATP + PC)	2 min	5 min
Reduction of the rapid-recovery phase	3 min	5 min
Muscle glycogen resynthesis	10 hr {after continuous exercise}	46 hr
	5 hr {after intermittent exercise}	24 hr
Liver glycogen replenishment	unknown	12–24 hr
Removal of lactic acid from blood and muscle	30 min {exercise-recovery}	1 hr
	1 hr {rest-recovery}	2 hr
Reduction of the slow-recovery phase	30 min	1 hr
Restoration of O_2 stores	10–15 sec	1 min

oxygen consumed during the rapid-recovery phase. The repayment of the rapid-recovery phase is completed in only a few minutes. The maximum size of the rapid-recovery phase ranges between 2 and 3 liters of oxygen, although much higher values have been recorded in trained athletes.

Restoration of the muscle and liver glycogen stores depleted during exercise is dependent upon the type of exercise performed (continuous versus intermittent) and may require several days for completion, during which time dietary intake of carbohydrates is necessary. Following continuous, exhausting exercise, muscle glycogen restoration is 60% completed in 10 hours of recovery and is fully completed within 46 hours. Following intermittent, exhausting exercise, restoration of muscle glycogen is 53% completed in 5 hours and is fully completed in 24 hours. Only small amounts of muscle and liver glycogen are restored within the immediate (1 to 2 hours) recovery period following maximal exercise of either type. The ATP energy for muscle and liver glycogen restoration

comes from the aerobic system, but does not involve, to a great extent, the oxygen consumed during the slow-recovery phase.

The lactic acid accumulated in blood and muscle during exercise is removed during the recovery period. The speed of lactic acid removal depends on whether one rests during recovery (rest-recovery) or performs light exercise (30 to 65% $\dot{V}O_2$max) during recovery (exercise-recovery). Lactic acid is removed faster during exercise-recovery. The fate of the lactic acid removed is (1) conversion to glucose and/or glycogen, (2) conversion to protein, and (3) oxidation to CO_2 and H_2O by the aerobic system. The major fate is oxidation, which occurs mainly in skeletal muscle, but also occurs in heart, kidney, liver, and brain tissues. Although at least part of the oxygen and ATP energy required for lactic acid removal probably comes from the slow-recovery phase, no quantitative relationship between the two has been determined. The maximal size of the slow-recovery phase is usually between 5 and 10 liters of oxygen.

Oxygen is stored in skeletal muscle in chemical combination with myoglobin. Although the stores are small, they are of importance during intermittent exercise because they are used during the work periods and are restored during the rest periods. Restoration of the O_2-myoglobin stores during recovery is rapid, requiring only a few seconds, and is dependent upon the availability (partial pressure) of oxygen. The oxygen is part of the rapid-recovery phase.

Questions

1. Describe the revision of post-exercise oxygen-consumption terminology.
2. Define recovery oxygen and its components.
3. How rapidly are the phosphagen stores (ATP + PC) replenished during recovery?
4. What is the relationship between restoration of the ATP and PC stores in the muscle and the rapid-recovery component?
5. How large is the rapid-recovery phase and what is the significance of its size?
6. Discuss the restoration of the muscle glycogen stores with respect to: (a) the type (continuous versus intermittent) of previous exercise performed; (b) the presence or absence of food intake during recovery; (c) the physiological factors related to the different rates of glycogen restoration; and (d) the energetics of glycogen replenishment.
7. What are the effects of exercise, diet, and recovery from exercise on liver glycogen stores?
8. What is meant by rest-recovery and exercise-recovery, and how do they influence the rate of lactic acid removed?
9. Discuss the fate of lactic acid removed during recovery. What organs and tissues are involved in this process?
10. What is the relationship between lactic acid removal and the rapid-recovery phase?
11. Explain the importance of the oxygen stores during intermittent exercise.
12. Suppose an athlete were to compete first in the 800-meter run, then about an hour or so later in the 1500-meter run. What would you as a coach tell the athlete concerning the fastest way to recover between events?

References

1. Astrand, I.: Lactate content in sweat. *Acta Physiol Scand.* 58:359–367, 1963.
2. Belcastro, A. N., Bonen, A.: Lactic acid removal rates during controlled and uncontrolled recovery exercise. *J Appl Physiol.* 39(6):932–936, 1975.
3. Bergstrom, J., Hermansen, L., Hultman, E., and Saltin, B.: Diet, muscle glycogen and physical performance. *Acta Physiol Scand.* 71:140–150, 1967.
4. Bonen, A., and Belcastro, A. N.: Comparison of self-selected recovery methods on lactic acid removal rates. *Med Sci Sports.* 8(3):176–178, 1976.
5. Bonen, A., Campbell, C. J., Kirby, R. L., and Belcastro, A. N.: A multiple regression model for blood lactate removal in man. *Pflugers Arch.* 380:205–210, 1979.
6. Bonen, A., Campbell, C. J., Kirby, R. L., and Belcastro, A. N.: Relationship between slow-twitch muscle fibers and lactic acid removal. *Can J Appl Sport Sci.* 3:160–162, 1978.
7. Brooks, G. A., Brauner, K. E., and Cassens, R. G.: Glycogen synthesis and metabolism of lactic acid after exercise. *Am J Physiol.* 224:1162–1166, 1973.
8. Brooks, G. A., Hittelman, K. J., Faulkner, J. A., and Beyer, R. E.: Temperature, liver mitochondrial respiratory functions, and oxygen debt. *Med Sci Sports.* 3(2):72–74, 1971.
9. Brooks, G. A., Hittelman, K. J., Faulkner, J. A., and Beyer, R. E.: Temperature, skeletal muscle mitochondrial functions, and oxygen debt. *Am J Physiol.* 220(4):1053–1059, 1971.
10. Brooks, G. A., Hittelman, K. J., Faulkner, J. A., and Beyer, R. E.: Tissue temperatures and whole-animal oxygen consumption after exercise. *Am J Physiol.* 221(2):427–431, 1971.

11. Cerretelli, P., Ambrosoli, G., Fumagalli, M.: Anaerobic recovery in man. *Europ J Appl Physiol.* 34:141–148, 1975.

12. Costill, D. L., Bowers, R. W., Branam, G., and Sparks, K.: Muscle glycogen utilization during prolonged exercise on successive days. *J Appl Physiol.* 31:834–838, 1971.

13. Costill, D. L., Sherman, W. M., Fink, W. J., Maresh, C., Witten, M., and Miller, J. M.: The role of dietary carbohydrate in muscle glycogen resynthesis after strenuous running. *Am J Clin Nutri.* 34:1831–1836, 1982.

14. Depocas, F., Minaire, Y., and Charonnet, J.: Rates of formation and oxidation of lactic acid in dogs at rest and during moderate exercise. *Can J Physiol Pharmacol.* 47:603–610, 1969.

15. diPrampero, P. E.: The alactic oxygen debt: its power, capacity and efficiency. In Pernow, B., and Saltin, B. (eds.): *Muscle Metabolism during Exercise.* New York, Plenum Press, 1971, pp. 371–382.

16. diPrampero, P. E., and Margaria, R.: Mechanical efficiency of phosphagen (ATP + PC) splitting and its speed of resynthesis. *Pflugers Arch.* 308:197–202, 1969.

17. diPrampero, P. E., and Margaria, R.: Relationship between O_2 consumption, high energy phosphates and the kinetics of the O_2 debt in exercise. *Pflugers Arch.* 304:11–19, 1968.

18. diPrampero, P. E., Peeters, L., and Margaria, R.: Alactic O_2 debt and lactic acid production after exhausting exercise in man. *J Appl Physiol.* 34:628–632, 1973.

19. Essen, B., Hagenfeldt, L., and Kaijser, L.: Utilization of blood-borne and intramuscular substrates during continuous and intermittent exercise in man. *J Physiol.* 265:480–506, 1977.

20. Fox, E. L.: Measurement of the maximal alactic (phosphagen) capacity in man. *Med Sci Sports.* 5:66, 1973.

21. Fox, E. L.: *Sports Physiology.* Philadelphia, W. B. Saunders, 1979, pp. 58, 78.

22. Fox, E. L., Robinson, S., and Wiegman, D.: Metabolic energy sources during continuous and interval running. *J Appl Physiol.* 27:174–178, 1969.

23. Gaesser, G. A., and Brooks, G. A.: Metabolism of lactate after prolonged exercise to exhaustion. *Med Sci Sports.* 1(1):76, 1979.

24. Gisolfi, C., Robinson, S., and Turrell, E. S.: Effects of aerobic work performed during recovery from exhausting work. *J Appl Physiol.* 21:1767–1772, 1966.

25. Gladden, L. B., Stainsby, W. B., McIntosh, B. R.: Norepinephrine increases canine skeletal muscle $\dot{V}O_2$ during recovery. *MSSE.* 14:471–476, 1982.

26. Hagberg, J. M., Mullin, J. P., and Nagle, F. P.: Effect of work intensity and duration on recovery O_2. *J Appl Physiol.* 48:540–544. 1980.

27. Hagerman, F. C., Connors, M. C., Gault, J. A., Hagerman, G. R., and Polinski, W. J.: Energy expenditure during simulated rowing. *J Appl Physiol.* 45(1):87–93, 1978.

28. Hagerman, F. C., Fox, E. L., Connors, M., and Pompei, J.: Metabolic responses of women rowers during ergometric rowing. *Med Sci Sports.* 6(1):87, 1974.

29. Harris, R. C., Edwards, R. H. T., Hultman, E., Nordesjo, L.-O., Nylind, B., and Sahlin, K.: The time course of phosphorylcreatine resynthesis during recovery of the quadriceps muscle in man. *Pflugers Arch.* 367:137–142, 1976.

30. Harris, R. C., Hultman, E., Kaijser, L., and Nordesjo, L.-O.: The effect of circulatory occlusion on isometric exercise capacity and energy metabolism of the quadriceps muscle in man. *Scand J Clin Invest.* 35:87–95, 1975.

31. Hermansen, L., Hultman, E., and Saltin, B.: Muscle glycogen during prolonged severe exercise. *Acta Physiol Scand.* 71:129–139, 1967.

32. Hermansen, L., Maehlum, S., Pruett, E. D. R., Vaage, O., Waldum, H., and Wessel-Aas, T.: Lactate removal at rest and during exercise. In Howald, H., and Poortmans, J. R. (eds.): *Metabolic Adaptation to Prolonged Physical Exercise.* Basel, Switzerland, Birkhauser Verlag, 1975, pp. 101–105.

33. Hermansen, L., and Stensvold, I.: Production and removal of lactate during exercise in man. *Acta Physiol Scand.* 86:191–201, 1972.

34. Hermansen, L., and Vaage, O.: Lactate disappearance and glycogen synthesis in human muscle after maximal exercise. *Am J Physiol.* 233(5):E422–E429, 1977.

35. Hill, A. V., Long, C. N. H., and Lupton, H.: Muscular exercise, lactic acid and the supply and utilization of oxygen. *Proc Roy Soc (London).* Series B, 96:438–475, 1924.

36. Hill, A. V., and Lupton, H.: The oxygen consumption during running. *J Physiol.* 56:xxxii–xxxiii, 1922.

37. Hubbard, J. L.: The effect of exercise on lactate metabolism. *J Physiol.* 231:1–18, 1973.

38. Hultman, E., and Bergstrom, J.: Muscle

glycogen synthesis in relation to diet studied in normal subjects. *Acta Med Scand.* 182:109–117, 1967.

39. Hultman, E., Bergstrom, J., and McLennan-Anderson, N.: Breakdown and resynthesis of phosphorylcreatine and adenosine triphosphate in connection with muscular work in man. *Scand J Clin Invest.* 19:56–66, 1967.

40. Hultman, E., and Nilsson, L. H. Liver glycogen in man: effect of different diets and muscular exercise. In Pernow, B., and Saltin, B. (eds.): *Muscle Metabolism during Exercise.* New York, Plenum Press, 1971, pp. 143–151.

41. Johnson, R. E., and Edwards, H. T.: Lactate and pyruvate in blood and urine after exercise. *J Biol Chem.* 118:427–432, 1937.

42. Karlsson, J., Bonde-Petersen, F., Hendriksson, J., and Knuttgen, H. G.: Effects of previous exercise with arms or legs on metabolism and performance in exhaustive exercise. *J Appl Physiol.* 38:763–767, 1975.

43. Karlsson, J., Funderburk, C. F., Essen, B., and Lind, A.: Constituents of human muscle in isometric fatigue. *J Appl Physiol.* 38:208–211, 1975.

44. Karlsson, J., and Saltin, B.: Oxygen deficit and muscle metabolites in intermittent exercise. *Acta Physiol Scand.* 82:115–122, 1971.

45. Kochan, R. G., Lamb, D. R., Lutz, S. A., Perrell, C. V., Reiman, E. M., and Schlender, R. R.: Glycogen synthetase activation in human skeletal muscle: effect of diet and exercise. *Am J Physiol.* 235:E660–666, 1979.

46. MacDougall, J. D., Ward, G. R., Sale, D. G., and Sutton, J. R.: Muscle glycogen repletion after high-intensity intermittent exercise. *J Appl Physiol.* 42:129–132, 1977.

47. Margaria, R., Cerretelli, P., diPrampero, P. E., Massari, C., and Torelli, G.: Kinetics and mechanism of oxygen debit contraction in man. *J Appl Physiol.* 18:371–377, 1963.

48. Margaria, R., Cerretelli, P., and Mangile, F.: Balance and kinetics of anaerobic energy release during strenuous exercise in man. *J Appl Physiol.* 19:623–628, 1964.

49. Margaria, R., Edwards, H. T., and Dill, D. B.: The possible mechanism of contracting and paying the oxygen debt and the role of lactic acid in muscular contraction. *Am J Physiol.* 106:687–714, 1933.

50. Nemoto, E. M., Hoff, J. T., and Severinghaus, J. W.: Lactate uptake and metabolism by brain during hyperlactacidemia and hypoglycemia. *Stroke.* 5:48–53, 1974.

51. Piehl, K.: Time course for refilling of glycogen stores in human muscle fibers following exercise-induced glycogen depletion. *Acta Physiol Scand.* 90:297–302, 1974.

52. Piiper, J., diPrampero, P.E., and Cerretelli, P.: Oxygen debt and high-energy phosphates in gastrocnemius muscle of the dog. *Am J Physiol.* 215:523–531, 1968.

53. Piiper, J., and Spiller, P.: Repayment of O_2 debt and resynthesis of high energy phosphates in gastrocnemius muscle of the dog. *J Appl Physiol.* 28:657–662, 1970.

54. Roberts, A. D., and Morton, A. R.: Total and alactic oxygen debts after supramaximal work. *Europ J Appl Physiol.* 38:281–289, 1978.

55. Rowell, L. B., Kraning, K. K., Evans, T. O., Kennedy, J. W., Blackmon, J. R., and Kusumi, F.: Splanchnic removal of lactate and pyruvate during prolonged exercise in man. *J Appl Physiol.* 21:1773–1783, 1966.

56. Spitzer, J. J.: Effect of lactate infusion on canine myocardial free fatty acid metabolism in vivo. *Am J Physiol.* 226:213–217, 1974.

57. Stainsby, W. N., and Barclay, J. K.: Exercise metabolism: O_2 deficit, steady level O_2 uptake and O_2 uptake for recovery. *Med Sci Sports.* 2:177–181, 1970.

58. Stamford, B. A., Weltman, A., Moffat, R., and Sady, S.: Exercise recovery above and below anaerobic threshold following maximal work. *J Appl Physiol.* 51:840–844, 1981.

59. Welch, H. G., Faulkner, J. A., Barclay, J. K., and Brooks, G. A.: Ventilatory response during recovery from muscular work and its relation with O_2 debt. *Med Sci Sports.* 2:15–19, 1970.

60. Yudkin, J., and Cohen, R. D.: The contribution of the kidney to the removal of a lactic acid load under normal and acidotic conditions in the conscious cat. *Clin Sci Mol Med.* 46:8P, 1974.

SELECTED READINGS

diPrampero, P. E.: The alactic oxygen debt: its power, capacity and efficiency. In Pernow, B., and Saltin, B. (eds.): *Muscle Metabolism during Exercise.* New York, Plenum Press, 1971, pp. 371–382.

Fox, E. L.: *Sports Physiology.* Philadelphia, W. B. Saunders, 1984, pp. 54–81.

Knuttgen, H. G.: Lactate and oxygen debt: an introduction. In Pernow, B., and Saltin, B. (eds.): *Muscle Metabolism during Exercise.* New York, Plenum Press, 1971, pp. 361–369.

Knuttgen, H. G.: Oxygen debt after submaximal physical exercise. *J Appl Physiol.* 29:651–657, 1970.

Margaria, R.: *Biomechanics and Energetics of Muscular Exercise.* Oxford, Oxford University Press, 1976, pp. 1–58.

Minaire, Y., and Forichon, J.: Lactate metabolism and glucose lactate conversion in prolonged physical exercise. In Howald, H., and Poortmans, J. (eds.): *Metabolic Adaptation to Prolonged Physical Exercise.* Basel, Switzerland, Birkhäuser Verlag, 1975, pp. 106–112.

Pirnay, F., and Crielaard, J. M.: Measuring anaerobic alactic capacity. *Med Sport* (Paris). 53(1):13–16, 1978.

chapter 4

Measurement of Energy, Work, and Power

The major concepts to be learned from this chapter are as follows:

- Energy, work, and power are functionally related, since energy is the capacity to perform work, and power is work per unit of time.
- The direct measurement of energy involves the measurement of heat production, whereas the indirect measure-

ment of energy in the human involves the measurement of oxygen consumption.

- The heat (caloric) equivalence of the oxygen consumed depends upon the foodstuff oxidized by the aerobic system.
- The measurement of the energy (oxygen) cost of anaerobic exercise involves measurement of resting and exercise and recovery (oxygen debt) oxygen consumption, whereas for aerobic exercise, only resting and exercise oxygen consumption are required.
- Heart rate, which can be measured by radio telemetry during actual playing of various sports activities, can be used to estimate energy cost of those activities.

One of the most valid means of determining a person's ability to perform physical exercise is to measure the maximal amount and rate of energy he or she can expend. This can be done indirectly by determining the maximal ability to consume oxygen while performing maximal exercise. The exercise is usually performed using a bicycle ergometer or treadmill, which permits variation of the workload from moderate to exhaustive (maximal). The amount of oxygen consumed by the individual during maximal work (usually expressed in liters*) can be converted into energy units such as **kilocalories (kcal)** or **kilojoules (kJ)**; work units such as **kilogram-meters (kg-m)** or **foot-pounds (ft-lb)**; and power units such as **kg-m per minute (kg-m/min), ft-lb per min** or **watts.**

Understanding energy expenditure, how it is measured, and how it relates to

work and power will make you much more knowledgeable about your subject, whether it be physical education or athletics, for as we learned in the last two chapters, it is *energy* and the way in which it is expended and restored that results in continued human movement.

Ergometry

In order to study the energetics of physical activity, suitable measurement devices that are reliable and valid are required. Such devices are named **ergometers** (ergo=work, meter=measure). Reliability is very important in that if we want to reproduce a work condition we can do so with a high degree of confidence. Thus, if the physiological response is different in a second test condition, we can ascribe that difference to something other than the ergometer itself. For example, if heart rate is lower at a given workload, following a ten-week training program, then we can say with confidence that the training program had an effect on the cardiovascular system of the subject. Several types of ergometers are available to the exercise physiologist.

Treadmill. Motor-driven treadmills consist of a running surface, similar to a conveyor belt and a means of controlling both speed and elevation for uphill running. Some models are adaptable to provide a simulated downhill run.

Stationary bicycle. Stationary bicycles consist of a means of providing resistance against pedaling. Resistance can be offered through mechanical loading (loading weights onto a platform or increasing tension on a belt) of a flywheel or through altering electrical resistance. Care must be taken in calibration of the bicycle.[18,20]

Swimming ergometer. Tethered swimming devices have been designed to provide a means of resistance in swimming so that the swimmer can remain in

---

*A liter equals about a quart.

one location in the pool. One such apparatus involves attaching a belt or harness to a swimmer. The belt is attached to a cable that runs through a pulley behind the swimmer. The cable then runs over a second pulley to a loading platform. In order to maintain his/her position in the water the swimmer must kick and/or stroke to maintain the load platform at a given point.[4] Heusner has modified the device so that very fine gradations in workload can be achieved.[14]

Other devices. The above-named devices are the most commonly available. There are several other types including rowing ergometers, staircase treadmills, and swimming flumes (a water tank in which a water current can be generated).

Energy, Work, and Power

In order to fully appreciate the whole of our subject, energy cost of performance, we need to know the meaning of and relationships among (1) energy, (2) work, and (3) power.

Energy

How often we have heard the expressions, "I haven't a bit of energy left," or "He is bursting at the seams with energy." Such everyday sayings carry a substance of meaning but fall short in defining energy. Actually, no one has ever seen energy or handled it. However, all have felt its effects. For example, a fall or being hit with an object causes pain. In other words, energy and its effects are all around us—the moving automobile, the sun, and the children and athletes on the playing field—all are illustrative of energy. Energy may be described as the *capacity to perform work.*

Generally, six forms of energy are recognized: mechanical, heat, light, chemical, electrical, and nuclear. Each can be converted from one form to another. The person exercising is converting chemical energy (food) to mechanical energy and heat—for every single human movement, whether it be merely a smile or the punting of a football, the energy (ATP) needed to perform it is derived from food. Our bodies also convert chemical energy into electrical energy: the stimulus to contract a muscle, for example, is electrical. The electrocardiogram is actually a recording on paper of the electrical activity of the heart muscle, just as the electromyogram is the tracing of the electrical impulses across the skeletal muscle.

The source of energy in a chemical reaction, which is our primary concern, comes from either breaking up a molecule or putting it back together. Regardless of which occurs, the same amount of energy (heat) will be involved in the reactions. For example, if hydrogen reacting with oxygen produces water and 68.4 kcal, it will require exactly 68.4 kcal to pull the water molecule apart to form hydrogen and oxygen. This is called the "first law of thermodynamics" and will be discussed later in more detail.

Work

The physicist defines work in a restricted sense, i.e., work is the application of a force through a distance. For example, if you raised a book weighing 1 kilogram (2.2 pounds) vertically 1 meter (3.3 feet), the work performed would have been 1 kilogram-meter (kg-m), or 7.3 foot-pounds (ft-lb). One kg-m would be defined as the work done when a constant force of 1 kilogram is exerted on a body that moves a distance of 1 meter, in the same direction as the force. Work may be expressed in the following formula:

$$W = F \times D$$

Where

W = work
F = force (remember, the force must be constant)

D = distance through which the force is moved (distance is the length of the path through which the body moves in the same direction as the force and while the force is acting on it)

Another example of work would be to perform a pull-up. If the person weighed 70 kg and if the bar were 0.75 meter (29.5 inches) above the chin, then the amount of work performed during the pull-up would be:

$$W = F \times D$$
$$W = 70 \text{ kg} \times 0.75 \text{ meter}$$
$$W = \textbf{52.5 kg-m.}$$

Work may be expressed in different terms. Table 4-1 contains a number of work and energy units that enable us to convert one to another depending upon how we wish to express our final measurement.

How many ft-lbs of work did the person performing the pull-up do?*

Power

Power is used to express work done in a unit of time. It may be written as:

$$\text{Power} = \frac{\text{Work}}{\text{Time}}$$

or

$$\text{Power} = \frac{F \times D}{t}$$

In the aforementioned example, if the book weighing 1 kg were raised 1 meter in 1 second, power would be expressed as 1

---

*Answer: 1 kg-m = 7.23 ft-lb. (Table 4-1); therefore, 52.5 kg-m = 379.6 ft-lb.

TABLE 4-1

Energy and Work Units

1 foot-pound	= 0.13825 kg-meter*
1 kg-meter	= 7.23 foot-pounds
1 kcal	= 3086 foot-pounds = 426.8 kg-meters
1 kcal	= 4.1855 kilojoules (kJ)
1 kJ	= 1000 joules (J) = 0.23892 kcal

*A kilogram-meter is the distance through which 1 kilogram (2.2 pounds) moves 1 meter (3.28 feet).

kg-m per second. By the same token, if the pull-up were performed in 0.5 second, the power produced would be:

$$P = W/t$$
$$P = 52.5 \text{ kg-m}/0.5 \text{ second}$$
$$P = \textbf{105 kg-m/sec}$$

Table 4-2 contains a number of ways in which power may be expressed.

It is important for us to understand from the above discussion both the meaning of energy, work, and power and that the six forms of energy can be converted from one to another. The importance of these concepts can be demonstrated when describing: (1) how work by a person can be measured directly through the amount of heat the body gives off while performing various tasks; (2) how measurement of heat is employed in determining energy values of food, i.e., how much energy or, more precisely, the number of kilocalories, in a soft drink, average sized potato, or slice of bread (we will see that this latter information is vital to the understanding of weight-control programs); and (3) how the exercise physiologist uses an indirect method of measuring energy by determining the amount of oxygen used.

TABLE 4–2

Relationships Among Power Units

	Horse-Power	kg-Meters/Minute	Foot-Pounds/Minute	Watts	kcal/Minute	kJ/Minute
1 horsepower	1.0	4,564.0	33,000.0	746.0	10,694	44.743
1 kg-meter/minute	0.000219	1.0	7.23	0.16345	0.00234	0.0098068
1 foot-pound/minute	0.00003	0.1383	1.0	0.0226	0.000324	0.0013562
1 watt	0.001341	6.118	44.236	1.0	0.014335	0.0599995
1 kcal/minute	0.09355	426.78	3086.0	69.759	1.0	4.1855
1 kJ/minute	0.02235	101.97	737.307	16.667	0.23892	1.0

Direct Measurement of Energy: Heat Production

When energy is expended by the human body in performing work, heat is liberated from the working muscles. Hence, the metabolism of foodstuffs (caloric value) should be equivalent to the amount of heat the body liberates. As was mentioned earlier, this demonstrates the first law of thermodynamics: *When mechanical energy is transformed into heat energy or heat energy into mechanical energy, the ratio of the two energies is a constant quantity (the principle of the conservation of energy).* It becomes a fact, then, that the expenditure of a fixed amount of energy will always result in the production of the same amount of heat. To demonstrate with animals this first law of thermodynamics, a scientist by the name of Max Rubner in the latter part of the 1800s built a chamber containing circulating water on the outside (Fig. 4-1). A dog was placed inside the chamber in order to measure both metabolism and heat production of the animal. Metabolism was indirectly determined by measuring the oxygen consumed by the dog in breaking down the foodstuffs. Heat production by the dog in the chamber (called a **bomb** calorimeter) was measured by noting the change (increase) in temperature of the circulating water. Each increase in water temperature of 1°C per kilogram of water is equivalent to 1 kcal of energy. The term *bomb* comes from the shape of the chamber (bomb) and *calorimeter* means the measurement of heat (expressed in calories).

The results of these early experiments demonstrated unequivocally that energy

Figure 4-1. Calorimeter for measuring heat energy. The calorimeter allows simultaneous measurement of metabolism and heat production. Oxygen consumption (indirect measurement of metabolism) equals heat production (direct measurement) by the animal as reflected in an increase of temperature of the circulating water.

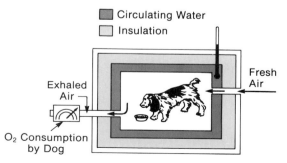

produced through the metabolism of foodstuffs is equal to the heat produced by the body. We can conclude, then, that energy expended by an individual doing any kind of work is exactly equal to the energy set free through body metabolism. For example, if we were to measure the oxygen consumption of an individual riding a bicycle or exercising in a human bomb calorimeter and then converted the oxygen utilized to heat equivalents or kilocalories (Table 4-3), we would find that the amount of energy as determined through the measurement of oxygen consumption would equal the amount of heat given off by the body during the exercise.

By the same token, if we were to determine the amount of energy contained in an average sized potato, soft drink, or medium-sized pizza, we would simply burn the food item in the calorimeter. The increase in temperature of the circulating water would be equivalent to the energy or caloric value of the food. It is in this manner that caloric values for various foods are determined.

The use of the bomb calorimeter is referred to as the **direct method** in the measurement of energy. This is true because heat production, a specific form of energy, is being directly determined. On the other hand, when we measure the oxygen consumption required in metabolizing food, we use an **indirect method** in determining energy.

Indirect Measurement of Energy: Oxygen Consumption

Many scientists have demonstrated that the amount of oxygen consumed at rest or while performing work when expressed in heat equivalents (kcal) will be equal to the heat produced by the body as determined directly in a calorimeter. The measurement of oxygen consumption is an indirect measure of energy, since heat is not measured directly.

In order to express the amount of oxygen consumed in heat equivalents (i.e., kilocalories), it becomes necessary to know what type of food (carbohydrate, fat, or

TABLE 4-3

Energy Equivalents of Food and Alcohol

Food	Energy (Bomb Calorimeter) kcal/g	Energy (Physiological Values)* kcal/g	O_2, kcal/liter	CO_2, kcal/liter	$R = \dfrac{\dot{V}CO_2}{\dot{V}O_2}$	O_2, liter/g	CO_2, liter/g
Carbohydrate	4.1	4.02	5.05	5.05	1.00	0.81	0.81
Protein	5.65	5.20	4.46	5.57	0.80	0.94	0.75
Fat	9.45	8.98	4.74	6.67	0.71	1.96	1.39
Alcohol	7.1	7.0	4.86	7.25	0.67	1.46	0.98
Mixed diet			4.83	5.89	0.82		

*In the body there is a loss of kcal to digestion as follows: carbohydrate, 2%; fat, 5%; protein, 8%; plus a 17% loss in urine. For alcohol there is a small loss in urine and exhaled air.

protein) is being metabolized. The reason for this deals with the energy equivalents of the particular food being metabolized. For example, when these foods are placed in a bomb calorimeter and 1 liter of oxygen is used in breaking down the foodstuffs, the following heat energy equivalents would be obtained (Table 4-3); carbohydrate (e.g., glycogen or glucose), 5.05 kcal; protein (e.g., meat), 4.46 kcal; and lipid (fat), 4.74 kcal. From the same table, in terms of kcal per gram of food metabolized, there is a slight difference in values between the results when the food is metabolized (physiologically) in the body compared with the bomb calorimeter. The small losses of energy as noted at the bottom of the table are due to digestion and some protein loss in the urine.

Note also from Table 4-3 that in terms of kilocalories per gram of food metabolized, fats (lipids) release 9.45 kcal of energy per gram, proteins, 5.65 kcal/g, and carbohydrates, 4.1 kcal/g. We drew your attention first to the energy released in terms of kilocalories per liter of oxygen because the hard-working athlete is confronted primarily with getting sufficient oxygen and only secondarily with the quantity of food. Why more heat or energy is liberated from fats as compared with carbohydrates on a per-gram basis is easy to explain. Remember, energy is released when water is formed (combining hydrogen and oxygen) during the metabolism of foods. There are more hydrogen atoms per oxygen atom in fat than in carbohydrates. For example, a typical carbohydrate, glucose, has the formula $C_6H_{12}O_6$ and a typical fat, palmitic acid, is $C_{16}H_{32}O_2$. As a consequence, there are more hydrogen atoms in fat to combine with oxygen in forming water (H_2O). Therefore, when the body uses a given amount of fat, more energy is released than when it metabolizes the same amount of carbohydrates. You can see from Table 4-3 that there are more than twice the number

of kilocalories in a gram of fat than in a gram of carbohydrate.

Because all proteins contain nitrogen in addition to carbon, hydrogen, and oxygen, they are not as rich in energy as is fat. This is true because when proteins are used, the body must get rid of the nitrogen and it is disposed of not as a free gas, like carbon dioxide, but rather as urea. It is excreted in the urine, and as a result, a portion of the energy from the protein molecule is lost.

The question that logically should confront us at this time is: If we have measured or been told the number of liters of oxygen used in performing a given exercise task, how do we know which food was being metabolized so that we might assign the proper caloric value to the oxygen being consumed? In the first place, it would be rare indeed if a person were using fat, protein, or carbohydrate exclusively. Rather, a person exercises on a mixed diet (predominantly carbohydrates and fats), and it is through measuring not only the oxygen consumed but also the carbon dioxide produced that permits us to know the mixture of foods being metabolized and hence to properly assign the correct caloric value to each liter of oxygen consumed (Table 4-4).

The Caloric Equivalence of Oxygen: The Respiratory Exchange Ratio *(R)*

The caloric value of 1 liter of oxygen consumed depends on which type of food is being metabolized. The ratio of the volume of carbon dioxide expired per minute ($\dot{V}CO_2$) to the volume of oxygen consumed during the same time interval ($\dot{V}O_2$) is called the **respiratory exchange ratio (R)**.* The *R*

---

*A cell respires while the animal breathes. It is usual to refer to $\dot{V}CO_2/\dot{V}O_2$ at the cellular level as the respiratory quotient *(RQ)* and at the lung level as the respiratory exchange ratio *(R)*.

TABLE 4-4

Caloric Equivalents (kcal/Liter of Oxygen) and Percentage of Total Calories Provided by Carbohydrate and Fat at Each Non-Protein R.

R	kcal/L of O_2	Percentage of Total Calories By	
		Carbohydrate	Fat
0.707	4.686	0.0	100.0
0.71	4.690	1.02	98.98
0.72	4.702	4.44	95.6
0.73	4.714	7.85	92.2
0.74	4.727	11.3	88.7
0.75	4.739	14.7	85.3
0.76	4.751	18.1	81.9
0.77	4.764	21.5	78.5
0.78	4.776	24.9	75.1
0.79	4.788	28.3	71.7
0.80	4.801	31.7	68.3
0.81	4.813	35.2	64.8
0.82	4.825	38.6	61.4
0.83	4.838	42.0	58.0
0.84	4.850	45.4	54.6
0.85	4.862	48.8	51.2
0.86	4.875	52.2	47.8
0.87	4.887	55.6	44.4
0.88	4.899	59.0	41.0
0.89	4.911	62.5	37.5
0.90	4.924	65.9	34.1
0.91	4.936	69.3	30.7
0.92	4.948	72.7	27.3
0.93	4.961	76.1	23.9
0.94	4.973	79.5	20.5
0.95	4.985	82.9	17.1
0.96	4.998	86.3	13.7
0.97	5.010	89.8	10.2
0.98	5.022	93.2	6.83
0.99	5.035	96.6	3.41
1.00	5.047	100.0	0.00

From Lusk, G. *Science of Nutrition,* 4th ed. Philadelphia, W. B. Saunders Co., 1928, p. 65.

can only be determined under conditions of steady-state exercise or rest.

Carbohydrate

At this time let us draw our attention to carbohydrate—a foodstuff that contains

hydrogen and oxygen in proper proportions to form water within the molecule (two hydrogen atoms for every oxygen atom). Because of this, all oxygen consumed can be employed in the oxidation of carbon. At the same time, remember that equal volumes of gases at the same temperature and pressure contain an equal number of molecules (Law of Avogadro). Therefore, on a pure diet of carbohydrate we would expect R to equal 1 or unity. For example:

$$C_6H_{12}O_6 + 6\ O_2 = 6\ CO_2 + 6\ H_2O$$
Glucose

$$R = \frac{\dot{V}CO_2}{\dot{V}O_2} = \frac{6\ CO_2}{6\ O_2} = 1$$

It can readily be observed that 6 moles of CO_2 are produced as a consequence of 6 moles of O_2 being used in the oxidation of glucose. The ratio $\frac{6\ CO_2}{6\ O_2} = 1$. One liter of oxygen will release 5.047 kcal of energy (heat), whether it is metabolized in the body or burned in the bomb calorimeter (Table 4-4).

Fat

When fat is oxidized, oxygen not only combines with carbon to form carbon dioxide but it also combines with hydrogen to form water. Therefore, we would expect R to be less than unity and so it is:

Fat (palmitic acid) $C_{16}H_{32}O_2$

Upon oxidation:

$$C_{16}H_{32}O_2 + 23\ O_2 \rightarrow 16\ CO_2 + 16\ H_2O$$

$$R = \frac{16\ CO_2}{23\ O_2} = 0.70$$

Although fat contains more than twice the chemical energy of carbohydrate per gram, it requires more oxygen to release each calorie of energy.

Protein

Proteins are completely burned in the bomb calorimeter, yielding 5.65 kcal per gram (Table 4-3). However, when metabolized in the body, the nitrogen and small amount of sulfur residue are excreted in the urine and feces, as previously mentioned. Consequently, less energy is available when the protein is metabolized in the body than when it is burned in the calorimeter, where complete oxidation of the nitrogen and sulfur takes place. As a consequence, the energy production in the body is about 5.20 kcal per gram of protein, whereas in the calorimeter it averages 5.65 kcal per gram of protein. Because of this factor, special consideration must be taken when employing R as representative of the food types being metabolized. This is of added significance when using R to assign the caloric value for each liter of oxygen the body is using.

It would be most convenient if the body metabolized only fats and carbohydrates, for then R would represent the relative proportions of the foods being used, since there is only a negligible loss of energy due to digestion. For example, an R of 1.00 would indicate to us that only carbohydrate was being burned; an R of 0.71, only fats; and any ratio between these two values would give us the relative combinations of the two foods being metabolized. In this manner, we could assign the proper caloric value to each liter of oxygen being consumed by the individual.

Fortunately, scientists before us have measured the excretion of nitrogen and have determined the amount of protein that was oxidized.* Subtracting the oxy-

gen required and the carbon dioxide produced when protein is oxidized from the total oxygen consumption yields an R value commonly referred to as the **nonprotein R.** Table 4-4 contains these nonprotein R values. With the help of this table, we need only to measure the oxygen consumed and the carbon dioxide produced in order to arrive at the proper caloric value for each liter of oxygen consumed. If this were not the case, nitrogen excretion values would have to be obtained and more cumbersome calculations made.

To measure the amount of energy expended in doing work, it is apparent that we must know the value of R if we are to determine the caloric value for the amount of oxygen consumed. As an illustration, let us assume that 2 liters of oxygen per minute were consumed during a 15-minute bicycle ride (a total of 30 liters of O_2). From Table 4-4, if the person's diet were carbohydrate ($R = 1.0$), the caloric value of the 30 liters of oxygen consumed would represent $30 \times 5.05 = 151.5$ kcal of energy expended. In cases in which R is not known, it can be assumed to be 0.83, which means a liter of oxygen consumed is equivalent to 4.83 kcal. (Can you convert the 151.5 kcal used in cycling to kg-m, ft-lb, watts, and horsepower? Also, approximately how much weight would be lost as a result of cycling, assuming 1 pound of fat is equivalent to 3500 kcal?*

Other Factors Affecting R

There are times when R can be affected by factors other than oxidation of food. The

---

*Lusk, G. The Science of Nutrition, 4th ed. Philadelphia. W. B. Saunders. 1918.

*Answers: From Table 4-1, 1 kcal = 426.8 kg-m = 3086 ft-lb, therefore, 151.5 kcal = 64,660.2 kg-m = 467,529 ft-lb. From Table 4-2, 1 kcal/min = 69.759 watts = 0.09355 horsepower, therefore, 151.5 kcal/15 min = 10.1 kcal/min = 704.6 watts = 0.945 horsepower. Weight loss = 151.5/3500 = 0.043 pound.

following factors are worthwhile to consider when interpreting R:

1. **Hyperventilation** (overventilating the lungs), which may be voluntary or may sometimes occur under psychological stress, results in excessive carbon dioxide loss. In such an instance, R would exceed unity.

2. During the first minute or so of submaximal exercise (aerobic) the apparent stimulating effects result in hyperventilation to the extent that the person blows off more carbon dioxide than he or she consumes oxygen, causing R to approach or exceed unity. After about 3 minutes the individual would more than likely be producing sufficient carbon dioxide as a result of the exercise to return R to within normal limits, more accurately reflecting the food being metabolized.

3. During short-term exhaustive exercise, R will exceed 1 as the buffering of lactic acid causes large quantities of CO_2 to be released (for more on acid-base balance, see Chapter 21). It is common practice in this case to consider R as equal to 1. In other words, carbohydrate is the primary food source and each liter of oxygen would be equivalent to 5.05 kcal.

4. During recovery from exercise, CO_2 is retained, resulting in a lowered R.

Measurement of Energy Cost of Exercise

Let us imagine we were given the problem of measuring the energy expenditure of a given exercise. How shall we proceed? The first thing we need to know is whether the exercise being performed is anaerobic or aerobic. If the exercise is anaerobic, i.e., involves both the aerobic and anaerobic energy systems throughout the duration of the exercise, then we need to measure the oxygen consumption ($\dot{V}O_2$) at rest, during exercise, and during recovery. If, however, the exercise can be performed in an aerobic steady state, then only the oxygen consumption at rest and during the steady-state period need be measured.

Resting oxygen consumption is necessary as this value must be deducted from the oxygen measured during exercise and recovery in order to determine the oxygen cost of the exercise alone. This is called the **net oxygen cost of exercise.** Recovery oxygen is needed because the amount of oxygen consumed during exercise reflects only the energy supplied through the aerobic system. The recovery oxygen, on the other hand, is used as an indicator of the amount of energy supplied during exercise through the anaerobic systems.* Therefore:

$$
\begin{aligned}
&\text{Net } O_2 \text{ Cost of Exercise} \\
&= \text{exercise } VO_2 + \text{recovery } VO_2 \\
&\quad - (\text{resting } \dot{V}O_2 \times \text{time})
\end{aligned}
$$

Net Oxygen Cost of Anaerobic Exercise

In exercises of maximal intensity in which the net O_2 cost of the exercise is to be determined, Douglas bags or meteorological balloons are most often used to collect the exhaled gas for purposes of volume measurement and analysis. The bags are rubber lined and covered with canvas and were named after a famous physiologist C. G. Douglas. In Figure 4-2 a schematic of a collection system is illustrated. Samples of expired air are collected during rest, exercise, and recovery. Several bags may be utilized to cover both exercise and recovery periods. Small gas samples are taken from each bag and analyzed for CO_2 and O_2 concentration. Following sample

---

*Whereas the recovery oxygen is still used in the calculation of the net oxygen cost of exercise, the validity of it, reflecting, in a quantitative way, the anaerobic energy released during exercise, is questionable (pp. 42 to 54).

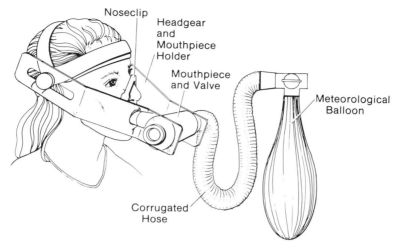

Figure 4-2. Illustration of a gas collection system utilizing a meteorological balloon.

analysis, the volume of each bag is determined by passing the gas through a gas meter (the small amount removed for CO_2 and O_2 analysis is added in). These measurements are needed in order to calculate the amount of oxygen consumed and carbon dioxide produced. While it will not be necessary at this time to go through the actual calculations of $\dot{V}O_2$ and $\dot{V}CO_2$, you can learn how to do this by reading Appendices C and D (p. 655–664).

In recent years a number of automated metabolic measurement devices have been developed incorporating computer technology. All input variables including barometric pressure, temperature, ventilation volume, and CO_2 and O_2 concentrations can be monitored continuously in any desired time frame, including breath-by-breath analysis. The advantage of this type of system is that results can be provided while the subject is still exercising or recovering. Figure 4-3 illustrates the input needed and a sample of the types of output or results.

For our present purposes, let us assume that upon analysis of the gas in the bal-

loons, we found that during a 5-minute rest period the subject consumed 1.5 liters of oxygen (0.3 liters per minute); during a 5-minute period of exhausting exercise, 17.0 liters of oxygen were consumed; and during a 45-minute recovery period, 25.0 liters of oxygen were consumed. How do we compute the net O_2 cost of the exercise?

During the 5-minute exercise period the subject consumed 17.0 liters of oxygen. From this amount must be subtracted what would have been consumed during the same period if the subject were resting; in other words, the exercise or net oxygen consumption is over and above that consumed during rest. Therefore, 17.0 liters − 1.5 liters = **15.5 liters** of net oxygen consumed during exercise.

From the oxygen debt (25 liters of O_2) we must also subtract that amount that would have been used if the subject were resting for that particular time period, or 25 liters − (45 minutes × 0.3 liters per minute), which equals **11.5 liters** of O_2 (net recovery oxygen).

Therefore, the *net oxygen cost of the exercise* would be equal to the exercise plus

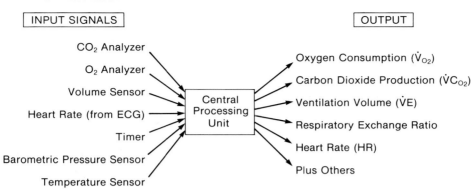

Figure 4-3. Electronically designed metabolic systems include all input signals from sensors and analyzers, a central processing unit for making rapid calculations, and an output device (screen or printer) with the metabolic data.

the recovery oxygen after the resting oxygen had been subtracted from each one, or:

$$\begin{aligned}
\text{net exercise } V_{O_2} &= 15.5 \text{ liters} \\
\text{net oxygen debt} &= \underline{11.5} \text{ liters} \\
\textbf{Net } \mathbf{O_2} \textbf{ Cost} &= \textbf{27.0 liters}
\end{aligned}$$

Assuming an R of 0.96, how many kilocalories of energy were expended?*

Net Oxygen Cost of Aerobic Exercise

If the exercise is submaximal and can be performed in an aerobic steady state, the measurement of net oxygen cost may be considerably simplified. You will recall that during submaximal exercise, a steady state of oxygen consumption occurs as noted in Figure 4-4. It indicates that at the time, all the energy required for the exercise is being supplied aerobically. Therefore, the net oxygen cost of the steady-state exercise can be determined simply by measuring the resting V_{O_2} and, for 1 minute, the oxygen consumed during the steady-state period.

*Answer: $R = 0.96 = 4.998$, or 5 kcal per liter O_2 consumed (Table 4-4); therefore, 5 kcal/liter $\times$ 27.0 liters = 135 kcal.

Recognizing these basic physiological considerations, let us proceed with the actual determination of the net O_2 cost while running for 10 minutes on a treadmill at 9.6 kilometers per hour (6 miles per hour) that can be performed in a steady state.

1. The resting $\dot{V}_{O_2}$ is determined as before.
2. The subject begins to exercise. No oxygen consumption measurements are made at this time since the steady-

Figure 4-4. Time course of oxygen consumption during rest, submaximal, aerobic exercise, and recovery. $\dot{V}_{O_2}$ (volume of oxygen used per unit of time) can be measured any time during steady state. Subtracting resting $\dot{V}_{O_2}$ from this amount permits us to report the net cost of the exercise in liters per minute.

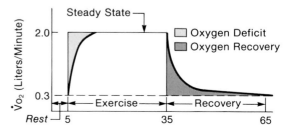

state period has not as yet been reached.

3. Once steady state is reached (usually within 3 to 4 minutes after exercise has started), oxygen consumption is measured over a 1-minute period (sometimes over 2 minutes). Again, Douglas bags or meteorological balloons are most often used to collect the subject's expired gas for determination of gas volume and O_2 and CO_2 concentrations.

4. The resting $\dot{V}O_2$ value is then subtracted from the steady-state $\dot{V}O_2$ value to determine the net oxygen cost of the exercise on a per minute basis.

5. Finally, for the total net oxygen cost, the net cost per minute is multiplied by the total time, in minutes, that the exercise was performed.

As an example, suppose that the steady-state $\dot{V}O_2$ determined during the 9.6 km/hr treadmill run mentioned previously was 2.8 liters per minute and the resting $\dot{V}O_2$ was 0.3 liters per minute. The net oxygen cost per minute would then be 2.8 − 0.3 = 2.5 liters. Since the exercise duration was 10 minutes, the total net oxygen cost of the exercise would be 2.5 liters per minute × 10 minutes = 25 liters.

Two other points need to be mentioned at this time. First, it is important to recognize that the net oxygen cost when expressed per minute is a *power* measure. By the same token, when the net oxygen cost is expressed for the total exercise period, it is a *work* measure. For example, in the anaerobic exercise (p. 72), the total net oxygen cost was 27 liters. Since the exercise lasted 5 minutes, the net power produced was 27 ÷ 5 = **5.4 liters** of O_2 per minute. In the aerobic exercise just mentioned, the net oxygen cost was 25 liters, about the same as that for the anaerobic exercise. However, the total aerobic exercise time was 10 minutes, and thus the net

power produced was 25 ÷ 10 = **2.5 liters** of O_2 per minute. Notice that this is less than half the power produced during the anaerobic exercise. In other words, even though the same total work was performed, the power or rate of work performed was much different between the two exercises. This points out the importance of understanding the difference between power and work and has strong implications for training.

Second, the maximal oxygen consumption (p. 34) is usually measured on a per minute basis. Thus, the proper term for expressing this is the maximal aerobic power. The measurement, both directly and indirectly, of the maximal aerobic power is described in detail in Appendix G.

The Concept of the MET

Recently, another unit used to express the energy or oxygen cost of exercise has been introduced.[1] It is called a MET, an acronym that stands for "**M**etabolic **E**quivalen**T**." One MET is defined as the amount of oxygen required per minute under quiet resting conditions. It is equal to 3.5 ml of oxygen consumed per kilogram of body weight per minute (ml/kg-min). Notice that because of the time factor, the MET is expressed with units of power. An exercise requiring 10 METS simply means that the oxygen cost of the exercise is 10 times 3.5, or 35 ml/kg-min. For a person who weighs 70 kg, this would represent a $\dot{V}O_2$ of 2.45 liters per minute (70 × 35 = 2450 ml, or 2.45 liters).

As an example of how to calculate METS consider the question, How many METS were required during the treadmill run mentioned previously? You will recall that the $\dot{V}O_2$ for this exercise was 2.8 liters per minute. Assuming that the subject weighed 70 kilograms, the oxygen cost on a per kilogram of body weight basis would be 2800 ml ÷ 70 kg = 40 ml/kg-min. Since 1 MET is equal to 3.5 ml/kg-min, this would represent an oxygen cost of $40 \div 3.5 = 11.4$ METS.

Computation of Efficiency

Per cent efficiency is defined as the ratio of work output over work input (energy expenditure) times 100, or:

$$\%EFF = \frac{\text{Useful work output}}{\text{Energy expended}} \times 100$$

In the physiological (metabolic) sense, we are interested in work performance expressed in kilocalories produced and the energy consumed in kilocalories. Thus:

$$\% EFF = \frac{\text{Work performed (kcal)}}{\text{Energy expended (kcal)}} \times 100$$

Fortunately, we can convert various work units into energy units. Thus work, expressed in ft-lb, kp-m, or kg-m, can be converted to kilocalories as can energy expenditure originally expressed in liters per minute.

All machines must be less than 100 per cent efficient because of friction. That is to say, the *useful* work output will always be less than the work input. The doctrine of the conservation of energy implies that although it is possible to convert one form of energy to another, *one can neither create nor destroy energy.* Remember, machines do *not* create or destroy energy; they merely convert it from one form to another. During the conversion, some energy is *always* lost (wasted). If this were not the case, we could develop a perpetual motion machine. A steam plant, for example, may operate at 5% or at even less efficiency because heat is lost up the smoke stack and through radiation, conduction, and exhaust steam. Turbines and automobile engines operate at about 20 to 25% efficiency, while a diesel engine may produce an output-input ratio of approximately 30 to 35%.

What is the efficiency of the human? Usually the performance of large muscle activities, such as walking, running, and cycling results in an efficiency of 20 to 25%. There are, of course, individual differences that are influenced by body size, fitness level, and skill in performing a given task. In addition, in activities in which there is considerable air or water resistance, such as ice-skating, rowing, and swimming, efficiencies are generally lower than 20%.[5,6,12,13,17] This is shown in Table 4-5. Notice that the efficiency of swimming freestyle is generally less than 10%.[17] Efficiency can also be dependent upon the speed with which a task is performed. For example, Figure 4-5 clearly demonstrates the influence of speed on efficiency in climbing stairs. Fifty steps per minute produces the highest efficiency (lowest energy cost).

It should also be mentioned at this time that there is a difference in running efficiencies between middle-distance and marathon runners.[9] This is shown in Figure 4-6. Efficiency is represented by the net oxygen cost of running at various speeds and is expressed as ml of oxygen per horizontal meter (m) run and per kg of body weight (ml/m-kg). Remember, the higher the net oxygen cost, the lower the efficiency. Marathon runners are about 5 to 10% more efficient on the average than middle-distance runners. This advantage, though small for runs of short duration, would be an important consideration during the $2\frac{1}{2}$ hours required to run a good marathon race. For example, a 10% greater efficiency would mean a savings of about 60 liters of oxygen consumed or 300 kcal of heat produced per marathon race! Also, note that the great half-mile and mile runner Jim Ryun is the most efficient of the middle-distance runners, and Derek Clayton, the most efficient among the marathon runners.

Cavanagh and Kram, in a recent review, discussed factors that affect effi-

TABLE 4-5

Efficiency While Performing Various Exercise Activities

Exercise Activity	Efficiency (per cent)		References
	Male	Female	
Horizontal walking	19.6–35.2	—	Donovan and Brooks[7]
Vertical walking	20.6–43.0	—	Donovan and Brooks[7]
Swimming (freestyle)	2.9–7.4	2.7–9.4	Pendergast et al.[18]
Rowing	13.0	—	Hagerman et al.[12]
Rowing	—	17.0	Hagerman et al.[13]
Rowing	10–20	—	diPrampero et al.[5]
Ice-skating	11.0	—	diPrampero et al.[6]
Cycling	24.4–34.0	—	Gaesser and Brooks[10]

ciency and economy of movement.[3] They identified structural factors and optimal phenomena. Structural factors include total body mass, distribution of body mass, variations in the distance of insertions of key muscles from joint centers, and variations in muscle fiber orientation and length.

Observations have been made on several types of human movement where bio-

mechanical variables have been manipulated. Such manipulations produce energy cost curves that have a point of least energy cost. Cavanagh and Kram characterized

Figure 4-5. Influence of speed in climbing stairs on energy cost and efficiency. The cost is lowest and efficiency highest when 50 steps per minute were climbed (shaded area). (Data from Lupton, H.[15])

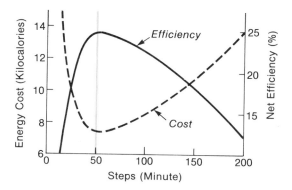

Figure 4-6. Differences in running efficiencies between middle-distance runners and marathon runners. Marathon runners are about 5 to 10% more efficient than middle-distance runners. Notice that the great miler J. Ryun is the most efficient of the middle-distance runners and that D. Clayton, the world's best marathoner, is the most efficient among the marathon runners. (Based on data from various sources as compiled by Fox and Costill.[9])

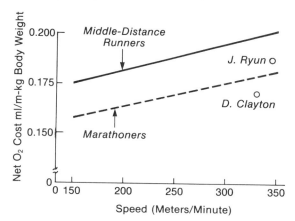

these points as "optimal phenomena." Some activities in which optimal phenomena have been observed include:[3]

1. The energetics of riding a bicycle at a constant power output are affected by seat height.
2. Maximal power output is also affected by seat height.
3. Pedal frequency affects energy cost at a constant power output. A mean value of 91 RPM was "chosen" by competitive cyclists.
4. A self-selected stride length in running at a given speed affects energy cost.
5. Analysis of running and walking at various downhill grades shows a minimum energy cost at a −5% grade.
6. A speed of walking exists at which the energy required to walk a given distance is minimized.

Measuring Efficiency on a Bicycle Ergometer

Figure 4-7 depicts a mechanically braked bicycle. A belt runs around the rim of a flywheel and can be provided with greater

Figure 4-7. Components of a mechanically braked bicycle ergometer. A weighted flywheel has a belt around its circumference. The belt is connected with a small spring on one end and has an adjustable tension lever on the other end. A pendulum balance indicates the resistance in kiloponds. The inset shows the pendulum at a resistance of 2 kiloponds.

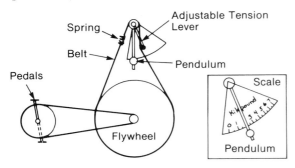

tension through an adjustable dial.[19] By increasing tension on the wheel more friction, and thus greater resistance, is provided. The bicycle gearing and wheel circumference have been designed so that one complete turn of the pedals moves a point on the rim 6 meters (the rim is 1.6 meters in circumference). With a metronome set at 100 counts per minute (50 RPM) a scale is provided that is graduated in **kiloponds (kp)**. One kp is the force acting on the mass of 1 kg at the normal acceleration of gravity. The braking power, in kp, multiplied by the distance pedaled in meters yields work in **kilopond-meters (kp-m)**. If the distance "traveled" is related to time then power can be expressed as kp-m/min. Power can also be expressed as **watts** and **kg-m/min**.

The relationship among the various work units, at 50 rpm is: 1 kp = 300kp-m (= 300 kg-m) = 723 ft-lb. The work units can be converted to energy units of kilocalories (kcal) or kilojoules (kJ).* 1 kcal = 3086 ft-lb = 486 kg-m = 4.1855 kJ.

There are several newer bicycle ergometers available that are electronically braked and allow for variations in pedal frequency. That is, if the subject pedals at a faster rate, the resistance will be lowered so that the total work output will be constant. The mechanically braked bicycle, described previously, represents an inexpensive, reliable research ergometer. For computing the efficiency we need to know both the work accomplished (output) and the work (energy) expended (input) by the subject.

In the following example, a subject exercises for 10 minutes on a bicycle ergometer at a resistance of 3 kp. The task is to determine efficiency for the 10-minute ride.

1. *Work output.* In order to determine work output we need to know the

---

*Joule is the international unit for work. 1 kp=9.80665 newtons (N). A Newton-meter is expressed in joules.

resistance (3 kp), the total time (10 min), the pedaling rate (50 rpm), and the distance the rim of the flywheel travels (6 meters per revolution).

a. Determine the work performed.

$$W = F \times D$$
$$W = (3 \text{ kp}) \times (50 \text{ rpm} \times 10 \text{ min} \times 6 \text{ m per rev})$$
$$W = (3 \text{ kp}) \times (3000 \text{ m})$$
$$W = 9000 \text{ kp-m}$$
or $$W = \textbf{9000 kg-m}$$

b. Convert to kilocalories.

$$1 \text{ kcal} = 426.8 \text{ kg-m}$$
$$\text{Total kcal} = 9000 \text{ kg-m} \div 426.8 \text{ kg-m/kcal}$$
$$\text{kcal} = \textbf{21.09}$$

2. *Work Input.* To determine work input, we need to know the R-value (in order to acquire the caloric equivalent of a liter of oxygen) and the total oxygen consumed. The R can be determined only under steady-state conditions, thus the work must be submaximal.

given: $R = 0.85$ From Table 4-4, 1 liter of $O_2 = 4.865$ kcal
$\dot{V}O_2 = 2.0$ L/min
exercise time = 10 minutes

c. Determine total oxygen consumed.

$$\text{total } \dot{V}O_2 = (2 \text{ L/min}) \times (10 \text{ min})$$
$$= \textbf{20 liters of oxygen}$$

d. Total calories consumed = $(20 \text{ L}) \times (4.865 \text{ kcal/liter})$
= **97.3 kcal**

e. $\%EFF = \dfrac{21.09 \text{ kcal}}{97.30 \text{ kcal}} \times 100 = \textbf{21.7\%}$

Many of the newer bicycles are calibrated to give a direct read-out in power units (i.e., watts or kilogram-meters per unit of time). Efficiency may still be computed as was previously mentioned, so long as the numerator and denominator are expressed in identical units (power or work).

Measuring Efficiency on a Treadmill

If the subject were walking or running horizontally on the treadmill he or she would not be performing "useful" work and therefore efficiency could not be computed. Sometimes this is difficult for a student to resolve because we know it requires *energy* to walk or run—but according to the physicist, we are not doing any *work*. Recall that work is moving an object through a distance. The subject walking along a horizontal is raising and lowering the center of gravity the same distance; therefore, one cancels the other. All the energy expended by the subject is degraded as heat without performing any useful work. The same is true if you hold a weight at arm's length in front of you; because you are not moving the weight, no useful work is being performed, even though you are expending energy. As a consequence, the treadmill must be positioned so the subject walks up a grade; in other words, the angle of the treadmill with the horizontal must be greater than 0 degrees. Usually the slope or incline of the treadmill is reported as per cent grade rather than in degrees. Per cent grade may be defined as units (feet) of rise per 100 horizontal units (feet); it may be determined by multiplying the tangent of the angle times 100, as can be observed in Table 4-6. To determine efficiency while walking or running on an elevated treadmill, the work output and work input are determined in the following ways.

1. *Work Output.* Work output is equal to the weight of the subject times the vertical distance he or she would have been raised in walking up the incline of the treadmill, i.e., work equals force (weight of

TABLE 4-6

Angles of Incline and Corresponding Per Cent Grade*

θ (Degrees)	Tangent θ	Sine θ	Per Cent Grade
1	0.0175	.0175	1.75
2	0.0349	.0349	3.49
3	0.0524	.0523	5.24
4	0.0699	.0698	6.99
5	0.0875	.0872	8.75
6	0.1051	.1045	10.51
7	0.1228	.1219	12.28
8	0.1405	.1392	14.05
9	0.1584	.1564	15.84
10	0.1763	.1736	17.63

*Note that the sine and the tangent are equal for the first two degrees; as the angle increases, the difference between sine and tangent increases.

subject) times distance. Measuring the weight of the subject poses no problem (e.g., 73 kg); however, computing vertical distance is somewhat more involved. Referring to Figure 4-8, the measurements and computations are made in the following manner:

The vertical distance X is equal to the sine of angle theta (θ) times B, which is the distance traveled along the incline, or:

$$X = (\text{Sine } \theta)(B)$$

For example, assume angle θ is 2 degrees. The angle may be measured with an inclinometer at point C, Figure 4-8. Sine θ of 2 degrees (from Table 4-5) equals 0.0349. The value of B is calculated by knowing the speed of the treadmill belt and duration of exercise. For example, the distance traveled on the incline while walking at 4.8 kilometers per hour (3 miles per hour) for 30 minutes (0.5 hour) is 2.4 km, or:

$$B = 4.8 \text{ km/hr} \times 0.5 \text{ hr} = \textbf{2.4 km}$$
$$\text{and}$$
$$X = 0.0349 \times 2.4 \text{ km} = \textbf{0.08376 km}$$

Changing X to meters:
0.08376 km $\times$ 1000 meters/km
= **83.76 meters**

Therefore, work output (W) becomes:

$$W = 73 \text{ kg (wt. of subj.)} \times 83.76 \text{ meters}$$
$$\text{(vert. dist.)}$$
$$= \textbf{6114.5 kg-m} \text{ of work accomplished}$$
$$\text{during 30 minutes}$$

For calculating efficiency, the work output may also be expressed in power units (work per unit of time). For power calculation, convert work output to work per unit of time, or:

$$\text{Power} = \frac{6114.5 \text{ kg-m}}{30 \text{ minutes}} = \textbf{203.8 kg-m/min}$$

2. *Work Input.* Work input during submaximal exercise (aerobic) can be ex-

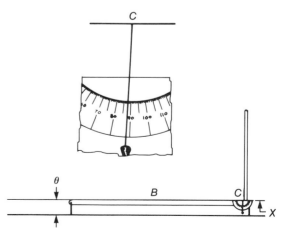

Figure 4-8. Determination of work output using inclined treadmill. Angle theta (θ) is determined by use of inclinometer at point C. The reading of 88 degrees at point C on the treadmill is equivalent to 2 degrees at angle θ (180 degrees − [90 degrees + 88 degrees] = 2 degrees). The vertical distance the subject would travel, X, is computed as outlined in the text.

pressed in terms of net oxygen consumption per unit of time. The subject must be in a steady state, as was previously discussed. Assuming the net $\dot{V}O_2$ of the subject while walking is 0.5 liter per minute, we must convert this measurement to identical units of power output; that is, liters of oxygen per minute must be expressed in kg-m per minute.

The first consideration is to convert liters of oxygen per minute to kilocalories per minute. This is done determining R and then referring to Table 4-4 to obtain the proper caloric equivalent. Or:

$$\text{Assuming } R = 0.82$$
$$1 \text{ liter of } O_2 = 4.83 \text{ kcal, or}$$

0.5 liter/minute $\times$ 4.83 kcal/liter
$$= \textbf{2.41 kcal/min}$$
1 kcal/min = **426.8 kg-m/min** (Table 4-2);
2.41 kcal/min $\times$ 426.8 kg-m/kcal
$$= \textbf{1028.5 kg-m/min}$$

$$\%EFF = \frac{203.8 \text{ kg-m/min}}{1028.5 \text{ kg-m/min}} \times 100 = \textbf{19.8\%}$$

Sometimes the efficiency of walking up an incline is represented as the ratio of useful work performed to the energy expended in walking up the grade less the energy expended walking the same distance on a horizontal plane, times 100.

$$\text{Efficiency} = \frac{(\text{vert. dist.})(\text{wt. of subj.})}{\text{energy exp. climbing} - \text{energy exp. horiz.}} \times 100$$

Modified Methods of Reflecting Energy Cost

Situations occur when the exercise scientist must employ a somewhat different approach in measuring energy expenditure. There are three methods that can yield satisfactory results; these are perhaps best illustrated with examples.

Measurement of Energy Cost for the 100-Meter Dash

One might consider it rather difficult to run along the track holding a Douglas bag in order to gather a sprinter's exhaled air. Instead, resting $\dot{V}O_2$ is determined; then, during the sprint, the subjects hold their breath until the finish, at which time they hold their nose and direct all exhaled air into a series of Douglas bags.

This method was employed in measuring the cost of the open and closed swimming turn.[8] The six male swimmers were tested in a postabsorptive state (12 hours following the last meal). Resting oxygen consumption was determined, then the swimmers swam 70 feet, performing either the closed or the open turn without taking a breath. Immediately upon completion of the swim, they exhaled into a Douglas bag for 15 minutes. Net energy cost of the exercise was determined by subtracting oxygen consumed during 15 minutes of rest from that obtained during the 15 minutes of recovery. The data showed no significant difference between the two turns in regard to the recovery oxygen, but the closed turn was performed significantly faster.

Measurement of Energy Cost for the 400-Meter Race

Again a difficult challenge arises: finding an experimenter physically qualified to run alongside an athlete with utensils in hand in order to collect that valued exhaled air! Furthermore, what athlete can hold his or her breath throughout the 400 meters? In this instance, the recovery oxygen alone may be used as a relative indication of the intensity of the exercise. After resting $\dot{V}O_2$ is determined, the stage is set so that immediately following the race, all exhaled air is collected. As before, the resting value subtracted from the recovery value represents the recovery oxygen.

This method was employed in comparing the oxygen debts accumulated in swimming the 400-yard free style, using the open and closed turns.[11] The subjects were five Ohio State University varsity swimmers who were actively engaged in competitive swimming. Upon entering the pool area in a postabsorptive state, the swimmers rested for 20 minutes. During the last 5 minutes of rest, exhaled air was directed into a Douglas bag. The subjects then entered the pool and were required to swim 400 yards in 4 minutes and 50 seconds, plus or minus 5 seconds. During recovery, expired air was collected for 30 minutes following the exercise. Average recovery oxygen for the open and closed turns were 4.7 and 5.1 liters of oxygen, respectively. Although the open turn resulted in a smaller recovery oxygen, the difference was not statistically significant.

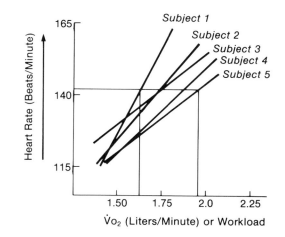

Figure 4-9. Relationships among workload, $\dot{V}O_2$, and heart rate. As the workload or $\dot{V}O_2$ increases, so does heart rate in a linear (straight line) manner. Notice the variability among subjects.

Measurement of Energy Cost Using Telemetry

The scientists of the National Aeronautics and Space Administration (NASA), prior to initiating programs designed to probe an organism's physiological reactions to space, devised instrumentation that could radio back to the space center such information as respiration, heart rate, and blood pressure. Today, the field of physiological radio transmission—i.e., **telemetry**—is so well advanced that most college laboratories are equipped for telemetering numerous physiological variables. Of special interest to us is the telemetering of heart rate, for under submaximal workloads this variable is linearly related to the work or power performed and to the amount of oxygen consumed per minute ($\dot{V}O_2$). Figure 4-9 graphically illustrates these relationships.

The use of telemetry allows us to estimate the $\dot{V}O_2$ of numerous physical and sports activities that otherwise would be impossible to determine. Of course, it also allows measurement of the heart rate during such activities, which in itself can be of value to physical educators, coaches, and others with respect to evaluating the intensity of an activity. In general, the higher the exercise heart rate, the greater the intensity of the exercise. However, the heart rate is also influenced by other factors, such as apprehension and excitement. Telemetering the heart rate of coaches while they were coaching, for example, revealed that the heart rate increased considerably (over 150 beats/min) during critical game situations even though physical activity was minimal.[17] Also, men about to be released in the X-15 experimental aircraft responded with extremely high heart rates, again even though the physical effort was of little consequence. The same was true of the astronauts when they were placed in critical situations, such as liftoff and moon landing.

If we were presented with the problem of evaluating energy cost while playing racquetball, or the delightful sport of curling,[2] we would proceed as follows:

1. Have each subject walk on the treadmill at gradually increasing workloads.
2. At each workload, measure heart rate and oxygen consumption.
3. Utilizing a statistical regression, plot this relationship on a graph, as indicated in Figure 4-9.

The subject is then fitted with a transmitter, as shown in Figure 4-10. This instrument, which is fitted about the subject's waist or chest, radios the heart rate to a recorder. Any time during the activity heart rate can be measured. In this manner, $\dot{V}O_2$ while playing can be indirectly determined. For example, if heart rate for subject 1 were 142 beats per minute then $\dot{V}O_2$ would equal about 1.6 liters per minute at that particular time (Fig. 4-9). Each person must be so "titrated," as the relationship is individual. For example, at the same heart rate (142 beats/min), the $\dot{V}O_2$ for subject five would be 1.96 liters/min. Incidentally, curlers utilize about 1000 kcal in a 2-hour curling match.

Ancillary Considerations in Measuring Energy Expenditure

The indirect physiological measurement of energy is quite well standardized in the laboratory. The methods we have already discussed are applicable in most cases. However, there are certain ancillary considerations that are well to keep in mind when measuring and interpreting the energy cost of activities.

Body Size and Energy Cost

A larger person in moving the body a given distance will expend more energy than will a smaller one. As a result, it is sometimes more appropriate to express energy expenditure in terms of body weight, particularly when making comparisons. For example:

Work: kilogram-meters per kilogram of body weight (kg-m/kg)
Energy: kilocalories per kilogram of body weight (kcal/kg)
Power: kilogram-meters per kilogram of body weight per minute (kg-m/kg-min^{-1})
Energy: $\dot{V}O_2$ in milliliters per kilogram of body weight per minute (ml/kg-min^{-1}), kilocalories per kilogram of body weight per minute (kcal/kg-min^{-1})

Notice that the body weight is usually expressed in kilograms, a metric unit not as familiar to us as pounds. A table con-

Figure 4-10. Subject fitted to transmitter for telemetering heart rate. The instrument picks up the subject's heart rate and transmits it to a receiver and recorder. This compact and light piece of equipment allows the subject to perform activity unencumbered and at a distance from the recording equipment.

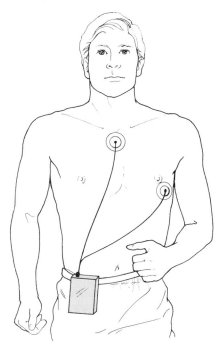

verting body weight from pounds to kilograms is given in Appendix E. One pound equals 0.4535 kilograms and one kilogram equals 2.205 pounds.

On occasion, body surface area rather than body weight is used for expressing energy per unit of body size. This is generally the case when expressing energy expenditure in heat equivalence (kcal) during heat balance studies. The reason for this is that the amount of heat gained and/or lost by the body is more a function of body surface area than just body weight. The body surface area is estimated from both the body weight and height. For example, a person who weighs 70 kg (154 pounds) and who is 180 centimeters in height (5 feet, 11 inches) has a body surface area of 1.87 square meters. The body surface area can be calculated from a nomograph, which is also contained in Appendix E.

Average Energy and Work Values

To be well oriented in the physiology of exercise, certain common energy values for various levels of exercise should be committed to memory. For example, one should remember that in sitting and reading this book, the amount of oxygen consumed is between 250 and 300 ml/min, or between 3.5 to 4.5 ml/kg-min^{-1}, and heat production is between 1.2 and 1.5 kcal/min. At the same time, about 6 to 8 liters of air are being ventilated per minute. The resting heart rate is between 70 and 80 beats per minute.

Knowing such values forms a base line for understanding intensity of work. For example, exercise requiring an oxygen consumption of 4.5 liters/min would mean little if one did not realize that 0.3 liter (300 ml) is required at rest. Exercise requiring such a high oxygen consumption is 15 times more intensive than is resting. So, too, a person ventilating 140 liters of air per minute is moving about 20 times more air

through the lungs than that required for resting metabolism.

Table 4-7 contains average energy and related values that permit us better understanding of the physiological requirements of performance. Memorizing a few of these values will be well worthwhile.

Summary

Energy, work, and power are functionally related. Energy is defined as the capacity to perform work, whereas work (W) is the application of a force (F) through a distance (D), or $W = F \times D$. Power (P) is the time (t) rate of performing work, or $P = W/t = (F \times D)/t$.

The direct quantification of energy in humans involves the measurement of heat production, whereas the indirect method involves the measurement of oxygen consumption. It is a known fact that energy produced through the metabolism of foodstuffs is equal to the heat produced by the body.

The oxygen consumed can be expressed in energy units, i.e., kilocalories (kcal), by knowing the respiratory exchange ratio (R). R is the ratio of the amount of carbon dioxide produced per minute ($\dot{V}CO_2$) over the oxygen consumed per minute ($\dot{V}O_2$), i.e., $R = \dot{V}CO_2/\dot{V}O_2$ and indicates which foodstuffs are being metabolized. If carbohydrate is being metabolized, then $R = 1$, and 1 liter of oxygen consumed equals 5.05 kcal of heat produced. If $R = 0.71$, then fat is being metabolized, and 1 liter of oxygen consumed equals 4.68 kcal of heat produced. Other factors that affect R besides the type of foodstuffs metabolized are: (1) hyperventilation (overventilation of the lungs), which leads to excessive carbon dioxide loss; (2) buffering of lactic acid during exhaustive exercise, which also leads to release of large quantities of CO_2; and (3) the retention of CO_2, which occurs during recovery from exhaustive exercise.

TABLE 4-7

Classification of Physical Work*

Classification of Work	Heart Rate (Beats per Minute)	Metabolic Rate				Ventilation		R	Lactic Acid in Multiples of Resting Value	Length of Time Work Can Be Sustained
		$\dot{V}o_2$ (liters/ minute)	$\dot{V}o_2$ (ml/ kg-min)	METS	Heat (kcal/ minute)	Volume (liters/ minute)	Rate (breaths/ minute)			
1. Light										
a. Mild	<100	<0.75	<10.5	<3	<4.0	<20	<14	0.85	Normal	Indefinite 8 hours daily on the job
b. Moderate	<120	<1.50	<21.0	<6	<7.5	<35	<15	0.85	Within normal limits	
2. Heavy										
a. Optimal	<140	<2.0	<28.0	<8	<10.0	<50	<16	0.9	1.5 ×	8 hours daily for few weeks (seasonal work, military maneuvers, etc.)
b. Strenuous	<160	<2.5	<35.0	<10	<12.5	<60	<20	0.95	2.0 ×	4 hours two or three times a week for a few weeks (special physical training)
3. Severe										
a. Maximal	<180	<3.0	<42.0	<12	<15.0	<80	<25	<1.0	5-6 ×	1 to 2 hours occasionally (usually in competitive sports)
b. Exhausting	>180	>3.0	>42.0	>12	>15.0	>120	>30	>1.0	6 × or more	Few minutes; rarely

*Modified from Wells et al.[20]

Determination of the energy (oxygen) cost of anaerobic exercise involves measurement of the oxygen consumed during rest, exercise, and recovery (oxygen debt). The total oxygen consumed during exercise and recovery minus the resting oxygen consumption is called the net oxygen cost of exercise. During aerobic exercise, only the resting and exercise steady-state oxygen consumption need be measured. In this case, the net oxygen cost is equal to the oxygen consumed during exercise minus the resting oxygen consumption. Another unit used to express the energy or oxygen cost of exercise is called the MET. One MET is defined as the amount of oxygen required per minute under quiet resting conditions and is equal to 3.5 ml of oxygen consumed per kilogram of body weight per minute ($ml/kg \cdot min^{-1}$).

Per cent efficiency is defined as the ratio of work output over work input (energy expenditure). The efficiency of large muscle activities, such as walking, running, and cycling, is usually 20 to 25%. Because of the water resistance, swimming has a very low efficiency, between 2 and 10%. Efficiency is most easily measured either on a bicycle ergometer or on an elevated treadmill.

Modified methods of reflecting energy cost include measuring only the recovery oxygen and estimating oxygen consumption from heart rate measurements. With the latter method, oxygen consumption can be estimated during the actual performance of activities, since heart rate can be measured through the transmission of radio waves (telemetry).

Energy expenditure of weight-bearing activities (e.g., walking or running) should be expressed relative to body size (body weight), whereas in heat balance studies, energy expenditure should be expressed in kilocalories per unit of body surface area.

Questions

1. Define, in words, energy, work, and power. Express work and power by formulae.
2. What is the principle of the conservation of energy?
3. Explain the difference between direct and indirect calorimetry.
4. What is the respiratory exchange ratio?
5. How is the respiratory exchange ratio used in the indirect measurement of energy?
6. What fundamental measurements are needed when indirectly measuring the energy expenditure of a given exercise?
7. Define the MET and explain how it is used.
8. Explain efficiency and indicate how the efficiency of a human is measured.
9. How might you proceed in measuring the energy cost of running the 100-yard dash?
10. What are the physiological considerations that allow you to estimate energy cost through telemetering heart rate?
11. How are body size and the performance of work related?
12. When should body surface area be used in expressing energy expenditure of exercise? Why?

References

1. American College of Sports Medicine. *Guidelines for Graded Exercise Testing and Exercise Prescription.* Philadelphia, Lea and Febiger, 1986.
2. Bowers, R. W., and Farrell, P. A.: How much does curling cost in calories? *Physician Sportsmed.* 4:37–39, 1976.
3. Cavanagh, P. R., and Kram, R.: Mechanical and muscular factors affecting the efficiency of human movement. *Med Sci Sports Exercise.* 17:326–331, 1985.
4. Costill, D. L.: Use of a swimming ergometer in physiological research. *Res Q.* 37:564–567, 1967.

5. diPrampero, P. E., Cortili, G., Celentano, F., and Cerretelli, P.: Physiological aspects of rowing. *J Appl Physiol.* 31(6):853–857, 1971.

6. diPrampero, P. E., Cortili, G., Mognoni, P., and Saibene, F.: Energy cost of speed skating and efficiency of work against air resistance. *J Appl Physiol.* 40(4):584–591, 1976.

7. Donovan, C. M., and Brooks, G. A.: Muscular efficiency during steady-state exercise. II. Effects of walking speed and work rate. *J Appl Physiol.* 43(3):431–439, 1977.

8. Fox, E. L., Bartels, R. L., and Bowers, R. W.: Comparison of speed and energy expenditure for two swimming turns. *Res Q.* 34: 322–326, 1963.

9. Fox, E. L., and Costill, D. L.: Estimated cardiorespiratory responses during marathon running. *Arch Environ Health.* 24: 315–324, 1972.

10. Gaesser, G. A., and Brooks, G. A.: Muscular efficiency during steady-rate exercise: effects of speed and work rate. *J Appl Physiol.* 38(6):1132–1139, 1975.

11. Hagerman, F. C.: *A Comparison of Oxygen Debts in Swimming the 400-Yard Freestyle While Using the Open and Closed Turns.* Master's Thesis, The Ohio State University, Columbus, Ohio, 1962.

12. Hagerman, F. C., Connors, M. C., Gault, J. A., Hagerman, G. R., and Polinski, W. J.: Energy expenditure during simulated rowing. *J Appl Physiol.* 45(1):87–93, 1978.

13. Hagerman, F. C., Fox, E. L., Connors, M., and Pompei, J.: Metabolic responses of women rowers during ergometric rowing. *Med Sci Sports.* 6(1):87, 1974.

14. Heusner, W. E.: Personal Communication, Michigan State University.

15. Lupton, H.: Analysis of effects of speed on mechanical efficiency of human movement. *J Physiol.* 57:337, 1923.

16. Lusk, G.: *Science of Nutrition,* 4th ed. Philadelphia, W. B. Saunders, 1928, p. 65.

17. McCafferty, W. B., Gliner, J. A., and Horvath, S. M.: The stress of coaching. *Physician Sportsmed.* 6(2):66–71, February, 1978.

18. Pendergast, D. R., diPrampero, P. E., Craig, A. B., Wilson, D. R., and Rennie, D. W.: Quantitative analysis of the front crawl in men and women. *J Appl Physiol.* 43(3): 475–479, 1977.

19. von Dobeln, W.: A simple bicycle ergometer. *J Appl Physiol.* 7:222, 1954.

20. Wells, J. G., Balke, B., and Van Fossan, D. D.: Lactic acid accumulation during work. A suggested standardization of work classification. *J Appl Physiol.* 10:51–55, 1957.

21. Wilmore, J. H., Constable, S. H., Stamford, P. R., Buono, M. J., Tsao, Y. W., Roby, F. B., Jr., and Ratliff, R. A.: Mechanical and physiological calibration of four cycle ergometers. *Med Sci Sports Exercise.* 14:322–325, 1982.

SELECTED READINGS

Briggs, G. M., and Calloway, D. H.: *Nutrition and Physical Fitness,* 10th ed. Philadelphia, W. B. Saunders, 1979, pp. 50–114.

Consolazio, C. F., Johnson, R. E., and Pecora, L. J.: *Physiological Measurements of Metabolic Functions in Man.* New York, McGraw-Hill, 1963, pp. 1–11.

Knuttgen, H. G.: Force, work, power, and exercise.: *Med Sci Sports.* 10(3):227–228, 1978.

Williams, K. R.: The relationship between mechanical and physiological energy estimates. *Med Sci Sports Exercise.* 17:317–325, 1985.

Neuromuscular refers to both the nervous and muscular systems. Therefore, in this section we will direct our attention to the structure and function of nerves, the nervous system, and muscles as they apply to the physical education and athletics. Our primary purpose in studying neuromuscular physiology is to learn how muscles respond to stimuli and, in particular, to gain some understanding about the way in which we learn motor skills. Such information should help us to become better teachers, coaches, and trainers, to say nothing of allowing us to better appreciate the complex communication system that belongs to each of us.

In Chapter 5, we will study the structure and function of skeletal muscles. The more than 600 skeletal muscles of the human body constitute about 40 per cent of the necessary total body weight. The muscles are useful, of course, because they are able to produce motion, the most fundamental function of the muscular and skeletal systems (musculoskeletal system). The action of muscles on the bony levers permits us to stand erect, carry out activities of daily living, perform a variety of sports activities, and impart movement to other objects. This motion in the musculoskeletal system is governed to a large extent by the strength and endurance of the muscles.

In Chapter 6, the structure and function of nerves and the nervous system will be studied. Basically there are two kinds of nerves: *sensory* and *motor*. Sensory nerves—also referred to as afferent nerves—convey information from the periphery (e.g., the skin) to the central nervous system (brain and spinal cord). Motor nerves—also called efferent nerves—convey information from the central nervous system to effector organs, such as the skeletal muscles.

Finally, in Chapter 7, we will look at some of the neuromuscular changes induced through weight resistance exercise programs. Only recently has this area of research yielded exciting new findings that relate directly to physical education and athletic programs.

NEUROMUSCULAR CONCEPTS

Skeletal Muscle: Structure and Function

The major concepts to be learned from this chapter are as follows:

- The structure of skeletal muscle forms the basis for understanding how it contracts.
- The basis for skeletal muscle function is the motor unit, defined as a single motor nerve and the muscle fibers it innervates.
- Muscular strength gradations are possible by varying the number of motor units contracting at any given time and by varying the frequency of contraction of individual motor units.
- There are basically two kinds of motor units: one containing fast-twitch (FT) muscle fibers and the other containing slow-twitch (ST) muscle fibers.
- FT fibers have a high anaerobic capacity and are used preferentially for sprintlike activities, whereas ST fibers have a high aerobic capacity and are used preferentially for endurance activities.
- Histochemical staining allows further subdivision of FT fibers into FT_A (oxidative-glycolytic), FT_B (glycolytic) and FT_C (unclassified) categories.
- Motor units are preferentially recruited during exercise following a motorneuron "size principle"; small ones first, large ones last.
- ST motor units are recruited for low intensity exercise, FT_A for more prolonged, higher intensity exercise, and FT_B for all-out, maximal efforts.
- With endurance training, the most common adaptation is an increase in the aerobic capacity of both ST and FT fibers and shifts to higher ratios of FT_A:FT_B fibers.
- The peak force generated by a muscle decreases and the peak power increases with increasing velocities of movement.

- For any given velocity of movement, the peak force and peak power produced are greater the higher the percentage distribution of FT fibers in the muscle.
- The most probable sites of local muscular fatigue are the neuromuscular junction, the muscle itself (contractile mechanism), and the central nervous system (brain and spinal cord).

For professional physical educators and coaches to adequately plan and conduct programs designed to increase muscular strength, endurance, and flexibility, they need a knowledge of the muscular system. They should know structure, both gross and microscopic, in order to understand function; and even though it remains a problem for future researchers to answer conclusively, the person dealing with movement should know the most recent views on how a muscle contracts and what causes a muscle to fatigue. The purpose of this chapter then, will be to discuss both the structure and function of skeletal muscle.

Structure—The Basis for Contraction

A great deal of information concerning how a muscle contracts has been gathered in the past 25 years. For the most part, information about the structural changes that occur when a resting muscle cell is actively contracted has been obtained by use of the electron microscope. It is, therefore, imperative that we understand in some detail the structure of muscle. Then the theory as to how a muscle contracts will be easier to comprehend.

Connective Tissues

Skeletal muscle is composed of many thousands of individual contractile fibers bound

TABLE 5-1

Structural Units of Skeletal Muscle and Their Corresponding Connective Tissues

Structural Unit	Connective Tissue
Muscle fiber or cell	Endomysium
Muscle bundle (fasciculus)	Perimysium
Entire muscle	Epimysium

together by a sheath of connective tissues. That portion of connective tissue that covers each muscle fiber or cell is called the **endomysium.** Just inside and attached to the endomysium is the muscle cell membrane or **sarcolemma.** Since the sarcolemma is *not* a connective tissue, we will talk more about it later. The inside of the muscle cell is composed of a specialized

protoplasm called **sarcoplasm** (*sarco* means "flesh"). The muscle cells (fibers) are grouped together to form muscle bundles or **fasciculi.** These bundles, containing various numbers of muscle fibers, are in turn held together by a connective tissue referred to as the **perimysium.** Encasing the entire muscle (or all the muscle bundles) is yet another connective tissue component, called the **epimysium.** The structural units of muscle and their associated connective tissues are given in Table 5-1 and illustrated in Figure 5-1.

Tendons

The intramuscular network of connective tissues coalesces and becomes continuous with the dense connective tissue of the tendons at each end of a muscle. These tendons are rigidly cemented to the outermost covering of bone, the *periosteum,* and

Figure 5-1. Relationship between connective tissues and the cell membrane (sarcolemma) of skeletal muscle.

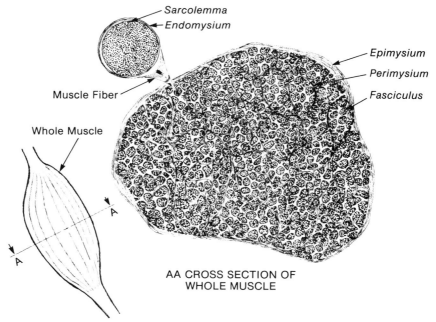

Sarcolemma

Endomysium

Epimysium

Perimysium

Fasciculus

Muscle Fiber

Whole Muscle

AA CROSS SECTION OF WHOLE MUSCLE

thereby serve to connect the skeletal muscles to the bony skeleton. The muscle fibers themselves do not come into direct contact with the skeleton; thus the tremendous tension developed by muscles is borne entirely by their tendinous attachments. There are several advantages to this arrangement. If muscle fibers were attached directly to bone they would be subject to considerable damage each time the muscle contracted. Tendons not only are much tougher than muscles but are also composed of "nonliving" fibers, which are metabolically inactive compared to muscle tissue. Furthermore, since tendons are stronger than muscles, a relatively small tendon can withstand the tension developed by a relatively large muscle.

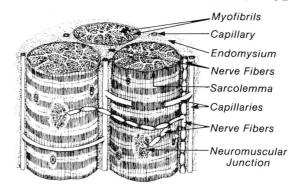

Figure 5-2. The nerves supplying a muscle contain both motor and sensory fibers and usually enter the muscle along with the blood vessels. They branch out repeatedly through the connective tissue framework of the muscle, thus reaching all the muscle fibers.

Blood Supply

Muscles are richly supplied with blood vessels. Arteries and veins enter the muscle along with the connective tissues and are oriented parallel to the individual muscle fibers. They branch repeatedly into numerous capillaries and venules, forming vast networks in and around the endomysium (Fig. 5-2). In this manner each fiber is assured of an adequate supply of freshly oxygenated blood from the arterial system and of the removal of waste products such as carbon dioxide via the venous system. In sedentary men and women, an average of 3 to 4 capillaries surround each muscle fiber, whereas in male and female athletes, 5 to 7 capillaries surround each fiber.[39,66]

The amount of blood required by skeletal muscle depends, of course, on its state of activity. During maximal exercise the muscles may require as much as 100 times more blood than when resting. Besides the large number of capillaries that supply each muscle fiber, there are other ways in which this blood-flow requirement can be met. For example, the alternating contraction and relaxation of active muscle cause periodic squeezing of the blood vessels. This pumping or milking action speeds up the flow of blood to the heart, thus increasing the amount of fresh blood that can be returned to the muscles. Constriction of the arteries supplying blood to the inactive areas of the body (such as the gut, kidney, and skin) and dilation of those to the active skeletal muscles also aid in regulating muscle blood flow. We will discuss these important muscle pump and shunting mechanisms again in Chapter 10.

Nerve Supply

The nerves supplying a muscle contain both **motor** (efferent) and **sensory** (afferent) **fibers**, and usually enter the muscle along with the blood vessels (see Fig. 5-2). They branch out repeatedly through the connective tissue framework of the muscle, thus reaching all the muscle fibers.

The motor nerves, which when stimulated cause the muscle to contract, originate in the central nervous system (spinal cord and brain). The point of termination of a motor nerve (axon) on a muscle fiber is known as the **myoneural** or **neuromus-**

cular junction or the **motor endplate** (p. 141). Motor nerves constitute about 60% of the nerves that enter the muscle. The sensory nerves, which make up the remaining 40%, convey information concerning pain and orientation of body parts from the muscle sense organs to the central nervous system. The muscle sense organs as well as other aspects of the nerve supply to muscle will be discussed in greater detail later in this chapter and in the next chapter.

Structure of the Muscle Cell (Fig. 5-3)

The scanning electron microscope provides us with detailed insights about the make-up and arrangement of muscle fibers. Although Figure 5-3 is for insect flight muscle, there is great similarity across various animal species including human beings.

To further appreciate the microscopic structure of a muscle cell, we can tease out a fiber from the sartorius muscle of a frog. After placing this single fiber under a light microscope, we can observe regularly alternating light and dark striations (Fig. 5-4). Because of these striations, skeletal muscle is sometimes referred to as striated or striped muscle. Inside the sarcolemma is the sarcoplasm, which we mentioned earlier. Subcellular components, such as nuclei and mitochondria, are suspended in this reddish, viscous fluid. The sarcoplasm also contains myoglobin, fat, glycogen, phosphocreatine, ATP, and hundreds of thread-like protein strands called **myofibrils.** It is within these myofibrils that the contractile units called **sarcomeres** (small boxes) are housed. The contractile unit contains **myofilaments** named **myosin** (thick ones) and **actin** (thin ones). These contractile proteins are found in a special arrangement to one another; i.e., each myosin is surrounded by six or more actins.

Figure 5-3. Scanning electron micrograph of insect flight muscle showing three very large muscle fibers or cells. The individual myofibrils making up the fibers are also clearly outlined. The inset in the upper right-hand corner is a light micrograph of the same tissue in transverse section (From Smith, D. S.: *Muscle.* New York, Academic Press, 1972, p. 10).

The Myofibrils

A closer look at the myofibrils (Fig. 5-4) reveals that they also are characterized by alternating light and dark areas. In fact, it is the geometrical arrangement of all these light and dark areas of the myofibrils juxtaposed that gives the fiber its overall striated appearance. The light areas are called **I bands,** the dark areas **A bands.** In the middle of each I band is a dark line, the **Z line** (from the German *zwischen,* meaning "between"). The bands, which are composed of protein filaments, are so named because of what happens to the velocity of a light wave as it passes through them. For example, when a light wave passes through the A band, its velocity is not equal in all directions, i.e., it is *anisotropic.* When

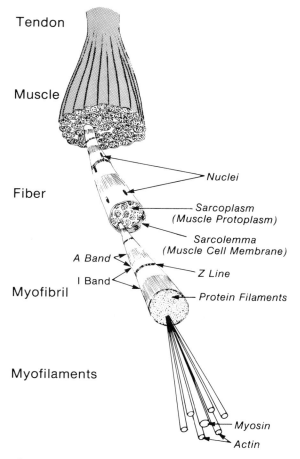

Tendon

Muscle

Fiber

Myofibril

Myofilaments

Nuclei

Sarcoplasm
(Muscle Protoplasm)

Sarcolemma
(Muscle Cell Membrane)

A Band

I Band

Z Line

Protein Filaments

Myosin

Actin

Figure 5-4. Skeletal muscle showing microscopic delineation of fiber, myofibril, and myofilaments. Note the striations in both the fiber and the myofibril; these alternating light and dark bands are caused by the geometric arrangement of the protein filaments, myosin and actin.

passed through the I band, the velocity of the emerging light is the same in all directions and thus is *isotropic*.

The Sarcoplasmic Reticulum and T-Tubules

As shown in Figure 5-5, surrounding the myofibrils is a netlike system of tubules and vesicles, collectively referred to as the **sarcoplasmic reticulum.** The **longitu-** **dinal tubules** are so named because they run parallel (longitudinally) to the myofibrils. The longitudinal tubules terminate at either end into vesicles or cisterns sometimes referred to as the **outer vesicles** or **cisterns** (see Fig. 5-5). This reticular pattern is repeated regularly along the entire length of the myofibrils. The outer vesicles of one reticular pattern are separated from those of another by a group of tubules called the **transverse tubules** (because they run transversely to the myofibril), the **T system,** or simply the **T-tubules.** The T-tubules, although functionally associated with the sarcoplasmic reticulum, are known to be anatomically separate from it. They are extensions or invaginations of the muscle cell membrane, the sarcolemma. The two outer vesicles and the T-tubule separating them are known as a **triad.** The fractional volume of the reticulum system and tubules has been determined to be about 5% of the total volume of a muscle fiber. With chronic exercise training, this volume increases by about 12% on the average.[9]

The entire function of the sarcoplasmic reticulum and T-tubules is not known. However, it is believed that the triad is of particular importance in muscular contraction. For example, it is thought that the T-tubules are responsible for spreading the nervous impulse from the sarcolemma inward to the deep portions of the fiber. The outer vesicles of the reticulum contain large amounts of calcium (Ca^{++}). As the impulse travels over the T-tubules and between the outer vesicles, Ca^{++} is released. We will discuss shortly the importance of both the spreading of the nervous impulse and the release of Ca^{++} in the actual contractile process. Right now, let's go on with the microscopic structure of muscle.

The Protein Filaments

The I and A bands are made up of two different protein filaments, a thinner fila-

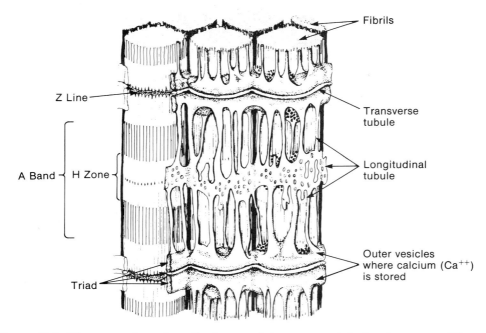

Figure 5-5. The sarcoplasmic reticulum and transverse tubules form a netlike system of tubules and vesicles surrounding the myofibrils. The outer vesicles store large quantities of calcium ions (Ca^{++}), one of the ingredients required for the contractile process. The transverse tubules are concerned with conduction of the nervous impulses deep into the myofibrils. The two outer vesicles and the transverse tubule separating them are known as a triad. (Modified and redrawn from Peachey.[60])

ment called **actin** and a thicker one called **myosin.** Their arrangement within the myofibrils is shown in Figures 5-4 and 5-6. As can be seen, the I band is composed entirely of the thinner actin filaments. You will also notice that they are not continuous within one **sarcomere,** i.e., between two Z lines. Rather, they are anchored to the Z lines at each end of the sarcomere and partly extend into the A band region. The latter band, although composed mainly of the thicker myosin filaments, therefore contains a small amount of actin. The so-called **H zone** is caused by the slight variation in shading resulting from the absence of actin filaments in the middle of the A band. The Z lines adhere to the sarco-lemma, lending stability to the entire structure, and presumably keep the actin filaments in alignment. The Z lines may also play a role in the transmission of nervous impulses from the sarcolemma to the myofibrils.

A closer look at the actin or thin filament is presented in Figure 5-7. The protein actin consists of globular (spheroidal) molecules linked together to form a double helix. Such a pattern is very similar in appearance to a twisted strand of beads. Although the thin filament is called the actin filament, it actually contains two other important proteins, **tropomyosin** and **troponin.** The tropomyosin is a long, thin molecule that lies on the surface of the

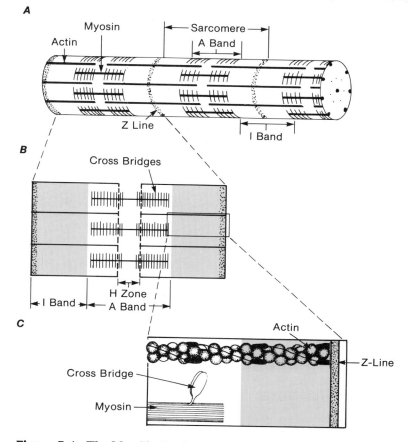

Figure 5-6. The Myofibril—the contractile unit of skeletal muscle. *A,* Note that the A band is composed of two protein filaments (actin and myosin). The I band contains actin filaments only. *B,* A closer look at the myosin filament, which projects in cross-bridging fashion toward the actin filament. The H zone (in the middle of the A band) is a result of the absence of actin filaments. *C,* A magnified view of a single myosin cross-bridge as it projects toward a single actin filament. (From Fox, E. L.[25])

actin strand. The ends of the tropomyosin molecules are embedded in globular molecules of troponin (Fig. 5-7).

The myosin filaments have tiny protein projections on each end which extend toward the actin filaments (Fig. 5-7). These are called **cross-bridges,** and as we shall see, together with the actin filaments they play a very important role in the contraction process.

The Sliding Filament Theory of Muscular Contraction

The structural arrangement of skeletal muscle presented above has led to a **sliding filament theory** of muscular contraction. As the name of the theory implies, one set of filaments is thought to slide over the other, thus shortening the muscle. This is illustrated in Figure 5-8. Note that the

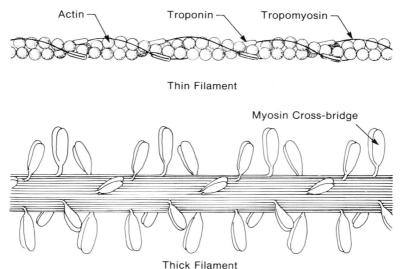

Thin Filament

Thick Filament

Figure 5-7. Close-up of actin (thin) and myosin (thick) filaments. The actin filament actually contains two other proteins important in the contractile process, troponin and tropomyosin. The head of the myosin filament is called the cross-bridge. (Modified and redrawn from Murray and Weber.[57])

lengths of the actin and myosin filaments do not change during contraction but rather the former merely slide over the latter toward the center of the sarcomere. This leads to a shortening of the I band but not of the A band and to disappearance of the H zone. The sliding filament theory proposes a mechanism somewhat analogous to the way in which a telescope shortens, i.e., the overall length of the telescope (muscle) decreases as one section (actin) slides over the other (myosin), with neither section itself shortening.

The exact manner in which this sliding process is effected has yet to be completely elucidated. However, it is thought that the myosin cross-bridges form a type of chemical bond with selected sites on the actin filaments. This forms a protein complex called **actomyosin.** When actomyosin is extracted from muscle and ATP is added, it will contract as it does in living muscle.

The mechanical and physiological events underlying the sliding filament theory of muscular contraction can be conveniently divided into five broad phases: (1) rest; (2) excitation-coupling; (3) contraction (shortening and tension development); (4) recharging; and (5) relaxation.

Rest (Fig. 5-9A)

Under resting conditions, the cross-bridges of the myosin filaments extend toward but do not interact with the actin filaments. An ATP molecule is bound to the end of the cross-bridge. At rest this complex is referred to as an *"uncharged" ATP cross-bridge complex.* As mentioned before, calcium (Ca^{++}) is stored in large quantities in the vesicles of the sarcoplasmic reticulum. In the absence of free Ca^{++}, the troponin of the actin filament inhibits the myosin cross-bridge from binding with actin; i.e., actin and myosin are said to be uncoupled.

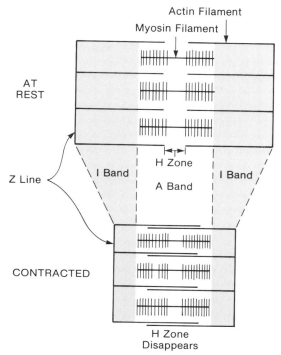

Figure 5-8. The sliding filament theory. When the sarcomeres of a muscle contract as compared to rest: (1) the H zone disappears because the actin filaments slide over the myosin filaments toward the center of the sarcomere; (2) the I band shortens because the actin filaments attached to the Z lines on either side of the sarcomere are pulled toward the center; (3) the A band does not change in length; and (4) neither the myosin nor the actin filaments change in length, because of the sliding or interdigitation mechanics. (From Fox, E. L.[25])

Excitation-Coupling (Fig. 5-9B)

When an impulse from a motor nerve reaches the motor endplate, acetylcholine is released, stimulating the generation of impulses (action potentials) in the sarcolemma of the muscle fiber (p. 141). These impulses are thought to be quickly spread throughout the fiber by way of the T-tubules. En route, they trigger the release of Ca^{++} from the vesicles of the reticulum.

The Ca^{++} is immediately bound (taken up) by the troponin molecules on the actin filaments. This results in what is referred to as the "turning on" of active sites on the actin filament. The turning on is a result of the Ca^{++} ions triggering changes in the conformation (structure) of both troponin and tropomyosin.[12] Simultaneously, but in an unknown manner, the "uncharged" ATP cross-bridge complex is changed into a "charged" ATP cross-bridge complex. The turning on by Ca^{++} of the active sites on the actin filament and the "charging" of the ATP cross-bridge complex mean that the two proteins are mutually attracted to each other. This results in a physical-chemical coupling of actin and myosin, i.e., in the formation of an actomyosin complex. Such a complex, as we will see, is force-generating.

Contraction (Fig. 5-9C)

The formation of actomyosin activates an enzyme component of the myosin filament called *myosin ATPase*. Myosin ATPase, as you might guess, causes ATP to be broken down into ADP and P_i (inorganic phosphate) with the release of large amounts of energy. This released energy allows the cross-bridge to swivel to a new angle[38] or to collapse[15] in such a way that the actin filament to which it is attached slides over the myosin filament toward the center of the sarcomere. Thus the muscle develops tension and shortens.

Recharging (Fig. 5-9D)

A single myosin cross-bridge may "make and break" with active sites on the actin filaments hundreds of times in the course of a one-second contraction. In order to do this, the myosin cross-bridge must be recharged. The first step in recharging is the breaking of the old bond between the actin and the myosin cross-bridge. This is accomplished by reloading the myosin cross-bridge with a new (resynthesized) ATP molecule. (The resynthesis of ATP was discussed in Chapter 2.) Once a new ATP is reloaded, the bond between the myosin cross-bridge and the active site on the actin filament is broken; the ATP cross-bridge is freed from the actin.* The cross-bridge as well as the active site are thus made available for recycling.

Relaxation (Fig. 5-9E)

When the flow of nervous impulses over the motor nerve innervating the muscle ceases, Ca^{++} is unbound from troponin and is actively pumped (calcium pump) back into storage in the outer vesicles of the sarcoplasmic reticulum. Removal of Ca^{++} "turns off" the actin filament, and the ATP cross-bridge complexes are no longer able to form a bond with the active sites. The ATPase activity of myosin is also turned off, and no more ATP is broken down. The muscle filaments return to their original positions, and the muscle relaxes.

---

*If ATP is not available, as is the case after death, the cross-bridges remain attached to the actin and the muscle is said to be in *rigor*.

Figure 5-9. Proposed mechanism of the sliding filament theory. *A,* At rest, uncharged ATP cross-bridges are extended, actin and myosin are uncoupled, and CA^{++} is stored in the reticulum. *B,* During excitation-coupling, stimulation releases Ca^{++}, which then binds to troponin, "turning on" actin active sites: actomyosin is formed. *C,* During contraction, ATP is broken down, releasing energy that swivels the cross-bridges; actin slides over the myosin, tension is developed, and the muscle shortens. *D,* During recharging, ATP is resynthesized and actin and myosin uncouple and are recycled. *E,* When stimulation ceases, Ca^{++} is restored in the reticulum by the calcium pump, and the muscle relaxes. (Modified and redrawn from Murray and Weber.[57])

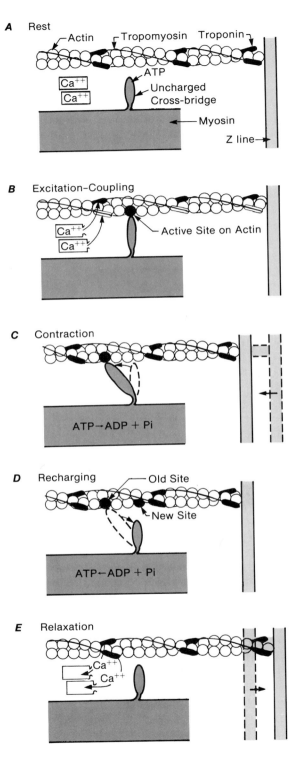

The contraction process described in Figure 5-9*C* is for **concentric** (shortening) contractions where the Z lines are pulled toward the middle of the sarcomere. This would be the type of contraction performed by the biceps muscles of the upper arm during the lifting or **positive work** (against gravity) portion of a chin-up. By contrast, during the lowering or **negative work** (assisted by gravity) portion, the actin filaments are viewed as sliding outward from the middle of the sarcomere. That is to say, controlled elongation of muscles back toward their original resting length also is possible. This is called **eccentric** (elongation) muscle contraction. In both cases the ATP cross-bridge complexes are made and broken as the actin filaments are either "pulled in" or "let out" depending on need. In the case of **isometric** or **static** "contractions," where there is no visible muscle shortening, the actins remain in their same relative position while ATP cross-bridges are recycled to provide tension.

By way of summary, the contractile events of a muscle can be compared to the firing of a gun.[57] The gun must first be loaded by placing an appropriate cartridge (ATP) in a specific chamber (myosin cross-bridge). This combination (uncharged ATP cross-bridge) is converted to a readied form by cocking the gun (charged ATP cross-bridge). When the trigger is squeezed (calcium turning on actin sites), the ATP is rapidly broken down, releasing large amounts of energy. Work is done on the bullet (myosin cross-bridge). The process is completed by ejection of the spent cartridge (ADP + P_i) and reloading with another cartridge (ATP).

Table 5-2 contains a summary of the sequence of events thought to occur during muscular contraction according to the sliding filament theory.

TABLE 5–2

Summary of Events Occurring During Muscular Contraction According to the Sliding Filament Theory

1. Rest	(a) Uncharged ATP cross-bridges extended
	(b) Actin and myosin uncoupled
	(c) Ca^{++} stored in sarcoplasmic reticulum
2. Excitation-coupling	(a) Nerve impulse generated
	(b) Ca^{++} released from vesicles
	(c) Ca^{++} saturates troponin, turning on actin
	(d) ATP cross-bridge "charged"
	(e) Actin and myosin coupled $\rightarrow$ actomyosin
3. Contraction	(a) ATP $\xrightarrow{\text{ATPase}}$ ADP + P_i + energy
	(b) Energy swivels cross-bridges
	(c) Muscle shortens $\rightarrow$ actin slides over myosin
	(d) Force developed
4. Recharging	(a) ATP resynthesized
	(b) Actomyosin dissociates $\rightarrow$ actin + myosin
	(c) Actin and myosin recycled
5. Relaxation	(a) Nerve impulse ceases
	(b) Ca^{++} removed by calcium pump
	(c) Muscle returns to resting state

Function of Skeletal Muscle

Of course, the main function of skeletal muscle is contraction, the result of which is movement. In physical education and athletics, it is generally the quality of the movement that is important. Therefore, it is appropriate at this time to discuss some of the basic functions of muscle as they relate to movement. For example, how is the strength graded within a given muscle? Do all muscle fibers have the same functional capacities? What is the relationship between the force produced by a muscle and the speed of movement? What factors are involved in muscular fatigue?

The Motor Unit

If we were to count the number of motor nerves entering a muscle and to calculate the number of muscle fibers within the muscle, we would find that a great difference exists between the two. There are about a quarter of a billion separate muscle fibers that make up the skeletal musculature in humans, but there are only about 420,000 motor nerves. Inasmuch as the number of muscle fibers greatly exceeds the number of nerve fibers and keeping in mind the fact that every muscle fiber is innervated, we see that the nerve fibers must necessarily branch repeatedly. In other words, a single motor nerve fiber innervates anywhere from 1 to 5 to 150 or more muscle fibers. All the muscle fibers served by the same motor nerve contract and relax at the same time, working as a unit. For this reason, the single motor nerve and the muscle fibers it supplies are called the **motor unit** (Fig. 5-10). The motor unit is the basic functional unit of skeletal muscle.

The ratio of muscle fibers innervated by a single motor nerve is not determined by the size of the muscle, but rather by the precision, accuracy, and coordination of its movement. Muscles that are called on to

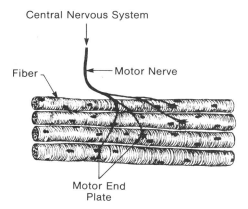

Figure 5-10. Motor unit of skeletal muscle. A single motor nerve from the central nervous system is shown innervating several muscle fibers through the motor endplates (neuromuscular junctions).

perform fine and delicate work, such as the eye muscles, may have as few as one muscle fiber in a motor unit; muscles used for rather heavy work, such as the quadriceps, may have hundreds or even thousands of muscle fibers per motor unit. By way of summary, a high **fiber:nerve ratio** is associated with gross movements requiring considerable force whereas a low **F:N** ratio exists where very precise, low force, or tension outputs are required of muscles.

A stimulated muscle or nerve fiber contracts or propagates a nerve impulse either completely or not at all. In other words, a minimal stimulus causes the individual muscle fiber to contract to the same extent that a stronger stimulus does. This phenomenon is known as the **all-or-none law.** Because a single neuron supplies many muscle fibers in the formation of the motor unit, it naturally follows that the motor unit will also function according to the all-or-none law. While this law of physiology holds true for the individual muscle fibers and motor units, it does not apply to the muscle as a whole. It is possible, therefore, for the muscle to exert forces of *graded* *strengths,* ranging from a barely perceptible contraction to the most vigorous type of contraction. This voluntary capability is called muscle strength **gradation.**

The Motor Unit and Strength Gradations

The capability of strength gradation is important to everyday activities as well as to physical education and athletics. Essentially, without the capability to vary the strength of muscular contractions, smooth, coordinated movement patterns would be virtually impossible. Can you imagine, for example, the outcome of brushing your teeth with the same muscular force applied as when lifting a 50-kilogram weight?

How is the strength of a muscle graded? There are basically two ways this is accomplished: (1) by varying the number of motor units contracting at any given time, referred to as **multiple motor unit summation;** and (2) by varying the frequency of contraction of individual motor units, referred to as **wave summation.**

Multiple Motor Unit Summation

As mentioned earlier, a motor unit adheres to the all-or-none law, i.e., given an adequate stimulus, it contracts maximally. It follows that the strength of a muscle can be graded depending upon whether one motor unit is contracting or several units are contracting simultaneously.

Actually, not only is the number of motor units contracting at any one time important in determining the final tension or strength developed by a muscle but the size or number of muscle fibers, i.e., the F:N ratio within each unit is also important. In most muscles, the number of fibers within a motor unit varies. For example, a muscle may have a total of 250 motor units with the smallest having as few as 25 fibers, the largest as many as 500 fibers, and the average having 200 fibers. Assuming that each fiber can produce a tension of 5 grams,

the smallest tension that can be produced by the muscle is 1 motor unit × 25 fibers × 5 grams = 125 grams, or ⅛ of a kilogram. By the same token, the largest tension that can be produced by the contraction of a single motor unit is 1 motor unit × 500 fibers × 5 grams = 2500 grams, or 2.5 kilograms. Therefore, depending only on the size of the motor unit and not the number, the strength of the muscle can be graded anywhere between .125(⅛) and 2.5 kilograms. The maximal tension of the muscle is developed when *all* the motor units contract, which in this case would result in a tension of 250 motor units × 200 fibers × 5 grams = 250,000 grams, or 250 kilograms. Thus, the full range of strength gradations of the muscle would be between ⅛ and 250 kilograms.

The relationship between the tension or strength of a muscle and the number of motor units contracting is shown in Figure 5-11.

Wave Summation

A motor unit responds to a single stimulus (nerve impulse) by giving a **twitch,** i.e., a

Figure 5-11. Multiple motor unit summation. The tension or strength of a muscle can be graded depending upon both the size and number of motor units contracting at any one time.

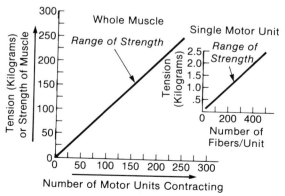

brief period of contraction followed by relaxation. A recording of such a twitch is shown in Figure 5-12. When a second stimulus is applied to the motor unit before it completely relaxes from the previous twitch, the two twitches are said to *summate* so that the tension developed by the motor unit is now greater than that produced by a single twitch alone. If the stimuli are repeated regularly at a high enough frequency, summation continues until the individual twitches are completely fused. Under these conditions, the motor unit is said to be in **tetanus,** with tension maintained at a high level as long as the stimuli continue or until fatigue sets in (Fig. 5-12). Note that the tension developed during tetanus as a result of wave summation can be 3 to 4 times greater than that for a single twitch.

Figure 5-12. Wave summation. A motor unit responds to a single stimulus (nerve impulse) by giving a twitch, i.e., a brief period of contraction followed by relaxation. When a second stimulus is applied to the motor unit before it completely relaxes from the previous twitch, the two twitches summate so that the tension developed is greater than that produced by a single twitch alone. If the stimuli are repeated, summation continues until the individual twitches are completely fused (tetanus). Eventually fatigue occurs and tension is reduced.

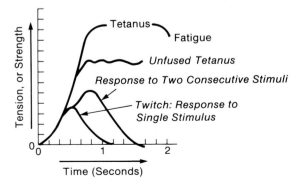

Asynchronous Summation of Motor Units—Smooth Contractions

During a maximal contraction, all of the motor units, and thus all of the fibers within a muscle, contract and summate more or less synchronously. However, during submaximal contractions, motor units contract and summate *asynchronously,* i.e., some are contracting (twitching) while others are relaxing. As each motor unit comes into play, it fuses with the twitches of the other already contracting units, thus producing a continued contraction of any given strength that is smooth and non-jerky.

It should be mentioned at this time that the degree of synchronization of motor units during various levels of muscular efforts is now being studied in humans in relation to weight resistance training.[54] Although this type of training appears to increase the synchronization of motor units, the significance of this change with respect to performance is not yet clearly understood.

Different Kinds of Motor Units—Fast-Twitch (FT) and Slow-Twitch (ST) Fibers

All skeletal muscle motor units function in the same general manner as described previously. However, not all motor units contain muscle fibers that have the same metabolic or functional capabilities. For example, whereas all motor units, and thus all muscle fibers, can perform under both aerobic and anaerobic conditions, some are better equipped biochemically and physiologically to work aerobically, and others are better equipped to work anaerobically. In humans the aerobic-type fibers (or motor units) have at different times been called type I, red, tonic, slow-twitch (ST), or slow-oxidative (SO); the anaerobic-type fibers have been called type II, white, phasic, fast-twitch (FT), or fast-glycolytic (FG).[17,18,29,55] A further subdivision of the

FT fibers into FT_A (IIA, fast-oxidative-glycolytic, FOG), FT_B (IIB, fast-glycolytic, FG), and FT_C (IIC, undifferentiated, unclassified, intermediate, interconversion) can also be made.[7,42,70] There is considerable recent research interest in the functional significance of this subdivision, which we will discuss in more detail later. For now, let's try to clear up some confusion by identifying the four main fiber types by abbreviation and by their principal mode of energy production: **ST (oxidative)**, **FT_A (oxidative-glycolytic)**, **FT_B (glycolytic)**, and **FT_C (unclassified)**. This system allows for a metabolic continuum that exists within muscles. This continuum ranges from fibers that are mainly oxidative, through combined oxidative-glycolytic ones, and on to those that are principally glycolytic. It also acknowledges the existence of some fibers that cannot be classified and about which we need to know more in terms of their functional role in exercise responses and training adaptations.

Method of Classifying Fiber Types

The classification of fiber types is done by histochemical analysis of a sample of muscle tissue obtained by a needle biopsy procedure. This procedure, which is relatively painless, involves the insertion of a pencil-size needle through a small incision in the skin and fascia. The incision is made under topical anesthesia. The needle is pushed into the muscle and a small window-like opening is filled with tissue. An internal cutting blade snips off the tissue, which usually weighs only 20 to 40 mg. The biopsy sample is then either mounted in an embedding medium and frozen or quickly frozen for later analysis using a liquid nitrogen isopentane solution. The analysis involves chemically staining the tissue for the presence of various oxidative and glycolytic enzymes as well as an enzymatic indicator

of muscle fiber contraction speed. This latter enzyme is myofibrillar adenosine triphosphatase or **myosin ATPase (m-ATPase)**.

When the stained muscle sample is viewed in cross section with a light microscope, it looks like the one shown in Figure 5-13. It should be pointed out at this time that all muscle fibers within any given motor unit are of the same type. For example, FT motor units contain only FT fibers and ST units only ST fibers. Also, as indicated in Figure 5-13, the fibers of FT and ST motor units are mixed together in the muscle giving a checkerboard appearance.

Carefully examine this slide (Fig. 5-13) prepared from the vastus lateralis muscle (outer thigh region) of a human subject. The vastus lateralis and the gastrocnemius (calf muscle) are commonly used in studies of human muscle fiber typing. What would you estimate the ratio of dark stained ST to lightly stained FT fiber areas to be? Perhaps 2:1 or about 66% ST and 33% FT? Check this by assuming for the moment

Figure 5-13. When a stained muscle sample is viewed in cross section, it has a checkerboard appearance, because the fibers of fast-twitch (FT) and slow-twitch (ST) motor units are mixed together in the muscle. In this human muscle sample from the vastus lateralis, the darkly stained fibers are ST and those lightly stained are FT.

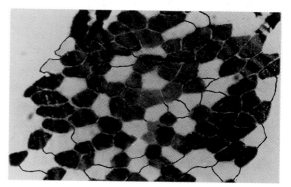

that all the fibers are the same general shape and have the same diameters. Count the approximate number of each fiber type. Do you get about 90 ST and 45 FT, a 2:1 ratio? Although an exercise scientist would project the slides to enlarge the fibers and then take great pains to measure their actual circumferences and calculate the areas occupied by the two major fiber types, you have done much the same thing. You have just "fiber typed" this muscle sample. It is clear that it is primarily comprised of ST fibers; probably from the leg of an endurance athlete or a person who might have a good chance of success in endurance events (see below).

As mentioned previously, FT fibers can be further subdivided.[6] To do this, slides of serial cross sections from the same muscle biopsy are preincubated in solutions that differ in their alkalinity (high pH like 10.4) or acidity (medium pH like 4.6 or low pH like 4.3). You should recall here the inverse relationship between pH and hydrogen ion concentrations in that a lower pH indicates a more acid solution and vice versa, i.e., a pH of 4.3 is more acid than a pH of 4.6. The serial slides, which can be viewed as slices of a loaf of bread, are then stained for myosin ATPase, an enzyme that identifies their contractile speed. In this case dark staining indicates stability of the m-ATPase within the muscle fiber. Likewise, intermediate staining indicates the presence of some stable enzyme whereas light staining indicates nearly complete breakdown or lability of the enzyme as a result of the specific preincubation treatment.

Figure 5-14 shows such a series of slides for human vastus lateralis muscle. Note that the slide A indicates four selected muscle fibers marked ST, FT_A, FT_B, and FT_C. These fibers all look similar when cut in thick section (40–50 μm), prepared with fixatives, and viewed under a light microscope. Also note the bar that indicates a length of 100 μm (100 micrometers or 1/10 of a millimeter). To gain a better "feel" for the actual diameters of the fibers, mark off one millimeter on a piece of paper and attempt to draw 10 distinct and separate pencil lines (simulating individual muscle fiber widths) within the boundaries. Use a very sharp pencil. Small, aren't they?

The second, B, third, C, and fourth, D, slides in Figure 5-14 were cut much thinner (only 10 μm) and were assayed for m-ATPase activity after three different preincubation pH treatments (4.3, 4.6, and 10.4) as shown. Note that the ST fiber stained dark after both high and intermediate acid treatments (pH 4.3 and 4.6) but stained light after the basic treatment (pH 10.4). The m-ATPase of the ST fiber was acid stabile but basic labile. Conversely, note that the FT_A fiber stained light after the acid treatments (pH 4.3 and 4.6) but dark after basic treatment (pH 10.4). The m-ATPase of the FT_A fiber was basic stabile and acid labile. Next, note that the FT_B fiber stained light after the high acid treatment (pH 4.3), intermediate after the intermediate acid treatment (pH 4.6), and dark after basic treatment (pH 10.4). The FT_B fiber is acid labile and basic stabile, just like the FT_A fiber, but displays a major difference in that its m-ATPase also shows some stability after exposure to intermediate acid (pH 4.6). Perhaps we can best recall that the FT_B fiber shows intermediate stain intensity after intermediate acid treatment. These relationships are summarized in Figure 5-15. Finally, note the uniqueness of the FT_C fiber in that it stained quite dark over the entire range of pH treatments. It appears that the m-ATPase of the FT_C fibers possess some of the stability characteristics common to the m-ATPase found in all of the other fiber types. This is what has led scientists to regard the FT_C fiber as an undifferentiated, less specialized fiber. Before becoming too concerned about these

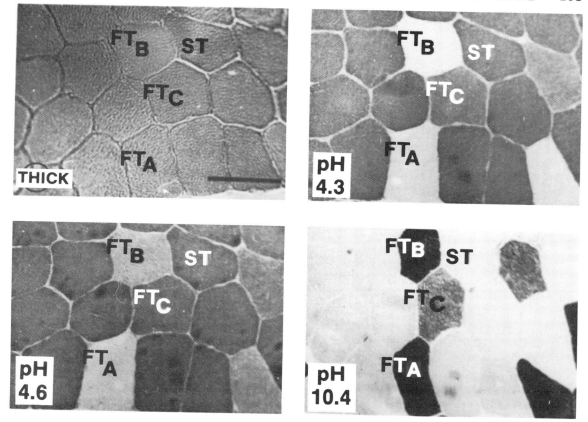

Figure 5-14. Serial cross sections of human vastus lateralis muscle fibers. Part *A* shows thick sections (40–50 μm) where all fibers appear to be the same. Other photos show the same muscle fibers stained for m-ATPase activity after different preincubation pH treatments; *B*, high acid of pH 4.3; *C*, intermediate acid of pH 4.6; and *D*, basic solution of pH 10.4. ST, FT$_A$, FT$_B$, and FT$_C$ fibers are identified. Bar=100 μm. (Modified from Staron, et al.[70])

fibers we should keep in mind that FT$_C$ fibers usually only make up 0 to 2% and no more than 5% of the total fiber population in human muscle.[70] For that reason, they are more of academic than practical interest to us here.

Other methods of muscle fiber-type classification have been attempted in addition to the m-ATPase pH lability method[6] and identification by differences in oxidative and glycolytic enzyme profiles. For example, the electron microscope has been

used to study differences in the number of "visible" individual bands that make up the M-band region at the middle of the sarcomere and the relative width of the Z-bands at the limits of the sarcomere.[69] Fiber sections were first viewed at a magnification of 10,000 times their original size. Photographs, called **electron micrographs,** were enlarged during printing to give final magnifications up to 225,000 times. Under such magnification the ST fibers can be seen to have 5 strong bands

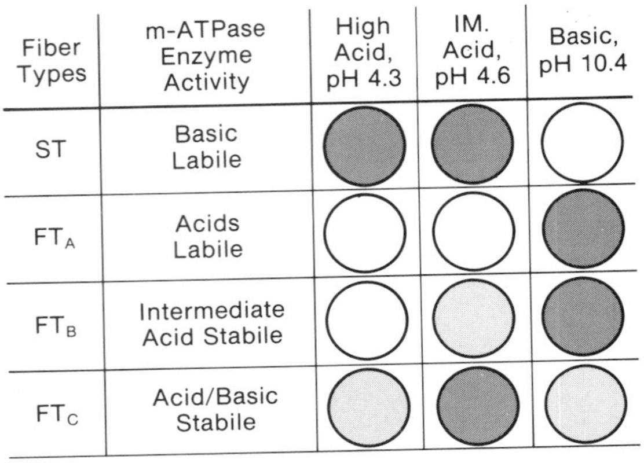

Fiber Types	m-ATPase Enzyme Activity	High Acid, pH 4.3	IM. Acid, pH 4.6	Basic, pH 10.4
ST	Basic Labile	●	●	○
FT$_A$	Acids Labile	○	○	●
FT$_B$	Intermediate Acid Stable	○	◐	●
FT$_C$	Acid/Basic Stable	◐	◐	◔

Figure 5-15. m-ATPase staining patterns reflecting labile/stabile characteristics for different fiber types after preincubation in high acid (pH 4.3), intermediate acid (pH 4.6), and basic (pH 10.4) solutions. Note "reverse staining" pattern for ST vs. FT$_A$ fibers, intermediate staining for FT$_B$ fibers in intermediate acid, and a wide range of pH stability for FT$_C$ fibers.

that make up the M-band and the presence of wide Z-bands—FT$_A$ fibers have 3 strong and 2 weak bands in their M-bands and intermediate width Z-bands and FT$_B$ fibers have only 3 strong bands in the M-band region and narrow Z-bands. Tibialis anterior muscle samples from the lower legs of human subjects were used in this study. Fiber typing for comparison of methods was done using m-ATPase pH lability and judgments of correct and incorrect allocation of different fiber types were based on these standards. When Z-band widths alone were used it was possible to allocate correctly only 70% of the fibers. This questionable record of allocation was improved to 95% when fibers were classified on the basis of M-banding appearance. It was recommended that the Z- and M-bands be used in combination as fiber-type discriminators and that the M-band structure be used if only one of the parameters is considered. In any case, there appears to be a

potential for classifying fibers on the basis of the presence and dimensions of subcellular structures as well as on the basis of metabolic enzyme profiles and enzymes related to contraction speed. It is clear that any of these methods of fiber typing require special laboratory techniques and the availability of expensive equipment.

Distribution of FT and ST Fibers

Studies of fiber distribution in postmorten samples of muscles from infants and young children through age 8 recently have been reported and summarized.[78] The predominant fiber type in limb and trunk muscles of the early fetus is the primitive, undifferentiated, FT$_C$ fiber. Fiber differentiation then occurs so that the histochemically identifiable ST, FT$_A$, and FT$_B$ fibers are eventually all present. The maturation rates for the various fiber types, however, are different. For example, ST fibers first appear after the 19th week of gestation but the great majority of fibers during the 20th through the 26th weeks are FT$_A$ and FT$_B$. That is to say, the ST fibers lag behind in their development before birth. By 36 weeks there are numerous FT$_A$ and FT$_B$ fibers and only a few of the original undifferentiated FT$_C$ fibers. You might say that all of the maturational differentiation that occurs in the womb occurs at the expense of the FT$_C$ fibers.

After birth, there is wide variation in the number of ST and FT fibers, a pattern that persists through the first year of life. Generally speaking, after the first year of life, more than 50% of the fibers are of the ST type. Thereafter the greatest changes are not in the distribution of fibers but in their size. Unlike adults, who display wide variation in fiber size for a given muscle, fiber diameters do not vary much in children. The quadriceps muscle of the anterior thigh is an exception with these fibers being consistently larger than those of other muscles after the age of 2 years. This difference is presumably due to the heavy loads placed on these muscles for locomotion and getting up and down. In normal children, ST fibers tend to be of similar size or larger than FT fibers and there is concern for muscle disease if they are smaller. As expected, fiber size correlates well with age; older children have larger muscle fiber diameters. There is no difference in muscle fiber size between boys and girls through age 8, and any gender differences may not become apparent until puberty. Adult fiber size is usually attained by the age of 12 to 15 years.

In summary, it can be said that differentiation of FT_C fibers into ST, FT_A, and FT_B fibers is a process that begins in the womb as neurological and muscular systems mature and as limb, diaphragm, and trunk muscles begin to function. After birth, there is a great increase in ST fibers so important to maintaining spinal posture, locomotion, and improved endurance. Once the fiber types are established in approximately equal percentages within muscles, i.e., about 50% ST and 50% FT, the major changes will be in fiber diameter, with adult fiber size attained in the early teen years. These developmental, maturation, and age-related concepts must be remembered when fiber typing is considered as a "screening" tool to identify potentially outstanding young athletes as discussed later.

The proportions of the different types of fibers in adult human muscles vary to a great extent. However, generally it can be said that the majority of our muscles contain an approximately equal mixture of FT and ST fibers, although there are specific muscles that are considered to be predominantly either FT or ST. For example, the soleus contains 25 to 40% more ST fibers than the other leg muscles, and the triceps contain 10 to 30% more FT fibers than the other arm muscles.[44]

A study of the per cent of FT fibers in muscle samples from four young men who had died suddenly indicates similar variability in distribution averages.[19] The soleus (24% FT) and vastus lateralis (57% FT) muscles of the leg were quite different in their compositions, whereas the biceps brachii (55% FT) and the lateral and long heads of the triceps brachii (60% FT) of the arm were quite similar. A difference in fiber type distribution within the same arm muscle was evident since the medial head of the triceps brachii contained only 40% FT fibers. In another study, comparisons of shoulder deltoideus to leg vastus lateralis and gastrocnemius muscles of elite orienteers showed that they contained approximately the same percentage of ST fibers, about 68%.[42] This is of interest because the legs receive a much greater training stimulus than the shoulder muscles in this gruelling sport which involves running over a wide variety of outdoor terrain. Marked differences existed, however, for FT_A and FT_B distributions in leg versus shoulder muscles. Leg muscles contained unequal distributions of about 26% FT_A and 3% FT_B fibers, while shoulder muscles contained more equal distributions of 14% FT_A and 17% FT_B. FT_C percentages were small in all muscles, ranging from 0 to 4%.

Taken collectively, these findings indicate that the composition of fiber types varies within different regions of the same muscle, between different muscles within the same person, and certainly among the same muscles of different people. Considerable variability also exists among FT fiber subgroups for muscles in different regions of the body. An awareness of these variations in fiber distributions is important as we consider such distributions in athletes and their potential impact on performance.

The distribution of FT and ST fibers in muscles of different groups of male and female athletes is shown in Figure 5-16. Although there is some degree of individual

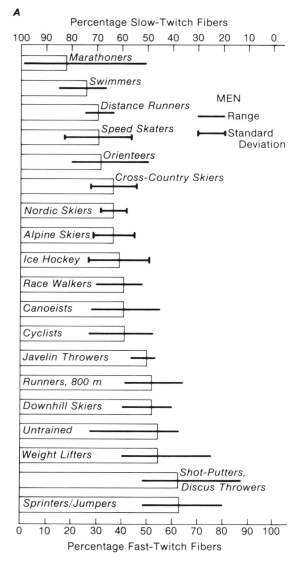

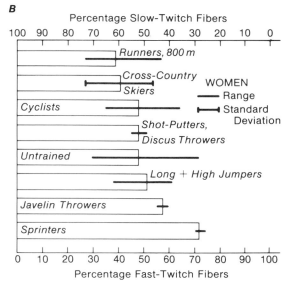

Figure 5-16. *A,* The distribution of fast-twitch (FT) and slow-twitch (ST) fibers in muscles of different groups of male and, *B,* female athletes. Although there is some degree of variation, on the average, endurance athletes tend to have greater percentages of ST fibers, whereas non-endurance athletes have greater percentages of FT fibers than their nonathletic counterparts. (Based on data from Burke et al.,[8] Costill et al.,[13] Gollnick et al.,[29] Komi et al.[48] and Thorstensson et al.[76])

variation, on the average, it can be seen that endurance athletes tend to have greater percentages of ST fibers, whereas nonendurance athletes have greater percentages of FT fibers than their nonathletic counterparts. In addition, the relationship between the maximal aerobic power (max $\dot{V}O_2$) of male athletes and male nonathletes and their percentage of distribu-

tion of ST fibers is given in Figure 5-17. Notice that the max $\dot{V}O_2$ is higher with higher percentages of ST fibers in both groups. This makes sense, because ST fibers have a greater potential for aerobic metabolism than do FT fibers. Notice also that for a given percentage of ST fibers above 40%, the max $\dot{V}O_2$ is higher in athletes. More will be said about this later.

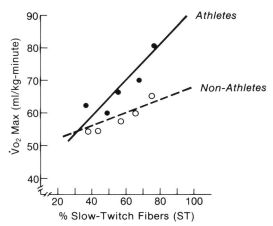

Figure 5-17. Relationship between maximal aerobic power (max $\dot{V}O_2$) of male athletes and male nonathletes and their percentage of distribution of slow-twitch (ST) muscle fibers. The max $\dot{V}O_2$ is higher with higher percentages of ST fibers in both groups; for a given percentage of ST fibers above 40 per cent, the max $\dot{V}O_2$ is higher in athletes. (Based on data from Bergh et al.[5])

There are two major questions that have been raised concerning the distribution of fiber types among athletes and the relationship between the percentage of ST fibers and the max $\dot{V}O_2$: (1) Does training cause a change in the percentage of distribution of ST and FT fibers and (2) is the increase in max $\dot{V}O_2$ that can be induced by training genetically limited by the percentage of ST fibers one is born with? The answer to the first question is still basically no.[31] The majority of evidence still suggests that the only way to effectively change a FT fiber to a ST fiber, or vice versa, is to cross-innervate the two fibers.[56] Cross-innervation means that the nerve originally innervating one fiber is transplanted to innervate the other. In other words, the motor nerve to a muscle has an influential effect (called a *trophic effect*) on the eventual functional capabilities of that muscle fiber. As we will discuss later, training

causes an increase in the size and functional capacities of the respective fiber types, but apparently does not cause conversion from one to another.

In answering the second question, it is known that both the distribution of fiber types and the magnitude of the max $\dot{V}O_2$ are genetically determined to a very large extent (p. 000). However, as shown in Figure 5-17, the max $\dot{V}O_2$ is higher for athletes than for nonathletes at any given percentage of ST fibers above 40%. This could be interpreted to mean that training also has a significant influence on the magnitude of the max $\dot{V}O_2$ over and above that set by the percentage of ST fibers. A direct answer to the second question is no, the genetic limit set on the percentage of distribution of ST fibers does not entirely limit the magnitude of the max $\dot{V}O_2$ resulting from training.

Functional Differences between FT and ST Fibers

As indicated earlier, ST fibers have a relatively large aerobic capacity and a relatively small anaerobic capacity compared with FT fibers. This is true even when the higher oxidative capabilities of the FT_A fibers are considered, i.e., an oxidative hierarchy exists with $ST > FT_A > FT_B$.[70] In fact, in humans, none of the FT subgroups has as high an oxidative capacity as the ST fibers.[20] These differences and other structural, biochemical, and functional relationships are shown in Table 5-3.

A remarkable aspect of the research underlying this summary is how well the structural and functional findings have consistently supported one another. This gives credence to the adage "anatomical structure supports function." Note first the sharp contrasts between characteristics for the ST versus combined FT_A and FT_B fibers. For the most part, they are opposites. A few exceptions are mitochondrial

TABLE 5-3

Structural and Functional Characteristics of Slow-Twitch (ST) and Fast-Twitch (FT$_A$ and FT$_B$) Muscle Fibers

Characteristics	Fiber Type		
	ST	FT$_A$	FT$_B$
NEURAL ASPECTS			
Motoneuron size	Small	Large	Large
Motoneuron recruitment threshold	Low	High	High
Motor nerve conduction velocity	Slow	Fast	Fast
STRUCTURAL ASPECTS			
Muscle fiber diameter	Small	Large	Large
Sarcoplasmic reticulum development	Less	More	More
Mitochondrial density	High	High	Low
Capillary density	High	Medium	Low
Myoglobin content	High	Medium	Low
ENERGY SUBSTRATES			
Phosphocreatine stores	Low	High	High
Glycogen stores	Low	High	High
Triglyceride stores	High	Medium	Low
ENZYMATIC ASPECTS			
Myosin-ATPase activity	Low	High	High
Glycolytic enzyme activity	Low	High	High
Oxidative enzyme activity	High	High	Low
FUNCTIONAL ASPECTS			
Twitch (contraction) time	Slow	Fast	Fast
Relaxation time	Slow	Fast	Fast
Force production	Low	High	High
Energy efficiency, "economy"	High	Low	Low
Fatigue resistance	High	Low	Low
Elasticity	Low	High	High

density, capillary density, myoglobin content, and triglyceride stores, where FT$_A$ fibers are more similar to ST fibers. Next, let's review the various characteristics of the fibers, keeping in mind the important known general relationship between structure and function.

The smaller motoneurons have a lower excitation threshold, which means the motor units comprised of ST fibers will be recruited first. This concept has been attributed to Henneman as the **size principle** of motor unit recruitment.[80] ST motor units are used during low-intensity exercise and the FT$_A$ motor units are recruited for higher intensity or more prolonged exercise. The FT$_B$ fibers are recruited for all-out force production or as other fibers display fatigue.[79] Motor nerve conduction velocity refers to the speed with which impulses travel down the axons of motor nerves. The slower velocities of ST fibers are consistent with their use for maintaining posture and slower, less intense movements where speed is not critical. On the other hand, the fast velocities of FT$_A$ and FT$_B$ fibers are consistent with quicker, more forceful muscle contractions where speed and power are critical to performance. For example, it is unlikely that the slow postural adjustments made by a basketball rebounder before a free throw will affect the outcome of a missed shot, but an explosive powerful vertical jump will. In this example, ST motor units and then FT motor units are preferentially recruited depending on need. Can you think of other examples?

The muscle fiber diameter characteristics in Table 5-3 best describe general differences in fiber size for limb and postural muscles. For example, postural muscles of the back contain many small, ST fibers whereas, the ST fibers of limb muscles are larger. In fact, in children and women, ST fibers in limb muscles may be as large or larger than FT fibers.[78] In men, the limb FT fibers are more hypertrophied and usually the same size or larger than the ST fibers. The generally larger size of the FT fibers allows them to contain more protein contractile filaments, which can produce higher forces. This larger size is accompanied by the development of a more extensive sarcoplasmic reticulum, the structural network so important to the rapid release of Ca^{++} throughout the length and breadth of the fiber. Other structural differences such as a higher mitochondrial density, i.e., more mitochondria per unit of cell volume, and higher myoglobin content in ST versus FT_B fibers reflects their differences in support of aerobic metabolism. ST fibers have a distinct advantage over FT fibers when it comes to production of ATP through oxidative processes because the mitochondria, capillaries, and myoglobin are all present in larger quantities. Additionally, the vascular beds of ST muscles have a higher blood flow at rest and do not show much increase in blood flow during exercise: they lack the functional vasodilatative response common to FT muscles. Note that FT_A fibers also have a high density of mitochondria and a substantial presence of capillaries and myoglobin to support the oxidative aspects of their metabolic function.

Perhaps it is not surprising that the energy substrates and enzyme differences (Table 5-3) between ST and FT fibers closely follow the descriptive scenario that is unfolding. The phosphocreatine stores are high in FT fibers where the demand for quick, high force outputs are common and are low in ST fibers where the reverse is true. Likewise, glycogen stores in FT fibers are higher than in ST fibers, although limb ST fibers may contain considerable amounts of intramuscular glycogen.[22] Generally speaking, the FT fibers are ready to deliver high force outputs and have the backup reserves to provide additional energy from stored PC or are capable and ready to provide ATP through glycolysis.

Conversely, the ST and FT_A fibers have higher quantities of stored triglycerides that they can use to produce ATP under more relaxed oxidative conditions. Not unexpectedly, the presence of oxidative and glycolytic enzymes and their specific activities reflect these differences in substrate availability. Note the reverse patterns for ST versus combined FT_A, FT_B fibers under the heading of enzymatic aspects (Table 5-3). At this point, it wouldn't make much sense to have high levels of substrate without the needed enzymes to speed reactions so they can be utilized effectively.

Finally, let's consider the functional aspects of different fiber types in Table 5-3. Note that the fast-twitch contraction times match up with high m-ATPase activity levels in FT fibers and slow times with low levels in ST fibers. Of course, these are the functional and related enzymatic bases upon which the fiber types are named. FT contraction times (to peak tension) are about twice as fast as ST times; 0.05 seconds versus 0.10 seconds and the relaxation times (return to one-half of peak tension) also are proportionally faster. The force output under repetitive electrical stimulation, which would be similar to an impulse volley during voluntary movement, is much greater for FT fibers because they wave summate and tetanize more quickly.[80] ST fibers, however, are more energy efficient, i.e., produce more force during dynamic contraction for the quantity of energy used. ST fibers also are more "economical," which means they produce more static or isometric force per unit of energy used.[62] Because of this and the many structural and metabolic support systems described above, the ST fibers are comparatively resistant to fatigue. Even the known differences in elasticity of the different fiber types fit the picture. ST fibers have more collagen, which is the building block of connective tissue.[50] This means that ST fibers are less elastic and stiffer than FT fibers. This does not really hinder the function of the ST fibers because they are contracting more slowly. Greater elasticity helps the FT fibers, however, since they can initiate rapid, forceful contractions without undue hindrance. This is referred to as a "higher compliance" of FT muscle. Once again, an impressive matchup between muscle structure and function exists.

The functional significance of the different biochemical and physiological characteristics of ST and FT fibers during exercise is indicated by the fact that FT fibers are preferentially recruited for performing short, high-intensity work bouts, such as sprinting. By the same token, ST fibers are preferentially recruited during long-term, endurance types of activity.[30,31] This is shown in Figure 5-18, in which the glycogen content of both fiber types of human muscle was qualitatively estimated during sprint and endurance exercises. The glycogen content decreased sooner and to a greater extent in the FT fiber during sprint bouts but sooner and to a greater extent in the ST fiber during endurance exercise, thus suggesting preferential recruitment.

One other factor is noticeable in Figure

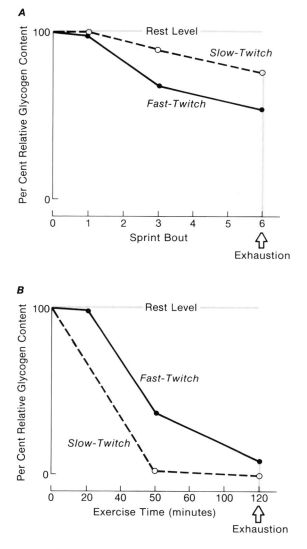

Figure 5-18. *A,* Glycogen content of slow-twitch and fast-twitch muscle fibers during sprintlike exercises and *B,* endurance-like exercises. The glycogen content decreased sooner and to a greater extent in the fast-twitch fiber during sprint bouts but sooner and to a greater extent in the slow-twitch fiber during endurance exercise. This suggests that the FT fibers are preferentially recruited for performing short high intensity work bouts, whereas the slow-twitch fibers are preferentially recruited during long-term endurance types of activities. (Based on data from Gollnick et al.[30,31])

5-18. The initial glycogen level does not limit sprintlike performance, since at exhaustion the glycogen content in both fiber types is still substantial. On the contrary, notice that the glycogen, particularly in the ST fibers, is completely used up after 2 hours of exhaustive endurance exercise. In this case, the initial glycogen level limits performance. More will be said about this later.

There has been further research on muscle glycogen depletion as evidence for preferential recruitment of ST, FT_A and FT_B fibers.[79] Subjects worked at 75% of their maximum oxygen uptake ($\dot{V}O_2$ max) on a treadmill or bicycle ergometer until they reached exhaustion. Muscle biopsies were taken from the lateral portion of the quadriceps. Not unexpectedly, the glycogen content of the combined FT_A and FT_B fibers at rest was 16% greater than the ST fibers. What was more surprising was that the ST and FT_A fibers showed the same glycogen depletion rates from the start of exercise, indicating that both fiber types were being recruited. The glycogen content of combined FT_A and FT_B, and FT_B alone, was unchanged at first. A later decrease in combined FT_A and FT_B and finally in FT_B indicated a difference in "threshold force" for recruiting these fibers. In summary, the intensity of the exercise was adequate to cause initial recruitment of both ST and FT_A fibers. Although the exercise intensity remained unchanged at 75% of max $\dot{V}O_2$, the effects of the fatigue required the recruitment of FT_B fibers so that work could be continued. These findings do not invalidate earlier observations that, generally speaking, ST fibers are recruited during low-intensity exercise and FT fibers during high-intensity exercise. More importantly, they indicate that ST fibers are always recruited first and depending on the intensity, duration, or fatigue that occurs, FT_A and FT_B fibers are called into play. For moderate-intensity exercise, ST and FT_A,

then FT_B are used if activity is continued. For high-intensity exercise, ST, FT_A, and FT_B are used in more rapid recruitment order. For all-out power performances, all fibers are recruited as quickly and completely as possible. Now let's consider some applications of these and other recent research findings related to muscle fiber types and typing.

Applications of Research

There has been much research interest in recent years in the area of muscle fiber typing, training adaptations within different fiber types, the impact of different types of training programs on fibers, and how fiber typing might be used as a screening tool. Before beginning this review of selected findings, the reader is reminded that the composition of fibers in adult muscles is determined by a process of differentiation and maturation that begins before birth and is not completed until the teenage years.[78] Furthermore, the distribution of fiber types can vary greatly within the same muscle, between different muscles within the same body, and among the same muscles from different people.[19,42] Also recall that during the process of preferential recruitment the ST fibers are always recruited regardless of exercise intensity, whereas the FT fibers are recruited only during prolonged activity leading to fatigue, or for higher intensity exercise and all-out power efforts.[33,79]

There has been a long-standing interest in characterizing the fiber-type profiles of athletes who excel in the performance of sprint versus endurance-type events. There has been little inconsistency in these reports, which indicates higher percentages of FT fibers in sprinters and higher percentages of ST fibers in endurance athletes. It follows that the muscle enzyme profiles of these athletes is consistently in the direction of greater anaerobic enzymes in the sprinters and greater aerobic enzymes in the endurance performers. Interest subsequently has been directed toward track and field athletes who compete in the middle-distance running events and jumping or throwing events that require explosive power. These latter athletes do not display clear distinctions in their muscle fiber makeup and in fact are represented by a wide range of fiber compositions.[13] These findings suggest that while training dictates the ultimate capacity for endurance, success in either sprint or distance running is in part determined by muscle fiber composition. Since middle-distance runners, jumpers, and throwers have relatively low muscle enzyme activities and highly variable fiber compositions, it is less likely that any clear predictions of performance success can be made on the basis of muscle fiber typing alone. We must look beyond genetic endowment.

What about differences between male and female athletes in terms of their comparative muscle fiber compositions and size of fibers? Female athletes have larger fibers than control subjects but smaller fibers than male athletes who perform similar events.[13,61] This holds for ST, FT_A, and FT_B fibers. By contrast, there are no apparent differences in fiber type distribution or histochemical properties between the sexes.[13,61] Generally speaking, the same high percentages of ST fibers and associated enzymes and high FT fibers and associated enzymes are present in sprinters and endurance runners, respectively, regardless of whether they are male or female. Studies of elite female track and field athletes confirm these earlier findings regarding fiber composition relative to specific events—comparative smaller size of fibers and difficulty in clearly characterizing middle-distance runners.[35] An additional finding is that in women, the size of ST relative to FT fibers tends to be greater than in men. The fiber size trends, however, with respect to event specialization are identical in women and men, i.e., events requiring greater power and less endurance are associated with a greater relative size of FT fibers. This relationship in relative size exists because the FT fibers are smaller in athletes specializing in endurance events and the ST fiber size is similar for the different types of athletes.[35] In summary, muscle fiber distribution and enzymatic characteristics are quite similar for men and women. Athletes of both sexes have larger fibers than control subjects, male athletes have larger fibers than female athletes, and female athletes tend to have larger ST to FT fiber size ratios.

Questions about what happens to the number of each fiber type with training have been of interest to coaches and trainers of recreational and competitive athletes alike. It now seems clear that any increase in muscle size is due to increases in the size of fibers (hypertrophy) rather than to any increase in fiber number due to splitting (hyperplasia).[34] That is to say, muscle fiber number is fixed early in life and any increases or decreases in muscle weight occur via hypertrophy or atrophy of existing fibers. Furthermore, it appears that the percentages of each fiber type are determined during the process of pre- and post-natal differentiation and maturation as discussed earlier.

There is limited evidence that some shifts in fiber types can be induced by specific training programs during the growing phase in juvenile research animals.[80] In this study, a static overload was placed on muscles by cutting the tendons of synergists while dynamic exercise was simulated by having animals jump to reach a food reward. The static overload enhanced conversion of FT_A to FT_C fibers while the dynamic exercise slowed this conversion process. A study of adult human subjects who cross-country skied 18.5 miles per day with a 25-kg backpack, 6 days per week for

8 weeks produced some similar results.[68] There was a 6% decrease in combined FT_A and FT_B fibers and a 4% increase in FT_C fibers in their triceps muscles. Such studies have kept alive the notion that FT_C fibers may be transitional fibers in the process of conversion of FT to ST fibers. While we must await further insight on this matter, the majority of evidence would indicate that ST fibers remain as ST fibers and FT fibers as FT fibers regardless of the type of training that is imposed. One exception is the experimental procedure of muscle-nerve cross-innervation mentioned earlier. A formerly fast-twitch muscle can be made to take on the structural, enzymatic, and metabolic characteristics of a slow-twitch muscle, and vice versa by cutting their respective nerves and cross attaching them. This procedure has helped us to understand the importance of nerve impulse patterns in determining the structure and function of muscles, the neurotrophic effect. At the same time, it has little potential for application and we are left with the impression that the distribution of ST and FT fibers cannot be altered to any significant degree by training.

This impression has led researchers to look more closely at substrate differences and metabolic shifts that might occur within fiber types with specific training that provide some advantages to athletes in different sports. For example, individual fibers teased out of freeze-dried samples of human muscles contained similar amounts of glycogen regardless of fiber type whereas the ST fibers contained more neutral fat in the form of triglycerides.[20] Other studies of muscle biopsies taken 4 to 6 seconds after static and dynamic exercise indicate that lactic acid accounts for most of the intracellular acids formed during exercise.[36] Phosphocreatine levels showed a nonlinear negative relationship to the level of lactic acid produced during exercise and lactate content was generally higher in FT fibers

after contraction. This means that as PC levels were being depleted during prolonged exercise, more FT fibers were being recruited. ATP was being synthesized through anaerobic metabolic pathways so that activity could be continued, but at the expense of producing increased amounts of intracellular lactic acid.

The importance of this likely rests with the observation that both the lactate threshold and workload that produce the onset of blood lactate accumulation, called W_{OBLA}, are higher in subjects who have large ST fiber percentages.[40,41] The advantage of this is that subjects with more ST fibers can use them to perform low-intensity exercise or the early phases of moderate- to high-intensity exercise and then recruit FT fibers as exercise is prolonged, the intensity is increased, or fatigue begins to occur. It is easy to see that having a larger percentage of ST fibers would provide an advantage for many sports. At the same time one might argue that having more FT fibers would provide an advantage for throwing, jumping, or other power sports. But we have already discussed that little, if anything, can be done to alter their numbers. This causes us to consider what might be done through training to alter the size and internal makeup of existing fibers to better meet the specific needs of different sports. This is the direction that has the greatest potential for application, so let's consider two specific aspects: metabolic shifts that can occur within muscle fibers as a result of training and the influence that progressive exercise training has on muscle fibers.

One of the most apparent metabolic shifts that occurs with training is a shift toward a greater oxidative potential and capacity. That such shifts occur in ST fibers regardless of the type of training relates, once again, to their being recruited on the initiation of all activities independent of intensity. Significant shifts toward oxidative metabolism also occur in FT_A and FT_B fibers. For example, female field hockey athletes have a higher percentage of oxidative (ST plus FT_A) fibers than untrained student controls, 83% vs. 46%.[61] The oxidative potential was increased in both ST and FT fibers in older male subjects who had not trained for two years prior to the study.[32] Subjects pedaled a bicycle ergometer at a workload that required 75% of maximum aerobic capacity for 1 hour per day, 4 days per week, over a 5-month period. A similar study indicates that part of the observed shifts might be due to a gradual conversion of FT_B fibers to FT_A fibers, which are more oxidative.[1] These findings, that FT fibers have the ability to adapt metabolically to high oxidative demands, hold for elite orienteers who have been shown to have higher ratios of FT_A to FT_B fibers.[42] It is of interest and perhaps not unexpected that with the described endurance training, the glycolytic capacity increased in only the FT fibers.[32] It is apparent from this that a real advantage to training is the shift in oxidative metabolic capacity that occurs within all fibers and some specific improvement in the glycolytic capacity of the FT fibers.

The impact of strength training programs on fiber types is of interest since it might help explain some of the highly variable responses that coaches, trainers, and rehabilitation specialists see when they put different people on the "same" program. Compared to distance runners, weight lifters have a significantly lower percentage of ST fibers, 40% vs. 70%, and a higher percentage of FT_A, 40% vs. 23%, and FT_B fibers, 22% vs. 4%.[70] Compared to control subjects, and irrespective of fiber type, weight lifters have more muscle fiber mitochondria but a lower intrafiber lipid content. This, plus the fact that control subjects have nearly twice as many FT_B fibers as weight lifters, may indicate the power of inactivity as a fiber type determinant.[70]

Inactive people have many glycolytic FT_B fibers that can change toward more oxidative FT_A fibers if they start a weight training program. Sounds like changes that take place with endurance training programs, doesn't it?

The above contrasts weight lifters to inactive control subjects but does not answer the question of what happens to inactive subjects when they are put on a weight training program. It appears that systematic strength training increases the FT- to ST-fiber area ratio, an indication of the specific affect of heavy training loads on FT muscle fibers.[75] The reader should keep in mind that the area represented by the different fiber types is being considered here. As mentioned earlier, inactive control subjects have greater numbers of FT_B fibers but they are small in size. This leaves relatively more potential for hypertrophy with strength training, i.e., increase size and area within the FT fiber pool. This is an important concept in the face of findings that 5 to 6 months of heavy resistance training produced a 98% increase in maximum elbow extension strength accompanied by increases in the fiber areas of both FT (39%) and ST (31%) fibers.[52] Once again, it is more difficult for the ST fibers to compete in the hypertrophy contest if they already are larger in the beginning. No correlation has been found between the magnitude of changes in fiber size and increases in maximal strength following heavy weight training.[52] This is consistent with earlier findings that showed only low to moderate correlations between maximum strength measurements and limb girth or estimated cross-sectional area. Dynamic strength increases relative to muscle crosssection, however, have been positively correlated to the relative content of FT fibers.[16] This latter finding supports the concept of specificity of training and indicates further that a high content of FT fibers in muscles may be a prerequisite for a successful strength training program. The best outcome likely will be achieved when subjects start with a high percentage of atrophied FT fibers and are trained with loads greater than 20 repetitions at 50% of their maximum strength, e.g., 6 repetitions at 80% of maximum. The fact that subjects vary so greatly from these ideal starting conditions provides a most plausible explanation for the wide variability in strength gains and hypertrophic change with standard weight training programs.

Limited data on bodybuilders indicates that they may differ from weight trainers in terms of functional strength.[67] As expected, bodybuilders have larger muscles than male and female physical education students. Yet their maximal strength expressed per unit of cross-sectional area is no greater. These findings are based on measures of maximal isokinetic torque of knee extensor and elbow flexor and extensor muscles made at angular velocities of 30, 90, and 180° per second. It is of interest to note that some of the bodybuilders had been using anabolic steroids and that they willingly submitted to needle biopsy measures of their thigh muscles but not to biopsy measures of their arm triceps muscles. It is apparent that more research is needed to sort out true differences in the structure and function of muscles of bodybuilders and weight trainers.

There is some evidence that the red muscles composed of ST oxidative fibers are more susceptible to exercise injuries than the white muscles composed of FT glycolytic fibers.[64] These data are from rats and mice that were exposed to a single bout of exercise by running them on a motor-driven treadmill for several hours. The differences in injury levels between the major muscle types is likely due to the process of selective recruitment discussed earlier. Increasing the duration of running increased the level of exercise injuries, whereas endurance training prior to the administra-

tion of the strenous exertion reduced the exercise injuries. In summary, it appears that ST fibers are injured more easily during the performance of low-intensity, long-duration exercise. Less is known about the fiber types that might be injured during high-intensity or all-out efforts.

The FT fibers are most involved in the aging process, i.e., these fibers display the greatest fiber atrophy seen in old age. This may be due to a selective degeneration of the largest and fastest conducting motoneurons, which innervate the high threshold fast twitch fibers as described by Rexed in 1944. These changes may ultimately be a reflection of progressive disuse as people purposely and unknowingly participate in less vigorous activities as they age.[51] There has been some study of the effects of strength training programs in reversing the progressive atrophy of the FT fibers. Eighteen sedentary males ranging in age from 22 to 65 years participated in a 60- to 80-minute, low-resistance, high repetition, circuit training program, twice a week for 15 weeks. Older subjects showed increases in fiber size for both ST and FT fibers but no significant improvements in isokinetic strength measures of their knee extensor muscles. This supports the contention that muscle fiber atrophy is not the primary explanation for strength declines in old age.[51]

A final research application that has been discussed much more than it has ever been practiced in the United States is the use of fiber typing as a screening and guidance measurement for young athletes. The idea would be to take muscle biopsy samples from children who show potential for elite sports performance and then, based on their having predominantly ST or FT fibers, guide them into sports where they have the best chance of excelling. Let's examine some reasons why this idea has intuitive merit but, at the same time, has never caught on in the U.S.A.

We should first recall that the number of ST and FT fibers are not fixed until some period during the teen years. This presents a problem because of individual variations in maturation rates so that there would be no assurance that the ratios of ST and FT fibers would truly reflect the numbers finally attained. This will remain a problem until adequate normative data are available to allow accurate prediction of final distributions from measurements made earlier in the young athlete's life. Second, the technical and logistical aspects of any meaningful broad screening approach must be considered. While muscle biopsy procedures are considered to be relatively safe in the hands of well-trained clinicians, there is some associated risk of soreness, swelling, hematoma, and infection. Consequently, the procedures would need to clear human subjects research review committees and signed consent would have to be obtained from the parents of minors. A combination of these factors would inhibit the implementation of any widespread screening and guidance program.

Even if screening and guidance programs could be conducted, there are many problems of interpretation that would need to be addressed. A major concern here would be the damaging effect that a misinterpretation caused by measurement error or a lack of our understanding could have in stifling the interest or motivation of an otherwise promising young athlete when they are told that they lack the "right stuff." Advocates of such programs would need to keep in mind the variability in fiber composition that exists in different regions of muscles and between different muscles of the same body. While some studies indicate that genetics may be operating in the process of selection and attraction of elite endurance athletes,[42] we should be mindful of a limited ability to predict running performance times on the basis of fiber composition.[24] In the former study, adult male elite orienteers had the same percentage of ST fibers in their lesser trained upper body muscles as they did in their more highly trained leg muscles. This suggests that training had not caused the high percentage of ST fibers (about 68%), but that individuals were "selected" with the best prerequisites for high oxidative capacity. The latter study reports only modest correlation coefficients of $r = -0.52$, -0.54, and -0.55 between ST percentages and performance times for running 1, 2, and 6 miles, respectively. Much stronger relationships existed between max $\dot{V}O_2$ measures and run times: $r = -0.84$, -0.87, and -0.88, and it was concluded that max $\dot{V}O_2$, not fiber composition, is the primary determinant of cross-sectional differences in running performance. Keep in mind that these studies are for adult athletes. In younger athletes, the added variability due to differences in levels of growth, development, and maturation would make future performance prediction even more complex and difficult.

The finding that distance running performance relates better to max $\dot{V}O_2$ than to muscle fiber composition points to a final major argument against the use of fiber typing for success prediction and guidance in competitive athletics. The point being that the magnitude of a max $\dot{V}O_2$ measurement reflects a number of physiological functional adaptations rather than a single morphological measurement. In fact, the magnitude even represents the level of motivation of the subject and their ability to endure exertional stress and pain related to fatigue. These individual characteristics, which are difficult, if not impossible, to quantitate, are the factors that often separate gold medal winners from other competitors who are of the same caliber. This, coupled with the fact that a considerable range of fiber composition percentages exist for any athletic group (see Figure 5-16) makes us wary of pre-selection and guidance solely on fiber typing. There are too many other factors operating that can influence performance.

Does this mean that efforts to screen and guide young athletes into activities where they have the best chance for success should be discontinued? The answer is no and it is clear that youth sports coaches do this each time they line up aspiring young athletes to determine who can best run sprints or longer distances. Likewise, as they note the developing somatotypes, heights, and weights of their young charges and make "eyeball measurements" of the childrens' parents, they are formulating screening and guidance strategies. In this regard, coaches might do well to explore more fully the existing genetic basis for performance by interviewing both the parents and grandparents about sports activities in which they innately excelled. The advantage of field tests like time trials for running, distance trials for jumping and throwing, and trials for regional body strength are obvious. First, they circumvent many of the administrative and logistical problems described above for clinical and laboratory tests. More importantly, they have a high level of face validity, i.e., they test aspects of performance that clearly can be related to the sports event itself. This is easily understood by the athletes and parents. Furthermore, test results reflect performance of the young athletes as a functioning organism at a particular point in time. This includes their levels of motivation, maturation, growth and development, and numerous other compensating factors that are integrated into a final performance score. Field tests are relatively easy to administer so that frequent retests can be conducted. All of this reduces the false-negative risk of screening a future champion out of a sport on the basis of their lacking a single genetic predictor of success like a favorable muscle fiber composition. Future applications of such clinical and laboratory tests may not reside

with the screening and guidance of youthful athletes but with the better understanding of differences in the performance levels of elite athletes. They already will have survived screening and self-selection trials but the objective remains of how to best assist them in achieving their full performance potential.

Muscle Force-Velocity and Power-Velocity Relationships

In physical education activities and athletics, muscular force and power are most often applied through a range of motion, e.g., during limb movement. Thus it is important to understand some of the basic concepts underlying the relationship between muscular force and speed (velocity) of movement and muscular power and speed of movement.

The Force-Velocity Curve: Influence of Fiber-Type Distribution

The relationship between muscular force and speed of movement is shown in Figure 5-19. Muscular force when applied over a range of motion is measured as torque.* In the figure, the peak torque an individual produced at the relatively slow speed of 57 degrees per second was used as a reference. All subsequent torque measurements were expressed as its fraction and denoted as % torque (vertical axis). The movement performed was leg extension. Two important features of the force-velocity relationship should be noted.

1. The peak torque generated by a muscle decreases with increasing velocities of movement. In other words, the greatest torque is produced at the slowest speeds of movement. This is true

---

*Torque is the product of force × the lever arm or moment arm distance.

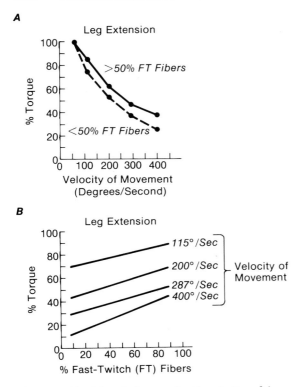

Figure 5-19. Muscle force-velocity relationships. *A,* The peak torque (force) generated by a muscle decreases with increasing velocities of movement, i.e., the greatest torque is produced at the slowest speeds of movement. *B,* At any given velocity of movement, the torque produced is greater the higher the percentage of distribution of fast-twitch (FT) fibers in the muscle. The data were obtained during leg extension movements. (Based on data from Coyle, et al.[14])

regardless of the fiber-type distribution (Fig. 5-19*A*).

2. At any given velocity of movement, the torque produced is greater the higher the percentage of distribution of FT fibers in the muscle (Fig. 5-19*A* and *B*). By the same token, at any given torque produced, the velocity of movement is greater the higher the percentage of distribution of FT fibers.

The preceding relationships point out that FT fibers are capable of producing greater peak muscular tension and a faster rate of tension development than are ST fibers. The biochemical and physiological properties related to these contractile dynamics are the fiber's myosin ATPase activities (p. 97) and their rates of calcium release and uptake from the sarcoplasmic reticulum (p. 97).[11] Both of these properties are higher within the FT fiber than in the ST fiber.[80] Note that FT fiber percentages are used as the basis for plotting changes in percent torque in Figure 5-19*B*. Other studies have shown no correlation between similar expressions of torque, and the percentage of ST fibers.[67] Likewise, there is no significant correlation between ST fiber percentages and decreases in torque with faster movement speeds as shown in Figure 5-19*A*.[67]

The preceding information also has some practical importance to physical education and athletics. For example, a high percentage of FT muscle fibers would seem advantageous for athletes who participate in power-type events. That this is actually the case can be seen from Figure 5-20, in which force-velocity curves for various groups of athletes are shown. Note that the curve for the power athletes (sprinters and high jumpers) is significantly above those of the other groups, whereas the curves for the endurance athletes (race walkers and orienteers) are significantly below the others. In fact, these latter curves are even below the curve for the untrained group.

It should also be noted that the sprinters and jumpers have the highest percentage of FT fibers (61%), whereas the race walkers (41%) and orienteers (33%) have the lowest. While this was expected, the percentage of FT fibers in the untrained group (56%) is very close to that of the sprinters and jumpers (61%), yet the magnitudes of the force-velocity curves are quite different. This suggests that training per

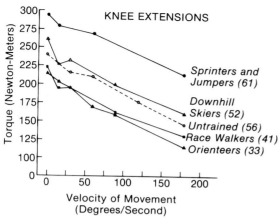

Figure 5-20. Muscle force velocity curves for various groups of athletes. The curve for the power athletes (sprinters and high jumpers), who have the greatest percentage of fast-twitch (FT) fibers (in parentheses), is significantly above those of the other groups, whereas the curves for the endurance athletes, who have the lowest percentage of FT fibers, are significantly below the others. The data were obtained during leg extension movements. (Based on data from Thorstensson, et al.[76])

se can significantly influence the force-velocity curve. (For more on training, see pp. 175–182).

The Power-Velocity Curve: Influence of Fiber-Type Distribution

Studies of elite female athletes indicate similar ST:FT fiber ratios.[35] Sprinters had 39:61, pentathletes 54:46, middle-distance runners 63:37, and distance runners 73:27 percentage ratios, respectively. Decreases in leg extensor torque-velocity plots were also related to whether the athletes had >50% or <50% FT fibers as was shown for other subjects in Figure 5-19A. Unlike earlier reports, there was no decline in torque when movement velocity was increased from 0 to 96°/sec. This is additional evidence that training can alter force-velocity curves toward an enhanced performance.

The relationship between muscular power and speed of movement is shown in Figure 5-21. The measurements were obtained during leg extension movements and are from the same group of subjects for which torque measurements are shown in Figure 5-19. It should be recalled that power is defined as the amount of work performed per unit of time. In the figure, it is the product of the percentage of torque produced and the velocity of the movement. As with the torque measurements, there are two points to notice.

1. The peak power generated by a muscle increases exponentially with increasing velocities of movement. This is to say, the increase in power is more rapid at lower speeds of movement

Figure 5-21. Muscle power-velocity relationships. The peak power generated by a muscle increases exponentially with increasing velocities of movement, and at any given velocity of movement, the peak power generated is greater the higher the percentage of distribution of fast-twitch (FT) fibers in the muscle. The data were obtained during leg extension movements. (Based on data from Coyle, et al.[14])

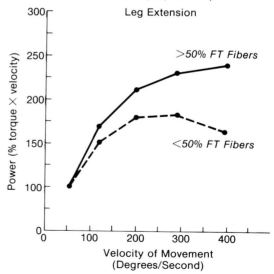

and less rapid at higher speeds. In fact, as shown by the lower curve, the power generated may level off or actually start to decrease at very high velocities of movement.

2. At any given velocity of movement, the peak power generated is greater the higher the percentage of distribution of FT fibers in the muscle. As mentioned before, this relationship is attributable to the biochemical and physiological differences between ST and FT fibers.

With respect to application, in Figure 5-22, power-velocity curves for various groups of athletes are presented. These are the same groups of athletes for which force-velocity curves are given in Figure 5-20. Again, it is clearly evident that peak muscular power is greater at any given velocity of movement for athletes who participate

in the so-called power events and who have relatively greater distributions of FT fibers. For example, the peak power generated at a velocity of movement of 180 degrees per second was found to be 81% greater in sprinters and jumpers than in orienteers.

Local Muscular Fatigue

Although much research has been devoted to muscular fatigue, neither the exact sites nor causes of fatigue are very well understood. Our brief discussion here will start with the influences of fiber-type distribution on fatigue and then will proceed to the possible sites and causes of local muscular fatigue.

Influence of Fiber-Type Distribution on Muscular Fatigue

Earlier, in Table 5-3 (p. 110), it was mentioned that FT fibers are more easily fatigued than are ST fibers. In humans, one of the ways in which muscle fatigue information is obtained is by recording the decrease in peak tension (torque) of a muscle group following a given number of repetitions of very rapid contractions performed through a range of motion. The decline in peak tension of the muscle is taken as a measure of fatigue. As an example, Figure 5-23 shows the results of such an experiment following 50 repetitions of knee extensions. Each repetition was performed at a fast speed of movement (180 degrees per second), and the muscle group studied was the vastus lateralis. It is clear from these results that muscular fatigue (as indicated by the magnitude of decline in peak tension) was greater (1) the greater the percentage of distribution of FT fibers in the muscle (Fig. 5-23A) and (2) the greater the FT fiber area of the muscle (Fig. 5-23B). Because of the biochemical and physiological differences between FT and ST fibers, the preceding information—as we will see next—is particularly important

Figure 5-22. Muscle power-velocity curves for various groups of athletes. Peak muscular power is greater at any given velocity of movement in athletes who participate in the so-called power events and who have relatively greater distributions of fast-twitch (FT) fibers (percentage in parentheses). The data were obtained during leg extension movements. (Based on data from Thorstensson et al.[76])

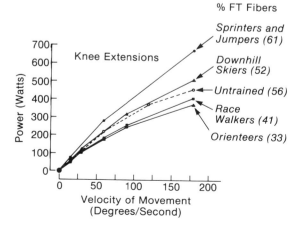

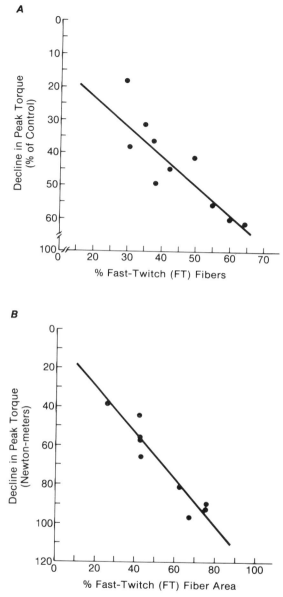

Figure 5-23. *A,* Muscular fatigue, as measured by decline in peak torque, is greater the greater the percentage distribution of fast-twitch (FT) fibers in the muscle and, *B,* the greater the percentage of distribution of the FT fiber area of the muscle. The data were obtained during leg extension movements. (Data in *A* from Thorstensson and Karlsson;[74] data in *B* from Tesch, et al.[72]

in helping to understand some of the causes of muscular fatigue.

Possible Sites and Causes of Muscular Fatigue

In the body, a muscle or muscle group may fatigue because of failure of any one or all of the different neuromuscular mechanisms involved in muscular contraction. For example, the failure of a muscle to contract voluntarily could be due to failure of the following:

1. The *motor nerve* innervating the muscle fibers within the motor units to transmit nervous impulses;
2. The *neuromuscular junction* to relay the nervous impulses from the motor nerve to the muscle fibers;
3. The *contractile mechanism* itself to generate a force; and
4. The *central nervous system,* i.e., the brain and spinal cord, to initiate and relay nervous impulses to the muscle.

Most research concerning local muscular fatigue has focused on the neuromuscular junction, the contractile mechanism, and the central nervous system. The possibility of the motor nerve as the site and cause of fatigue is not very great.

1. *Fatigue at the Neuromuscular Junction.* There is some evidence both for[10,49,71] and against[10,21,22,49,53,59] the idea that local muscular fatigue is caused by failure at the neuromuscular junction. This type of fatigue appears to be more common in FT motor units[49,71] and may account, in part, for the greater fatigability of FT fibers compared with ST fibers. Failure of the neuromuscular junction to relay nervous impulses to the muscle fibers is most likely due to a decreased release of the chemical transmitter, acetylcholine, from the nerve ending. (More on acetylcholine and chemical transmitters is given on p. 139.)

2. *Fatigue Within the Contractile Mech-*

anism. Several factors have been implicated in fatigue of the contractile mechanism itself. Some of them are as follows:

(a) *Accumulation of Lactic Acid.* Fatigue due to lactic acid accumulation has been suspected for many years.[23,37,45,46,47] However, only recently has a relationship between intramuscular lactic acid accumulation and decline in peak tension (a measure of fatigue) been established.[22,72] This relationship is shown in Figure 5-24A for isolated frog sartorius muscle[22] and in Figure 5-24B for intact human vastus lateralis muscle.[72] Whereas establishment of these relationships does not in itself prove conclusively that lactic acid causes fatigue, it does lend considerable support, which has been lacking in the past, to the idea. For example, in the classic experiments conducted by A. V. Hill and colleagues over 50 years ago[37] from which the hypothesis that lactic acid causes muscular fatigue originated, lactic acid accumulation in the muscle was never even measured!

The lactic acid accumulation in the human vastus lateralis is represented as the ratio of lactic acid concentrations in FT and ST fibers (horizontal axis of Fig. 5-24B). This means that as the ratio increases, more lactic acid is being produced in FT fibers in comparison with ST fibers. This greater ability to form lactic acid might be one contributing factor to the higher anaerobic performance capacity of the FT fibers.[72] Notice also that as the lactic acid FT:ST ratio increases, the peak tension of the muscle decreases. This may be interpreted to mean that the greater fatigability of FT fibers is related to their greater ability to form lactic acid.

The idea that lactic acid accumulation is involved in the fatigue process is further strengthened by the fact that there are at least two physiological mechanisms whereby lactic acid could hinder muscle function. Both mechanisms depend on the effects lactic acid has on intracellular pH or hydrogen ion (H^+) concentration. With

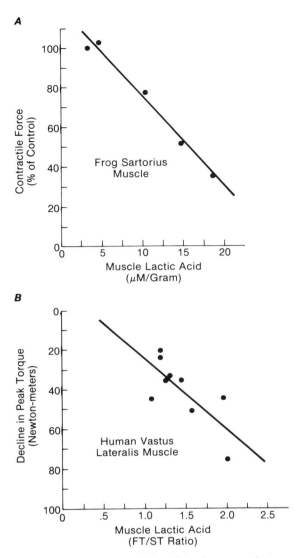

Figure 5-24. *A,* Relationship between intramuscular accumulation of lactic acid and decline in peak tension (a measure of muscular fatigue) for isolated frog sartorius muscle and, *B,* for intact human vastus lateralis muscle. (Data in *A* from Fitts and Holloszy;[22] data in *B* from Tesch et al.[72])

increases in lactic acid, H^+ concentration increases and pH decreases. (More on pH and acid-base balance is presented in Chapter 21, p. 596.) On one hand, an increase in H^+ concentration hinders the excitation-coupling process (Fig. 5-9*B*) by decreasing the amount of Ca^{++} released from the sarcoplasmic reticulum[27] and interfering with the Ca^{++}-troponin binding capacity.[58] On the other hand, an increased H^+ concentration also inhibits the activity of phosphofructokinase, a key enzyme involved in anaerobic glycolysis.[77] Such an inhibition slows glycolysis, thus reducing the availability of ATP for energy.

(b) *Depletion of ATP and PC Stores.* Since ATP is the direct source of energy for muscular contraction, and PC is used for its immediate resynthesis, intramuscular depletion of these phosphagens results in fatigue. However, studies with humans[46,47]

have been conclusive that exhaustion cannot be attributed to critically low phosphagen concentrations in muscle. A similar conclusion was reached from a study conducted on isolated frog sartorius muscle.[22] Some of the results of this study are shown in Figure 5-25. As can be seen, the largest decrease in the concentration of ATP and PC occurred in the first 2 minutes of contraction, before there was a decline in peak tension of the muscle. When the muscle was fully fatigued (after 15 minutes of contraction), there was still 76% of the resting concentration of ATP available to the muscle. In addition, notice that the concentrations of both ATP and PC increased very

Figure 5-25. Relationship between muscular fatigue (decline in peak force) and intramuscular concentrations of ATP and PC in isolated frog muscle. The largest decrease in the concentration of ATP and PC occurred in the first 2 minutes of contraction before there was a decline in peak tension of the muscle. When the muscle was fully fatigued (about 15 minutes of contraction), there was still 76% of the resting concentration of ATP available to the muscle. (Based on data from Fitts and Holloszy.[22])

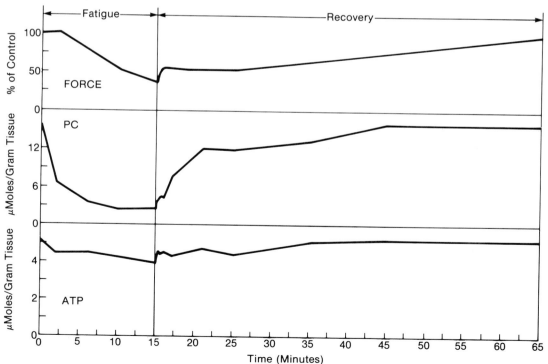

rapidly within the first several minutes of recovery, but that muscular force changed very little. This further indicates that phosphagen availability and muscular fatigue are not highly correlated.

Despite the preceding information, the possibility that ATP and PC might still be involved in the fatigue process cannot be completely dismissed. For example, it has been suggested that during contractile activity, the concentration of ATP in the region of the myofibrils might decrease more markedly than in the muscle as a whole.[22] Therefore, ATP could be limited within the contractile mechanism even though there is only a moderate decrease in total muscle ATP content. Another possibility is that the energy yield in the breakdown of ATP rather than the amount of ATP available is limiting for muscular contraction. For example, the amount of energy liberated when 1 mole of ATP is broken down to ADP + Pi has been calculated to decrease almost 15%, from 12.9 kilocalories (kcal) at rest to as low as 11.0 kcal after exhaustive exercise.[63] The reason for this decrease might be related in part to large increases in intracellular H^+ ion concentration, primarily due to lactic acid accumulation.

(c) *Depletion of Muscle Glycogen Stores.* Earlier, it was mentioned that during prolonged exercise (e.g., 30 minutes to 4 hours) the muscle glycogen stores within some of the fibers (mainly ST fibers) are nearly completely depleted (Fig. 5-18). It is thought that such severe glycogen depletion is a cause of contractile fatigue.[65] This is thought to be true even though plenty of free fatty acids and glucose (from the liver) are still available as fuels to the muscle fibers. Apparently, these other fuels cannot fully cover the energy demand of the glycogen-depleted muscle fibers.[65] As with lactic acid and fatigue, a definite cause-and-effect relationship between muscle glycogen depletion and muscular fatigue

has not been determined. Other factors related to fatigue during prolonged exercise were mentioned in Chapter 2 (p. 32).

(d) *Other Factors.* Some additional but less well-understood factors that may contribute to muscular fatigue are lack of oxygen[28,82] and inadequate blood flow[4] to the muscle fibers.

3. *The Central Nervous System and Local Muscular Fatigue.* Perhaps the most recent research into the role of a central nervous system component in local muscular fatigue is that conducted by Dr. Erling Asmussen and associates.[2,3] He and his staff performed a very clever series of experiments in which repeated bouts of exhaustive work consisting of rhythmical lifting of weights were performed with either the elbow flexor muscles or the flexors of the middle finger. Pauses lasting 2 minutes spent either at complete rest (control) or while physically active were alternated between the work bouts. The active pause periods consisted of performing what was referred to as "diverting activities," i.e., physical activity performed with non-fatigued muscles. The results of one of these experiments[3] are shown in Figure 5-26. The amount of work performed when diverting activities were used during the pause periods was 22% greater than when complete rest was used. Further experiments in the same series of studies[2] showed that similar results were obtained when (1) the diverting activities were performed simultaneously with the exhaustive bouts of work; (2) the circulation to the muscles involved in both the exhaustive and diverting exercises was occluded; (3) mental work was used as the diverting activity; and (4) exhausting work was performed with open compared with closed eyes (more work was performed with the eyes open). These results led to the conclusion that recovery from local muscular fatigue is influenced by a central nervous system factor that is independent of the local blood flow.

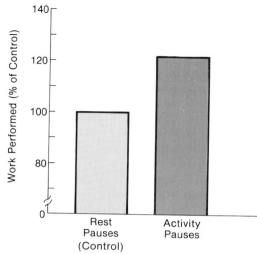

Figure 5-26. Repeated bouts of exhaustive work consisting of rhythmical lifting of weights were performed with either the elbow flexor muscles or the flexors of the middle finger. Pauses lasting 2 minutes spent either at complete rest (control) or while physically active were alternated between the work bouts. The amount of work performed when active pause periods were used was 22% greater than when complete rest periods were used. (Based on data from Asmussen and Mazin.[3])

Physiologically, how might such a mechanism work? Although the exact mechanism is not known, it is proposed that as a muscle fatigues, the local disturbances that occur within its internal environment are signaled back to the central nervous system (brain) via sensory nerves. In turn, the brain sends out inhibitory signals to the nerve cells in the motor system, resulting in a declining muscular work output. During a rest pause, the local disturbances tend to be restored in the muscles, and the fatigue gradually diminishes or disappears. If a diverting activity is performed during a pause period, other signals from the periphery or from the brain itself will impinge on the facilitatory areas of the brain. Consequently, facilitatory impulses

will be sent to the motor system leading to better muscular performance or to a faster recovery from fatigue.[2] The local disturbances in the contractile mechanism of the muscle that initiates this series of events are most likely those discussed earlier (i.e., lactic acid accumulation and depletion of ATP + PC and muscle glycogen).

As has been indicated from the preceding discussion, local muscular fatigue is complex, having several etiologies, and is not as yet well understood. The most likely causes of muscular fatigue are summarized in Table 5-4.

Summary

The connective tissues of skeletal muscle are the endomysium, surrounding the fibers or cells, the perimysium, surrounding the bundles, and the epimysium, encasing the entire muscle. The cell membrane of the muscle fiber is called the sarcolemma. The connective tissues become continuous with the connective tissue of the tendons, which connect the skeletal muscles to the bony skeleton.

Muscles are richly supplied with blood vessels. On the average, three to four capillaries surround each fiber in sedentary men and women, whereas five to seven surround each fiber in male and female athletes.

Muscles contain both motor and sensory nerves. Motor nerves originate in the central nervous system (brain and spinal cord) and when stimulated, cause the muscles to contract. The termination of a motor nerve on a muscle fiber is known as the neuromuscular junction. Sensory nerves convey information concerning pain and orientation of body parts from the muscle to the central nervous sytem.

Each muscle fiber or cell contains hundreds of threadlike protein strands called myofibrils, within which the contractile unit is housed. The light and dark stria-

TABLE 5–4

Summary of Possible Sites and Physiological Mechanisms Involved in Local Muscular Fatigue

Site of Fatigue	Proposed Mechanism
1. Neuromuscular junction	(a) Decreased release of acetylcholine at nerve ending
2. Contractile mechanism	(a) Decreased Ca^{++} released from sarcoplasmic reticulum and reduced Ca^{++}-troponin binding capacity due to increased H^+ concentration caused by lactic acid accumulation
	(b) Depletion of ATP + PC stores and/or decreased energy yield per mole of ATP broken down
	(c) Depletion of muscle glycogen stores
	(d) Lack of oxygen and inadequate blood flow
3. Central nervous system	(a) Local disturbances caused by contractile fatigue signals brain to send inhibitory signals to the motor system resulting in further decline in muscular work output

tions of the myofibrils are called the I and A bands, respectively. The bands contain two protein filaments, actin and myosin. Actin filaments also contain the proteins troponin and tropomyosin. Myosin filaments have tiny protein projections called cross-bridges, which extend toward the actin filaments.

The sarcoplasmic reticulum is a network of tubules surrounding each myofibril. It aids in spreading the nervous impulse throughout the muscle and in storing and releasing calcium (Ca^{++}), both of which are important in the contractile and recovery processes.

Muscular contraction, according to the sliding filament theory, results when the actin filaments are pulled over the myosin filaments, thus producing tension and shortening of the muscle. Both shortening and tension development are dependent upon (1) the breakdown of ATP for energy; (2) Ca^{++}-troponin binding for activation of the actin filaments; and (3) the coupling of myosin to actin (formation of actomyosin).

The single motor nerve and the muscle fibers it supplies are called the motor unit, and it is the basic functional unit of skeletal muscle. The motor unit functions according to the all-or-none law, meaning that it contracts maximally or not at all. Strength gradations are possible by (1) varying the number of motor units contracting at any given time, called multiple motor unit summation; and (2) by varying the frequency of contraction of individual motor units, called wave summation.

The muscle fibers within a given motor unit may be either fast-twitch (FT) or slow-twitch (ST) fibers, but not both. Generally speaking, motor units comprised of FT fibers can be further subdivided into FT_A, FT_B, and FT_C categories, which represent an aerobic to anaerobic metabolic continuum. ST fibers have the highest aerobic capacity while FT_A fibers are both oxidative and glycolytic. FT_B fibers have only a high capacity for anaerobic, glycolytic metabolism. FT_C fibers are an unclassified, nondifferentiated type, which are very few in number.

During exercise there is preferential recruitment of fiber types based on the "size principle" of their motorneurons; small ones first, large ones last. ST fibers are recruited first for low-intensity, endurance exercise. FT$_A$ fibers and then FT$_B$ fibers are recruited as exercise duration is extended, intensity is increased, or fatigue occurs. All available fibers are recruited for all-out power efforts. Sprint athletes tend to have a predominance of FT fibers and endurance athletes a predominance of ST fibers. Middle-distance runners, throwers, and jumpers display a wider range of fiber type compositions. Major adaptations with endurance training include increases in the aerobic capacity of ST and FT$_A$ fibers and a shift toward a higher ratio of FT$_A$ to FT$_B$ fibers. Weight training produces some similar effects but also stimulates FT fibers to enlarge. In neither case do fibers switch from one fiber type to the other, nor do they increase in number. The muscle fiber distributions and enzymatic characteristics of male and female athletes are quite similar.

Heredity strongly influences final adult muscle fiber composition in a process that begins before birth, shows considerable change during the first year of life, and is completed during the teenage years. This and other logistic, safety, and cost factors along with concern over the validity and reliability of the measurement results, inhibit the widespread use of fiber typing as a useful tool to screen and guide young athletes into sports that are "best" for them.

The peak force generated by a muscle decreases and the peak power increases with increasing velocities of movement. For any given velocity of movement, the peak force and peak power produced are greater the higher the percentage of distribution of FT fibers in the muscle.

The most probable sites of local muscular fatigue are the neuromuscular junction, the muscle itself (contractile mechanism), and the central nervous system. Fatigue at the neuromuscular junction, which might be more common in FT fibers, is probably due to a decreased release of chemical transmitter, acetylcholine, from the nerve ending. Fatigue within the contractile mechanism may be caused by one or more of the following: (1) the accumulation of lactic acid, (2) depletion of ATP and PC stores, (3) depletion of muscle glycogen stores, and (4) lack of oxygen and inadequate blood flow. Recovery from local muscular fatigue is quickened by a central nervous system factor that involves irradiation of facilitatory impulses of the motor system.

Questions

1. What are the structural units and associated connective tissues of skeletal muscle?
2. Describe the nerve and blood supplies to muscle.
3. Draw and label a diagram of a sarcomere. Include the I band, A band, H zone, and Z lines.
4. Describe the structure and function of the sarcoplasmic reticulum and T-tubule system.
5. What proteins make up the thick and thin filaments? What is their functional significance?
6. Define the sliding filament theory of muscular contraction.
7. Describe in detail how the myosin cross-bridges are thought to form a bond with selected sites on the actin filaments during an isotonic contraction.
8. Describe the structure and function of the motor unit.
9. How is the strength of a muscle graded?
10. Explain how our movements are smooth and nonjerky.
11. What are the major functional differences between FT and ST muscle fibers or motor units?
12. Discuss the distribution of muscle fiber types in various groups of athletes.
13. What is the functional significance of FT and ST fibers with respect to sprint and endurance exercises?
14. What is the "size principle" of motor unit recruitment?

15. What relationships exist between exercise intensity and the "types" of motor units recruited?
16. Describe the force-velocity and power-velocity curves. How does fiber-type distribution affect these curves?
17. Discuss some of the causes of local muscular fatigue.

References

1. Andersen, P., and Henriksson, J.: Training induced changes in the subgroups of human type II skeletal muscle fibres. *Acta Physiol Scand*. 99:123–125, 1977.
2. Asmussen, E., and Mazin, B.: A central nervous component in local muscular fatigue. *Europ J Appl Physiol*. 38:9–15, 1978.
3. Asmussen, E., and Mazin, B.: Recuperation after muscular fatigue by "diverting activities." *Europ J Appl Physiol*. 38:1–7, 1978.
4. Barclay, J. K., and Stainsby, W. N.: The role of blood flow in limiting maximal metabolic rate in muscle. *Med Sci Sports*. 7(2): 116–119, 1975.
5. Bergh, U., Thorstensson, A., Sjödin, B., Hulten, B., Piehl, K., and Karlsson, J.: Maximal oxygen uptake and muscle fiber types in trained and untrained humans. *Med Sci Sports*. 10(3):151–154, 1978.
6. Brooke, M. H., and Kaiser, K. K.: Three "myosin adenosine triphosphatase" systems: the nature of their pH lability and sulfhydryl dependence. *J. Histochem Cytochem*. 18:670–672, 1970.
7. Brooke, M. H., and Kaiser, K. K.: Muscle fibre types: how many and what kind? *Arch Neurol*. 23:369–379, 1970.
8. Burke, F., Cerny, F., Costill, D., and Fink, W.: Characteristics of skeletal muscle in competitive cyclists. *Med Sci Sports*. 9: 109–112, 1977.
9. Cirrito, J. F.: *Fractional Volumetric Changes in the Ultra Structure of Sarcoplasmic Reticulum in Rat Skeletal Muscle due to Chronic Exercise*. Doctoral Dissertation, The Ohio State University, Columbus, Ohio, 1979.
10. Clamann, H. P., and Broecker, K. T.: Relationship between force and fatigability of red and pale skeletal muscles in man. *Am J Phys Med*. 58(2):70–85, 1979.
11. Close, R. I.: Dynamic properties of mammalian skeletal muscles. *Physiol Rev*. 52(1):129–197, 1972.
12. Cohen, C.: The protein switch of muscle contraction. *Sci Am* 233(5):36–45, 1975.
13. Costill, D., Daniels, J., Evans, W., Fink, W., Krahenbuhl, G., and Saltin, B.: Skeletal muscle enzymes and fiber composition in male and female track athletes. *J Appl Physiol*. 40:149–154, 1976.
14. Coyle, E. F., Costill, D. L., and Lemes, G. R.: Leg extension power and muscle fiber composition. *Med Sci Sports*. 11(1):12–15, 1979.
15. Davies, R.: A molecular theory of muscle contraction: calcium dependent contractions with hydrogen bond formation plus ATP-dependent extensions of part of the myosin-actin cross-bridges. *Nature*. 199:1068–1074, 1963.
16. Dons, B., Bollerup, K., Bonde-Petersen, F., and Hancke, S.: The effect of weight lifting exercise related to muscle fiber composition and muscle cross-sectional area in humans. *Eur J Appl Physiol*. 49:95–106, 1979.
17. Dubowitz, V., and Pearse, A.: A comparative histochemical study of oxidative enzymes and phosphorylase activity in skeletal muscle. *Histochemistry*. 2:105–117, 1960.
18. Edström, L., and Nyström, B.: Histochemical types and sizes of fibers of normal human muscles. *Acta Neurol Scand*. 45: 257–269, 1969.
19. Elder, G. C. B., Bradbury, K., and Roberts, R.: Variability of fiber type distributions within human muscles. *J Appl Physiol: Respirat Environ Exercise Physiol*. 53(6): 1473–1480, 1982.
20. Essén, B., Jansson, E., Henriksson, J., Taylor, A. W., and Saltin, B.: Metabolic characteristics of fibre types in human skeletal muscle. *Acta Physiol Scand*. 95: 153–165, 1975.
21. Fitts, R. H., and Holloszy, J. O.: Contractile properties of rat soleus muscle: effects of training and fatigue. *Am J Physiol*. 233(3): C86–C91, 1977.
22. Fitts, R. H., and Holloszy, J. O.: Lactate and contractile force in frog muscle during development of fatigue and recovery. *Am J Physiol*. 231(2):430–433, 1976.
23. Fletcher, W. W., and Hopkins, F. G.: Lactic acid in mammalian muscle. *J Physiol* (London). 35:247–303, 1907.
24. Foster, C., Costill, D. L., Daniels, J. T., and Fink, W. J.: Skeletal muscle enzyme activ-

ity, fiber composition and $\dot{V}O_2$ max in relation to distance running performance. *Europ J Appl Physiol.* 39:73–80, 1978.

25. Fox, E. L.: *Sports Physiology.* Philadelphia, W. B. Saunders, 1979, pp. 89, 90, 106–107.

26. Fridén, J., Sjöström, M., and Ekblom, B.: Muscle fibre type characteristics in endurance trained and untrained individuals. *Eur J Appl Physiol.* 52:266–271, 1984.

27. Fuchs, F., Reddy, V., and Briggs, F. N.: The interaction of cations with the calcium-binding site of troponin. *Biochim Biophys Acta.* 221:407–409, 1970.

28. Gladden, L. B., MacIntosh, B. R., and Stainsby, W. N.: O_2 uptake and developed tension during and after fatigue, curare block, and ischemia. *J Appl Physiol.* 45(5): 751–755, 1978.

29. Gollnick, P., Armstrong, R., Saubert, C., Piehl, K., and Saltin, B.: Enzyme activity and fiber composition in skeletal muscle of untrained and trained men. *J Appl Physiol.* 33(3):312–319, 1972.

30. Gollnick, P., Armstrong, R., Saubert, C., Sembrowich, W., Shepherd, R., and Saltin, B.: Glycogen depletion patterns in human skeletal muscle fibers during prolonged work. *Pflugers Arch.* 344:1–12, 1973.

31. Gollnick, P., Armstrong, R., Sembrowich, W., Shepherd, R., and Saltin, B.: Glycogen depletion pattern in human skeletal muscle fiber after heavy exercise. *J Appl Physiol.* 34(5):615–618, 1973.

32. Gollnick, P. D., Armstrong, R. B., Saltin, B., Saubert, C. W., IV, Sembrowich, W. L., and Shepherd, R. E.: Effect of training on enzyme activity and fiber composition of human skeletal muscle. *J Appl Physiol.* 34(1):107–111, 1973.

33. Gollnick, P. D., Piehl, K., and Saltin, B.: Selective glycogen depletion pattern in human muscle fibers after exercise of varying intensity and at varying pedal rates. *J Physiol.* 241:45–47, 1974.

34. Gollnick, P. D., Timson, B. F., Moore, R. L., and Riedy, M.: Muscular enlargement and number of fibers in skeletal muscles of rats. *J Appl Physiol.* 50(5):936–943, 1981.

35. Gregor, R. J., Edgerton, V. R., Perrine, J. J., Campion, D. S., and DeBus, C.: Torque-velocity relationships and muscle fiber composition in elite female athletes. *J Appl Physiol.* 47(2):388–392, 1979.

36. Harris, R. C., Sahlin, K., and Hultman, E.: Phosphagen and lactate contents of m.

37. Hill, A. V., and Kupalov, P.: Anaerobic and aerobic activity in isolated muscle. *Proc Roy Soc* (London). Series B, 105:313–322, 1929.

38. Huxley, H.: The mechanism of muscular contraction. *Science.* 164(3886):1356–1366, 1969.

39. Inger, F.: Maximal aerobic power related to the capillary supply of the quadriceps femoris muscle in man. *Acta Physiol Scand.* 104:238–240, 1978.

40. Ivy, J. L., Withers, R. T., Van Handel, P. J., Elger, D. H., and Costill, D. L.: Muscle respiratory capacity and fiber type as determinants of the lactate threshold. *J Appl Physiol.* 48(3):523–527, 1980.

41. Jacobs, I., and Kaiser, P.: Lactate in blood, mixed skeletal muscle, and FT or ST fibres during cycle exercise in man. *Acta Physiol Scand.* 114:461–466, 1982.

42. Jansson, E., and Kaijser, L.: Muscle adaptation to extreme endurance training in man. *Acta Physiol Scand.* 100:315–324, 1977.

43. Jansson, E., Sjödin, B., and Tesch, P.: Changes in muscle fibre type distribution in man after physical training: a sign of fibre type transformation? *Acta Physiol Scand.* 104:235–237, 1978.

44. Johnson, M. A., Polgar, J., Weightman, D., and Appleton, D.: Data on distribution of fibre types in thirty-six human muscles. An autopsy study. *J Neurol Sci.* 18:111–129, 1973.

45. Karlsson, J., Bonde-Petersen, F., Henriksson, J., and Knuttgen, H. G.: Effects of previous exercise with arms or legs on metabolism and performance in exhaustive exercise. *J Appl Physiol.* 38:763–767, 1975.

46. Karlsson, J., and Saltin, B.: Lactate, ATP, and CP in working muscles during exhaustive exercise in man. *J Appl Physiol.* 29(5): 598–602, 1970.

47. Karlsson, J., and Saltin, B.: Oxygen deficit and muscle metabolites in intermittent exercise. *Acta Physiol Scand.* 82:115–122, 1971.

48. Komi, P., Rusko, H., Vos, J., and Vihko, V.: Anaerobic performance capacity in athletes. *Acta Physiol Scand.* 100:107–114, 1977.

49. Komi, P. V., and Tesch, P.: EMG frequency spectrum, muscle structure, and fatigue

during dynamic contractions in man. *Europ J Appl Physiol.* 42:41–50, 1979.

50. Kovanen, V., Suominen, H., and Heikkinen, E.: Collagen of slow twitch and fast twitch muscle fibres in different types of rat skeletal muscle. *Europ J Appl Physiol.* 52:235–242, 1984.

51. Larsson, L.: Physical training effects on muscle morphology in sedentary males at different ages. *Med Sci Sports Exercise.* 14(3):203–206, 1982.

52. MacDougall, J. D., Elder, G. C. B., Sale, D. G., Moroz, J. R., and Sutton, J. R.: Effects of strength training and immobilization on human muscle fibres. *Europ J Appl Physiol.* 43:25–34, 1980.

53. Merton, P. A.: Voluntary strength and fatigue. *J Physiol* (London). 123:553–564, 1954.

54. Milner-Brown, H. S., Stein, R. B., and Lee, R. G.: Synchronization of human motor units: Possible roles of exercise and supraspinal reflexes. *Electroenceph Clin Neurophysiol.* 38:245–254, 1975.

55. Morris, C.: Human muscle fiber type grouping and collateral re-innveration. *J Neurol Neurosurg Psychiatr.* 32:440–444, 1968.

56. Munsat, T. L., McNeal, D., and Waters, R.: Effects of nerve stimulation on human muscle. *Arch Neurol.* 33:608–617, 1976.

57. Murray, J., and Weber, A.: The cooperative action of muscle proteins. *Sci Am.* 230(2): 58–71, 1974.

58. Nakamura, Y., and Schwartz, S.: The influence of hydrogen ion concentration on calcium binding and release by skeletal muscle sarcoplasmic reticulum. *J Gen Physiol.* 59:22–32, 1972.

59. Nilsson, J., Tesch, P., and Thorstensson, A.: Fatigue and EMG of repeated fast voluntary contractions in man. *Acta Physiol Scand.* 101:194–198, 1977.

60. Peachey, L.: The sarcoplasmic reticulum and transverse tubules of frog's sartorious. *J Cell Biol.* 25(3) (Part 2):209–231, 1965.

61. Prince, F. P., Hikida, R. S., and Hagerman, F. C.: Muscle fiber types in women athletes and non-athletes. *Pflugers Arch.* 371:161–165, 1977.

62. Rall, J. A.: Energetic aspects of skeletal muscle contraction: implications of fiber types. *Exercise Sport Sci Rev.* 13:33–74, 1985.

63. Sahlin, K., Palmskog, G., and Hultman, E.: Adenine nucleotide and IMP contents of the quadriceps muscle in man after exercise. *Pflugers Arch.* 374:193–198, 1978.

64. Salminen, A.: Lysosomal changes in skeletal muscles during the repair of exercise injuries in muscle fibers. *Acta Physiol Scand.* 124 (Suppl 539):5–31, 1985.

65. Saltin, B.: Adaptive changes in carbohydrate metabolism with exercise. In Howald, H., and Poortmans, J. (eds.): *Metabolic Adaptation to Prolonged Physical Exercise.* Basel, Switzerland, Birkhäuser Verlag, 1975, pp. 94–100.

66. Saltin, B., Henriksson, J., Nygaard, E., and Andersen, P.: Fiber types and metabolic potentials of skeletal muscles in sedentary man and endurance runners. *Ann NY Acad Sci.* 301:3–29, 1977.

67. Schantz, P., Randall-Fox, E., Hutchison, W., Tydén, A., and Åstrand, P.-O.: Muscle fibre type distribution, muscle cross-sectional area and maximal voluntary strength in humans. *Acta Physiol Scand.* 117:219–226, 1983.

68. Schantz, P., Billeter, R., Henriksson, J., and Jansson, E.: Training-induced increase in myofibrillar ATPase intermediate fibers in human skeletal muscle. *Muscle Nerve.* 5:628–636, 1982.

69. Sjöström, M., Kidman, S., Larsén, K. H., and Ängquist, K.-A.: Z- and M- band appearance in different histochemically defined types of human skeletal muscle fibers. *J Histochem Cytochem.* 30(1):1–11, 1982.

70. Staron, R. S., Hikida, R. S., Hagerman, F. C., Dudley, G. A., and Murray, T. F.: Human skeletal muscle fiber type adaptability to various workloads. *J Histochem Cytochem.* 32(2):146–152, 1984.

71. Stephens, J., and Taylor, A.: Fatigue of maintained voluntary muscle contraction in man. *J Physiol* (London). 220:1–18, 1972.

72. Tesch, P., Sjödon, B., Thorstensson, A., and Karlsson, J.: Muscle fatigue and its relation to lactate accumulation and LDH activity in man. *Acta Physiol Scand.* 103:413–420, 1978.

73. Thomson, J. A., Green, H. J., and Houston, M. E.: Muscle glycogen depletion patterns in fast twitch fibre subgroups of man during submaximal and supramaximal exercise. *Pflugers Arch.* 379:105–108, 1979.

74. Thorstensson, A., and Karlsson, J.: Fatiguability and fibre composition of human skeletal muscle. *Acta Physiol Scand.* 98:318–322, 1976.

75. Thorstensson, A.: Muscle strength, fibre types and enzyme activities in man. *Acta Physiol Scand.* (Suppl 443):7–45, 1976.

76. Thorstensson, A., Larsson, L., Tesch, P.,

and Karlsson, J.: Muscle strength and fiber composition in athletes and sedentary men. *Med Sci Sports.* 9:26–30, 1977.

77. Trivedi, B., and Danforth, W. H.: Effect of pH on the kinetics of frog muscle phosphofructokinase. *J Biol Chem.* 241:4110–4112, 1966.

78. Vogler, C., and Bove, K. E.: Morphology of skeletal muscle in children. *Arch Pathol Lab Med.* 109:238–242, 1985.

79. Vøllestad, N. K., Vaage, O., and Hermansen, L.: Muscle glycogen depletion in type I and subgroups of type II fibers during prolonged severe exercise in man. *Acta Physiol Scand.* 122:433–441, 1984.

80. Vrbova, G.: Influence of activity on some characteristic properties of slow and fast mammalian muscles. *Exercise Sport Sci Rev.* 7:181–213, 1979.

81. Watt, P. W., Goldspink, G., and Ward, P. S.: Changes in fiber type composition in growing muscle as a result of dynamic exercise and static overload. *Muscle Nerve.* 7:50–53, 1984.

82. Wilson, B. A., and Stainsby, W. N.: Relation between oxygen uptake and developed tension in dog skeletal muscle. *J Appl Physiol.* 45(2):234–237, 1978.

SELECTED READINGS

Buchthal, F., and Schmalbruch, H.: Motor unit of mammalian muscle. *Physiol Rev* 60(1): 90–142, 1980.

Close, R. I.: Dynamic properties of mammalian skeletal muscles. *Physiol Rev.* 52(1):129–197, 1972.

Cohen, C.: The protein switch of muscle contraction. *Sci Am.* 233(5):36–45, 1975.

Ebashi, S.: Muscle contraction and pharmacology. *Trends Pharmacol Sci.* 1:29–31, 1979.

Essén, B., Jansson, E., Hendriksson, J., Taylor, A. W., and Saltin, B.: Metabolic characteristics of fibre types in human skeletal muscle. *Acta Physiol Scand.* 95:153–165, 1975.

Fitts, R. H.: The effects of exercise-training on the development of fatigue. *Ann NY Acad Sci.* 301:424–430, 1977.

Huxley, A., and Simmons, R.: Proposed mechanism of force generation in skeletal muscle. *Nature.* 233(5321):533–538, 1971.

Huxley, H.: The mechanism of muscular contraction. *Sci Am.* 213(6):18, 1965.

Huxley, H.: The structural basis of muscular contraction. *Proc Roy Soc Med.* 178:131–149, 1971.

Marston, S. B., Tregear, R. T., Rodger, C. D., and Clarke, M. L.: Coupling between the enzymatic site of myosin and the mechanical output of muscle. *J Mol Biol.* 128(2):111–126, 1979.

The mechanism of muscular contraction. *Cold Springs Harbor Symp Quant Biol.* XXXVII: 1–706, 1972.

Weber, A., and Murray, J.: Molecular control mechanisms in muscle contraction. *Physiol Rev.* 53(3):612–673, 1973.

Wilkie, D. R.: *Muscle.* New York, St. Martin's Press, 1968.

chapter 6

Nervous Control of Muscular Movement

The major concepts to be learned from this chapter are as follows:

- The central nervous system comprises the brain and spinal cord.
- The basic functional and anatomical unit of a nerve is the neuron, which consists of a cell body, or soma, several short nerve fibers called dendrites, and a larger nerve fiber called an axon.
- A nervous impulse or action potential is an electrical disturbance at the point of stimulation of a nerve that is self-propagated the entire length of the axon.
- A simple reflex arc involves a sensory signal traveling by way of an afferent, or sensory, nerve to the spinal cord and stimulating an efferent, or motor nerve, causing a muscular response.
- The connection of one nerve to another is called a synapse, whereas the connection of a nerve to a muscle is a special synapse called a neuromuscular junction.

- Nervous impulses are relayed from nerve to nerve and from nerve to muscle by excitatory chemical transmitter substances released at the ends of the nerve.
- Proprioceptors are muscle sense organs that transmit information about limb position to the central nervous system.
- The learning of a motor skill is specific and takes place in the cerebral cortex and the cerebellum.

Absolutely nothing on this earth is more complex than the nervous system. Neuroanatomists and physiologists spend their entire professional careers attempting to untangle a tiny part of this complex system. Understandably, therefore, we as coaches, physical educators, trainers, and exercise leaders will study only the most pertinent parts of this complex field.

For purpose of study we may first divide the nervous system into the sensory, central, and motor portions. Sensory nerves receive stimuli from such areas as the surface of the skin (pain, cold, heat, and pressure), the eyes, nose, ears, and tongue.

The spinal cord, which extends from the base of the skull to the second lumbar vertebra, and the brain compose the central portion of the nervous system, which is called the **central nervous system (CNS).** The primary functions here are to integrate incoming stimuli, to modify these stimuli, if necessary, to execute motor movements, to store information (memory), and to generate thoughts or ideas.

Connections are made from the CNS to the motor portion of the nervous system. It is here that muscles receive their incoming signals and execute the desired motor event, whether it be kicking a football or throwing a baseball.

The **autonomic nervous system** (meaning self-controlled, or functioning independently) is generally considered by itself and is that portion of the nervous system that helps to control activities such as those involving movement and secretion by the visceral organs, urinary output, body temperature, heart rate, adrenal gland secretion, and blood pressure. Although involuntary, many of these functions are influenced by emotions. For example, secretions and movements of the digestive organs, movement of the bowels, and secretion of sweat are modified during periods of excitement. All of us have experienced increases in heart rate as we become scared or emotionally aroused. Breaking out into a cold sweat is another example of an involuntary act (one which we cannot turn on or off at will) caused by an excited emotional state such as fear. Autonomic nervous system control over blood vessels in leg muscles of humans also exists.[14] This system helps to regulate blood pressure during rest and is of considerable interest because of its possible implications to hypertension or high blood pressure. More on the autonomic nervous system can be found on pp. 273–281 and pp. 331–334.

We might suggest at this time that the overall organization of the nervous system performs three basic functions: (1) *excitability,* which results in a signal from a receptor—for example, the retina of the eye becomes excited from a light source, and the inner ear is stimulated by a sound wave; (2) *conduction* takes place as the stimulus or signal is transmitted over nerve fibers, either to the CNS (sensory) or from the CNS (motor) to effector organs, such as skeletal muscle; and (3) *integration* and *regulation,* which take place within the CNS. Here numerous stimuli or signals are received, sorted out, and integrated into controlled, coordinated motor responses. The response may be to throw a ball, to volley in tennis, or simply reflexively to remove your finger from a hot stove.

It is our purpose in this chapter to describe how excitation takes place, the method whereby stimuli or signals are conducted, and how the CNS integrates all messages into coordinated performance. This information will give us a better understanding of how a motor skill is learned, how it is stored, and how it is recalled when the appropriate stimulus is applied.

Basic Structure of the Nerve

The basic functional and anatomical unit of a nerve is the **neuron,** or **nerve cell.** Its structure is shown in Figure 6-1. The neuron consists of (1) a **cell body,** or **soma;** (2)

Figure 6-1. A nerve cell (neuron) composed of an axon, the long fiber that conducts impulses away from the cell body; the soma or body of the cell, containing the nucleus; and the dendrites, numerous short projections from the body of the cell that receive impulses from other neurons.

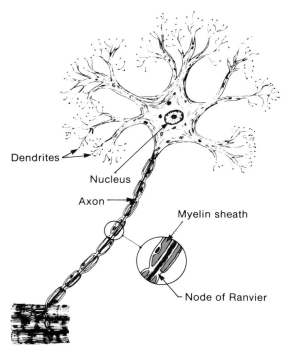

Dendrites

Nucleus

Axon

Myelin sheath

Node of Ranvier

several short nerve fibers called **dendrites;** and (3) a longer nerve fiber called an **axon.** Although technically both dendrites and axons are nerve fibers, the term "nerve fiber" is generally used in reference to an axon. The dendrites transmit nerve impulses toward the cell body, whereas the axon transmits them away from the cell body.

In large nerve fibers, such as those innervating most skeletal muscles, the axon is surrounded by a **myelin sheath** (Fig. 6-1). The sheath is composed mainly of lipid (fat) and protein. Nerve fibers containing a myelin sheath are referred to as **medullated fibers,** whereas those devoid of the sheath are called **nonmedullated fibers.** The myelin sheath is not continuous along the entire length of the fiber, but rather is laid down in segments with small spaces between segments. These spaces are called the **nodes of Ranvier.** We will later see that the myelin sheath and the nodes of Ranvier play important roles in how quickly the nerve impulse is transmitted along the axon.

Basic Function of the Nerve

The information sent from the periphery to the CNS by the afferent nerves is concerned with various kinds of sensations— heat, light, touch, smell, pressure, and so on. The connections of the sensory nerves with the CNS serve to supply us with the perception of these various sensations and to trigger, under certain circumstances, appropriate motor responses. An example of the latter would be the rapid *reflex* withdrawal of your finger from a lighted candle.

To complete such a reflex response, motor nerves are required. These nerves originate in the CNS and terminate in effector organs, such as skeletal muscles. When stimulated, the motor nerves cause the muscles in which they terminate to contract. Thus, in brief, when you accidentally place your finger on a hot object, the heat-sensitive receptors located in the skin send information via the sensory nerve to the CNS. Once in the CNS (in this case, in the spinal cord), the sensory nerve relays the information to the appropriate motor nerve, which in turn sends information to the muscles in the hand; the muscles contract, and the finger is automatically and rapidly withdrawn from the hot object (Fig. 6-2).

The Nerve Impulse

The information transmitted and relayed by the sensory and motor nerves is in a form of electrical energy referred to as the **nerve impulse.** A nerve impulse can be thought of mainly as an electrical disturbance at the point of stimulation of a nerve that is self-propagated along the entire length of the axon. The actual means by which a nerve impulse is generated and propagated in response to a **stimulus**—a change in the environment which modifies the activity of cells—may be summarized as follows: when a nerve fiber is at rest,

sodium ions (Na^+) are most heavily concentrated on the outside of the nerve membrane, causing it to be electrically positive, while the inside of the nerve is electrically negative (Fig. 6-3A). Thus a potential difference exists between the inside and outside of the nerve fiber. This is referred to as the **resting membrane potential.** When a stimulus is applied to the nerve, the nerve membrane becomes highly permeable to sodium ions, and they leak into the inside of the nerve. As a result, the outside of the nerve now becomes negative and the inside positive (Fig. 6-3B). In other words, an adequate stimulus causes a *reversal of polarity* of the nerve. Such a reversal in polarity is referred to as an **action potential.**

In addition to the action potential, a local flow of current is created in the membrane at the site where the stimulus was applied. This current is self-regenerating, in that it flows to adjacent areas of the nerve, causing each area to also undergo a reversal of polarity, which in turn evokes a new action potential and a local flow of current (Fig. 6-3C). This process is repeated over and over again until the action poten-

Figure 6-2. The reflex arc. When your fingers touch a flame, the pain receptors in the fingers receive the stimulus, which is then transmitted by means of the afferent (sensory) nerve fiber to the spinal cord. The efferent (motor) fiber then transmits impulses to the appropriate muscles, and the hand is withdrawn from the flame.

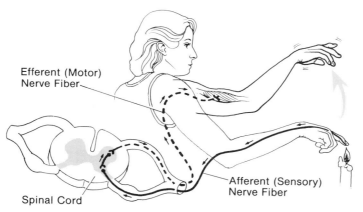

Efferent (Motor) Nerve Fiber

Afferent (Sensory) Nerve Fiber

Spinal Cord

A Rest

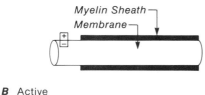

Myelin Sheath
Membrane

B Active

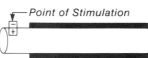

Point of Stimulation

C Propagation

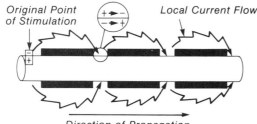

Original Point of Stimulation

Local Current Flow

Direction of Propagation

Figure 6-3. Generation and propagation of the nerve impulse. *A,* at rest, the outside of the nerve is positive. *B,* A stimulus causes a reversal of polarity or action potential and a local flow of current. *C,* The local flow of current evokes a new action potential and flow of current in adjacent areas of the axon (From Fox, E. L.[5])

tial has been propagated the entire length of the nerve fiber.

On some nerve fibers there is a myelin sheath (mentioned earlier); this sheath insulates that part of the nerve it surrounds from electrical disturbances. Therefore, a nerve impulse can be neither generated nor propagated over that part of the fiber covered by the myelin. Instead, the nerve impulse is propagated only at the nodes of Ranvier, that is, from node to node the entire length of the fiber. This jumping from node to node, referred to as **saltatory conduction,** serves to greatly increase the conduction velocity of the nerve impulse.

For example, the conduction velocity of large medullated fibers typical of those innervating skeletal muscles is 60 to 100 meters per second (135 to 225 miles per hour). In nonmedullated fibers of the same diameter, conduction velocity is only 6 to 10 meters per second (13.5 to 22.5 miles per hour).

Nerve-to-Nerve Synapses

The preceding discussion was concerned with how an action potential is transmitted along a single nerve fiber (axon), such as a motoneuron, that innervates a skeletal muscle. Since there are literally billions of nerve cells within the nervous system, the next question to answer is how is nervous information, such as an action potential, passed on from one nerve to another?

The connection of an axon of one nerve to the cell body or dendrites of another is called a **synapse.** Although not pointed out before, go back to Figure 6-1 for a moment, and notice the black dots located on the end of the axon of the neuron. These represent what are called **synaptic knobs.** These knobs are important in relaying nervous information from one neuron to another. For example, in Figure 6-4 a close-up view of a nerve-to-nerve synapse is shown. The axon of a presynaptic neuron approaches the soma of a postsynaptic neuron (called an axon-somatic synapse). The nervous information is relayed across the **synaptic cleft** or gap, by means of a **chemical transmitter substance.** The chemical transmitter is stored in *vesicles* within the synaptic knobs. Mitochondria are also found within the knobs, as ATP generated by the aerobic system is required to synthesize new transmitter substance. Continuous synthesis of transmitter substance is necessary, since only a relatively small amount can be stored in the vesicles at any one time.

As an impulse reaches the synaptic

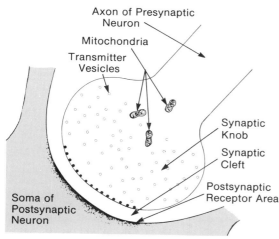

Figure 6-4. Close-up view of a nerve-to-nerve synapse. The axon of a presynaptic neuron approaches the soma of a postsynaptic neuron. The nervous information is relayed across the synaptic cleft by means of a chemical transmitter substance stored in vesicles within the knobs. Mitochondria are also found within the knobs, as ATP generated by the aerobic system is required to synthesize new transmitter substance.

cleft, the chemical transmitter is discharged, and, depending upon the kind of transmitter released, either the postsynaptic membrane (neuron) is excited and an electrical potential is created, or the postsynaptic membrane is inhibited and is said to become *hyperpolarized*. In the first case, the increase in electrical potential (millivolts) in the postsynaptic neuron from its resting membrane potential is called the **excitatory postsynaptic potential (EPSP).** If the voltage increase is adequate (increase of about 11 millivolts above the resting potential), the neuron will fire, sending the impulse, or stimulus, on its way. If the EPSP is less than 11 millivolts, the neuron will not discharge; consequently, the stimulus will be lost. The minimal electrical level at which a neuron will fire

(transmit an impulse) is called the *threshold for excitation.*

In the second case, where the chemical transmitter causes hyperpolarization, the postsynaptic neuron is actually inhibited from eliciting an action potential. In other words, an **inhibitory postsynaptic potential (IPSP)** is said to be created within the neuron. Hyperpolarization refers to the strengthening of the resting membrane potential, thus making it more difficult for an action potential to be elicited.

Excitatory and Inhibitory Transmitter Substances

One of the excitatory transmitters is probably **acetylcholine (ACh).** As we will see next, ACh is also the excitatory chemical transmitter at the neuromuscular junction. Other excitatory transmitter substances include: (1) **norepinephrine,** (2) **dopamine,** and (3) **serotonin.** At least two chemical substances are thought to be inhibitory transmitters: (1) **gamma-aminobutyric acid (GABA),** which is suspected to be the main inhibitory transmitter in the brain; and (2) **glycine,** a simple amino acid,* which is thought to be the main inhibitory transmitter in the spinal cord. Both excitatory and inhibitory transmitters work in the same general manner, causing a change in permeability in the membrane of the postsynaptic neuron. The excitatory transmitters increase the membrane's permeability to sodium ions (Na^+), whereas the inhibitory transmitters increase the permeability to potassium (K^+) and chloride (Cl^-) ions. It should be recalled (p. 137) that an influx of Na^+ to the neuron, if great enough, elicits an action potential. On the other hand, an increased permeability to only K^+ and Cl^- leads to strengthening of

---

*Amino acids are the building blocks of protein (see Chapter 19).

the resting membrane potential (hyper-polarization).

Spatial and Temporal Summation

Each stimulus received at the synaptic cleft may not by itself be strong enough to affect the postsynaptic neuron. However, provided a minimal number of stimuli are received from various presynaptic terminals (axons) simultaneously or within a short time period of one another, they will summate, causing excitation or inhibition of the postsynaptic neuron. The additive effect of these various stimuli is called **spatial summation.** If successive discharges from the *same* presynaptic terminal occur within about 15 milliseconds of one another, they too will summate and, if strong enough, will cause a neuronal effect. This is called **temporal summation.**

Excitation versus Inhibition

Most neurons are constantly bombarded with excitatory and inhibitory stimuli (Fig. 6-5). The net effect of these stimuli on the neuron is determined by their algebraic sum, since the two types of stimuli oppose each other. For example, if excitatory stimuli outnumber inhibitory stimuli to the extent that the threshold for excitation of the postsynaptic neuron is reached, then an action potential is elicited, and the impulse continues on its way. However, if this difference between the two stimuli is not great enough to reach the threshold, the neuron will not fire, and the stimulus is not passed on. Recall here the discussion of the size principle of motor unit recruitment and that the excitation threshold for ST and FT fibers is different; smaller motoneurons to ST units fire first, then larger motoneurons to FT units.

Examples of excitation are numerous and are quite familiar to most of us: the contraction of a muscle results from excitation of its motoneuron. The reflex arc men-

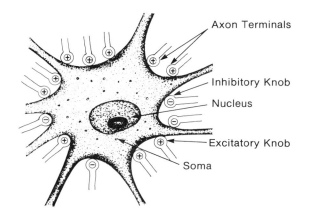

Figure 6-5. Most neurons are constantly bombarded with excitatory (+) and inhibitory (−) stimuli. The net effect of these stimuli on the neuron is determined by their algebraic sum, since the two types of stimuli oppose each other.

tioned earlier, for instance, involved sensory stimuli exciting a motoneuron so that the finger was rapidly withdrawn from the heat source. In addition, as pointed out in the last chapter, the central nervous system component of muscular fatigue is thought to function as a result of the facilitatory (excitatory) influence of the CNS on the motor system.

The function of inhibitory neurons is not only to allow us to overcome excitatory impulses that we consciously wish to oppose, but also, more importantly, to exclude unimportant nonconscious stimuli, especially those elicited through the sensory receptors. Just imagine the number of impulses that would have to be processed by the CNS if inhibition were absent. To mention a few:

1. Continual sensations of pressure from sitting, standing, and lying.
2. Sensations of touch from our clothing.
3. Innumerable sounds we do not care to be bothered with.
4. Light alone sends tremendous numbers of impulses to the retina that are

of no concern (we see only what we wish to see).

5. Stimulation from minor variations in heat and cold are ignored by the CNS through the inhibitory neuronal mechanism.

6. Odors are about us constantly and perhaps only those coming from the kitchen before dinner are worthy of processing; many others are inhibited and should be.

Stop for a moment and look about you; listen and then ponder the countless number of stimuli coming to the CNS from the environment and from your peripheral nerve endings that should be inhibited. Inhibition of extraneous impulses allows you to concentrate on the contents of this book, thus enabling you to become a better exercise physiologist, coach, trainer, physical educator or fitness specialist—we hope! Without the inhibitory mechanism the poor brain probably would be stimulated right out of its cranium!

Later in this chapter (p. 147), we will discuss another example of the inhibitory mechanism, the Golgi tendon organs, which when stimulated cause inhibition of muscular contraction. Also, in the next chapter we will look at the idea that under most circumstances, muscular strength is inhibited by the CNS.

Nerve-to-Muscle Synapse— The Neuromuscular Junction

Figure 6-6 illustrates anatomical features of a motor nerve embedded into a muscle fiber. This union is called the **neuromuscular** or **myoneural junction** or **motor endplate.** Transmission of the neuronal impulse across the synaptic cleft is made possible through the secretion of the chemical transmitter, acetylcholine. As the stimulus reaches the muscle fiber, cholinesterase is secreted, which deactivates the acetylcholine by chemically breaking it

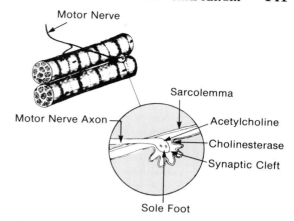

Figure 6-6. The neuromuscular junction. The point at which the motor nerve fiber invaginates the muscle fiber is called the endplate (enlargement). Transmission of the neuronal impulse across the synaptic cleft is made possible through the secretion of acetylcholine. The cholinesterase breaks down acetylcholine, thus preventing further excitation of the muscle following stimulation for that immediate time period.

down. This prevents further excitation of the muscle fiber following stimulation for that immediate time period.

The manner in which a stimulus is transmitted from the nerve to the muscle fiber is very similar, as you will see, to the way in which an impulse is transmitted from nerve to nerve through the neuronal synapse. Apparently, the major difference is that there is no inhibition mechanism at the neuromuscular junction.

As mentioned in the last chapter, a muscle fiber receives only one nerve fiber. However, the large fibers of an efferent (motor) nerve divide into numerous smaller fibers servicing as many as 200 muscle fibers. An individual nerve fiber plus all the muscle fibers it innervates is called a *motor unit.* As an impulse arrives at the neuromuscular junction, acetylcholine is released; the impulse is then able to cross the synapse, creating a potential in the muscle fiber (Fig. 6-7). Such a potential, as we just learned in our discussion of the neuronal synapse, is called an *excitatory postsynaptic potential* (EPSP). The motoneuron activating the muscle fiber may receive impulses from several nerve fibers (Fig. 6-7). If the postsynaptic potential is too small the muscle fiber will not contract; but when the EPSP rises to a certain level, discharge takes place and the muscle fiber contracts.

As previously illustrated in the description of the neuronal synapse, this progressive increase in size of the EPSP as a result of a number of impulses is called *spatial summation*. In addition, successive dis-

charges from the same presynaptic terminal will summate, eliciting an increased EPSP, provided that the discharges occur in rapid succession (within 15 milliseconds of each other). As before, this mechanism is called *temporal summation*.

To illustrate, suppose impulse A is initiated in the brain and impulse B comes from a pain receptor in the skin. For example, you decide to get a tan from a sun lamp and in a few minutes impulses from A + B inform you that the heat is too great; you turn off the lamp or perhaps move farther from it. However, you might fall asleep while under the lamp, in which case im-

Figure 6-7. Diagram demonstrating measurement of a nerve impulse. One electrode is placed in the soma, the other on the efferent nerve fiber. Upon stimulation from either neuron A and/or neuron B, the impulse is amplified and printed on the recorder. For example, the impulse from neuron A is recorded and appears in the insert as does the impulse from neuron B; the combined effect results in the summation of both impulses (A + B).

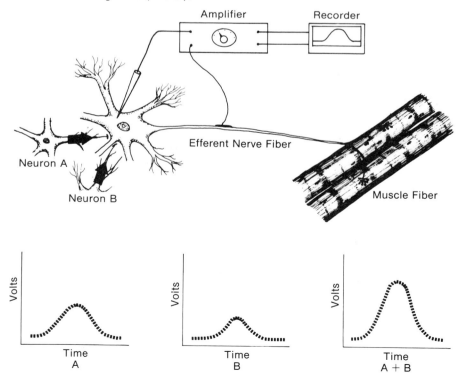

pulse A, which originated in the brain, could not be activated. Impulse B is not sufficiently strong by itself to arouse muscular activity (i.e., to create an adequate EPSP to fire the neuron). Consequently, you remain asleep while the sun lamp continues slowly to bake your tissue. When you do awaken, in all probability you will have received serious burns.

By inhibiting activation of brain cells, sleep, anesthetics, and too much alcohol prevent adequate stimulation of recipient neurons.

Before leaving this area let's consider the impulse firing rates of single motor units within various muscles of the human body. These rates are highly variable with an average of 30 ± 10 impulses per second (Hz units, pronounced Hertz) for the biceps brachii and an average of 10 ± 3 Hz for the soleus muscle.[2] Remember that the biceps muscle of the arm commonly contains 50% or more of FT fibers and that the soleus is primarily comprised of ST fibers. The impulse frequencies also match up well with the general type of muscle being stimulated, i.e., a high firing rate for the fast muscle and a low rate for the slow muscle. The discharge frequencies for individual motor units of the tibialis anterior muscle of the lower leg are approximately 10 Hz.[10] Other studies of the thumb adductor pollicis muscle indicate that maximal electrical stimulation through the ulnar nerve at high rates of 50 to 80 Hz produced rapid fatigue whereas a stimulation rate of 20 Hz produced fatigue curves similar to those for maximal voluntary contractions.[3] The maximum discharge frequency of this latter muscle also has been shown to relate closely to the percentage of **maximum voluntary contraction (MVC)** that is being performed. The average discharge frequency ranges from 35–55 Hz.[12] In summary, it can be said that motor units receive impulse volleys at a rate that relates to the makeup of their constituent fiber types

with an overall range between approximately 10 and 60 Hz. It is not surprising that these reports would indicate a higher rate of firing when more force is being applied. We have discussed that this is one important way to gradate the strength of muscle contractions.

Muscle Sense Organs

There are several types of sense organs in muscle. The pain resulting from exercising too vigorously after long disuse (muscle soreness, p. 172) or from torn muscle fibers are good examples of muscle sense organs at work. These pain receptors, which are few in number, are found not only in the muscle fibers themselves but also in blood vessels (arteries, but *not* veins) that supply the muscle cells and in the connective tissues mentioned in the last chapter that surround the fibers.

Proprioceptors

Other kinds of sense organs found within the muscles and joints are called **proprioceptors.** The function of proprioceptors is to conduct sensory reports to the CNS from (1) muscles, (2) tendons, (3) ligaments, and (4) joints. These sense organs are concerned with **kinesthesis** or **kinesthetic sense** that, in general, unconsciously tells us where our body parts are in relation to our environment. Their contributions enable us to execute a smooth and coordinated movement, no matter whether we are putting a golf ball, hitting a home run, or simply climbing an unfamiliar flight of stairs without stumbling. They also help us to maintain a normal body posture and muscle tonus. The tendency for the lower jaw to drop, the head to fall forward, and the knees to buckle because of the effects of gravity are all counterbalanced by the so-called antigravity muscles, which relay information regarding position in space.

How do these sense organs or proprioceptors function? We can begin to answer this question by first describing how each type of sense organ sends specific sensory information to the CNS. For our purposes there are three important muscle sense organs concerned with kinesthesis: muscle spindles, Golgi tendon organs, and joint receptors.

The Muscle Spindle

Muscle spindles are perhaps the most abundant type of proprioceptor found in muscle. Briefly, **muscle spindles** send information to the CNS concerning the degree of stretch of the muscle in which they are embedded. This provides the muscles with information, for example, as to the exact number of motor units necessary to contract in order to overcome a given resistance; the greater the stretch, the greater the load and the greater the number of motor units required. The spindles are important in the control of posture and, with the help of the gamma system, in voluntary movements.

Structure of the Spindle

The structure of the muscle spindle is given in Figure 6-8. It is nothing more than several modified muscle fibers contained in a capsule, with a sensory nerve spiraled around its center. These modified muscle cells are called **intrafusal fibers** to distinguish them from the regular or **extrafusal fibers.** The center portion of the spindle is not capable of contracting, but the two ends contain contractile fibers. The thin motor nerves innervating the ends are of the gamma type and are thus called **gamma motor neurons** or **fusimotor neurons.** When they are stimulated, the ends of the spindle contract. The larger motor nerves innervating the regular or extrafusal fibers are called **alpha motor nerves.** When they are stimulated, the muscle contracts in the usual sense.

Function of the Spindle

As mentioned before, the spindle is sensitive to length or stretch. Therefore, because the spindle fibers lie parallel to the regular fibers, when the whole muscle is stretched, the center portion of the spindle is stretched also. This stretching activates the sensory nerve located there, which then sends impulses to the central nervous system. In turn, these impulses activate the alpha motor neurons that innervate the regular muscle fibers, and the muscle contracts. If the muscle shortens when it contracts, the spindle also shortens, thus stopping its flow of sensory impulses; the muscle then relaxes.

The spindle is sensitive to both the *rate* of change in length and to the *final length* attained by the muscle fibers. The functional significance of these two types of sensitivity can be illustrated by a muscle engaged in a steady contraction, as when the elbow is flexed steadily against a load (for example, when holding a book). The type of stretch placed on the muscle because of the load is called *tonic stretch* and is concerned with the final length of the muscle fibers. If the load is light, the fibers will be stretched only moderately, and the frequency of discharge of the sensory impulses from the spindle will be low. Thus, only a few motor units are called upon in keeping the load steady.

If there is an unexpected increase in the load being held, such as by adding another book, the muscle will be stretched again. This is evidenced by the fact that the forearm will be lowered owing to the added load. The ensuing reflex contraction initiated by the spindle will reposition the forearm to its original level. However, there will be some overcompensation; that is, at first the contraction will be greater than needed. The greater and more abrupt the increase in load, the greater the frequency of discharge of the spindle, the greater the

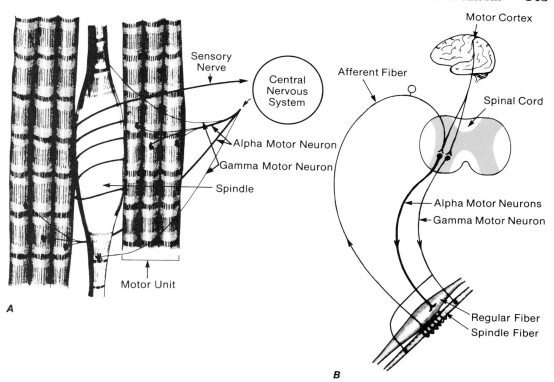

Figure 6-8. *A,* Structure of the muscle spindle; *B,* Connections to the central nervous system of the muscle spindle. The spindle is sensitive to stretch. It can be stretched when the entire muscle is stretched or when the gamma motor neurons are stimulated by the motor cortex (gamma loop). In either case, sensory impulses from the spindle are sent to the spinal cord, stimulating the alpha motor neurons, and the muscle contracts. Also, direct stimulation of the alpha motor neurons from the motor cortex is possible.

contraction, and the greater the overcompensation. In other words, with this type of stretch, called *phasic stretch,* the spindle is responding to the rate or velocity of the change in length and not to the length *per se.* Another example of phasic stretch is given below (stretch reflex).

The Gamma System

There is one other way in which the spindle can be stretched. You will recall (Fig. 6-8) that the contractile ends of the spindle fibers are supplied with motor nerves called gamma motor neurons. These gamma neurons can be stimulated directly by the motor centers located in the cerebral cortex of the brain via their pyramidal tract nerve connections to the spinal cord. Look ahead to p. 150 and Figure 6-13. When stimulated in this manner, the ends of the spindle contract, thus *stretching* the center portion and stimulating the sensory nerve. In other words, the muscle spindle can be activated by itself, apart from the rest of the muscle. This kind of setup provides a very sensitive system for the execution of smooth, voluntary movements. Furthermore, it has been suggested that the gamma neurons have a recruitment order much the same as the motoneurons of alpha motor neurons.[4] While all the functional interrelationships in producing precise voluntary movements are not completely understood, this combined recruitment is called **alpha-gamma coactivation.**

For an example of how the gamma system (sometimes called the gamma loop) works, let's go back to the person voluntarily holding a book in a fixed position (elbow flexed to 90 degrees). We stated that the tonic stretch on the entire muscle created by the load provides information that keeps the load (book) in a relatively fixed position. However, in addition, the gamma neurons are stimulated by impulses sent down directly from the motor cortex. The ends of the spindle contract, the sensory nerve sends impulses back to the central nervous system, and additional information is provided concerning the number of motor units that is required to maintain the original voluntarily initiated position. This additional information provides the refinement that is needed for a smooth rather than a jerky movement.

In summary, there are three ways that the muscle spindle can activate the alpha motor neurons that cause the muscle to contract: (1) by tonic stretch, (2) by phasic stretch, and (3) by the gamma system or gamma loop. All of these controls work together to provide for effective, coordinated, and smooth movement.

Muscle Spindles, Muscle Tone, and the Stretch Reflex

Place your forearm upon the desk in a completely relaxed and slightly flexed position. In feeling the muscles, even though relaxed, you will notice a resiliency rather than a flabbiness. Maintaining this relaxation, have a partner gently extend your forearm (a little powder on the desk will minimize resistance). Your partner will observe a small amount of muscular resistance not related to conscious effort, assuming of course that you are maintaining complete relaxation. This characteristic of resiliency and resistance to stretch in the relaxed resting muscle is called **muscular tonus,** or **tone.**

Now, if you were to sever the efferent or motor nerves (ventral roots) that service this muscle, it would lose tonus and become *flaccid*. Furthermore, if the dorsal roots containing sensory fibers from this muscle were cut, tonus would be obliterated also. Such experiments clearly illustrate that muscular tonus is maintained through reflex activity of the nervous system and is *not* a property of the isolated muscle. However, some scientists[1] have evidence to suggest that there are at least two components of muscle tone: (1) *active*—as just mentioned, due to partial contraction of the muscles through activity of the nervous system; and (2) *passive*—due to the natural elasticity or turgor of muscular and connective tissues, which is independent of nervous innervation. Incidentally, muscles with more than normal tone are referred to as *spastic*.

The basic neural mechanism for maintenance of active muscle tonus is the **stretch reflex,** or the **muscle spindle reflex.** As we have just learned, when a muscle is stretched, impulses are discharged from the muscle spindles. As shown in Figure 6-8, afferent fibers from these spindles enter the spinal cord and form a synapse with the motor nerve cells located there. Axons from these motor neurons conduct impulses to the motor endplates in the same muscle fibers, and this activation produces increased tension, or tonus, in the muscle fibers.

You might test your neuromuscular stretch reflexes by exerting a quick forceful tap with a rubber hammer to the tendon. The following is a list of several spinal cord segments associated with their respective muscles:

MUSCLE	CORD SEGMENTS
Biceps brachii	C5-C6 (fifth and sixth cervical vertebrae)
Triceps brachii	C6-C7
Quadriceps	L2, L3, L4 (second, third, and fourth lumbar vertebrae)

Biceps reflex.   Flex your forearm 90 degrees and have a partner support it; have the partner place his or her thumb over the tendon of insertion of the biceps (tubercle of radius). Now strike the thumb with a mallet; the force is transferred to your biceps tendon. The biceps muscle will contract, flexing the forearm.

Triceps reflex.   Support your arm in a similar fashion as in the biceps reflex. The triceps tendon of insertion (olecranon process of ulna) is struck directly with a mallet. The triceps will contract, extending the forearm.

Patellar reflex.   Sit comfortably on the edge of a table, with your legs dangling and relaxed. Strike the patellar tendon with a sharp blow. The quadriceps femoris muscles will contract, causing extension of the leg.

Stimulation of the spindles by rapping the tendon with a sharp blow conveys information to the CNS, where motor stimuli are relayed to the appropriate muscle and contraction of the muscle is initiated. A positive response (i.e., lack of contraction for the specified muscle) is indicative of a malfunction or lesion at the level of the CNS servicing that particular muscle. Likewise, the absence of limb reflexes might indicate a disruption of normal function in the sensory afferent or motor efferent nerve systems due to injury or disease. Team physicians and trainers frequently conduct basic reflex tests to determine whether or not an injured athlete has experienced nerve damage. Similar reflex testing can be used to check for CNS hyperexcitability or depression caused by the possible presence of drugs and medications in the body.

Golgi Tendon Organs

Golgi tendon organs are proprioceptors encapsulated in tendon fibers and are located near the junction of the muscle and tendon fibers (musculotendinous junction). Their structure is shown in Figure 6-9. Like the spindles, the tendon organs are sensitive to stretch. However, they are much less sensitive than the spindles and therefore

Figure 6-9. The Golgi tendon organ. When a contracted muscle is forcefully stretched, the sensory nerve of the tendon organ is stimulated. Impulses are sent to the spinal cord, where a synapse is made with an inhibitory interneuron that inhibits the alpha motor neuron, and the muscle relaxes.

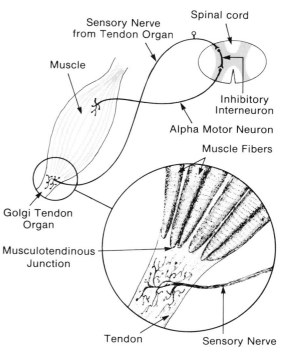

require a strong stretch before they are activated. Actually, because of their location with respect to the muscle fibers, the Golgi tendon organs are activated mainly by the stretch placed upon them by the contraction of the muscles in whose tendons they lie. Given such a stretch, sensory information is sent to the central nervous system, causing the contracted muscle to relax. In other words, in contrast to the spindles, which are facilitatory (i.e., they cause contraction), stimulation of the tendon organs results in *inhibition* of the muscles in which they are located. This can be interpreted as a protective function in that during attempts to lift extremely heavy loads that could cause injury, the tendon organs effect a relaxation of the muscles.

A good example of the tendon organs in action is given by arm-wrestling. It has been suggested that the loss of the contest occurs when the tendon organ inhibition overcomes the voluntary effort to maintain contraction.[11] In addition, the "breaking point" in muscle strength testing might be related to inhibition caused by the tendon organs. If this is the case, maximal strength would be dependent upon the ability to oppose voluntarily the inhibition of the tendon organs.[11]

It should be pointed out that the spindles and tendon organs work together, the former causing just the right degree of muscular tension to effect a smooth movement and the latter causing muscular relaxation when the load is potentially injurious to the muscles and related structures.

Joint Receptors

The joint receptors are found in tendons, ligaments, periosteum (bone), muscle, and joint capsules. They supply information to the central nervous system concerning the joint angle, the acceleration of the joint, and the degree of deformation brought about by pressure. The names of some of the joint receptors are the *end bulbs of Krause,* the *Pacinian corpuscles,* and *Ruffini end organs.* All of this information plus that from other receptors (e.g., sight and sound) is used to give us a sense of awareness of body and limb position, as well as to provide us with automatic reflexes concerned with posture.

The Nervous System and Motor Skills

Now we will direct our attention to the motor responses that are fundamental to the execution of motor skills. Figure 6-10 is a cross-sectional diagram of the essential anatomical parts of the spinal cord. The afferent nerve enters the spinal column through the *dorsal* (rear) *root* and forms synaptic junctions with several neurons (called *internuncial neurons*). The efferent nerve leaves the spinal cord by way of the *ventral root* (front) to the effector muscle. Injury to the ventral root (efferent) fibers affects the muscle or muscles supplied with these motor fibers. Severing of the nerve results in total paralysis.

The majority of afferent fibers entering the spinal cord do not form a synapse with an efferent fiber and leave at the same

Figure 6-10. Essential anatomical parts of the spinal cord. The afferent (sensory) nerve enters the cord through the dorsal root and synapses with internuncial neurons. The efferent (motor) nerve leaves the cord by way of the ventral root to the effector muscle.

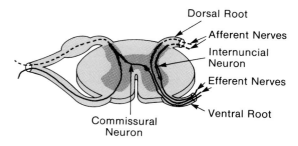

Dorsal Root
Afferent Nerves
Internuncial Neuron
Efferent Nerves
Ventral Root
Commissural Neuron

level, as depicted in the common reflex arc; rather, they split into ascending and descending branches which travel up and down the cord (Fig. 6-11). These long reflex paths connect receptors of the feet with those of the hand, and by the same token, the splitting of the ascending and descending fibers allows impulses to be received and discharged as required by the complexity of the movement. Such a vast array of interneurons and connections from the toe to the brain permit the CNS to function as a coordinating unit regardless of movement complexity.

Simple movements, such as removing a finger from a heated surface, are handled by the spinal cord reflex pattern, whereas the more complicated movements involve higher levels of the cord and brain. Generally speaking, the motoneurons in the spinal cord effect the contraction patterns of the muscles, and the higher centers program the *sequences* of contraction.

Voluntary Control of Motor Functions

The cerebral cortex and the cerebellum are the centers employed in learning new skills. These areas of the brain initiate voluntary control of movement patterns. Figure 6-12 illustrates the motor area of the brain. The dark shading represents the *pyramidal,* or *Betz, cells.* Upon electrical stimulation to this area, motor movements are elicited— hence the term **primary motor cortex.**

The *pyramidal tract* or *corticospinal tract* is made up of the long axons of the pyramidal cells and is the route used to send impulses from the motor cortex down to the motoneurons of the spinal cord, referred to as the anterior, or lower, motoneurons. From here, they form spinal nerves and are distributed to their terminations in skeletal muscles (Fig. 6-13). Most of the pyramidal tract fibers cross over before entering the spinal cord so that the right motor cortex controls the muscles of the

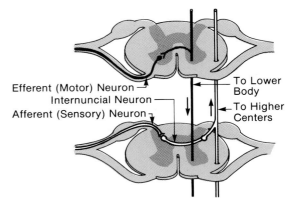

Efferent (Motor) Neuron
Internuncial Neuron
Afferent (Sensory) Neuron
To Lower Body
To Higher Centers

Figure 6-11. The majority of afferent fibers entering the cord do not form synapses with efferent fibers and leave at the same level of the cord; rather, they split into ascending and descending branches, which travel up and down the cord.

left side of the body and vice versa. The presence of this anatomical relationship is very apparent in stroke victims. Damage to the right brain is seen as muscular dysfunction on the left side of the body.

Figure 6-14 illustrates the area of the body affected when particular portions of the motor cortex are stimulated. The size of the area represented is related to the discreteness of movement. For example, the tongue, thumb, fingers, lips, and vocal cords are represented by large areas where only minimal stimuli are required to contract a single muscle or perhaps even a single fasciculus. In the abdominal area, however, groups of muscles rather than single muscles are contracted upon stimulation of the pyramidal area.

Premotor Area for Learning Specialized Motor Skills

The area just forward to the motor area, the **premotor area,** is probably the "sports skills area" of the brain. It is believed that this area is especially concerned with the

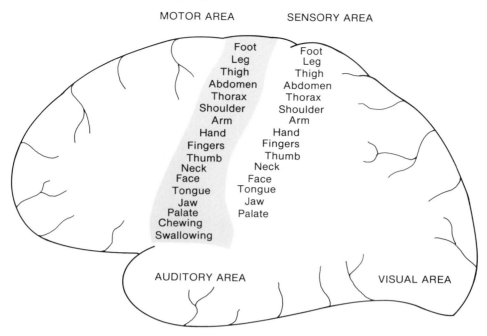

Figure 6-12. The motor area of the brain (cortex). The dark shading represents the pyramidal or Betz cells. Upon electrical stimulation to this area, motor movements are elicited—hence the term, primary motor cortex.

Figure 6-13. The neural pathways of the pyramidal and extrapyramidal tracts. (Modified and redrawn from Gatz.[6])

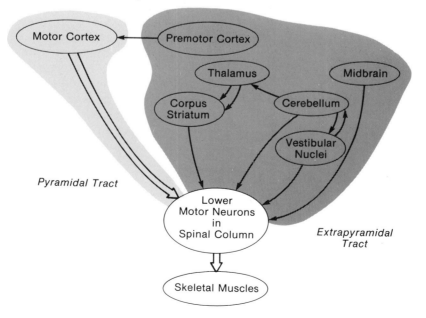

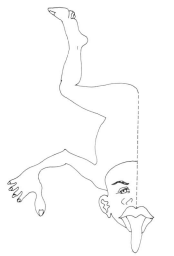

Figure 6-14. When particular portions of the motor cortex are stimulated, certain areas of the body are affected. The size of the area represented is related to the discreteness of movement. For example, the tongue, thumb, big toe, and lips are represented by large areas where only minimal stimuli are required to contract a single muscle.

ing a football is initiated. Impulses are transmitted downward through the pyramidal tract to excite the appropriate muscles. Impulses are also simultaneously transmitted to the cerebellum (Fig. 6-15). As the signals arrive at the muscles, proprioceptors (muscle spindles, Golgi tendon organs, and joint receptors) send the "punting" signal back to the cerebellum. The cerebellum then compares the two sets of

Figure 6-15. When a voluntary movement such as punting a football is initiated, impulses are transmitted downward through the pyramidal tract (P) and eventually to the muscles (E). Impulses are also transmitted to the cerebellum (c). As the signals arrive at the muscles, proprioceptors send the "punting" signal back to the cerebellum (d). The cerebellum then compares the two sets of information and elicits an impulse (correction factor) from the motor cortex, where the original stimulus was initiated; the movement is then executed.

acquisition of specialized motor skills. If a small area is removed, coordinated skill movements are difficult to develop.

The *extrapyramidal tract* is the route used to send impulses from the premotor area down to the lower motoneurons of the spinal cord (Fig. 6-13). En route, the premotor area also has several subcortical connections, such as the thalamus, corpus striatum, and the cerebellum. This latter part of the brain, as we will see next, is responsible for the coordination of movement patterns involving large groups of muscles.

The Cerebellum

The **cerebellum** receives information when a motor stimulus has occurred regardless of the stimulus source. For example, a voluntary movement such as punt-

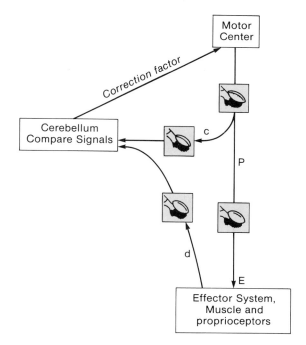

information and elicits an impulse (correction factor) from the motor cortex, where the original stimulus was initiated; the movement is then executed.

Here we have an example of one of the many fascinating but extremely complicated feedback circuits that begin in the motor cortex and return to it via proprioceptors and the cerebellum. This servomechanism type of feedback has been compared to control systems such as those used in industry, guided missiles, automatic pilot mechanisms, and antiaircraft guns. For example, the guided missile continuously transmits radar signals which are received and fed to a computer. The computer, which is analogous to the cerebellum, monitors the signals and compares them to a prewritten program. In this manner, it can detect any errors in the missile's path and radio a correction signal. In somewhat the same fashion, the cerebellum compares the information from the motor cortex to the execution of the football punt. The "error" is calculated by the cerebellum, and a correction is immediately relayed to the motor cortex.

Dampening Effect

It is in the preceding manner that the cerebellum exerts a dampening effect on such pendular movements as the golf swing and throwing and kicking a ball. As the arm or leg moves, momentum is developed with a resulting tendency for the limb to overshoot its mark. The dampening or "correcting" effect is administered by the cerebellum so that the limb stops at the intended position.

Similarly, the cerebellum predicts eventual limb position. The incoming information from the proprioceptors is used by the cerebellum to guide all body parts during the performance of a skill. Through the motor cortex the cerebellum exerts control over both the antagonist and agonist muscles.

Perception of Speed

The cerebellum also allows us to perceive the speed with which we approach objects and with which objects approach us. Without such perception, we would bang into walls and chairs and would miss the shuttlecock or tennis lob. For example, the football player, performing an agility run through a maze of blocking dummies, is guided by the cerebellum so that he does not run into a dummy but rather cuts sharply to either the right or the left at the appropriate time.

Two other variables that the brain takes into account are the speed of limb movements and the effect of gravity on limb positioning.[13] Consideration of these variables is important to programming the proper sequence of muscular contractions and relaxations needed to produce a desired limb movement in sports.

In addition, the cerebellum aids in establishing equilibrium through interpreting changes as revealed by the semicircular canals in the ears. Just as the cerebellum aids in predicting the speed with which we approach an object, it also predicts body positions as a consequence of rotational movements of the head. For example, **tonic neck reflexes** are useful to young children under the age of 4 to 6 months to help them correct losses of balance. These reflexes also are present in persons with certain neurological dysfunctions or those who are well below average in motor skills and coordination. They apparently are not present in normal adults even during the performance of selected activities that would be expected to elicit them.[7]

Sensory Input and Motor Skills

A currently prevalent theory suggests that in the sensory area of the brain, a skill that has been practiced a sufficient number of times becomes memorized and that when the individual wishes to perform the given skill, he or she calls upon this particular motor pattern, which is immediately "replayed." Psychologists have referred to these memorized motor patterns as **engrams.** An engram is a permanent trace left by a stimulus in the tissue protoplasm. By practicing the tennis forehand stroke, for example, this stimulus, over a period of practice sessions, changes the protoplasmic configuration of certain cells in the sensory portion of the brain. The resulting realignment is an engram, or a motor memory pattern, for that special skill. The engram now becomes a part of the person's sensory portion of the brain and upon the appropriate stimulus can be recalled for use immediately.

The sensory engram involves a proprioceptor feedback servomechanism. Neuronal pathways from proprioceptors pass through the cerebellum to the sensory areas of the cerebral cortex and then to the motor cortex. Each center can modify the response to the muscles that perform the motor act. Once learned, the engram is stored and becomes available for use whenever the act is to be performed. In drinking from a glass, the proprioceptors from fingers, hand, and arm convey messages to the CNS. Here the previously stored engram is used as the model. When and if deviations from the stored engram occur, a correction is made through the release of additional motor signals from the motor cortex as "told" to it by the cerebellum.

Engrams for extremely rapid movements are stored in the motor area of the brain and are referred to as **motor engrams.** Engrams stored in the sensory portion of the brain, which are for slower motor acts, operate through the feedback servomechanism previously described in our discussion of the cerebellum; engrams in the motor area (frontal lobe) can be effected without sensory feedback. Typing or rapid movements at the keyboard do not allow sufficient time for a servomechanistic feedback.

Henry's Memory Drum [8,9]

Research has cast doubt on the widely accepted theory that motor ability is completely general. This theory states that if one excels in a certain sport, the ability shown there will carry over into other activities. The range of skills displayed by the high school athlete who excels in a number of sports has been cited, although perhaps erroneously, as proof of this theory. Relying on the "obvious," we have permitted ourselves to conclude that motor ability is truly general or nonspecific, whereas the contrary is probably true. Athletes who excel in several sports may owe more to their motivation and to their numerous activity experiences than to any carry-over of acquired skills from one sport to another. Also, they may be endowed with many specific sports aptitudes rather than any great amount of general motor ability.

Research by Franklin Henry and his colleagues at the University of California has shown that the simple ability to perform a given neuromotor skill is no indication that the performer will be equally capable of performing other such skills; i.e., motor ability is *specific* to a task rather than *general*.[8,9] His reasoning led to the theory that neuromotor coordination patterns are stored in the mind on what we might call a memory drum. Whenever a specific movement pattern is needed, the stimulus causes the storage center or memory drum to "play back" the particular learned skill. Hence, the movement is performed automatically. Such learned skills as playing the piano, running, walking, throwing, and eating are all performed without conscious thought; the memory drum simply plays them back on demand.

The entire process might be likened to the functioning of an electronic computer. According to this theory, the program (or recorded movement pattern) has been learned previously and stored on the memory drum (motor memory), ready to be selected and released when needed. Such a program consists of a set of nonconscious instructions that direct the necessary nerve impulses to the appropriate muscles in a coordinated sequence, thus causing the desired movement. The "read-out time," or performance times, varies somewhat, depending on the length and complexity of the movement. A program in process of being "read out" cannot be changed before it has been completed, in conformity with the all-or-none law of physiology. Some of the findings that lend support to this theory are as follows:

1. Individual differences in ability to make a fast arm movement are about 70% specific to the particular movement being made. For example, a person who can perform a certain arm movement rapidly is not necessarily able to perform other movements of the same arm with equal speed.
2. Reaction time lengthens with increased movement complexity.
3. Little or no relationship exists between static strength and speed of movement. This seems to indicate that speed of movement depends more upon the quality of the impression of the memory drum than on the muscular strength of the limb.
4. A fast limb movement, once underway, cannot be changed in its direction, nor can it be stopped partway through unless it was originally programmed to be stopped rather than completed.
5. Motor-oriented programming results in slower movement and greater reaction latency than sensory-oriented programming. For instance, concentration on the movement to be made (motor orientation) rather than on the starting signal (sensory orientation) tends to result in *slower* reaction time, as conscious control of motor move-

ment interferes with the reading out of the programmed impulses.
6. The component parts of a skill are first learned discretely and are gradually combined into a continuous pattern on the memory drum. When a skill deteriorates, as is the case in aging or long disuse, one notices that the combined pattern breaks up and reverts to the separate movements.
7. Research over a period of many years has shown that the relationship between motor skills is usually quite low.

Summary

The central nervous system (CNS) comprises the brain and spinal cord, the latter extending from the base of the skull to the second lumbar vertebra.

Generally considered by itself, the autonomic nervous system helps to control secretions, urinary output, temperature, sweating, heart rate, breathing rate, blood pressure, and other involuntary acts.

The basic functional and anatomical unit of a nerve is the neuron, which consists of a cell body, or soma, several short nerve fibers called dendrites, and a longer nerve fiber called an axon.

The information transmitted and relayed by nerves is in a form of electrical energy that is referred to as the nerve impulse or action potential. A nerve impulse is an electrical disturbance at the point of stimulation of a nerve that is self-propagated along the entire length of the axon.

A finger being quickly withdrawn from a hot flame as a consequence of a painful sensation exemplifies a simple reflex arc. The sensory signal travels by way of an afferent, or sensory, nerve fiber to the spinal cord and makes contact with a motor nerve fiber; the appropriate muscles are stimulated, and the hand is withdrawn.

The connection of an axon of one nerve to the cell body or dendrites of another is called a synapse. When an impulse arrives at the synapse, a chemical transmitter substance is released from the synaptic knobs at the end of the axon. If it is an excitatory transmitter, such as acetylcholine (ACh), the impulse is passed on to the adjoining nerve fiber; if it is an inhibitory transmitter, such as gamma-aminobutyric acid (GABA), the impulse is inhibited and not passed on. Such an inhibitory mechanism permits the CNS to select or reject stimuli.

At the neuromuscular junction, where the motor nerve invaginates the muscle fiber, a similar synaptic arrangement exists. However, all sufficiently strong stimuli are transmitted across the neuromuscular junction by the transmitter ACh, as inhibition does not occur here.

In muscles (muscle spindles), tendons (Golgi tendon organs), ligaments, and joints (joint receptors) are located proprioceptors that transmit information about limb positions to the CNS. These are also called the kinesthetic receptors, because they aid in performing body movements.

The learning of a motor skill is a complex and not completely understood process. It takes place in the cerebral cortex and the cerebellum. Signals dealing with the particular skill originate in the motor cortex and are transmitted to the muscles. A "copy" of this information to the muscles is also fed to the cerebellum. As movement of the muscles is initiated, proprioceptors relay the program status back to the cerebellum, which sends a corrected signal to the brain if necessary; the skill is then completed.

Henry's memory drum theory of neuromotor reaction provides some hypotheses about how skills are memorized. Most important evidence supports the concept of specificity, which states that learning of motor skills is specific rather than general. There is little if any carry-over from one sport to another unless skills are nearly identical.

Questions

1. What are considered to be the three basic functions of the nervous system?
2. Diagram and label the parts of a nerve cell.
3. Describe how a nerve transmits a nervous impulse along its axon.
4. What is a reflex arc?
5. How are signals transmitted from one nerve fiber to another?
6. How does inhibition at the neuronal synapse occur? Of what value is the inhibitory mechanism?
7. Diagram the myoneural junction and the related anatomical parts.
8. Explain how a signal is transmitted across the myoneural junction.
9. What are proprioceptors, where are they located, and how do they function?
10. Explain muscle tonus.
11. What is the stretch reflex, and how might we test for it?
12. Where is the "sports skill area" of the brain located?
13. Outline the manner in which a voluntary skill is performed.
14. What is meant by the dampening effect exerted through the cerebellum?
15. Define an engram.
16. Outline Henry's memory drum theory of motor learning.

References

1. Basmajian, J. V.: *Muscles Alive* 3rd ed. Baltimore, Williams and Wilkins, 1974.
2. Bellemare, F., Woods, J. J., Johansson, R., and Bigland-Ritchie, B.: Motor-unit discharge rates in maximal voluntary contractions of three human muscles. *J Neurophysiol.* 50(6):1380–1392, 1983.
3. Bigland-Ritchie, B., Jones, D. A., and Woods, J. J.: Excitation frequency and muscle fatigue: electrical responses during human voluntary and stimulated contractions. *Exper Neurology.* 64:414–427, 1979.
4. Burke, D., Hagbarth, K. E., and Skuse,

N. F.: Recruitment order of human spindle endings in isometric voluntary contractions. *J Physiology* (London). 285:101–112, 1978.

5. Fox, E. L.: *Sports Physiology* 2nd ed. Philadelphia, W. B. Saunders, 1984, p. 72.
6. Gatz, A.: *Manter's Essentials of Clinical Neuroanatomy and Neurophysiology* 3rd ed. Philadelphia, F. A. Davis, 1966, p. 121.
7. Geddes, D., and O'Grady, W.: Manifestation of tonic neck reflexes in normal adults during physical activity. *Am Corr Ther J.* 33:184–187, 1979.
8. Henry, F. M.: Influence of motor and sensory sets on reaction latency and speed of discrete movements. *Res Q.* Oct., 1960.
9. Henry, F. M., and Rogers, D. E.: Increased response latency for complicated movements and a "memory drum" theory of neuromotor reaction. *Res Quart.* Oct., 1960.
10. Kato, M., Murakami, K., Takahashi, K., and Hirayama, H.: Motor unit activities during maintained voluntary muscle contraction at constant levels in man. *Neurosci Letters.* 25:149–154, 1981.
11. O'Connell, A., and Gardner, E.: *Understanding the Scientific Bases of Human Movement.* Baltimore, Williams and Wilkins, 1972, p. 209.
12. Petrofsky, J. S., and Phillips, C. A.: Discharge characteristics of motor units and the surface EMG during fatiguing isometric contractions at submaximal tensions. *Aviat Space Environ Med.* 56:581–586, 1985.
13. Ross, E. D., and Muhlbauer, M.: Speed of movement, gravity, and the neural coordination of muscular actions. *Electromyogr Clin Neurophysiol.* 23:385–392, 1983.
14. Svendenhag, J., Wallin, B. G., and Sundlöf, G.: Skeletal muscle sympathetic activity at rest in trained and untrained subjects. *Acta Physiol Scand.* 120:499–504, 1984.

SELECTED READINGS

Axelrod, J.: Neurotransmitters. *Sci Am.* 230(6): 59–71, 1974.

Eyzaguirre, C.: *Physiology of the Nervous System.* Chicago, Year Book Medical, 1969.

Gatz, A.: *Clinical Neuroanatomy and Neurophysiology,* 3rd ed. Philadelphia, F. A. Davis, 1966.

Guyton, A. C.: *Textbook of Medical Physiology,* 5th ed. Philadelphia, W. B. Saunders, 1976, pp. 112–159, 608–625, 678–693.

Hodgkin, A.: *The Conduction of the Nervous Impulse.* Springfield, Ill., Charles C Thomas, 1964.

Lester, H. A.: The response to acetylcholine. *Sci Am.* 236(2):107–118, 1977.

Llinãs, R. R.: The cortex of the cerebellum. *Sci Am.* 232(1):56–71, 1975.

Loeb, G. E.: The control and responses of mammalian muscle spindles during normally executed motor tasks. *Exercise Sport Sci Rev.* 12:157–204, 1984.

Merton, P.: How we control the contraction of our muscles. *Sci Am.* 226(5):30–37, 1972.

O'Connell, A., and Gardner, E.: *Understanding the Scientific Bases of Human Movement.* Baltimore, Williams and Wilkins, 1972, pp. 193–232.

Ruch, T., and Patton, H. D.: *Physiology and Biophysics. The Brain and Neural Function,* 20th ed. Philadelphia, W. B. Saunders, 1979, pp. 53–156.

Suzuki, S., and Hutton, R. S.: Postcontractile motoneuronal discharge produced by muscle afferent activation. *Med Sci Sports.* 8(4): 258–264, 1976.

chapter 7

Development of Muscular Strength, Endurance, and Flexibility

The major concepts to be learned from this chapter are as follows:

- When a muscle shortens while lifting a constant load, the tension developed over a range of motion depends on the length of the muscle, the angle of pull of the muscle on the skeleton, and the speed of shortening.
- Muscular strength and endurance can be significantly improved with properly planned weight resistance exercise programs.
- Increases in strength and endurance are accompanied by such physiological changes as increased muscle size (hypertrophy), small biochemical alterations, and adaptations within the nervous system.
- The physiological principle upon which strength and endurance development depend is called the overload principle.
- Acute muscular soreness is caused by lack of adequate blood flow (ischemia), whereas delayed muscular soreness is probably caused by disruption of the connective tissues.
- Weight training is specific in that gains in strength and muscular endurance will improve skill performance to the greatest extent when the training program consists of exercises that include the muscle groups and that simulate the movement patterns used during the skill.
- Flexibility, the range of motion about a joint, is related to health, and to some extent, to athletic performance.

Our purpose in this chapter will be to investigate the concepts involved in the development of muscular strength and endurance training programs, and to discuss joint flexibility as it relates to physical performance.

Coaches, physical educators, and trainers have always had an interest in muscular strength, endurance, and flexibility. Such interest has frequently centered on the following questions:

1. What is the most effective way in which strength, endurance, and flexibility may be gained?
2. How long will these gains last, and how may they best be maintained?
3. What physiological and biochemical changes do muscles undergo when they increase in strength and endurance?
4. Does strength development result in more rapid muscular contractions and therefore in increased power output for the individual?
5. Do weight-training programs and flexibility exercises positively affect sports performance?

Weight-Training Programs

In this section, we will concentrate on the various kinds of weight-training and progressive-resistance exercise (**PRE**) programs that have been used for the development of muscular strength and endurance. We will start with some basic definitions and will then proceed to a discussion of the physiological changes induced by such programs. Finally, we will attempt to answer some of the questions posed earlier, relating strength and endurance to physical performance.

Muscular Strength: Definition and Types of Contractions

Muscular strength may be defined as *the force or tension a muscle or, more correctly, a muscle group can exert against a resistance in one maximal effort.* There are four basic types of muscular contraction: **isotonic, isometric, eccentric,** and **isokinetic** (Table 7-1).

TABLE 7-1

Summary of the Types of Muscular Contraction

Type of Contraction	Definition
Isotonic, dynamic, or concentric	The muscle shortens with varying tension while lifting a constant load.
Isometric or static	Tension develops but there is no change in the length of the muscle.
Eccentric	The muscle lengthens while contracting (developing tension).
Isokinetic	The tension developed by the muscle while shortening at constant speed is maximal over the full range of motion.

Isotonic Contraction

Isotonic contraction is one of the most familiar types of contraction. It is sometimes referred to as a **concentric contraction** or a **dynamic contraction.** Concentric simply means that a muscle shortens during contraction. Actually, the term dynamic contraction is more accurate, because "isotonic" literally means same or constant *(iso)* tension *(tonic).* In other words, an isotonic contraction supposedly is one that produces the same amount of tension while shortening as it overcomes a constant resistance. However, this is not true for intact muscles, because the tension exerted by a muscle as it shortens is affected by several important factors, three of which are (1) the initial length of the muscle fibers, (2) the angle of pull of the muscle on the bony skeleton, and (3) the speed of shortening. The last factor was discussed previously (p. 119), since speed of shortening is affected by the percentage of distribution of fast- and slow-twitch fibers within a given muscle. Therefore, only the first two factors will be discussed here.

  1. *Muscle Length-Tension Relationships.* As shown in Figure 7-1, an isolated muscle can exert its maximal force or tension while in a stretched position. The

range of peak tension is slightly greater than the resting length of the muscle as it would be positioned in the body. As the muscle shortens, less tension can be exerted. For instance, at about 60% of its resting length, the amount of tension that a muscle can exert approaches zero. The

Figure 7-1. Relationship between tension developed during contraction and muscle length in an isolated muscle. Outside the body, the muscle is strongest at slightly greater than resting length.

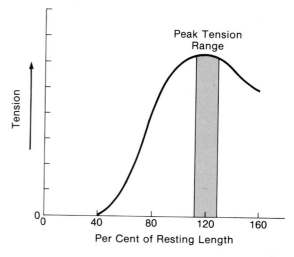

physiological reason for this is explained in Figure 7-2 as follows: with excessive shortening (Fig. 7-2*A*), there is an overlap of actin filaments such that the filament from one side interferes with the coupling potential of the cross-bridges on the other side. Since there are fewer cross-bridges "pulling" on the actin filaments, less tension can be developed. In Figure 7-2*B*, the length of the muscle (sarcomere) is optimal so that all cross-bridges can connect with the actin filaments, and maximal tension can be developed. In Figure 7-2*C*, the sarcomere is stretched to such an extent that the actin filaments are pulled completely out of the range of the cross-bridges. Consequently, the bridges cannot connect, and no tension can be developed.

Figure 7-2. Relationship between the length of a sarcomere and the tension developed. *A,* With excessive shortening, there is an overlap of actin filaments such that the filament from one side interferes with the coupling potential of the cross-bridges on the other side, and no tension is developed. In *B,* the length of the sarcomere is optimal, and all cross-bridges connect with the actin filaments, producing maximal tension. In *C,* the sarcomere is stretched so that the actin filaments are beyond the range of the cross-bridges, and no tension is developed. (Modified and redrawn from Gordon et al.[57])

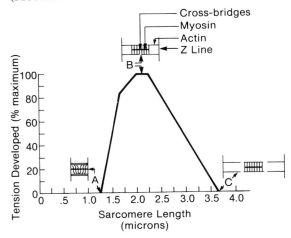

2. *Angle of Pull of Muscle.* From the previous discussion, we might conclude that a person can lift the heaviest load when the muscle is at resting stretched length. However, this is not true, because the intact mechanical system with which we lift objects involves the use of both muscles for force and the use of bones for levers. It is the arrangement of muscles and bones *together* that determines the final effect. Such an effect is shown in Figure 7-3, which depicts the force or tension exerted by various intact muscle groups throughout their range of joint motion. If we let the joint angle represent the angle of pull of the muscle on the bone to which it is attached,* we see that for the elbow (forearm) flexor muscles, for instance, the strongest force is exerted between joint angles of 100 and 140 degrees; (180 degrees is complete extension). At a joint angle of 180 degrees (the position of resting stretch), the muscle group can exert only 64 pounds (29 kilograms) of force. The same thing can be seen of the other muscle groups in the figure. Note the great variability in the shapes of the curves for different muscle groups.

The preceding information has some applications to weight-training programs. First, remember that a dynamic (isotonic) contraction is one in which the muscle shortens while lifting a *constant* resistance, with the muscular tension varying somewhat over the full range of joint motion. Second, the tension required of a muscle to lift an object must be greater than the weight of the object. It follows then that the heaviest constant weight that can be lifted through a full range of joint motion can be no heavier than the weight that can be lifted at the weakest point of the muscle. As an example, look at Figure 7-3 again. Notice that the weakest point of the forearm

---

*The joint angle generally, but not always, accurately reflects the angle of pull of the muscle on the bone.

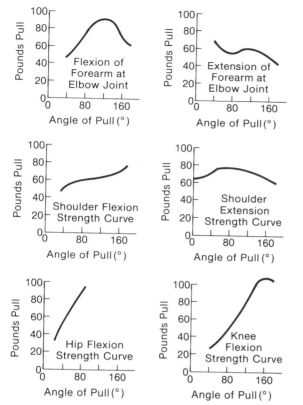

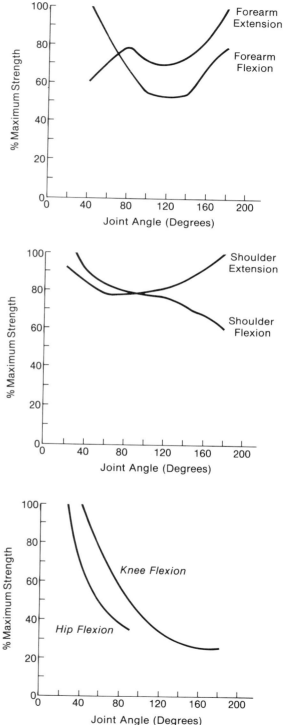

Figure 7-3. Relationship between tension (pounds pull) developed during contraction and angle of pull of the muscle (as indicated by joint angle) on the bone to which it is attached. In this case, strength is not always greatest at resting length (180°). For example, the elbow flexor muscles are strongest between 100° and 140°.

flexor muscles through a range of motion between 40 and 180 degrees is 48 pounds pulled at 40 degrees. Therefore, the heaviest load that can be lifted over that range of forearm flexion is 48 pounds. When this is done, it is easy to see from Figure 7-4 that

Figure 7-4. When lifting a constant load through a range of joint motion (isotonic contraction), the muscle is maximally contracted only at its weakest point in the range.

the muscle is maximally contracted only at the joint angle of 40 degrees, or at its weakest point. At its strongest point (115 to 120 degrees), the muscle is contracted to only 53% of its maximum.

This same concept applies to other muscle groups, as is also shown in Figure 7-4. Notice that the knee flexor muscle group, for instance, is taxed to only 25% of its maximum at joint angles between 140 and 180 degrees. This is a definite disadvantage with respect to strength training programs that involve only isotonic contractions using constant loads, such as lifting free weights (e.g., barbells).

Recognizing this problem, manufacturers of weight-training equipment have developed new machines to compensate for this disadvantage in weight training while lifting constant loads. One of these manufacturers (Nautilus/Sports Medical Industries) uses an odd-shaped cam (Fig. 7-5) to compensate for the variations in muscular tension at different joint angles. It does this by changing the lever (moment) arm of the machine so that the load varies accordingly. This variation in load provides for maximal or at least near maximal muscular tension throughout the full range of joint motion. Other manufacturers (e.g., Universal Gym) have also developed variable resistance machines that provide for production of near maximal isotonic tension over a range of motion.

Isometric Contraction

The term **isometric** literally means same or constant *(iso)* length *(metric)*. In other

Figure 7-5. The Nautilus hip and back machine. A cam compensates for the variations in muscular force at different joint angles by changing the lever (moment) arm; as a result, the muscles exert maximal or near maximal force throughout the full range of motion. (Courtesy Nautilus Sports/Medical Industries, DeLand, Fla.)

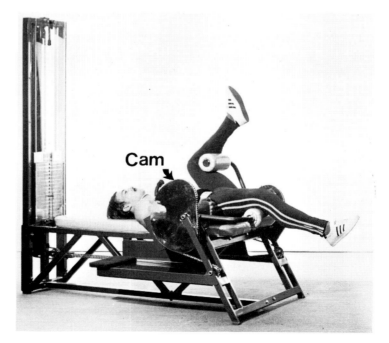

words, a muscle that contracts isometrically is one in which tension is developed, but there is no change in the external length of the muscle. The reason the muscle does not shorten is because the external resistance against which the muscle is pulling is greater than the maximal tension (internal force) the muscle can generate. Observe the use of the term pull rather than push. Although it is true that you may attempt to push a heavy, immovable object, the isometric force is always applied by muscles "pulling" on the bones. In an isotonic contraction where the muscle shortens, the internal force generated by the muscle exceeds that of the external force. Another term used for isometric contraction (although isometric is accurate in its literal derivation) is **static contraction.**

Eccentric Contraction

This type of contraction refers to the *lengthening* of a muscle during contraction, i.e., during the development of active tension. A good example of an eccentric contraction is as follows: Flexing your elbow, have someone try to extend your forearm by pulling down on your wrist. At the same time, resist the pull by attempting to flex your elbow. As your forearm is extended, the elbow flexor muscles will lengthen while contracting. This, by definition, is an eccentric contraction. Eccentric contractions are used in resisting gravity, e.g., walking down a hill or down steps. They also are often used in wrestling where one competitor will resist the efforts of the other to forcefully move their arm or leg but eventually may lose out in the struggle.

Isokinetic Contraction

During an **isokinetic contraction,** the tension developed by the muscle as it shortens at constant *(iso)* speed *(kinetic)* is *maximal* at all joint angles over the full range of motion. Such contractions are common

during sports performances; a good example is the arm stroke during freestyle swimming. The application of full tension in either a sports performance setting or during clinical or laboratory testing is, of course, dependent on the motivation level of the performer.

Although isokinetic and isotonic contractions are both concentric, i.e., involve shortening, the two are not identical. As just mentioned, maximal tension can be developed throughout the full range of motion during isokinetic contractions but not during isotonic contractions. In addition, in an isotonic contraction the speed of movement is not controlled and is relatively slow. This is something of a limitation, for as mentioned in an earlier chapter, it is more and more apparent that muscular power, i.e., both strength and speed of contraction, is a major success factor in many athletic performances (pp. 119–122).

To perform a controlled isokinetic contraction, special equipment is required (Fig. 7-6). Basically, the equipment contains a speed governor so that the speed of movement is constant no matter how much tension is produced in the contracting muscles. Therefore, if one attempts to make the movement as quickly as possible, the tension generated by the muscles will be maximal throughout the full range of motion, but the speed of movement will be constant. This feature, which is unique to truly isokinetic apparatus, is called **accommodating resistance.** The movement speed on many isokinetic devices can be preset and can vary between 0 and approximately 300 degrees of motion per second. Many movement speeds during actual athletic performances exceed 200 degrees per second. Most of the isokinetic machines also have devices for read-out that record either force or torque. Some also simultaneously record joint angles so the points of low- and high-force outputs throughout the range of limb movement can be identified. This is a

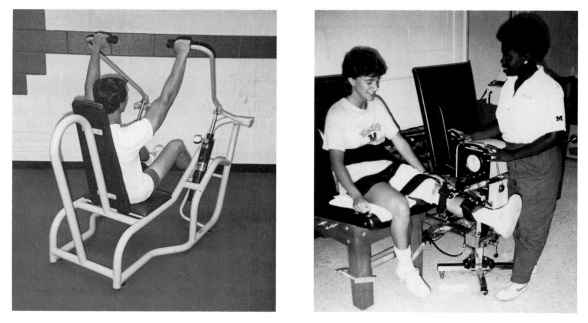

Figure 7-6. Isokinetic strength training and testing equipment. The Hydra-Fitness chest press machine, *A*, uses a hydraulic oil displacement system to provide partial accommodating resistance. The Cybex knee flexion-extension test machine, *B*, uses electric servo-breaking to provide nearly complete accommodating resistence so that the muscles shorten at constant speed and can be maximally loaded throughout the full range of motion. (Courtesy Hydra-Fitness Industries, Belton, TX and Cybex, Division of Lumex, Inc. Ronkonkoma, NY.)

particular advantage, since a read-out provides for scientific evaluation and research and can serve as a training monitor during actual training and injury rehabilitation sessions.

There also are strength training machines that provide partial accommodating resistance (Fig. 7-7). Most of them operate on the principle of hydraulics, i.e., forced oil displacement through an adjustable orifice in a closed cylinder similar to a car's shock absorber. The greater the force applied to the system, the greater the resistance offered by the oil as it is squeezed from one chamber to another. The difference between this and isokinetics, in the strictest sense of the word, is that the hydraulic machines can be pushed and pulled at different rates of speed depending

on the strength of the user. This is in contrast to the fully accommodating resistance of the true isokinetic machines where the apparatus moves only at a fixed, pre-set speed, regardless of the amount of force applied against it.

The strength of intact muscle groups can be measured in a variety of ways. The techniques and apparatus parallel the different types of contractions, i.e., isometric, isotonic, eccentric, and isokinetic. The three latter test modes are called dynamic since they involve movement, whereas isometric tests are frequently called static tests. Examples of static tests are those which use a cable tensiometer or electronic force transducer (strain gauge) attached in series with an immoveable linkage system. Maximum force is measured at joint angles

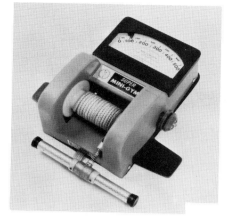

Figure 7-7. Isokinetic-type strength-training machines that provide partial accommodating resistance. The Mini-Gym, *A*, uses a centrifugal clutch as the speed governor. The multi-station Universal machine, *B*, uses a sliding fulcrum to alter the resistance of weight blocks. (Courtesy, MGI Strength/Fitness Systems, Independence, MO, and Universal Fitness and Leisure Inc. Cedar Rapids, IA.)

that approximate the most favorable angle for a given muscle group and joint. Isokinetic tests are usually conducted at different speed settings on Cybex equipment where a zero speed setting can also be used to measure static strength at different joint angles. Isotonic tests often involve repeated trials at lifting free or machine weights to determine the maximum weight that can be lifted only once. This is called one repetition maximum or 1 RM. Because of its simplicity and control over shifts in body position, the bench press 1 RM test using either free or machine weights is a popular test of isotonic strength. Similar tests can be conducted for other muscle groups and the results used to design starting weight-training programs, usually at 80 to 90% of 1 RM. Tests of eccentric strength require special apparatus to measure dynamic force during muscle elongation. Each testing method has its advantages and disadvantages as well as its proponents and opponents. A comparison of isometric, isotonic, and isokinetic methods of testing the strength of knee and elbow flexor and extensor muscles of the same subjects yielded similar results. The average correlation among the three testing modes was quite high, $r = 0.78$, suggesting that a similar phenomenon termed maximal voluntary strength was being measured.[74]

From both a theoretical and practical viewpoint, isokinetic contractions and, therefore, isokinetic measurements and training programs appear to be most suited for improving muscular strength and endurance for athletic performances. Further details of such programs and their effects will be discussed later in this chapter.

Muscular Endurance Defined

As with strength, there are four kinds of local muscular endurance depending upon which of the four types of contraction are used. Local muscular endurance is usually defined as the ability or capacity of a muscle group to perform repeated contractions (either isotonic, isokinetic, or eccentric) against a load or to sustain a contraction (isometric) for an extended period of time. Dynamic endurance tests may be of the **absolute** or **fixed load** type where all subjects are required to lift a common amount of weight, say 50 lb, at a set cadence until they fatigue and can no longer keep up the pace. This is in contrast to **relative load** endurance tests where subjects are assigned a fixed percentage of their maximum strength, say 20 to 50% of 1 RM or of peak isometric tension. They are then timed for their ability to endure a given lifting cadence in dynamic tests, or to sustain a predetermined level of static force in isometric tests.

However, muscular endurance may also be defined as the opposite of muscular fatigue, i.e., a muscle that fatigues rapidly has a low endurance capacity and vice versa. Some of the factors that contribute to local muscular fatigue, including the influence of fast- and slow-twitch fiber distribution, were discussed in an earlier chapter (p. 122) and should be reviewed now. In this chapter we will limit our discussion as to how local muscular endurance can be increased through weight-resistance training programs.

Physiological Changes Accompanying Increased Strength

Muscular exercise is such a common experience that the more striking effects are evident to all. One need go no farther than the school playground to hear the familiar challenge, "Show us your muscle," and to witness the youngsters flexing their arms to compare biceps. Indeed, muscle enlargement with a corresponding increase in strength is a commonly observed phenomenon; (it was first shown scientifically as early as 1897).[97]

Hypertrophy

The enlargement of muscle that results from weight-training programs is mainly due to an increase in the cross-sectional area of the individual muscle fibers. This increase in fiber diameter is called **hypertrophy;** a reduction in size is called **atrophy** or **hypotrophy.** In untrained muscle, the fibers vary considerably in diameter. The objective of a strengthening exercise program can be thought of as to bring the smaller muscle fibers up to the size of the larger ones. Rarely do the hypertrophied fibers exceed the cross-sectional area of the already existing larger ones, but a great many more attain this size. The relationship between the strength of a muscle and its cross-sectional area is shown in Figure 7-8. Notice that it is the same for men and women. (For more on this, see p. 391.)

Hypertrophy of individual muscle fibers is attributable to one or more of the following changes:[53]

1. Increased number and size of myofibrils per muscle fiber.[54,58,88]
2. Increased total amount of contractile protein,[58,89] particularly in the myosin filament.[101]
3. Increased capillary density per fiber.
4. Increased amounts and strength of connective, tendinous, and ligamentous tissues.[123,124]

The changes that contribute most to hypertrophy following weight-training programs are probably the first three listed

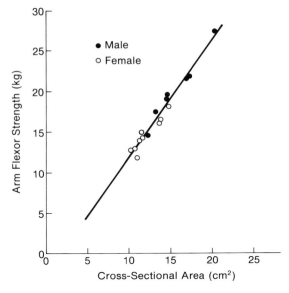

Figure 7-8. Relationship between the strength of the arm flexor muscles and their cross-sectional area. Notice that the relationship is the same for both males and females. (Based on data from Ikai and Fukunaga.[68])

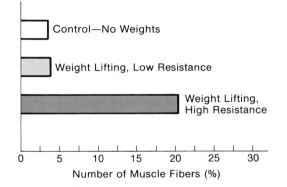

Figure 7-9. Effects of longitudinal fiber splitting on number of muscle fibers. A 20% increase in the number of muscle fibers was found in cats following a 5-day-per-week, 34-week-long program of weight lifting. Note that the fiber splitting is apparently intensity related in that it occurred only after a high-resistance program. (Based on data from Gonyea.[55])

previously. Also, an increased number of capillaries per fiber (number 3) is likely to be most closely associated with increased muscular endurance.

The finding of **longitudinal fiber splitting** in chronically exercised (weight lifting) animals[45,55,56,65] is an interesting phenomenon and deserves further comment. For nearly 85 years, the increased size of a muscle, as a result of weight training, has been attributed solely to an increase in the diameter of the muscle fibers already present (hypertrophy) and *not* to an increase in the number of fibers (hyperplasia). Observation of fiber splitting, of course, casts some doubt on earlier theories about increases in muscle size. For example, studies were reported, Figure 7-9,[55,56] in which a 20% increase in the number of fibers was found in cats following a five-day-per-week, 34-week-long program of weight lifting. It is important to note that

fiber splitting, in this case, was apparently intensity related in that it occurred only after a high-resistance program. Also, although fiber splitting has been shown in several different animals (e.g., rats and cats), it has not as yet been shown to occur in humans following weight-training programs.[88]

More recent studies indicate that increases in the size and strength of human muscles are related to muscle fiber hypertrophy rather than hyperplasia as a result of fiber splitting.

Hypertrophy and Testosterone Levels

It is a popular belief that a large muscle mass and hypertrophy resulting from weight-training programs are related to high levels of the male sex hormone **testosterone**. This is particularly true regarding the so-called masculinizing effect of weight training in females. While these ideas may be popular, they are not supported by scientific fact. For example, correlations among serum testosterone, body composition, and muscular strength were all nonsignificant in both high school and college men and women.[46] In another study,[62] similar nonsignificant correlations were found, and in addition, it was concluded that chronic androgen (testosterone) levels do not change significantly in adult men or women during the course of weight-lifting programs. Although blood levels of testosterone are elevated following single bouts of maximal exercise,[49,115] including weight lifting,[46] no physiological significance of this response is apparent.

Since the preceding studies were conducted only on adults, the question may be raised as to whether or not there is a difference in the response of pre- and postpubescent children to strength-training programs. In this case, blood levels of testosterone would be different in a more physiological or functional sense. From this type of study,[126] it was found that for prepubescent boys no consistent pattern of strength change was noted following a weight-training program. On the other hand, in postpubescent boys there were significant increases in strength in all muscles tested. These results suggest that the presence of testosterone may at least be a prerequisite for promoting strength gains and that weight-training programs for the purpose of increasing muscular strength in prepubescent children are not effective. Obviously, more research along these lines is required to clarify this and related issues.

Biochemical and Muscle Fiber Compositional Changes

The following biochemical and fiber compositional changes in skeletal muscle have been shown to occur following weight-training programs:

1. Increases in concentrations of muscle creatine (by 39%), PC (by 22%), ATP (by 18%), and of glycogen (by 66%).[90]

2. Increase[30,76] or no change[30,122] in glycolytic enzyme activities (phosphofructokinase, or PFK; lactate dehydrogenase, or LDH; muscle phosphorylase; and hexokinase).

3. Little or no consistent change in the ATP turnover enzyme activities, such as myokinase and creatine phosphokinase.[30,76,122]

4. Small but significant increases in aerobic, Krebs Cycle enzyme activities, e.g., malate dehydrogenase, or MDH, and succinic dehydrogenase, or SDH.[30,76]

5. No interconversion of fast- and slow-twitch fibers.[30,42,122]

6. A decrease in the volume (density) of mitochondria due to increases in size of the myofibrils and the sarcoplasmic volume.[89]

7. A selective hypertrophy of fast-twitch fibers as evidenced by an increase in the FT:ST fiber area.[30,42,122]

Two major conclusions seem warranted based on the previous changes. First, the biochemical changes are small and for the most part inconsistent. Therefore, it is highly likely that other changes are mostly responsible for improved muscle function following weight training. While these other changes have not been precisely identified, they probably involve adaptations within the nervous system,[108] including changes in the recruitment pattern[121] and synchronization[94] of motor units.

Second, it appears that a high percentage of distribution of fast-twitch fibers is a prerequisite for maximal gains from strength-training programs. This is suggested by the selective hypertrophy of fast-twitch fibers, which reflects their preferential use during the strength-training exercises. In addition, as shown in Figure 7-10, it has been found that the increase in isotonic strength per unit of muscle cross-

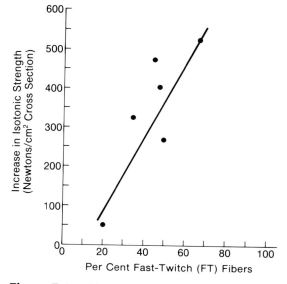

Figure 7-10. The increase in isotonic strength per unit of muscle cross-sectional area is positively correlated with the percentage of distribution of fast-twitch (FT) muscle fibers. (Based on data from Dons et al.[42])

sectional area is positively correlated with the percentage of distribution of fast-twitch fibers.[42] This relationship may also help explain why the individual response to training varies considerably, and why there is a lack of consistency in the weight-training literature regarding the relative effects of different training programs.[42]

Stimulus for Strength and Endurance Gains

What causes a muscle to increase in strength and endurance? We have already indicated that certain physiological and biochemical changes correlate somewhat with an increased capacity of the muscle to exert maximal force as well as to exert submaximal force over an extended period of time. In other words, one of the reasons is related to the increased size and biochemical adaptations of the muscle. In

turn, we know that chronic stress or use of the muscles, as would be the case with regularly scheduled weight-training programs, is the ultimate stimulus for increased levels of strength and endurance.

All of the changes described thus far can be said to have occurred in the muscle tissue itself. What about the nervous system? Is it not true that within the body, a muscle voluntarily contracts through the control of the central nervous system? It is interesting that little research has been conducted along these lines. However, there is some evidence to suggest that changes in the central nervous system act as stimuli for gains in both strength and endurance. A good example of this was mentioned in the discussion of the Golgi tendon organs (p. 148). Here we said that the breaking point of strength testing could very well be limited by the inhibiting influence of these proprioceptors.

Another example is given by true stories of extraordinary feats of muscular strength and endurance. These feats usually occur under exceptional circumstances, i.e., during frightening or "life-and-death" situations. Nevertheless, they may be interpreted to mean that under normal circumstances, strength and endurance are *inhibited* by the central nervous system.[69] Such feats could be explained on the basis that normally it is not possible, because of central nervous system inhibitions, to activate all of the motor units available within a muscle or muscle group. Under extreme circumstances, such inhibitions would be removed and thus all motor units activated. A reduction in central nervous system inhibition with concomitant increases in strength and endurance would also seem to be a reasonable change that could be "learned" through weight-training programs. The effects of this learning could be reflected in a combination of neural reflex facilitation and removal of reflex-mediated inhibition of motor neurons at the spinal cord level. Each change would result in an expansion of the recruitable motor neuron pool. Such expansion would translate into increases in maximum strength performance independent of any changes in the muscles themselves.

Weight Training and Body Composition Changes

For the average college-age man and woman, body composition changes following a weight-training program will consist of (1) little or no change in total body weight, (2) significant losses of relative and absolute body fat, and (3) a significant gain in lean body weight (presumably muscle mass). For example, 5 weeks of one-leg isokinetic strength training produced the following changes in 10 middle-aged women: increases in thigh muscle thickness, relative number of FT fibers, relative area of FT_B fibers, and a decrease of subcutaneous adipose tissue.[78] The fat changes were determined by ultrasound and skinfold caliper measurements. Since fat-cell size did not change, it was concluded that the decrease in thickness of the subcutaneous fat layer was due to geometrical factors related to hypertrophy of the underlying muscles. These findings were therefore not viewed as evidence in support of the concept of spot fat reduction or local emptying of fat depots in the areas of exercising muscles.[78] More is said about these changes in Chapter 14 (page 393).

The Overload Principle

The physiological principle on which strength and endurance development depends is known as the **overload principle.** This principle states simply that the strength, endurance, and hypertrophy of a muscle will increase only when the muscle performs for a given period of time at its maximal strength and endurance capac-ity, i.e., against workloads that are above those normally encountered. As early as 1919, Lange[80] expressed in the scientific literature the first views on the relationship between muscle hypertrophy and the overload phenomenon:

> Only when a muscle performs with greatest power, i.e., through the overcoming of greater resistance in a unit of time than before, would its functional cross section need to increase. . . . If, however, the muscle performance is increased merely by working against the same resistance as before for a longer time, no increase in the contractile substance is necessary.

One of the first experimental demonstrations in humans of the overload principle was made by Hellebrandt and Houtz.[61] Some of their results are shown in Figure 7-11. It is clear that the gains in strength and endurance are most pronounced when the muscle is exercised in

Figure 7-11. The overload principle. Gains in strength and endurance are most pronounced when the muscle is exercised in the overload zone, i.e., with resistances above those normally encountered by the muscle. (Based on data from Hellebrant and Houtz.[61])

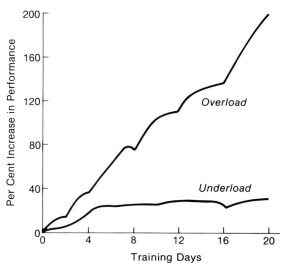

the overload zone, i.e., with resistances far above those normally encountered. Underload, in this case, refers to resistances below those normally encountered by the muscle.

The overload principle, when applied to weight-training programs, means that the resistance against which the muscle works should be increased throughout the course of the program as the muscle gains in strength and endurance. For this reason, the original version of the overload principle, as first stated by Lange, has been modified to what we now call the principle of **progressive-resistance exercise (PRE)**. In fact there is some preference for this term to describe all types of resistance-training methods including devices that can be stretched or compressed, calisthenics that are progressive, as well as weight training.

A unique study of chronic overload training of 11 international caliber jumpers and throwers has been reported.[20] They wore weighted vests equal to 13% of their body weight all day except while sleeping. After a three-week period of overload the subjects showed significant improvements in vertical jumping ability from a squat position, following drops from 20 to 100 cm heights and for a 15-second endurance test period. These improvements were lost within 4 weeks after removal of the vests.[20]

Specificity of Weight Training

Experience has taught successful coaches that in order to increase the performance of their athletes, a *specific* training program must be planned for each athlete. In other words, the training programs must be relevant to the demands of the event for which the athlete is being trained. Such demands include (1) the predominant energy system(s) involved and (2) the movement patterns and the specific muscle groups involved. The first demand will be discussed in more detail in Chapter 12 (p. 288). The second demand means that gains in strength and endurance will improve skill performance to the greatest extent when the training program consists of progressive-resistance exercises that include the muscle groups and simulate the movement patterns most often used during the actual execution of that skill. For example, weight-training exercises for improvement in swimming the breast stroke should focus on those muscles and their movement patterns associated with the breast stroke. The same rule would apply to other swimming events and to other events or skills within other sports and activities.

The specificity of weight training is demonstrable in other ways. You will recall from Chapter 5 that fast-twitch fibers are preferentially recruited for sprintlike activities, including weight lifting, and slow-twitch fibers for endurance exercises. It is easy to see that in order to maximally improve performance in either of these activities, training must be specific to increasing the functional capabilities of the respective fiber types. The information presented earlier on fiber type and the force-velocity curve (p. 119) bears this out. Also, strength training has been shown to be somewhat specific to the joint angle at which the muscle group is trained.[10,50,87] In other words, a muscle group trained, for example, at a joint angle of 115 degrees will not necessarily show increased strength at other joint angles. Specificity is further evidenced by the fact that isometric programs will increase isometric strength more than they will isotonic strength and vice versa.[13,44] The importance of specificity of training speed as it translates to performance power will be discussed in the section on isokinetic training.

A further aspect of specificity of weight training and exercise is the matter of **cross training** or **transfer** of training effects to other regions of the body. The basic question is whether strengthening the legs will transfer to the arms and shoulders so these areas also become stronger? Will continuing to train the arms protect against losses in leg strength? There is some evidence that leg exercise influences the EMG activity of arm biceps muscles so they appear as though they also had been contracting.[132] This would support the existence of an electrophysiological transfer effect. There is less evidence that exercising with one region of the body (e.g., the arms) can promote retention of training effects derived from training a different region (e.g., the legs).[100] Any strength gains by transfer effects would likely be small so it is appropriate to think of PRE training benefits as being specific to body regions and not generally transferable.

Finally, there is some evidence that simultaneously training for strength and endurance will interfere with strength development.[64] In one study there were three exercise groups comprised of adult males and females: a strength-training group that weight trained 30 to 40 minutes per day, 5 days per week; an endurance-training group that rode stationary bicycle ergometers for 40 minutes per day, 6 days per week; and a combination strength and endurance group that did both workouts each day. After 10 weeks the strength group showed no improvement in $\dot{V}O_2$ max and the endurance group showed no improvement in strength. The combination group showed improvements in $\dot{V}O_2$ max at 10 weeks and in strength up to the 7th week. Thereafter strength gains leveled off and actually declined during the 9th and 10th weeks. Simultaneously training for both strength and endurance reduced the subjects' capacity to develop strength, but did not affect their ability to improve their cardiorespiratory endurance by approximately 20%. Similar improvements in $\dot{V}O_2$ max, i.e., 25%, have been shown for young female subjects who performed various

cross-country runs, 45 minutes per day, 3 days per week over 24 weeks.[70] No strength measures were made in this latter study and the training adaptations in muscle fibers, capillary support, and mitochondria were all specific to an enhanced aerobic power.

Specificity of training is obviously important and should be taken into account when planning a weight-training program, whether it be for improvement of athletic or recreational performance.

Muscular Soreness

At one time or another, all of us have experienced muscular soreness, particularly with weight-training programs. Generally, two types of muscle soreness are recognized: (1) **acute soreness** and (2) **delayed soreness.**

Acute Soreness

This type of muscular soreness and pain that, as its name implies, occurs *during* and *immediately following* the exercise period, is thought to be associated with lack of adequate blood flow to the active muscles **(ischemia).** Perhaps the most conclusive scientific evidence pointing to ischemia as the primary cause of acute soreness was gathered over 30 years ago.[43] Some of these data are presented in Figure 7-12. In *A,* a sustained isometric contraction of the finger flexor muscles was performed at the same time that the circulation to those muscles was occluded. Notice how the pain (soreness) increased not only during the contraction period but also for nearly a minute after the contraction was stopped, but with the circulation still occluded. When blood flow was restored, the muscle pain decreased rather rapidly. In *B,* the same kind of experiment was conducted but with the circulation to the active muscles intact. Under these conditions, muscular pain followed fairly well the intensity of

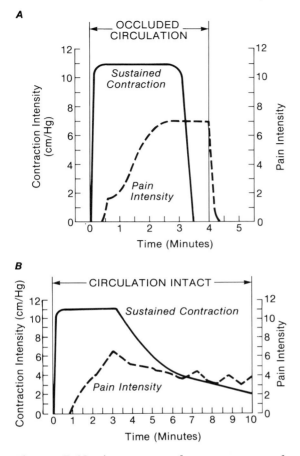

Figure 7-12. Acute muscular soreness and muscle ischemia. *A,* A sustained isometric contraction of the finger flexor muscles was performed at the same time that the circulation to those muscles was occluded (ischemia). The pain (soreness) increased during and was maintained after the contraction period then decreased when blood flow was restored. *B,* The same experiments as in *A* but with the circulation to the active muscles intact. Muscular pain followed fairly well the intensity of the contraction. (Based on data from Dorpat and Holmes.[43])

the contraction. For example, the pain increased to a maximum when the intensity of the contraction was maximal, then declined slowly along with the contraction intensity.

From the preceding experiments, the following conclusions concerning acute muscular soreness were made:

1. Muscular pain is produced during contractions in which the tension generated is great enough to occlude the blood flow to the active muscles (ischemia).
2. Because of the ischemia, metabolic waste products, such as lactic acid and potassium, cannot be removed and thus accumulate to the point of stimulating the pain receptors located in the muscles.
3. The pain continues until either the intensity of the contraction is reduced or the contraction ceases altogether, and blood flow is restored allowing removal of the accumulated waste products.

Delayed Muscular Soreness

Acute soreness, although often an annoyance, does not pose much of a problem because it is short-lived (acute) and is alleviated when exercise is discontinued. The more serious problem is delayed muscular soreness, i.e., the pain and soreness that occurs 24 to 48 hours after exercise sessions have stopped.

From experiments designed to induce delayed muscular soreness,[75,117] it has been found that the degree of soreness is related to the type of muscle contraction performed. In one typical experiment, the results of which are shown in Figure 7-13, muscle soreness was induced with weightlifting exercises as follows: male and female subjects performed two sets of exhaustive contractions of the elbow flexor muscles with barbells. During eccentric contractions, the barbell was only actively lowered, whereas during isotonic contractions, it was only actively raised. During isometric contractions, the barbell was held stationary. As shown in Figure 7-13, mus-

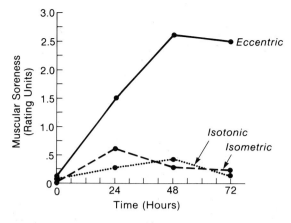

Figure 7-13. Delayed muscle soreness is most pronounced following eccentric contractions and is least pronounced following isotonic and isometric contractions. (Based on data from Talag.[117])

cle soreness was found to be most pronounced following eccentric contractions and was least pronounced following isotonic contractions. The soreness following isometric contractions was only slightly greater than that following isotonic contractions, but it was still considerably below that found after eccentric contractions. Also, in all cases the soreness was delayed, the greatest delay being 24 to 48 hours after exercise.

Although not shown in Figure 7-13, it was found in this experiment that muscular strength decreased appreciably following eccentric contractions and remained depressed throughout the duration of the soreness period. No significant decrease in strength was noted during the soreness period following isotonic or isometric contractions. Little or no delayed muscle soreness was noted following exercise involving isokinetic contractions, and there was no decrease in strength.

What causes delayed muscular soreness and how can it be avoided? The exact cause (or causes) of muscle soreness are not known. However, three different theories have been advanced.

1. *The Torn Tissue Theory.*[67] This theory proposes that tissue damage, such as the tearing of muscle fibers, could explain muscle soreness.
2. *The Spasm Theory.*[39,41] In this theory, three stages of action are suggested: (a) exercise causes ischemia within the active muscles; (b) ischemia leads to the accumulation of an unknown "pain substance" (or P substance) that stimulates the pain nerve endings in the muscle; and (c) the pain brings about a reflex muscle spasm that causes ischemia, and the entire cycle is repeated.
3. *The Connective Tissue Theory.*[8,75] This theory suggests that the connective tissues, including the tendons, are damaged during contraction, thus causing muscular pain.

In studies designed specifically to investigate these theories,[1,2] it was concluded that delayed muscular soreness is most likely related to disruption of the connective tissue elements in the muscles and tendons. Some of the results of this study are shown in Figure 7-14. One of the products of breakdown of connective tissue is a substance called *hydroxyproline*. An increase in the urinary excretion of hydroxyproline indicates damage to the connective tissues. Therefore, urinary excretion of hydroxyproline was monitored in subjects over several days as follows: on a control day when no exercise was performed, on an exercise day during which some of the subjects experienced muscular soreness and some did not, and 24 and 48 hours following exercise. It can be seen that hydroxyproline excretion was higher on the exercise day and after 24 and, particularly, 48 hours after exercise in those subjects who had soreness than in those who did not. In addition, a more detailed analysis of the

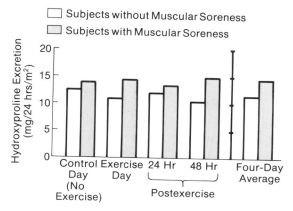

Figure 7-14. Hydroxyproline excretion was higher on the exercise day and after 24 and, particularly, 48 hours after exercise in subjects who had muscular soreness than in those who did not. These results suggest that delayed muscular soreness is most likely due to disruption of the connective tissue elements in the muscles and tendons. (Based on data from Abraham.[2])

data showed a significant correlation between the day of maximal hydroxyproline excretion and the day when the subjects reported their greatest soreness.

The connective tissue theory appears consistent with the findings mentioned earlier of greatest soreness following eccentric contractions.[75,116] You will recall that during eccentric contractions, the muscle lengthens under tension thus stretching the connective tissue components associated with both the tendons and the muscle fibers. In contrast, during concentric contractions (isotonic and isokinetic), the majority of stretch is put on the connective tissues associated with tendons. Furthermore, the tension developed during maximal eccentric contractions is greater than that possible during other types of contractions. This greater tension could possibly cause more damage to the connective tissues.

The following suggestions have been made to prevent muscle soreness:

1. Stretching appears to help not only the prevention of soreness but also the relief of it when present.[40] Stretching exercises should be performed, however, without bouncing or jerking, since this may further damage the connective tissues. More about stretching exercises is presented later in this chapter.

2. A gradual progression in the intensity of exercise usually helps in reducing the possibility of excessive muscular soreness. Such a progression in a weight-training program involves using relatively light weights at the start of the program and then gradually increasing the load as gains in strength are made.

3. It has been proposed that ingestion of 100 milligrams per day of vitamin C (about twice the daily recommended dosage) for a period of 30 days will prevent or at least reduce subsequent muscle soreness.[112] However, the value of consuming such a quantity of vitamin C (ascorbic acid) has not been entirely established through scientific experimentation.

Strength and Endurance Programs

Because there are four basic kinds of muscular contraction (see Table 7-1), it is not surprising to find that there are also four basic types of strength and endurance programs, each structured around one of the basic contractions. In answering some of the questions posed earlier, we will consider each type of program. A fifth type of training program that combines a prestretch of muscle-tendon units followed by an isotonic contraction also will be considered. This combination program is called **plyometrics**.

Isotonic Programs

One of the first isotonic progressive resistance programs advocated was that of DeLorme and Watkins in 1948.[36,37] In setting forth their method of exercises for maximal development of strength, they first established the idea of a **repetition maximum (RM).** A repetition maximum is the maximal load that a muscle group can lift over a given number of repetitions before fatiguing. In their program they used a 10-repetition maximum (10 RM), i.e., the maximal load that can be lifted over 10 repetitions. For each muscle group to be trained, the exercise program consisted of a total of 30 repetitions per training session divided into three *sets* of 10 repetitions each as follows:

Set 1 = 10 repetitions at a load of ½ 10 RM*
Set 2 = 10 repetitions at a load of ¾ 10 RM
Set 3 = 10 repetitions at a load of 10 RM

A set is the number of repetitions performed consecutively without resting (in this case, one set = 10 repetitions). From day to day the subject tries to increase the number of repetitions while maintaining the same resistance load. When more than 10 repetitions are possible, the load is increased to a new 10 RM load. The most important part of this program is set 3, i.e., 10 repetitions at the full 10 RM load. This represents the greatest resistance for the muscle group. Variations in the warm-up repetitions (sets 1 and 2) do not affect the results appreciably.

DeLorme and Watkins also recommended the training frequency to be 4 consecutive days per week. They found by experience that 5 days per week was usually the heaviest schedule that could be employed without developing serious signs of delayed recovery from the training sessions. These findings have been verified in that training 3, 4, or 5 days per week produced significantly greater gains in 1 RM bench-press performances than did training only 1 or 2 days per week.[52] Some caution in generalizing these results may be warranted since the subjects performed 18 sets of 1 RM during each workout. This can be viewed as an unusually large number of sets. In fact, when 3 sets of 6 to 8 RM were studied, subjects made similar strength gains lifting 2 days (Tuesday and Thursday) as opposed to 3 days per week (Monday, Wednesday, and Friday).[59] It is now common practice to recommend that PRE training be performed 3 or 4 days per week on alternate rather than consecutive days.

Further research using the principles set forth by DeLorme and Watkins was conducted later concerning the optimum number of sets and repetitions that would most effectively increase strength.[11,13-15, 17,18] These studies employed programs with a training frequency of 3 days per week over a duration of 8 to 12 weeks. Some of the results are shown in Figure 7-15. It can be seen that the greatest improvement in strength is obtained from three sets, each with a 6 RM load.[15] Generally, it can be said that the optimal number of repetitions maximum lies somewhere between three and nine.[17,131] When different numbers of sets are combined with different RM loads, several equivalent programs for strength can be developed.[11] This is apparent when comparing the mean strength gains from the various programs shown in Figure 7-15.

We can conclude that there is no *single* combination of sets and repetitions that yields optimal strength gains for everyone. Although there is some disagreement regarding the details of a strength-training program, there is one agreement in principle: *If you want to develop strength, use progressive-resistance exercises in the overload zone.*

---

*If the 10 RM load were 100 pounds, a ½ 10 RM load would equal 50 pounds.

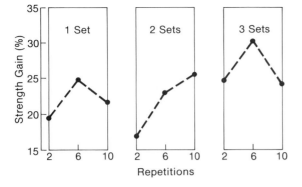

Figure 7-15. Strength gains resulting from isotonic weight-training programs consisting of various sets and repetitions. All programs were performed 3 days per week for 12 weeks. When different numbers of sets are combined with different repetition maximum (RM) loads, several equivalent programs for strength can be developed. (Based on data from Berger.[15])

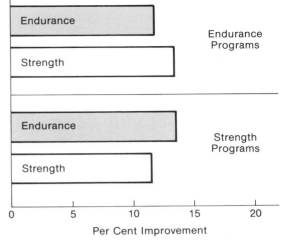

Figure 7-16. Both muscular strength and endurance were developed equally from either a low-repetition, high-load program (so-called strength program) or a high-repetition, low-load program (so-called endurance program). (Based on data from Clarke and Stull[26] and Stull and Clarke.[114])

So far we have discussed only isotonic weight-training programs that have been shown to improve strength. What about muscular endurance? The "old rule"—strength = low repetitions and high loads, and endurance = high repetitions and low loads—appears still to be valid; but it needs first to be clarified and second to be extended. Clarification involves the term "low load." We must remember that the progressive overload principle is also a requisite for improvement of muscular endurance. Prolonged repetitions of "underloaded" muscles (Fig. 7-11) have little effect on endurance.[61]

Extension of the rule is based on the fact that both strength and endurance have been shown to be equally developed from either a low-repetition and high-load program or a high-repetition and low-load program.[26,35,114] This can be seen in Figure 7-16. In this case, both the so-called endurance and strength programs consisted of three training sessions per week for 6 or 7 weeks. Each training session of the "endurance" program[26] consisted of elbow flexion at a rate of 40 repetitions per minute with a load of 11 pounds until exhaustion was reached. The strength program[114] consisted of arm curls performed according to the DeLorme-Watkins progression outlined on page 176. It should be noted, however, that this progression involved a total of 30 repetitions and as such may not be considered as a low-repetition program. For example, it was later found that isotonic strength could be improved significantly more with a weight-training program involving 12 repetitions of an 80% maximum load than with 20 repetitions of a 50% maximum load.[42] Isotonic endurance, on the other hand, increased significantly more in the latter program.

These findings were verified by reports that maximum strength gains of 20% over 9 weeks resulted from lifting 3 sets of 6 to 8 RM, 3 days per week.[6] Surprisingly, this high-resistance, low-repetition training yielded similar improvements in absolute-load endurance compared to the medium-resistance, medium-repetitions (2 sets, 30 to 40 RM) and low-resistance, high-repetition (1 set, 100 to 150 RM) training. The medium- and low-resistance groups excelled on relative-load endurance tests with 22 and 28% gains while the high-resistance training group decreased by 7% after training.

One of the implications that can be made from these findings is that the same strength and endurance gains may be achieved in a more economical way by higher intensity, lower repetition techniques. Programs involving a very high number of repetitions with a very low resistance require more time. If time is a factor, the overload technique heretofore considered characteristic of strength training would be preferable.[114] Likewise, it is apparent that gains in absolute endurance are related more strongly to strength improvements than vice versa. Since strength, power, and absolute endurance are needed more than relative-load endurance in sports, it makes sense for competitive athletes to train for strength using high resistance and low repetitions. This is not to say that other factors such as safety, subject limitations, and special needs would not indicate the preferential use of lower intensity, higher repetition programs for middle-age and older subjects or in rehabilitation settings.

Isometric Programs

Just as DeLorme and Watkins did for isotonic programs, Hettinger and Müller[63] in 1953 provided the impetus for the scientific inquiry into and establishment of isometric resistance-training programs. Their original studies claimed that maximal strength could be gained at a rate of about 5% per week merely by isometrically contracting a muscle group for 6 seconds at $2/3$ maximal tension once a day for 5 days per week. Strength gain was unaffected by increasing either the tension (even to maximum) or the number and duration of the contractions. Such findings revolutionized the entire concept of strength-training programs.

Their findings concerning strength development and the amount of tension and number and duration of isometric contractions stimulated a great deal of further research both in Europe and in the United States. The results of these studies proved to be inconsistent. Some findings confirmed Hettinger and Müller's original results,[97,103] others did not.[7,86,98,129] Most interestingly, one of the latter studies was done by Müller himself.[98] This time his results showed that maximal isometric strength could be developed best by training 5 days per week, with each training session consisting of 5 to 10 maximal contractions held for 5 seconds each.

Again, we see that several types of isometric training programs will yield substantial strength gains. There does not seem to be just one program that will be best for everyone. Probably the program outlined by Müller in his last study and reported previously should provide almost everyone with satisfactory results. In addition, it is generally agreed that muscular endurance can be increased through isometric exercises.[24,27,28,104] However, once again the design of such a program varies considerably. For example, when isometric exercises are used in a rehabilitation program, they may follow the application of heat treatments. It is of interest that 20 minutes of diathermy heat has been reported to cause an initial decrease in static strength measures followed by an increase 30 minutes after the heat is removed.[23]

At least two factors related to isometric training programs need to be mentioned at this time. First, we said earlier that the development of strength and endurance is specific to the joint angle at which the muscle group is trained.[87] This, of course, implicates isometric training in particular because of its static nature. Thus, if strength and endurance at different joint angles are desired and if isometric programs are used, the exercises must be performed at all specified joint angles.

The second factor deals with the changes in blood pressure that accompany weight-training exercises. Most muscular contractions and, in particular, isometric contractions involve what is called a **Valsalva maneuver.** A Valsalva maneuver means making an expiratory effort with the glottis* closed. Since air cannot escape, intrathoracic pressure increases appreciably (even to the point where it can cause the venae cavae, which return blood to the heart, to collapse). This elevated intrathoracic pressure causes systolic and diastolic blood pressures to increase beyond values normally seen during exercise in which a Valsalva maneuver does not occur. Even though the Valsalva maneuver can be avoided by exhaling while lifting or sustaining an isometric contraction, most physicians advise against weight training in general and isometrics in particular as an activity for the postcoronary patient.

Evidence for the specificity of isometric versus dynamic training exists from a unique study of intact adductor pollicus (thumb) muscles of human subjects. After 3 months of comparable isometric (10 daily 5-second contractions) or dynamic (100 daily 0.5-second lifts) training, the subject's ulnar nerves were stimulated using supramaximal electrical stimulation. One of the advantages of this type of stimulation is that all muscle fibers are made to contract and the variable effects of subject motivation are removed. Isometric train-

ing produced greater improvements in maximal tetanic tension whereas dynamic training produced greater increases in the peak rate of tension development. Once again it is clear that, generally speaking, static strength can be increased best by isometric training and dynamic strength best by dynamic training.

Finally, the relative-load endurance time is known to be much decreased for both static and dynamic exercise when loads exceed 15 to 20% of maximum voluntary contraction levels.[60] The decreases relate to the greater and more prolonged occlusion of blood flow to working muscles. If the dynamic exercise is performed slowly, there is not much difference in static and dynamic fatigue curves since the occlusion of blood flow is similar. As expected, both faster dynamic contractions and intermittent isometric contractions, i.e., contract, relax, contract, as contrasted to sustained isometric contractions, will enhance endurance times.[60]

Eccentric Programs

Weight-training programs structured around eccentric contractions are not common. Furthermore, they have not been adopted for use by coaches. What little information is available concerning eccentric programs indicates that while strength gains can be made through such programs,[81] by comparison with other programs they are not any more effective.[72,110] Their use, however, is advocated in therapy and rehabilitation.[105] Furthermore, as mentioned earlier, delayed muscular soreness is greatest following eccentric contractions, a definite disadvantage.

On the other hand, there is more recent evidence that the specific benefit of longer term eccentric training is remarkable. Eight weeks of eccentric training on a modified bicycle ergometer produced only slight improvements in dynamic concentric mus-

---

*The glottis is the space or opening between the vocal cords.

cle strength but an enormous 375% improvement in eccentric work capacity.[48] After training there was little evidence of soreness and disruption of myofibrillar materials that had been caused by single maximal bouts of eccentric exercise prior to training. It appears that the tissues adapt to repeated bouts of eccentric training just as they do for other modes of training. These and future findings may cause coaches and trainers to look more closely at the potential benefits of eccentric training for events like gymnastics and wrestling. Especially if concerns over muscular soreness can be overcome.

Isokinetic Programs

These are the newest type of weight-training programs. Because of this, fewer research studies have been conducted using such programs.[85,95,96,118] In theory, isokinetic exercises should lead to the greatest improvement in muscular performance. For example, as mentioned earlier, the isokinetic principle permits development of maximal muscular tension throughout the full range of joint movement. In other words, a greater number of motor units are activated. As a result, greater demands (greater overload) than were previously possible can be placed on the muscles being exercised.

Examples of the strength gains possible with isokinetic training programs are given in Figures 7-17 and 7-18. In Figure 7-17, the isokinetic strength gains are shown following a 7-week, 4-day-per-week training program in which the subjects performed maximal extensions and flexions of the knee at a constant velocity of 180 degrees per second. One leg was trained with a 6-second work bout repeated 10 times, with 114 seconds of rest between each work bout. The other leg was trained with a 30-second work bout repeated 2 times with 20 minutes of rest between

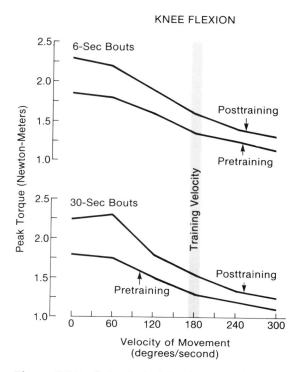

Figure 7-17. Gains in isokinetic strength (knee flexion) following a 7-week, 4-day-per-week training program in which one leg was trained using 6-second bouts of work and the other 30-second bouts. The magnitude of the increase in strength was the same for each leg, and each program produced a "speed specificity" in that maximal gains in strength were made at velocities of movement equal to or slower than the training velocity of 180 degrees per second. (Based on data from Lesmes et al.[85])

bouts. Three important points to notice are as follow:

1. The increase in strength for knee flexion (and extension, although not shown in Fig. 7-17) was the same in the leg trained with 6-second bouts of work as the one trained with 30-second bouts.
2. Each leg was trained exactly 60 seconds per day, 4 days per week for a total of 7 weeks. Therefore, the total

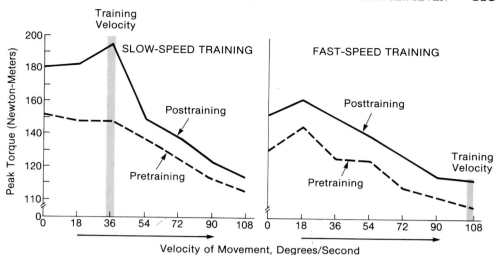

Figure 7-18. Gains in isokinetic strength (knee extension) following a 6-week, 3-day-per-week training program consisting of a 2-minute period of knee extensions and flexions either at a slow speed (36 degrees per second) or fast speed (108 degrees per second) of movement. Note the speed specificity, i.e., maximal increases in strength occurring only at speeds of movement equal to or slower than the training velocity. (Based on data from Moffroid and Whipple.[95])

training time was only 4 minutes per week × 7 weeks = 28 minutes for the entire program. This suggests that large volumes of training are not necessary to improve muscular strength using isokinetic contractions.

3. Each of the training programs produced similar gains in strength at velocities of movement equal to or slower, but not faster, than the training velocity of 180 degrees per second. This "speed specificity" is of practical value to athletes, as it suggests that athletic strength training should take place at speeds approximating or exceeding those used during their actual sport. The importance of this idea is also emphasized in Figure 7-18.

The results presented in Figure 7-18 agree very well with the findings just described. The isokinetic training program used in this case consisted of a continuous 2-minute period of repeated knee extensions and flexions either at a constant slow speed of 36 degrees per second or at a constant fast speed of 108 degrees per second. The subjects exercised 3 days per week for a total of 6 weeks. Again note the speed specificity, i.e., the improvement in knee extensor strength occurring only at speeds of movement equal to or slower than the training velocity. Although not shown in Figure 7-18, the speed specificity principle was also found to hold true for improvement in muscular endurance. In other words, training at a fast speed increased muscular endurance at fast speeds more than slow-speed training increased muscular endurance at slow speeds.[95]

The total training time of this program was 6 minutes per week × 6 weeks = 36 minutes. The strength gains are comparable in magnitude (percentage) to those obtained from the 28-minute program, again emphasizing that volume of training may not be necessary with isokinetic contractions.

These basic findings have been verified and refined for college-age male[34] and female[3] subjects and for adolescent male subjects.[111] Fast-speed training produced the greatest improvements in isokinetic strength, power, and endurance as well as for field tests including the vertical jump, standing broad jump, and 40-yard dash. High-speed training apparently has a limited transfer effect toward static endurance performance at 20% of maximum voluntary contraction.[109] It does produce significant gains in power for moving light to medium loads whereas slow-velocity isokinetic training has been shown to produce added power for moving heavy loads.[73] There is also limited evidence that power outputs may be improved by high-speed isokinetic training at performance speeds faster than those used in training.[73] These findings contradict earlier indications that significant gains are made only at or below the speeds used for training. Future research will likely resolve this discrepancy.

Some interesting similarities and differences exist between isokinetic and isotonic or isometric test results. For example, there is little or no correlation between isokinetic peak strength and isokinetic relative endurance.[9] This lack of relationship is based, of course, on the assumption that subjects are highly motivated to perform continuous repetitions at an all-out effort to a predetermined point of fatigue, say 75% of maximum torque. These findings are similar to isotonic or static relative load endurance tests where the motivational levels of the subjects also enters in. One major difference for isokinetic tests is that peak knee extension torques have been found to occur at a speed of 96 degrees per second rather than at an isometric speed setting of 0 degrees per second (no movement). This has led to the suggestion that the force-velocity curves for in-vivo human muscles are not the same as those for isolated animal muscles.[102]

Numerous coaches have adopted the isokinetic idea and have developed specific weight-training programs structured entirely around isokinetic contractions. One of these coaches is Dr. James Counsilman, head swimming coach at Indiana University. He suggests that since swimmers contract their arm muscles isokinetically when pulling through the water, it is important that their weight-training programs on land also be isokinetically oriented.[31-33,125]

Special equipment is needed for isokinetic exercises, clinical testing, rehabilitation programs, and research. Equipment manufacturers such as MGI Strength/Fitness Systems have developed numerous isokinetic machines and methods that may be used for strength and endurance development in such specific activities as swimming, running, throwing, putting the shot, volleyball, football, jumping, and kicking. Cybex, a division of Lumex, Inc., has developed various pieces of equipment for isokinetic strength assessment and injury rehabilitation.*

Comparison among Programs

Thus far we have considered the changes in muscular strength and endurance brought about as a result of each of the programs separately. Which program is the best? Again, there is no simple answer to the question. There are research design problems associated with equating the various programs in such a way that the only differing factor is the type of contraction. Further complications result because of specificity. In an attempt to answer the

---

*For information write to the following addresses: MGI Strength/Fitness Systems, 1026 S. Powell Road, Independence, MO. 64050; and Cybex, Division of Lumex, Inc., 2100 Smithtown Avenue, Ronkonkoma, NY. 11779.

question, some results from comparative studies are presented in Figure 7-19. Figure 7-19*A* presents a comparison of strength gains resulting from various isotonic programs and one type of isometric program.[14] The exact designs of the isotonic programs are given in the figure. The isometric program consisted of two maximal contractions held for 6 to 8 seconds; each contraction was at a different joint angle. The subjects were college-age men; the training frequency and duration were 3 days per week and 12 weeks, respectively, for all programs. Only one isotonic program was superior to the isometric program. By the same token, the isometric program was superior to only one isotonic program. In other words, the two types of programs are quite comparable in this case.

Figure 7-19*B* provides a comparison of isokinetic, isotonic, and isometric programs.[118] The subjects in this study were patients with varying degrees of rehabilitative problems. The training frequency and duration were 4 days per week and 8 weeks, respectively. The programs were consistent with the normal clinical programs, e.g., the isotonic program followed the DeLorme-Watkins technique. In this case, it is easy to conclude that the isokinetic program was clearly superior to the other programs in both strength and endurance gains.

A survey of studies comparing isotonic and isometric training programs has been conducted by Clarke[28] and is summarized as follows:

1. Motivation is generally superior with isotonic exercises, as they are self-testing in nature. However, isometrics may be performed anywhere, whereas some isotonics may place considerable demands on available space and may require special equipment.
2. Both isometric and isotonic forms of exercise improve muscular strength.

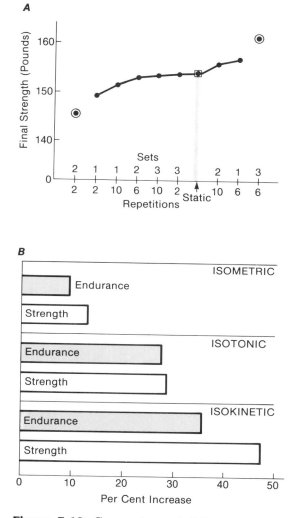

Figure 7-19. Comparison of different weight training programs. *A,* Comparison of strength gains resulting from various isotonic programs and one isometric program. All programs were performed 3 days per week for 12 weeks. Only one isotonic program (circled dot to the right) was superior to the isometric program, and the isometric program was superior to only one isotonic program (circled dot at left). *B,* Comparison of isokinetic, isotonic, and isometric programs. All programs were performed 4 days per week for 8 weeks. The isokinetic program was superior to the other programs in both strength and endurance gains. (Data in *A* from Berger;[13] data in *B* from Thistle et al.[118])

Most studies do not favor one method over another; however, some investigators have reported greater gains for trainees using the isotonic form.

3. Muscular endurance is developed more effectively through isotonic exercise than through isometric exercise. Recovery from muscular fatigue is faster after isotonic exercise than after isometric exercise.

4. Isometric training at one point in the range of joint motion develops strength significantly at that point but not at other positions. Isotonic exercises produce a more uniform development of strength.

Getting back to the problem of the best program, one has to ask the question, "Best for what?" For the physical educator the answer might be designing a weight-training program for students or a particular group in the community. For the coach, it most likely will involve designing a program that will improve performance of a particular athletic skill. These programs will of course be different. However, both can best be designed by considering (1) the overload principle, (2) the specificity of training, and (3) the availability of equipment.

The interested reader is encouraged to review an article entitled "A Hypothetical Model for Strength Training."[113] This article includes a discussion of the concept of "periodization," which means that strength-training workouts are matched to the athlete's season so that peak strength is attained at the most appropriate time. A basic tenet of periodization is a shift from low-intensity, high-repetition training during the early season preparation phase to high-intensity, low-repetition training during the late season competition phase. It is of interest that a stimulus for this work was the observation that competitive weight lifters rarely use the 3 set, 6 RM method for year-round training.

A summary of the advantages and disadvantages of isokinetic, isometric, and isotonic weight-training programs is presented in Table 7-2. The type of muscular training with the best overall rating is the isokinetic program.

Circuit Training

A different kind of training program that may also be effective in improving strength and in preparing athletes for competition is *circuit training*. This type of program consists of a number of "stations" where a given exercise is performed, usually within a specified time. Once the exercise is completed at one station, the trainee moves rapidly to the next station, performing another exercise also within a prescribed time period. The circuit is completed once the exercises at all stations are performed.

The exercises at the various stations consist mainly of weight-resistance exercises, but running, swimming, cycling, calisthenics, and stretching exercises may also be included. Circuit training, therefore, may be designed to increase muscular endurance, flexibility, and if running, swimming, or cycling is involved, to increase some cardiorespiratory endurance as well.

The circuit should include exercises that will develop the particular capabilities required in the sport for which the athlete is training. For example, circuits that consist mainly of weight-resistance exercises are good for sports in which muscular strength is a major factor and cardiorespiratory endurance a minor factor—sports such as gymnastics, wrestling, swim sprints, running sprints, competitive weight lifting, and football. The weight-resistance exercises should, of course, emphasize development of those muscles most used in the performance of the particular sport.

Regardless of which sports the circuits are designed for, they should consist of

TABLE 7-2

Summary of Advantages and Disadvantages of the Three Most Common Types of Resistance Training Programs*

Criterion	Comparative Rating		
	Isokinetic	Isometric	Isotonic
Rate of strength gain	Excellent	Poor	Good
Rate of endurance gain	Excellent	Poor	Good
Strength gain over range of motion	Excellent	Poor	Good
Time per training session	Good	Excellent	Poor
Expense	Poor	Excellent	Good
Ease of performance	Good	Excellent	Poor
Ease of progress assessment	Poor	Good	Excellent
Adaptability to specific movement patterns	Excellent	Poor	Good
Least possibility of muscle soreness	Excellent	Good	Poor
Least possibility of injury	Excellent	Good	Poor
Skill improvement	Excellent	Poor	Good

*Modified from Lamb.[79]

between 6 and 15 stations, requiring a total time of between 5 and 20 minutes to complete. Usually, each circuit is performed several times in one training session. Only 15 to 20 seconds rest should be allowed between stations. For the weight-resistance stations, the load should be adjusted so that the working muscles are noticeably fatigued after performing as many repetitions as possible within a designated time period (e.g., 30 seconds). This load should be increased periodically in order to ensure progressive overload. In addition, the sequence of exercises should be arranged so that no two consecutive stations consist of exercises involving the same muscle groups. Training frequency should be 3 days per week, with a duration of at least 6 weeks.

As previously mentioned, circuit training may be designed to increase muscular strength and power, muscular endurance, flexibility, and, to a limited extent, cardio-respiratory endurance. However, it should be emphasized that the physiological effects are to a large extent dependent upon the type of circuit that is set up. For example, it has been shown that circuits consisting only of weight-resistance exercises produce substantial gains in strength but only minimal gains in cardiorespiratory endurance.[4,51,130] The latter is affected least of all if the circuits have only five or six stations.[4]

Although an increase in cardiorespiratory endurance can and does result from circuit training, especially when endurance activities are included in the stations, the magnitude of the increase is generally not as great as that from endurance programs consisting entirely of running, swimming, or cycling. The physiological reason for this is not entirely known. This is particularly puzzling, since heart rates during circuit weight training have been shown to be substantially elevated (138 to 186 beats per minute) and maintained throughout completion of the circuit.[4,51] (An elevated heart rate is one criterion for realizing a cardiovascular training effect; for more on this, see Chapters 12 and 13). One possibility, however, is that during weight training, a reduction in muscle blood flow caused by high levels of intramuscular pressure during contraction may result in a lessened stimulus for biochemical and vascular adaptations at the local muscular level.[4] This idea is supported by the studies mentioned earlier (p. 168) in which only small biochemical changes have been found following several weeks of weight training. In contrast, a substantial biochemical adaptation at the local muscular level has been noted following run training (p. 324).

From the rather limited research thus far available, it may be concluded that circuit training appears to be an effective training technique for altering muscular strength and endurance, and, to a limited extent, flexibility and cardiorespiratory endurance. The use of circuit training, particularly for off-season programs, therefore, may be recommended for athletes whose sports require high levels of muscular strength, power, and endurance and lower levels of cardiorespiratory endurance.[130]

Weight Training and Sports Performance

Several of the questions asked at the beginning of this chapter were concerned with strength development and increases in speed of contraction and sports performance. Although a few studies suggest little or no improvement in speed of contraction, most show that strengthening exercises do indeed increase both speed and power of contraction.[16,25,91,133] Incidentally, the fact that speed of contraction is improved by strength training provides evidence that the term "muscle-bound" has no scientific merit. In addition, research generally demonstrates that specific sports skills, such as speed in running, swimming, throwing, speed and force of offensive football charge, and jumping, all can be improved significantly through weight-training programs.[22,119,120]

In a review of the research completed on strength development and motor and/or sports improvement, Clarke[29] reached the following conclusions:

1. Both isometric and isotonic forms of strength training can produce improvements in many motor and sports performances. Although the evidence is at times conflicting, it is generally accepted that progressive weight-training programs are superior.
2. Some studies did not provide adequate overload in applying both isometric and isotonic strength training. In general, exercises confined to single static contractions of short duration or isotonic efforts limited to a single bout were not effective in developing either strength or motor skills. Strenuous resistance exercises of either form are needed for best results.
3. Fear of muscle-bound effects from weight training may be laid to rest. The majority of studies show that speed of movement may be enhanced rather than retarded as a consequence of strength development.
4. Exercise programs designed to strengthen muscles primarily involved in a particular sport can be used as supplements to regular practice in effectively improving the athlete's skills and motor fitness.

Earlier it was mentioned that a fifth type of strength training, plyometrics, would be discussed. This method of training primarily has been used by track and field jumpers, volleyball and basketball players, gymnasts, and other athletes who must project their bodies upward against the force of gravity. Currently, there are efforts to apply the basic plyometrics training concepts to other competitive and recreational sports, e.g., baseball and skiing. A basic example of plyometric training would be athletes who drop down from a platform, land on the balls of their feet, and as their body weight is settling down through their heels, force themselves to explosively jump back onto the platform. The controlled settling of body weight puts an eccentric load on the calf muscles and Achilles tendons and induces a stretch on the muscle-tendon unit. One effect of this is the storage of energy in the elastic components. A second effect is the pre-stretch that operates on the stretch receptors (muscle spindles) located within the calf muscles. The pre-stretch results in afferent impulses being sent via reflex pathways to facilitate the calf muscle motoneurons located in the spinal cord. Theoretically, the explosive muscular power should be enhanced because it is a combination of stored energy and recruitment of facilitated motoneurons and their associated motor units.

While the clear benefits of this training over and above those derived from isotonic, isokinetic, or more conventional methods needs additional documentation, there appears to be three main potential advantages. First, the athletes may learn to better time their voluntary muscle contractions to match up with any release of stored elastic energy. Timing would mean everything here. Second, more forceful muscle contractions because of pre-stretch facilitation may allow a greater adaptive stimulus to promote strength gains. Third, the exercises are a natural form of training for jumpers and others who might apply the pre-stretch principle without violating other biomechanical principles. Also the plyometric drills can be designed to be progressive in intensity, duration, and frequency as the athlete improves. Watch for much more research on this in the sports science literature.

Retention of Strength and Endurance

Once desired strength and endurance levels have been attained with a weight-training program, how do we retain them? Do we have to continue with the same type of weight-training program for an indefinite time? The answer to the last question is no. Let's see why.

It is generally agreed that strength and endurance, once developed, subside at slower rates than they were developed. This can be observed from Figure 7-20. There are two important points to note in Figure 7-20A. First, strength gained during a 3-week isotonic training program consisting of 3 sets at a 6 RM load, 3 days per week, was not lost during a subsequent 6-week period of no training (detraining). Second, strength was further improved during a subsequent 6-week training program involving only one set at a 1 RM load performed once a week.[12] Other studies using both isotonic and isometric programs have confirmed these results.[93,97,104,106] In one study, 45% of the strength gained from a 12-week program was still retained after 1 year.[93]

In Figure 7-20B, the retention of muscular endurance is shown. The training program consisted of 3 sessions per week for 8 weeks, with each session comprising an exhausting bout of elbow flexions at a work rate of 40 repetitions per minute against an 11-pound load. Endurance was lost most rapidly during the first few weeks of the detraining period. However, after 12 weeks of detraining, the loss of endurance was stable and 70% of that gained was still retained.

This information emphasizes that the most difficult phase of the weight-training program is the *development* of strength and endurance. Once this has been accomplished, they are relatively easy to retain. As little exercise as once per week or once every 2 weeks will maintain strength and

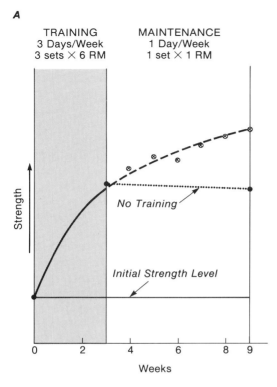

A

TRAINING
3 Days/Week
3 sets × 6 RM

MAINTENANCE
1 Day/Week
1 set × 1 RM

Strength

No Training

Initial Strength Level

Weeks

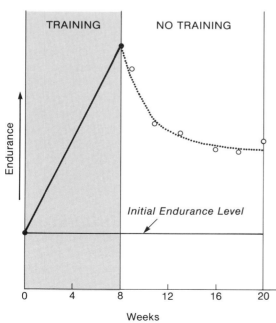

B

TRAINING

NO TRAINING

Endurance

Initial Endurance Level

Weeks

endurance, provided maximal contractions are used. Specific examples of weight-training programs for various sports activities are contained in the book *Sports Physiology*.[47]

Flexibility

Along with strength and endurance, flexibility is also an important component of muscular performance. In studying flexibility, we will concentrate our discussion around four topics: (1) definitions, (2) structural limits to flexibility, (3) development of flexibility, and (4) flexibility and performance. A review concerning the physiology of flexibility has been written by Holland.[66]

Definition of Flexibility

Two kinds of flexibility, **static** and **dynamic,** have been described.[39]

Static Flexibility

The *range of motion about a joint* is defined as static flexibility. Static flexibility can be

Figure 7-20. Retention of strength and endurance. *A,* The strength gained during a 3-day-per-week, 3-week isotonic training program (three sets of 6 RM) was not lost during a subsequent 6-week period of no training (dotted line); and strength was further improved during a subsequent 6-week training program involving only one set at a 1 RM load performed once a week.

B, Retention of muscular endurance. The program was performed 3 days per week for 8 weeks with each session consisting of an exhausting bout of elbow flexions at a work rate of 40 repetitions per minute against an 11-pound load. Although endurance was lost most rapidly during the first few weeks of the detraining (no training) period, after 12 weeks of no training, 70% of the endurance gained was still retained. (Data in *A* from Berger;[17] data in *B* from Syster and Stull[116] and Waldman and Stull.[127])

measured most reliably with an instrument called a flexometer.[84] As shown in Figure 7-21, it has a weighted 360-degree dial and a weighted pointer that are independently controlled by gravity. While in use, the flexometer is strapped to the segment being tested. When the dial is locked at one extreme position (e.g., full extension of the elbow), the reading of the pointer on the dial is the arc through which the movement has taken place. It is called static flexibility because when the dial is actually read, there is no joint motion.

Dynamic Flexibility

This type of flexibility is defined as the *opposition or resistance of a joint to motion.* In other words, it is concerned with the forces that oppose movement over any range rather than the range itself. This type of flexibility is more difficult to measure and as such has been given little attention in physical education and athletics.

Structural Limits to Flexibility

The structural limits to flexibility are (1) bone, (2) muscle, (3) ligaments and other structures associated with the joint capsule, (4) tendons and other connective tissues, and (5) skin. Limitations by bony structures are confined to certain joints, for example the hinge-type joint, such as the elbow. However, in all the joints, including the hinge, the so-called soft tissues provide the major limitation to the range of joint movement.

The relative importance of the soft tissues with respect to limiting flexibility is given in Table 7-3. These particular data were obtained from the wrist joints of cats, but they are applicable to humans.[71] The joint capsule and associated connective tissues plus the muscle provide the majority of resistance to flexibility. It should be mentioned that the values were obtained from the mid-range of joint motion. At the extremes of joint motion, the tendons have a more limiting effect. Since flexibility can be modified through exercise, so also can these soft-tissue limitations. The reason for this, at least in part, is related to the *elastic* nature of some of the tissues.

Development of Flexibility

Flexibility is significant in performing certain skills. Also, recent advances in physical medicine and rehabilitation indicate that flexibility is important to general health and physical fitness. For example, flexibility exercises have been successfully prescribed for relief of dysmenorrhea, gen-

Figure 7-21. The Leighton flexometer. (From Mathews.[92])

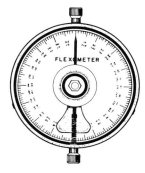

TABLE 7-3

Relative Contribution of Soft-Tissue Structures to Joint Resistance*

Structure	Resistance to Flexibility (Percentage of Total)
1. Joint capsule	47
2. Muscle	41
3. Tendon	10
4. Skin	2

*Based on data from Johns and Wright.[71]

eral neuromuscular tension, and low back pains.[19,77] For athletes, if they maintain a satisfactory degree of flexibility, they will be less susceptible to certain muscular injuries.

Types of Exercise

The best exercises to use for flexibility are the so-called stretching exercises. A number of these are shown in Figures 7-22 to 7-31. Many variations, which involve similar joints and muscle groups, can also be used. A book on stretching exercises for various sports has been published.[5]

Methods of Stretching

Stretching exercises can be performed in one of three ways: (1) *statically,* (2) *ballistically,*[38,129] and (3) *contract-relax.*[107,128] Static stretching involves stretching without "bobbing" or forcing, followed by holding the final stretched position for a given amount of time. Ballistic stretching involves "bobbing" or active movements. The final stretched position is not held.

Figure 7-22. Standing floor touch. Place feet astride and bend at the waist, with knees slightly bent and arms and head hanging loosely. Concentrate on relaxing your muscles, and try to touch the floor. This static exercise is good for stretching the muscles of the upper back, buttocks, and upper and lower legs.

Figure 7-23. Sitting toe touch. Sit on the floor with the feet spread and reach first for one foot, then the other. Each time you reach, attempt to touch and hold your chest to the thigh of the leg along which you are reaching. Although this static exercise develops flexibility in the same muscle groups as does the standing floor touch, it places more emphasis on stretching the upper-back muscles.

Contract-relax (C-R) stretching involves stretching to the limits of motion, doing a static contraction against opposition for a few seconds, relaxing and stretching further. This also has been called proprioceptive neuromuscular facilitation or the PNF method. While all three types of stretching will improve flexibility, the static method might be preferred because (1) there is less danger of tissue damage, (2) the energy

Figure 7-24. Chest stretch. Lie face down, with your legs and feet straight and the arms spread. Raise the chest from the floor. Concentrate on arching the upper part of the chest. Hold this static position for 6 seconds. This exercise is excellent for people who have a tendency to slump, because it stretches the muscles of the anterior shoulders and chest.

Figure 7-25. Alternate toe touch. Stand with feet astride, bend from the waist, and touch the right hand to the left toe and hold. Come to an erect standing position before touching the left hand to the right toe. Continue the exercise, alternating sides. Alternate toe touching stretches the muscles of the shoulders, back, buttocks, and legs. This is a ballistic stretching exercise.

requirement is less, and (3) there is prevention and/or relief from muscular distress and soreness.[38,40]

Numbers (1) and (3) in the preceding paragraph are related to the muscle sense organs mentioned in the last chapter (p.

164). In static stretching, or in the C-R method, the Golgi tendon organs are stretched, resulting in *inhibition* of contraction or, in other words, in relaxation of the muscles involved in the stretch. As a result, the stretch is greater and less pain-

Figure 7-26. Waist bend. Stand with feet astride and the hands on the hips. Bend forward, head up, and try to attain a position whereby the upper part of the body is parallel to the floor; hold. This static exercise is excellent for stretching the muscles of the lower back, upper back, and neck.

Figure 7-27. Overhead toe touch. Lie on your back and raise your feet straight in the air, supporting your hips with your hands. Point your toes and touch first one foot, hold, then the other, to the floor above your head. This ballistic exercise is excellent for flexibility of the hip joint, upper back, and neck muscles.

Figure 7-28. Treading. Stand erect, with your weight on your right foot. Place the ball of your left foot on the floor and transfer the weight to it gradually. Alternate by placing the ball of the right foot on the floor and transferring the weight to it from the left foot. Gradually increase the tempo to a slow run. This ballistic exercise is excellent for flexibility of and for developing proper use of the ankle.

Figure 7-29. Lower-leg stretch. Stand 3 feet in front of a wall, with feet 2 inches apart. Place outstretched hands on the wall, keeping feet flat on the floor. Move your feet away from the wall, but keep them flat on the floor. This static exercise is excellent for stretching the muscles of the lower leg and is practiced by many runners and skiers.

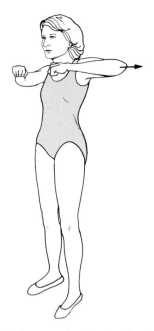

Figure 7-30. Upper-chest stretch. Stand erect, with feet shoulder-width apart, hands in front, and elbows raised to the side. While keeping your head up, pull the elbows back. Hold this static position. Excellent for stretching the anterior shoulder muscles. A good exercise for people with round upper back.

ful. With ballistic stretching, the bouncing and jerking cause activation of the muscle spindles, which in turn causes *contraction* of the muscles under stretch. In this case the stretching is hindered and can be more painful.

Design of the Program

The frequency and duration of the static program should be 2 to 5 days per week for 15 to 60 minutes each day. Within 5 weeks, improvement should be noted.[38] The stretched position should be held for longer periods as the program progresses. For example, at first hold the position for 20 seconds, then after several sessions increase the holding time by 10 seconds more

Figure 7-31. Spinal stretch. Place hands and knees on the floor and hunch your back. Bend your elbows, come slightly forward, and lower your chest toward the floor; return to original position. This exercise will develop flexibility of the spinal column.

up to a minute. Start by performing each exercise 3 times, then progress to 5. These general guidelines are based on a program that would include 10 different stretching exercises. At first, 10 minutes of actual stretching is performed in a 15 minute workout (10 exercises × 20 sec × 3 reps); later, 50 minutes of stretching is performed in one hour (10 exercises × 60 sec × 5 reps).

Although static stretching programs are recommended from the standpoint of safety and minimization of soreness, the C-R programs appear to be superior for improving flexibility. For example, shoulder, trunk, and hamstring muscle areas were compared in college men who had trained 3 days per week over 6 weeks using static, ballistic, or PNF methods.[107] Only the PNF group had flexibility increases greater than the control subjects. Similar findings have been published for plantar flexor, hip adductor, and hip extensor muscle areas. That is to say, C-R methods were superior to ballistic methods practiced 3 days per week over a 30-day period.[128] Such findings

may result in a progressive shift toward more widespread use of C-R and PNF methods.

Flexibility and Performance

Earlier, we mentioned that flexibility aids the performance of certain skills. Figure 7-32 presents flexion and extension flexibility measurements (with the flexometer) of seven different athletic groups.[82,83] The following factors concerning flexibility are evident from the figure.

Specificity of Flexibility

The range of motion about a joint is specific in two ways. First, there is a tendency

Figure 7-32. Flexion and extension flexibility measures of seven different athletic groups. For further information, see text. (Based on data from Leighton.[83,84])

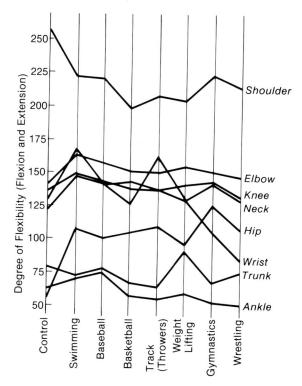

toward a specific pattern of flexibility and selected sporting events. For example, shot-putters and discus throwers have greater flexibility in the wrist than do wrestlers. Second, flexibility is joint-specific. In other words, a high degree of flexibility in one joint does not necessarily indicate a high flexibility in other joints. For example, gymnasts can be seen to have above-average flexibility in the hip but are below average in the ankle.

Stability versus Flexibility

Certain joints are structurally very weak. As a result, they are prone to injury. The shoulder is one of these joints. The reason is that the glenoid fossa of the scapula, into which the head of the humerus fits, is very shallow. Its main stability is provided by the surrounding musculature. You will notice that shoulder flexibility in all of the athletic groups shown in Figure 7-32 is below average. This probably reflects an increased muscular strength, which in this case limits flexibility. However, notice that in most other joints, flexibility is at least average or above in those athletes for whom strength is especially important (throwers, weight lifters, gymnasts, and wrestlers). This further refutes the concept of "muscle-bound."

It should also be mentioned here that excessive flexibility is often indicative of proneness to injury, particularly in contact sports. Thus, flexibility measurements might prove to be a useful screening tool for young prospective football players.[99]

Warm-up, Warm-down, and Flexibility

Although this is not shown by the figure, it is probably true that performance of stretching or warm-up exercises that increase flexibility can prevent serious injury during subsequent athletic competition. Also, stretching exercises are excellent as part of a warm-down or cool-down program.

Summary

Muscular strength is the force that a muscle or muscle group can exert against a resistance in one maximal effort. There are four types of muscular contraction: isotonic, isometric, eccentric, and isokinetic.

With isotonic contractions (muscle shortening while lifting a constant load), the tension developed over the range of motion is related to (1) the length of the muscle fibers, (2) the angle of pull of the muscle on the bony skeleton, and (3) the speed of shortening. As a result, the tension developed during lifting of a constant load varies over the full range of joint motion with the muscle stressed maximally only at its weakest point in the range. This is in contrast to an isokinetic contraction in which the tension developed by the muscle as it shortens at constant speed is maximal at all joint angles.

An isometric contraction is one in which tension is developed but there is no change in the external length of the muscle. An eccentric contraction refers to the lengthening of a muscle during contraction.

Local muscular endurance is usually defined as the ability of a muscle group to perform repeated contractions (either isotonic, isokinetic, or eccentric) against a load or to sustain a contraction (isometric) for an extended period of time. However, muscular endurance may also be defined as the opposite of muscular fatigue.

Physiological changes that accompany increased strength are as follows:

1. Hypertrophy—an increase in the size of the muscle due to an increased size of muscle fibers (mainly fast-twitch) and myofibrils, an increased total amount of protein, an increased number of capillaries, and increased amounts of connective, tendinous, and ligamentous tissues.
2. Biochemical changes—including in-

creased concentrations of creatine, PC, ATP, and glycogen and a decreased volume of mitochondria, but only small changes in anaerobic and aerobic enzyme activities.

3. Adaptations within the nervous system—including changes in recruitment pattern and synchronization of motor units.

The physiological principle upon which strength and endurance development depends is called the overload principle. It states that strength and endurance increase only when a muscle performs at its maximal capacity. With weight-training programs, the resistance against which the muscle works should be increased periodically as gains in strength are made. This is the principle of progressive-resistance exercises, or **PRE.**

Weight training is specific in that gains in strength and muscular endurance improve skill performance to the greatest extent when the training program consists of exercises that include the muscle groups and simulate the movement patterns used during the skill. Also, strength training is specific to the joint angle at which the muscle is trained (isometrics) and to the type of contraction used.

There are two types of muscular soreness—acute and delayed. Acute soreness is due to muscle ischemia (lack of adequate blood flow). Delayed soreness (onset 24 to 48 hours after exercise) could be due to torn muscle tissue or muscle spasms but is more likely due to disruption of the connective tissues, including the tendons. There is no known prevention or cure for soreness; however, stretching exercises may relieve it when present and may sometimes prevent or delay its onset. Delayed muscular soreness is greatest following eccentric contractions and is least following isokinetic contractions.

With isotonic strength programs, there is no single combination of sets (number of repetitions performed consecutively) and repetition maximums (maximal load that can be lifted a given number of repetitions before fatiguing) that yields optimal strength gains. However, most programs should include between one and three sets with repetition maximums between three and nine. Although improvement in strength and muscular endurance can be greater with low repetitions and high resistances, and high repetitions and low resistances, respectively, equal increases in strength and endurance have been found with either program.

Isometric programs can significantly increase strength by training 5 days per week, with each training session consisting of 5 to 10 maximal contractions held for 5 seconds each. Isometric endurance can also be improved, but the design of such a program varies considerably.

Eccentric exercise programs, in comparison with isotonic and isometric programs, are not any more effective in developing strength and endurance. They may excel, however, in developing eccentric contraction strength.

Isokinetic programs are speed specific, i.e., they cause maximal gains in strength and endurance at velocities of movement equal to or slower, but usually not faster, than the training velocity. Gains in isokinetic strength and endurance can be made with programs consisting of as little exercise as 1 minute per day, 4 days per week, for 7 weeks (total time = 28 minutes). In theory and in comparison with other programs, isokinetic programs should lead to the greatest improvement in muscular performance. Once gained, strength and endurance are retained for relatively long periods of time.

Circuit training consists of a number of stations where a given weight-lifting exercise is performed within a specified time. It, too, is an effective training technique for improving muscular strength, muscular endurance, and to a lesser extent, flexibility and cardiovascular endurance.

Although a few studies suggest little or no improvement in speed of contraction, most show that weight-training programs do increase both speed and power of contraction. Specific sports skills can also be significantly improved through weight-training programs.

Flexibility, the range of motion about a joint, is related to health, and, to some extent, to athletic performance. Regularly scheduled programs involving stretching exercises (2 to 5 days per week, 15 to 60 minutes per day) will improve flexibility within a few weeks.

Questions

1. Define strength and the following types of contractions: (a) isotonic, (b) isometric, (c) eccentric, and (d) isokinetic.
2. Identify the factors that affect the tension of a muscle undergoing an isotonic contraction in the body, and explain how they affect them.
3. Define muscular endurance.
4. What structural and biochemical changes are brought about within a muscle as a consequence of a weight-training program?
5. What stimulates gains in strength and endurance?
6. Explain the overload principle. How are the overload principle and progressive resistance related?
7. Give several examples of the specificity of weight training.
8. What causes muscular soreness, and how can it be relieved or prevented?
9. Describe how you would structure a weight-training program around (a) isotonic exercises, (b) isometric exercises, and (c) isokinetic exercises.
10. Compare the effectiveness of the previous programs.
11. Define circuit training and describe how you would design such a program.
12. How does weight training affect sports performance?
13. How can strength and endurance be retained and/or maintained?
14. What are the structural limitations to flexibility?
15. How can flexibility be gained, and why is it important to health and physical performance?

References

1. Abraham, W. M.: Exercise-induced muscle soreness. *Physician Sportsmed.* 7(10): 57–60, 1979.
2. Abraham, W. M.: Factors in delayed muscle soreness. *Med Sci Sports.* 9(1):11–20, 1977.
3. Adeyanju, K., Crews, T. R., and Meadors, W. J.: Effects of two speeds of isokinetic training on muscle strength, power and endurance. *J Sports Med.* 23:352–356, 1983.
4. Allen, T. E., Byrd, R. J., and Smith, D. P.: Hemodynamic consequences of circuit weight training. *Res Q.* 47(3):299–306, 1976.
5. Anderson, R. A.: *Stretching.* P. O. Box 2734, Fullerton, Ca. 92633, 1975.
6. Anderson T., and Kearney, J. T.: Effects of three resistance training programs on muscular strength and absolute and relative endurance. *Res Q Exer Sport.* 53(1): 1–7, 1982.
7. Asa, M.: *The Effects of Isometric Exercise on the Strength of Skeletal Muscle.* Doctoral Dissertation, Springfield College, 1959.
8. Asmussen, E.: Observations on experimental muscle soreness. *Acta Rheumatologica Scand.* 1:109–116, 1956.
9. Barnes, W. S.: The relationship between maximum isokinetic strength and isokinetic endurance. *Res Q Exer Sport.* 51(4): 714–717, 1980.
10. Belka, D.: Comparison of dynamic, static, and combination training on dominant wrist flexor muscles. *Res Q.* 39:244–250, 1968.
11. Berger, R.: Comparative effects of three weight training programs. *Res Q.* 34:396–398, 1963.
12. Berger, R.: Comparison of the effect of

various weight training loads on strength. *Res Q.* 36:141–146, 1965.

13. Berger, R.: Comparison of static and dynamic strength increases. *Res Q.* 33:329–333, 1962.

14. Berger, R.: Comparison between static training and various dynamic training programs. *Res Q.* 34:131–135, 1963.

15. Berger, R.: Effect of varied weight training programs on strength. *Res Q.* 33:168–181, 1962.

16. Berger, R.: Effects of dynamic and static training on vertical jumping ability. *Res Q.* 34:419–424, 1963.

17. Berger, R.: Optimum repetitions for the development of strength. *Res Q.* 33:334–338, 1962.

18. Berger, R., and Hardage, B.: Effect of maximum loads for each of ten repetitions on strength improvement. *Res Q.* 38:715–718, 1967.

19. Billing, H., and Loewendahl, E.: *Mobilization of the Human Body.* Palo Alto, California, Stanford University Press, 1949.

20. Bosco, C., Zanon, S., Rusko, H., DalMonte, A., Bellotti, P., Latteri, F., Candeloro, N., Azzaro, E., Pozzo, R., and Bonomi, S.: The influence of extra load on the mechanical behavior of skeletal muscle. *Europ J Appl Physiol.* 53:149–154, 1984.

21. Byrd, R., and Hills, W.: Strength, endurance, and blood flow responses to isometric training. *Res Q.* 42:357–361, 1971.

22. Campbell, R.: Effects of supplemental weight training on the physical fitness of athletic squads. *Res Q.* 33:343–348, 1962.

23. Chastain, P. B.: The effect of deep heat on isometric strength. *Phys Ther.* 58(5):543–546, May, 1978.

24. Clarke, D.: Adaptations in strength and muscular endurance resulting from exercise. In Wilmore, J. (ed.): *Exercise and Sport Sciences Reviews,* vol. 1. New York, Academic Press, 1973, pp. 73–102.

25. Clarke, D., and Henry, F.: Neuromuscular specificity and increased speed from strength development. *Res Q.* 32:315–325, 1961.

26. Clarke, D., and Stull, G.: Endurance training as a determinant of strength and fatigability. *Res Q.* 41:19–26, 1970.

27. Clarke, H. (ed.): Development of muscular strength and endurance. *Phys Fit Res Digest.* Series 4, No. 1, Jan., 1974.

28. Clarke, H. (ed.): Isometric versus isotonic exercises. *Phys Fit Res Digest.* Series 1, No. 1, July, 1971.

29. Clarke, H. (ed.): Strength development and motor-sports improvement. *Phys Fit Res Digest.* Series 4, No. 4, Oct., 1974.

30. Costill, D. L., Coyle, E. F., Fink, W. F., Lesmes, G. R., and Witzmann, F. A.: Adaptations in skeletal muscle following strength training. *J Appl Physiol.* 46(1):96–99, 1979.

31. Counsilman, J.: Isokinetic exercise. *Athletic J.* 52(6): Feb., 1972.

32. Counsilman, J.: Isokinetic exercise: a new concept in strength building. *Swimming World.* 10:4, 1969.

33. Counsilman, J.: New approach to strength building. *Scholastic Coach.* March, 1971.

34. Coyle, E. F., Feiring, D. C., Rotkis, T. C., Cote III, R. W., Roby, F. B., Lee, W., and Wilmore, J. H.: Specificity of power improvements through slow and fast isokinetic training. *J Appl Physiol: Respirat Environ Exercise Physiol.* 51(6):1437–1442, 1981.

35. DeLateur, B., Lehmann, J., and Fordyce, W.: A test of the DeLorme axiom. *Arch Phys Med Rehabil.* 49:245–248, 1968.

36. DeLorme, T., and Watkins, A.: *Progressive Resistance Exercise.* New York, Appleton-Century-Crofts, 1951.

37. DeLorme, T., and Watkins, A.: Techniques of progressive resistance exercise. *Arch Phys Med Rehab.* 29:263–273, 1948.

38. deVries, H.: Evaluation of static stretching procedures for improvement of flexibility. *Res Q.* 33:222–229, 1962.

39. deVries, H.: *Physiology of Exercise for Physical Education and Athletics,* 3rd ed. Dubuque, Iowa, W. C. Brown, 1980.

40. deVries, H. A.: Prevention of muscular distress after exercise. *Res Q.* 32:468–479, 1961.

41. deVries, H. A.: Quantitative electromyographic investigation of the spasm theory of muscle pain. *Am J Phys Med.* 45:119–134, 1966.

42. Dons, B., Bollerup, K., Bonde-Petersen, F., and Hancke, S.: The effects of weight-lifting exercise related to muscle fiber composition and muscle cross-sectional area in humans. *Europ J Appl Physiol.* 40:95–106, 1979.

43. Dorpat, T. L., and Holmes, T. H.: Mechanisms of skeletal muscle pain and fatigue. *Arch Neurol Psych.* 74:628–640, 1955.

44. Duchateau, J., and Hainaut, K.: Isometric or dynamic training: differential effects of mechanical properties of a human muscle. *J Appl Physiol: Respirat Environ Exercise Physiol.* 56(2).296-301, 1984.

45. Edgerton, V.: Morphology and histochemistry of the soleus muscle from normal and exercised rats. *Am J Anat.* 127:81-88, 1970.

46. Fahey, T. D., Rolph, R., Moungmee, P., Nagel, J., and Mortara, S.: Serum testosterone, body composition, and strength of young adults. *Med Sci Sports.* 8(1): 31-34, 1976.

47. Fox, E. L.: *Sports Physiology.* Philadelphia, W. B. Saunders, 1979.

48. Friden, J., Seger, J., Sjöström, M., and Ekblom, B.: Adaptive response in human skeletal muscle subjected to prolonged eccentric training. *Int J Sports Med.* 4: 177-183, 1983.

49. Galbo, H., Hummer, L., Petersen, I. B., Christensen, N. J., and Bie, N.: Thyroid and testicular hormone responses to graded and prolonged exercise in man. *Europ J Appl Physiol.* 36:101-106, 1977.

50. Gardner, G.: Specificity of strength changes of the exercised and nonexercised limb following isometric training. *Res Q.* 34:98-101, 1963.

51. Gettman, L. R., Ayres, J. J., Pollock, M. L., and Jackson, A.: The effect of circuit weight training on strength, cardiorespiratory function, and body composition of adult men. *Med Sci Sports.* 10(3):171-176, 1978.

52. Gillam, G. M.: Effects of frequency of weight training on muscle strength enhancement. *J Sports Med.* 21:432-436, 1981.

53. Goldberg, A., Etlinger, J., Goldspink, D., and Jablecki, C.: Mechanism of work-induced hypertrophy of skeletal muscle. *Med Sci Sports.* 7(3):185-198, 1975.

54. Goldspink, G.: The combined effects of exercise and reduced food intake on skeletal muscle fibers. *J Cell Comp Physiol.* 63:209-216, 1964.

55. Gonyea, W. J.: The role of exercise in inducing skeletal muscle fiber number. *J Appl Physiol.* 48(3):421-426, 1980.

56. Gonyea, W. J., Ericson, G. C., and Bonde-Petersen, F.: Skeletal muscle fiber splitting induced by weightlifting exercise in cats. *Acta Physiol Scand.* 99:105-109, 1977.

57. Gordon, A. M., Huxley, A. F., and Julian, F. J.: Variation in isometric tension with sarcomere length in vertebrate muscle fibers. *J Physiol* (London). 184:170-192, 1966.

58. Gordon, E.: Anatomical and biochemical adaptations of muscle to different exercises. *JAMA.* 201:755-758, 1967.

59. Gregory, L. W.: Some observations on strength training and assessment. *J Sports Med.* 21:130-137, 1981.

60. Hagberg, M.: Muscular endurance and surface electromyogram in isometric and dynamic exercise. *J Appl Physiol: Respirat Environ Exercise Physiol.* 51(1):1-7, 1981.

61. Hellebrandt, F., and Houtz, S.: Mechanisms of muscle training in man: experimental demonstration of the overload principle. *Phys Ther Rev.* 36:371-383, 1956.

62. Hetrick, G. A., and Wilmore, J. H.: Androgen levels and muscle hypertrophy during an eight week weight training program for men/women. *Med Sci Sports.* 11(1):102, 1979.

63. Hettinger, T., and Müller, E.: Muskelleistung und Muskeltraining. *Arbeitsphysiol.* 15:111-126, 1953.

64. Hickson, R. C.: Interference of strength development by simultaneously training for strength and endurance. *Europ J Appl Physiol.* 45:255-263, 1980.

65. Ho, K., Roy, R., Taylor, J., Heusner, W., Van Huss, W., and Carrow, R.: Muscle fiber splitting with weightlifting exercise. *Med Sci Sports.* 9(1):65, 1977.

66. Holland, G.: The physiology of flexibility: a review of the literature. *Kinesiology Review.* 1968, pp. 49-62.

67. Hough, T.: Ergographic studies in muscular soreness. *Am J Physiol.* 7:76-92, 1902.

68. Ikai, M., and Fukunaga, T.: Calculation of muscle strength per unit cross-sectional area of human muscle by means of ultrasonic measurements. *Int Z Angew Physiol.* 26:26-32, 1968.

69. Ikai, M., and Steinhaus, A.: Some factors modifying the expression of human strength. *J Appl Physiol.* 16:157-163, 1961.

70. Ingjer, F.: Effects of endurance training on muscle fibre atp-ase activity, capillary supply and mitochondrial content in man. *J Physiol.* 294:419-432, 1979.

71. Johns, R., and Wright, V.: Relative impor-

tance of various tissues in joint stiffness. *J Appl Physiol.* 17:824–828, 1962.

72. Johnson, B. L., Adamczyk, W., Tennoe, K. O., and Stromme, S. B.: A comparison of concentric and eccentric muscle training. *Med Sci Sports.* 8(1):35–38, 1976.

73. Kanehisa, H., and Miyashita, M.: Effect of isometric and isokinetic muscle training on static strength and dynamic power. *Europ J Appl Physiol.* 50:365–371, 1983.

74. Knapik, J. J., Wright, J. E., Mawdsley, R. H., and Braun, R. H.: Isokinetic, isometric and isotonic strength relationships. *Arch Phys Med Rehab.* 64:77–80, 1983.

75. Komi, P. V., and Buskirk, E. R.: The effect of eccentric and concentric muscle acitivity on tension and electrical activity of human muscle. *Ergonomics.* 15:417–434, 1972.

76. Komi, P. V., Viitasalo, J. T., Rauramaa, R., and Vihko, V.: Effect of isometric strength training on mechanical, electrical, and metabolic aspects of muscle function. *Europ J Appl Physiol.* 40:45–55, 1978.

77. Kraus, H., and Raab, W.: *Hypokinetic Disease.* Springfield, Ill., Charles C Thomas, 1961.

78. Krotkiewski, M., Aniansson, A., Grimby, G., Björntorp, P., and Sjöström, L.: The effect of unilateral isokinetic strength training on local adipose and muscle tissue morphology, thickness, and enzymes. *Europ J Appl Physiol.* 42:271–281, 1979.

79. Lamb, D. R.: *Physiology of Exercise,* 2nd ed. New York, MacMillan, 1984.

80. Lange, L.: *Uber funktionelle Anpassung.* Berlin, Springer Verlag, 1919.

81. Laycoe, R., and Marteniuk, R.: Learning and tension as factors in static strength gains produced by static and eccentric training. *Res Q.* 42:299–306, 1971.

82. Leighton, J.: Flexibility characteristics of four specialized skill groups of college athletes. *Arch Phys Med Rehab.* 38:24–28, 1957.

83. Leighton, J.: Flexibility characteristics of three specialized skill groups of champion athletes. *Arch Phys Med Rehab.* 38:580–583, 1957.

84. Leighton, J.: Instrument and technic for measurement of range of joint motion. *Arch Phys Med Rehab.* 36:571–578, 1955.

85. Lesmes, G. R., Costill, D. L., Coyle, E. F., and Fink, W. J.: Muscle strength and power changes during maximal isokinetic training. *Med Sci Sports.* 10(4):266–269, 1978.

86. Liberson, W., and Asa, M.: Further studies of brief isometric exercises. *Arch Phys Med Rehab.* 40:330–336, 1959.

87. Lindh, M.: Increase of muscle strength from isometric quadriceps exercises at different knee angles. *Scand J Rehab Med.* 11:33–36, 1979.

88. MacDougall, J. D., Sale, D. G., Elder, G., and Sutton, J. R.: Ultrastructural properties of human skeletal muscle following heavy resistance training and immobilization. *Med Sci Sports.* 8(1):72, 1976.

89. MacDougall, J. D., Sale, D. G., Moroz, J. R., Elder, G. C. B., Sutton, J. R., and Howald, H.: Mitochondrial volume density in human skeletal muscle following heavy resistance training. *Med Sci Sports.* 11(2):164–166, 1979.

90. MacDougall, J. D., Ward, G. R., Sale, D. G., and Sutton, J. R.: Biochemical adaptation of human skeletal muscle to heavy resistance training and immobilization. *J Appl Physiol.* 43(4):700–703, 1977.

91. Masley, J., Hairabedian, A., and Donaldson, D.: Weight training in relation to strength, speed and coordination. *Res Q.* 24:308–315, 1952.

92. Mathews, D.: *Measurement in Physical Education,* 4th ed. Philadelphia, W. B. Saunders, 1973.

93. McMorris, R., and Elkins, E.: A study of production and evaluation of muscular hypertrophy. *Arch Phys Med Rehab.* 35:420–426, 1954.

94. Milner-Brown, H. S., Stein, R. B., and Lee, R. G.: Synchronization of human motor units: possible roles of exercise and supraspinal reflexes. *Electroenceph Clin Neurophysiol.* 38:245–254, 1975.

95. Moffroid, M. T., and Whipple, R. H.: Specificity of speed and exercise. *J Am Phys Ther Assoc.* 50:1699–1704, 1970.

96. Moffroid, M., Whipple, R., Hofkosh, J., Lowman, E., and Thistle, H.: A study of isokinetic exercise. *Phys Ther.* 49:735–746, 1968.

97. Morehouse, C.: Development and maintenance of isometric strength of subjects with diverse initial strengths. *Res Q.* 38:449–456, 1967.

98. Müller, E., and Rohmert, W.: Die Geschwindigkeit der Muskelkraft-Zunahme bei isometrischem Training. *Arbeitsphysiol.* 19:403–419, 1963.

99. Nicholas, J. A.: Injuries to knee ligaments. Relationship to looseness and tightness in football players. *JAMA*. 212:2236-2239, 1970.

100. Pate, R. R., Huges, R. D., Chandler, J. V., and Ratliffe, J. L.: Effects of arm training on retention of training effects derived from leg training. *Med Sci Sports*. 10(2):71-74, 1978.

101. Penman, K.: Ultrastructural changes in human striated muscle using three methods of training. *Res Q*. 40:764-772, 1969.

102. Perrine, J. J., and Edgerton, V. R.: Muscle force-velocity and power-velocity relationships under isokinetic loading. *Med Sci Sports*. 10(3):159-166, 1978.

103. Rarick, G., and Larsen, G.: Observations on frequency and intensity of isometric muscular effort in developing static muscular strength in post-pubescent males. *Res Q*. 29:333-341, 1958.

104. Rasch, P.: Isometric exercise and gains of muscle strength. In Shephard, R. (ed.): *Frontiers of Fitness*. Springfield, Ill., Charles C Thomas, 1971, Chapter 5.

105. Rasch, P.: The present status of negative (eccentric) exercise: a review. *Am Corr Ther J*. 28:77, 1974.

106. Rasch, P., and Morehouse, L.: Effect of static and dynamic exercises on muscular strength and hypertrophy. *J Appl Physiol*. 11:29-34, 1957.

107. Sady, S. P., Wortman, M., and Blanke, D.: Flexibility training: ballistic, static or proprioceptive neuromuscular facilitation? *Arch Phys Med Rehab*. 63:261-263, 1982.

108. Sale, D. G., MacDougall, J. D., Upton, A. R. M., and McComas, A. J.: Effect of strength training upon motoneuron excitability in man. *Med Sci Sports*. 11(1):76, 1979.

109. Seaborne, D., and Taylor, A. W.: The effect of speed of isokinetic exercise on training transfer to isometric strength in the quadriceps muscle. *J Sports Med*. 24:183-188, 1984.

110. Singh, M., and Karpovich, P.: Effect of eccentric training of agonists on antagonistic muscles. *J Appl Physiol*. 23:742-745, 1967.

111. Smith, M. J., and Melton, P.: Isokinetic versus isotonic variable-resistance training. *Am J Sports Med*. 9:275-279, 1981.

112. Staton, W. M.: The influence of ascorbic acid in minimizing post-exercise soreness in young men. *Res Q*. 23:356-360, 1952.

113. Stone, M. H., O'Bryant, H., and Garhammer, J.: A hypothetical model for strength training. *J Sports Med*. 21:342-351, 1981.

114. Stull, G., and Clarke, D.: High-resistance, low-repetition training as a determiner of strength and fatigability. *Res Q*. 41:189-193, 1970.

115. Sutton, J. R., Colemean, M. J., Casey, J., and Lazarus, L.: Androgen responses during physical exercise. *Br Med J*. 1:520-522, 1973.

116. Syster, B., and Stull, G.: Muscular endurance retention as a function of length of detraining. *Res Q*. 41:105-109, 1970.

117. Talag, T. S.: Residual muscular soreness as influenced by concentric, eccentric, and static contractions. *Res Q*. 44(4):458-469, 1973.

118. Thistle, H., Hislop, H., Moffroid, M., and Lowman, E.: Isokinetic contraction: a new concept of resistive exercise. *Arch Phys Med Rehab*. 48:279-282, 1967.

119. Thompson, C., and Martin, E.: Weight training and baseball throwing speed. *J Assoc Phys Ment Rehab*. 19:194, 1965.

120. Thompson, H., and Stull, G.: Effects of various training programs on speed of swimming. *Res Q*. 30:479-485, 1959.

121. Thorstensson, A.: Muscle strength, fibre types, and enzyme activities in man. *Acta Physiol Scand*. (Suppl 443), 1977.

122. Thorstensson, A., Hultin, B., von Döbeln, W., and Karlsson, J.: Effect of strength training on enzyme activities and fibre characteristics in human skeletal muscle. *Acta Physiol Scand*. 96:392-398, 1976.

123. Tipton, C. M., Martin, R. K., Matthes, R. D., and Carey, R. A.: Hydroxyproline concentrations in ligaments from trained and nontrained rats. In Howald, H., and Poortmans, J. R. (eds.): *Metabolic Adaptation to Prolonged Physical Exercise*. Basel, Switzerland, Birkhäuser Verlag, 1975, pp. 262-267.

124. Tipton, C. M., Matthes, R. D., Maynard, J. A., and Carey, R. A.: The influence of physical activity on ligaments and tendons. *Med Sci Sports*. 7(3):165-175, 1975.

125. Van Oteghen, S.: Isokinetic conditioning for women. *Scholastic Coach*. Oct., 1974.

126. Vrijens, J.: Muscle strength development in the pre- and post-pubescent age. *Med Sport* (Basel). 11:152-158, 1978.

127. Waldman, R., and Stull, G.: Effects of various periods of inactivity on retention of newly acquired levels of muscular endurance. *Res Q*. 40:393-401, 1969.

128. Wallin, D., Ekblom, B., Grahn, R., and Nordenborg, T.: Improvement of muscle flexibility: a comparison between two techniques. *Am J Sports Med.* 13:263–268, 1985.

129. Walters, C., Stewart, C., and LeClaire, J.: Effect of short bouts of isometric and isotonic contractions on muscular strength and endurance. *Am J Phys Med.* 39:131–141, 1960.

130. Wilmore, J. H., Parr, R. B., Girandola, R. N., Ward, P., Vodak, P. A., Barstow, T. J., Pipes, T. V., Romero, G. T., and Leslie, P.: Physiological alterations consequent to circuit weight training. *Med Sci Sports.* 10(2):79–84, 1978.

131. Withers, R.: Effect of varied weight-training loads on the strength of university freshmen. *Res Q.* 41:110–114, 1970.

132. Wolf, E., Blank, A., Shochina, M., and Gonen, B.: Effect of exercise of the lower limbs on the non-exercised biceps brachii muscle. *Am J Phys Med.* 63:113–121, 1984.

133. Zorbas, W., and Karpovich, P.: The effect of weight lifting upon the speed of muscular contractions. *Res Q.* 22:145–148, 1951.

SELECTED READINGS

Fox, E. L.: *Sports Physiology* (2ed) Philadelphia, Saunders College Publishing, 1984, pp. 123–161.

Hinson, M. N., Smith, W. C., and Funk, S.: Isokinetics: a clarification. *Res Q.* 50(1):30–35, 1979.

Hooks, G.: *Weight Training in Athletics and Physical Education.* Englewood Cliffs, N.J., Prentice-Hall, 1974.

Ianuzzo, C. D., and Chen, V.: Metabolic character of hypertrophied rat muscle. *J Appl Physiol.* 46(4):738–742, 1979.

Jesse, J. P.: Misuse of strength development programs in athletic training. *Physician Sportsmed.* 7(10):46–52, 1979.

Komi, P. V., and Karlsson, J.: Physical performance, skeletal muscle enzyme activities, and fibre types in monozygous and dizygous twins of both sexes. *Acta Physiol Scand.* (Suppl 462), 1979.

O'Shea, J. P.: *Scientific Principles and Methods of Strength Fitness,* 2nd ed. Reading, Mass., Addison-Wesley, 1976.

Riley, D. P.: *Strength Training: By the Experts.* West Point, N.Y., Leisure Press, 1977.

I n Chapter 2, we discussed the importance of oxygen with respect to the production of ATP energy. For this function, oxygen must be transported from the environment to the muscles, where it is then consumed by the mitochondria. The transport of oxygen (and the removal of carbon dioxide) necessarily involves the respiratory and circulatory systems (cardiorespiratory system). It is in the respiratory system that movement of air into and out of the lungs takes place, along with the exchange of oxygen and carbon dioxide between lungs and blood. In the circulatory system, the transport of oxygen and carbon dioxide by the blood occurs, as does gas exchange between blood and muscle.

In this section, we shall study the functional components of the respiratory and circulatory systems, both at rest and during exercise. Specifically, we shall discuss the changes they undergo and the various mechanisms by which these changes are mediated and regulated. Finally, we shall point out how these cardiorespiratory responses differ between trained and untrained subjects. This information should prove to be a valuable contribution to your professional preparation.

CARDIO-RESPIRATORY CONSIDERATIONS

Pulmonary Ventilation

The major concepts to be learned from this chapter are as follows:

- The movement of air into and out of the lungs is called ventilation, or pulmonary ventilation.
- Changes in ventilation are controlled by chemical and neurogenic stimuli.
- During exercise, ventilation may be 15 to 30 times greater than at rest.

- Exercise capacity is not normally limited by ventilation.
- During exercise, ventilation is useful in detecting an increased rate of anaerobic metabolism (anaerobic threshold).
- Alveolar ventilation, ventilation of the tiny air sacs (alveoli) in the lungs, assures adequate oxygenation of and carbon dioxide removal from the blood.
- Ventilation is brought about through

activity of the respiratory muscles, which are skeletal muscles located within the thoracic (rib) cage, but not in the lungs themselves.

In this chapter, we will study the means by which air is moved into and out of the lungs. This rhythmic to-and-fro movement of air is called **pulmonary ventilation.** In studying the materials which follow, you will find it helpful to refer frequently to Appendix B. In this appendix have been included both a standardized list of cardio-respiratory symbols and typical values for pulmonary function tests most often used by cardiorespiratory physiologists.

Minute Ventilation

As we all know, ventilation is composed of two phases, one that brings air into the lungs, called *inspiration* or *inhalation,* and one that lets air out into the environment, called *expiration* or *exhalation.* **Minute ventilation** refers to how much air we either inspire *or* expire (but not both) in one minute. Most often it refers to the amount expired $(\dot{V}E)$* rather than inspired $(\dot{V}I)$. This amount can be determined by knowing (a) the tidal volume (TV), i.e., how much air we expire in one breath, and (b) the respiratory frequency (f), i.e., how many breaths we take in one minute. In other words:

$\dot{V}E$	=	TV	$\times$	f
minute ventilation (liters per min)	=	tidal volume (liters)	$\times$	respiratory frequency (breaths per min)

Ventilation at Rest

Under normal resting conditions, minute ventilation varies considerably from person to person. Usually, we ventilate between 4 and 15 liters per minute (BTPS)† at rest. This varies with body size and is smaller in women and larger in men. Tidal volume and respiratory frequency vary even more than minute ventilation. This is easy to understand, since there are many combinations of tidal volume and frequency that yield the same minute ventilation. At rest, typical values for tidal volume and frequency are 400 to 600 milliliters (ml) and 10 to 25 breaths per minute, respectively.

Ventilation during Exercise

Minute ventilation increases during exercise. For the most part, this increase is directly proportional to increases in the amounts of oxygen consumed and carbon dioxide produced per minute by the working muscles. This is shown in Figure 8-1 for trained and untrained young men. Minute ventilation, $(\dot{V}E_{BTPS})$, is disproportional to oxygen consumption $(\dot{V}O_{2STPD})$ only at or near maximal values (Fig. 8-1A). However, this is not the case with respect to carbon dioxide production $(\dot{V}CO_{2STPD})$ (Fig. 8-1B). This indicates that minute ventilation is perhaps regulated more to the need for carbon dioxide removal than to oxygen consumption, at least under maximal exercise.[26] The fact that ventilation increases much more than $\dot{V}O_2$ (indicated by the curved portion of the lines in Fig. 8-1A) also tells us that minute ventilation does not normally limit the capacity (max $\dot{V}O_2$) of the cardiorespiratory system.

One other point to note in Figure 8-1 is that trained subjects tend to have lower

---

*The procedures for measuring $\dot{V}E$ are given in Chapter 4.

†The procedures for measuring BTPS and STPD are given in Appendix C.

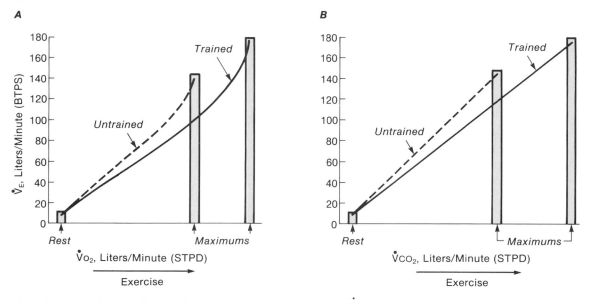

Figure 8-1. Effects of exercise on minute ventilation ($\dot{V}_{E_{BTPS}}$) in trained and untrained subjects. The close relationship of $\dot{V}_E$ and $\dot{V}_{O_2}$ is shown in A and to $\dot{V}_{CO_2}$ in B. Note that $\dot{V}_E$ is disproportional to $\dot{V}_{O_2}$ but not to $\dot{V}_{CO_2}$ at maximal and near maximal values.

minute ventilations during exercise at given workloads or oxygen consumptions ($\dot{V}_{O_2}$, Fig. 8-1A) and at given carbon dioxide productions ($\dot{V}_{CO_2}$, Fig. 8-1B). This lower ventilatory response to exercise, while common in most athletes,[3,18] is most pronounced in endurance athletes.[16] The physiological reason for this is not entirely known; however, it is suggested to be related to diminished peripheral chemoreceptor function,[3,17] and genetic and familial influences.[4,23] (Peripheral chemoreceptors will be studied in more detail in Chapter 11, p. 270). At any rate, regardless of its cause, it has been suggested that the low ventilatory response to exercise may be linked to outstanding endurance athletic performance.[16]

Maximal ventilation (max $\dot{V}_E$) due to exercise can reach values as high as 180 and 130 liters per minute (BTPS) in male and female athletes, respectively. This rep-

resents about a 25- to 30-fold increase over resting values. Such large increases are made possible by increases in both depth (tidal volume) and frequency of breathing. In untrained men and women, where $\dot{V}_{O_2}$, $\dot{V}_{CO_2}$, and working capacities are lower, max $\dot{V}_E$ is also lower. Along with this lower max $\dot{V}_E$ is a lower ventilatory efficiency, i.e., as previously indicated, untrained men and women have a greater $\dot{V}_E$ at a given $\dot{V}_{O_2}$ than trained men and women (Fig. 8-1A).

Ventilation not only varies with workload, but it also varies before, during, and after exercise at any given workload. As shown in Figure 8-2, these changes are as follows.[9]

Changes before Exercise

Immediately before exercise begins, ventilation increases. This increase obviously

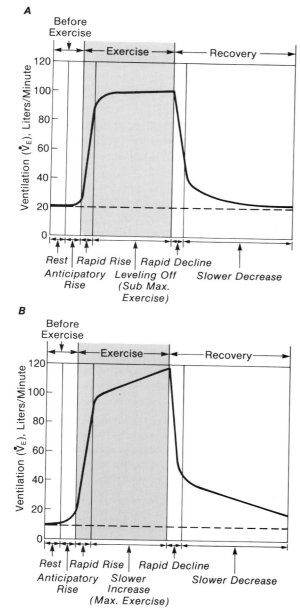

Figure 8-2. Minute ventilation ($\dot{V}E$) increases even before exercise begins. Immediately after exercise starts, ventilation increases rapidly, then either levels off (submaximal exercise as shown in *A*) or continues to increase (maximal exercise as shown in *B*). During recovery, ventilation decreases more rapidly at first, then gradually toward resting values.

cannot be due to anything resulting from the exercise. Therefore, it is most likely due to stimulation from the cerebral cortex resulting from anticipation of the ensuing exercise bout.

Changes during Exercise

During exercise, there are two major changes in ventilation:

1. A very rapid increase within only a few seconds after the start of exercise. This is probably related to nervous stimulation arising from the joint receptors resulting from the movement generated by the working muscles.
2. The rapid rise in ventilation soon ceases and is replaced by a *slower rise,* which in submaximal exercise (Fig. 8-2*A*) tends to level off, i.e., reach a steady-state value. (The ventilations shown in Figure 8-1, up to maximum, are steady-state values.) In maximal exercise (Fig. 8-2*B*), this leveling off, or steady state, does not occur; rather, ventilation continues to increase until the exercise is terminated. These changes are thought to be stimulated by chemical stimuli, mainly from the carbon dioxide in the blood produced during exercise.

Changes during Recovery

During the recovery period from exercise, there are again two major changes:

1. As soon as exercise is stopped, there is a sudden decrease in ventilation. This is because motor activity has stopped, and so has the nervous stimulation arising from receptors located in the muscles and joints.
2. After the sudden decrease in ventilation, there is a gradual or slower decrease toward resting values. The more severe the work, the longer it takes for ventilation to return to resting levels.

This change is probably related to the decrease in stimulation resulting from a decrease in carbon dioxide production.

A summary of these ventilatory changes is given in Table 8-1. We will discuss their control in more detail in Chapter 11.

Ventilation and the Anaerobic Threshold

The **anaerobic threshold** is defined as that intensity of workload or oxygen consumption in which anaerobic metabolism is accelerated.[8,28,29] You will recall from Chapter 2 that an increase in anaerobic metabolism results in accumulation of lactic acid in the muscles and blood; from Chapter 5, you will recall that lactic acid is a prime suspect as a cause of muscular fatigue. This, plus the fact that the anaerobic threshold is considerably different for trained and untrained subjects, has generated some interest in its applications to athletic training, particularly endurance training.[15] These applications will be discussed later in Section 4. Right now our interest lies in the relationship between the anaerobic threshold and the minute ventilation.

One of the ways to detect the anaerobic threshold is, of course, to measure the blood lactic acid periodically during continuous and progressively increasing exercise loads, such as those performed on a bicycle ergometer or on a motor-driven treadmill. However, this technique requires drawing multiple blood samples, which may be uncomfortable to the subjects and which requires a certain amount of time for chemical analysis of the blood samples. A faster and more comfortable way to detect the anaerobic threshold is by observing the minute ventilation and other gas exchange variables, such as carbon dioxide production, during a progressive exercise test.[8] These variables increase linearly, i.e., in a straight-line fashion, with increasing workloads until the anaerobic threshold is reached. At this point, their rate of increase is greatly accelerated; this is shown in Figure 8-3. Notice how $\dot{V}E$ and $\dot{V}CO_2$ start to rise sharply at the anaerobic threshold. Notice also how these changes coincide with the steep increase in blood lactic acid.

Thus we see that minute ventilation is a reliable and relatively easily obtained indicator of the onset of anaerobic metabolism during exercise. The physiological significance of the increased minute ventilation at the anaerobic threshold has to do with buffering the increase in lactic acid and will be discussed in more detail in Chapter 21, page 596.

TABLE 8-1

Ventilatory Changes Before, During, and After Exercise

Phase	Change	Control
1. Pre-exercise	Moderate increase	Cerebral cortex
2. During exercise		
a. Immediate	Rapid increase	Muscles and joints
b. Later	Steady-state or slower rise	Chemical (CO_2)
3. Recovery		
a. Immediate	Sudden decrease	Cessation of movement
b. Later	Slower decrease toward rest	Decrease in CO_2

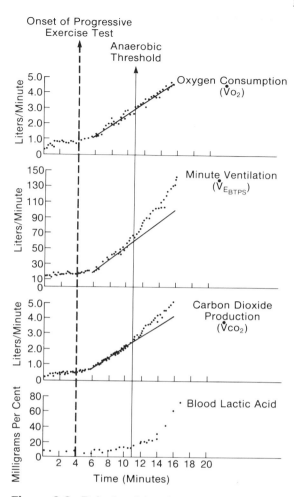

Figure 8-3. Relationship of minute ventilation to the anaerobic threshold. Minute ventilation ($\dot{V}_{E_{BTPS}}$) and carbon dioxide production ($\dot{V}_{CO_2}$) start to rise sharply at the anaerobic threshold (thin vertical line), coinciding with the steep rise in blood lactic acid. The dashed vertical line denotes the start of the progressive exercise test. (Based on data from Davis et al.[8])

Alveolar Ventilation and Dead Space

Not all the fresh air we inspire per minute takes part in gas exchange with the capillaries that perfuse the lungs (referred to as pulmonary capillary blood). Only that por-

tion of fresh air that reaches the alveoli, called **alveolar ventilation,** assures adequate oxygenation of and carbon dioxide removal from the pulmonary capillary blood. The **alveoli** (singular, **alveolus**) are those tiny, terminal air sacs in the lungs that are in intimate contact with the pulmonary capillaries (Fig. 8-4). The volume of fresh air that remains in the respiratory passages (nose, mouth, pharynx, larynx, trachea, bronchi, and bronchioles) and does not participate in gas exchange is referred to as **anatomical dead space.**

The size of the anatomical dead space is difficult to measure in humans, particularly during exercise. However, estimates have indicated that an average resting value is around 0.15 liter in men and about 0.10 liter in women.[5] Since dead space varies somewhat with body size, a rough estimate of dead space in milliliters (ml) is the body weight expressed in pounds. For example, if you weigh 167 pounds, your respiratory dead space should be close to 167 ml or 0.167 liter. Of the 0.5 liter of air inspired per breath (tidal volume) at rest, 70% [(0.5 liter − 0.15 liter)/0.5 liter × 100] ventilates the alveoli and 30% remains in the dead space. During exercise, dilation of the respiratory passages may cause anatomical dead space to double, but since tidal volume also increases, an adequate alveolar ventilation, and therefore gas exchange, is maintained.

Alveolar ventilation, then, is dependent on three factors: (1) depth of breathing (tidal volume); (2) rate of breathing (frequency); and (3) size of the dead space. Minute ventilation alone does not indicate whether or not alveolar ventilation is adequate. For example, in Figure 8-5A and B, resting minute ventilation is 6.0 liters per minute. However, in Figure 8-5A, tidal volume (TV) is 0.5 liter and respiratory frequency is 12 breaths per minute (0.5 liter per breath × 12 breaths per minute = 6.0 liters per minute). In Figure 8-5B, however,

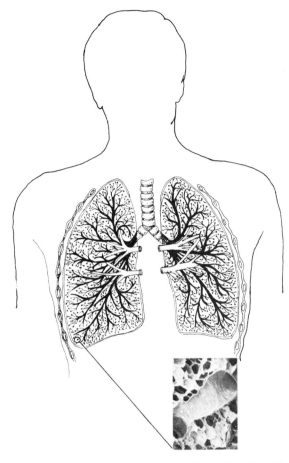

Figure 8-4. Fresh air that reaches the alveoli, called alveolar ventilation, assures adequate oxygenation of and carbon dioxide removal from the pulmonary capillary blood. The alveoli are tiny air sacs in the lungs that are in contact with the pulmonary capillaries. The inset is a scanning electron micrograph of a section of lung tissue showing many small alveoli and a much larger bronchiole. The pulmonary capillaries run in the walls of the alveoli and are not visible. (Micrograph by J. A. Nowell and W. S. Taylor, from West.[30])

TV is 0.25 liter and frequency is 24 breaths per minute (0.25 × 24 = 6.0 liters per minute). If anatomical dead space (DS) in each case is 0.15 liter then 0.35 liter of fresh air (0.5 − 0.15) will enter the alveoli per breath

in A, but only 0.10 liter (0.25 − 0.15) will enter the alveoli in B. This means that alveolar ventilation in A will be 4.2 liters per minute (0.35 × 12), and sufficient exchange of gases at the alveolar-capillary membranes will be assured. On the other hand, alveolar ventilation in B will be reduced to only 2.4 liters per minute ([0.25 − 0.15] × 24), and gas exchange will be inadequate.

These relationships point out why doubling DS during exercise does not lead to decreased alveolar ventilation, provided that TV and frequency increase proportionally. For example, if during moderate exercise minute ventilation = 40 liters per minute, TV = 1.6 liters per breath, DS = 0.3 liter per breath, and frequency = 25 breaths per minute, alveolar ventilation would be:

$$(1.6 - 0.3) \times 25 = 32.5 \text{ liters per minute.}$$

This indicates that 80% of the fresh air inspired per minute ventilates the alveoli.

Other Lung Volumes and Capacities

There are a number of other lung volumes with which you should become familiar. Most are used as measures of pulmonary function; therefore, knowledge of them will enable you to better understand respiratory physiology. Furthermore, a few are easily measured with nothing more than a spirometer, and thus you may wish to periodically test the pulmonary function of your athletes.

Table 8-2 contains a list of eight lung volumes or capacities, their definitions, and the approximate changes they undergo during exercise. Also, schematic representations of these volumes at rest, together with their spirographic tracings,* are

---

*Residual volume (and thus functional residual capacity and total lung capacity) cannot be measured directly with a spirometer. Its measurement is more complex and involves gas dilution or wash-out methods.

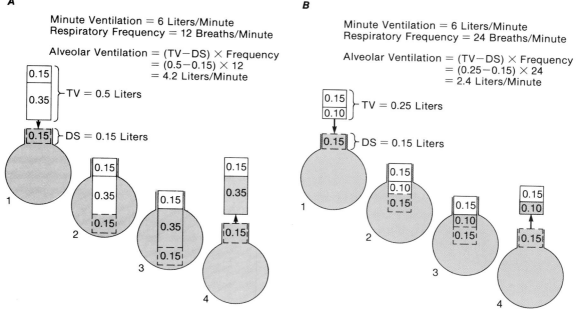

Figure 8-5. Effects of tidal volume (TV) and frequency of breathing (*f*) on alveolar ventilation. The large circles represent alveoli; the necks of the circles represent the respiratory passages or dead space volume (DS); the open blocks, fresh air (high in O_2 low in CO_2); shaded areas, alveolar gas (low in O_2 and high in CO_2). Numbers inside blocks represent gas volumes, in liters. In *A* and *B*, both minute ventilation and dead space are equal. However, in *A* more fresh air reaches the alveoli than in *B* because the breaths are deeper but not as frequent. The numbers under the alveoli designate respiratory phases: (1) pre-inspiration; (2) inspiration; (3) end-inspiration; and (4) end-expiration. (Modified and redrawn from Comroe et al.[6])

shown in Figure 8-6*A* and *B* for untrained and trained young men. In Figure 8-6*C* is shown a cutaway drawing of a spirometer from which spirographic tracings, like the one in Figure 8-6*A* and *B*, are made. A spirometer consists of two metal containers, one inverted over the other. The inverted container is made airtight by sealing it in a column of water. As the person exhales into the spirometer, the inverted container, called the *bell,* moves up, whereas upon inhalation, the bell moves down. The up-and-down movements of the bell, which represent the volume of air breathed, are recorded on a rotating chart or drum attached to the spirometer. This recording is referred to as a spirographic tracing.

As mentioned earlier, the increase in TV during exercise contributes in part to an increase in minute ventilation. During maximal exercise, TV may be five to six times greater than at rest. The increase in TV results from utilization of both the inspiratory reserve volume (IRV) and the expiratory reserve volume (ERV), but probably more of the former than of the latter.

The slight decreases in total lung capacity (TLC) and in vital capacity (VC) during exercise are related to an increase in pulmonary blood flow. This increases the amount of blood in the pulmonary capillaries and thus reduces the available gas volume space. As a result residual volume (RV) and functional residual capacity

TABLE 8–2

Definitions of Lung Volumes and Capacities and Their Changes During Exercise as Compared with Rest

Lung Volume or Capacity	Definition	Changes During Exercise
Tidal volume (TV)	Volume inspired or expired per breath	Increase
Inspiratory reserve volume (IRV)	Maximal volume inspired from end-inspiration	Decrease
Expiratory reserve volume (ERV)	Maximal volume expired from end-expiration	Slight decrease
Residual volume (RV)	Volume remaining at end of maximal expiration	Slight increase
Total lung capacity (TLC)	Volume in lung at end of maximal inspiration	Slight decrease
Vital capacity (VC)	Maximal volume forcefully expired after maximal inspiration	Slight decrease
Inspiratory capacity (IC)	Maximal volume inspired from resting expiratory level	Increase
Functional residual capacity (FRC)	Volume in lungs at resting expiratory level	Slight increase

(FRC) will be slightly increased during exercise. This in turn means that the oxygen and particularly the carbon dioxide levels in the alveoli will fluctuate less and tend toward more constant values. For example, the increased carbon dioxide produced by the working muscles is diluted as it mixes with the large FRC, causing less pronounced changes in alveolar carbon dioxide levels. We shall see later that changes in carbon dioxide are important in the regulation of pulmonary ventilation.

As shown in Figure 8-6, the various lung volumes measured under resting conditions for the most part (with the exception of TV) are larger in trained than in untrained men.[1] The same holds true for women, although the absolute values are lower by approximately 25%. The majority of these changes can be attributed to the fact that training results in improved pulmonary function and therefore in larger lung volumes. This is true though it has been shown that body size is directly proportional to TLC and VC especially, and that athletes as a group are generally taller and heavier than are their nonathletic counterparts. It should be mentioned, however, that there is very little, if any, correlation between athletic performance and these lung volumes in young (13- to 17-year-old) boys and girls, provided that body size is taken into consideration.[7] Swimmers as a rule have developed larger vital capacities than their matched counterparts. Larger vital capacities in swimmers are usually attributed to the observation that swimmers undergo a form of resistance training while exhaling in the water.

Dynamic Lung Measures

It is impractical to try to distinguish athletic prowess on the basis of static lung

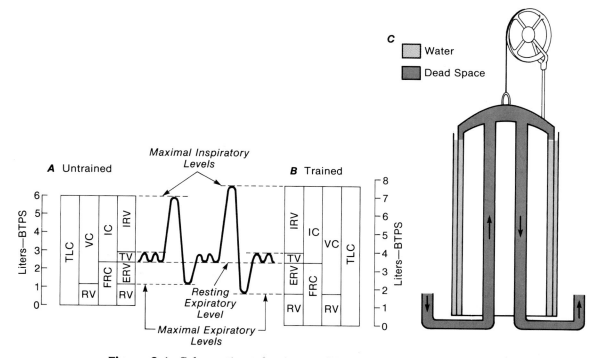

Figure 8-6. Schematic and spirographic tracings of lung volumes and capacities. Various lung volumes at rest (except TV) are generally smaller in untrained, *A*, than in trained individuals, *B. C* represents a cutaway drawing of a spirometer from which spirographic tracings are made. It consists of two metal containers, one inverted over and fitted into the other. As a person exhales into the spirometer, the inverted container, called a bell, rises; upon inhalation, the bell moves down. Up and down movements of the bell are recorded on a kymograph and referred to as a spirogram. For definitions and key to abbreviations see Table 8-2. (Data for untrained subjects from Comroe et al.[6] and data for trained subjects from Holmgren.[11])

volumes and capacities previously described. There is a variety of dynamic lung function tests which, as with the static tests, have limited application for the athlete. However, they do have clinical application in the diagnosis of pulmonary diseases. Among the dynamic lung function tests the following are described and discussed briefly.

Forced Vital Capacity (FVC)

FVC may be characterized as a vital capacity test carried out as rapidly as possible.

In other words, the subject exhales as rapidly and completely as possible following a maximal inspiration. Beyond the FVC test, clinicians are interested not only in the total amount of air moved (liters) but also the rate of flow. For example, the forced expiratory volume in 1 second (FEV_1) represents the air expired in the first second of the test. $FEV_{1,2}$ would represent the volume of air moved between the first and second second. Normally, $FEV_1 =$ 80 to 83% of the FVC. With airway obstructions, the value may drop to 40% or even 20% of the FVC.

Maximum Voluntary Ventilation (MVV)

The maximum ventilation a subject can reach depends upon the integrity of the entire respiratory anatomy, including the respiratory muscles and their control and resistance in the lungs. A timed maximal ventilation of either 12 or 15 seconds is recorded and then converted to liters per minute. For example, if a 12-second test is conducted, the volume recorded is multiplied by 5 (12 seconds × 5 = 60 seconds) and the result reported in liters per minute, BTPS. The resultant value is usually larger than maximal ventilation levels recorded during all-out exercise.

Importance of Pulmonary Volumes and Capacities

You will note from Figure 8-6 that the pulmonary capacities are represented by combinations of the various pulmonary volumes. For example, vital capacity (VC) equals inspiratory reserve volume (IRV) plus tidal volume (TV) plus expiratory reserve volume (ERV). Can you determine other capacities?

The various volumes and capacities are affected not only by body size and build but also by body position. When a person lies down most volumes will decrease. This observation is attributable to two factors. First, the abdominal contents tend to push against the diaphragm as a consequence of the influence of gravity in the supine position and, secondly, there is an increase in pulmonary blood volume as a result of altered hemodynamic pressures.

Residual volume, as mentioned earlier, acts as a reservoir in reducing large fluctuations of carbon dioxide and oxygen in the pulmonary blood flow. In other words, the removal of carbon dioxide from the blood is maintained within nominal limits and, at the same time, oxygen continues to diffuse into the blood.

Vital capacity is affected by body position, strength of the respiratory muscles, and distensibility of the lungs and thoracic cage (compliance). In addition, when the thoracic cage is immersed in water, such as in underwater weighing (see Chapter 20), vital capacity is slightly reduced. A number of disease states decrease vital capacity as well, including paralysis of respiratory muscles (polio, spinal cord injuries), tuberculosis, chronic asthma, pulmonary cancer, chronic bronchitis, pulmonary vascular congestion and edema.

In general, we see very little, if any, change in the various lung volumes in response to exercise training with the possible exception of swimming.

Second Wind

A phenomenon usually associated with ventilation is called "second wind." All of us in physical education and athletics have probably experienced the second wind at one time or another. It is generally characterized by a sudden transition from a rather ill-defined feeling of distress or fatigue during the early portion of prolonged exercise to a more comfortable, less-stressful feeling later in the exercise. This apparent distress is sensed, so to speak, in a variety of ways, for example, intense breathlessness (dyspnea), rapid, shallow breathing, chest pain, throbbing headache or vertigo and pain in various muscles.[12]

Physiologically, no one knows exactly what causes second wind. In one of the few studies designed to investigate this problem,[12] it was found that second wind was experienced at different times during exercise by different subjects (between 2 and 18 minutes during a 20-minute treadmill run). Also, in 90% of the subjects, second wind was associated with more comfortable breathing, in 70% with relief or partial relief of muscular fatigue or pain in the legs, and in 35% with simultaneous relief from both leg and chest pain. These variable responses lead to the conclusion that second wind does exist.

What then causes second wind? A review of this phenomenon by Dr. R. Shephard of the University of Toronto revealed several possible causes:[25] (1) relief from breathlessness caused by slow ventilatory adjustments early in the exercise; (2) removal (oxidation) of lactic acid accumulated early in the exercise because of delayed blood flow changes in the working muscles; (3) adequate warm-up; (4) relief from local muscle fatigue, particularly of the respiratory muscles; and (5) psychological factors. Until more definite information is available, it appears that the coach and the athlete alike can do little to accelerate the occurrence of second wind.

Stitch in the Side

This phenomenon is also very familiar to most athletes. A stitch in the side is usually described as a sharp pain in the side or rib cage. Like second wind, it occurs early during exercise (generally during running and swimming), subsiding as exercise continues. However, for some athletes the pain is so severe that they must either slow down or stop exercising altogether. While the exact cause of such pain is not known for sure, it has been suggested that lack of oxygen (hypoxia) in the respiratory muscles (particularly the diaphragm and intercostal muscles) due to insufficient blood flow (ischemia) is involved. Unfortunately, there is no simple remedy.

Ventilatory Mechanics

Movement of air into and out of the lungs results from changes in intrapulmonary pressure (i.e., the pressure inside the lung), which is produced by variations in the size of the **thoracic cage** or **cavity.** Such variations result from periodic contractions of the respiratory muscles.

Movements of the Thoracic Cage—The Respiratory (Ventilatory) Muscles

In Figure 8-7 are shown the position of the lungs within the thoracic cavity, and the main respiratory muscles, the **diaphragm** and **intercostal muscles.** It should be pointed out that the lungs themselves are passive contributors to the respiratory movements in that they contain no respiratory muscles.

Muscles of Inspiration

During quiet (resting) inspiration, the size of the thoracic cage is increased longitudinally by contraction of the **diaphragm muscle,** and transversely and dorsoventrally by contraction of the **external intercostal muscles.** The diaphragm, the principal muscle of inspiration, is a large, dome-shaped muscle innervated by the left and right phrenic nerves. Stimulation of these nerves during inspiration causes the diaphragm to contract or flatten; i.e., its domed portion is lowered. Since it separates the thoracic and abdominal cavities, the longitudinal diameter of the former is increased, and the diameter of the latter is decreased. The abdomen therefore protrudes slightly during inspiration. It has been estimated that contraction of the diaphragm contributes between one-fourth and three-fourths of the tidal volume.[10,27] The intercostal muscles (insert, Fig. 8-7) lie between successive ribs (*intercostal* means "between ribs") and consist of two layers. The fibers of the external layer (the external intercostal muscles) are so arranged that when they contract the ribs are lifted and rotated, thus increasing the transverse and dorsoventral diameters of the thoracic cavity. These changes in size of the thoracic cage are also shown schematically in Figure 8-7).

The much larger inspired volumes produced by exercise are made possible by contraction of accessory inspiratory mus-

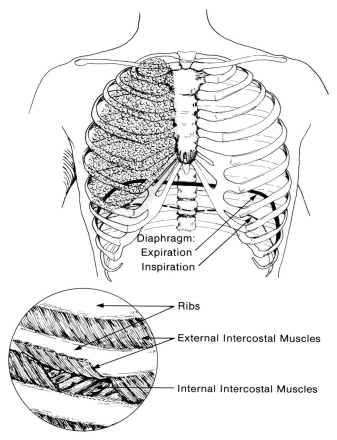

Diaphragm:
Expiration
Inspiration

Ribs

External Intercostal Muscles

Internal Intercostal Muscles

Figure 8-7. The ventilatory muscles. The diaphragm and the intercostal muscles (insert) are the principal muscles of respiration. The shaded area represents increases in size of the thoracic cage during inspiration.

cles, all of which further increase the size of the rib cage.[10] For example, contraction of the **scalene muscles** elevates the first two ribs, and contraction of the **sternocleido-mastoid muscles** elevates the sternum (front of thorax). During maximal exercise, contraction of the **trapezius** and **extensors of the back and neck** are also thought to facilitate inspiratory movements.

Muscles of Expiration

Relaxation of the diaphragm and external intercostal muscles during quiet expiration permits the thoracic cage to return to its original size. In other words, expiration under these conditions is passive and independent of the expiratory muscles. This is so because during inspiration the elastic tissues of the lungs and the walls of the thorax are stretched, thus storing in them potential energy. Therefore, reduction in the size of the thoracic cage during normal expirations is the result of the elastic recoil of these tissues through the release of this stored energy. We shall discuss this in more detail later.

During exercise, expiration is usually active, that is, it is facilitated by contractions of the expiratory muscles, the most important of which are the **abdominal muscles**.[10] These contractions, besides flexing the trunk, depress the lower ribs and increase the pressure inside the abdomen, forcing the diaphragm upward into the thoracic cavity. The **internal intercostal muscles** are also muscles of expiration. Their fibers (insert, Fig. 8-7) and movements are diametrically opposed to those of the external intercostals; when active, they lower the ribs, moving them closer together. All of these actions aid in reducing the size of the thorax and therefore facilitate the act of expiration.

The Respiratory Muscles and Training

Since the respiratory muscles are skeletal muscles, both their strength and endurance can be significantly increased following training programs. This is particularly true if the training programs are limited to the ventilatory muscles.[2,13,14] Such changes in strength and endurance have been suggested to be important in the control of ventilation and, as mentioned earlier, in the lower ventilatory response to exercise observed in athletes.[14] Increases in the strength and endurance of the respiratory muscles as a result of training could also help explain the larger lung volumes found in athletes, as previously pointed out.

A summary of the major respiratory muscles and their actions during rest and exercise is contained in Table 8-3.

Oxygen Cost of Ventilation

The ventilatory muscles must overcome the elastic recoil of the lungs and thorax and the resistance to airflow offered by the respiratory passages. At rest, the work required in overcoming these forces is minimal because tidal volume and respiratory frequency are also minimal. Furthermore, expiration is passive. Under these conditions, the amount of oxygen consumed by the ventilatory muscles constitutes no more than 1 to 2% of the total body oxygen consumption.

During exercise, increases in tidal volume, and frequency and involvement of more respiratory muscles necessarily mean that the oxygen cost of ventilation also increases. In fact, oxygen consumption of

---

TABLE 8-3

The Major Respiratory Muscles During Rest and Exercise

Respiratory Phase	Muscles Acting During Rest	Action	Muscles Acting During Exercise
Inspiration	Diaphragm	Flattens	Diaphragm
	External intercostals	Raises ribs	External intercostals
		Elevates first and second ribs	Scaleni
		Elevates sternum	Sternocleidomastoids
Expiration	None	Lowers ribs	Internal intercostals
		Depresses lower ribs and forces diaphragm into thorax	Abdominals

the respiratory muscles during heavy exercise may constitute 8 to 10% of the total oxygen consumed by the body.[19,24] It has been suggested that the increase in total body oxygen consumption above a certain ventilatory rate (around 120 liters per minute) is used exclusively by the respiratory muscles and thus is not available to the other skeletal muscles for performance of mechanical work.[21,24] Others have suggested that this is true once the cardiac output (amount of blood pumped by the heart in one minute) has reached its limit rather than when ventilation reaches a certain level.[20] In either case, with these limits so high, from a practical viewpoint the oxygen cost of ventilation *per se* does not normally limit most exercise and athletic performances.

Oxygen Cost of Ventilation and Training

It was mentioned earlier that trained individuals have a higher ventilatory efficiency than do untrained persons. A higher ventilatory efficiency means that the amount of air ventilated at the same oxygen consumption level is lower. The O_2 cost of ventilation increases greatly with increasing ventilation. Therefore, a lower ventilation, particularly over a prolonged effort (e.g., the marathon), would mean less oxygen to the respiratory muscles and more to the working skeletal muscles.

Oxygen Cost of Ventilation and Smoking

All of us have heard and perhaps used the phrase "smoking causes shortness of breath." The phrase, though colloquial, is essentially correct from a physiological standpoint. Chronic smoking of cigarettes results in increased airway resistance. This in turn means that the respiratory muscles must work harder and thus consume more oxygen in ventilating a given amount of air. As shown in Figure 8-8, during heavy exercise the oxygen cost of ventilation in

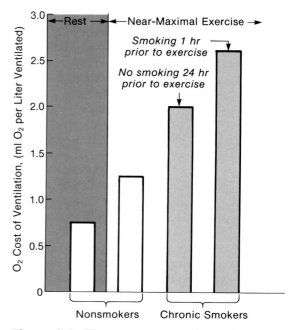

Figure 8-8. The oxygen cost of ventilation in chronic cigarette smokers is greatly increased during near-maximal exercise, particularly if a few cigarettes are smoked within an hour prior to exercise. Abstinence from smoking 24 hours before exercise decreases the cost of ventilation but does not decrease it to the nonsmokers levels. (Based on data from Rode and Shepard[22] and Shepard.[24])

chronic smokers was found to be on the average two times that of nonsmokers.[22] This was true when only a few cigarettes were smoked within 1 hour prior to the exercise. In the heaviest smoker (20 to 30 cigarettes per day for 27 years), the difference was nearly four times that of nonsmokers! If no cigarettes were smoked by the smokers for 24 hours prior to exercise, the oxygen cost of ventilation was about 25% lower, but still about 60% higher than in nonsmokers.[22,24]

This information has two practical implications:

1. The added cost of ventilation caused by the chronic smoking of cigarettes

can rob the working muscles of a large percentage of their potential oxygen supply. During maximal exercise, this could lead to a corresponding reduction in performance, and during submaximal exercise to an increase in anaerobic metabolism (LA system) and thus early fatigue.

2. A large part of the increase in the oxygen cost of ventilation in chronic smokers can be substantially reduced by a relatively short period of abstinence from cigarettes (24 hours). Therefore, athletes who cannot or will not "kick the habit" permanently can help their performance by not smoking on the day of competition.

Pressure Changes

We have already stated that ventilation of the lungs is a result of changes in intrapulmonary pressure. The magnitude of these pressure changes and how they are reflected in the lungs by movements of the thoracic cage are related to the anatomical relationships among the thoracic walls, the diaphragm, and outer surfaces of the lungs.

The Pleural Cavity

The lungs are not directly attached to the walls of the thorax. Rather, they are "connected" by a thin film of fluid, called **serous fluid,** which covers and is secreted by the inner surfaces of two thin serous membranes, collectively known as the **pleurae** (singular, **pleura**). The outer surface of one pleura has two "components"—the part that lines the thoracic wall, which is called the **parietal pleura** (*parietal* means "wall"), and the part that covers the diaphragm, which is called the **diaphragmatic pleura.** The outer surface of the other pleura covers the lungs; this is the **visceral pleura** (*visceral* pertains to internal organs). The "potential space" between these two pleurae is called the **pleural cavity.** The thin film of serous fluid is located within this cavity. These relationships are shown in Figure 8-9.

This type of "connection" between the thoracic wall, the diaphragm, and the lungs is similar to that between two thin, flat pieces of glass held together by a film of water. While each piece of glass slides easily over the other (the water lubricates the two surfaces), the force required to pull the surfaces apart is considerable. Consequently, lifting one carries the other with it. Through this fluid connection, any movements and resulting pressure changes that occur in the thorax will be reflected directly in the lungs.

Intrapulmonary and Intrapleural Pressures

Expansion of the thorax also expands the lungs. Whenever a volume of gas is suddenly expanded, the gas molecules become farther apart, reducing their pressure. Thus, during inspiration, intrapulmonary pressure is reduced below atmospheric pressure and air flows into the lungs. As air fills the lungs, intrapulmonary pressure rises, and when it is equal again to atmospheric pressure (at end-inspiration), airflow ceases. The opposite is true during expiration. Passive or active compression (or both) of the thorax raises intrapulmonary pressure above atmospheric pressure and air flows out of the lungs. At end-expiration, intrapulmonary pressure is again equal to atmospheric pressure, and there is no movement of air.

Changes in intrapleural (or intrathoracic) pressure are similar to those that take place inside the lung. However, intrapleural pressure is *always* lower than intrapulmonary and atmospheric pressures. For example, at the end-expiratory position, intrapleural pressure is about 5 mm Hg lower than atmospheric pressure. The rea-

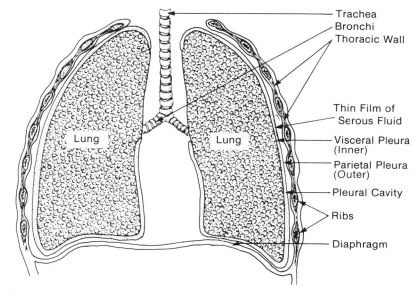

Figure 8-9. The pleural cavity.

son for this is related to the elastic tissues of the lungs and thoracic walls. You will recall that stretching these elastic tissues during quiet inspiration provides all the energy required for the subsequent expiration.

The elastic tissues of the lungs tend to collapse them, i.e., to pull them away from the thoracic wall. This creates the partial vacuum or subatmospheric pressure in the pleural cavity. If this collapsing force were not restrained by an equal and opposite force, the lungs would indeed completely collapse. Such a restraining force is presented by the elasticity of the thoracic walls. In our example (end-expiratory position), the walls of the thorax tend to spring out with the same force as that tending to collapse the lungs. In other words, the elastic forces of the thoracic walls and lungs are equal but opposite at this time. If at any time the restraining force of the thoracic wall is lost (such as would occur by the entrance of air into the pleural cavity), the lung will collapse. This is called a **pneumothorax** (p. 463).

The intrapulmonary pressure, intrapleural pressure, and lung volume changes during inspiration and expiration at rest are summarized in Figure 8-10.

Figure 8-10. Changes in intrapulmonary ("within the lungs") and intrapleural ("between the lung wall and thoracic wall") pressures and lung volume during inspiration and expiration at rest.

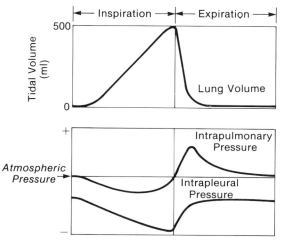

Summary

The movement of air into and out of the lungs is called pulmonary ventilation. Ventilation is composed of two phases: inspiration and expiration. Minute ventilation is the amount of air we either exhale or inhale in 1 minute. At rest, this amounts to between 4 and 15 liters. During maximal exercise, this can increase to over 150 liters. Ventilation changes before, during, and after exercise.

The anaerobic threshold is that intensity of workload or oxygen consumption in which anaerobic metabolism (lactic acid accumulation) is accelerated. It can be detected by monitoring the minute ventilation periodically during a progressive exercise test. Ventilation and carbon dioxide production increase sharply and out of proportion when the anaerobic threshold is reached.

Alveolar ventilation assures adequate oxygenation of and carbon dioxide removal from the pulmonary capillary blood. The volume of air that remains in the respiratory passages and does not participate in gas exchange is called anatomical dead space. Alveolar ventilation is dependent upon the depth and frequency of breathing and the size of the dead space.

Training improves pulmonary function, as evidenced by the fact that athletes have greater resting and exercising lung volumes than nonathletes. However, these volumes do not necessarily correlate highly with athletic performance.

Second wind is thought to be related to adjustments in ventilation and metabolism made at some time early in exercise. Its exact cause, however, is not known. Stitch in the side is a sharp pain in the rib cage that also occurs early in exercise. It may be caused by ischemia of the respiratory muscles, for which there is no simple remedy.

The principal muscles of inspiration are the diaphragm and the external intercostal muscles at rest, with added help from the scalene and sternocleidomastoid muscles during exercise. Expiration is passive during rest, and is facilitated by the abdominal and internal intercostal muscles during exercise. The strength and endurance of the respiratory muscles can be increased through exercise training programs.

At rest, the oxygen cost of ventilation is negligible. During maximal exercise, the cost increases greatly, but still is not considered to be a limiting factor to performance. On the other hand, chronic cigarette smoking can increase the oxygen cost of ventilation to a point at which it may limit exercise and athletic performance.

Air rushes into the lungs when the intrapulmonary and intrapleural pressures decrease due to contraction of the inspiratory muscles. During expiration, these pressures are reversed and air is forced out of the lung back to the environment.

Questions

1. What are the phases of ventilation and what two factors comprise the minute ventilation?
2. How much air do we expire per minute at rest and during maximal exercise?
3. Describe the nature and control of the ventilatory changes: (a) immediately before exercise, (b) during exercise, and (c) during recovery from exercise.
4. What is the anaerobic threshold, and how is it related to ventilation?
5. Define alveolar ventilation and dead space, and explain their roles in providing adequate ventilation?
6. Alveolar ventilation depends on what three factors?
7. Define the various lung volumes and discuss how each changes with exercise.
8. Discuss the possible causes of second wind and stitch in the side.
9. Name the respiratory muscles at rest and during exercise. How are they affected by exercise training programs?

10. Discuss the role of the cost of ventilation with respect to limiting athletic performance. Include the effects of cigarette smoking.
11. Describe the intrapulmonary and intrapleural pressure changes and the movement of air into and out of the lungs at rest.

References

1. Bachman, J., and Horvath, S.: Pulmonary function changes which accompany athletic conditioning programs. *Res Q.* 39: 235–239, 1968.
2. Bradley, M. E., and Leith, D. E.: Ventilatory muscle training and the oxygen cost of sustained hyperpnea. *J Appl Physiol.* 45(6):885–892, 1978.
3. Byrne-Quinn, E., Weil, J. V., Sodal, I. E., Filley, G. F., and Grover, R. F.: Ventilatory control in the athlete. *J Appl Physiol.* 30(1): 91–98, 1971.
4. Collins, D. D., Scoggin, C. H., Zwillich, C. W., and Weil, J. V.: Hereditary aspects of decreased hypoxic response. *J Clin Invest.* 21:105–110, 1978.
5. Comroe, J.: *Physiology of Respiration.* Chicago, Year Book Medical, 1974.
6. Comroe, J., Forster, R., DuBois, A., Briscoe, W., and Carlsen, E.: *The Lung,* 2nd ed. Chicago, Year Book Medical, 1962.
7. Cumming, G.: Correlation of athletic performance with pulmonary function in 13 to 17 year old boys and girls. *Med Sci Sports.* 1(3):140–143, 1969.
8. Davis, J. A., Vodak, P., Wilmore, J. H., Vodak, J., and Kurtz, P.: Anaerobic threshold and maximal aerobic power for three modes of exercise. *J Appl Physiol.* 41(4): 544–550, 1976.
9. DeJours, P.: *Respiration.* New York, Oxford University Press, 1966.
10. Grimby, G., Bunn, J., and Mead, J.: Relative contribution of rib cage and abdomen to ventilation during exercise. *J Appl Physiol.* 24(2):159–166, 1968.
11. Holmgren, A.: Cardiorespiratory determinants of cardiovascular fitness. *Can Med Assoc J.* 96:697–702, 1967.
12. Lefcoe, N., and Yuhasz, M.: The 'second wind' phenomenon in constant load exercise. *J Sports Med Phys Fit.* 11:135–138, 1971.
13. Leith, D. E., and Bradley, M. E.: Ventilatory muscle strength and endurance training. *J Appl Physiol.* 41(4):508–516, 1976.
14. Leith, D. E., Philip, B., Gabel, R., Feldman, H., and Fencl, V.: Ventilatory muscle training and ventilatory control. *Am Rev Respir Dis.* 119(2):99–100, 1979.
15. MacDougall, J. D.: The anaerobic threshold: its significance for the endurance athlete. *Can J Appl Sport Sci.* 2:137–140, 1977.
16. Martin, B. J., Sparks, K. E., Zwillich, C. W., and Weil, J. V.: Low exercise ventilation in endurance athletes. *Med Sci Sports.* 11(2): 181–185, 1979.
17. Martin, B. J., Weil, J. V., Sparks, K. E., McCullough, R. E., and Grover, R. F.: Exercise ventilation correlates positively with ventilatory chemoresponsiveness. *J Appl Physiol.* 45(4):557–564, 1978.
18. Miyamura, M., Yamashina, T., and Honda, Y.: Ventilatory responses to CO_2 rebreathing at rest and during exercise in untrained subjects and athletes. *Jap J Physiol.* 26: 245–254, 1976.
19. Otis, A.: The work of breathing. In Fenn, W., and Rahn, H. (eds.): *Handbook of Physiology.* Sec. 3, Respiration, vol. 1. Washington, D.C., American Physiological Society, 1964, p. 463.
20. Ouellet, Y., Poh, S., and Becklake, M.: Circulatory factors limiting maximal aerobic exercise capacity. *J Appl Physiol.* 27:874–880, 1969.
21. Riley, R.: Pulmonary function in relation to exercise. In Johnson, W. (ed.): *Science and Medicine of Exercise and Sports.* New York, Harper and Brothers, 1960, pp. 162–177.
22. Rode, A., and Shephard, R.: The influence of cigarette smoking upon the oxygen cost of breathing in near-maximal exercise. *Med Sci Sports.* 3(2):51–55, 1971.
23. Scoggin, C. H., Doekel, R. D., Kryger, M. H., Zwillich, C. W., and Weil, J. V.: Familial aspects of decreased hypoxic drive in endurance athletes. *J Appl Physiol.* 44(3):464–468, 1978.
24. Shephard, R.: The oxygen cost of breathing during vigorous exercise. *Q J Exp Physiol.* 51:336–350, 1966.
25. Shephard, R.: What causes second wind? *Physician Sportsmed.* 2(11):37–42, 1974.
26. Sutton, J. R., and Jones, N. L.: Control of pulmonary ventilation during exercise and mediators in the blood: CO_2 and hydrogen ion. *Med Sci Sports.* 11(2):198–203, 1979.
27. Wade, O.: Movements of the thoracic cage

and diaphragm in respiration. *J Physiol* (Lond.), 124:193-212, 1954.

28. Wasserman, K., and McIlroy, M. B.: Detecting the threshold of anaerobic metabolism. *Am J Cardiol.* 14:844-852, 1964.

29. Wasserman, K., Whipp, B. J., Koyal, S. N., and Beaver, W. L.: Anaerobic threshold and respiratory gas exchange during exercise. *J Appl Physiol.* 35(2):236-243, 1973.

30. West, J. B.: *Respiratory Physiology—The Essentials.* Baltimore, Williams and Wilkins, 1974, p. 4.

SELECTED READINGS

American College of Sports Medicine: Symposium on ventilatory control during exercise. *Med Sci Sports.* 11(2):190-226, 1979.

Campbell, E.: *The Respiratory Muscles and Mechanics of Breathing.* Chicago, Year Book Medical, 1958.

Dempsey, J. A., and Reed, C. E. (eds.): *Muscular Exercise and the Lung.* Madison, Wisconsin, University of Wisconsin Press, 1977.

Dressendorfer, R. H., Wade, C. E., and Bernauer, E. M.: Combined effects of breathing resistance and hyperoxia on aerobic work tolerance. *J Appl Physiol.* 42(3):444-448, 1977.

Grimby, G.: Respiration in exercise. *Med Sci Sports.* 1(1):9-14, 1969.

Guyton, A. C.: *Textbook of Medical Physiology,* 5th ed. Philadelphia, W. B. Saunders, 1976, pp. 516-529.

Milic-Emili, J., Petit, J., and Deroanne, R.: Mechanical work of breathing during exercise in trained and untrained subjects. *J Appl Physiol.* 17:43-46, 1962.

Roussos, C., Fixley, M., Gross, D., and Macklem, P. T.: Fatigue of inspiratory muscles and their synergic behavior. *J Appl Physiol.* 46(5):897-904, 1979.

West, J. B.: *Respiratory Physiology—The Essentials.* Baltimore, Williams and Wilkins, 1974.

chapter 9

Gas Exchange and Transport

The major concepts to be learned from this chapter are as follows:

- Gas exchange between the lungs and blood (alveolar-capillary membrane) and between the blood and tissues (tissue-capillary membrane) takes place through diffusion, a physical process involving the random movement of molecules.
- The single most important factor affecting gas diffusion is the partial pressure gradient of the gases involved. Partial pressure refers to the pressure exerted by a single gas in a gas mixture or in a liquid.
- The partial pressure of oxygen is highest in the lungs and lowest in the tissues, whereas the partial pressure of carbon dioxide is highest in the tissues and lowest in the lungs.
- Diffusion of a gas always takes place from an area of higher to an area of lower partial pressure.

- During exercise, the diffusion of oxygen and carbon dioxide across the alveolar-capillary and tissue-capillary membranes increases.
- Oxygen and carbon dioxide are transported by the blood, mainly in chemical combination with hemoglobin.

We saw from the last chapter that pulmonary ventilation (more accurately, alveolar ventilation) supplies the alveoli with fresh air, which is high in oxygen and low in carbon dioxide. Venous blood, on the other hand, is low in oxygen and high in carbon dioxide. Thus, gas exchange between the air in the alveoli and the venous blood (referred to as the alveolar-capillary membrane) loads and unloads the blood with oxygen and carbon dioxide, respectively. After transportation via the circulation, oxygen and carbon dioxide are again exchanged, this time between the tissues (e.g., muscle) and the arterial blood (the tissue-capillary membrane). Here oxygen in the blood is given up to the tissues and carbon dioxide in the tissues is given up to the blood. It is the main purpose of this chapter to study both how the gases are exchanged and how they are carried in the blood.

Gas Exchange—Diffusion

Gas exchange at the alveolar-capillary and tissue-capillary membranes takes place through the physical process of diffusion. **Diffusion** can be defined as the random movement of molecules—in this case, gas molecules. This random movement (sometimes called Brownian motion) is caused by the kinetic energy of the molecules. *Gases tend to diffuse from an area of higher concentration to one of lower concentration.*

Partial Pressure of Gases

We need at this time to delve a bit further into the concept of diffusion. Specifically, we need to know what the **partial pressures** of oxygen (PO_2) and carbon dioxide (PCO_2) mean with respect to gas exchange. Gases consist of discrete particles or molecules. These tiny molecules, although separated by relatively large distances, will occasionally collide with each other (and with the walls of their container) because, as just indicated, each molecule is in a state of random motion. The pressure exerted by a gas is dependent on the number of such collisions; e.g., the greater the number of collisions, the greater the pressure will be. The term "partial pressure" is used to express the pressure of each gas in a gas mixture, such as exists in the alveoli or in a liquid, such as the blood.

Partial Pressure of Gases in a Gas Mixture

From what we have said thus far, a higher partial pressure of a gas represents an area of greater molecular activity than does an area in which the partial pressure of that same gas is lower. This means that gases will diffuse from an area of higher to an area of lower partial pressure. The same is true concerning concentration differences; a greater concentration of gas represents greater molecular activity than does one of lower concentration. The relationship between concentration and partial pressure of a gas in a gas mixture is shown in Figure 9-1. Container *A* holds 100% oxygen. The PO_2 is 760 mm Hg, the same as the total (barometric) pressure since oxygen is the only gas present. Container *B* holds an equal volume of mixed gases, 20% O_2 and 80% N_2, which is also at a total pressure of 760 mm Hg. Each of the gases in the mixture will exert a pressure proportional to its respective concentration, the sum of which will equal the total pressure. In other words, the PO_2 and PN_2 are the same as

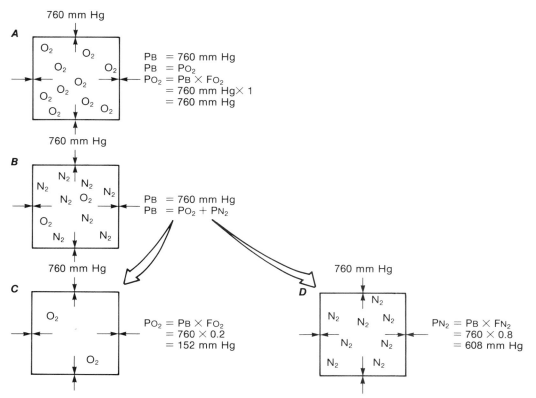

Figure 9-1. Partial pressure of gases in a gas mixture. The partial pressure of a gas is equal to the barometric pressure (P_B) times the fractional concentration of that gas. In container *A*, the partial pressure of oxygen (PO_2) is equal to P_B because it makes up the entire volume (100%); i.e., its fractional concentration (FO_2) is 1.00. In a mixture, such as the O_2 and N_2 in container *B*, each gas exerts a partial pressure proportional to its concentration as though it alone, *C* and *D*, occupied the entire volume. In this case, $PO_2 + PN_2 = P_B$.

those which each gas would exert if it alone occupied the entire container. If oxygen alone occupied the entire container (Fig. 9-1*C*), the number of collisions would be only 20% of that possible in Figure 9-1*A*, and the PO_2 would be correspondingly reduced to 20% of 760 mm Hg (760 × 0.2), or 152 mm Hg. The same holds true for nitrogen, as shown in container *D*; i.e., the PN_2 is given by 80% of 760 (760 × 0.8), or 608 mm Hg. The sum of the two partial pressures equals the total pressure.

The partial pressure of a gas in a gas mixture is, then, dependent on (1) the total (barometric) pressure and (2) the fractional concentration of that gas. If at any time either of these is changed independently of the other, the partial pressure will also change. *The most important factor determining gas exchange is the partial pressure gradients of the gases involved.* For example, you shall see in Chapter 17 that the concentration of oxygen at altitude is the same as that at sea level. However, since the total pressure is lower, the P_{O_2} is lower and the taking up of oxygen in the blood is reduced. By the same token, increasing total pressure without reducing the concentration of oxygen (as in scuba diving with air) can increase the P_{O_2} to toxic levels.

Partial Pressure of Gases in a Liquid (Blood)

As mentioned before, gases dissolved in a liquid, such as blood, also exert a partial pressure. This process is illustrated in Figure 9-2 as follows: When the liquid in container A is first exposed to a gas mixture in which the P_{O_2} is equal to 100 mm Hg, the oxygen molecules in the gas phase continually strike the surface of the liquid, with some of them entering the liquid. Those gas molecules that enter the liquid are said to be dissolved in the liquid. Since the process is just beginning, however, not many oxygen molecules have had time to enter the liquid, and the P_{O_2} in the liquid is still zero. Given more time, more oxygen molecules will dissolve in the liquid (container B). Not only are the gas molecules from the gas mixture striking the surface from above and entering the liquid, but also the gas molecules dissolved in the liquid are striking from below the surface and entering the gas mixture. In other words, there is an exchange of the oxygen molecules in the gas mixture with those in the liquid. In our example (container B), only half as many oxygen molecules are escaping from the liquid to the gas mixture as are escaping from the gas mixture to the liquid. Therefore, the P_{O_2} in the liquid (50 mm Hg) is half of that in the gas mixture (100 mm Hg). After a sufficient amount of time (container C), the number of oxygen molecules escaping from the gas mixture to the liquid and from the liquid to the gas mixture will be equal, and the P_{O_2} in both phases will also be equal at 100 mm Hg. At this point, the liquid is *saturated* with the gas, and the gas molecules in both phases are said to be in *equilibrium*.

Figure 9-2. Partial pressure of gases in liquids. The liquid in the container is exposed to a gas mixture with a P_{O_2} of 100 mm Hg. In container A, the process of equilibration has just begun and the P_{O_2} of the liquid is still zero. In container B, the process is half completed and the P_{O_2} of the liquid is 50 mm Hg. In container C, equilibration is complete and the P_{O_2} of the liquid is 100 mm Hg, the same as that of the gas mixture. For further explanation, see text. (Modified and redrawn from Guyton.[3])

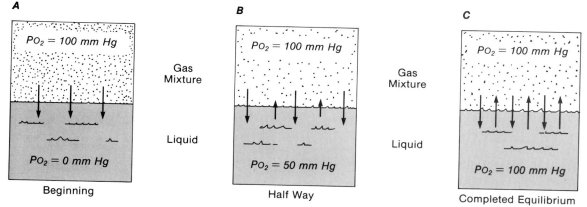

Just as in a gas mixture, the most important factor determining diffusion of a gas in a liquid is the partial pressure gradients of the gases involved. This also applies to the diffusion of gases from a gas mixture to a liquid and vice versa (e.g., the alveolar-capillary membrane).

PO_2 and PCO_2 Gradients in the Body

As emphasized previously, in order for oxygen to diffuse from the alveoli ultimately into the tissues, the PO_2 must be higher in the former than in the latter; i.e., a pressure gradient must exist. The opposite is true for carbon dioxide to diffuse into the blood; i.e.,

the PCO_2 gradient must decrease from the tissues to the alveoli. This is shown in Figure 9-3A. The decrease in PO_2 from inspired to tracheal air results from addition of water vapor as air enters the respiratory passages. The partial pressure of water vapor (PH_2O) at body temperature is 47 mm Hg and is independent of the total pressure (see Appendix C). Therefore, the pressure available for oxygen, carbon dioxide, and nitrogen (not shown) is $760 - 47$ mm Hg, or 713 mm Hg, and the PO_2 is decreased by about 10 mm Hg. The PCO_2 is less affected by PH_2O because its concentration in inspired air is negligible. As moist air enters the alveoli, the PO_2 decreases and the PCO_2

Figure 9-3. PO_2 and PCO_2 gradients and gas exchange. A, the PO_2 and PCO_2 of inspired air, tracheal air, alveolar gas, venous and arterial blood, and tissue (skeletal muscle) are shown. Exchange (via diffusion) of these gases at the alveolar-capillary and tissue-capillary membranes is always from an area of higher to one of lower partial pressure.

Illustration continued on the following page.

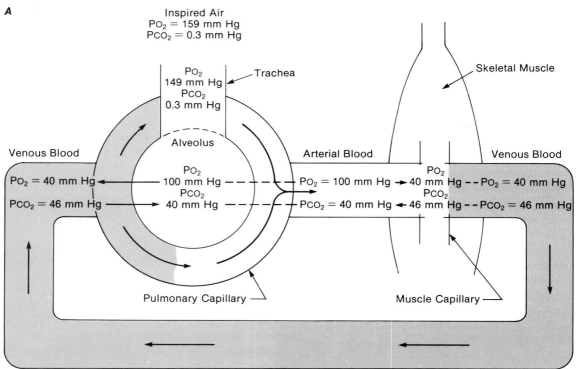

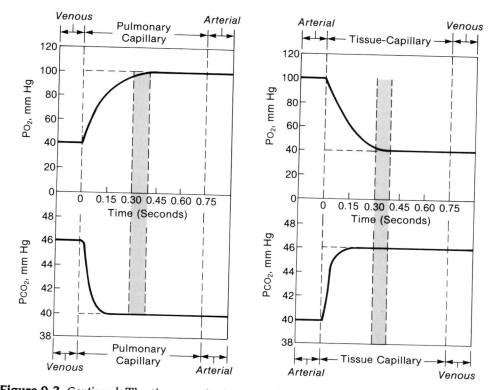

Figure 9-3. *Continued* The time required to complete these exchanges is shown in *B*. At rest, blood remains in the pulmonary and tissue capillaries for about 0.75 second and during maximal exercise between 0.3 and 0.4 seconds (shaded area).

increases markedly. This results from dilution by the rather large functional reserve volume (p. 212), in which the PO_2 and PCO_2 are about 98 and 40 mm Hg, respectively. After mixing, alveolar PO_2 averages 100 mm Hg and PCO_2, 40 mm Hg. The partial pressures of oxygen and carbon dioxide in the mixed venous blood perfusing the alveoli are 40 and 46 mm Hg, respectively.

The partial pressure differences between gases in the alveoli and in venous blood mean that oxygen will diffuse into venous blood and carbon dioxide into the alveoli. Consequently, venous blood PO_2 increases and PCO_2 decreases to values approximating those in the alveoli; venous blood is thus arterialized. Blood remains in

the pulmonary capillaries for about 0.75 second under resting conditions, as shown in Figure 9-3*B*. However, the transition from venous to arterial blood is virtually completed within half that time (shaded area). This corresponds to about the length of time blood remains in the pulmonary capillaries during maximal exercise. The PO_2 and PCO_2 of arterial blood during exercise, then, are maintained or are only slightly reduced, compared with resting values, even though the velocity of blood coursing through the capillaries is greatly increased.

A similar situation exists at the tissue-capillary membranes (Fig. 9-3*A*). The PO_2 of arterial blood is higher than that in the tissues and oxygen diffuses from blood to tissue. The opposite is true for carbon dioxide; the higher PCO_2 in the tissues promotes diffusion of carbon dioxide from the tissues to the blood. Consequently, arterial blood is changed back to venous blood and the entire process of gas exchange is repeated over and over. Presumably, the transition from arterial to venous blood also occurs within a few tenths of a second, and is the exact opposite of the transition from venous to arterial blood (Fig. 9-3B). It should be mentioned that the greater the metabolic activity of the tissue, the lower will be the PO_2 and the higher the PCO_2 in venous blood draining that particular tissue. For example, during exercise the PO_2 will be lower and the PCO_2 higher in the venous blood from an active skeletal muscle than in venous blood from an inactive tissue, such as the kidney or skin.

Other Factors Affecting Gas Exchange

Besides partial pressure gradient, gas exchange can be affected by several other factors. These include (1) the length of the diffusion path; (2) the number of red blood cells or their hemoglobin concentration, or both; and (3) the surface area available for diffusion. Figure 9-4A depicts the diffusion path for oxygen and carbon dioxide at the alveolar-capillary and tissue-capillary membranes. Normally, it is very short, even during exercise. Membrane fibrosis and interstitial edema caused by certain diseases lengthen the path, and diffusion is impaired. You will notice that the diffusion pathways include red blood cells, the transporting vehicles for both oxygen and carbon dioxide. Therefore, variations in their number would obviously affect overall gas exchange.

The surface area available for diffusion at the alveolar-capillary membranes is determined by the number of functional capillaries in contact with ventilated al-

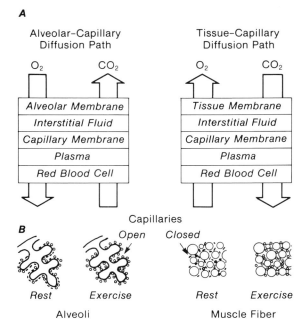

Figure 9-4. *A,* Diffusion paths of O_2 and CO_2 at the alveolar-capillary (left) and tissue-capillary (right) membranes. Normally, the lengths of these paths do not limit diffusion. *B,* Surface area available for diffusion at these membranes is determined by the number of open capillaries in contact with ventilated alveoli (left) and muscle fibers (right). Note the large increase in open capillaries during exercise.

veoli. For example, in Figure 9-4B, the alveoli on the left side of the diagram are all open and are thus ventilated, but not all the capillaries supplying them are open. This is probably a normal situation under resting conditions. An increase in surface area and in diffusion capacity during exercise might occur by increasing the number of open capillaries. In a similar manner, the diffusing surface at the tissue-capillary membranes may be increased by increasing the number of functional tissue capillaries. It has been estimated that an actively contracting muscle has at least 10 times as many open capillaries as a resting muscle (Fig. 9-4B).

Diffusion Capacity during Exercise

We just indicated that during exercise there is an increase in surface area and thus in the diffusion of oxygen and carbon dioxide across both the alveolar-capillary and tissue-capillary membranes. The diffusion capacity for oxygen at the alveolar-capillary membrane is shown in Figure 9-5 for trained and untrained young men. This same pattern of change with exercise also applies to trained and untrained females; however, the diffusion values are of somewhat lower magnitude.[4] Diffusion capacity is defined as the volume of gas that diffuses through the membrane each minute for a pressure difference of 1 mm Hg (ml/min/mm Hg). It can be seen that the diffusion capacity for oxygen increases in nearly a linear (straight-line) manner with increasing exercise loads, leveling off at near maximal efforts.

The trained athletes indicated in Figure 9-5 were male swimmers. In general, it can be said that athletes tend to have larger diffusion capacities at rest and during exercise than nonathletes. This is particularly true for endurance athletes. For example, in Figure 9-6, notice that the diffusion capacity of marathon runners at rest is almost as high as that for untrained men during maximal exercise.[5] Likewise, during maximal exercise the diffusion capacities of oarsmen[10] and endurance swimmers[6,8] are much higher than their untrained counterparts. It is thought that diffusion capacity *per se* is not directly affected by training,[8-10] but, rather, training induces larger lung volumes (p. 212) and thus, in turn, provides a greater alveolar-capillary surface area.[6]

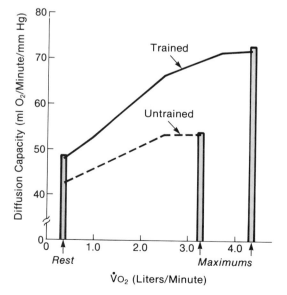

Figure 9-5. The pulmonary diffusing capacity for O_2 increases during exercise in both trained and untrained subjects. (Based on data from Magel and Andersen.[6])

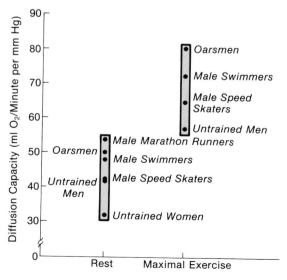

Figure 9-6. In general, the pulmonary diffusing capacity for O_2 in athletes, particularly endurance athletes, is greater at rest and during maximal exercise compared to nonathletes. (Data for untrained females from Fox et al.[2]; untrained males and swimmers from Magel and Andersen[6] and Newman et al.[8]; speed skaters from Maksud et al.[7]; oarsmen from Reuschlein et al.[10]; and marathon runners from Kaufmann et al.[5])

Gas Transport

The oxygen that diffuses from the alveoli to the pulmonary-capillary blood is transported to the tissues, where it is consumed. By the same token, the carbon dioxide that diffuses from the tissues to the tissue-capillary blood is transported to the alveoli, from where it is exhaled. The transport of these gases is the primary function of the cardiovascular or circulatory system. The circulating liquid of this system, the blood, serves as the transport vehicle, the blood vessels act as highways, and the heart provides the force which constantly keeps the blood circulating throughout the lungs and various tissues of the body.

Transport of Oxygen by Blood

Oxygen is carried both by **plasma** (the liquid portion of the blood) and by **hemoglobin** contained in red blood cells. Oxygen that diffuses into plasma does not undergo any chemical reactions; rather, it is *dissolved* in plasma and is carried in physical solution. The amount carried in this way is, under normal conditions, very small. On the other hand, oxygen that diffuses into the red blood cells *combines chemically* with hemoglobin (Hb) to form what is called **oxyhemoglobin (HbO$_2$).** This binding process increases the oxygen carrying capacity of blood by about 65 times.

Dissolved Oxygen

The *solubility* (dissolving power) of oxygen in plasma is relatively low. Therefore, very little dissolved oxygen can be transported by plasma to the tissues. For example, at rest, dissolved oxygen contributes only 3 to 4% of the total of 250 to 300 ml of oxygen required per minute. The percentage is even lower during maximal exercise, when it constitutes less than 2% of the total oxygen required by the working muscles. The amount of oxygen dissolved in plasma is dependent not only on its solubility, but, as mentioned before, also on its partial pressure. However, even if arterial PO$_2$ is increased by breathing pure oxygen, the amount of oxygen dissolved would still supply only 38% of the total oxygen required at rest and 12% during maximal exercise.

The role played by dissolved oxygen in meeting tissue oxygen demands is therefore not very impressive. What physiological role, if any, does it then play? We can answer this question by first saying that the partial pressure of oxygen in both venous and arterial blood results from the oxygen that is dissolved in plasma. Second, a similar situation exists at the tissues; i.e., tissue PO$_2$ results from the oxygen dissolved in the tissue fluids. The importance of PO$_2$ in gas exchange has already been pointed out. Later, you will see that decreases in arterial and tissue PO$_2$ (such as those that occur at altitude) cause increases in ventilation and red blood cell production, respectively. Both of these changes increase the overall oxygen-carrying capacity of the blood when it is vitally needed. These examples illustrate why the concept of dissolved oxygen is an important consideration; its significance is equally great under conditions of exercise and rest.

Oxyhemoglobin (HbO$_2$)

The hemoglobin found in red blood cells is a complex molecule containing *iron* (heme) and *protein* (globin). This is shown schematically in Figure 9-7. Hemoglobin's affinity for or ability to combine with oxygen is related to the heme component. Each heme group, of which there are four in each hemoglobin molecule, is capable of combining chemically with one O$_2$ molecule. This means that one Hb molecule is capable of maximally combining with four O$_2$ molecules, i.e.:

$$Hb_4 + 4\,O_2 \rightleftharpoons Hb_4(O_2)_4$$

More simply we can write:

$$Hb + O_2 \rightleftharpoons HbO_2$$

In terms of amount, this turns out to be 1.34 ml of O_2 per gram of Hb. Thus, one gram of Hb becomes *saturated* with O_2 when it combines with 1.34 ml of O_2.

O_2 capacity of Hb. Once we know both the saturation point of hemoglobin and the Hb concentration in blood, we can calculate what is referred to as the **O_2 capacity of Hb:**

O_2 capacity of Hb (ml O_2/100 ml blood)
= Hb concentration (grams Hb/100 ml blood)
    $\times$ (1.34 ml O_2/gram Hb)

Figure 9-7. The hemoglobin molecule is composed of a protein called globin and four iron-containing groups called heme. Oxygen is carried by the heme groups, and carbon dioxide is carried by globin.

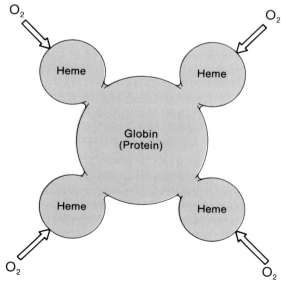

Hemoglobin concentration is determined by rupturing the red blood cells so that Hb dissolves uniformly in the fluid portion of the blood sample. The amount of light passed through this fluid is inversely related to the amount of Hb present. At rest and at sea level, there are about 15 grams of Hb present in every 100 ml of blood (for males, 16 grams per 100 ml, and for females, 14 grams per 100 ml). Therefore, under these conditions, the O_2 capacity of Hb is $15 \times 1.34 = 20.1$ ml O_2/100 ml blood, or 20.1 volumes per cent.*

During exercise, the Hb concentration of blood increases anywhere from 5 to 10%. This is so, at least in part, because fluid shifts from the blood into the active muscle cells, and *hemoconcentration* results.[1] It is exaggerated during prolonged work in the heat because of further shifts of fluids from the blood to the cell due to excessive sweating. A 10% hemoconcentration during exercise means that there will be about 16.5 grams of Hb per 100 ml blood instead of the normal 15 grams. The O_2 capacity of Hb would in this case increase from 20.1 to 22.1 volumes per cent, a definitely advantageous change.

Per cent saturation of Hb. There is one more concept concerning Hb that we need to discuss at this time. This is the **per cent saturation of Hb with O_2,** abbreviated **%So$_2$.** It relates the amount of O_2 *actually* combined with Hb to the O_2 capacity of Hb:

$$\%SO_2 = \frac{O_2 \text{ actually combined with Hb}}{O_2 \text{ capacity of Hb}} \times 100$$

For example, if your O_2 capacity is 20 volumes per cent and the amount of oxygen actually combined with Hb is 10 vol-

---

*Volumes per cent (vol %) in this case means milliliters of O_2 per 100 ml blood.

umes per cent, then %SO$_2$ is 10/20 × 100 = 50%. A %SO$_2$ of 100 means that the O$_2$ actually combined with Hb is equal to the O$_2$ capacity of Hb. Use of %SO$_2$ takes into account individual variations in Hb concentration. The hemoconcentration that occurs during exercise is a good example. In this case, if %SO$_2$ is 50%, then the amount of O$_2$ actually combined with Hb would be 22 × 0.5 = 11 volumes per cent, rather than 10 volumes per cent. The increase in number of red blood cells, and thus in Hb concentration, during acclimatization to altitude (p. 469) is also another good example of why %SO$_2$ is used.

The Oxyhemoglobin Dissociation (or Association) Curve

Up to now, we have neglected the factors that affect the saturation of Hb with O$_2$. Actually, there are four such factors: (1) the partial pressure of oxygen in the blood; (2) the temperature of the blood; (3) the pH (acidity) of the blood; and (4) the amount of carbon dioxide in the blood. The first of these factors, the PO$_2$ of blood, is of course paramount. However, we will see shortly that the other three factors are also extremely important, particularly during exercise.

The relationships of these factors to %SO$_2$ are shown in Figure 9-8. The amount of O$_2$ combined with Hb at the various per cent saturations is also shown, on the right ordinate. These values are based on a Hb concentration of 15 grams per 100 ml of blood. Such curves are called **oxyhemoglobin (HbO$_2$) dissociation curves.** (They may also be called association curves, but are preferably referred to as dissociation curves.) Use of the HbO$_2$ dissociation curve tells us a great deal about gas transport. Let us see just what kinds of information it can tell us.

The HbO$_2$ curve at rest. We can start with the single curve shown in Figure

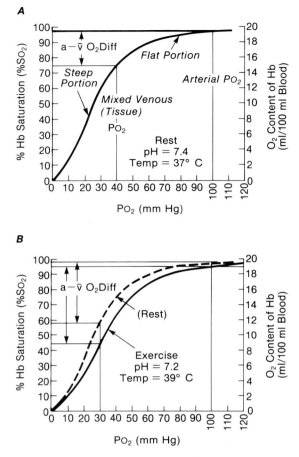

Figure 9-8. Oxygen transport. The oxyhemoglobin dissociation curve: *A,* at rest and, *B,* during exercise. Such curves give the relationship between PO$_2$ and how much oxygen associates or dissociates with hemoglobin. During exercise, the curve "shifts" downward and to the right and facilitates the diffusion of oxygen into muscle. For further explanation, see text.

9-8*A.* This curve is applicable under normal resting conditions, i.e., with blood pH of 7.4, and with temperature of 37°C. Also, keep in mind that at rest the arterial blood PO$_2$ is 100 mm Hg, whereas the mixed venous blood PO$_2$ is 40 mm Hg. The first two things we should notice are that the higher the PO$_2$, the greater is the *associa-*

tion of O_2 with Hb (HbO_2); and the lower the PO_2, the greater is the *dissociation* of O_2 from Hb (Hb + O_2). For example, at a PO_2 of 100 mm Hg, the Hb in arterial blood is 97.5% saturated with O_2. In terms of amount, arterial blood holds 20 × 0.975 = 19.5 volumes per cent of O_2. Therefore, this amount of O_2 is transported to the tissues by each 100 ml of arterial blood flowing to them.* At a PO_2 of 40 mm Hg, venous blood returning from the various tissues is only 75% saturated; it then holds 20 × 0.75 = 15 volumes per cent of O_2. The difference between the two, called the **arteriovenous oxygen difference (a-$\bar{v}O_2$ diff),** represents how much oxygen is extracted or consumed by the tissues from each 100 ml of blood perfusing them. In our present example, the a-$\bar{v}O_2$ diff is 19.5 − 15.0 = 4.5 ml of O_2 per 100 ml of blood flow. Most of the oxygen transported by Hb during rest is thus kept in reserve. This will come in handy during exercise, as we shall soon see.

The third thing we should notice is the shape of the curve. The upper part of the curve is almost flat. This means that a large change in PO_2 in this portion of the curve is associated with only a small change in the amount of O_2 held by Hb. For example, if arterial blood PO_2 were *increased* from the normal 100 mm Hg (as by breathing pure O_2 at sea level), only 0.5 volume per cent of O_2 is added to Hb. This plus the additional dissolved O_2 represent only an 11% increase in the amount of O_2 transported to the tissues. This serves to point out that, normally, arterial PO_2 is maintained at close to optimal levels. Use of pure O_2 at sea level during exercise,

therefore, will not greatly increase O_2 transport. On the other hand, if arterial PO_2 were *decreased,* e.g., from 100 to 70 mm Hg (as by ascent to altitude), %SO_2 would decrease from 97.5 to only 93%, a difference of 1 ml of O_2/100 ml blood. In this case, the flat upper part of the curve indicates protection against inadequate oxygenation of blood despite large decreases in PO_2. During maximal exercise (at sea level), arterial blood PO_2 rarely decreases by more than 5 mm Hg.

The steep middle and lower portions of the curve likewise reflect protective functions, but of a different kind. In this portion of the curve (below a PO_2 of about 50 mm Hg), a small change in PO_2 is associated with a large change in Hb saturation. Therefore, a small decrease in *tissue* PO_2 enables the tissues to extract a relatively large amount of O_2. For example, if tissue PO_2 decreased from 40 to 10 mm Hg, %SO_2 decreases from 75 to 13%, respectively, a difference of 13.5 ml of O_2 per 100 ml blood that can be extracted by the tissues. The steep middle and lower portions of the curve, then, protect the tissues by favoring dissociation of O_2 from Hb despite small decreases in PO_2. During exercise, it has been shown that the PO_2 of active skeletal muscles may be lower than 5 mm Hg.

The HbO_2 curve during exercise. A fourth consideration is how pH, temperature, and CO_2 affect the HbO_2 dissociation curve. Increases in blood acidity (which decreases pH), temperature, and CO_2 cause a shift of the HbO_2 dissociation curve to the right.[11,12] This is shown in Figure 9-8*B* (solid line). The curve represented by the dashed line is the same as that in Figure 9-8*A,* and is included as a basis for comparison. During exercise, increased CO_2 and lactic acid production lowers blood pH and increased heat production raises body temperature. Therefore, the "shifted" curve in Figure 9-8*B,* is applicable under exercise conditions.

---

*The *total* amount of O_2 transported to the tissues per 100 ml of blood flow is 19.8 volumes per cent; 19.5 volumes per cent via HbO_2 plus 0.3 volume per cent dissolved in plasma. For the total O_2 content of arterial and venous blood at rest and during exercise, see Table 9-1, page 240.

What does this shift mean? A close look at the curve reveals that the greatest amount of shift occurs in the steep middle and lower portions, e.g., between 20 and 50 mm Hg P_{O_2}. On the other hand, between 90 and 100 mm Hg P_{O_2}, very little shift occurs. During exercise, these changes are extremely important for two reasons: (1) because more O_2 is made available to the tissues at a given tissue P_{O_2}, and (2) because the loading of blood with O_2 is not greatly affected. For example, suppose that during exercise arterial blood P_{O_2} equaled 100 mm Hg, and mixed venous blood P_{O_2} equaled 30 mm Hg. If there were no shift in the HbO_2 dissociation curve, the a-$\bar{v}O_2$ diff—i.e., the amount of O_2 given up to the tissues—would be $19.5 - 11.6 = 7.9$ ml per 100 ml of blood flow. With the shift to the right, as indicated in Figure 9-8*B*, the a-$\bar{v}O_2$ diff would be $19.0 - 8.8 = 10.2$ ml of O_2 per 100 ml of blood. This represents nearly a 30% increase in the amount of O_2 available to the tissues. During maximal exercise, this shift plus the greatly lowered P_{O_2} of the active muscles may increase the a-$\bar{v}O_2$ diff 3 to 3.5 times that at rest (Fig. 9-9).

HbO_2 and Cigarette Smoking. In the last chapter, the effect of cigarette smoking on airway resistance was mentioned. Cigarette smoking also affects the amount of oxygen that can be carried by hemoglobin. One of the by-products of smoke from a burning cigarette is *carbon monoxide* (CO). Carbon monoxide has a 210 to 250 times higher affinity for Hb than does oxygen. This means that the partial pressure of CO need be only $\frac{1}{250}$ of that of O_2 in order to combine equally with Hb. Therefore, when both CO and O_2 are present, such as would be the case when a smoker inhales after taking a puff, CO is much quicker to combine with Hb. Once CO has combined with Hb, it is not possible for HbO_2 to be formed, because CO combines with the same chemical unit of Hb (heme) that ordinarily would combine with oxy-

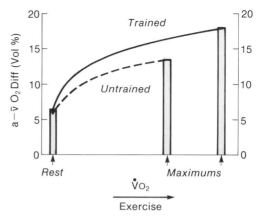

Figure 9-9. Effects of exercise on arteriovenous oxygen difference (a-$\bar{v}O_2$ diff) for trained and untrained subjects. During exercise, the muscles extract a greater amount of O_2 from a given quantity of arterial blood. Training improves this capacity.

gen. As a result, the oxygen-carrying capacity of blood is reduced. In heavy, chronic smokers, the reduction can amount to as much as 10%.

Transport of Carbon Dioxide by Blood

Like oxygen, carbon dioxide is carried by the blood in physical solution (dissolved) and in chemical combination. Also, as in O_2 transport, the amount of dissolved CO_2 constitutes only a small percentage (about 5%) of the total transported; the majority (95%) is carried in chemical combination. However, the chemical reactions that CO_2 undergoes (principally in the red blood cells) are quite different from those of oxygen. In blood, CO_2 reacts chemically with water to form a weak acid, **carbonic acid,** and with blood proteins (principally, the globin of Hb) to form **carbamino compounds.**

Dissolved Carbon Dioxide

What was said concerning dissolved O_2 is also applicable to dissolved CO_2. Briefly:

1. The amount of CO_2 dissolved in blood (arterial and venous) and in tissues is dependent on its solubility and partial pressure.
2. Dissolved CO_2 is relatively unimportant as a transporting mechanism.
3. Dissolved CO_2 determines blood and tissue P_{CO_2} and therefore is important in cardiorespiratory regulating mechanisms.

Transport of CO_2 in Chemical Combination

By far the majority of CO_2 is transported in chemical combination. As was previously mentioned, CO_2 combines with blood water to form carbonic acid, and with blood proteins to form carbamino compounds.

Carbonic acid and the bicarbonate ion. As CO_2 diffuses into tissue-capillary blood, it immediately reacts with water in plasma and red blood cells to form carbonic acid (H_2CO_3) according to the following reaction:

$$CO_2 + H_2O \rightleftharpoons H_2CO_3$$

In order for this reaction to occur with any great speed, an enzyme called **carbonic anhydrase** is required. In plasma, this enzyme is absent, but in red blood cells, it is highly concentrated. Therefore, the formation of carbonic acid takes place principally within the red blood cells.

As quickly as carbonic acid is formed, it ionizes; i.e., it dissociates into a *hydrogen ion (H+)* and a **bicarbonate ion (HCO_3^-)** as follows:

$$H_2CO_3 \rightleftharpoons H^+ + HCO_3^-$$

The complete reaction, then, is more accurately written as:

$$CO_2 + H_2O \rightleftharpoons H_2CO_3 \rightleftharpoons H^+ + HCO_3^-$$

Thus, as shown by this reaction, CO_2 is carried in the blood in the form of bicarbonate ions. The double arrows in the equation mean that the reactions are reversible. It proceeds to the right as CO_2 is added (by diffusion) to tissue-capillary blood, and it proceeds to the left when CO_2 diffuses from the blood into the alveoli. The *formation* of HCO_3^- occurs mostly within the red cell because of the presence of carbonic anhydrase, as mentioned earlier. However, HCO_3^- is *transported* primarily by plasma. This is because as the concentration of HCO_3^- increases in the red cell (but not in plasma) it diffuses into the plasma.*

The H^+ ions formed when H_2CO_3 dissociates will increase the acidity of venous blood if they are not buffered. (This is one of the reasons why an increase in CO_2 production is associated with an increase in acidity.) The small amount of free H^+ ions formed in plasma are buffered, i.e., taken out of circulation, by plasma proteins. Inside the red cell, where most of the H^+ ions are formed, Hb serves as the buffer. It is interesting to note that Hb is a better buffer than is HbO_2. This means that, as O_2 dissociates from Hb and diffuses into the tissues, buffering of H^+ ions is facilitated. In turn, more HCO_3^- can be formed and more CO_2 carried without a substantial change in blood acidity. Furthermore, remember that an increase in blood acidity shifts the HbO_2 dissociation curve to the right. This favors not only the release of O_2 for tissue use, but also the presence of Hb, which is the better buffer. The increases in both O_2 consumption and CO_2 production during exercise point out the importance of these mutually beneficial changes.

More about acid-base balance and buf-

---

*As HCO_3^- diffuses from the red cell into plasma, chloride ion (Cl$^-$) diffuses from plasma into the red cell. This is called the "chloride shift" and serves to maintain the ionic balance between the red cell and the plasma.

fering mechanisms can be found in Chapter 21 (p. 596).

Carbamino compounds. Plasma proteins and Hb, besides serving as buffers, also play another important role in CO_2 transport. This role involves their direct chemical reaction with CO_2, forming what are referred to as carbamino compounds. In these reactions, H^+ ions are also formed and must be buffered, as we previously described.

Formation of carbamino compounds takes place mainly in the red blood cells, by the reaction of CO_2 with Hb. In this case, the carbamino compound formed is called **carbaminohemoglobin.** Inside the red cells, CO_2 reacts with the protein fraction (globin) of the Hb molecule and *not* with the heme, or iron, group, as is the case with O_2. This means that Hb is capable of chemically combining with, and thus transporting, O_2 and CO_2 simultaneously. However, Hb is capable of combining with more CO_2 than HbO_2 can. Therefore, as in the case of the bicarbonate ion mechanism, the unloading of O_2 to the tissues facilitates the loading of CO_2 in tissue-capillary blood, and vice versa.

The transport mechanisms for CO_2 as it diffuses from the tissues into tissue-capillary blood are summarized in Figure 9-10. It should be remembered that as CO_2 diffuses from the pulmonary-capillary blood to the alveoli, all reactions are reversed, and free CO_2 is exhaled. For example, as previously mentioned, the diffusion of CO_2 carried in the form of the bicarbonate ion from the blood to the alveoli occurs as the last reaction given on page 237 proceeds from right to left.

The carbon dioxide dissociation curve. As should be expected, the partial pressure of carbon dioxide determines the total amount of CO_2 combined with the blood regardless of whether it is in the form of bicarbonate ions, carbamino compounds, or simply dissolved. The relationship of the P_{CO_2} and the total CO_2 content

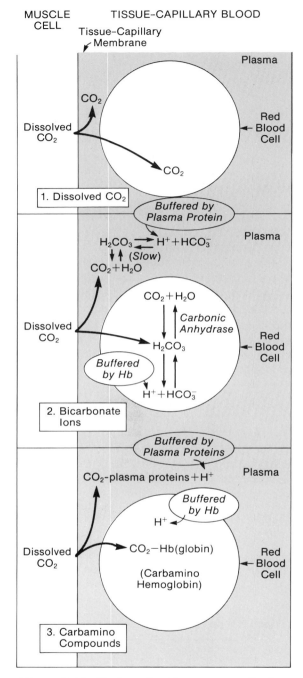

Figure 9-10. Carbon dioxide transport. Carbon dioxide is transported in physical solution as dissolved CO_2 (1) and in chemical combination as bicarbonate ions (2) and carbamino compounds (3).

of the blood is called the **carbon dioxide dissociation curve** and is shown in Figure 9-11. Notice that its shape is somewhat different and its physiological range narrower than the O_2 dissociation curve. However, its interpretation is the same; i.e., as the P_{CO_2} increases, the total amount of CO_2 combined with the blood also increases.

Total O_2 and CO_2 Contents of Blood

The O_2 and CO_2 contents of blood at rest and during heavy exercise are shown in Table 9-1. As can be seen, gas transport *per unit volume of blood flow* (in this case, per 100 ml of blood) increases during exercise. Some of the mechanisms facilitating this increase have already been pointed out. However, these changes alone cannot fully account for the large increases in O_2 consumed and CO_2 produced by the working muscles on a *per unit of time basis*. For example, as indicated in Table 9-1, $\dot{V}O_2$ at rest is 0.246 liter per minute and during exercise is 3.2 liters per minute. This repre-

sents a 13-fold increase. Yet, during exercise, the amount of O_2 extracted by the tissues on an equal blood flow basis (as indicated by the a-$\bar{v}O_2$ diff) is only 3.4 times that at rest (15.86/4.62). This is enough to increase $\dot{V}O_2$ to only $0.246 \times 3.4 = 0.84$ liter per minute. Thus, in order to fully meet the gas transport demands of exercise, blood flow must also be increased.

Summary

Gas exchange at the alveolar-capillary and tissue-capillary membranes occurs through the process of diffusion (random motion of molecules) and is primarily dependent on the partial pressure gradients of the gases involved. Gases always diffuse from an area of higher to an area of lower partial pressure. The partial pressure of a gas is the pressure of a single gas either in a gas mixture or in a liquid and depends on the amount of gas present and the total barometric pressure of the gas system.

Besides being affected by partial pressure gradients, gas exchange can be affected by: (1) the length of the diffusion path; (2) the number of red cells, or their hemoglobin concentration, or both; and (3) the surface area available for diffusion.

During exercise the diffusion capacity increases because of opening of more alveoli and capillaries, thus increasing the surface area. Generally, athletes have larger diffusion capacities at rest and during maximal exercise than nonathletes.

Oxygen is carried in small amounts in plasma and in large amounts by the red blood cells. In the plasma, it is carried in solution and is responsible for the partial pressure of oxygen in the blood. In the red cell, it is chemically united with hemoglobin. Four factors affect the saturation of Hb with O_2: (1) the partial pressure of O_2 in the blood; (2) the temperature of the blood; (3) the pH of the blood; and (4) the amount of CO_2 in the blood. During exercise, changes in these factors favor the release

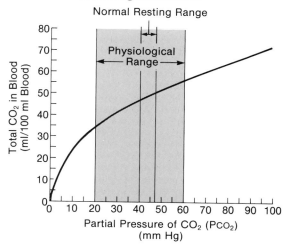

Figure 9-11. The carbon dioxide dissociation curve. As the partial pressure of carbon dioxide (P_{CO_2}) increases, so does the total amount of CO_2 combined with the blood. The physiological range of the curve is rather narrow, particularly under normal resting conditions.

TABLE 9-1

Oxygen and Carbon Dioxide Content of Blood at Rest and During Heavy Exercise

Transport Mechanisms	O_2 or CO_2 Content (Milliliters per 100 ml Whole Blood)		
	Arterial Blood	Mixed Venous Blood	Difference
Rest ($\dot{V}O_2$ = 0.246 liter per minute; $\dot{V}CO_2$ = 0.202 liter per minute)			
Total O_2	19.8	15.18	4.62
Dissolved	0.3	0.18	0.12
As HbO_2	19.5	15.0	4.5
Total CO_2	48.0	51.8	3.8
Dissolved	2.3	2.7	0.4
As HCO_3^-	43.5	45.9	2.4
As carbamino compounds	2.2	3.2	1.0
Heavy exercise ($\dot{V}O_2$ = 3.20 liters per minute; $\dot{V}CO_2$ = 3.03 liters per minute)			
Total O_2	21.2	5.34	15.86
Dissolved	0.3	0.06	0.4
As HbO_2	20.9	5.28	15.62
Total CO_2	45.0	60.0	15.0
Dissolved	2.1	3.1	1.0
As HCO_3^-	40.8	53.2	12.4
As carbamino compounds	2.1	3.7	1.6

Hb concentration + 15 grams per 100 ml whole blood at rest; 16.5 grams per 100 ml whole blood during exercise (10% hemoconcentration).

of O_2 to the working muscles. The relationships among these factors may be shown by what is called the oxyhemoglobin dissociation curve.

Carbon monoxide (CO) combines much more rapidly with Hb and to the same chemical unit of Hb as does O_2. Since CO is a by-product of cigarette smoke, cigarette smoking can significantly reduce the O_2-carrying capacity of the blood.

Like oxygen, carbon dioxide is carried both in physical solution and in chemical combination. By far the greater amount of CO_2 is transported in chemical combination, just as with oxygen. Carbon dioxide combines with water in the blood to form carbonic acid and with blood proteins including Hb to form carbamino compounds.

Questions

1. What is meant by the partial pressure of a gas?
2. Describe the relationship between partial pressure and concentration of gases in a gas mixture.
3. Discuss the partial pressure of a gas in a liquid.
4. What is the physiological significance of dissolved oxygen and carbon dioxide?

5. Discuss all factors affecting gas exchange.
6. How does diffusion capacity change during exercise?
7. Compare the diffusion capacity of athletes and nonathletes.
8. What effect does training have on diffusion capacity?
9. Explain how the P_{O_2} and the P_{CO_2} of arterial blood during exercise are maintained even though the velocity of the blood through the capillaries is greatly increased.
10. What is meant by: (a) the O_2 capacity of Hb and (b) the per cent saturation of Hb?
11. Explain the significance of the oxyhemoglobin dissociation curve with respect to gas exchange and transport.
12. Explain how cigarette smoking can reduce the O_2-carrying capacity of the blood.
13. During exercise, there are increases in blood acidity, temperature, and CO_2. How do these factors affect the dissociation curve?
14. Describe the ways in which CO_2 is transported.
15. Relate CO_2 transport to acid-base balance.

References

1. Åstrand, P., Cuddy, T., Saltin, B., and Stenberg, J.: Cardiac output during submaximal and maximal work. *J Appl Physiol.* 19:268–274, 1964.
2. Fox, E., Cohen, K., and Stevens, D.: Unpublished data, 1975.
3. Guyton, A. C.: *Textbook of Medical Physiology,* 6th ed. Philadelphia, W. B. Saunders, 1981.
4. Holmgren, A., and Åstrand, P.: D_L and the dimensions and functional capacities of the O_2 transport system in humans. *J Appl Physiol.* 21(5):1463–1470, 1966.
5. Kaufmann, D., Swenson, E., Fencl, J., and Lucas, A.: Pulmonary function of marathon runners. *Med Sci Sports.* 6(2):114–117, 1974.
6. Magel, J., and Andersen, K.: Pulmonary diffusing capacity and cardiac output in young trained Norwegian swimmers and untrained subjects. *Med Sci Sports.* 1(3):131–139, 1969.
7. Maksud, M., Hamilton, L., Coutts, K., and Wiley, R.: Pulmonary function measurements of Olympic speed skaters from the U.S. *Med Sci Sports.* 3(2):66–71, 1971.
8. Newman, F., Smalley, B., and Thompson, M.: A comparison between body size and lung function of swimmers and normal school children. *J Physiol* (London). 156:9P, 1961.
9. Reddan, W., Bongiorno, F., Burpee, J., Reuschlein, P., Gee, J., and Rankin, J.: Pulmonary function in endurance athletes. *Fed Proc.* 22:396, 1963.
10. Reuschlein, P., Reddan, W., Burpee, J., Gee, J., and Rankin, J.: Effect of physical training on the pulmonary diffusing capacity during submaximal work. *J Appl Physiol.* 24(2):152–158, 1968.
11. Shappell, S., Murray, J., Bellingham, A., Woodson, R., Detter, J., and Linfant, C.: Adaptation to exercise: Role of hemoglobin affinity for oxygen and 2,3-diphosphoglycerate. *J Appl Physiol.* 30(6):827–832, 1971.
12. Thompson, J., Dempsey, J., Chosy, L., Shahidi, N., and Reddan, W.: Oxygen transport and oxyhemoglobin dissociation during prolonged muscular work. *J Appl Physiol.* 37(5):658–664, 1974.

SELECTED READINGS

Comroe, J.: *Physiology of Respiration,* 2nd ed. Chicago, Year Book Medical, 1974.

Comroe, J., Forster, R., DuBois, A., Briscoe, W., and Carlsen, E.: *The Lung,* 2nd ed. Chicago, Year Book Medical, 1962, pp. 111–161.

Dempsey, J. A., and Reed, C. E. (eds.): *Muscular Exercise and the Lung.* Madison, Wisconsin, University of Wisconsin Press, 1977.

Forster, R.: Exchange of gases between alveolar air and pulmonary capillary blood: Pulmonary diffusing capacity. *Physiol Rev.* 37: 391–452, 1957.

Slonim, N., and Hamilton, L.: *Respiratory Physiology,* 2nd ed. St. Louis, C. V. Mosby, 1971, pp. 76–96.

Weibel, E.: Morphological basis of alveolar capillary gas exchange. *Physiol Rev.* 53(2): 419–495, 1973.

West, J.: *Respiratory Physiology—The Essentials.* Baltimore, Williams and Wilkins, 1974, pp. 23–88.

chapter 10

Blood Flow and Gas Transport

The major concepts to be learned from this chapter are as follows:

- The heart is two muscular pumps in one: the left heart that pumps blood to the body tissues and the right heart that pumps blood to the lungs.
- The individual cardiac muscle fibers are interconnected so that they function (contract) together as one fiber.
- Cardiac tissue has the property of auto-rhythm, i.e., the ability to self-generate nervous impulses in a rhythmical fashion.
- Two major circulatory changes that occur during exercise are an increase in cardiac output, i.e., in the amount of blood pumped by the heart, and a re-distribution of blood flow away from inactive organs toward the active skeletal muscles.
- Cardiac output is made up of two functional components: the stroke volume—the amount of blood pumped per beat—and the heart rate. Both increase during exercise.
- The redistribution of blood flow during exercise involves vasoconstriction of the arterioles supplying the inactive areas of the body and vasodilation in the active muscles caused by increases in local temperature, CO_2, and lactic acid levels and a decrease in O_2.
- The oxygen transport system involves the stroke volume, the heart rate, and

the arterial, mixed venous oxygen difference.

- The study of physical laws, as they relate to blood flow, is called hemodynamics.

As mentioned in the last chapter, in order to fully meet the gas transport demands during exercise, two major blood flow changes are necessary: (1) *an increase in* **cardiac output,** *i.e., in the amount of blood pumped per minute by the heart;* and (2) *a* **redistribution of blood flow** *from inactive organs to the active skeletal muscles.* The object of this chapter will be to provide an understanding of these and other related changes. Our discussion of cardiac output and blood flow changes will be limited to the **left heart and systemic circuit,** i.e., to the flow of arterial blood to and venous blood from the body tissues such as the working muscles. Remember, however, that these changes are equally great in the flow of blood to and from the lungs, i.e., in the **right heart and pulmonary circuit.** It is easy to visualize what would happen if the outputs of the left and right heart were not equal. In cases in which this does occur, as in cardiac patients with left heart failure, blood accumulates in the lungs, causing pulmonary edema, pneumonia, and even death, if the patient is not treated immediately.

Blood Flow Changes

As previously mentioned, the transport of gases to and from the working muscles involves an increase in cardiac output and a redistribution of blood away from the inactive organs toward the active muscles. Let's see what these changes are and how they are controlled. We will start with a review of the heart and cardiac cycle.

The Heart and Cardiac Cycle

The heart is a muscular pump that circulates the blood through the circulatory system. Two major areas that need discussing here are (1) the anatomy and physiology of the heart and (2) the cardiac cycle, the electrical and mechanical activities of the heart muscle.

Anatomy and Physiology of the Heart

Figure 10-1 shows an illustration of a human heart. It consists of four chambers, the left and right **atria** (singular = **atrium**) and the left and right **ventricles.** Usually, the heart is considered to be two pumps, the left heart consisting of the left atrium and ventricle and the right heart consisting of the right atrium and ventricle. As briefly mentioned earlier, the left side pumps blood through the systemic circuit to the body tissues, such as the skeletal muscles; the right side pumps blood to the lungs via the pulmonary circuit.

1. *Heart Valves and Direction of Blood Flow.* The direction of blood flow is shown by arrows in Figure 10-1. Its direction is controlled by unidirectional valves that are strategically located throughout the heart. Blood from the head and upper extremities and from the trunk and lower extremities returns via the superior and inferior **vena cava,** respectively, to the right atrium. From there it goes to the right ventricle. As the right ventricle contracts, the **tricuspid valve** closes, preventing blood from backflowing to the atrium. At the same time, the **pulmonary valve** opens, channeling the blood out the pulmonary arteries toward the lungs. On returning from the lungs (by the pulmonary veins), the blood empties into the left atrium and then into the left ventricle. The valve arrangement here is the same as in the right ventricle, except that the names are different: the **mitral valve** closes to prevent backflow into the atrium, and the

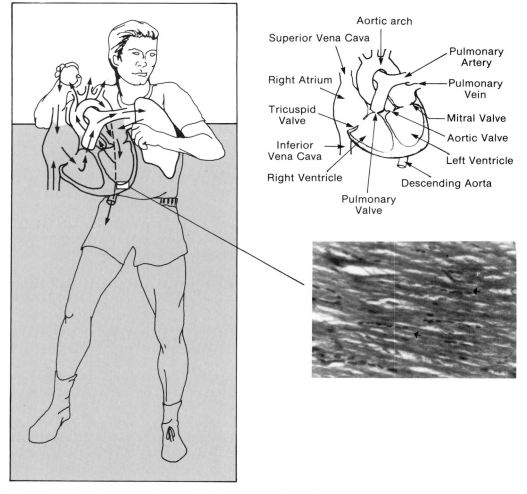

Figure 10-1. The human heart. The heart consists of four main chambers, the left atrium and left ventricle (left heart) and the right atrium and right ventricle (right heart). The flow of blood is indicated by arrows. The left heart pumps blood to the body tissues and the right heart to the lungs. Inset: microscopic structure of the heart muscle (myocardium) showing the intercalated discs and syncytial arrangement of fibers. (Inset courtesy Dr. Julianne Chase, The Ohio State University.)

aortic valve opens, directing the blood to the body tissues. Incidentally, if a valve is damaged or does not close properly, blood regurgitates, causing a noise. This type of noise is referred to as a "heart murmur."

2. *Microscopic Structure of Heart Muscle.* A closer look at the heart muscle,

called the myocardium, is shown in the inset of Figure 10-1. In some ways, heart muscle is similar to skeletal muscle. For example, it is striated, containing myofibrils and actin and myosin protein filaments. In fact, the actual contraction of the myocardium is thought to occur according to the sliding filament theory of muscular contraction as outlined in Chapter 5.

However, in other ways, the heart muscle is quite different from skeletal muscle. In cardiac muscle, all of the individual fibers or cells are anatomically interconnected. This is shown in the inset of Figure 10-1. Notice that the myocardial fibers are connected end-to-end by what are referred to as **intercalated discs.** These discs are actually nothing more than cell membranes. Because all of the fibers of heart muscle are interconnected, the heart acts as if it were one large fiber. For example, the entire heart muscle follows the all-or-none law (p. 100), whereas with skeletal muscle, only the individual fibers and motor units follow this law. Such an arrangement is referred to as a *functional syncytium,* functional in the sense that when one fiber contracts, all fibers contract, and a syncytium by the fact that all the cells interconnect. Actually, there are two functional syncytia, one for the atria and one for the ventricles. What this means is that first the atria contract together and then the ventricles. It is easy to see that this type of arrangement is most effective in producing the pumping action required of the heart.

3. *Conduction System of the Heart.* The heart has an inherent contractile rhythm. That is to say, if all nerves supplying the heart are severed, the heart still continues to generate nervous impulses causing it to contract in a rhythmical fashion. Usually, this *autorhythm* originates in a specialized area of tissue referred to as the **sinoatrial node (S-A node);** however, all heart tissue has this property. The S-A node is located in the posterior wall of the right atrium, as illustrated in Figure 10-2. Because the normal heartbeat is initiated in the S-A node, it is sometimes referred to as the **pacemaker** of the heart.

From the S-A node, the cardiac or nervous impulse spreads throughout the atria.

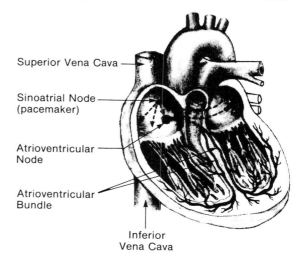

Superior Vena Cava

Sinoatrial Node (pacemaker)

Atrioventricular Node

Atrioventricular Bundle

Inferior Vena Cava

Figure 10-2. The electrical conduction system of the heart. The S-A node is considered the pacemaker of the heart since the cardiac impulse is normally initiated there. (Modified and redrawn from Landau.[19])

Therefore, the atria contract first, emptying their contents into the ventricles. Next the impulse from the atria activates another specialized area of the heart referred to as the **atrioventricular node (A-V node).** It is located also in the right atrium at the atrioventricular junction (Fig. 10-2). From the A-V node extends a bundle of this same type of special conducting tissue, called the **atrioventricular bundle, (Bundle of His),** into the right *(right bundle branch)* and left *(left bundle branch)* ventricles. These bundles give off many branches that eventually reach throughout the entire ventricular myocardium, causing it to contract.

4. *Blood Supply to the Heart.* Like any living tissue, the cardiac muscle also requires a blood supply to provide it with oxygen and to remove waste products. The blood supply to the heart is referred to as the **coronary circulation** and is shown in Figure 10-3. The heart muscle is supplied

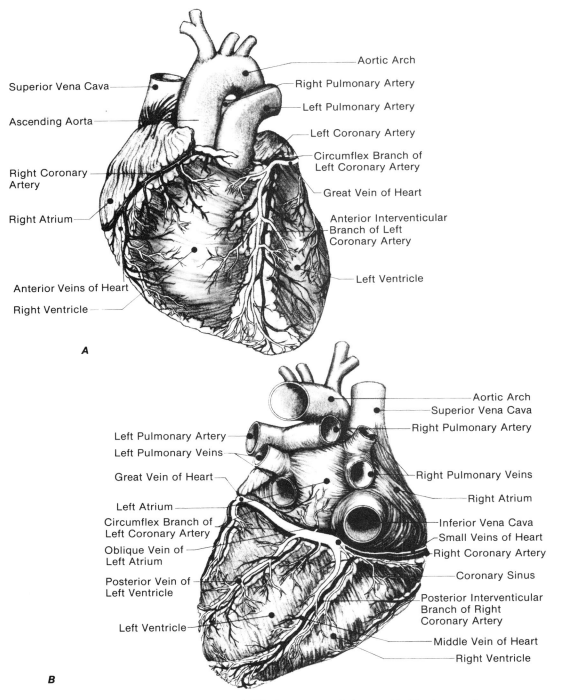

Labels in figure A (top):

Superior Vena Cava

Ascending Aorta

Right Coronary Artery

Right Atrium

Anterior Veins of Heart

Right Ventricle

Aortic Arch

Right Pulmonary Artery

Left Pulmonary Artery

Left Coronary Artery

Circumflex Branch of Left Coronary Artery

Great Vein of Heart

Anterior Interventicular Branch of Left Coronary Artery

Left Ventricle

A

Labels in figure B (bottom):

Left Pulmonary Artery

Left Pulmonary Veins

Great Vein of Heart

Left Atrium

Circumflex Branch of Left Coronary Artery

Oblique Vein of Left Atrium

Posterior Vein of Left Ventricle

Left Ventricle

Aortic Arch

Superior Vena Cava

Right Pulmonary Artery

Right Pulmonary Veins

Right Atrium

Inferior Vena Cava

Small Veins of Heart

Right Coronary Artery

Coronary Sinus

Posterior Interventricular Branch of Right Coronary Artery

Middle Vein of Heart

Right Ventricle

B

Figure 10-3. The coronary circulation. *A,* The heart muscle is supplied by two major arteries, the left and right coronary arteries. *B,* The arteries give off many branches as they encircle the heart, eventually anastomosing (joining) on the posterior surface of the heart. (Modified and redrawn from Landau.[19])

by two major arteries, the **left coronary artery** and the **right coronary artery.** They originate from the aorta, just beyond (above) the aortic valve, and encircle the heart. They *anastomose,* i.e., join together, on the posterior (back) surface of the heart (Fig. 10-3*B*). All along the way, branches are given off such that the entire myocardium is supplied with a rich network of vascular tissue. The major branch of the left coronary artery is called the *circumflex branch,* whereas that of the right coronary artery is simply referred to as the *branch of the right coronary artery.*

The coronary veins run alongside the arteries (Fig. 10-3). They eventually all drain into a very large vein referred to as the **coronary sinus,** which in turn deposits the venous blood directly into the right atrium of the heart.

The Cardiac Cycle

The **cardiac cycle** refers to the electrical and mechanical changes (pressure and volume changes) that occur in the heart during the course of a single heartbeat, i.e., during contraction and relaxation of the myocardium. The contractile phase of the cardiac cycle is referred to as **systole** and the relaxation phase as **diastole.** Since the electrical changes lead to the mechanical changes, they will be considered first.

1. *Electrical Changes—The EKG.* The conduction system of the heart and the flow of the nervous impulse throughout the myocardium have already been described. This electrical activity can be graphically recorded as a function of time. Such a recording is called an **electrocardiogram,** or, more simply, an **EKG.** The EKG is recorded by placing **electrodes** on the surface of the body that are connected to an amplifier and recorder called an *electrocardiograph.* Thus the electrical activity of the heart is "picked up" from the body surface by the electrodes and is amplified and recorded, as a function of time, on a graph.

An example of a normal, resting EKG for one complete heartbeat or cardiac cycle is shown in Figure 10-4. Each wave or change in shape of the EKG is related to a specific electrical change in the heart. These are as follows:

(a) The **P wave** results from the depolarization of the atria.
(b) The **QRS complex** reflects the depolarization of the ventricles. It follows about 0.15 to 0.16 seconds after the P wave.
(c) The **T wave** is created as a result of the repolarization of the ventricles. When the atria are repolarized, a wave is also created, but it is of low magnitude and, as a result, is obscured by the large QRS complex.

Because the electrodes are always placed on the body surface at standardized positions, any variation in the change in elec-

Figure 10-4. Normal, resting EKG for one complete heartbeat or cardiac cycle. The P wave results from atrial depolarization, the QRS complex from ventricular depolarization, and the T wave from ventricular repolarization.

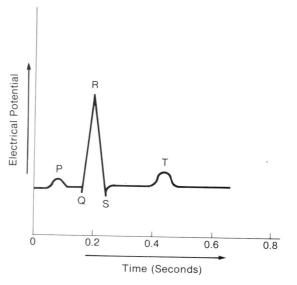

trical activity may indicate changes in the functional capabilities of the heart. Therefore, the EKG is a useful clinical tool for detecting cardiac disorders.

2. *Mechanical Events—Pressure and Volume Changes.* As previously mentioned, the heart alternately contracts and relaxes in a rhythmical fashion due to the changes in electrical activity as just described. During this cycle (systole and diastole), both the pressure and volume of blood within the atria and ventricles fluctuate as shown in Figure 10-5. The upper three curves depict the pressure changes of the aorta, left ventricle, and left atrium, respectively. The single middle curve shows

Figure 10-5. Electrical and mechanical changes in the left heart during the cardiac cycle. The upper three curves depict pressure changes in the aorta, left ventricle, and left atrium, respectively. The middle curve shows changes in the volume of blood in the left ventricle; the bottom curves represent the EKG and phonocardiogram recordings, respectively. The numbered, vertical lines correspond to different, important events of the cycle, which are detailed in Table 10-1. (Modified and redrawn from Landau.[19])

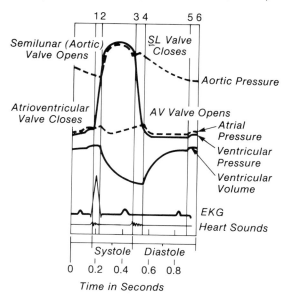

the changes in blood volume that take place in the left ventricle, whereas the bottom two curves represent the EKG and *phonocardiogram* recordings, respectively.

The phonocardiogram is a recording of the sounds made by the heart during the cardiac cycle. These sounds are thought to be a result of the vibrations created by the *closing* of the heart valves. There are at least two such sounds. The first occurs when the A-V valves close at the beginning of systole; the second occurs when the aortic valve closes at the end of systole.

The most important features of the events of the cardiac cycle are summarized in Table 10-1. The line numbers given in the table refer to the numbers shown in Figure 10-5. Remember, these changes are for the *left heart.* However, they are essentially the same for the right heart, except that the pressures within the pulmonary arteries and right ventricle are much lower, only about one-sixth of that in the aorta and left ventricle.

Cardiac Output during Exercise

As mentioned earlier, cardiac output is defined as the amount of blood pumped per minute by the heart, specifically, by the left ventricle. The increase in cardiac output that occurs during exercise is shown in Figure 10-6A for trained and untrained male subjects. As would be expected, this increase is closely related to $\dot{V}O_2$ (and thus to workload) over the entire range from rest to maximal values. At rest, there is little difference in cardiac output between trained and untrained subjects, with average values ranging between 5 and 6 liters per minute. However, during exercise requiring a given $\dot{V}O_2$, the cardiac outputs of untrained subjects are sometimes slightly higher than[5,6,14,32] and sometimes the same as[16,27] those of trained subjects.

Maximal cardiac outputs in trained male subjects can reach values in excess of

TABLE 10-1

Summary of Events During the Cardiac Cycle

Line Numbers (Refer to Figure 10-5)	Phase of Cardiac Cycle	Pressure Changes	Valve Position	Ventricular Volume Changes	Heart Sounds
1	Beginning of ventricular systole	Ventricular pressure greater than atrial pressure	A-V valve closes, aortic valve closed	—	—
1-2	Isometric ventricular contraction	Ventricular pressure rises rapidly; little change in aortic and atrial pressures	A-V and aortic valves closed	No change	First heart sound
2	—	Ventricular pressure greater than aortic pressure	Aortic valve opens	—	—
2-3	Ventricular ejection	Ventricular and aortic pressures reach peaks, then begin to decrease; little change in atrial pressure	Aortic valve open, A-V valve closed	Rapid decrease	—
3	Beginning of diastole	Ventricular pressure less than aortic pressure	Aortic valve closes	—	—
3-4	Isometric relaxation	Ventricular pressure decreases rapidly; little change in aortic and atrial pressures	Aortic and A-V valves closed	No change	Second heart sound
4	—	Ventricular pressure lower than atrial pressure	A-V valve opens	—	—
4-5	Diastole	Little change in ventricular and atrial pressures; aortic pressure decreasing gradually	A-V valve open, aortic valve closed	Rapid increase	—
5-6	Diastole-atrial contraction	Small increases in ventricular and atrial pressures; little change in aortic pressure	A-V valve open, aortic valve closed	Small increase	—

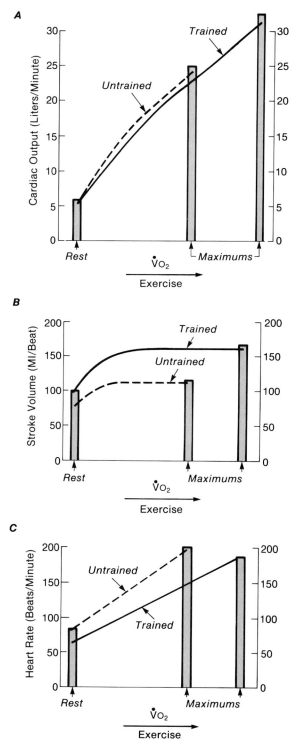

Figure 10-6. *A,* Cardiac output, *B,* stroke volume, and, *C,* heart rate during exercise in trained and untrained subjects. Cardiac output and heart rate are closely related to $\dot{V}O_2$ over the entire range from rest to maximal exercise (in the upright position); maximal stroke volume is usually reached at submaximal $\dot{V}O_2$ or exercise. Cardiac output is the product of stroke volume times heart rate.

30 liters per minute. This represents a five to sixfold increase over resting values. In fact, it is not unusual to find that highly trained athletes who excel in endurance events and who have exceptionally high aerobic capacities have maximal cardiac outputs near 40 liters per minute.[7] By the same token, untrained male subjects, who have lower work and aerobic capacities, have lower maximal cardiac outputs (about 20 to 25 liters per minute). In general, we can say that the higher the maximal cardiac output, the higher the maximal aerobic power (max $\dot{V}O_2$), and vice versa.

The changes in cardiac output described above for men are similar to those for women.[1,18] However, it should be mentioned that in comparison with men, women tend to have a slightly higher cardiac output when performing work at the same level of oxygen consumption.[1,10] This difference amounts to between 1.5 and 1.75 liters per minute; in other words, the cardiac output will be 1.5 to 1.75 liters per minute higher on the average in women than in men for a given oxygen consumption.[1,10] The reason for this is probably due to the women's lower oxygen-carrying capacity of blood, resulting from their lower levels of hemoglobin (p. 386). Also, the maximal cardiac output of both trained and untrained women is generally lower than that of their male counterparts.

These large increases in cardiac output during exercise are brought about through increases in (1) **stroke volume,** i.e., the amount of blood pumped by the heart per stroke or beat; and (2) **heart rate,** the number of times the heart beats per minute. Mathematically, the relationship of cardiac output ($\dot{Q}$) to stroke volume (SV) and heart rate (HR) is as follows:

$$\underset{\substack{\text{(liters per} \\ \text{minute)}}}{\dot{Q}} = \underset{\substack{\text{(liters per} \\ \text{beat)}}}{SV} \times \underset{\substack{\text{(beats per} \\ \text{minute)}}}{HR}$$

For example, if during heavy exercise stroke volume were 160 ml (0.16 liter) per beat and heart rate were 185 beats per minute, cardiac output would be:

$$\dot{Q} = 0.16 \text{ liter/beat} \times 185 \text{ beat/min}$$
$$= \textbf{29.6 liters/min}$$

Stroke Volume

The relationship of stroke volume to exercise $\dot{V}O_2$ is shown in Figure 10-6B. Stroke volume increases during the progression from rest to moderate work, but does not necessarily increase from moderate to maximal work. Thus, in most cases, stroke volume becomes maximal at a submaximal workload when $\dot{V}O_2$ is only about 40% of maximum. This applies both to trained and untrained male and female subjects.

The resting, upright* stroke volume of untrained male subjects averages between 70 and 90 ml per beat with maximal values ranging between 100 and 120 ml per beat. For trained men, both resting and maximal values are higher, averaging about 100 to 120 ml and 150 to 170 ml per beat, respectively. For the highly trained male endurance athletes mentioned earlier, maximal stroke volume may reach or even exceed 200 ml per beat.[6] Thus, it should be noted that the primary contributor to the endurance athletes' much larger cardiac output is brought about by an increased maximum stroke volume. Maximum heart rates are similar in both trained and untrained individuals whereas maximum stroke volume may be doubled in the athlete.

---

*Stroke volume is lower in the upright, or sitting, position compared with the lying, or supine, position. In the upright position, more blood pools in the extremities and thus less returns to the heart. As a result, stroke volume decreases. Since most exercise is performed in the upright position, this will be the position of reference unless otherwise stated.

For women, the values for stroke volume are generally lower than those for men under all conditions. For example, at rest, the stroke volume may be between 50 to 70 ml per beat in untrained females and between 70 and 90 ml per beat after training. Maximal stroke volumes for untrained and trained females are usually between 80 and 100 ml and 100 and 120 ml per beat, respectively. At a submaximal workload requiring the same oxygen consumption, stroke volume will be lower in the female than in the male. Since stroke volume is maximal during submaximal exercise, this difference can be explained by the smaller heart volume of the female.

The mechanism whereby stroke volume is increased during exercise was for a long time thought to be a result of **Starling's law of the heart.** This law states that stroke volume increases in response to an increase in the volume of blood filling the heart ventricle during *diastole* (ventricular relaxation). The increase in *diastolic volume* causes a greater stretch on the cardiac fiber, which in turn promotes a more forceful ventricular systole (contraction). As a result, more blood is ejected, and stroke volume increases. However, more recently it has been shown that diastolic volume does not increase during exercise,[3,11,30] and so the significance of this mechanism with respect to increasing the stroke volume is now questionable. Actually, the major role of Starling's law, both at rest and during exercise, is in keeping the outputs of the left and right ventricles in pace with each other, so that blood flow through the systemic and pulmonary circuits is maintained equally.

How, then, does stroke volume increase during exercise? The answer to this question lies in the fact that at rest only about 40 to 50% of the total diastolic volume is ejected during each ventricular systole. (This is the ejection fraction.) This means that, without increasing diastolic volume,

a stronger contraction could as much as double stroke volume by more completely emptying the ventricles.[21,31] In this case, the stronger ventricular contraction, often referred to as an increased **myocardial contractility,** is mediated through nervous and hormonal influences. These will be discussed in greater detail later.

Heart Rate

Figure 10-6C shows that heart rate increases linearly with increasing workload or $\dot{V}O_2$ in both trained and untrained subjects. However, in some cases, this increase may lessen just before maximal values are reached. It should be remembered that once stroke volume becomes maximal (which is usually at submaximal workloads), further increases in cardiac output are possible only through increases in heart rate. Here it is interesting to note that the same nervous and hormonal influences that increase stroke volume also increase heart rate.

Training has a very pronounced effect on heart rate, even at rest. For example, in highly trained athletes of either sex, resting heart rates may be as low as or lower than 40 beats per minute. In contrast, resting heart rates for untrained but healthy individuals may be as high as 90 beats per minute. A slow resting heart rate is characteristic of the trained individual (p. 332).

During exercise, the heart rate of a trained subject is also lower at any given $\dot{V}O_2$ than is that of his or her untrained counterpart. However, under these conditions the female has a higher heart rate. This is so because as mentioned before, she also has a greater cardiac output and smaller stroke volume for the same oxygen consumption. (Remember, $\dot{Q} = SV \times HR$). In addition, training may also reduce maximal heart rate, e.g., from 200 to about 185 to 190 beats per minute. However, this effect is neither as consistent nor as pronounced as that at a given $\dot{V}O_2$. This is because training also increases work capacity (and max $\dot{V}O_2$); therefore, maximal heart rates in trained subjects are reached at comparatively higher workloads and $\dot{V}O_2$ levels.

It should be pointed out that a relatively slow heart rate, coupled with a relatively large stroke volume, indicates an efficient circulatory system. This is true because for a given cardiac output the heart does not beat as often. For example, consider a trained subject whose cardiac output during exercise is 20 liters per minute. With a stroke volume of 150 ml per beat, the heart rate would be:

$$HR = \dot{Q}/SV \text{ (since } \dot{Q} = SV \times HR)$$
$$= 20 \text{ liters per minute}/0.15 \text{ liter per beat}$$
$$= \textbf{133 beats per minute}$$

On the other hand, an untrained subject with the same cardiac output but with a stroke volume of only 120 ml per beat would have a heart rate of 167 beats per minute. This also applies under resting conditions. For a given cardiac output, a slower beating heart with a larger stroke volume requires less oxygen.

Measurement of heart rate, either in the laboratory (with an electrocardiograph) or in the field by counting the pulse,* is relatively simple. This simplicity, plus the relationships of heart rate to $\dot{V}O_2$, workload, and training, has made it the single most often used index of circulatory function during exercise. As a coach and physical educator, you can use heart rate responses (1) as a guide to the severity of any given exercise; (2) in assessing the effects of training; and (3) based on results of the first two, in developing the most effective

training programs employing the progressive overload principle (Chapter 12). It must be emphasized, however, that such criteria should be confined to use on an individual basis since heart rate responses to exercise can and do vary considerably from one person to another.

Cardiac Output during Prolonged Exercise

Changes in cardiac output, stroke volume, and heart rate for short-term exercise (5 to 10 minutes) are shown in Figure 10-7A. These changes are similar in pattern to those described earlier for oxygen consumption (p. 72) and pulmonary ventilation (p. 207). There is a sharp rise at the onset of exercise followed by a more gradual rise and then a leveling or steady-state plateau. These steady-state levels were shown for several submaximal efforts in Figure 10-6.

During prolonged submaximal work, i.e., work over 30 minutes' duration, cardiac output is maintained over the course of the exercise, but stroke volume and heart rate are not.[8,28] As shown in Figure 10-7B, stroke volume gradually decreases and heart rate gradually increases as the exercise progresses. This is sometimes referred to as "cardiovascular drift."[15,17,23,29] Since the changes are opposite in direction and equal in magnitude, cardiac output remains fairly constant. Thus, in prolonged efforts, it is not surprising to find near maximal heart rates by the end of the performance. As an example, it has been estimated that during a 2½-hour marathon race, in which the energy requirements are about 75% of maximum, heart rate was maximal for as long as 1 hour or so.[9]

Venous Return

Regardless of the mechanisms that increase cardiac output during exercise, the heart can pump only as much blood as it

---

*Even your own students (athletes) can measure their heart rates during practice sessions (Chapter 12).

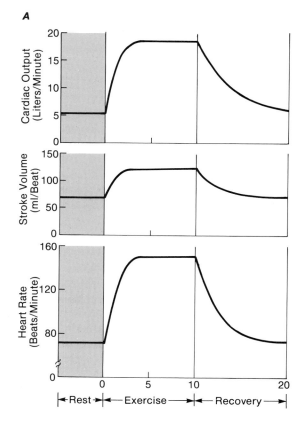

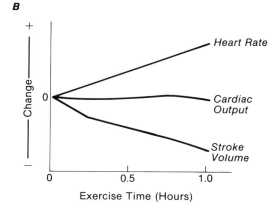

Figure 10-7. *A,* Pattern of change in cardiac output (top), stroke volume (middle), and heart rate (bottom) during short-term (5 to 10 minutes) submaximal exercise. There is a sharp rise at the onset of exercise followed by a steady state, then a sharp decline as exercise stops. *B,* During prolonged exercise (30 minutes or more), heart rate increases steadily while stroke volume decreases. This is referred to as "cardiovascular drift." Since these changes are equal in magnitude and opposite in direction, cardiac output remains stable.

receives. For this reason, cardiac output is ultimately dependent on the amount of blood returned to the right heart via the systemic venous system, or, in other words, upon the **venous return.** Thus, an increase in cardiac output of 30 liters per minute or more during maximal exercise means that the venous return must also increase by that amount.

Several mechanisms contribute to increasing the venous return during exercise: the muscle pump, the respiratory pump, and venoconstriction.

1. *The Muscle Pump.* The **muscle pump** was mentioned briefly in Chapter 5; it is a result of the mechanical pumping action produced by rhythmical muscular contractions. As the muscles contract, their veins are compressed and the blood within them is forced toward the heart. Blood is prevented from flowing backwards because the veins in the limbs contain numerous valves, which permit flow only toward the heart. When the muscles relax, blood fills the veins again and with the next contraction, more blood is forced toward the heart. The muscle pump is important when standing and when walking, running, and performing other, similar exercises during which the muscles alternatively contract and relax. During weight lifting or other types of exercises that require *sustained* muscular effort, the pump cannot operate and venous return is actually hindered.

2. *The Respiratory Pump.* Another, similar mechanical action that promotes

venous return is provided by the **respiratory pump.** With this pump, the veins of the thorax and abdomen are emptied toward the heart during inspiration and refilled during expiration. The reason for this is that the intrathoracic pressure decreases during inspiration (becomes more subatmospheric; p. 219), and this serves to aspirate the blood in the thoracic veins toward the right heart. The lowering of the diaphragm during inspiration increases abdominal pressure and the veins contained within this cavity are also emptied during inspiration. These pressure effects are reversed during expiration, and the veins fill again with more venous blood. Thus, merely by breathing, venous return is enhanced. This pump is more effective the greater the respiratory rate and depth, such as is the case during exercise.

3. *Venoconstriction.* A third way in which venous return is facilitated during exercise is through **venoconstriction,** i.e., by reflex constriction of the veins draining the muscles. Venoconstriction reduces the volume capacity of the systemic venous system, and, as a result, blood is forced out toward the heart. As we have indicated, this reflex is one of the many that is initiated and controlled by the central nervous system during exercise.

Distribution of Blood Flow

In Figure 10-8 are shown the approximate percentages of the total cardiac output distributed to the skeletal muscles, in comparison with other organs, at rest and during exercise. At rest, approximately 20% of the total systemic flow is distributed to the muscles; the majority goes to the visceral organs (gastrointestinal tract, liver, spleen, and kidneys), the heart, and the brain. However, during exercise there is a redistribution of blood flow so that the active muscles receive the greatest proportion of the cardiac output.[12,23,24] In fact, during

maximal exercise the working muscles may receive as much as 85 to 90% of the total blood flow. This means that, with a cardiac output of 25 liters per minute, more than 22 liters of blood would go to the muscles.

As we mentioned in Chapter 5, this redistribution of blood flow results from (1) reflex vasoconstriction of the arterioles supplying the inactive areas of the body, especially those of the visceral organs and skin; (2) reflex vasodilation of the arterioles supplying the active skeletal muscles, particularly before and at the very beginning of exercise; and (3) vasodilation in the active muscles caused by increases in local temperature, CO_2, and lactic acid levels and by a decrease in O_2, particularly as the exercise continues. As might be suspected, these nervous reflexes are coordinated with the nervous and hormonal reflexes mentioned earlier, which increase stroke volume, heart rate, and venous return. Blood flow to the heart (since it too is an active muscle) likewise increases during exercise as a result of vasodilation,[20] whereas that to the brain is maintained at resting levels.[33] It will be pointed out in Chapter 18, that in the heat or when rectal temperature reaches a critical level, blood flow to the skin increases greatly and the amount of blood available to the working muscles is correspondingly reduced.

In the last chapter (p. 235), we said that the difference in oxygen content between the arterial and mixed venous blood (a-$\bar{v}O_2$ diff) represents the amount of oxygen extracted or consumed by the tissues. The more oxygen extracted, the greater is the difference and vice versa. The magnitude of the a-$\bar{v}O_2$ diff is also affected by the distribution of blood flow. This is true because tissues that are more metabolically active (e.g., working skeletal muscle) extract more oxygen from the blood than less active tissues (e.g., skin, gastrointestinal tract, and kidney). If more blood is distributed to the tissues that extract more oxygen and

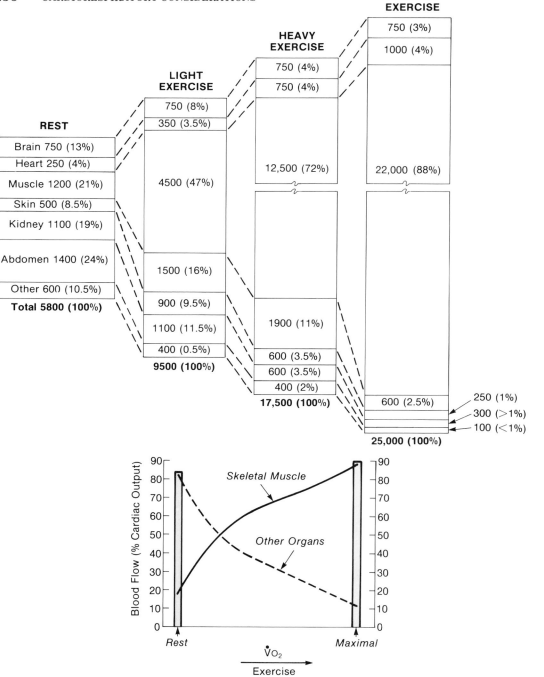

Figure 10-8. Distribution pattern of cardiac output through the various organs of the body during rest and exercise. Cardiac output to each area is expressed in milliliters and as a percentage of the total blood flow. The insert illustrates the percentage of blood flow to the muscles versus the combination of all other organs. (Modified from Chapman and Mitchell.[4])

less to those that extract less, then the a-$\bar{v}O_2$ diff will be increased.

Training leads to a larger a-$\bar{v}O_2$ diff in young men,[26] especially during maximal exercise. However, in young women and older men and women, the a-$\bar{v}O_2$ diff does not increase much with training.[16,18] The reason for this is not known. The increase seen in young men is apparently caused by a greater extraction of oxygen by the working muscles.[23]

The significance of the redistribution of blood flow with respect to gas transport is impressive. For example, it can be calculated that an additional 540 ml of oxygen can be transported to the working muscles per minute during maximal exercise without an additional increase in cardiac output.[23] This amounts to about 15% of the total maximal oxygen consumption in normal male subjects.

Blood Flow to the Myocardium

As we have stated, blood flow to skeletal muscle may increase 22 liters or more from a resting value of about 1.2 liters per minute. This response supports the great need for oxygen in the working muscles. However, in the heart muscle (myocardium), blood flow increases from a resting level of 250 ml up to about 1000 ml during maximal work. Also, cardiac muscle has an a-$\bar{v}O_2$ difference of 150 ml/liter of blood at rest. In other words, cardiac muscle extracts about 70 to 75% of the available oxygen at rest while skeletal muscle extracts only about 25% of the available oxygen with an a-$\bar{v}O_2$ difference of 50 ml/liter of blood.

Thus, not only does blood flow increase dramatically in skeletal muscle during exercise, the extraction of oxygen also increases greatly. Cardiac muscle, on the other hand, is limited in both how much more oxygen can be extracted (a-$\bar{v}O_2$ difference) and the increase in blood flow. Note from Figure 10-8 that the percentage

of cardiac output distributed to the myocardium remains at about 4% of the total distribution.

Other Features of Blood Distribution

Referring to Figure 10-8, notice some other features of the distribution of blood during exercise: (1) Blood flow to the brain remains constant throughout rest and various levels of exercise. (2) Blood flow to the kidneys diminishes but does not cease. (3) Blood flow to the skin increases as exercise intensity increases but at maximal work levels it decreases. As we will see in Chapter 18, this observation has important implications in heat stress.

The Oxygen Transport System

The increase in cardiac output and the redistribution of blood flow that occur during exercise can best be summarized by developing the concept of the **oxygen transport system**. The components of the system and their interrelationships are as follows:

$\dot{V}O_2$ (oxygen transported)	= SV (stroke volume)	× HR (heart rate)	× a-$\bar{v}O_2$ diff (arterio-venous O_2 difference)

You will remember that the stroke volume times the heart rate is equal to the cardiac output. Also, as just mentioned, the a-$\bar{v}O_2$ diff reflects how much oxygen is extracted by the tissues and the redistribution of blood flow between inactive and active muscles.

Some examples of the system at rest and during maximal exercise for trained and untrained male subjects and endurance athletes are given in Table 10-2. Notice how each component contributes toward increasing the amount of oxygen transported to the muscles. Using the un-

TABLE 10-2

Components of the Oxygen Transport System at Rest and During Maximal Exercise for Trained and Untrained Subjects and Endurance Athletes

Condition	$\dot{V}O_2$ (ml/Min)	=	Stroke Volume (Liters/Beat)	×	Heart Rate (Beats/Min)	×	a-$\overline{v}O_2$ Diff (ml/Liter)
1. Untrained							
a. Rest	300	=	0.075*	×	82	×	48.8
b. Maximal exercise	3100	=	0.112	×	200	×	138.0
2. Trained							
a. Rest	300	=	0.105	×	58	×	49.3
b. Maximal exercise	3440	=	0.126	×	192	×	140.5
3. Endurance athletes							
a. Maximal exercise	5570	=	0.189	×	190	×	155.0

*Usually expressed in ml per beat, e.g., 0.075 liters per beat = 75 ml per beat. (Data for untrained and trained subjects from Ekblom et al.,[6] data for endurance athletes from Ekblom and Hermansen.[7])

trained subjects as an example, the oxygen transported during maximal exercise is 10 times greater than that found during rest. This increase is accomplished by a 1.5-fold increase in stroke volume, a 2.4-fold increase in heart rate, and a 2.8-fold increase in the a-$\overline{v}O_2$ diff ($1.5 \times 2.4 \times 2.8 = 10$). Also, notice the differences between the trained subjects and the highly trained endurance athletes. The blood flow changes in the trained subjects resulted from a 16-week, 3 days per week training program. The endurance athletes on the other hand, were international competitors in long-distance and cross-country running and cycling. They were members of the Swedish National teams and had been training for several years. The biggest difference is in the magnitude of the stroke volume. The 16 weeks of training caused about a 13% increase in stroke volume. However, the stroke volume in the endurance athletes is 70% higher than that of the untrained subjects! Such a large difference clearly points out that the most important component of the oxygen transport system is the stroke volume.

Circulatory Mechanics— Hemodynamics

So far we have discussed only some of the physiological mechanisms that modify blood flow during exercise. Full comprehension of how these mechanisms produce such changes requires a basic understanding of *the physical laws that govern blood flow*. The study of these physical laws, as they relate to blood flow, is called **hemodynamics.**

There are two major hemodynamic factors that we need to consider: (1) **blood pressure,** i.e., the driving force that tends to move blood through the circulatory system, and (2) **resistance to flow,** i.e., the opposition offered by the circulatory system to this driving force (sometimes referred to as **total peripheral resistance**). The relationship of these factors to blood flow or to cardiac output is as follows:

Cardiac output ($\dot{Q}$) = Blood pressure (P)/Resistance (R)

This is the basic hemodynamic equation. We shall be using it and its two other algebraic forms, $P = \dot{Q} \times R$ and $R = P/\dot{Q}$ later on in this chapter. Right now, let us discuss blood pressure and resistance in more detail.

Blood Pressure

As we have mentioned, pressure is the force that moves the blood through the circulatory system. However, more important is the concept that, as does any other fluid, **blood flows from an area of high pressure to one of low pressure.** For example, as shown in Figure 10-9, blood flows from the left ventricle of the heart into the aorta (the main artery of the systemic circuit) because as the ventricle contracts it exerts a pressure that is higher than that in the aorta (Fig. 10-5 and Table 10-1). Blood

flows from the aorta through the remaining systemic blood vessels (arteries, arterioles, capillaries, venules, and veins, in that order) and finally to the right heart for the same reason—because of the *pressure differential* along the systemic vascular tree. This is true for pulmonary blood flow as well, except that here the pressures are lower in magnitude.* In other words, blood always flows from an area of high pressure to one of lower pressure.

Systolic and Diastolic Pressures

It is also important to note from Figure 10-9 that the pressure fluctuates in the arteries. The highest pressure obtained is called the **systolic pressure** and the lowest the **diastolic pressure.** As blood is ejected into the arteries during ventricular systole, the pressure increases to a maximum (systolic pressure); as blood drains from the arteries during ventricular diastole, the pressure decreases to a minimum (diastolic pressure). These pressure fluctuations are minimized, and in fact are absent in the capillaries, because the *arteries are elastic* rather than rigid. Thus, their walls stretch during systole and recoil during diastole. The elasticity of the arteries plus an added resistance to flow (mainly in the arterioles) assures a steady flow of blood in the capillaries. This has real meaning, because we know that it is in the capillaries that diffusion of gases and other nutrients takes place.

Mean Arterial Pressure

The average of the systemic systolic and diastolic pressures during a complete cardiac cycle (systole plus diastole) is called the **mean arterial pressure.** The mean arterial pressure is one of the most impor-

Figure 10-9. Blood pressure differential along the systemic vascular tree. Blood always flows from an area of high pressure to one of low pressure. Note also that the pressure (and thus the flow of blood) fluctuates in the arteries and arterioles, but that it is steady in the capillaries. Systolic pressure is the highest pressure obtained, diastolic the lowest; the average of the two is the mean arterial pressure.

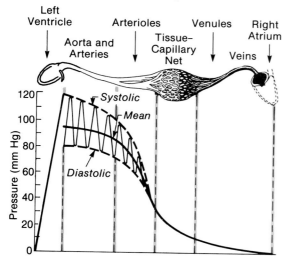

---

*Even though the pressure differential in the pulmonary circuit is lower than that in the systemic circuit, blood flow is the same because pulmonary resistance is also lower ($\dot{Q} = P/R$).

tant circulatory pressures because it, more than any other, *determines the rate of blood flow through the systemic circuit.* In our basic hemodynamic equation ($\dot{Q}$ = P/R), therefore, it is the mean arterial pressure (P_{mean}) that is important.†

Determination of P_{mean} is not simple. In fact, it is not merely the value halfway between systolic and diastolic pressure, because diastole usually lasts longer than systole. However, it is reasonably accurate to assume that P_{mean} is the diastolic pressure plus one-third of the difference between the systolic and diastolic pressures *(pulse pressure).* Mathematically then:

$$P_{mean} = \text{diastolic pressure} + \tfrac{1}{3}\text{pulse pressure}$$

As an example, if the systolic pressure were 125 millimeters of mercury (mm Hg) and the diastolic pressure 80 mm Hg, then P_{mean} would be estimated to be:

$$
\begin{aligned}
P_{mean} &= 80 \text{ mm Hg} + (1/3 \times 45 \text{ mm Hg}) \\
&= 80 \text{ mm Hg} + 15 \text{ mm Hg} \\
&= \textbf{95 mm Hg}
\end{aligned}
$$

Resistance to Flow

Resistance to blood flow is caused by friction between the blood and the walls of the blood vessels. The greater this friction, the greater the resistance to flow. Vascular friction depends on (1) the viscosity (or thickness) of the blood, (2) the length of the blood vessel, and (3) the diameter of the blood vessel. For example, an increase in the number of red blood cells, such as

occurs at high altitude, increases blood viscosity, which in turn causes greater vascular friction and resistance to flow. By the same token, the longer the vessel, the greater the vascular surface in contact with the blood and the greater the resistance.

On the other hand, when the diameter of the vessel decreases (vasoconstriction), resistance to flow increases. This is so because with a smaller diameter, a greater portion of the blood in the vessel is in contact with the walls, and the greater will be the friction. The opposite is true during vasodilation. Actually, *resistance varies inversely to the fourth power of the vessel radius.* In other words, if the radius (which is one-half the diameter) of the vessel doubles, resistance decreases 16 times; if the radius is halved, resistance increases 16 times! Referring once again to the relationship $\dot{Q} = P_{mean}/R$, we see that for a given P_{mean}, substantial blood flow changes can be effected by relatively small adjustments in blood vessel diameter. For this reason, vasoconstriction and vasodilation, which occur primarily in the arterioles, control to a very large extent blood flow through the circulatory system.

Changes in Pressure and Resistance during Exercise

Shown in Figure 10-10 are the systemic blood pressures *(A)* and resistance *(B)* at rest and during exercise. Systolic and diastolic pressures at rest average around 125 and 80 mm Hg, respectively, with a mean pressure of about 95 mm Hg. Although resistance to flow cannot be directly measured in humans, it can be calculated from the relationship $R = P_{mean}/\dot{Q}$. Therefore, if cardiac output at rest is 5 liters per minute, the resistance to flow must be 95 mm Hg/5 liters per minute = 19 mm Hg/liter per minute (Fig. 10-10B).

During exercise, blood pressure in-

---

†As was mentioned earlier, it is the pressure differential that determines the rate of blood flow. However, the pressure differential for the entire systemic circuit is P_{mean} minus the pressure in the right atrium. Since the latter is zero, P_{mean} can be used.

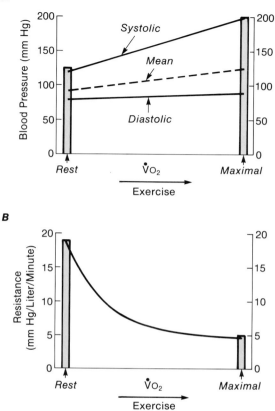

Figure 10-10. *A,* Changes in blood pressure and, *B,* resistance to flow during exercise. Blood pressure increases linearly during exercise as a result of an increase in cardiac output (heart rate and stroke volume), whereas resistance decreases because of vasodilation in the active muscles.

creases as a result of the accompanying increase in cardiac output or, more specifically, of increases in stroke volume and heart rate brought about by nervous and hormonal influences, as we have previously indicated. Actually, as shown in Figure 10-10*A,* this affects systolic pressure more than diastolic or mean pressure. The reason for this is that during exercise there

is a simultaneous decrease in resistance as a result of vasodilation of the arterioles supplying blood to the active skeletal muscles. This means that more blood will drain from the arteries through the arterioles and into the muscle capillaries, thus minimizing changes in diastolic pressure. In turn, changes in mean arterial pressure will also be minimized. In other words, P_{mean} increases with increasing cardiac output, but decreases with decreasing resistance.

The changes in resistance during exercise are impressive. For example, at maximal exercise, with P_{mean} equal to 126 mm Hg and cardiac output to 30 liters per minute, resistance would be $126/30 = 4.2$ mm Hg/liter per min. This represents a 4.5-fold decrease from that at rest.

Hypertension and Exercise

Hypertension refers to high blood pressure, both systolic and diastolic. High blood pressure is associated with a variety of circulatory diseases and, as such, it has been estimated that 12% of all persons die as a direct result of hypertension. Moreover, one out of every five persons can expect to have high blood pressure at some time during their lives.[13]

From our basic hemodynamic equation, we know that the mean arterial pressure is equal to cardiac output times resistance ($P_{mean} = \dot{Q} \times R$). It is easy to see that hypertension is a result of either an increased cardiac output and/or an increased resistance. An increased resistance can be caused by a number of factors, most of which involve the kidneys. However, the most common form of high blood pressure in humans is called **essential hypertension.** It has no known cause and therefore no known cure. It is significant to point out that in this respect, continuous exercise has been shown to reduce resting and exercise blood pressure, particularly in older men[2,22] and women.[18] More about this will be said in Chapters 13 and 15.

Summary

The heart is a muscular pump that circulates the blood through the circulatory system. The direction of blood flow is controlled by unidirectional valves located in the heart. The myocardium (heart muscle) is a syncytium, i.e., all of its fibers are interconnected. Thus the heart contracts as though it were one fiber.

The heart has an inherent contractile rhythm that originates in the sinoatrial node (S-A node) in the right atrium and then spreads to the atrioventricular node (A-V node) and then throughout the heart muscle.

The left and right coronary arteries are the major arteries supplying blood to the heart. They branch repeatedly throughout the entire myocardium. The major vein of the heart is called the coronary sinus.

The cardiac cycle refers to the electrical and mechanical changes that occur in the heart during contraction (systole) and relaxation (diastole). The electrical activity can be recorded from the surface of the body in the form of an electrocardiogram (EKG). The mechanical events involve mainly pressure changes in the aorta, left atrium, and left ventricle.

In order to fully meet the gas transport demands during exercise, two major blood flow changes are necessary: (1) an increase in cardiac output and (2) a redistribution of blood flow from inactive organs to the active skeletal muscles.

The increase in cardiac output ($\dot{Q}$) with exercise is brought about through increases in stroke volume (SV) and in heart rate (HR). Their mathematical relationship is: $\dot{Q} = SV \times HR$. The increase in stroke volume, which reaches maximal levels during submaximal exercise, is a result of greater emptying of the left ventricle. Heart rate increases linearly with increasing workload and $\dot{V}O_2$ in both trained and untrained subjects.

A slow heart rate coupled with a relatively large stroke volume, which is characteristic of the athlete, indicates an efficient circulatory system. For a given cardiac output, a slower-beating heart with a larger stroke volume requires less oxygen.

Cardiac output is ultimately dependent upon the venous return. During exercise, the muscle and respiratory pumps plus venoconstriction help in increasing the venous return.

The redistribution of blood flow that occurs during exercise so that the active muscles receive the greatest proportion of the cardiac output results from (1) reflex vasoconstriction of the arterioles supplying the inactive areas of the body (visceral organs and skin); (2) reflex vasodilation of the arterioles supplying the active muscles, particularly before and at the beginning of exercise; and (3) vasodilation in the active muscles caused by increases in local temperature, CO_2, and lactic acid levels, and a decrease in O_2, particularly as the exercise continues.

The oxygen transport system ($\dot{V}O_2$) is composed of the stroke volume, the heart rate, and the arterial-mixed venous oxygen difference (a-$\bar{v}O_2$ diff). Mathematically, it is defined as: $\dot{V}O_2 = SV \times HR \times$ a-$\bar{v}O_2$ diff. The main difference in the oxygen transport system between trained and untrained subjects is a larger stroke volume.

The study of the physical laws that govern blood flow is called hemodynamics. The two main hemodynamic factors are blood pressure and resistance to flow. The average of the systolic and diastolic pressures during a complete cycle, called mean arterial pressure, determines the rate of blood flow through the systemic circulation. Resistance to flow is caused by friction between the blood and the walls of the vessels. During exercise, blood pressure increases and resistance decreases.

Questions

1. Describe some important anatomical and physiological features of the heart.
2. Define and discuss the cardiac cycle.
3. What is an EKG and how is it recorded?
4. What major blood flow changes occur during exercise?
5. How much could we increase our oxygen consumption if the preceding changes did not occur?
6. Give some values for cardiac output at rest and during maximal exercise for (a) untrained men and women and (b) trained men and women.
7. Describe the changes in stroke volume and heart rate during exercise.
8. Describe the differences and similarities between changes in stroke volume and heart rate during short- and long-term exercise.
9. Explain how the blood flow is redistributed during exercise.
10. How is the redistribution of blood flow related to the a-$\bar{v}O_2$ diff?
11. What are the physiological components of the oxygen transport system? Give an example of how they are interrelated.
12. Define blood pressure and explain how and why it changes during exercise.
13. What is resistance to flow and how is it related to hypertension?

References

1. Åstrand, P., Cuddy, T., Saltin, B., and Stenberg, J.: Cardiac output during submaximal and maximal work. *J Appl Physiol.* 19:268–274, 1964.
2. Boyer, J., and Kasch, F.: Exercise in therapy in hypertensive men. *JAMA.* 211:1668–1671, 1970.
3. Braunwald, E., Godblatt, A., Harrison, D., and Mason, D.: Studies on cardiac dimensions in intact unanesthetized man. III. Effects of muscular exercise. *Circ Res.* 13:448, 1963.
4. Chapman, C. B., and Mitchell, J. H.: The physiology of exercise. *Sci Am.* 212(5):88–96, May 1965.
5. Clausen, J.: Effects of physical conditioning. A hypothesis concerning circulatory adjustment to exercise. *Scand J Clin Lab Invest.* 24:305, 1969.
6. Ekblom, B., Åstrand, P., Saltin, B., Stenberg, J., and Wallström, B.: Effect of training on circulatory response to exercise. *J Appl Physiol.* 24(4):518–528, 1968.
7. Ekblom, B., and Hermansen, L.: Cardiac output in athletes. *J Appl Physiol.* 25(5):619–625, 1968.
8. Ekelund, L., and Holmgren, A.: Circulatory and respiratory adaptation during long-term, nonsteady state exercise, in the sitting position. *Acta Physiol Scand.* 62:240–255, 1964.
9. Fox, E., and Costill, D.: Estimated cardio-respiratory responses during marathon running. *Arch Environ Health.* 24:315–324, 1972.
10. Freedson, P., Katch, V. L., Sady, S., and Weltman, A.: Cardiac output differences in males and females during mild cycle ergometer exercise. *Med Sci Sports.* 11(1):16–19, 1979.
11. Gorlin, R., Cohen, L., Elliott, W., Klein, M., and Lane, F.: Effect of supine exercise on left ventricular volumes and oxygen consumption in man. *Circulation.* 32:361, 1965.
12. Grimby, G.: Renal clearance during prolonged supine exercise at different loads. *J Appl Physiol.* 20:1294–1298, 1965.
13. Guyton, A.: *Textbook of Medical Physiology,* 4th ed. Philadelphia, W. B. Saunders, 1971, p. 304.
14. Hanson, J., Tabakin, B., Levy, A., and Nedde, W.: Long-term physical training and cardiovascular dynamics in middle-aged men. *Circulation.* 38:783–799, 1968.
15. Hartley, L. H.: Central circulatory function during prolonged exercise. *Ann NY Acad Sci.* 301:189–194, 1977.
16. Hartley, L., Grimby, G., Kilbom, Å., Nilsson, N., Åstrand, I., Ekblom, B., and Saltin, B.: Physical training in sedentary middle-aged and older men. III. Cardiac output and gas exchange at submaximal and maximal exercise. *Scand J Clin Lab Invest.* 24:335–344, 1969.
17. Johnson, J. M.: Regulation of skin circulation during prolonged exercise. *Ann NY Acad Sci.* 301:195–212, 1977.
18. Kilbom, Å., and Åstrand, I.: Physical train-

ing with submaximal intensities in women. II. Effect on cardiac output. *Scand J Clin Lab Invest.* 28:163-175, 1971.

19. Landau, B. R.: *Essential Human Anatomy and Physiology.* Glenview, Ill., Scott, Foresman, 1976.

20. Messer, J., Wagman, R., Levine, H., Neill, W., Krasnow, N., and Gorlin, R.: Patterns of human myocardial oxygen extraction during rest and exercise. *J Clin Invest.* 41:725-742, 1962.

21. Michielli, D. W., Stein, R. A., Krasnow, N., Diamond, J. R., and Horwitz, B.: Effects of exercise training on ventricular dimensions at rest and during exercise. *Med Sci Sports.* 11(1):82, 1979.

22. Pollock, M., Miller, H., Janeway, R., Linnerud, A., Robertson, B., and Valentino, R.: Effects of walking on body composition and cardiovascular function of middle-aged men. *J Appl Physiol.* 30(1):126-130, 1971.

23. Rowell, L.: Human cardiovascular adjustments to exercise and thermal stress. *Physiol Rev.* 54(1):75-159, 1974.

24. Rowell, L., Blackmon, J., and Bruce, R.: Indocyanine green clearance and estimated hepatic blood flow during mild to maximal exercise in upright man. *J Clin Invest.* 43:1677-1690, 1964.

25. Rowell, L., Blackmon, J., Martin, R., Mazzarella, J., and Bruce, R.: Hepatic clearance of indocyanine green in man under thermal and exercise stresses. *J Appl Physiol.* 20:384-394, 1965.

26. Saltin, B.: Physiological effects of physical conditioning. *Med Sci Sports.* 1(1):50-56, 1969.

27. Saltin, B., Blomqvist, G., Mitchell, J., Johnson, R., Wildenthal, K., and Chapman, C.: Response to exercise after bed rest and after training. *Circulation.* 38 (Suppl. 7): 1-78, 1968.

28. Saltin, B., and Stenberg, J.: Circulatory response to prolonged severe exercise. *J Appl Physiol.* 19:833-838, 1964.

29. Sawka, M. N., Knowlton, R. G., and Critz, J. B.: Thermal and circulatory responses to repeated bouts of prolonged running. *Med Sci Sports.* 11(2):177-180, 1979.

30. Simon, G., Dickhuth, H. H., Starger, J.,

Essig, C., Kindermann, W., and Keul, J.: The value of echocardiography during physical exercise. *Int Sport Sci.* 1(11) (Abstr.):900, 1980.

31. Slutsky, R., Karliner, J., Ricci, D., Schuler, G., Pfisterer, M., Peterson, K., and Ashburn, W.: Response of left ventricular volume to exercise in man assessed by radionuclide equilibrium angiography. *Circulation.* 60(3):565-571, 1979.

32. Tabakin, B., Hanson, J., and Levy, A.: Effects of physical training on the cardiovascular and respiratory response to graded upright exercise in distance runners. *Br Heart J.* 27:205-210, 1965.

33. Zobl, E., Talmers, F., Christensen, R., and Baer, L.: Effect of exercise on the cerebral circulation and metabolism. *J Appl Physiol.* 20:1289-1293, 1965.

SELECTED READINGS

Berne, R., and Levy, M.: *Cardiovascular Physiology,* 2nd ed. St. Louis, C. V. Mosby, 1972.

Burton, A.: *Physiology and Biophysics of the Circulation.* Chicago, Year Book Medical, 1965.

Carlsten, A., and Grimby, G.: *The Circulatory Response to Muscular Exercise in Man.* Springfield, Ill., Charles C Thomas, 1966.

Guyton, A.: *Circulatory Physiology: Cardiac Output and Its Regulation.* Philadelphia, W. B. Saunders, 1963.

Keul, J.: The relationship between circulation and metabolism during exercise. *Med Sci Sports.* 5(4):209-219, 1973.

Marshall, R., and Shepherd, R.: *Cardiac Function in Health and Disease.* Philadelphia, W. B. Saunders, 1968.

Rowell, L.: Circulation. *Med Sci Sports.* 1(1): 15-22, 1969.

Rowell, L.: Human cardiovascular adjustments to exercise and thermal stress. *Physiol Rev.* 54(1):75-159, 1974.

Rushmer, R.: *Cardiovascular Dynamics,* 4th ed. Philadelphia, W. B. Saunders, 1976.

Vanfraechem, J. H. P.: Stroke volume and systolic time interval adjustments during bicycle exercise. *J Appl Physiol.* 46(3):588-592, 1979.

chapter 11

Cardio-Respiratory Control

The major concepts to be learned from this chapter are as follows:

- During rest and exercise, control of the respiratory and circulatory systems is complex.
- Control of respiration and circulation involves the cardiovascular and respiratory areas, which are located in the brain.
- Both humoral and neural stimulation of these areas aids in regulating important cardiorespiratory variables, such as arterial blood pressure and arterial blood PO_2, PCO_2, and H^+ concentration.
- The response of the cardiorespiratory system during exercise is initially matched to the intensity and type of muscle contractions (static versus dynamic), to the active muscle mass, and later to the fatigue that might be occurring.
- During exercise, primary neural drives to the cardiorespiratory areas include descending impulses from the motor cortex, ascending impulses from muscle ergoreceptors, and vagal afferent impulses from the lungs, i.e., "CO_2 flow" receptors.
- Cardiovascular adjustments primarily are made by an increase in sympathetic neural activity and a decrease in

parasympathetic activity. Ventilatory adjustments by activation of the phrenic and intercostal nerves to the diaphragm and intercostal muscles. These responses may be called the exercise pressor reflex and exercise-induced hyperpnea.

- Precise regulation is attempted through feedback error impulses sent from peripheral and central chemoreceptors to signal a need for additional systematic adjustments. The regulation is never perfect.

Control of the cardiorespiratory system is a difficult job. This is true even under resting conditions, but most of all during exercise. For example, we have seen that many respiratory and circulatory adjustments are necessary during exercise in order to meet the increased metabolic demands of the working muscles. Furthermore, to do this most efficiently, all of these adjustments must be controlled and coordinated with each other.

Basically, this difficult job is carried out by the central nervous system through the combined efforts of the *respiratory* and *cardiovascular areas* located in the brain. These areas constantly receive information concerning the adequacy of gas exchange and transport, either directly or from a variety of receptors located throughout the body. Then, using this information as a basis, they elicit, if necessary, regulatory changes in pulmonary ventilation and blood flow.

Summary of the Cardiorespiratory System

Let us begin our discussion of cardiorespiratory control by summarizing the function of this system. We see from Figure 11-1 that the respiratory system first of all provides a means whereby air is moved into and out of the lungs. This rhythmic to-and-fro movement of air is called *pulmonary*

Figure 11-1. The cardiorespiratory system. The respiratory and circulatory systems work intimately together in meeting, under all conditions, the gaseous exchange and transport requirements of the cells.

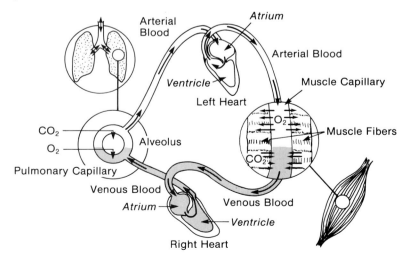

ventilation. Next, the oxygen brought in from the outside environment through pulmonary ventilation is made available to the blood by a vast network of capillaries surrounding the 600 million or so tiny closed air sacs or *alveoli* found in the lungs. The blood contained within the capillaries is *venous blood,* which is relatively low in oxygen and high in carbon dioxide content. At the *alveolar-capillary membranes,* oxygen diffuses from the air in the alveoli to the blood in the capillaries, whereas carbon dioxide diffuses in the opposite direction. Thus, the venous blood brought to the alveoli of the lungs via the right heart returns to the left heart as *arterial blood,* high in oxygen and low in carbon dioxide. The alveolar-capillary membranes, then, represent a functional union between the respiratory and circulatory systems.

The next important job, which is the transporting of arterial blood to the body tissues (and ultimately the carrying of venous blood away from the body tissues), is carried out by the left heart and its associated blood vessels. We should remember that the heart represents two pumps, each with its own circuit of blood vessels. The right heart and its blood vessels, as we have already pointed out, are primarily responsible for transporting venous blood to and arterial blood from the lungs (alveoli). This is called the *pulmonary circuit* or *pulmonary circulation.* Maintaining an adequate flow of arterial blood to and venous blood from the body tissues, on the other hand, is the primary function of the left heart and blood vessels. This is called the *systemic circuit* or *systemic circulation.*

Referring again to Figure 11-1, arterial blood in the pulmonary circuit is returned to the left heart, which then pumps it to all the body tissues—for instance, in our example, to the skeletal muscles. At this level, another vast network of capillaries is found. You will recall from Chapter 5 that skeletal muscle is richly supplied with capillary beds, which come into close contact with the individual muscle fibers. It is at these *tissue-capillary membranes* that a second exchange of gases occurs. This time, oxygen diffuses from the blood in the capillaries to the cells of the tissues, and carbon dioxide diffuses in the opposite direction. The exchange of gases at the tissue-capillary membranes converts arterial blood to venous blood. The venous blood is then returned to the right heart, where the entire process of exchange and transportation of gases is repeated over and over again.

Finally, the oxygen delivered via the cardiorespiratory system is utilized by the cells for purposes of supplying energy in the form of ATP. Oxygen utilization and carbon dioxide production by the cell (the aerobic pathway) were discussed in Chapter 2. Now let's answer the question, How is all this controlled?

The Respiratory and Cardiovascular Areas

The respiratory and cardiovascular areas consist of *networks of nerve cells and their connections.* They are located in the brain stem, mainly in an area called the **medulla oblongata.** Anatomically, it is rather difficult to distinguish one area from the other. However, physiologically, it has been shown that electrical stimulation of certain areas in the brain stem primarily affects respiration, whereas stimulation of nearby but different areas primarily affects circulation. The effect on respiration is mainly a change in pulmonary (alveolar) ventilation, i.e., in the rate and particularly in the depth of breathing. Circulatory effects involve changes in heart rate, stroke volume (force of contraction), the distribution of blood to various organs (vasoconstriction and vasodilation), and venous return (venoconstriction). Although these areas affect one system more than the other, they are neurally interconnected, so that each is informed of the other's activity. Therefore, stimulation of one area will, via its connection with the other, affect both ventilation and blood flow. This, of course, makes sense since the end-result functions of these two systems are one and the same.

As we mentioned earlier, the respiratory and cardiovascular areas receive, evaluate, and send information so that the metabolic needs of each cell are maintained adequately at all times. As part of a control system and under most conditions, this is their main function.

Stimulation of the Cardiorespiratory Areas

The areas are stimulated by a variety of information received from all parts of the body, as shown to the left of Figure 11-2. Stimulation refers to an increase in the activity of the nerve cells and connections that make up the areas. As we will see later, this increased activity initiates the regulatory changes in ventilation and blood flow.

Classification of Stimuli

The many *stimuli* shown in Figure 11-2 can be grouped into two classifications, *humoral* and *neural*. Humoral stimuli origi-

Figure 11-2. Nervous control of the cardiorespiratory system. Various kinds of information (stimuli) from all parts of the body are sent to the respiratory and circulatory areas located in the brain stem. Then, using this information, the areas elicit, if necessary, regulatory changes in pulmonary ventilation and blood flow.

STIMULI (INPUT) RESPONSE (OUTPUT)

Mental Conditions

Motor Command

Contraction

Venous Blood Pressure

Ventilatory Muscles

Ventilation Rate and Depth

Heart

Cardiac Output Rate and Stroke Volume

CO_2, O_2, H^+

Cardiorespiratory Control Areas

(Respiratory Area)
(Cardiovascular Area)

Arterial Blood Pressure

Arterioles and Veins

Vasodilation Vasoconstriction

Stretch

Venoconstriction

Adrenal Medulla

e.g., Pain and Body Temperature

Secretion

Other Information

Epinephrine

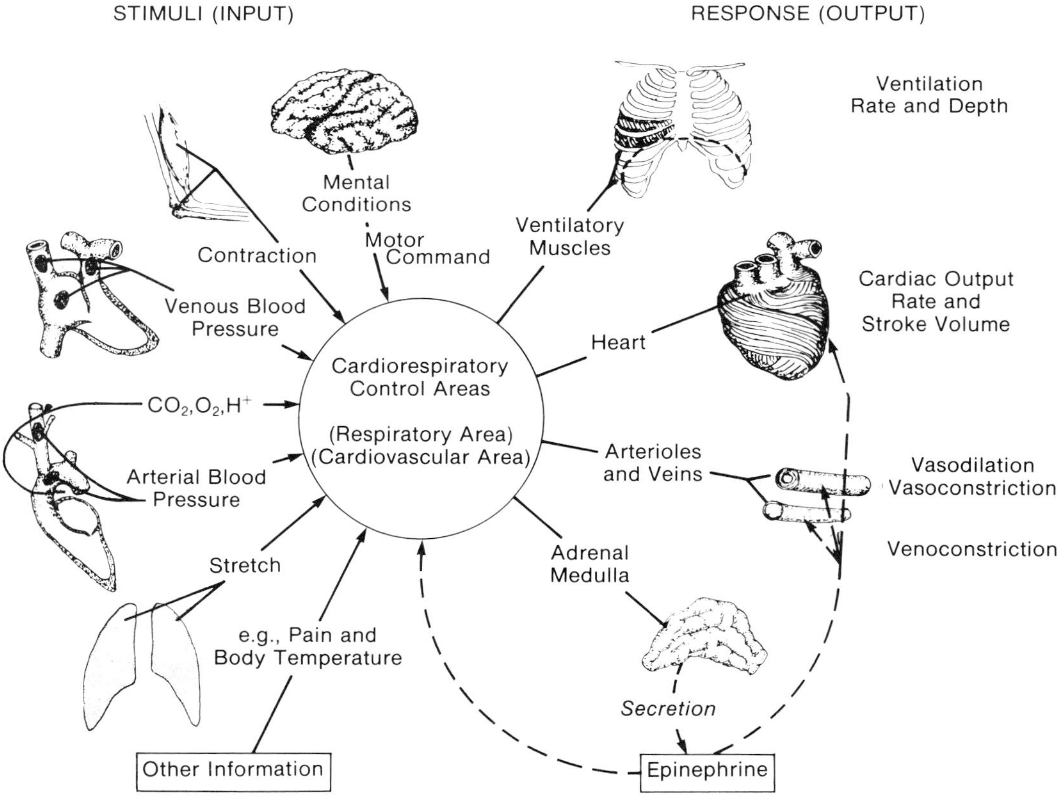

nate from changes in the physical and chemical properties of blood from their normal values at rest. Thus, the areas are supplied with important information concerning changes in: (1) arterial and venous blood pressures and blood temperature (physical changes), and (2) arterial blood PO_2, PCO_2, and H^+ concentration (chemical changes). Neural stimuli, on the other hand, are independent of changes in the properties of blood; rather, they originate from changes that take place in higher brain centers, the lungs, the muscles, joints, tendons, skin, and respiratory passages. The information they provide the areas is concerned with (1) mental conditions, e.g., emotions, and particularly the activity of the motor cortex; (2) inflation and deflation (stretch) of the lungs; (3) muscle contraction and limb movement or tension development; and (4) intense pain or general discomfort and the presence of respiratory irritants (hence, the cough and sneeze reflexes). While all of these neural stimuli are important, we will be most interested in those from the motor areas of the cortex, the lungs, and the muscles, joints, and tendons.

Action on the Cardiorespiratory Areas

As indicated in Table 11-1, stimuli may act upon the cardiorespiratory areas either *directly* or *indirectly*, or both. In the first case, the areas are stimulated directly either via the circulating blood due to increases in temperature, PCO_2, and H^+ concentration, or via nervous impulses from higher brain centers. Indirect stimulation of the areas occurs *reflexly* via sensory nerves originating in specialized receptors, to which the areas are connected. In this case, the areas are stimulated by an increase in the number of sensory nerve impulses initiated by the receptors as a result of increases in blood temperature, arterial and venous blood pressures, and arterial

blood PCO_2 and H^+ concentrations, a decrease in arterial blood PO_2, inflation and deflation of the lungs, and limb movement. The names and locations of the receptors are given in Table 11-1 and are schematically shown in Figure 11-2. Note that increases in blood temperature and arterial blood PCO_2 and H^+ concentration act on the areas both directly and indirectly. This of course provides additional sensitivity and precision to the controlling mechanism.

Effects on Ventilation and Blood Flow

As previously mentioned, stimulation of the cardiorespiratory areas initiates regulatory changes in ventilation and blood flow. Some of these changes, along with their respective stimuli, are contained in Table 11-1. We shall want to study these, as they relate to the control of the cardiorespiratory system both at rest and during exercise. However, before doing so, it is essential that we understand something about the nervous connections between the areas on the one hand, and the cardiorespiratory apparatus on the other.

Innervation of the Cardiorespiratory Apparatus

The innervation of the cardiorespiratory system is shown schematically to the right of Figure 11-2. The motor nerves connected to the ventilatory muscles (page 215) are called *somatic motor nerves* (*somatic* means "body"). We know that when they are stimulated they affect both the rate and depth of respiration. In addition, they belong to the *voluntary* nervous system, like those innervating the other skeletal muscles. This explains why we have some voluntary control over ventilation, i.e., why we can alter our ventilatory behavior at will (just as we can alter our motor behavior at will).

The motor nerves innervating the heart and blood vessels, on the other hand, are

TABLE 11-1

Action of Humoral and Neural Stimuli on the Cardiorespiratory Areas and Their Effects on Respiration and Circulation

Stimuli	Action on Cardiorespiratory Areas				Effects		
	Direct (Central)	Indirect (Reflex)	Receptors		Respiration	Circulation	
			Name	Location	Ventilation (Rate and Depth)	Heart (Rate and Force)	Blood Vessels
1. Humoral							
a. Physical							
1. Increased blood temperature	✓	✓	Thermoreceptors	Hypothalamus	Increased	Increased	Vasodilation in active muscles and skin
2. Increased arterial blood pressure		✓	Pressoreceptors, baroreceptors, or stretch receptors	Carotid arteries, aortic arch	Decreased	Decreased	Vasodilation
3. Increased venous blood pressure		✓		Vena cavae, right atrium	Increased	Increased	Vasoconstriction
b. Chemical							
1. Increased arterial blood P_{CO_2}, H^+	✓	✓	Chemoreceptors	Carotid arteries, aortic arch	Increased	Increased	Vasoconstriction
2. Decreased arterial blood P_{O_2}		✓			Increased	Increased	Vasoconstriction

Stimulus		Receptor	Location	Respiration		Circulation
3. Increased norepineph-rine and epinephrine from adrenal medulla	—	—	—	—	Increased	Vasodilation in active muscles; vasoconstric-tion in inac-tive muscles
2. Neural a. Impulse trans-mission from higher brain centers	√			Increased	Increased	Vasodilation in active muscles; vasoconstric-tion in active muscles
b. Inflation and deflation of lungs	√	Stretch receptors, or mechano-receptors	Lungs (bronchi, bronchioles, alveoli)	Inflation: Inhibits inspira-tion	Increased	Vasoconstriction
				Deflation: Stimulates inspira-tion	Unknown	Unknown
c. Muscle contraction 1. Mechanical 2. Metabolic	√	Ergoreceptors mechanoreceptors metaboreceptors	Muscles, joints, and tendons	Increased	Increased	Vasodilation in active muscles; vasoconstric-tion in inac-tive muscles

quite different. This is evidenced by the fact that we do not usually have voluntary control over the circulatory system. These particular motor nerves belong to the *involuntary,* or **autonomic nervous system** and are collectively referred to as autonomic nerves. Those which, when stimulated, cause increased heart rate and stroke volume (greater force of contraction) are called *cardioaccelerator nerves* because of their function, or *sympathetic nerves* because they belong to the *sympathetic division* of the autonomic nervous system. Other autonomic nerves that innervate the heart, the *vagus nerves,* belong to the *parasympathetic division* of the autonomic nervous system. When they are stimulated, heart rate decreases, just the opposite of what happens when the sympathetic nerves are stimulated. This again provides additional precision to the controlling mechanism. For example, increases in heart rate and stroke volume result from either a decreased rate of stimulation of the vagus nerves or an increased rate of stimulation of the sympathetic cardioaccelerator nerves, or both. During exercise, both of these occur simultaneously.*

The motor nerves innervating the smooth muscles of the blood vessels also belong to the autonomic nervous system. They include: (1) sympathetic nerves that go to virtually all arterioles and veins, and which when stimulated cause vaso- and venoconstriction *(sympathetic vasoconstrictor nerves);* and (2) sympathetic nerves that connect *only* to the arterioles of skeletal and heart muscles, and which when stimulated cause vasodilation *(sympathetic vasodilator nerves).*† The latter

nerves are thought to be most active in the alarm or defense reactions and before and at the very beginning of exercise. As mentioned in Chapter 10, during exercise, vasodilation in the working muscles is brought about mainly by locally produced "vasodilator metabolites." Thus the sympathetic vasoconstrictor nerves and the local vasodilator metabolites released by the working muscles are in large part responsible for the redistribution of blood away from inactive tissues toward the active muscles and for the increase in venous return that occurs during exercise.

The effects caused by stimulation of these various motor nerves result from the release of chemical transmitter substances at the nerve endings (see Chapter 6 for more on chemical transmitters). For example, increases in heart rate, stroke volume, and vasoconstriction are caused by the release of *norepinephrine* from the ends of the sympathetic cardioaccelerator and vasoconstrictor nerves when they are stimulated. We mention this here because of the importance of a group of specialized gland cells found in the medullae (central portions) of the adrenal glands. These cells are similar to the sympathetic nerves just mentioned in that they also release norepinephrine, plus another, similar chemical called *epinephrine* (adrenalin). These two chemicals (in this case called *hormones*) are secreted when their sympathetic nerves are stimulated and are carried in the circulating blood. This occurs during alarm or fright and most importantly before and during exercise. The effects of these hormones on the heart and blood vessels are identical or almost identical to those produced when the sympathetic nerves innervating these tissues are directly stimulated (Table 11-1). In addition, these hormones increase the metabolic rate of the tissues and the rate and depth of ventilation.

A different chemical, called *acetylcholine,* is released at the ends of the vagus

---

*At rest, the heart is primarily under the influence of the vagus nerves. The slow resting heart rates of trained subjects are thought to result from increased vagal stimulation (tone). However, the mechanism responsible for this is unknown.

†There are also parasympathetic vasodilator nerves, but they supply only the tongue, salivary glands, external genital organs, urinary bladder, and rectum.

and sympathetic vasodilator nerves and the somatic nerves innervating the ventilatory muscles.

Cardiorespiratory Control at Rest and during Exercise

One of the most important functions of any physiological control system is to maintain certain variables at optimal levels. For example, in Chapter 18, we will see how the thermoregulatory system strives to maintain an optimal body temperature over a wide range of climatic conditions, both at rest and during exercise. In this respect, the cardiorespiratory control system is no different; it too strives to maintain certain variables at optimal levels under all conditions.

From our previous discussions, it is obviously quite difficult to single out any one or even a few cardiorespiratory variables that are, at all times, preferentially maintained at optimal levels. These preferences change, depending on the metabolic needs of the cells from one moment to the next. Actually, with our present knowledge, it is virtually impossible to give an adequate overall explanation of how given levels of ventilation and blood flow are achieved and controlled so as to exactly meet the metabolic needs of any cell under any condition.[19] Furthermore, the respective roles of the many stimuli involved in this control and their interactions are not yet completely known. At best, all we can say is that the final outcome is determined by the stimuli that predominate at any given moment.

All of this serves well to illustrate how complex and how little understood is the control of the cardiorespiratory system. Nevertheless, there are several important concepts concerning this control that we can point out, among them how arterial blood pressure, and arterial blood PO_2, PCO_2, and H^+ concentration are maintained at optimal levels at rest and during exercise. We have chosen these particular variables because more is known about their control than about any others.

Control at Rest

The most important factors in maintenance of arterial blood pressure, PO_2, PCO_2, and H^+ concentration at optimal levels under resting conditions are changes in these variables themselves. As indicated in Table 11-1, changes in them initiate cardiorespiratory adjustments that affect these changes inversely. For example, an *increased* arterial pressure (e.g., above the 100 mm Hg normally required at rest) causes decreases in heart rate, stroke volume (force of contraction), and resistance to blood flow (vasodilation). We know from our discussion of hemodynamics that these circulatory adjustments will in turn lead to a *decrease* in arterial pressure.* By the same token, a decrease in pressure below the normal, by causing the opposite circulatory adjustments, will lead to an increase in pressure. This regulatory adjustment is mediated by the **carotid baroreceptors** that are sensitive to transluminal (across the walls) stretch of these elastic vessels. There is evidence that the baroreflex operates to support arterial blood pressure during the transition from rest through the first minutes of exercise[12] and later serves to make fine response adjustments.[17] In either case, when the pressure returns to its normal (optimal) level, the original stimulus (i.e., a change in pressure)—and thus the whole process—is "turned off." This type of control is sometimes referred to as a **negative feedback mechanism.**

The same type of control mechanism limits changes in the normal levels of arterial blood PO_2, PCO_2, and H^+ concentration. For instance, a decreased PO_2 or an in-

---

*Remember: $P_{mean} = \dot{Q} \times R$, and $\dot{Q} = SV \times HR$; therefore, $P_{mean} = SV \times HR \times R$.

creased PCO_2, and H^+ concentration, or both, causes an immediate increase in alveolar ventilation by increasing primarily the depth of respiration (Table 11-1). This affects the levels of these variables in the opposite direction.

One other aspect of ventilatory control needs to be mentioned here. Note that inflation and deflation of the lungs does not affect total ventilation, as do the other stimuli. Inflation of the lungs during inspiration causes expiration (i.e., it inhibits inspiration), whereas deflation of the lungs during expiration stimulates inspiration. In other words, these reflexes, initiated via the pulmonary stretch receptors, automatically reinforce the maintenance of a normal respiratory rhythm of inspiration followed by expiration. They provide us the luxury of a normal ventilatory rhythm without continuous conscious effort. This is their main function. They are not directly involved with maintenance of PO_2, PCO_2, and H^+ concentration simply because they are not equipped to supply the respiratory areas with this type of information.

Control during Exercise

At rest, adjustments in ventilation and blood flow regulate or maintain arterial blood pressure, PO_2, PCO_2, and H^+ concentration at optimal levels. This is also true during exercise, for this is the main function of the cardiorespiratory control system under any condition. However, there is one big difference—at rest, changes in these regulated variables are the predominant stimuli that initiate such adjustments; during exercise, other stimuli predominate. This is easy to see, for many reasons.

First, we know from experience that heart rate and ventilation, for example, increase even before exercise begins, long before changes in pressure or in PO_2, PCO_2, and H^+ concentration can occur. In addi-

tion, we now know, from a physiological standpoint, that an increase in heart rate (and in stroke volume) increases arterial blood pressure. If this increased pressure (which is optimal under these conditions), were the predominant stimulus at any time during exercise, heart rate and stroke volume would decrease rather than increase. Likewise, vasodilation would occur in *all* tissues rather than mainly in the active muscles, and the redistribution of blood flow to the latter, which we also know occurs, would not be possible.

Second, changes in arterial blood PO_2, PCO_2, and H^+ concentration would have to be quite pronounced in order to account fully for the large increase in pulmonary ventilation that occurs during exercise. The fact of the matter is that these variables change very little during exercise. This is true except during very heavy or maximal exercise. Under these conditions, PO_2 decreases and H^+ increases, primarily because of lactic acid formation. In this case, these changes—particularly in H^+ concentration—do cause an additional increase in ventilation (Figure 8-1A). On the other hand, arterial blood PCO_2 decreases during heavy exercise, and this would tend to decrease ventilation.

Which stimuli, then, predominate during exercise? Unfortunately, all of the stimuli have not as yet been determined. However, there are several that are known to be of primary importance in maintaining certain cardiorespiratory variables at optimal levels. These stimuli include: (1) increased activity of the motor cortex, (2) muscle contraction and limb movement or static tension development, (3) increased H^+ concentration (lactic acid formation) and "CO_2 flow" to the lungs, (4) increased blood temperature, and (5) increased secretion of norepinephrine and epinephrine from the adrenal medulla. Their effects on ventilation and blood flow are given in Table 11-1. Most of these stimuli (particularly the first four) supply information concerning the intensity of exercise rather than the level or magnitude of any particular cardiorespiratory variable. This enables the resulting adjustments in ventilation and blood flow to keep in approximate pace with the increased gas exchange and transport requirements of the working muscles.

Models of Cardiorespiratory Control

The response of the cardiovascular system during exercise is matched to the type and intensity of the activity being performed. For example, during static contractions the increases in arterial blood pressure match the intensity of effort which, in turn, is directly related to the active muscle mass and the percentage of maximal voluntary contraction. On the other hand, during dynamic exercise, the increase in cardiac output matches the intensity of effort, which is directly related to the oxygen uptake of active skeletal muscles. In general, these cardiovascular responses to static and dynamic exercise are brought about by an increased activity of the sympathetic nervous system and a decreased activity of the parasympathetic nervous system.[16]

Now let's take a closer look at how these adjustments of the autonomic nervous system are mediated during exercise. For this, refer to Figure 11-3. The model[14] in Figure 11-3 places equal importance for regulation of the cardiovascular system during static and dynamic exercise on both direct neural control and reflex neural control. The central control is referred to as "central command" and shows the presence of descending impulses from the higher motor centers of the cerebrum onto the cardiovascular areas of the medulla. Thus, when an individual anticipates the start of exercise or indeed begins to send impulses to recruit motor units to produce muscle contractions, there also are impulses sent to the cardiovascular areas.

This results in an almost immediate increase in the outflow of impulses down the sympathetic nerve fibers, which connect to the SA node region of the heart. The release of norepinephrine at the SA node causes an increase in heart rate. A simultaneous reduction in parasympathetic activity results in a reduced release of acetylcholine at the SA node, which likewise contributes to a rapid response of faster heart rate during the initial seconds of exercise. Note also the release of norepinephrine to the ventricles and other regions of the heart, which increases myocardial contractility to produce a larger stroke volume. Cardiac output is thereby increased[1] and combined with the constriction of selected blood vessels[3] causes the systolic blood pressure to rise, the so-called "exercise pressor reflex."[13]

Other neural impulses impinge on the cardiovascular area after muscle contractions begin and either movement or static tension is produced. These impulses originate in special receptors found in muscles and joints that collectively are called ergoreceptors. One type of ergoreceptor is sensitive to the mechanical effects of muscular contractions and appropriately are called mechanoreceptors.[2] The afferent fibers for the mechanoreceptors are type III fibers,[10] which have Paciniform corpuscles as their sensory endings. These fibers travel in the dorsal root to the cord and follow ascending spinal pathways to the cardiovascular area. The mechanoreceptors along with the descending impulses from the cerebral motor regions provide information to the cardiovascular area regarding the mass of skeletal muscle involved in the exercise being performed. Collectively the central command impulses and mechanoreceptor mediated reflex impulses initiate the cardiovascular responses and determine the starting level of the efferent activity of the autonomic nervous system to the heart and blood vessels.

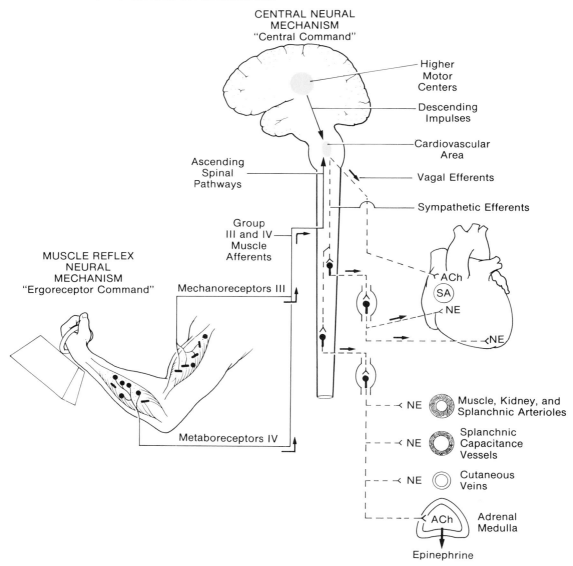

Figure 11-3. Control over the cardiovascular system during exercise. Both descending impulses from the motor region of the cerebrum ("central command") and ascending impulses from muscle receptors ("ergoreceptor command") impinge on the cardiovascular area of the medulla. This results in reduced parasympathetic activity to the heart and an increase in sympathetic activity to the heart, blood vessels, and adrenal medulla. The end result is an increase in cardiac output and increase in blood pressure, which combine to give the "exercise pressor reflex." See text for details. (Redrawn from Mitchell, et al.[14])

The second type of ergoreceptors are called metaboreceptors. They serve as a feedback system from the exercising skeletal muscle to monitor the effectiveness of blood flow in meeting increased metabolic needs. The terminal ends of these receptors are free nerve endings, which sometimes are called nociceptors (activated by noxious stimuli and responsible for muscle pain). Their afferent nerve fibers are unmyelinated, are relatively slow conducting, and are classed as type IV sensory fibers. They travel the same spinal route to the medullary cardiovascular area as the type III fibers from the mechanoreceptors. The difference is that during light-intensity dynamic exercise the metabolic neural reflex mechanism may not be activated. During higher intensity dynamic exercise or during static contractions where blood flow is either partly or totally occluded this neural reflex mechanism may quickly signal that a shortage of blood flow exists. This flow error message arrives at the cardiovascular area and elicits an appropriate level of autonomic efferent regulation of the heart and blood vessels as described before for the mechanoreceptors.

Before leaving this area of cardiovascular regulatory responses to exercise it is appropriate to summarize some of the experimental evidence that supports the presence of redundant neural control mechanisms. The term redundant here means that either mechanism could function to produce the exercise pressor effect independent of the other mechanism. This proves to be the case. For example, Figure 11-4 shows that the heart rate and blood pressure responses are the same for static contractions induced by electrical stimulation (no central mechanism, only ergoreceptor command) and those changes produced through voluntary contractions (central and ergoreceptor commands). This is evidence for the presence of a muscle reflex neural mechanism operating with-

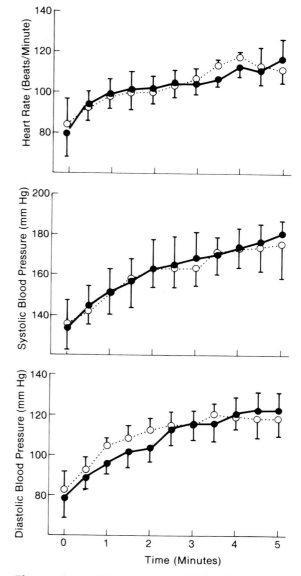

Figure 11-4. Heart rate and blood pressure response to static exercise voluntary contraction (●—●) and electrical-induced contractions (○--○). Values are mean ± standard deviation ($n = 6$). (From original work of Hultman and Sjöholm, *Acta Physiol Scand.* 115:499, 1982.[14])

out any known contribution of central command. In other studies of static and dynamic exercise the sensory input from working muscles was blocked by spinal anesthesia. This eliminated the effectiveness of neural reflex command influences from the ergoreceptors. The observation that increases in cardiac output during dynamic exercise were still related to oxygen consumption provides solid evidence for the independent effectiveness of the central command mechanism.

Further evidence for the effectiveness of central command has resulted from studies where neuromuscular function was partially blocked with decamethonium. It can be reasoned that partial blockade would require more motor impulses to be sent to motoneurons to finally recruit enough motor units to produce a desired static tension, say 10 or 30% of maximum voluntary contraction. Likewise, it can be reasoned that if a central command mechanism is present the cardiovascular area will be impacted by more descending impulses during static contractions under partial blockade than under normal conditions. This should result in a more pronounced HR and BP response during static contractions at the same absolute force production. This all proved to be true in experiments conducted on human subjects. Normally, either central or reflex neural mechanisms can elicit the observed cardiovascular responses, and the two mechanisms work in concert. Thus, the appropriate response may be elicited by either mechanism and they are truly redundant, because they appear to influence the same neural circuits in the central nervous system. When there is a disproportionate signal from the central neural mechanism as compared to the reflex neural mechanism, the larger of the two seems to dictate the HR and BP response.

Control mechanisms for the pulmonary or ventilatory system during exercise are shown in Figure 11-5. Note first that there are similarities between this control model[7] and that shown for cardiovascular

regulation in Figure 11-3. For example, both the respiratory and the cardiovascular areas of the medulla receive redundant[18] descending impulses from higher motor regions of the cerebrum and ascending impulses from the mechano- and metaboreceptors of active muscles. These descending and ascending impulses plus a third source of input from the lung itself are considered primary drives to hyperpnea, i.e., an increase in the rate and depth of breathing. Sensors in the lung itself detect changes in "CO_2 flow," which is defined as the product of cardiac output ($\dot{Q}$) times the concentration of CO_2 in mixed venous blood ($C\bar{v}CO_2$). The C-fiber endings of the afferent vagal nerves that return from the lung are likely the sensors and carriers of information regarding any increase or decrease in CO_2 flow to the lung during rest and low-intensity exercise. Note that the adjustment in rate and depth of breathing is made via an increased neural activity to the intercostal muscles and diaphragm.

The control model in Figure 11-5 also shows several error detection feedback impulses that impinge on the respiratory area. These are from lung and airway receptors, intercostal and diaphragm muscle spindles, peripheral chemoreceptors in the carotid bodies, and central chemoreceptors in the medulla itself. The feedback from the lung, airway receptors, and chest wall are concerned with optimization of mechanical events such as flow, pressure, volume, and tension relationships via control of breathing pattern and lung volume. The peripheral chemoreceptors[9] are affected by arterial blood PO_2 and $[H^+]$ whereas the central chemoreceptors respond to extracellular cerebral fluid acidity, i.e., $[H^+]$.

The prevailing concept of neurohumoral regulation of exercise-induced hyperpnea is inherent in this model.[7] For example, "CO_2 flow" serves as a humoral or blood-borne substance that can drive ven-

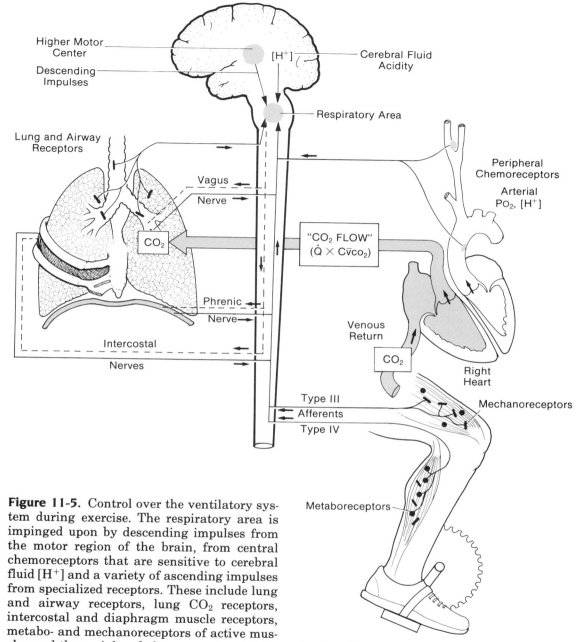

Figure 11-5. Control over the ventilatory system during exercise. The respiratory area is impinged upon by descending impulses from the motor region of the brain, from central chemoreceptors that are sensitive to cerebral fluid [H$^+$] and a variety of ascending impulses from specialized receptors. These include lung and airway receptors, lung CO$_2$ receptors, intercostal and diaphragm muscle receptors, metabo- and mechanoreceptors of active muscles and the peripheral chemoreceptors. This results in reduced parasympathetic activity to the bronchioles and increased volleys of impulses to the diaphragm and intercostal muscles via the phrenic and intercostal nerves. The end result is exercise-induced hyperpnea, an increase in the rate and depth of breathing and regulation of arterial P$_{O_2}$, P$_{CO_2}$, and pH. See text for details. (Redrawn from Demsey, et al. model.[7])

tilation under varying conditions of rest where little movement or effort is involved. At the onset of exercise, neural impulses from the cerebral motor centers would produce a rapid adjustment in ventilation that would approximate the magnitude of muscle force production and metabolic rate. As exercise is continued, this central neural regulation would be supported by additional neural drives from the mechano- and metaboreceptors. The effectiveness of the adjustments in ventilation would be indicated by the closeness of matchup between the production of CO_2 by active muscles and the impact of hyperpnea in regulating arterial PCO_2 and its associated $[H^+]$ yield. Apparently there is not a precise matching of the primary stimuli to breathe during exercise and an ideal response such as fully regulated arterial PCO_2, which is referred to as isocapnic hyperpnea. Chemofeedback from peripheral and central receptors provide an additional stimulus when primary stimuli are insufficient, and serve as a guard against hyperventilation when primary stimuli are excessive.[6,7] The precision of the adjustment via chemoreceptor feedback is likely only about ±5 to 10% but this imprecision is tolerated well by the organism during the performance of even high-intensity exercise.

There is some evidence that control over ventilation through the respiratory area can provide some protections during heavy exercise. For example, the hyperventilation and blowing off of CO_2 may be a protection against metabolic acidosis but at the same time an effort to protect against hypoxemia by increasing the delivery of more O_2-rich air to the alveoli. The drive for hyperventilation that rises nonlinearly during higher work rates may be coincident with an increased output from CNS locomotor centers in an effort to compensate for the quickly declining efficiency of limb muscles that are undergoing fatigue. This would be a neurally based rather than a humorally based drive that might be viewed as a last effort to continue the exercise or survival efforts. The observation that an inappropriately low or no hyperventilatory response occurs during high work rates in some trained athletes may be due to a reflex inhibition of the inspiratory drive to prevent respiratory muscle fatigue. The benefits of this protection strategy may be short lived, however, due to the acid buildup (acidosis) and hypoxemia (reduced arterial blood O_2).

At this point the reader is well aware that there are both neural and humoral factors that exert control and regulation of the cardiorespiratory system through specialized areas in the brain stem. The neural control mechanisms, both central and reflex commands, have been emphasized for the cardiovascular system, but it is apparent that the epinephrine and norepinephrine released by the adrenal medulla is a circulating humoral substance with tremendous regulatory effect on the entire cardiorespiratory system. It also should be apparent that because the stimulatory impulses that arrive at the medullary areas are very often one and the same, that both the cardiovascular and ventilatory system are coordinated and matched in the timing and magnitude of their respective responses during exercise. This is as one would expect and as every observer of their own physiological responses at the beginning of exercise is aware; two of the most immediately noticeable and measurable indications that exercise is being performed are the increases in HR and breathing rate. Later, during steady-state exercise, the performer is often aware of an even, leveled off, breathing pattern and a measurably stable HR. When higher intensity challenges such as hills during a run are encountered, the runner is once again aware of the faster and deeper breathing patterns and pounding HR, which subside after the challenge has been met. At the point of impending fatigue or exhaustion, the unwelcomed perceptions of "being behind" in breathing and unable to "catch up" are felt, which translates into hyperventilation. The HR and blood pressure would be near their peak levels at this point as the organism makes every effort to endure and survive the experience. All of this without the performer having to think about it or attempt to make voluntary adjustments attests to the magnificent complexity and precision of the cardiorespiratory regulatory mechanisms.

Physical training has been shown to affect some of the cardiovascular and ventilatory control mechanisms we have just reviewed. For example, the well-known bradycardia of training may be mediated through different mechanisms at rest and during exercise.[8] The resting bradycardia is due to enhanced parasympathetic control, whereas, the exertional bradycardia is the result of a decreased sympathetic drive. Training may alter the responsiveness and impact of muscle receptors in exerting a regulatory role over exercise bradycardia.[5] Trained persons also may be able to attenuate their exercise HR responses (tachycardia) when given visual feedback during heavy exercise.[15] Other differences between trained and control subjects exist in the area of ventilatory control since trained subjects have lower $\dot{V}E$ increases per unit of metabolic rate such as $\dot{V}O_2$ uptake or $\dot{V}CO_2$ production;[11] that is to say, a relatively low ventilatory response to chemical stimuli. Furthermore, hypoxic and hypercapnic ventilatory drives have been shown to be inversely related to $\dot{V}O_2$ max measures.[4] As is often the case, these training adaptations support the observation of improved tolerance to endure exercise, when the mechanistic drives in lesser trained individuals have forced them to slow up or stop activity.

Other Control Mechanisms

Nervous control of the cardiorespiratory system is paramount to the overall functional efficiency of this system; for this reason, we have studied it in some detail. However, we must not forget about those cardiorespiratory adjustments that are *not* controlled by the central nervous system. For example, remember that increases in blood temperature, acidity, and CO_2 beneficially shift the HbO_2 dissociation curve to the right during exercise. Furthermore, these same factors, plus a lowered PO_2 (collectively referred to as vasodilator metabolites), also promote local vasodilation of the arterioles supplying blood to the active muscles, an adjustment made by the smooth muscles themselves in response to changes in their local environment. We can also mention the increase in venous return resulting from the mechanical actions of the muscle and respiratory pumps, and the hemoconcentration caused by fluid shifts between the active muscles and the blood. All of these adjustments represent a type of control mechanism that is equally important to the overall efficiency of the cardiorespiratory system, particularly during exercise.

Summary

During both rest and exercise, control of the cardiorespiratory system is extremely complex. The essential constituents for such control are found in the respiratory and circulatory areas located in the brain stem. Both humoral and neural stimulation of these areas aids in regulating, at all times, such important cardiorespiratory variables as arterial blood pressure and arterial blood PO_2, PCO_2, and H^+ concentration.

Innervation of the cardiorespiratory apparatus involves both the voluntary nervous system (supplying the respiratory muscles) and the involuntary or autonomic nervous system (supplying the heart and blood vessels).

At rest, the most important factors in maintenance of blood pressure, PO_2, PCO_2, and H^+ concentration are changes in these variables themselves (negative feedback).

During exercise, the predominant stimuli are (1) increased activity of the motor cortex, (2) muscle contraction and limb movement or static tension development, (3) increased H^+ concentration and "CO_2 flow" to the lungs, (4) increased blood temperature, and (5) secretion of norepinephrine and epinephrine from the adrenal medulla. Other mechanisms include shifts in the HbO_2 dissociation curve and in local vasodilation in the muscles.

Questions

1. Where are the respiratory and circulatory areas located and what are their main functions?
2. Describe the difference between neural and humoral stimuli and give examples of each.
3. Describe the difference between direct and indirect stimulation of the cardiorespiratory area and give examples of each.
4. Discuss the innervation of the cardiorespiratory apparatus.
5. Outline how ventilation and blood flow are regulated during rest and exercise. How do they differ?

References

1. Asmussen, E., and Nielsen, M.: Cardiac output during muscular work and its regulation. *Physiol Rev.* 35:778-800, 1955.
2. Asmussen, E., Johansen, S., Jørgensen, M., and Neilsen, M.: On the nervous factors controlling respiration and circulation during exercise. *Acta Physiol Scand.* 63:343-350, 1965.
3. Bevegard, B., and Shepherd, J.: Regulation of the circulation during exercise in man. *Physiol Rev.* 47:178-213, 1967.
4. Bryne-Quinn, E., Weil, J. V., Sodal, I. E., Filley, G. F., and Grover, R. F.: Ventilatory control in the athlete. *J Appl Physiol.* 30(1): 91-98, 1971.
5. Clausen, J., Trap-Jensen, J., and Lassen, N.: The effects of training on the heart rate

during arm and leg exercise. *Scand J Clin Lab Invest.* 26:295-301, 1970.
6. Dempsey, J. A., Mitchell, G. S., and Smith, C. A.: Exercise and chemoreception. *Am Rev Respir Dis.* 129-Suppl S31-S34, 1984.
7. Dempsey, J. A., Virduk, E. H., and Mitchell, G. S.: Pulmonary control systems in exercise: update. *Fed Proc.* 44(7):2260-2270, 1985.
8. Frick, M., Elovainio, R., and Somer, T.: The mechanism of bradycardia evoked by physical training. *Cardiologia.* 51:46-54, 1967.
9. Hildebrandt, J. R., and Hildebrandt, J.: Cardiorespiratory responses to sudden release of circulatory occlusion during exercise. *Respir Physiol.* 38(1):83-92, 1979.
10. Kalia, N., Senapati, J., Parida, B., and Panda, A.: Reflex increase in ventilation by muscle receptors with non-medulated fibers (C fibers). *J Appl Physiol.* 32:189-193, 1972.
11. Martin, B. J., Sparks, K. E., Zwillich, C. W., and Weil, J. V.: Low exercise ventilation in endurance athletes. *Med Sci Sports.* 11(2): 181-185, 1979.
12. Melcher, A., and Donald, D. E.: Maintained ability of carotid baroreflex to regulate arterial pressure during exercise. *Am J Physiol.* (Heart Circ. Physiol. 10):H838-H849, 1981.
13. Mitchell, J. H., Kaufman, M. P., and Iwamoto, G. A.: The exercise pressor reflex: its cardiovascular effects, afferent mechanisms, and central pathways. *Ann Rev Physiol.* 45:299-42, 1983.
14. Mitchell, J. H.: Cardiovascular control during exercise: central and reflex neural mechanisms. *Am J Cardiol.* 55:34D-41D, 1985.
15. Perski, A., Tzankoff, S. P., and Engel, B. T.: Central control of cardiovascular adjustments to exercise. *J Appl Physiol.* 58(2): 431-435, 1985.
16. Stone, H. L., and Liang, I. Y. S.: Cardiovascular response and control during exercise. *Am Rev Respir Dis.* 129:Suppl S13-S16, 1984.
17. Walgenbach, S. C., and Donald, D. E.: Inhibition by carotid baroreflex of exercise-induced increases in arterial pressure. *Circ Res.* 52:253-262, 1983.
18. Weissman, M. L., Wasserman, K., Huntsman, D. J., and Whipp, B. J.: Ventilation and gas exchange during phasic hindlimb exercise in dog. *J Appl Physiol.* 46(5):878-884, 1979.

19. Whipp, B. J., Ward, S. A., and Wasserman, K.: Ventilatory responses to exercise and their control in man. *Am Rev Respir Dis.* 129:Suppl S17–S20, 1984.

SELECTED READINGS

American College of Sports Medicine: Symposium on ventilatory control during exercise. *Med Sci Sports.* 11(2):190–226, 1979.

Berne, R., and Levy, M.: *Cardiovascular Physiology,* 2nd ed. St. Louis, C. V. Mosby, 1972, pp. 237–253.

Burton, A.: *Physiology and Biophysics of the Circulation,* 2nd ed. Chicago, Year Book Medical, 1972.

Carlsten, A., and Grimby, G.: *The Circulatory Response to Muscular Exercise in Man.* Springfield, Ill., Charles C Thomas, 1966.

Caro, C. G. (ed.): *Advances in Respiratory Physiology.* Baltimore, Williams and Wilkins, 1966.

Comroe, J.: *Physiology of Respiration,* 2nd ed. Chicago, Year Book Medical, 1974.

Comroe, J., Forster, R., Dubois, A., Briscoe, W., and Carlsen, E.: *The Lung,* 2nd ed. Chicago, Year Book Medical, 1962.

Cunningham, D., and Lloyd, B. (eds.): *The Regulation of Human Respiration.* Philadelphia, F. A. Davis, 1963.

DeJours, R.: *Respiration.* New York, Oxford University Press, 1966.

Dempsey, J. A., and Reed, C. E. (eds.): *Muscular Exercise and the Lung.* Madison, Wis., University of Wisconsin Press, 1977.

Rushmer, R.: *Cardiovascular Dynamics.* Philadelphia, W. B. Saunders, 1961.

Slonim, N., and Hamilton, L.: *Respiratory Physiology,* 2nd ed. St. Louis, C. V. Mosby, 1971, pp. 123–142.

West, J. B.: *Respiratory Physiology—The Essentials.* Baltimore, Williams and Wilkins, 1974.

Whipp, B. J.: The hyperpnea of dynamic muscular exercise. In Hutton, R. S. (ed.): *Exercise and Sport Sciences Reviews,* vol. 5. Santa Barbara, Journal Publishing Affiliates, 1978, pp. 295–311.

Over the past century, there have been massive assaults on athletic performance records. As an example, the world's best running performances in the 100-meter, 400-meter, 1500-meter, and marathon (42.2 kilometers, or 26.2 miles) races from 1900 to the present have fallen sharply with an average improvement of just under 25 per cent. Similar record-breaking trends are common in competitive swimming as well as in most other sports activities.

One of the many factors that undoubtedly has contributed to this phenomenon is improvement in training techniques and methods. This fact is dramatically emphasized when the performance records and training methods of race-horses are examined. Improvement in horseracing performance is just under 8 per cent over the past 100 years, whereas their training methods over the same period have not changed at all. By the same token, other factors important for the improvement of performance, such as nutrition, genetics, and the type of running surface, have all been improved for both man (except genetics) and animal over the same time period. The threefold greater improvement in performance of man, then, may be taken as a measure of the importance of sound training techniques and methods.

It will be the purpose of this section to review these training techniques and methods and to examine the scientific and physiological principles upon which their success is based. Chapter 12 will present basic considerations and an overview of current training methods used by coaches and physical educators. Chapter 13 will discuss the physiological effects of these methods on the human body. Two other important aspects of exercise and training, the influences of gender and age and the relationship to fitness and health will be considered in Chapter 14 and Chapter 15.

PHYSICAL TRAINING

Methods of Physical Training

The major concepts to be learned from this chapter are as follows:

- The basic tenets in any training program are (1) to recognize the major energy system utilized to perform a given activity, and (2) then, through the overload principle, to construct a training program that will develop that particular energy system more than will any other.

- The primary energy system for any activity can be estimated on the basis of its performance time. The overload principle as applied to aerobic (endurance) and anaerobic (sprint) training programs requires that the training intensity be near maximal.

- Training intensity can be best judged either from the heart rate response to exercise or from the anaerobic threshold and, to a lesser extent, from the training frequency and duration.

- Athletes should train all year using off-season, preseason, and in-season training programs.
- Warm-up and cool-down activities and procedures are important in the overall safety and effectiveness of training programs.
- Training programs are available that develop primarily either the aerobic and anaerobic or all three energy systems.

A major objective of physical educators and coaches is to construct the most effective *individualized* conditioning or training programs for their students and athletes. It is, therefore, the purpose of this chapter to outline fundamental principles that will help you do just that.

The principles underlying the development of muscular strength, endurance, and flexibility have been discussed in Chapter 7. This presentation will stress the relationship between the particular activity or event you wish to improve and the primary energy source(s) involved. By recognizing which of the energy sources are being employed to the greatest extent during a given activity, you will be able to prescribe the most effective conditioning regimen. These regimens are sometimes referred to as sprint and endurance training programs because they can be designed to develop either anaerobic (sprint) or aerobic (endurance) capacities.

In starting our discussion, we will outline several general considerations that are applicable to all training and conditioning programs. Then we will move on to the details of specific training regimens, each of which contributes in a unique way to the full development of the energy and

performance capabilities of your students and athletes.

General Considerations

There are four general considerations that are important to all training programs: (1) the basic principles of training; (2) the various training phases; (3) preliminary activity or warm-up; and (4) warm- or cool-down.

Training Principles

You learned that to develop strength and muscular endurance requires working the muscle at an increasing resistance. As a consequence, the muscle hypertrophies and gains in strength and endurance. In other words, a number of physiological adaptations take place that lead to a greater energy potential within each muscle cell. Thus our basic tenets in any conditioning or training program are to: (1) recognize the major energy source utilized to perform a given activity; and (2) then, through the overload principle, construct a program that will develop that particular energy source more than will any other.

Specificity of Training

Tenet (1) mentioned previously is closely related to what is usually referred to as specificity of training. We mentioned this concept earlier in conjunction with weight-training programs (p. 171). It needs to be emphasized again that all training programs *must* be specific to developing the energy system or systems predominantly used during performance of the sports activity in question. It should also be pointed out that specificity applies equally to general conditioning programs. In such a case, however, we might be interested in improving fitness only and not necessarily sports performance. In most sports events, one or two energy systems usually are considered when planning the training program. With persons seeking general conditioning, all three systems may be involved, with emphasis perhaps being placed on the system that best meets that person's fitness needs. For example, people recovering from coronary and other related cardiorespiratory diseases would want to emphasize the oxygen system. Development of exercise training programs for health purposes will be discussed later in this Section (Chapter 15). Also, the specificity of training effects will be presented in the next chapter.

Determining the Predominant Energy System

How does one know which energy system(s) predominates in various activities and sports? The answer to this question is given by the information contained in Table 12-1. The table illustrates the relationship between track running events and the primary energy-yielding components involved. From this information, it becomes apparent that you as the coach, if training marathon runners, would devote 5% of the training regimen to development of the ATP-PC and lactic acid systems, whereas 95% of the time would be spent on developing the oxygen system.

Table 12-1 was constructed for track events. However, you will notice that the time of performance has been included; this was done for a special reason. Regardless of the event, the time of performance is related to the energy-yielding systems involved. That is to say, if we were discussing a swimming event requiring 4 to 5 minutes, reference to the table shows us that the per cent emphasis for training would be as follows: 20% speed, 25% oxygen system, and 55% anaerobic capacity. The point we wish to make is that *the energy sources for a given activity are time-dependent.* Whether a person is chopping wood, shoveling snow, performing calisthenics, running, or swimming for a continuous period of time, the primary source of energy will be dependent upon the performance time.

Using the information given in Table 12-1, it is possible to analyze a number of sports with regard to the per cent emphasis

TABLE 12-1

Per Cent of Training Time Spent in Developing the Three Energy Sources for Various Track Events*

Event	Time of Performance (Minutes:Seconds)	Speed (ATP-PC Strength)	Aerobic Capacity (Oxygen System)	Anaerobic Capacity (Speed + Lactic Acid System)
Marathon	135:00 to 180:00	—	95%	5%
6 mile	30:00 to 50:00	5	80	15
3 mile	15:00 to 25:00	10	70	20
2 mile	10:00 to 16:00	20	40	40
1 mile	4:00 to 6:00	20	25	55
880 yards	2:00 to 3:00	30	5	65
440 yards	1:00 to 1:30	80	5	15
220 yards	0:22 to 0:35	98	—	2
100 yards	0:10 to 0:15	98	—	2

*Adapted from Wilt.[47]

that should be placed on training the various energy systems. The results of these analyses are given in Table 12-2. Two points concerning the table need to be emphasized. First, notice how the energy systems have been grouped, i.e., ATP-PC and LA, LA-O_2, and O_2. This has been done because it is not as yet possible to identify the exact percentage contribution of any one energy system to any one sport or sport activity. The one exception to this might be the aerobic or oxygen (O_2) system. It has been studied more than the others, and more information concerning its energy contribution to various sports is available. At any rate, the groups of the energy systems should be thought of as representing anaerobic contributions (ATP-PC and LA); anaerobic and aerobic contributions (LA-O_2); and aerobic conditions (O_2).

The second point concerns the accuracy of the percentage contributions of the energy systems. These are only estimates and are not exact, mainly because scientific information of this kind is not yet available. However, this should not affect the usefulness of the table, for with these guidelines, specific training programs can be constructed that will lead to maximum increases in performance. We will talk more about this a little later in this chapter. If your favorite sport or activity is not listed in Table 12-2, you can do your own analysis using the information on performance times contained in Table 12-1.

The Overload Principle—Intensity, Frequency, and Duration of Training

Our second tenet concerns the overload principle. As you will recall from Chapter 7, the progressive overload principle implies that the exercise resistance is near maximal and that it is gradually increased as the person's fitness capacity improves throughout the course of the training program. In weight training this was accomplished by establishing the repetition maximum (p. 175). With training programs consisting of running, cycling, or swimming, the **intensity, frequency,** and **duration** of the program rather than the amount of weight lifted are used as the means of progressive overload.

Determining intensity of training. This is probably the most important of the three factors in applying the overload principle. For example, as will be pointed out in the next chapter, the intensity of the training program is directly related to improvement in the maximal aerobic power (max $\dot{V}O_2$).[15-17]

How can the intensity of the training program be determined? The easiest method to use is the **heart rate method.** It has been determined that the magnitude of the heart rate response to an exercise load can be used as an indicator of the overload that is being placed on the body in general and the cardiorespiratory system specifically.[12,27]

Intensity of training is generally determined by monitoring the heart rate. The significance of this is to realize that heart rate monitoring is an indirect way of estimating oxygen utilization by the body (see Table G-4, p. 683). Within a wide range of values, oxygen consumption and heart rate are related in a linear (straight line) fashion. At very low and very high work levels the linear relationship breaks down. Maximum heart rate is achieved before maximum oxygen consumption. When compared on a percentage of maximum basis, 70% of maximum heart rate represents only 60% of maximum aerobic capacity, while 85% of maximum heart rate represents about 80% of maximum aerobic capacity. When maximum heart rate is achieved, the level of oxygen consumption is still rising (see Fig. 12-1). The higher the heart rate response, the greater the intensity of the exercise. Therefore, the idea of determining a **target heart rate (THR)** to be reached

TABLE 12-2

Various Sports and Their Predominant Energy System*

Sports or Sport Activity	% Emphasis According to Energy Systems		
	ATP-PC and LA	LA-O_2	O_2
1. Baseball	80	20	—
2. Basketball	85	15	—
3. Fencing	90	10	—
4. Field hockey	60	20	20
5. Football	90	10	—
6. Golf	95	5	—
7. Gymnastics	90	10	—
8. Ice hockey			
a. Forwards, defense	80	20	—
b. Goalie	95	5	—
9. Lacrosse			
a. Goalie, defense, attack men	80	20	—
b. Midfielders, man-down	60	20	20
10. Rowing	20	30	50
11. Skiing			
a. Slalom, jumping, downhill	80	20	—
b. Cross-country	—	5	95
c. Pleasure skiing	34	33	33
12. Soccer			
a. Goalie, wings, strikers	80	20	—
b. Halfbacks, or link men	60	20	20
13. Swimming and diving			
a. 50 yd, diving	98	2	—
b. 100 yd	80	15	5
c. 200 yd	30	65	5
d. 400, 500 yd	20	40	40
e. 1500, 1650 yd	10	20	70
14. Tennis	70	20	10
15. Track and field			
a. 100, 220 yd	98	2	—
b. Field events	90	10	—
c. 440 yd	80	15	5
d. 880 yd	30	65	5
e. 1 mile	20	55	25
f. 2 miles	20	40	40
g. 3 miles	10	20	70
h. 6 miles (cross-country)	5	15	80
i. Marathon	—	5	95
16. Volleyball	90	10	—
17. Wrestling	90	10	—

*Modified from Fox and Mathews.[19]

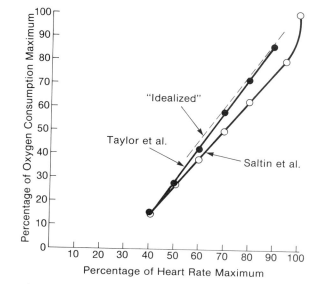

Figure 12-1. The relationship between heart rate and oxygen consumption expressed as a percentage of the maximum for each. Note the linear relationship between the two variables. Data from Saltin et al.[41] are represented by the open circles, and those from Taylor[44] are represented by closed circles. Authors generally state that the relationship shows 70% of HR_{max} = 60% of max VO_2 and 85% of HR_{max} = 80% of max VO_2. Presumably the basis for this statement is taken from observations similar to the Taylor data. The "idealized" relationship is depicted by the dashed line.

during endurance training sessions has been developed. One of the following two methods of determining the THR may be used:

1. *The Maximal Heart Rate Reserve Method.* This method was developed by Karvonen[27] and consists of calculating what is referred to as the **heart rate reserve (HRR).** The HRR is simply the difference between the resting heart rate (HR_{rest}) and the maximal heart rate (HR_{max}) or:

$$
\begin{array}{cccc}
\text{HRR} & = & HR_{max} & - & HR_{rest} \\
\text{(heart rate} & & \text{(maximal} & & \text{(resting} \\
\text{reserve)} & & \text{heart rate)} & & \text{heart rate)}
\end{array}
$$

For example, suppose your resting heart rate were 65 beats per minute and your maximal heart rate, 200 beats per minute. Your HRR would then be 200 − 65 = 135 beats per minute. The THR can then be determined as a percentage of the HRR plus the HR_{rest}. Using the HRR from our previous example, a THR of 75% of the HRR would be calculated as follows:

$$
\begin{aligned}
\text{HRR} &= 200 - 65 \\
&= 135 \text{ beats/min} \\
75\% \text{ THR} &= (0.75 \times 135) + 65 \\
&= 101.25 + 65 \\
&= \mathbf{166 \text{ beats/min}}
\end{aligned}
$$

The exercise during the training program, then, should be intensive enough to cause the heart rate to reach 166 beats per minute. What would the THR be for a 90% HRR?*

2. *The Maximal Heart Rate Method.* In this method, the THR is calculated from the maximal heart rate only. For example, a 75% THR for an athlete with a HR_{max} of 200 beats per minute would simply be calculated as:

$$75\% \text{ THR} = 0.75 \times 200$$
$$= \textbf{150 beats/min}$$

The relationship between the two methods is shown in Table 12-3. Several points should be particularly noticed. First, the difference between the two methods is greater the lower the THR. For example, a THR of 186 beats/min represents a 90% HRR and a 93% HR_{max}. On the other hand, a THR of 146 beats/min represents a 60% HRR and a 73% HR_{max}. Second, the lowest THR (60% HRR or 73% HR_{max}) is considered *threshold.*[27] What this means is that a THR below this level will not always provide a great enough overload to stimulate improvements in endurance capacity or endurance performance. For young high school and college age athletes (men and women), the THR for endurance training programs should be between 80 and 90% HRR or 85 to 95% HR_{max}. The physiological reason for this will be discussed in following paragraphs (p. 294). Lower THRs would be associated with older, nonathletic people as will be discussed in a later chapter (p. 435).

In order to use the previous methods for determining endurance training intensity, the resting and maximal heart rates must be known. The resting heart rate may be determined by palpating the radial artery (at the wrist), the temporal artery (in

---

*Answer: 90% THR = (0.9 × 135) + 65
= 121.5 + 65
= 186 beats/min

TABLE 12-3

Relationship of the Target Heart Rate (THR) Calculated as a Percentage of the Maximal Heart Rate Reserve (HRR) and of the Maximal Heart Rate (HR_{max})

THR* (Beats/Min)	Per Cent HRR	Per Cent HR_{max}
186	90	93
180	85	90
173	80	87
166	75	83
160	70	80
153	65	76
146	60	73

*HR_{rest} = 65 beats/min and HR_{max} = 200 beats/min.

front of the ear), or the carotid artery (in the neck). These methods are shown in Figure 12-2. Only light pressure should be used, particularly at the carotid artery. The reason for this is to avoid closing off the artery completely and/or causing a reflex slowing of the heart rate and triggering occasional cardiac abnormalities.[46]

One method for determining resting heart rate is to take it early in the morning after getting out of bed and sitting upright for a few minutes. Count the number of beats during a full minute and record the result on a 3 × 5 card. An alternative method is to take the count for 15 seconds and multiply the result by 4. Repeat this process for 3 to 5 days and compute the average. This will be your resting heart rate.

Direct determination of the maximal heart rate is difficult and involves exercising the person to a maximal level while at the same time determining the heart rate with an electrocardiograph. However, reasonable estimates for males and females

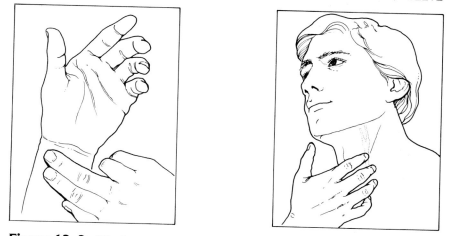

Figure 12–2. The heart rate may be determined by palpating the radial artery (at the wrist) or the carotid artery (in the neck).

based on age may be made from the following formula:

$$HR_{max} = 220 - age$$

As an example, a 20-year-old person would have an estimated HR_{max} of $220 - 20 = 200$ beats per minute.

In order to check whether your athletes are attaining their predetermined THRs, it is a good idea to teach them to take their pulses occasionally during the training sessions. Although it is not possible to take the pulse accurately during exercise, the pulse count obtained in a 6- or 10-second span immediately following exercise is a reasonable indicator of what the heart rate was during exercise. Remember, a 6-second count would be multiplied by 10, and a 10-second count by 6 in order to convert to beats per minute.

Besides the heart rate method, there is another way in which the exercise intensity may be determined for endurance training programs. This method is based on the concept of *anaerobic threshold.* You will recall from Chapter 8 that the anaer-

obic threshold is that workload intensity or oxygen consumption in which anaerobic metabolism is accelerated. In other words, it is that workload intensity in which lactic acid begins to rapidly accumulate in the blood and muscles. Several researchers have recently advocated that the workload intensity at or slightly above the anaerobic threshold should be used by endurance athletes during their training sessions.[28,30-32] There are two methods whereby the workload intensity at the anaerobic threshold can be determined; both require use of laboratory equipment.

1. *Minute Ventilation and the Anaerobic Threshold Method.* You will recall from Chapter 8 that the anaerobic threshold can be detected by observing the minute ventilation during a progressive exercise test. Minute ventilation increases linearly with increasing workloads until the anaerobic threshold is reached. At this time, the rate of increase in ventilation is greatly accelerated.

An example of how to use this information in determining a training intensity for endurance runners is shown in Figure 12-3. The athlete runs at different speeds on a

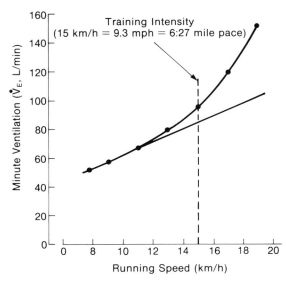

Figure 12-3. One method of detecting the anaerobic threshold involves monitoring the minute ventilation during a progressive exercise test (e.g., running on a treadmill at various speeds as shown here). The workload intensity at or slightly above the anaerobic threshold can be used as the exercise intensity during endurance-training sessions.

motor-driven treadmill in a laboratory. After several minutes of running at each speed, minute ventilation is measured. Afterward, a graph is constructed by plotting minute ventilation against speed of running (Fig. 12-3). Notice how ventilation increases in a straight-line fashion for the first three running speeds and then begins to increase rapidly. The running speed at which ventilation increases abruptly represents the exercise intensity at or slightly above the anaerobic threshold and can be used as the runner's exercise intensity during his or her training sessions. In the example, the training intensity would be 15 kilometers per hour (km/h), or 9.3 mph, or a 6-minute, 27-second mile pace.

2. *Blood Lactic Acid and the Anaerobic Threshold Method.* In this method, blood lactic acid during two or more differ-

ent exercise loads must be determined. In addition, a blood lactic acid concentration of 4 millimoles per liter (mmol/L)* is considered to be the level at which the anaerobic threshold is reached.[30,32]

Again, a graph is constructed, in this case, plotting blood lactic acid concentration against running speed as shown in Figure 12-4. The running speed at which 4 mmol/L of blood lactic acid is found is the suggested exercise intensity for the training sessions. In this example, three athletes are plotted: Runner 1 is an example of a beginner who is totally untrained; runner 2, an experienced but only average competitor; and runner 3, a highly experienced, international competitor. The training intensities are different among the runners as might be expected.

Although the previous examples were for endurance runners, the same kind of procedure can be applied in determining the training intensity for endurance swimmers and cyclists by plotting ventilation or blood lactic acid levels against swimming speed and cycling speed, respectively.

The physiological differences between the heart rate method and the anaerobic threshold method in determining endurance training intensity lies in the different systems being stressed. For example, with the heart rate method, training intensity is judged mainly by the degree of stress placed on the cardiorespiratory system. With the anaerobic threshold method, the degree of stress placed on the metabolic system of the skeletal muscles is the major factor upon which the intensity of the exercise is determined. On an individual basis, a given degree of stress placed on one system does not guarantee the same degree of stress placed on the other system.

Which method, then, should be used?

---

*1 mmol of lactic acid = 9 milligrams (mg) per 100 ml of blood, referred to as mg %; therefore, 4 mmol = 36 mg %.

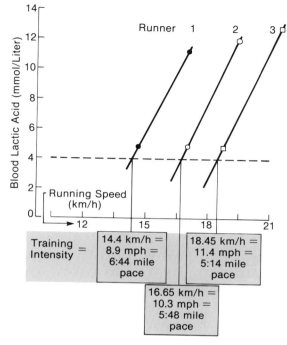

Figure 12-4. Another method for detecting the anaerobic threshold involves measurement of the blood lactic acid levels at different exercise intensities, such as running on a treadmill at various speeds as shown here. The running speed at which 4 mmol/L of blood lactic acid (dashed line) is found is the suggested exercise intensity for the endurance-training sessions. Runner 1 is an example of a beginner who is totally untrained; runner 2, an experienced but only average competitor; and runner 3, a highly experienced international competitor.

First, it must be recognized that either one of the heart rate methods is easier to use than is either of the anaerobic threshold methods. From a practical standpoint, this certainly is an advantage. Second, little research is presently available to help answer this question. However, it has been shown that when the anaerobic threshold method involving measurement of blood lactic acid is used to determine training intensity (Fig. 12-4), the average heart rate will be 91% of the HR_{max}.[30] Furthermore, at an exercise intensity requiring a heart rate of 80% of the HR_{max}, only 55% of the subjects will be working at or above their anaerobic threshold.[28] Therefore, it can be recommended that in order to assure adequate cardiorespiratory and metabolic stresses during endurance training in the majority of people, the heart rate during the training sessions should be greater than 85% of the HR_{max} or 80% of the HRR (Table 12-4).

Re-examining the data of Saltin et al.[41] by plotting percentage of max $\dot{V}O_2$ versus both the HRR method and the HR_{max} method confirms the concept of providing cardiorespiratory stress or metabolic stress. Figure 12-5 shows how the two heart rate methods relate to percentage of max $\dot{V}O_2$. One must be sensitive to which heart rate method is used for determining exercise intensity. As pointed out previously, the lower the percentage heart rate level the greater the discrepancy between the HRR and HR_{max} method.

TABLE 12–4

Percentage of Subjects at or Above Anaerobic Threshold During Exercise at Different Percentages of the Maximal Heart Rate (Per Cent HR_{max}) and the Maximal Heart Rate Reserve (Per Cent HRR)*

Per Cent of Subjects at or Above Anaerobic Threshold	Per Cent HR_{max}	Per Cent HRR
0	60	40
3	70	55
55	80	70
75	85	80
100	>90	85

*Based on data from Katch et al.[28] and Kindermann et al.[30]

Specific endurance programs will be identified later in this chapter. What about sprint or anaerobic training programs? How should the intensity of these programs be judged? With sprint programs, the heart rate response during training is not as important as with the endurance programs, but will generally be 180 beats per minute or higher. The sprints will be performed at a faster pace, well above anaerobic threshold. They may require only 10 to 20 seconds to perform but will demand many repetitions. These kinds of programs will also be identified later in this chapter.

Determining frequency and duration of training. Generally, the more frequent and longer the training program, the greater will be the fitness benefits. This is particularly true with respect to endurance training.[17,39] For example, more frequent (2 versus 4 days per week) and longer duration (7 versus 13 weeks) endurance interval training programs have been shown to produce less cardiorespiratory stress during submaximal exercise[17] (p. 350).

Figure 12-5. Comparative illustration of the HRR (○) and the HR_{max} (●) methods for estimating the metabolic response to exercise. The lower the heart rate percentage, the greater is the discrepancy between the two methods.

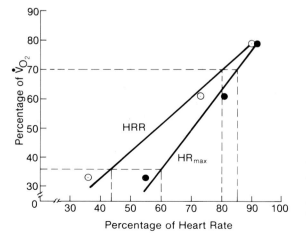

It can be recommended that the training frequency for endurance programs be between 3 and 5 days per week, and for sprint or anaerobic training programs, 3 days per week. This rule of thumb would hold true for most sports with the exception of track and swimming; here, the training frequencies are usually 5 days per week for sprinters and 6 to 7 days per week for endurance athletes. As will be pointed out in the next chapter, one training session per day is recommended since 2 or even 3 workouts per day do not lead to greater fitness or performance gains.

A summary of and guidelines for the factors involved in the overload principle as applied to aerobic (endurance) training programs and anaerobic (sprint) programs of running are given in Table 12-5. It should be emphasized that of the three training factors—intensity, frequency and duration—intensity is probably the most important with respect to assuring the proper overload, particularly for endurance training programs.

It should be emphasized that the previous guidelines and information pertaining to training intensity are applicable mainly for endurance training, i.e., for training programs designed to improve the aerobic or oxygen transport system.

Training Phases

It is usual to classify the total training period of athletes into three phases: off-season, preseason, and in-season. It is also usual for the training programs to vary considerably from phase to phase. Here is what we recommend.

Off-season training. Training programs during the off-season are generally nonspecific. Most often they require only that the athlete keep moderately active and, perhaps of most concern, keep his or her body weight at or reasonably near "playing weight."

TABLE 12-5

Guidelines for Estimating Intensity, Frequency, Duration, and Distance of Aerobic (Endurance) and Anaerobic (Sprint) Training Programs of Running

Training Factor	Aerobic Training	Anaerobic Training
Intensity	Heart rate = 80 to 90% HRR; or = 85 to 95% HR_{max}	Heart rate = 180 beats/min or greater
Frequency	4–5 days/week	3 days/week
Sessions/day	One	One
Duration	12–16 weeks or longer	8–10 weeks
Distance/workout	3–5 miles	1½–2 miles

It is suggested that an off-season training program consists of some or all of the following:

1. A weight-training program with emphasis placed on increasing strength, muscular endurance, and power in those muscle groups most directly involved in the specific athletic event. Such a program should be based on the principles outlined in Chapter 7.

2. An informal (in other words, not required) 8-week running program of *low intensity* performed no more than twice a week. This kind of program could be administered concurrently with the weight-training program. For example, if the latter were conducted on Monday, Wednesday, and Friday, the running program could be performed on Monday and Wednesday or Wednesday and Friday. It makes little difference whether the running program is performed before or after the weight-training program.

3. Participation in sports activities and recreational games purely for relaxation, pleasure, and enjoyment.

4. Limited participation in the athlete's specific sport in order to develop his or her skill; for example, in basketball such skills would include shooting ac-

curacy, ball-handling (dribbling, passing), pivoting, and so on.

Preseason training. During the preseason phase (i.e., the 8 to 10 weeks prior to competition), training programs should be designed to increase to a maximum the capacities of the energy systems that are predominant when performing a specific athletic event. *It is during this phase of athletic training that a specific high-intensity program should be used.* Such programs have been detailed by Fox.[19,22] It is hoped, however, that with the information contained in this book, and specifically in this chapter, you will be able to construct your own training program that will best fit the needs of your athletes. The off-season weight-training program should also be continued during preseason training.

In-season training. Traditionally, in-season training programs for most sports emphasize skill development. It is generally thought that drills, scrimmages, and competition will maintain the increases in energy capacities that were obtained during the preseason training program. For the majority of athletes who compete regularly, this is probably true. However, for some of the "regulars" and for most of those athletes who do not compete every week, some maintenance program might include some of the following:

1. One or two days of training per week, with a program similar to that used in the preseason.
2. Weight training with one workout per week, alternating the upper body and the lower body workouts on a weekly basis (e.g., one week, upper body; the next, lower body).
3. Utilizing drills not only to improve skill but also to help maintain fitness. To do this, the drills should be intense and long enough in duration to stress the muscle groups involved.

Table 12-6 contains a summary of the kinds of programs recommended for the various training phases.

Preliminary Exercise (Warm-Up)

It has been said that record performances among athletes have occurred without so-called warm-up. Also, some scientific studies have shown that performances without prior warm-up were no different than those after warm-up.[26,35,43] On the other hand, there are also scientific studies that show that prior to a heavy workout or competitive performance, preliminary exercises, or warm-up, should be performed.[1,5,6,24,34,36-38]

There are many physiological reasons for performing warm-up exercises. For example, increased body and muscle temperatures promote increases in (1) enzyme activity and thus in the metabolic reactions associated with the energy systems[5,34]; (2) increases in blood flow and oxygen availability[4]; and (3) decreases in contraction and reflex times.[45] Some of these changes are shown in Figure 12-6. Notice how oxygen consumption (peak $\dot{V}O_2$) and heart rate during maximal exercise are directly related to muscle temperature. The higher the temperature, the higher the $\dot{V}O_2$ and heart rate. Also notice that although work time was not increased at the highest muscle temperature, blood lactic acid was considerably reduced. In addition, abrupt, intensive exercise may be as-

---

TABLE 12-6

Recommended Programs for the Various Training Phases*

Training Phase		
Off-Season	**Preseason**	**In-Season**
1. Weight training 8 weeks, 3 days/week	1. Running† high intensity, 8 weeks, 3 days/week	1. Running† high intensity, 1 or 2 days/week
2. Informal running, low intensity, 8 weeks, 1 to 2 days/week	2. Weight training 2 to 3 days/week	2. Weight training, 1 day/week
3. Participation in other sports and games	3. Viewing films, learning strategies, some skill drills	3. Skill drills
4. Limited practice in specific sport for skill development		4. Scrimmages
		5. Regular competitive performances

*Modified from Fox and Mathews.[19]

†The training program should be specific; e.g., swimmers would use a swimming program.

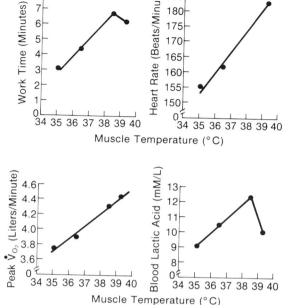

Figure 12-6. Oxygen consumption (peak $\dot{V}O_2$) and heart rate during maximal exercise are directly related to muscle temperature. The higher the temperature, the higher the $\dot{V}O_2$ and heart rate. Although work time is not increased at the highest muscle temperature, blood lactic acid is considerably reduced. (Based on data from Bergh and Ekblom.[5])

sociated with inadequate blood flow to the heart.[5] Preliminary exercise prevents this danger. The following preliminary exercises are recommended: (1) stretching exercises for flexibility; (2) calisthenics for development of arm, shoulder, and abdominal strength; and (3) brief, formal activity that you will use during the work interval, thereby placing the body in readiness for maximal effort.

Stretching exercises. Flexibility (stretching) exercises, such as reaching toward the floor without bending the knees, or alternate toe touching, should be performed several times before each workout. These exercises are done (1) to increase the range of motion about a joint, enabling better skill performance; (2) as a precautionary measure against tearing muscle fibers and connective tissues, and thus against muscular stiffness and soreness; and (3) as insurance against development of muscular tension in the low back, across the shoulders, and throughout the neck regions. A number of flexibility exercises were given in Chapter 7 (p. 190). Several or all of these should be performed at least 10 times prior to the workout.

Calisthenics. Calisthenics should be performed after the stretching routines. Calisthenics are active, that is, they involve muscular contractions. Therefore, they will cause further increases in body and muscle temperatures. Calisthenic exercises should include the major muscle groups, particularly those directly involved in the sport for which the athlete is training. Athletes may unintentionally overdo calisthenics; they should be reminded that exercised muscle groups should not be fatigued following the calisthenic routine. The total time needed for this particular phase of the warm-up period will be only 5 to 10 minutes.

For each body area, there are calisthenics involving the appropriate muscle contractions. For example, for the neck, the bridge can be used; for the shoulders and groin, jumping jacks are suitable; for the ankle, toes, and gastrocnemius muscle, toe raises and running in place can be used; for the quadricep muscles, half-squats are good; for the shoulders, arms and chest, pushups are appropriate; and for the abdominal muscles, bent-knee sit-ups, and bent-knee leg raises can be used.

Formal activity. The last phase of the warm-up should consist of performing the activity utilized in the sport for which one is training. For example, in a warm-up for baseball, formal activities would include throwing, catching, fielding, and batting. This kind of practice serves at least two purposes: (1) it ensures that physiological factors, such as muscle temperature and blood flow, are optimal in the muscles directly used during the sport; and (2) it provides a warm-up for hand-to-eye coordination and other neuromuscular mechanisms that also are directly involved in the sport.

Warm-Down or Cool-Down

It is a common practice of athletes and others who engage in regular physical exercise to warm- or cool-down, i.e., perform light or mild exercise immediately following competition and training sessions. There are at least two important physiological reasons for such a practice.

1. As pointed out in Chapter 3, blood and muscle lactic acid levels decrease more rapidly during exercise-recovery than during rest-recovery. Thus, warm-down would promote faster recovery from fatigue.
2. Mild activity following heavy exercise keeps the muscle pump going and thereby prevents the blood from pooling in the extremities, particularly the legs. As you will recall (p. 253), the muscular pump promotes venous return by the milking action caused by the alternate contraction and relaxation of the active muscle. Preventing the pooling of blood not only reduces the possibility of delayed muscular stiffness and soreness, but also reduces the tendency for fainting and/or dizziness.

Specific warm-down procedures or activities are not as yet available. However, it can be recommended that warm-down activities be similar to warm-up activities, but be performed in reverse order. Thus, formal activity would immediately follow the training session or competition. As examples, several laps of jogging or walking would follow hard running, and free-throw or field goal shooting might follow a hard basketball scrimmage. Following this, some light calisthenics might be performed and then some stretching exercises. The formal activity and stretching exercises should be considered the most important phase of the warm-down procedure.

Training Methods

As mentioned in the introduction to this section, much of the improvement in sports performances over the past century can be attributed to refinement of the training methods used by coaches and athletes. Such methods have involved programs for improving both aerobic (endurance) and anaerobic (sprint) energy capacities and performances. Let's see what these methods are and how and why they are so successful in improving performance.

Interval Training

Interval training, as the name implies, is a series of repeated bouts of exercise alternated with periods of relief. Light or mild exercise usually constitutes this relief period. In order to understand why this method of training has been so successful, we will start with a discussion of energy production and fatigue during intermittent work.

Energy Production and Fatigue during Intermittent Work

The information we learned from Chapter 2 concerning energy production during exercise applies, of course, both to work performed intermittently and work performed continuously. However, for our purposes, there is one very important difference.

To illustrate this difference, suppose you ran continuously for as long and as hard as you could for one minute; then, on another occasion, suppose you ran intermittently, running just as hard as you did continuously, but for only 10 seconds at a time with 30 seconds of rest between each run. If you repeated this six times, you would have performed the same amount of work at the same intensity intermittently as you did continuously (i.e., six runs at 10 seconds each equals one minute of running—but *the degree of fatigue following intermittent running would be considerably less.*

Why? The reason for this can be explained physiologically. The answer lies in the different interaction between the phosphagen (ATP-PC) system and anaerobic glycolysis (LA system) during intermittent as compared to continuous running. Comparatively, the energy supplied via anaerobic glycolysis (LA system) will be less and that via the phosphagen (ATP-PC) system will be more in the intermittent runs.[21,33] What this means is that there will be *less lactic acid* accumulated and thus *less fatigue* associated with the intermittent work. This will be true no matter how intense the intermittent work bouts or how long they last.

Replenishing ATP and PC. How is it possible that the ATP-PC system can supply more ATP and the LA system less ATP during the series of intermittent runs as compared to the continuous run? Didn't we already indicate that the stores of ATP + PC are exhausted after only a few seconds of all-out running? Yes, we did; however, remember that between each intermittent run there is a *period of relief*. The question that needs answering, then, is, what, in terms of energy production, is occurring during the relief intervals?

You will recall from Chapter 3 that during the relief intervals, a portion of the muscular stores of ATP and PC that were depleted during the preceding work intervals will be replenished via the aerobic system.[23,33,42] This is shown in Figure 12-7. In other words, during the relief intervals,

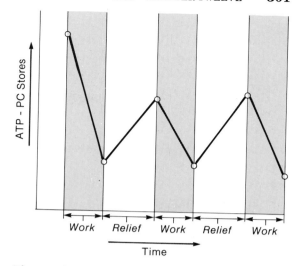

Figure 12-7. During the relief intervals of intermittent work, a portion of the muscular stores of ATP and PC that were depleted during the preceding work intervals will be replenished via the aerobic system. (From Fox and Mathews.[19])

part of the rapid-recovery phase (see Chapter 2) is complete. In addition, a portion of the O_2-myoglobin stores will also be replenished.[2,3,7] Thus, during each run that follows a relief interval, the replenished ATP and PC and O_2-myoglobin stores will again be available as an energy source. Consequently, energy from the LA system will be "spared," so to speak, by that amount, and lactic acid will not accumulate as rapidly or to as great an extent (Fig. 12-8). In contrast, during a continuous run, the stored ATP-PC will be exhausted within a matter of a few minutes or seconds and will not be replenished until the work is terminated.[23,25] In this case, energy in the form of ATP from the LA system will be called on early in the run, and LA will rapidly accumulate to high levels.

All of this has real meaning when applied to training, for *the savings in fatigue accompanying intermittent work can be converted to an increase in the intensity of*

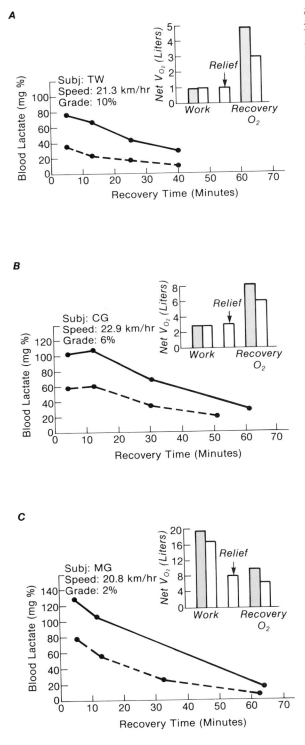

work performed. This is the single most important feature of intermittent work and as such is the key to the interval training system. It has been shown that an intermittent work level as much as two and one-half times the intensity of the continuous level can be performed before blood lactic acid levels in each are comparable.[2,7,15,21,33]

The interaction between the ATP-PC and the LA systems during intermittent work also varies slightly according to the type or activity level of the relief interval used. Our discussion thus far has centered on intermittent work using complete rest intervals. During actual interval training, it is recommended that the relief intervals consist of either light or mild work. Later, we will learn when it is best to use one or the other. Right now, the primary difference between intermittent work of the same intensity and duration performed with complete rest intervals as compared with light or mild work-relief intervals is that the blood lactic acid levels will be higher with the latter.[21] This is so because the work performed during the relief interval blocks or partially blocks the replenish-

Figure 12-8. *A,* Blood lactate during recovery from a continuous run (solid line) and interval runs (dashed line) involving the same amount of work. In the continuous run the subject ran for 30 seconds; in the interval run he ran three intervals of 10 seconds each with 20 seconds of rest-relief between intervals. Net O_2 consumption (VO_2) during work, during the rest-relief intervals, and after work (O_2 debt) for the continuous (hatched bar) and interval (open bar) runs are also shown. *B,* Similar measurements during and after a continuous run of 60 seconds' duration and an interval run of five 12-second runs with 20 seconds of rest-relief between intervals. *C,* A continuous run of 300 seconds' duration and an interval run of five 60-second runs with 60 seconds of rest-relief between intervals. Symbols the same as in *A.* (From Fox et al.[21])

ment of the ATP-PC stores.[21] Without as much of these stores being renewed, a greater proportion of the energy needed during the work intervals must be supplied via the LA system. In this way, the accumulation of lactic acid will be greater; the harder the work during the relief interval, the greater will be this lactic acid accumulation.

Specifically, in regard to the development of the energy systems, intermittent work or the interval-training system accomplishes the following:

1. It allows the stores of ATP + PC to be used over and over. This, in turn, provides an adequate stimulus for promoting an increase in the energy capacity of this system and aids in delaying the onset of fatigue by not delving so deeply into anaerobic glycolysis.
2. With proper regulation of the duration and type of relief interval, the involvement of anaerobic glycolysis will be maximal and thus improved.
3. By performing longer work intervals with many repetitions and brief relief intervals, the oxygen transport system is stressed and the aerobic energy system is improved.

Interval-Training Terms

There are several terms peculiar to describing interval training with which you should be familiar.

Work interval. The portion of the interval-training program that consists of the high intensity work effort, for example, a 220-yard run at a prescribed time.

Relief interval. The time between work intervals as well as between sets. The relief interval may consist of (1) light activity such as walking (referred to as rest-relief); (2) mild to moderate exercise such as jogging (referred to as work-relief); or (3) a combination of (1) and (2). The relief interval usually is expressed in relationship to the work interval; together they form the work-relief ratio and may be expressed as follows: 1:½; 1:1; 1:2; or 1:3. A ratio of 1:½ implies that the time of the relief interval is equal to half the time of the work interval; 1:1 indicates that the relief and work intervals are equal; 1:2 indicates that the relief interval is twice as long as the work interval; and 1:3 indicates that the relief interval is three times as long as the work interval. Principles enabling us to note proper work-relief ratios will be explained later in the chapter. With longer work intervals usually a 1:½ or 1:1 work-relief ratio is prescribed; with middle duration intervals a 1:2 ratio, and with shorter work intervals, because of the high intensity, a 1:3 work-relief ratio is prescribed.

Sets. A series of work and relief intervals. For example, six 220-yard runs at a prescribed time with designated relief intervals.

Repetitions. The number of work intervals within one set. For example, six 220-yard runs may constitute one set and six repetitions.

Training time. The rate at which the work is to be accomplished during the work interval. For example, each 220-yard run might be performed in 33 seconds.

Training distance. The distance of the work interval, e.g., 220 yards.

Frequency. The number of times per week for the workout.

Interval training prescription. Contains pertinent information concerning an interval training workout. It will usually include the number of sets, the number of repetitions, the distance or performance time of the work interval, the training time, and the time of the relief interval. As an example, one set from a prescription for a running program may be written as follows:

Set 1   6 × 220 at 0:33 (1:39)

where:

6 = number of repetitions
220 = training distance in yards
$0:33$ = training time in minutes and seconds
$(1:39)$ = time of relief interval in minutes and seconds

See Figure 12–9.

Interval-Training Variables

The overload principle as applied to interval training is accomplished through the manipulation of five variables:

1. Rate and distance of work interval;
2. Number of repetitions during each workout;
3. Relief interval or the time between work intervals;
4. Type of activity during relief interval; and
5. Frequency of training per week.

There are many advantages to the interval training system as compared to other methods of training. Among these are

1. A precise control of the stress;
2. A systematic day-to-day approach, enabling one to easily observe progress;
3. More rapid improvement in energy potential than in other methods of conditioning; and
4. A program that can be performed almost anywhere and that requires no special equipment.

Selecting the Type of Work for the Work Interval

Interval-training prescriptions for athletes employ a work interval in which the exercise is specific to that athlete's sport. Swimmers would structure or have their programs developed in accordance with their specific swimming needs, whereas track athletes would employ running.

The type of work chosen for general conditioning is based mainly on preference, since improving a specific sports skill might not be of primary concern. A person could select a single activity that he or she most enjoys, or several activities, e.g., swimming, jogging, jumping rope, cycling, or calisthenics.

Figure 12-9. Interpretation of an interval-training program prescription involving running. (From Fox and Mathews.[19])

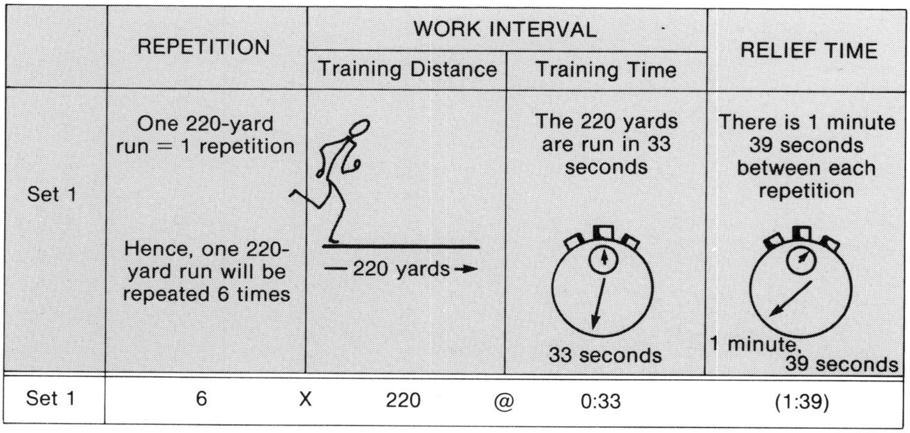

| | REPETITION | WORK INTERVAL | | RELIEF TIME |
		Training Distance	Training Time	
Set 1	One 220-yard run = 1 repetition Hence, one 220-yard run will be repeated 6 times	← 220 yards →	The 220 yards are run in 33 seconds 33 seconds	There is 1 minute 39 seconds between each repetition 1 minute, 39 seconds
Set 1	6 X 220	@	0:33	(1:39)

Manipulation of Variables

The variables mentioned previously may be considered in the following manner when constructing the interval program.

Rate and distance of work interval. Interval training prescriptions are made up of long-duration work intervals performed at low intensities, medium-duration intervals performed at moderate intensities, and short work efforts performed at higher intensities. Prescription content depends upon which energy systems are to be enhanced. Thus, for most activities, the interval-training prescription can best be written by considering the performance time of the work interval. You will recall that knowing the performance time of an activity allows us to determine the predominant energy system involved (p. 288). Understanding the relationship between the predominant energy system and performance time is fundamental in learning how to construct the work intervals of interval training programs.

How is a sufficient rate of work determined? There are several methods by which the proper intensity of the work interval can be calculated.

1. As mentioned earlier in this chapter, one method, applicable regardless of the type of work or activity used, is based on the *heart rate* response during the work interval. The target heart rate (THR) for most interval-training work intervals should be calculated as a percentage of the maximal heart rate reserve (HRR) or maximal heart rate (HR_{max}) as explained on page 289. For young high school and college age athletes and students, this will be between 80 and 90% of the HRR or between 85 to 95% of the HR_{max}. Another useful rule of thumb involving exercise heart rate and interval-training work intervals is to keep the work hard enough to raise the heart rate to at least 180 beats per minute. For most young athletes and students, either of these heart rate methods should provide adequate guidelines for assuring the proper work interval intensity.

2. A second method, again applicable regardless of the type of work, is based on the number of work intervals (repetitions) that can be performed per workout. At a given work rate, if a selected number of repetitions cannot be performed (because of exhaustion), the work rate is too intensive. On the other hand, if more than the selected number of repetitions can be performed, then that work rate is too easy. As an illustration, suppose you are using 440 yards as your training distance. The speed of each 440-yard run, therefore, should permit between 6 to 8 repetitions before undue exhaustion.

3. Wilt[47] has worked out a method for determining a sufficient work rate when structuring the interval-training prescription for running that might be easier than those mentioned above. The times for training distances between 55 and 220 yards should be between 1.5 and 5 seconds slower, respectively, than the best time for those distances measured from running starts. For example, if a person can run 55 yards from a running start in 6 seconds, the training time for this distance would be 6 + 1.5 = 7.5 seconds. For training distances of 110 and 220 yards, add 3 and 5 seconds, respectively, to the best times taken from running starts.

For training distances of 440 yards, the rate of work would be 1 to 4 seconds less (i.e., the person runs faster) than one-fourth the time required to run a mile. As an illustration, if a person ran the mile in 6 minutes, the average time for each 440 yards would be 90 seconds (360 seconds divided by 4 = 90 seconds). Therefore, the training time would be between 90 − 4 = 86 and 90 − 1 = 89 seconds.

If the training distance is over 440 yards, each 440 yards of that distance should be run at an average speed of 3 to 4 seconds slower than the average 440-yard time in the mile run. For example, in running 880 yards as the training distance, the 6-minute miler would run each 440 yards of the 880 yards in an average time of $90 + 3 = 93$ to $90 + 4 = 94$ seconds.

This method can also be applied to swimming. However, the training distances for swimming programs will be approximately one-fourth those used for running programs. A summary of how to determine a sufficient work rate for running and swimming programs is given in Table 12-7.

Number of repetitions. The number of repetitions of the work interval is the factor that determines the length of the workout. A total workout distance of between 1.5 and 2 miles will be necessary to achieve maximum improvement. If you should decide to use a training distance of 220 yards on a particular day, it would be necessary to have 12 to 16 repeats. This is the basis upon which the number of repetitions was determined in number 2 mentioned previously.

Duration and type of relief interval. There are two important considerations when dealing with the relief interval: (1) the time (duration) of the relief interval; and (2) the type of activity during the relief interval.

1. *Time of Relief Interval.* Recovery heart rate following the work interval is a good indication as to whether or not the individual is physiologically ready for the next interval or next set. For example, for men and women less than 20 years old, both athletic and nonathletic, the heart rate should drop to at least 140 beats per minute between repetitions and to 120 beats per minute between sets.[18] Determination of heart rate (pulse) should be made periodically throughout the relief interval by taking 6- or 10-second counts and multiplying by 10 or 6 to convert to beats per minute (p. 293).

Since it is not always possible to use heart rate as a guide for determining the duration of the relief interval, the work-relief ratio, described earlier (p. 303), can be used. This will guarantee that heart rates

TABLE 12-7

Guidelines for Determining a Sufficient Work Rate for Running and Swimming Interval-Training Programs*

Training Distance (Yards)		Work Rate
Run	Swim	
55	15	1½ ⎫
110	25	3 ⎬ seconds slower than best times from moving starts
220	55	5 ⎭
440	110	1 to 4 seconds faster than average 440 (run) or 110 (swim) than best times in mile (run) or 440 (swim)
660–1320	165–330	3 to 4 seconds slower than average 440 (run) or 110 (swim) than best times in mile (run) or 440 (swim)

*From Fox and Mathews.[19]

will have recovered to or near the 120 to 140 beats per minute values. With longer work intervals (880 yards and over) usually a 1:1 or 1:½ work-relief ratio is prescribed; with middle duration intervals (440 to 660 yards) a 1:2 ratio is used; and with shorter work intervals, because of the high intensity, a 1:3 work-relief ratio is prescribed.

Knowing these work-relief ratios facilitates administration of the interval training program, particularly to groups, as it does not become necessary to time the pulse following each work effort. However, occasional 6-second checks must be made toward the end of the relief interval so that work intensity can be increased, decreased, or maintained.

2. *Type of Relief Interval.* What you do during the relief intervals is important, for it also relates to the energy system you may wish to develop. The type of activity may consist of:

(a) Rest, i.e., moderate moving about such as walking, or flexing arms and legs; termed **rest-relief.**
(b) Light or mild exercise including rapid walking and jogging; termed **work-relief.**
(c) A combination of (a) and (b).

Rest-relief intervals should be used with interval-training programs designed to modify the ATP-PC energy system. This is so because, during rest-relief intervals, ATP-PC is restored to the muscles and can be used over and over, since it is the major source of energy for the short exhaustive work intervals. When one is stressing modification of the lactic acid system, work-relief intervals should intervene between work intervals. As you may recall, mild work will inhibit or partially block complete restoration of the ATP-PC energy system. As a consequence, the lactic acid system, rather than the ATP-PC system, is used during subsequent work intervals. Such practice (work-relief) encourages improvement of the lactic acid system. The key to modification of the oxygen system is prevention of lactic acid buildup. Therefore, a rest-relief interval should be used with a program designed for improvement of the oxygen system.

The Group Interval-Training Program

Interval training is the method most commonly used by track and swimming coaches to improve the condition and performance of their athletes. As has been stressed, the programs are individually tailored to assure that each athlete receives maximum benefits, depending upon his or her condition and event. Thus the interval training program for the sprinter differs from that for the miler; as a matter of fact, in all likelihood it will also differ from one sprinter to another or from one miler to another. For all sports, interval training is a very effective way to train your athletes.[19]

Of considerable additional importance to the physical educator is the interval-training program that, with a minimal amount of time, can also be used to improve the condition of the average person. To do this requires construction of the prescriptions (workouts) on a group basis. Appendix F contains an example of such a program for an 8-week period for both men and women and contains procedures to follow in administering such a group program.

Summary of the Interval-Training System

Before going on to other kinds of training methods, let's summarize the interval-training system.

1. Determine which energy system(s) needs to be increased.
2. Select the type of activity (exercise) to be used during the work interval.
3. Using Tables 12-8 and 12-9, write the training prescriptions according to the

TABLE 12-8

Pertinent Information for Writing Interval Training-Prescriptions Based on Training Times*

Major Energy System	Training Time (Min:Sec)	Repetitions Per Workout	Sets Per Workout	Repetitions Per Set	Work-Relief Ratio	Type of Relief Interval
ATP-PC	0:10	50	5	10		Rest-relief (e.g., walking, flexing)
	0:15	45	5	9		
	0:20	40	4	10	1:3	
	0:25	32	4	8		
ATP-PC-LA	0:30	25	5	5		Work-relief (e.g, light to mild exercise, jogging)
	0:40–0:50	20	4	5	1:3	
	1:00–1:10	15	3	5		
	1:20	10	2	5	1:2	
LA-O$_2$	1:30–2:00	8	2	4	1:2	Work-relief
	2:10–2:40	6	1	6		
	2:50–3:00	4	1	4	1:1	Rest-relief
O$_2$	3:00–4:00	4	1	4	1:1	Rest-relief
	4:00–5:00	3	1	3	1:½	

*Modified from Fox and Mathews.[19]

TABLE 12-9

Pertinent Information For Writing Interval-Training Prescriptions Based on Training Distances*

Major Energy System	Training Distance Yards		Repetitions Per Workout	Sets Per Workout	Repetitions Per Set	Work-Relief Ratio	Type of Relief Interval
	Run	Swim					
ATP-PC	55	15	50	5	10	1:3	Rest-relief (e.g., walking, flexing)
	110	25	24	3	8		
ATP-PC-LA	220	55	16	4	4	1:3	Work-relief (e.g., light to mild exercise, jogging)
	440	110	8	2	4	1:2	
LA-O$_2$	660	165	5	1	5	1:2	Work-relief
	880	220	4	2	2	1:1	Rest-relief
O$_2$	1100	275	3	1	3	1:½	Rest-relief
	1320	330	3	1	3	1:½	

*Modified from Fox and Mathews.[19]

information appearing in the row opposite the major energy systems you wish to be improved. The number of repetitions and sets, the work-relief ratio, and the type of relief interval are all given in the tables. For any activity selected, the training times given in Table 12-8 (second column) may be used. However, if the activity is either running or swimming, it is more common to use training distance as shown in the second column of Table 12-9.

4. Provide for an increase in intensity (progressive overload) throughout the training program.

Examples of prescriptions, for interval training workouts based on Tables 12-8 and 12-9 for a sprinter and a miler are given in Table 12-10.

Although interval training is an excellent system for athletes of any sport as well as for nonathletes interested in general fitness, it is not the only training method available today. Some of the training methods presented below are also effective in improving specific fitness levels required for many sports and activities. Generally, as was the case with interval training, these methods were developed mainly by track-and-field and swimming coaches to meet the specific needs of their athletes. However, again as with interval training, with some adaptations these methods can be used to bring about the specific changes required to improve the fitness and health of those who use them.

Continuous Running

This method, as the name implies, involves continuous running (or swimming) for relatively long distances. Wilt[47] classifies continuous-running programs into two categories, *continuous slow-running training* and *continuous fast-running training*. A third category, *jogging,* can be added. In all cases, the aerobic or oxygen system is the predominant source of energy, and therefore continuous running programs develop endurance capacity (max $\dot{V}O_2$).

Continuous Slow-Running

This means running for long distances at a slow speed or pace. This type of running is sometimes referred to as LSD, i.e., long, slow distance or endurance and aerobic power training.[11] The pace will vary from runner to runner. Examples of paces might be 8 minutes per mile for an inexperienced runner or athlete, and 6 minutes per mile for the international class competitor.[47] No matter what the exact pace, the intensity of the run should be great enough to bring the heart rate to within 70 to 75% of the HRR or about 80 to 85% of the HR_{max}.

The distance covered is also important in this type of training and should be related to the runner's specialty event. Generally, runners should cover between 2 to 5 times the distance of their racing event. For example, a miler would cover 2 to 5 miles; a 3-miler, 6 to 12 miles; and a 6-miler, 12 to 18 miles.[47] Because running such distances is monotonous on a track, they are usually covered over natural terrain (e.g., golf courses or roads).

Continuous slow-running is also used

TABLE 12-10

Examples of Interval-Training Prescriptions for a Sprinter and a Miler

Type of Runner	Prescription
Sprinter	Set 1 4 × 220 at 0:27 (1:21)*
	Set 2 8 × 110 at 0:13 (0:39)
	Set 3 8 × 110 at 0:13 (0:39)
Miler	Set 1 1 × 1320 at 3:45 (1:52)
	Set 2 2 × 1100 at 2:58 (1:29)

*Read as follows: four 220-yd runs at a pace of 27 sec with 1 min and 21 sec work-relief between runs.

by marathon (26.2 miles) and ultramarathon (52.5 miles) runners. How does one prepare to run a 52.5-mile race? For one such runner, Ted Corbitt,[8] a typical weekly workout schedule would include a 30-mile run on Sunday, 20 miles each on the other mornings (Monday through Saturday), and an additional 11.6 to 13 miles each evening. This requires an average of 4 hours each day. Several times each month, Ted runs 62 miles in one day. In a month of training, he is able to cover more than 800 miles, more than most family cars accumulate in the same period! Most of his training distance is covered at a rate of between 7 and 8 minutes per mile, since very little emphasis is placed on speed.

Continuous Fast-Running

This differs from continuous slow-running in that the pace is faster, resulting in earlier fatigue, and less distance is covered. As an example, the intensity of the run should be such that the THR approaches 80 to 90% of the HRR or 85 to 95% of the HR_{max}. In addition, an 880-yard runner might run ¾ to 1½ miles, repeating the distance one to four times; a 6-miler might run 8 to 10 miles at a steady but fast pace, or run 4 to 5 miles on 2 to 3 occasions.[47] Between repeats, the runners should perform 5 minutes of walking and jogging.

As previously mentioned, continuous slow- and fast-running are used by distance runners. As has also been emphasized, total mileage or distance covered per workout and per week for the endurance athlete is an important overload factor. While the monthly distance covered by Ted Corbitt may be best suited for him, Costill[9] recommends that the average competitive distance runner cover between 320 and 360 miles per month. As shown in Figure 12-10, he further suggests that the distances be broken down weekly and in cycles of 4 weeks each. The greatest distance in either

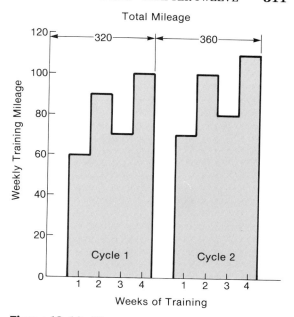

Figure 12-10. The average competitive distance runner might cover between 320 and 360 miles per month. The distances might be broken down weekly and in cycles of 4 weeks each. The greatest distance covered in a cycle should be in the second and fourth weeks. (Based on data from Costill.[9])

cycle should be covered in the second and fourth weeks. Notice also that the second cycle shows a progressive overload feature. For example, the total distance covered during each week of the second cycle is greater than during the corresponding week of the first cycle.

Jogging

This is a term used to include all speeds of running, but it usually refers to slow continuous running.[40] Recently, jogging has gained a great deal of popularity, particularly among adults seeking fitness for health reasons. For example, the improvement in the circulatory and respiratory systems resulting from jogging programs serves as a prophylaxis against coronary disease (Chapter 15).

Jogging programs, like competitive programs, vary a great deal. A reasonable basic schedule to follow is contained in Table 12-11. Whenever the goal of one step is achieved, no matter how long it takes, the jogger should proceed to the next step. The frequency of the training sessions should be 3 days per week, jogging 2 miles at each session.

Repetition Running

Repetition running is similar to interval training but differs in (1) the length of the work interval, and (2) the degree of recovery between repetitions.[47] The lengths of the work intervals in repetition running are usually between 880 yards and 2 miles, and recoveries between repetitions are more complete (e.g., a recovery heart rate well below 120 beats per minute). The main object of repetition running for the competitive track athlete is to stimulate the duration of stress encountered under racing conditions.

There are basically two forms of repetition running:[29,47]

1. Running one-half the race distance at or faster than race pace. This is repeated so as to accumulate from 1.5 to 2 times the race distance. For example, a 4-minute 30-second (4:30) miler would run 3 to 4 repeats of ½ mile each

---

TABLE 12-11

A Basic Jogging Schedule for Men and Women*

Steps	1 Mile Check Time (Min:Sec)	Total Target Time for 2 Miles (Min:Sec)
1. Slow walk	20:00	40:00
2. Alternate ¼-mile slow walk and ¼-mile fast walk	18:00	36:00
3. Fast walk	16:00	32:00
4. Alternate 330-yd fast walk and 110-yd slow jog	14:30	29:00
5. Alternate 220-yd fast walk and 220-yd slow jog	13:00	26:00
6. Alternate ¼-mile fast walk and ¼-mile slow jog	13:00	26:00
7. Alternate ½-mile slow jog and ¼-mile fast walk	11:30	23:00
8. Alternate ¾-mile slow jog and ¼-mile fast walk	11:30	23:00
9. Slow jog	10:00	20:00
10. Alternate ¼-mile fast jog and ¼-mile slow jog	9:30	19:00
11. Alternate ¼-mile slow jog and ¼-mile fast jog	9:00	18:00
12. Alternate ½-mile slow jog and ½-mile fast jog	9:00	18:00
13. Alternate ½-mile fast jog and ¼-mile slow jog	8:30	17:00
14. Alternate ¼-mile slow jog and ¾-mile fast jog	8:30	17:00
15. Fast jog	8:00	16:00
16. Alternate ¼-mile fast jog and ¼-mile faster jog	7:30	15:00
17. Alternate ½-mile fast jog and ½-mile faster jog	7:30	15:00
18. Faster jog	7:00	14:00

*Modified from Roby and Davis.[40]

at a pace of between 2:10 and 2:15. Remember, the recovery between repetitions should be nearly complete.

2. Running three quarters of the race distance at slightly slower than race pace. Again, repetitions should allow 1.5 to 2 times the race distance. For example, a 10-minute 2-miler might run 2 to 3 repeats of 1½ miles, each at a speed of about 7:48. The pace is determined by taking the average race pace for each ¼ mile plus 3 seconds (in our example, $75 + 3 = 78$ seconds average per 440 yards $\times$ 6 quarter-miles = 7:48 per 1½ miles).

Repetition running develops either aerobic or anaerobic capacities, depending on whether the pace is slow or fast, respectively.

Speed Play or Fartlek Training

Speed play or fartlek (a Swedish word meaning "speed play") training is said to be the forerunner of the interval-training system. It involves alternating fast- and slow-running over natural terrain. It can be thought of as an informal interval-training program in that neither the work nor relief intervals are precisely timed. Furthermore, the proportions of fast- and slow-running are left entirely up to the runners as they feel the need or urge to run them. Such a program will develop both aerobic and anaerobic capacities. An example of training schedule for one workout using the fartlek method is as follows:[10]

1. Warm up by running easily for 5 to 10 minutes.
2. Run at a fast, steady speed over a distance of ¾ to 1¼ miles.
3. Walk rapidly for 5 minutes.
4. Practice easy running, broken by sprints of 65 to 75 yards, repeating until fatigue becomes evident.
5. Run easily, injecting 3 to 4 swift steps occasionally.
6. Run at full speed uphill for 175 to 200 yards.
7. Run at a fast pace for 1 minute.
8. Finish the routine by running 1 to 5 laps around the track, depending on the distance run in competition.

Another example of a fartlek workout would be:[47]

1. Jog 10 minutes as a warm-up.
2. 4 minutes brisk calisthenics.
3. 1 to 2 × ¾ to 1¼ miles at a fast, steady pace that might be described as ¾ full speed. Walk 5 minutes after each.
4. 4 to 6 × 150-yard acceleration sprints (jog 50 yards, stride 50 yards, and sprint 50 yards, and walk 50 yards after each).
5. 4 to 6 × 440 yards at slightly faster than racing effort. Jog 440 yards after each.
6. Walk 10 minutes.
7. Continuous slow-running for 2 minutes.
8. Walk 5 minutes.
9. 8 to 12 × 110 yards at 1½ to 2½ seconds slower than best effort, jogging 110 yards after each. Walk 5 minutes.
10. Jog 1 mile as a warm-down.

Sprint Training

This type of training is used by sprinters to develop speed (ATP-PC system) and muscular strength.[47] Here, repeated sprints at *maximal* speed are performed. About 6 seconds are required to accelerate to maximum speed from a static start. Therefore, the sprinter should run at least 60 yards on each sprint in order to experience moving at top speed.[47] Also, because each sprint should be performed at top speed, recovery between repetitions must be complete.

Interval Sprinting

Interval sprinting is a method of training whereby an athlete alternately sprints 50 yards and jogs 60 yards for distances up to 3 miles.[47] For example, over 440 yards, the sprinter would perform four 50-yard sprints, jogging 60 yards after each; repeat 12 times. Because of fatigue setting in after the first few sprints, the athlete will not be able to run subsequent sprints at top speed. This factor, plus the relatively long distances covered per training session (up to 3 miles), makes this type of training system suitable for the development of the aerobic system.

Acceleration Sprints

As the name implies, acceleration sprints involve a gradual increase in running speed from jogging to striding and finally to sprinting.[13,47] The jogging, striding, and sprinting intervals may consist of 50-yard, 110-yard, or 120-yard segments. In each case, recovery should consist of walking. For example, a sprinter may jog 50 yards, stride 50 yards, sprint 50 yards, walk 50 yards, and then repeat. Because recovery between repetitions is nearly complete, this type of training develops speed and strength. Also, it is a good method to use in cold weather, since the runs are graduated from easy to hard, thus lessening the chances of muscular injury.[13,47]

Hollow Sprints

Hollow sprints involve use of two sprints interrupted by a *hollow* period of either jogging or walking. These sprints are performed in repeats; one repetition might include sprinting 60 yards, jogging 60 yards, then walking 60 yards. Similar intervals might include distances up to but not beyond 220 yards.

Application of Training Methods to Various Sports

A summary of the prescription content for the various training methods is presented in Table 12-12. Although the prescriptions are for different track athletes, they may be applied to other sports and activities within minimal adaptations. For example, acceleration sprints, hollow sprints, interval training, and sprint training methods might be modified for the football player as follows:

1. Prescribe sprint distances of only 40 to 50 yards.
2. Prescribe backward and lateral running.
3. Prescribe stop-and-go sprinting (i.e., the runner sprints for 5 yards, then stops and reaches out to touch the ground, then sprints 5 more yards, reaches out and touches the ground, and so on, for a total of 40 to 50 yards).

It should be noticed that these particular variations include movement patterns that are specifically involved in football skills. It is thought that such training induces changes that are quite distinct from the training's effects on anaerobic metabolism.[14] As will be pointed out in the next chapter, the effects of training for high power output activities on anaerobic metabolism are not impressive, yet improvements in performance can be substantial. Obviously, some other changes induced by training must come into play. Possible factors that dictate performance changes in high power output activities are changes in motor unit recruitment patterns or chemical alterations at the neuromuscular junction.[14] Therefore, repeated performance of a specific motor skill or movement pattern involved in a high power activity should contribute greatly to improvement in performance. Any variations in prescriptions for football or other sports should take this aspect of training into account.

Which training method should be used for which sport? The answer to this lies in how well the various training methods develop the different energy systems. This

TABLE 12-12

Sample Prescriptions for Various Training Methods*

Training Method	Type of Athlete	Sample Prescription
Acceleration sprints	Sprinter	Jog 50 to 120 yards, stride 50 to 120 yards, walk 50 to 120 yards, repeat
Continuous fast-running	Half-miler	Run ¾ to 1½ miles at a steady, fast pace (e.g., 6-minute-mile pace); repeat 1 to 4 times
	6-miler	Run 8 to 10 miles at a steady, fast pace
Continuous slow-running	Miler	Run 3 to 5 miles at a steady, slow pace (e.g., 7½-minute-mile pace)
	3-miler	Run 6 to 12 miles at a steady, slow pace
	6-miler	Run 12 to 18 miles at a steady slow pace
Hollow sprints	Sprinter	Sprint 60 yards, jog 60 yards, walk 60 yards; repeat until fatigued
Interval sprinting	Middle-distance	Alternate 50-yard sprints with 60-yard jogs; repeat up to 3 miles
Interval training	Sprinter	Set 1 4 × 220 @ 0:27 (1:21)* Set 2 8 × 110 @ 0:13 (0:39) Set 3 8 × 110 @ 0:13 (0:39)
	Miler	Set 1 1 × 1320 @ 3:45 (1:52) Set 2 2 × 1100 @ 2:58 (1:29)
Jogging	Recreational	Jog 2 miles in 14 minutes
Repetition running	Miler	Run 3 to 4 repeats of ½ mile at a pace of 2:10 to 2:15
Speed play (fartlek)	Middle-distance and distance	Jog 5 to 10 minutes; run ¾ to 1¼ miles at a fast, steady pace; walk 5 minutes; alternate jog-sprint (65 to 75 yards); sprint uphill for 175 to 200 yards; jog for ¾ to 1¼ miles
Sprint training	Sprinter	Repeat full-speed sprints of 60 to 70 yards with complete recovery between repeats

*From Fox[20]; read as follows: four 220-yd runs at a pace of 27 sec with 1 min and 21 sec relief (walking) between runs.

information, combined with knowing the energy system or systems most used during the performance of a given sport, will enable the coach and physical educator to select the best training method for improving performance in a specific sport or sports activity.

Information relative to the various sports and activities and their predominant energy systems was presented earlier in Table 12-2 (p. 290). Table 12-13 contains information relating the various training methods to the development of the energy systems. Notice that the energy systems are grouped the same as in Table 12-2, i.e., ATP-PC and LA, LA and O_2, and O_2. Also notice that there are several methods that develop the same energy systems to approximately the same degree. For example, acceleration sprints and hollow sprints develop mainly the anaerobic energy systems to the same degree. Interval-training prescriptions on the other hand, may be designed to develop mainly the two anaerobic

TABLE 12-13

Various Training Methods and Development of the Energy Systems*

Training Method	Per Cent Development		
	ATP-PC and LA	LA and O_2	O_2
Acceleration sprints	90	5	5
Continuous fast-running	2	8	90
Continuous slow-running	2	5	93
Hollow sprints	85	10	5
Interval sprinting	20	10	70
Interval training	10–80	10–80	10–80
Jogging	—	—	100
Repetition running	10	50	40
Speed play (fartlek)	20	40	40
Sprint training	90	6	4

*Modified from Fox.[20]

systems, or mainly the aerobic system, or all three systems equally.

The percentages given in Table 12-13 are only approximations since exact information of this kind is not as yet available. The same applies to Table 12-2. Nevertheless, selection of a suitable training method for a particular sport can be facilitated by matching the information concerning the energy systems in Table 12-2 with that in Table 12-13. As an example, suppose you wanted to train someone to run 2 miles. From Table 12-2, you can find the approximate degree of usage of the energy systems during a 2-mile run. Table 12-13 may then be consulted so you can determine which training methods develop the energy systems to this degree. Two methods, interval training and speed play, develop each system in the appropriate range, and another method, repetition running, approximates the development the runner will need. By looking back at Table 12-2, you can see that any one of these three methods

might also be appropriate for use in training a 400-meter freestyle swimmer or a rower. Remember, however, for the swimmer the mode of exercise would be swimming (not running), and for the rower, rowing.

Suggested training methods that are appropriate for various sports and sports activities are given in Table 12-14. This table was constructed from the information given in Tables 12-2 and 12-13.

Summary

The basic tenets in any conditioning or training program are: (1) to recognize the major energy source utilized in performing a given activity and (2) then, through the overload principle, to construct a program that will develop that particular energy source more than will any other. The primary energy system for any activity can be estimated on the basis of its performance time.

TABLE 12–14

Suggested Sprint and Endurance Training Methods for Various Sports and Sports Activities

Sport or Sport Activity	Acceleration Sprints	Continuous Fast-Running	Continuous Slow-Running	Hollow Sprints	Interval Sprinting	Interval Training	Jogging	Repetition Running	Speed Play (Fartlek)	Sprint Training
Baseball				✓		✓				✓
Basketball				✓		✓				✓
Fencing	✓			✓		✓				✓
Field hockey						✓				
Football	✓			✓		✓				✓
Golf	✓									✓
Gymnastics	✓			✓		✓				✓
Ice Hockey*										
Forwards, defense				✓		✓				
Goalie	✓					✓				✓
Lacrosse										
Goalie, defense, attack men				✓		✓				
Midfielders, man-down						✓				
Recreational sports			✓			✓	✓			
Rowing*						✓		✓	✓	
Skiing*										
Slalom, jumping, downhill				✓		✓				
Cross-country		✓	✓							
Soccer										
Goalie, wings, strikers				✓		✓				
Halfbacks, link men						✓				

Table continued on the following page.

TABLE 12-14

Suggested Sprint and Endurance Training Methods for Various Sports and Sports Activities (*Continued*)

Sport or Sport Activity	Acceleration Sprints	Continuous Fast-Running	Continuous Slow-Running	Hollow Sprints	Interval Sprinting	Interval Training	Jogging	Repetition Running	Speed Play (Fartlek)	Sprint Training
Softball				✓		✓				
Swimming and diving*										
50-m freestyle, diving	✓									✓
100-m, 100-yd (all strokes)					✓	✓				
200-m, 220-yd (all strokes)						✓				
400-m, 440-yd freestyle						✓		✓	✓	
1500-m, 1650-yd freestyle					✓	✓				
Tennis						✓				
Track and field	✓									
100-m, 100-yd	✓									✓
200-m, 220-yd	✓				✓	✓				✓
Field events					✓	✓				✓
400-m, 440-yd					✓	✓				
800-m, 880-yd						✓				
1500-m, 1 mile						✓		✓	✓	
2 miles						✓		✓	✓	
3 miles, 5000-m					✓	✓				
6 miles, 10,000-m		✓			✓	✓				
Marathon		✓	✓							
Volleyball	✓				✓	✓				✓
Wrestling	✓				✓	✓				✓

*Rather than running, the mode of exercise during the training sessions should be that used in the sport. (From Fox.[22])

The overload principle requires that the training intensity be near maximal. For endurance-training programs, training intensity can be judged either from (1) the heart rate response to exercise or from (2) the anaerobic threshold. With the heart rate method, the target heart rate (THR) should be between 80 and 90% of the maximal heart rate reserve (HRR) plus the resting heart rate (HR_{rest}) or between 85 and 95% of the maximal heart rate (HR_{max}). The HRR is defined as the difference between the HR_{max} and the HR_{rest}. The HR_{max} may be estimated from the equation, $HR_{max} = 220 - age$. The HR_{rest} may be determined by palpation of an artery, such as the carotid in the neck.

With the anaerobic threshold method, the intensity of exercise at or slightly above the anaerobic threshold can be used during endurance training. The anaerobic threshold is the work intensity at which anaerobic metabolism (accumulation of lactic acid) begins to rapidly accelerate. It can be detected either by monitoring minute ventilation or blood lactic acid concentration during a progressive exercise test. During exercise at the anaerobic threshold, the heart rate is on the average 91% of the HR_{max}.

For anaerobic (sprint) training programs, the heart rate should be 180 beats per minute or more. The anaerobic threshold will usually be exceeded during anaerobic training since sprints are performed at a maximal pace.

Other important overload factors are training frequency and training duration. More frequent and longer-duration programs are more important aspects of endurance training than of sprint training.

Off-season training should consist mainly of weight training and low-intensity running. Preseason training should contain weight training and high-intensity aerobic or anaerobic training programs, and in-season training should consist of some running, weight training, drills, scrimmages, and competitive performances.

Warm-up prior to any training session promotes increased body and muscle temperatures which in turn promote increases in muscle metabolism, blood flow, oxygen availability, and decreases in muscle contraction and reflex times. Warm-up activities should include stretching exercises, calisthenics, and formal activity. Warm-down or cool-down should include similar activities but performed in reverse order. Warm-down hastens recovery and reduces the possibility of dizziness and fainting after heavy exercise.

The interval training system involves repeated bouts of hard work alternated with periods of lighter work or rest. Intermittent work delays fatigue and allows for maximal intensity during the work intervals. Manipulation of the rate and distance of the work interval, the number of repetitions, and the time and type of relief interval provides for a training program that can meet the needs of many athletes and non-athletes.

Other training methods include continuous slow-running (LSD), continuous fast-running, jogging, and interval sprinting primarily for development of the oxygen system; and sprint training, acceleration sprints, and hollow sprints primarily for development of the ATP-PC and LA systems. Interval training, repetition running, and speed play (fartlek) training improve both aerobic and anaerobic systems.

Questions

1. Discuss the basic tenets of any conditioning or training program.
2. How can one determine which energy system(s) predominates in any sport or activity?
3. What is meant by the overload principle as

applied to aerobic and anaerobic training programs?

4. Discuss and compare the ways in which training intensity can be determined.

5. What are the phases of athletic training, and what kinds of programs should they contain?

6. Why are warm-up and warm-down programs important from a physiological standpoint?

7. Describe the ingredients of good warm-up and warm-down programs.

8. Define interval training.

9. Physiologically, explain why intermittent work, and thus the interval-training system, is successful in improving all three energy systems.

10. There are five variables you may manipulate in fulfilling the requirements of a good interval-training program. Describe each one.

11. Discuss the method by which you might estimate the training times in running 55 to 1320 yards in an interval-training program.

12. In an interval-training program, on what do the time and type of relief interval depend?

13. Discuss several different training programs that develop primarily the aerobic system.

14. Discuss several different training programs that develop primarily the anaerobic systems.

References

1. Asmussen, E., and Boje, O.: Body temperature and capacity for work. *Acta Physiol Scand.* 10:1–22, 1945.

2. Åstrand, I., Åstrand, P., Christensen, E., and Hedman, R.: Intermittent muscular work. *Acta Physiol Scand.* 48:448–453, 1960.

3. Åstrand, I., Åstrand, P. O., Christensen, E. H., and Hedman, R.: Myohemoglobin as an oxygen-store in man. *Acta Physiol Scand.* 48:454–460, 1960.

4. Barnard, R., Gardner, G., Diaco, N., MacAlpin, R., and Kattus, A.: Cardiovascular responses to sudden strenuous exercise— heart rate, blood pressure, and ECG. *J Appl Physiol.* 34(6):833–837, 1973.

5. Bergh, U., and Ekblom, B.: Physical performance and peak aerobic power at different body temperatures. *J Appl Physiol.* 46(5):885–889, 1979.

6. Carlile, F.: Effects of preliminary passive warming-up on swimming performance. *Res Q.* 27:143–151, 1956.

7. Christensen, E., Hedman, R., and Saltin, B.: Intermittent and continuous running. *Acta Physiol Scand.* 50:269–287, 1960.

8. Costill, D., and Fox, E.: The ultra-marathoner. *Distance Running News.* 3(4):4–5, 1968.

9. Costill, D. L.: *A Scientific Approach to Distance Running.* Los Altos, Calif., Track and Field News, 1979.

10. Cretzmeyer, F., Alley, L., and Tipton, C.: *Track and Field Athletics,* 8th ed. St. Louis, C. V. Mosby, 1974.

11. Daniels, J., Fitts, R., and Sheehan, G.: *Conditioning for Distance Running.* New York, John Wiley, 1978.

12. Davis, J. A., and Convertino, V. A.: A comparison of heart rate methods for predicting endurance training intensity. *Med Sci Sports.* 7(4):295–298, 1975.

13. Dintiman, G.: *What Research Tells the Coach about Sprinting.* Washington, D.C., American Alliance for Health, Physical Education, and Recreation, 1974.

14. Edgerton, V. R.: Neuromuscular adaptation to power and endurance work. *Can J Appl Sport Sci.* 1:49–58, 1976.

15. Fox, E. L.: Differences in metabolic alterations with sprint versus endurance interval training. In Howald, H., and Poortmans, J. (eds.): *Metabolic Adaptation to Prolonged Physical Exercise.* Basel, Switzerland, Birkhäuser Verlag, 1975, pp. 119–126.

16. Fox, E. L., Bartels, R., Billings, C., Mathews, D., Bason, R., and Webb, W.: Intensity and distance of interval training programs and changes in aerobic power. *Med Sci Sports.* 5:18–22, 1973.

17. Fox, E. L., Bartels, R., Billings, C., O'Brien, R., Bason, R., and Mathews, D.: Frequency and duration of interval training programs and changes in aerobic power. *J Appl Physiol.* 38(3):481–484, 1975.

18. Fox, E. L., Klinzing, J., and Bartels, R. L.: Interval training: metabolic changes as related to relief-interval heart rates of 120 and 140 beats per minute. *Fed Proc.* 36(3):449, 1977.

19. Fox, E. L., and Mathews, D.: *Interval Training: Conditioning for Sports and General Fitness.* Philadelphia, W. B. Saunders, 1974.

20. Fox, E. L.: Physical training: methods and effects. *Orthop Clin N Am.* 8:533–548, 1977.

21. Fox, E. L., Robinson, S., and Wiegman, D.: Metabolic energy sources during continuous and interval running. *J Appl Physiol.* 27:174–178, 1969.

22. Fox, E. L.: *Sports Physiology.* Philadelphia, W. B. Saunders, 1985.

23. Hultman, E., Bergstrom, J., and McLennan Anderson, N.: Breakdown and resynthesis of phosphorylcreatine and adenosine triphosphate in connection with muscular work in man. *Scand J Clin Invest.* 19:56–66, 1967.

24. Inger, F., and Strømme, S. B.: Effects of active, passive or no warm-up on the physiological response to heavy exercise. *Europ J Appl Physiol.* 40:273–282, 1979.

25. Karlsson, J., and Saltin, B.: Lactate, ATP and CP in working muscles during exhaustive exercise in man. *J Appl Physiol.* 29:598–602, 1970.

26. Karpovich, P., and Hale, C.: Effect of warming-up upon physical performance. *JAMA* 162:1117–1119, 1956.

27. Karvonen, M., Kentala, E., and Mustala, O.: The effects of training on heart rate. A longitudinal study. *Ann Med Exper Biol Fenn.* 35:307–315, 1957.

28. Katch, V., Weltman, A., Sady, S., and Freedson, P.: Validity of the relative per cent concept for equating training intensity. *Europ J Appl Physiol.* 39:219–227, 1978.

29. Kennedy, R.: *Track and Field for College Men.* Philadelphia, W. B. Saunders, 1970.

30. Kindermann, W., Simon, G., and Keul, J.: The significance of the aerobic-anaerobic transition for the determination of work load intensities during endurance training. *Europ J Appl Physiol.* 42:25–34, 1979.

31. MacDougall, J. D.: The anaerobic threshold: its significance for the endurance athlete. *Can J Appl Sport Sci.* 2:137–140, 1977.

32. Mader, A., Liesen, H., Heck, H., Philippi, H., Rost, R., Schürch, P., and Hollmann, W.: Zur Beurteilung der sportartspezifischen Ausdauerleistungsfähigkeit im Labor. *Sportarzt Sportmed.* 27:80–88, 109–112, 1976.

33. Margaria, R., Oliva, R., diPrampero, P., and Cerretelli, P.: Energy utilization in intermittent exercise of supramaximal intensity. *J Appl Physiol.* 26:752–756, 1969.

34. Martin, B. J., Robinson, S., Wiegman, D. L., and Aulick, L. H.: Effect of warm-up on metabolic responses to strenuous exercise. *Med Sci Sports.* 7(2): 146–149, 1975.

35. Mathews, D., and Snyder, H.: Effect of warm-up on the 440-yard dash. *Res Q.* 30: 446–451, 1959.

36. Michael, E., Skubic, V., and Rochelle, R.: Effect of warm-up on softball throw for distance. *Res Q.* 28:357–363, 1957.

37. O'Connor, H.: Warm-up as an aid to track performance. *Scholastic Coach.* 25, 1955.

38. Pacheco, B.: Improvement in jumping performance due to preliminary exercise. *Res Q.* 28:55–63, 1957.

39. Pollock, M. L.: The quantification of endurance training programs. In Wilmore, J. H. (ed.): *Exercise and Sport Sciences Reviews,* vol. 1. New York, Academic Press, 1973, pp. 155–158.

40. Roby, F., and Davis, R.: *Jogging for Fitness and Weight Control.* Philadelphia, W. B. Saunders, 1970.

41. Saltin, B., Blomquist, B., Mitchell, J. H., Johnson, Jr., R. L., Wildenthal, K., and Chapman, C. B.: Responses to exercise after bed rest and training. *Circulation.* 38:1–78, 1968. Also in American Heart Association Monograph no. 23:VII-1 to VII-78. AHA. 1968.

42. Saltin, B., and Essen, B.: Muscle glycogen, lactate, ATP, and CP in intermittent exercise. In Pernow, B., and Saltin, B. (eds.): *Muscle Metabolism during Exercise.* New York, Plenum Press, 1971, pp. 419–424.

43. Skubic, V., and Hodgkins, J.: Effect of warm-up activities on speed, strength, and accuracy. *Res Q.* 28:147–152, 1957.

44. Taylor, H. L., Haskell, W., Fox, Jr., S. M., and Blackburn, H.: Exercise tests: a summary of procedures and concepts of stress testing for cardiovascular diagnosis and function evaluation. In Blackburn, H. (ed.): *Measurement in Exercise Electrocardiography.* Springfield, Ill., Charles C Thomas, 1969, pp. 259–305.

45. Tipton, C., and Karpovich, P.: Exercise and the patellar reflex. *J Appl Physiol.* 21(1): 15–18, 1966.

46. White, J. R.: EKG changes using carotid artery for heart rate monitoring. *Med Sci Sports.* 9(2):88–94, 1977.

47. Wilt, F.: Training for competitive running. In Falls, H. (ed.): *Exercise Physiology.* New York, Academic Press, 1968, pp. 395–414.

SELECTED READINGS

Armbruster, D., Allen, R., and Billingsley, H.: *Swimming and Diving,* 6th ed. St. Louis, C. V. Mosby, 1973.

Counsilman, J.: *The Science of Swimming.* Englewood Cliffs, N.J., Prentice-Hall, 1968.

Doherty, J.: *Modern Track and Field,* 2nd ed. Englewood Cliffs, N.J., Prentice-Hall, 1963.

Doherty, J.: *Modern Training for Running.* Englewood Cliffs, N.J., Prentice-Hall, 1964.

Fox, E. L., and Mathews, D.: *Interval Training: Conditioning for Sports and General Fitness.* Philadelphia, W. B. Saunders, 1974.

Fox, E. L.: Methods and effects of physical training. *Pediatric Ann.* 7(10):66–94, 1978.

Fox, E. L.: Physical training: methods and effects. *Ortho Clin N Am.* 8:533–548, 1977.

Fox, E. L.: *Sports Physiology.* Philadelphia, W. B. Saunders, 1979, pp. 192–241.

Shaffer, T. E., and Fox, E. L.: Guidelines to physical conditioning for sports. *Pediatric Basics.* 18:10–14, 1977.

chapter 13

Physiological Effects of Physical Training

The major concepts to be learned from this chapter are as follows:

- Training induces physiological changes in almost every system of the body, particularly within the skeletal muscles and the cardiorespiratory system.
- The changes resulting from training are influenced by the frequency, duration, and, particularly, by the intensity of the training program, and by heredity.
- The effects of training are specific to the type of exercise performed, the muscle groups involved, and to the type of training program used.

- The specificity of training and exercise has two broad physiological bases—metabolic and neuromuscular.
- The effects of training are lost after several weeks of detraining.
- Training effects can be maintained with maintenance programs consisting of one or two days of exercise per week.
- Previous training does not significantly influence the magnitude or rate of gain of training effects induced by subsequent training programs.

In the previous chapter we discussed some basic principles related to construction of physical training programs. These programs, when applied over a sufficient time period, cause physiological changes that lead to greater energy-yielding capabilities and improved physical performances.

The purpose of this chapter is to explore these changes with respect to the physiological mechanisms involved as well as to the relevant training factors.

Training Effects

The effects of training can be studied most easily by classifying the changes as follows: (1) those occurring at the tissue level, that is, biochemical changes; (2) those occurring systemically, that is, those affecting the circulatory and respiratory systems, including the oxygen transport system; and (3) other changes such as those concerned with body composition, blood cholesterol and triglyceride levels, blood pressure changes, and changes with respect to heat acclimatization.

It should be pointed out at this time that not all of the following training effects can be expected from a single training program. Training effects are specific to the type of training regimen used, whether it is an aerobic (endurance) or anaerobic (sprint) program. The specificity of training effects will be discussed in detail later in this chapter.

Biochemical Changes

Much new information concerning the effects of physical training at the cellular or biochemical level has been made available only recently. Excellent reviews concerning these changes have been written by Gollnick and Hermansen[65] and Holloszy.[81-86]

Aerobic Changes

There are three major aerobic adaptations that occur in skeletal muscle, mainly as a result of endurance training programs.

1. *Increased Myoglobin Content.* Myoglobin content in skeletal muscle has been shown to be substantially increased following training.[120] The training program involved rats and consisted of treadmill running, 5 days per week for 12 weeks. This response is specific in that the myoglobin increased only in those muscles involved in the training program (leg muscles). Further, Hickson[75] has shown, in rats, that myoglobin increases are associated with the frequency of training. With exercise at 2 days, 4 days, and 6 days per week, myoglobin levels increased 14, 18, and 26%, respectively.

As was mentioned earlier (p. 54), myoglobin is an oxygen-binding pigment similar to hemoglobin. In this respect, it acts as a store for oxygen. However, this is considered a minor function in contributing to the improvement of the aerobic system. Its main function is in aiding the delivery (diffusion) of oxygen from the cell membrane to the mitochondria where it is consumed.

2. *Increased Oxidation of Carbohydrate (Glycogen).* Training increases the capacity of skeletal muscle to break down

glycogen in the presence of oxygen (oxidize) to $CO_2 + H_2O$ with ATP production. In other words, the capacity of the muscle to generate energy aerobically is improved. Evidence for this change is an increase in the maximal aerobic power (max $\dot{V}O_2$). More will be said about this later.

There are two major subcellular adaptations that contribute to the muscle cells' increased capacity to oxidize carbohydrate following training: (1) increases in the number, size, and membrane surface area of skeletal muscle mitochondria,[33,66,80,89,99] and (2) an increase in the level of activity or concentration of the enzymes involved in the Krebs Cycle and electron transport system.[9,12,36,63,67,80,121] Several studies[66,80,87,89,99] have shown increases in both the number and size of mitochondria following training. For example, as shown in Figure 13-1A, in one study involving humans,[99] there was a 120% increase in the number of mitochondria in the vastus lateralis muscle following a 28-week, 5-day-per-week training program of distance running and calisthenics. The increase in mitochondrial size (Fig. 13-1B) is not as large as is the increase in number, averaging in humans between 14 and 40% greater in athletes versus non-athletes.[87,99] This too is probably a specific response, occurring only in those muscle fibers involved in the training program.

With respect to (1) mentioned previously, it should be mentioned that the

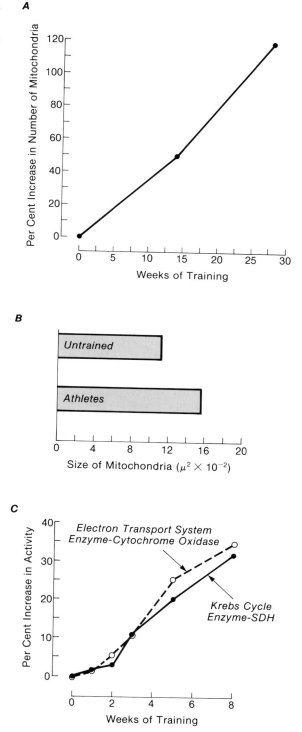

Figure 13-1. Major subcellular adaptations that contribute to the muscle cells' increased capacity to oxidize carbohydrate following training are *A,* an increased number; *B,* size of muscle mitochondria; and *C,* an increased level of activity of the enzymes involved in the Krebs Cycle (e.g., succinate dehydrogenase, or SDH) and electron transport system (cytochrome oxidase). (Data in *A* and *B* from Kiessling et al.[99]; data in *C* from Hendricksson and Reitman.[72])

number of mitochondria per myofibril is less in women than in men.[87,89] The significance of this difference is not immediately apparent. However, it would appear to represent a definite biochemical limitation with respect to the overall maximal aerobic power of the female.

You will recall from Chapter 2 that the many metabolic reactions involved in the Krebs Cycle and electron transport system are controlled by the presence of specific enzymes. An increased level of activity of these enzymes as a result of training means that more ATP can be produced in the presence of oxygen. The levels of activity of these enzymes in rat skeletal muscle have been shown to double in the course of a 12-week, five-day-per-week training program.[80] In humans, as shown in Figure 13-1C, the increase in just 8 weeks of training is nearly 40%.[72]

Aside from the increased ability of muscle to oxidize glycogen, there is also an increase in the amount of glycogen stored in the muscle following training.[67,68] You will recall from Chapter 2 (p. 26), that human skeletal muscle normally contains between 13 and 15 grams of glycogen per kilogram of muscle. After training, this amount has been shown to increase 2.5 times[67] (Fig. 13-2). This increase in glycogen storage is due, at least in part, to the fact that training causes increased activities of the enzymes responsible for glycogen synthesis and breakdown (glycogen cycle enzymes).[158,159]

The initial level of muscle glycogen is directly related to aerobic or endurance capacity (p. 543). It is easy to see how the mitochondrial and enzyme changes mentioned above plus the increased glycogen storage in the muscles work together in effectively improving all aspects of the aerobic capabilities of the muscle.

2. *Increased Oxidation of Fat.* Like glycogen, the breakdown (oxidation) of fat to $CO_2 + H_2O$ with ATP production in the

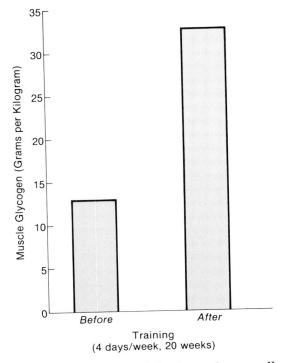

Figure 13-2. Human skeletal muscle normally contains between 13 and 15 grams of glycogen per kilogram of muscle. After training, this amount has been shown to increase as much as 2.5 times. (Based on data from Gollnick et al.[67])

presence of oxygen is increased following training.[64,120,126] It should be remembered that fat can and does serve as a major source of fuel for skeletal muscle during endurance exercises. Thus, an increased capacity to oxidize fat is a definite advantage in increasing the performance of such activities. Actually, at a given submaximal workload, the trained person oxidizes more fat and less carbohydrate than does the untrained person.[64,73,94,144,145] During exercise with heavy but submaximal workloads, a greater fat oxidation would mean less glycogen depletion, less lactic acid accumulation, and less muscular fatigue.[36]

The increase in the muscles' capacity to oxidize fat following endurance training is related to three factors: (1) an increase in the intramuscular stores of triglycerides, the storage form of fat[87,121,159]; (2) an increased release of free fatty acids from adipose tissue, i.e., the availability of fats as a fuel is increased[19]; and (3) an increase in the activities of the enzymes involved in the activation, transport, and breakdown of fatty acids.[112] In relation to (1), rather large increases in muscle triglyceride stores have been demonstrated in humans following endurance training. An example is shown in Figure 13-3. In this study,[87] the intramuscular fat stores were 1½ times greater in endurance-trained male athletes compared to their untrained counterparts. Also of interest is to note that intramuscular fat stores between untrained men and women are the same.

In relation to (2), it has recently been shown that increased availability of fats made possible by their increased dietary intake can have a significant positive effect on endurance performance.[32,79] This response is apparently related to the glycogen-sparing effect mentioned earlier, resulting from greater fat oxidation. More will be said about the dietary effects of fat consumption in a later chapter. The last factor, (3), includes both the enzymes necessary to break down the large fat molecules into smaller units in preparation for entry into the Krebs Cycle and electron transport system (called beta oxidation) as well as the enzymes mentioned earlier that work within these latter series of reactions themselves.

The effects of training on the aerobic potential of skeletal muscles are summarized in Figure 13-4.

Anaerobic Changes

The anaerobic changes in skeletal muscle resulting from training involve increased capacities of (1) the phosphagen (ATP-PC) system; and (2) anaerobic glycolysis, i.e., the lactic acid system.

1. *Increased Capacity of the Phosphagen (ATP-PC) System.* The capacity of the ATP-PC system is enhanced by two major biochemical changes: (a) increased levels of muscular stores of ATP and PC; and (b) increased activities of key enzymes involved in the ATP-PC system.

Muscular stores of ATP have been shown to increase approximately 25% (from 3.8 to 4.8 mM/kg of wet muscle) following a training program of distance running for 7 months for 2 to 3 days per week.[97] Also, the concentration of PC in the muscles of boys 11 to 13 years of age increased nearly 40% after 4 months of training.[44] Since these phosphagens represent the most rapidly available source of energy for the muscle, their increased storage correlates well with the improved execution of activities requir-

Figure 13-3. Intramuscular fat stores have been found to be as much as 1½ times greater in endurance-trained, male athletes compared with their untrained counterparts. Also notice that intramuscular fat stores between untrained men and women are the same. (Based on data from Hoppeler et al.[87])

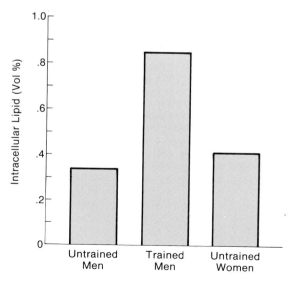

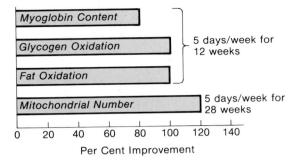

Figure 13-4. The effects of training on the aerobic potential of skeletal muscle include increases in myoglobin, glycogen and fat oxidation, and the size and number of mitochondria. (Based on data from Pattengale and Holloszy[128]; Holloszy[80]; Molé et al.[120]; and Kiessling et al.[99])

ing only a few seconds to perform that is also a consequence of physical training.

As mentioned previously, training alters several key enzymes of the ATP-PC system.[156,162] You will remember that in the ATP-PC system, ATP is continually turned over, i.e., broken down and resynthesized. The breakdown of ATP is facilitated by an enzyme called ATPase, whereas its resynthesis is facilitated by the enzymes myokinase (MK) and creatine kinase (CPK). Myokinase catalyzes the reactions involved in replenishing ATP from ADP, and creatine kinase catalyzes the reactions involved in replenishing ATP from phosphocreatine (PC). In a recent study on humans,[162] the activities of these enzymes were found to increase following 8 weeks of sprint training as follows: ATPase, 30%; MK, 20%; and CPK, 36%. Thus, not only is the storage of ATP and PC increased by training, but also their rates of turnover are also enhanced. These mutually beneficial changes clearly demonstrate that the rapid release of energy by the muscle cell is alterable through proper (mainly sprint) training programs.

2. *Increased Glycolytic Capacity.* Not nearly as much information concerning the effects of training on anaerobic glycolysis (lactic acid system) is available compared to that for the aerobic system. Nevertheless, a number of well-designed studies have indicated that several of the key enzymes that control glycolysis are significantly altered by physical training. For example, the activity of one such enzyme, phosphofructokinase (PFK), which is important in the early reactions of glycolysis, doubled following endurance training in one study[68] and increased by 83% in another.[44] In 11- to 13-year-old boys, PFK increased 20%.[49] Other important glycolytic enzymes have also been reported to increase following training.[7,147,156] In addition, it has been shown that activities of important glycolytic enzymes are much higher in sprint athletes than in endurance athletes.[33]

The significance of increased glycolytic enzyme activities is that they speed up the rate and quantity of glycogen broken down to lactic acid. Therefore, the ATP energy derived from the lactic acid system is increased also and thus contributes to the improved performance of activities that depend heavily on this system for energy. Evidence for an increased glycolytic capacity following training is also demonstrable by the ability to accumulate significantly greater quantities of blood lactic acid following maximal exercise (p. 345).

The changes in the ATP-PC and lactic acid system enzymes as a result of training are shown in Figure 13-5.

Relative Changes in Fast- and Slow-Twitch Fibers

The changes just noted do not all occur to the same degree in the slow-twitch and fast-twitch fibers. There is, in other words, a specific response in fast- and slow-twitch fibers with respect to the changes induced

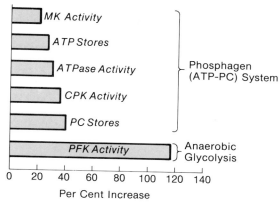

Figure 13-5. The effects of training on the anaerobic potential of skeletal muscle include increases in the activities of the ATP turnover enzymes—ATPase, myokinase (MK), and creatine kinase (CPK)—in muscular stores of ATP and PC, and in glycolytic capacity. (Based on data from Thorstensson et al.[162]; Karlsson et al.[97]; Eriksson et al.[44]; and Gollnick et al.[67])

by training. Some of these specific changes are as follows:

1. In the case of aerobic changes, it is fairly well agreed that the aerobic potential of skeletal muscle following training is increased equally in both fibers.[6,68] This means that the inherent differences in oxidative capacity between the fiber types is not altered by training. In other words, the slow-twitch fiber has a higher aerobic capacity compared to the fast-twitch fiber after as well as before training.

2. Changes in the glycolytic capacity of human skeletal muscle appear to be more specific, being greater in fast-twitch fibers.[48,67]

3. Evidence suggests that there is a selective hypertrophy of fast- and slow-twitch fibers. For example, slow-twitch fibers occupy a greater area of the muscle in endurance athletes than do fast-twitch fibers.[33,68] By the same

token, fast-twitch fibers occupy a greater area in sprinters, shot-putters, and discus throwers (Fig. 13-6). This information implies a selective hypertrophy dependent upon the kind of training and/or sports activities performed by the athletes.

4. Most available evidence suggests that there is no interconversion of fast- and

Figure 13-6. Training produces a selective hypertrophy of fast- and slow-twitch skeletal muscle fibers. The slow-twitch fibers of endurance athletes occupy a greater area of the muscle than do fast-twitch fibers. However, fast-twitch fibers occupy a greater area in sprinters, shot-putters and discus throwers. (Based on data from Costill et al.[33])

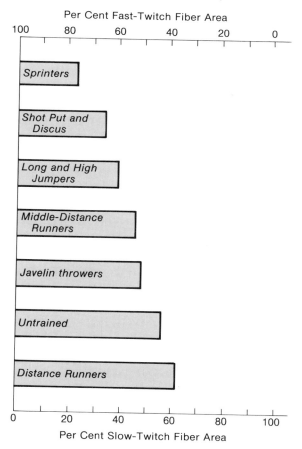

slow-twitch fibers as a result of physical training.[44,67,146] Evidence indicates that with aerobic training there is a gradual conversion of type FT_B (fast-glycolytic) to type FT_A (fast-oxidative-glycolytic) fibers but no gross changes in the ratio between type ST and type FT fibers. In one study, subjects trained for 8 weeks on a bicycle working at 81% of their aerobic capacity. Following training, type FT_A fibers were observed to have increased to 75% from 65% of the total of type FT fibers. The percentage of type ST (slow-oxidative) fibers remained the same as before.[2] However, another study[87] has presented evidence to suggest that the percentage of fast-twitch fibers increased and the percentage of slow-twitch fibers decreased following anaerobic training. Just the opposite was reported following aerobic training, i.e., slow-twitch fibers increased and fast-twitch fibers decreased. Nevertheless, the majority of evidence is still in favor of no fiber type interconversions due to training.

A summary of the biochemical changes in skeletal muscle resulting from physical training is given in Table 13-1.

Cardiorespiratory (Systemic) Changes

The cardiorespiratory (systemic) changes induced by training include those that affect mainly the oxygen transport system. As pointed out in Chapter 10, the oxygen transport system involves many circulatory, respiratory, and tissue level factors, all working together for one common goal—to deliver oxygen to the working muscles. First we will discuss some changes that are demonstrable under resting conditions, and then we will outline the

---

TABLE 13-1

Biochemical Changes in Skeletal Muscle Induced by Physical Training

Aerobic changes
  Increased myoglobin content
  Increased oxidation of glycogen
    Increased number and size of mitochondria
    Increased activity of Krebs Cycle and ETS enzymes
    Increased muscular stores of glycogen
  Increased oxidation of fat
    Increased muscular stores of triglycerides
    Increased availability of fats as fuel
    Increased activity of enzymes involved in activation, transport, and breakdown of fatty acids

Anaerobic changes
  Increased capacity of the ATP-PC system,
    Increased muscular stores of ATP and PC
    Increased activities of the ATP turnover enzymes
  Increased glycolytic capacity
    Increased glycolytic enzyme activities

Relative change in fast- and slow-twitch fibers
  Increased aerobic capacity equal in both fibers
  Increased glycolytic capacity greater in fast-twitch fiber
    Selective hypertrophy, fast-twitch—sprint training; slow-twitch—endurance training
    No fiber type interconversion

systemic changes that are prominent during submaximal and maximal exercise. Several very thorough review articles pertaining to cardiovascular changes and physical training have been written by Rowell,[138] Clausen,[29] Scheuer and Tipton,[149] and Barnard.[8]

Cardiorespiratory Changes at Rest

There are five main changes resulting from training that are apparent at rest: (1) changes in heart size; (2) a decreased heart rate; (3) an increased stroke volume; (4) increased blood volume and hemoglobin; and (5) changes in skeletal muscles.

1. *Changes in Heart Size.* It has been known for a long time[102] that the size (volume) of the heart is greater in athletes than in nonathletes. However, until recently, not much was known concerning the details of this cardiac hypertrophy because the technique commonly used for its measurement (chest X-ray) is not capable of delineating exact dimensional characteristics of the heart. At present, a noninvasive* technique called echocardiography provides a sensitive means for assessing, among other factors, the size of the cavity of the ventricles and the thickness of the ventricular wall.[45] One or both of these factors could account for an increase in heart size. Using this method, the following has been found concerning cardiac dimensions of male and female athletes and nonathletes:[38,40,122,124,137,139,155,167,173]

(a) The cardiac hypertrophy of endurance athletes (e.g., distance runners, swimmers, and field hockey players) is characterized by a *large ventricular cavity* and a *normal thickness* of the ventricular wall. This means that the volume of

blood that fills the ventricle during diastole is also larger. We will soon see that this effect causes the stroke volume capabilities of the endurance athlete to be greater than those of the nonathlete as well as those of the nonendurance athlete.

(b) The cardiac hypertrophy of nonendurance athletes, that is, athletes engaged in high-resistance or isometric types of activities such as wrestling and putting the shot, is characterized by a *normal-sized ventricular cavity* and a *thicker ventricular wall*. Therefore, even though the magnitude of the cardiac hypertrophy in these athletes is the same as in endurance athletes, their stroke volume capabilities are no different from those of their nonathletic counterparts.

Previously, it was thought that heredity plays a dominant role in determining heart size. However, it is clear from the previous information that differences in cardiac hypertrophy are related to the type of sport or activity performed or trained for by the athlete, thus indicating that heart size is influenced by training. This idea is also supported by the recent finding that heart volume is not as genetically dependent as is, for example, the maximal oxygen consumption.[106] In addition, the heart volumes of nonathletes have increased significantly following several months of physical training.[58] The fact that heart volume does not always increase following physical training[42,59] suggests that the training program must be intense and that it probably should be maintained over a long period of time, perhaps even years, before the change is effected.

The previous information gathered from echocardiography has also provided insight into the types of stimuli required to elicit changes in cardiac function. For ex-

---

*Noninvasive refers to measurements made from outside the body rather than those made by "invading" the body with hypodermic needles or catheters, for example.

ample, training for endurance activities usually requires prolonged efforts during which the cardiac output is sustained at high levels.[53] The response to this type of stimulus, which may be called volume stress, is cardiac hypertrophy through an increase in the size of the ventricular cavity. On the other hand, athletes who participate in and train for brief but powerful activities such as wrestling and putting the shot are not subjected to volume stress but rather to intermittently elevated arterial blood pressure similar to that generated during straining. The cardiac hypertrophy in response to this stimulus is a thickening of the ventricular wall.

It was mentioned in Chapter 7 that hypertrophy of skeletal muscle is accompanied by an increase in capillary density. So too is cardiac hypertrophy.[39,111,160,161] Such an effect provides for better blood flow to the heart and most likely serves as a prophylactic treatment against coronary heart disease.

The different types of cardiac hypertrophy resulting from physical training are shown in Figure 13-7.

2. *Decreased Heart Rate.* The resting **bradycardia** (decreased heart rate) resulting from training is (a) most evident when athletic and nonathletic subjects are compared (Fig. 13-8A); (b) less evident but still clear-cut when sedentary subjects undergo a training program; and (c) least distinct when athletes are studied in the untrained versus the trained state.[57] This information points out that (a) the training bradycardia is dependent upon a long time period (maybe years) of intensive training, and (b) the magnitude of the decrease in resting heart rate produced by training is less when the level of fitness is greater. It should also be noted (Fig. 13-8A) that the magnitude of the resting bradycardia is the same in endurance and nonendurance athletes. Apparently, neither the different training programs nor the different types

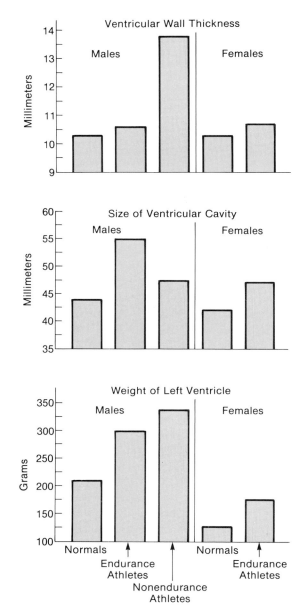

Figure 13-7. The cardiac hypertrophy of endurance athletes is characterized by a large ventricular cavity with a normal thickness of the wall. On the other hand, the cardiac hypertrophy of nonendurance athletes is characterized by a thicker ventricular wall with a normal-sized ventricular cavity. (Male data from Morganroth et al.[122]; female data from Zeldis et al.[173])

A

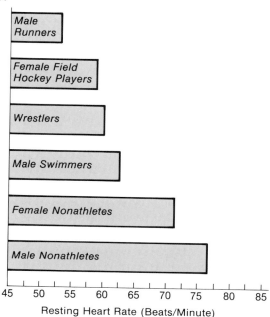

Male Runners

Female Field Hockey Players

Wrestlers

Male Swimmers

Female Nonathletes

Male Nonathletes

Resting Heart Rate (Beats/Minute)

B

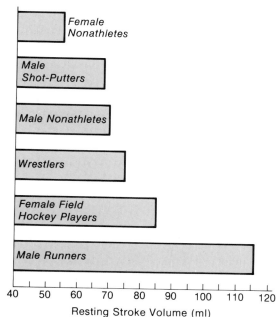

Female Nonathletes

Male Shot-Putters

Male Nonathletes

Wrestlers

Female Field Hockey Players

Male Runners

Resting Stroke Volume (ml)

of cardiac hypertrophy resulting from them significantly influences the magnitude of the bradycardia.

What causes this training bradycardia at rest? You will recall (p. 275) that the heart is supplied by two major autonomic nerves, the sympathetic nerves, which, when stimulated, increase the heart rate, and the vagus nerves (parasympathetic nerves), which decrease the rate when stimulated. With this dual nervous system, the heart rate can be decreased either by (a) an increased parasympathetic (vagal) tone or influence; (b) a decreased sympathetic influence (drive); or by (c) a combination of (a) and (b). Evidence to support all three sides has been presented.[57,91,152,164,165,172]

However, there is also another factor that must be considered when discussing training-induced bradycardia—the *intrinsic rate of the atrial pacemaker or S-A node*.[5,152,153] (The S-A node was discussed in Chapter 10, p. 245). If the intrinsic rate of the pacemaker is decreased with exercise training, then the heart rate would be slower independently of the influences of the autonomic nervous system. Taking this into account together with the nervous influences mentioned previously, the resting bradycardia resulting from exercise training most likely involves two major components.[5]

(a) A reduction or slowing in the intrinsic rate of the atrial pacemaker, the S-A node. This in turn could be related to the increased amounts

Figure 13-8. *A,* Training induces a resting bradycardia (a decreased heart rate). *B,* Training induces an increased resting stroke volume. Note that the magnitude of the bradycardia is the same in endurance and non-endurance athletes but that the increase in stroke volume is most pronounced in endurance athletes. (Male data from Morganroth et al.[122]; female data from Zeldis et al.[173])

of acetylcholine (the parasympathetic neurotransmitter) found in atrial tissue following exercise training[5] and to the decreased sensitivity of cardiac tissue to *catecholamines,* which is also known to occur following training.[153] (The catecholamines are a class of chemicals including the sympathetic neurotransmitters, epinephrine, and norepinephrine.)

(b) An increase in parasympathetic (vagal) predominance on the pacemaker rate as a result of a decrease in sympathetic activity. In other words, the increased parasympathetic influence is thought to be secondary to the primary decrease in sympathetic nervous system activity caused by exercise training.

3. *Increased Stroke Volume.* Since the resting cardiac output is approximately the same for trained and nontrained subjects, it is easy to see (since $\dot{Q} = SV \times HR$) that the resting stroke volume of athletes or trained subjects will be higher than that of their nonathletic counterparts[13,122] (Fig. 13-8*B*). Notice that the increased stroke volume is most pronounced in endurance athletes. As mentioned earlier, these athletes have an increased ventricular cavity, thus allowing more blood to fill the ventricle during diastole, resulting in a larger stroke volume. Another contributing factor to an increased resting stroke volume following training is an increased myocardial contractility[118,131,135] (p. 252). The increase in contractility may in turn be related to increases in ATPase activity within the heart muscle,[14,15,148] and/or to an enhanced extracellular calcium availability leading to enhanced interaction with the contractile elements.[8,163]

The change in resting stroke volume as a result of training is most pronounced when athletes are compared to nonathletes.

This again points out that this effect probably requires a long-term intensive training program. Therefore, in some studies in which previously untrained subjects have been trained for only several months, an increased resting stroke volume does not always occur.[42]

4. *Changes in Blood Volume and Hemoglobin.* Both the total blood volume and the total amount of hemoglobin increase with training.[101,125] An example of such changes is given in Table 13-2. That the total blood volume and hemoglobin levels are important with respect to the oxygen transport system is evidenced by the fact that they both are closely correlated with the max $\dot{V}O_2$ (see Fig. 14-10, p. 386). Blood volume and hemoglobin also play important roles during exercise at altitude (Chapter 17). In addition, since deep body heat is carried by the blood to the periphery, where it can then be dissipated, blood volume is important during exercise in the heat (Chapter 18).

Note should be made of the fact that *hemoglobin concentration* does not usually change with training (Table 13-2). If anything, it decreases slightly. For example, the normal hemoglobin concentration for males is 15 grams per 100 ml of blood on the average. In a group of highly trained endurance runners, the average hemoglobin concentration was only 14.3 gm/100 ml blood.[43]

5. *Changes in Capillary Density and Hypertrophy of Skeletal Muscle.* As previously indicated, hypertrophy of skeletal muscle resulting from weight-training programs is generally accompanied by an increase in capillary density. Capillary density refers to the number of capillaries that surround a skeletal muscle fiber. Long-term endurance training for competition in running, swimming, or cycling, for instance, sometimes causes muscular hypertrophy and almost always an increased capillary density in skeletal muscle.[1,3,23,74,92]

TABLE 13–2

Changes in Hemoglobin and Blood Volume Following Physical Training in Males*

Variable	Training State		Per Cent Change
	Before	After	
Total hemoglobin			
gm	805	995	+24
gm/kg body wt	11.6	13.7	+17
Total blood volume			
liters	5.25	6.58	+ 25
ml/kg body wt	75.0	90.1	+20
Hemoglobin concentration			
gm/100 ml blood	15.3	15.1	−1.3

*Based on data from Kjellberg et al.[101]

This effect is shown in Figure 13-9, which indicates that the muscle fibers of highly trained endurance athletes (max $\dot{V}O_2$ = 71.4 ml/kg-min) were found to be 30% larger than those of a group of untrained subjects (max $\dot{V}O_2$ = 50.2 ml/kg-min) of the same age. In addition, for the athletes it was determined that each muscle fiber was surrounded on the average by 5.9 capillaries, whereas for the untrained subjects, the average fiber was surrounded by only 4.4 capillaries (Fig. 13-9C). The supply of oxygen and other nutrients to, and the removal of waste products from, the muscle are all enhanced because there are more capillaries per fiber.

The number of capillaries surrounding each skeletal muscle fiber is related to two factors: (a) the size or diameter of the muscle fiber,[23,92] and (b) the fiber type or number of mitochondria per muscle fiber.[1,3,92] The relationship between fiber diameter and number of capillaries around each fiber is shown in Figure 13-10A. Notice that this relationship holds for both trained and untrained subjects. In relation to fiber type, it should be remembered that slow-twitch fibers have more mitochondria than do fast-twitch fibers. Therefore, as shown in Figure 13-10B, the number of capillaries surrounding slow-twitch fibers is greater than in either FT_A or FT_B fibers. Again, notice that this holds true for both untrained and trained subjects.

A summary of the changes induced by physical training at rest is given in Table 13-3.

Changes during Submaximal Exercise

Several important changes in the functioning of the oxygen transport and related systems following training are evidenced during steady-state, submaximal exercise. These major changes, as shown in Figure 13-11, are as follows:

1. *No Change or Slight Decrease in Oxygen Consumption.* The oxygen consumption during exercise at a given submaximal work load is the same[55,145] or slightly lower[42,56] before as compared to after training. The decrease is due to an increase in mechanical efficiency (skill) and is most pronounced in comparisons of highly trained athletes and untrained individuals. Such a difference is also evident

A

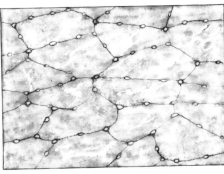

B

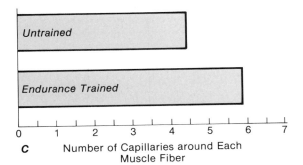

C   Number of Capillaries around Each
Muscle Fiber

Figure 13-9. Training results in hypertrophy of skeletal muscle and increased capillary density. The muscle fibers of *B,* highly trained endurance athletes, are 30 per cent larger and, *C,* are surrounded by more capillaries than *A,* the fibers of the untrained subjects. (Data in *A* and *B* from Hermansen and Wachtlova[74]; data in *C* from Brodal et al.[23])

between good and average runners (see Fig. 4-5, p. 75).

2. *Decrease in Muscle Glycogen Utilization (Glycogen Sparing).* During prolonged, submaximal exercise at a given workload or oxygen consumption, the amount of muscle glycogen utilized is less following training.[98,141] This effect is sometimes referred to as **glycogen sparing** and is probably related to the muscles' increased ability to use (oxidize) free fatty acids as a metabolic fuel, thus sparing glycogen. In turn, increased fatty acid oxidation is a result of some of the biochemical alterations discussed earlier. Gollnick and Saltin[69] have presented a rather complete theory concerning how the increase in oxidative enzymes could operate to alter the choice of substrate during submaximal work in a manner such that the oxidation of fatty acids increases, glycogen depletion and lactic acid production are reduced, and work capacity is enhanced. The reader is referred to Gollnick and Saltin for more details.[69]

It may be recalled that depletion of muscle glycogen stores has been implicated in muscular fatigue.[140] Therefore, the glycogen-sparing effect appears to be an important factor in delaying fatigue and in increasing endurance performance.

3. *Decrease in Lactic Acid Production (Increase in Anaerobic Threshold).* Training is associated with a decrease in the accumulation of lactic acid during a given submaximal exercise.[42,50,56,97] This is an important change, since most work, including that performed during training sessions, is to a large extent submaximal. This factor is illustrated in distance running, which requires submaximal effort over extended periods of time. Not only must these runners have a highly developed maximal aerobic power (max $\dot{V}O_2$), but also in order to be successful they must be able to employ a large fraction of that power with minimal accumulation of lactic

A

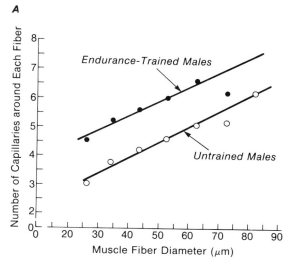

TABLE 13-3

Changes At Rest Induced by Training

Cardiac hypertrophy
  Increased ventricular cavity (endurance
    athletes)
  Increased myocardial thickness
    (nonendurance athletes)
Decreased heart rate
  Decreased intrinsic atrial rate
  Increased parasympathetic (vagal) tone
  Decreased sympathetic influence
Increased stroke volume
  Cardiac hypertrophy
    Increased myocardial contractility
Increased blood volume and hemoglobin
Increased skeletal muscle hypertrophy and
  capillary density

B

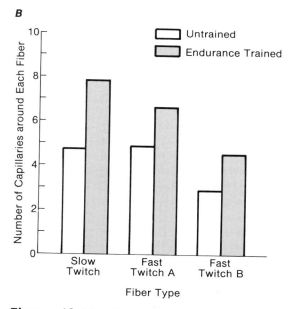

Figure 13-10. The number of capillaries surrounding each skeletal muscle fiber is related to: *A,* the size or diameter of the muscle fiber (the larger the diameter, the greater the number of capillaries); and *B,* the fiber type or number of mitochondria per muscle fiber, since slow-twitch fibers have more mitochondria than fast-twitch fibers. (Data in *A* from Brodal et al.[23]; data in *B* from Inger.[92])

acid.[34] This allows the runners to maintain a fast pace throughout the race without experiencing early fatigue.

A decreased lactic acid accumulation during exercise following training also means that the anaerobic threshold has increased.[37] This is illustrated in Figure 13-12. Note that the anaerobic threshold (the work intensity at which lactic acid begins to accumulate) is around 60% of the max $\dot{V}O_2$ in untrained subjects, but is about 75% of the max $\dot{V}O_2$ in trained distance runners. Note also that the anaerobic threshold of Derek Clayton, at the time the world's fastest marathoner, is very close to 85% of his max $\dot{V}O_2$.

The physiological mechanisms responsible for a decreased accumulation of lactic acid during submaximal exercise following training are not entirely known. However, there are several possibilities as follows:

(a) As explained above, a greater utilization of fatty acids as a metabolic fuel to fulfill the energy requirements of the exercise would result in less glycogen usage and

STEADY-STATE, SUBMAXIMAL WORK

A   METABOLIC CHANGES

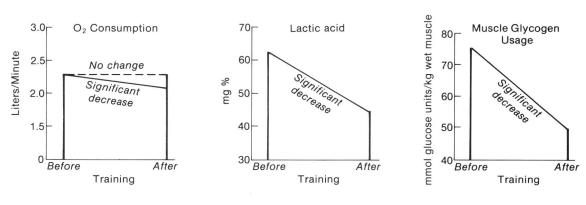

B   TOTAL BLOOD FLOW CHANGES

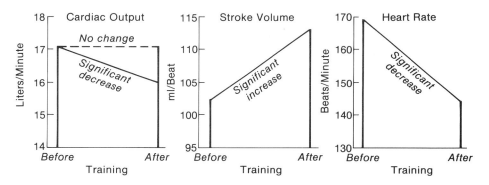

C   LOCAL BLOOD FLOW CHANGES

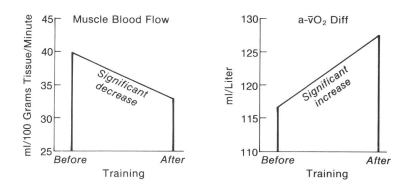

Figure 13-11. Important changes in the functioning of the oxygen transport and related systems during submaximal work following training include no change or slight decrease in oxygen consumption; decreased lactic acid production; decreased muscle glycogen usage; no change or slight decrease in cardiac output; increased stroke volume; decreased heart rate; and a decreased blood flow per kilogram of working muscle. (Based on data from Ekblom et al.[42]; Frick et al.[58]; Grimby et al.[70]; and Karlsson et al.[98])

thus less lactic acid production by the muscles. (Remember, lactic acid is a by-product of glycogen breakdown). This would be a better possibility during prolonged exercises, such as long-distance running, in which there is sufficient time for a significantly greater fatty acid oxidation, rather than during short-term exercises.[52]

(b) A smaller oxygen deficit incurred at the beginning of exercise due to a more rapid increase in oxygen consumption could also lead to less lactic acid accumulation.[97] Such a training effect has been shown to occur.[26,71,76]

(c) A greater use (oxidation) of any lactic acid produced as a metabolic fuel during exercise would also result in a lowered overall lactic acid accumulation. Again this would appear to be a more important factor during prolonged exercise because of the time factor.

(d) Another possible mechanism concerning lowered lactic acid levels following training could be a result of some of the biochemical changes discussed earlier. For example, it has been suggested[81,85] that since training increases the number and size of muscle mitochondria, the steady-state oxygen consumption that balances the breakdown of ATP to ADP + Pi during exercise will be attained at lower concentrations of ADP plus Pi. In other

words, as shown in Figure 13-13, with more mitochondria, the oxygen as well as the ADP and Pi required per mitochondrion will be less after training as compared with before training. Since the levels of both ADP and Pi control the rate of glycolysis (the higher the levels of ADP and Pi, the greater the rate of glycolysis), their lower levels after training would cause the rate of lactic acid production to

Figure 13-12. The anaerobic threshold (the work intensity at which lactic acid begins to accumulate) is around 60% of the max $\dot{V}O_2$ in untrained subjects, but about 75% of the max $\dot{V}O_2$ in trained distance runners. Note also that the anaerobic threshold of Derek Clayton, formerly the world's fastest marathoner, is very close to 85% of his max $\dot{V}O_2$.

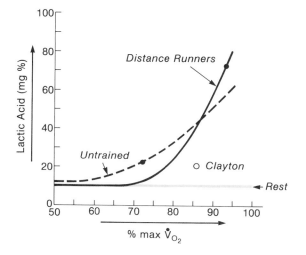

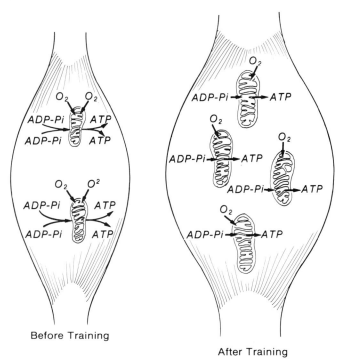

Before Training

After Training

Figure 13-13. With more mitochondria, the oxygen as well as the ADP and Pi required per mitochondrian will be less for a given submaximal exercise load after training as compared with before training. Since the levels of ADP and Pi control the rate of glycolysis (the higher the levels, the greater the rate of glycolysis), their lower levels after training would cause the rate of lactic acid production to be slower.

be slower during exercise at the same workload. This hypothesis appears to be the most plausible and takes into account some of the other possibilities mentioned previously.

4. *No Change or Slight Decrease in Cardiac Output.* During submaximal exercise at a given load or $\dot{V}O_2$, the cardiac output of trained subjects is sometimes slightly lower than and sometimes the same as that of untrained subjects (p. 248). The reason for this discrepancy is not known. However, it may be related to the type, intensity, and duration of the training programs involved.

5. *Increased Stroke Volume.* The stroke volume is increased during submaximal exercise at a given workload following training.[13,56,58,143] As in the case of the increased resting stroke volume, this exercise effect is related mainly to the increased size of the ventricular cavity and to an increased myocardial contractility also promoted by training; the greater the amount of blood filling the cavity and the greater the force of contraction (contractility), the greater will be the stroke volume. It should also be remembered that one of the most important components of the oxygen transport system is the stroke volume (p. 257).

6. *Decreased Heart Rate.* Perhaps the most consistent and pronounced

change associated with training is a decreased heart rate during submaximal exercise following training.[42,54-58,98,117,172] As in the case of the resting bradycardia, this decrease is most pronounced in comparisons of nonathletic subjects and highly trained athletes. It should also be pointed out again that a slower-beating heart is more efficient, requiring less oxygen than a faster-beating heart at the same cardiac output level.[10]

The exercise bradycardia, like the resting bradycardia, is thought to be caused by modifications within the heart muscle itself and within the autonomic nervous system. For example, evidence for a decreased sympathetic drive during exercise in humans is shown in Figure 13-14. Plasma levels of norepinephrine and epinephrine (catecholamines) and the heart rate response to a given submaximal exercise load are plotted against weeks of training. It is clearly evident that during the first 2 or 3 weeks of training, the reduction in heart rate paralleled the decreases in plasma norepinephrine and epinephrine. Notice that with further training, however, the plasma catecholamines tended to level off, yet heart rate continued to fall. This suggests that other factors, such as an increased parasympathetic (vagal) tone or a slowing of the intrinsic rate of the atrial pacemaker, might also be involved in the exercise bradycardia. Nevertheless, a decreased sympathetic drive during exercise could have two origins:[29]

(a) An *intracardiac* or *central mechanism,* that is, an effect directly on the heart muscle itself, may be responsible. For example, we have already seen that training causes increases in myocardial contractility and hypertrophy leading to an increased stroke volume during submaximal work. Thus, at the same or slightly decreased cardiac

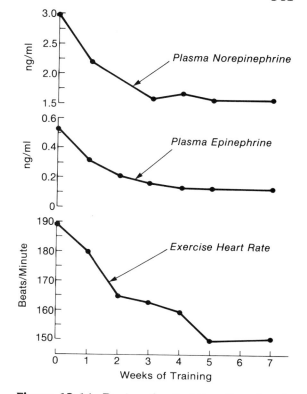

Figure 13-14. During the first 2 or 3 weeks of training, the reduction in heart rate parallels the decreases in plasma catecholamine (norepinephrine and epinephrine) levels. However, with further training, the catecholamines tend to level off yet heart rate continues to fall. (Based on data from Winder et al.[172])

output, the need for a higher heart rate through sympathetic stimulation is greatly reduced.[57]

(b) An *extracardiac* or *peripheral mechanism,* that is, an indirect effect resulting from alterations in the trained skeletal muscles, may be the cause. For example, we know from Chapter 11 (p. 281) that sympathetic stimulation to the heart can be modified by nervous impulses arising from the muscles and joints and by descending impulses from the motor cortex. A reduced heart rate resulting from these kinds of modifications would mean that the training effect on the heart is secondary to the biochemical changes occurring in the trained skeletal muscles.[30,56,117]

7. *Changes in Muscle Blood Flow.* Contrary to what you might think, blood flow per kilogram of working muscle is *lower* in trained than in untrained individuals at the same absolute submaximal workload.[70,81,103] The working muscles compensate for the lower blood flow in the trained state by extracting more oxygen.[81] This is evidenced by a greater arterial-mixed venous oxygen difference (a-$\bar{v}O_2$ diff) and may be related to the biochemical changes mentioned earlier that occur in the skeletal muscles.

As previously mentioned, the total blood flow (i.e., cardiac output) either remains the same or is slightly lower after training during exercise at the same workload as before training. In the case where the cardiac output is the same, a decreased muscle blood flow would mean that more blood is made available for the nonexercising areas such as the skin. During exercise in the heat, this would be an advantage with respect to heat elimination. On the other hand, a reduced blood flow to the muscles would account for the reduction in cardiac output sometimes observed.

All of the previous submaximal exercise changes induced by training tend to reduce the relative stress imposed on the oxygen transport and related systems. In other words, a given amount of submaximal exercise becomes "more submaximal" as a result of physical training. A summary of the changes induced by training during submaximal exercise is given in Table 13-4.

Changes during Maximal Exercise

It is common knowledge that physical training greatly increases maximal working capacity. Some of the physiological changes that are necessary to bring about such an improvement are shown in Figure 13-15.

TABLE 13-4

Changes During Submaximal Exercise Induced by Training

No change or slight decrease in $\dot{V}O_2$
Decreased muscle glycogen utilization
   Increased fatty acid oxidation
Decreased lactic acid production; increased anaerobic threshold
   Increased fatty acid oxidation
   Decreased oxygen deficit
   Increased use of lactic acid as metabolic fuel
   Increased number and size of mitochondria
No change or slight decrease in cardiac output
Increased stroke volume
   Cardiac hypertrophy
   Increased myocardial contractility
Decreased heart rate
   Decreased sympathetic drive
   Decreased intrinsic atrial rate
Decreased blood flow per kg of active muscle
   Increased oxygen extraction by muscles

MAXIMAL EXERCISE

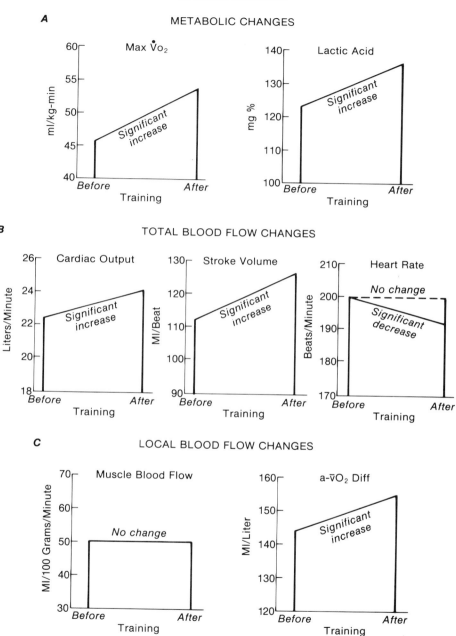

Figure 13-15. Important changes in the functioning of the oxygen transport and related systems during maximal work include the following: increased max $\dot{V}_{O_2}$; increased lactic acid production; increased cardiac output; increased stroke volume; no change or slight decrease in heart rate; no change in muscle blood flow per kilogram of working muscle; and an increased a-$\bar{v}_{O_2}$ diff. (Based on data from Ekblom et al.[42] and Grimby et al.[70])

1. *Increased Maximal Aerobic Power (max $\dot{V}O_2$).* The effects of training on the amount of oxygen that can be consumed per minute during maximal exercise has been studied extensively; there is little doubt that it is increased with training.[42,50,52,54,59,72,132,143,146] The magnitude of the increase in max $\dot{V}O_2$ varies considerably and is dependent upon a number of factors, as we will point out later. An average improvement of between 5 and 20%, however, can be anticipated for college-age men or women students following 8 to 12 weeks of training.[132] The max $\dot{V}O_2$ is highest in athletes who compete and train for endurance types of activities.[142]

As you probably know by now, the max $\dot{V}O_2$ is a measure of the functional capacity of the oxygen system, or the cardiorespiratory system, or the oxygen transport system. It is considered by most exercise physiologists to be the single most accurate measure of endurance fitness. In Appendix G several methods are presented for both direct and indirect measurement of the max $\dot{V}O_2$.

As indicated in an earlier chapter, the physiological factors involved in the oxygen transport system or max $\dot{V}O_2$ are:

$$\max \dot{V}O_2 = SV \times HR \times a\text{-}\overline{v}O_2 \text{ diff}$$

Thus, the increase in max $\dot{V}O_2$ is brought about by two main changes: (a) an increased oxygen delivery to the working muscles through an increased cardiac output (cardiac output $= SV \times HR$); and (b) an increased oxygen extraction from the blood by the skeletal muscles. The causes of an increased maximal cardiac output will be discussed below. You will recall that an increased oxygen extraction is related to the enzymatic and other biochemical changes that occur within the muscles and that are also a result of training. Current information indicates that the changes in cardiac output and oxygen extraction contribute about equally to the increase in max $\dot{V}O_2$.[41,42,138]

A logical question to ask at this time is, which factor limits max $\dot{V}O_2$, the cardiac output or the ability of the skeletal muscles to extract oxygen from the blood? The answer is not entirely clear, but the present information appears to implicate the cardiac output. For example, an increased cardiac output implies an increased supply of blood and oxygen to the working muscles. However, as will be pointed out below, the blood supply per kilogram of active muscle during maximal exercise does not change following training. Therefore, the increased cardiac output does not represent an increased oxygen supply to individual muscle fibers but, rather, to a larger working muscle mass.

On the other hand, the oxygen extraction by individual muscle cells is increased during maximal exercise as reflected by an increased arterial-mixed venous oxygen difference (Fig. 13-15). It would appear reasonable to suggest from this information that since training results in increased extraction of oxygen by individual muscle fibers in the absence of an increased oxygen supply, the max $\dot{V}O_2$ is limited by the circulatory supply of oxygen to the working muscles. This should at least be the case during the kind of maximal exercise used for assessing the max $\dot{V}O_2$ (e.g., bicycle riding or treadmill running to exhaustion in 4 to 8 minutes). For more arguments on this answer, see references 83 and 138.

2. *Increased Cardiac Output.* As was just indicated, the maximal cardiac output increases with training. The magnitude of change is similar to that of the max $\dot{V}O_2$. The maximal attainable cardiac output and the max $\dot{V}O_2$ are directly related (Fig. 13-16*A*); the former is a factor in

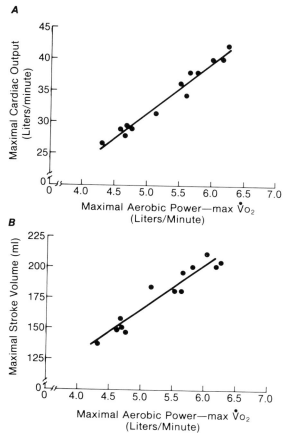

Figure 13-16. A, the maximal attainable cardiac output and the max $\dot{V}O_2$ are directly related; the former is a factor in determining the latter. B, The maximal attainable stroke volume is a major determinant of the magnitude of the cardiac output and thus the max $\dot{V}O_2$. (Based on data from Ekblom and Hermansen.[43])

lowing training is entirely due to an increase in stroke volume.

3. *Increased Stroke Volume.* The increase in maximal stroke volume resulting from training is related to the cardiac hypertrophy and increased myocardial contractility described earlier. A larger ventricular volume coupled with an increased force of contraction allows for a maximal output of blood with each beat.

The single most important feature that distinguishes the athlete who has been training for several years from the sedentary person who has been training for only a few months is the magnitude of the stroke volume.[43,141] In other words, as shown in Figure 13-16B, the stroke volume is a major determinant of the magnitude of the cardiac output and thus of the max $\dot{V}O_2$.

4. *No Change or Slight Decrease in Heart Rate.* The maximal attainable heart rate is either unchanged or decreases slightly following training. Although the decrease in maximal heart rate is particularly evident in athletes engaged in endurance training,[142] short-term training of previously sedentary subjects can also cause a slight (3 to 10 beats/minute) but significant decrease in maximal heart rate.[42,54,55]

A decrease in maximal heart rate with training is probably related to three factors: (a) an increased heart volume due to cardiac hypertrophy; (b) a decreased sympathetic drive; and (c) a decreased intrinsic pacemaker rate.

5. *Increased Lactic Acid Production.* One of the biochemical changes induced by training is an increase in the glycolytic (lactic acid system) capacity. This increase is evidenced by the ability to produce greater quantities of blood lactic acid during exhaustive maximal work. Thus more ATP energy can be generated through this metabolic pathway, thereby improving the performance or working capacity of activi-

determining the latter. As would be expected, maximal cardiac output is greatest in highly trained endurance athletes[43] (p. 248).

The cardiac output, you will recall, is the product of stroke volume and heart rate. Since the maximal heart rate is either unchanged or slightly decreased following training, the increased cardiac output fol-

ties that rely heavily on this system for energy.

6. *No Change in Muscle Blood Flow.* Even during maximal exercise, the blood flow per kilogram of muscle is no different for the trained or untrained individual.[70] This should not be interpreted to mean that the blood flow to the *entire* working muscle mass is lower after training. In fact, it has been shown that the blood flow to the total working musculature is indeed greater during maximal work following training.[143] How can this apparent contradiction be resolved? As explained previously, the answer lies in the fact that since the maximal work load is greater after training, it is likely that the total muscle mass required to perform the work is also greater. In other words, the increased blood flow is distributed over a larger muscle mass, thus keeping the flow per kilogram of muscle constant.[141]

A summary of the changes induced by physical training during maximal work is given in Table 13-5.

TABLE 13-5

Changes During Maximal Work Induced by Training

Increased max $\dot{V}O_2$
   Increased total blood flow (cardiac output)
   Increased oxygen extraction by muscles
Increased lactic acid production
   Increased glycolytic enzyme activities
Increased cardiac output
   Increased stroke volume
Increased stroke volume
   Cardiac hypertrophy (ventricular cavity)
   Increased myocardial contractility
No change or slight decrease in heart rate
   Increased heart volume
   Decreased sympathetic drive
   Decreased intrinsic pacemaker rate
No change in blood flow per kg working muscle
   Blood flow distributed over larger muscle
     mass

Respiratory Changes

So far, we have discussed cardiorespiratory changes resulting from training that are concerned mainly with circulatory functions. What about respiration? In Chapter 8, we presented several respiratory changes that appear to be a result of physical training (p. 205). Let's review them now:

1. Maximal minute ventilation is increased following training. Since ventilation is not a limiting factor for the max $\dot{V}O_2$, the increase in maximal ventilation should be considered secondary to the increase in max $\dot{V}O_2$. Nevertheless, the increase is brought about by increases in both tidal volume and breathing frequency.

2. Training causes an increased ventilatory efficiency. A higher ventilatory efficiency means that the amount of air ventilated at the same oxygen consumption level is lower than in untrained individuals. Since the oxygen cost of ventilation increases greatly with increasing ventilation, a greater ventilatory efficiency, particularly over a prolonged effort (e.g., the marathon) would result in less oxygen to the respiratory muscles and more to the working skeletal muscles.

3. The various lung volumes measured under resting conditions (with the exception of tidal volume) are larger in trained than in untrained individuals. The majority of these changes can be attributed to the fact that training results in improved pulmonary function and therefore in larger lung volumes. It should be mentioned, however, that there is little, if any, correlation between athletic performance and these lung volume changes.

4. Athletes tend to have larger diffusion capacities at rest and during exercise than do nonathletes. This is particu-

larly true for endurance athletes (see Fig. 9-6, p. 231). It is thought that diffusion capacity per se is not directly affected by training but rather that the larger lung volumes of athletes provide a greater alveolar-capillary surface area.

Other Training Changes

Besides biochemical changes and changes in the cardiorespiratory system, training produces other important alterations. Some of these are concerned with (1) body composition; (2) blood cholesterol and triglyceride levels; (3) blood pressure; (4) heat acclimatization; and (5) connective tissue changes.

Changes in Body Composition

The changes in body composition induced by training are as follows: (1) a decrease in total body fat; (2) no change or slight increase in lean body weight; and (3) a small decrease in total body weight.[16,133,134,171] For the most part, these changes, particularly that of fat loss, are more pronounced for obese men and women than for the already "lean" individual.

In discussing changes in body composition, it is important to keep in mind that loss of body fat is dependent upon the balance between calories taken in and calories expended (Chapters 19 and 20). The significance of this observation is that the caloric cost of running and walking is independent of speed. In terms of how many calories are expended, it is not how *fast* you run or walk, but rather how *far* you travel. Also, it is important to note that (1) more calories are expended when running rather than walking a given distance[47,90] and (2) women expend more calories per kilogram of body weight than do men either walking or running a given distance.[22,90] The approximate caloric expenditures for

walking and running various distances are given in Table 13-6.

Changes in Cholesterol and Triglyceride Levels

Regular exercise programs cause decreases in both blood cholesterol and triglyceride levels. This change is particularly apparent in individuals who initially have very high blood levels prior to training.[115]

Of recent interest are the specific kinds of cholesterol found in the blood, referred to as **high-density lipoproteins (HDL), low-density lipoproteins (LDL),** and **very low-density lipoproteins (VLDL).** They are called lipoproteins because cholesterol is a lipid and is carried in the blood in chemical combination with certain proteins. The changes in these various lipoproteins due to exercise training will be discussed in Chapter 15 (p. 000).

TABLE 13-6

Caloric Expenditures for Walking and Running Various Distances for Men and Women*

| Distance | | Caloric Expenditure, kcal/kg Body Wt† | | | |
| | | Walking | | Running | |
miles	km	Men	Women	Men	Women
0.5	0.8	0.54	0.58	0.79	0.87
1.0	1.6	1.08	1.15	1.57	1.73
1.5	2.4	1.62	1.73	2.36	2.60
2.0	3.2	2.16	2.30	3.14	3.46
2.5	4.0	2.70	2.88	3.93	4.33
3.0	4.8	3.24	3.45	4.71	5.19
3.5	5.6	3.78	4.03	5.50	6.06
4.0	6.4	4.32	4.60	6.28	6.92
4.5	7.2	4.86	5.18	7.07	7.79
5.0	8.0	5.40	5.75	7.85	8.65

*Based on data from Howley and Glover.[90]

†To find your total caloric expenditure, multiply the value in the table by your body weight in kilograms (1 kg = 2.2 lb).

Changes in Blood Pressure

Following training, blood pressure at the same absolute workload is lower than before training.[100] Furthermore, individuals with hypertension (p. 261) show significant reductions in resting diastolic and systolic blood pressure as well.[21,115]

Changes in Heat Acclimatization

Heat acclimatization involves physiological adjustments that allow us to work more comfortably in the heat. As will be pointed out in Chapter 18 (p. 480), physical training promotes a high degree of heat acclimatization even if the training sessions are not carried out in hot environments. For example, interval training produces 50% of the total physiological adjustment resulting from heat acclimatization.

The increased heat acclimatization promoted by physical training apparently is stimulated by the large amounts of heat produced during the training sessions. This causes increases in skin and body temperatures comparable to those encountered while working in hot environments.

Changes in Connective Tissues

The connective tissues include bone, ligaments and tendons, and joints and cartilage. Reviews of the effects of training on the connective tissues have been written by Booth and Gould[18] and Tipton et al.[166]

1. *Changes in Bone.* The bone changes produced by physical training are related to the intensity of the training program.[18] For example, in growing animals and with low-intensity programs, there is either no effect or a stimulating effect on the growth of bone length and girth, with no effect on bone density. On the other hand, in growing animals and with high-intensity programs, bone growth (length and girth) is inhibited, thus increasing bone density. Other changes in bone due to training involve increases in bone enzyme activity, increased breaking strength, and in some cases (e.g., following weight training), bone hypertrophy.

2. *Changes in Ligaments and Tendons.* Physical training has been shown to increase the breaking strength of both ligaments and tendons. In addition, the strength of ligamentous and tendinous attachments to bone have been shown to increase following training. This may be interpreted to mean that greater stresses can be sustained and thus there is less chance of injury.

3. *Changes in Joints and Cartilage.* Perhaps the most consistent training-induced change in joints and cartilage is an increase in the thickness of cartilage in all joints. Unfortunately, the significance of this effect during exercise or with respect to arthritis is not known.

A summary of the changes induced by training on respiration and other systems is given in Table 13-7.

Factors Influencing Training Effects

The effects of training are influenced by many factors, including (1) the intensity of the training sessions; (2) the frequency per week of the training sessions and the duration of the training programs; (3) the type of training program, i.e., the specificity of training effects; (4) genetic limitations; (5) the mode of exercise used during the training program; and (6) maintenance of training effects.

Intensity of Training

Several studies have shown that with continuous types of training programs, intensity of the training sessions is of paramount importance in guaranteeing maximal gains in fitness.[4,35,46,150,152] With interval training we have also found this to be true.[31,54,55,112] For example, as shown in Fig-

TABLE 13-7

Changes Induced by Training on Respiration and Other Systems

Respiratory changes
  Increased maximal minute ventilation
    Increased tidal volume
    Increased breathing frequency
  Increased ventilatory efficiency
  Increased lung volumes
  Increased diffusion capacity
Other changes
  Changes in body composition
    Decreased total body fat
    No change or slight increase in lean body
      weight
    Decreased total body weight
  Decreased blood cholesterol and triglyceride
    levels
  Decreased exercise and resting blood
    pressures
  Increased heat acclimatization
  Increased breaking strength of bone,
    ligaments, and tendons

ure 13-17*A,* as the intensity of the training program is increased, the improvement in max $\dot{V}O_2$ is likewise increased.

Two other points are apparent from Figure 13-17*A.* First, the intensity factor as given on the abscissa (horizontal axis) is in relation to the individual's initial fitness level, in this case to the initial max $\dot{V}O_2$. In other words, intensity is relative; what is intense for one person may be easy for another. This is one reason that different people respond differently to similar training programs. Actually, the gains in max $\dot{V}O_2$ are inversely related to the initial max $\dot{V}O_2$ levels, irrespective of the intensity of the training program.[55,107,141] This effect is shown in Figure 13-17*B.* Thus, the lower the initial max $\dot{V}O_2$, the greater the improvement with training.

Second, the improvement in max $\dot{V}O_2$ is greater in women than in men at the same relative intensity[31] (Fig. 13-17*A*). The reason for this is not immediately appar-

ent. However, it does not seem to be caused by the lower initial max $\dot{V}O_2$ of the women, since as shown in Figure 13-17*B,* the relationship between improvement in max $\dot{V}O_2$ and initial max $\dot{V}O_2$ is the same for men and women. Because of the limited number of training studies conducted on women thus far, the significance of this interesting trend will have to await more extensive studies using women subjects. For now we can say that women respond to training at least as well, if not better, than do men (Chapter 14).

So far we have discussed training intensity in relation to changes produced in max $\dot{V}O_2$ only. What about other training-induced changes? Are they also related to intensity? For the most part, the answer to the latter question is yes. For example, the biochemical changes and bone changes referred to earlier are more pronounced in more intensive training programs. Also, as has been emphasized throughout our discussion, the magnitude of most training effects is greatest in the athlete whose competitive training program is very intensive and least in the sedentary individual who has trained only moderately.

We need to point out at this time that there is at least one exception to this intensity rule. The exercise bradycardia induced by training does not appear to be related to training intensity; instead, it is related to the frequency and duration of the training programs. More will be said about this later.

The positive relationship between training intensity and the magnitude of the training effect has been implied for many years. As mentioned in the last chapter, there is a *threshold intensity* of training above which significant gains in fitness occur. This threshold level of intensity varies from individual to individual and is, as has been indicated, related to the initial level of fitness (max $\dot{V}O_2$) of the participant. For example, it has already been

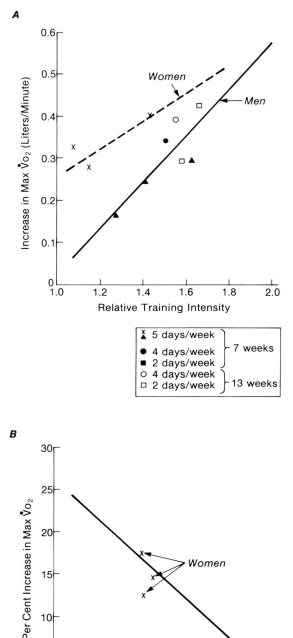

Figure 13-17. *A,* The intensity of the training sessions is of paramount importance in guaranteeing maximal gains in fitness; as the intensity of the training program is increased, the improvement in max $\dot{V}O_2$ is likewise increased. Note that the improvement in max $\dot{V}O_2$ is greater in females than in males at the same relative intensity. *B,* The gains in max $\dot{V}O_2$ are inversely related to the initial max $\dot{V}O_2$ levels, irrespective of the intensity of the training program; the lower the initial max $\dot{V}O_2$, the greater the improvement with training. (Based on data from Fox et al.[55] and Cohen and Fox.[31])

pointed out that training intensity can be judged either by the heart rate response to exercise or by the anaerobic threshold. Each of these factors is altered by training and as such each is related to the initial fitness level of the trainee.

Frequency and Duration of Training

Very few, if any, longitudinal training studies have been conducted; that is, studies in which the same subjects are observed over a prolonged period of time. This particular research design is the only real way to approach the problem of training frequency and duration.

Most of the information concerning the influence of training frequency and duration on training effects has come from studies conducted over relatively short periods of time.[35,55,62,93,107,119,132,133,151] Although the results are not clear-cut, most studies show that frequency and duration have some effect on the magnitude of the training results. This is shown in Figure 13-18. The changes in max $\dot{V}O_2$ induced by walking/running programs of 30 minutes duration with frequencies of either 1, 3, or 5 days per week are compared with the changes in max $\dot{V}O_2$ elicited by walking/running programs performed 3 days per week with durations of either 15, 30, or 45 minutes per training session. All programs,

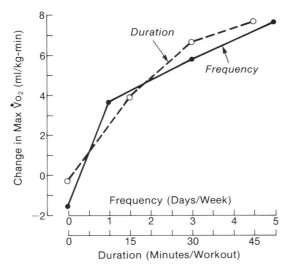

Figure 13-18. Interaction between frequency and duration of training and gains in max $\dot{V}O_2$. For example, a program consisting of a frequency of 1 day per week and a duration of 30 minutes resulted in a gain in max $\dot{V}O_2$ comparable to that following a program consisting of a frequency of 3 days per week and a duration of 15 minutes. (Based on data from Milesis et al.[119] and Gettman et al.[62])

regardless of duration or frequency, were conducted over a 20-week period and were of equal intensities (88% of the maximum heart rate reserve). Notice the interaction between frequency and duration with respect to improvements in max $\dot{V}O_2$. For example, a program consisting of a frequency of 1 day per week and a duration of 30 minutes resulted in a gain in max $\dot{V}O_2$ comparable to that following a program consisting of a frequency of 3 days per week and a duration of 15 minutes. This information suggests that frequency and duration of training programs can be "traded off," so to speak, to produce comparable training effects, provided each is of the same intensity and is conducted over the same length of time.

However, we have found with interval training that frequencies between 2 and 5 days per week and durations between 7 and 13 weeks do not significantly affect the gains made in max $\dot{V}O_2$ (Fig. 13-19). It is quite clear from interval training studies using college-age males[54,55] and females[4,112] that the gain in max $\dot{V}O_2$ is a function of intensity rather than of frequency or duration (see Fig. 13-17A). Others[133] who have used interval training, but with older men as subjects, have shown that max $\dot{V}O_2$ is greater in more frequent and longer training. Thus age may have a significant influence on this particular training benefit.

Perhaps the most significant effect of frequency and duration is on submaximal exercise heart rate. We mentioned earlier that the exercise bradycardia resulting from training is related to the training frequency and duration rather than to the intensity.[54,55] This observation is illustrated in Figure 13-20, in which the combined effects of frequency and duration of train-

Figure 13-19. With interval training programs, training frequencies between 2 and 5 days per week and training durations between 7 and 13 weeks do not significantly affect the gains made in max $\dot{V}O_2$. (Based on data from Fox et al.[54,55])

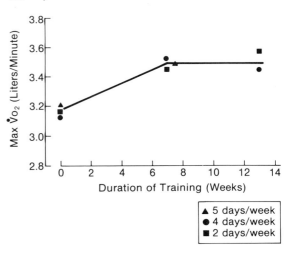

ing are expressed as the total oxygen cost during the training program (horizontal axis); the more frequent and longer the training program, the greater the total cost. This effect has also been shown by others.[133] Decreased circulatory stress during the performance of submaximal exercise might prove to be the most important and practical benefit of more frequent and longer duration training programs.

A question often raised concerning training frequency is do multiple daily

Figure 13-20. The most significant effect of training frequency and duration is an exercise bradycardia (decreased submaximal-exercise heart rate). The combined effects of frequency and duration of training are expressed as the total oxygen cost during the training program; the more frequent and longer the training program, the greater the total cost. (Based on data from Fox et al.[55])

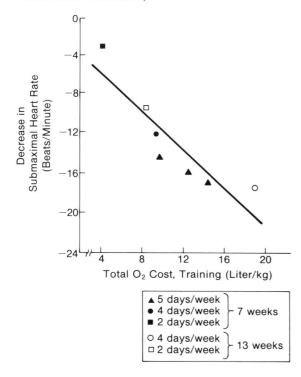

workouts lead to greater fitness and performance gains? This question is of particular importance to track and swimming coaches, some of whom advocate two and even three workouts per day. There is no scientific evidence to suggest that multiple daily workouts lead to greater fitness and performance gains. For example, in the few studies conducted on this subject,[123,169] measurement of several physiological functions (max $\dot{V}O_2$, heart rate, vital capacity, and hemoglobin concentration) plus mile-run times indicated no advantage of two or three workouts per day over one workout per day. In fact, in one of the studies[123] it was even suggested that performances are poorer when the frequency per day of workouts is greater. Therefore, from both a physiological and performance standpoint, multiple daily workouts are not recommended.

Since longitudinal training studies are not available, information concerning prolonged training durations, such as would be the case with many athletes, must come from cross-sectional studies. A cross-sectional study in this case is one in which a comparison is made among different groups of subjects, each of whom has been trained for various durations. Such a comparison is given in Table 13-8. Notice that the greatest difference is in the magnitude of the stroke volume. As mentioned in Chapter 10, this is perhaps the most significant difference between the highly trained endurance athlete and the sedentary individual. How much of this difference is due to duration of training or for that matter to any facet of training cannot be determined precisely. While both frequency and duration and intensity of training undoubtedly influence the magnitude of the stroke volume for the champion athlete, genetics, as we will soon see, also is a significant factor. This, of course, points out one of the major drawbacks of cross-sectional studies.

TABLE 13–8

Cross-Sectional Comparison of the Effects of Training Duration*

Variable Maximal Values	Training Duration		
	4 Months	Several Years	Many Years (Champion Athletes)
$\dot{V}O_2$, liters/minute	3.44	4.93	5.57
$\dot{Q}$, liters/minute	24.2	28.9	36.0
SV, ml	112.0	155.0	189.0
HR, beats/minute	192	186	190
a-$\bar{v}O_2$ diff, ml/liter	143.1	171.0	156.0
heart volume, ml	798	1070	1140

*Based on data from Ekblom et al.,[42] Ekblom and Hermansen,[43] and Saltin.[144]

Specificity of Training Effects

We mentioned in the previous chapter that all training programs must be constructed so as to develop the specific physiological capacities required to perform a given sports skill or activity. This is called specificity of training. The specificity of training is best exemplified by the following examples.

Specificity and Type of Exercise

The max $\dot{V}O_2$ of a group of nonathletic men was measured using five different types of maximal exercise: (1) leg cycling in the supine position, (2) cycling in a sitting position, (3) arm cranking while standing, (4) walking uphill on a motor-driven treadmill, and (5) stepping up and down on a 16-inch (40.6 cm) high bench. The results are shown in Figure 13-21A. It is easy to see that the max $\dot{V}O_2$ of the men varied according to the type of maximal exercise performed. For instance, walking uphill on a treadmill to exhaustion elicited the highest max $\dot{V}O_2$, whereas arm cranking elicited the lowest. This difference was considerable, amounting to just under 18%. The smallest difference (arm cranking versus supine cycling) was 2%.

Similar results have been reported by others on nonathletic men[114,129,136] as well as on trained athletic men and women.[157] The specificity of the max $\dot{V}O_2$ response in athletes is shown in Figure 13-21B. Here the max $\dot{V}O_2$ of three different groups of athletes, rowers, cyclists, and skiers, was determined while they ran on a treadmill and while they performed their specific sport. Again, it is quite clear that the max $\dot{V}O_2$ was higher when performing the specific sport activity than when running.

Muscle Group Specificity

A group of male college students was tested on a bicycle ergometer once while performing submaximal exercise with the arms (pedaling with the arms) and once while performing submaximal exercise with the legs (pedaling with the legs), both before and after 5 weeks of daily interval training. For half of the students, training consisted of pedaling the bicycle with the arms only, whereas the other half pedaled the bicycle with the legs only.[56,117] The results are shown in Figure 13-22. Notice the speci-

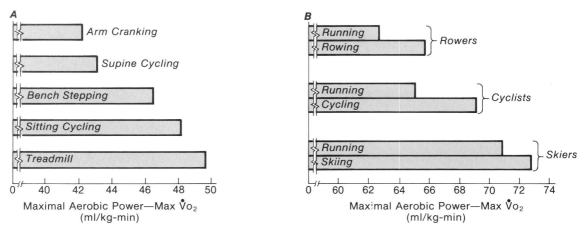

Figure 13-21. Examples of specificity of training and exercise. *A*, In a group of untrained men, the max V̇O₂ varied according to the type of maximal exercise performed. For instance, walking uphill on a treadmill to exhaustion elicited the highest max V̇O₂, whereas arm cranking elicited the lowest. *B*, The max V̇O₂ of three different groups of athletes, rowers, cyclists, and skiers, was determined while they ran on a treadmill and while they performed their specific sport activity. The max V̇O₂ was higher when performing the specific sport activity than when running. (Data in *A* from Bouchard et al.[20]; data in *B* from Stromme et al.[157])

ficity of responses. The magnitudes of the posttraining changes were always greater when the exercise was performed with the trained rather than the untrained muscle groups (limbs). Again, these results emphasize the specific nature of the physiological changes induced by training. As pointed out earlier, they also indicate that the controlling mechanisms for such changes are to a large extent mediated by the skeletal muscles.[29,56,117,146,168]

Specificity of Training Programs

Two groups of male college students were trained using the interval training method. One group participated in a sprint program consisting of repeated bouts of short (30 seconds) fast runs. The other group used an endurance program consisting of repeated bouts of longer (2 minutes) but slower runs.[50,52] The results, as shown in Figure 13-23, were as follows:

1. Both groups improved by approximately the same magnitude in max V̇O₂.
2. After training, the endurance group had a much greater *decrease* in lactic acid production during exercise at the same submaximal workload than did the sprint group.
3. The capacity of the ATP-PC system significantly increased in the sprint group but not in the endurance group.
4. Neither group increased the capacity of the lactic acid system.

These results indicate yet another type of specificity. For example, although the max V̇O₂ for each group was not much different, the lower accumulation of lactic acid induced by the endurance training would be a definite advantage for athletes training for endurance events, because there would be less fatigue. By the same token, the sprint program would be advan-

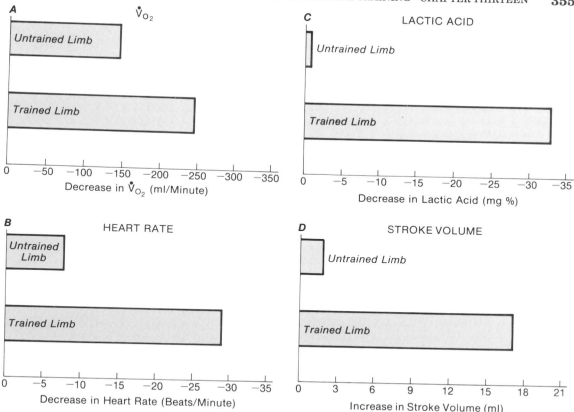

Figure 13-22. Training effects are specific to the muscle groups used during the training program. Notice that the magnitudes of the posttraining changes were always greater when the exercise was performed with the trained rather than with the untrained muscle groups (limbs). (Based on data from Fox et al.[56])

tageous for those training for sprints because of the increased capacity of the ATP-PC system. Also, it is significant that neither type of program is suitable for increasing the capacity of the lactic acid system. Apparently, the type of program needed for such a change would involve repeated bouts of runs between 60 and 90 seconds.[50]

Other examples of the specificity of sprint and endurance training effects have been demonstrated both in animals[63,77] and in humans.[146] An excellent review of the specificity of training effects at the subcellular (biochemical) level of adaptation

has been written by McCafferty and Horvath.[116]

Physiology of Specificity of Training and Exercise

As suggested by the above examples, the specificity of training and exercise has two broad physiological bases—*metabolic* and *neuromuscular*. The metabolic base has in turn two major components, the energy systems and the cardiorespiratory system. The energy systems, as has been repeatedly emphasized, have different capacities and powers. Because of these differences, the

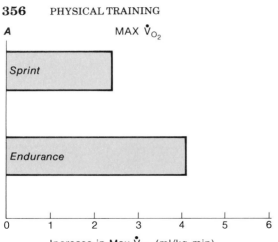

A MAX $\dot{V}_{O_2}$

Sprint

Endurance

0 1 2 3 4 5 6
Increase in Max $\dot{V}_{O_2}$ (ml/kg-min)

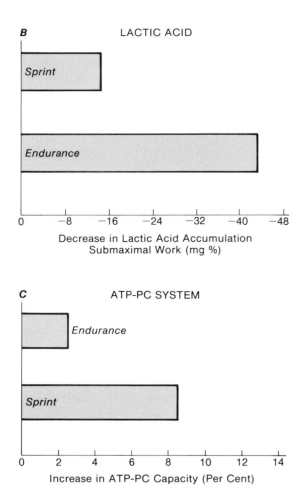

B LACTIC ACID

Sprint

Endurance

0 −8 −16 −24 −32 −40 −48
Decrease in Lactic Acid Accumulation
Submaximal Work (mg %)

C ATP-PC SYSTEM

Endurance

Sprint

0 2 4 6 8 10 12 14
Increase in ATP-PC Capacity (Per Cent)

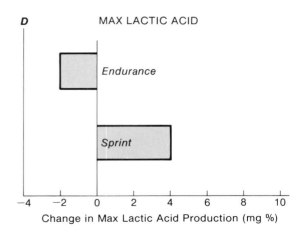

D MAX LACTIC ACID

Endurance

Sprint

−4 −2 0 2 4 6 8 10
Change in Max Lactic Acid Production (mg %)

Figure 13-23. Training effects are specific to the type of training program used. In comparing sprint and endurance training programs: *A,* both groups improved by the same magnitude in max $\dot{V}o_2$; *B,* after training, the endurance group had a greater decrease in lactic acid production during submaximal exercise than did the sprint group; *C,* the capacity of the ATP-PC system was increased in the sprint group only; and *D,* neither group increased the capacity of the lactic acid system. (Based on data from Fox.[50,52])

intensity and duration of exercise dictate the predominant energy system stressed during any given exercise. Low-intensity, long-duration exercises depend heavily on the aerobic system, and high-intensity, short-duration exercises on the anaerobic systems. The more a particular energy system is stressed, the greater the improvement potential in performance of activities involving that energy system can be expected. Thus with training programs, it is essential to use the kind of exercise that stresses the primary energy system or systems used during the performance of the activity for which the athlete is training.

The cardiorespiratory or oxygen transport system is involved mainly with the aerobic energy system, being responsible for the transport and exchange of oxygen and carbon dioxide between the environment and the working muscles. Because of this function, the cardiorespiratory system is more important during the performance of low-intensity, long-duration exercises and less important during high-intensity, short-duration exercises. Again, the importance of using the right kind of exercise in a training program with respect to promoting specific changes in the cardiorespiratory system is obvious.

The neuromuscular base stems from the different motor units or fiber types found in skeletal muscle and from their specific recruitment patterns during the performance of various kinds of exercises. The latter is controlled mainly by the central nervous system, i.e., the brain and spinal cord. The two basic fiber types, slow-twitch (ST) and fast-twitch (FT), also have a metabolic specificity. You will recall that ST fibers have a high aerobic capacity and a low anaerobic capacity, whereas FT fibers have a low aerobic capacity and a high anaerobic capacity. Therefore, ST fibers are recruited for low-intensity, long-duration exercises and FT fibers for high-intensity, short-duration exercises. This level of specificity dictates that exercises used during training should involve the same muscle groups and simulate as closely as possible the movement patterns required during the actual performance of the activity for which the athlete is being trained. The improvement in skill is another reason for including such exercises.

A summary of the major physiological factors involved in the specificity of training and exercise is presented in Figure 13-24. Notice the interaction among the various components (indicated by double-headed arrows).

Genetic Limitations

In Chapter 5 (p. 102) and earlier in this chapter (p. 331), it was mentioned that certain physiological and functional capacities are to a large extent limited by genetic make-up. For example, even with the best possible training program, the improvement in functional capabilities is ultimately going to be limited by genetic potential. This fact has been scientifically demonstrated as follows.[105] One monozygous (identical) twin who was well trained athletically was compared to the other twin, who was sedentary. The results showed that the max $\dot{V}O_2$ of the trained twin was 37% greater than that of the untrained twin. However, the magnitude of the max $\dot{V}O_2$ after training was still within the normal range of values, thus suggesting a genetic limitation.

How heritable are some of the physiological functions that we have been discussing? Again, the information that allows us to answer this question has become available only recently. It has been estimated[104,106] that the max $\dot{V}O_2$ is 93.4% genetically determined in males and 95.9% in both males and females together. This kind of estimate is based on differences in intrapair variability measures of the max $\dot{V}O_2$ of monozygous (identical) twins and dizygous (fraternal) twins. As shown in Figure 13-25A, the intrapair (twin A versus twin B) variability in max $\dot{V}O_2$ for dizygous twins is much greater than for monozygous twins, as indicated by the wide scatter of points about the diagonal line. If the max $\dot{V}O_2$ values were exactly the same for twin A and twin B, the points would fall on the line. The heritability of the max $\dot{V}O_2$ is not significantly influenced by either sex or age.[104,106]

Another important physiological variable that has a very high genetic component in both males and females is the percentage distribution of slow-twitch and fast-twitch fibers in skeletal muscle.[108,110] This is shown in Figure 13-25B. As with max $\dot{V}O_2$, the scatter of points about the line is much greater for the dizygous twins

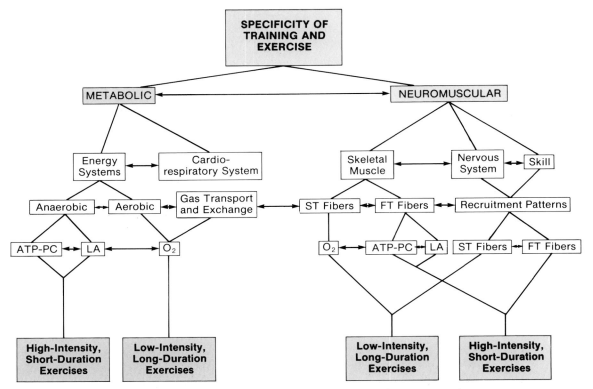

Figure 13-24. A summary of the major physiological factors in the specificity of training and exercise. Note the interaction among the various components as indicated by double-headed arrows.

than for the monozygous twins. In terms of percentage, fiber type distribution is estimated to be 99.5% genetically determined in males and 92.2% in females.[110]

In the same manner, the capacity of the lactic acid system and the maximal heart rate have been found to be genetically determined to the extent of 81.4 and 85.9%, respectively.[104] Again, neither age nor sex has a significant influence on the heritability. Other functions that were studied but that did not show significant heritability tendencies are given in Table 13-9.

There is an old saying, "Sprinters are born, not made." As we have seen, this statement has some scientific support in that the capacity of the lactic acid system is in part genetically determined. Also, from studies of the heritability of the max $\dot{V}O_2$ and fiber-type distribution, it seems appropriate to add a new saying: "Distance runners are born, not made."

Mode of Exercise

Most exercise activities, when used in a training program structured on the principles set forth in the preceding chapter, will lead to substantial gains in fitness. For example, increases in fitness have been demonstrated for such activities as walk-

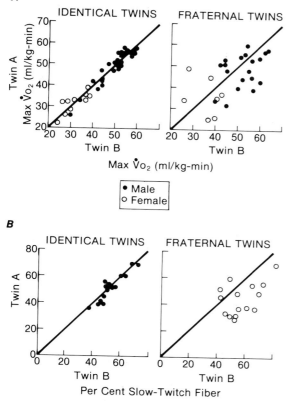

Figure 13-25. *A,* The max $\dot{V}O_2$ is genetically determined to a great extent. This is shown by the fact that the intrapair (twin A versus twin B) variability in max $\dot{V}O_2$ for dizygous (fraternal) twins is much greater than for monozygous (identical) twins, as indicated by the wide scatter of points about the diagonal line. If the max $\dot{V}O_2$ values were exactly the same for twin A and twin B, the points would fall on the line. *B,* Fiber type distribution is also genetically determined to a great extent. (Data in *A* from Klissouras et al.[104,106]; data in *B* from Komi et al.[110])

ing, jogging, running, bicycling, swimming, bench stepping, calisthenics, and skipping rope.

An interesting question in this regard is which mode of exercise leads to the greatest gains in fitness? In answering

this question, we must first be concerned with two factors: (1) the frequency, duration, and most importantly, the intensity of the programs; and (2) the specificity of the training results. In other words, as we have seen, the outcome of any training program is greatly influenced by these factors. However, if these factors are held constant, we can answer the question more accurately.

A comparison of training effects on middle-aged males using either running, walking, cycling, jogging, or tennis as an exercise mode is given in Table 13-10.[133,170] The training intensities of the various programs, as judged by the heart rate response during the training sessions, were comparable except in the tennis group. Here the intensity was much lower, which undoubtedly explains why the improvement in max $\dot{V}O_2$ was also much lower compared to the other groups. In addition, the influence of specificity was eliminated by testing the subjects according to their training exercise mode. As can be seen, improvement in max $\dot{V}O_2$ is quite comparable for all exercise modes (with the exception of the tennis group as mentioned above). Similar results were obtained for other related functions, including a significant decrease in per cent body fat for all programs. This information emphasizes again that provided the training program is conducted according to sound principles, its fitness benefits can be realized, regardless of the type of exercise.

Detraining, Retraining, and Maintenance of Training Effects

Several important questions in any training procedure are: (1) How fast are the benefits gained from training lost once training is stopped? (2) How can the benefits gained from training be best maintained? and (3) Does prior training facilitate the magnitude and speed of the training effects gained during retraining? The following information should help you in attempting to answer these questions.

Detraining

It is well agreed that most training benefits are lost within a relatively short period of time after training has stopped. Some selected changes with detraining are shown in Figure 13-26. The speed of the complete detraining effect is, however, somewhat variable, requiring anywhere from several weeks to several months. For example, sizable decreases (6 to 7%) have been noted in max $\dot{V}O_2$, physical working capacity, total hemoglobin, and blood volume following just 1 week of complete bed rest.[60] In addition, in rats it has been shown that one half of the absolute increase in cytochrome c

TABLE 13-9

Heritability Estimates for Various Physiological Functions

Function	Sex	Heredity Estimate (Per Cent)	Reference
1. Oxygen transport			
a. Maximal aerobic power	M	93.4	Klissouras[104]
(max $\dot{V}O_2$)	M & F	95.9	Klissouras et al.[106]
b. Maximal heart rate (HR_{max})	M	85.9	Klissouras[104]
c. Heart volume	M & F	n.s.*	Klissouras et al.[106]
d. Maximal O_2 pulse			
(max $\dot{V}O_2/HR_{max}$)	M & F	n.s.	Klissouras et al.[106]
e. Maximal minute ventilation			
(max $\dot{V}E$)	M & F	n.s.	Klissouras et al.[106]
f. Ventilation equivalence			
(max $\dot{V}E$/max $\dot{V}O_2$)	M & F	n.s.	Klissouras et al.[106]
2. Muscle function			
a. Fiber type	M	99.5	Komi et al.[110]
	F	92.2	Komi et al.[110]
b. Muscular power	M	99.2	Komi et al.[109]
	F	n.s.	Komi et al.[109]
	M & F	97.8	Karlsson et al.[96]
c. Maximal lactic acid			
concentration	M	81.4	Klissouras[104]
d. Strength	M & F	n.s.	Komi et al.[109] and Karlsson et al.[96]
e. Enzyme activities	M & F	n.s.	Komi et al.[110] and Karlsson et al.[96]
3. Neuromuscular function			
a. Patellar reflex time	M	97.5	Komi et al.[109]
	F	n.s.	Komi et al.[109]
b. Reaction time	M	85.7	Komi et al.[109]
	F	n.s.	Komi et al.[109]
c. Nerve conduction velocity	M & F	n.s.	Komi et al.[109]
d. Chronaxie†	M & F	n.s.	Karlsson et al.[96]

*Genetic component not significant.

†The minimum time at which a current (stimulus) of a certain strength will excite muscular contraction.

TABLE 13-10

Comparison of Training Effects on Middle-Aged Males Using Different Modes of Exercise*

Mode of Exercise	Intensity of Training (Per Cent HR_{max})	Type of Test	Per Cent Increase in max $\dot{V}O_2$
Running	90	Treadmill	11.7
Walking	87	Treadmill	12.4
Cycling	87	Bicycle	23.6
Cycling	82	Bicycle	17.4
Jogging	84	Treadmill	13.3
Tennis	65	Treadmill	5.7

*Based on data from Pollock et al.[134] and Wilmore et al.[170] All training programs were 3 days per week for 20 weeks.

(one of the electron transport system enzymes) caused by training will be lost in just 7 days.[17] At this rate, the activity of the enzyme would be at pretraining values in about 1 month. A similar time course of response for other muscle enzymes in humans has also been demonstrated.[72]

The rate of decline of other fitness benefits is probably similar to the enzyme rate, i.e., being completely lost after 4 to 8 weeks of detraining.[24,25,28,29,61,126,127,154]

Maintenance

One way to maintain effectively the benefits gained from training would be to train on a regular basis throughout the year, year after year. However, this remedy is least desirable from the standpoint of economy of time on the part of the participant. Furthermore, a number of beneficial training effects can be maintained for several months with reduced training frequencies.

With interval training, we have found that a reduction in training frequency, but *not* intensity, can be effective in maintaining the max $\dot{V}O_2$. For example, as shown in Figure 13-27A, reducing the training frequency from 3 days per week to 2 days per week completely maintains the max $\dot{V}O_2$ for at least a 10-week period.[126,127] This agrees with earlier findings that gains in max $\dot{V}O_2$ following interval training programs with frequencies of 2 and 4 days per week are the same.[55,112] On the other hand, a reduction in training frequency from 3 to only 1 day per week retards, but does not totally prevent, a decline in max $\dot{V}O_2$. As shown in Figure 13-27A, the max $\dot{V}O_2$ after 10 weeks of a 1-day-per-week maintenance program was over 7% lower than at the end of the regular training program. Although the previously mentioned studies[126,127] were conducted with female subjects, similar findings on male subjects have also been reported.[24,27,28]

What other training benefits can be maintained by interval training maintenance programs? One of the most important benefits that can be maintained is the ability to perform a given submaximal workload with less accumulation of lactic acid. As shown in Figure 13-27B, this effect can be maintained for up to 16 weeks. As before, the prescription for the one maintenance workout per week should be the same as, or nearly to, that used during the

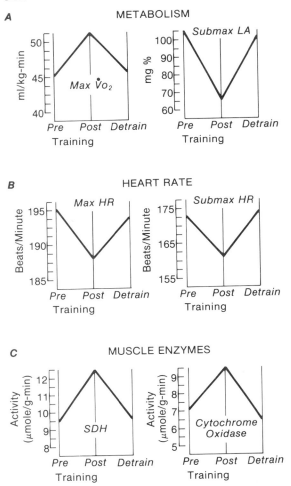

Figure 13-26. It is well agreed that most training benefits, including metabolic, cardio-respiratory, and muscle enzyme changes, are lost within 4 to 8 weeks after training stops (detraining). (Based on data from Fox et al.[52,55] and Henricksson and Reitman.[72])

final week of the regular training program. Notice also that this benefit can be maintained by intermittent exposure to altitude (hypoxia).[11] During the exposures, no exercise is necessary (p. 475). Also of interest is the fact that the lower lactic acid accumulation cannot be maintained with a main-tenance program consisting of a training frequency of only once every 2 weeks.

Reduction in training level is also an important factor to consider. In one study, subjects who trained aerobically for 40 minutes a day, 6 days a week, for 10 weeks improved max $\dot{V}O_2$ between 10 and 20%. One-half of the group then reduced training time to 26 minutes per day and the other half exercised for 13 minutes per day for an additional 15 weeks. The previously demonstrated gains in max $\dot{V}O_2$ were retained by both groups. Additionally, both groups maintained their ability to perform "short-term" endurance work at a high intensity. However, the 13-minute group had a decreased "long-term" endurance. The authors concluded that some aspects of the endurance trained state are not regulated uniformly.[78] Gollnick and Saltin have proposed that observed changes in oxidative enzymes of 100% or more are more related to increased endurance capacity than to improved aerobic capacity.[69] Thus, without an elevated max $\dot{V}O_2$, long endurance capacity is limited but, on the other hand, merely having a high max $\dot{V}O_2$ does not ensure long endurance capacity.

Retraining

It is an old wives' tale that states that both the magnitude and rate of gain of training effects are increased in persons who have previously participated in training programs. Scientific studies, although not numerous, do not support this idea.[88,130] The effects of retraining on max $\dot{V}O_2$ are shown in Figure 13-28. The female subjects were trained on a bicycle ergometer, 2 days per week for 7 weeks. At the end of training, their max $\dot{V}O_2$ was increased by 13.8% on the average. This was followed by a 7-week period of detraining during which time the subjects resumed their normal pretraining activities and during which time their max $\dot{V}O_2$'s declined to within 3% of pretraining

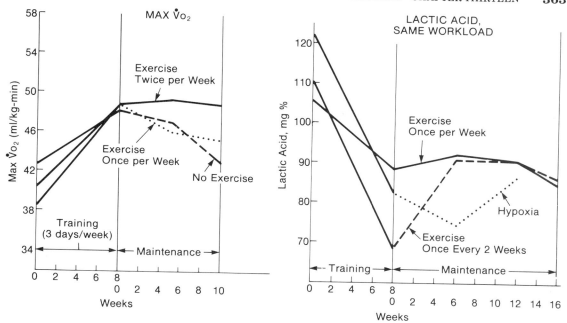

Figure 13-27. *A*, The gains in max $\dot{V}O_2$ following a 3-day-per-week interval training program can be completely maintained with a maintenance program of the same intensity but with a frequency of only 2 days per week. A 1-day-per-week program retards, but does not totally prevent, a decline in max $\dot{V}O_2$. *B*, One of the most important benefits retained by a maintenance training program is the ability to perform a given submaximal workload with less accumulation of lactic acid. This effect can be maintained by exercise once per week or by weekly exposures to hypoxia. (Data in *A* from Otto[126] and Otto et al.[129]; data in *B* from Chaloupka,[27] Chaloupka and Fox,[28] and Bason et al.[11])

values. Immediately following the detraining period, the subjects were retrained, again for 7 weeks, using the same training program as before. As can be seen from the figure, the magnitude and rate of increase of max $\dot{V}O_2$ were similar to that induced by the initial training period. Thus there was no indication of a beneficial or positive transfer from one training period to the other.

The previous information pertains to training-retraining programs administered over a period of 21 weeks and to previously untrained, nonathletic subjects. What about the highly trained athlete who may

be forced into brief periods of inactivity as a result of minor injuries? A partial answer to this question is shown in Figure 13-29. In this study,[88] six male competitive runners were used as subjects. They were tested for various physiological and performance variables at the peak of their training (day zero in Fig. 13-29), after 15 days of detraining,* and after 15 days of retraining. It is

---

*For the first 7 days of the detraining period, a walking plaster cast was placed on the right leg, immobilizing the muscles of the calf. For the remaining 8 days of detraining, the subjects performed their normal daily activities, except no strenuous physical activity was performed.

clear from the figure that significant decreases in muscle enzyme activity (succinate dehydrogenase, SDH; and lactic dehydrogenase, LDH), endurance performance, and max $\dot{V}O_2$ were induced during the 15 days of detraining. Of equal importance is to note that a 15-day retraining period did not in all cases return the physiological or performance capacities to their previous levels. This further confirms the idea that prior training does not in itself convey a positive influence on the gains and maintenance of training benefits. It also points out that a relatively brief layoff by highly trained athletes can significantly decrease performance.

Figure 13-28. At the end of training, the max $\dot{V}O_2$ of a group of female students was increased by 13.8% on the average. After a 7-week period of detraining, the average max $\dot{V}O_2$ was decreased to within 3% of the pretraining value. Following another 7 weeks of training, the average max $\dot{V}O_2$ increased to the same extent and at the same rate as in the initial training period. Thus there was no indication of a beneficial or positive transfer from one training period to the other. (Based on data from Pedersen and Jorgensen.[120])

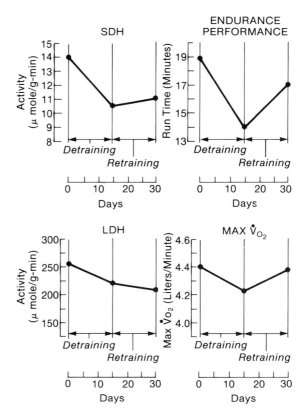

Figure 13-29. Six male competitive runners were tested at the peak of their training (day zero), after 15 days of detraining, and after 15 days of retraining. Significant decreases in muscle enzyme activity (succinate dehydrogenase, or SDH, and lactic dehydrogenase, or LDH), endurance performance, and max $\dot{V}O_2$ were induced during the 15 days of detraining. Fifteen days or retraining did not return all of the variables to their previous levels. These results suggest that brief layoffs by highly trained athletes can significantly decrease performance. (Based on data from Houston et al.[88])

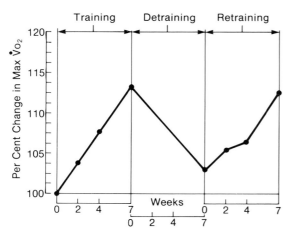

Summary

Biochemical alterations induced by training are as follows:

1. Increased myoglobin content.

2. Increased oxidation of carbohydrate (glycogen).
3. Increased oxidation of fat.
4. Increased muscular stores of ATP and PC.
5. Increased glycolytic (lactic acid system) capacity.

Systemic (oxygen transport system) changes induced by training include the following:

1. At rest
   a. Cardiac hypertrophy
   b. Decreased heart rate
   c. Increased stroke volume
   d. Increased blood volume and hemoglobin
   e. Hypertrophy of skeletal muscle
2. During submaximal exercise
   a. No change or slight decrease in max $\dot{V}O_2$
   b. Decreased muscle glycogen utilization
   c. Decrease in lactic acid accumulation
   d. No change or slight decrease in cardiac output
   e. Increased stroke volume
   f. Decreased heart rate
   g. Lower blood flow per kilogram of active muscle
3. During maximal exercise
   a. Increased max $\dot{V}O_2$
   b. Increased lactic acid accumulation
   c. Increased cardiac output
   d. Increased stroke volume
   e. No change or slight decrease in heart rate
   f. No change in muscle blood flow per kilogram of muscle

Respiratory changes induced by training include:

1. Increased pulmonary ventilation.
2. Increased ventilatory efficiency.
3. Increased lung volumes.
4. Increased diffusion capacity.

Other changes resulting from training are:

1. Decreased body fat.
2. Decreased blood levels of cholesterol and triglycerides.
3. Decreased blood pressure during rest and exercise.
4. Increased heat acclimatization.
5. Increased breaking strength of bone, ligaments, and tendons.

The effects of training are influenced by many factors. Generally, the greater the intensity, frequency, and duration of the training program, the greater will be the improvement in most functions. Training effects are specific to the type of training program used, e.g., running versus bicycling, sprint versus endurance, and arm versus leg training. Genetic limitations are also influential in determining the final magnitude of the training effect. The max $\dot{V}O_2$, muscle fiber types, the lactic acid capacity, and the maximal heart rate are to a large extent genetically determined.

Most modes of exercise (e.g., walking, jogging, running, bicycling, and swimming), when used in a training program structured on sound principles, will lead to substantial and equal gains in fitness.

Most of the beneficial effects of training return to pretraining levels within 4 to 8 weeks of detraining. Some training benefits, such as an increased max $\dot{V}O_2$ and a decreased lactic acid production during submaximal exercise, can be maintained for several months with maintenance programs consisting of 1 or 2 days of exercise per week.

Contrary to popular belief, prior training does not hasten the rate nor increase the magnitude of training benefits gained from subsequent training programs. Brief detraining periods by athletes, such as those caused by minor injuries, can significantly decrease performance.

Questions

1. What are the major aerobic adaptations that occur in skeletal muscle as a result of training?
2. How does an increased myoglobin concentration resulting from training enhance the aerobic system?
3. Discuss the major subcellular adaptations that contribute toward the muscle cells' increased capacity to oxidize carbohydrate and fat following training.
4. List two major anaerobic adaptations that occur in skeletal muscle as a result of training.
5. Discuss the relative biochemical changes resulting from training in slow- and fast-twitch muscle fibers.
6. Discuss the major systemic changes resulting from training that are apparent at rest.
7. What are the major differences between cardiac hypertrophy in endurance and nonendurance athletes?
8. What physiological mechanisms are responsible for the resting bradycardia induced by training?
9. List the changes in the oxygen transport system following training that are evidenced during steady-state submaximal exercise.
10. What mechanisms may be responsible for the decreased lactic acid accumulation during submaximal work following training?
11. Discuss the intracardiac and extracardiac mechanisms as related to exercise bradycardia.
12. List the training effects that are responsible for increases in maximal working capacity.
13. Discuss the respiratory and other changes induced by training.
14. In what manner do training intensity, frequency, and duration influence training effects?
15. Give three examples of the specificity of training effects.
16. Discuss the physiology of the specificity of training.
17. In what manner does heredity influence training effects?
18. Which mode of exercise leads to the greatest gains in fitness?
19. Discuss the time course of the decrease in most training benefits during detraining.
20. What factors should be considered in the development of a maintenance program?
21. Explain how brief periods of detraining-retraining affect performance.

References

1. Andersen, P.: Capillary density in skeletal muscle of man. *Acta Physiol Scand.* 95:203–205, 1975.
2. Andersen, P., and Henriksson, J.: Training induced changes in the subgroups of human type II skeletal muscle fibres. *Acta Physiol Scand.* 99:123–125, 1977.
3. Andersen, P., and Henriksson, J.: Capillary supply of the quadriceps femoris muscle of man: adaptive response to exercise. *J Physiol.* 270:677–690, 1977.
4. Atomi, Y., Ito, K., Iwasaki, H., and Miyashita, M.: Effects of intensity and frequency of training on aerobic work capacity of young females. *J Sports Med.* 18(1):3–9, 1978.
5. Badeer, H. S.: Resting bradycardia of exercise training: a concept based on currently available data. In Roy, P.-E., and Rona, G. (eds.): *The Metabolism of Contraction.* Baltimore, University Park Press, 1975, pp. 553–560.
6. Baldwin, K., Klinerfuss, G., Terjung, R., and Holloszy, J.: Respiratory capacity of white, red, and intermediate muscle: adaptive response to exercise. *Am J Physiol.* 222:373–378, 1972.
7. Baldwin, K., Winder, W., Terjung, R., and Holloszy, J.: Glycolytic capacity of red, white, and intermediate muscle: adaptive response to running. *Med Sci Sports.* 4:50, 1972.
8. Barnard, R. J.: Long-term effects of exercise on cardiac function. In Wilmore, J. H., and Keough, J. F. (eds.): *Exercise and Sport Sciences Reviews.* New York, Academic Press, 1975, pp. 113–133.
9. Barnard, R., Edgerton, V., and Peter, J.: Effects of exercise on skeletal muscle. I. Biochemical and histological properties. *J Appl Physiol.* 28:762–766, 1970.
10. Barnard, R. J., MacAlpin, R., Kattus, A. A., and Buckberg, G. D.: Effect of training on myocardial oxygen supply/demand balance. *Circulation.* 56(2):289–291, 1977.

11. Bason, R., Fox, E., Billings, C., Klinzing, J., Ragg, K., and Chaloupka, E.: Maintenance of physical training effects by intermittent exposure to hypoxia. *Aerospace Med.* 44(10):1097-1100, 1973.

12. Benzi, G., Panceri, P., DeBernardi, M., Villa, R., Arcelli, E., d'Angelo, L., Arrigoni, E., and Berte, F.: Mitochondrial enzymatic adaptation of skeletal muscle to endurance training. *J Appl Physiol.* 38(4): 565-569, 1975.

13. Bevegard, S., Holmgren, A., and Jonsson, B.: Circulatory studies in well trained athletes at rest and during heavy exercise, with special reference to stroke volume and the influence of body position. *Acta Physiol Scand.* 57:26-50, 1963.

14. Bhan, A. K., Malhotra, A., and Scheuer, J.: Biochemical adaptations in cardiac muscle: effects of physical training on sulfhydryl groups on myosin. *J Mol Cellular Cardiol.* 7:435-442, 1975.

15. Bhan, A. K., and Scheuer, J.: Effects of physical training on cardiac myosin ATPase activity. *Am J Physiol.* 228:1178-1182, 1975.

16. Boileau, R., Buskirk, E., Hortsman, D., Mendez, J., and Nichols, W.: Body composition changes in obese and lean men during physical conditioning. *Med Sci Sports.* 3(4):183-189, 1971.

17. Booth, F. W., and Holloszy, J. O.: Cytochrome c turnover in rat skeletal muscles. *J Biol Chem.* 252:416-419, 1977.

18. Booth, F. W., and Gould, E. W.: Effects of training and disuse on connective tissue. In Wilmore, J. H., and Keough, J. E. (eds.): *Exercise and Sport Sciences Reviews.* New York, Academic Press, 1975, pp. 83-112.

19. Borensztajn, J., Rone, M., Babirak, S., McGarr, J., and Oscai, L.: Effects of exercise on lipoprotein lipase activity in rat heart and skeletal muscle. *Am J Physiol.* 229:394-397, 1975.

20. Bouchard, C., Godbout, P., Mondor, J.-C., and Leblanc, C.: Specificity of maximal aerobic power. *Europ J Appl Physiol.* 40: 85-93, 1979.

21. Boyer, J., and Kasch, F.: Exercise therapy in hypertensive men. *JAMA.* 211:1668-1671, 1970.

22. Bransford, D. R., and Howley, E. T.: Oxygen cost of running in trained and untrained men and women. *Med Sci Sports.* 9(1):41-44, 1977.

23. Brodal, P., Inger, F., and Hermansen, L.: Capillary supply of skeletal muscle fibers in untrained and endurance-trained men. *Am J Physiol.* 232(6):H705-H712, 1977.

24. Brynteson, P., and Sinning, W.: The effects of training frequencies on the retention of cardiovascular fitness. *Med Sci Sports.* 5(1):29-33, 1973.

25. Case, H.: *Detraining Following High Volume Interval Training.* Doctoral Dissertation, The Ohio State University, 1971.

26. Cerretelli, P., Pendergast, D., Paganelli, W. C., and Rennie, D. W.: Effects of specific muscle training on VO_2 on-response and early blood lactate. *J Appl Physiol.* 47(4):761-769, 1979.

27. Chaloupka, E.: *The Physiological Effects of Two Maintenance Programs Following Eight Weeks of Interval Training.* Doctoral Dissertation. The Ohio State University, Columbus, Ohio, 1972.

28. Chaloupka, E., and Fox, E.: Physiological effects of two maintenance programs following eight weeks of interval training. *Fed Proc.* 34(3):443, 1975.

29. Clausen, J. P.: Effect of physical training on cardiovascular adjustments to exercise in man. *Physiol Rev.* 57(4):779-815, 1977.

30. Clausen, J., Trap-Jensen, J., and Lassen, N.: The effects of training on the heart rate during arm and leg exercise. *Scand J Clin Invest.* 26:295-301, 1970.

31. Cohen, K., and Fox, E.: Intensity and distance of interval training programs and metabolic changes in females. Unpublished manuscript, 1975.

32. Costill, D. L., Coyle, E., Dalsky, G., Evans, W., Fink, W., and Hoppes, D.: Effects of elevated plasma FFA and insulin on muscle glycogen usage during exercise. *J Appl Physiol.* 43(4):695-699, 1977.

33. Costill, D. L., Daniels, J., Evans, W., Fink, W., Krahenbuhl, G., and Saltin, B.: Skeletal muscle enzymes and fiber composition in male and female track athletes. *J Appl Physiol.* 40(2):149-154, 1976.

34. Costill, D., Thomason, H., and Roberts, E.: Fractional utilization of the aerobic capacity during distance running. *Med Sci Sports.* 5(4):248-252, 1973.

35. Davies, C., and Knibbs, A.: The training stimulus: the effects of intensity, duration and frequency of effort on maximum aer-

obic power output. *Int Z Angew Physiol.* 29:299–305, 1971.

36. Davies, K. J. A., Packer, L., and Brooks, G. A.: Biochemical adaptation of mitochondria, muscle, and whole-animal respiration to endurance training. *Arch Biochem Biophys.* 209:539–554, 1981.

37. Davis, J. A., Frank, M. H., Whipp, B. J., and Wasserman, K.: Anaerobic threshold alterations caused by endurance training in middle-aged men. *J Appl Physiol.* 46(6): 1039–1046, 1979.

38. DeMaria, A. N., Neuman, A., Lee, G., Fowler, W., and Mason, D. T.: Alterations in ventricular mass and performance induced by exercise training in man evaluated by echocardiography. *Circulation.* 57:237–244, 1978.

39. Eckstein, R.: Effect of exercise and coronary artery narrowing on coronary collateral circulation. *Circ Res.* 5:230–238, 1957.

40. Ehsani, A. A., Hagberg, J. M., and Hickson, R. C.: Rapid changes in left ventricular dimensions and mass in response to physical conditioning and deconditioning. *Am J Cardiol.* 42:52–56, 1978.

41. Ekblom, B.: Effect of physical training on the oxygen transport system in man. *Acta Physiol Scand.* 328(Suppl):1–45, 1969.

42. Ekblom, B., Åstrand, P., Saltin, B., Stenberg, J., and Wallstrom, B.: Effect of training on circulatory response to exercise. *J Appl Physiol.* 24(4):518–528, 1968.

43. Ekblom, B., and Hermansen, L.: Cardiac output in athletes. *J Appl Physiol.* 25(5): 619–625, 1968.

44. Eriksson, B., Gollnick, P., and Saltin, B.: Muscle metabolism and enzyme activities after training in boys 11–13 years old. *Acta Physiol Scand.* 87:485–497, 1973.

45. Falsetti, H. L.: Invasive and noninvasive evaluation of exercise in humans. *Med Sci Sports.* 9(4):262–267, 1977.

46. Faria, I.: Cardiovascular response to exercise as influenced by training of various intensities. *Res Q.* 41:44–50, 1970.

47. Fellingham, G. W., Roundy, E. S., Fisher, A. G., and Bryce, G. R.: Caloric cost of walking and running. *Med Sci Sports.* 10(2):132–136, 1978.

48. Fink, W., Costill, D., Daniels, J., Pollock, M., and Saltin, B.: Muscle fiber composition and enzyme activities in male and female athletes. *Physiologist.* 18(3):213, 1975.

49. Fournier, M., Ricci, J., Taylor, A. W., Ferguson, R. J., Montpetit, R. B., and Chaitman, B. R.: Skeletal muscle adaptation in adolescent boys: Sprint and endurance training and detraining. *Med Sci Sport Exer.* 14:453–456, 1982.

50. Fox, E.: Differences in metabolic alterations with sprint versus interval training programs. In Howald, H., and Poortmans, J. (eds.): *Metabolic Adaptation to Prolonged Physical Exercise.* Basel, Switzerland, Birkhauser Verlag. 1975, pp. 119–126.

51. Fox, E. L.: Physical training: methods and effects. *Orthop Clin N Am.* 8(3):533–548, 1977.

52. Fox, E. L., Bartels, R. L., Klinzing, J., and Ragg, K.: Metabolic responses to interval training programs of high and low power output. *Med Sci Sports.* 9(3):191–196, 1977.

53. Fox, E., and Costill, D.: Estimated cardiorespiratory responses during marathon running. *Arch Environ Health.* 24:315–324, 1972.

54. Fox, E., Bartels, R., Billings, C., Mathews, D., Bason, R., and Webb, D.: Intensity and distance on interval training programs and changes in aerobic power. *Med Sci Sports.* 5(1):18–22, 1973.

55. Fox, E., Bartels, R., Billings, C., O'Brien, R., Bason, R., and Mathews, D.: Frequency and duration of interval training programs and changes in aerobic power. *J Appl Physiol.* 38(3):481–484, 1975.

56. Fox, E., McKenzie, D., and Cohen, K.: Specificity of training: metabolic and circulatory responses. *Med Sci Sports.* 7(1): 83, 1975.

57. Frick, M., Elovainio, R., and Somer, T.: The mechanism of bradycardia evoked by physical training. *Cardiologia.* 51:46–54, 1967.

58. Frick, M., Konttinen, A., and Sarajas, S.: Effects of physical training on circulation at rest and during exercise. *Am J Cardiol.* 12:142–147, 1963.

59. Frick, M., Sjogren, A., Persasalo, J., and Pajunen, S.: Cardiovascular dimensions and moderate physical training in young men. *J Appl Physiol.* 29(4):452–455, 1970.

60. Friman, G.: Effect of clinical bed rest for seven days on physical performance. *Acta Med Scand.* 205(5):389–393, 1979.

61. Fringer, M. N., and Stull, G. A.: Changes in cardiorespiratory parameters during periods of training and detraining in

young adult females. *Med Sci Sports.* 6(1): 20–25, 1974.

62. Gettman, L. R., Pollock, M. L., Durstine, J. L., Ward, A., Ayres, J., and Linnerud, A. C.: Physiological responses of men to 1, 3, and 5 day per week training programs. *Res Q.* 47(4):638–646, 1976.

63. Gillespie, A. C., Fox, E. L., and Merola, A. J.: Enzyme adaptations in rat skeletal muscle after two intensities of treadmill training. *Med Sci Sport Exer.* 14(6):461–466, 1982.

64. Gollnick, P. D.: Free fatty acid turnover and the availability of substrates as a limiting factor in prolonged exercise. *Ann NY Acad Sci.* 301:64–71, 1977.

65. Gollnick, P., and Hermansen, L.: Biochemical adaptations to exercise: anaerobic metabolism. In Wilmore, J. (ed.): *Exercise and Sports Sciences Reviews.* New York, Academic Press, 1973, pp. 1–43.

66. Gollnick, P., and King, D.: Effects of exercise and training on mitochondria of rat skeletal muscle. *Am J Physiol.* 216:1502–1509, 1969.

67. Gollnick, P., Armstrong, R., Saltin, B., Saubert, C., Sembrowich, W., and Shepherd, R.: Effect of training on enzyme activity and fiber composition of human skeletal muscle. *J Appl Physiol.* 34(1):107–111, 1973.

68. Gollnick, P., Armstrong, R., Saubert, C., Piehl, K., and Saltin, B.: Enzyme activity and fiber composition in skeletal muscle of untrained and trained men. *J Appl Physiol.* 33(3):312–319, 1972.

69. Gollnick, P. D., and Saltin, B.: Significance of skeletal muscle oxidative enzyme enhancement with endurance training. *Clin Physiol.* 2:1–12, 1982.

70. Grimby, G., Haggendal, E., and Saltin, B.: Local xenon 133 clearance from the quadriceps muscle during exercise in man. *J Appl Physiol.* 22(2):305–310, 1967.

71. Hagberg, J. M., Hickson, R. C., Ehsani, A. A., and Holloszy, J. O.: Faster adjustment to and recovery from submaximal exercise in the trained state. *J Appl Physiol.* 48(2):218–224, 1980.

72. Henriksson, J., and Reitman, J. S.: Time course of changes in human skeletal muscle succinate dehydrogenase and cytochrome oxidase activities and maximal oxygen uptake with physical activity and inactivity. *Acta Physiol Scand.* 99:91–97, 1977.

73. Hermansen, L., Hultman, E., and Saltin, B.: Muscle glycogen during prolonged severe exercise. *Acta Physiol Scand.* 71:129–139, 1967.

74. Hermansen, L., and Wachtlova, M.: Capillary density of skeletal muscle in well-trained and untrained men. *J Appl Physiol.* 30(6):860–863, 1971.

75. Hickson, R. C.: Skeletal muscle cytochrome c and myoglobin, endurance, and frequency of training. *J Appl Physiol.* 51:746–749, 1981.

76. Hickson, R. C., Bomze, H. A., and Holloszy, J. O.: Faster adjustment of O_2 uptake to the energy requirement of exercise in the trained state. *J Appl Physiol.* 44(6):877–881, 1978.

77. Hickson, R. C., Heusner, W., and Van Huss, W.: Skeletal muscle enzyme alterations after sprint and endurance training. *J Appl Physiol.* 40:868–872, 1976.

78. Hickson, R. C., Kanakis, C. K., Jr., Moore, A. M., and Rich, S.: Reduced training duration effects on aerobic power, endurance, and cardiac growth. *J Appl Physiol.* 53:225–229, 1982.

79. Hickson, R. C., Rennie, M. J., Conlee, R. K., Winder, W. W., and Holloszy, J. O.: Effects of increased plasma fatty acids on glycogen utilization and endurance. *J Appl Physiol.* 43:829–833, 1977.

80. Holloszy, J.: Effects of exercise on mitochondrial oxygen uptake and respiratory enzyme activity in skeletal muscle. *J Biol Chem.* 242:2278–2282, 1967.

81. Holloszy, J.: Biochemical adaptations to exercise: aerobic metabolism. In Wilmore, J. (ed.): *Exercise and Sports Sciences Reviews.* New York, Academic Press, 1973, pp. 45–71.

82. Holloszy, J.: Adaptation of skeletal muscle to endurance exercise. *Med Sci Sports.* 7(3):155–164, 1975.

83. Holloszy, J. O., and Booth, F. W.: Biochemical adaptations to endurance exercise in muscle. *Ann Rev Physiol.* 38:273–291, 1976.

84. Holloszy, J. O., Booth, F. W., Winder, W. W., and Fitts, R. H.: Biochemical adaptations of skeletal muscle to prolonged physical exercise. In Howald, H., and Poortmans, J. R. (eds.): *Metabolic Adaptation to Prolonged Physical Exercise.* Basel, Switzerland, Birkhauser Verlag, 1975, pp. 438–447.

85. Holloszy, J., Oscai, L., Mole, P., and Don,

I.: Biochemical adaptations to endurance exercise in skeletal muscle. In Pernow, B., and Saltin, B. (eds.): *Muscle Metabolism during Exercise.* New York, Plenum Press, 1971, pp. 51-61.

86. Holloszy, J. O., Rennie, M. J., Hickson, R. C., Conlee, R. K., and Hagberg, J. M.: Physiological consequences of the biochemical adaptations to endurance exercise. *Ann NY Acad Sci.* 301:440-450, 1977.

87. Hoppeler, H., Luthi, P., Claassen, H., Weibel, E. R., and Howald, H.: The ultrastructure of the normal human skeletal muscle: a morphometric analysis on untrained men, women, and well-trained orienteers. *Pflugers Arch.* 344:217-232, 1973.

88. Houston, M. E., Bentzen, H., and Larsen, H.: Interrelationships between skeletal muscle adaptations and performance as studied by detraining and retraining. *Acta Physiol Scand.* 105:163-170, 1979.

89. Howald, H.: Ultrastructural adaptation of skeletal muscle to prolonged physical exercise. In Howald, H., and Poortmans, J. R. (eds.): *Metabolic Adaptation to Prolonged Physical Exercise.* Basel, Switzerland, Birkhauser Verlag, 1975, pp. 372-383.

90. Howley, E., and Glover, M.: The caloric costs of running and walking one mile for men and women. *Med Sci Sports.* 6(4): 235-237, 1974.

91. Hughson, R. L., Sutton, J. R., Fitzgerald, J. D., and Jones, N. L.: Reduction of intrinsic sinoatrial frequency and norepinephrine response of the exercised rat. *Can J Physiol Pharmacol.* 55:813-820, 1977.

92. Inger, F.: Capillary supply and mitochondrial content of different skeletal muscle fiber types in untrained and endurance-trained men: a histochemical and ultrastructural study. *Europ J Appl Physiol.* 40:197-209, 1979.

93. Jackson, J., Sharkey, B., and Johnston, L.: Cardiorespiratory adaptations to training at specified frequencies. *Res Q.* 39:295-300, 1968.

94. Jansson, E., and Kaijer, L.: Muscle adaptation to extreme endurance training in man. *Acta Physiol Scand.* 100:315-324, 1977.

95. Jansson, E., Sjodin, B., and Tesch, P.: Changes in muscle fibre type distribution in man after physical training. *Acta Physiol Scand.* 104:235-237, 1978.

96. Karlsson, J., Komi, P. V., and Viitasalo, J. H. T.: Muscle strength and muscle characteristics in monozygous and dizygous twins. *Acta Physiol Scand.* 106:319-325, 1979.

97. Karlsson, J., Nordesjo, L., Jorfeldt, L., and Saltin, B.: Muscle lactate, ATP, and CP levels during exercise after physical training in man. *J Appl Physiol.* 33(2): 199-203, 1972.

98. Karlsson, J., Nordesjo, L.-O., and Saltin, B.: Muscle glycogen utilization during exercise after physical training. *Acta Physiol Scand.* 90:210-217, 1974.

99. Kiessling, K., Piehl, K., and Lundquist, C.: Effect of physical training on ultrastructural features in human skeletal muscle. In Pernow, B., and Saltin, B. (eds.): *Muscle Metabolism during Exercise.* New York, Plenum Press, 1971, pp. 97-101.

100. Kilbom, A.: Physical training with submaximal intensities in women. I. Reaction to exercise and orthostasis. *Scand J Clin Invest.* 28:141-161, 1971.

101. Kjellberg, S., Rudhe, U., and Sjostrand, T.: Increase of the amount of hemoglobin and blood volume in connection with physical training. *Acta Physiol Scand.* 19:146-151, 1949.

102. Kjellberg, S., Rudhe, U., and Sjostrand, T.: The amount of hemoglobin and the blood volume in relation to the pulse rate and cardiac volume during rest. *Acta Physiol Scand.* 19:136-145, 1949.

103. Klassen, G., Andrew, G., and Becklake, M.: Effect of training on total and regional blood flow and metabolism in paddlers. *J Appl Physiol.* 28(4):397-406, 1970.

104. Klissouras, V.: Heritability of adaptive variation. *J Appl Physiol.* 31(3):338-344, 1971.

105. Klissouras, V.: Genetic limit of functional adaptability. *Int Z Angew Physiol.* 30: 85-94, 1972.

106. Klissouras, V., Pirnay, F., and Petit, J.: Adaptation to maximal effort: genetics and age. *J Appl Physiol.* 35(2):288-293, 1973.

107. Knuttgen, H., Nordesjo, L., Ollander, B., and Saltin, B.: Physical conditioning through interval training with young male adults. *Med Sci Sports.* 5:220-226, 1973.

108. Komi, P. V., and Karlsson, J.: Physical performance, skeletal muscle enzyme activities, and fibre types in monozygous

and dizygous twins of both sexes. *Acta Physiol Scand.* (Suppl) 462, 1979.

109. Komi, P. V., Klissouras, V., and Karvinen, E.: Genetic variation in neuromuscular performance. *Int Z Angew Physiol.* 31: 289-304, 1973.

110. Komi, P. V., Viitasalo, J. H. T., Havu, M., Thorstensson, A., Sjodin, B., and Karlsson, J.: Skeletal muscle fibres and muscle enzyme activities in monozygous and dizygous twins of both sexes. *Acta Physiol Scand.* 100:385-392, 1977.

111. Leon, A., and Bloor, C.: Effects of exercise and its cessation on the heart and its blood supply. *J Appl Physiol.* 24(4):485-490, 1968.

112. Lesmes, G. R., Fox, E. L., Stevens, C., and Otto, R.: Metabolic responses of females to high intensity interval training of different frequencies. *Med Sci Sports.* 10(4): 229-232, 1978.

113. Longhurst, J. C., Kelley, A. R., Gonyea, W. J., and Mitchell, J. H.: Echocardiographic left ventricular masses in distance runners and weight lifters. *J Appl Physiol.* 48(1):154-162, 1980.

114. Magel, J. R., Foglia, F., McArdle, W. D., Gutin, B., Pechar, G. S., and Katch, F. I.: Specificity of swim training on maximum oxygen intake. *J Appl Physiol.* 38:151-155, 1974.

115. Mann, G., Garrett, H., Farhi, A., Murray, H., and Billings, F.: Exercise to prevent coronary heart disease. *Am J Med.* 46: 12-27, 1969.

116. McCafferty, W. B., and Horvath, S. M.: Specificity of exercise and specificity of training: a subcellular review. *Res Q.* 48(2):358-371, 1977.

117. McKenzie, D. C., Fox, E. L., and Cohen, K.: Specificity of metabolic and circulatory responses to arm or leg interval training. *Europ J Appl Physiol.* 39:241-248, 1978.

118. Michielli, D. W., Stein, R. A., Krasnow, N., Diamond, J. R., and Horwitz, B.: Effects of exercise training on ventricular dimensions at rest and during exercise. *Med Sci Sports.* 11(1):82, 1979.

119. Milesis, C., Pollock, M. L., Bah, M. D., Ayres, J. J., Ward, A., and Linnerud, A. C.: Effects of different durations of physical training on cardiorespiratory function, body composition, and serum lipids. *Res Q.* 47(4):716-725, 1976.

120. Mole, P., Oscai, L., and Holloszy, J.: Adaptation of muscle to exercise: increase in

levels of palmityl CoA synthetase, carnitine palmityltransferase, and palmityl CoA dehydrogenase, and in the capacity to oxidize fatty acid. *J Clin Invest.* 50: 2323-2330, 1971.

121. Morgan, T., Cobb, L., Short, F., Ross, R., and Gunn, D.: Effects of long-term exercise on human muscle mitochondria. In Pernow, B., and Saltin, B. (eds.): *Muscle Metabolism during Exercise.* New York, Plenum Press, 1971, pp. 87-95.

122. Morganroth, J., Maron, B., Henry, W., and Epstein, S.: Comparative left ventricular dimensions in trained athletes. *Ann Intern Med.* 82:521-524, 1975.

123. Mostardi, R., Gandee, R., and Campbell, T.: Multiple daily training and improvement in aerobic power. *Med Sci Sports.* 7(1):82, 1975.

124. Nutter, D., Gilbert, C., Heymsfield, S., Perkins, J., and Schlant, R.: Cardiac hypertrophy in the endurance athlete. *Physiologist.* 18(3):336, 1975.

125. Oscai, L., Williams, B., and Hertig, B.: Effect of exercise on blood volume. *J Appl Physiol.* 24(5):622-624, 1968.

126. Otto, R. M.: *Metabolic Responses of Young Women to Training and Maintenance/ Detraining.* Doctoral Dissertation, The Ohio State University, Columbus, Ohio, 1977.

127. Otto, R. M., Fox, E. L., and Stevens, C. J.: Metabolic responses of young women to training and maintenance/detraining. *Med Sci Sports.* 10(1):52, 1978.

128. Pattengale, P., and Holloszy, J.: Augmentation of skeletal muscle myoglobin by a program of treadmill running. *Am J Physiol.* 213:783-785, 1967.

129. Pechar, G., McArdle, W., Katch, F., Magel, J., and DeLuca, J.: Specificity of cardiorespiratory adaptation to bicycle and treadmill training. *J Appl Physiol.* 36(6): 753-756, 1974.

130. Pedersen, P., and Jorgensen, J.: Maximal oxygen uptake in young women with training, inactivity, and retraining. *Med Sci Sports.* 10(4):233-237, 1978.

131. Penpargkul, S., and Scheuer, J.: The effect of physical training upon the mechanical and metabolic performance of the rat heart. *J Clin Invest.* 49:1859-1868, 1970.

132. Pollock, M.: The quantification of endurance training programs. In Wilmore, J. (ed.): *Exercise and Sport Sciences Reviews,* vol. 1. New York, Academic Press, 1973, pp. 155-188.

133. Pollock, M., Cureton, T., and Greninger, L.: Effects of frequency of training on working capacity, cardiovascular function, and body composition of adult men. *Med Sci Sports.* 1(2):70–74, 1969.

134. Pollock, M., Dimmick, J., Miller, H., Kendrick, Z., and Linnerud, A.: Effects of mode of training on cardiovascular function and body composition of adult men. *Med Sci Sports.* 7(2):139–145, 1975.

135. Ritzer, T. F., Bove, A. A., and Carey, R. A.: Left ventricular performance characteristics in trained and sedentary dogs. *J Appl Physiol.* 48(1):130–138, 1980.

136. Roberts, J., and Alspaugh, J.: Specificity of training effects resulting from programs of treadmill running and bicycle ergometer riding. *Med Sci Sports.* 4(1): 6–10, 1972.

137. Roeske, W. R., O'Rourke, R. A., Klein, A., Leopold, G., and Karliner, J. S.: Noninvasive evaluation of ventricular hypertrophy in professional athletes. *Circulation.* 53:286–292, 1975.

138. Rowell, L. B.: Human cardiovascular adjustments to exercise and thermal stress. *Physiol Rev.* 54(1):75–159, 1974.

139. Rubal, B. J., Rosentswieg, J., and Hamerly, B.: Echocardiographic examination of women collegiate softball champions. *Med Sci Sport Exer.* 13:176–179, 1981.

140. Saltin, B.: Adaptive changes in carbohydrate metabolism with exercise. In Howald, H., and Poortmans, J. R. (eds.): *Metabolic Adaptation to Prolonged Physical Exercise.* Basel, Switzerland, Birkhauser Verlag, 1975, pp. 94–100.

141. Saltin, B.: Physiological effects of physical training. *Med Sci Sports.* 1(1):50–56, 1969.

142. Saltin, B., and Åstrand, P.: Maximal oxygen uptake in athletes. *J Appl Physiol.* 23:353–358, 1967.

143. Saltin, B., Blomqvist, G., Mitchell, J., Johnson, R., Wildenthal, K., and Chapman, C.: Response to exercise after bedrest and after training. *Circulation.* (Suppl 7), 1968.

144. Saltin, B., Hartley, L., Kilbom, A., and Åstrand, I.: Physical training in sedentary middle-aged and older men. II. Oxygen uptake, heart rate and blood lactate concentrations at submaximal and maximal exercise. *Scand J Clin Invest.* 24:323–334, 1969.

145. Saltin, B., and Karlsson, J.: Muscle glycogen utilization during work of different intensities. In Pernow, B., and Saltin, B. (eds.): *Muscle Metabolism during Exercise.* New York, Plenum Press, 1971, pp. 289–299.

146. Saltin, B., Nazar, K., Costill, D. L., Stein, E., Jansson, E., Essen, B., and Gollnick, P. D.: The nature of the training response; peripheral and central adaptations to one-legged exercise. *Acta Physiol Scand.* 96:289–305, 1976.

147. Saubert, C., Armstrong, R., Shepherd, R., and Gollnick, P. D.: Anaerobic enzyme adaptations to spring training in rats. *Pflugers Arch.* 341:305–312, 1973.

148. Scheuer, J., Penpargkul, S., and Bhan, A. K.: Experimental observations on the effects of physical training upon intrinsic cardiac physiology and biochemistry. *Am J Cardiol.* 33:744–751, 1974.

149. Scheuer, J., and Tipton, C. M.: Cardiovascular adaptations to physical training. *Ann Rev Physiol.* 39:221–251, 1977.

150. Sharkey, B., and Holleman, J.: Cardiorespiratory adaptations to training at specified intensities. *Res Q.* 38:698–704, 1967.

151. Shephard, R.: Intensity, duration and frequency of exercise as determinants of the response to a training regimen. *Int Z Angew Physiol.* 26:272–278, 1968.

152. Sigvardsson, K., Svanfeldt, E., and Kilbom, A.: Role of the adrenergic nervous system development of training-induced bradycardia. *Acta Physiol Scand.* 101: 481–488, 1977.

153. Smith, D. C., and El-Hage, A.: Effect of exercise training on the chronotropic response of isolated rat atria to atropine. *Experientia.* 34(8):1027–1028, 1978.

154. Smith, D. P., and Stransky, F. W.: The effect of training and detraining on the body composition and cardiovascular response of young women to exercise. *J Sports Med.* 16:112–120, 1976.

155. Snoeckx, L. H. E. H., Abeling, H. F. M., Lanbreghts, J. A. C., Smitz, J. J. F., Verstappen, F. T. J., and Reneman, R. S.: Echocardiographic dimensions in athletes relative to their training programs. *Med Sci Sport Exer.* 14:428–434, 1982.

156. Staudte, H., Exner, G., and Pette, D.: Effects of short-term, high intensity (sprint) training on some contractile and metabolic characteristics of fast and slow muscle of the rat. *Pflugers Arch.* 344:159–168, 1973.

157. Stromme, S. B., Ingjer, F., and Meen, H. D.: Assessment of maximal aerobic power in specifically trained athletes. *J Appl Physiol.* 42(6):833-837, 1977.

158. Taylor, A., Thayer, R., and Rao, S.: Human skeletal muscle glycogen synthetase activities with exercise and training. *Can J Physiol Pharmacol.* 50:411-412, 1972.

159. Taylor, A. W.: The effects of exercise and training on the activities of human skeletal muscle glycogen cycle enzymes. In Howald, H., and Poortmans, J. R. (eds.): *Metabolic Adaptation to Prolonged Physical Exercise.* Basel, Switzerland, Birkhauser Verlag, 1975, pp. 451-462.

160. Tepperman, J., and Pearlman, D.: Effects of exercise and anemia on coronary arteries of small animals as revealed by the corrosion-cast technique. *Circ Res.* 9:576-584, 1961.

161. Terjung, R., and Spear, K.: Effects of exercise on coronary blood flow in rats. *Physiologist.* 18(3):419, 1975.

162. Thorstensson, A., Sjodin, B., and Karlsson, J.: Enzyme activities and muscle strength after "sprint training" in man. *Acta Physiol Scand.* 94:313-318, 1975.

163. Tibbits, G., Koziol, B. J., Roberts, N. K., Baldwin, K. M., and Barnard, R. J.: Adaptation of the rat myocardium to endurance training. *J Appl Physiol.* 44(1):85-89, 1978.

164. Tipton, C.: Training and bradycardia in rats. *Am J Physiol.* 209:1089-1094, 1965.

165. Tipton, C., Barnard, R., and Tcheng, T.: Resting heart rate investigations with trained and nontrained hypophysectomized rats. *J Appl Physiol.* 26(5):585-588, 1969.

166. Tipton, C. M., Matthes, R. D., Maynard, J. A., and Carey, R. A.: The influence of physical activity on ligaments and tendons. *Med Sci Sports.* 7(3):165-175, 1975.

167. Underwood, R. H., and Schwade, J. L.: Non-invasive analysis of cardiac function of elite distance runners—echocardiography, vectorcardiography, and cardiac intervals. *Ann NY Acad Sci.* 301: 297-309, 1977.

168. Van Handel, P. J., Costill, D. L., and Getchell, L. H.: Central circulatory adaptations to physical training. *Res Q.* 47(4): 815-823, 1976.

169. Watt, E., Buskirk, E., and Plotnicki, B.: A comparison of single vs. multiple daily training regimens: some physiological considerations. *Res Q.* 44(1):119-123, 1973.

170. Wilmore, J., Davis, J., O'Brien, R., Vodak, P., Walder, G., and Amsterdam, E.: A comparative investigation of bicycling, tennis, and jogging as modes for altering cardiovascular endurance capacity. *Med Sci Sports.* 7(1):83, 1975.

171. Wilmore, J., Royce, J., Girandola, R., Katch, F., and Katch, V.: Body composition changes with a 10-week program of jogging. *Med Sci Sports.* 2(3):113-117, 1970.

172. Winder, W. W., Hagberg, J. M., Hickson, R. C., Ehsani, A. A., and McLane, J. A.: Time course of sympathoadrenal adaptation to endurance exercise training in man. *J Appl Physiol.* 45(3):370-374, 1978.

173. Zeldis, S. M., Morganroth, J., and Rubler, S.: Cardiac hypertrophy in response to dynamic conditioning in female athletes. *J Appl Physiol.* 44(6):849-852, 1978.

SELECTED READINGS

Cutilletta, A. F., Edmiston, K., and Dowell, R. T.: Effect of a mild exercise program on myocardial function and the development of hypertrophy. *J Appl Physiol.* 46(2):354-360, 1979.

Daniels, J. T., Yarbrough, R. A., and Foster, C.: Changes in maxVO₂ and running performance with training. *Europ J Appl Physiol.* 39:249-254, 1978.

Fox, E. L.: Methods and effects of physical training. *Pediatric Ann.* 7(10):690-703, 1978.

Fox, E. L.: Physical training: methods and effects. *Orthop Clin N Am.* 8(3):533-548, 1977.

Fox, E. L.: Physiological effects of training. In *Encyclopedia of Physical Fitness,* Stull, G. A., and Cureton, T. K. (eds.): *Encyclopedia of Physical Education, Fitness, and Sports: Training, Environment, Nutrition, and Fitness.* Salt Lake City, Brighton Publishing, 1980, pp. 83-96.

Fox, E. L.: *Sports Physiology.* Philadelphia, W. B. Saunders, 1979, pp. 192-241.

Hickson, R. C., Hammons, G. T., and Holloszy, J. O.: Development and regression of exercise-induced cardiac hypertrophy in rats. *Am J Physiol.* 236(2):H268-H272, 1979.

Krieger, D. A., Tate, C. A., McMillin-Wood, J.,

and Booth, F. W.: Populations of rat skeletal muscle mitochondria after exercise and immobilization. *J Appl Physiol.* 48(1):23–28, 1980.

Saltin, B., and Rowell, L. B.: Functional adaptations to physical activity and inactivity. *Fed Proc.* 39:1506–1513, 1980.

Shaffer, T. E., and Fox, E. L.: Guidelines to physical conditioning for sports. *Pediatric Basics.* 18:10–14, 1977.

Tipton, C. M., and Scheuer, J. (eds.): Symposium on experimental preparations to study the effects of training on the cardiovascular system. *Med Sci Sports.* 9(4):219–267, 1977.

Wolfe, L. A., Cunningham, D. A., Rechnitzer, P. A., and Nichol, P. M.: Effects of endurance training on left ventricular dimensions in healthy men. *J Appl Physiol.* 47(1):207–212, 1979.

chapter 14

Exercise and Training in Females

The major concepts to be learned from this chapter are as follows:

- Athletic performance differences between men and women are due in large part to differences in body size and composition.
- The capacities of the energy systems of the female are less than those of the male.
- The absolute strength of females is about two-thirds that of males.
- Relative strength gains in females are the same or even better than in males following similar weight-resistance training programs.
- Strength-training programs for females do not cause excessive muscular bulk or produce a masculinizing effect.
- Comparable physiological and biochemical changes leading to greater working capacity can be produced in both sexes following similar physical training programs.
- Mild exercise does not have a significant effect on menstrual disorders. However, heavy, intensive training and competition induce amenorrhea (cessation of menstruation) in some athletes.
- Female athletes should be allowed to train and compete in any sport during menstruation, provided that they know that no unpleasant symptoms will occur and that their performances will not be greatly affected.
- Serious injuries to either the breasts or external and internal reproductive organs are rare in females, even in contact sports.

The purpose of this chapter is to emphasize some of the physiological responses of girls and women to both exercise and physical training. It should be made clear from the outset that, in general, the responses of females to exercise and training are *basically* no different from those described elsewhere for boys and men. After all, it must be remembered that the cellular mechanisms controlling most physiological and biochemical responses to exercise are the same for both sexes. However, there are some differences but they should be recognized mainly as differences in magnitude rather than mechanism.

First, we will take a good look at the performance records of men and women. A comparison of these records will provide a basis for our discussion of exercise and training in females with respect to: (1) body size and body composition, (2) the energy systems, (3) muscular strength and function, (4) physical trainability, and (5) gynecological considerations.

Performance Records

Table 14-1 contains the world's best performances in selected track and field and freestyle swimming events for men and women. Data from the 1979 and 1985 world records are included. The difference in performance between men and women is shown as the performance ratio. The performance ratio is nothing more than the women's record divided by the men's record. For example, in the 100-meter dash, the time of :10.76 is divided by the time of :09.93 to yield a ratio of 1.084. An equal performance in any event would yield a ratio of 1.00. The performance ratios in Table 14-1 are all greater than 1.00, meaning that the men's records exceed the women's.

In Figure 14-1, the performance ratios have been plotted, event by event. Notice that, except for the 200-meter dash, the 1985 ratios for track and field events have been lowered while those in swimming have been elevated. The true meaning of

TABLE 14-1

World-record performances in track and field and freestyle swimming for men and women. Performance ratios for 1985 and 1979 records are presented

Track and Field				
Event	Men	Women	1985 Ratio (1979)*	Change
100 m	:09.93	:10.76	1.084 (1.093)	↓
200 m	:19.72	:21.71	1.101 (1.101)	⟷
400 m	:43.86	:47.99	1.094 (1.108)	↓
800 m	1:41.73	1:53.28	1.114 (1.122)	↓
1500 m	3:29.45	3:52.47	1.110 (1.113)	↓
Mean			1.101 (1.107)	↓
Mile	3:46.31	4:16.71	1.134	
High Jump	7ft 10.75in	6ft 9.5in	1.163 (1.164)†	⟷
Long Jump	29ft 2.5in	24ft 5.0in	1.196 (1.255)†	↓
Marathon**	2:07:12	2:21:06	1.109	
Freestyle Swimming				
100 m	:48.95	:54.79	1.119 (1.121)	↓
200 m	1:47.44	1:57.75	1.096 (1.076)	↑
400 m	3:48.32	4:06.28	1.079 (1.064)	↑
800 m	7:52.33	8:24.62	1.068 (1.059)	↑
1500 m	14:54.75	16:04.49	1.078 (1.069)	↑
Mean			1.088 (1.078)	↑

*Women's time divided by men's time.

†Men's jump divided by women's jump.

**Only a world's best time is recognized, there is no world record.

these observations is yet to be realized, but one could speculate that across a variety of running events, the ratio will "settle" at about 1.10. For freestyle swimming, the ratio may settle at about 1.08. Of the two jumping events included, note the dramatic improvement in the performance ratio for the high jump event (1.255 in 1979 to 1.196 in 1985).

Also included in Table 14-1 is the world's best time in the marathon event with a performance ratio of 1.109. Figure 14-2 illustrates marathon performance from a slightly different perspective. Re-

sults of a recent well-known marathon are examined via a distribution curve. Included are results for 11,410 men and 2,132 women, representing approximately 90% of the finishers for both sexes. The mean time for the men was 4 hours 09 minutes and 31 seconds (249.52 minutes), and that for the women was 4 hours 27 minutes and 55 seconds (267.95 minutes), yielding a ratio of 1.074. Approximately 30% of the women finishers were better than the average of the male finishers.

In summary, the following points should be noted:

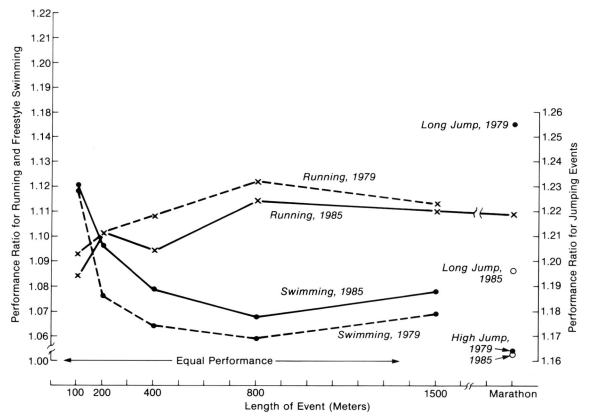

Figure 14-1. World's best performances by men and women in track and field and freestyle swimming are given by the performance ratio, i.e., dividing the men's performance time by the women's. The 1979 ratios (prior edition of this text) and the 1985 ratios are presented for comparison. See text for further discussion.

1. The overall performance by women is closer to men in swimming than either running or jumping.
2. In running, except for the 100-meter dash, the ratio is similar across all running events illustrated.
3. Similarly, in the swimming events from 400 meter to 1500 meter, the performance ratios were relatively constant.
4. The highest ratios are in the 100-meter freestyle and the jumping events.
5. The lowest ratios are in the 100-meter dash in running and distance events in swimming.
6. When a large number of participants were observed in a marathon, the ratio of mean performances was relatively low.

With these observations in mind, let us continue our discussion to determine, physiologically, why we see such performance differences.

Body Size and Body Composition

From Figure 14-3, compared with the average adult male, the average adult female:

1. is 3 to 4 inches *shorter;*
2. is 25 to 30 pounds *lighter* in total body weight;
3. has 10 to 15 pounds *more adipose tissue* (fat);
4. has 40 to 45 pounds *less fat-free weight* (mainly muscle, bone, and organs).

In general, these differences refer to both nonathletic and athletic men and women.[91] Also, from Figure 14-3, notice that the biggest female athletes (discus throwers and shot-putters), though considerably larger than their nonathletic counterparts, are about the size of the average nonathletic male.

Weight and Height

At least some of the performance differences illustrated in Table 14-1 can be explained on the basis of body weight and height differences. Looking at the long jump and high jump events the absolute performance differences are quite large. However, if the distances jumped are "corrected" for body weight, the performances are very similar for both events (Table 14-2). The performance ratio favors the female world-record holder in the high jump on the basis of height jumped per kilogram of body weight. Height of the athlete tends to even out performance as well. Although such comparisons may not be completely valid, they do point out some influence of body size on absolute performance.

Figure 14-2. Distribution curve of performances by men and women in a recent major marathon competition. The vertical lines represent the mean performances by each sex. Refer to the text for further discussion.

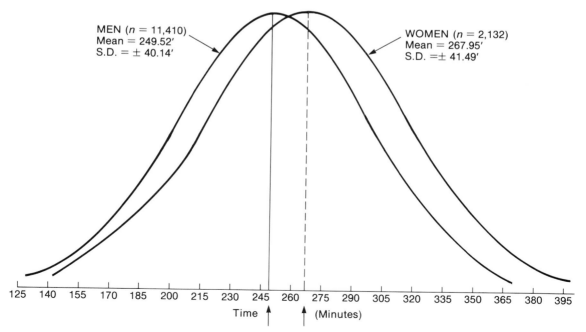

MEN (*n* = 11,410)
Mean = 249.52′
S.D. = ± 40.14′

WOMEN (*n* = 2,132)
Mean = 267.95′
S.D. = ± 41.49′

125 140 155 170 185 200 215 230 245 260 275 290 305 320 335 350 365 380 395

Time ↑ ↑ (Minutes)

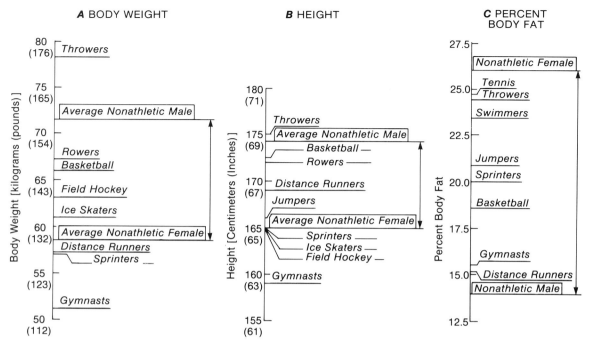

Figure 14-3. The heights, weights, and relative body fats (%) are presented for a variety of female athletes. The average values for nonathletic females and nonathletic males are included for comparison. Not all of the athletic groups represented are elite performers. (Based on data from references 13, 27, 45, 54, 70, 80, 83, 85, 108, 115, 116, and 134.)

Body Fat

It was mentioned earlier that in swimming the performance of women is closer to that of men than in running. In swimming, sex differences in body composition tend to be less disadvantageous to the female athlete, whereas in running, the men have the advantage. In water, the greater body fat of the female leads to less body drag, which, in turn, leads to less energy expenditure per unit of distance swum.[103] In other words, women swimming over the same distance as men require 20% less energy per unit body weight. However, in running, the extra body fat of the female becomes a burden by virtue of the fact that it increases the workload without making any metabolic contribution.

Possible Body Structure Differences

The average female has a wider pelvis than the average male. In running, particularly sprinting, this means that the female must shift her pelvis more in order to keep the center of gravity over the weight-bearing foot.[67] As a result, there is greater hip muscle involvement and thus, a decreased mechanical efficiency during running. Theoretically, this should limit the running ability of the female with respect to the male. However, research findings show that the relationship between width of the hips and running speed is very low and as such should not be a significantly limiting factor from a practical standpoint.[99,124] This point is well illustrated by the performance ratios shown in

Figure 14-1. As already pointed out, the women's performance is closer to the men's in the sprints, in which such a limitation would be more apparent than in the other running events.

Age and Body Size Differences

It is well known that body size differences are minimal in young children, i.e., before the onset of puberty.[5,41] Thus, it should be instructive with respect to the effects of body size on performance to examine the performance of young athletes before puberty through age 18. Records for age-group swimmers afford such an opportunity.[119,120]

Freestyle swimming performances for boys and girls from age 10 through 18 are shown in Figure 14-4. Events range from the sprints through distance events. Performance ratios were established for each event from the best freestyle performances by United States swimmers. The 50-yard and 50-meter events were combined and averaged as were the other events of near equal distance. For example, in the 50-yard and 50-meter sprints the performance ratios were 0.998 and 0.990, respectively.

The mean ratio for the 50 then is 0.994. Long distances in each age group were combined as a single event. Thus the 1000-yard for 10-year-olds, the 2000-yard for 12-year-olds, and the 3000-yard for 14- and 16-year-olds were treated as a single event in Figure 14-4.

Notice that for the 10- and 12-year-old swimmers, performance ratios cluster about the equal performance line (1.00). In three instances (the 50, 1000, and 2000) the girls performance exceeds that of the boys. Other pertinent observations are that the performance ratios increase with maturation and that there is less disadvantage for girls in the events of 200 yards/meters and longer. In the power events of the 50 and 100 yard/meter distances, the ratio increases linearly with age.

Performance-Matched Physiological Characteristics

What are the physiological characteristics and responses of performance-matched males and females? To provide some insight into this question, Pate, Barnes, and Miller[100] reported the results of a study in

TABLE 14-2

Observations on World-Record Performances in the Jumping Events Taking Height and Weight Into Account

Event	Record	Height and Weight of Record Holder*		Jump Per cm of Height	Jump Per kg of Weight
Women's High Jump	81.5 in.	177 cm	58 kg	0.46 in.	1.41 in.
Men's High Jump	94.75 in.	191 cm	72 kg	0.50 in.	1.32 in.
Women's Long Jump	293 in.	181 cm	70 kg	1.62 in.	4.6 in.
Men's Long Jump†					
(C. Lewis)	346.25 in.	188 cm	80 kg	1.84 in.	4.9 in.
(B. Beamon)	350.5 in.	196 cm	76 kg	1.79 in.	4.6 in.

*Personal communication with Dave Johnson, Statistician, *Track and Field News*.

†B. Beamon is the world-record holder from the Mexico City Olympics and C. Lewis has consistently recorded performances in the high 28-foot range.

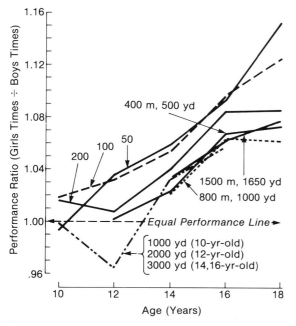

Figure 14-4. Performance ratios of boys and girls by age group in freestyle swimming events, e.g., the 50-yard and 50-meter sprint ratios of 0.998 and 0.990 are combined to yield an average of 0.994. At the younger ages, when body size differences are minimal, girls performances are equal to or better than the boys. The performance ratios increase with age until about age 16 for the distance events, but continue to increase for the sprints through age 18. (See references 119, 120.)

which male and female participants were matched, for laboratory studies, on the basis of a 24.2-meter (15-mile) road race. In the laboratory setting, all subjects were given a graded treadmill test with assessments for max $\dot{V}O_2$, maximum heart rate, respiratory exchange ratio (R), hematocrit and hemoglobin, lactic acid, and 2,3-diphosphoglyceric acid (2,3-DPG facilitates the dissociation of oxygen from hemoglobin). Additionally, body composition was assessed by hydrostatic weighing. There were no significant differences in max $\dot{V}O_2$ (55.8 and 55.1 ml/kg/min for females and

males respectively), maximum heart rate (186 and 189 beats/min), respiratory exchange ratio, and other measures. Body compositions were nearly the same (17.8% for females and 16.3% for males). Both resting and exercise hematocrit, as well as hemoglobin levels, were greater in males. The males were heavier and taller than the females.

Postexercise lactic acid levels were quite similar. 2,3-DPG concentration was similar in both groups. However, when 2,3-DPG was expressed relative to hemoglobin levels, the females had a higher concentration.

Thus, it can be concluded that when males and females have similar training patterns and performances, most of their physiological characteristics are similar. Other studies have shown results similar to this study.[20,128] One practical implication for results of this nature is that in either physical education or athletic settings where performance and conditioning are based upon aerobic capacity, men and women not only can but should be placed in common groupings.

The Energy Systems

Of the three energy systems discussed in Chapter 2, only the oxygen (aerobic) system has gained much attention with respect to the female.[6,30,33,107] Even in this, the research is scanty. Almost no research has been conducted with respect to the female's anaerobic capacities (ATP-PC and LA systems). In view of this limited research, a discussion of the energy systems with respect to performance differences might well prove to be enlightening.

The ATP-PC System

It has been shown that the muscular concentrations of ATP and PC in females are the same as those in males,[64] i.e., about 4 mM/kg muscle for ATP and 16 mM/kg muscle for CP (p. 17). However, because of the smaller total skeletal muscle mass in the female, there is less total phosphagen available for use during exercise. Comparisons of the functional capacities of the ATP-PC system between men and women can be made in three ways: first, by alactacid oxygen debt measurements; second, by the Margaria Anaerobic Power Test; and third, by the performance ratios.

Rapid-Recovery Phase (Alactacid O₂ Debt)

You will recall (p. 42) that the maximal rapid-recovery phase of recovery oxygen is associated with regeneration of the total muscular stores of ATP and PC that were depleted during exhaustive exercise. In Figure 14-5 are shown some comparative values for the maximal alactacid oxygen debt capacity between men and women. It can be seen that the lowest values are associated with untrained females and males, whereas the highest values are related to the highly trained oarswomen and oarsmen of the U.S. National Team. The differences between men and women would be closer if the values were expressed per unit of muscle mass rather than total body weight.

Anaerobic Power Test

The stair-climbing test, described in Appendix G, takes only a fraction of a second and as such indirectly reflects the ability to rapidly utilize the stores of ATP and PC in the leg muscles. These power measurements are shown in Figure 14-6 for males and females from 6 to 25 years old. Notice that there is very little difference between the sexes. Also, though not shown in the figure, the maximal anaerobic power decreases after the age of 25 years for both men and women. The power values are expressed relative to body weight; the total power capability for the average male would be around 2.1 horsepower (HP) and

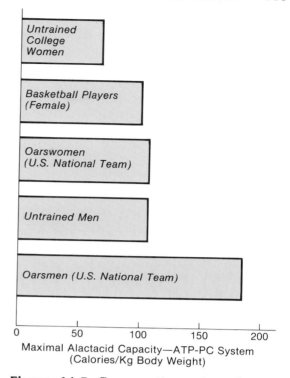

Figure 14-5. Comparative values for the maximal alactacid oxygen debt capacity between men and women. The lowest values are associated with untrained females and males, whereas the highest values are related to the highly trained oarsmen and oarswomen of the U.S. National Team. (Based on data from Cohen,[17] Diehl,[27] Fox,[42,43] and Hagerman et al.[54,55])

for the average female, 1.7 HP. This difference is due again to the smaller body size of the female.

Performance Ratios

With respect to the performance ratios (see Fig. 14-1), it is interesting to note that the best running events for the female in comparison with those of the male are the 100- and 200-meter sprints. You will recall that these types of events rely heavily on the muscular stores of ATP and PC for their primary source of energy. This also tends

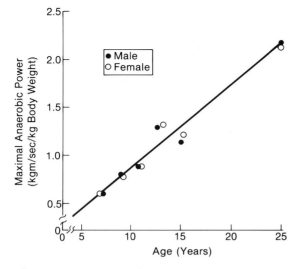

Figure 14-6. Anaerobic (ATP + PC) power in males and females. Notice that both men and women fit the same line, indicating that there is very little, if any, difference between genders. (Based on data from references 25, 69, and 87.)

to support the idea that the muscular concentrations of ATP and PC in females are not much different from those of males, and as such should not significantly hinder female performance in those events that require short-term, but high-intensity, efforts. The lower total stores of ATP and PC in females appear to be due mainly to their smaller total muscle mass.

The Lactic Acid System (Anaerobic Glycolysis)

Females tend to have lower levels of lactic acid in their blood following maximal exercise than do males.[6,17,22,33,54,71] Such low lactic acid levels strongly suggest that the capacity of the lactic acid system is also lower in the female. This can be seen in Figure 14-7, in which the capacity of the LA system is shown for men and women, both trained and untrained. The values, though expressed as cal/kg of total body weight, are based on blood lactic acid levels following maximal exercise.

As with the ATP-PC system, one of the reasons for a lower LA capacity in the female is the smaller total muscle mass. If the values given in Figure 14-7 were expressed per kilogram of total muscle mass, the differences between the sexes would be smaller.

The Oxygen (Aerobic) System

As with the two anaerobic capacities mentioned previously, the maximal aerobic

Figure 14-7. The capacity of the lactic acid system for men and women, both trained and untrained. Again, the lactic acid capacity is lower in females than in males. While this may be related in part to lesser muscle mass, it points out that females might be at a slight disadvantage when competing in those events that involve the lactic acid system to a large extent. (Based on data from references 6, 17, 22, 27, 33, 42, 54, 55, 71, and 108.)

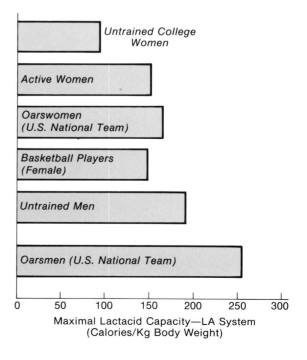

power (max $\dot{V}O_2$) of females is also smaller than that of males (by about 15 to 25%). This is shown in Figure 14-8, in which two points are worth noting:

1. The difference in max $\dot{V}O_2$ between male and female is negligible at the younger ages and most pronounced during the adult, middle-age years. This relationship stems from the fact that, as mentioned, earlier, body size and composition differences between males and females are minimal prior to puberty and maximal during adulthood.

2. The difference in max $\dot{V}O_2$ between the sexes is smallest when expressed relative to a body size dimension such as body weight (Fig. 14-8B). Again, this goes back to sex differences in body size and composition. Since the metabolism of the working skeletal muscles dictates the size of the max $\dot{V}O_2$, differences between male and female are minimal when max $\dot{V}O_2$ is expressed relative to lean body mass[21,25,28,31] and to an even lesser extent when related to active muscle mass.[21] The latter relationship is shown in Figure 14-9. In this case, the max $\dot{V}O_2$ was measured on a bicycle ergometer and the active muscle estimated by leg volume measurements. Leg volume is a measure of the volume of leg bone plus the volume of leg muscle. Since leg bone volume does not account for much of the total, leg volume primarily reflects leg muscle volume or mass. Notice how little difference there is between males and females at all ages when max $\dot{V}O_2$ is expressed in ml O_2 per liter of leg volume and per minute. Also, the insert shows the relationship between max $\dot{V}O_2$ in liters per minute and leg volume in liters; both males and females fit the same line.

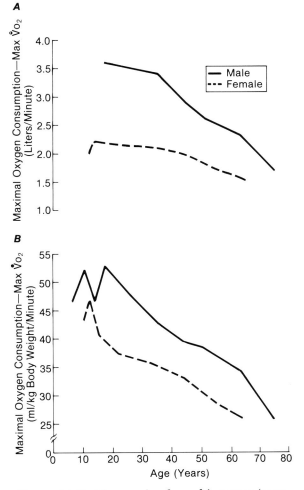

Figure 14-8. The maximal aerobic power (max $\dot{V}O_2$) of males and females from 6 to 75 years of age. In *A*, the values are expressed in liters of oxygen without respect to body size. Note the large gender difference. In *B*, differences are reduced when max $\dot{V}O_2$ is expressed relative to total body weight. (Based on data from references 33, 108, and 109.)

In the real world of athletic performance the only meaningful relationship discussed in the preceding points is between max $\dot{V}O_2$ and total body weight. This is so because in most exercises and sports activities, movement of the total body

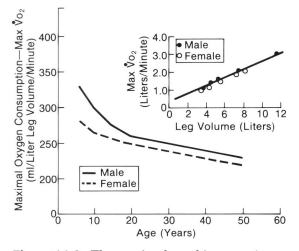

Figure 14-9. The maximal aerobic power (max $\dot{V}O_2$) of males and females from 5 to 50 years of age. In this case, max $\dot{V}O_2$ was measured on a bicycle ergometer and the active muscle mass estimated by leg volume measurements. Notice how little difference there is between sexes when max $\dot{V}O_2$ is expressed in ml of oxygen per liter of leg volume. The inset shows the relationship between max $\dot{V}O_2$ in liters per minute and leg volume in liters; both males and females fit the same line. (Based on data from Davies et al.[25])

weight of the athlete comprises the largest part of the workload. Therefore, there is little question that the female is at a disadvantage in terms of max $\dot{V}O_2$ (Fig. 14-8*B*).

Hemoglobin, Blood Volume, and Heart Volume

As you already know, hemoglobin (Hb) is the compound found in red blood cells that carries most of the oxygen from the lungs to the skeletal muscles. Also, the greater the blood volume, the greater the Hb. Thus, both Hb and blood volume are directly related to the amount of oxygen transported, and hence to the functional size of the aerobic or oxygen system, i.e., to the max $\dot{V}O_2$. This is shown in Figure 14-10*A* and *B*.

Notice that the relationships for the male (solid lines) and for the female (broken lines) are the same. This means that everything else being equal, the max $\dot{V}O_2$ of the female would equal that of the male if each

Figure 14-10. *A,* The total amount of hemoglobin and, *B,* the blood volume are directly related to the amount of oxygen transported to the muscles, and hence to the functional size of the aerobic or oxygen system (max $\dot{V}O_2$). These relationships are the same for men and women. (Based on data from Åstrand et al.[7,8])

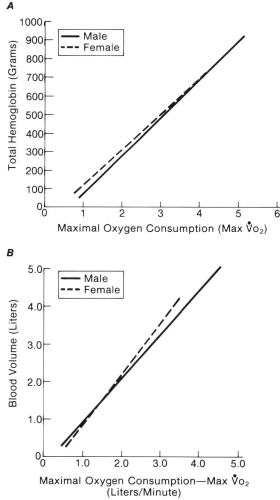

were to have the same total Hb and total blood volume.

The total amount of Hb, total blood volume, and Hb concentration for males and females are shown plotted against age in Figure 14-11. Again, it is clear that differences in these variables are minimal at the younger ages before puberty and are maximal after puberty, being much lower in the female. For example, total Hb and blood volume are about 25% lower in untrained adult females compared to untrained adult males and about 12% lower after each is trained (Table 14-3).

The lower Hb concentration of the adult female is sometimes associated with *iron deficiency anemia*.[136] Anemia represents a subnormal Hb concentration and indicates a negative iron balance (more iron being lost than taken in). You should recall that iron is an essential Hb component (p. 237). Iron deficiency in some adult females is related to menstrual bleeding. This problem as it relates to exercise tolerance, will be discussed later in this chapter (p. 405).

The amount of blood capable of being pumped by the heart, i.e., the size of the heart, is also an important factor in determining how much oxygen can be transported to the muscles. Therefore, the relationship between heart size (heart volume) and the max $\dot{V}O_2$ is quite good, as is shown in Figure 14-12. Notice once again that the data for both men (filled circles) and women (unfilled circles) fall on the same line. The fact that females have on the average a smaller heart volume than men (see Table 14-3) undoubtedly contributes to their smaller max $\dot{V}O_2$.

Figure 14-11. *A,* Total hemoglobin, *B,* blood volume, and *C,* Hb concentration for males and females as a function of age. Differences in these variables are minimal at the younger ages before puberty and are maximal after puberty, being much lower in females. (Based on data from reference 7.)

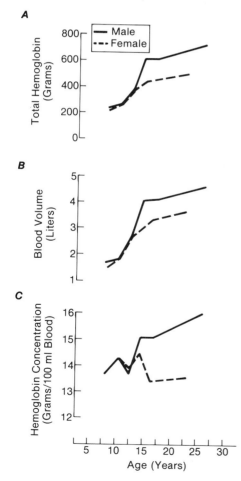

Performance Ratio

For a final look at the oxygen systems, let's go back to the performance ratios. It can be seen (Fig. 14-1, p. 377) that for the swimming events involving the oxygen system (400, 800, and 1500 meters), and in which the body size difference is effectively reduced by the water, the women's performance is closer to the men's than under any other set of conditions. From a practical standpoint, this illustrates very nicely the influence of differences in body size and the functional capacities of the female.

TABLE 14–3

Normal Values of Hemoglobin (Hb), Blood Volume (BV), and
Heart Volume (HV) for Trained and Untrained Men and Women

Subjects	Mean Age (yr)	Hb (grams)	Hb (g/kg)	Hb Concentration (g/100 ml blood)	BV (liters)	BV (liters/kg)	HV (ml)	HV (ml/kg)
Untrained								
Females	37.6	555	8.5	13.6	4.07	62.1	560	8.5
Males	24.0	805	11.6	15.3	5.25	75.0	785	11.2
Trained								
Females	26.0	800	12.5	14.1	5.67	88.6	790	12.3
Males	36.0	995	13.7	15.1	6.58	90.1	930	12.7

Based on data from Kjellberg et al.[72,73]

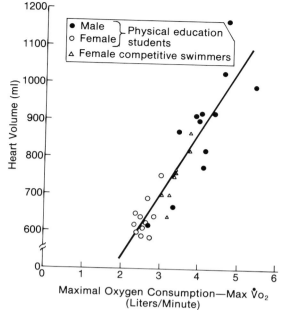

Figure 14-12. Heart volume is directly related to the amount of oxygen transported to the muscles, and hence to the functional size of the aerobic system (max $\dot{V}O_2$). (Based on data from Åstrand.[7,8])

Strength

There are two important questions relative to muscular strength and the female that need answering:

1. What is the magnitude of the difference in strength in various muscle groups between male and female?
2. Does the female have the same potential as the male for strength development, general body composition changes, and muscular hypertrophy (muscle bulk) following a weight training program?

Strength Differences

Strength differences between male and female should be examined from the standpoint of (1) absolute strength, (2) strength in relation to body size and composition, and (3) strength in relation to muscle size. An excellent review of the comparative muscular strength of males and females has been written by Laubach.[77]

Absolute Strength

Differences between the sexes in absolute strength, e.g., in the amount of weight lifted, are shown in Figure 14-13. The differences are expressed in terms of a strength ratio; i.e., the absolute strength of the female was divided by the absolute strength of the male—a ratio less than one means

Figure 14-13. Differences between the sexes in absolute muscular strength. The differences are expressed in terms of a strength ratio (strength of females divided by strength of males); a ratio less than one means the men are stronger. General muscular strength in the female is two-thirds that of the male but varies according to the muscle group compared. (Based on data from Hettinger[62] and Wilmore.[132])

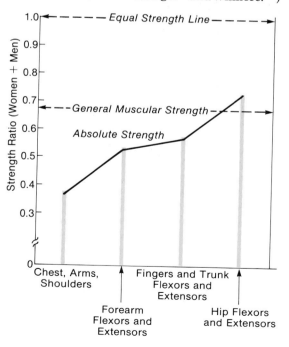

the men are stronger. General muscular strength in the female is approximately two-thirds that of the male.[62,77] However, notice that the strength differences vary among the different muscle groups. For example, in comparison with men, women are weaker in the chest, arms and shoulders and strongest in the legs.[62,77,132] The reason for this is more than likely related to the fact that both sexes use their legs to a similar degree, e.g., standing, walking, running, climbing stairs, and cycling. On the other hand, females, at least heretofore in American society, have had little opportunity to use their upper limb muscles.

Strength Relative to Body Size

Just like the other functional capacities so far discussed, strength differences between male and female are reduced when related to body size. Figure 14-14 shows the strength ratio when strength in both sexes is expressed (1) in terms of total body weight and (2) in terms of lean body mass. Notice that leg strength per unit lean body weight is actually slightly greater in the female than in the male. It should be remembered that lean body weight more closely approximates total muscle mass than does total body weight since lean body weight is calculated as total body weight minus total fat weight.

The fact that leg strength when expressed per unit of lean body weight is the same in males and females was recently confirmed for isokinetic strength[3] as is shown in Figure 14-15. Notice, however, that while both isometric (zero degrees per second in the figure) and isokinetic knee extensor strength at slow speeds of movement (e.g., 60 degrees per second) were not different between sexes; isokinetic strength at faster speeds of movement (180 and 300 degrees per second) was significantly greater in males. This difference in strength at fast speeds of movement was also de-

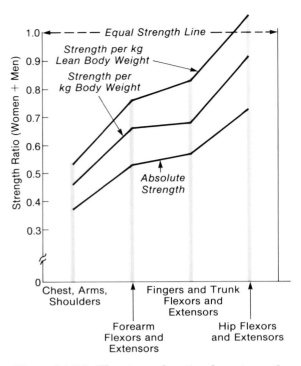

Figure 14-14. The strength ratio when strength in both sexes is expressed in terms of total body weight and lean body mass. Strength differences between male and female are reduced when strength is related to body size. (Based on data from Wilmore.[132])

monstrable using a jump-reach test (inset Fig. 14-15).

The reasons for these differences are not known but may be related to differences in muscle fiber type or fiber recruitment patterns between the sexes. Remember, fast-twitch fibers are generally recruited when performing fast, intensive movements. At any rate, these findings might suggest the need for different or at least modified strength training techniques for females.[3] More research along these lines is warranted.

In addition to total and lean body weights, strength is also related to height.[4] This is particularly true in children of both sexes. For example, there is little or no difference in the strength of the leg muscles in boys and girls from 7 to 17 years of age when expressed relative to body height.

Strength and Muscle Size

So far as is known, strength relative to muscle size (expressed as the cross-sectional area of the muscle) is the same for the male and the female.[62,66] In other words, the quality of the muscle fibers as far as the ability to exert force is concerned, is independent of sex. This is shown in Figure 14-16. In Figure 14-16A, the strength of the arm flexors is plotted against the cross-sectional area of the flexors. It is easy to see

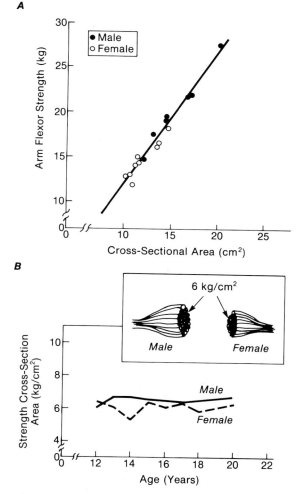

Figure 14-15. Isometric (0 degrees/sec) and isokinetic knee extensor strength at slow speeds of movement (e.g., 60 degrees/sec) are not different between sexes. However, isokinetic strength at faster speeds of movement (e.g., 180 and 300 degrees/sec) is significantly greater in males. This difference in strength at fast speeds of movement is also demonstrable using a jump-reach test (inset). (Based on data from Anderson et al.[3])

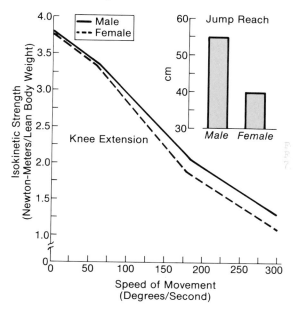

Figure 14-16. In *A*, the strength of the arm flexors is plotted against their cross-sectional area; both males and females fit the same line. In *B*, strength per unit cross-sectional area is shown for males and females. Again, there is little or no difference in strength. The inset shows that the force exerted by equally sized muscles is the same in both sexes. (Based on data from Ikai and Fukunago.[66])

that the relationship between muscle strength and muscle size (cross-sectional area) is excellent. Also, note how both males (filled circles) and females (unfilled circles) fit the same line. In Figure 14-16B, strength per unit of cross-sectional area (i.e., the absolute strength of the muscle fibers divided by their cross-sectional area) is shown for males and females of various ages. Again, there is little or no difference between the sexes and little or no difference according to age, at least between 12 and 20 years of age. This means that although the male usually has a larger muscle than the female, the force exerted by equal-sized muscles is the same in both sexes (Fig. 14-16*B* inset).

The preceding information, though interesting, is again only practical from the standpoint of absolute strength, i.e., strength without respect to muscle or body size. As mentioned before, this is true because in those activities that are at least partially dependent upon strength (such as sprinting or accelerating and jumping), the entire body is involved. The performance ratios tend to bear this out. For example, females are relatively poor in the jumping events. However, when the heights jumped are adjusted according to body size, both sexes are about equal (p. 379). The same applies to the 100-meter dash. The men's speed per unit of body size is 8.4 meters/min per kg body weight, and for the women, 9.5 meters/min. The women are slightly faster when expressed relative to body size.

Effects of Weight Training

One of the concepts most misunderstood by physical educators, coaches, and parents alike is the effect of a weight-training program. This is particularly true regarding the female. The common concept is that although a weight-training program increases strength, it also produces bulging muscles that turn into fat when the program is no longer continued. Let's see what the true story is.

Strength Development

It is true that muscular strength in both men and women increases following a weight-training program.[13,61,62,90,132] This is shown in normal college-age students in Figure 14-17. The per cent increase in strength for the females in all but one muscle group (the arms) was the same or better than in the males. Although part of this greater relative strength gain can be explained on the basis of the lower initial strength levels of the females, these results

Figure 14-17. Both men and women increase in muscular strength following a weight training program. The per cent increase in strength for females in most muscle groups is the same or even better than for males. (Based on data from Wilmore.[132])

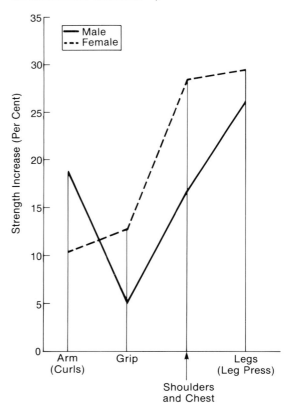

indicate that the female can make substantial gains in strength through weight-lifting activities. This is an important point, since earlier information indicated that women were less trainable than men with respect to muscular strength.[61] The strength gains shown here were made over a 10-week period, 2 days per week, using the progressive-resistance principle. For example, the initial weights were chosen so that the subjects could perform only 7 to 9 repetitions. When the subjects increased in strength to the point where the same weights could be lifted 14 to 16 repetitions, additional weight was added so that only 7 to 9 repetitions could again be performed.

Figure 14-18 also shows the effects of a weight-training program on strength gains, but this time for female athletes. The female athletes were nationally prominent track-and-field and throwing-event athletes between the ages of 16 and 23 years. The important point here is that these females are much stronger than normal females but their strength gains are still very substantial, particularly after 6 months of training. This information suggests that weight-training programs can and should be used by female athletes who wish to improve their performance in those activities demanding a great deal of strength.

Weight Training and Body Composition Changes

For the average college-age male and female, body composition changes following a weight-training program are as follows[90,132]:

1. Little or no change in total body weight.
2. Significant losses of relative and absolute body fat.
3. A significant gain in lean body weight (presumably muscle mass).

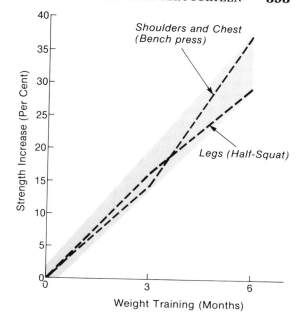

Figure 14-18. The increase in strength in female athletes. These females are much stronger than nonathletic females; yet their strength gains are still very substantial. (Based on data from Brown and Wilmore.[13])

An example of these changes is shown in Figure 14-19. Notice that while the changes are similar in both sexes, changes in absolute and relative body fat tend to be slightly greater in the female. On the other hand, the increase in lean body weight (muscle mass) tends to be less in the female than in the male. The changes shown in Figure 14-19 were obtained on the same subjects whose strength gains are shown in Figure 14-17 (10 weeks of training, 2 days per week).

Similar changes in body composition have been observed in female athletes following a season of training and competition.[13,27,80,115]

Muscular Hypertrophy

As discussed in Chapter 7, gains in muscular strength are usually accompanied by

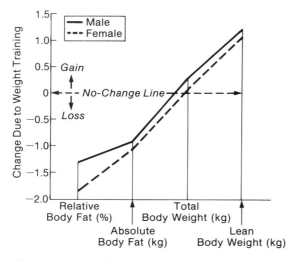

Figure 14-19. Following a weight-training program you could expect, in both sexes, to find little change in total body weight, a loss of body fat, and a gain in muscle mass. Losses in body fat tend to be slightly greater in the female, whereas gains in muscle mass tend to be slightly greater in the male. (Based on data from Wilmore.[132])

an increase in the size of individual muscle fibers. While this is true for both the male and female, *it is much less pronounced in the female.*[13,90,131,133] This can be seen from Figure 14-20, where increases in muscular girth are shown for those same subjects whose body composition and strength changes are shown in Figure 14-19 and 14-17, respectively. In every case, increases in muscular girth (circumference) were greater in the male than in the female. Also, the largest increase in muscular size exhibited by the females was 0.6 centimeter or *less than a quarter of an inch!* Such small increases in girth clearly point out that muscular hypertrophy in the female as a result of weight-training programs will certainly not lead to excessive muscular bulk or produce a masculinizing effect. Muscular hypertrophy is regulated mainly by the hormone testosterone, which is

about 10 times higher in the blood of normal men than in normal women.[39,61] Other factors to consider are[44] (1) the smaller amount of muscle mass in females and (2) their greater subcutaneous fat stores, which tend to "soften" the muscular relief and definition characteristic of the male. Thus, regardless of strength gains, muscular hypertrophy appears to be less in females than in males.

Physical Trainability

Our discussion of the trainability of the female will be limited mainly to those changes occurring following a physical training program consisting of activities such as running, jogging, swimming, or bicycling. The trainability of the female with respect to muscular strength was just discussed.

Training Frequency, Duration, and Intensity

What is presently known concerning training frequency, duration, and intensity has

Figure 14-20. Gains in strength are usually accompanied by increases in muscular size (girth). While this is true for both sexes, it is much less pronounced in the female. (Based on data from Wilmore.[132])

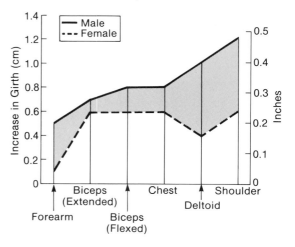

been discussed earlier (p. 348). Again, most of that information was obtained from research on males. The studies conducted on females[9,17,34,36,49,57,71,78,97,110,130] tend to support the idea that most of this information is applicable to the female.

Briefly, the following can be said concerning the frequency, the duration, and the intensity of training programs designed for females.

Frequency

For the average, college-age female, significant physiological changes can be realized from training programs conducted as few as 2 or 3 times per week.[9,49,71,110] Female athletes usually train 5, even 6, times per week. Although the physiological benefits of more frequent training sessions per week are questionable,[44] more frequent training sessions in this case may be necessary from a skill and/or strategy standpoint.

Duration

Significant improvement in fitness has been produced in young sedentary females with as little as 4 weeks of training with 5 training sessions per week.[34] Also, 6 to 7 weeks of training with 2 or 3[9,71,78,97,102,110,130] or 5[17] training sessions per week, and 10 weeks with 2 days per week,[49] and 14 weeks with 3 days per week[36] have likewise led to significant improvements in aerobic and anaerobic capacities.

Intensity

Of all the information obtained on physical training, for both men and women, the intensity of training appears to be most critical in bringing about significant change. There is a *threshold intensity* above which there is significant improvement and below which there is not. This threshold level of intensity varies from individual to individual and is related to

the initial level of fitness (conditioning) of the participant (p. 348). The determination of proper training intensities based on heart rate and anaerobic threshold measures was given in Chapter 12 (p. 289). It is valid for the female.

Physiological Changes Following Training

At the risk of stating the obvious, females benefit from training just as males do and this benefit is brought about through similar physiological changes.[71] This is true for maximal work performance as well as for submaximal efforts.

Changes and Maximal Work Capacity

A summary of the physiological changes induced by physical training during maximal exercise is shown in Figure 14-21. These changes were obtained on nonathletic normal females (Swedish) between the ages of 19 and 31 years of age.[71] The training programs consisted of riding the bicycle ergometer 2 to 3 days per week for 7 weeks. Each training session lasted 30 minutes and consisted of 6 intervals of bicycling at about 70% capacity for 3 minutes with 2-minute relief intervals. The changes included:

1. A significant increase in the maximal capacity of the oxygen system, i.e., the maximal aerobic power (max $\dot{V}O_2$). Closely related to this change are increases in total blood volume, total hemoglobin, and heart volume (see Table 14-3).
2. A significant increase in the accumulation of lactic acid in the blood following maximal exercise.
3. A significant increase in the maximal cardiac output and stroke volume. These results have been confirmed in other studies involving young females.[9,17,34,36,49,57,78,89,98,110,130] In addition, the anaerobic capacity of females has

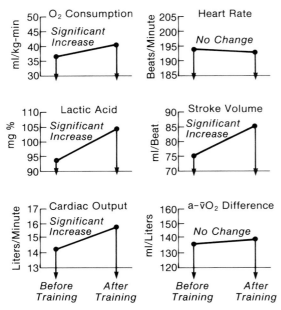

Figure 14-21. The physiological changes induced by physical training during maximal work in females are similar to those in males. (Based on data from Kilbom.[71])

Changes and Submaximal Exercise Capacity

As mentioned above, the physiological changes resulting from a physical training program appear to be essentially the same in both sexes with respect to submaximal exercise responses. As illustrated in Figure 14-23, when performing submaximal work of the same intensity before and after physical training (2 to 3 days per week of cycling for 7 weeks), the most consistent differences are[71]

1. Little or no change in steady-state $\dot{V}O_2$.
2. A significant decrease in lactic acid accumulation following exercise.
3. A significant decrease in heart rate.

been shown to increase significantly following a 6-week training program conducted 3 days per week.[129]

The magnitude of the training changes appears comparable with that of males. For example, it has been found that the increase in maximal aerobic power is similar in females and males following identical programs of 7 weeks of interval training with 2 training sessions per week.[44,46,76,110] This is shown in Figure 14-22. Notice that the gain in max $\dot{V}O_2$ expressed as ml O_2/kg body weight per minute (ml/kg-min) was the same; however, because the initial max $\dot{V}O_2$ of the females on the average was lower than that of the males (34.8 versus 44.2 ml/kg-min, respectively), the per cent increase in max $\dot{V}O_2$, as indicated inside the bars, was higher for the females.

Figure 14-22. The increase in max $\dot{V}O_2$ is similar in females and males following identical programs of interval training. Expressed in ml per kilogram of body weight per minute, the gain in max $\dot{V}O_2$ is the same; however, because the initial max $\dot{V}O_2$ of the females was lower, the per cent increase was larger for the females. (Based on data from Fox et al.[44] and Romero.[110])

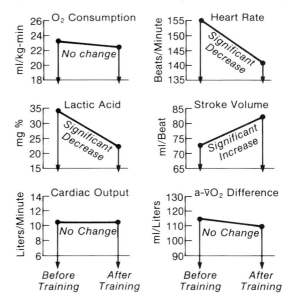

4. A significant increase in stroke volume.

5. Little or no change in cardiac output or arterial mixed venous blood O_2 difference.

It should be noticed that the preceding changes are all in the direction of making submaximal exercise a little more submaximal. In other words, training makes submaximal work easier and thus produces less physiological stress. This is an important consideration because most work, including that done during training sessions, is submaximal.

Biochemical Changes

As mentioned in Chapter 13, much new information concerning the effects of physical training at the cellular or biochemical level has only recently been made available. These changes, though determined mostly on male subjects, should be applicable to the female. Also, such changes are presumed to be specific to the type of training program; e.g., so-called sprint-training programs mainly bring about anaerobic changes (ATP + PC and LA systems), whereas endurance programs mainly bring about aerobic changes (oxygen system). Since the biochemical changes were discussed in detail earlier (p. 324), only a brief outline will be presented here.

Anaerobic Changes

1. An increase in the capacity of the ATP-PC system, by increased stores of ATP and PC in skeletal muscle.

2. An increase in the LA system as reflected by:
   a. an increase in glycogen content of skeletal muscle and
   b. an increase in glycolytic enzyme activity of skeletal muscle (mainly in fast-twitch fibers).

3. A selective hypertrophy mainly of fast-twitch muscle fibers.

Aerobic Changes

1. An increase in skeletal muscle myoglobin content.

2. An increase in the capacity of skeletal muscle to utilize (oxidize) carbohydrate and fat (i.e., in the presence of oxygen to break down sugar and fat to $CO_2 + H_2O$ with ATP production). This is facilitated by:
   a. an increase in the number and size of the mitochondria in skeletal muscle fibers and
   b. an increase in the concentration and activity of the enzymes involved in the Krebs Cycle, the electron transport system (p. 22), and the activation, transport, and breakdown of fatty acids.

Figure 14-23. The physiological changes induced by physical training during submaximal work (in this case, 75 watts) in females are similar to those in males. (Based on data from Kilbom.[71])

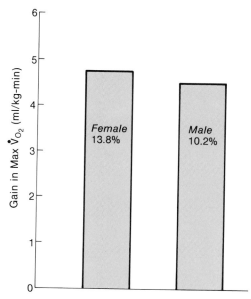

Gain in Max $\dot{V}_{O_2}$ (ml/kg-min)

Female 13.8%

Male 10.2%

3. A selective hypertrophy mainly of slow-twitch muscle fibers.

With respect to 2a, it is important to mention that the number of mitochondria per myofibril is less in females than males.[63] Although the significance of this difference is not immediately apparent, it would appear to represent a definite biochemical limitation with respect to the overall maximal aerobic power of the female.

Body Composition Changes

The changes in body composition resulting from physical training are similar to those described earlier following weight training. In other words, females can expect (1) a sizable decrease in body fat (e.g., 2.5 to 3.0 kg), (2) a small increase in lean body weight, and (3) a small decrease in total body weight after a physical training program consisting of jogging, walking, and running.[92,93] These changes, particularly fat loss, are more pronounced for the obese than for the "lean" female. In addition, it is evident that modifications in diet must also be involved in a comprehensive weight-loss program in order to obtain an optimal weight-loss level (see Chapter 20).

Other Training Changes

With short-term, moderate intensity training programs (7 weeks, 2 to 3 times per week), significant decreases in blood cholesterol, serum iron, and resting as well as exercise systolic and diastolic blood pressures have been noted in young and middle-aged females.[71] The changes in cholesterol and blood pressure are beneficial. However, the lower iron values are not. They probably indicate greater iron consumption through the formation of new red blood cells. Although several other studies[46,101,137] have not confirmed this finding such a change should be kept in mind, especially in the training of females who already

have large iron losses through menstruation.[121] More about this problem will be discussed later in this chapter in conjunction with the menstrual cycle.

Changes with Detraining

As you would expect, a period of detraining following a period of training results in a reversal of almost all the changes indicated previously for both men and women. This holds true in general for both the nonathlete and athlete. For example, Figure 14-24 shows the decrease in maximal aerobic power (max $\dot{V}O_2$) after various weeks of detraining for a group of nonathletic college-age females (solid lines) and young (15- to 17-year-old) female track athletes (dashed line). Notice that the max $\dot{V}O_2$ for

Figure 14-24. Decrease in max $\dot{V}O_2$ after various weeks of detraining for two groups of nonathletic college-age females (solid lines) and a group of young female track athletes (dashed line). The max $\dot{V}O_2$ for all groups decreased at about the same rate. (Based on data from Drinkwater and Horvath,[33] Otto,[97] and Pedersen and Jorgensen.[102])

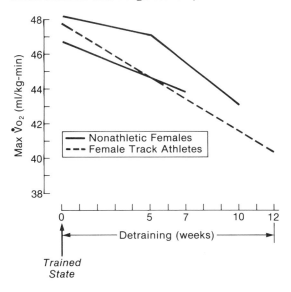

both groups decreased at about the same rate.

It should also be mentioned here that maintenance of training gains in females has been shown to be the same as in males. In other words, a maintenance training program that requires the same intensity of work but less frequent training sessions per week than did the regular training program will maintain many of the benefits of training.[97,98]

Gynecological Considerations

There are two important gynecological considerations as they relate to exercise that must be discussed here, namely: (1) menstruation and (2) pregnancy, childbirth, and injuries to the reproductive organs. Excellent reviews of these factors have been written by Ryan[111] and Thomas.[121,122]

Menstruation

The primary focus regarding the menstrual cycle in athletics is on the development of either an irregular pattern (oligomenorrhea) or cessation extending beyond 90 days (amenorrhea). Primary amenorrhea is defined as the delay of menarche beyond 16 years of age while secondary amenorrhea is the absence of menstruation in women who have been previously menstrual.[79]

The menstrual (ovulatory) cycle is a complex physiological phenomenon. Wells[126] and Hale[56] present a very good discussion of the physiology of menstruation and responses during sports participation.[127] Several types of secondary amenorrhea can be identified, including: (1) hypothalamic chronic anovulation, (2) pituitary chronic anovulation, (3) inappropriate feedback to the hypothalamus or pituitary, and (4) other endocrine or metabolic dysfunctions.[79] Athletic amenorrhea has been placed in the general category of chronic anovulation. Along with the possible or-

ganic and psychogenic factors leading to secondary amenorrhea, it is difficult for researchers to show a clear cause-and-effect relationship between specific factors of sports participation and secondary amenorrhea. However, let us proceed with a discussion of some of the possible relationships and factors.

Age of Menarche

The age at which menstruation begins *(menarche)* is significantly higher in the American female athlete than in her nonathletic counterpart. For example, as shown in Figure 14-25, both high school and college athletes attained menarche significantly later than nonathletes, and the various groups of national and Olympic athletes attained menarche significantly later than the high school and college athletes. These results clearly indicate later menarche for national- and international-caliber athletes and suggest a relationship between delayed menarche and more advanced competitive levels.[86] In one study involving competitive swimmers, athletes who were more successful reported delayed menarche when compared with their less successful counterparts.[118]

On the other hand, age of menarche for Hungarian athletes has been found to be little affected by athletic competition.[37] In addition, in Swedish swimmers,[8] the age of menarche was slightly earlier than in nonathletes whereas in other young swimmers (10 to 12 years), more advanced sexual maturity, as indicated by breast and pubic hair development, was found in the finalist of a national age group competition compared to the semifinalist.[10] These results suggest the possibility that there may be different maturity relationships for different sports and competitive levels among female athletes of different countries.[86] However, it is significant to point out that most of this information, in contrast to the

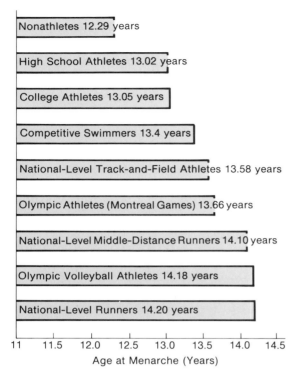

Figure 14-25 bar chart labels:
Nonathletes 12.29 years
High School Athletes 13.02 years
College Athletes 13.05 years
Competitive Swimmers 13.4 years
National-Level Track-and-Field Athletes 13.58 years
Olympic Athletes (Montreal Games) 13.66 years
National-Level Middle-Distance Runners 14.10 years
Olympic Volleyball Athletes 14.18 years
National-Level Runners 14.20 years

Age at Menarche (Years)
11 11.5 12.0 12.5 13.0 13.5 14.0 14.5

Figure 14-25. The age at which menstruation begins (menarche) is significantly higher in the American female athlete than in her nonathletic counterpart. As indicated, both high school and college athletes attained menarche later than nonathletes, and the various groups of national and Olympic athletes attained menarche later than the high school and college athletes (Based on data from Feicht et al.,[40] Malina et al.,[86] Stager et al.,[118] and Wakat and Sweeney.[126])

recent information gathered in Figure 14-25, was obtained nearly 25 years ago. At that time, training and competition in women's athletic programs were much different in scope and intensity than they are today, a factor which undoubtedly would have an influence on the results.

At any rate, given the fact that menarche is later in most highly skilled female athletes, two questions arise: (1) what causes the late menarche and (2) what is its

significance? Regarding the cause, it has been shown[12] that exercise causes a large increase in *prolactin,* one of the hormones secreted by the pituitary gland and responsible for readying the breasts for nursing (lactation). In the adolescent athlete, this could create what is referred to as a "prolactin impregnation" on the maturing ovary, an effect sufficient to delay further maturation of the ovary by another hormone called *follicle-stimulating hormone.* This in turn could result in delayed menarche or in a transient amenorrhic (absence of the menses) condition somewhat similar to the one observed in the nursing mother.[12]

The association of later attainment of menarche and success in sports has been suggested to have two main significances, one dealing with physiological aspects and the other with sociological aspects.[86]

1. The physical and physiological characteristics associated with later maturation in females are, in many respects, more suitable for successful athletic performance. For example, the later maturing female has longer legs, narrower hips, less weight per unit height, and less relative body fat than does her earlier-maturing counterpart. On the contrary, in swimming, earlier rather than later maturation may be more beneficial since greater strength and body fat would tend to enhance swimming performance in the female. This would correlate well with the aforementioned findings of a slightly earlier age of menarche in Swedish swimmers, and the more sexually developed age-group swimming finalist.

2. In American culture, the mature female is, so to speak, "socialized" away from sports competition.[86] As a result, late-maturing girls tend to perform at higher levels than their early-maturing peers of the same age later in ado-

lescence (e.g., 14 to 15 years). In other words, once the female has developed the full sexual characteristics of the adult woman, her interests, through social pressures, are directed away from sport and toward family and/or career goals. While this is changing, it is still a significant factor today.

Exercise and Menstrual Disorders

Based on information gathered many years ago, the conclusion was that exercise does not appear to affect menstrual disorders significantly. For example, in 1963,[8] it was reported that in a group of Swedish elite female swimmers, 81% had regular menstruation at about 4-week intervals. Both the duration of menstruation and the blood loss were no different from that normally found in young girls. In 1964, out of 557 Hungarian female athletes, 84% showed no change in their menstrual cycles due to sports participation. Of the 16% who did show signs of change, 30% were favorable, whereas 70% were unfavorable. The unfavorable changes were more frequent in the younger than in the older age groups.[37] The menstrual cycle was found to be rhythmic in 61 of 66 female athletes who participated in the 1964 Olympic Games.[137]

The preceding conclusion that exercise does not significantly affect menstrual disorders needs to be amended based on recent research findings. This is particularly true for female athletes involved in high-intensity training and competition, such as in sports like long-distance running, gymnastics, swimming, and professional ballet dancing.[2,23,24,40,58,114] For example, approximately one-third of female distance runners develop *amenorrhea,* i.e., a cessation of menstruation during their training and competitive seasons.[23,24] This is shown in Figure 14-26. In *A,* the incidence of amenorrhea was 34% in a group of runners, 23% in a group of joggers, and only 4% in the non-running control group. In this study, run-

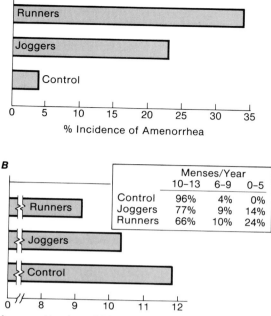

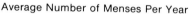

Figure 14-26. *A,* Approximately one-third of female distance runners develop amenorrhea (cessation of menstruation) during their training and competitive seasons. *B,* The average number of menses per year is lower in runners and joggers than in controls. Further evaluation of the menstrual patterns of female runners is given in the inset. (Based on data from Dale et al.[24])

ners were defined as those females who ran more than 30 miles per week and combined long, slow-distance running with speed work. Joggers, on the other hand, were defined as those females who ran slow and easy and only 5 to 30 miles per week. The average number of menses per year for controls was 11.85, for joggers 10.32, and for runners 9.16 (Figure 14-26*B*).

Further evaluation of the menstrual patterns of female runners is given in the inset of Figure 14-26*B.* Note that as many as 24% of the runners had 5 or fewer menses per year. Also, although not shown in the figure, the incidence of amenorrhea appears to be significantly greater in those female runners and joggers with late onset of menarche, who had not experienced pregnancy, or who had taken contraceptive hormones.[2,24,37,40,127]

The exact cause of amenorrhea in female athletes is not known. However, whatever the cause, it appears to be related to the intensity of training. For example, as shown in Figure 14-27, the incidence of amenorrhea in female middle-distance runners was found to be directly related to their weekly training mileage.[40,82] This can be interpreted to mean that the amenorrhea is caused by the training or competition itself, or by some other factors related to chronic exercise training, such as loss of body weight,[23,24] or general psychological stress.[58] In the case of the training itself, it is important to point out that the more intense training could lead to better performance and thus more stress.[40]

Excessive weight loss through a reduc-

tion of the body fat stores has been shown to be associated with amenorrhea.[50,51,117,125] Since fat stores of many female athletes, particularly long-distance runners and gymnasts, are much lower than nonathletes', this remains a possible cause of amenorrhea in these athletes. However, it should be emphasized that there is probably no single amount of body fat loss, or training for that matter, that will induce amenorrhea in every female. Instead, each female probably has a different threshold for amenorrhea, which may be related to any of the previously mentioned factors.[24]

Finally, the question of what happens to these kinds of menstrual disorders once exercise training and competition is stopped needs to be answered. As might be expected, the complete answer to this question is not yet available. However, based on the results of one study involving a group of young female swimmers,[38] it appears that once competition and training are stopped, the menses resumes a normal pattern, and the childbearing functions of the female are normal in every respect. Presumably, this would apply to other sports as well.

Dysmenorrhea (painful menstruation) is probably neither aggravated nor cured by sports participation. If anything, it may be less common in those women who are physically active than in those who are not.[37,74,111,138] However, 30% of a group of competitive swimmers stated that swimming caused pain in the lower part of the abdomen.[8] At any rate, dysmenorrhea, if not severe, should not hinder performance—at least from a physiological standpoint. However, it is recognized that psychological factors also play an important role.

Figure 14-27. The incidence of amenorrhea in female middle-distance runners is directly related to their weekly training mileage. (Modified and redrawn from Feicht et al.[40])

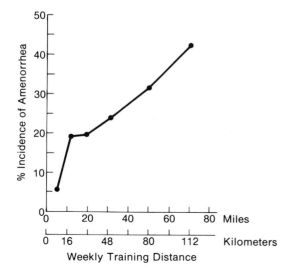

Performance and Menstruation

In Table 14-4 is a compilation of findings obtained from a variety of female athletes relative to their performance during men-

TABLE 14-4

Performance During Menstruation

Caliber of Performance	Reference	Sport	Performance			
			Better %	No Change %	Poorer %	Variable
Olympics	76	Track and field	29	63	8	—
Olympics	65	Variety	19	43	38	—
Olympics	137	Variety	3	37	17	28
Unspecified	37	Variety	13–15	42–48	31–38	—
Unspecified	7	Swimming	4	48	48	—

struation. In general, these results show that for the majority of young athletes, physical performance itself is not materially affected by the menstrual period. However, there is considerable individual variation. Of those female athletes reporting poorer performances during menstruation, a large percentage were endurance athletes (e.g., tennis players and rowers). Performances for volleyball and basketball players and swimmers and gymnasts were better than for the endurance athletes, but were still below normal. Performances by track-and-field athletes, especially sprinters, were not affected nearly so much by menstruation as were the performances by other athletes.[37] Gold-medal performances have been reported in swimming and track and field.[68]

From a physiological standpoint, metabolic and cardiovascular responses at rest and during maximal exercise are not systematically affected during different phases of the menstrual cycle. An example of this is shown in Figure 14-28. In this study,[47,48] metabolic and cardiovascular responses were determined at rest and during exercise on eight trained female athletes and nine untrained females during the following three phases of the menstrual cycle: (1) 7 days after ovulation (premen-

strual phase), (2) 3 days after the onset of bleeding (menstrual phase), and (3) 13 days after the onset of bleeding (postmenstrual phase). As can be seen, none of the responses, either at rest or during exercise, was significantly affected by the different phases of the cycle. Similar results have been found by others,[1,106] although some minor physiological fluctuations at rest, but not during exercise, have also been reported.[52]

Training and Competition during Menstruation

Whether or not female athletes should train and/or compete during their menstrual flow (menses) is again an individual matter. As shown in Table 14-5, 69% of the Olympic sportswomen surveyed at the Tokyo games always competed during menstruation. However, only 34% trained during menstruation.[138] Out of the 31% who sometimes competed during menstruation, all competed in major meets, especially those involving team competition. A similar trend was found for a group of young female swimmers; out of 27 girls, only 7 trained during menstruation; whereas all competed if an event coincided with their menstruation.[8]

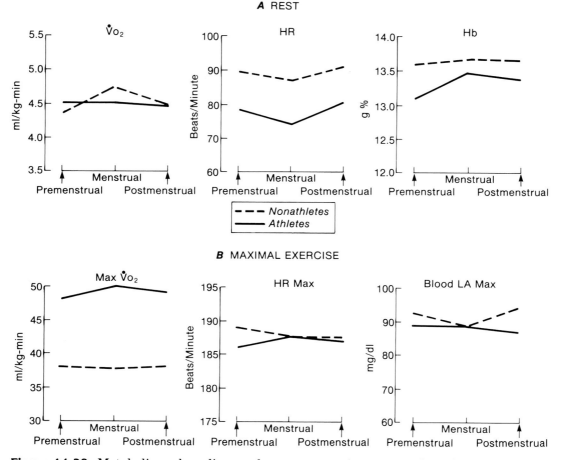

Figure 14-28. Metabolic and cardiovascular responses, *A,* at rest and, *B,* during maximal exercise are not systematically affected during the premenstrual phase (7 days after ovulation), the menstrual phase (3 days after the onset of bleeding), and the postmenstrual phase (13 days after the onset of bleeding) of the menstrual cycle. (Based on data from Fox et al.[47] and Martin.[88])

From a medical standpoint, there is some disagreement regarding sports participation during menses. Some physicians believe that participation (training and competition) should not be allowed in those sports in which there is a greater incidence of menstrual disorders. As mentioned above, these are sports such as long-distance running, skiing, gymnastics, tennis, and rowing. It should be mentioned here that nearly all physicians advise against swimming while menstruating.[8,37] This is interesting, since it has been determined that during menstruation, there is no bacterial contamination of the water in the pool[111] and no sign of any enhanced bacterial infections of the reproductive organs of the swimmers.[8] In addition, Dr. A. J. Ryan has suggested that the use of the intravaginal tampon has made it both convenient and comfortable for most female swimmers during menstruation.[111]

TABLE 14-5

Survey of Olympic Sportswomen Concerning Participation in Training and Competition During Menstruation*

	Participation During Menstruation (%)		
	Always	Sometimes	Never
Training	34	54	12
Competition	69	31	

*Data from Zaharieva.[138]

From the preceding information, it is reasonable to suggest that female athletes should be allowed to train and compete in any sport during menstruation provided they know through experience that no unpleasant symptoms will occur and that their performance will not be greatly affected. It might be further observed that with the level of competition in modern sport, the athlete cannot afford the luxury of missing three or four days of practice. For the majority of competitive athletes, the thought of missing training is not even considered. In addition, it is equally reasonable that no female athlete should be forced or ordered to train or compete during menstruation if, by doing so, she feels uncomfortable and performs very poorly during this time.

Menstruation and Iron Deficiency

Hemoglobin's ability to combine with oxygen is related to its iron (heme) component (p. 232). Thus adequate body stores of iron are necessary in order to prevent what is referred to as *iron-deficiency anemia*. Anemia refers to a decreased number of red blood cells. In iron-deficiency anemia, the decreased number of red blood cells is linked to iron deficiency since the majority of iron taken in is used for the production of new hemoglobin.

As mentioned earlier in this chapter, there is some evidence to suggest that females are more susceptible to iron deficiency than are males due to the loss of iron through menstruation. In particular, female athletes may be further affected because of the possibility of a greater iron need during physical training.[15,26,35,60] For example, some studies[11,71] have shown significant decreases in serum iron in females following physical training while others[35] have shown significant decreases in iron stores. On the other hand, studies have also been reported that show no significant alterations in serum iron levels, hemoglobin concentration, or iron-binding capacity in females following physical training.[46,137] This has been found to be true with and without oral iron supplementation.[19,101]

With respect to iron deficiency and oral iron supplementation in female athletes, the following conclusion from a study conducted by Pate, Maguire, and Van Wyk[101] is appropriate:

> We conclude that there is no basis for recommending that all women athletes routinely ingest oral iron supplements for prophylactic purposes. However, certain individual athletes (those who are iron deficient and/or anemic) may require dietary iron supplementation. We recommend that coaches, trainers, and team physicians maintain a constant awareness that a significant percentage of women are iron deficient and consequently are at increased risk of developing anemia. We suggest that tests of Hb and iron storage be included in the medical screening of women athletes and that such tests be repeated whenever an athlete experiences an unexplained drop-off in endurance performance.

The Breast, Reproductive Organs, Pregnancy, and Childbirth

Earlier, we mentioned that weight training in the female was widely misunderstood by physical educators, coaches, and parents alike. So, too, is the concept of what effects physical activity and athletic participation have on injuries to the breasts and reproductive organs and on pregnancy and childbirth.

Injuries to the Breast and Reproductive Organs

Actually, injuries to the reproductive organs are less frequent and less severe in the female than in the male. The most common injury in the female is to the breasts. For example, repeated blows to the breast can lead to contusions and hemorrhages into the loose fatty tissue. This, in turn, may result in fat necrosis (death of fatty tissue), a condition which clinically is difficult to differentiate from carcinoma or cancer.[74] It is advisable for females to use breast protectors in most sports where there may be body contact. In noncontact sports, it is also advisable to wear a good supportive bra in order to minimize the up and down and lateral excursions of the breasts resulting from running and jumping.[112]

Injuries to the female genital organs, though rare, are usually confined to minor contusions and lacerations of the external genitalia.[111] The internal organs, i.e., the uterus, fallopian tubes, and ovaries are extremely well protected by virtue of their position deep within the bony pelvis. The only known serious injury to these organs was rupture of the vaginal wall resulting from the forceful entry of water into the vagina following a fall in water skiing.[104] This can result in salpingitis (inflammation of a fallopian tube), pelvic peritonitis (inflammation of the serous membrane lining the pelvis), and vaginal hemorrhage from ruptured uterine arteries. In this regard, it is suggested that rubber wet suits be worn by females when water skiing. Otherwise, participation in physical activities and athletics does not predispose the female to serious or permanent injury to the breasts or reproductive organs.

It should be mentioned here that, in general, female athletes sustain the same injuries in relatively the same numbers as do male athletes, with perhaps only injuries related to the patella (knee) and joints occurring more often in females.[59,131]

Pregnancy and Childbirth

There are two schools of thought concerning the effects of athletic participation on pregnancy and childbirth.[37] One opinion is that because of the hypertrophy of the pelvic musculature accompanying sports participation, the muscles become less extensible and thus cause difficulties during labor and delivery. The other theory emphasizes the favorable effects on labor and delivery of stronger abdominal muscles. Several surveys have been conducted in order to clarify this issue[37,138]; the results are given in Table 14-6. In general, it is quite clear that female athletes tend to have fewer pregnancy- and childbirth-related complications than do normal non-athletic women.

There are three more questions relevant to pregnancy and childbirth that need attention: (1) Should female athletes compete during pregnancy? (2) How is performance affected after childbirth? (3) What

TABLE 14-6

Effects of Athletic Participation on Pregnancy and Childbirth

Variable	Athlete Versus Nonathlete
Complications of pregnancy	Fewer
Duration of labor	Shorter
Number of cesarean sections	Fewer
Tissue ruptures during delivery	Fewer
Spontaneous abortions	Fewer

effects do oral contraceptives (birth control pills) have on performance?

In answering the first question, championship-level athletes have been known to compete during the first 3 or 4 months of their pregnancies and some even up to a few days prior to the onset of labor.[37,121] It was reported recently that one runner was 6½ months into her pregnancy while recording a time of 4 hours in the first U.S. Olympic Marathon Trials. Ten weeks later she delivered a healthy son.[96] Also, the female bronze medalist in swimming in the 1952 Olympics was pregnant.[109] Further, exercise has been shown *not* to constitute a more severe physiological stress during pregnancy than before, provided lifting activities are minimized.[75] Indeed it is recognized that physicians frequently prescribe various forms of exercise during pregnancy.[112] In a case study,[29] the max $\dot{V}O_2$ of a female was followed before, during, and after pregnancy. The results are shown in Figure 14-29. Although the max $\dot{V}O_2$ fell during pregnancy, this was probably a function of the training mileage, which also fell. Two important points to note are: (1) the max $\dot{V}O_2$ increased during pregnancy by about 10% and (2) the max $\dot{V}O_2$ returned to control values after parturition (postpartum). It was concluded that during normal pregnancy and lactation, max $\dot{V}O_2$ and endurance performance can be improved by physical training without harmful effects on the mother or child.[29]

This preceding information shows that pregnancy per se does not always adversely affect athletic participation or exercise performance. It also shows that the opposite is true; i.e., athletics or exercise per se do not adversely affect pregnancy. Nevertheless, it must be emphasized that the advisability of participation in athletics and exercise programs during pregnancy should be determined on an individual basis and always with the approval of a physician.

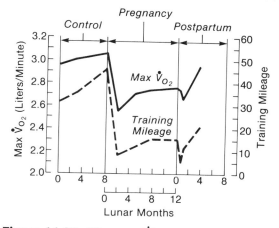

Figure 14-29. The max $\dot{V}O_2$ of a female before (control), during, and after (postpartum) pregnancy. Although the max $\dot{V}O_2$ fell during pregnancy, this was probably a function of the training mileage, which also fell. Note that the max $\dot{V}O_2$ increased by 10% during pregnancy and returned to control values after pregnancy. (Based on data from Dressendorfer.[29])

With respect to performance following childbirth, 46% of the female athletes who participated in the Tokyo Olympics (1964) and continued athletic competition after delivery, bettered their results by the end of the first year after childbirth; 31% more bettered their performances between the first and second year after childbirth.[138] Similar results were obtained from other groups of sportswomen.[95,105] Apparently, childbirth does not limit athletic performance. Furthermore, it has been shown that mild to heavy exercise does not influence max $\dot{V}O_2$, coronary blood flow in response to stress, or myocardial structure in the male offspring of rats trained during pregnancy.[135] In other words, there appears to be no harmful effects of exercise during pregnancy on the offspring.

Birth control pills have now been used by a great majority of females for a considerable amount of time. Yet the effects of these chemicals (hormones) on athletic performance are still unknown. One study, however, has indicated that females who take birth control pills are less active than those who don't take them.[94] Another more recent study[136] has indicated that both muscular endurance and total force output are nearly 20% lower in females who use oral contraceptives compared to those who do not (Fig. 14-30). Although much more research is needed to clarify this issue, some medical authorities feel that in light of the already-known metabolic effects of these pills, it would be surprising to find no alterations in performance.[121]

Guidelines for Female Participation in Sports

To assist those who may be involved in making decisions regarding participation in sport by girls and young women, the Committee on Pediatric Aspects of Physical Fitness, Recreation, and Sports offers the following guidelines[18]:

Figure 14-30. Both muscular endurance and total force output are nearly 20% lower in females who use oral contraceptives compared with those who do not use them. (Based on data from Wirth and Lohman.[136])

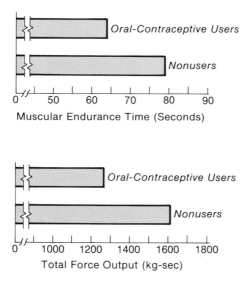

1. There is no reason to separate prepubescent children by sex in sports, physical education, and recreational activities.
2. Girls can compete against girls in any sports activity if matched for size, weight, skill, and physical maturation, as long as the customary safeguards for protection of health and safety in sports and competitive athletics are followed.
3. Girls can attain high levels of physical fitness through strenuous conditioning activities to improve their physical fitness, agility, strength, appearance, endurance, and sense of psychic well-being. These have no unfavorable influences on menstruation, future pregnancy, and childbirth.
4. Postpubescent girls should not participate against boys in heavy collision sports because of the grave risk of serious injury due to their lesser muscle mass per unit of body weight.
5. The talented female athlete may participate on a team with boys in an appropriate sport provided that the school or community offers opportunities for all girls to participate in comparable activities.

With respect to female participation in long-distance running, the American College of Sports Medicine offers the following opinion[2]:

It is the opinion of the American College of Sports Medicine that females should not be denied the opportunity to compete in long-distance running. There exists no conclusive scientific or medical evidence that long-distance running is contraindicated for the healthy, trained female athlete. The American College of Sports Medicine recommends that females be allowed to compete at the national and international level in the same distances in which their male counterparts compete.

Summary

The purpose of this chapter was to emphasize some of the physiological responses of girls and women to both exercise and physical training.

With respect to world records in track and field and freestyle swimming, performances by men are better than by women. However, the performance of women is closer to men in swimming than in running or jumping. In running, women's performance is closest to men's in sprints, whereas in swimming it is closest in the distance events.

On the average, women are shorter and lighter, with more fatty tissue and less muscle mass than men. This is also true when female athletes are matched against male athletes for any given sport. Some of the performance differences between men and women can thus be explained by these body composition and size differences. This is brought out by the fact that performance and body size differences between prepubescent boys and girls are minimal.

Females have the same concentrations of muscular $ATP + PC$ as men, but because of their lesser total muscle mass, the total body stores of these phosphagens are smaller. However, female performances in the shortest events (running 100 meters), in which $ATP + PC$ are important sources of energy, are close to the men's performances.

Women tend to have lower levels of lactic acid in their blood following maximal exercise than men. Again, one reason for this is the female's lesser muscle mass. However, the worst events for females compared with those of males, involve performance times of around 1 to 4 minutes. This indicates that females may be at a real disadvantage when competing in those events that involve the LA system to a large extent.

The maximal aerobic power (max $\dot{V}O_2$) of the female is lower than that of the male. Once again, this difference appears to be due mainly to body size factors, including less hemoglobin and blood volume, and a smaller heart volume. This is illustrated by the fact that differences in max $\dot{V}O_2$ are negligible in young boys and girls, when body size differences are also minimal. When max $\dot{V}O_2$ is expressed relative to body size, particularly with respect to active muscle mass, differences in aerobic power between sexes are small. Performances by females in distance events are relatively good, especially in swimming. In running, since the female must use her total body weight, she is clearly at a disadvantage with respect to max $\dot{V}O_2$.

Although the absolute strength of the female is only about two-thirds that of the male, the quality of the muscle fibers, so far as the ability to exert force is concerned, is independent of sex. With respect to strength development, relative strength increases in the female are the same or even better than in males following similar weight-training programs. Also, from a weight-training program, females can expect little or no change in total body weight, a decrease in body fat, and an increase in muscle size (hypertrophy). The latter is much less pronounced in the female compared with that of the male, presumably because of lower levels of testosterone. Strength-training programs for females do not cause excessive muscular bulk or produce a masculinizing effect.

Present information concerning physical training indicates that training frequency, duration, and intensity have similar effects on both sexes. In other words, comparable physiological and biochemical changes leading to greater working capacity can be produced in both sexes following similar training programs. Minimally, such programs should be 7 to 8 weeks in duration with 2 or 3 training sessions per week and should be intensive enough to raise the heart rate above 70% of the maximum.

Mild exercise does not appear to have a significant effect on menstrual disorders. In fact, dysmenorrhea is less common in physically active womem than in those who are sedentary. However, heavy intensive training has been found to induce amenorrhea (cessation of menstruation) in some athletes, particularly long-distance runners and gymnasts. The amenorrhea is temporary and uncomplicating and disappears upon cessation of heavy training. In addition, some female athletes may be particularly susceptible to iron deficiency anemia because of heavy blood loss during menstruation and a demanding physical training program.

For the majority of young athletes, performance is not materially affected by the menstrual period. Therefore female athletes should be allowed to train and compete in any sport during menstruation provided that they know that no unpleasant symptoms will occur and that their performances will not be greatly affected.

Serious injuries to either the breats or external and internal reproductive organs are rare in females even in contact sports. Complications of pregnancy and childbirth are fewer in female athletes than in non-athletes. Pregnancy per se does not adversely affect athletic participation or exercise performance and vice versa. Following childbirth, performance returns or even exceeds previous levels within a year or two. Although the effects of birth control pills on exercise are not exactly known, it is felt that they could alter performance.

Questions

1. What track events and freestyle swimming events do women perform best in comparison with men?
2. Describe the differences in body composition and size between men and women and between boys and girls.
3. How are the preceding differences in body composition and size related to running and swimming performances in adult men and women and in boys and girls?
4. Discuss the similarities and differences between men and women in the physiological capacities of:
   a. The ATP-PC system.
   b. The LA system.
   c. The oxygen system.
5. Relate the similarities and differences in the capacities of the energy systems between the sexes to performance potential.
6. Which muscle groups are strongest and weakest in the female compared with those of the male?
7. Which body size dimensions best relate to muscular strength in both sexes?
8. Compare strength gains and body composition changes in men and women following similar weight-training programs.
9. In talking to a group of parents, the question of "muscular bulk" is raised with respect to weight training in females. What would you tell them?
10. Design a physical training program for females that would bring about significant physiological change.
11. What physiological and biochemical changes occur in females as a result of physical training?
12. What are the effects of training and athletic participation on menstruation?
13. What is iron-deficiency anemia and why are female athletes more susceptible to it than males?
14. What are the effects of training and athletic participation on pregnancy and childbirth?
15. What effect does childbirth have on subsequent athletic performance?

References

1. Allsen, P. E., Parson, P., and Bryce, G. R.: Effect of the menstrual cycle on maximum oxygen uptake. *Physician Sportsmed.* 5:53–55, 1977.
2. American College of Sports Medicine. Opinion statement on the participation of the female athlete in long-distance running. *Sports Med Bull.* 15(1):1,4–5, 1980.

3. Anderson, M. D., Cote, R. W., Coyle, E. F., and Roby, F. B.: Leg power, muscle strength, and peak EMG activity in physically active college men and women. *Med Sci Sports.* 11(1):81–82, 1979.

4. Asmussen, E.: Muscular performance. In Rodahl, K., and Horvath, S. (eds.): *Muscle as a Tissue.* New York, McGraw-Hill, 1962, pp. 161–175.

5. Asmussen, E., and Heeboll-Nielsen, K.: Physical performance and growth in children: influence of sex, age and intelligence. *J Appl Physiol.* 8:371–380, 1956.

6. Åstrand, I.: Aerobic work capacity in men and women with specific reference to age. *Acta Physiol Scand.* 49(Suppl):169, 1960.

7. Åstrand, P. O.: *Experimental Studies of Physical Working Capacity in Relation to Sex and Age.* Copenhagen, Ejnar Munksgaard, 1952.

8. Åstrand, P. O., Eriksson, B., Nylander, I., Engstrom, L., Karlbert, P., Saltin, B., and Thoren, C.: Girl swimmers. *Acta Paediat.* (Suppl)147, 1963.

9. Atomi, Y., Ito, K., Iwasaki, H., and Miyashita, M.: Effects of intensity and frequency of training on aerobic work capacity of young females. *J Sports Med.* 18(1):3–9, 1978.

10. Bar-Or, O.: Predicting athletic performance. *Physician Sportsmed.* 3:80–85, 1975.

11. Bottiger, L. E., Nyberg, A., Åstrand, I., and Åstrand, P. O.: Iron administration to healthy, physically very active students. *Nord Med.* 85:396–398, 1971.

12. Brisson, G. R., Volle, M. A., Desharnais, M., DeCarnfel, D., and Audet, A.: Exercise-induced blood prolactin responses and sports habits in young women. *Med Sci Sports.* 11(1):91, 1979.

13. Brown, C., and Wilmore, J.: The effects of maximal resistance training on the strength and body composition of women athletes. *Med Sci Sports.* 6:174–177, 1974.

14. Brynteson, P., and Sinning, W.: The effects of training frequencies on the retention of cardiovascular fitness. *Med Sci Sports.* 5:29–33, 1973.

15. Buskirk, E. R., and Haymes, E. M.: Nutritional requirements for women in sport. Women and Sports: A National Research Conference. *Pa. State HPER Series.* 2:339–374, 1972.

16. Chaloupka, E.: *The Physiological Effects of Two Maintenance Programs following Eight Weeks of Interval Training.* Doctoral Dissertation. The Ohio State University, Columbus, Ohio, 1972.

17. Cohen, K.: *Metabolic Alterations with Sprint Versus Endurance Interval Training in Females.* Doctoral Dissertation. The Ohio State University, Columbus, Ohio, 1975.

18. Committee on Pediatric Aspects of Physical Fitness, Recreation, and Sports: Participation in Sports by Girls. *Pediatrics.* 55:563, 1975.

19. Cooter, G. R., and Mowbray, K. W.: Effects of iron supplementation and activity on serum iron depletion and hemoglobin levels in female athletes. *Res Q.* 49:114–117, 1978.

20. Costill, D. L., Fink, W. J., Getchell, L. H., Ivy, J. L., and Witzmann, F. M. Lipid metabolism in skeletal muscle of endurance trained males and females. *J Appl Physiol.: Respir Environ Exer Physiol.* 47(4):787–792, 1979.

21. Cotes, J., Davies, C., Edholm, O., Healy, M., and Tanner, J.: Factors related to the aerobic capacity of 46 British males and females ages 18–28 years. *Proc Roy Soc Lond B.* 74:91–114, 1969.

22. Cranford, M.: *Blood Lactate Concentrations in Female Athletes Performing Various Types and Intensities of Work.* Doctoral Dissertation, The Ohio State University, Columbus, Ohio, 1972.

23. Dale, E., Gerlach, D. H., Martin, D. E., and Alexander, C. R.: Physical fitness profiles and reproductive physiology of the female distance runner. *Physician Sportsmed.* 7(1):83–95, 1979.

24. Dale, E., Gerlach, D. H., and Wilhite, A. L.: Menstrual dysfunction in distance runners. *Obstet Gynecol.* 54(1):47–53, 1979.

25. Davies, C., Barnes, C., and Godfrey, S.: Body composition and maximal exercise performance in children. *Hum Biol.* 44:195–215, 1972.

26. DeWyn, J. F., DeJongste, J. L., Mosterd, W., and Willebrand, D.: Hemoglobin, packed cell volume, serum iron and iron binding capacity of selected athletes during training. *J Sports Med.* 11:42–51, 1972.

27. Diehl, P.: *Effects of a Season of Training and Competition on Selected Physiological Parameters in Female College Basketball Players.* Doctoral Dissertation. The Ohio State University, Columbus, Ohio, 1974.

28. Dobeln, Von, W.: Human standard and

maximal metabolic rate in relation to fat-free body mass. *Acta Physiol Scand.* 37(Suppl 126):1-79, 1956.

29. Dressendorfer, R. H.: Physical training during pregnancy and lactation. *Physician Sportsmed.* 6(2):74-75,78,80, Feb., 1978.

30. Drinkwater, B.: Aerobic power in females. *J Phys Educ Rec.* 46:36-38, 1975.

31. Drinkwater, B.: Physiological responses of women to exercise. In Wilmore, J. (ed.): *Exercise and Sport Sciences Reviews,* vol. 1. New York, Academic Press, 1973.

32. Drinkwater, B., and Horvath, S.: Detraining effects on young women. *Med Sci Sports.* 4:91-95, 1972.

33. Drinkwater, B., Horvath, S., and Wells, C.; Aerobic power of females, ages 10 to 68. *J Gerontol.* 30(4):385-394, 1975.

34. Edwards, A.: The effects of training at pre-determined heart rate levels for sedentary college women. *Med Sci Sports.* 6:14-19, 1974.

35. Ehn, L., Carlmark, B., and Hoglund, S.: Iron status in athletes involved in intense physical activity. *Med Sci Sports.* 12(1):61-64, 1980.

36. Eisenman, P. A., and Golding, L. A.: Comparison of effects of training on $\dot{V}O_2$ max in girls and young women. *Med Sci Sports.* 7(2):136-138, 1975.

37. Erdelyi, G.: Gynecological survey of female athletes. *J Sports Med.* 2:174-179, 1962.

38. Eriksson, B. O., Engstrom, I., Karlberg, P., Lunden, A., Saltin, B., and Thorne, C.: Long-term effect of previous swim-training in girls, a 10-year follow-up of the "Girl Swimmers." *Acta Paediat Scand.* 67:285-292, 1978.

39. Fahey, T. D., Rolph, R., Mongmee, R., Nagle, J., and Mortara, S.: Serum testosterone, body composition, and strength of young adults. *Med Sci Sports.* 8(1):31-34, 1976.

40. Feicht, C. B., Johnson, T. S., Martin, B. J., Sparks, K. E., and Wagner, W. W.: Secondary amenorrhea in athletes. *Lancet.* 2(8100):1145-1146; Nov. 25, 1978.

41. Forbes, G.: Growth of the lean body mass during childhood and adolescence. *J Pediat.* 64:822-827, 1964.

42. Fox, E.: Differences in metabolic alterations with sprint versus endurance interval training. In Howald, H., and Poortmans, J. (eds.): *Metabolic Adaptations to Prolonged Physical Exercise.* Basel, Switzerland, Birkhauser Verlag, 1975, pp. 119-126.

43. Fox, E.: Measurement of the maximal alactic (phosphagen) capacity in man. *Med Sci Sports.* 5:66, 1973.

44. Fox, E., Bartels, R., Billings, C., O'Brien, R., Bason, R., and Mathews, D.: Frequency and duration of interval training programs and changes in aerobic power. *J Appl Physiol.* 38(3):481-484, 1975.

45. Fox, E., Billings, C., Bartels, R., Bason, R., and Mathews, D.: Fitness standards for male college students. *Int Z Angew Physiol.* 31:231-236, 1973.

46. Fox, E., and Cohen, K.: Unpublished data, 1975.

47. Fox, E. L., Martin, F. L., and Bartels, R. L.: Metabolic and cardiorespiratory responses to exercise during the menstrual cycle in trained and untrained subjects. *Med Sci Sports.* 9(1):70, 1977.

48. Freedson, P., Katch, V. L., Sady, S., and Weltman, A.: Cardiac output differences in males and females during mild cycle ergometer exercise. *Med Sci Sports.* 11(1):16-19, 1979.

49. Fringer, M., and Stull, G.: Changes in cardiorespiratory parameters during periods of training and detraining in young adult females. *Med Sci Sports.* 6(1):20-25, 1974.

50. Frisch, R. E.: Fatness and the onset and maintenance of menstrual cycles. *Res Reprod.* 9:1, 1977.

51. Frisch, R. E., and McArthur, J. W.: Menstrual cycles: fatness as a determinant of minimum weight for height necessary for this maintenance or onset. *Science.* 185:949-951, Sept. 13, 1974.

52. Garlick, M. A., and Bernauer, E. M.: Exercise during the menstrual cycle. *Res Q.* 39(3):533-542, 1968.

53. Gisolfi, C. V., and Cohen, J. S.: Relationships among training, heat acclimation, and heat tolerance in men and women: the controversy revisited. *Med Sci Sports.* 11(1):56-59, 1979.

54. Hagerman, F., Fox, E., Conners, M., and Pompei, J.: Metabolic responses of women rowers during ergometric rowing. *Med Sci Sports.* 6(1):87, 1974.

55. Hagerman, F., and Fox, E.: Unpublished data, 1974.

56. Hale, R. W.: Factors important to women engaged in vigorous physical activity. In

Strauss, R. H. (ed.): *Sports Medicine.* Philadelphia, W. B. Saunders, 1984.

57. Hanson, J., and Nedde, W.: Long-term physical training effect in sedentary females. *J Appl Physiol.* 37:112–116, 1974.

58. Harris, D. (quoted in): Secondary amenorrhea linked to stress. *Physican Sportsmed.* 6(10):24, 1978.

59. Haycock, C. E., and Gillette, J. V.: Susceptibility of women athletes to injury: myths vs. reality. *JAMA* 236(2):163–165, 1976.

60. Haymes, E. M.: Iron deficiency and the active women. *DGWS Research Reports: Women in Sports.* Washington, D.C., AAHPER Press, 1973, 2:91–97.

61. Hetrick, G. A., and Wilmore, J. H.: Androgen levels and muscle hypertrophy during an eight week weight training program for men/women. *Med Sci Sports.* 11(1):102, 1979.

62. Hettinger, T.: *Physiology of Strength.* Springfield, Ill., Charles C Thomas, 1961.

63. Hoopeler, H., Luthi, P., Claassen, H., Weibel, E. R., and Howald, H.: The ultrastructure of the normal human skeletal muscle. A morphometric analysis on untrained men, women, and well-trained orienteers. *Pflugers Arch.* 344:217–232, 1973.

64. Hultman, E., Bergstrom, J., and McLennan Anderson, N.: Breakdown and resynthesis of phosphorylcreatine and adenosine triphosphate in connection with muscular work in man. *Scand J Clin Lab Invest.* 19:56–66, 1967.

65. Ingman, O.: Menstruation in Finnish top class sportswomen. In *Sports Medicine-International Symposium of the Medicine and Physiology of Sports and Athletes.* Helsinki, Finnish Association of Sports Medicine, 1952.

66. Ikai, M., and Fukunaga, T.: Calculation of muscle strength per unit cross-sectional area of human muscle by means of ultrasonic measurements. *Int Z Angew Physiol.* 26:26–32, 1968.

67. James, S., and Brubaker, C.: Biochemical and neuromuscular aspects of running. In Wilmore, J. (ed.): *Exercise and Sport Sciences Reviews,* vol. 1. New York, Academic Press, 1973, pp. 189–216.

68. Jokl, E.: Some clinical data on women athletes. *J Assoc Physical Mental Rehab.* 10(2):48–49, 1956.

69. Kalamen, J.: *Measurement of Maximum Muscular Power in Man.* Doctoral Dissertation, The Ohio State University, Columbus, Ohio, 1968.

70. Katch, F., Michael, E., and Jones, E.: Effects of physical training on the body composition and diet of females. *Res Q.* 40:99–104, 1969.

71. Kilbom, A.: Physical training in women. *Scand J Clin L Invest.* 28(Suppl):119, 1971.

72. Kjellberg, S., Rudhe, U., and Sjostrand, T.: Increase of the amount of hemoglobin and blood volume in connection with physical training. *Acta Physiol Scand.* 19:146–151, 1949.

73. Kjellberg, S., Rudhe, U., and Sjostrand, T.: The amount of hemoglobin and the blood volume in relation to the pulse rate and cardiac volume during rest. *Acta Physiol Scand.* 19:136–145, 1949.

74. Klafs, C., and Lyon, M.: *The Female Athlete,* 2nd ed. St. Louis, C. V. Mosby, 1978.

75. Knuttgen, H., and Emerson, K., Physiological response to pregnancy at rest and during exercise. *J Appl Physiol.* 36:549–553, 1974.

76. Kral, J., and Markalous, E.: The influence of menstruation on sports performance. In Mallwitz, A. (ed.): *Proceedings of the 2nd International Congress on Sports Medicine.* Leipzig, Theime, 1937.

77. Laubach, L.: Comparative muscular strength of men and women: a review of the literature. *Aviat Space Environ Med.* 47(5):534–542, 1976.

78. Lesmes, G. R., Fox, E. L., Stevens, C., and Otto, R.: Metabolic responses of females to high intensity interval training of different frequencies. *Med Sci Sports.* 10(4):229–232, 1978.

79. Loucks, A. B., and S. M. Horvath: Athletic amenorrhea: a review. *Med Sci Sports Exer.* 17(1):56–72, 1985.

80. Lundegren, H.: Changes in skinfold and girth measures of women varsity basketball and field hockey players. *Res Q.* 39:1020–1024, 1968.

81. McNab, R., Conger, P., and Taylor, P.: Differences in maximal and submaximal work capacity in men and women. *J Appl Physiol.* 27:644–648, 1969.

82. Mahle, J., and Cushman, S.: Menstrual patterns in female runners. *Physician Sportsmed.* 10(9):60–72, 1982.

83. Maksud, M., Wiley, R., Hamilton, L., and Lockhart, B.: Maximal $\dot{V}O_2$, ventilation,

and heart rate of Olympic speed skating candidates. *J Appl Physiol.* 29:186-190, 1970.

84. Malina, R., Harper, A., Avent, H., and Campbell, D.: Age at menarche in athletes and non-athletes. *Med Sci Sports.* 5(1):11-13, 1973.

85. Malina, R., Harper, A., Avent, H., and Campbell, D.: Physique of female track and field athletes. *Med Sci Sports.* 3:32-38, 1971.

86. Malina, R. M., Spirduso, W. W., Tate, C., and Baylor, A. M.: Age at menarche and selected menstrual characteristics in athletes at different competitive levels and in different sports. *Med Sci Sports.* 10(3):218-222, 1978.

87. Margaria, R., Aghemo, P., and Rovelli, E.: Measurement of muscular power (anaerobic) in man. *J Appl Physiol.* 21:1662-1664, 1966.

88. Martin, F. L.: *Effects of the Menstrual Cycle on Metabolic and Cardiorespiratory Responses.* Doctoral Dissertation, The Ohio State University, Columbus, Ohio, 1976.

89. Massicotti, D. R., Avon, G., and Corrivean, G.: Comparative effects of aerobic training on men and women. *J Sports Med.* 19(1):23-32, 1979.

90. Mayhew, J., and Gross, P.: Body composition changes in young women with high resistance weight training. *Res Q.* 45:433-440, 1974.

91. Medved, R.: Body height and predisposition for certain sports. *J Sports Med.* 6:89-91, 1966.

92. Moody, D., Kollias, J., and Buskirk, E.: The effect of a moderate exercise program on body weight and skinfold thickness in overweight college women. *Med Sci Sports.* 1:75-80, 1969.

93. Moody, D., Wilmore, J., Girandola, R., and Royce, J.: The effects of a jogging program on the body composition of normal and obese high school girls. *Med Sci Sports.* 4(4):210-213, 1972.

94. Morris, N., and Udry, J.: Depression of physical activity by contraceptive pills. *Am J Obstet Gynecol.* 104:1012-1014, 1969.

95. Noack, H.: Duet. Med. Wochenschr. Cited by Thomas, C. Special problems of the female athlete. In Ryan, A., and Allman, F. (eds.): *Sports Medicine.* New York, Academic Press, 1974, pp. 347-373.

96. O'Brian, R.: Rising expectations. *Runner.* 8(4):56-61, 1985.

97. Otto, R. M.: *Metabolic Responses of Young Women to Training and Maintenance Detraining.* Doctoral Dissertation, The Ohio State University, Columbus, Ohio, 1977.

98. Otto, R. M., Fox, E. L., and Stevens, C. J.: Metabolic responses of young women to training and maintenance/detraining. *Med Sci Sports.* 19(1):52, 1978.

99. Oyster, N., and Wooten, E.: The influence of selected anthropometric measurements on the ability of college women to perform the 35 yard dash. *Med Sci Sports.* 3:130-134, 1971.

100. Pate, R. R., Barnes, C., and Miller, W.: A physiological comparison of performance-matched female and male distance runners. *Res Q Exer Sport.* 56(3):245-250, 1985.

101. Pate, R. R., Maguire, M., and Van Wyk, J.: Dietary iron supplementation in women athletes. *Physician Sportsmed.* 7(9):81-88, 1979.

102. Pedersen, P., and Jorgenson, K.: Maximal oxygen uptake in young women with training, inactivity, and retraining. *Med Sci Sports.* 10(4):233-237, 1978.

103. Pendergast, D. R., diPrampero, P. E., Craig, A. B., Wilson, D. R., and Rennie, D. W.: Quantitative analysis of the front crawl in men and women. *J Appl Physiol.* 43(3):475-479, 1977.

104. Pfanner, D.: Salpingitis and water-skiing. *Med J Australia.* 1:320, 1964.

105. Pfeiffer, W.: Top performance of women and their influence on constitution, fertility, and proceedings of birth. *Rev Anal Educ Phys Sports.* 8:2, 1966.

106. Phillips, M.: Effect of the menstrual cycle on pulse rate and blood pressure before and after exercise. *Res Q.* 39(2):327-333, 1968.

107. Flowman, S. A., Drinkwater, B. L., and Horvath, S. M.: Age and aerobic power in women: a longitudinal study. *J Gerontol.* 34(4):512-520, 1979.

108. Robinson, P.: *The Physiological Effects of Chronic Heavy Physical Training on Female Age-Group Swimmers.* Doctoral Disseration, The Ohio State University, Columbus, Ohio, 1974.

109. Robinson, S.: Experimental studies of physical fitness in relation to age. *Arbeitsphysiol.* 19:251-323, 1938.

110. Romero, L.: *The Effects of an Interval Training Program on Selected Physiological Variables in Women.* Master's Thesis, The Ohio State University, Columbus, Ohio, 1970.

111. Ryan, A.: Gynecological consideration. *J Phys Educ Res.* 46(10):40–44, 1975.

112. Schuster, K.: Equipment update: jogging bras hit the street. *Physician Sportsmed.* 7(4):125–128, 1979.

113. Shangold, M. M.: The problem: exercise during pregnancy. *Physician Sportsmed.* 8(4):40, April, 1980.

114. Shangold, M., Freeman, R., Thysen, B., and Gatz, M.: The relationship between long-distance running, plasma progesterone, and luteal phase length. *Fertil Steril.* 31(2):130–133, 1979.

115. Sinning, W.: Body composition, cardiorespiratory function and rule changes in women's basketball. *Res Q.* 44:313–321, 1973.

116. Sinning, W., and Lindberg, G.: Physical characteristics of women gymnasts. *Res Q.* 43:226–234, 1972.

117. Speroff, L., and Redwine, D.: Exercise and menstrual function. *Physician Sportsmed.* 8(5):42–52, 1980.

118. Stager, J. M., Robershaw, D., and Miescher, E.: Delayed menarche in swimmers in relation to age at onset of training and athletic performance. *Med Sci Sports Exer.* 16(6):550–555, 1984.

119. *Swimmers World.* 26(1):47–52, 1985.

120. *Swimmers World.* 26(9):43–48, 1985.

121. Thomas, C. L.: Special problems of the female athlete. In Ryan, A., and Allman, F., (eds.): *Sports Medicine.* New York, Academic Press, 1974, pp. 347–373.

122. Thomas, C. L.: Factors important to women participants in vigorous athletics. In Strauss, R. H. (ed.): *Sports Medicine and Physiology.* Philadelphia, W. B. Saunders, 1979, pp. 304–319.

123. Thorsen, M.: Body structure and design: factors in the motor performance of college women. *Res Q.* 35(3)(Suppl):418–432, 1964.

124. Trussell, J.: Menarche and fatness: reexamination of the critical body composition hypothesis. *Science.* 200:1506–1513, 1978.

125. Wakat, D. K., and Sweeney, K. A.: Etiology of athletic amenorrhea in cross-country runners. *Med Sci Sports.* 11(1):91, 1979.

126. Wells, C. L.: *Women, Sport, and Performance: A Physiological Perspective.* Champaign, Ill., Human Kinetics Publishers, 1985.

127. Wells, C. L., Hecht, L. H., and Krahenbuhl, G. S.: Physical characteristics and oxygen utilization of male and female marathon runners. *Res Q Exer Sport.* 52(3):281–285, 1981.

128. Wells, C. L., and Plowman, S. A.: Sexual differences in athletic performance: biological or behavioral? *Physician Sportsmed.* 11(8):52–63, 1983.

129. Weltman, A., Moffatt, R. J., and Stamford, B. A.: Supramaximal training in females: effects on anaerobic power output, anaerobic capacity and aerobic power. *J Sports Med.* 18:237–244, 1978.

130. Whiteside, P. A.: Men's and women's injuries in comparable sports. *Physician Sportsmed.* 8(3):130–135,138,140, 1980.

131. Wilmore, J.: Alterations in strength, body composition and anthropometric measurements consequent to a 10-week weight training program. *Med Sci Sports.* 6:133–138, 1974.

132. Wilmore, J.: Body composition and strength development. *J Phys Educ Rec.* 46(1):38–40, 1975.

133. Wilmore, J., and Brown, C.: Physiological profiles of women distance runners. *Med Sci Sports.* 6:178–181, 1974.

134. Wilson, N. C., and Gisolti, C. V.: Effects of exercising rats during pregnancy. *J Appl Physiol.* 48(1):34–40, 1980.

135. Wirth, J. C., and Lohman, T. G.: The relationship of muscle endurance to the use of oral contraceptives and vitamin B-6 status. *Med Sci Sports.* 11(1):113, 1979.

136. Wirth, J. C., Lohman, T. G., Avallone, J. P., Shire, T., and Boileau, R. A.: The effect of physical training on serum iron levels of college-age women. *Med Sci Sports.* 10(3):223–226, 1978.

137. Zaharieva, E.: Survey of sportwomen at the Tokyo Olympics. *J Sports Med.* 5: 215–219, 1965.

chapter 15

Exercise and Training for Health and Fitness

The major concepts to be learned from this chapter are as follows:

- Two major health problems in the United States and the world are cardiovascular diseases and obesity. Regular exercise training can help reduce their risks.
- The major cause of coronary heart disease is atherosclerosis, a disease that causes a narrowing of the lumen of the coronary and other arteries.
- A heart attack occurs when an artery is blocked, depriving the heart tissue of blood and oxygen.
- The three primary risk factors of coronary heart disease are cigarette smoking, high blood pressure, and high blood levels of cholesterol (lipids).

- A stroke occurs when there is interference with the blood supply to the brain.
- The mechanisms by which physical activity may reduce the occurrence or severity of coronary heart disease include increases in cardiovascular efficiency and decreases in blood lipids and blood pressure.
- The exercise prescription includes a medical evaluation and consideration of the frequency of training, the intensity of training, the duration of exercise, and the mode of exercise.

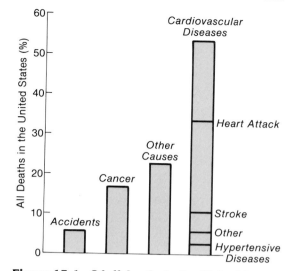

Figure 15-1. Of all deaths in the United States, more than half are due to cardiovascular diseases.

There is little doubt that proper habitual exercise training is a significant factor in reducing the severity of cardiovascular and other diseases among the peoples of the world, particularly the United States. Of all deaths in the United States, more than half are due to cardiovascular diseases. As shown in Figure 15-1, cardiovascular diseases and their incidences in the United States include: (1) heart attack, 34%; (2) stroke, 11%; (3) hypertensive diseases, 3%; and (4) others, 6%. It is encouraging that death rates due to coronary artery disease, which were at their peak in the mid-1960s, have steadily declined. The total overall reduction has been estimated at 25%. The reductions are believed to be due to a combination of improved treatment and primary prevention programs, which include exercise.

Another major health problem in the United States is obesity (overfatness). The degree of a person's obesity is somewhat difficult to define. In this discussion, however, we will consider obesity to mean anyone who weighs 20% more than their "ideal" body weight (>1.2 × IBW = obesity). As with cardiovascular diseases, more than 50% of all adults are afflicted with obesity. The incidence of cardiovascular

disease is statistically and physiologically related to obesity. For example, the obese individual has a mortality rate from cardiovascular disease that is 2½ times greater than the individual with an average or below-average body composition or weight.[39] Obese people also are more prone to have hypertension and diabetes which, when taken together, form a high-risk triad with a higher overall risk than the simple sum of the individual factors. The reasons for this will be made clearer as the known relationships between risk factors and coronary heart disease are reviewed and the additive nature of their presence in any individual is emphasized. Since the major causes of obesity are overeating and physical inactivity,[50] this means that chronic exercise training can significantly reduce both the problems of obesity and cardiovascular diseases.

Over the past 15 years, thousands of adult fitness programs have surfaced throughout the country. Many times these programs are at least in part the responsibility of physical educators and/or exercise physiologists. Therefore, it is the purpose of this chapter to discuss the essentials of adult exercise programs designed specifically for the improvement and maintenance of cardiovascular health and proper body composition.

Causes and Risk Factors of Cardiovascular Diseases

To start our discussion of exercise and health, a brief overview of some of the causes and risk factors associated with cardiovascular diseases will be presented.

As mentioned previously, the most common types of cardiovascular diseases are (1) **heart attack** or **coronary heart disease** (2) **stroke** or **apoplexy** and (3) **hypertensive diseases.**

Causes of Heart Attack

Of the total deaths in the United States due to cardiovascular disease, heart attack or coronary heart disease accounts for about 65% of them. This means that heart attack alone accounts for 35% of all deaths in the United States!

The major cause of coronary heart disease is **atherosclerosis,** a slow, progressive disease involving the narrowing of the lumen of the coronary arteries (for a review of the coronary arteries, see Fig. 10-3, p. 246). This narrowing is in turn caused by fatty substances, calcium, and other cellular sluffings being deposited on the inside wall of the arteries. Besides the narrowing effect, the arteries so afflicted become stiff or hardened, thus the term "hardening of the arteries." As shown in Figure 15-2, the narrowing is progressive and in its early stages may produce a variety of symptoms. These may include numbness of body regions, reduced organ functions, chest pain (angina) at rest and during exertion, occasional limping (intermittent claudication), and an inability to think clearly. In advanced stages, the blood flow through the artery can be completely stopped, resulting in localized tissue dying (necrosis), stroke, heart attack (myocardial infarction), kidney failure, lameness, and even death.

When complete blockage occurs in the heart, the part of the heart muscle supplied

Figure 15-2. The narrowing of the lumen of an artery by atherosclerosis is progressive. Narrowing may produce warning symptoms as shown. In an advanced stage, the blood flow through the artery can be completely blocked (occluded) resulting in permanent tissue and organ damage or even death.

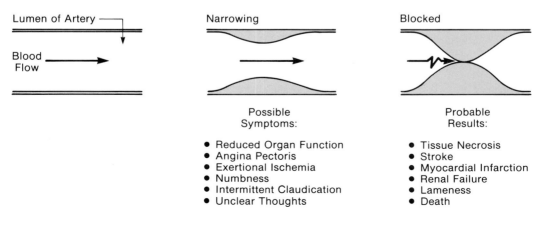

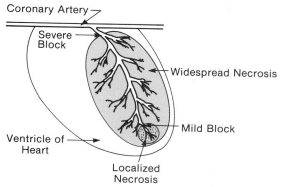

Figure 15-3. A heart attack occurs when the blood flow through a coronary artery is blocked. If the block is toward the end of the artery, the heart attack may not be too severe since the amount of heart tissue involved would be minimal. However, if the block is more toward the beginning of the artery, the amount of tissue involved would be large and the heart attack severe.

with blood by that artery dies; a heart attack is said to have occurred. The severity of the heart attack is determined by the exact location of the block within the artery. For example, as shown in Figure 15-3, if the block is toward the end of the artery, then the heart attack may not be too severe since the amount of heart tissue involved would be minimal. However, if the block is more toward the beginning of the artery, the amount of tissue involved would be large and the heart attack severe.

Blockage can occur in vessels of the body other than the heart. Certain branching portions of the arterial system are more prone to placque deposition than others, for example, the sharp right angular portions of the renal arteries from the descending aorta to the kidneys and the Y-bifurcation of the descending aorta to form the femoral arteries to the legs. As shown in Figure 15-4, the branch point of the carotid

Figure 15-4. This plug of placque, nearly an inch long, was surgically removed from the branching point of a carotid artery. Despite the size of the obstruction, the stroke patient survived.

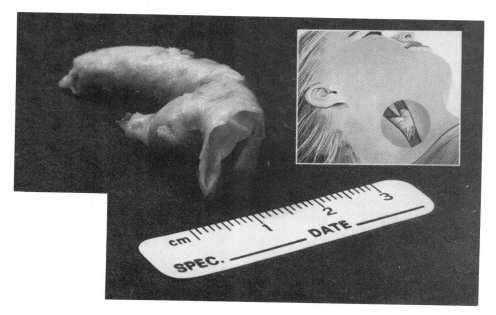

artery is another common site of athero-sclerotic placque formation.

Because atherosclerosis is a relatively slow-developing disease, it is generally thought of as an "old age" disease. However, this is not necessarily true. For example, autopsies performed on American soldiers killed in the Korean and Vietnam wars have revealed moderately advanced stages of atherosclerosis in the majority of these young men.[21,51] The beginning stages of atherosclerosis have even been found in children less than 5 years of age,[40] and 62% of children between the ages of 7 and 12 years have been found to have at least one coronary heart disease risk factor.[30,69]

Risk Factors Associated with Heart Attack

It was stated earlier in this chapter that chronic exercise training is a significant factor in reducing the severity of heart attacks. Thus one risk factor that has been identified with heart attacks is physical inactivity, or sedentary living. How to prescribe properly an exercise program for the purpose of reducing the risk of heart attack will be discussed in detail later in this chapter. Right now, what are some of the other known risk factors associated with heart attack? The most commonly identified risk factors are as follows: (1) age; (2) heredity; (3)obesity (body weight); (4) tobacco smoking; (5) exercise; (6) cholesterol or per cent fat in the diet; (7) blood pressure; (8) gender; and (9) stress.

Age

Generally, the older you are, the greater your risk for heart attack. For example, between the ages of 25 and 34, the death rate due to heart attack is about 10 in every 100,000 white males; at ages 55 to 64, this increases 100-fold to nearly 1000 deaths in every 100,000 males.

Heredity

Heredity appears to play some role in the risk of heart attack. For example, people who suffer a heart attack, particularly at an early age, have a family history of early-age heart attacks. By the same token, those who do not have heart attacks generally belong to families in which heart attacks rarely strike.

The exact way in which heredity plays a role in heart attack is not known at this time. Rather than being genetically linked, there is the possibility that family life-styles, including eating habits and physical exercise patterns, are more important in developing the tendency toward heart attack. In other words, parents who rarely exercise on a regular basis tend to raise children who also rarely exercise. Obesity is another good example; obese parents frequently raise obese children.

Obesity

As mentioned previously, the risk of heart attack increases as the proportion of body fat increases. People who are considered 20% or more overfat have a mortality rate from cardiovascular disease that is 2½ times greater than that of people with average or below-average body weight. Remember, the most common causes of obesity itself are overeating and lack of exercise. Weight loss through exercise and dieting is an effective remedy for obesity. Weight loss and obesity are discussed in more detail in Chapter 20.

Tobacco Smoking

The more cigarettes smoked per day and the longer one smokes, the greater the risk of coronary heart disease and lung cancer. As shown in Figure 15-5, a more than one-pack-a-day smoker has over twice the risk of heart attack compared with the non-smoker. Although the link between lung cancer and smoking is quite well known

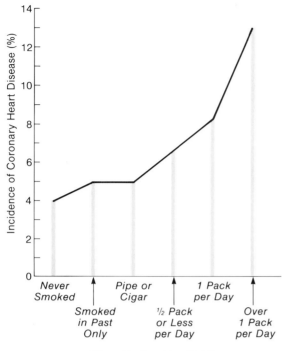

Figure 15-5. Per cent incidence of coronary heart disease in relation to cigarette smoking. A more than one-pack-a-day smoker has over twice the risk of heart attack compared with the nonsmoker. (Based on data from Loviglio.[47])

among the general public, smoking's link to coronary heart disease is not. Actually, the risk of coronary heart disease is greater in smokers than is the risk of lung cancer.

The exact physiological link between smoking and coronary heart disease is not known. However, it is thought that cigarette smoking, although not causing atherosclerosis, may initiate small blood clots that eventually may block a coronary artery already narrowed by atherosclerosis.

Exercise

Many studies have been conducted in hopes of finding conclusive evidence for the idea that increased physical activity decreases the risk of coronary heart disease. Most of these studies, however, have failed to do so. Instead, the majority of studies have only been able to *infer* that exercise and coronary heart disease are related. Nevertheless, so many studies have arrived at this same assumption that it is strongly accepted as fact.

One of the first studies to infer that exercise and coronary heart disease are related was done in 1953 in England on groups of bus drivers and bus conductors.[52] The results showed that the incidence of heart disease in the sedentary bus drivers was twice that of the more active bus conductors. While the drivers sat most of their working day, the conductors walked up and down the double-decker buses. Since this study nearly 35 years ago, many similar studies using different groups of subjects* have come to the same conclusion: *the risk of heart attack is less the more physically active you are.*

Blood Cholesterol (Lipid) Levels

The American diet is typically very rich in foods containing large amounts of *animal fats* and *cholesterol*. Animal fats, in turn, are rich in saturated fats (see Fig. 19-3, p. 530 for definition of saturated fats). Both cholesterol and these fats make up the atherosclerotic deposits on the inner lining of the arteries. In this way, high blood levels of cholesterol and triglycerides (saturated fats) are related to a high incidence of coronary heart disease. Such a relationship is shown in Figure 15-6. Note that the incidence of coronary heart disease of a person with a total blood cholesterol of over 259 mg% is nearly five times that of a person with a total blood cholesterol of under 200 mg%. Likewise, a person with a

---

*For excellent reviews, see references 25, 26, and 33.

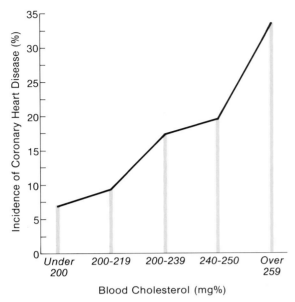

Figure 15-6. Per cent incidence of coronary heart disease in relation to total blood cholesterol levels. Note that the incidence of coronary heart disease of a person with a blood cholesterol of over 259 mg% is nearly 5 times that of a person with a blood cholesterol of under 200 mg%. (Based on data from Loviglio.[47])

total cholesterol of 220 mg% is at 2 times greater risk than someone with 180 mg%. This latter value of 180 mg% is often recommended as a health goal or standard that people should strive to achieve. The blood levels of cholesterol and saturated fats can be reduced by avoiding foods rich in these substances and by substituting vegetable fats (unsaturated fats) for animal fats (for more on saturated and unsaturated fats, see p. 529). As will be pointed out later, chronic exercise, in some but not all instances, also has been shown to reduce total blood cholesterol levels.

As mentioned in Chapter 13, total cholesterol can be separated into its subfractions on the basis of differences in their molecular densities. Not all of the subfractions of cholesterol are considered to be risk factors. In fact, the *high-density lipoprotein cholesterol (HDL)* fraction is thought to be *protective* against coronary heart disease. As will be pointed out later in this chapter, regular exercise programs have been shown to increase the HDL fraction. One of the reasons why HDLs are not harmful is that they do not collect or adhere to the inner linings of arteries. In fact, they may actually help break down the fatty deposits already present. The fatty atherosclerotic deposits are composed of *low-density* lipoprotein *(LDL)* and *very low density (VLDL)* lipoprotein cholesterol fractions. The LDL is the primary carrier of cholesterol in the bloodstream, whereas the principal lipid components of VLDL are triglycerides. The possible mechanisms by which HDL cholesterol decreases atherosclerosis include: (1) a reversal of cholesterol transport from peripheral cells to the liver for removal from the body, and (2) inhibition of LDL cholesterol uptake by cells at the LDL receptor sites.[31] Therefore, an overall low total cholesterol level, with low LDL and VLDL fractions plus a high HDL fraction, appears to be a healthy balance with respect to blood cholesterol. Ratios of 4.0 (total cholesterol:HDL cholesterol) or alternatively, 0.25 (HDL cholesterol:total cholesterol) have been suggested as healthful standards. The reader is referred to a recent review summary of the effects of physical activity on these lipid and lipoprotein subfractions.[31]

Blood Pressure (Hypertension)

High blood pressure or *hypertension* (p. 261) is another risk factor associated with coronary heart disease. As shown in Figure 15-7, an individual with a systolic blood pressure of over 150 mm Hg has over twice the risk of coronary heart disease than does someone with a pressure below 120 mm Hg. It is estimated that 15% of the entire United States' population suffers

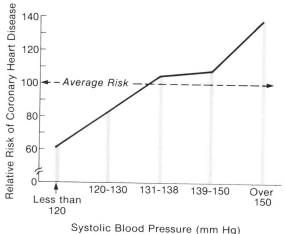

Figure 15-7. Relative risk of coronary heart disease in relation to systolic blood pressure. An individual with a systolic blood pressure of over 150 mm Hg has over twice the risk of coronary heart disease than does someone with a pressure below 120 mm Hg. (Based on data from the American Heart Association.[5])

from hypertension. For adults in the United States, about 20% of white males and females have hypertension, and about 30% of black males and females are hypertensive. Of these, the majority are classified as "essential," meaning that no known cause (and, therefore, no known cure) can be identified as causing the hypertension. Another astonishing fact is that essential hypertension in young children and young adults is on the increase in the United States.[11]

For more information on black and minority health issues in the United States, readers are referred to the report of the Secretary of the U.S. Department of Health and Human Services Task Force published in August of 1985. This report, entitled "Black and Minority Health" is available through the U.S. Government Printing Office; request document number 491-313/44706.

As mentioned in Chapter 13 (p. 348), habitual exercise training has been shown to be effective in reducing blood pressure to nearly normal values.

Gender

The incidence of coronary heart disease is greater in young males than in young females. For example, the death rate of white males between the ages of 35 and 44 years is six times that of white females of the same age. However, with older age, the incidence of coronary heart disease is about the same in men and women.

Physiologically, the lower death rate due to heart disease among young females is probably related to the production of *estrogen*. For whatever reason, this hormone is "protective" against coronary heart disease. For example, administration of estrogen to males who have previously suffered from a heart attack decreases the number of subsequent attacks. After *menopause* (cessation of menstruation), the estrogen level drops dramatically and, therefore, explains the comparable risk of coronary heart disease of the older female to the older male.

Understandably, there is little that a man can do about being at higher risk for coronary heart disease (CHD) because of his gender. This also is true for one's age and hereditary profile (family history of early coronary heart disease). These risk factors, when present, are viewed as permanent rather than modifiable. That is to say, an individual can alter his life-style, diet, exercise habits, etc., and consequently modify a number of the other risk factors. The permanent risk factors remain as a reminder that these individuals are always at some elevated risk for reasons over which they have no control and which are no fault of their own. At the same time, these higher risk individuals must be taught that they can exert considerable control over a majority of risk factors, particularly the "big three," which we will identify later.

Stress

All of us are under "pressure" or under stress at one time or another. While this in itself is not necessarily bad, the biggest problem is how we manage it. Two basic types of behavior in response to stress have been identified: *type A* and *type B*. Type A behavior is characterized by high levels of aggression, competition, and drive. For example, a type A individual always seems to be "racing the clock" no matter what it is he or she is doing. This type of behavior has been scientifically linked with increased risk of coronary heart disease.[27,28] Type B behavior, on the other hand, is just the opposite of type A, i.e., easygoing and seemingly never in a hurry to beat the clock. The risk of coronary heart disease is much less with type B behavior than with type A.

The "Big" Three Risk Factors

Of all the previously mentioned risk factors, the three most important ones are (1) cigarette smoking, (2) high blood pressure, and (3) high blood levels of cholesterol. The danger of heart attack with none or a combination of these risk factors is shown in Figure 15-8. Note that the individual risk factors are additive, i.e., 1.3× higher risk for cigarettes and cholesterol and 3.7× higher risk for cigarettes and blood pressure. If all three primary risk factors are present, the danger of a heart attack is 5 times that when none are present!

What Is Your Coronary Heart Disease Risk?

The American Heart Association has published a gamelike test, called RISKO, that can be used to estimate your coronary heart

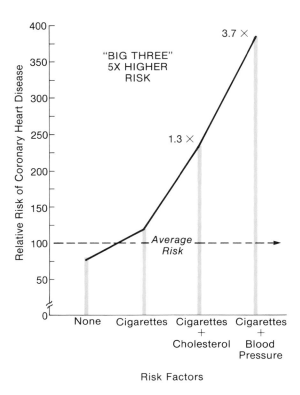

Figure 15-8. Relative risk of coronary heart disease in relation to the "big" three risk factors. If all three primary risk factors are present, the danger of a heart attack is 5 times (1.3 + 3.7) that when none are present. (Based on data from the American Heart Association.[5])

disease risk. The test is shown in Table 15-1. Here are the rules:

> The purpose of RISKO is to give you an estimate of your chances of suffering heart attack.
>
> The game is played using Table 15-1 by marking squares which—from left to right—represent an increase in your RISK FACTORS. These are medical conditions and habits associated with an increased danger of heart attack. *Not all risk factors are measurable enough to be included in this game.*
>
> *Rules.* Study each Risk Factor and its row. Find the box applicable to you and

circle the number in it. For example, if your age is 37, circle the number in the box labeled 31 to 40. After checking out all the rows, add the circled numbers. This total—your score—is an estimate of your risk.

If You Score:

6-11—Risk well below average.
12-17—Risk below average.
18-24—Risk generally average.
25-31—Risk moderate.
32-40—Risk at a dangerous level.
41-62—Danger urgent. See your doctor now.

Heredity. Count parents, grandparents, brothers, and sisters who have had heart attack and/or stroke.

Tobacco Smoking. If you inhale deeply and smoke a cigarette way down, add one to your classification. Do *not* subtract because you think you do not inhale or smoke only a half-inch on a cigarette.

Exercise. Lower your score one point if you exercise regularly and frequently.

Cholesterol or Saturated Fat Intake Level. A cholesterol blood level determination is best. If you can't get one from your doctor, then estimate honestly the percentage of solid fats you eat. These are usually of animal origin—lard, cream, butter, and beef and lamb fat. If you eat much of this, your cholesterol level probably will be high. The U.S. average, 40% total fat (animal plus vegetable) in a person's diet, is too high for good health.

Blood Pressure. If you have no recent reading but have passed an insurance or industrial examination, the chances are you have an upper reading (systolic blood pressure) of 140 or less.

Sex. This line takes into account the fact that men have between 6 and 10 times more heart attacks than women of childbearing age.

Stroke and Hypertensive Diseases

According to the American Heart Association, a *stroke* occurs when there is interference with the blood supply to the brain. In order to function, brain cells must have a continuous and ample supply of oxygen-rich blood, which if completely stopped, causes the cells to die. One of the frequent causes of stroke is the blocking of one of the arteries that supplies blood to a section of the brain by a clot that forms inside the artery. This is a condition called *cerebral (brain) thrombosis.* A clot is not likely to occur in a healthy artery. However, in arteries damaged by atherosclerosis, clots are apt to form around the deposits formed on the inner wall of the artery.

Stroke also occurs when an atherosclerotic artery in the brain bursts, flooding the surrounding tissue with blood. This is called a *cerebral hemorrhage.* Cells nourished by the artery are deprived of blood and cannot function. The accumulation of blood from the burst artery soon forms a clot. By displacing or destroying brain tissue, it may interfere with brain function, causing physical disability.

A cerebral hemorrhage is more likely to occur when a person suffers from a combination of atherosclerosis and high blood pressure. For example, the risk of stroke if you are a 45-year-old male, smoke cigarettes, and have a high blood cholesterol and high blood pressure is over 10 times that of a male of the same age with none of these risk factors. Hemorrhage of an artery in the brain may also be caused by a head injury or by a burst *aneurysm.* Aneurysms are blood-filled pouches that balloon out from a weak spot in the artery wall and are often associated with high blood pressure. Aneurysms do not always cause trouble, but when one bursts in the brain, the result is a stroke.

The result of a stroke is usually *hemiparesis* (paralysis of one side of the body). It also may result in *aphasia* (loss of the power of expression or understanding communications) or in loss of memory. The effects may be slight or severe, temporary or permanent, depending on which brain

TABLE 15-1

Cardiac Risk Index

1 Age	10 to 20	21 to 30	31 to 40	41 to 50	51 to 60	61 to 70
	1	**2**	**3**	**4**	**6**	**8**
2 Heredity	No known history of	1 relative over 60 with cardiovascular disease	2 relatives over 60 with cardiovascular disease	1 relative under 60 with cardiovascular disease	2 relatives under 60 with cardiovascular disease	3 relatives under 60 with cardiovascular disease
	1	**2**	**3**	**4**	**6**	**8**
3 Weight	More than 5 lbs below standard weight	−5 to +5 lbs standard weight	6–20 lbs overweight	21–35 lbs overweight	36–50 lbs overweight	51–65 lbs overweight
	0	**1**	**2**	**3**	**5**	**7**
4 Tobacco smoking	Nonuser	Cigar and/or pipe	10 cigarettes or less a day	20 cigarettes a day	30 cigarettes a day	40 cigarettes or more a day
	0	**1**	**2**	**4**	**6**	**10**

5 Exercise	Intensive occupational and recreational exertion **1**	Moderate occupational and recreational exertion **2**	Sedentary work and intense recreational exertion **3**	Sedentary work and moderate recreational exertion **5**	Sedentary work and light recreational exertion **6**	Complete lack of all exercise **8**
6 Cholesterol or % fat in diet	Cholesterol below 180 mg% **1**	Cholesterol 181–205 mg% **2**	Cholesterol 206–230 mg% **3**	Cholesterol 231–255 mg% **4**	Cholesterol 256–280 mg% **5**	Cholesterol 281–330 mg% **7**
	No animal or solid fats in diet **1**	10% animal or solid fat in diet **2**	20% animal or solid fat in diet **3**	30% animal or solid fat in diet **4**	40% animal or solid fat in diet **5**	50% animal or solid fat in diet **7**
7 Blood pressure	100 upper reading **1**	120 upper reading **2**	140 upper reading **3**	160 upper reading **4**	180 upper reading **6**	200 or over upper reading **8**
8 Sex	Female under 40 **1**	Female 40–50 **2**	Female over 50 **3**	Male **5**	Stocky male **6**	Bald stocky male **7**

Total score _____

RISKO is reprinted courtesy of Michigan Heart Association. © Michigan Heart Association.

cells have been damaged and how widespread the damage is. Effects also depend on how well the body can repair its system of blood supply or how rapidly other areas of the brain tissue can take over the work of the damaged cells.

Prevention of stroke through modification of risk factors is particularly important since injured brain cells cannot regenerate. Regular exercise can reduce the risk of stroke because of its effects on blood cholesterol and blood pressure.

Effects of Exercise and Training on Health and Fitness

Not all of the changes caused by exercise training mentioned in Chapter 13 are necessarily related to a decreased risk of cardiovascular diseases. In fact, the 1984 data of Paffenbarger and colleagues shown in Table 15-2 suggest that physical activity benefits may not be limited to the primary prevention of coronary heart disease. They show that persons who exercise also have a lower incidence of stroke, respiratory diseases, all cancers, and deaths from all causes than persons who do not exercise. A more recent report about this subject group indicates that exercise participation lengthens lifespan—a previously suspected but undocumented finding. It will be the purpose here, however, to review those training-induced changes that are most closely linked to improvement in cardiovascular function and thus to the reduction in coronary heart disease risk the rationale being that coronary heart disease still

---

TABLE 15-2

Cause-specific death rates per 10,000 man-years of observation, adjusted for differences in age, cigarette smoking and hypertension among 16,936 Harvard alumni, 1962-1978, by physical activity index. Note the lower rates in subjects who expended more kcal/week in physical activity. (From Paffenbarger, et al. *JAMA*. 252:491-495, 1984.[55])

Cause of Death	Physical Activity Index (kcal Per Wk)			One-Tail Test for Trend, *p*
	<500	500-1,999	2,000+	
All causes (*n* = 1,413)	84.8	66.0	62.1	<0.001
Total cardiovascular diseases (*n* = 840)	39.5	30.8	21.4	<0.001
Coronary heart disease (*n* = 441)	25.7	21.2	16.4	0.002
Stroke (*n* = 103)	6.5	5.2	2.4	0.001
Total respiratory diseases (*n* = 60)	6.0	3.2	1.5	0.001
Total cancers (*n* = 446)	25.7	19.2	19.0	0.026
Lung (*n* = 89)	6.2	3.7	4.0	0.116
Colorectal (*n* = 58)	2.2	2.3	3.5	0.091*
Pancreas (*n* = 41)	1.8	2.4	1.0	0.085
Prostate (*n* = 36)	2.2	1.5	1.8	0.359
Total unnatural causes (*n* = 146)	8.7	7.1	6.9	0.032
Accidents (*n* = 78)	3.6	3.9	3.0	0.147
Suicides (*n* = 68)	5.1	3.2	2.9	0.049

*Opposite trend.

TABLE 15-3

Mechanisms by Which Physical Activity May Reduce the Occurrence or Severity of Coronary Heart Disease*

Increase	Decrease
Coronary collateral vascularization	Serum lipid levels
Vessel size	Triglycerides
Myocardial efficiency	Cholesterol
Efficiency of peripheral blood distribution and return	Glucose intolerance
Electron transport capacity	Obesity-adiposity
Fibrinolytic capability	Platelet stickiness
Red blood cell mass and blood volume	Arterial blood pressure
Thyroid function	Heart rate
Growth hormone production	Vulnerability to dysrhythmias
Tolerance to stress	Neurohormonal overreaction
Prudent living habits	"Strain" associated with psychic "stress"
Joie de vivre ("joy of living")	

*From Fox, S. M., Naughton, J. P., and Haskell, W. L.: Physical activity and the prevention of coronary heart disease. *Ann Clin Res.* 3:404–432, 1971.

remains the number 1 killer of young and middle-aged American citizens.

Table 15-3 lists those mechanisms by which physical activity may reduce the occurrence or severity of coronary heart disease. Because some of these have already been discussed in considerable detail in Chapter 13, only coronary collateral vascularization, vessel size, fibrinolytic capability, serum lipid levels, blood pressure, and vulnerability to dysrhythmias will be mentioned in further detail here.

Coronary Collateral Vascularization

When a coronary artery supplying blood to a portion of the heart muscle (myocardium) is blocked, changes may occur in the arterial network that enable blood from other arteries to supply the affected area of the myocardium. In addition, small collateral arteries may form a natural bypass from one side of the blocked artery to the other. Apparently, these changes are caused by myocardial hypoxia, as evidenced by autopsy studies.[12,59,72]

Studies that directly confirm an increase in coronary collateral vascularization with exercise training are not numerous. In fact, most have been able to generate only indirect evidence for such an effect.[24,26,41] Perhaps the most direct study in support of exercise-induced collateralization was done on dogs some 30 years ago.[20] In this study, it was shown that coronary collateral vascularization was developed around artificially induced coronary artery constrictions in direct proportion to the amount of exercise performed. In sedentary dogs with the same degree of arterial constriction, the vascularization was not as great.

In a more recent study on humans,[16] two out of six patients with coronary heart disease showed some definite increased collateralization. However, it could not be determined whether these changes were in response to some extension of the occlusive disease or to the exercise program itself.

Before any definite conclusions can be made regarding exercise and increased coronary collateral vascularization, more research is needed.

Vessel Size

It has been known for a long time that the size of the coronary vasculature in rats is increased following regular exercise programs.[10,62,63] Such an increase facilitates coronary blood flow. No studies to date have demonstrated an increased vessel size in humans. However, autopsy studies on Clarence DeMar, the famous marathon runner, showed his coronary arteries to be two to three times normal size.[17] Since DeMar regularly ran marathon races up to the age of 69 years, it is tempting to attribute his huge coronary vessels to regular exercise training. The fact that genetics may have also been involved cannot be completely ruled out.

Blood Clotting Capability

A blood clot may lodge in a coronary artery and cause a heart attack. If the clot blocks an artery in the brain, a stroke results. If the clot is formed in the artery it blocks, it is called a *thrombus*. If it is formed in one artery, then carried to another which it then blocks, it is called an *embolus*. In either case, blood clots have serious consequences.

The clotting of blood involves a complicated series of chemical reactions, the initiation of which is triggered by damaged or traumatized tissue. A good example of damaged tissue is the inner lining of atherosclerotic arteries. The atherosclerotic plaque is rough, and as the blood flows over it, the clotting mechanism is initiated. If either the time required for clotting and/or the time required to dissolve a clot (referred to as *fibrinolysis*) is altered, the rate and number of blood clots formed would also be altered. Obviously, a slower rate of blood clotting coupled with a

faster rate of fibrinolysis would be beneficial with respect to the risk of heart attack.

Exercise has been shown to speed up both blood coagulation and the rate of fibrinolysis.[7,38,68] These changes are opposite in effect and, if equal in magnitude, offsetting. Under these conditions, exercise would appear not to have any beneficial effect on the formation of blood clots. However, research on this topic is sparse, and more is needed before a final answer can be determined.

Blood Cholesterol (Lipid) Levels

Recent research has shown that exercise not only lowers total blood cholesterol, but also increases the fraction of cholesterol known as high-density lipoproteins (HDL) and decreases the low-density lipoprotein (LDL) fraction. As mentioned previously, HDL cholesterol is thought to be protective against coronary heart disease whereas LDL is not.

Several studies have shown exercise training to cause decreases in total blood cholesterol, triglycerides, and LDL concentrations and an increase in HDL cholesterol in both men and women.[22,23,37,43,45,58,60,70,71] An example of the results of one such study is shown in Figure 15-9. In this study, the subjects were active men, ages 35–49 years, who averaged 39 miles of running per week. The nonrunners who served as the control group were of the same age span but did not exercise on a regular basis.

The results of some other training studies have been less consistent, particularly with regards to any significant reductions in total cholesterol and triglycerides.[29,65] Some of these inconsistencies may be due to the fact that the effects of training may occur only as a consequence of changes in body habitus (build or composition that might predispose one to disease), diet, smoking, alcohol intake, and use of

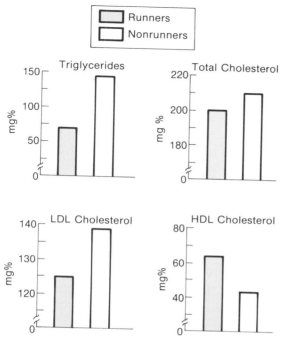

Figure 15-9. Chronic exercise training causes decreases in total blood cholesterol, triglycerides, and low-density lipoprotein (LDL-cholesterol) concentrations, and an increase in high-density lipoprotein (HDL-cholesterol) concentration in both men and women. In this study, the subjects were active men, ages 35 to 49 years, who averaged 39 miles of running per week. (Based on data from Wood et al.[71])

medications. Although it has been difficult to establish a clear independent relationship between exercise or fitness and some lipids, the following summary statement seems warranted. Evidence to date suggests that individuals with higher cholesterol, LDL, and triglyceride levels, as well as those with lower HDL levels, have favorable changes in these measurements after either endurance or resistive exercise training.[31]

Considerable interest has developed in the area of endurance-training effects on serum lipid levels in children. Little training effect on lipid profiles has been found in these studies.[46,67] This is not surprising since they involved relatively short training periods and the children had rather "normal" lipid levels before training was initiated. One study of more intensive training on school-age children has shown different results.[54] Children (20 boys, 18 girls, mean age 14.5 years) from a sport school participated in ten 45-minute periods per week of basketball and light athletics (short-distance running, long jump, high jump, etc.). A control group of 35 children (17 boys, 18 girls, mean age 14.5 years) from a standard school had only two 45-minute periods of physical exercise each week, mainly gymnastics and team games. The more active group displayed a significantly higher mean plasma HDL concentration and lower triglyceride levels. Although the difference in the intensity aspects of training are emphasized in this study, it is clear that the sport school children received a much greater overall stimulus through differences in training frequency, 10 versus 2 weekly sessions. This means that their accumulative duration of training was 5 times greater. The length of the study period was not reported but is likely one academic year since students were in their "third year" of sport or standard school.

Blood Pressure

It was mentioned in Chapter 13 that exercise training causes a decrease in blood pressure, particularly in those subjects who are hypertensive.[13,14,42,49] The results of one of these studies is shown in Figure 15-10. Notice that blood pressure at rest as well as during exercise was reduced following 6 months of exercise training. Before training, the subjects were considered borderline hypertensives; after training, they had normal blood pressures.

In a recent review of the literature concerning the effects of exercise on blood pressure, the following conclusions were noted:[15]

1. In epidemiological surveys, men in physically active occupations had lower systolic and diastolic blood pressures than did those in sedentary work.
2. Men identified as physically fit by a bicycle ergometer test had lower systolic and diastolic blood pressures than did those identified as unfit.
3. Two studies showed decreases (one did not) in both blood pressures from participation in exercise regimens of the walk-jog type. In one of these studies, the subjects had multiple coronary heart attack risk factors, including high blood pressure.
4. In one study, hypertensive men lowered their blood pressures following participation in isometric exercise over a period of 5 to 8 weeks.
5. Two studies reported improved blood pressure of postcoronary patients with elevated blood pressures as a result of aerobic-type training over a period of 3 to 8 months; matched control groups did not improve.
6. As might be expected, the effects of exercise on systolic and diastolic blood pressures of hypertensive individuals are greater than for those with blood pressures within the normal range.
7. One investigator[65] concluded that the physiological advantages from lowering blood pressure through exercise in hypertensive populations are sufficient to encourage the inclusion of exercise within most therapeutic programs designed to manage this disease.

Vulnerability to Cardiac Dysrhythmias

Cardiac dysrhythmias, or disturbances in the rhythm (beating) of the heart, may lead to serious cardiac problems, including heart attack and even death. It has been suggested that regular exercise tends to reduce the susceptibility of the heart to rhythm disturbances.[35] The physiological mechanism involved is not clear; however, it may be related to a lesser production of epinephrine and other catecholamines.

The Exercise Prescription

Now that we know how and why chronic exercise training improves cardiovascular health and reduces the risk of coronary heart disease, how should an exercise program designed to do just that be constructed?

First of all, the point has been well made that exercise programs should be individualized and specific to the group for which they are designed. Table 15-4 reflects

Figure 15-10. Chronic exercise training causes a decrease in blood pressure, particularly in those subjects who are hypertensive. Note that following exercise training (6 months in this case), the blood pressure is lowered at rest as well as during exercise. (Based on data from Choquette and Ferguson.[14])

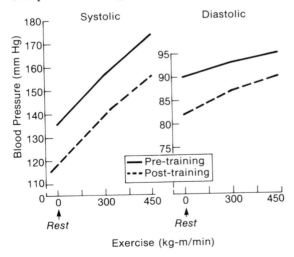

TABLE 15-4

Major health-fitness goals and specific physical activity plans for different age groups. (From Haskell et al. _Public Health Reports._ 100:202, 1985.[34])

Major Health-Fitness Goals	Physical Activity Plan*
Youth (1-14 years) • Optimal physical growth and development • Good psychological adjustment • Develop interest and skills for active lifestyle as adult • Reduction of coronary heart disease risk factors	T Emphasis on large muscle, dynamic exercise; moving body over distance and against gravity; some heavy resistive activity and flexibility exercise I Moderate to vigorous intensity D Total of more than 30 minutes per day in 1 or more sessions F Every day G Increased activity to and from school
Young adults (15-24 years) • Optimal physical growth and development • Good psychological adjustment • Reduction of coronary heart disease • Develop interest and skills for active lifestyle as adult	T Emphasis on large muscle, dynamic strength and flexibility exercise I Moderate to vigorous intensity (more than 50% max $\dot{V}_{O_2}$) D Total of more than 30 minutes per session (more than 4 kilocalories per kg of body weight) F At least every other day G Increased activity to and from school
Adults (25-65 years) • Prevention and treatment of coronary heart disease • Prevention and treatment of type II diabetes • Maintenance of optimal body composition • Enhance psychological status • Retain musculoskeletal integrity	T Emphasis on large muscle dynamic exercise; some heavy resistive and flexibility exercises I Moderate intensity (more than 50% max $\dot{V}_{O_2}$) D Total of more than 30 minutes per session (more than 4 kilocalories per kg of body weight) F At least every other day G Lower level activities (e.g., walking) every day
Older adults (over 65 years) • Maintain general functional capacity • Retain musculoskeletal integrity • Enhance psychological status • Prevent and treat coronary heart disease and type II diabetes	T Emphasis on moving about, flexibility, and and some resistive exercises I Moderate intensity (overload with slow progression) D Based on capacity of individual, up to 60 minutes per day in multiple sessions F Every day G Lower level activities (e.g., walking) every day

*T = type of exercise; I = intensity; D = duration or amount; F = frequency of exercise session; G = goal.

the latest thinking on this matter from a public health standpoint.[34] Note that major health-fitness goals are identified for four different age groups ranging from youth (1–14 years) to older adults (over 65 years). Also that a physical activity plan is specifically defined for each group. These plans are described in the language of exercise prescriptions, i.e., type, intensity, duration, frequency, and goals. It is acknowledged that the dose-response relationships are not presently known for all possible changes induced by exercise training. We do know a considerable amount about coronary heart disease, however, and it is prudent for us to continue to prescribe exercise on this basis alone. Let's look at how the exercise prescriptions are designed on an individual basis.

Medical Evaluation

The first step of an exercise prescription is a complete medical evaluation. While it is advisable for anyone who plans to participate in a regular physical exercise program to have a medical examination, this is particularly true for persons of any age who have symptoms of coronary heart disease or who are 35 years or older but asymptomatic, i.e., have no symptoms of coronary heart disease.

The medical examination should be thorough and should include the following:[1]

1. *A comprehensive medical history questionnaire or review.* The review should include both family and personal histories and current health habits such as smoking, diet, exercise, and so on. Special emphasis should be directed toward any history of chest pain, cardiac dysrhythmia, or cardiovascular diseases.
2. *A physical examination.* Emphasis here should be placed on identifying symptoms and signs of cardiopulmonary and other problems that would contraindicate exercise testing. Examination of the bones and joints should also be included.
3. *Twelve-lead resting electrocardiogram (EKG).*
4. *Resting systolic and diastolic blood pressure.*
5. *Blood analyses.* Fasting blood glucose, cholesterol, and triglyceride determinations are recommended but not essential.
6. *A graded, EKG-monitored exercise test (unless medically contraindicated).* The stress test can be performed using either a bicycle ergometer or a motor-driven treadmill. It should be graded in intensity, starting with a light load, then increasing gradually until the maximum working capacity is reached. The initial exercise test for anyone 35 years or older should be monitored by a physician. A complete review of exercise stress testing can be found in references 1, 3, and 4 and the book by Pollock et al., 1984, listed in the selected readings.

The objectives of exercise testing are listed in Table 15-5.

Quantity and Quality of the Exercise Program

The questions, "how much exercise is enough?" and "what type of exercise is best for developing and maintaining fitness?" are frequently asked. There are four factors that must be considered in order to answer these questions: (1) frequency of training, (2) intensity of training, (3) duration of training, and (4) mode of activity. Most of these factors were discussed in considerable detail in Chapter 12. Therefore, they will be only briefly mentioned

TABLE 15-5

Objectives of Exercise Testing*

To establish a diagnosis of overt or latent heart disease

To evaluate cardiovascular functional capacity, particularly as a means of clearing individuals for strenuous work or exercise programs

To determine the physical work capacity in kilogram-meters per minute (kg-m/min) or the functional capacity in METS†

To evaluate responses to conditioning and/or preventive programs

To serve as the basis for exercise prescription

To assist in the selection and evaluation of appropriate modes of treatment

To increase individual motivation for entering and adhering to exercise programs

---

*From the American Heart Association[3,4] and the American College of Sports Medicine.[1]
†For an explanation of METS, see page 436.

here, emphasizing their uses in an adult fitness program.

The American College of Sports Medicine makes the following recommendations for the quantity and quality of training for developing and maintaining cardiorespiratory fitness and body composition in the healthy adult.[2] These recommendations have provided the bases for the "standard of practice" for exercise prescription in the United States. The reader is directed to an excellent review on this subject by Kirkendall published in 1984.[44]

Frequency of Training

You should exercise 3 to 5 days per week; e.g., Monday, Wednesday, and Friday; or Tuesday, Thursday, and Saturday; or Monday through Friday. This recommendation is based on the findings that participants will improve in fitness if they exercise only one day per week but will improve even more if they exercise 3 to 5 days per week.[56]

After this frequency there is a "diminishing return" plateau for 6 and 7 days per week, and the risk of injury from overuse increases. Nonconsecutive days are recommended to allow recovery from the exercise sessions.

Intensity of Exercise

The exercise should be hard enough so that your target heart rate (THR) will be between 60 and 90% of your maximum heart rate reserve (HRR), or so that your metabolism will be between 50 and 85% of your maximum oxygen consumption (max $\dot{V}O_2$). Determination of the THR from the HRR was explained earlier in Chapter 12 (p. 292). Therefore, this procedure will not be further discussed other than to say that direct determination of the maximal heart rate (HR_{max}) should be used in the calculation of the THR whenever possible. The reason for this is that HR_{max} varies greatly from person to person. If HR_{max} cannot be determined directly, then estimates based on the formula 220 − age or those HR_{max} values given in Table 15-6 may be used. Note that on the average, maximum heart rates decrease by about 10 beats per minute per decade of life. The reader should be aware that the full range of deviation of heart rate (3 times the standard deviation of ±3.3) is about 10 beats/minute in either direction. That is to say, if a 50-year-old person's HR_{max} was estimated to be 170 beats/minute, we are confident that his or her known "true" HR_{max} would be somewhere between 160 and 180 beats/minute. This imprecision is built into the exercise prescription and is the main reason for directly determining HR_{max} whenever possible. Included in the table are THRs of 60%, 70%, and 90% of the HRR. For these calculations, a resting heart rate of 75 beats per minute was assumed. Similar calculations are shown in Figure 15-11 as THR zones for subjects of various ages, 20

TABLE 15-6

Average Maximum Heart Rates by Age and Recommended Target Heart Rates (THR) for Normal Asymptomatic Participants During Exercise*

Age (Yrs)	20-29	30-39	40-49	50-59	60-69
HR_{max}	195	185	180	170	160
Peak THR $0.9(HR_{max} - 75) + 75$	183	174	170	161	152
Average THR $0.7(HR_{max} - 75) + 75$	159	152	149	141	135
Lowest THR $0.6(HR_{max} - 75) + 75$	147	141	138	132	126

*Modified from the American College of Sports Medicine.[1]

through 70 years. The American Heart Association also has published THR standards for men over the age of 50 years.[6]

Direct and indirect determinations of max $\dot{V}O_2$ are presented in Appendix G. Once the max $\dot{V}O_2$ and the oxygen consumption ($\dot{V}O_2$) for various workloads and running speeds are known, the percentage of max $\dot{V}O_2$ can be calculated as the ratio:

$$\text{per cent max } \dot{V}O_2 = [\dot{V}O_2 / \text{max } \dot{V}O_2] \times 100$$

As mentioned earlier, based on these measurements, the intensity of exercise during training should be between 50 and 85% of max $\dot{V}O_2$. This latter method of determining training intensity is much more difficult than is the heart rate method. However, the exercise intensity may be estimated from the individual's *functional metabolic capacity* as measured in METS. In this case, the proper training intensity would be between approximately 70 and 90% of the maximal functional capacity.

Figure 15-11. Target heart rate zone showing THR for different age subjects at 60%, 75% and 90% of heart rate reserve (HRR). Based on the Karvonen equation and using a maximum heart rate (MHR_{est}) of 220 − age and a resting HR (RHR) of 75 beats per minute. (Karvonen, et al. *Ann Med Exper Biol Fennise.* 35:307, 1957.)

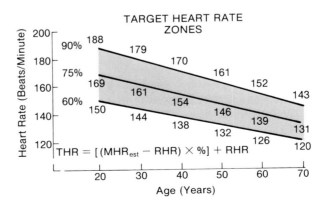

For example, a person with a maximal functional capacity of 10 METS would exercise at an intensity between 7 and 9 METS.

The MET method is easier than using oxygen consumption since the MET can be estimated on the bicycle ergometer from body weight and workload and on the treadmill from per cent grade and speed of walking or running. The energy expenditure in METS during bicycle ergometry is given in Table 15-7, whereas that for treadmill exercise is presented in Table 15-8. As an example of how to use the tables, suppose a male weighing 70 kg were administered an exercise stress test on the bicycle ergometer. Suppose further that the maximal workload attained were 1350 kilogram meters per minute (kg-m/min) or 225 watts (W). From Table 15-7, his maximal functional capacity would be 12.2 METS. The exercise intensity that he should use during training then would be between 70 and 90% of 12.2 or between 8.54 and 11.0 METS. If he were going to exercise on the bicycle ergometer, his workload would be between 900 and 1200 kg-m/min (150–200 W).

Traditionally, THRs calculated as 60% of HHR have been used as the low end of the training intensities that will produce significant improvements in fitness. There is interest in determining the true "threshold" intensity that will still be effective but is even safer to prescribe. This is particularly true for older persons, the extremely low-fit, and those who have disease or mobility impairments. The results of these studies have been both varied and surprising. For example, young male subjects improved their max $\dot{V}O_2$ by 19% after 20 weeks of bicycle ergometer training at 80 to 85% of their maximum heart rates.[18] Middle-aged subjects who performed at the same intensity improved by only 8%. This is in contrast to middle-aged men who improved their max $\dot{V}O_2$ levels by a full 17% after a 12-week, home-based walking and jogging

program.[32] Although training intensity assignments were based on per cent of baseline max $\dot{V}O_2$ in the latter study, conversions to maximum HR show that assignments were similar in each study, i.e., approximately 80 to 85%. The two-fold greater improvement in middle-aged subjects of the latter study can not be attributed to differences in training intensity. The explanation likely rests in differences in max $\dot{V}O_2$ levels at the start of training. Subjects in the former study were comparatively fit with relative max $\dot{V}O_2$ levels of 49.8 ml/kg $\cdot$ min^{-1}, whereas, the latter group had pretraining levels of only 32.2 ml/kg $\cdot$ min^{-1}.

Let's return to the matter of threshold intensity or, stated as a question, how low can the intensity prescription be and still be effective? As part of the second study just described, middle-aged subjects also trained at 42 to 60% of baseline max $\dot{V}O_2$, which corresponded to 60 to 70% HR$_{max}$ and 35 to 45% HRR. Even with this seemingly low intensity assignment, the subjects still improved their max $\dot{V}O_2$ by 8%.[32] These findings indicate that the threshold may be as low as 40% of HRR for sedentary, healthy, middle-aged adults. Other studies support a similar 45% of HRR threshold for younger (20 to 30 years) sedentary males[29] and an even lower 30 to 45% of HRR threshold for sedentary older people (60s to 70s).[8] Additional research will eventually disclose the true threshold intensity. At this time it appears that exercise can be effectively and safely prescribed for sedentary men and women of various ages using THRs as low as 35% of HRR.

Duration of Exercise

The exercise should be performed continuously at the proper intensity for 15 to 60 minutes per day. Duration is dependent on the intensity of the activity, thus lower intensity activity should be conducted over

TABLE 15-7

Energy Expenditure in METS During Bicycle Ergometry*

Body Weight		Work Rate on Bicycle Ergometer (kg-m/min and watts)												
(kg)	(lb)	75	150	300	450	600	750	900	1050	1200	1350	1500	1650	1800 (kg-m/min)
		12	25	50	75	100	125	150	175	200	225	250	275	300 (watts)
20	44	4.0	6.0	10.0	14.0	18.0	22.0							
30	66	3.4	4.7	7.3	10.0	12.7	15.3	17.9	20.7	23.3				
40	88	3.0	4.0	6.0	8.0	10.0	12.0	14.0	16.0	18.0	20.0	22.0		
50	110	2.8	3.6	5.2	6.8	8.4	10.0	11.5	13.2	14.8	16.3	18.0	19.6	21.1
60	132	2.7	3.3	4.7	6.0	7.3	8.7	10.0	11.3	12.7	14.0	15.3	16.7	18.0
70	154	2.6	3.1	4.3	5.4	6.6	7.7	8.8	10.0	11.1	12.2	13.4	14.0	15.7
80	176	2.5	3.0	4.0	5.0	6.0	7.0	8.0	9.0	10.0	11.0	12.0	13.0	14.0
90	198	2.4	2.9	3.8	4.7	5.6	6.4	7.3	8.2	9.1	10.0	10.9	11.8	12.6
100	220	2.4	2.8	3.6	4.4	5.2	6.0	6.8	7.6	8.4	9.2	10.0	10.8	11.6
110	242	2.4	2.7	3.4	4.2	4.9	5.6	6.3	7.1	7.8	8.5	9.3	10.0	10.7
120	264	2.3	2.7	3.3	4.0	4.7	5.3	6.0	6.7	7.3	8.0	8.7	9.3	10.0

*From: American College of Sports Medicine: *Guidelines for Graded Exercise Testing and Prescription*, 3rd ed. Philadelphia, Lea and Febiger, 1986.

TABLE 15-8

Approximate Relative Energy Expenditure in METS During Walking or Running Treadmill Tests*

Speed of Walking								
Grade %	km/h mph	2.7 1.7	3.2 2.0	4.0 2.5	4.8 3.0	5.5 3.4	5.6 3.5	6.4 4.0	6.8 4.2
0		1.7	2	2.5	3	3.4	3.5	4.6	5
2.5		2.3	2.7	3.3	4	4.5	4.7	6	6.5
5.0		2.9	3.4	4.2	5	5.7	5.9	7.3	7.9
7.5		3.4	4	5	6	6.9	7.1	8.7	9.3
10.0		4	4.7	5.9	7	8	8.3	10	10.8
12.0		4.5	5.3	6.6	7.9	9	9.2	11.1	11.9
12.5		4.6	5.4	6.8	8	9.2	9.5	11.4	12.2
14.0		4.9	5.8	7.3	8.7	10	10.2	12.2	13
15.0		5.2	6.1	7.6	9	10.3	10.7	12.8	13.6
16.0		5.4	6.4	8	9.5	10.8	11.1	13.3	14.2
17.5		5.8	6.8	8.5	10	11.5	11.8	14.1	15
20.0		6.3	7.5	9.3	11	12.7	13	15.5	16.5

Speed of Running				
Grade %	km/h mph	9.7 6.0	11.3 7.0	12.9 8.0	14.5 9.0
0		10	11.5	12.8	14.2
2.5		11.4	12.7	14.1	15.4
5.0		12.7	14	15.4	16.7
7.5		13.9	15.3	16.6	18
10.0		15.2	16.5	17.9	19.3
12.5		16.5	17.8	19.2	20.5

*From: American College of Sports Medicine: *Guidelines for Graded Exercise Testing and Prescription.* 3rd ed. Philadelphia, Lea and Febiger, 1986.

a longer period of time. Because of the importance of the "total fitness" effect and the fact that it is more readily attained in longer duration programs and because of the potential hazards and compliance problems associated with high-intensity activity, lower-to-moderate intensity activity of longer duration is recommended for the nonathletic adult (e.g., exercise at a THR of 70% HRR for 60 minutes rather than at a THR of 90% for 15 minutes).

An interesting study of the effects of different durations of similar intensity (85% HR_{max}) jogging on body fat, cholesterol, and triglyceride levels has been reported.[66] Untrained male university students were randomly assigned to control or exercise subgroups who jogged either 1.6,

3.2, or 4.8 km, 3 times a week for 12 weeks. Since body fat decreased similarly in all groups and triglycerides decreased only in the 4.8 km group, which had the highest pretraining levels, it appears that differences in training duration exerted little effect in this study.[66] This may indicate the primary importance of intensity and the more secondary impact of duration in the overall exercise prescription. It also may support the viewpoint that, in the formulation of exercise prescriptions, duration is the primary factor that can be adjusted to ensure progression.[44]

Mode of Exercise

The type of exercise to be used during training should have the following characteristics: (1) involve large muscle groups, e.g., the legs; (2) can be maintained continuously; and (3) be rhythmical and aerobic in nature. Examples of exercises fitting these characteristics are (1) running–jogging; (2) walking–hiking; (3) swimming; (4) skating, both ice- and roller-skating; (5) bicycling, both on the open road and on an ergometer; (6) rowing, actual or simulated; (7) cross-country skiing; (8) rope skipping; (9) dancing, aerobic dancing, ballet, and disco dancing; and (10) bench stepping. The selection of the proper activity is important in that it provides motivation for the participant to continue exercising on a regular basis. For example, interval training may appeal more to some participants than continuous endurance training. There is recent evidence that either approach will improve max $\dot{V}O_2$ measures provided that the total work completed is equalized.[9]

Various endurance game activities are also suitable as an exercise mode provided they fit the preceding characteristics. Tennis, for example, when played well, can be an effective endurance conditioner. Handball, racketball, paddle ball, and badminton can also be effective exercise modes provided they are played vigorously and on a regular basis.

Some concern also should be shown for matching the activity to best meet the needs and lifestyle of the participant. For example, body fat changes have been induced by a variety of training modes including cycle ergometers,[19] running,[61] and jogging.[66] There is evidence that simply performing an office-based bicycle ergometer test will stimulate some middle-aged participants to pursue other activities apart from fitness classes enough to significantly improve their fitness.[57] It also is known that middle-aged women who have previously participated in supervised walk–jog conditioning programs may regress to their pre-program fitness levels when left to exercise on their own.[48] The potential effectiveness of home-based exercise training programs based on low intensity walking and jogging[32] and the use of solid-state microprocessor systems to monitor compliance[53] are potentially exciting innovations. These approaches allow for the selection of one or more training modalities so long as the prescribed TRHs are achieved.

A summary of the quantity and quality of the exercise program for healthy adults is given in Table 15-9. It should be re-emphasized here that such a program is for *healthy, asymptomatic* adults. Individuals who are symptomatic for cardiovascular disease or for whom a complete exercise program is not medically advised should be placed in a modified program. For the cardiovascularly diseased patient, such modifications can be found in the handbook written by the American Heart Association[4] and by the American College of Sports Medicine.[1]

Warm-Up and Warm-Down

Prior to engaging in the aerobic portion of the exercise program, the participant

TABLE 15-9

Summary of the Quantity and Quality of The Exercise Program for Healthy Adults*

Frequency of training	3 to 5 days per week
Intensity of training	60 to 90% of HRR or 50 to 85% of max $\dot{V}O_2$
Duration of training	15 to 60 minutes of continuous aerobic activity
Mode of activity	Any activity that uses large muscle groups, that can be maintained continuously, and is rhythmical and aerobic in nature

*As recommended by the American College of Sports Medicine.[2]

should warm-up, then following the workout, warm-down. As mentioned in Chapter 12 (p. 300), three types of warm-up and warm-down activities are recommended: (1) stretching exercises for flexibility and for possible protection against serious injury; (2) calisthenics for development of muscular strength and muscular endurance; and (3) brief formal activity of the type used in the aerobic program. Of these three activities, the first two should be considered the most important for the warm-up, whereas the first and third should be considered the most important for the warm-down. Stretching exercises should be used that include most of the major muscle groups and joints of the body, e.g., the neck, back, upper and lower legs, chest, hips, groin, spine, shoulders, arms, ankles, abdomen, and feet. Each stretching exercise should be repeated 5 or 6 times and performed without bobbing or jerking and with the final stretched position held for 20 or 30 seconds. Examples of stretching exercises are presented in chapter 7 (p. 190).

Improvement in muscular strength and muscular endurance of the legs usually will accompany the aerobic portion of the exercise program, since most of the activities involve the large leg muscles. Therefore, exercises for improving muscular strength and endurance should concentrate on the upper body, i.e., the neck, abdomen, the arms, and the shoulders. Either calisthenics or weight-resistance exercises may be used for this purpose (Chapter 7).

The stretching exercises and formal activity used for the warm-down prevents the blood from pooling in the extremities, thus reducing the possibilities of dizziness and even fainting. Severe muscular soreness may also be reduced as a result of the warm-down.

Summary

Two major health problems in the United States and in the world are cardiovascular diseases and obesity. Regular exercise training can help reduce their risk.

The major cause of coronary heart disease is atherosclerosis, a disease that causes a narrowing of the lumen of the coronary and other arteries. When a coronary artery is completely blocked, the heart tissue normally supplied with blood from that artery dies. A heart attack is said to have occurred. Although atherosclerosis is thought of as an "old age" disease, moderate to severe stages of atherosclerosis have been found in young children.

Risk factors associated with coronary heart disease include: (1) age; (2) heredity; (3) obesity; (4) tobacco smoking; (5) lack of exercise; (6) high blood cholesterol (lipid) levels; (7) high blood pressure (hypertension); (8) sex; and (9) stress. The big three risk factors are cigarette smoking, high blood pressure, and high blood levels of cholesterol.

A stroke occurs when there is interference with the blood supply to the brain. A frequent cause of stroke is the blocking of one of the arteries that supplies blood to a section of the brain by a blood clot that forms inside the artery. Stroke also occurs when an atherosclerotic artery in the brain bursts, flooding the surrounding tissue with blood (cerebral hemorrhage). The result of a stroke is usually paralysis of one side of the body (hemiparesis). Regular exercise can reduce the risk of stroke because of its effects on atherosclerosis and blood pressure.

The mechanisms by which physical activity may reduce the occurrence or severity of coronary heart disease are increases in: (1) coronary collateral vascularization; (2) vessel size; (3) myocardial efficiency; (4) efficiency of peripheral blood distribution and return; (5) electron transport capacity; (6) fibrinolytic capability; (7) red blood cell mass and blood volume; (8) thyroid function; (9) growth hormone production; (10) tolerance to stress; (11) prudent living habits; and (12) *joie de vivre* ("joy of living"); and decreases in: (1) blood cholesterol and triglyceride levels; (2) glucose intolerance; (3) obesity; (4) platelet stickiness; (5) arterial blood pressure; (6) heart rate; (7) vulnerability to dysrhythmias; (8) neurohormonal overreaction; and (9) "strain" associated with psychic "stress."

The exercise prescription includes a medical evaluation and consideration of the frequency of training, the intensity of training, the duration of exercise, and the mode of exercise. The medical evaluation should include a complete medical history; a physical examination; a 12-lead resting EKG, resting blood pressure, blood analysis; and a graded, EKG-monitored exercise test. The frequency of training should be 3 to 5 days per week. The intensity of training should be 60 to 90% of the HRR or 50 to 85% of the max $\dot{V}O_2$; the duration of exercise should be 15 to 60 minutes; and the mode of exercise should be any activity that uses large muscle groups, can be maintained continuously, and is rhythmical and aerobic in nature.

Training intensity as low as 35 of HRR may be effective in low-fit or older populations.

The exercise program should be preceded by a warm-up period and followed by a warm-down period.

Questions

1. Discuss the death rate due to cardiovascular disease compared with all other deaths.
2. Discuss the major cause of coronary heart disease.
3. Discuss each of the known risk factors for coronary heart disease. What are the "big" three risk factors?
4. What is stroke, what is it caused by, and how may its risk be reduced?
5. What are the mechanisms by which regular exercise training may reduce the occurrence or severity of coronary heart disease?
6. Discuss the three different forms of cholesterol or lipoproteins.
7. What is meant by exercise prescription?
8. What should a medical evaluation include?
9. Describe the ways in which a proper exercise intensity can be determined.
10. What kinds of activities should a good warm-up and warm-down include? Why?
11. How do the physical activity plans for improving health and fitness in specific age groups differ?

References

1. American College of Sports Medicine.: *Guidelines for Graded Exercise Testing and Prescription*, 3rd ed. Philadelphia, Lea and Febiger, 1986.
2. American College of Sports Medicine.: The recommended quantity and quality of exercise for developing and maintaining fitness in healthy adults. *Med Sci Sports.* 10(3):vii–x, 1978.
3. American Heart Association, The Committee on Exercise.: *Exercise Testing and*

Training of Apparently Healthy Individuals: A Handbook for Physicians. New York, American Heart Association, 1972.

4. American Heart Association, The Committee on Exercise.: *Exercise Testing and Training of Individuals with Heart Disease or at High Risk for its Development: A Handbook for Physicians.* New York, American Heart Association, 1975.

5. American Heart Association.: *Heart Facts—1978.* Dallas, Texas, American Heart Association, 1977.

6. American Heart Association.: *Exercise and Your Heart.* Dallas, Texas, American Heart Association, 1984, p. 17.

7. Astrup, T.: The effects of physical activity on blood coagulation and fibrinolysis. In Naughton, J., and Hellerstein, H. K. (eds.): *Exercise Testing and Exercise Training in Coronary Heart Disease.* New York, Academic Press, 1973, pp. 169-192.

8. Badenhop, D. T., Cleary, P. A., Schaal, S. F., Fox, E. L., and Bartels, R. T.: Physiological adjustments to higher- or lower-intensity exercise in elders. *Med Sci Sports Exer.* 15(6):496-502, 1983.

9. Bhambhani, Y., and Singh, M.: The effects of three training intensities on $\dot{V}O_2$ max and $\dot{V}E/\dot{V}O_2$ ratio. *Can J Appl Sport Sci.* 10(1): 44-51, 1985.

10. Bloor, C. M., and Leon, A. S.: Interaction of age and exercise on the heart and its blood supply. *Lab Invest.* 22:160-164, 1970.

11. Blumenthal, S., Epps, R. P., Heavenrich, R., Lauer, R. M., Lieberman, E., Mirkin, B., Mitchell, S. C., Naito, V. B., O'Hare, D., Smith, W. M., Tarazi, R. C., and Upson, D.: Report of the task force on blood pressure control in children. *Pediatrics.* 59(5):Part II, 1977.

12. Blumgart, H. L., Schlesinger, M. J., and Davis, D.: Studies on relation of clinical manifestations of angina pectoris, coronary thrombosis and myocardial infarction to pathologic findings with particular reference to significance of collateral circulation. *Am Heart J.* 19:1-91, 1940.

13. Boyer, J., and Kasch, F.: Exercise therapy in hypertensive men. *JAMA.* 211:1668-1671, 1970.

14. Choquette, G., and Ferguson, R. J.: Blood pressure reduction in "borderline" hypertensives following physical training. *Can Med Assoc J.* 108:699-703, 1973.

15. Clarke, H. H. (ed.): Update: exercise and some coronary risk factors. *Phys Fit Res Digest.* Ser. 9, no. 3, July, 1979.

16. Connor, J. F., La Camera, F., Swanick, E. J., Oldham, M. J., Holzaepfel, D. W., and Lyczkowskyj, O.: Effects of exercise on coronary collateralization—angiographic studies of six patients in a supervised exercise program. *Med Sci Sports.* 8(3):145-151, 1976.

17. Currens, J. H., and White, P. D.: Half a century of running: clinical, physiologic and autopsy findings in the case of Clarence DeMar (Mr. Marathon). *N Engl J Med.* 265:988-993, 1961.

18. Denis, C., Dormois, D., and Lacour, J. R.: Endurance training, $\dot{V}O_2$max, and OBLA: a longitudinal study of two different age groups. *Int J Sports Med.* 5(4):167-173, 1984.

19. Despres, J. P., Bouchard, C., Tremblay, A., Savard, R., and Marcotte, M.: Effects of aerobic training on fat distribution in male subjects. *Med Sci Sports Exer.* 17(1):113-118, 1985.

20. Eckstein, R. W.: Effects of exercise and coronary heart narrowing on coronary collateral circulation. *Circ Res.* 5:230-235, 1957.

21. Enos, W. F., Holmes, R. H., and Beyer, J.: Coronary disease among United States soldiers killed in action in Korea. *JAMA.* 152:1090-1093, 1953.

22. Erkelens, D. W., Albers, J. J., Hazzard, W. R., Frederick, R. E., and Bierman, E. L.: High-density lipoprotein-cholesterol in survivors of myocardial infarction. *JAMA.* 242(20):2185-2189, 1979.

23. Farrell, P. A., and Barboriak, J. J.: Time course in alterations of plasma lipids and lipoproteins during endurance training. *Med Sci Sports Exer.* 12(2):93, 1980.

24. Ferguson, R. J., Petitclerc, R., Choquette, G., Chaniotis, L., Gauthier, P., Huot, R., Allard, C., Jankowski, L., and Campeau, L.: Effect of physical training on treadmill exercise capacity, collateral circulation and progression of coronary disease. *Am J Cardiol.* 34:764-769, 1974.

25. Fox, S. M., and Haskell, W. L.: Physical activity and the prevention of coronary heart disease. *Bull NY Acad Med.* 44:950-965, 1968.

26. Fox, S. M., Naughton, J. P., and Haskell, W. L.: Physical activity and the prevention of coronary heart disease. *Ann Clin Res.* 3:404-432, 1971.

27. Friedman, M., and Rosenman, R. H.: Association of specific overt behavior patterns with blood and cardiovascular findings. *JAMA*. 169:1286-1296, 1959.

28. Friedman, M., and Rosenman, R. H.: *Type A Behavior and Your Heart*. New York, Alfred A. Knopf, 1974.

29. Gaesser, G. A., and Rich, R. G.: Effects of high- and low-intensity exercise training on aerobic capacity and blood lipids. *Med Sci Sport Exer*. 16(3):269-274, 1984.

30. Gilliam, T. B., Catch, V. L., Thorland, W., and Weltman, A.: Prevalence of coronary heart disease risk factors in active children, 7 to 12 years of age. *Med Sci Sports*. 9(1):21-25, 1977.

31. Goldberg, L., and Elliot, D. L.: The effect of physical activity on lipid and lipoprotein levels. *Med Clin N Am*. 69(1):41-55, 1985.

32. Gossard, D., Haskell, W. L., Taylor, C. B., Mueller, J. K., Rogers, F., Chandler, M., Ahn, D. K., Miller, N. H., and DeBusk, R. F.: Effects of low- and high-intensity home-based exercise training on functional capacity in healthy middle-aged men. *Am J Cardiol*. 57:446-449, 1986.

33. Hartung, G. H.: Physical activity and coronary heart disease risk—a review. *Am Corr Ther J*. 31:110-115, 1977.

34. Haskell, W. L., Montoye, H. J., and Orenstein, D.: Physical activity and exercise to achieve health-related physical fitness components. *Public Health Reports*. 100:202-211, 1985.

35. Hellerstein, H. K.: Exercise therapy in coronary disease. *Bull NY Acad Med*. 44:1028-1047, 1968.

36. Henritze, J., Weltman, A., Schurrer, R. L., and Barlow, K.: Effects of training at and above the lactate threshold on the lactate threshold and maximal oxygen uptake. *Europ J Appl Physiol*. 54:84-88, 1985.

37. Hicks, R. W., Morton, M. L., Brammell, H. L., Johnson, R. W., Keller, N. L., and Mathias, M. M.: Effect of exercise and dietary counseling on blood lipids in healthy males. *Med Sci Sports Exer*. 12(2):93, 1980.

38. Hyers, T. M., Martin, B. J., Pratt, D. S., Dreisin, R. B., and Franks, J. J.: Enhanced thrombin and plasmin activity with exercise in man. *J Appl Physiol*. 48(5):821-825, 1980.

39. Kannel, W. B.: Medical evaluation for physical exercise programs. In Morse, R. L. (ed.): *Exercise and the Heart*. Springfield, Ill., Charles C. Thomas, 1972.

40. Kannel, W. B., and Dawber, T. R.: Atherosclerosis as a pediatric problem. *J Pediatrics*. 80:544-554, 1972.

41. Kattus, A. A., and MacAlpin, R. N.: Exercise therapy for angina pectoris. *Circulation*. (Suppl 2) 32:122, 1965.

42. Kilbom, Å.: Physical training with submaximal intensities in women. I. Reaction to exercise and orthostasis. *Scand J Clin Invest*. 28:141-161, 1971.

43. Kinsman, T. E., Weber, H., and Anderson, N. O.: Lipoprotein changes in men training at different intensities. *Med Sci Sport Exer*. 12(2):93, 1980.

44. Kirkendall, D. T.: Exercise prescription for the healthy adult. *Primary Care*. 11(1):23-31, 1984.

45. Lewis, S., Haskell, W. L., Wood, P. D., Manoogian, N., Bailey, J. E., and Pereira, M.: Effects of physical activity on weight reduction in obese middle-aged women. *Am J Clin Nutri*. 29:151-156, 1976.

46. Linder, C. W., and DuRant, R. H.: Exercise, serum lipids, and cardiovascular disease risk factors in children. *Pediatr Clin North Am*. 29:1341-1354, 1982.

47. Loviglio, L.: What's your risk: A layman's guide to cardiovascular disease. *Bostonia* (Boston University Alumni Magazine), 52:1, Winter, 1978.

48. MacKeen, P. C., Franklin, B. A., Nicholas, W. C., and Buskirk, E. R.: Body composition, physical work capacity and physical activity habits at 18-month follow-up of middle-aged women participating in an exercise intervention program. *Int J Obesity*. 7:61-71, 1983.

49. Mann, G., Garrett, H., Farhi, A., Murray, H., and Billings, F.: Exercise to prevent coronary heart disease. *Am J Med*. 46:12-27, 1969.

50. Mayer, J.: *Overweight: Causes, Cost and Control*. Englewood Cliffs, N.J., Prentice-Hall, 1968.

51. McNamara, J. J., Molot, M. A., Stremple, J. F., and Cutting, R. T.: Coronary artery disease in combat casualties in Vietnam. *JAMA*. 216:1185-1187, 1971.

52. Morris, J. N., Heady, J. A., Raffle, P. A. B., Roberts, C. G., and Parks, J. W.: Coronary heart disease and physical activity of work. *Lancet*. 2:1053-1057, 1953.

53. Mueller, J. K., Gossard, D., Adams, F. R., Taylor, C. B., Haskell, W. L., Kraemer, H. C., Ahn, D. K., Burnett, K., and DeBusk, R. F.: Assessment of prescribed increases in

physical activity: application of a new method for microprocessor analysis of heart rate. *Am J Cardiol.* 57:441–445, 1986.

54. Niżankowska-Blaz, T., and Abramowicz, T.: Effects of intensive physical training on serum lipids and lipoproteins. *Acta Paediatr Scand.* 72:357–359, 1983.

55. Paffenbarger, R. S., Hyde, R. T., Wing, A. L., and Steinmetz, C. H.: A natural history of athleticism and cardiovascular health. *JAMA.* 252:491–495, 1984.

56. Pollack, M. L., Schmidt, D. H., and Jackson, D. S.: Measurement of cardiorespiratory fitness and body composition in the clinical setting. *Comp Ther.* 6:12–27, 1980.

57. Rodnick, J. E., and Frischer, A.: Changes in cardiovascular fitness following physical fitness classes. *J Fam Prac.* 20(4):367–371, 1985.

58. Rotkis, T. C., Coté, R., Coyle, E., and Wilmire, J. H.: Relationship between high density lipoprotein cholesterol and weekly running mileage. *Med Sci Sport Exer.* 12(2):93–94, 1980.

59. Schlesinger, M. J.: An injection plus dissection study of coronary artery occlusions and anastomoses. *Am Heart J.* 15:528–568, 1938.

60. Schwane, J. A., and Cundiff, D. E.: Relationships among cardio-respiratory fitness, regular physical activity and plasma lipids in young adults. *Metabolism.* 28(7):771–776, 1979.

61. South-Paul, J. E., and Tenholder, M. F.: The assessment of improved physiologic function with a short term exercise program in mildly to moderately obese people. *Mil Med.* 150(3):135–137, 1985.

62. Stevenson, J. A. F., Feleki, V., Rechnitzer, P., and Beaton, J. R.: Effect of exercise on coronary tree size in the rat. *Circ Res.* 15:265–269, 1964.

63. Tepperman, J., and Pearlman, D.: Effects of exercise and anemia on coronary arteries of small animals as revealed by the corrosion-cast technique. *Circ Res.* 9:576–584, 1961.

64. Thomas, S. G., Cummingham, D. A., Thompson, J., and Rechnitzer, P. A.: Exercise training and "ventilation threshold" in elderly. *J Appl Physiol.* 59(5):1472–1476, 1985.

65. Tipton, C. M., Matthes, R. D., Callahan, A., Tcheng, T.-K., and Lais, L.: The role of chronic exercise on resting blood pressures of normotensive and hypertensive rats. *Med Sci Sports.* 9(3):168–177, 1977.

66. Toriola, A. L.: Influence of 12-week jogging on body fat and serum lipids. *Br J Sports Med.* 18(1):13–17, 1984.

67. Valimaki, I., Hursti, M. L., Pihlaskoski, L., and Viikari, J.: Exercise performance and serum lipids in relation to physical activity in school children. *Int J Sports Med.* 1: 132–138, 1980.

68. Vogt, A., and Straub, P. W.: Lack of fibrin formation in exercise-induced activation of coagulation. *Am J Physiol.* 236(4): H577–H579, 1979.

69. Wilmore, J. H., and McNamara, J. J.: Prevalence of coronary heart disease risk factors in boys 8 to 12 years of age. *J Pediatrics.* 84:527–533, 1974.

70. Wood, P. D., and Haskell, W. L.: The effect of exercise on plasma high density lipoproteins. *Lipids.* 14(4):417–427, 1979.

71. Wood, P. D., Haskell, W., Klein, H., Lewis, S., Stern, M. P., and Farquhar, J. W.: The distribution of plasma lipoprotein in middle-aged male runners. *Metabolism.* 25(11): 1249–1257, Nov., 1976.

72. Zoll, P. M., Wessler, S., and Schlesinger, M. J.: Interarterial coronary anastomoses in the human heart with particular reference to anemia and relative anoxia. *Circulation.* 4:797–815, 1951.

SELECTED READINGS

American College of Sports Medicine: Symposium on exercise in the post-coronary patient. *Med Sci Sports.* 11(4):362–385, 1979.

Amsterdam, E. A., Wilmore, J. H., and DeMaria, A. N. (eds.): *Exercise in Cardiovascular Health and Disease.* New York, Yorke Medical Books, 1977.

deVries, H. A.: Tips on prescribing exercise regimens for your older patient. *Geriatrics.* 34(4):75–77, 80–81, 1979.

Ellestad, M. H.: *Stress Testing, Principles and Practice.* Philadelphia, F. A. Davis, 1975.

Falls, H. B., Baylor, A. M., and Dishman, R. K.: *Essentials of Fitness.* Philadelphia, Saunders College, 1980.

Fu, F. H.: Training heart rate: A comparison of four prescriptions. *Can J Public Health.* 69(5):389–392, 1978.

Getchell, B.: *Physical Fitness: A Way of Life,* 2nd ed. New York, John Wiley, 1979.

Kannel, W. B., and Sorlic, P.: Some health

benefits of physical activity: the Framingham study. *Arch Intern Med.* 139(8):857–861, 1979.

Naughton, J., and Hellerstein, H. K. (eds.): *Exercise Testing and Exercise Training in Coronary Heart Disease.* New York, Academic Press, 1973.

Pollock, M. L.: Exercise—a preventive prescription. *J School Health.* 49(4):215–219, 1979.

Pollock, M. L., Wilmore, J. H., and Fox, S. M.: *Health and Fitness through Physical Activity.* John Wiley, 1978.

Pollock, M. L., Wilmore, J. H., and Fox, S. M., III: *Exercise in Health and Disease: Evaluation and Prescription for Prevention and Rehabilitation.* Philadelphia, W. B. Saunders, 1984.

Wasserman, K., Hansen, J. E., Sue, D. Y., and Whipp, B. J.: *Principles of Exercise Testing and Interpretation.* Philadelphia, Lea and Febiger, 1987.

Wyndham, C. H.: The role of physical activity in the prevention of ischaemic heart disease. *S Afr Med J.* 56(1):7–13, 1979.

I f you had knowledge of how, physiologically, a player practicing football can die from heat stroke, you would never knowingly contribute to such a casualty. As a matter of fact you, being informed, could greatly influence other teachers and coaches. If all were informed, there would be no deaths in physical education and athletics attributed to heat stroke. By the same token, understanding the physiological sequence in drowning prepares you to handle emergency treatment with a greater depth of understanding. Also, scuba diving and performance at high-terrestrial altitude can be potentially dangerous if the physical educator and coach do not have a thorough understanding of the effects of changes in barometric pressure on physiological responses. These are several illustrations as to why you should be informed regarding certain physiological principles, many of which take place at the cellular level. The knowledge contained in this section will help you better understand important problems that will confront you as a physical educator and coach.

We will start this section by studying the physical processes of diffusion and osmosis as they relate to both sea water and freshwater drowning (Chapter 16). Next, application of these and other principles will be discussed in conjunction with scuba diving and performance at altitude (Chapter 17). Finally, the ever-present threat of serious heat problems in athletics will be thoroughly explored (Chapter 18).

ENVIRONMENTAL ASPECTS

Diffusion, Osmosis, and Drowning

The Cell
Diffusion
Facilitated Diffusion
Osmosis
Electrical Forces
Active Transport

Physiology of Drowning
Drowning in Fresh Water
Drowning in Sea Water
Emergency Treatment
Implications
Summary

The major concepts to be learned from this chapter are as follows:

- Particles and materials move into and out of cells through the processes of diffusion, facilitated diffusion, osmosis, electrical potential, and active transport.
- The sequence of events occurring during salt- (sea-) water drowning are different from those occurring during freshwater drowning.
- During saltwater drowning, water moves into the lungs causing pulmonary edema, red blood cells undergo plasmolysis (shrink), blood pressure and heart rate fall, and death ensues.
- During freshwater drowning, water moves through osmosis into the blood stream, red blood cells undergo hemolysis (rupture), blood electrolytes and proteins are diluted, and ventricular fibrillation causes death.

Life is maintained at the cellular level, and is dependent primarily on the movement of food, electrolytes, and waste products into and out of the cell. When this delicate equilibrium is interrupted, serious consequences prevail and death may occur if the situation is not remedied immediately. Comprehending the principles of cellular exchange is extremely important if the physical educator and coach are to be knowledgeable about their professions. For example, the principles of cellular exchange are important in understanding respiration, cellular metabolism, heat stroke, and the sequential events in drowning, as well as important aspects of athletic injuries. The sequential events in drowning will be the principal focus of this chapter.

The Cell

The interior of the cell is composed of organic and inorganic materials dissolved in H_2O: these substances are constantly involved in a myriad of chemical reactions to produce energy and hence maintain life. Outside of every cell is the **interstitial fluid,** whose composition is quite similar to the interior of the cell. Food moves from the blood through the interstitial fluid and into the cell, while waste materials come from the cell through the interstitial fluid into the blood. Forces are constantly at work to maintain this dynamic equilibrium.

Diffusion, facilitated diffusion, osmosis, electrical potential, and **active transport** are the forces that allow this delicate balance between the inside and the outside of the cell to be maintained.

Diffusion

Each molecule is in constant vibration, and as a result, the molecules contained within a given volume will be constantly colliding with one another. The vibrating and colliding result in a mixing of the molecules throughout the system. The movement is caused by the kinetic energy of the particle. This randomness of movement, or *diffusion,* is an excellent mixing device and is the most important means by which particles move into and out of the cell. In diffusion, particles always move from a region of higher concentration to one of lower concentration. For example, oxygen moves from the capillary to the interstitial fluid (lymph surrounding the cell) and from the interstitial fluid into the cell. By the same token, carbon dioxide (CO_2) moves from the cell through the interstitial fluid and into the capillaries. There are by far a greater number of oxygen molecules in the blood moving about in random fashion—this is the reason why more will diffuse toward the cell. By the same token, CO_2 is produced in the cell and the random motion of these molecules will result in their greater diffusion out of the cell through the interstitial fluid and into

the capillaries. When the concentration of molecules is greater on one side of a membrane than on the other, a *diffusion gradient* exists. One might say that the oxygen has a "downhill grade" toward the cell, whereas CO_2 would have a "downhill grade" toward the capillary. Figure 16-1 diagrammatically portrays this phenomenon.

Facilitated Diffusion

Each cell is surrounded by a membrane within which is contained a matrix. The matrix is composed of lipids (fats), and therefore is called a lipid matrix (Fig. 16-2). As we have just seen, in ordinary or free diffusion, carbon dioxide, oxygen, and other compounds such as fatty acids and alcohol (1) pass through the pores of the outer membrane, (2) dissolve into the matrix, (3) diffuse to the inner membrane, and (4) finally pass through the membrane wall into the interior of the cell.

Sugars, such as glucose, however, *do not* dissolve in the lipid matrix. Consequently, they must find some other means

Figure 16-1. Diffusion between cell and capillary. Because of a higher concentration of CO_2 in the cell, more CO_2 moves toward the capillary; on the other hand, a greater concentration of O_2 in the capillary causes more O_2 to move toward and into the cell by diffusion. Water, CO_2, and O_2 pass freely into and out of the cell.

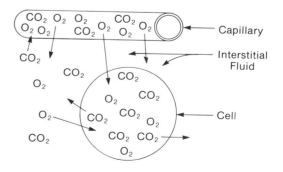

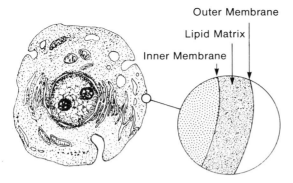

Figure 16-2. The membrane of a cell is composed of a lipid (fat) matrix.

of diffusing to the inner membrane wall. It is thought that this is accomplished with the help of an unknown carrier substance. Figure 16-3 shows how it works. The carrier substance (let's call it X) combines with glucose just inside the outer membrane of the matrix, forming a compound we can call glucose X. Since this compound is soluble (dissolvable) in the lipid matrix, the glucose can now diffuse across to the inner membrane of the matrix. At this point, the carrier substance breaks away and glucose passes to the inside of the cell. The carrier substance then diffuses back across the matrix where it can once again transport more glucose to the inside of the cell. This process is called *facilitated diffusion* because, as we have seen, the carrier substance facilitates the transport or diffusion of glucose into the cell.

Osmosis

Small molecules and other particles, such as CO_2 and O_2, pass into and out of the cell membrane through pores, with ease, as was discussed previously. However, certain molecules are too large to find passage through the pores of the cell membrane and as a result, too little or too much water moving into or out of the cell may cause it

to swell or shrink. The reason for this may be explained in the following manner. Consider a cell with only water on the inside and outside. As water molecules pass easily into and out of the cell through diffusion, there will be an equal number of molecules on either side of the cell membrane—i.e., a diffusion gradient does not exist. Now suppose there were a number of large nondiffusible particles (too large to get through the pores) on the outside of the membrane, which would prevent the water molecules from entering the cell. In this situation, the water molecules on the inside would remain continuously in motion and gradually move to the outside of the cell by diffusion. The condition whereby there are a greater number of molecules bombarding one side of the cell membrane than the other is called *osmosis*. Osmosis is a special case of diffusion that occurs when you have: (1) a semipermeable membrane, and (2) a liquid containing particles on either side of the membrane.

Figure 16-3. Facilitated diffusion. A carrier substance (X) combines with glucose just inside the outer membrane of the matrix, forming a compound called glucose X. The glucose (now soluble) diffuses across to the inner membrane of the matrix. The carrier then breaks away, and glucose passes into the cell.

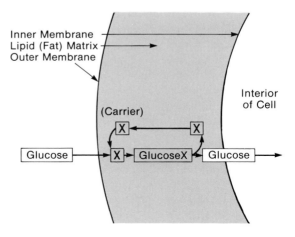

Osmosis can be demonstrated using a U-tube with a semipermeable membrane that separates water and a solution of sodium chloride (NaCl). The relatively large sodium (Na^+) and chloride (Cl^-) ions find it difficult to move through the membrane. Because of the presence of these ions about the membrane, fewer water molecules will come into contact with the membrane and fewer will diffuse through to the other side. The side containing water molecules alone will lose more of these molecules by diffusion as there is nothing to impede their progress through the cell membrane. Water will diffuse to the side of the membrane containing a larger number of Na^+ and Cl^- ions and the fewer number of water molecules. In other words, the water diffuses from a higher to a lower concentration. As a consequence of the diffusion of water, pressure will gradually increase on the other side of the membrane containing the greater number of Na^+ and Cl^- ions because of the weight of the additional amount of water. The buildup in pressure will stop when the force tending to drive the molecules into the compartment is equalized by the force tending to drive them out. This is a hydraulic pressure, which overcomes the tendency of water to diffuse into the compartment of higher concentration of ions. This force is called the *osmotic pressure*.

Figure 16-4 depicts two U-tubes with a

Figure 16-4. U-tubes with semipermeable membranes separating the solutions. Solutions A_1 and A_2 contain an equal number of Na^+ and Cl^- ions. Water will pass in both directions through the semipermeable membrane in equal amounts; the solutions are isotonic to each other. Solution B_1 contains fewer Na^+ and Cl^- ions than solution B_2. More water molecules will therefore diffuse to solution B_2. This will continue until the same number of water molecules are diffusing from B_2 and B_1, and vice versa. The point at which there exists an equilibrium in diffusion is dependent upon the osmotic pressure, P.

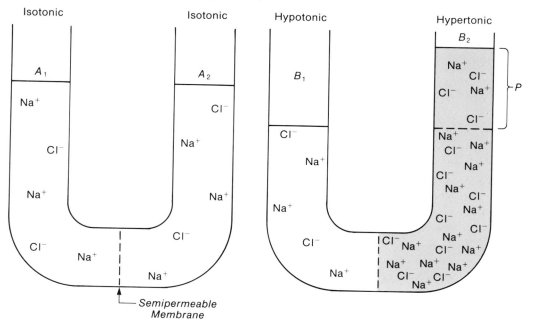

semipermeable membrane separating the solutions. In Figure 16-4, the solutions (A_1 and A_2) on either side of the membrane contain an equal number of Na^+ and Cl^- ions. The membrane is not permeable to these ions; however, water will pass through from one side to the other in equal amounts. As a result, the solutions are said to be *isotonic* to each other. In Figure 16-4, side B_1 contains fewer Na^+ and Cl^- ions as compared to side B_2. Gradually more water molecules will diffuse to B_2. Solution B_2 is said to be *hypertonic* to side B_1, which in turn is *hypotonic* to side B_2. Practical application of this principle can be observed using red blood cells in three separate saline solutions: (1) a solution isotonic to the internal mixture of the cell; (2) a solution hypertonic to the internal mixture of the cell; (3) a solution hypotonic to the internal mixture of the cell. Can you deduce what would happen to the cell in each of the three conditions? Figure 16-5 contains three test tubes with the aforementioned solutions. Observe what has happened in each instance to the red blood cell. Does this demonstration help explain why a physician uses an isotonic solution when making injections into the blood stream?

Electrical Forces

When certain compounds, such as NaCl, are placed in water they ionize. That is, the sodium breaks away from the chlorine, resulting in a positively charged sodium ion (cation) or Na^+ and a negatively charged chloride ion (anion) or Cl^-. Like charges repel and unlike charges attract. The outstanding difference between the intracellular fluid and the interstitial fluid is the concentration of ions. Sodium, calcium, and chloride concentrations are many times greater outside the cell; on the other hand, potassium, magnesium, and phosphate concentrations are greater inside the cell. As a result of the distribution

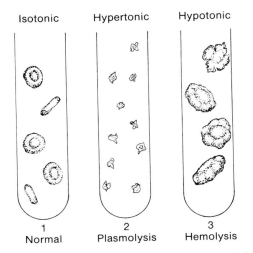

Figure 16-5. Three test tubes containing isotonic, hypertonic, and hypotonic solutions. In test tube 1, the solution is isotonic, and therefore the cells retain their normal size and shape. In tube 2, the solution is hypertonic to the interior of the cells, causing them to shrink (plasmolysis). In tube 3, the solution is hypotonic, causing the cells to swell (hemolysis).

of these ions, the inside of the cell has a negative charge (between -75 and -95 millivolts), whereas the electrical potential of the interstitial fluid is zero. This *electrochemical force* on the inside of the cell tends to attract the positively charged cations into the cell and drive the negatively charged anions out of the cell. For example, K^+ would tend to diffuse from the cell because of its high concentration, but the influence of the internal negative charge would cause the K^+ to remain within the cell. These two forces (diffusion gradient and electrochemical force) are almost equal, but are sufficiently unequal to favor the movement of K^+ from the cell. The opposite is true for Cl^-. Chloride ion has a high interstitial concentration, which would cause diffusion into the cell, but the electric forces are sufficient to keep the Cl^- from entering the cell. In other words, the chloride ions inside the cell are in electrochemical equilibrium with those on the outside.

Active Transport

Sodium is a large ion because it attracts water molecules about its surface. Consequently, even though it is a cation, it experiences difficulty in penetrating the pores of the cell. Although there is a small leakage of sodium into the cell, the number of ions inside the cell remains small, which suggests that a mechanism is in operation that actively removes sodium from the cell. Remember, when sodium moves from the inside to the outside of the cell it is going against the concentration gradient ("uphill," for sodium is in greater concentration outside the cell). It is also moving against the electrochemical force because the inside of the cell is electrically negative, and unlike charges attract. The explanation for this suggests the presence of an enzyme active in cellular metabolism, which affords the energy to move sodium from the interior of the cell. Exactly how this comes about is unknown, but it is observed that as sodium leaves the cell, K^+ enters. This phenomenon, which is referred to as the **sodium-potassium pump,** maintains an equilibrated movement of Na^+ and K^+ against the diffusion gradient and the electrochemical forces.

Diffusion, both free and facilitated, osmosis (hydraulic pressure), electrochemical potential, and active transport are the forces that move materials into and out of the cell. This is a dynamic process going on continuously. The time factor for a given particle to diffuse from the capillary to the cell and vice versa is measured in microseconds at the cellular level. Upsetting this equilibrium, as was mentioned earlier, results in serious physiological consequences.

Physiology of Drowning

Exploring the physiology of drowning will permit us to see how adverse consequences upset the delicate ionic balance at the cellular level and can cause death if the process is not immediately checked. It should be obvious to us that the sequential events that occur when a person drowns in fresh water will not be the same as those that occur when one drowns in sea water. The reason for this is simply that fresh water is hypotonic, whereas sea water is hypertonic, to the blood. Let us apply what we have learned thus far.

Drowning in Fresh Water

Even though it is commonly believed that manual resuscitative methods are effective in expelling water from the airway, research has shown that this is not true.[4] Experiments in which dogs have been submerged in fresh water have resulted in the following observations: (1) the dog holds his breath; (2) large amounts of water are swallowed; (3) vomiting occurs; (4) terminal gasping accompanied by flooding of lungs with water (in the neighborhood of 1.5 liters) takes place; and (5) death ensues. This sequence of events is rapid, but survival was usually noted if interruption of the events occurred prior to the stage of terminal gasping. In this case, spontaneous survival was most common, with resuscitative efforts contributing little.[1]

Further experiments have demonstrated that drowning in fresh water results in large volumes of water passing rapidly from the lungs into the blood. It has been found that after 2 minutes of submergence, a dog's blood could contain 51% of the aspirated water.[7] This dilution of blood *(hemodilution)* as a result of increased water volume is called *hypervolemia.* From our knowledge of osmosis we can readily follow the adverse physiological consequences that occur during fresh-water drowning:

1. The water as it enters the alveoli is hypotonic to the blood (Fig. 16-6A);

Figure 16-6. Alveoli with surrounding capillaries. *A,* During freshwater drowning, water moves into the capillary by osmosis, diluting the blood and electrolytes and rupturing the cells. *B,* During saltwater drowning, blood water moves from the capillaries into the alveoli, causing edema, concentration of blood electrolytes, and cell shrinkage. (Adapted from Redding et al.[2])

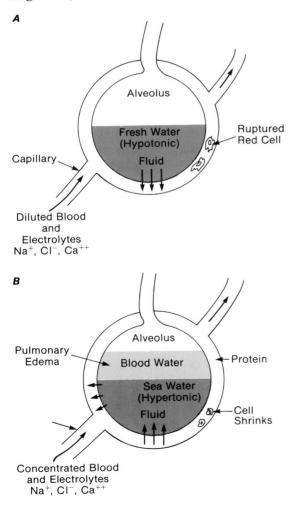

therefore, through osmosis it will move into the bloodstream. The inaccuracy of such a statement as "The person couldn't have drowned because there wasn't any water in his lungs" should be apparent when drowning occurs in *fresh water.*

2. The blood is diluted and becomes hypotonic to the cell. It follows that water will diffuse into the red blood cells, causing them literally to burst. This is termed *hemolysis* (see Fig. 16-5), and it occurs in such massive proportions that it eliminates the oxygen-carrying capacity of the red blood cells.

3. The dilution of the blood electrolytes (sodium, chloride, and calcium, in particular) and of plasma proteins, coupled with low oxygen concentration, precipitates *ventricular fibrillation* (irregularity in force and rhythm of the heart, or quivering of the muscle fibers, causing inefficient emptying). It has been demonstrated that fibrillation results from low plasma sodium accompanied by low oxygen tension, both of which occur in freshwater drowning.[6]

Experimentally, a group of scientists prevented ventricular fibrillation in freshwater drowning by intravenous administration of 37% sodium chloride solution. However, if the heart were already fibrillating, immediate administration of the saline failed to reverse the condition. Because the onset of fibrillation is so rapid after submergence in fresh water, the investigators abandoned the technique as not being practical as a resuscitative measure.[6]

Drowning in Sea Water

As we mentioned earlier, seawater drowning precipitates a different sequence of events because the water (3.5% salts) is hypertonic to blood (0.9% salts).

In saltwater drowning:

1. Sea water enters the alveoli and salts diffuse into the blood, while water from the blood (blood water) moves into the lungs (Fig. 16-6*B*).
2. The withdrawal of water from the blood causes a rapid rise in plasma sodium concentration.
3. The number of red blood cells per cubic centimeter of blood (hematocrit value) rapidly increases. The cells undergo plasmolysis, i.e., they shrink (see Fig. 16-5).
4. The lungs become full of blood water (pulmonary edema), the systolic blood pressure falls (hypotension), bradycardia (slowing of heart) occurs, and death ensues.

Emergency Treatment

Investigators have noted that spontaneous breathing movements often did not stop until the heart failed.[3] After immersion in sea water, dogs recovered when water being taken into their lungs was stopped and before profound hypotension occurred. Furthermore (as we have already mentioned), recovery also occurred when freshwater flooding of the lungs did not lead to ventricular fibrillation.

It has been concluded that spontaneous survival is likely in victims of near drowning who are apneic (i.e., who have stopped breathing). The following care should be given in such an emergency:[2]

1. Reoxygenation should be started immediately by means of exhaled air methods (e.g., mouth-to-mouth resuscitation).
2. Reoxygenation should be continued as soon as possible by means of intermittent positive pressure breathing (IPPB) apparatus with 100% oxygen.
3. For seawater victims, once IPPB therapy is started it should be continued until a blood specimen demonstrates plasma deficiencies have been corrected.
4. Intermittent positive pressure breathing treatment using oxygen combined with closed chest cardiac massage is recommended when fibrillation occurs from freshwater drowning. This is preliminary to external electrical defibrillation.
5. Finally, delayed death after freshwater near-drowning may be averted through subsequent judicious management by the attending physician of massive hemolysis, hypovolemia, electrolyte imbalances and myocardial failure.

Implications

What does this mean to you, the physical educator, should you be at the scene of a near drowning? Your training should allow you to perform mouth-to-mouth resuscitation and, if necessary, closed chest cardiac massage prior to arrival of the emergency squad. The individual should be transported to the hospital, where competent medical attention will permit observation and complete evaluation of the patient's condition before being discharged.

Another potential subject of interest stemming from our discussion of drowning is how to decrease the hazard of drowning in private and public swimming pools (fresh water). For example, we learned that in both fresh- and salt- (sea-) water drownings, gas exchange is prevented. In addition, drowning in fresh water causes hemolysis and hemodilution (hypotonic solution), and drowning in salt water results in plasmolysis and hemoconcentration (hypertonic solution). We saw how the latter changes were instrumental in the eventual death of the drowning victim.

We also learned, however, that in an isotonic solution, blood cells, for instance, are not damaged; i.e., they retain their normal size and shape. In other words, there is no net movement of large amounts of water into or out of the cell (see Fig. 16-5). What this implies is that the survival time may be longer if drowned in an isotonic solution* rather than in either fresh or sea water. In mice, this has actually been demonstrated. As shown in Figure 16-7, the survival time of mice (as judged by the time of the last gasp) was significantly increased when drowned in an isotonic solution rather than in either fresh or salt water.[5] While this significant increase amounted to only 15 seconds, remember that these data apply to mice; in humans, because of their much larger size, the increase in survival time would most likely be much greater. Even at that, with at least 15 more seconds: Is it possible that more lives could be saved if our swimming pools

_____
*An isotonic solution for humans would contain 0.9% NaCl. (Remember, the salt content of sea water is 3.5%.)

Figure 16-7. Survival times of mice drowned in fresh water, sea water, and an isotonic solution. The survival time is significantly greater in the isotonic solution. (Based on data from Standish and Miller.[5])

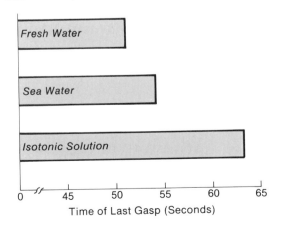

were isotonic rather than hypotonic? Although it is recognized that there would be technical and perhaps costly problems associated with maintaining an "isotonic pool," it nevertheless provides some "food for thought."

Summary

Particles move into and out of cells through the processes of diffusion, facilitated diffusion, osmosis, electrical potential, and active transport. Diffusion is the random movement of molecules caused by their kinetic energy. In facilitated diffusion, a carrier substance facilitates the diffusion process. Osmosis is the diffusion through a semipermeable membrane of a solvent such as water from a lower to a more concentrated solution. An electrical potential is created between the inside and outside of the cell due to ionic concentration differences. Active transport is the movement of substances or materials against their concentration gradients by the expenditure of metabolic energy.

The sequence of events in drowning in fresh water are:

1. Water that enters the alveoli is hypotonic to blood; through osmosis it moves into the blood stream.
2. The blood is diluted and becomes hypotonic to the cell; hemolysis (rupturing of red blood cells) occurs.
3. The dilution of the blood electrolytes and of plasma proteins, coupled with low oxygen concentration, precipitates ventricular fibrillation and death.

The sequential events in drowning in sea water are:

1. Sea water enters the alveoli and salts diffuse into the blood while water from the blood moves into the alveoli.
2. Plasma sodium concentration increases rapidly.

3. The concentration of red blood cells increases and undergo plasmolysis (shrinkage).
4. Pulmonary edema sets in, systolic blood pressure and heart rate fall, and death ensues.

The question of the possibility of saving more lives through "isotonic swimming pools" is raised.

Questions

1. Indicate how oxygen and carbon dioxide move into and out of the cell.
2. Describe the difference between diffusion and osmosis.
3. Why does a physician use a solution isotonic to the blood when making injections into a vein?
4. Why is there a tendency for potassium to remain within the cell and sodium to remain outside the cell?
5. What are the prime forces that move materials into and out of a cell?
6. What are the sequential events in drowning? Where must these events be interrupted if survival is to occur?
7. What are the adverse physiological consequences of drowning (a) in fresh water, and (b) in salt water?
8. If you were present at the scene of a near drowning, what considerations should be taken into account to ensure the best care for the person involved?
9. Explain physiologically how an isotonic swimming pool could potentially save lives from drowning.

References

1. Fainer, D., Martin, C., and Ivy, A.: Resuscitation of dogs from fresh water drowning. *J Appl Physiol.* 12:417–426, 1957.
2. Redding, J., Cozine, R., Voigt, G., and Safar, P.: Resuscitation from drowning. *JAMA.* 178(12):1136–1139, 1961.
3. Redding, J., Voigt, G., and Safar, P.: Resuscitation from drowning: laboratory evaluation. *Anesthesiology.* 21:113–114, 1959.
4. Safar, P.: Failure of manual artificial respiration. *J Appl Physiol.* 14:84–88, 1959.
5. Standish, M., and Miller, J.: Drowning in fresh water, Ringer's solution, and sea water: effects of hypothermia. *Fed Proc.* 28(2):792, 1969.
6. Swann, H.: *Studies in Resuscitation.* Air Force Technical Report No. 6696, Wright Air Development Center, Wright-Patterson Air Force Base, Ohio, 1951.
7. Swann, H., and Spafford, N.: Body salt and water changes during fresh and sea water drowning. *Texas Rep Biol Med.* 9:356–382, 1951.

SELECTED READINGS

American Medical Association: Standards for cardiopulmonary resuscitation (CPR) and emergency cardiac care (ECC). Supplement to *JAMA.* Feb. 18, 1974.

chapter 17

Scuba and Performance at Altitude

The major concepts to be learned from this chapter are as follows:

- When the pressure on a given volume of gas is increased, the volume decreases (Boyle's law).
- When the temperature of a given volume of gas is increased, the volume increases (Charles's law).
- Scuba (self-contained underwater breathing apparatus) diving is an ex-

cellent sport and can be performed without accident, provided that physiological concepts are understood and applied.

- At altitudes over 5000 feet (1524 meters), the ability to perform endurance activities is decreased due to hypoxia, i.e., the lowered partial pressure of oxygen in the air.
- Endurance performance at altitude may sometimes be improved with con-

tinued stay at altitude due to the acclimatization process.

- Acclimatization to altitude involves: (1) increasing pulmonary ventilation, (2) increasing red blood cell and hemoglobin concentrations, (3) eliminating bicarbonate in the urine, and (4) tissue changes.
- Training at altitude might enhance endurance performance at sea level but only in unconditioned, nonathletic individuals.
- For the highly trained athlete, the training intensity required for maintenance of peak performances cannot be achieved at altitude.

Scuba (self-contained underwater breathing apparatus) diving, in addition to being fun, offers a wonderful opportunity to learn a great deal about physiology in a very exciting and interesting manner. The physiology of just one dive could actually fill a textbook, and the importance of this information is dramatically illustrated by the fact that if the knowledge is not applied, a single dive could be fatal.

It is not unusual in this jet age for athletic teams to be suddenly whisked to competitions in cities that are at much greater altitudes than the place where the athletes trained. The day of the competition will be too late to wonder about the effects of low pressure and the advisability of administering oxygen to your team; one must plan well in advance.

You are the most logical person in a community to serve as a knowledgeable reference source for those who wish to learn about scuba and performance at altitude. The purpose of this chapter is to provide the knowledge that will allow you to fulfill this function.

Effects of Changes in Pressure and Temperature on Gas Volumes

Comprehension of the physiological factors associated with physical performance below the sea and at altitude requires knowledge of the gas laws. Familiarity with these laws will help us to make valid judgments regarding how the individual may be physiologically affected, whether skiing in Squaw Valley (altitude of 6000 or more feet) or donning scuba gear and searching the ocean floors.

Effects of Pressure Changes on Gas Volume

It is quite interesting to note that when you increase the pressure on a given volume of gas, the volume diminishes. Whereas, when you increase the pressure on a given volume of water, the volume remains just about the same. If, for example, a given amount of gas is subjected to twice the pressure, the volume will be *reduced* by one-half. By the same token, if the pressure should be diminished by one-half, the volume will *double*. Water volume is not affected by pressure changes, whereas gas volumes are significantly altered. You will realize shortly that these are important considerations for us to be aware of, particularly in scuba diving. The gas law that relates pressure and volume of a gas is called **Boyle's law.**

Effects of Temperature Changes on Gas Volume

Gas volume is affected not only by pressure but also by temperature. Heating a gas causes it to expand. As a matter of fact, if you hold pressure on the gas constant and raise the temperature from 0°C to 100°C, the volume increases almost 37%. However, temperature change has an insignificant effect on the volume of water, just as does pressure change. The gas law that relates temperature and volume of a gas is called **Charles's law.**

A more comprehensive treatment of the gas laws appears in Appendix C.

Weight of Air and Water

Air has weight and at sea level exerts 14.7 pounds of pressure per square inch (psi). This 14.7 psi is equal to a barometric pressure of 760 millimeters of mercury (mm Hg) and is also referred to as one atmosphere of pressure. As we ascend in altitude, the amount of air above us decreases and, as a result, the pressure diminishes. For example, at 5000 feet the pressure is reduced to 12.2 psi; at 10,000, 10.1 psi, and at 15,000, 8.3 psi. At 60,500 feet, only 1 psi of pressure is exerted by air.

On the other hand, as we descend below the surface of the sea, we have in addition to the 14.7 psi of pressure exerted by the atmosphere, the weight of the water above us. Sea water, because of the salt content, weighs 64 pounds per cubic foot, while fresh water weighs 62.4 pounds per cubic foot. The density* of water, i.e., its weight per cubic foot, remains constant as one descends to the ocean depths because, as was mentioned earlier, water is essentially noncompressible. Because of this factor, the weight of water is proportional to the depth. That is, at 33 feet under the surface the weight of water alone will be equal to one atmosphere, or 14.7 psi of pressure. Why is this so?

If the weight of sea water equals 64 pounds per cubic foot, and a diver descends to 33 feet, what is the pressure (or weight of the water) on the diver at this depth in terms of pounds per square inch?

$$33 \text{ feet} \times 64 \text{ pounds per cubic foot} = 2112 \text{ pounds per square foot}$$
1 square foot contains (12 inch × 12 inch) or 144 square inches

*Density equals the mass per unit volume.

Converting pounds per square foot to pounds per square inch:

$$\frac{2112 \text{ pounds per square foot}}{144 \text{ square inches per square foot}} = 14.7 \text{ psi}$$

Therefore, at a depth of 33 feet, the water would cause a pressure on the diver of 14.7 psi. The total pressure on the diver, or what is referred to as the absolute pressure, will be equal to 29.4 psi because to the weight of the water must be added the weight of the atmosphere (14.7 psi + 14.7 psi = 29.4 psi). Figure 17-1 depicts the increased pressure as one descends to 99 feet.

Physical and Physiological Principles of Scuba

We have learned: (1) that gas volume is affected by both pressure and temperature;

Figure 17-1. Depth and pressure relationships. As the diver descends from the surface of the water at sea level to a depth of 99 feet, the absolute pressure increases from 14.7 psi to 58.8 psi.

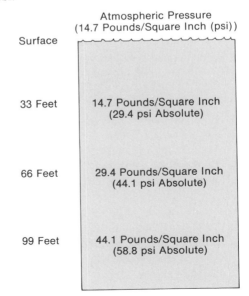

Atmospheric Pressure
(14.7 Pounds/Square Inch (psi))

Surface

33 Feet — 14.7 Pounds/Square Inch (29.4 psi Absolute)

66 Feet — 29.4 Pounds/Square Inch (44.1 psi Absolute)

99 Feet — 44.1 Pounds/Square Inch (58.8 psi Absolute)

(2) that air has weight, and that the greater the altitude, the less it weighs; (3) that water is noncompressible (at 5000 feet below the surface a cubic foot of water weighs the same as at the surface); and (4) why, at 33 feet below the surface of the sea, the water pressure is equivalent to one atmosphere. It is imperative for us to remember that the body contains air cavities, the most important being the lungs; and that the body (with the exception of air cavities) is essentially water and therefore noncompressible.

Air Embolus (Fig. 17-2)

The term **embolus** comes from the Greek meaning "plug"; it is used in physiology to refer to any material that enters the blood stream and obstructs a blood vessel. We may consider the alveoli of the lungs as millions of small balloons. Let us suppose that, at a depth of 33 feet, a diver inhales a volume of air from his or her tank, holds the breath, and then proceeds to the surface. If the diver should be foolish enough to do this, the lungs would rupture and death would result. This is true because, as we have learned, gas volume is affected by pressure; the volume of gas the diver inhaled at a depth of 33 feet would double by the time he or she reached the surface, causing the alveoli to rupture.

   Even under 5 feet of water, if a volume of air is breathed from the scuba tank and the breath is held while surfacing, overdistension of the lungs will occur. This in turn can cause rupture of the alveoli and perhaps pulmonary hemorrhage. The more severe rupture results in shattering of lung tissue, capillaries, and veins, and free air may be forced into the capillaries, forming emboli. The emboli may then enter the mainstream of the circulatory system, and the bubbles of air may find their way into the arteries of the heart and brain. As a consequence, circulatory blockage by the emboli and even death may occur. Proba-

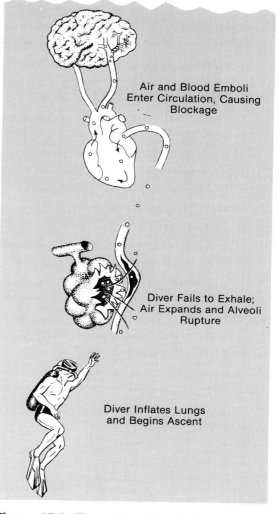

Figure 17-2. Formation of emboli as a diver ascends without exhaling.

bly the single most important consideration when giving scuba instruction is that *a diver must exhale as he or she surfaces. NEVER HOLD YOUR BREATH!*

Spontaneous Pneumothorax (Spontaneous Entrance of Air into the Pleural Cavity, Fig. 17-3)

Following rupture of lung tissue (alveoli), an accumulation of air or gas in the pleural

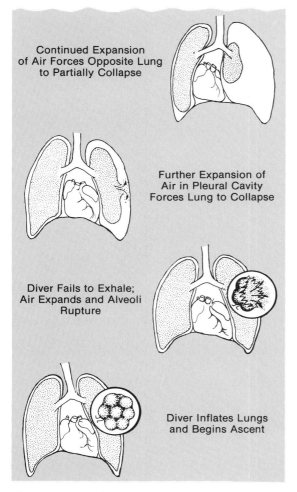

Continued Expansion of Air Forces Opposite Lung to Partially Collapse

Further Expansion of Air in Pleural Cavity Forces Lung to Collapse

Diver Fails to Exhale; Air Expands and Alveoli Rupture

Diver Inflates Lungs and Begins Ascent

Figure 17-3. Spontaneous pneumothorax, caused by diver's failure to exhale during ascent.

cavity (intrathoracic space) may occur. This is referred to as a **pneumothorax.** As the diver continues to ascend, the pressure decreases, and the air that is in the pleural cavity, as a consequence of the lung rupture, will continue to expand, causing the ruptured lung to collapse. In addition, the increasing volume of air will cause the collapsed lung and the heart to be pushed toward the opposite side of the chest. As a

consequence, the diver may go into shock, and if the pneumothorax is sufficiently severe, death may result. Treatment requires surgical intervention with a syringe and needle to remove the air pocket.

Nitrogen Narcosis (Raptures of the Deep, Fig. 17-4)

Nitrogen narcosis is dependent primarily on the depth of the dive and secondarily on the length of time at that depth. Nitrogen narcosis affects the central nervous system: first there is a sense of dizziness, then a slowing of mental processes, euphoria, and a fixation of ideas. The exact cause of these symptoms is difficult to explain. However, it is felt that because nitrogen is quite soluble in fatty tissue, the deeper the dive (i.e., exceeding 100 feet), the more nitrogen is forced into solution within the body. Its effects on the central nervous system are similar to those of alcohol. As a consequence, the "martini rule" has been formulated: 100 feet has the same effect as one martini on an empty stomach; 200 feet, two to three martinis; 300 feet, four martinis; and 400 feet, "tee many martoonis!"

One must recognize that the effects are quite individualistic and some people may be affected at moderate depths (50 feet or less)—the severity of the symptoms is unique to the individual. The U.S. Navy suggests the maximum depth for scuba should be set at 200 feet, with a practical limiting depth of 130 feet.[23]

The Bends (Fig. 17-5)

Nitrogen is inert, that is, this gas does not take part in respiratory exchange. The amount inhaled is equal to the amount exhaled.[13] As a diver descends, the pressure about the diver increases; this increased pressure will force nitrogen into solution within the blood. The deeper the dive, the greater the length of time for the dive, and the greater the exercise intensity,

Figure 17-4. Nitrogen narcosis. Nitrogen has a narcotic effect on the nervous system similar to that of alcohol. Prolonged stay at depth may produce a euphoric condition such as is illustrated by the diver chasing the mermaid.

Figure 17-5. Bends. Increased pressure forces nitrogen into solution. Decreased pressure releases this nitrogen from solution into the blood and causes formation of gas bubbles in the tissues.

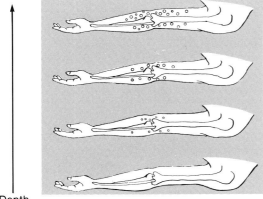

the more nitrogen will go into solution. The same principle prevails in carbonation of soft drinks. The carbon dioxide (CO_2) is forced into the liquid under high pressure and the bottle is capped. When the cap is removed, the CO_2 escapes into the air in the form of bubbles because of the decreased pressure. Very rapid ascent by a diver to regions of lower pressure is similar to removal of the cap from the soda bottle in that the dissolved gas (nitrogen) is liberated in the form of bubbles. These nitrogen bubbles (gas emboli) may cause the **bends,** i.e., circulatory blockage and tissue damage. Exercise hastens the onset of the bends in that it is analogous to shaking a bottle of soda, causing a rapid and large release of gas bubbles. Pain is usually felt at the joints or ligaments and tendons first, within 24 hours following exposure; indeed, 85% of those suffering from the bends will have symptoms within 4 to 6 hours. Other symptoms besides pain in the legs or arms include dizziness, paralysis, shortness of breath, fatigue, and collapse with unconsciousness.

There is only one way in which the bends may be successfully treated and that is by recompression. The individual is placed into a chamber into which air is pumped, elevating the pressure and hence forcing the nitrogen bubbles back into solution. The diver then undergoes slow decompression, which allows the nitrogen to gradually come from solution (without the formation of bubbles) and be exhaled.

It is obvious that those responsible for the welfare of divers should be aware of the location of the nearest recompression chamber.

The prevention of the bends requires a thorough knowledge of the recommended ascent patterns for divers from various depths who had been submerged for various durations. These data can be found in the United States Navy Diving Manual.[23]

Oxygen Poisoning (Fig. 17-6)

Breathing of 100% oxygen, and the depth and duration of the dive are factors in the production of **oxygen poisoning.** As was mentioned earlier, increasing the pressure of a gas over a liquid will cause more of the gas to go into solution. If oxygen is forced into solution, the tissues would first use the oxygen in solution as it is more readily available than is the oxygen carried by the red cell. At the same time, if the red cells are adequately loaded with oxygen, carbon dioxide, which is continually being formed, cannot be removed. Remember that the red cell carries oxygen from the alveoli to the cells and transports CO_2 from the cells to the alveoli. Because the red cell cannot dispose of the oxygen, it cannot as readily take on the CO_2, causing a buildup of CO_2 in body tissues. Excess CO_2 and O_2 in the tissues disturbs cerebral blood flow, result-

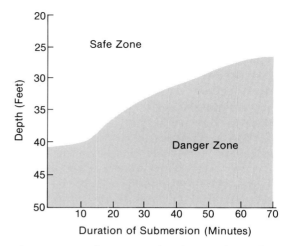

Figure 17-6. Oxygen poisoning is dependent upon duration of submersion and depth of dive.

ing in the following symptoms of oxygen poisoning: tingling of fingers and toes, visual disturbance, acoustic hallucinations, sensations of abnormality, confusion, muscle twitching, unpleasant respiratory sensations, nausea, vertigo, lip twitching, and convulsions.

There is no place in amateur diving for the use of pure oxygen. One might ask why pure oxygen is ever used. Consider the Navy's UDT (Underwater Demolition Team) given a project to destroy an enemy vessel. If you were the person on watch and observed bubbles coming toward your ship, what might you surmise? Quite obviously someone is "up to no good!" Navy divers must use a closed breathing system so that bubbles of expired air do not come to the surface, revealing their presence. The unit works by employing a chemical to absorb the CO_2 produced, and returning, hopefully, only oxygen and nitrogen to the tank. Unfortunately, a good chemical for ridding the expired air of all CO_2 has not as yet been perfected. The result is a possible buildup of CO_2, which may cause the diver eventually to lose consciousness.

Squeeze (Fig. 17-7)

When the face mask is donned at the surface it contains air at surface pressure. As the diver descends, the water pressure outside increases, causing considerable pressure differential between the inside and outside of the mask. Exhaling occasionally into the mask from the tank will equilibrate the two pressures. If equilibration does not take place, there will be extravasation of blood into the conjunctivae of the eyes; indeed, extreme pressure differential would have a tendency to **"squeeze"** the eyes from their sockets. *A person should never wear goggles to dive, as there is no way in which to equilibrate the pressures.*

Aerotitis

The eustachian tube is a small channel connecting the middle ear cavity and the back of the throat. When ascending or descending in altitude, one may experience a popping in the ears. The purpose of this tube is to equilibrate the pressure within the ear cavity with the outside. When this passageway is blocked (e.g., because of infection), equilibration is impossible. If you are diving and continue to descend, **aerotitis** may develop in which case there will be pain, congestion of mucous membranes, hemorrhage, bleeding into the middle ear, and possible rupture of the eardrum. Consequently, you should never dive when you have a serious upper respiratory infection because of the possibility of a mucus plug forming in the eustachian tube and preventing equilibration of pressure. As a matter of fact, if during any dive pain is experienced in the ear, the dive should be aborted and the diver should return at once to the surface.

We are well aware that the skull contains a number of sinuses anatomically in communication with our surroundings. The sinuses contain air cavities, and should mucus block the passageways to the outside, pressure changes cannot take place. In such an instance, should you dive or ascend to heights, pain and bloody transudate may ensue.

Underwater Breathing Systems

One of the newer types of breathing systems in open circuit scuba is the cryogenic (relating to production of very low temperature) gear, which uses liquid air (at temperature of −317.8°F). A great deal more air can be carried liquified than in compressed gaseous form. As a result, one tank will last several hours and weighs approximately one-half of the standard 72 cubic foot bottle. A heat exchanger and a pressure regulator raise the very low liquid air temperature and pressure to those of the surrounding water.

The scuba gear that permits diving to depths of 1000 feet uses a helium-oxygen

Figure 17-7. Squeeze is caused by failure to equilibrate pressures. When the diver fails to equilibrate the pressure between the inside and outside of the mask, extravasation of blood into the conjunctivae of the eyes may occur. This is why goggles should not be worn while diving.

system. Helium replaces the nitrogen to eliminate problems of the bends and at the same time dilutes the oxygen to avoid oxygen toxicity. The amount of oxygen to be mixed with helium must be regulated with the depth of the dive. By means of regulator valves, the partial pressure of oxygen must approximate that in the air at sea level (21% of 760 mm of Hg). For example, at 100 feet the breathing mixture would be approximately 5% oxygen and 95% helium; whereas at 650 feet, the mixture would be 1% oxygen and 99% helium.

The cryogenic gear using liquid air will undoubtedly replace the present scuba equipment used by the sports diver. Whereas the deep diving gear is extremely expensive (several thousand dollars), it has been developed for use mostly by the Navy in such exploits as the Navy's Sealabs and the Tektite project.

Performance at Altitude

It is an established fact that at altitudes of over 5000 feet (1524 meters), the ability to perform physical work is affected—the higher the altitude, the more severe the effects. This is illustrated by the data shown in Figure 17-8. In the past, it has been established that there is a reduction in endurance capacity as measured by maximal oxygen consumption of 3 to 3.5% for every 1000 feet ascended above 5000 feet.[9] More recently, it has been proposed that impairment may begin as one ascends from sea level to moderate altitudes below 5000 feet. The concept of a threshold for aerobic impairment may be misleading.[21] Also notice in the figure that work performance and max $\dot{V}O_2$ are reduced by 60% or more at extremely high altitudes, i.e., at around 25,000 feet.[19] Although such reductions in physical performance are quite large as they stand, it should be pointed out that these values were obtained on acclimatized and very fit mountain climbers. Acclimati-

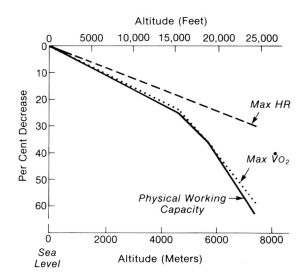

Figure 17-8. At altitudes of about 3000 feet (914 meters), small decrements in maximal oxygen consumption can be observed. At 5000 feet (1524 meters) and above, the decrement in max $\dot{V}O_2$ is 3 to 3.5% for every 1000 feet ascended. Physical working capacity and max $\dot{V}O_2$ are reduced by 60% or more at extremely high altitudes. (Based on data from Squires and Buskirk[21] and Pugh[9]).

zation, as we will presently discuss, refers to certain physiological adjustments that are brought about through continued exposure to altitude and which significantly improve performance. For the unacclimatized person, additional oxygen is essential above 18,000 feet (5488 meters).

It is important to point out at this time that although more than approximately 15 million people live at an altitude higher than 10,000 feet (3000 meters), most athletic competition in the United States takes place in areas located below this altitude. This means that since the effects of altitudes below 5000 feet are not great, from a practical standpoint, we need to be concerned mainly with the effects on athletic competition of altitudes between 5000 and 10,000 feet.

Altitude Acclimatization

The longer you remain at altitude, the better becomes your performance, but it never quite reaches the values that are obtained at sea level. As we have just mentioned, the improved performance during stay at altitude is brought about through **acclimatization.** The number of weeks to acclimatize depends on the altitude—i.e., for 9000 feet, about 7 to 10 days; for 12,000 feet, 15 to 21 days; and for 15,000 feet, 21 to 25 days. These are only approximations; a great deal depends on the individual. As a matter of fact, a few people will never acclimatize and continue to suffer **mountain** or **altitude sickness**[14,16] while at altitude. This happens even with people who were born and raised at altitude. Suddenly, for unknown reasons, they lose their acclimatization and suffer from mountain sickness. The symptoms of altitude sickness include pulmonary edema, nausea, vomiting, headache, rapid pulse, and anorexia (loss of appetite).

A word of warning: severe cases of mountain sickness cause symptoms not unlike pneumonia, even at an altitude of 10,000 feet; i.e., fever and congestion of the lungs (pulmonary edema). In more than one instance the diagnosis has been that these persons were suffering from pneumonia and they were given antibiotics, while the persons were left at altitude. As a result, the patients have died. Emergency treatment of severe mountain sickness consists of administering oxygen or removal to lower altitude or both. Services of a physician should be obtained at once.

Physiology of Acclimatization

As we ascend above sea level, the barometric pressure (P_B) decreases as the weight of the atmosphere becomes less. The *percentage* of oxygen in the air remains 20.93, but the number of oxygen molecules per unit volume decreases. This means that, when at altitude, in order to receive the same number of molecules in a breath of air that we receive at sea level, we must breathe more air. The main reason for lessened performance at altitude is a consequence of the lowered oxygen partial pressure (P_{O_2}). This lowered P_{O_2} results in **hypoxia,** i.e., lack of adequate oxygen. Apparently, hypoxia stimulates the acclimatization mechanisms. Depending upon altitude and duration of stay, among the important physiological changes that take place during acclimatization to altitude are[17]

1. *Increased pulmonary ventilation (hyperventilation).* This response is immediate (within a few hours) upon arrival at altitude, being more pronounced during the first few days, then stabilizing after about a week at altitude. The most important result of hyperventilation is an increased alveolar P_{O_2}. This ensures a greater saturation of hemoglobin (Hb) with oxygen (see Fig. 9-8, p. 234). Also, you may remember that with hyperventilation, excessive amounts of CO_2 are "blown off," thus decreasing both the alveolar P_{CO_2} and the H^+ concentration (increased pH).

2. *Increased number of red blood cells and hemoglobin concentration.* This too is rapid during the first few weeks at altitude, with the increase becoming more gradual thereafter. The function of this response is to increase the oxygen content of the arterial blood.

3. *Elimination of bicarbonate (HCO_3^-) in the urine.* This adjustment requires several days. Although this mechanism per se does not enhance oxygen availability, its main function is to maintain blood pH at near normal values. Remember, with hyperventilation and loss of CO_2, the blood pH will tend to increase; elimination of bicarbonate is offsetting, causing a decrease in pH.

4. *Tissue level changes.* These changes include (a) increased muscle and

tissue capillarization; (b) increased myoglobin concentration; (c) increased mitochondrial density; and (d) enzyme changes that enhance the oxidative capacity. Unlike the previously mentioned acclimatization processes, these cellular changes take more time. In fact, they are seen most developed in the long-time resident of high-altitude regions.

These are major physiological changes that greatly aid in delivering oxygen to the tissues when oxygen is hard to come by (i.e., under hypoxic conditions). When the person returns from a 3- to 4-week sojourn at altitude, he or she will lose these changes brought about by acclimatization within a period of about 2 to 4 weeks.

Conditioned versus Nonconditioned Persons

Studies have shown that on first arriving at altitude, conditioned subjects have no greater advantage over their nonconditioned contemporaries beyond what they would have at sea level.[5] Fit persons will be able to perform more work, just as they can at sea level, than the unfit, but at a diminished level. They will not acclimatize any more rapidly; nor will they be any more immune to the discomforts of mountain sickness.[6] As a matter of fact, in our altitude studies[5,6] the most highly trained person became so ill at 12,500 feet we had to remove him to a lower altitude, where he stayed for 2 days. We then returned him to 12,500 feet for another 2 weeks, during which time he was a little better off, but not much.

Athletic Performance at Altitude

Several studies involving both high school and college athletes have been conducted. The results provide important information regarding the effects of training and acclimatization on competitive athletic performances. However, before discussing these results, it should be pointed out that altitude mainly affects endurance or aerobic activities rather than sprint or anaerobic events. This makes sense because as has already been emphasized, hypoxia significantly reduces oxygen availability.

The Lexington–Leadville Study[15]

The primary purpose of this very interesting study with high school athletes was to determine whether lifelong acclimatization to altitude would give the native an advantage over the newcomer in regard to track performance. Two groups of athletes were studied:

1. Five members of the track team of Lafayette High School, Lexington, Kentucky (altitude, 300 meters or 1000 feet); and
2. Five athletes from Lake County High School, Leadville, Colorado (altitude, 3100 meters or 10,200 feet).

The Leadville students had to be selected from other sports (skiing, basketball, or football) as the high school had no organized track team. They did, however, have 4 months of training prior to a track meet with the Kentucky high school track team. Table 17-1 contains the physical and

TABLE 17-1

Average Physical and Physiological Characteristics of High School Athletes*

	Athletes Native to 3100 Meters	Athletes Native to 300 Meters
Age	17 years	17 years
Height	176 cm	175 cm
Weight	68 kg	66 kg
Max $\dot{V}O_2$ (low altitude)	66 ml/kg-min	68 ml/kg-min

*From Grover et al.[15]

physiological characteristics of these young athletes. The interesting thing to note is the high maximum oxygen consumption values these young men obtained while running on a treadmill. The data may be compared with those appearing in Figure 14-8*B,* page 385.

The experiment consisted of having two track meets between the teams, one in Leadville and the other in Lexington. In Leadville, the competition was held on the twentieth day of residence at altitude for the Kentucky team. Table 17-2 contains the running times for the track events at both altitudes. The Kentucky team (who incidentally were the Kentucky State Champions in 1964) was superior and won the competition at both low and high altitudes. It is apparent from these track times that hypoxia as a consequence of altitude affects the long-term resident just as it does the newcomer during strenuous activity. The athlete or team that is highly successful in competition at sea level should be equally successful at altitude.

The faster times obtained by the Kentucky team in the 220- and 440-yard sprints at altitude may be due in part to the lessened atmospheric density at 3100 meters (about $\frac{1}{3}$ less dense than that at sea level). At any rate, these results clearly indicate that anaerobic events are not adversely affected by moderate altitude.

The Pennsylvania State University Study[8]

A study of equal interest was conducted by E. Buskirk and others of Pennsylvania State University. They took several members of Penn State's track team to Nunoa, Peru, which is at an altitude of 13,000 feet (4000 meters). Figure 17-9 shows the average decreases in running performance experienced by the runners. The running times were obtained after 40 to 57 days at altitude, that is, after acclimatization had occurred. Notice also that as was the case with the high school runners, the decreases in performance were most pronounced in the longer events, where the oxygen system is the predominant energy pathway.

Following 3 weeks of residence at altitude, the runners began participating in soccer with the Indian natives. After 5 weeks of residence the trackmen were as good as the natives, with four of the runners eventually playing on the winning team! During a track meet held at 13,000

TABLE 17-2

Running Times for Track Events at 300 and 3100 Meters*

Running Distances		Lexington Team Altitude (meters)		Leadville Team Altitude (meters)	
		300	3100	300	3100
Yards	Meters	Time (min:sec)		Time (min:sec)	
220	201	0:24.0	0:22.4	0:25.7	0:27.0
440	402	0:54.0	0:51.0	1:03.5	0:52.5
880	804	2:10.0	2:11.5	2:24.7	2:30.0
1760	1608	4:49.0	5:10.9	5:23.5	5:35.0

*From Grover, et al.: Muscular exercise in young men native to 3,100 m altitude. *J Appl Physiol.* 22(3):555–564, 1967.

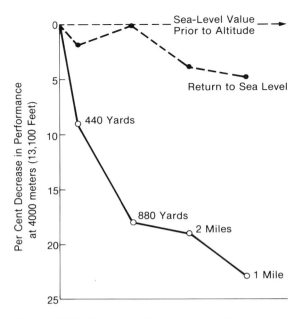

Figure 17-9. Decreases in running performances at 13,000 feet (4000 meters). Notice that the decreases in performance are most pronounced in the longer events where the oxygen system is the predominant energy pathway. Notice also that the performances did not exceed their prealtitude values upon returning to sea level. (Based on data from Buskirk et al.[8])

feet, the runners won over the best times for the Indians by 1 minute in the 1-mile event and by 2 minutes in the 2-mile event. These results again point out that altitude affects the working capacity of the native in much the same manner as it does the newcomer to altitude.

It is of further interest to note from Figure 17-9 that upon return to sea level the athletes' performances were not improved as a result of training at altitude. As a matter of fact, performances in the 1-mile and 2-mile events were slower the third and fifteenth days after return from altitude.

The Michigan–Penn State Study[12]

In another study by Dr. Buskirk and associates, 12 athletes, some of whom were top-rated middle-distance runners, were studied at various altitudes over a 5- to 6-week period. The results of their time-trials at an altitude of 7500 feet (2300 meters) are shown in Figure 17-10. Three points are worth noting: First, all performances were not quite as good as at sea level. Second, the decrease in performance was related, once again, to the duration of

Figure 17-10. Decreases in running performances at 7500 feet (2300 meters). These results indicate that even at moderate altitude, physical performance, particularly if it relies heavily on the aerobic system, will be impaired and will not always improve with acclimatization. (Based on data from Faulkner et al.[12])

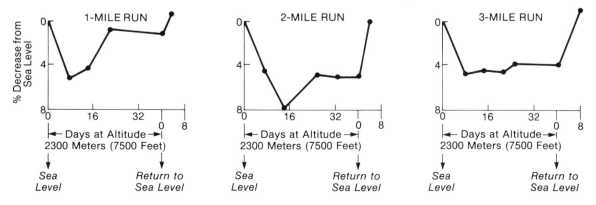

the event; the longer the race, the greater the oxygen needed and the poorer the performance. Third, the 2-and 3-mile performances were *not* improved with acclimatization as was the performance in the mile run. In relation to this, it is interesting that the maximal aerobic power also did not improve with acclimatization.

These results indicate that even at moderate altitude (7500 feet), physical performance, particularly if it relies heavily on the aerobic system, will be impaired and will not always improve with acclimatization.

The California–Colorado Study[1]

In this study, 12 middle-distance runners, each having recently completed a competitive track season, were divided into two groups. One group trained for 3 weeks at sea level (Davis, California) running 19.3 km (12 miles) per day. The other group trained with an identical training program at an altitude of 2300 meters or 7500 feet (Colorado Springs, Colorado). The two groups then exchanged sites and followed similar training programs for an additional 3 weeks. Periodically, the runners ran 2-mile competitive time trials and had their maximal aerobic powers (max $\dot{V}O_2$) determined on a motor-driven treadmill. The results are shown in Figure 17-11. Three features are observable: (1) both the max $\dot{V}O_2$ and 2-mile performance were significantly decreased at days 1 and 3 of altitude; (2) only a slight (2%) improvement in max $\dot{V}O_2$ and the 2-mile performance was made after 18 to 20 days of acclimatization to altitude; and (3) performances equaled but did not exceed their prealtitude values upon returning to sea level. The authors concluded that there is no potentiating effect of hard endurance training at 2300 meters over equivalently severe sea-level training on sea-level max $\dot{V}O_2$ or on 2-mile

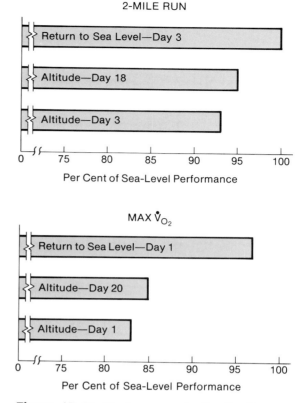

Figure 17-11. Performance in the 2-mile run and maximal aerobic power (max $\dot{V}O_2$) during exposure to an altitude of 7500 feet (2300 meters). Note that (1) both max $\dot{V}O_2$ and 2-mile performances were significantly decreased at day 1 of altitude; (2) only a slight (2%) improvement in max $\dot{V}O_2$ and the 2-mile run was made after 18 to 20 days of acclimatization; and (3) performances equaled but did not exceed their prealtitude values upon returning to sea level. (Based on data from Adams et al.[1])

performances in already well-conditioned middle-distance runners.[1]

The Ohio State Studies[5,6,7]

We studied 25 young college men at Columbus, Ohio (altitude, 750 feet or 230 meters) and at the Barcroft Research Station, White Mountain, California (altitude,

12,470 feet or 3800 meters). The following conclusions were reached:

1. The physical fitness of healthy individuals, measured at sea level, is not a sufficient index of their ability to perform hard physical work at high terrestrial altitudes.
2. Physical fitness appears to bear no relationship to the occurrence of symptoms of acute altitude sickness. The extremely fit person is as likely to become ill as is the sedentary person.
3. Ability to perform hard physical work at high altitudes improves markedly during 3 weeks of continuous residence at such altitudes. It does not, however, approach sea-level work capacity during this period of time.
4. Some subjects, regardless of physical condition, do not tolerate altitude well and may be expected to become ineffective or ill.
5. All healthy individuals, other than those with a predisposition to altitude sickness, can work steadily for one-half hour or more at a level that is roughly half their sea-level capacity at 12,500 feet immediately after arrival. Only a minority will be able to sustain one-half hour of work at two-thirds of their sea-level work capacity even after 8 days at altitude.

The Oxygen Dissociation Curve and Altitude

What factors limit performance at altitude? You will recall from Chapter 9 (p. 234) our discussion on the oxygen dissociation curve. Briefly, the alveolar partial pressure of oxygen provides the pressure head for the diffusion of oxygen into the alveolar capillaries as blood passes through the lungs. As we ascend to altitude, barometric pressure decreases and, as a consequence, so does the partial pressure of oxygen in the alveolae. This phenomenon is presented in Table 17-3. As air enters the alveolae, we must subtract the partial pressure of water (47 mmHg at a temperature of 37°C). Assuming an alveolar oxygen concentration of 14.75%, we can see the effect on the partial pressure of oxygen in the lungs (pAO_2).

At sea level, arterial blood is approximately 96 to 98% saturated with oxygen. At the conclusion of exhaustive exercise, the arterial saturation is somewhat diminished. Further, as one ascends to altitude, arterial saturation at rest is lower. However, more importantly, the level of saturation of arterial blood following exhaustive work is further diminished. This is illustrated in Figure 17-12 where the difference between rest and exercise arterial oxygen saturation was 5.1, 9.4, and 10.8% at sea

---

TABLE 17-3

Effect of Increasing Altitude on the Partial Pressure of Oxygen in the Lungs (pA_{O_2})

Altitude	Barometric Pressure (mm Hg)	P_B −47 (mm Hg)	Alveolar Oxygen Fraction	pA_{O_2} (mm Hg)
Sea level	760	713	.1475	105
5000 feet	638	591	.1475	87
7200 feet	586	539	.1475	79.5
10000 feet	530	483	.1475	71.2

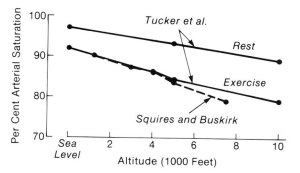

Figure 17-12. Changes in arterial oxygen saturation (SaO_2) with different altitudes. Resting and postexercise data from Tucker et al.[22] and postexercise data from Squires and Buskirk.[21]

level, 5000 feet, and 10,000 feet, respectively.[22] Also shown in Figure 17-12 are the postexercise data from another study involving different altitudes.[21] Note the remarkable agreement between the two studies for the level of arterial oxygen saturation following exercise.[21,22] One may conclude from these data that not only is the resting arterial saturation for oxygen lowered at altitude but also that saturation is progressively less complete during more intense work at higher altitudes.

Training and Altitude

When Mexico City (elevation, 7400 feet or 2250 meters) was named as the site for the 1968 Olympic games, coaches immediately asked: How can we train our athletes to best withstand any effects of altitude on their performance? Should they train only at altitude? If so, at what altitude and for how long? Should they train intermittently at altitude and at sea level? Because the answers to these questions were not available, a great deal of research was initiated.

From a theoretical viewpoint, training at altitude could produce more rapid and even greater physiological changes than could training at sea level only. The reason for this is that altitude hypoxia is a stress that produces physiological changes (acclimatization) similar to those caused by physical training. For example, total blood volume, hemoglobin, red blood cell count, mitochondrial concentration, and muscle enzyme changes have all been shown to be enhanced in both types of stress. To a certain extent, this idea has been supported experimentally. For example, in several well-controlled studies using nonathletes,[3,20] greater increases in maximal aerobic power and endurance time were seen when the training sessions were conducted at altitude (7400 to 11,300 feet) rather than at sea level. In addition, we have shown that some effects of 8 weeks of interval training can be maintained for an additional 12 weeks by use of two 3-hour exposures to a simulated altitude of 15,000 feet (4572 meters). During the exposures, the subjects did not perform any exercise, but merely rested.[4] Other studies[2,11] have shown improved performances at sea level after training at altitude. Some of the results are given in Table 17-4. However, in these studies, it was not determined whether the increased sea-level performances were due to altitude exposure per se or to the fact that the subjects eventually increased their fitness level during the conditioning at altitude. In other words, it is possible that their performances would have been improved with further training even at sea level.

It can be seen from Figures 17-9, 17-10, and 17-11 that in studies involving highly trained athletes, performance on return from altitude was not much different from prior performance at sea level; if anything, some were poorer. This would indicate that for the highly trained athlete, training at and acclimatization to altitude does not improve performance. Also, as already pointed out, maximal aerobic power and performance of these athletes do not al-

TABLE 17-4

Time Trials in Running Before, During, and After Training at an Altitude of 7500 Feet (2300 Meters)*

Event	Time at Sea Level (Min:Sec)	Day 3	Time at Altitude (Min:Sec) Day 14	Day 21	Time on Return to Sea Level (Min:Sec) Day 1	Day 21
880-yard run	2:41	2:48	2:38	2:37	2:32	2:32
1-mile run	6:07	6:30	—	6:15	5:49	5:38
2-mile run	13:08	13:45	13:09	—	12:22	11:57

*Based on data from Faulkner, Daniels, and Balke.[11]

ways improve with altitude acclimatization. One of the major reasons for this might be that the training programs required for these athletes cannot be sustained at altitude at an intensity and duration commensurate with that at sea level.[18] This can be seen from Figure 17-13, which gives the intensity of the training workouts for six collegiate runners at various altitudes. Even though their coach was present at all workouts, it is clear that altitude greatly reduced their training efforts.

Training at altitude, therefore, appears to be helpful for unconditioned, nonathletic subjects but not necessarily for highly trained athletes. However, if you wish to train your athletes at altitude for whatever reason, the following guidelines may prove to be helpful:[10]

1. Adequate training facilities and training atmosphere must be available.
2. The bulk of time spent at altitude should be at moderate altitude (6500 to 7500 feet).
3. Short exposure to higher altitude should be included regularly during the general training period at moderate elevation.
4. Steady altitude exposures should be limited to periods of 2 to 4 weeks, with intermittent sea-level or lower elevation trips scheduled to assure maintenance of muscular power and normal competitive rhythm and intensity of effort.
5. Training at altitude should emphasize maintenance of muscular power yet be

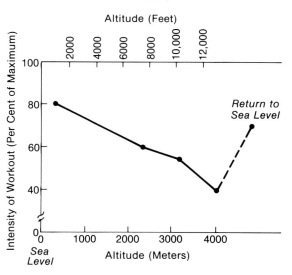

Figure 17-13. Intensity of training workouts for six collegiate runners at various altitudes. Even though their coach was present at all workouts, it is clear that altitude greatly reduced their training efforts. (Based on data from Kollias and Buskirk.[18])

geared to include normal or near normal overall amounts of work.

6. Important sea-level efforts should be scheduled about 2 weeks after leaving altitude.

Summary

Scuba is an excellent sport and can be performed without accident, provided that the physiological concepts are understood and applied. Following is a list of guidelines that should be strictly adhered to if one wishes to dive:

1. Receive competent instruction before going out on your own;
2. Never dive alone;
3. Never dive when you have a serious upper respiratory infection;
4. Do not dive using pure oxygen;
5. Never ascend faster than do the smallest bubbles from your exhaled air;
6. Follow very carefully the Navy decompression tables for depths greater than 30 feet;
7. Know your equipment well;
8. If you are easily disturbed emotionally, seek some other sport. Panic causes accidents;
9. Practical limiting depth is 130 feet.

At altitudes over 5000 feet (1524 meters), the ability to perform physical work is decreased due to hypoxia (lowered PO_2). However, physical performance at moderate altitude may sometimes be improved with continued stay at altitude due to the acclimatization process. This involves (1) increased pulmonary ventilation (hyperventilation), (2) increased red blood cell and hemoglobin concentrations, (3) elimination of bicarbonate (HCO_3^-) in the urine and (4) in those chronically exposed to altitude, tissue level changes. Increased physical fitness does not alone acclimatize the individual to altitude.

Altitude mainly affects endurance or aerobic activities rather than sprint or anaerobic events. This is because the major problem at altitude is hypoxia, which significantly reduces oxygen availability.

Training at altitude might enhance performance at sea level but only in unconditioned, nonathletic individuals. For the highly trained athlete, the training intensity required for maintenance of peak performances cannot be achieved at altitude.

Questions

1. Discuss the effects of increasing and decreasing the pressure, while holding temperature constant, on (a) a given volume of water, and (b) a given volume of gas.
2. At 33 feet below the surface of the sea, the weight of water above the diver will be equal to 1 atmosphere. Why is this true?
3. Describe how a diver may suffer air embolism.
4. What is spontaneous pneumothorax, and how is it treated?
5. What is the effect of nitrogen narcosis on a diver?
6. How may one avoid developing the bends during a dive?
7. What are the physiological principles underlying oxygen poisoning while diving?
8. How does one prevent squeeze while diving?
9. What is the importance of the eustachian tube for one who descends below the surface of the sea or ascends to altitude?
10. Define acclimatization to altitude and discuss the physiology involved.
11. How is performance affected at altitude?
12. How does training at altitude affect performance at altitude and at sea level?

References

1. Adams, W. C., Bernauer, E. M., Dill, D. B., and Bomar, J. B.: Effects of equivalent sea-level and altitude training on $\dot{V}O_2$max and running performance. *J Appl Physiol.* 39(2):262–266, 1975.

2. Balke, B., Nagle, F., and Daniels, J.: Altitude and maximum performance in work and sports activity. *JAMA.* 194:646-649, 1965.

3. Banister, E. W., and Woo, W.: Effects of simulated altitude training on aerobic and anaerobic power. *Europ J Appl Physiol.* 38:55-69, 1978.

4. Bason, R., Fox, E., Billings, C., Klinzing, J., Ragg, K., and Chaloupka, E.: Maintenance of physical training effects by intermittent exposure to hypoxia. *Aerospace Med.* 44(10):1097-1100, 1973.

5. Billings, C., Bason, R., Mathews, D., and Fox, E.: Cost of submaximal and maximal work during chronic exposure at 3,800 m. *J Appl Physiol.* 30(3):406-408, 1971.

6. Billings, C., Brashear, R., Mathews, D., and Bason, R.: Medical observations during twenty days at 3800 meters. *Arch Environ Health.* 18:987-995, 1969.

7. Billings, C., Mathews, D., Bartels, R., Fox, E., Bason, R., and Tanzi, D.: *The Effects of Physical Conditioning and Partial Acclimatization to Hypoxia on Work Tolerance at High Altitudes.* Columbus, Ohio, Ohio State University Research Foundation Report RF 2002-4, June, 1968.

8. Buskirk, E., Kollias, J., Akers, R., Prokop, E., and Picon-Reátegui, E.: Maximal performance at altitude and on return from altitude in conditioned runners. *J Appl Physiol.* 23(2):259-266, 1967.

9. Buskirk, E., Kollias, J., Picon-Reátegui, E., Akers, R., Prokop, E., and Baker, P.: Physiology and performance of track athletes at various altitudes in the United States and Peru. In Goddard, R. (ed.): *The International Symposium on the Effects of Altitude on Physical Performance.* Chicago, The Athletic Institute, 1967.

10. Daniels, J.: Effects of altitude on athletic accomplishment. *Mod Med.* June 26:73-76, 1972.

11. Faulkner, J., Daniels, J., and Balke, B.: Effects of training at moderate altitude on physical performance capacity. *J Appl Physiol.* 23(1):85-89, 1967.

12. Faulkner, J., Kollias, J., Favour, C., Buskirk, E., and Balke, B.: Maximum aerobic capacity and running performance at altitude. *J Appl Physiol.* 24(5):685-691, 1968.

13. Fox, E., and Bowers, R.: Steady-state equality of respiratory gaseous N_2 in resting man. *J Appl Physiol.* 35:143-144, 1973.

14. Green, I. D., and Fletcher, R. F. (eds.): Acute mountain sickness. *Postgrad Med J.* 55(645):441-515, 1979.

15. Grover, R., Reeves, J., Grover, E., and Leathers, J.: Muscular exercise in young men native to 3,100 m altitude. *J Appl Physiol.* 22(3):555-564, 1967.

16. Houston, C. S.: High altitude illness: disease with protein manifestations. *JAMA.* 236(19):2193-2195, 1976.

17. Hurtado, A.: Acclimatization to high altitudes. In Weihe, W. (ed.): *The Physiological Effects of High Altitude.* New York, MacMillan, 1964, pp. 1-17.

18. Kollias, J., and Buskirk, E.: Exercise and altitude. In Johnson, W., and Buskirk, E. (eds.): *Science and Medicine of Exercise and Sports,* 2nd ed. New York, Harper and Row, 1974, pp. 211-227.

19. Pugh, L.: Muscular exercise at great altitudes. In Weihe, W. (ed.): *The Physiological Effects of High Altitude.* New York, MacMillan, 1964, pp. 209-210.

20. Roskamm, H., Landry, F., Samek, L., Schlager, M., Weidemann, H., and Reindell, H.: Effects of a standardized ergometer training program at three different altitudes. *J Appl Physiol.* 27(6):840-847, 1969.

21. Squires, R. W., and Buskirk, E. R.: Aerobic capacity during acute exposure to simulated altitude, 914 to 2286 meters. *Med Sci Sports Exer.* 14(1):36-40, 1982.

22. Tucker, A., Stager, J. M., and Cordain, L.: Arterial O_2 saturation and maximum O_2 consumption in moderate-altitude runners exposed to sea level and 3,050 m. *JAMA.* 252(20):2867-2871, 1984.

23. U.S. Navy Diving Manual. Washington, D.C., Department of Navy, 1970.

SELECTED READINGS

Bentz, R. L.: Development of the Navy Mark 14 Underwater Breathing Apparatus. *Nav Eng J.* 91(2):91-98, 1979.

Crosbie, W. A., Reed, J. W., and Clarke, M. C.: Functional characteristics of the large lungs found in commercial divers. *J Appl Physiol.* 46(4):639-645, 1979.

Davies, C. T. M., and Sargeant, A. J.: Effects of hypoxic training on normoxic maximal aerobic power output. *Europ J Appl Physiol.* 33:227-236, 1974.

Fox, E. L.: *Sports Physiology.* Philadelphia, W. B. Saunders, 1979, pp. 185-188.

Goddard, R. (ed.): *The International Symposium on the Effects of Altitude on Physical Performance.* Chicago, The Athletic Institute, 1967.

Heath, D., and Williams, D. R.: The lung at high altitude. *Invest Cell Pathol.* 2(3):147–156, 1979.

Hegnauer, A. (ed.): *Biomedicine Problems of High Terrestrial Elevations.* Natick, Mass., U.S. Army Research Institute of Environmental Medicines, January, 1969.

Humpeler, E., Inama, K., and Deetjen, P.: Improvement of tissue oxygenation during a 20 days-stay at moderate altitude in connection with mild exercise. *Klin Wochenschr.* 57(6):267–272, 1979.

Hurtado, A.: Animals in high altitudes: resident man. In *Handbook of Physiology, Section H, Adaptation to the Environment.* Washington, D.C., American Physiological Society, 1964.

Luce, J. M.: Respiratory adaptations and maladaptation to altitude. *Physician Sportsmed.* 7(6):54–59, 62–65, 68–69, 1979.

Maher, J. T., Jones, L. G., and Hartley, L. H.: Effects of high-altitude exposure on submaximal endurance capacity of men. *J Appl Physiol.* 37(6):895–898, 1974.

Margaria, R. (ed.): *Exercise at Altitude.* New York, Excerpta Medica Foundation, 1967.

Miles, S.: *Underwater Medicine.* Philadelphia, J. B. Lippincott, 1962.

Pugh, L.: Athletes at altitude. *J Physiol.* 192: 619–646, 1967.

Rattner, B. A., Gruenau, S. P., and Altland, P. D.: Cross-adaptive effects of cold, hypoxia, or physical training on decompression sickness in mice. *J Appl Physiol.* 47(2): 412–417, 1979.

Strauss, R. H. (ed.): *Diving Medicine.* New York, Grune & Stratton, 1976.

Weihe, W. (ed.): *The Physiological Effects of High Altitude.* New York, MacMillan, 1964.

chapter 18

Heat Balance: Exercise in the Heat and Cold

The major concepts to be learned from this chapter are as follows:

- Body heat balance is achieved when heat loss equals heat production (gain).
- The body loses heat through convection, conduction, radiation, and evaporation of sweat. Heat is gained by the body mainly through metabolism, but it may also be gained from the environment through radiation, convection, and conduction.
- The major function of the thermoregulatory system is to maintain a relatively constant internal body temperature (37° C) at rest as well as during exercise.
- The seriousness of overexposure to heat while exercising is exemplified not only by a decrease in work performance, but also by a predisposition to serious heat illnesses and even death.
- Heat illnesses in athletics can be significantly reduced through (1) adequate water and electrolyte replacement (2) acclimatization to heat and (3) awareness of the limitations imposed by the combination of exercise, clothing, and environmental heat.
- Exercise in the cold does not usually present a serious hazard.

Over a 3-year period seven **heat stroke** deaths were reported among high school football players and five among college players.[20] Information about the fatalities is assembled in Table 18-1. Three colleges failed to respond to the inquiry; as a consequence, data on only nine players are presented.

All players (including the three not shown) were interior linemen, and seven of the nine were stricken during the first two days of practice. All were clothed in full football equipment. The temperature and relative humidity at the time of the fatalities are indicated in Figure 18-1. The line drawn from 100% relative humidity and 60° F (15.6° C) to 40% relative humidity and 89° F (31.7° C) indicates that the deaths occurred under conditions ranging from

TABLE 18-1

Description of Heat Stroke Victims*

Position	Date	Hour	Practice Session	Age (Years)	Height (Feet, Inches)	Weight (Pounds)
Guard-Tackle (1)†	9/25/61	2-4 PM	5th week	17	5'11"	190
Tackle (2)	8/21/59	4:00 PM	2nd day	16	6'1"	185
Tackle (3)	8/29/60	3:30 PM	1st day	15	6'1"	180
Guard (4)	8/27/62	5:00 PM	2nd day	15	5'10"	165
Tackle (5)	8/22/62	10:00 AM	1st day	15	6'1½"	244
Tackle (6)	10/8/62	4:15 PM	7th week	15	5'10"	190
Guard (7)	8/22/59	10:00 AM	1st day	15	5'8"	180
Guard (8)	9/1/62	5:50 PM	1st day	19	5'11"	190
Center (9)	9/2/62	10:00 AM	1st day	20	6'0"	200

*From Fox, et al.[20]

†The numbers in parentheses correspond to the circled numbers in Figure 18-1.

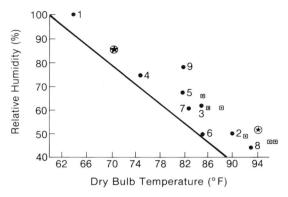

Figure 18-1. Dry bulb temperatures and relative humidity at the time of heat stroke incidences in football players (●, ✪) and Marine recruits (⊡). Note that football casualty number 1 occurred at a temperature of 64° F and relative humidity of 100%. Although temperature was low, heat could not be lost through evaporation because the atmosphere was saturated with water vapor (● = data from Fox et al.,[20] ✪ = data from Sohal et al.,[77] and ⊡ = data from O'Donnell and Clowes.[57])

either high temperature (dry bulb) and low relative humidity to low temperature and high relative humidity. It should also be noted that five of the casualties were not permitted water during practice but were required to take salt tablets, a practice that is far from being physiologically sound!

More recent data concerning heat stroke occurrences in high school football players[75] and in Marine recruits engaged in heavy physical exercise[55] are also shown in Figure 18-1. Although all of the Marine recruits survived, the two high school football players were less fortunate; they died. It is easily seen that these incidences of heat stroke also occurred under either high dry bulb temperature and low relative humidity or low dry bulb temperature and high relative humidity.

The deaths of these young men were in vain, for all were preventable. Why did they happen? Lack of knowledge as well as misinformation on the part of the coaches contributed to the fatalities. It is our intention in this chapter to ensure you well against contributing toward such accidents.

We will discuss what you must understand in order to maintain a team at top level of performance while at the same time eliminating the dangers of heat illness. To do so, you should realize, first of all, which basic physiological mechanisms prevail in heat illness; second, how the environmental or weather conditions can significantly contribute to heat illness; and third, which symptoms occur and which vital emergency procedures are required if such accidents should occur. We shall presently make use of the knowledge gained in Chapter 16, especially that regarding movement of water and electrolytes into and out of the cell.

Obviously, during physical activity an athlete sweats. The sweating rate will depend on many factors, among them: (1) the intensity of the activity; (2) the environmental conditions; (3) the physical fitness of the athlete, (4) how accustomed the athlete is to working in the heat (heat acclimatization), and (5) the type and amount of clothing worn.

Before considering these relevant factors, let us in a very general manner examine the sequential events that culminate in heat stroke. We can then return and discuss each of the factors mentioned previously, along with the important considerations that will enable us to protect our athletes.

1. Sweat is hypotonic to the blood; that is, it contains more water than salt.
2. We know from Chapter 16 that if one loses more water than salt, the liquid surrounding the cell becomes hypertonic to the interior of the cell.
3. As a consequence, the water from the interior of the cell will flow out of the cell to maintain osmotic equilibrium.

4. If the athlete continues to sweat without replacing water, a critical physiological situation will ensue. To maintain the osmotic equilibrium, water must move from the blood. This is true because of the lowered diffusion gradient existing outside the blood vessels. As the blood volume diminishes because of the water moving out, a high concentration of electrolytes will exist in the remaining blood volume.

5. As water loss becomes excessive, sweating is either diminished or stops to maintain blood volume. Internal body temperature soars. A conclusive symptom of heat stroke is a body temperature exceeding 105° F (40.5° C). In the Marine recruits referred to earlier, the body temperatures ranged between 106° F (41.1° C) and 110° F (43.3° C). The average body temperature was 107.2° F or 41.8° C.

6. A high concentration of electrolytes in the blood will interfere with the normal rhythm of the heart, precipitating ventricular fibrillation, heart failure, and death.

This, to be certain, is a simplified outline of the primary physiological factors involved in heat stroke casualty. However, this information will permit us to discuss intelligently measures that will aid us in averting trouble.

Heat Balance

The heat stroke fatalities listed in Figure 18-1 were all interior linemen. Even the three about whom we failed to obtain complete information played this position. Why are these men most vulnerable? The answer is that they expend a significantly greater amount of energy than do the other players. All of this energy, as you will recall, is liberated as heat from within the body. In order to maintain a constant body temperature, this heat must be dissipated;

if it is not, it will be stored by the body, causing the temperature to climb. This is shown schematically in Figure 18-2.

Let us examine the concept of heat balance in a little more detail. As we sit or otherwise use little energy, our body temperature remains at 37° C (98.6° F). In other words, the energy we expend in performing light activity is constantly being liberated by the body to the environment so that we maintain heat balance; as a result, our body temperature remains constant.

Heat Exchange

The body gains or loses heat through **convection, conduction, radiation,** and **evaporation.**

Convection

Convection is defined as the transfer of heat from one place to another by the motion of a heated substance. For example, a fan blowing over the surface of the skin removes air warmed by the body and replaces it with cooler air. Holding your arm out the window of a moving auto produces the same results. As long as cooler air blows across the surface of the body, heat can be lost. The individual who is

Figure 18-2. Heat balance. When heat gain and heat loss are equal, the amount of heat stored does not change, and therefore body temperature remains constant. When heat gain is greater than heat loss, body temperature will increase and when heat loss exceeds heat gain, body temperature will decrease.

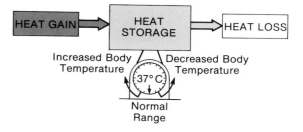

running can lose heat by convection just as one can lose heat by standing in a breeze. The amount of heat lost depends on the speed and temperature of the air flow over the surface of the body. Convection also occurs when blood carries heat from the muscles to the core and, then, to the skin. *Convection is directly related to the temperature difference between two areas.*

Conduction

Conduction is the transfer of heat between two objects of different temperatures that are in direct contact with each other. The direction of heat flow is always from the warmer to the cooler object. When we touch a piece of ice, for example, heat is conducted from the surface of the hand to the ice, whereas when we touch a hot stove, heat is transferred from the stove to the hand. *Conduction is directly related to the temperature difference between two surfaces in contact with one another.*

Radiation

This accounts for about 60% of the heat loss from a nude person resting quietly in a room at 70° F. The principle of *radiation* is based upon the fact that molecules within a body are constantly vibrating, and as a consequence, heat in the form of electromagnetic waves, in the infrared range, is continuously being given off. Radiation, then, is the transfer of heat between objects through electromagnetic waves. When we are seated in the classroom, for example, we are radiating heat to the walls of the room, while at the same time heat is being radiated from the walls to us. We gain heat through radiation when surrounding objects are warmer than our bodies; we lose heat through radiation when our body temperatures are warmer than surrounding objects. A person seated in a sweat box with the temperature set at 120° F would obviously gain more heat from the radiating light bulbs than he or she could lose through radiation.

By the same token, on the athletic field a considerable amount of heat can be gained from the sun through radiation. This is especially true (1) when there is little or no cloud cover, and (2) between 12:00 noon to 4:00 P.M., as a result of the position of the sun (during this period the radiation from the sun is more concentrated).

Evaporation

The major portion of heat loss during exercise is through *evaporation* of sweat from the surface of the skin. Even during resting, what is referred to as *insensible perspiration* aids in ridding the body of the excessive heat being produced. A small amount of extracellular fluid is continually diffusing through the skin and evaporating. As it evaporates rapidly, we do not notice the moisture, hence the term "insensible."

Evaporation is the term applied when changing a liquid to a vapor. Energy is required for this change and is extracted from the immediate surroundings. This extraction of energy results in cooling. When we work hard and sweat profusely, our bodies will be cooled *only* if the sweat evaporates; that is, if it changes into a vapor at the surface of the skin. If the sweat cannot evaporate and merely falls to the ground, no cooling of the body can take place. For every gram of sweat evaporated, the body can lose approximately 0.580 kcal of heat.

Heat Production (Gain)

The unit of heat energy most commonly used is the calorie, which we already defined as the heat required to raise the temperature of 1 gram of water 1° C. The kilocalorie (kcal), as the name implies, is the amount of heat required to raise the temperature of 1 kg of water 1° C. The **specific heat** of water (the heat required to change the temperature of a unit mass of water one degree) is therefore 1 kcal per kilogram of water per degree centigrade (1 kcal/kg/°C). The specific heat of the body tissues (collectively) is 0.83 kcal/kg/°C. That is to say, a person weighing 70 kg (154 pounds) must "store" 58 kcal of heat (0.83 × 70) to increase the body temperature 1°C.

As you will recall, the amount of heat or energy produced during metabolism is dependent upon the food being oxidized. A person weighing 70 kg who is resting quietly consumes between 250 and 300 ml of oxygen per minute. The caloric equivalent of one liter of oxygen ranges between 4.69 and 5.05 kcal, depending, of course, on the food being metabolized. We realize that a resting person usually oxidizes about sixty-six per cent fat and thirty-three per cent carbohydrate ($R = 0.82$), which means that for each liter of oxygen consumed, 4.83 kcal of heat will be produced (see Chapter 4). Heat production of a resting person as a consequence of metabolism would be about 1.45 kcal (0.3 liter of O_2 × 4.83 kcal per liter) per minute, or 87 kcal per hour. If no heat were lost, body temperature would increase approximately 1.5° C in 1 hour or rise from 37.0° C (normal) to 38.5° C (that is, 98.6° F to 101.3° F). This increase usually does not occur at rest because under most environmental conditions of temperature and relative humidity the 87 kcal per hour of heat produced can be easily dissipated through convection, conduction, radiation, and evaporation. However, on an extremely hot day the potential rise in body temperature of an athlete whose heat production may be ten to fifteen times that at rest is staggering.

Let us assume that an athlete consumes, on the average, 2 liters of oxygen per minute doing an activity for 1 hour. At the end of this hour the oxygen consumption would equal 120 liters (60 minutes × 2 liters per minute). Each liter of oxygen, assuming R equals 0.82, would be equivalent to 4.83 kcal of heat energy. The total heat energy produced would equal 580 kcal (120 liters × 4.83 kcal per liter). If no heat were lost at all, how high would the body temperature rise because of the stored heat? Remember, the specific heat of body tissue is 0.83 kcal/kg/°C. If the person weighed 80 kg, the temperature would increase 1° C for each 66.4 kcal of heat produced (0.83 kcal/kg/°C × 80 kg). As the person produced 580 kcal in 1 hour, the temperature would rise 8.7° C (580 divided by 66.4)! This simple calculation should make us keenly aware of the extreme importance of maintaining heat balance during activity. If there was no means of heat loss, we would gain 0.5 to 0.6° C every hour. In a matter of a few hours we would attain a body temperature that would no longer support life, even at rest.

In addition, heat can be gained by the body from the environment through radiation, convection, and conduction. This occurs when both the air and the objects surrounding the body are warmer than the body.

The heat stroke cases plotted in Figure 18-1 were the direct cause of the body's inability to lose heat. At this time it would be wise for us to learn the fascinating manner in which a person regulates his or her internal temperature. The understanding of the physical means of losing heat (conduction, convection, radiation, and evaporation), coupled with the knowledge of the thermoregulatory mechanisms, will enable us to manage our athletes judiciously during periods of environmental stress.

Mechanisms of Heat Exchange

For purposes of discussing the interactions of conduction, convection, radiation, and evaporation we need to be aware of the **core-shell** model of heat production and transfer. The *core* of the body may be described as the deep body tissues of the head, neck, and brain. Core temperature, usually represented by rectal temperature, is maintained within a very narrow range of 2° to 3° C. The *shell* represents tissue below the surface of the skin, which may vary over a range of 11° C or more dependent upon the thermal stress. There is not a clear anatomical landmark that separates the core and the shell.

Figure 18-3 depicts the interactions of the various components of the heat exchange system. Key points to remember are (1) heat flows down the *temperature gradient* from muscle to the core to the skin via convection; (2) some heat is conducted directly to the surface of the skin from both muscle and the core; (3) transfer of heat from the skin to the environment depends

Figure 18-3. Avenues of heat transfer are depicted in the rectangles. Heat production increases dramatically in the muscle with exercise. Internally, conduction and convection are important in the transfer of heat both from muscle to core to shell to skin and from muscle to shell to skin. Externally, during heavy exercise, evaporation accounts for practically all of the heat transfer. Other external mechanisms important at rest include radiation, convection, and conduction. Important factors include ΔT (temperature difference between the skin and the air) and ΔP_v (vapor pressure difference between skin and air).

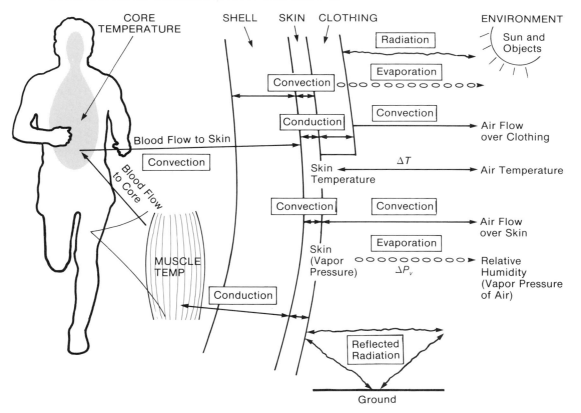

upon (a) the temperature gradient between the skin and the air for both convection and radiation and (b) the rate of evaporation, which is dependent upon the difference vapor pressure between the skin and the environment.[1,54,80]

The rate of convective transfer of heat from muscle to core to skin is also dependent upon the rate of blood flow. When blood vessels (both skin and muscle) are vasodilated little resistance is offered to blood flow and heat transfer takes place rather rapidly. Then if the temperature gradient between the skin and the environment is maintained, heat loss is facilitated (Fig. 18-3). Also, the temperature gradient between the shell and the core must remain at least 2° F; otherwise, the shell will act as an insulating layer.

Increased sweating makes the skin wet, thus raising its vapor pressure. If the relative humidity is low, evaporative heat loss is enhanced. If relative humidity is high, then the difference between skin and environmental vapor pressure is low and heat cannot be dissipated effectively. This later condition, especially during exercise, will exaggerate heat storage.

Temperature Regulation

The function of the thermoregulatory system is to maintain a relatively constant internal body temperature. At rest and during exercise the system strives to keep the temperature at 37° C, which is called the **reference temperature.**

The thermoregulatory system uses the following basic components in carrying out its function: (1) **thermal receptors** or sensors, i.e., organs sensitive to thermal stimuli (heat and cold); (2) **thermal effectors** or organs that respond to the stimuli sensed by the receptors and which produce regulatory or corrective changes; and (3) a **thermal regulatory center** located in the central nervous system that coordinates the incoming information from the receptors with the outgoing regulatory action of the effector organs.

Thermal Receptors

The human body has at least two major thermal receptor areas; one is located in the *hypothalamus* of the brain (central receptors), the other in the *skin* (peripheral receptors). Both receptor areas contain two types of sensors, one sensitive to heat, the other to cold. The receptors in the hypothalamus are sensitive to small temperature fluctuations (within 0.2 to 0.5° F) of the arterial blood perfusing them, whereas the skin receptors respond to fluctuations in environmental temperature.

The receptors in the skin, both those that sense cold and those that sense warmth, are thought to consist mainly of free nerve endings. They are located throughout the body surface, usually with more cold receptors than warm. It was once thought that specialized nerve endings, such as the *end bulbs of Krause* (sensitive to cold) and the *brushes of Ruffini* (sensitive to heat) also served as thermal receptors. This now seems doubtful. At any rate, both the central and peripheral receptors are neurally connected to the cortex as well as to the regulatory center in the hypothalamus. The cortical connections, from which we consciously perceive warm and cold sensations, provide us with a means for voluntary regulation, such as seeking shaded or sunny areas, initiating or avoiding physical exercise, removing or adding clothing, and stretching out or curling up in warm or cool environments, respectively. Regulation initiated from the hypothalamus is reflex in nature and thus involuntary.

Thermal Effectors

The thermal effector organs are the *skeletal muscles,* the *smooth muscles encircling* *the arterioles* that supply blood to the skin, eccrine* *sweat glands,* and certain *endocrine glands.* In a cold environment, the muscles effect shivering, which increases metabolic heat production; at the same time, the arterioles supplying blood to the skin constrict (cutaneous vasoconstriction). In a warm or hot environment, cutaneous vasodilation and sweating occur, as opposed to vasoconstriction and shivering. The importance of vasomotor control (by dilation and constriction) of the arterioles supplying blood to the skin stems from the fact that heat from the body core must first be transported—by circulatory conduction and convection—to the surface before it can be lost to the environment by conduction, convection, radiation, and evaporation. For example, with cutaneous vasoconstriction, skin blood flow is decreased and, hence, so is the transfer of heat from the body core. The opposite is true for cutaneous vasodilation; increased blood flow allows dissipation of more deep body heat to the environment. The secretion of sweat, so important in preventing overheating in humans because it eventually vaporizes, comes from an estimated 2,500,000 sweat glands. These glands are very widely distributed over the body surface, being more heavily concentrated on the palms of the hands, soles of the feet, the neck, and the trunk.

The endocrine glands involved in temperature regulation are the *thyroid* and the *adrenal medulla.* Over several weeks' exposure to cold, metabolic heat production is increased due to increased output of *thy-*

---

*There are two kinds of sweat glands in the body. The eccrine sweat glands, which are the most numerous, secret a dilute, watery sweat that is involved in thermal regulation as mentioned above. The apocrine sweat glands secrete a thicker sweat that is not used for thermal regulation. Rather, this kind of sweat is secreted in response to emotional stress. The apocrine sweat glands are found mainly in the pubic and axillary (underarm) areas.

roxin from the thyroid gland. Also during cold exposure, increased levels of *epinephrine* and *norepinephrine* from the adrenal medulla cause increased heat production along with increased heat conservation through cutaneous vasoconstriction.

The Thermal Regulatory Center

The responses previously described are coordinated by the thermal regulatory center located in the *hypothalamus.* The role of this center is somewhat analogous to that of a thermostat in a house. The temperature of the room (internal body temperature) is measured by a thermometer (receptor organs) and compared to a set point (37° C). If the measured temperature deviates from the set point, the thermostat (hypothalamic center) automatically relays information to the heating or cooling systems (effectors), which correct the temperature to the set point value through the mechanisms we have already described. The return to the set point value then automatically shuts off the effector system.

Although the regulatory center responds to both the central and peripheral thermal receptors mentioned earlier, it does so in different ways. We said that the central receptors initiate appropriate effector action after the internal body temperature is compared with a set point temperature, which is usually 37° C or 98.6° F. The set point, however, can be changed and this is thought to be the major role of the peripheral receptors in temperature regulation. For example, when the skin is warmed, the set point is reduced. In effect, this causes sweating and cutaneous vasodilation and thus body cooling to occur sooner. The opposite is true when the skin is exposed to cold; that is, the set point is increased and increases in heat conservation and heat production occur sooner.

A summary of the thermoregulatory system is shown in Figure 18-4.

RECEPTORS   EFFECTORS

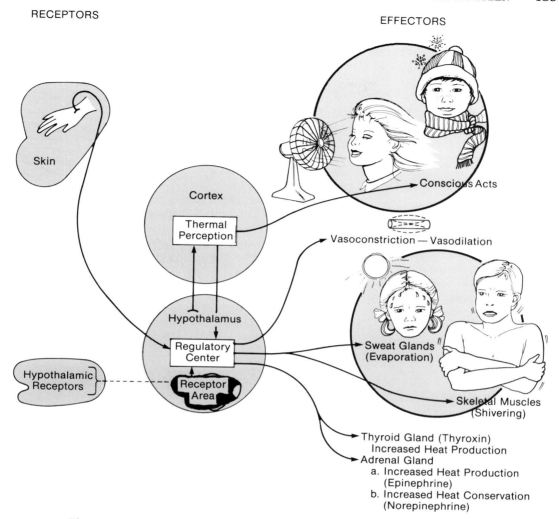

Figure 18-4. A summary of the thermoregulatory system. The internal body temperature is measured by receptor organs and compared to a set point (37° C). If the temperature deviates from the set point, the hypothalamic center automatically relays information to the effector organs, which correct the temperature to the set point value through the mechanisms shown on the right. The return to the set point value then automatically shuts off the effector system. The cortical connections provide us with a means for voluntary regulation of body temperature.

Exercise in the Heat and Heat Disorders

The principal means by which the body loses heat during exercise or exposure to heat are (1) circulatory adjustments of in- creased skin blood flow resulting from cuta- neous vasodilation, and (2) evaporative cooling resulting from increased secretion of sweat. Internal body heat produced mainly by the liver and skeletal muscles is carried by the blood (circulatory convection) to the surface, where conduction, convection, radiation, and particularly evaporation take place (review Fig. 18-3). The cooled blood then returns to the warmer core and the cycle is repeated. The body temperature changes that occur during exercise in a comfortable environment (room temperature) are shown in Figure 18-5. Internal or rectal temperature increases to a new level during the first 30 minutes or so of work, and remains at this new level until work is terminated. At the same time, skin temperature decreases slightly primarily as a result of increased convective and evaporative cooling. The net result of these changes is an increase in the *thermal gradient* between the skin and the core, which facilitates heat loss in the manner previously described.

In a cold or cool environment, exercise that can be maintained for an hour or more is seldom limited by an excessive increase

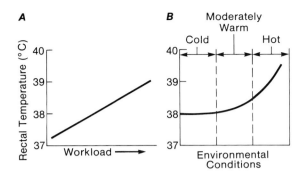

Figure 18-6. *A,* relationship between rectal temperature and work rate in a cool environment. Although environmental conditions remain constant, as the work rate increases, the rectal temperature increases proportionately. *B,* at a constant work rate, the rise in rectal temperature is the same in a cool to moderately warm environment, but it rises disproportionately in a hot environment because of the added resistance to heat loss.

in internal or rectal temperature. Under these environmental conditions, nearly all the metabolic heat produced can be easily dissipated by the circulatory and sudomotor (sweating) adjustments referred to earlier. Even in severe, short-term work, when heat production may well exceed the heat dissipating capacity made possible by these adjustments, exhaustion usually results from the buildup of anaerobic metabolites (mainly lactic acid) before rectal temperature can reach a limiting or dangerous level. It is important to note that the elevation of rectal temperature during exercise, although proportional to the intensity of work (and therefore to metabolic rate), is independent of environmental temperatures ranging from cold to moderately warm (Fig. 18-6).

Exercise in the Heat

As stated earlier, environmental heat reduces the thermal gradient between the environment and the skin surface, and

Figure 18-5. Rectal and skin temperatures during and following 60 minutes of running at 6 miles per hour. Note that during exercise, rectal temperature increases while skin temperature decreases, thus increasing the thermal gradient between skin and core. Environmental conditions were 25° C and 35% relative humidity.

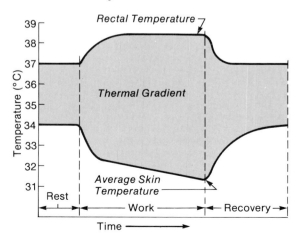

between the skin surface and the body core, thus imposing an added resistance to body heat loss. We have seen that body heat can actually be gained when the temperature of the environment is greater than that of our skin. By the same token, increased humidity imposes a heat loss barrier to the evaporative mechanism by decreasing the vapor pressure gradient between the moisture in the air and the sweat on our skin. Such a heat-loss barrier causes an excessive increase in rectal temperature and severely limits the capacity for work.

Circulatory System and
Sweating Mechanism

The reduced thermal and vapor pressure gradients of hot, humid environments greatly increase the demands placed upon the circulatory system and sweating mechanism. This is evidenced by greater increases in heart rate and sweating during exercise in hot as compared to cool environments (Table 18-2). More blood must be circulated and more sweat secreted by the sweat glands in order to lose any given quantity of heat. Note should also be made of the effects of hot, dry environments on the magnitude of these responses. Even though the temperature is high, the low relative humidity considerably reduces the heat stress because evaporation of sweat is more efficient (Table 18-2). The major circulatory demands while working in the heat are (1) a large blood flow through the working muscles is necessary to provide for the increased respiratory exchange of O_2 and CO_2, and to carry away the increased heat produced there; and (2) as previously indicated, a large skin blood flow is also necessary to cool the blood and supply the sweat glands with water. Excellent reviews of the circulatory adjustments during exercise in the heat have been written by Rowell[68] and Wyndham.[84]

Water and Salt Requirements

The high sweat rates required for adequate evaporative cooling during exposure to heat (0.5 to 2.0 liters per hour) can lead to excessive losses of water (dehydration) and of salt and other electrolytes. When this occurs, work performance and tolerance to heat are greatly reduced; hyperthermia (excessive internal body temperature) with predisposition to serious heat disorders is eminent.[9,15,29,61,69,71,80]

The most serious consequence of profuse sweating is loss of body water. This leads to a decrease in blood volume[41,70] and, if severe enough, to a decrease in sweating rate and evaporative cooling. The decrease

---

TABLE 18-2

Effects of Environmental Heat Loads on Sweat Rate and Heart Rate Responses During 15 Minutes of Moderate Work*

Dry Bulb Temperature, °C	Wet Bulb Temperature,†°C	Relative Humidity, Per Cent	Sweat Rate, Liters Per Hour	Heart Rate, Beats Per Minute
22	14.7	45	0.4	150
35	26.0	50	1.0	155
35	33.4	90	1.6	165

*Based on data from Fox.[21]

†For a definition of wet bulb temperature, see p. 503

in blood volume and evaporative cooling, in turn, cause added circulatory strain with eventual circulatory collapse and an excessive rise in rectal temperature. Figure 18-7 shows clearly the effects of progressive water and salt deficiencies during intermittent marching in the heat for a 6-hour period. The best replacement fluid is one that contains as much salt and water as is lost through sweating; that is, about 1 to 2 grams of salt per liter of water. Several such types of replacement fluids—which have been flavored for palatability—are available commercially. When these liquids are used, salt tablets should *not* be taken. Salt tablets should not be taken by the athlete unless a clinical test shows an electrolyte deficiency. Fluids should be administered during as well as after prolonged work bouts in the heat. Adequate hydration by voluntary intake (thirst mechanism) alone takes several days. Therefore, during day-to-day heat exposures it might

be necessary to insist on the drinking of some liquid even though there is no apparent thirst.

Heat Disorders in Athletics

The seriousness of overexposure to heat while exercising is exemplified not only by a decrease in work performance, but also by a predisposition to heat illness.[39] These disorders are categorized in ascending severity as: (1) heat cramps, (2) heat syncope, (3) heat exhaustion—either salt-depletion or water-depletion, and (4) heat stroke. Figure 18-8 schematically depicts the events associated with the various heat disorders. Special note is made of the possibility of *exercise-induced hypothermia.* Exercise-induced hypothermia is relatively rare, but does occur (see page 515).

1. *Heat Cramps.* Heat cramps are characterized by muscle spasms or twitching in the arms, legs, and, possibly, abdomen and usually occur in the unacclimatized individual.

2. *Heat Syncope.* Heat syncope is characterized by a general weakness and fatigue, hypotension (low blood pressure), occasionally blurred vision, pallor (paleness), syncope (brief loss of consciousness), and elevated skin and core temperature. Heat syncope usually occurs in the unacclimatized.

3. *Heat Exhaustion (Water Depletion).* Water-depletion heat exhaustion is characterized by reduced sweating, although there is a large weight loss, dry tongue and mouth ("cotton-mouth"), thirst, elevated skin and core temperature, weakness, loss of coordination, and dullness. Another sign is that the urine is very concentrated and almost an orange color. Water-depletion heat exhaustion can occur in the acclimatized individual.

4. *Heat Exhaustion (Salt Depletion).* Salt-depletion heat exhaustion is characterized by headache, dizziness, fatigue,

Figure 18-7. Effects of progressive water loss (and salt deficiency) during intermittent marching in the heat. When water consumption equals sweat loss (water balance), rectal temperature is lowest, compared to no replacement and water ad libitum. Environmental conditions were 100° F and 35 to 45% relative humidity. (Adapted from Pitts et al.[61])

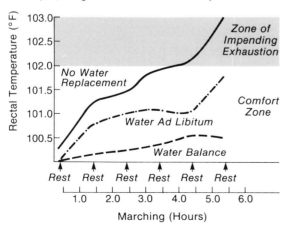

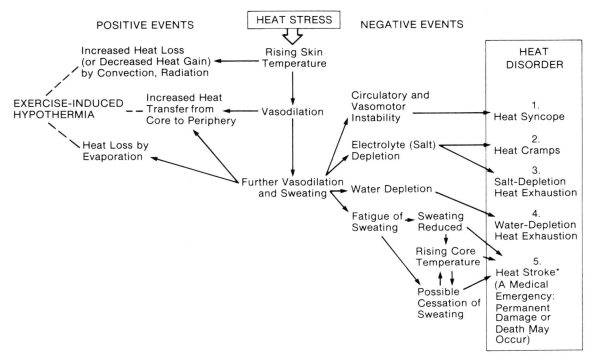

Figure 18-8. When an athlete is exposed to a heat stress during exercise, a number of events occur including elevated skin temperature, vasodilation, and sweating. Generally, these are positive and facilitate heat loss, which helps to minimize a rise in core temperature. Prolonged effort or extreme conditions, however, can lead to a variety of heat disorders. On the extreme left is depicted a parodoxical circumstance, hypothermia. Under the proper conditions, heat loss may be exaggerated leading to mild hypothermia.[43,55]

nausea, possible vomiting and diarrhea, syncope, and muscle cramps. Salt-depletion heat exhaustion is insidious in that it usually takes 3 to 5 days to develop. It can occur in an acclimatized individual.

5. *Heat Stroke.* We cannot emphasize the following too much: HEAT STROKE IS A LIFE-THREATENING, MEDICAL EMERGENCY. The sweating mechanism has become fatigued although some sweating may still be occurring. Additionally there are elevated skin and core temperatures (core temperature may well exceed 105° F or 40.5° C), muscle flaccidity, involuntary limb movement, seizures and coma, vomiting and diarrhea, and tachy-

cardia (rapid, shallow heart beat). The individual may be irrational and hallucinating if not in a coma. Heat stroke may occur to any individual under the proper conditions. The appearance of any one of these features should be taken seriously and emergency procedures begun immediately. The athlete should not be left alone to "rest."

The most frequent common denominators for all of these conditions are (1) heat exposure, (2) loss of water and electrolytes, and (3) heat storage, usually reflected by a high core temperature (hyperthermia). However, the single most important factor, from a clinical standpoint, is loss of body water. It is also important to point out that inattention to heat cramps, heat syncope, and heat exhaustion can lead to heat stroke and finally to death because of irreversible damage to the central nervous system. Even in those who do recover from heat stroke there often is some permanent damage to the thermoregulatory center in the hypothalamus. As a result of this damage, the hypothalamus loses some of its integrity or ability to regulate body temperature. This leads to decreased heat conductance from the body core to the periphery and explains why many who have survived heat stroke are more prone to future heat disorders.[71]

Normally, a person will voluntarily stop working and seek shelter from the heat when heat cramps, heat exhaustion, or syncope, sets in. However, highly competitive athletes are more vulnerable to heat disorders in general and heat stroke in particular for several reasons: (1) they are highly competitive (motivated) and therefore more likely to overextend themselves; (2) they have a sense of immortality; (3) they sometimes are required to wear heavy protective equipment, which adds resistance to heat dissipation; and (4) incomprehensible as it may seem, the coach may deny them water during prolonged contests or practice sessions, which lowers their resistance to heat tolerance. These factors, either singularly or combined, are as pertinent to environmental conditions that are usually considered "comfortable" as they are to hot environments. For example, rectal temperatures equal to or greater than 40° C (104° F) are not uncommon, even in athletes who compete at environmental temperatures as low as 5° to 16° C (41° to 61° F).

Football

As discussed earlier, the seriousness of the problem of heat disorders in athletics is best illustrated by the frequency of heat stroke deaths among football players. These deaths resulted from a combination of the factors mentioned above and therefore could have been prevented by a well-informed coach or team physician. You will recall that information about nine of twelve deaths reported between 1959 and 1962 revealed that: (1) all victims were interior linemen, who are probably required to work hardest and longest; (2) most were stricken during the first 2 days of preseason practice, indicating that they were probably not in good physical condition (see Table 18-1); (3) environmental conditions ranged from high temperature and low relative humidity to low temperature and high humidity (see Fig. 18-1); (4) all players were dressed in full uniform which, by virtue of its weight (6 kg or 13 pounds), increases the effective workload (metabolism) and interferes with heat dissipation; and (5) most were not permitted to drink water during practice, but were required to take salt tablets. Unfortunately, these situations are typical of those that have existed throughout the United States during preseason football practice, both in high school and college. It is hoped that today's coaches are well informed concerning the need for fluid intake during practice. There is no evidence available that shows water intake is detrimental to physical performance.

If it is not obvious to you why these men died needlessly of heat stroke, consider the following illustration. Nine men ran on a treadmill for 30 minutes at 9.6 km/hr (6 mph) under three conditions: (1) in shorts only; (2) in a football uniform; and (3) in shorts plus a backpack weighing the same as the uniform (13 pounds). The temperature of the room for all runs was only 23.9° C (78° F), with a relative humidity of 35%—in other words, a normally comfortable situation. As shown in Figure 18-9A the increase in rectal temperature

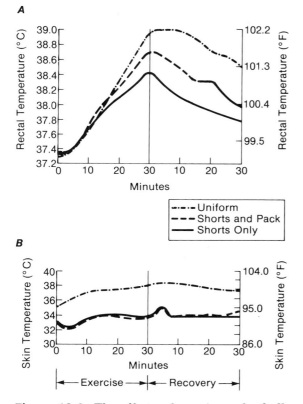

Figure 18-9. The effects of wearing a football uniform on rectal and skin temperatures during 30 minutes of running at 6 miles per hour. *A,* The uniform retards heat loss, causing rectal temperature to climb during exercise and remain elevated during recovery. *B,* Skin temperatures while wearing the uniform also rise considerably owing to reduction in evaporative cooling. Environmental conditions were 78° F and 35% relative humidity. (Adapted from Mathews, Fox, and Tanzi.[44])

while wearing the uniform was 1.5 times greater (average, 39.0° C) than when only shorts were worn.[43]

The weight of the uniform alone, as shown by the increase in rectal temperature while carrying the pack, was as important a factor as was the heat loss barrier imposed by the clothing and protective pads of the uniform. The heat loss barrier of the uniform showed its effect by the excessively high skin temperatures of those areas covered by both pads and clothing, compared with conditions obtained by shorts and shorts plus pack (Fig. 18-9*B*). In other words, the uniform prevented the evaporation of sweat, greatly impairing body cooling. Comcomitant with this was a twofold greater loss of body water because of profuse sweating and a significantly higher heart rate or circulatory strain—both of which reduce tolerance to heat.

Perhaps even more startling was the slow return of rectal temperature during recovery in the uniform, as compared with the other conditions. This is an extremely important point to remember. For example, a 16-year-old boy reported to his first football practice on a hot day and was required to wear a complete uniform. After a period of time, he felt ill. The coach placed him in the shade but did not remove his uniform; practice was then resumed and the boy was left unattended. About 2 hours later the boy was found unconscious. He was then taken to the hospital, where he died of heat stroke.

Other Sports

Serious heat disorders in athletics are not confined to football. Football was merely used as an example. Any sport or physical activity is potentially hazardous for heat illness. This includes wrestling, where the athlete loses large quantities of water in order to "make weight," and track-and-field events, particularly those held outdoors.[8,31,32,35] For example, in the 1956 Olympic Games, the marathon was run on a hot (30° C or 85° F), humid day. One of the United States marathoners reported that at the start of the race, Emil Zatopek, the great Czechoslovakian runner, said "Today we die!" It was not surprising that a French Algerian, who was heat acclimatized because of his native climate won that particular marathon race.[8] In addition, heat stroke in novice long-distance runners (10 km or more) is quite common.[31,32]

With the advent and unprecedented growth of jogging and subsequent development of both "fun runs" and races, literally millions of people are participating. Many races are held during the hot-weather months and thus provide a potential for heat illness.[79] Concerned by hot-weather conditions under which distance races and fun runs are sometimes held, the American College of Sports Medicine has issued a new Position Stand on Prevention of Thermal Injuries During Distance Running.[2] This replaces a statement issued in 1975.[35] The updated stand (1984) is divided into four sections dealing with (1) the Medical Director, (2) race organization, (3) medical support, and (4) competitor education. We will highlight components of the ACSM position stand featuring race organization and competitor education.

Race Organization

1. Races should be organized to avoid the hottest summer months and the hottest part of the day. As there are great regional variations in environmental conditions, the local weather history will be most helpful in scheduling an event to avoid times when an unacceptable level of heat stress is likely to prevail. Organizers should be cautious of unseasonably hot days in the early spring, as entrants will almost certainly not be heat acclimatized.

2. The environmental heat stress prediction for the day should be obtained from the meteorological service. It can be measured as wet bulb globe temperature (WBGT), which is a temperature/humidity/radiation index. If WBGT is above 28° C (82° F), consideration should be given to rescheduling or delaying the race until safer conditions prevail. If below 28°C, participants may be alerted to the degree of heat stress by using color-coded flags at the start of the race and at key positions along the course (see p. 504).

3. All summer events should be scheduled for the early morning, ideally before 8:00 A.M., or in the evening after 6:00 P.M., to minimize solar radiation.

4. An adequate supply of water should be available before the race and every 2 to 3 km during the race. Runners should be encouraged to consume 100 to 200 ml at each station.

5. Race officials should be educated as to the warning signs of an impending collapse. Each official should wear an identifiable arm band or badge and should warn runners to stop if they appear to be in difficulty.

6. Adequate traffic and crowd control must be maintained at all times.

7. There should be a ready source of radio communications from various points on the course to a central organizing point to coordinate responses to emergencies.

Competitor Education

Recognizing that all runners are not well versed in the hazards of thermal stress, the ACSM recognizes that distributing guidelines before the race, providing publicity in the press, and holding clinics and seminars may be valuable. Persons particularly prone to heat illness include the obese, the unfit, the dehydrated, those unacclimatized, those with previous history of heat stroke, and anyone who runs while ill. Children are more susceptible than adults. Specific points include the following:

1. Adequate training and fitness are important for full enjoyment of the run and also to prevent heat-related injuries.
2. Prior training in the heat will promote heat acclimatization and thereby reduce the risk of heat injury. It is wise to do as much training as possible at the time of day at which the race will be held.
3. Fluid consumption before and during the race will reduce the risk of heat injury, particularly in longer runs such as the marathon.
4. Illness prior to and at the time of the event should preclude competition.
5. Participants should be advised of the early symptoms of heat injury. These include clumsiness, stumbling, excessive sweating (and also cessation of sweating), headache, nausea, dizziness, apathy, and any gradual impairment of consciousness.
6. Participants should be advised to choose a comfortable speed and not to run faster than conditions warrant.
7. Participants are advised to run with a partner, each being responsible for the other's well being.

Even ordinary activities, such as cutting the grass on an extremely warm day, can induce heat illness if proper precautions are not taken. In any case, the basic principles underlying prevention of heat disorders are common to all situations.

Prevention of Heat Disorders

The occurrence of heat disorders can be greatly reduced by: (1) adequate salt and water replacement; (2) acclimatization to heat; and (3) awareness of the limitations imposed by the combination of exercise, clothing, and environmental heat.

Salt and Water Replacement

As we have seen, water and salt replacement during and following work in the heat is absolutely essential (see Fig. 18-6). It is not unusual for an athlete to lose 5 to 15 pounds (mostly water loss, i.e., sweat) during each practice session or during a game. Such large weight losses can occur even when water is available on the field. For example, it has been shown that a college football player (tackle) lost 14 pounds during one fall preseason practice in spite of offering water on the field.[49] It was further shown that the largest weight losses occurred in the tackles, the least in the quarterbacks. These considerable weight losses serve to illustrate the need for the coach to keep daily weight records to prevent progressive day-to-day dehydration. The athletes should be weighed before and after each practice session. If a weight loss of greater than 2% exists before the next scheduled practice, the player should be excused from any further sessions until this weight deficit is reduced. For example, an athlete who normally weighs 200 pounds and who weighs in for the next day's practice at 196 pounds should not practice that day.

Water Replacement

The availability of water should be unrestricted at all times during scheduled practices and games. The "superhydrated" athlete suffers no impairment of efficiency.[6,29] However, large amounts of water should not be imbibed at any one time since the athlete may feel uncomfortable under these conditions. The best procedure is to schedule frequent water breaks as well as to encourage the drinking of water ad libitum.

For athletic teams, water consumption can be facilitated by maintaining several water stations strategically located around the practice field. This allows the player convenient access to water. Frequent trips to the "bucket" and drinking small amounts are ideal. This procedure is physiologically more sensible than having a break every hour or so, during which the athlete might gulp copious amounts of water; also, it allows for more efficient use of practice time. Ice water buckets, pressurized garden-spray containers, and thermos jugs are containers that can be properly located and adequately maintained.[49]

What the athlete should drink. During competition and training in hot and/or humid weather, coaches and athletes should follow the "drinking" guidelines outlined in Table 18-3. Many liquids may be imbibed to replace lost water and satisfy thirst, but what is needed most is a drink that will provide for hydration without "lying in the stomach" for too long. A cold drink that is hypotonic and has a concentration of sugar below that which retards gastric emptying is ideal. As shown in Figure 18-10, liquids with high concentrations of glucose (sugar) significantly retard gastric emptying.[14] In the study[14] shown in the figure, the subjects drank 400 ml (13.5 ounces) of liquid containing various concentrations of sugar. After 15 minutes, the residue remaining in the stomach was removed and measured through a gastric tube. A 2.5% glucose solution emptied at about the same rate as no sugar at all. However, notice how the 5% and 10% solutions drastically retarded gastric emptying. Thus the ideal drink should contain less than 2.5% sugar. Having made these observations, we must emphasize that water is the best and most available drink.

TABLE 18-3

Guidelines for Fluid Intake for Athletes

Content of Drink
    The drink should be:
        hypotonic (few solid particles per unit of water)
        low in sugar content (less than 2.5 grams per 100 ml of water)
        cold (roughly 45–55°F, or 8–13°C)
        palatable (it will be consumed in volumes ranging from 100 to 400 ml, or 3 to 10 ounces)

Amount to be Ingested before Competition
    Drink 400–600 ml (13.5 to 20 ounces) of water or the above drink 30 minutes before the start of competition.

Amount to be Ingested during Competition
    During the competition, 100 to 200 ml (3 to 6.5 ounces) of the above drink should be taken at 10 to 15 minute intervals throughout the activity.

Post-Competition Diet
    Following the competition, modest salting of foods and the ingestion of drinks with essential minerals can adequately replace the electrolytes (sodium and potassium) lost in sweat.

Detection of Dehydration
    The athlete should keep a record of his or her early morning body weight (taken immediately after rising, after urination, and before breakfast) to detect symptoms of a condition of chronic dehydration.

Value of Drink(s)
    Drinks are of significant value in races lasting more than 50 to 60 minutes.

---

*Text appearing beneath each heading is from Costill.[13]

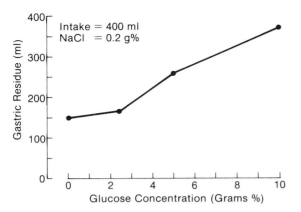

Figure 18-10. Liquids with high concentrations of glucose (sugar) significantly retard gastric emptying. A 2.5% glucose solution empties at about the same rate as a solution with no sugar at all. However, 5% and 10% solutions drastically retard gastric emptying. (Based on data from Costill and Saltin.[14])

Also, contrary to popular belief, cold (8°–13° C or 45°–55° F) drinks *do not* cause stomach cramps. Such cramps are probably related to the volume taken in rather than to temperature. Fluid replacement is of significant value mainly in activities lasting 50 to 60 minutes or longer.

Water loss versus fat loss. Water has *no* caloric value; the drinking of water in large amounts therefore *does not* result in obesity. Nor does loss of water play *any* role in the loss of body fat. Thus deliberately causing excessive water loss through sweating for purposes of losing weight is uncalled for. Such a practice is in fact very hazardous; persons who garb themselves in sweatsuits, rubber jackets, and other similar clothing on hot days run the risk of serious heat illness and other health problems. They may think they are "melting off" pounds, but this has nothing to do with real weight loss. Real weight loss is the loss of body fat, and *body fat does not melt*. As previously indicated, it is increased physical activity that aids in the loss of body fat—a loss that takes place over a considerable period of time. Remember, the single most important aspect of loss of body fat is this: *caloric intake (calories due to food) must be less than caloric output (energy spent during activity)*.

The Body Weight Chart. The thirst mechanism—that is, the natural desire for drinking water—is not always adequate to the task of replacing a sufficient amount of fluid, particularly during day-to-day exposure to high environmental heat and/or humidity. Therefore, continued measurements of daily body weight (which mainly reflect water loss) should be taken. The body weight should be recorded before and after practice or training so that possible excessive water loss may be detected. A 3% weight (water) deficit is cause for concern if it is not made up in a 24- to 48-hour period. Figure 18-11 contains an example of a chart that may be used for measuring weight as needed (instructions for using the chart are included in the figure).

Salt Replacement

A person normally consumes 7 to 15 grams of salt each day, which is more than adequate. As was previously mentioned, some salt is lost through sweating and when excessive, supplemental salt is required.

There are basically two ways to supplement your body with salt: (1) through the food you eat (diet); and (2) through taking salt tablets. Probably the safest and best way to supplement salt is through the diet. In other words, during prolonged excessive sweating, you should make an effort to salt your food a little more than you normally do. If this is done consistently, the salt that was lost in the sweat should be adequately replaced. The taking of salt tablets is usually not necessary with most sports activities. Too often salt tablets are taken in excess and without drinking sufficient water. Such a practice can actually *promote* rather than prevent the possibil-

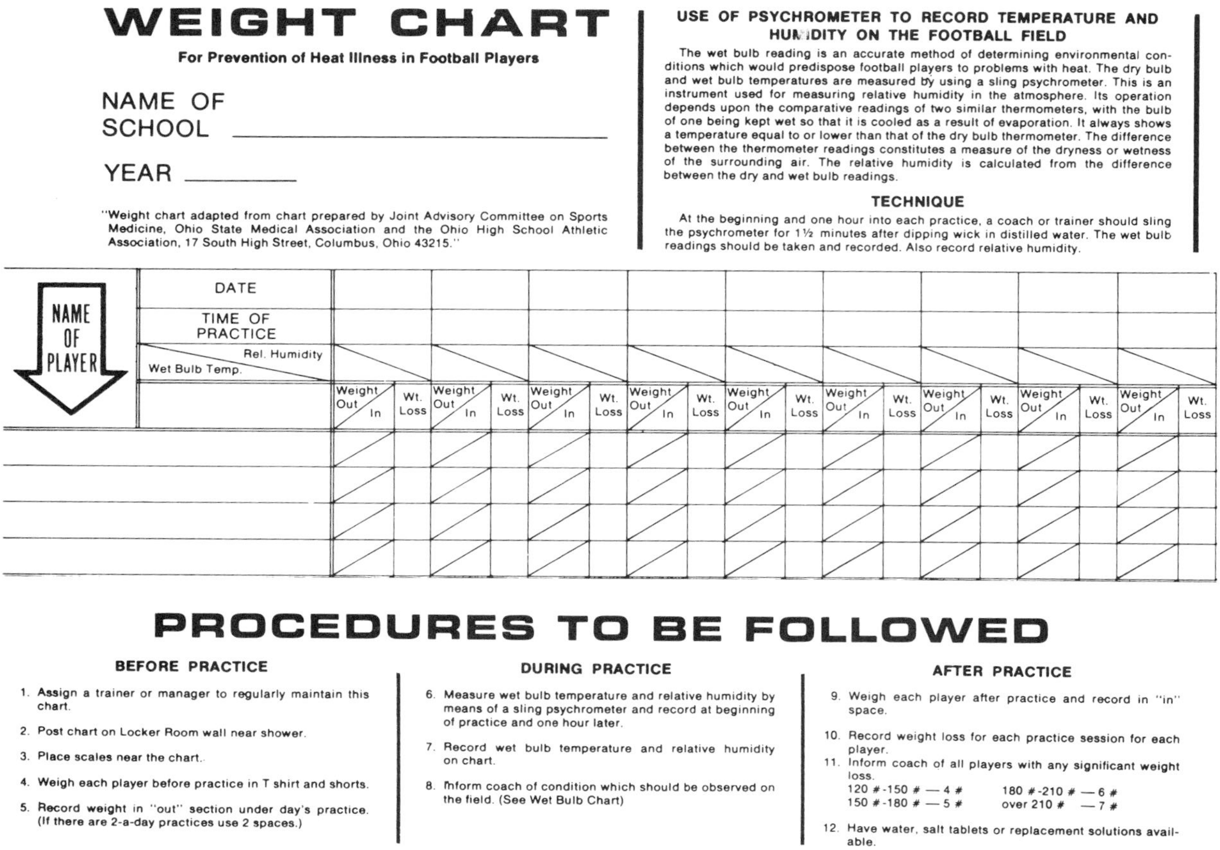

WEIGHT CHART
For Prevention of Heat Illness in Football Players

NAME OF
SCHOOL _____

YEAR _____

"Weight chart adapted from chart prepared by Joint Advisory Committee on Sports Medicine, Ohio State Medical Association and the Ohio High School Athletic Association, 17 South High Street, Columbus, Ohio 43215."

USE OF PSYCHROMETER TO RECORD TEMPERATURE AND HUMIDITY ON THE FOOTBALL FIELD

The wet bulb reading is an accurate method of determining environmental conditions which would predispose football players to problems with heat. The dry bulb and wet bulb temperatures are measured by using a sling psychrometer. This is an instrument used for measuring relative humidity in the atmosphere. Its operation depends upon the comparative readings of two similar thermometers, with the bulb of one being kept wet so that it is cooled as a result of evaporation. It always shows a temperature equal to or lower than that of the dry bulb thermometer. The difference between the thermometer readings constitutes a measure of the dryness or wetness of the surrounding air. The relative humidity is calculated from the difference between the dry and wet bulb readings.

TECHNIQUE

At the beginning and one hour into each practice, a coach or trainer should sling the psychrometer for 1½ minutes after dipping wick in distilled water. The wet bulb readings should be taken and recorded. Also record relative humidity.

NAME OF PLAYER

DATE									
TIME OF PRACTICE									
Rel. Humidity									
Wet Bulb Temp.									
Weight Out/In	Wt. Loss	Weight Out/In	Wt. Loss	Weight Out/In	Wt. Loss	Weight Out/In	Wt. Loss	Weight Out/In	Wt. Loss

PROCEDURES TO BE FOLLOWED

BEFORE PRACTICE

1. Assign a trainer or manager to regularly maintain this chart.
2. Post chart on Locker Room wall near shower.
3. Place scales near the chart.
4. Weigh each player before practice in T shirt and shorts.
5. Record weight in "out" section under day's practice. (If there are 2-a-day practices use 2 spaces.)

DURING PRACTICE

6. Measure wet bulb temperature and relative humidity by means of a sling psychrometer and record at beginning of practice and one hour later.
7. Record wet bulb temperature and relative humidity on chart.
8. Inform coach of condition which should be observed on the field. (See Wet Bulb Chart)

AFTER PRACTICE

9. Weigh each player after practice and record in "in" space.
10. Record weight loss for each practice session for each player.
11. Inform coach of all players with any significant weight loss.
   120 # -150 # — 4 #   180 # -210 # — 6 #
   150 # -180 # — 5 #   over 210 # — 7 #
12. Have water, salt tablets or replacement solutions available.

Figure 18-11. Example of a body-weight chart including instructions for its use. (Modified from Murphy.[48])

ity of serious heat injury. Provided extra salt (from the "shaker") is supplied during meals, salt tablets are not recommended for most athletes.

Acclimatization to Heat

Tolerance and ability to work comfortably in the heat are increased through heat acclimatization.[4,9,46,68,84,85] It improves the circulatory and sweating responses (Table 18-4), which facilitate heat dissipation, and thus minimize changes in skin and rectal temperature. Acclimatization is accomplished by a progressive exercise program performed in the heat for 5 to 8 days. Merely resting in the heat produces little, if any, tolerance to heat. An example of such a program would be 20 minutes of light work (in shorts) followed by 20 minutes of rest on the first day. Each day the work period, workload, and uniform dress can be increased. On the last day, the work period may be 30 minutes long at full speed and in complete uniform, with rest periods of 10 to 15 minutes. During the rest periods, water or a commercial electrolyte solution should be administered since—in addition to the factors already mentioned—withholding liquids significantly retards the acclimati-

TABLE 18-4

Physiological Adjustments While Working in the Heat Following Acclimatization

Physiological Mechanisms	Physiological Adjustments
Circulatory System	
Pulse rate	Decreased
Skin blood flow	(1) time of response increased
	(2) decreased skin blood flow (dry heat); no change in skin blood flow (humid heat)
Blood volume	Increased
Blood pressure	Adequately regulated
Sweating Mechanism	
Sweat rate	Increased and more rapid response
Evaporation	Increased
Salt loss in sweat	Decreased
Subjective Symptoms	
Nausea	Decreased
Dizziness	Decreased
Syncope (fainting)	Decreased
Discomfort	Decreased

zation process. Such a program serves two purposes: (1) it enhances physical conditioning; and (2) it provides acclimatization to heat.

The relationship between physical conditioning and heat acclimatization is interesting and deserves further comment.[17,26, 28,37,52,58,59,62,63,67,73,74] It has been shown that a training program conducted indoors or outdoors during the winter months promotes a high degree of heat acclimatization even though the subjects had not been exposed to environmental heat since the preceding summer.[26,62,63] It has been estimated that training produces at least 50 to 65% of the total physiological adjustment resulting from heat acclimatization.[26,51,58] An example of this is shown in Figure 18-12. As can be seen, when subjects were neither trained nor acclimatized, the sweating response did not start until a relatively high internal body temperature was reached (37.7° C). On the other hand, when the subjects were

Figure 18-12. In untrained and unacclimatized subjects, the sweating response starts at a relatively high body temperature (37.7° C). When subjects are trained, the onset of sweating occurs at a lower temperature (37.5° C), and when subjects are both trained and acclimatized, sweating begins at an even lower body temperature (37.2° C). Furthermore, not only is the onset of sweating faster under these latter conditions, but its rate of increase is also greater (as evidenced by the steepness of the slopes of the lines). (Based on data from Nadel.[51])

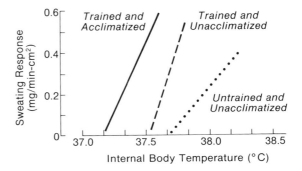

physiologically trained, the onset of sweating occurred at a lower internal temperature (37.5° C) and at the lowest temperature (37.2° C) when the subjects were both trained and acclimatized to the heat. Furthermore, not only was the onset of sweating faster under these latter conditions, but its rate of increase was also greater (as evidenced by the steepness of the slopes of the lines). This faster onset and greater rate of sweating reduce the skin temperature, promoting greater body cooling. The great elevation in metabolic rate and therefore in heat production during training causes rectal temperatures to increase close to 40° C at the end of each workout. Such high rectal temperatures undoubtedly serve as a stimulus for the improvement of the circulatory and sweating adjustments characteristic of the acclimatized individual.

It should be mentioned at this time that it was once thought that men and women differed in their responses to high environmental temperatures, particularly during exercise.[16,53,60] The biggest difference was in the females' lower sweating rate and lower evaporative heat loss. However, it is now thought that these differences were in part due to the higher level of cardiovascular fitness of the male subjects compared with the female subjects. When this factor is equated, there appear to be no major differences in thermal responses between the sexes.[17,27,83] In other words, given the same relative workload in the same hot environment, thermoregulation is the same in both men and women.

Clothing and Environment

In spite of consideration for the previous precautions, heat disorders can occur when the exercise load is superimposed on heat-loss resistances induced by environmental conditions or the wearing of necessary protective equipment and clothing required in some activities, or both (see Fig. 18-3). For example, we know a nude man exercising in a hot, saturated environment cannot lose a significant amount of heat since all avenues of heat loss are blocked. We have also seen that neither can an exercising person lose a significant amount of heat even in a moderate environment when most of his or her surface (skin) is covered with protective equipment impermeable to sweat (see Fig. 18-9B). A high school football player died from heat stroke during a preseason practice session in which he was required to wear, beneath a full uniform, a rubber sweat suit! Is there any wonder why he died? Regardless of acclimatization and complete hydration, an athlete can suffer heat illness while wearing full equipment if the environmental conditions are severe and the workload is heavy.

Clothing

The padding of the football uniform covers 50% of the body, seriously limiting heat loss through evaporative cooling.[44] There are certain considerations of dress that you as the coach can take into account to aid in heat dissipation when weather conditions warrant:

1. Have your athletes wear short sleeve netted jerseys, loose fitting and light in color, and no stockings;
2. Remove helmets when feasible;
3. Use conservative taping on exposed skin surfaces; and
4. During rest periods, remove as much clothing as feasible to expose skin surface, e.g., raise jersey to expose abdominal area.

Environment

Sufficient information is now available for constructing several environmental guidelines. These guidelines enable the coach and others to make reasonable estimates of the severity of the climatic conditions as they may affect the athletes.

1. *The Football Weather Guide.* The football weather guide shown in Figure 18-13 was constructed from the weather data gathered at the time of the heat stroke fatalities shown in Figure 18-1. Note that any combination of environmental conditions in Zone 1 would be considered safe. Under conditions obtained in Zone 2, all players should be carefully observed for symptoms of heat illness, for example, nausea, profuse sweating, lack of good color, headache, and lack of coordination. When conditions meet those of Zone 3, practice should be postponed, or only moderately light workouts in shorts should be permitted. Unacclimatized players should be closely observed for the symptoms previously mentioned. Note that all the heat stroke fatalities plus the marine survivors referred to earlier occurred in this zone. It should be mentioned that the marines were wearing the usual fatigue uniforms and were engaged in heavy exercise.

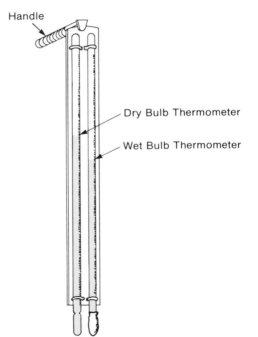

Figure 18-14. Sling psychrometer. This instrument, composed of a dry bulb and a wet bulb thermometer, is used to measure relative humidity.

Figure 18-13. Football weather guide for prevention of heat illness. The combination of relative humidity and air temperature in Zone 1 can be considered safe; for Zone 2, use caution; for Zone 3, use extreme caution when working in a football uniform.

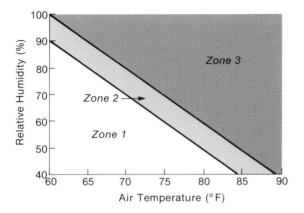

2. *The WBT Index.* Perhaps the simplest measurement of environmental heat stress is the **wet bulb temperature (WBT).** The WBT is obtained by first wetting a wick wrapped around the bulb of a thermometer and then determining the effects of evaporation of moisture in the wick on the thermometer's temperature reading. The thermometer used in this assessment is called a **wet bulb thermometer.** Together with a regular thermometer (dry bulb), it is contained in a device called a *sling psychrometer,* which is used to produce evaporation. Actual measurement of the WBT involves dipping the wick of the wet bulb thermometer into water, after which the psychrometer housing the thermometer (Fig. 18-14) is spun by its handle for 1½ minutes (a process known as "sling-

ing"). As the water in the wick evaporates, the bulb of the thermometer is cooled, just as your skin is cooled when sweat evaporates. The amount of evaporation depends upon wind currents and, more importantly, the amount of water vapor in the air. Therefore, a high wet bulb temperature would reflect considerable moisture in the air (high relative humidity) with little evaporation possible. A low wet bulb temperature, on the other hand, would reflect little moisture (low relative humidity) with a high rate of evaporation possible. The wet bulb temperature never exceeds the dry bulb temperature; when they are equal, the air is completely saturated with water vapor (relative humidity is 100%), and no evaporation is possible. The calculation of relative humidity from wet and dry bulb temperatures is given in Table 18-5.

The following wet bulb temperatures have been suggested by Murphy and Ashe[50] as guides to the degree of environmental stress on persons wearing heavy, protective clothing, such as a football uniform:

WET BULB TEMPERATURE	PRECAUTIONS
Less than 60° F	No precaution necessary
61 to 66° F	Alert observation of all squad members, particularly those who lose considerable weight
67 to 72° F	Insist water be given on field
73 to 77° F	Alter practice schedule to provide rest periods every 30 minutes, in addition to previous precautions
78° F or higher	Practice postponed or conducted in shorts

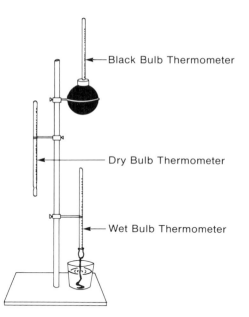

Figure 18-15. An instrument that simultaneously measures solar radiation (black bulb or globe thermometer), air temperature (dry bulb thermometer), and relative humidity computed via the wet bulb thermometer in conjunction with the dry bulb thermometer. A combination of the three temperatures recorded is used in computing the wet bulb globe (WBGT) index.

3. *The Wet Bulb Globe Temperature.* The **wet bulb globe temperature (WBGT)** consists of (a) ordinary air temperature (measured with a dry bulb thermometer), (b) temperature as affected by wind and humidity (measured with a wet bulb thermometer), and (c) temperature as affected by radiant heat from the sun (measured with a black globe thermometer). Figure 18-15 shows the combination of thermometers used to take the WBGT. WBGT Index indicators are available commercially, however, you could make your own unit with the assistance of your chemistry or physics teacher. Equipment needed includes 3 thermometers, a ring stand and 3 clamps, a wick (which can be made from

TABLE 18-5

Relative Humidity From Wet and Dry Bulb Thermometers (Celsius Scale) (Dry Bulb, t °C.; Wet Bulb, t' °C.)*

t \ $t - t'$	1.0	2.0	3.0	4.0	5.0	6.0	7.0	8.0	9.0	10.0	11.0	12.0	13.0	14.0	15.0
16	90	81	71	63	54	46	38	30	23	15	8				
17	90	81	72	64	55	47	40	32	25	18	11				
18	91	82	73	65	57	49	41	34	27	20	14	7			
19	91	82	74	65	58	50	43	36	29	22	16	10			
20	91	83	74	66	59	51	44	37	31	24	18	12			
21	91	83	75	67	60	53	46	39	32	26	20	14	6		
22	92	83	76	68	61	54	47	40	34	28	22	17	9	6	
23	92	84	76	69	62	55	48	42	36	30	24	19	11	8	
24	92	84	77	69	62	56	49	43	37	31	26	20	13	10	5
25	92	84	77	70	63	57	50	44	39	33	28	22	15	12	8
26	92	85	78	71	64	58	51	46	40	34	29	24	17	14	10
27	92	85	78	71	65	58	52	47	41	36	31	26	19	16	12
28	93	85	78	72	65	59	53	48	42	37	32	27	21	18	13
29	93	86	79	72	66	60	54	49	43	38	33	28	22	19	15
30	93	86	79	73	66	61	55	50	44	39	35	30	24	21	17
31	93	86	80	73	67	61	56	51	45	40	36	31	25	22	18
32	93	86	80	74	68	62	57	51	46	41	37	32	27	24	20
33	93	87	80	74	68	63	57	52	47	42	38	33	28	25	21
34	93	87	81	75	69	63	58	53	48	43	39	35	29	26	23
35	94	87	81	75	69	64	59	54	49	44	40	36	30	28	24
36	94	87	81	75	70	64	59	54	50	45	41	37	32	29	25
37	94	87	82	76	70	65	60	55	51	46	42	38	33	30	26
38	94	88	82	76	71	66	61	56	51	47	43	39	34	31	27
39	94	88	82	77	71	66	61	57	52	48	43	39	35	32	28
40	94	88	82	77	72	67	62	57	53	48	44	40	36	33	29

Example: (t) Dry Bulb = 27°
(t') Wet Bulb = 20°
$t - t'$ = 7°
R.H. = 52%

*Condensed from U.S. Weather Bureau Bulletin No. 1071.

gauze), and a copper toilet bowl float. The float should be painted flat black.

The assembled device is placed in the open, away from trees, buildings, or other objects that cast shadows or influence air movement. Readings should not be made for at least 30 minutes after the unit is in place. To compute the WBGT, the following formula is used:

$$WBGT\,(°F) = (0.7 \times wb) + (0.2 \times g) + (0.1 \times db)$$

where

wb = wet bulb temperature
g = black globe temperature (radiant energy)
db = dry bulb temperature

If, for example, the wet bulb temperature is 75° F, the black globe temperature is 110° F, and the dry bulb temperature is 85° F, then:

$$WBGT = (75 \times .7) + (110 \times .2) + (85 \times .1)$$
$$= 83° F$$

A wet bulb globe temperature of 83° F is quite high. It falls in the upper range of the WBGT Index, which, like the WBT Index, is designed to identify conditions of heat stress. Specifically, the WBGT Index was developed by the armed forces for use in determining stress on unconditioned trainees participating in physical activity while wearing army fatigues.

The ACSM position stand suggests a flag warning system, similar to that used by the military, to be used at race sites to alert participants to potential risk of thermal stress.[2] Table 18-6 represents the various thermal stress risk levels. Keep in mind that the WBGT Index takes into

TABLE 18-6

The American College of Sports Medicine recommended flag
warning system for alerting participants to the potential
risk of various thermal conditions. This system is based
upon the WBGT Index, which takes into account temperature,
radiation, and relative humidity.[2]

Flag/Status	WBGT Index	Comment
1. Red/High risk	23° to 28°C (73° to 82°F)	This signal would indicate that all runners should be aware that heat injury is possible and that any person particularly sensitive to heat or humidity probably should not run.
2. Amber/Moderate risk	18° to 23°C (65° to 73°F)	It should be remembered that the air temperature, probably humidity, and almost certainly the radiant heat at the beginning of the race will increase during the course of the race if conducted in the morning or early afternoon.
3. Green/Low risk	Below 18°C (65°F)	This is no guarantee that heat illness will not occur but indicates only that risk is low.
4. White/Low risk	Below 10°C (50°F)	Low risk for hyperthermia but possible risk for hypothermia.

account temperature (dry bulb), relative humidity (wet bulb), and radiation (globe). You will note that the highest warning level is for a WBGT Index of 23° to 28° C (73° to 82° F). If the WBGT Index is at 88° F, it would be advisable not to participate. These precautions apply to tennis, track and field, soccer, field hockey, training workouts, and those activities in which heavy protective clothing is not a problem.

Emergency Care in Heat Illness

When an athlete exhibits symptoms of heat illness, which have been previously discussed, *immediate* emergency procedures must be initiated. If not, heat stroke, a much more dangerous clinical situation, will follow heat exhaustion. It is not the prerogative of the coach to make a diagnosis, but rather to act at once:

1. All clothing should be removed without delay;
2. Immediate cooling with whatever means available—hose, ice water, and cold shower are examples;
3. An emergency vehicle should be called and hospital notified of a possible heat casualty; and
4. En route, ice water through use of sponge or towels should be continuously applied.

For your knowledge, hospital treatment may consist of immersing the nude athlete in a tub of ice water while attendants rub extremities. Meanwhile, the physician will administer fluids and such drugs as the clinical situation dictates. A rectal thermometer is used to record body temperature continuously, which may go as high as 110° F. When the temperature descends to around 102° F, the patient is removed to a bed and covered with blankets. Should the patient remain in the cold bath too long, body temperature will rap-

idly fall to dangerously low levels, precipitating shock, which might be lethal.

A wise coach and athletic director will not find it necessary to use the protocol outlined previously. If an emergency should occur, a prearranged plan for prompt emergency care and medical assistance regardless of the illness or injury should be available. This includes immediate access to a phone, as well as presence of assistants who are familiar with well-thought-out and rehearsed, printed emergency procedures.

Figure 18-16 is a 10-point fluid replacement and heat guide. The large, colorful chart may be obtained free of charge by writing Stokely-Van Camp, Inc., P.O. Box 1113, Indianapolis, Indiana 46206. It would be wise to post such a chart in the locker room or training facility for all participants, coaches, trainers, and athletes to study.

Exercise in the Cold

Activities in the cold can be classified under two general headings: (1) sporting events, and (2) wilderness experiences. Each presents its own unique interactions between the environment and the participant. Sporting events such as alpine and nordic skiing, running, some football contests, and other outdoor sporting events rarely present serious problems to the athlete. This is so for several reasons, including: (1) exposure time in the elements is limited, (2) access to shelter is readily available, (3) adequate protective clothing for heat conservation is worn or available, and (4) exercise generates large increases in heat production. Spectators to sporting events in the cold are usually more uncomfortable than the athletes.

On the other hand, wilderness experiences such as hiking, backpacking, mountain climbing, and ski-touring in isolated areas can increase the possibility of cold injury and even death from overexposure.

1 ACCLIMATIZATION — GETTING YOUR MEN IN CONDITION

Get your athlete in condition by getting him used to working in heat. Start with light exercise in gym shorts and gradually increase workout time and clothing to full uniform over a 5 day period. Workout sessions starting with 1 hour and working up to 2 hours in 5 days is recommended. Consider 10 minute breaks every 20 minutes of workout.

Day	1	2	3	4	5
Time in Minutes	60	80	100	110	120
Gear	Shorts	Shorts	Pants	Pants & Helmet	Full Gear
Workout	Calisthenics & Jogging	Calis. & Sprints	Sprints & Drills	Sprints & Drills	Practice

2 WEIGHT CHARTS — KEY TO GOOD TRAINING PRACTICE

The weight charts are prepared to help you in your work. Set up a procedure of lining up your men for weigh-in and weigh-out before and after practice or workout. The difference in weight is the athlete's loss of sweat. Replacement of fluid loss is important. Replacement is necessary for performance. At least 80% replacement must be achieved before next practice session.

Wt. Before – Wt. After = Wt. Loss = Sweat = Fluid replacement needed.

3 WEIGHT LOSS CHECK — FOCUS ON REHYDRATION NEED

The weight loss check is a convenient, reliable way of keeping tabs on the athlete's rehydration needs. If an athlete is given adequate access to fluids (Gatorade thirst quencher, water) by providing water breaks and encouraged to drink, he may be able to diminish his dehydration and replenish his fluid requirements. Such athletes will not show large losses in weight. If an athlete's weight loss is high, then his rehydration needs are great and should be satisfied. It is better to drink frequently, replace the fluid needed gradually, and maintain maximum rehydration throughout practice workout and game performance.

4 WATER REPLACEMENT — MAJOR INGREDIENT OF SWEAT

What goes out as sweat must be put back in the form of a fluid replacement. Since sweating to keep our body temperature from becoming excessive, it is in line to sweat, to minimize body temperature rise. Rehydrating the body of fluid lost is one of the best ways of insuring a continued cycle of performance. Rehydration must be encouraged — fluid replacement made available to make up for the fluid lost in sweat.

5 SALT REPLACEMENT — THE OTHER INGREDIENTS OF SWEAT

Along with water, when one sweats one loses electrolytes and body salts, primarily sodium chloride. In rehydrating the athlete with the water lost, we must replenish the lost salts as well. Gatorade has been formulated to supply those body salts in their proper ratios with respect to water and rehydration. If you drink water, however, make certain you use the proper ratio of water to salt tablets in order to keep the concentrations in balance. It is easier to stick to Gatorade and have the properly prepared, physiologically sound fluid replacement for your needs. No salt tablets should be used if one is drinking Gatorade.

6 WORK-HEAT RELATIONSHIP — ELEMENTARY BUT BASIC FACTS

Work produces heat and increases body temperature. If we were not able to lose the heat produced, our body temperature could go from 98.6°F (normal body temperature) to as high as 114 F (fatal to humans) in one hour. Fortunately, our body has a built-in temperature regulator and control. Our body sweats, loses water and salts and cools the skin while evaporation is taking place. Under normal conditions this cycle and regulation is adequate. In periods of heavy work and/or heavy uniform and insulation, the regulation system needs a helping hand to be able to maintain reasonable temperature control. The properly hydrated athlete in top shape is able to perform to his capacity. Remember that even a 3% weight loss is sufficient to show up significant performance loss. The percent weight loss can easily be calculated.

$$\frac{\text{Wt. loss of athlete}}{\text{Wt. before workout}} \times 100 = \text{Percent wt. loss}.$$

If you want the athlete's best performance, keep a sharp lookout on his heat-work relationship. Give him fluid replacement to help keep that temperature in control. Rehydrate him continually.

7 WEATHER EFFECTS — THE OVERLOOKED FACTOR

Hot and humid days can materially contribute to taking the zing out of your athlete's performance. On such days, the dehydration of the athlete is greater. His chances of heat illness are greater and your needs for rehydration are more acute. The use of the wet bulb thermometer is a means of quickly determining what the conditions are on the field during practice or a game. The sling psychrometer (about $15.00) may be purchased at any industrial supply company and assigned to a student manager, trainer or assistant coach. Careful observations of the wet bulb temperature and following the recommendations on the chart, can minimize dehydration. Frequent drinking breaks, fluid drinking encouragement, as well as allowing the body to dissipate heat, will be needed. The higher the temperature, the greater the humidity of the day, the greater is the degree of dehydration. Rehydrate your athletes — do it with Gatorade. It works.

8 DANGER SYMPTOMS — KEEP A SHARP LOOKOUT

They say an ounce of prevention is worth a pound of cure. A coach or trainer who is on the lookout for the danger signs will not only catch a situation before it becomes dangerous, but will also recognize that something must be corrected if it is producing such dangerous conditions. He then takes steps to correct the situation. Watch out for Muscle Cramps, Heat Exhaustion, Heat Stroke, Heat Fatigue and Sloppy Coordination. They all spell danger.

9 PROPER DRESS — EVERY LITTLE BIT HELPS

Particularly in football, the athlete is forced to wear heavy clothing which retards heat dissipation and acts as an insulator. Whenever and wherever it is possible, the body should be given a chance to throw off heat and become cooler. Clothing which can breathe and ventilate rather than insulate, can be helpful. Loosening the garments when not in action will help to cool. Keep using every means to bring your athlete close to normal body condition.

10 EMERGENCY MEASURES

If you practice good performance habits you will cut down on dangerous incidents. When an emergency occurs, however, be prepared to handle it with professional efficiency. Have a telephone handy. Give quick, effective treatment on the spot by cooling the body, removing clothing and applying cold applications such as a sponge, towel or bath in cold water or ice. Transport to a hospital immediately while applying the cold applications. Give the doctor the background information so that he can quickly anticipate what must be done. Even with all this, you must orient and teach all your personnel to carry out such a program when the necessity arises.

Figure 18-16. 10 point fluid replacement guide. (Courtesy of Stokely-Van Camp, P.O. Box 1113, Indianapolis, IN 46206.)

One unusual event, the Four Inns walking competition, has been recorded in which three competitors died as a result of exposure to the cold.[64] The event involved a 45-mile competitive hike between elevations of 650 to 2000 feet. The weather was wet with drizzle and rain, cold with temperatures between 0° C (32° F) and 7° C (45° F), and windy (28 mph and higher). Needless to say these are not desirable conditions. The record time was reported to be about 7.5 hours, however, typical times for completing the course are from 9.5 to 20 hours. We will refer to the conditions of this competition later.

Responses to Cold

In the resting individual, a number of physiological and behavioral responses can be witnessed in response to cold exposure. Physiological responses include: (1) peripheral vasoconstriction which shunts blood away from the surface of the skin to the core; (2) nonshivering thermogenesis, which involves either sympathetic stimulation or increased adrenal hormone circulation stimulating greater metabolic activity in skeletal muscle; (3) shivering, which involves uncontrolled, synchronous muscular contraction—shivering can elevate heat production up to 4 to 5 times resting levels but generally is less than this; and (4) piloerection ("goosebumps"), which may produce insignificant amounts of heat and is generally considered to be a vestigial response in humans.

Behavioral responses include: (1) wearing appropriate attire, (2) avoiding the cold by remaining indoors, and (3) altering activity level to generate more heat production. In other words, we try to avoid the cold whenever we can! However, in the event that we must or desire to exercise in the cold there are a number of questions to be addressed. Do the lungs ever freeze? How much heat is lost through the head? What is the effect of the cold on oxygen consumption? What is wind chill and why is it important? These and other questions will be addressed over the next several pages.

Do the Lungs Ever Freeze?

Anyone who exercises in the cold and produces high ventilation rates has experienced varying levels of throat irritation. Over the years, the myth has persisted that this is a sign that the lungs are about to freeze. The evidence suggests otherwise. The danger of lung tissue freezing under weather conditions experienced in any athletic setting is very remote.[11] What is the evidence?

In general, air is "conditioned" in the upper respiratory passageways, which involves both temperature elevation to within 2 or 3% of body temperature and increasing moisture content also to within 2 to 3% of full saturation.[30] A number of studies have been performed in which cool to cold air has been introduced into the respiratory system and monitored.[34,47,82]

Moritz and Weisiger,[47] using anesthetized dogs, introduced air at temperatures between −50° C (−58° F) and −100° C (−148° F). They were able to demonstrate that the temperature, recorded with a thermocouple at the level of the bifurcation of the trachea, had risen to 18° C (65° F). In other words, the air temperature was well above freezing values before reaching the smaller bronchi and other lung tissue. Webb,[82] using a very sensitive thermocouple system, measured the temperature of both inspired and expired air as it passed through the nasal passages in resting human subjects. Sensors were positioned at depths of 1, 5, and 9 cm in the nasal pathway. Air was introduced at three different temperatures, −24.5° C, 7° C, and 25° C. The results are seen in Figure 18-17. Webb's study showed that (1) under all conditions, the air temperature at a depth of 9 cm reached at least 25.4° C, (2) the air was warmed significantly as it passed each measurement site, and (3) in exhalation, the air temperature was higher at each corresponding site compared with inhalation.

Hartung et al.[34] measured inspired and expired air temperatures in subjects exercising at two workloads of 60 and 75% of aerobic capacity for 10 minutes. Expired air temperature was measured at a point just beyond the outlet of a breathing valve.

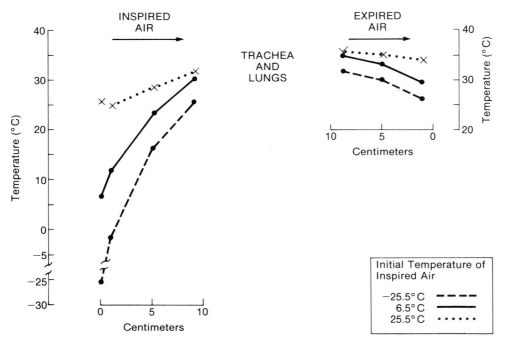

Figure 18-17. Air is rapidly warmed as it enters the nasal passage. Regardless of the temperature of inspired air from −25° C to 25° C, by the time it reached 9 cm into the nasal passage it had been warmed to at least 25° C. The left side of the figure represents inspired air and its pattern of warming. The right side of the figure shows expired air cooling slightly but remaining at higher temperatures at each measurement site. This illustrates, in part, the conditioning of inspired air.[82]

Even when air at −35° C was inhaled, the temperature of expired air at the highest workload and ventilation rates was 23.2° C (74° F). One could speculate, on the basis of Webb's data (Fig. 18-17), that the air was even warmer before it reached the measurement site.

Now that we have established that lung tissue does not feeze what, then, is the reason for throat irritation during prolonged exercise in the cold? We mentioned earlier that air is "conditioned" as it enters the respiratory passages. Conditioning occurs when both heat and moisture are rapidly added to the incoming air via the mucosal linings of the trachea. Likewise, as exhaled air leaves the airways, part of the heat and moisture is returned to the mucosa. Because there is a net loss of moisture from mucosal tissue, the tissue becomes dryer and irritated.

Heat Loss from the Head

Another belief is that the loss of heat through the head represents a major source of heat loss during exercise (up to 50% during exercise). What are the facts? Two studies will be cited. Froese and Burton[23] have shown that from 32° C to −21° C heat loss from the head is linear with temperature. In other words, the lower the temperature, the greater the heat loss. The authors have presented an equation for calculating heat loss from the head area as follows:

$$H = 284.8 - (7.55)(T)$$

where

$$H = \text{kcal/m}^2/\text{hr}$$
$$T = \text{air temperature in } °C$$
$$284.8 = \text{a constant}$$

According to the calculations of Froese and Burton,[23] at a temperature of 0° C about 38% of resting heat production could be lost through the head. Nunneley et al.[56] estimated that head cooling removes about 30% of the heat produced at rest and at a work level of 50% of aerobic capacity removes about 19% of the heat produced. The surface area of the head is approximately 0.12 m². This represents approximately 7 to 9% of the body surface area.

What conclusions may we draw from these observations? While the head does not normally serve to remove 50% of the heat production of the body, it certainly can account for a significant level of heat loss in a cold environment. The simple solution of wearing a woolen watch cap can significantly reduce body heat loss through the head. By the same token, the individual who is exercising in the cold and is becoming too warm can remove the cap to promote heat loss.

Oxygen Consumption

What is the influence of exercising in the cold on oxygen consumption? Is the energy cost of performing in the cold different than under normal conditions? At submaximal workloads it has been found that the energy cost of a particular work task is greater, while at maximal workloads there appears to be no difference between working in the cold and in normal temperatures. Horvath[38] states, "It would appear that a critical level of heat production is required before the incidental influence of cold-induced shivering can be counteracted." Investigators have made observations under a variety of conditions including normal core temperature with exposure to cold and lowered core temperature while performing either submaximal or maximal work.

Pugh[65] showed that when oxygen consumption was 2.1 liters per minute or higher, there was no difference in energy cost between a comfortable temperature and one at 5° C in wet clothing. However, at work levels requiring less than 2.0 liters of oxygen per minute the energy consumption was 15 to 20% higher in the cold environment. Incidentally, the conditions in Pugh's experiment were similar to those reported in the Four Inns walking competition (p. 508). The energy cost of vigorous walking is generally less than 2.0 liters of oxygen per minute. The unfavorable weather conditions in combination with the submaximal oxygen consumption levels apparently led to an unusually rapid depletion of energy stores precipitating an early onset of fatigue for many of the performers.

Strømme et al.[78] compared oxygen consumption patterns between 5° C and 27° C environments. Subjects rode stationary bicycles at 0 resistance, 300, and 600 kg-m/min. Estimates from a figure in their study show that pedalling at 0 resistance the ride in 5° C "cost" about 0.9 liters of oxygen per minute while at 27° C the "cost" was about 0.6 L/min. At 300 kg-m/min, the respective values were about 1.0 L/min and 1.2 L/min. Strømme et al.[78] estimated a "crossover" point of about 1.2 to 1.4 L/min of oxygen consumption.

Hellstrøm et al.[36] reported similar results when they observed subjects riding at 300 and 900 kpm on a stationary bicycle. The low work level induced a relatively higher oxygen consumption in the cold environment. At the higher work level there was no difference in oxygen consumption in the cold environment versus normal conditions. Claremont et al.[10] had subjects riding a stationary bicycle at workloads of

55% of their aerobic capacity. While riding at a temperature of 0° C, oxygen consumption was higher than when riding at 35° C (29.7 ml/kg-min vs. 26.6 ml/kg-min).

Bergh[5] cooled the core temperature of subjects by immersion in a cold bath. With core temperature at 34° C, it was observed that the oxygen consumption of a standardized workload that required 2.0 L/min at normal core temperature now required 2.6 L/min., an increase of 30%.

Thus, there is a consistent pattern of higher energy costs associated with light to moderate workloads in the cold. Applications of this observation would include advising athletes who are about to perform in the cold to stay as warm as possible until the competition begins and to advise older persons and children to take extra precautions if they are going to be exposed to cold conditions.

Maximal work capacity. Very little evidence is available concerning the effects of cold weather on aerobic capacity with a normal core temperature. However, based upon the information presented in the above paragraphs,[5,10,78] it would be logical to assume that there would be no effect on aerobic capacity. Matsui et al.[45] have reported just that. There were no significant changes in aerobic capacity over the course of an entire year. Subjects were tested two times each month for an entire year, once at the ambient temperature (ranging from 3° C to 25° C) and once at a constant room temperature of 18° C. Subjects were also tested in a climate-controlled chamber at 5° C, 18° C, and 35° C. At no time were there any meaningful differences in maximal oxygen consumption.

When core temperature is lowered by submersion in cold water followed by a standard maximal test the results are different.[17] Performers showed a decreased maximal oxygen consumption that was related to the decreased core temperature. That is, the lower the core temperature, the

greater was the decrease in maximal oxygen consumption. The decrease was 5 to 6% in aerobic capacity for each 1° C decrease in core temperature.

Muscular Strength and Endurance

Within the normal physiologic range of muscle temperature, which prevails in athletic activities, there is no apparent effect on muscular strength or endurance. Outside the physiologic range there may be some differential effects. Falls,[18] Haymes and Wells,[33] and Horvath[38] present reviews of these effects.

Wind Chill

The most immediate threat to an athlete exposed to the cold is the influence of wind on the rate of surface skin cooling. Heat loss from the body is expressed in kilocalories per square meter of body surface area per hour (kcal/m²/hr). The expression "wind chill" dates from the work of Siple[76] and Siple and Passel.[75] Wind chill simply is another name for the dry, convective cooling power of the atmosphere. Exposure to the cold and wind can manifest basically two conditions: freezing of human flesh (frostbite) and hypothermia (lowering of body temperature). We will discuss the more rapidly developing of the two (frostbite) first since, in extreme conditions, frostbite can occur in less than one minute following exposure.

Frostbite

Frostbite occurs when skin temperature reaches between −2° C and −6° C (28.4° F to 21.2° F). For a variety of reasons, including vasomotor activity and metabolism, an environmental temperature lower than −29° C (−20° F) is required to freeze exposed areas such as ear lobes, fingers, and facial skin. Toes may also suffer frostbite if they are inadequately protected. The keys to the occurrence of frostbite, and hypothermia for that matter, are the rate of heat loss from the skin and time of exposure to the elements.

Siple and Passel[75] developed the following formula for calculating heat loss:

$$K_0 = [(\sqrt{100V}) + 10.5 - V][33 - T]$$

where

K_0 = heat loss in kcal/m²/hr
V = wind velocity in meters/sec
T = environmental temperature in °C
10.5 = a constant
33 = the assumed normal skin temperature in °C
(Note: 1 mph = 0.447 meters/sec)

Based upon the above formula and a classification scale listed by Gates[25] (see Table 18-7), we have developed a chart similar to those developed for the military with five "comfort/distress" zones.[81] In Figure 18-18, Zone I represents heat loss rates of up to 800 kcal/m²/hr and normally poses no threat. Zone II (between 800 and 1200 kcal/m²/hr) is described as "cold" and can become unpleasant with prolonged exposure. Zone III (between 1200 and 1400 kcal/m²/hr) is described as "bitterly cold" and can result in cold injury if exposure is prolonged. Zone IV (1400 to 2000 kcal/m²/hr) represents the conditions under which exposed flesh may begin to freeze,[75] and Zone V (2000 kcal/m²/hr) represents

---

TABLE 18-7

Wind Chill Factor Expressed in kcal/m²/hr. and Relative Comfort/Discomfort Exclusive of the Effects of Relative Humidity. The Zones Refer to the Areas in Figure 18-17. The Last Two Columns Give Actual Dry Bulb Temperatures at Wind Speeds of 5 MPH and 10 MPH.[12, 25]

Wind Chill Factor (kcal/m²/hr)				Dry Bulb Temp (°F) With a Breeze	
Midpoint	Range	Zone	Level of Comfort/Discomfort	5 MPH	10 MPH
50	25–75		Hot	87	88
112	75–150		Warm	83	84
225	150–300		Pleasant	74	77
400	300–500		Cool	61	64
600	500–700	I	Very cool	45	51
800	700–900	II	Cold	29	38
1000	900–1100	II	Very cold—unpleasant for skiing on an overcast day	14	25
1200	1100–1300	III	Bitterly cold—unpleasant for skiing on a sunny day	−2	11
1400	1300–1660	IV	Exposed flesh may freeze	−17	−2
2000	1660–2300	V	Exposed flesh freezes in one minute or less	−63	−43
2300	2300–	V+	Exposed flesh freezes in 30 seconds or less	−90	−62

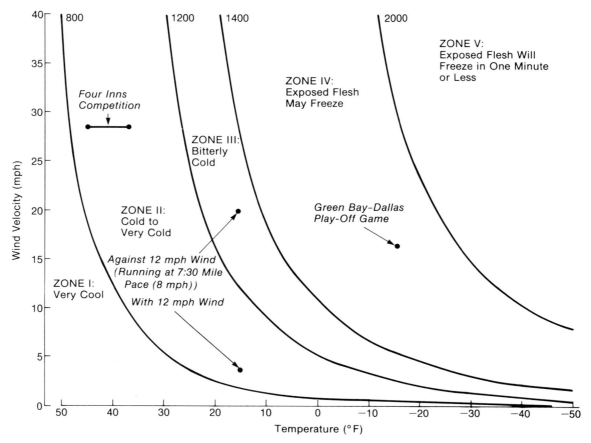

Figure 18-18. Thermal comfort/discomfort zones similar to those used by the military. Four isobars representing heat loss rate of 800, 1200, 1400, and 2000 kcal/m/hr divide the graph into five zones.[75,81]

conditions under which exposed flesh will freeze in less than one minute.[75]

It can be seen that at a temperature of 0° F, it would take a wind of only 10 mph to threaten a person with frostbite. We must hasten to add that the chart in Figure 18-18 is calculated for low activity levels. An athlete who is very active would probably be able to tolerate lower temperatures and higher winds before experiencing frostbite. It is not uncommon for runners who are adequately clothed to train when the temperature is −20° F. Other factors moderating the onset of frostbite include: (1) the

radiant effect of the sun, (2) the amount of insulating clothing, (3) wetness of the clothing, and (4) relative humidity.

Hypothermia

Prolonged exposure in cold or bitterly cold conditions can lead to hypothermia. Hypothermia is diagnosed when core temperature has reached 95° F. Recall the conditions from the Four Inns walking competition in which the temperature was recorded between 0° C and 7° C with wind velocities of 28 to 30 mph. An additional complicating factor was that there was rain, which reduced the insulating capability of the participants' clothing. The combination of cold, windy, and wet conditions along with clothing that lost its insulating power and low metabolic heat production rates proved a disastrous combination.

Another illustration of the importance of being aware of weather conditions is given in the following hypothetical case. A runner is exercising at a 7:30 mile pace (8 mph) with a 12-mph wind and temperature of 15° F. When running with the wind, the effective wind velocity is 4 mph (12 mph − 8 mph). When the wind chill formula of Siple and Passel[74] is applied, a heat loss rate of approximately 937 kcal/m²/hr is calculated, which is generally well tolerated by properly clothed runners. However, when the runner turns into the wind, the effective wind velocity becomes 20 mph (12 mph + 8 mph). The calculated heat loss rate is now 1335 kcal/m²/hr. Examination of Figure 18-18 shows that the athlete is now in a much more precarious situation. Modifying factors that are protective to the runner in this scenario include a relatively higher metabolic rate (at a 7:30 mile pace, metabolism is about 10 to 12 mets) and proper clothing.

Ironically, runners may experience hypothermia in what we may consider to be very comfortable conditions. Nash[55] reported that following the 1985 Boston Marathon, 250 persons were treated for hyperthermia while 75 were treated for hypothermia. The environmental conditions were described as being warm (76° F), sunny, and humid! How can hypothermia occur under these conditions? The runners affected are usually slower runners meaning that their rate of heat production is not as great as the front runners. Other necessary factors are that the runners have become dehydrated, with reduced total blood volume, and there must be an opportunity for increased heat loss such as in-creased evaporation, increased convection, and sudden cooling by being sprayed with cold water or by the development of a cloud cover. Fluid replacement by intravenous injection and ingestion of drinking water generally alleviated the hypothermia within 30 minutes to 1 hour.

On December 31, 1967 a National Football League playoff game was played in Green Bay, Wisconsin, between the Green Bay Packers and Dallas Cowboys. The weather conditions were remarkable with a temperature of −14° F and a northwest wind of 16 to 18 mph. On the wind chill chart (Fig. 18-18), this places the weather conditions in zone IV, which represents high potential for frostbite. It was reported that among the players there was no hypothermia and only "a couple of cases of minor frostbite."* Of course, the players were wearing extra protective clothing and had various heaters and other warming devices on the sidelines. No report was available on the 50,000 fans.

Tolerance to Cold

Why do some people seem to tolerate the cold better than others? Frisancho,[22] discussing this topic, identifies four factors. They include differences in body surface area, subcutaneous fat levels, age, and physical fitness. Gender should also be included as a discussion point.[33]

1. *Body Surface Area.* The size and shape of the body affect the amount of heat required to maintain a constant internal temperature. When the ratio of the surface area to body weight is considered, a smaller person is required to produce more heat to maintain body temperature than is a larger person.

2. *Subcutaneous Fat.* The subcutaneous fat layer serves as the most impor-

---

*Personal communications, Scott Berchstold, Public Relations, Green Bay Packers.

tant source of natural insulation in humans. Thermal conductivity is relatively low in subcutaneous fat because it is not well vascularized. Thin persons are more prone to shivering than more obese individuals. Thicker subcutaneous fat layers are an advantage to persons, such as channel swimmers, who swim in colder waters.

3. *Age.* Young adults are better able to tolerate cold than are older persons.

4. *Physical Fitness.* Whether increased levels of physical fitness affects tolerance to cold is unclear. However, if we assume increased vascularization, increased total muscle mass, as well as increased aerobic capacity, we can speculate that physical fitness enhances our ability to tolerate the cold.

5. *Gender.* Factors related to subcutaneous fat thickness, aerobic capacity, relative energy expenditure during work, and body surface area to mass ratio confound trying to answer the question of whether men and women tolerate cold differently. When men and women were matched for both skinfold thickness and aerobic capacity there were no apparent differences in skin and core temperature responses at the same workloads.[33]

Acclimation and Acclimatization

Buskirk[7] has defined acclimation as a physiological change that reduces the strain of experimentally induced stressful changes in specific climatic factors. Acclimation may be observed under controlled acute exposure either in laboratory chambers or in the environment. Acclimatization, on the other hand, represents physiological changes occurring within the individual that allows him/her to adjust to changes in the natural environment.

Acclimation to cold includes both heat-conserving (peripheral vasoconstriction) and heat-producing mechanisms (nonshivering thermogenesis, shivering, piloerection, and/or increased physical activity).

Have you ever wondered why your hands or cheeks suddenly appear flushed, sometimes, when you are exposed to the cold? A seeming paradoxical response to cold is the hunting response of Lewis.[3,42] As we have stated, the initial vasomotor response to cold exposure is peripheral vasoconstriction where blood flow is diverted from the skin surface. If skin temperature reaches about 3° to 4° C, peripheral vasodilation suddenly occurs. The skin becomes reddened and a feeling of warmth prevails. This is an "attempt" to warm the skin surface and is indeed successful. Local skin temperature will rise to 11° or 12° C for a period of time, then vasoconstriction reoccurs. Continued exposure sees a continued fluctuation between vasodilation and vasoconstriction.

Most of the scientific literature seeking to clarify the process of acclimatization focuses upon native populations. Frisancho[22] reviews studies on Australian Aborigines, Kalahari Bushmen, Alacaluf Indians (Southern Chile), Norwegian Lapps, Eskimos, and others. Kang et al.[40] and Rennie et al.[66] have studied the Ama, Korean women who regularly do free dives in water at temperatures as low as 10° C. Acclimatization is evidenced in these populations.

Does the athlete acclimate to the cold? Yes. Does the athlete acclimatize to the cold? Probably. Because of the nature of our western culture with modern conveniences and well-designed clothing, we actually live in a microclimate that is generally quite comfortable. Therefore the process of acclimatization is difficult to ascertain. Intuitively, one could say that some acclimatization occurs among athletes who exercise through seasonal climatic changes.

Training in the Cold

The primary concern of the athlete exercising in the cold is to maintain a comfortable microclimate and body temperature. Dress becomes an important matter. Dependent upon the level of heat produced by a specific activity, the athlete will dress appropriately. Under the same climatic conditions a downhill skier will dress seeking more insulation than a runner.

Gagge, Burton, and Bazett[24] introduced the concept of a standardized insulating unit, the "clo." One clo is the amount of insulating material required to keep a person comfortable equivalent to sitting in a room at 70° F, with a relative humidity less than 50% and with an air movement of 20 feet per minute! In a cold environment, as heat production increases, the required clo value of the insulating clothing decreases. As clothing becomes wet, its insulating capability is dramatically reduced. Again, we remind you of the circumstances surrounding the Four Inns walking competition (p. 508).

Lightweight clothing that is worn in layers represents a sensible approach to dress for activity in the cold where the athlete will be expending large amounts of energy (6 mets or more). Materials that "wick" moisture away from the surface of the skin to the outer layers of the garment are recommended. When frostbite is a threat, the athlete should wear some sort of protective covering over the face. Claremont,[11] an experienced cold-weather runner, suggests that a piece of light terry cloth draped across the face, bridging the nose and fastened to the head cover, is effective. This arrangement allows free movement of air at the high ventilation rates experienced by runners. The greater threats to the winter runner are associated with ice- and snow-covered surfaces.

Summary

Heat balance is obtained when the same amount of heat is lost as is produced or gained. Heat is lost from the body through convection, conduction, radiation, and evaporation. Convection is defined as the transfer of heat from one place to another by the motion of a heated substance (e.g., air). Conduction is heat exchange between two objects of different temperatures in direct contact with each other. Radiation involves the transfer of heat between objects through electromagnetic waves. Heat loss through evaporation is the result of changing a liquid (e.g., sweat) to a vapor. Heat is gained by the body mainly through metabolism, but heat may also be gained by the body from the environment through radiation, convection, and conduction.

The function of the thermoregulatory system is to maintain a relatively constant internal body temperature at rest as well as during exercise. The basic components of the thermoregulatory system are (1) thermal receptors located in the hypothalamus of the brain and in the skin; (2) thermal effectors or organs such as the skeletal muscles, the smooth muscles of the arterioles, the sweat glands, and the endocrine glands; and (3) a thermal regulatory center located in the hypothalamus that coordinates the incoming information from the receptors with the outgoing regulatory action of the effector organs.

The principal means by which the body loses heat during exercise or exposure to heat are (1) circulatory adjustments of increased skin blood flow resulting from cutaneous vasodilation, and (2) evaporative cooling resulting from increased secretion of sweat. Internal body heat produced mainly by the liver and skeletal muscles is carried by the blood (circulatory convection) to the surface, where conduction, convection, radiation, and, particularly, evaporation take place. The cooled blood then returns to the warmer core, and the cycle is repeated.

The seriousness of overexposure to heat while exercising is exemplified not only by a decrease in work performance, but also by a predisposition to heat illness. These disorders are categorized in order of ascending severity as (1) heat cramps, (2) heat syncope, (3) heat exhaustion (both water-depletion and salt-depletion), and (4) heat stroke. The most frequent common denominators for all of these are (1) heat exposure, (2) loss of water, and (3) heat storage, usually reflected by high internal body temperature. However, the single most important factor, from a clinical standpoint, is loss of body water. It is also important to point out that inattention to heat cramps, heat syncope, and heat exhaustion can lead to heat stroke and, finally, to death because of irreversible damage to the central nervous system.

Heat disorders in athletics can be significantly reduced through (1) adequate water and electrolyte replacement, (2) acclimatization to heat, and (3) awareness of the limitations imposed by the combination of exercise, clothing, and environmental heat.

Individuals respond to the cold through both physiological and behavioral means. Physiological responses include peripheral vasoconstriction, nonshivering thermogenesis, shivering, and piloerection. Behavioral responses include wearing appropriate attire, avoiding the cold, and altering physical activity levels.

Lung tissue is not normally in danger of freezing because air is conditioned before it reaches lung tissue. The exposed head can be a significant heat loss source although, during exercise, it probably does not exceed 20% of total heat loss. The energy cost of submaximal work is elevated due to shivering while the person exercises. Maximal oxygen consumption is not affected unless the core temperature is reduced.

Wind chill is an important concept because it gives a means by which heat loss from the body can be calculated. Wind velocity and temperature are the key factors in calculating wind chill. Two consequences of exposure to the cold are frostbite and hypothermia. Human flesh freezes when its temperature reaches between $-2°$ and $-6°$ C. Hypothermia can occur under conditions that can be characterized as mild. Factors important to cold tolerance include body surface area, subcutaneous fat stores, age, and physical fitness. Any gender differences appear to be related to these factors.

Athletes may acclimatize to the cold season through daily exposure. With proper clothing, an athlete can train successfully in cold environments.

Questions

1. Outline the sequential physiological events that occur during heat stroke.
2. Describe the manner by which the body loses heat.
3. Describe in detail how the body may gain heat.
4. How does the thermoregulatory system maintain a relatively constant temperature?
5. Explain the principal means by which we lose heat during exercise or exposure to heat.
6. Explain how salt and water depletion during exercise can lead to serious heat disorders.
7. What procedures would you follow to ensure the athlete against heat illness during stressful environmental conditions?
8. Describe the effects of cold exposure on the energy cost of work.
9. Can the lungs freeze during exercise in the cold? Explain your answer.
10. What is wind chill and why is it important to understand?
11. How would you regulate salt and water replacement as a consequence of exercising in the heat?
12. List the "drinking" guidelines for athletes.
13. Why may the highly competitive athlete be more vulnerable to heat disorders?
14. Describe the pertinent aspects of the experiment discussed in the text that demonstrated the effects of wearing a football uniform on heart rate, water loss, and core temperature.

15. Discuss the weather guides that may be used to estimate severity of climatic conditions.
16. Define wet bulb temperature, globe temperature, and relative humidity.
17. What are the emergency procedures for a heat stroke casualty?
18. Discuss exposure to cold during exercise.

References

1. Adams, T., and Iampietro, P. F.: Temperature regulation. In Falls, H. B. (ed.): *Exercise Physiology.* New York, Academic Press, 1968.
2. American College of Sports Medicine Position Stand: Prevention of thermal injuries during distance running. *Physician Sportsmed.* 12(7):43-51, 1984.
3. Bangs, C. C.: Cold injuries. In Strauss, R. H. (ed.): *Sports Medicine.* Philadelphia, W. B. Saunders, 1984.
4. Bass, D., Kleeman, C., Quinn, M., Henschel, A., and Hegnauer, A.: Mechanisms of acclimatization to heat in man. *Medicine.* 34:323-380, 1955.
5. Bergh, U.: Human power at subnormal body temperature. *Acta Physiol Scand.* (Suppl no. 478) 1-39, 1980.
6. Blyth, C., and Burt, J.: Effects of water balance on ability to perform at high ambient temperatures. *Res Q.* 32:301-307, 1961.
7. Buskirk, E. R.: Temperature regulation with exercise. In Hutton, R. S. (ed.): *Exercise and Sport Sciences Reviews,* Vol. 5. Santa Barbara, Journal Publishing Affiliates, 1977.
8. Buskirk, E., and Bass, D.: Climate and exercise. In Johnson, W., and Buskirk, E. (eds.): *Science and Medicine of Exercise and Sports,* 2nd ed. New York, Harper and Brothers, 1974, pp. 190-205.
9. Buskirk, E., Iampietro, P., and Bass, D.: Work performance and dehydration; effects of physical condition and heat acclimatization. *J Appl Physiol.* 12:189-194, 1958.
10. Claremont, A. D., Nagle, F., Redden, W. D., and Brooks, G. A.: Comparison of metabolic, temperature, heart rate and ventilatory responses to exercise at extreme ambient temperatures (0 and 35° C). *Med Sci Sports Exer.* 7(2):150-153, 1975.
11. Claremont, A. D.: Taking winter in stride. *Physician Sportsmed.* 4:65-68, 1976.
12. Consolazio, C. F., Johnson, R. E., and Pecora, L. J.: *Physiological Measurements of Metabolic Function in Man.* New York, McGraw-Hill, 1963.
13. Costill, D. L.: Fluids for athletic performance: why and what you should drink during prolonged exercise. In *The New Runners Diet.* Mountain View, Calif., World Publications, August, 1977.
14. Costill, D. L., and Saltin, B.: Factors limiting gastric emptying during rest and exercise. *J Appl Physiol.* 37(5):679-683, 1974.
15. Craig, E., and Cummings, E.: Dehydration and muscular work. *J Appl Physiol.* 21: 670-674, 1966.
16. Cunningham, D. J., Stolwijk, J. A. J., and Wenger, C. B.: Comparative thermoregulatory responses of resting men and women. *J Appl Physiol.* 45(6):908-915, 1978.
17. Drinkwater, B. L., Denton, J. E., Kupprat, I. C., Talag, T. S., and Horvath, S. M.: Aerobic power as a factor in women's response to work in hot environments. *J Appl Physiol.* 41:815-821, 1976.
18. Falls, H. B.: Heat and cold applications. In Morgan, W. P.: *Ergogenic Aids and Muscular Performance.* New York, Academic Press, 1972.
19. Fortney, S. M., and Senay, L. C.: Effect of training and heat acclimation on exercise responses of sedentary females. *J Appl Physiol.* 47(5):978-984, 1979.
20. Fox, E. L., Mathews, D., Kaufman, W., and Bowers, R.: Effects of football equipment on thermal balance and energy cost during exercise. *Res Q.* 37:332-339, 1966.
21. Fox, E. L., Weiss, H. S., Bartels, R. L., and Hiatt, E. P.: Thermal responses of man during rest and exercise in a helium oxygen environment. *Arch Environ Health.* 13:23-28, 1966.
22. Frisancho, A. R.: *Human Adaptation,* St. Louis, C. V. Mosby, 1979.
23. Froese, G., and Burton, A. C.: Heat loss from the human head. *J Appl Physiol.* 10:235-241, 1957.
24. Gagge, A. P., Burton, A. C., and Bazett, H. C.: A practical system of units for the description of the heat exchange of man with his environment. *Science.* 94(2445): 428-430, 1941.
25. Gates, D. M.: *Man and His Environment: Climate.* New York, Harper and Row, 1972.
26. Gisolfi, C. V.: Work-heat tolerance derived

from interval training. *J Appl Physiol.* 35:349–354, 1973.

27. Gisolfi, C. V., and Cohen, J. S.: Relationships among training, heat acclimation, and heat tolerance in men and women: the controversy revisited. *Med Sci Sports.* 11(1):56–59, 1979.

28. Gisolfi, C. V., Wilson, N. C., and Claxton, B.: Work-heat tolerance of distance runners. *Ann NY Acad Sci.* 301:139–150, 1977.

29. Greenleaf, J., and Castle, B.: Exercise temperature regulation in man during hypohydration and hyperhydration. *J Appl Physiol.* 30:847–853, 1971.

30. Guyton, A. C.: *Textbook of Medical Physiology,* 6th ed. Philadelphia, W. B. Saunders, 1981, p. 486.

31. Hanson, P. G.: Heat injury in runners. *Physician Sportsmed.* 7(6):91–96, 1979.

32. Hanson, P. G., and Zimmerman, S. W.: Exertional heatstroke in novice runners. *JAMA.* 242(2):154–157, 1979.

33. Haymes, E. M., and Wells, C. L.: *Environment and Human Performance.* Champaigne, Ill., Human Kinetics Publishers, 1986.

34. Hartung, G. H., Myhre, L. G., and Nunneley, S. A.: Physiological effects of cold air inhalation during exercise. *Aviat Space Environ Med.* 51:591–597, 1980.

35. Heat peril in distance runs spurs ACSM guideline alert. *Physician Sportsmed.* 3(7): 85–87.

36. Hellstrøm, B., Berg, K., and Lorentzen, V.: Human peripheral re-warming following exercise in the cold. *J Appl Physiol.* 29: 191–199, 1970.

37. Henane, R., Flandrois, R., and Charbonnier, J. P.: Increase in sweating sensitivity by endurance conditioning in man. *J Appl Physiol.* 43:822–828, 1977.

38. Horvath, S. M.: Exercise in a cold environment. In Miller, D. I. (ed.): *Exercise and Sport Sciences Reviews,* Vol. 9. Philadelphia. The Franklin Institute Press, 1981.

39. Hubbard, R. W.: Effects of exercise in the heat on predisposition to heatstroke. *Med Sci Sports.* 11(1):66–71, 1979.

40. Kang, B. S., Song, S. H., Suh, C. S., and Hong, S. K.: Changes in body temperature and basal metabolic rate of the Ama. *J Appl Physiol.* 18(3):483–488, 1963.

41. Kozlowski, S., and Saltin, B.: Effects of sweat loss on body fluids. *J Appl Physiol.* 19:1119–1124, 1964.

42. Lewis, T.: Vasodilation in response to strong cooling. *Heart.* 15:1177–81, 1931.

43. Licht, S. (ed.): *Medical Climatology.* New Haven, Elizabeth Licht, 1964.

44. Mathews, D., Fox, E. L., and Tanzi, D.: Physiological responses during exercise and recovery in a football uniform. *J Appl Physiol.* 26:611–615, 1969.

45. Matsui, H., Shimaoka, K., Miyamura, M., and Kobayashi, K.: Seasonal variation of aerobic work capacity in ambient and constant temperature. In Folinsbee, L. J., et al. (eds.): *Environmental Stress: Individual Adaptations.* New York, Academic Press, 1978, pp. 279–292.

46. Mitchell, D., Senay, L. C., Wyndham, C. H., van Rensburg, A. J., Rogers, G. G., and Strydom, N. B.: Acclimatization in a hot, humid environment: energy exchange, body temperature, and sweating. *J Appl Physiol.* 40:768–778, 1976.

47. Moritz, A. R., and Weisiger, J. R.: Effects of cold air on the air passages and lungs. *Arch Int Med.* 75:233–240, 1945.

48. Murphy, R. J.: Heat illness and athletics. In Strauss, R. H. (ed.): *Sports Medicine and Physiology.* Philadelphia, W. B. Saunders, 1979, pp. 320–326.

49. Murphy, R. J.: The problem of environmental heat in athletics. *Ohio State Med J.* 59, No. 8, 1963.

50. Murphy, R. J., and Ashe, W.: Prevention of heat illness in football players. *JAMA.* 194:650–654, 1965.

51. Nadel, E. R.: Temperature regulation during exercise. In Houdus, Y., and Guieu, J. D. (eds.): *New Trends in Thermal Physiology.* Paris, Masson, 1978, pp. 143–153.

52. Nadel, E. R., Pandolf, K. B., Roberts, M. F., and Stolwijk, J. A. J.: Mechanisms of thermal acclimation to exercise and heat. *J Appl Physiol.* 37:515–520, 1974.

53. Nadel, E. R., Roberts, M. F., and Wenger, C. B.: Thermoregulatory adaptations to heat and exercise: comparative responses of men and women. In Folinsbee, L. J., et al. (eds.): *Environmental Stress: Individual Human Adaptations.* San Francisco, Academic Press, 1978, pp. 29–38.

54. Nadel, E. R.: Control of sweating rate while exercising in the heat. *Med Sci Sports Exer.* 11(1):31–35, 1979.

55. Nash, H. L.: Treating thermal injury: disagreement heats up. *Physician Sportsmed.* 13(7):134–144, 1985.

56. Nunneley, S. A., Troutman, S. J., and Webb, P.: Head cooling in work and heat stress. *Aerospace Med.* 42:64–68, 1971.

57. O'Donnell, T., and Clowes, G.: The circulatory abnormalities of heat stroke. *N Engl J Med.* 287(15):734–737, 1972.

58. Pandolf, K. B.: Effects of physical training and cardiorespiratory physical fitness on exercise-heat tolerance: recent observations. *Med Sci Sports.* 11(1):60–65, 1979.

59. Pandolf, K. B., Burse, R. L., and Goldman, R. F.: Role of physical fitness in heat acclimatization, decay and reinduction. *Ergonomics.* 20:399–408, 1977.

60. Paolone, A. M., Wells, C. L., and Kelly, G. T.: Sexual variations in thermoregulation during heat stress. *Aviat Space Environ Med.* 49:715–719, 1978.

61. Pitts, G., Johnson, R., and Consolazio, F.: Work in the heat as affected by intake of water, salt and glucose. *Am J Physiol.* 142:253–259, 1944.

62. Piwonka, R., and Robinson, S.: Acclimatization of highly trained men to work in severe heat. *J Appl Physiol.* 22:9–12, 1967.

63. Piwonka, R., Robinson, S., Gay, V., and Manalis, R.: Pre-acclimatization of men to heat by training. *J Appl Physiol.* 20:379–383, 1965.

64. Pugh, L. G. C.: Death from exposure in Four Inns walking competition, March 14–15, 1964. *Lancet.* (May 30):1210–1212, 1964.

65. Pugh, L. G. C.: Cold stress and muscular exercise, with special reference to accidental hypothermia. *Br Med J.* 2:333–337, 1967.

66. Rennie, D. W., Covino, B. G., Howell, B. J., Song, S. H., Kang, B. S., and Kong, S. K.: Physical insulation of Korean diving women. *J Appl Physiol.* 17:961–966, 1962.

67. Roberts, M. F., Wenger, C. B., Stolwijk, J. A. J., and Nadel, E. R.: Skin blood flow and sweating changes following exercise training and heat acclimation. *J Appl Physiol.* 43:133–137, 1977.

68. Rowell, L.: Human cardiovascular adjustments to exercise and thermal stress. *Physiol Rev.* 54(1):75–159, 1974.

69. Saltin, B.: Aerobic and anaerobic work capacity after dehydration. *J Appl Physiol.* 19:1114–1118, 1964.

70. Saltin, B.: Aerobic work capacity and circulation at exercise in man. *Acta Physiol Scand.* 62(Suppl. 230):1–52, 1964.

71. Saltin, B.: Circulatory response to submaximal and maximal exercise after thermal dehydration. *J Appl Physiol.* 19:1125–1132, 1964.

72. Shapiro, Y., Magazanik, A., Vdassin, R., Ben-Baruch, G. M., Shvartz, E., and Shoenfeld, Y.: Heat intolerance in former heatstroke patients. *Ann Intern Med.* 90(6):913–916, 1979.

73. Shvartz, E., Bhattacharya, A., Sperindle, S. J., Brock, P. J., Sciaraffa, D., and Van Beaumont, W. J.: Sweating responses during heat acclimation and moderate conditioning. *J Appl Physiol.* 46(4):675–680, 1979.

74. Shvartz, E., Shapiro, Y., Magazanik, A., Meroz, A., Birnfeld, H., Mechtinger, A., and Shibolet, S.: Heat acclimation, physical fitness, and responses to exercise in a temperate and hot environment. *J Appl Physiol.* 43:678–683, 1977.

75. Siple, P. A., and Passel, C. F.: Measurement of dry atmospheric cooling in subfreezing temperatures. *Proc Am Philosophical Soc.* 89:177–199, 1945.

76. Siple, P. A.: *Adaptation of the Explorer to the Climate of Anarctica.* Dissertation. Worcester, Mass., Clark University, 1939.

77. Sohal, R., Sun, S., Colcolough, H., and Burch, G.: Heat stroke: an electron microscopic study of endothelial cell damage and disseminated intravascular coagulation. *Arch Intern Med.* 122:43–47, 1968.

78. Strømme, S., Lange Andersen, K., and Elsner, R. W.: Metabolic and thermal responses to muscular exertion in the cold. *J Appl Physiol.* 18(4):756–763, 1963.

79. Sutton, J. R.: Heat illness. In Strauss, R. H. (ed.): *Sports Medicine.* Philadelphia, W. B. Saunders, 1984.

80. Taylor, H., Henschel, A., Mickelson, O., and Keys, A.: The effect of sodium chloride intake on the work performance of man during exposure to dry heat and experimental heat exhaustion. *Am J Physiol.* 140:439, 1943.

81. Temperature/windchill index. *U.S. Army Aviation Digest.* 10(2):42, 1964. U.S. Government Printing Office.

82. Webb, P.: Air temperature in respiratory tracts of resting subjects in the cold. *J Appl Physiol.* 4(11):378–82, 1951.

83. Wells, C. L.: Responses of physically active and acclimatized men and women to exercise in a desert environment. *Med Sci Sports Exer.* 12(1):9–13, 1980.

84. Wyndham, C. H.: The physiology of exercise under heat stress. *Ann Rev Physiol.* 35:193–220, 1973.

85. Wyndham, C. H., Rogers, G. G., Senay, L. C., and Mitchell, D.: Acclimatization in a hot, humid environment: cardiovascular adjustments. *J Appl Physiol.* 40:779–785, 1976.

SELECTED READINGS

Bass, D., and Henschel, A.: Responses of body fluid compartments to heat and cold. *Physiol Rev.* 36:128–144, 1956.

Benzinger, R.: Heat regulation: homeostasis of central temperature in man. *Physiol Rev.* 49:671–759, 1969.

Burch, G. E., Knochel, J. P., and Murphy, R.: Stay on guard against heat syndromes. *J Patient Care.* 13(12):67, 69, 73–76, 78–80, 1979.

Fox, E. L.: *Sports Physiology.* Philadelphia, W. B. Saunders, 1979, pp. 282–300.

Gisolfi, C. V., and Wenger, C. B.: Temperature regulation during exercise: old concepts, new ideas. In Terjung, R. J. (ed.): *Exercise and Sport Sciences Reviews,* vol. 12. Lexington, The Collamore Press, 1984.

Gisolfi, C. V. (ed.): Symposium on the thermal effects of exercise in the heat. *Med Sci Sports.* 11(1):30–71, 1979.

Kerslake, D.: *The Stress of Hot Environments.* Cambridge, England, Cambridge University Press, 1972.

McMurray, R. G., and Horvath, S. M.: Thermoregulation in swimmers and runners. *J Appl Physiol.* 46(6):1086–1092, 1979.

Mustafa, K. Y., and Mahmoud, N. E.: Evaporative water loss in African soccer players. *J Sports Med.* 19(2):181–183, 1979.

Nadel, E. R. (ed.): *Problems with Temperature during Exercise.* New York, Academic Press, 1977.

Nunneley, S.: Physiological responses of women to thermal stress: a review. *Med Sci Sports.* 10(4):250–255, 1978.

Robinson, S.: Temperature regulation in exercise. *Pediatrics.* 32:691–702, 1963.

Rowell, L. B.: Human cardiovascular adjustment to exercise and thermal stress. *Physiol Rev.* 54(1):75–159, 1974.

Sutton, J. R., and Hughson, R. L.: Heatstroke in road races (letter to editor): *Lancet.* 1(8123): 983, 1979.

Wyndham, C. H.: The physiology of exercise under heat stress. *Ann Rev Physiol.* 35: 193–220, 1973.

Young, K. C.: The influence of environmental parameters on heat stress during exercise. *J Appl Meteorol.* 18:886–897, 1979.

I n this section, the relationships among nutrition, body composition, body weight control, and exercise performance will be highlighted. The importance of these relationships is made obvious by the fact that good nutrition is essential to proper growth and development. Too often, coaches think of good nutrition only during the season of their sport. As we will learn in this section, good nutrition is critical at all times for effective athletic performance.

Closely associated with nutrition are the problems of obesity and body weight control. Obesity in the American population is of epidemic proportions. Its major cause is a lack of physical activity. It has been said that if you intend to maintain an average body weight and at the same time to lead a sedentary way of life, you will have to literally starve yourself for the majority of your life. How true this is.

Basic to the understanding of obesity and nutrition are the principles of body weight control. These principles apply to the nonathlete as well as to the athlete, but for different reasons. The nonathlete, as was just mentioned, must always be concerned with the problem of obesity, whereas the athlete is more concerned with gaining muscle mass or fat-free weight. In either case, the "do's and don'ts" of body weight control must be learned and thoroughly understood by the physical educator and coach.

To start this section, we will discuss the relationship between nutrition and exercise performance (Chapter 19) and then proceed to exercise, obesity, and body weight control (Chapter 20).

section **6**

NUTRITION AND BODY WEIGHT CONTROL

Nutrition and Exercise Performance

The major concepts to be learned from this chapter are as follows:

- Carbohydrates, fats, proteins, vitamins, minerals, and water are essential to the diet.
- Carbohydrates, fats, and proteins are referred to as energy nutrients since they are used as food fuels for metabolism.
- The protein requirement during heavy exercise and training is not significantly increased in adults.

- Vitamins are parts of enzymes or coenzymes that are vital for metabolism. However, vitamin and mineral supplementation above the daily minimum requirement does not increase exercise performance.
- The athletes' food requirements are the same as for the nonathlete, except that more calories are needed.
- Carbohydrates should be the major constituent of the pregame meal and should be consumed no later than 2½ hours before exercise or competition.
- Large amounts of sugar in liquid and pill form should be avoided 30 to 45 minutes before exercise is to begin. However, during prolonged exercise, some liquid glucose in low concentration should be imbibed.
- Endurance performance is positively correlated with the amount of glycogen stored in the working muscles. Muscle glycogen storage can be greatly increased by several diet and/or exercise procedures.

Athletic performance improves with wise nutrition and crumbles with nutritive deficiency. Inadequate water intake has by far the most immediate and serious debilitating effect on performance. An athlete's exploits can be not only improved through proper nutritional practices but harmed through malpractice.

In a survey of the nutritional practices of coaches in the Big Ten Conference,[65] 78% of the coaches felt a need for more nutritional information, yet 69% of them rarely read about nutrition. In another study,[4] it was found that the majority of coaches and trainers surveyed had up-to-date information about water replacement, but were totally uninformed about sound nutritional practices. These situations are probably typical of many coaches throughout the United States. The surveys vividly point out that scientific information aimed at the coach concerning nutrition and its effects on exercise and athletic performance is greatly needed. Our essential concern in this chapter, therefore, will be to fulfill this need.

Nutrients

Essential to the diet are (1) carbohydrates, (2) fats, (3) proteins, (4) vitamins, (5) minerals, and (6) water. Carbohydrates, fats, and proteins are the only sources of food energy; hence, they are called the **energy nutrients.** Devoid of carbon, minerals and water are the inorganic nutrients. Vitamins play a metabolic role in every single cell of the body, with the B complex being particularly important in energy metabolism.

Carbohydrates

Simple and complex sugars are chemical compounds that comprise the nutritional group referred to as *carbohydrates*. Simple sugars such as glucose and fructose **(monosaccharides),** double sugars such as sucrose and maltose **(disaccharides),** and complex sugars such as starch and glycogen **(polysaccharides)** are among the important carbohydrates. All sugars are reduced to the simple sugar, glucose, through digestion before being absorbed. Starch and glycogen are complex sugars containing numerous glucose molecules. Plants store sugar in the form of starch, whereas in humans, a limited amount of sugar is stored as glycogen in the liver and in the muscles. Glycogen is depleted during intensive muscular activity (p. 29).

Structure of Carbohydrates

All carbohydrates contain atoms of carbon (C), hydrogen (H), and oxygen (O). The distinguishing structural feature of carbohydrates is that there are two hydrogen atoms per atom of oxygen. For example, the chemical formula of the simple sugars glucose, fructose, and galactose is $C_6H_{12}O_6$. Even though these sugars have the same formula, they are different because of the different arrangement of atoms within each molecule. This is shown in Figure 19-1. Notice that each sugar has the same numbers of carbon, hydrogen, and oxygen atoms, but that their arrangement within each molecule is different.

Fuel Forms of Carbohydrates

It was mentioned previously that carbohydrates serve as major food fuels for the metabolic production of ATP. There are two forms of carbohydrates used for this

Figure 19-1. The simple sugars, glucose and fructose, have the same chemical formula, $C_6H_{12}O_6$; however, they are different because of the different arrangement of the same atoms within each molecule.

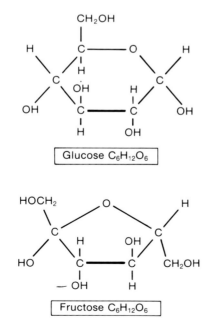

Glucose $C_6H_{12}O_6$

Fructose $C_6H_{12}O_6$

purpose: (1) **blood glucose** and (2) **intramuscular stores of glycogen.** Blood glucose levels are regulated mainly through the glycogen stored in the liver. For example, when blood glucose is low, glycogen from the liver is broken down to glucose by a process called **glycogenolysis** and is dumped into the blood stream. From here it is carried to the skeletal muscles and other organs that need it for metabolism. Just the opposite occurs when blood glucose is high, i.e., glucose is taken up by the tissues with the help of a hormone called **insulin.** If taken up by the liver, it can either be used for metabolism or can be converted to glycogen through a process referred to as **glycogenesis.** After being converted to glycogen, it is then stored in the liver. If the glucose is taken up by skeletal muscles and other tissues, it is used for metabolic purposes. If the glycogen stores are filled, excess glucose (sugars) can be converted to fats and can be stored within the fat cells located throughout the body.

The muscular stores of glycogen are used directly by muscles for metabolism. As such, these stores do not contribute directly to the maintenance of the blood glucose levels. However, the blood glucose levels can be affected by muscle glycogen metabolism indirectly as follows: when anaerobic glycolysis occurs within the muscles, some of the lactic acid formed diffuses into the blood. From there some of it is carried to the liver where it is converted to glucose and is then (1) dumped back into the blood as blood glucose, (2) used by the liver as a metabolic fuel, or (3) converted to glycogen and stored as liver glycogen.

Food Sources of Carbohydrates

Some common food sources of carbohydrates are baked beans, bread, cakes, cereals, dried fruits, fresh fruits, honey, pancakes, pastries, potatoes, spaghetti, syrup, vegetables (legumes), and waffles.

Fats

Forty to forty-five per cent of the total energy intake in the United States is made up of fat nutrients. Unquestionably, eating such a large quantity of fat contributes toward excessive obesity and cardiovascular diseases such as atherosclerosis.[59] Most nutritionists agree that 25% fat in our daily diet would be an adequate amount.

Fats or lipids are found in the body mainly as **triglycerides, phospholipids,** and **cholesterol.** Triglycerides are stored in the fat cells located throughout the body and within the skeletal muscles. They represent the fat form that is used as a food fuel in aerobically manufacturing ATP energy (see p. 22). Our discussion at this time, therefore, will focus exclusively on this form of fat.

Structure of Fats

When fats are metabolized, they must first be broken down from the triglyceride molecule. The basic structure of triglycerides consists of one molecule of a compound called *glycerol* and three molecules of **free fatty acids (FFA).** Free fatty acids are the usable fuel form of the triglyceride molecule. Although there are numerous free fatty acids, the three most common fatty acids are *stearic acid, oleic acid,* and *palmitic acid.* The structure of palmitic acid is shown in Figure 19-2. Note that like carbohydrates, free fatty acids contain atoms of carbon, hydrogen, and oxygen. The number and arrangement of these atoms distinguish a free fatty acid from other compounds containing the same kinds of atoms (e.g., carbohydrates). For example, as shown in the figure, palmitic acid contains a long chain of 16 carbon atoms, each of which is *saturated* with hydrogen atoms. A free fatty acid whose carbon atoms are saturated with hydrogen atoms is referred to as a **saturated fatty acid.** Consumption of large amounts of saturated fats is

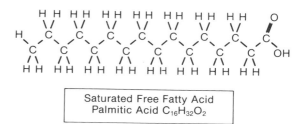

Saturated Free Fatty Acid
Palmitic Acid $C_{16}H_{32}O_2$

Figure 19-2. The chemical structure of the common saturated fatty acid, palmitic acid. Fatty acids contain long chains of carbon atoms (C) linked together with hydrogen atoms (H) and oxygen atoms (O) also linked to the carbon atoms.

not recommended since this is thought to lead to high blood cholesterol levels, atherosclerosis, cardiovascular disease, and obesity.

Unsaturated fats are those fatty acids whose carbon atoms are not saturated with hydrogen atoms. Instead, some of the carbon atoms are chemically linked to each other with a *double bond,* thus decreasing the number of bonding links for the hydrogen atoms. The structural difference between saturated and unsaturated free fatty acids is shown in Figure 19-3. In this example, with the same number of carbon atoms, the number of hydrogen atoms bound to the saturated fat is 11 compared with only 7 for the unsaturated fat. The symbol R represents the remainder of the fatty acid molecule.

Food Sources of Fatty Acids

Saturated fats are usually in a solid form at room temperature. They include most of the animal fats, i.e., the fats in meats such as beef, pork, and lamb. Eggs and dairy products also contain high levels of saturated fats. Unsaturated fats are in the liquid state at room temperatures. They are found in vegetable oils such as peanut oil, corn oil, cottonseed oil, and soybean oil.

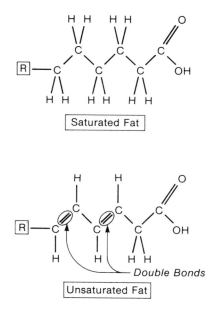

Saturated Fat

Unsaturated Fat

Figure 19-3. The structural difference between saturated and unsaturated fatty acids is that the former are saturated with hydrogen atoms whereas the latter are not. The fewer number of hydrogen atoms and the presence of double bonds in unsaturated fatty acids provide evidence of this difference. The symbol R represents the remainder of the fatty acid molecule.

Other sources of fat are bacon, butter, margarine, and salad oils.

Proteins

Protein has a wide variety of physiological functions that are considered essential to health and physical performance.[64] Although the role of protein in providing energy has not been considered important for most forms of muscular activity, it is becoming increasingly clear that protein catabolism is increased by endurance activity (greater than 60 minutes) and may contribute between 5 and 15% of the energy needs.[21,40] In the following, we will discuss the structure of protein, food sources of pro-

tein, and protein requirement during heavy exercise and training.

Structure of Proteins

Proteins are more complex and larger molecules than either carbohydrates or fats. In addition to carbon, hydrogen, and oxygen, proteins contain nitrogen; many also contain sulfur, phosphorus, and iron. Proteins are the building blocks of tissue, and as such, form a vital part of the nucleus and protoplasm of all cells. In addition, all enzymes found in the body are proteins.

The basic structural units of proteins are **amino acids.** In proteins, the amino acids are chemically bonded into long chains by what are referred to as *peptide linkages*. There are 22 different kinds of amino acids in the body. The structure of one of these is given in Figure 19-4. The nitrogen component of the amino acid (NH_2) is referred to as an *amino radical* or *group*. This chemical group plus the *carboxyl group* ($COOH$) distinguishes amino acids from other compounds containing the same atoms. Of the 22 known amino acids, 9 are referred to as *essential amino acids*. They are essential because they cannot be synthesized within the body. Therefore, their only source is through the diet.

Figure 19-4. The chemical structure of the amino acid isoleucine. The nitrogen component of amino acids (NH_2) is referred to as an amino group whereas the COOH component is called a carboxyl group.

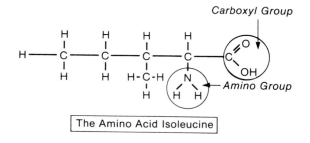

The Amino Acid Isoleucine

The essential amino acids are histadine, isoleucine, leucine, lysine, methionine, phenylalanine, threonine, tryptophan, and valine.

The nonessential amino acids are so named because they may be synthesized in the body as well as being provided by food intake. Some nonessential amino acids include alanine, arginine (essential in rats), aspartic acid, cystine, glutamic acid, glutamine, glycine, hydroxyproline, proline, serine, and tyrosine.

Food Sources of Proteins

Foods that are richest in essential amino acids are animal proteins and milk. Plant proteins contain some but not many of the essential amino acids. Therefore, to meet the protein needs with plant protein not only requires more but also a wide variety of vegetables. Common sources of protein are cereal, cheese, eggs, fish, lean meat, liver, milk (low-fat milk is preferable), nuts, poultry, soya beans, yeast (brewers), and vegetables (legumes).

Protein Requirement during Heavy Exercise and Training

The normal adult daily protein requirement is about 0.8 gram per kilogram of body weight. For example, the daily protein requirement of a person weighing 75 kg (165 pounds) would be 75 kg × 0.8 g/kg = 60 g (2.1 oz). This amount of protein is easily obtained from a well-balanced diet in which 10 to 15% of the calories taken in are from protein sources. If our 75-kg person has a daily caloric requirement of 3000 kcal, a well-balanced diet would supply between 75 and 112 grams of protein.*

Contrary to what many coaches and athletes believe, the protein requirement during heavy exercise is not significantly increased in adults.[16,19,22,45,50,52,53] The requirements may be 1 to 1.5 grams per kilogram of body weight as compared with 0.8 grams per kilogram of body weight. This amount of protein is easily supplied in the average American diet.[23] If the athlete is interested in promoting muscle growth, the only known stimulus is resistance exercise (see Chapter 7). Further, the maximum muscle mass that can be added is approximately 1 pound per week. It has been estimated that the increased protein intake required for this to occur is only 15 grams per day and an additional 400 kcal per day.[12] Ingested protein in excess of metabolic requirements will be stored as fat and will not result in any further increase in muscle mass. Thus, amounts of protein sufficient to meet the body's ordinary demands will also be sufficient during periods of increased physical activity—even during heavy weight training involving increases in muscle mass.

It should be noted that since the protein requirement is estimated on a body weight basis, it provides for greater protein intake with increases in muscle mass. For example, an active male football player who weighs 115 kg (253 pounds) would have a daily protein requirement of 115 grams. If his daily caloric requirement were 5000 kcal, a well-balanced diet containing 10 to 15% of its calories in the form of protein would provide him with between 138 and 187 grams of protein. He would easily meet his requirement.

The consumption of excessive quantities of protein, particularly in the forms of pills and powders, during athletic training is neither required nor recommended. In fact, it may be contraindicated in many sports since a large protein diet may cause dehydration and constipation.

---

*10% of 3000 kcal = 300 kcal, and 15% = 450 kcal. One gram of protein contains 4 kcal. Therefore, 300/4 = 75 grams, and 450/4 = 112 grams of protein.

Protein as an Energy Source during Prolonged Exercise

Cathcart, in 1925, suggested that physical activity increases, "if only in small degree," the metabolism of protein.[13] More recently, authors have provided further evidence of the role of protein in activity.[21,24,43] The role of protein metabolism as an energy source has mostly been ignored and declared insignificant. However, with prolonged exercise (60 minutes at 60 to 70% of aerobic capacity) some amino acids are oxidized during exercise to provide amino groups ($-NH_2$). Sixteen amino acids have been identified as glucogenic with leucine, isoleucine, and valine the most readily available. Leucine, for example, is degraded to $-NH_2$ and CO_2. The NH_2 radical combines with pyruvic acid to form alanine. Alanine is transferred from the muscle, via the circulation, to the liver where it is deaminated to form urea and pyruvic acid. The pyruvic acid is then converted to liver glycogen and glucose. The glucose then can be recirculated to the working muscle to provide energy for muscular contraction. This process is called the "glucose-alanine" cycle. Figure 19-5 illustrates the glucose-alanine cycle.[28]

The process of protein metabolism is significant in at least three ways: (1) amino acid conversion to Krebs Cycle intermediates enhances the rate of oxidation of acetyl-CoA generation from glucose and fatty acids; (2) increased conversion of amino acids to glucose helps prevent hypoglycemia; and (3) oxidation of some specific amino acids may provide energy for muscular contraction.

A summary of the food nutrients and their richest sources and functions is listed in Table 19-1.

Vitamins and Minerals

Most **vitamins** serve as essential parts of enzymes or coenzymes that are vital to the

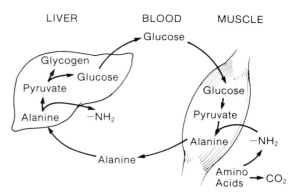

Figure 19-5. The glucose-alanine cycle provides a small amount of energy for muscular contraction during prolonged work. Amino acid breakdown provides an amino group (NH_2) that interacts with pyruvate to form alanine. Alanine is transferred to the liver where it can be converted to pyruvate then glycogen and glucose. Glucose is then transported to the working muscle where it can be utilized as an energy substrate. (Modified from Felig and Wahren.[28])

metabolism of fats and carbohydrates. Thus, although vitamins do not in themselves yield energy, they are essential to life (i.e., they are nutrients).

Vitamins are classified as **water-soluble** or **fat-soluble.** The water-soluble vitamins are *vitamin C (ascorbic acid)* and the *B-complex vitamins.* These are *not* stored in the body and therefore must be constantly supplied in the diet. Since they are not stored, when taken in excess (above that required), they will be passed in the urine. The fat-soluble *vitamins, A, D, E,* and *K,* are stored in the body, principally in the liver but also in fatty tissue. While this means that these vitamins need not be supplied each day, it also means that excessive accumulations can cause toxic effects.

A deficiency of vitamins can lead to serious illness, chronic disease, and even death. However, deficiencies, particularly in the United States, are very rare. The minimum daily requirements of vitamins

TABLE 19-1

Some Principal Food Nutrients and Their Sources and Functions*

Nutrient	Rich Food Sources	Functions
Protein	Meat, fish, eggs, legumes, nuts, and cereal	Growth and repair of tissue, synthesis of hormones, antibodies and enzymes, milk production during lactation, and relatively poor energy source
Fats	Oils, margarine and butter, well-larded meats, mayonnaise and salad dressing, nuts, chocolate, and peanut butter	Good energy source, efficient storage of energy, carriers of fat-soluble vitamins (A, D, E, and K), satiety value, and flavor
Carbohydrate	Cereal grain products, sugar and honey, pastries, and dried fruits	Excellent energy source and flavor

*Modified from Smith,[57] p. 18.

are small and can be easily met through a varied diet. Although most fats, carbohydrates, and protein foods contain vitamins, the richest sources are green leafy vegetables.

Minerals are inorganic compounds found in trace amounts in the body and are also important to proper bodily function. *Calcium, phosphorus, potassium, sodium, iron,* and *iodine* are a few of the more important required minerals. Mineral deficiencies are generally uncommon today.

Although iodine is artificially added to common table salt ("iodized" salt is the result), most minerals occur naturally in a large variety of foods. For example, milk is rich in calcium, as are other dairy products, *and* in potassium, as are dried fruits and wheat germ. Most animal protein foods are good sources of phosphorus, and lean meats, particularly liver, provide enough iron to meet most requirements (iron supplements are discussed below). Common table salt supplies us with sodium.

Iron

Iron is an important mineral in the diet of both female and male athletes.[15,24,43,51] As

an essential constituent of hemoglobin, myoglobin, and several enzymes in the metabolic pathways, iron deficiency can be a contributor to diminished performance, especially in endurance events. Iron deficiency can occur with or without anemia. Clark identifies groups of individuals who are susceptible to iron deficiency.[14] They include (1) menstruating women, (2) dieters, (3) endurance athletes, (4) those who do not eat red meat, (5) lacto-ovo vegetarians, and (5) "nature-food" eaters.

The Recommended Daily Allowance (RDA) for iron is 18 mg for women and growing teenagers and 10 mg for adult men. Americans ingest about 5 to 6 mg of iron per 1000 kcal of food. Thus athletes who are on a restricted diet for weight-control purposes—such as dancers, ice skaters, distance runners, and gymnasts—can incur an iron deficiency.

In warm weather, runners and other athletes can lose 2 to 5 kg of water through sweating. Sweat contains approximately 0.4 mg of iron per liter of water. Thus the athlete may lose 0.8 to 2 mg of iron just by sweating alone.

Is it necessary for the athlete to take an

iron supplement? Not really. By pursuing a dietary practice that includes the following, it is possible to acquire adequate iron intake and absorption[14]:

1. Include foods that are rich in vitamin C. Vitamin C helps the body absorb iron.
2. Include breads, cereals, and pastas that have been "fortified" or "enriched" or have iron listed among the ingredients.
3. Avoid drinking tea when eating iron-rich foods. The tannic acid in tea can reduce iron absorption.
4. Eat meats, preferably lean, red meats and the dark meat of chicken and turkey. Animal protein contains heme-iron, which is more readily bioavailable; that is, more easily absorbed. Vegetable sources of iron are not as easily absorbed. Interestingly, heme-iron from red meats enhances the absorption of non–heme-iron.

Iron supplementation may be in order for some athletes who have diminished iron storage.[47] However, excessive iron intake is not recommended for at least two reasons: (1) chronic over-indulgence in iron intake can be toxic and liver damage may occur, and (2) excessive iron intake has not been shown, objectively, to improve performance. In any event, if iron-deficiency is suspected by the athlete or coach, a medical examination is strongly recommended to confirm the condition. Following confirmation, medically supervised treatment should be started.

Calcium

Calcium is the most abundant mineral found in the body. Approximately 99% of the body's calcium is found in bone and teeth as an integral part of their respective structures. The remaining 1% is found in the blood and other areas of the body. Calcium has many important functions in addition to its structural function. It plays an important role in blood clotting, muscle tone and irritability, nerve transmission, normal heart activity (myocardial rhythm), and activation of several metabolic enzymes. The Recommended Daily Allowance for calcium is about 1 gram per day for adults. Only about 20 to 40% of ingested calcium is absorbed by the body. Generally, calcium deficiency is not a problem in the United States. However, a lifetime of low calcium intake may contribute to a gradual demineralization and weakening of bone tissue. Bone, as a living, dynamic tissue, is constantly being "remodeled" throughout life. With the combination of low calcium intake and ongoing calcium needs over a prolonged period, calcium levels may gradually diminish. This is true especially for postmenopausal women. Resistance exercise appears to discourage calcium loss and to increase bone mass.

In sports, in rare instances, some female athletes may be subject to early stages of osteoporosis. The combination of chronic endurance activity generating high sweat rates (calcium is excreted in sweat) and low calcium intake through a restricted diet can lead to osteoporosis.

Sources for calcium include milk (2 cups per day will meet calcium needs), green leafy vegetables, cheeses, turnip greens, and citrus fruits. Recently, it has been reported that commercially available antacids can provide calcium (200 mg per tablet). However, the absorption rate is not as high as that found in calcium-rich foods.

Use of Vitamin and Mineral Supplements by Athletes

With respect to exercise, there does not appear to be an excessive demand for most vitamins or minerals during periods of increased physical activity. The one exception might be the requirement for iron, which is found in red blood cells and is responsible for the oxygen-carrying ability of the blood. As mentioned in Chapter 14, levels of iron in the blood of women have been found to be significantly decreased after heavy physical training;[39,66] thus, female athletes, especially those who have heavy menstrual blood losses, may wish to consider supplementing their diet with extra iron. A note of caution is needed here: overdoses of iron can be toxic. Therefore, the athlete contemplating taking iron supplements should first consult a physician.

Use of vitamin and mineral supplements is fairly common among athletes (as well as the general population). For example, it has been reported that 85% of the Olympic athletes use vitamin and mineral supplements. Although some of these athletes have indicated that the supplements have improved their performances, little scientific evidence is available to support their contentions.[10,48,55,56,57] Furthermore, those authorities who recommend vitamin supplements for athletes usually do so only on theoretical grounds (the value of *extra* vitamins is inferred from the fact that

meeting the *basic* vitamin requirement is essential to life).

It may be concluded that supplementing the diet with amounts of vitamins and minerals above the minimum daily requirements does not increase physical performance. Furthermore, the minimum daily requirements are easily met through a *varied, normal diet.*

Food Requirements

The amount of food necessary each day depends upon a person's energy needs. These energy needs are directly related to: (1) periods of rapid growth, (2) age, and (3) physical activity. During the rapid growing years (12–22 years for boys and 12–18 years for girls), there is a gradual increase in the minimal daily food requirements (Table 19-2). As we become older, our daily energy needs decrease (Fig. 19-6). The biggest difference in food requirements for the athlete versus the nonathlete is the total number of calories consumed; the athlete will require more.

The per cent contributions toward the

TABLE 19-2

Recommended Daily Dietary Allowances Established by The National Academy of Sciences*

	Age (Yrs)	Weight (Lb)	(kg)	Height (In)	Kilocalories	kcal/Lb
Males	10–12	77	35.0	55	2,500	33
	12–14	95	43.1	59	2,700	28
	14–18	30	59.0	67	3,000	23
	18–22	147	66.7	69	2,800	19
Females	10–12	77	35.0	56	2,250	29
	12–14	97	44.0	61	2,300	24
	14–16	114	51.8	62	2,400	21
	16–18	119	54.0	63	2,300	19
	18–22	128	58.1	64	2,000	16

*From Nutrition for the Athlete: American Association for Health, Physical Education and Recreation, Washington, D.C., 1971, p. 9.

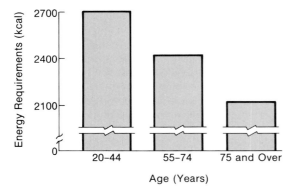

Figure 19-6. Daily energy requirements for men ages 20 to 75 years. When body weight is considered, the greatest energy decline occurs at about 60 years of age. (Based on data from McGandy, R. B., et al.[42])

total caloric intake for each of the three foodstuffs are[25]

Protein	10 to 15%
Fat	29 to 30%
Carbohydrate	55 to 56%

For example, athletes requiring 5000 kcal per day could have their diet divided as follows:

Protein	500 to 750 kcal
Fat	1450 to 1500 kcal
Carbohydrate	2750 to 2800 kcal

Selecting Foods

Many years ago, the United States Department of Agriculture suggested four basic food groups from which meals should be selected each day to ensure minimal nutrition.[46] They are (1) milk, (2) meat, (3) cereals, and (4) vegetables and fruit.

More recently, the American Association for Health, Physical Education and Recreation, in collaboration with the Amer-

ican Dietetic and Nutrition Foundation, published *Nutrition for the Athlete*.[45] The essential food groups in this fine booklet are listed as: milk, meat (fish, poultry, cheese, or eggs), dark green or deep yellow vegetables, citrus fruits, other fruits and vegetables, bread (enriched or whole grain bread), cereal or potatoes, and fats (butter, margarine, or other fat spreads).

Table 19-3 contains an extensive list of these foods.

Number of Meals

The spacing of and number of meals eaten per day that would prove most satisfactory have been scientifically studied in humans, but have yielded somewhat conflicting results. For example, it has been suggested that eating fewer and larger meals (e.g., 2 to 3 per day) impairs glucose tolerance[26,27,61,67,68] and increases body weight and body fat content.[24] On the other hand, several well-controlled studies with humans have not substantiated these contentions.[9,29,41,60,61,69] Although no definite conclusions can be made regarding the effects of the number of meals per day, it would appear that eating more than 3 meals per day would either have no effect or a beneficial effect on metabolism.

Based on the preceding information, nutritive nibbling—not just nibbling—interspersed among the three main meals is suggested in order to increase the consumption of the added calories most athletes require. Foods without nutritive value should be limited. Always of concern is the problem of obesity when nibbling gets out of hand. Table 19-4 contains a number of snack foods with their caloric equivalents.

A very active person, such as the athlete requiring 5000 or 6000 kcal per day, may be better advised to eat five meals, as follows:

TABLE 19-3

Foods that Within a Group May Be Exchanged or Substituted for Each Other*

Milk

(1 cup whole milk contains 12 grams carbohydrate, 8 grams protein, 10 grams fat, and 170 calories; 1 cup of skim milk contains 80 calories; 1 cup cocoa made with milk contains approximately 200 calories)

1 cup whole milk	¼ cup powdered milk
1 cup skim milk	1 cup buttermilk
½ cup evaporated milk	1 cup cocoa

Meat Group

(1 ounce contains 7 grams protein, 5 grams fat, and 75 calories)

1 ounce lean beef, lamb, pork, liver, chicken†	3 medium sardines
1 ounce fish—cod, haddock, perch, etc.	1 slice cheese
1 hot dog	¼ cup cottage cheese
¼ cup tuna, salmon, crab, lobster	1 egg
5 small oysters, shrimp, clams	2 tablespoons peanut butter

†1 average serving of meat or fish (such as a pork chop or 2 meatballs) is about 3 ounces

Dark Green or Deep Yellow Vegetables (½ cup is one serving)

Greens and lettuce have very little carbohydrate content. The other vegetables contain approximately 7 grams carbohydrate and 2 grams protein and 35 calories

Broccoli†	Pepper	Greens†	Kale
Carrots	Pumpkin	Beet greens	Mustard
Chicory†	Tomatoes†	Chard	Spinach
Escarole†	Watercress†	Collard	Turnip greens
	Winter squash	Dandelion	Lettuce†

†Low Calories Vegetables.

Citrus Fruits or Substitute (½ cup is one serving)

The carbohydrate is averaged to approximately 10 grams per ½ cup and 40 calories

Orange	Grapefruit juice†	Tangerine
Orange juice	Cantaloupe†	Tomato juice†
Grapefruit†		

†Represent low calorie fruits and vegetables

Other Fruits and Vegetables

Fruits (½ cup is approximately 10 grams carbohydrate and 40 calories)

Apple	Figs	Pineapple
Applesauce	Grapes	Plums
Apricots	Grape juice (¼ cup)	Raisins (2 tablespoons)
Banana (½ small)	Honeydew melon	Pineapple juice (1/3 cup)
Raspberries	Mango	Prunes (2 medium)
Blueberries	Papaya	Watermelon†
Cherries	Peach	
Dates	Pear	

(Continued)

TABLE 19-3

Foods that Within a Group May Be Exchanged or Substituted for Each Other* *(Continued)*

Vegetables (½ cup is one serving)
The vegetables without the dagger contain approximately 7 grams carbohydrate, 2 grams protein, and 35 calories

Asparagus†	Cucumbers†	Radishes†
Beets	Eggplant†	Rutabagas
Brussels sprouts†	Mushrooms†	Sauerkraut†
Cabbage†	Okra†	String beans†
Cauliflower†	Onions	Summer squash†
Celery†	Peas, green	Turnips

†Represents low calorie fruits and vegetables

Bread Group
(1 slice of bread or 1 substitute contains 15 grams carbohydrate, 2 grams protein, and 70 calories)

½ hamburger bun	½ cup spaghetti, noodles, macaroni, etc.	⅔ cup parsnips
½ hot dog bun		1 small potato
1 cup popcorn	2 graham crackers	½ cup mashed potato
2½″ wedge pizza	5 saltines	15 potato chips—1 ounce bag
1 slice enriched bread	6 round, thin crackers	6 pretzels, medium, or 20 thin sticks
1 biscuit or roll	½ cup beans or peas (dried or cooked)	
1 small muffin		8 French fries
1 small piece cornbread	(Lima or navy beans, split pea, cowpeas, etc.)	½ cup sweet potatoes or yams
½ cup cooked cereal	¼ cup baked beans	1½″ cube sponge or angel cake (no icing)
¾ cup ready-to-eat cereal	⅓ cup corn	½ cup ice cream (omit 2 fat servings)
	½ cup rice or grits	

Fat Group
(1 teaspoon fat contains 5 grams fat and 45 calories)

Bacon	1 slice	Cream cheese	1 tablespoon
Butter or margarine or fat spread	1 teaspoon	French dressing	1 tablespoon
Cream (light)	2 tablespoons	Mayonnaise	1 teaspoon
Cream (heavy—40%)	1 tablespoon	Oil or cooking fat	1 teaspoon

Sugars
(1 teaspoon contains 5 grams carbohydrate and 20 calories)

Sugar	Syrup
Jelly	Hard candy
Honey	Carbonated beverage (¼ cup)

Salt used in the home should be iodized.

*From Nutrition for the Athlete: American Association for Health, Physical Education and Recreation, Washington, D.C., 1971.

TABLE 19-4

Snack Foods and Their Approximate Energy Values in Kilocalories (kcal)*

Snack Food	kcal
Milk shake (fountain size)	400
Malted milk shake (fountain size)	500
Sundaes	215–325
Sodas	260
Hamburger (including bun)	360
Hot dog (including bun)	210
Pizza (4″-5″ section)	135
Popcorn, lightly buttered (½ cup)	75
Nuts (3 tbsp. chopped, or 30 peanuts)	150
Pound cake (1⅜″ slice)	140
Cup cake with frosting (2¾″ diam.)	185
Layer cake with frosting (2″ slice)	370–445
Pancake (4″ diam.)	60
Waffle (medium, 4½″ x 5½″ x ½″)	215
Add 20 kcals for each teaspoon syrup or sweetening	
Add 45 kcals for each teaspoon butter or other fat spread	
Brownies (2″ x 2″ x ¾″)	140
Plain cookie (3″ diam.)	120
Pie (⅛ of a 9″ pie)	275–345
Fruit juice (1 cup)	110–165

*From Nutrition for the Athlete: American Association for Health, Physical Education and Recreation, Washington, D.C. 1971, p. 19.

	kcal %	TOTAL kcal
First breakfast	21	1050
Second breakfast	14	700
Lunch	27	1350
Dinner	23	1150
Snacks	15	750
	100	5000

Diet before Activity: The Pregame Meal

From what has already been stated, you should realize that there are no foods that, when consumed several hours prior to physical activity, will lead to "super" performances. Proper nutrition, as emphasized throughout, is an ongoing, year-round task. However, there are certain foods that should probably be avoided on the day of competition. For example, fats and meats are generally digested slowly. If consumed 3 to 4 hours or less before an athletic event, they may cause a feeling of fullness, hindering performance. Other food categories to avoid might include gas-forming foods, "greasy" foods, and highly seasoned foods.

What should the pregame meal consist of? Carbohydrates should be the major constituent of the pregame meal and should be consumed no later than 2½ hours before competition. The reasons for this are that carbohydrates are easily digested and help maintain the blood glucose levels. This latter effect makes one feel better. The pregame meal can also include moderate portions of such foods as fruits, cooked vegetables, gelatin desserts, and fish (or lean meats, provided the advice given previously is heeded).

Ingestion of Large Amounts of Glucose (Sugar) before Exercise

Although carbohydrates should make up the major contents of the pregame meal, a note of caution is necessary: *consumption of large amounts of sugar or glucose, particularly in liquid or pill form, less than an hour before exercise is not recommended.*[18,30] An example of the physiological reasons for this is shown in Figure 19-7. In this study,[18] 75 grams of glucose were ingested 45 minutes before the start of 30 minutes of moderate-to-heavy treadmill exercise (70% max VO_2).

The following findings should be noted:

1. The ingestion of glucose at rest caused a 38% increase in blood glucose levels at the start of exercise (Fig. 19-7A).
2. The ingestion of glucose at rest also caused a 3.3-fold increase in blood insulin levels at the start of exercise (Fig. 19-7B).
3. As a result of the high insulin levels, blood glucose is progressively reduced throughout the exercise period leading to hypoglycemia or low blood glucose levels (Fig. 19-7A). This causes a feeling of fatigue and reduces the availability of blood-borne glucose as a metabolic fuel. In turn, there was a 17% greater utilization of muscle glycogen (inset of Fig. 19-7).

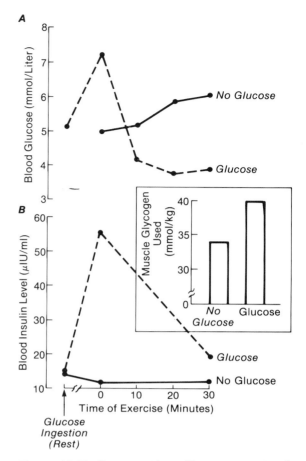

Figure 19-7. Consumption of large amounts of sugar (75 grams in 300 ml water or a 25% solution) 45 minutes before the start of exercise will actually cause blood glucose to be less available because of the insulin response. Greater dependence is thereby placed on muscle glycogen as a metabolic fuel. Consequently, muscle glycogen is depleted faster during endurance activities. This could lead to early muscle fatigue. (Based on data from Costill et al.[18])

The conclusion to be drawn from these results is that consumption of large amounts of sugar within an hour of exercise will actually cause blood glucose to be less available, thereby placing greater dependence on muscle glycogen as a metabolic fuel. Consequently, muscle glycogen is depleted faster; in endurance activities, this could lead to early muscular fatigue.

Provided their sugar concentration is not excessive (not greater than 2.5 grams per 100 ml of liquid), liquids may be imbibed up to 30 minutes before physical activity without hindering performance.[31,][32,63] Water is perhaps the best liquid, but fruit and vegetable juices are suitable, as are uncarbonated, fruit-flavored drinks.

Liquid Pregame Meals

An increasingly popular pregame meal with both coaches and athletes is the liquid meal. There are several liquid formulas commercially available today that can serve as excellent pregame meals (e.g., Ensure, Ensure Plus, Nutriment, Sustagen, and SustaCal). Available in a variety of flavors to suit most tastes, liquid meals are well balanced nutritionally (most contain large amounts of carbohydrates plus fat and protein). Besides being palatable and nutritious, liquid meals are easily digested and are emptied quickly from the stomach. As both "liquid" and "meals," they contribute to hydration and to energy intake. From a physiological standpoint, it has been shown that liquid meals (Ensure Plus) can be substituted for a solid diet containing the same calories without decreasing daily exercise performance.[31,32] There are subjective efforts as well: the athlete drinking a liquid meal will have a feeling of satiety and relief from hunger. At the very least, the occasional unpleasant sensations associated with pregame meals (nervous indigestion, diarrhea, nausea, vomiting, and abdominal cramps) are minimized when liquid meals are used.

In using the liquid pregame meal, it is important to remember that a period of adjustment will more than likely be needed, since, for most athletes, a liquid meal will be a new experience. Therefore, the coach should introduce the liquid meal early in the season, explaining to the athletes its nutritional advantages. Of course, any athlete who cannot (or will not) adjust to such a meal should not be forced to do so.

It should be emphasized that the pregame "menu" is not entirely based on strict "do's" and "don't's." The basic requirement is a relative one: the athlete's diet on the day of competition should not be drastically different from that normally consumed (so long as it is remembered that nervousness and tension during intense competition may so affect the digestive system that the foods normally eaten without discomfort may now cause distress). Provided the athlete does not overeat or does not eat foods that will cause gastrointestinal discomfort, performance will not be affected per se by the foods consumed at the pregame meal.

Guidelines to follow in planning the pregame diet are given in Table 19-5.

Diet during Activity: Replacement of Sugar and Water

It is fairly common to find that athletes, particularly endurance athletes, ingest glucose (usually in liquid form) during prolonged exercise. Does this practice improve performance? It is generally agreed that ingestion of some liquid glucose during prolonged physical exercise will help spare muscle glycogen and delay or prevent hypoglycemia or low blood sugar levels.[1,17,36,49,62] Both the glycogen sparing effect and the deterrent effect on hypoglycemia should help reduce and/or delay fatigue. An example of this is shown in Figure 19-8. The subjects in this study[36] were orally given 12.5 grams of liquid glucose every 15 minutes for the first 90 minutes of a 2-hour exercise period consisting of riding a bicycle ergometer. As is indicated in Figure 19-8A, blood glucose was maintained at

TABLE 19-5

Guidelines to Follow in Planning the Pregame Diet*

Energetics of the diet
Energy intake should be adequate to ward off any feelings of hunger or weakness during the entire period of the competition. Although pre-contest food intakes make only a minor contribution to the immediate energy expenditure, they are essential for the support of an adequate level of blood sugar, and for avoiding the sensations of hunger and weakness.

Timing of the diet
The diet plan should ensure that the stomach and upper bowel are empty at the time of competition.

Fluid content of the diet
Food and fluid intakes prior to and during prolonged competition should guarantee an optimal state of hydration.

Blandness of the diet
The pre-competition diet should offer foods that will minimize upset in the gastrointestinal tract.

Psychological aspects of the diet
The diet should include food that the athlete is familiar with, and is convinced will "make him win."

*Recommendations under each heading are from Smith[57] p. 118.

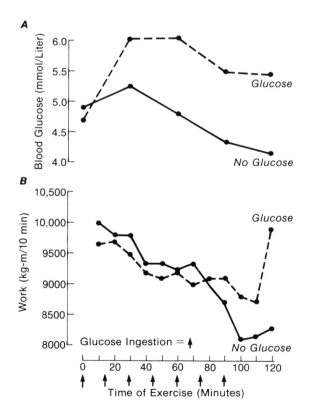

much higher levels when glucose was consumed than when no glucose was given. The total work performed during the 2-hour ride was not much different between trials until the last 30 minutes of exercise (Fig. 19-8*B*). During this time, the total work produced, was on the average, 11% greater than in the no-glucose trial. It was concluded that ingestion of liquid glucose during long-duration exercise is effective in maintaining elevated blood glucose levels, which in turn reduce fatigue during the latter part of exercise.

Remember, when glucose is made available to an athlete during prolonged exer-

Figure 19-8. *A,* It is generally agreed that ingestion of some liquid glucose during prolonged physical exercise will help spare muscle glycogen and delay or prevent hypoglycemia or low blood sugar levels. This in turn helps reduce and/or delay fatigue as demonstrated by an 11% greater work output during the last 30 minutes of exercise, *B*. (Based on data of Ivy et al.[36])

cise, it should be provided in low concentrations. The stomach can empty only a limited amount of glucose in a short period of time (p. 498). If too much glucose is present, the rate of gastric emptying is retarded, and glucose is absorbed into the blood more slowly. Thus ingestion of high concentrations of glucose actually delays its utilization as a metabolic fuel. As mentioned in the last chapter, the recommended concentration of glucose is 2.0 to 2.5 grams per 100 ml of water.

With respect to replacement of fluids, whether it be a liquid glucose solution or just plain water, it is important to remember that it is not possible to ingest fluids as rapidly as they are lost (mainly through sweating) during most endurance events. For example, only about 800 ml per hour of fluid can be emptied by the stomach during distance running, whereas losses amount to 2½ times that or 2 liters per hour.[7] Therefore, endurance athletes must be careful not to ingest fluids at a greater rate than 800 ml per hour. Otherwise, the fluid retained in the stomach may cause discomfort and may possibly hinder performance.

Diet following Activity

Following endurance events, serious effort should be made to replace fats, proteins, carbohydrates, vitamins, minerals, and water. One will be in better physiological condition if the athlete waits an hour or so after exercising before eating a large meal; however, a liquid nutrient may be consumed a few minutes following exertion in order to stabilize blood glucose. If competition is to be renewed the next day, care must be taken to replenish the energy stores—muscle and liver glycogen (see below). Easily digestible foods should be selected and may include cream and butter for fat content; carbohydrates in the form of bread, puddings, rice; proteins such as fish, soft-boiled eggs, cheese, and other

milk products; and fresh fruit and juices, which are excellent for vitamin C, energy, and liquid replacement.

Can Diet Affect Performance?

Carbohydrate is the prime source of energy during exhaustive work; both fat and carbohydrate are the sources of energy during steady-state activities. The carbohydrate molecule contains more oxygen than does fat. Add to this the fact that carbohydrate is a more efficient precursor of energy than fat (requires less oxygen to produce the same amount of energy); this makes it the preferable energy-producing food. Studies conclusively demonstrate that diets lacking in carbohydrates have deleterious effects on work performance.[2,5,34] One study showed that hard work was reduced by 50% with a high fat diet and increased 25% over that with a normal diet when a high-carbohydrate diet was consumed.[5]

As shown in Figure 19-9, muscle glycogen content is positively related to endurance performance.[5] Muscle biopsy studies have been used to show the effects of diet on muscle glycogen stores. The procedure involves use of a special needle that is inserted into a muscle under local anesthesia. A portion of the muscle is removed for later analysis. One of the studies[5] went as follows:

Men were administered three diets, following which they performed on a bicycle ergometer to exhaustion. Time to exhaustion on a normal diet was 114 minutes; on a high-protein, high-fat diet it was 57 minutes; and on a high-carbohydrate diet it was 167 minutes. The glycogen content of the quadriceps femoris muscle following the mixed diet was 17.5 grams per kilogram of wet muscle before exercise; following three days of a carbohydrate-free diet, it was only 6.3 grams, whereas after the same period of time on a high carbohy-

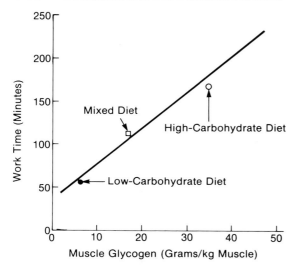

Figure 19-9. Effects of a mixed diet, a low-carbohydrate diet, and a high-carbohydrate diet on the initial glycogen content of the quadriceps femoris muscle and the duration of exercise on a bicycle ergometer; the higher the initial muscle glycogen content, the longer the duration of exercise. (Based on data from Bergström et al.[5])

drate diet, it was 35.1 grams per kilogram of muscle.

Muscle Glycogen-Loading or Supercompensation

The amount of glycogen resynthesized in skeletal muscle can be increased to values much higher than normal by following one or more of the following diet and/or exercise procedures.[5,6,7,34,35,38,45,54]

1. The first of these procedures is the simple dietary manipulation we have just described. Endurance athletes who consume a high-carbohydrate diet for 3 or 4 days after several days on a normal mixed diet may increase their glycogen stores from the normal 15 grams to around 25 grams per kilogram of muscle. During the period

of the high-carbohydrate diet, no exhausting exercise should be performed.

2. A second procedure for loading the muscle with glycogen combines exercise and diet. In this procedure, the muscles that are to be loaded are first exhausted of their glycogen stores through exercise; the individual then follows a high-carbohydrate diet for a few days. This routine has been shown to double the glycogen stores. An example of this is shown in Figure 19-10. Again, no exhausting exercise should be performed during the time period of the high-carbohydrate diet.

3. A third procedure for glycogen-loading calls for exercise and *two* special diets. Exercise is once again used to induce glycogen depletion. The individual then follows a diet very *low* in carbohydrates but high in fat and protein for 3 days, after which a high-

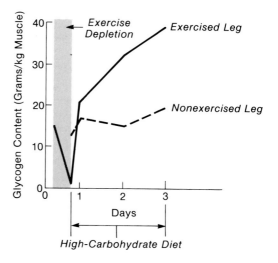

Figure 19-10. The amount of muscle glycogen stored can be increased by first depleting the muscle of its glycogen through exercise, then for 3 days thereafter, consuming a high-carbohydrate diet. (Based on data from Bergström and Hultman.[7])

carbohydrate diet is followed for an additional 3 days. Exhausting exercise may be performed during the period of the diet that is high in fat and protein but not during the high-carbohydrate diet. This procedure has been shown to increase the glycogen stores (in the depleted muscles) to levels approaching 50 g/kg. This conceivably could result in as much as 700 grams of stored glycogen, or 2800 kcal of ready energy. An average amount for all the muscles of the body would be about 400 grams of glycogen (p. 26).

Examples of high- and low-carbohydrate diets, suitable for this procedure and, as needed, for the others, are given in Table 19-6.

A degree of caution should be observed whenever glycogen-loading is attempted. Of the procedures described above, the third is most difficult to follow, particularly on a weekly basis. In addition, this procedure, in which exercise-induced depletion of glycogen is followed by a fat and protein diet, causes a feeling of fatigue. Therefore, for weekly competitions either

TABLE 19-6

Diets for Enhanced Muscle Glycogen Storage*

Days 4-6 Before an Event	Days 1-3 Before an Event
High-Energy, Low-Carbohydrate Diet	Very High-Energy, High-Carbohydrate Diet
Breakfast	
½ grapefruit or ½ c grapefruit juice or berries	1 c orange or pineapple juice
2 eggs	Hot cereal as desired
Generous serving bacon, ham or sausage	Eggs and hot cakes
Butter or margarine as desired	Generous serving bacon, ham or sausage
1 thin slice whole wheat bread	Butter or margarine as desired
1 c whole milk or half and half	2-4 slices whole grain bread
	Chocolate or cocoa as desired
Luncheon and Dinner	
Clear bouillon or ½ c tomato juice	Cream or legume soup or chowder
Large serving fish, poultry, or liver (>6 oz)	Large serving fish, poultry, or liver (>6 oz)
Mixed green (only) salad or 1 c cooked green vegetable	Added beans or fruits
Salad dressing, butter or margarine as desired	Salad dressing, butter or margarine as desired
1 c whole milk or half and half	1 c whole milk, half and half, or milkshake
Artificially sweetened gelatin with whipped cream (no sugar)	2-4 slices whole grain bread or rolls or potato
	Pie, cake, pudding, or ice cream
Snacks	
Cheddar cheese	Fruits, especially dates, raisins, apples, bananas
Nuts	More milk or milkshakes
1 slice whole grain bread	Cookies or candy
Artificially sweetened lemonade	

*From Bogert, Briggs, and Calloway: *Nutrition and Physical Fitness,* 9th ed. Philadelphia, W. B. Saunders, 1973, p. 487.

of the other two procedures is suggested; the more difficult method of glycogen-loading might be reserved for more important competitions such as conference championships.

Another precaution with glycogen-loading that has just recently been pointed out is the possibility of a reduced niacin intake during the carbohydrate-rich diet.[37] Niacin is a vitamin that functions in the body as a coenzyme* for the oxygen system. In this same study,[37] a decreased max $\dot{V}O_2$ (about 8 to 10%) following the carbohydrate-rich diet was also observed. It was concluded that the reduced niacin intake during the glycogen-loading procedure may hamper maximal aerobic power. While this is a possibility, more research is needed for verification.

Whatever the procedure used, glycogen-loading results in an increased muscular storage of water. A feeling of stiffness and heaviness is thus often associated with loading of the muscle. For example, increasing the glycogen stores from 15 g/kg to 40 g/kg in 20 kilograms of muscle would mean an increase in glycogen of 1 pound, and an increase in water of 3 pounds, for a total increase in weight of 4 pounds. For some athletes, this may be enough to create a feeling of heaviness or stiffness that may hinder rather than help performance, as it may cause muscular cramping and premature fatigue. This is one reason why glycogen-loading is not recommended for sprinters and other nonendurance athletes. The other reason, of course, is that the *muscle glycogen stores do not normally limit high-intensity, short-duration activities.*

One aspect of glycogen-loading that all coaches must be especially wary of is the possibility of harmful side effects. There have been some clinical reports of myoglo-

binuria (myoglobin in the urine) in athletes who persistently use glycogen-loading,[3] and chest pain and electrocardiographic changes similar to those observed in patients with heart disease have been described as well.[32] These side effects are potentially very serious (myoglobinuria may lead to acute kidney failure); if encountered, the athlete should seek medical help immediately.

A summary of the glycogen-loading procedures is shown in Figure 19-11. On the balance, the simple procedure of increasing carbohydrate intake for 3 or 4 days prior to endurance competition is preferred and adequate for most sporting events.

Effects of a Fatty Meal on Endurance Performance

One other point concerning endurance exercise and diet needs mentioning. You will recall that fat is an important fuel during the performance of endurance exercise. The effect of diet on the muscular storage and usage of fats during endurance exercise has not been extensively researched. However, a few studies of fat usage in relation to glycogen usage *have* been conducted recently, with interesting results.[18,33] For example, in one study[18] seven men were analyzed during 30 minutes of treadmill exercise to determine the effects of increased availability of blood-borne free fatty acids (FFA) on the utilization of muscle glycogen. The free fatty acids were made available by first having the subjects consume a "fatty" meal 4½ to 5 hours before the exercise was to begin. Then, 30 minutes prior to exercise, heparin, an anticoagulant, was injected into a vein in the forearm to promote the breakdown of the blood triglycerides, thus elevating the free fatty acids. The results are shown in Figure 19-12. As you can see, more fat and less muscle glycogen were used when a fatty

---

*A coenzyme facilitates the action of an enzyme. The niacin-based coenzymes act as hydrogen acceptors for some of the oxidative reactions of the Krebs Cycle.

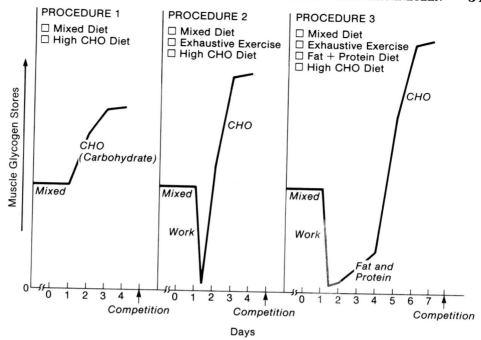

Figure 19-11. Summary of muscle glycogen-loading procedures. (Modified and redrawn from Saltin and Hermansen.[54])

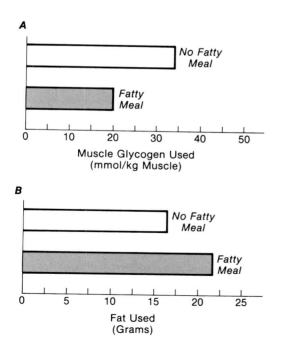

meal preceded the 30-minute exercise period than when no fatty meal was consumed.

The preceding results suggest that since muscle glycogen is spared when free fatty acids are made available, fatigue will be delayed and endurance prolonged. Direct confirmation of this idea has been obtained in studies of rats.[33]

It is extremely important to emphasize that use of the experimental dietary regi-

Figure 19-12. Effects of a fatty meal on fat and muscle glycogen usage. Less muscle glycogen, *A*, and more fat, *B*, were used when a fatty meal preceded the 30 minute exercise period than when no fatty meal was consumed. As a result, muscle glycogen is spared and fatigue is delayed and endurance is prolonged. (Based on data from Costill et al.[18])

men just described is *not* advised, because (1) heparin was involved and, in fact, was injected, and (2) large "fatty" meals prior to competition might cause considerable gastrointestinal discomfort. Dietary manipulations involving large intakes of fat must be proved safe and effective by further research before their general use is allowed.

Summary

Carbohydrates, fats, proteins, vitamins, minerals, and water are essential to the diet. Carbohydrates, fats, and proteins are called the energy nutrients since they are used as food fuels during metabolism.

Carbohydrates are the simple (monosaccharides) and complex (polysaccharides) sugars. They are stored in muscles and liver as glycogen and are found in the blood as blood glucose. Glycogen and blood glucose are the two forms of food fuels.

Fats are found in the body as triglycerides, phospholipids, and cholesterol. Triglycerides are stored in the skeletal muscles and in the fat cells and are made up of glycerol and free fatty acids (FFA). FFA are the food fuel form. When the carbon atoms of FFA are chemically saturated with hydrogen atoms, they are referred to as a saturated fatty acid; when they are not, they are referred to as an unsaturated fatty acid. Consumption of large amounts of saturated fats is discouraged.

Proteins are not normally used as a food fuel. They consist of aggregates of amino acids and are the building blocks of tissue. There are 22 different amino acids in the body, 9 of which are referred to as essential amino acids. Essential amino acids cannot be synthesized by the body; as a result, their only source is through the diet. Contrary to popular belief, the protein requirement during heavy exercise and training is not significantly increased in adults.

Vitamins are essential parts of enzymes or coenzymes that are vital to the metabolism of fats and carbohydrates. However, again contrary to popular belief, vitamin supplementation above the daily minimum requirement does not increase exercise performance.

Mineral deficiencies are uncommon today. The only mineral that may need supplementation during chronic exercise and training is iron in some female athletes.

The biggest difference in food requirements for the athlete versus the nonathlete is the total number of calories consumed; the athlete will need more. Foods should be selected each day from the following food groups: (1) milk, (2) meat, (3) cereals, and (4) vegetables and fruits. Athletes who require a large daily caloric intake may need to eat 5 or 6 meals per day.

Carbohydrates should be the major constituent of the pregame meal and should be consumed no later than 2½ hours before competition. Fruits, cooked vegetables, gelatin desserts, and fish may also be included in the pregame meal. Liquid meals for some athletes are suitable as the pregame meal. Fats and spicy foods should be excluded from the pregame meal.

Large amounts of sugar in liquid and pill form should be avoided 30 to 45 minutes before exercise is to begin. These large amounts actually cause less glucose to be available and cause a more rapid depletion of muscle glycogen stores. Early fatigue is the result.

During prolonged endurance exercise (several hours or more), some liquid glucose should be imbibed. The glucose concentration, however, should not be more than 2.5 grams per 100 ml of liquid since absorption from the stomach is hindered by high concentrations of glucose. Consumption of low concentrations of liquid glucose prevents low blood sugar levels (hypoglycemia), dehydration, and delays fatigue.

Water intake during endurance exercise is encouraged, but should not exceed 800 ml per hour since this is the maximum rate that the stomach can empty during exercise.

Muscle glycogen storage can be greatly increased by several diet and/or exercise procedures. The greatest glycogen stores can be attained first by depleting the muscles of their glycogen through exercise, then consuming a low-carbohydrate meal (i.e., high fat and protein) for several days. This is then followed by consumption of high-carbohydrate meals for an additional 2 or 3 days. However, overloading muscles with glycogen may result in a feeling of heaviness or stiffness in the muscles. Consequently, such a practice is not advisable for sprinters or those athletes participating in events of short duration (30 minutes or less). Other possible side effects include myoglobinuria (myoglobin in the urine), chest pain, and electrocardiographic changes.

Questions

1. Is there a difference between the diet of an athlete and the diet of a nonathlete? Explain.
2. What are the essential dietary nutrients? Describe their chemical structure.
3. What is the difference between saturated and unsaturated fats?
4. Describe the four basic food groups as suggested by the United States Department of Agriculture.
5. Are there special suggestions you could make in recommending a pregame diet?
6. What would you tell an endurance athlete concerning the intake of fluids (including sugar) before and during competition?
7. Following competition, should one's diet be modified? Explain.
8. Explain how diet can affect your performance.
9. Explain how you would increase the muscle glycogen stores of your endurance athletes.
10. What is known concerning a fatty meal and exercise performance?

References

1. Ahlborg, G., and Felig, P.: Influence of glucose ingestion on fuel-hormone response during prolonged exercise. *J Appl Physiol.* 41(5):683–688, 1976.
2. Åstrand, P.-O.: Diet and athletic performance. *Fed Proc.* 26:1772, 1967; *Nutr Today.* 3(2):9, 1968.
3. Bank, W. J.: Myoglobinuria in marathon runners: possible relationships to carbohydrate and lipid metabolism. *Ann NY Acad Sci.* 301:942–948, 1977.
4. Bentivegna, A., Kelley, E. J., and Kalenak, A.: Diet, fitness, and athletic performance. *Physician Sportsmed.* 7(10):99–102, 105, 1979.
5. Bergström, J., Hermansen, L., Hultman, E., and Saltin, B.: Diet, muscle glycogen and physical performance. *Acta Physiol Scand.* 71:140–150, 1967.
6. Bergström, J., and Hultman, E.: Muscle glycogen synthesis after exercise: an enhancing factor localized to the muscle cells in man. *Nature.* 210(5033):309–310, 1966.
7. Bergström, J., and Hultman, E.: Nutrition for maximal sports performance. *JAMA.* 221(9):999–1006, 1972.
8. Bogert, J., Briggs, G., and Calloway, D.: *Nutrition and Physical Fitness,* 9th ed. Philadelphia, W. B. Saunders, 1973.
9. Bortz, W. M., Wroldsen, A., Issekutz, B., and Rodahl, K.: Weight loss and frequency of feeding. *N Engl J Med.* 274:376–379, 1966.
10. Bourne, G. H.: Nutrition and exercise. In Falls, H. B. (ed.): *Exercise Physiology.* New York, Academic Press, 1968, pp. 155–171.
11. Buskirk, E.: Obesity: a brief overview with emphasis on exercise. *Fed Proc.* 33(8):1948–1950, 1974.
12. Buskirk, E. L.: Diet and athletic performance. *Postgrad Med.* 61(1):229–236, 1972.
13. Cathcart, E. P.: The influence of muscle work on protein metabolism. *Physiol Rev.* 5:225–243, 1925.
14. Clark, N.: Increasing dietary iron. *Physician Sportsmed.* 13(1):131–132, 1985.
15. Clement, D. B., and Asmundson, R. C.:

Nutritional intake and hematological parameters in endurance runners. *Physician Sportsmed.* 10(32):37–43, 1982.

16. Consolazio, C. F., Johnson, H. L., Nelson, R. Q., Dramise, J. G., and Skala, J. H.: Protein metabolism of intensive physical training in the young adult. *Am J Clin Nutr.* 28:29–35, 1975.

17. Costill, D. L., Bennett, A., Branam, G., and Eddy, D.: Glucose ingestion at rest and during prolonged exercise. *J Appl Physiol.* 34:764–769, 1973.

18. Costill, D. L., Coyle, E., Dalsky, G., Evans, W., Fink, W., and Hoopes, D.: Effects of elevated plasma FFA and insulin on muscle glycogen usage during exercise. *J Appl Physiol.* 43(4):695–699, 1977.

19. Darling, R. C., Johnson, R. E., Pitts, G. C., Consolazio, R. C., and Robinson, P. F.: Effects of variations in dietary protein on the physical well-being of men doing manual work. *J Nutr.* 28:273–281, 1955.

20. Dohm, G. L.: Protein metabolism in exercise. In Fox, E. L. (ed.): *Nutrition Utilization during Exercise: Ross Symposium.* Columbus, Ohio, Ross Laboratories, 1983, pp. 8–13.

21. Dohm, G. L., Kasperak, G. J., Tapscott, E. B., and Barakat, H. A.: Protein metabolism during endurance exercise. *Fed Proc.* 44(2):348–52, 1985.

22. Durnin, J. V. G. A.: Protein requirements and physical activity. In Parizková, J., and Rogozkin, V. A. (eds.): *Nutrition, Physical Fitness, and Health.* Baltimore, University Press, 1978, pp. 53–60.

23. Elliot, D. L., and Goldberg, L.: Nutrition and exercise. *Med Clin North Am.* 69(1):71–82, 1985.

24. Ehn, L., Carlmark, B., and Hoglund, S.: Iron status in athletes involved in intense physical activity. *Med Sci Sports Exer.* 12(1):61–64, 1984.

25. *Encyclopedia of Sport Sciences and Medicine.* The American College of Sports Medicine, New York, Macmillan, 1971.

26. Fabry, P., Fodar, J., Hejl, Z., Braun, T., and Zvolankova, K.: The frequency of meals: its relation to overweight, hypercholesterolemia, and decreased glucose-tolerance. *Lancet.* Sept. 19, pp. 614–615, 1964.

27. Fabry, P., and Tepperman, J.: Meal frequency—a possible factor in human pathology. *Am J Clin Nutr.* 23:1059–1068, 1970.

28. Felig, P., and Wahren, J.: Interrelationship between amino acid and carbohydrate metabolism during exercise: the glucose-alanine cycle. In Pernow, B., and Saltin, B. (eds.): *Muscle Metabolism during Exercise: Advances in Experimental Medicine and Biology,* Vol. 11. Plenum Press, 1971, pp. 205–214.

29. Finkelstein, B., and Fryer, B. A.: Meal frequency and weight reduction of young women. *Am J Clin Nutr.* 24:465–468, 1971.

30. Foster, C., Costill, D. L., and Fink, W. J.: Effects of pre-exercise feedings on endurance performance. *Med Sci Sports.* 11(1):1–5, 1979.

31. Fox, E. L., Keller, J., Bartels, R., Vivian, V., Chase, J., Delio, D., Burke, E., and Toner, M.: Multiple daily exercise: solid vs. liquid diets. *Med Sci Sports.* 11(1):102, 1979.

3′. Girandola, R. N., Bulbulian, R., Hecker, A., and Wiswell, R.: Effects of liquid and solid meals and time of feeding on $\dot{V}O_2$ max. *Med Sci Sports.* 11(1):101, 1979.

33. Hickson, R. C., Rennie, M. J., Conlee, R. K., Winder, W. W., and Holloszy, J. O.: Effects of increased plasma fatty acids on glycogen utilization and endurance. *J Appl Physiol.* 43:829–833, 1977.

34. Hultman, E.: Studies on muscle metabolism of glycogen and active phosphate in man with special reference to exercise and diet. *Scand J Clin Invest.* 19(Suppl 94):1–63, 1967.

35. Hultman, E., and Bergström, J.: Muscle glycogen synthesis in relation to diet studied in normal subjects. *Acta Med Scand.* 182:109–117, 1967.

36. Ivy, J. L., Costill, D. L., Fink, W. J., and Lower, R. W.: Influence of caffeine and carbohydrate feedings on endurance performance. *Med Sci Sports.* 11(1):6–11, 1979.

37. Jette, M., Pelletier, O., Parker, L., and Thoden, J.: The nutritional and metabolic effects of a carbohydrate-rich diet in a glycogen supercompensation training regimen. *Am J Clin Nutr.* 31(12):2140–2148, 1978.

38. Karlsson, J., and Saltin, B.: Diet, muscle glycogen and endurance performance. *J Appl Physiol.* 31(2):203–206, 1971.

39. Kilbom, A.: Physical training in women. *Scand J Clin Invest.* 28(Suppl 119):1–34, 1971.

40. Lemon, P. W. R., and Nagle, N. J.: Effects of exercise on protein and amino acid metabolism. *Med Sci Sport Exer.* 13(3):141–149, 1981.

41. Macdonald, I., Coles, B. L., Brice, J., and

Jourdan, M. H.: The influence of frequency of sucrose intake on serum lipid, protein and carbohydrate levels. *Br J Nutr.* 24: 413-423, 1970.

42. McGandy, R. B., Barrows, Jr., C. H., Spanias, A., et al.: Nutrient intake and energy expenditures in men of different ages. *J Geront.* 21(4):581-587, 1966.

43. Martin, D. E., Vroon, D. H., May, D. F., and Pilbeam, S. P.: Physiological changes in elite male distance runners training for Olympic competition. *Physician Sportsmed.* 14(1):152-171, 1986.

44. Mirkin, G.: Carbohydrate loading: a dangerous practice. *JAMA.* 223(13):1511-1512, 1973.

45. *Nutrition for the Athlete.* American Association for Health, Physical Education and Recreation, Washington, D.C., 1971.

46. Page, L., and Phippard, E.: *Essentials of an Adequate Diet.* Home Economics Research Report No. 3, Washington, D.C., U.S. Department of Agriculture, Government Printing Office, 1957.

47. Pate, R. R., Maguire, M., and Van Wyk, J.: Dietary iron supplementation in women athletes. *Physician Sportsmed.* 7(9):81-89, 1979.

48. Percy, E. C.: Ergogenic aids in athletics. *Med Sci Sports.* 10(4):298-303, 1978.

49. Pirnay, F., Lacroix, M., Mosora, F., Luyckx, A., and Lefebvre, P.: Glucose oxidation during prolonged exercise evaluated with naturally labeled (^{13}C) glucose. *J Appl Physiol.* 43(2):258-261, 1977.

50. Pitts, G. C., Consolazio, F. C., and Johnson, R. E.: Dietary protein and physical fitness in temperate and hot environments. *Am J Physiol.* 27:497-508, 1944.

51. Plowman, S. A., and McSwegin, P. C.: The effects of iron supplementation in female cross-country runners. *J Sports Med Phys Fit.* 21:407-416, 1981.

52. Rasch, P. J.: Protein and the athlete. *Phys Educ.* 17(4):143-144, 1960.

53. Rasch, P. J., and Pierson, W. R.: Effect of a protein dietary supplement on muscular strength and hypertrophy. *Am J Clin Nutr.* 11:530-532, 1962.

54. Saltin, B., and Hermansen, L.: Glycogen stores and prolonged severe exercise. In Blix, G. (ed.): *Nutrition and Physical Activity.* Uppsala, Sweden, Almqvist and Weksells, 1967.

55. Sharman, I. M., Down, M. G., and Sen, R. N.: The effects of vitamin E on physiological function and athletic performance in adolescent swimmers. *Br J Nutr.* 26:265-276, 1971.

56. Shephard, R. J., Campbell, R., Pimm, P., Stuart, D., and Wright, G.: Do athletes need vitamin E? *Physician Sportsmed.* 2(9):57-60, 1974.

57. Smith, N. J.: *Food for Sport.* Palo Alto, Bull Publishing Co., 1976, pp. 44-48.

58. Smith, E. L.: Bone changes in the exercising older adult. In Smith, E. L., and Serfass, R. C. (eds.): *Exercise and Aging: The Scientific Basis.* Hillsdale, N.J., Enslow Publishers, 1981.

59. Stamler, J., Wentworth, D., and Neaton, J. D.: Is relationship between serum cholesterol and risk of premature death from coronary heart disease continuous or graded? *JAMA.* 256(20):2823-2828, 1986.

60. Swindells, Y. E., Holmes, S. A., and Robinson, M. F.: The metabolic response of young women to changes in the frequency of meals. *Br J Nutr.* 22:667-680, 1968.

61. Wadhwa, P. S., Young, E. A., Schmidt, K., Elson, C. E., and Pringle, D. J.: Metabolic consequences of feeding frequency in man. *Am J Clin Nutr.* 26:823-830, 1973.

62. Wahren, J.: Glucose turnover during exercise in man. *Ann NY Acad Sci.* 301:45-55, 1977.

63. *Water Deprivation and Performance of Athletes.* Food and Nutrition Board, Division of Biological Sciences Assembly of Life Sciences, National Research Council, National Academy of Sciences, May, 1974.

64. Williams, H. H.: *Nutrition for Fitness and Sport.* Dubuque, Iowa, William C. Brown, 1983.

65. Wolf, E. M., Wirth, J. C., and Lohman, T. G.: Nutritional practices of coaches in the Big Ten. *Physician Sportsmed.* 7(2): 113-114, 116-117, 119, 122-124, 1979.

66. Yoshimura, H.: Anemia during physical training. *Nutr Rev.* 28:251, 1970.

67. Young, C. M., Frankel, D. L., Scanlan, S. S., Simko, V., and Lutwak, L.: Frequency of feeding, weight reduction and nutrient utilization. *J Am Diet Assoc.* 59:473-480, 1971.

68. Young, C. M., Hutter, L. F., Scanlan, S. S., Rand, C. E., Lutwak, L., and Simko, V.: Metabolic effects of meal frequency on normal young men. *J Am Diet Assoc.* 61:391-398, 1972.

69. Young, C. M., Scanlon, S. S., Topping, C. M., Simko, V., and Lutwak, L.: Frequency of feeding, weight reduction, and

body composition. *J Am Diet Assoc.* 59: 466–472, 1971.

SELECTED READINGS

Ahlborg, B., Bergström, J., Ekelund, L., and Hultman, E.: Muscle glycogen and muscle electrolytes during prolonged physical exercise. *Acta Physiol Scand.* 70:129–142, 1967.

Bergström, J., and Hultman, E.: A study of the glycogen metabolism during exercise in man. *Scand J Clin Invest.* 19:218–228, 1967.

Bergström, J., and Hultman, E.: Synthesis of muscle glycogen in man after glucose and fructose infusion. *Acta Med Scand.* 182: 93–107, 1967.

Hultman, E.: Muscle glycogen in man determined in needle biopsy specimens. Method and normal values. *Scand J Clin Invest.* 19:209–217, 1967.

Katch, F. I., and McArdle, W. D.: *Nutrition, Weight Control, and Exercise.* Boston, Houghton Mifflin, 1977.

Pařizkova, J., and Rogozkin, V. A. (eds.): *Nutrition, Physical Fitness, and Health.* Baltimore, University Park Press, 1978.

Smith, N. J.: *Food for Sport.* Palo Alto, Bull Publishing Co., 1976.

Strauzenberg, S. E., Schneider, F., Donath, R., Zerbes, H., and Kohler, E.: The problem of dieting in training and athletic performance. *Bibl Nutr Dieta.* 27(27):133–142, 1979.

Williams, M.: *Nutritional Aspects of Human Physical and Athletic Performance.* Springfield, Ill., Charles C. Thomas, 1976.

chapter 20

Exercise, Body Composition, and Weight Control

The major concepts to be learned from this chapter are as follows:

- Body composition is significantly related to physical activity.
- Endomorphy (fat component), mesomorphy (muscle component), and ectomorphy (lean component) describe the somatotype or body build of a person. Each of us has a degree of all three components.
- Athletes and other active people tend to have higher mesomorphic and ectomorphic components and a lower endomorphic component than do nonathletes or sedentary individuals.
- Lack of exercise and excessive caloric intake is the primary cause of obesity in all age groups.
- The degree of obesity is dependent upon the fat content of each fat cell and on the total number of fat cells.
- Total body fat can be estimated by measuring the specific gravity of the body through underwater weighing and by measuring skinfold thicknesses to estimate body density.
- Energy balance means consuming the same amount of energy through food intake as is being expended by activity.
- When more energy is consumed than expended (positive energy balance), body weight is gained. When less energy is consumed than expended (negative energy balance), body weight is lost.
- Making weight in wrestling is a potentially hazardous practice that can be made considerably safer by predicting with anthropometric measures each wrestlers' minimal wrestling weight.

In this chapter there are two major areas of concentration: (1) the relationship of body composition to exercise performance and (2) the principles involved in body weight control. Included in this latter category will be the estimation of minimal wrestling weights for high school and college wrestlers.

Body Composition

Body composition as related to exercise performance is generally assessed by two basic methods: (1) the somatotype and (2) the body fat determination.

The Sheldon Somatotype

Somatotyping deals with the body type or physical classification of the human body. The terms **endomorph, mesomorph,** and **ectomorph** are used to describe a person in terms of his or her somatotype. According to Sheldon, included in these three body components are the following characteristics.[52]

Endomorphy

The first component is *endomorphy* and is characterized by roundness and softness of the body. In layman's terms, endomorphy is the "fatness" component of the body. Anteroposterior diameters as well as lateral diameters tend toward equality in the head, neck, trunk, and limbs. Features of this type are predominance of abdomen over thorax, high square shoulders, and short neck. There is a smoothness of contours throughout, with no muscle relief.

Mesomorphy

The second component is mesomorphy and is characterized by a square body with hard, rugged, and prominent musculation. The bones are large and covered with thick muscle. Legs, trunks, and arms are usually massive in bone and heavily muscled throughout. Outstanding characteristics of this type are forearm thickness and heavy wrist, hand, and fingers. The thorax is large and the waist is relatively slender. Shoulders are broad, the trunk is usually upright, and the trapezius and deltoid muscles are quite massive. The abdominal muscles are prominent and thick. The skin appears coarse and acquires a deep tan readily, retaining it for a long time. Many athletes have a large degree of this component.

Ectomorphy

The third component, ectomorphy, includes, as predominant characteristics, linearity, fragility, and delicacy of body. This is the leanness component. The bones are small and the muscles thin. Shoulder droop is seen consistently in the ectomorph. The limbs are relatively long and the trunk short; however, this does not necessarily mean that the individual is tall. The abdomen and the lumbar curve are flat, while the thoracic curve is relatively sharp and elevated. The shoulders are mostly narrow and lacking in muscle relief. There is no bulging of muscle at any point on the physique. The shoulder girdle lacks muscular support and padding, and the scapulae tend to wing out posteriorly.

Sheldon's choice of the three body types was made because they exhibit the characteristics of the extreme variants found in the population. Once the components were classified, 4000 males were photographed

Figure 20-1. 2-6-2 Somatotype: When you watch a baseball game, with possibly 30 players appearing on the field in the course of the afternoon, you can approximately somatotype most of them merely by playing the averages. Probably two-thirds of the players are 2-6-2's, 2-6-3's, or 4-6-2's. If it were professional football, the same somatotypes would almost surely predominate, but there would be more 7's in mesomorphy, and playing in the lines would be six or eight of the heavier extremes such as 3-7-1, 4-7-1, and even 5-6-1 (a heavyweight wrestler somatotype). (Sheldon,[52] p. 120.)

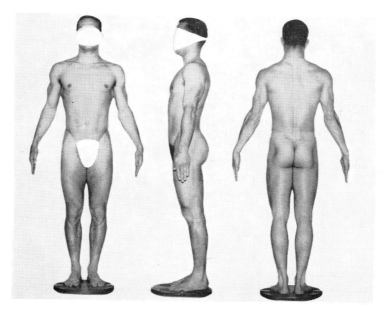

and classified in accordance with the characteristics of the three basic components. On the basis of this analysis, it was determined that the pure type does not exist, but that each person is made up in part of all three components. That is, each one exhibits in his or her body makeup a portion of all three components.

Sheldon's method of somatotyping requires a photograph of the individual in three planes (Fig. 20-1). From these three pictures, a number of measurements are taken and, with the aid of tables developed by Sheldon, the somatotype is determined. Numbers one through seven designate the degree of each of the three components; numeral one represents the least amount of the component, while numeral seven the greatest or maximal amount. Thus a somatotype of 7—1—1 would indicate extreme endomorphy (fatness); 1—7—1 extreme mesomorphy (muscular); and 1—1—7, extreme ectomorphy (thinness).

Heath-Carter Anthropometric Somatotype

Although much of the previous description deals primarily with males, recently Heath and Carter have contributed extensively to the field of somatotyping for both men and women. They suggest that there are essentially three methods of obtaining a somatotype rating: (1) an anthropometric rating without a somatotype photograph; (2) photoscopic or inspectional ratings by experienced somatotypers, when age, height and weight, and a standard somatotype photograph are available; and (3) a combination of these two methods, which is the procedure used by Heath and Carter.[11,12,28,57]

Endomorphic Component of the Heath-Carter Somatotype

To obtain the first component, *endomorphy,* the somatotype rating form shown in Figure 20-2 is used.* First sum the obtained values from the following skinfold measurements: triceps, subscapular, and suprailiac. Procedures for the skinfold measurements are shown in Figure 20-3. The sum in our example equals 43.4 mm. The closest value on the total skinfold scale is circled (43.5). Also, the first component for that column is circled (4½).

Mesomorphic Component of the Heath-Carter Somatotype

The second component, *mesomorphy,* is determined also using Figure 20-2 as follows:

1. Place an arrow above the column containing the subject's height (or closest approximation).* The height in our example is 64.8 inches; therefore, the arrow has been placed between 64.0 and 65.5.
2. For the two bone measurements (humerus and femur breadth), circle the closest figure in the appropriate row. Where a decision must be made to circle either a higher or a lower number, circle the one which is closer to the height column (noted by arrow). For example, 6.05 cm width of the humerus occurs at the mid-point between 5.93 and 6.07; consequently, 6.07 cm, the upper limit, was circled.
3. Subtract the triceps skinfold from the biceps circumference. To do this, first convert the triceps to centimeters by moving the decimal point one place to the left; e.g., 29.8 cm − 2.4 cm (24 mm) = 27.4 cm.

---

*The somatotype rating form may be obtained from Rapid Print, 7609 El Cajon Blvd., La Mesa, California, 92041.

*The height scale is continuous with a distance of 1½ inches between each half column. Place your arrow (if necessary, between columns) to represent as accurately as possible the exact height.

HEATH-CARTER SOMATOTYPE RATING FORM

NAME D. C. AGE 23-6 SEX: M (F) NO: 96

OCCUPATION Phys. Ed. Student ETHNIC GROUP Cauc. DATE May, 1987

PROJECT: A.T.P. MEASURED BY: L.C.

Skinfolds (mm):
Triceps = 24.0
Subcapular = 10.4
Supraliac = 8.9
TOTAL SKINFOLDS = 43.4
Calf = 17.1

TOTAL SKINFOLDS (mm)

Upper Limit	10.9	14.9	18.9	22.9	26.9	31.2	35.8	40.7	46.2	52.2	58.7	65.7	73.2	81.2	89.7	98.9	108.9	119.7	131.2	143.7	157.2	171.9	187.9	204.0
Mid-point	9.0	13.0	17.0	21.0	25.0	29.0	33.5	38.0	43.5	49.0	55.5	62.0	69.5	77.0	85.5	94.0	104.0	114.0	125.5	137.0	150.5	164.0	180.0	196.0
Lower Limit	7.0	11.0	15.0	19.0	23.0	27.0	31.3	35.9	40.8	46.3	52.3	58.8	65.8	73.3	81.3	89.8	99.0	109.0	119.8	131.3	143.8	157.3	172.0	188.0
FIRST COMPONENT	½	1	1½	2	2½	3	3½	4	4½	5	5½	6	6½	7	7½	8	8½	9	9½	10	10½	11	11½	12

Height (in.) = 64.8
Bone: Humerus (cm) = 6.05
Femur = 9.35
Muscle: Biceps (cm) 29.8 − 2.4 = 27.4
- (triceps skinfold)
Calf* = 36.4
- (calf skinfold)
*38.1 − 1.7 =

Height	55.0	56.5	58.0	59.5	61.0	62.5	64.0	65.5	67.0	68.5	70.0	71.5	73.0	74.5	76.0	77.5	79.0	80.5	82.0	83.5	85.0	86.5	88.0	89.5
Humerus	5.19	5.34	5.49	5.64	5.78	5.93	6.07	6.22	6.37	6.51	6.65	6.80	6.95	7.09	7.24	7.38	7.53	7.67	7.82	7.97	8.11	8.25	8.40	8.55
Femur	7.41	7.62	7.83	8.04	8.24	8.45	8.66	8.87	9.08	9.28	9.49	9.70	9.91	10.12	10.33	10.53	10.74	10.95	11.16	11.37	11.58	11.79	12.00	12.21
Biceps	23.7	24.4	25.0	25.7	26.3	27.0	27.7	28.3	29.0	29.7	30.3	31.0	31.6	32.2	33.0	33.6	34.3	35.0	35.6	36.3	37.1	37.8	38.5	39.3
Calf	27.7	28.5	29.3	30.1	30.8	31.6	32.4	33.2	33.9	34.7	35.5	36.3	37.1	37.8	38.6	39.4	40.2	41.0	41.8	42.6	43.4	44.2	45.0	45.8

SECOND COMPONENT ½ 1 1½ 2 2½ 3 3½ 4 4½ 5 5½ 6 6½ 7 7½ 8 8½ 9

Weight (lb.) = 137.0
Ht. / $\sqrt[3]{\text{Wt.}}$ = 12.56

Upper limit	11.99	12.32	12.53	12.74	12.95	13.15	13.36	13.56	13.77	13.98	14.19	14.39	14.59	14.80	15.01	15.22	15.42	15.63
Mid-point	and	12.16	12.43	12.64	12.85	13.05	13.26	13.46	13.67	13.88	14.01	14.29	14.50	14.70	14.91	15.12	15.33	15.53
Lower limit	below	12.00	12.33	12.54	12.75	12.96	13.16	13.37	13.56	13.78	13.99	14.20	14.40	14.60	14.81	15.02	15.23	15.43
THIRD COMPONENT	½	1	1½	2	2½	3	3½	4	4½	5	5½	6	6½	7	7½	8	8½	9

	FIRST COMPONENT	SECOND COMPONENT	THIRD COMPONENT	
Anthropometric Somatotype	4½	5	2	BY: L. C.
Anthropometric plus Photoscopic Somatotype				RATER:

Figure 20-2. Heath-Carter Somatotype Rating Form.

4. Now subtract the calf skinfold from the calf circumference. Again, change the calf skinfold to centimeters by moving the decimal point one place to the left; e.g., 38.1 cm − 1.7 cm (17 mm) = 36.4 cm.
5. Circle these two corrected measurements (27.4 and 36.4) in their proper rows; e.g., 27.7 and 36.3 are circled.
6. Using the arrow marked in the height row as the starting column (in our example, both 6.07 and 27.7 appear in the most extreme left column), count the number of columns each other circled or value deviates from this starting point (each column equals one-half unit). In our example, both the humerus and the biceps measurements deviate zero units (since they are immediately next to the arrow column), while the femur measurement deviates +1.5 units and the calf measurement deviates + 2.5 units. The average deviation of these measurements equals the total divided by four:

$$\frac{0 + 0 + 1.5 + 2.5}{4} = 1.0$$

This represents the average deviation from the height column.

7. Take the average deviation from the height column (+1.0 in our example) and add 4. This value gives the ob-

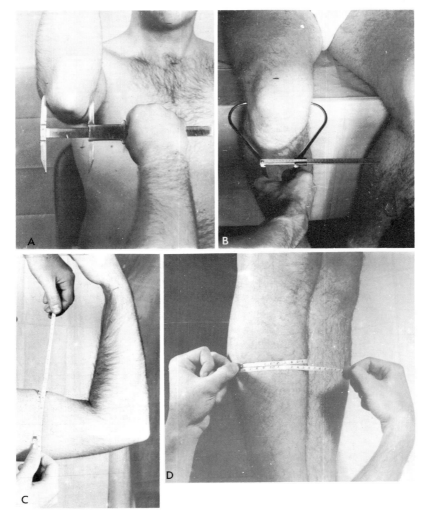

Figure 20-3. Measurements necessary for Heath-Carter somatotype. *A,* humerus breadth; *B,* femur breadth; *C,* biceps circumference; *D,* calf circumference.

Illustration continued on the following page

tained final value of 5.0 for the second component. Next, circle 5.0 in the second component row of Figure 20-2.

Ectomorphic Component of the Heath-Carter Somatotype

The third component, ectomorphy, is obtained by computing the ponderal index, i.e., the height divided by the cube root of the weight (Fig. 20-4), and recording this value. Circle the closest value and note the somatotype in the third component row under the column (Fig. 20-2). In our example, the component 2 appears directly below the 12.54. The complete somatotype equals 4.5—5.0—2. This person is classified as an endo-mesomorph.

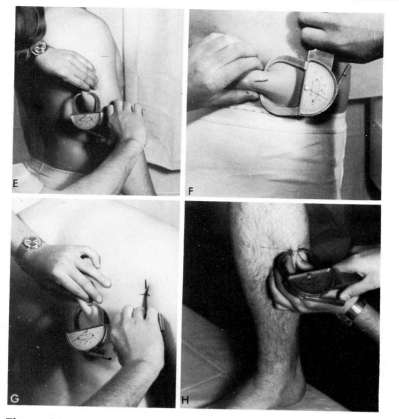

Figure 20-3. *Continued. E,* Skinfold: triceps; *F,* skinfold: suprailiac; *G,* skinfold: subscapular; *H,* skinfold: calf. (Courtesy, E. Churchill et al.[13])

Somatotype and Physical Activity

Somatotyping has been used to describe the type of physique that is most susceptible to various diseases. For example, a number of studies indicate heavily muscular men (mesomorphs) and endo-mesomorphs have a greater predisposition toward coronary artery disease than do ectomorphic types.[44,58]

Physical educators manifest an interest in somatotyping as a means of relating body type to success in various sports.[57,62] Figures 20-5 and 20-6 depict the somatotypes of men and women athletes and the various sports in which they excel. In relation to nonathletes (reference population), most athletes, males and females alike, are more muscular, i.e., have a larger mesomorphic component and are leaner, i.e., have a greater ectomorphic component. For example, Carter, in reporting on male Olympic athletes, describes the mean somatotype for marathon runners as 1.4—4.3—3.5; pole vaulters, 1½—4.8—3.2; and swimmers 2—5—3. These somatotypes would be noted collectively as meso-ectomorphs because of the higher mesomorph and ectomorph ratings.[15] The mean somatotype of a varsity football team was found to be 4.2—6.3—1.4, which is endo-mesomorphic.[12]

Height
(in.)

Weight
(lb)

$Ht/\sqrt[3]{W}$

Figure 20-4. Ponderal index $\dfrac{Ht.}{\sqrt[3]{W}}$.

Female swimmers and hockey and softball players are usually endo-mesomorphs. Female gymnasts and skiers are ecto-mesomorphic, while basketball players appear to be endo-mesomorphs. Like the males, female physiques in track and field vary in accordance with the event. Sprinters contain more massive musculature along with those participating in throwing events, while the lithe (limber) body prevails in the distance and jumping events.

Body Fat

Differences in performance between the men and women can be partially explained by the greater percentage of fat contained in the female body (p. 380). Body fat of the adult male averages 15 to 17% of the body weight, while the average female body contains about 25% fat. Fat cells do not manufacture ATP for use by the muscles; their primary purpose is to store lipids. Consequently, the greater percentage of fat is detrimental (performancewise) in two ways: (1) the cells do not contribute toward energy production, and (2) it costs energy to move the fat. For example, an average female weighing 60 kilograms (132 lbs) would possess 15 kilograms (33 lbs) of fat, while the male of the same weight would possess 9 to 10 kilograms (20 to 22 lbs) of fat. During performance, the female would be carrying 5–6 kilograms (11–13 lbs) more of non-energy-producing tissue than her male contemporary.

Physically active people possess considerably less total body fat than their inactive contemporaries. Table 20-1 contains the results of a number of studies reporting the percentage of fat among male and female athletes.

Buskirk[9] has suggested the following skinfold measurements for classifying male athletes in terms of body fat (see Fig. 20-7 for how to make the skinfold measurements):

1. *Subscapula.* Below tip of right scapula; skinfold lifted along long axis of body.
2. *Abdomen.* Five cm lateral from umbilicus avoiding abdominal crease; skinfold lifted on axis with umbilicus.
3. *Triceps.* Back of upper arm over triceps, midway on upper arm; skinfold lifted parallel with the long axis of arm with arm pendant.

According to Buskirk, the subscapular skinfold is the single best fold to measure.

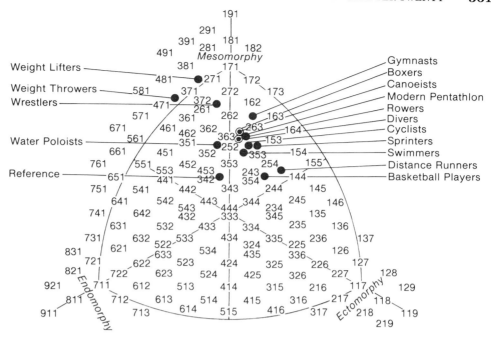

Figure 20-5. Somatotype distribution of mean somatotypes for various male sports groups and nonathletes (reference group). (From deGaray et al.[15])

Figure 20-6. Somatotype distribution of mean somatotypes for various female sports groups and nonathletes (reference group). (From deGaray et al.[15])

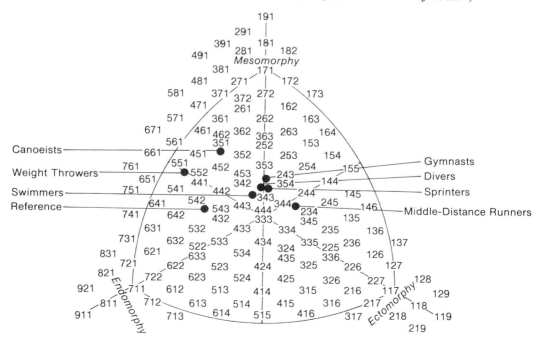

TABLE 20-1

Per Cent Body Fat Among Athletes*

Sport	Male	Female
Track and field		
Runners	6.3–7.5	15.2–19.2
Discus and javelin	16.3	25.0
Shotput	16.5–19.6	28.0
Sprinters	—	19.3
Weight lifting	9.8	—
Power	15.6	—
Olympic	12.2	—
Body building	8.4	—
Wrestlers	5.0–10.7	—
Swimmers	5.0–8.5	26.3
Skiers	7.4	—
Baseball	11.8–14.2	—
Football	13.9	—
Defensive backs	9.6–11.5	—
Offensive backs	9.4–12.4	—
Linebackers	13.4–14.0	—
Quarterbacks and kickers	14.4	—
Offensive linemen	15.6–19.1	—
Defensive linemen	18.2–18.5	—
Gymnasts	4.6	9.6–23.8
Jockeys	14.1	—
Ice hockey	15.1	—
Basketball	9.7	20.8–26.9
Volleyball	—	25.3
Tennis	15.2	—
Nonathletes	16.8	25.5

*Compiled from various sources by Wilmore et al.[74]

Classification values can be adjusted in accordance with coaches' and physicians' judgments. Table 20-2 contains standards for such skinfold measurements that may be applied to male athletes.

Skinfold measurements at the same sites may also be used for classifying female athletes. Some standards are shown in Table 20-3.

Several methods have been employed to estimate the body's fat content. Measuring the specific gravity is perhaps one of the more valid, but difficult, methods; estimating fat content from a number of anthropometric measures is an easier, though less valid, method. A more recent method called electrical impedance has been marketed during the past few years but the validity of this approach remains to be proven. Early reports are that the reliability and objectivity of the instruments are quite good and the simplicity of the procedures speak in their favor. The method involves the application of surface elec-

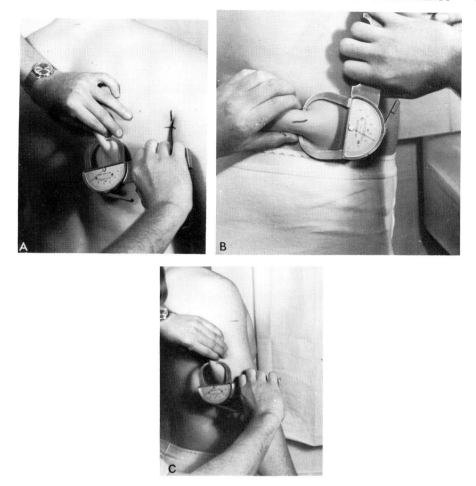

Figure 20-7. Skinfold measurements for predicting minimal athletic weight values. *A,* Skinfold: subscapular; *B,* skinfold: 5 cm lateral from umbilicus; *C,* skinfold: triceps. (Courtesy, E. Churchill et al.[13])

TABLE 20-2

Classification of Skinfold Measurements for Male Athletes*

Classification		Triceps (mm)	Subscapular (mm)	Abdomen (mm)	Sum (mm)
Lean	<7% fat	<7	<8	<10	<25
Acceptable	7–15% fat	7–13	8–15	10–20	25–48
Overfat	>15%	>13	>15	>20	>48

*From Buskirk.[9]

TABLE 20-3

Classification of Body Fat From Skinfold Thicknesses for Female Athletes*

Classification	Body Fat	Skinfold Thickness (mm)			
		Triceps	Subscapular	Abdomen	Sum
Lean	<12%	<9	<7	<7	<23
Acceptable	12–25%	9–17	7–14	7–15	23–46
Overfat	>25%	>17	>14	>15	>46

*Based on data from Hall.[27]

trodes on the body, the input of subject data such as gender, age, height, and weight into a computer, and the measurement of electrical impedance between the electrodes. Standard equations are preprogrammed into the software so that an estimation of the subject's percentage of body fat and related variables are printed out. There is an ongoing effort to refine this method and to improve on its validity index.

Measurement of Body Fat: Specific Gravity

Specific gravity (SG) of a body may be defined as the ratio of its **density (D)** to the density of water. Density of a body is spoken of in terms of **mass (M)** per unit **volume (V).**

$$D = \frac{M}{V}$$

For example, the density of water is equal to 1 gram per cubic centimeter (1 gm/cc) because one cubic centimeter (cc) weighs 1 gram; the density of gold is 19.3 gm/cc. The specific gravity of gold is 19.3. Note that the numbers representing specific gravity are called pure numbers. They have no units, but merely represent the ratio of the density of a substance to that of water.

Archimedes' Principle

One may determine the density of an object by using Archimedes' principle, which states that an object immersed in a fluid loses an amount of weight equivalent to the weight of the fluid that is displaced.

$$D = \frac{\text{weight of object in air}}{\text{weight of water displaced}}$$

Thus, by weighing an object in air, then immersing the object in water and measuring the weight of the water displaced, the density of that object could be determined. Note also that the density could be determined indirectly, (i.e., without collecting and weighing displaced water) by measuring the change in weight when the object is fully immersed.

$$D = \frac{\text{weight of object in air}}{\text{weight of} \atop \text{object in air} - \text{weight of} \atop \text{object in water}}$$

As a simple illustration, what would be the density of an object weighing 200 gm in air and 120 gm in water?

$$D = \frac{200 \text{ gm}}{200 \text{ gm} - 120 \text{ gm}} = 2.5$$

The density of the object is two and one-half times greater than the density of water; consequently, it would sink. Incidentally, since the density of water is one, what is the specific gravity of this object? 2.5 is the correct answer since specific gravity = D/D = 2.5/1.0 = 2.5.

The volume would be equal to 80 cc since the weight of the water displaced equals 80 gm (1 cc of water weighs 1 gm).

Specific Gravity of the Human Body

Figure 20-8 illustrates a human body volumeter for measuring the body's density.

One could measure either the weight of the water displaced by the body or the weight of the body when completely submerged. Fewer technical difficulties are encountered using body weight totally submerged; however, the lungs must be as nearly deflated as possible (maximal expiration) during the underwater weighing, with correction made for the residual volume. The air remaining in the lungs following a maximal expiration (the residual volume) may be estimated for males by multiplying the vital capacity (BTPS) by the constant 0.24 and for females, by the constant 0.28.[70] These values will approximate 1300 ml for males and 1000 ml for females. Although these approximations can be made, a more precise estimation of true body density is

Figure 20-8. Human body volumeter for measuring body density. One could measure either weight of the water displaced by the body or the weight of the body when completely submerged. (Photos by Tom Malloy, Courtesy, Department of Photography, The Ohio State University.)

possible when residual volume is measured directly.

Once the body weight in air, the weight while totally submerged, and the residual volume are determined, body density (gm/cc) may be computed by the following formula:[8]

$$D_b = \frac{W_a}{K - (RV + 100)}$$

where

D_b = body density (gm/cc)
W_a = weight in air in grams
K = weight in air minus weight in water divided by the density of water at the weighing temperature
RV = residual volume in cc
100 = estimate of G.I. gas in cc

The amount of fat may be computed by either of the following formulae:

Brozek[8] formula
$$\text{per cent fat} = \left(\frac{4.570}{D_b} - 4.142\right) \times 100$$

Siri[71] formula
$$\text{per cent fat} = \left(\frac{4.95}{D_b} - 4.50\right) \times 100$$

The following data illustrate calculation of body density and percentage of fat (note data are converted to grams [gm] and cubic centimeters [cc]).

1. *Brozek Formula—Male:*
Ht.—72.1 inches = 183.13 centimeters
= 18.31 decimeters
Weight in air = 200 lb = 90.91 kg
= 90,910 gm
Weight in water = 4.78 lb = 2.17 kg
= 2,170 gm
Density of water at 32° C = .9951 gm/cc

Vital capacity (BTPS) = 6000 cc
Residual volume = 0.24 × vital capacity
= 0.24 × 6000 cc = 1440 cc
R.V. + G.I. gas = 1440cc + 100cc
= 1540cc

$$K = \frac{90,910 - 2,170}{.9951} = \frac{88,740}{.9951} = \mathbf{89,176.97}$$

$$D_b = \frac{90,910}{89,176.97 - (1440 + 100)} = \frac{90,910}{87,636.97}$$

$$= \mathbf{1.0373 \ gm/cc}$$

The amount of fat (%) may be computed as follows:

$$\text{per cent fat} = \left(\frac{4.570}{1.0372} - 4.142\right) \times 100$$
$$= (4.405 - 4.142) \times 100$$
$$= 0.263 \times 100 = \mathbf{26.3\%}$$

2. *Siri Formula:*
Using the same preceding information, the per cent body fat using the Siri formula would be:

$$\text{per cent fat} = \left(\frac{4.95}{1.0362} - 4.50\right) \times 100$$
$$= (4.772 - 4.500) \times 100$$
$$= .272 \times 100 = \mathbf{27.2\%}$$

As can be seen, the difference in the estimation of body fat between the two formulae is relatively small.

Measurement of Body Fat:
Skinfold Measurements

Sloan and Weir, using measurements from two skinfold thicknesses, derived formulas for predicting body density in young men

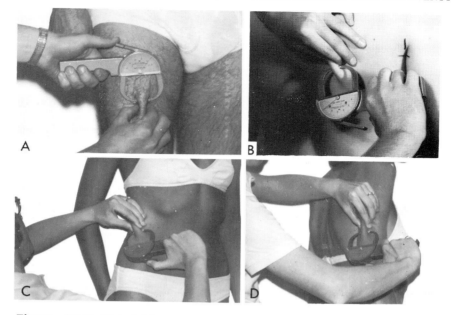

Figure 20-9. Skinfold measurements required for use with the Sloan-Weir nomogram. *A,* Skinfold: thigh (men); *B,* skinfold: subscapular (men); *C,* skinfold: suprailiac (women); *D,* skinfold: triceps (women).

18 to 26 years and women 17 to 25 years of age.[55] In young men, the best predictions were found to come from a vertical skinfold in the anterior midline of the thigh, halfway between the inguinal ligament and the top of the patella, and the subscapular skinfold running downward and laterally in the natural fold of the skin from the inferior angle of the scapula. In young women, the best predictions were found to come from a vertical skinfold over the iliac crest in the midaxillary line and from a vertical skinfold on the back of the arm halfway between the acromion and olecranon processes measured with the elbow extended. These measurements are shown in Figure 20-9.

By using the formula developed by Brozek et al.,[8] Sloan and Weir could relate total body fat to body density and thus predict body fat from these two skinfold measurements. The formulas and example of the computations appear in Table 20-4,

while Figure 20-10 contains the nomograms.

Specificity of Skinfold Measurements and Body Density Estimates

It needs to be emphasized that predictions of body density from equations derived from skinfold and other anthropometric measurements are specific to the population from which the equations were originally derived.[27,33,54,73] This means that accurate predictions of body density for men or women differing in age and fitness level cannot be made from one set of equations, such as those presented by Sloan and Weir (Table 20-4). These latter equations were derived from random samples taken from average, college-age male and female populations. Therefore, they may be used most accurately for persons fitting this classification only. For athletes or those with a better-than-average fitness level or of dif-

TABLE 20–4

Sloan-Weir Formulas for Predicting Body Density and Total Body Fat*

	Female	Male
Height	174 cm	178 cm
Weight	59 kg	75.9 kg
Thigh skinfold	—	18 mm
Subscapular skinfold	—	8.5 mm
Suprailiac skinfold	19 mm	—
Triceps skinfold	15 mm	—
Actual density (measured by underwater weighing)	1.0524 gm/ml	1.0678 gm/ml
Predicted density	1.0478 gm/ml	1.0693 gm/ml
Fat	21.9%	13.2%

Men: $1.1043 - (0.00133 \times \text{thigh skinfold}) - (0.00131 \times \text{subscapular skinfold})$
   $= 1.1043 - .0349 = 1.0692$ gm/ml (with standard error of estimate = 0.0069 gm/ml)
Women: $1.0764 - (0.00081 \times \text{suprailiac skinfold}) - (0.00088 \times \text{triceps skinfold})$
   $= 1.0764 - .0286 = 1.0478$ gm/ml (with standard error of estimate = 0.00822 gm/ml)

Fat Percentage = $4.570/\text{Body density} - 4.142 \times 100$.

*Data by Sloan and Weir[55] and recalculated by L. Laubach, University of Dayton, Dayton, Ohio.

Figure 20-10. Sloan-Weir nomograms (left=men, right=women) for prediction of body density and total body fat from two skinfold measurements; see text and Fig. 20-9 for details. (From Sloan and Weir.[55])

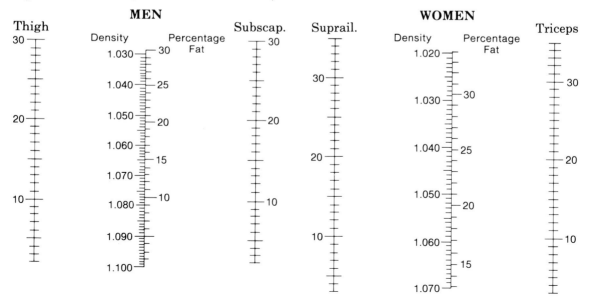

ferent age groups, the equations will not accurately predict the body density and thus the percentage of body fat.

Equations for predicting body composition of nonathletic males and females of different age groups are given in Table 20-5. For those equations that predict body density, the percentage of body fat can be estimated by using either the Brozek or Siri formula. For those equations predicting lean weight (i.e., total body weight minus fat weight), the percentage of body fat can be determined by subtracting the lean weight from the total body weight, then dividing by the total body weight and, finally, multiplying by 100. In other words:

$$\text{per cent fat} = \frac{\text{total body weight} - \text{lean weight}}{\text{total body weight}} \times 100$$

Equations for predicting body density of college-age female athletes engaged in specific sports are presented in Table 20-6. Note that the equations are all different in that they are based on different skinfolds and/or anthropometric measures. This very nicely points out the specificity of this type of estimation.

Body Weight Control

In discussing body weight control, we will start with a few words about obesity, then present guidelines for losing fat weight and gaining lean or fat-free weight, and then finish with the problem of making weight in wrestling.

Obesity

An unvarnished tale states, "most people become obese because of *physical inactivity*."[40] Such is true for teenagers as well as adults. A study in California revealed 14% of high school seniors (boys and girls) were obese. The need for physical education in

---

TABLE 20-5

Equations Based on Sex and Age for Determining Body Composition*

Age (Yr)	Equation	Reference
Females		
9–12	Density = 1.079 − (0.043 × log of scapula skinfold†)	Parízková[43]
13–16	Density = 1.102 − (0.058 × log of scapula skinfold†)	Parízková[43]
17–35	Lean weight (kg) = 8.63 + [0.68 × weight (kg)] − [0.16 × scapula skinfold] − [0.10 × triceps skinfold] − [0.05 × thigh skinfold]	Wilmore and Behnke[73]
Males		
9–12	Density = 1.094 − (0.054 × log of scapula skinfold†)	Parízková[43]
13–16	Density = 1.131 − (0.083 × log of triceps skinfold†)	Parízková[43]
17–35	Lean weight (kg) = 10.26 + [0.793 × weight (kg)] − [0.368 × abdominal skinfold]	Wilmore and Behnke[72]
36–67	Lean weight (kg) = 6.14 + [0.84 × weight (kg)] − [0.63 × midaxillary skinfold]	Lewis et al.[37]

*Modified from Wilmore.[71]

†Take the log of the skinfold from a table of logarithms and multiply it by the designated constant.

TABLE 20-6

Estimation of Body Density in Female Athletes From Anthropometric Measurements*

Sport	Equation†
Field Hockey	Density = 0.98876 − (0.00382 × triceps skinfold) − (0.00495 × calf girth) + (0.03636 × bihumeral diameter) + (0.00896 × bifemoral diameter)
Competitive Swimming	Density = 1.40716 − (0.00339 × hip girth) + (0.03318 × bitalar diameter) + (0.00170 × thigh girth) + (0.03557 × bihumeral diameter) − (0.00200 × height) − (0.01046 × bi-iliac diameter) + (0.00116 × subscapular skinfold) − (0.00091 × bust girth)
Synchronized Swimming	Density = 1.19144 − (0.00269 × calf skinfold) − (0.00028 × height) + (0.00162 × suprailiac skinfold) − (0.00321 × thigh girth) + (0.00043 × bust girth) + (0.00217 × calf girth) − (0.00031 × weight)
Volleyball	Density = 1.01010 + (0.01103 × flexed biceps girth) − (0.00177 × hip girth) − (0.00145 × triceps skinfold) + (0.00141 × subscapular skinfold) − (0.02248 × bistyloid diameter)
Gymnastics‡	Density = 1.02462 + (0.002024 × neck circumference) − (0.001435 × suprailiac skinfold) − (0.001039 × abdominal skinfold)

*Based on data from Hall.[27]

†Units for body density are gm/cc; skinfold thicknesses, mm; girth and height, cm; and weight, kg.

‡Based on data from Sinning.[54]

elementary, junior, and senior high schools can be substantiated on this verity alone.

Obesity is related to a number of diseases including diabetes, coronary heart disease, psychological disturbances, kidney disease, hypertension, stroke, liver ailments, and mechanical difficulties (particularly, back and foot problems). As a consequence, life expectancy is significantly reduced among the obese population. Excessive obesity may result in as high as 100% increase in mortality over that which might be expected!

What is Obesity?

Authorities generally concur that the normal body weight between the ages of 25 and 30 years should not be exceeded throughout life. Table 20-7 contains suggested weights based upon a sample of college men and women. A weight in excess

TABLE 20-7

Suggested Weights for Heights of College Men and Women*

Height (In.)†	Median Weight (Lbs)†			
	Men		Women	
	Normal	Obese	Normal	Obese
60			109 ± 9	>136
62			115 ± 9	>144
64	133 ± 11	>166	122 ± 10	>152
66	142 ± 11	>177	129 ± 10	>161
68	151 ± 14	>189	136 ± 10	>170
70	159 ± 14	>199	144 ± 11	>180
72	167 ± 15	>209	152 ± 12	>190
74	175 ± 15	>219		
76	182 ± 16	>228		

*From Bogert, J., et al.[6] p. 512.

†Measurements—nude.

±refers to weight range between 25th and 75th percentile of each height category. For example, 50% of the women sampled at 60 inches weighed between 100 and 118 lbs.

of 15% of that regarded as normal would be considered tending toward obesity, whereas 25% above normal is grossly obese.

Buskirk,[10] in addressing the question, "Who is fat?" claims that obesity is difficult to define in quantitative terms. Obesity refers to the above-average amount of fat contained in the body, this in turn being dependent upon lipid content of each fat cell and on the total number of fat cells. Methods for estimating fat content of the body were just discussed.

Adipocytes (fat cells) probably increase in number up to early adolescence. Lack of exercise and overeating may stimulate their formation. Obesity, then, is a combination of the number of adipocytes and their lipid content.[63] Obese people have a larger number of fat cells that contain a greater volume of lipids than their lean contemporaries (Fig. 20-11). As a consequence, physical educators should seriously consider that:

1. Prevention of obesity results in greater success than treatment. This is particularly true during preadolescence. Evidence suggests that overeating

Figure 20-11. Obese people have a larger number of fat cells (right), which contain a greater volume of lipids (left), than their lean contemporaries. (Based on data from Hirsch and Knittle.[29])

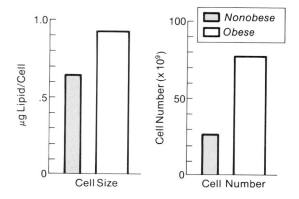

during this period may cause adipocyte hyperplasia (an increase in the number of fat cells), thus planting the garden in which obesity may grow and bloom.

2. Exercise keeps total body fat content low and may reduce the rate at which adipose cells accumulate.

3. If a given food intake does not allow weight reduction, then physical activity must be increased for a negative energy balance to occur.

4. Activities must be selected requiring considerable energy expenditure but at the same time within the physical and skill capabilities of the individual.

5. Living habits are developed early, and so the sooner control programs are initiated, the better.

Energy Balance and Weight Control

The quantity of food required by an individual above that which is necessary for body maintenance and growth depends upon the amount of physical activity that he or she experiences. Just as an automobile traveling 60 miles each day requires more gasoline than one traveling 30 miles per day, a person walking 20 miles a day requires more food than a person walking 2 miles each day. For body weight to remain constant, food intake must equal energy needs. If, in fact, too much food is consumed, we will gain weight or be in what is referred to as a **positive energy balance.** On the other hand, if our energy needs exceed that produced by the food we eat, a **negative energy balance** occurs. In this case, the body consumes its own fat, and then protein, with a concomitant loss in body weight.

Table 20-8 contains a number of sports

TABLE 20-8

Median Energy Consumption and Corresponding Daily Food Requirements (in Kilocalories)*

Selected Disciplines 1	Expenditure of Energy/kg of Body Weight/ Day (kcal) 2	Average Body Weight (kg) 3	Normative Daily Net Needs Based on Computed Energy Requirements (Column 2 × Column 3) (kcal) 4	Nutritional, Physiological, Optimal Daily Gross Requirements, With 10% Added for Consumption (kcal) 5
Group A				
Cross-country skiing	82.14	67.5	5,550	6,105†
Crew racing	69.21	80.0	5,550	6,105
Canoe racing	72.72	75.0	5,450	5,995
Swimming	69.87	76.0	5,300	5,830†
Bicycle racing	80.39	68.0	5,450	5,995
Marathon racing	79.07	68.0	5,400	5,940
Average values (men)			5,450	5,995†

Rounded-off norm: 6,000 kcal

Also belonging to sports of group A are skiing (Norwegian combination); middle-distance racing; walking; ice racing; modern pentathlon; equine sports; and touring (Alpine climbing).

TABLE 20–8

Median Energy Consumption and Corresponding Daily Food Requirements (in Kilocalories)* (*Continued*)

Selected Disciplines 1	Expenditure of Energy/kg of Body Weight/ Day (kcal) 2	Average Body Weight (kg) 3	Normative Daily Net Needs Based on Computed Energy Requirements (Column 2 × Column 3) (kcal) 4	Nutritional, Physiological, Optimal Daily Gross Require- ments, With 10% Added for Consumption (kcal) 5
Group B				
Soccer	72.28	74.0	5,350	5,885
Handball	68.06	75.0	5,100	5,610
Basketball	67.93	75.0	5,100	5,610
Field hockey	69.18	75.0	5,200	5,720
Ice hockey	71.87	68.0	4,900	5,390
Average values (men)			5,130	5,643

Rounded-off norm: 5,600 kcal

Also belonging to group B are rugby; water polo; volleyball; tennis; polo; and bicycle polo.

Group C				
Canoe slalom	67.16	68.0	4,550	5,005
Shooting	62.71	72.5	4,550	5,005
Table tennis	59.96	74.0	4,450	4,895
Bowling	62.69	75.0	4,700	5,170
Sailing	63.77	74.0	4,700	5,170
Average values (men)			4,590	5,049

Rounded-off norm: 5,000 kcal

Also belonging to group C are circuit cycle racing (1,000–4,000 meters); fencing; ice sailing; and gliding.

Group D				
Sprinting	61.77	69.0	4,250	4,675
Running: short to middle distances	65.62	65.0	4,250	4,675
Pole vault	57.83	73.0	4,200	4,620
Diving	69.24	61.0	4,200	4,620
Boxing (middle and welter weight: to 63.5 kg)	67.25	63.0	4,250	4,675
Average values (men)			4,230	4,653

Rounded-off norm: 4,600 kcal

Also belonging to group D are hurdle races; broad- and high jump; hop-skip-and-jump; ballet; swimming; figure skating; figure roller skating; skiing; ski jump; bob sled; and tobogganing.

TABLE 20-8

Median Energy Consumption and Corresponding Daily Food Requirements (in Kilocalories)* *(Continued)*

Selected Disciplines 1	Expenditure of Energy/kg of Body Weight/ Day (kcal) 2	Average Body Weight (kg) 3	Normative Daily Net Needs Based on Computed Energy Requirements (Column 2 × Column 3) (kcal) 4	Nutritional, Physiological, Optimal Daily Gross Requirements, With 10% Added for Consumption (kcal) 5
Group E				
Group I				
Judo (light-weight)	79.92	62.5	4,550	5,005
Weight lifting (light-weight)	69.15	67.5	4,650	5,115
Javelin	56.95	76.0	4,350	4,785
Gymnastics with apparatus	67.14	65.0	4,350	4,785
Steeplechase	63.96	68.0	4,350	4,785
Ski: Alpine competition	71.29	67.5	4,800	5,280
Average values (men)			4,508	4,959
Rounded-off norm: 5,000 kcal				
Group II				
Hammerthrow	62.46	102.0	6,350	6,985
Shot put and discus	62.47	102.0	6,350	6,985
Rounded-off norm: 7,000 kcal				

Also belonging to group E are wrestling; automobile rallies; motor racing; gymnastics; acrobatics; parachute jumping; equine sports shows; decathlon; and bicycle gymnastics.

*From *Encyclopedia of Sport Sciences and Medicine,*[2] pp. 1128–1129.

†Deviations of a few per cent from the median values are, in the field of biology, to be taken as basically insignificant.

with their respective energy requirements in kcal* per day. Table 20-9 contains a few sports and exercises in terms of total kcal expended per minute. Of what value is this information to us? By knowing the energy

*To convert from kcal to liters of oxygen consumed, divide kcal by 5.

cost of the activity, we can more judiciously plan our diets to maintain proper energy balance and thus body weight control.

For example, a man weighing 68 kilograms and participating in bicycle racing would expend 5450 kcal (plus 10% utilized in digestion) or 5995 kcal per day (Table 20-8). A person playing golf uses 5 kcal per

TABLE 20-9

Approximate Energy Cost of Various Exercises and Sports

Sport or Exercise	Total Calories Expended Per Minute of Activity
Climbing	10.7–13.2
Cycling 5.5 mph	4.5
9.4 mph	7.0
13.1 mph	11.1
Dancing	3.3–7.7
Football	8.9
Golf	5.0
Gymnastics	
Balancing	2.5
Abdominal exercises	3.0
Trunk bending	3.5
Arms swinging, hopping	6.5
Rowing 51 str/min	4.1
87 str/min	7.0
97 str/min	11.2
Running	
Short-distance	13.3–16.6
Cross-country	10.6
Tennis	7.1
Skating (fast)	11.5
Skiing, moderate speed	10.8–15.9
Uphill, maximum speed	18.6
Squash	10.2
Swimming	
Breaststroke	11.0
Backstroke	11.5
Crawl (55 yd/min)	14.0
Wrestling	14.2

*From *Nutrition for the Athlete*,[42] p. 26.

minute (Table 20-9). If that person were to play for three hours, he or she would have expended 900 kcal of energy (5 kcal per min times 180 min).

These data are approximations and depend upon a number of factors, including the physical condition of the person, his or her degree of skill, and the degree of effort employed. For example, (Table 20-9), 7.1 kcal per minute are expended for playing tennis. A novice might spend considerable time walking after balls, while the expert engages in vigorous rallies. The same would be true for golf. Terrain, skill, and body weight are also important considerations related to the energy cost of the activity. Usually, it costs you more in the rough than on the fairway—in more ways than one!

Negative Energy Balance and Weight Loss

The average daily caloric requirement for young adult nonathletic males is about 3000 kcal, and that for young adult nonathletic females is about 2000 kcal. If the daily caloric expenditure through physical activity for the male were also 3000 kcal, then his body weight would remain constant. However, if he were to climb for an hour each day without changing his caloric intake, he would be expending between 642 and 792 kcal more than he takes in; his body weight would decrease. The magnitude of the decrease may be calculated in terms of how long it would take one pound of pure fat, which contains about 3500 kcal, to be lost. In this case, it would take 4½ to 5½ days for the pound of fat to be lost (3500/642 = 5½ and 3500/792 = 4½).

For highly active male and female athletes, the daily caloric requirements might be as high as 5000 to 6000 kcal and 3500 to 4500 kcal, respectively. Although these might appear to be excessively high, remember that athletes' daily energy expenditures are also high (e.g., running a 26.2 mile marathon requires about 2500 to 2800 kcal).

Positive Energy Balance and Weight Gain

If our average man from the preceding example were consuming 3500 kcal and expending only 3000 kcal, then he would be in positive energy balance as previously mentioned and would gain body weight. The question to answer is whether he would gain fat weight or fat-free weight. If he were not engaged in an exercise program, the weight gain would be mainly in the form of stored fat.[21] In this case, it would require an excess caloric intake of 3500 kcal to gain one pound of fat. With a +500 kcal balance per day, this would take 7 days.

On the other hand, if an exercise program is undertaken at the same time during positive energy balance, the weight gain would be mainly in the form of lean (muscle) weight or fat-free weight. In this case, it requires about 2500 kcal of excess intake to gain one pound of lean or fat-free

weight. Assuming the same +500 kcal balance per day as before, this would take 5 days.

Figure 20-12 may help in summarizing the relationship of food consumption and energy expenditure (energy balance) to body weight control. Although this model is simplistic and may not represent all of the factors that might be considered in energy balance equations, it does accu-

Figure 20-12. Relationship of food consumption, energy expenditure, and body weight.

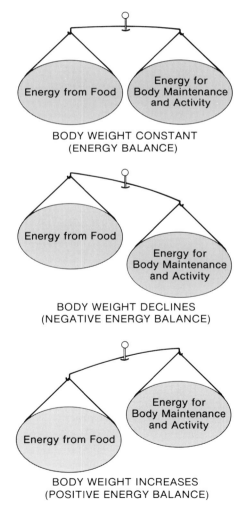

BODY WEIGHT CONSTANT
(ENERGY BALANCE)

BODY WEIGHT DECLINES
(NEGATIVE ENERGY BALANCE)

BODY WEIGHT INCREASES
(POSITIVE ENERGY BALANCE)

rately represent the concept of "calories in = calories out." This describes most people, i.e., excessive or overeating produces fatness while semistarvation and malnutrition produce decreases in body fat and body cell mass.[53] Some factors that are not considered in the most basic forms of the energy balance equations are differences in muscle tone, very small differences in basal energy requirements, prolonged effects of exercise on resting caloric expenditure, and individual differences in the thermic effect of food.[77] The eventual inclusion of these and other factors will yield energy balance equations that are more precise in a scientific sense but may not prove to be more useful in clinical applications.

Guidelines for Losing Body Fat

While male athletes who have an estimated body fat of less than 7% (see Table 20-2) and female athletes of less than 12% (see Table 20-3) should not be concerned about losing fat (except under medical advisement), many nonathletes and other athletes *will* find it necessary to shed body fat. For athletes, this is especially true at the beginning of the season. At the same time, these "overfat" athletes may want to gain, or at least maintain, their fat-free weight. The following guidelines should be helpful in achieving these goals:

1. Remember, it requires an excess expenditure of 3500 kcal in order to lose one pound of pure fat.
2. It is recommended that the caloric deficit not exceed 2000 to 2500 kcal/day. This is equivalent to a loss of 4 pounds of fat per week. An ideal loss is 2 to 3 pounds per week, which is equivalent to a caloric deficit of 1000 to 1500 kcal/day. An attempt to estimate daily or weekly caloric intake and expenditure should be made.
3. The caloric deficit should represent both an increased expenditure and a

reduced caloric intake. A caloric deficit that is solely the result of diet restriction will also cause fat-free weight loss.
4. For most active athletes, the lower limit of a restricted diet is a 2000-kcal intake per day. Caloric reductions below this level should be medically supervised. An example of a 2000-kcal diet is presented in Table 20-10. Note that all of the essential nutrients are provided in amounts adequate for most athletes.

Guidelines for Gaining Fat-Free Weight

For most people, gaining weight is easy. Unfortunately, the gain is mostly in body fat, which can lead to health problems. Ideally, increases in weight should reflect gains in fat-free weight. Such gains are often desired by athletes, since fat-free weight is generally positively correlated with athletic performance. However, for many athletes, gaining or at least maintaining fat-free weight during the long, difficult season is a real problem. One way of handling this problem is to follow the guidelines for gaining fat-free weight presented as follow:

1. As previously mentioned, in order to gain weight, caloric intake must be greater than caloric expenditure. In order to gain one pound of fat-free weight (muscle), an excess intake of about 2500 kcal is required. An excess of this size should *not* be taken in in one day.
2. It is recommended that the daily caloric intake not exceed expenditure by more than 1000 to 1500 kcal. On the basis of 5 diet days per week, this would mean a gain of *2 to 3 pounds per week*.
3. An estimate of how many calories are being taken in and how many are being expended daily or weekly should

TABLE 20-10

Example of a Low-Calorie (2000 kcal) Diet in Five Meals*

Breakfast

½ cup orange juice
1 soft-boiled egg
1 slice whole wheat toast
2 teasp. margarine
1 glass skim milk or other
   beverage

Total kilocalories: 345

Lunch

1 hamburger (3 oz.) on a roll
   with relish
½ sliced tomato
1 glass skim milk
1 medium apple

Total kilocalories: 510

Dinner

1 serving of baked
   chicken marengo
   (½ breast)
¾ cup rice
5-6 Brussel sprouts
1 bowl of green salad
   with French dressing
1 small piece gingerbread
1 cup skim milk or other
   beverage

Total kilocalories: 660

Snack

1 banana

Total kilocalories: 100

Snack

1 carton fruit-flavored
   yogurt
1 cup grape juice

Total kilocalories: 385

Daily total kilocalories: 2000

*From Smith.[56]

be made. This is not easy, but it can be done with the help of the athlete's parents and perhaps the home economics teacher or school dietician.

4. Note that calories needed to *maintain* weight must be added to excess intake for an accurate picture of the diet of an athlete on a weight-gain plan. In this regard, an intake of 6000 kcal a day is a realistic diet for young male athletes, since their average daily caloric expenditure may be about 5000 kcal. An example of a 6000-kcal diet is given

in Table 20-11. Note the quality of the food—low levels of large-bulk foods (such as cereals, grains, beverages, and salads), low amounts of animal fats, and an abundance of low-bulk carbohydrates.

5. To ensure that the excess calories will be laid down primarily as muscle, a vigorous training program, particularly of weight training, should be undertaken during the high caloric diet period. The skinfold measures mentioned earlier can be used to deter-

mine whether any excess fat is being added.

Examples of programs of weight gain and weight reduction are given in Table 20-12.

Making Weight in Wrestling

Understanding the somatotype and anthropometry has important applications to physical education and athletics. Some of these have already been discussed. Another one is making weight in wrestling. Since it is a rather serious problem, let's discuss it in some detail.

The Committee on Medical Aspects of Sports has posed several questions raised by the wrestling community[14]:

1. What are the hazards of indiscriminate and excessive weight reduction?
2. How much weight can a wrestler lose safely?
3. What are defensible means of losing weight?

TABLE 20-11

Example of a High-Calorie (6000 kcal) Diet in Six Meals*

Breakfast
½ cup orange juice
1 cup oatmeal
1 cup low-fat milk
1 scambled egg
1 slice whole wheat toast
1½ teasp. margarine
1 tablespoon jam
Total kilocalories: 665

Snack
1 peanut butter sandwich
1 banana
1 cup grape juice

Total kilocalories: 485

Lunch
5 fish sticks with tartar sauce
1 large serving, French fries
1 bowl of green salad with avocado and French dressing
1 cup lemon sherbet
2 granola cookies
1 cup low-fat milk
Total kilocalories: 1505

Snack
1 cup mixed dried fruit
1½ cup malted milk

Total kilocalories: 660

Dinner
1 cup cream of mushroom soup
2 pieces oven-baked chicken
1 candied sweet potato
1 dinner roll and margarine
1 cup carrots and peas
½ cup cole slaw
1 piece cherry pie
1 beverage
Total kilocalories: 1615

Snack
1 cup cashew nuts
1 cup cocoa

Total kilocalories: 1045

Daily Total kilocalories: 5975

*From Smith.[56]

TABLE 20-12

Examples of Fat-Free Weight (FFW) Gain and Fat Reduction Programs

Athlete	Present Body Composition	Means of Achieving Goal			Goal (after 3 months)
		Daily Caloric Intake	Daily Caloric Expenditure	Difference between Intake and Expenditure	
Football player	Total body weight: 200 pounds Fat: 10% FFW: 180 pounds	6000 kcal; see Table 20-11	4940 kcal, including calories spent in training*	6000 − 4940 = 1060 kcal *excess*	Total body weight: 225 pounds Fat: 8% FFW: 207 pounds
Field hockey player	Total body weight: 127 pounds Fat: 25% FFW: 95 pounds	2000 kcal; see Table 20-10	3000 kcal, including calories spent in training†	3000 − 2000 = 1000 kcal *deficit* (500 from re-stricted diet, 500 from exercise)	Total body weight: 112 pounds Fat: 15% FFW: 95 pounds

*Training for the football player interested in gaining fat-free weight might include repeated 40-yard sprints (2 days per week) and weight resistance training (3 days per week).

†Training for the field hockey player interested in losing body fat might include jogging 3 miles per day, calisthenics, and weight resistance training (2 days per week).

4. What weigh-in plan would best serve the purpose intended?

Excessive weight loss results in impaired competitive abilities;[48] extreme weight reduction seriously affects health. The wrestler uses a combination of food restriction, liquid deprivation, and dehydration in order to lose weight. Vomiting, the use of hot boxes, rubberized apparel, and exercise are among other practices employed. In a recent review of the literature, The American College of Sports Medicine[3] concluded that the simple and combined effects of these practices are generally associated with: (1) a reduction in muscular strength, (2) a decrease in work performance times (the athlete cannot work as long), (3) lower plasma and blood volumes, (4) a reduction in cardiac functioning during submaximal work conditions, (5) a lower oxygen consumption, especially when food restriction is a critical part of the weight reduction plan, (6) an impairment of thermoregulatory processes, (7) a decrease in renal blood flow and in the volume of fluid being filtered by the kidney, (8) a depletion of liver glycogen stores, and (9) an increase in the amount of electrolytes being lost from the body. Some studies have shown that weight losses caused by dehydration of 3% or more result in diminished athletic performance. Prolonged semistarvation diets, unbalanced diets, and excessive sweating combined with dehydration may cause severe harm to the athlete.

The amount of weight that a wrestler can safely lose should be related to his *effective weight level* (the weight level that yields his best performance) rather than the minimal weight, according to the Committee on the Medical Aspects of Sports. It is difficult to define scientifically the limits of safe weight control. Argument is in favor of a good preparticipation medical examination. Such a plan involves the weight history, which allows the physician a more valid judgment regarding how much weight a boy can safely lose.

The Committee is quick to emphasize that there is no alternative to:

1. A balanced diet at a sustaining caloric level.
2. Adequate fluid intake.
3. High energy output for attaining and maintaining an effective competitive weight.

Finally, the Committee suggests the weight of the wrestling candidates can best be assessed through a natural approach:

1. Educate youth who are interested in athletics regarding the importance of periodic medical examinations and the advantages of a general, year-round conditioning program for cardiovascular-pulmonary endurance, muscular fitness, and nutritional readiness.
2. Building on this orientation, assist any aspiring wrestler in an intensive conditioning program related to the demands of wrestling for at least four weeks, preferably six, without emphasis on weight level.
3. At the end of this period and without altering his daily training routine, take his weight in a prebreakfast, post-micturition state.
4. Consider this weight his minimal effective weight for competition as well as certification purposes.
5. Educate the boy and his parents in the concept of defensible weight control to avert fluctuation from his effective weight level.

The Iowa Studies

Tipton and colleagues at the University of Iowa have performed extensive studies concerning the effect of weight loss in high school wrestlers. Their studies show[64]:

1. A large number of young athletes lose an excessive amount of weight in a relatively short period of time. This holds true for all classes below 175 pounds. The lightest lose the highest percentage (circa 10%) of body weight during a 17-day period [Fig. 20-13].
2. The majority of weight loss occurs immediately preceding the date of certification.
3. Weight-losing methods were suggested by either coach or teammate.
4. Of the 835 boys measured, the average percentage of fat is 8%, whereas the state finalists ($n = 224$) had a 4 to 6% body fat content.

Dr. Tipton is particularly concerned with the lack of professional supervision dealing with the method or amount of weight which an athlete should lose. He recommends a body weight containing 7% fat (not less than 5% without medical supervision) and one that does not exceed 7% loss of the initial weight. Ideally, one would predict minimal weight at the beginning of the school year; then under professional guidance, a proper and gradual weight reduction could take place.

Predicting Minimal Weight Values

Research by Tipton et al.[61] resulted in an equation that allows prediction of minimal weight values. Several anthropometric measurements are obtained 6 to 8 weeks before the start of the wrestling season. The minimal weights are computed; the results are then used as a screening device along with the physician's judgment concerning the proper minimal weight for the particular boy.

Anthropometric Measurements (Fig. 20-14)

1. *Chest Diameter.* Subject stands with both hands on the crests of the ilium. Calipers are placed in the axillary region with ends placed on the second or third rib. At the end of expiration, the measurement is obtained.
2. *Chest Depth.* Subject stands with right hand behind head. One end of the caliper is placed on the tip of the xiphoid process while the other end is placed over the vertebrae of the twelfth rib. Measurement is taken at the end of expiration.
3. *Bi-iliac Diameter.* Distance between most lateral projections of the crests of the ilium is measured.
4. *Bitrochanteric Diameter.* Distance between the most lateral projections of the greater trochanters is measured.
5. *Wrist Diameter.* Distance between the styloid processes of the radius and ulna is measured. Measure both wrists and use their sum.

Figure 20-13. During a 17-day period, 6.8 pounds or 4.9% of the body weight was lost, most of which occurred during the last 10 days. An average increase of 13.6 pounds above the certification weight occurred at the end of the season. (From Tipton and Tcheng.[64])

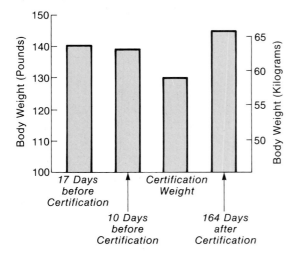

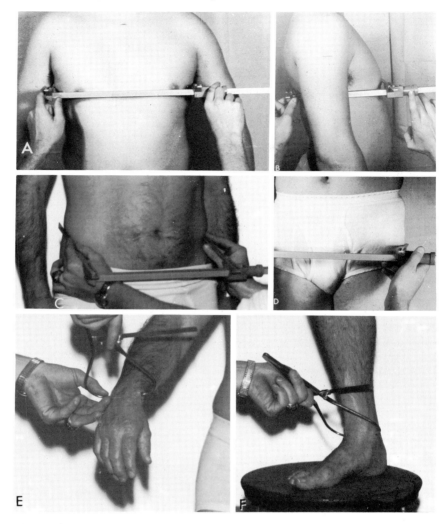

Figure 20-14. Measurements required for predicting minimal wrestling weight for high school males. *A,* Chest diameter; *B,* chest depth; *C,* bi-iliac diameter; *D,* bitrochanteric diameter; *E,* wrist diameter; *F,* ankle diameter. (*A, B, D,* courtesy of E. Churchill et al.[13])

6. *Ankle Diameter.* The foot is placed on a stool or chair with caliper ends placed over malleoli at an angle of 45 degrees. Measure both ankles and use their sum.

Data from the preceding anthropometric measures may then be substituted in one of two formulas, the long form or the short form.

Long form. Minimal weight = 1.84 × (height, inches) + 3.28 × (chest diameter, cm) + 3.31 × (chest depth, cm) + 0.82 × bi-iliac diameter, cm) + 1.69 × (bitrochanteric diameter, cm) + 3.56 × (both wrists, cm) + 2.15 × (both ankles, cm) − 281.72. A correlation of .933, with a standard error of estimate of 8.7 pounds was found between this equation and the actual weight of the finalists.

Short form. Minimal weight = 2.05 × (height, inches) + 3.65 × (chest diameter, cm) + 3.51 (chest depth, cm) + 1.96 × (bitrochanteric diameter, cm) + 8.02 × (left ankle, cm) − 282.18. A correlation of .923 with a standard error of estimate of 8.9 pounds was found between this equation and the actual weight of the finalists.

We measured an Ohio State Big Ten finalist at the beginning of the wrestling season with the following results:
Weight = 150 lbs
Height = 71 in.
Chest diameter = 25.4 cm
Chest depth = 18.5 cm
Bitrochanteric diameter = 32.3 cm
Bi-iliac diameter = 25.7 cm
Wrist diameter (sum of both wrists) = 11.4 cm
Ankle diameter (sum of both ankles) = 14.2 cm

Minimal Weight (Long Form)

$$
\begin{aligned}
(1.84) \times (71 \text{ in}) &= 130.64 \\
(3.28) \times (25.4) &= 83.31 \\
(3.31) \times (18.5) &= 61.24 \\
(.82) \times (25.7) &= 21.07 \\
(1.69) \times (32.3) &= 54.59 \\
(3.56) \times (11.4) &= 40.58 \\
(2.15) \times (14.2) &= \underline{30.53} \\
& 421.96 \\
& \underline{-281.72}
\end{aligned}
$$

Minimal weight = 140.24 lbs

The boy's predicted minimal weight equals 140.24 lbs. Weighing 150 lbs at the beginning of the season, this wrestler could lose a maximum of 10 lbs. He actually wrestled at a body weight of 142 pounds.

Minimal Weight (Short Form)

$$
\begin{aligned}
(2.05) \times (71 \text{ in}) &= 145.55 \\
(3.65) \times (25.4) &= 92.71 \\
(3.51) \times (18.5) &= 64.94 \\
\end{aligned}
$$

$$
\begin{aligned}
(1.96) \times (32.3) &= 63.31 \\
(8.02) \times (7.1) &= \underline{56.94} \\
& 423.45 \\
& \underline{-282.18}
\end{aligned}
$$

Minimal weight = 141.27 lbs

You can see that the short form produces results almost identical to those of the long form.

ACSM Guidelines for Weight Loss in Wrestlers

The American College of Sports Medicine (ACSM)[3] suggests that the potential health hazard created by the procedures that are used by wrestlers to "make weight" can be eliminated if state and national organizations will:

1. Assess the body composition of each wrestler several weeks in advance of the competitive season. Individuals with a fat content less than 5% of their certified body weight should receive medical clearance before being allowed to compete.

2. Emphasize the fact that the daily caloric requirements of wrestlers should be obtained from a balanced diet and determined on the basis of age, body surface area, growth, and physical activity levels. The minimal caloric needs of wrestlers in high schools and colleges will range from 1200 to 2400 kcal/day; therefore, it is the responsibility of coaches, school officials, physicians, and parents to discourage wrestlers from ingesting less than their minimal needs without prior medical approval.

3. Discourage the practice of fluid deprivation and dehydration. This can be accomplished by:
   a. Educating the coaches and wrestlers . . . [so that they are aware of] the physiological consequences and medical complications that can occur as a result of these practices.

  b. Prohibiting the single or combined use of rubber suits, steam rooms, hot boxes, saunas, laxatives, and diuretics to 'make weight.'
  c. Scheduling weigh-ins just prior to competition.
  d. Scheduling more official weigh-ins between team matches.
4. Permit more participants per team to compete in those weight classes (119–145 pounds) which have the highest percentages of wrestlers certified for competition.
5. Standardize regulations concerning the eligibility rules at championship tournaments so that individuals can participate only in those weight classes in which they had the highest frequencies of matches throughout the season.
6. Encourage local and county organizations to systematically collect data on the hydration state of wrestlers and its relationship to growth and development.

Exercise and Training Effects

In this section we will review some research findings as they pertain to several subtopics in the general area of body composition and weight control. Namely, we will concentrate on the effects of exercise, either acute bouts or short-term activity programs, the effects of longer term training, differences that exist between groups of athletes, and some findings related to children and older adults. To begin, the reader is referred to reviews on the measurement of body composition in clinical settings,[47] and future directions for body composition research in sports and exercise programs.[75]

As indicated earlier, there is a definite place for exercise and an increased expenditure of energy in activities of daily living as part of programs to assist people to lose weight.[22] The exercise should be of long duration and low intensity so as to maximize energy expenditure and promote a negative caloric "balance."[26] That is to say, the activities should be aerobic and should promote the liberation and metabolism of the person's own stored energy sources. At the same time the programmed activities must be safe and take into consideration some specific concerns and precautions related to obese persons.[23,24] The effects of aerobic exercise such as walking and jogging have been found to be reliable and directly related to energy expenditure.[19] At the same time, comparisons of the results of exercise and other forms of weight control suggests that the weight losses due to exercise are quite small.[19] The multitude of positive, beneficial "side effects" that accompany participation in exercise sessions during an overall weight-loss program tend to more than compensate for the arguments that it takes a lot of exercise to "burn off a pound of fat."

Exercise Classes

Aerobic dancing at an intensity of 70% of maximum heart rate for 30 minutes during the first week and progressing to 90 minutes by the 13th week produced only small reductions in the body weights of previously sedentary female college students.[32] Estimations of per cent body fat decreased more predictably and dramatically but it didn't matter whether the students danced two or three times per week, the same effects were seen. A second study reports contradictory results in that a 10-week period of aerobic dance classes, (3 classes per week, 45 minutes per class) failed to produce any reductions in either body weight or per cent fat.[66] The training intensity was not reported but was adequate to produce improvements in cardiorespiratory measurements. The underlying reason for the failure of this aerobic dance activity to produce reductions in per cent body fat was not apparent but the short duration of the study has been suggested.

This argument is countered by the report that male physical education students who exercised at various team games and sports for 20 to 30 hours per week were heavier and had higher body fat percentages at the end of a three year period of study.[68]

Reductions in body fat and body weight have been reported for participants who have engaged in a variety of other activities. For example, participants in a 4-week, intensive Alpine climbing expedition lost both body fat and lean body mass.[4] Likewise, six sedentary obese men, ages 19 to 31, lost a significant amount of body weight and fat during the completion of 16 weeks of vigorous walking 90 minutes per day, 5 days per week, on a treadmill at speeds up to 3.2 mph on a 10% grade.[36] It was estimated that they expended about 1100 kcal per session or about 88,000 kcal during the experimental period. This would be equivalent to 25 lbs of fat. The subjects actually lost an average of 5.7 kg (11.5 lbs) so by any rough accounting of caloric balance it is apparent that no attempt was being made to "influence their diet." It is of interest to note that, when there is no attempt to control dietary intakes, exercise-induced reductions in body weight and body fat are not closely related to exercise intensity[60] (bicycle ergometer, 45 min/day, 5 days/week, 12 weeks, 540 kpm/min versus 900 kpm/min), or duration[65] (jogging 1.6 km, 3.2 km, or 4.8 km, 3 days/week, 85% HR_{max}, 12 weeks). Finally, exercising in cool water (17 to 22° C, bicycle ergometer, 5 times per week, 30 to 40% of maximum oxygen consumption, 8 weeks) was well tolerated by obese women but did not reduce their body weight, body fat, fat-free body weight, or caloric intake.[51]

Training Programs

The effects of exercise in supervised and unsupervised training programs have been studied. These results are more consistent since subjects in all cases lost body weight, body fat, and showed reductions in skinfolds in studies where these important measurements were made. For example, 16 young female swimmers (mean age 15.8 years) decreased their percentage of body fat from 21.9 to 19.8% during 7 weeks of training where they swam an average of 12,806 yards per week and worked out an average of 4 days per week.[59] Fat percentage losses were a bit greater, 17.3 to 14.6%, for 13 sedentary male subjects (mean age 24.3 years) who participated in a 20-week aerobic training program (bicycle ergometer, 40 to 45 minutes per session, 4 to 5 times per week, progressing from 60 to 85% of HRR).[16] The sum of seven skinfolds was significantly reduced with most of the reductions occurring in trunk rather than extremity measures. This latter finding was interpreted to mean that exercise-induced fat losses are not due to a preferential depletion of subcutaneous fat layers. Similar losses in body fat from 25.8 down to 23.2% occurred in 22 women runners (mean age 28.4 years, range 23 to 37) who increased their running by 30 miles per week over a 4 to 7 month period.[49] These reductions in body fat were accompanied by small increases in lean body weight from 42.3 to 43.0 kg.

Estimations of per cent body fat of 87 male and 57 female army trainees were made using four skinfold measurements and the regression equations of Durnin and Wormsley (*Br J Nutr*. 32:77–92, 1974).[45] After seven weeks of basic training the estimated body fat had decreased by 11% in males (from 16.3 to 14.5%) and 7% in females (28.2 to 26.2%). The fat losses were greatest in personnel who had the highest starting levels, i.e., those who had the most to lose. A contrasting study of the effects of marathon-run training on young men (mean age 21.7 years) who started with relatively low body fat percentages of 13.4 has been reported.[31] The subjects participated in a 16-week special training program where they ran 50 to 70 miles per week to prepare them to run a certified marathon. Their body fat dropped to 10.8% and the sum of six skinfolds decreased from 70.1 to 52.6 mm. It was concluded that transition from moderate to extreme endurance training levels in normal young men is accompanied by significant reductions in body fat.

Finally, a study of lean and obese middle-aged female subjects who participated in the same supervised, 12-week aerobic training program has been reported.[25] The program was structured along ACSM guidelines (walking-jogging 15 to 25 minutes, 4 days per week, 75% max $\dot{V}O_2$). Normal-weight subjects decreased their body fat from 24.7 to 23.9%, obese subjects reduced from 38.0 to 36.2% and the sum of 10 skinfolds decreased significantly in both groups. This moderate-intensity physical conditioning program affected both obese and leaner women in a similar fashion. An 18-month follow-up of a subsample of these subjects indicated that they regained body weight and body fat to pretraining levels.[38] Since only half of the well-intentioned subjects were exercising on their own, it was concluded that the majority of middle-aged women who have participated in supervised walk-jog conditioning interventions will regress to their preprogram levels of fitness and fatness when left to exercise ad libitum (take it as you will). This is the principle reason why good exercise leaders always will be in demand.

Sports Specific Responses

Body composition differences among athletes who compete in different sports has been an area of research interest for the past three decades. These efforts are driven by questions such as: which athletes have the lowest body fat percentages and which have the highest?, which athletes have the greatest amount of lean muscle mass and how does this contribute to their performance?, and how do "average" performers compare to elite athletes? The review by Wilmore[75] covers these questions well and includes height, weight, and body fat percentages for 20 different sports, from 20 different reports published since 1980. Fat percentage levels ranged from 4.6 and 5.0 for male gymnasts and wrestlers up to 26 and 28% for female swimmers, basketball players, and discus or shot putters. The lowest values for female athletes were between 9.6 and 11% for gymnasts and pentathalon competitors.

Since this report a variety of other athletes have been described including Nigerian female athletes by sport,[39] and elite American athletes by sport.[20] The latter report is based on 528 male and 298 female athletes participating in 26 and 15 different Olympic events. Generally speaking, participants in sports where their body weight is supported have higher per cent fat values (canoe and kayak—males 13%, females 22%) than athletes who have to meet a weight class (boxing or wrestling, males 7 to 8%), perform very anaerobically (100 and 200 meters—males 6%, females 14%), or extremely aerobically (marathon, males 6%). The athletes with the highest lean body masses were participants in sports where body size is a definite advantage (basketball—males 84 kg, females 55 kg; volleyball—males 75 kg, females 58 kg). Other reports exist for rugby union or club players[5] (11 to 18% depending on position), female ballet and modern dancers[17] (18 to 26%), speed skaters[46] (non-Olympic 8.1, Olympic 6.8%), college football players by position[69] (defensive backs 7.3%, offensive linemen 14.8%), and 9- to 12-year-old experienced wrestlers[50] (controls 20%, wrestlers 13%). Lean body mass has been measured in 30 middle-aged male marathon runners who were found to be slightly taller and lighter in weight than a comparison group.[1] More importantly, their total body calcium and potassium levels were higher, which supports the concept that rigorous exercise prevents the involutionary loss of skeletal and lean body mass. Finally, high school basketball officials have been reported to be overweight with average body densities of 1.047 and 22% body fat levels.[30]

Children and Fatness

A final topic we will address is that of children, their body composition and changes that occur during the process of aging. It is well known that obese children often become obese adults, that dramatic changes in body composition and fatness can occur during the peripubertal years, and that many children are at risk for disease and the unhappy status of being overly fat. Part of the problem might relate to differences between the perceptions that obese and slim children have of physical education and other school activities.[76] Obese children evaluated endurance activities more negatively and flexibility-coordination activities more positively than slim children. The slim–obese differences were independent of but paralleled similar differences between boys and girls with slim children's perceptions being similar to those of boys'. Both of these differences present problems for physical education teachers who wish to foster endurance activity among girls and obese children to help them regulate and lose body weight and fat.

Girls at an age of 8.75 years have a higher percentage of body fat than boys, 24.3% (range 14.7 to 41.6%) versus 20.1% (range 11.7 to 34.3%).[35] Fatness levels in girls could not be related to longitudinal activity scores obtained from the age of 6 months, whereas there was a negative correlation between activity scores of boys at age 3 and 4 years and their fatness levels at age 8. Per cent fat levels in obese adolescents (mean 12.7 years, range 10 to 16 years) are higher for girls (42.2%) than for boys (39.3%).[34] Physical work capacities determined at a selected heart rate of 170 beats per minute (PWC_{170}) are not related to per cent body fat in male youths between the ages of 15 and 19 years.[67] Meredith has alerted us that there may be differences in the body weight and other somatic dimensions of rural compared to urban children in different countries of the world.[41]

Aging and Fatness

Currently, there is much interest in the matter of aging, the aging process and the influence of exercise on older populations. Durnin[18] has addressed the topic of body composition and energy expenditure in elderly people (defined as being 60 to 75 years of age). Changes in body mass and body composition accompany aging, and these changes will reduce the total energy expenditure and the need for a large food intake. Height is known to decrease by as much as 5 to 7 cm between the ages of 30 and 70 years for some groups, with larger reductions in industrial communities and among less-privileged socioeconomic classes. While there remains some uncertainty, it is likely that the skeletal mass and the mineral content of the skeleton decrease and the fat mass of the body increases in elderly people. There also is a change in the ratio of fat between the subcutaneous layers and adipose tissue deposits on the trunk of the body, with more of the fat being deposited in the deeper regions in older people.

BMR measures are lower in older persons but much of this might be due to the shifts in lean to fat components, which favor a lowered metabolic rate. The body composition of most elderly people will be more influenced by differences in energy expenditure related to their leisure time activity levels than to whether they still work at a sedentary job. Other considerations include whether or not they suffer from degenerative diseases of the cardio-respiratory or bone and joint systems, which makes it uncomfortable or even painful for them to be more active. They also may have experienced a reduction in the mechanical efficiency of their limbs or in control over their balance, which occurs more often with aging. The housewife is particularly at high risk for becoming less active and consequently fatter from age 45 on. In a traditional home setting, after the children are raised and have left, her work does not stop but becomes progressively less. This means that her energy expenditure starts to decrease at age 45 to 50, and falls proportionally more than that of a man up to the age of 70 years. Durnin[18] suggests that it might be more important to emphasize what the levels of physical activity and energy expenditure of elderly persons ought to be rather than to spend more time in assessing what they currently are. He suggests that we should "actively" encourage physical activity in the elderly which, in turn, will be accompanied by an increase in their energy expenditure, less fatness, and at the same time promote the need to ingest adequate amounts of essential dietary nutrients. In essence, an activity-driven metabolic system that is truly in a harmonious balance.

Summary

Endomorph, mesomorph, and ectomorph are the terms employed in describing the somatotype or body type of a person. Endomorph refers to fat; mesomorph to muscle; and ectomorph to a body that is lean. Each of us has a degree of all three body-type components. Athletes and other active people tend to have higher mesomorphic and ectomorphic components than do nonathletes or sedentary individuals.

Two methods commonly used to describe somatotypes are the Sheldon method, which requires a photograph, and the Heath-Carter method, which uses anthropometric measures.

In addition to studying body types as they are associated with athletic performance, body types have also been related to disease entities; for example, a number of studies associated coronary artery disease more with the mesomorph than with the ectomorph.

Fat content of the body is significantly associated with physical activity. Athletes and other active people are less obese than sedentary individuals. Lack of exercise is the prime cause of obesity in all age groups. Obesity refers to the above-average amount of fat contained in the body, this in turn being dependent upon the lipid (fat) content of each adipocyte (fat cell) and on the total number of fat cells. The prevention of obesity through regular exercises and proper diet is more successful than is treatment for it.

Two methods are commonly employed in estimating fat content of the body: (1) measuring the specific gravity of the person and (2) measuring skinfolds to estimate body density. The density of the body can be measured by hydrostatic (underwater) weighing. This is the most accurate method of estimating body density, but it is also the most difficult from a technical standpoint. Estimates of body density from skinfold measures are less accurate and more specific than underwater weighing but are a less difficult and practical method. Body fat can be estimated from body density measures using one of two equations: per cent fat = (4.57/body density) $- 4.142 \times 100$ or per cent body fat $= (4.95/\text{body density}) - 4.50 \times 100$.

Energy balance means consuming the same amount of energy through food intake as is being expended by activity. When more energy is consumed than expended, the person is said to be in a positive energy balance and body weight is gained. When less energy is consumed than expended, the person is said to be in a negative energy balance and body weight is lost. The weight gained may be in the form of fat or fat-free (lean or muscle) weight. The latter is possible when a person is in a positive energy balance while participating in an exercise program at the same time.

Considerable attention is being given to the serious malpractices associated with "making weight" in wrestling. This is particularly true for high school wrestlers. Tipton and colleagues have suggested a method using anthropometric measurements whereby minimal wrestling weight can be predicted.

Questions

1. Define endomorphy, mesomorphy, and ectomorphy.
2. According to Sheldon's rating form, what would be the somatotype of an extreme endomorph?
3. How do the somatotypes of marathon runners compare with those of football players, according to Carter?
4. Would you consider that female and male somatotypes in comparable sport events are similar?
5. Explain how the difference in track performance between men and women might be partially attributed to the body's fat content.
6. Illustrate how density determinations are used to compute body fat.
7. How are the Sloan-Weir nomograms used to predict body fat? Can body density estimates be accurately determined on ath-

letes and children from the Sloan-Weir nomograms? Explain.

8. Compute the percentage of fat using both the Brozek and Siri formulae of a person whose body density equals 1.0456 g/cc.
9. Explain and give an example of a person in a positive energy balance.
10. Explain and give an example of a person in negative energy balance.
11. The Committee on the Medical Aspect of Sports suggests that the weight of a wrestler can best be assessed through a natural approach. What are some of their suggestions?
12. What are the results of Tipton's studies dealing with weight loss among high school wrestlers?
13. What procedures might be used in predicting minimal weight values for high school wrestlers?
14. According to the American College of Sports Medicine, how can the hazards of weight loss in wrestlers be eliminated?

References

1. Aloia, J. F., Cohn, S. H., Babu, T., Abesamis, C., Kalici, N., and Ellis, K.: Skeletal mass and body composition in marathon runners. *Metabolism.* 27(12):1793–96, 1978.
2. American College of Sports Medicine: *Encyclopedia of Sport Sciences and Medicine.* New York, Macmillan, 1971.
3. American College of Sports Medicine: Position stand on weight loss in wrestlers. *Med Sci Sports.* 8(2):xi–xiii, 1976.
4. Baker, S. J.: An intensive alpine climbing expedition and its influence on some anthropometric measurements. *Br J Sports Med.* 14(2,3):126–130, 1980.
5. Bell, W.: Body composition and maximal aerobic power of rugby union forwards. *J Sports Med.* 20:447–451, 1980.
6. Bogert, J., Briggs, G., and Calloway, D.: *Nutrition and Physical Fitness,* 9th ed. Philadelphia, W. B. Saunders, 1973.
7. Brozek, J.: Techniques for measuring body composition. Quartermaster Research and Engineering Center. (A.D. <286506), Natick, Mass. January, 1959, p. 95.
8. Brozek, J., Grande, F., Anderson, J., and Keys, A.: Densitometric analysis of body

composition: revision of some quantitative assumptions. *Ann NY Acad Sci.* 110:113–140, 1963.

9. Buskirk, E. R.: Nutrition for the athlete. In Ryan, A., and Allman, F. (eds.): *Sports Medicine.* New York, Academic Press, 1974, p. 146.

10. Buskirk, E. R.: Obesity: a brief overview with emphasis on exercise. *Fed Proc.* 33(8): 1948–1951, 1974.

11. Carter, J., and Heath, B.: Somatotype methodology and kinesiology research. *Kinesiol Rev.* 1971, pp. 10–19.

12. Carter, J., and Phillips, W.: Structural changes in exercising middle-aged males during a 2-year period. *J Appl Physiol.* 27(6):787–794, 1969.

13. Churchill, E., McConville, J., Laubach, L., and White, R.: Anthropometry of U.S. Army Aviators—1970. Technical Report 72-52-CE. Natick, Mass. United States Army Natick Laboratories, Dec., 1971.

14. Committee on Medical Aspects of Sports. Wrestling and weight control. *JAMA.* 201(7):131–133, 1967.

15. deGaray, A., Levine, L., and Carter, J. (eds.): *Genetic and Anthropological Studies of Olympic Athletes.* New York, Academic Press, 1974, p. 55.

16. Després, J. P., Bouchard, C., Tremblay, A., Savard, R., and Marcotte, M.: Effects of aerobic training on fat distribution in male subjects. *Med Sci Sports Exer.* 17(1):113–118, 1985.

17. Dolgener, F. A., Spasoff, T. C., and St. John, W. E.: Body build and body composition of high ability female dancers. *Res Q Exer Sport.* 51(4):599–607, 1980.

18. Durnin, J. V. G. A.: Body composition and energy expenditure in elderly people. *Biblthca Nutri Dieta.* 33:16–30, 1983.

19. Epstein, L. H., and Wing, R. R.: Aerobic exercise and weight. *Addictive Behaviors.* 5:371–388, 1980.

20. Fleck, S. J.: Body composition of elite American athletes. *Am J Sports Med.* 11(6):398–403, 1983.

21. Forbes, G. B.: Body composition as affected by physical activity and nutrition. *Fed Proc.* 44:343–347, 1985.

22. Foss, M. L.: Exercise prescription and training programs for obese subjects. In Bjorntorp, P., Cairella, M., and Howard, A. N. (eds.): *Recent Advances in Obesity Research: III.* London, John Libbey, 1981.

23. Foss, M. L., and Strehle, D. A.: Exercise testing and training for the obese. In Storlie, J., and Jordan, H. A. (eds.): *Nutrition and Exercise in Obesity Management.* New York, Spectrum Publications, 1984.

24. Foss, M. L.: Exercise concerns and precautions for the obese. In Storlie, J., and Jordan, H. A. (eds.): *Nutrition and Exercise in Obesity Management.* New York, Spectrum Publication, 1984.

25. Franklin, B., Buskirk, E., Hodgson, J., Gahagan, H., Kollias, J., and Mendez, J.: Effects of physical conditioning on cardio-respiratory function, body composition and serum lipids in relatively normal-weight and obese middle-aged women. *Int J Obesity.* 3:97–100, 1979.

26. Franklin, B., and Rubenfire, M.: Losing weight through exercise. *JAMA.* 244(4): 377–379, 1980.

27. Hall, L. K.: *Anthropometric Estimations of Body Density of Women Athletes in Selected Athletic Activities.* Doctoral Dissertation. The Ohio State University, Columbus, Ohio, 1977.

28. Heath, B., and Carter, J.: A modified somatotype method. *Am J Phys Anthropol.* 27(1):57–74, 1967.

29. Hirsch, J., and Knittle, J. L.: Cellularity of obese and nonobese human adipose tissue. *Fed Proc.* 29(4):1516–1521, 1970.

30. Holland, J. C., and Cherry, R. B.: Aerobic capacity, body composition, and heart rate response curves of high school basketball officials. *J Sports Med.* 19:63–72, 1979.

31. Johnson, G. O., Thorland, W. G., Crabbe, J. M., Dienstbier, R., and Fagot, T.: Effects of a 16-week marathon training program on normal college males. *J Sports Med.* 22: 224–230, 1982.

32. Johnson, S., Berg, K., and Latin, R.: The effect of training frequency of aerobic dance on oxygen uptake, body composition and personality. *J Sports Med.* 24:290–297, 1984.

33. Katch, F. I., and McArdle, W. D.: Prediction of body density from simple anthropometric measurements in college-age men and women. *Human Biol.* 45:445–454, 1973.

34. Katch, V., Rocchini, A., Becque, D., Marks, C., and Moorehead, K.: Basal metabolism of obese adolescents: age, gender and body composition effects. *Int J Obesity.* 9:69–76, 1985.

35. Ku, L. C., Shapiro, L. R., Crawford, P. B., and Huenemann, R. L.: Body composition

and physical activity in 8-year-old children. *Am J Clin Nutr.* 24:2770-2775, 1981.

36. Leon, A. S., Conrad, J., Hunninghake, D. B., and Serfass, R.: Effects of a vigorous walking program on body composition, and carbohydrate and lipid metabolism of obese young men. *Am J Clin Nutr.* 32:1776-1787, 1979.

37. Lewis, S., Haskell, W. L., Klein, H., Halpern, J., and Wood, P. O.: Prediction of body composition in habitually active middle-aged men. *J Appl Physiol.* 39:221-225, 1975.

38. MacKeen, P. G., Franklin, B. A., Nicholas, W. C., and Buskirk, E.: Body composition, physical work capacity and physical activity habits at 18-month follow-up of middle-aged women participating in an exercise intervention program., Internat. *J Obesity.* 7:61-71, 1983.

39. Mathur, D. N., and Salokun, S. O.: Body composition of successful Nigerian female athletes. *J Sports Med.* 25:27-31, 1985.

40. Mayer, J.: *Overweight: Causes, Cost, and Control.* Englewood Cliffs, N.J. Prentice-Hall, 1968.

41. Meredith, H. V.: Comparative findings on body size of children and youths living at urban centers and in rural areas. *Growth.* 43:95-104, 1979.

42. *Nutrition for the Athlete:* American Alliance for Health, Physical Education, Recreation, and Dance. Washington, D.C., 1971.

43. Pařizková, J.: Total body fat and skinfold thickness in children. *Metabolism.* 10:794-801, 1961.

44. Parnell, R.: Etiology of coronary heart disease. *Br Med J.* 1:232, 1959.

45. Patton, J. F., Daniels, W. L., and Vogel, J. A.: Aerobic power and body fat of men and women during army basic training. *Aviat Space Environ Med.* 492-496, 1980.

46. Pollack, M. L., Foster, C., Anholm, J., Hare, J., Farrell, P., Maksud, M., and Jackson, A. S.: Body composition of Olympic speed skating candidates. *Res Q Exer Sport.* 53(2):150-155, 1982.

47. Pollack, M. L., Schmidt, D. H., and Jackson, A. S.: Measurement of cardiorespiratory fitness and body composition in the clinical setting. *Com Ther.* 6(9):12-27, 1980.

48. Ribisl, P.: When wrestlers shed pounds quickly. *Physician Sportsmed.* 2(7):30-35, 1974.

49. Rotkis, T., Boyden, T. W., Pamenter, R. W.,

Stanforth, P., and Wilmore, J.: High density lipoprotein cholesterol and body composition of female runners. *Metabolism.* 30(10):994-995, 1981.

50. Sady, S. P., Thomson, W. H., Savage, M., and Petratis, M.: The body composition and physical dimension of 9- to 12-year old experienced wrestlers. *Med Sci Sports Exer.* 14(3):244-248, 1982.

51. Sheldahl, L. M., Buskirk, E. R., Loomis, J. L., Hodgson, J. L., and Mendez, J.: Effects of exercise in cool water on body weight loss. *Int J Obesity.* 6:29-42, 1982.

52. Sheldon, W.: *Atlas of Men.* New York, Harper and Brothers, 1954.

53. Shizgal, H. M.: The effect of malnutrition on body composition. *Surg Gynecol Obstet.* 152:22-26, 1981.

54. Sinning, W. E.: Anthropometric estimation of body density, fat, and lean body weight in women gymnasts. *Med Sci Sports.* 10(4):243-249, 1978.

55. Sloan, A., and Weir, J.: Nomograms for prediction of body density and total body fat from skinfold measurements. *J Appl Physiol.* 28(2):221-222, 1970.

56. Smith, N. J.: *Food for Sport.* Palo Alto, Bull Publishing, 1976.

57. Sodhi, H. S.: A study of morphology and body composition on Indian basketball players. *J Sports Med.* 20:413-422, 1980.

58. Spain, D., Nathan, D., and Gellis, M.: Weight, body type and the prevalence of coronary atherosclerotic heart disease in males. *Am J Med Sci.* 245:63-72, 1963.

59. Stransky, A. W., Mickelson, R. J., van Fleet, C., and Davis, R.: Effects of a swimming training regimen on hematological, cardiorespiratory and body composition changes in young females. *J Sports Med.* 19:347-354, 1979.

60. Swenson, E. J., and Conlee, R. K.: Effects of exercise intensity on body composition in adult males. *J Sports Med.* 19:323-326, 1979.

61. Tcheng, T.-K., and Tipton, C.: Iowa wrestling study: anthropometric measurements and the prediction of a "minimal" body weight for high school wrestlers. *Med Sci Sports.* 5(1):1-10, 1973.

62. Thorland, W. G., Johnson, G. O., Fagot, T. G., Tharp, G. D., and Hammer, R. W.: Body composition and somatotype characteristics of Junior Olympic athletes. *Med Sci Sports Exer.* 13(5):332-338, 1981.

63. Tipton, C. M. (ed.): The influence of exer-

cise on the morphology and metabolism of the isolated fat cell. *Fed Proc.* 33(8):1947–1968, 1974.

64. Tipton, C. M., and Tcheng, T.-K.: Iowa wrestling study. *JAMA.* 214(7):1269–1274, 1970.
65. Toriola, A. L.: Influence of 12-week jogging on body fat and serum lipids. *Br J Sports Med.* 18(1):13–17, 1984.
66. Vaccaro, P., and Clinton, M.: The effects of aerobic dance conditioning on the body composition and maximal oxygen uptake of college women. *J Sports Med.* 21:291–294, 1981.
67. Watson, A. W. S., and O'Donovan, D. J.: The effects of five weeks of controlled interval training on youths of diverse pre-training condition. *J Sports Med.* 17:139–146, 1977.
68. Watson, A. W. S.: A three-year study of the effects of exercise on active young men. *Eur J Appl Physiol.* 40:107–115, 1979.
69. White, J., Mayhew, J. L., and Piper, F. C.: Prediction of body composition in college football players. *J Sports Med.* 20:317–324, 1980.
70. Wilmore, J.: The use of actual, predicted and constant residual volumes in the assessment of body composition by underwater weighing. *Med Sci Sports.* 1(2):87–90, 1969.
71. Wilmore, J. H.: Athletic Training and Physical Fitness. Boston, Allyn and Bacon, Inc., 1976.
72. Wilmore, J. H., and Behnke, A. R.: An anthropometric estimation of body density and lean body weight in young men. *J Appl Physiol.* 27(1):25–31, 1969.
73. Wilmore, J. H., and Behnke, A. R.: An anthropometric estimation of body density and lean body weight in young women. *Am J Clin Nutr.* 23:267–274, 1970.
74. Wilmore, J. H., Brown, C. H., and Davis, J. A.: Body physique and composition of the female distance runner. *Ann NY Acad Sci.* 301:764–776, 1977.
75. Wilmore, J. H.: Body composition in sport and exercise: directions for future research. *Med Sci Sports Exer.* 15(1):21–31, 1983.

76. Worsley, A., Coonan, W., Leitch, D., and Crawford, D.: Slim and obese children's perceptions of physical activities. *Int J Obesity.* 8:201–211, 1984.
77. Zahorska-Markiewicz, B.: Thermic effect of food and exercise in obesity. *Eur J Appl Physiol.* 44:321–235, 1980.

SELECTED READINGS

Benke, A. R., and Wilmore, J. H.: *Evaluation and Regulation of Body Build and Composition.* Englewood Cliffs, N.J., Prentice-Hall, 1974.

Bray, G. A. (ed.): *Obesity in America.* U.S. Department of Health, Education, and Welfare, NIH Publication No. 79-359, 1979.

Briggs, G. M., and Calloway, D. H.: *Nutrition and Physical Fitness,* 10th ed. Philadelphia, W. B. Saunders, 1979.

Brownell, K. D., and Foreyt, J. P. (eds.): *Handbook of Eating Disorders.* New York, Basic Books, 1986.

Buskirk, E. R.: Obesity. In Downey, J. A., and Darling, R. C. (eds.): *Physiological Basis of Rehabilitation Medicine.* Philadelphia, W. B. Saunders, 1971, pp. 229–242.

Clark, N.: *The Athlete's Kitchen.* New York, Bantam Books, 1981.

deGaray, A. L., Levine, L., and Carter, J. E. L. (eds.): *Genetic and Anthropological Studies of Olympic Athletes.* New York, Academic Press, 1974.

Fox, E. L.: *Sports Physiology.* Philadelphia, W. B. Saunders, 1979, pp. 242–281.

Katch, F. I., and McArdle, W. D.: *Nutrition, Weight Control, and Exercise.* Boston, Houghton Mifflin, 1977, pp. 69–181.

Smith, N. J.: *Food for Sport.* Palo Alto, Bull Publishing, 1976, pp. 51–72, 127–142.

Storlie, J., and Jordan, H. A. (eds.): *Book 1: Evaluation and Treatment of Obesity, Book 2: Nutrition and Exercise in Obesity Management, Book 3: Behavioral Management of Obesity.* New York, Spectrum Publications, 1984.

T he activity of all cells takes place within a fluid environment. This internal environment, referred to as the *milieu intêrieur* by the French physiologist, Claude Bernard, must be precisely regulated with respect to content, temperature, and hydrogen ion concentration. Exercise, as well as environmental factors, tends to temporarily unbalance or disrupt the homeostatic mechanisms that at rest normally maintain a constant internal environment. For example, in Section 5, we studied how particles move into and out of cells, how arterial blood oxygen content is regulated under high and low barometric pressures, and how body temperature is controlled under warm and cold environments.

In this section, we will study, first, how the hydrogen ion content (pH) of the internal environment is regulated at rest and during exercise (Chapter 21); second, how the endocrine system aids in the overall homeostatic regulation of the internal environment, again under resting and exercising conditions (Chapter 22); and third, what influence, if any, drugs and other so-called ergogenic aids have on these and other regulating mechanisms during exercise and athletic performance (Chapter 23).

SPECIAL CONSIDERATIONS

Exercise and Acid-Base Balance

The major concepts to be learned from this chapter are as follows:

- An acid is a chemical compound that in solution gives up hydrogen ions (H^+); a base is one that gives up hydroxyl ions (OH^-).
- A buffer system consists of a weak acid and the salt of that weak acid. The most common buffer system in the body consists of carbonic acid and sodium bicarbonate.
- The symbol "pH" refers to the power of the hydrogen ion and is equal to the negative log of the hydrogen ion concentration.
- The respiratory system aids in the regulation of the H^+ ion concentration by changing the rate and depth of ventilation.
- The kidney tubules help regulate the pH of the body fluids by regulation of the bicarbonate ion concentration.

- During heavy exercise of short duration, both muscle and blood pH decrease considerably.

As the internal environment (body fluids) becomes more acidic, muscles lose their contractility. During the metabolism of food, acid metabolites are released within the body; during exercise even more acid is produced. If acids were allowed to accumulate, serious illness and, finally, death would result. So, too, if tissue fluids become too basic (alkaline), illness and death would be consequential.

The body's maintenance of a proper acid-base internal environment occurs through three basic mechanisms:

1. Contained within the body fluids are chemicals called **buffers.** These sub-

stances react with the acids and bases to maintain a proper acid-base balance; a buffer dampens or diminishes the effect when either an acid or a base is added to the body fluids.

2. The **kidney** through a sensor system will excrete urine that is either acidic or basic in order to maintain the correct acid-base environment; and

3. The **respiratory mechanism** aids in regulating the acid-base balance by the amount of carbon dioxide retained or released.

Acids and Bases

An **acid** is a chemical compound that in solution gives up *hydrogen ions (H+);* a **base** is one that gives up *hydroxyl ions (OH−)* when placed in solution. For example:

ACIDS	BASES
$HCl \rightleftharpoons H^+ + Cl^-$ (hydrochloric acid)	$NaOH \rightleftharpoons Na^+ + OH^-$ (sodium hydroxide)
$H_2SO_4 \rightleftharpoons H^+ + SO_4^-$ (sulfuric acid)	$KOH \rightleftharpoons K^+ + OH^-$ (potassium hydroxide)

Strong acids give up relatively more H^+ ions than weak acids; strong bases release more OH^- ions than weak bases.

Aqueous (water) solutions contain both H^+ and OH^- ions. An acid solution contains more H^+ ions, whereas the basic solution contains more OH^- ions. Pure water is neutral since it contains an equal number of H^+ ions and OH^- ions:

$$H_2O \rightleftharpoons H^+ + OH^-$$

Consequently, the determinant regarding whether a solution is acidic or basic simply

amounts to *the concentration or number of H+ ions present.* If the number of H^+ ions exceeds the number of OH^- ions, then the solution is acidic; when the number of OH^- ions exceeds the number of H^+ ions, the solution is basic.

Buffers

A *buffer system* consists of two parts: (1) a weak acid and (2) the salt of that weak acid. Its primary purpose is to maintain a given H^+ ion concentration. Examples of buffers are acetic acid (weak acid) and sodium acetate (salt), carbonic acid (weak acid) and sodium bicarbonate (salt).

In the buffering game, an acid reacts with a salt, resulting in the formation of a stronger salt and a weaker acid. For example, lactic acid (LA) reacting with sodium bicarbonate ($NaHCO_3$) forms sodium lactate (NaLA) and carbonic acid (H_2CO_3):

$$LA + NaHCO_3 \rightarrow NaLA + H_2CO_3$$

In the blood, carbonic acid is weak, for it does not yield many H^+ ions; also carbonic acid dissociates into water and carbon dioxide, both of which can be readily excreted:

$$H_2CO_3 \rightleftharpoons H_2O + CO_2$$

Sodium bicarbonate ($NaHCO_3$) easily buffers the strong hydrochloric acid (HCl) with formation of a strong salt (NaCl) and a weak acid (H_2CO_3):

$$NaHCO_3 + HCl \rightarrow NaCl + H_2CO_3$$
$$\text{or}$$
$$\text{Bicarbonate + strong acid} \rightarrow \text{salt + weak acid}$$

Here, the excessive hydrogen ions dissociated from HCl are by and large removed from the solution in forming carbonic acid. Remember this acid is weak, for it does not dissociate as readily as HCl (i.e., it does not yield as many H⁺ ions).

Such a buffering system exemplifies the one way in which the body fluids do not become too acidic or basic.

pH (*Power of the Hydrogen Ion*)

To express alkalinity or acidity of a solution, one determines the number of H⁺ ions present. This resulting number is expressed as the pH of that solution or power of the hydrogen ion. Because of the small numbers with which we must deal (e.g., the number of moles* of hydrogen ions contained in 1 liter of water), the pH of a liquid is expressed as a negative logarithm to the base 10:

$$pH = -\log [H^+]$$

where [H⁺] equals grams of H⁺ ions present in one liter of solution.

The concentration of hydrogen ions in pure water is approximately 10^{-7} mole per liter (.0000007 mole per liter). Therefore:

$$
\begin{aligned}
pH &= -\log [10^{-7}] \\
&= -(-7) \text{ (the log of } 10^{-7} = -7) \\
&= \mathbf{7}
\end{aligned}
$$

The pH of pure water equals 7; a pH greater than 7 (fewer hydrogen ions) would be considered alkaline; a pH of 7, neutral; and a pH less than 7, acidic.

Adding an acid to a solution lowers its pH because the number of free hydrogen ions increases, while adding an alkali re-

duces the concentration of the H⁺ ions because the number of OH⁻ ions increases, hence increasing the pH.

The range of blood pH in the body compatible with life is between 7.0 and 7.7 during rest. Exercise will cause the muscle pH to shift toward the acid side; it may go as low as 6.4 to 6.6 during exhausting exercise.[3,4] Such a low pH is only transitory, for the body's buffering power including the kidney and respiratory systems will become operable and return the pH to normal.

In addition to the bicarbonate buffering system (e.g., sodium bicarbonate—$NaHCO_3$), there are the phosphate and protein buffering systems. All the systems work in a similar manner. The phosphate buffers (e.g., disodium phosphate—Na_2HPO_4) are concentrated in the kidneys, while the proteins (e.g., hemoglobin) are contained in the cells and plasma. Since most buffering is performed within the cells, the protein buffers are very important.

Respiratory Regulation of pH

As mentioned in Chapter 11, the respiratory area of the medulla oblongata in the brain and the chemoreceptors in the aortic arch are sensitive to changes in the hydrogen ion concentration of the blood. An increase in CO_2 within the body fluids (which combines with water to form carbonic acid) decreases the pH; elimination of CO_2 will cause the pH to rise. The increased H⁺ ion concentration stimulates the respiratory system, thus increasing ventilation (hyperventilation) and removing (blowing off) the CO_2. Conversely, a lowered H⁺ ion concentration will depress the respiratory mechanism. Alterations in the rate and depth of respiration, i.e., in alveolar ventilation, can immediately effect changes in body fluid pH. For example, as the blood pH falls below normal resting levels (7.4), respiration is strongly

---

*A mole is the amount of a substance with a weight equal to its molecular weight in grams. One mole of H_2O equals 18 gm. [H = 1; O = 16; therefore, $1 \times 2 + 16 = 18$.]

stimulated and hyperventilation occurs. As just mentioned, hyperventilation causes CO_2 to be eliminated, which in turn raises the body fluid pH. As shown in Figure 21-1, hyperventilation at a rate twice normal (rest), will cause the blood and body fluid pH to increase as much as 0.25 pH unit. On the other hand, when alveolar ventilation is reduced to one-half normal, such as is the case when the blood pH is above 7.4, the pH decreases by about 0.25 pH unit. At a blood pH of 7.2, ventilation increases fourfold; at a blood pH of 7.5, ventilation is reduced by about one half. The power of the respiratory buffering system is one to two times as great as that of all the chemical buffers discussed previously.[1]

Alkali Reserve

The degree to which the pH of the body fluids is affected by the buildup of carbon dioxide (CO_2), and subsequent formation of carbonic acid depends upon the amount of bicarbonate (HCO_3^-) available for the buffering operation. Actually, the pH of the

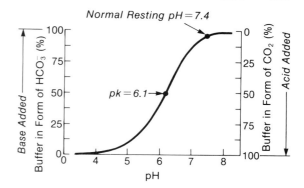

Figure 21-2. A buffer system. An increase in the concentration of HCO_3^- (bicarbonate) ion (base added) causes a rise in pH of the solution, and an increase in dissolved CO_2 (acid added) decreases the pH. (Modified and redrawn from Guyton.[1])

body fluids is related to *the ratio of the concentration of bicarbonate ions to the amount of dissolved carbon dioxide.* By formula:

$$pH = pK + \log \left[\frac{HCO_3^-}{CO_2} \right]$$

The abbreviation "pK" refers to a constant of a buffer, which for the bicarbonate buffer system is equal to 6.1 This means that when the concentration of HCO_3^- ions is equal to the amount of dissolved CO_2, the pH of the solution (in this case, the body fluids) will be 6.1.* Normally at rest, the ratio of HCO_3^- ions to CO_2 is 20:1, for a pH of 7.4. As shown in Figure 21-2, an increase in the concentration of HCO_3^- ions (base added) causes a rise in pH, while an increase in dissolved CO_2 (acid added) decreases the pH. In the body, the amount of bicarbonate ions available for buffering is called the **alkali reserve**.

Figure 21-1. Hyperventilation at a rate twice normal (rest) will cause the blood and body fluid pH to increase as much as 0.25 pH units. On the other hand, when alveolar ventilation is reduced to one-half normal, the pH decreases by about 0.25 pH units. (Modified and redrawn from Guyton.[1])

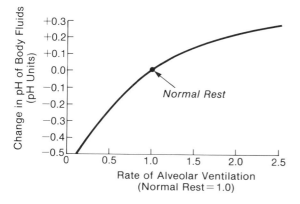

---

*When the concentrations of HCO_3^- ions and dissolved CO_2 are equal, the ratio HCO_3^-:$CO_2 = 1$; the log of $1 = 0$; therefore, pH = pK = 6.1.

Some have conjectured that by taking doses of bicarbonate to increase the alkali reserve, fatigue during heavy, prolonged work or athletic events would be forestalled. Hopefully, this would be brought about by the increased capacity to buffer lactic acid. While the research on this subject is not completely consistent, some studies have shown this to be true. More will be said about this in the last chapter (p. 641).

The Kidney and Acid-Base Balance

The kidney regulates the H^+ ion concentration through a complicated series of chemical reactions and active transport mechanisms. The principal way in which the kidney regulates the H^+ ion concentration is by increasing or decreasing the bicarbonate ion concentration.

The renal mechanism involved in regulating the bicarbonate ion concentration is shown schematically in Figure 21-3. The important steps in this mechanism are as follow:

1. Carbon dioxide from the extracellular fluids and from the epithelial cells of the kidney tubules combines with water (in the presence of the enzyme, carbonic anhydrase) to form carbonic acid ($CO_2 + H_2O \rightarrow H_2CO_3$) within the tubule cells.

2. As mentioned previously, carbonic acid dissociates into a bicarbonate ion (HCO_3^-) and a hydrogen ion (H^+). The H^+ ion is *actively transported or secreted* into the lumen of the kidney tubules and is eventually excreted in the urine as water. The HCO_3^- ion dif-

Figure 21-3. Renal mechanism for regulation of body fluid pH. The mechanism involves active transport or secretion of H^+ ions into the urine (center and right) and conservation of HCO_3^- ions (center and left). (Modified and redrawn from Guyton.[1])

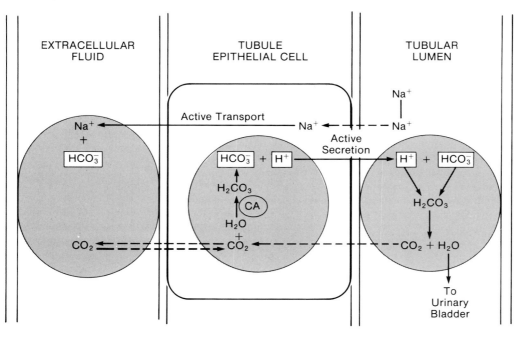

fuses into the extracellular fluid and is thus returned to the body, or conserved.

3. In the kidney tubular lumen, the secreted H^+ ions combine with bicarbonate ions that are also in the lumen to again form carbonic acid. The carbonic acid breaks down to CO_2 and H_2O. The CO_2 diffuses into the tubule cells and/or the extracellular fluid. The water, as mentioned previously, is excreted into the urine. It should also be pointed out that sodium ions (Na^+) in the tubule are conserved by active transport into the extracellular fluids. This exchange of Na^+ ions for H^+ ions maintains electrical balance between the tubular and extracellular fluids.

It is interesting to note that the HCO_3^- ions found in the tubular lumen fluid are not the same ions that are conserved in the extracellular fluid (Fig. 21-3). In other words, the bicarbonate ion concentration is regulated more or less indirectly through the amount of hydrogen ions secreted by the kidney tubules and by the amount of CO_2 metabolically produced. Also, it requires several hours, maybe 10 to 20 hours, for the kidneys to respond effectively in regulating the bicarbonate ion concentration.

Alkalosis and Acidosis

When there are excessive bicarbonate ions in the extracellular fluids, the condition is called alkalosis. These ions enter the tubules and pass on into the urine accompanied by sodium or some other positive ion (e.g., potassium or K^+). Removal of bicarbonate ions from the extracellular fluid shifts the pH toward the acidic side.

When there is an increase in CO_2 in the extracellular fluid, acidosis occurs. In this case there is an excessive number of hydrogen ions being secreted in the tubules;

these combine with the tubular buffers and are then excreted in the urine.

Acid-Base Balance Following Heavy Exercise

During maximal exercise of short duration, large changes occur in the acid-base metabolic chemistry caused primarily by the production of lactic acid. Anaerobic work, which produces lactic acid, causes the blood and muscle pH to decrease. The amount of lactic acid produced depends upon: (1) the amount of time, (2) the work intensity, and (3) the muscle mass involved.[2] Within minutes during continuous anaerobic work, lactic acid levels may approximate 180 mg%, with blood pH values nearing 7.0 and muscle pH nearing 6.4.[4] Intermittent work may cause the blood pH to reach 6.80 (one of the lowest values ever recorded) with lactic acid values around 280 mg%.[3]

These values are excessive when one considers that during rest a blood pH of less than 7.4 indicates acidosis, while a blood pH greater than 7.4 indicates alkalosis. The lower limit of blood pH compatible with life (not exercising) for a few minutes is 7.0 and the upper limit about 7.7.[1]

The plasma bicarbonate concentration (normal values 23 to 28 millimoles (mM/liter—women lower than men) has been recorded as low as 2.6 mM/liter. Figure 21-4 illustrates the relationship of blood pH, blood lactate concentration, and plasma bicarbonate following exhaustive work from data by Osnes and Hermansen.[3]

Figure 21-5A illustrates the relationship between blood pH and blood lactate concentration as a consequence of brief, strenuous exercise. Note that the blood pH values decline toward 6.80 as the blood lactic acid increases to 288 mg%. These are the lowest and highest values, respectively, ever recorded. Figure 21-5B shows the rela-

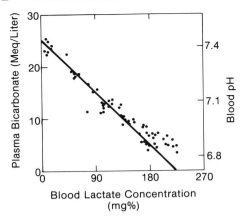

Figure 21-4. Relationship between blood pH, blood lactate (lactic acid), and plasma bicarbonate following exhausting exercise. (Based on data from Osnes and Hermansen.[3])

tionship between muscle pH and muscle lactic acid and pyruvic acid concentrations. Notice that four subjects had muscle pH values below 6.6, whereas one subject had a pH of 6.4! These, too, are the lowest values ever recorded during exercise.

Summary

An acid is a chemical compound that in solution gives up hydrogen ions (H^+); a base is one that gives up hydroxyl ions (OH^-). When the concentration of H^+ ions exceeds the concentration of OH^- ions, the solution is acidic; when the concentration of OH^- ions exceeds the concentration of H^+ ions, the solution is basic.

A buffer system consists of a weak acid and the salt of that weak acid. The most common buffer system in the body consists of carbonic acid (H_2CO_3, a weak acid) and sodium bicarbonate ($NaHCO_3$, salt of the weak acid). The amount of bicarbonate ion (HCO_3^-) available for buffering is called the alkali reserve.

The symbol "pH" refers to the power (concentration) of the hydrogen ion in solu-

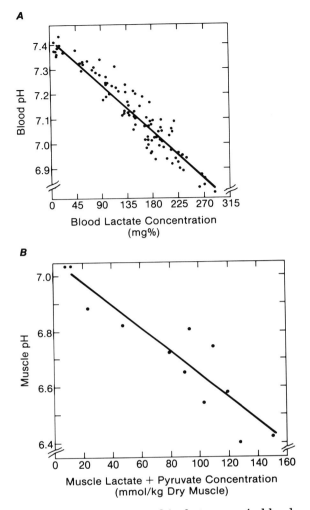

Figure 21-5. Relationship between, *A*, blood pH and, *B*, muscle pH and blood lactic acid concentration as a consequence of brief, exhausting exercise. Note that the blood pH values decline toward 6.8 and the muscle pH toward 6.4 as the blood lactic acid increases to 288 mg%. (Data in *A* from Osnes and Hermansen[3] and data in *B* from Sahlin et al.[4])

tion and is equal to the negative log of the hydrogen ion concentration (pH = −log [H^+]). A solution with a pH below 7.0 is considered acidic, whereas a pH above 7.0 is considered basic.

The respiratory system aids in the regulation of the H^+ ion concentration by changing the rate and depth of ventilation. When body fluid pH increases, ventilation decreases, retaining CO_2, and when body fluid pH decreases, ventilation increases (hyperventilation), blowing off CO_2.

The kidney tubules help regulate the pH of the body fluids by regulating the bicarbonate ion concentration in the body. They do this indirectly by secretion of H^+ ions into the lumen of the tubules.

Immediately following heavy exercise of short duration, both muscle and blood pH can drop to well below 7.0, while the lactic acid concentration in muscle and blood can rise to very high levels (close to 300 mg% in blood). At the same time, the plasma bicarbonate concentration may fall as low as 2.6 mM/L (normal rest = 25 mM/L).

Questions

1. Define an acid; a base.
2. Describe how a buffer works.
3. What is meant by the power of the hydrogen ion (pH)?
4. Explain how respiration aids in regulating acid-base balance.
5. What is the alkali reserve?
6. Explain the kidney's function in acid-base regulation.
7. Immediately following heavy exercise of short duration, what happens to the following: blood and muscle pH, plasma bicarbonate, and blood lactate?

References

1. Guyton, A. C.: *Textbook of Medical Physiology,* 5th ed. Philadelphia, W. B. Saunders, 1976.
2. Hermansen, L.: Lactate production during exercise. In Pernow, B., and Saltin, B. (eds.): *Muscle Metabolism during Exercise.* New York, Plenum Press, 1971, pp. 401–407.
3. Osnes, J., and Hermansen, L.: Acid-base balance after maximal exercise of short duration. *J Appl Physiol.* 32(1):59–63, 1972.
4. Sahlin, K., Harris, R. C., Nylind, B., and Hultman, E.: Lactate content and pH in muscle samples obtained after dynamic exercise. *Pflügers Arch.* 367:143–149, 1976.

SELECTED READINGS

Davenport, H.: *The ABC of Acid-Base Chemistry,* 4th ed. Chicago, The University of Chicago Press, 1958.

Guyton, A. C.: *Textbook of Medical Physiology,* 5th ed. Philadelphia, W. B. Saunders, 1976, pp. 485–500.

Hills, A. G.: *Acid-Base Balance.* Baltimore, Williams and Wilkins, 1973.

Jones, N. L., Sutton, J. E., Taylor, R., and Toews, C. J.: Effect of pH on cardiorespiratory and metabolic responses to exercise. *J Appl Physiol.* 43(6):959–964, 1977.

Sahlin, K., Alvestrand, A., Brandt, R., and Hultman, E.: Acid-base balance in blood during exhaustive bicycle exercise and the following recovery period. *Acta Physiol Scand.* 104:370–372, 1978.

Exercise and the Endocrine System

The major concepts to be learned from this chapter are as follows:

- A hormone is a chemical substance secreted into the body fluids by an endocrine gland and has a specific effect on the activities of other organs.
- An endocrine gland is ductless and secretes a hormone directly into the blood or lymph.
- The predominant hormonal control system is the negative feedback mechanism. In this mechanism, the secretion of the hormone is turned off or decreased due to the end result of the response caused by that hormone.
- Exercise and training have an effect on blood levels of most hormones.

As mentioned in the introduction to this section, the internal environment in which all cells function must be precisely regulated with respect to content, temperature, and hydrogen ion concentration. Such a task is indeed difficult, requiring many homeostatic mechanisms, some of which have already been mentioned.

However, there are two major control systems around which all homeostatic mechanisms function: (1) the nervous system, some functions of which have already been presented in other parts of this book; and (2) the *endocrine system,* a system, which by way of chemical substances called *hormones* controls specific cellular functions and responses. The purpose of this chapter will be to describe the hormonal or endocrine system with respect to maintenance of homeostasis during both resting and exercising conditions. The impact of training on circulating blood levels of selected hormones also will be considered.

Characteristics of Hormone Action

A **hormone** can be defined as a discrete chemical substance secreted into the body fluids by an endocrine gland and that has a specific effect on the activities of other cells, tissues, and organs. The cell, tissue, or organ upon which a hormone has an effect is called a **target cell, or target tissue, or target organ,** respectively.

The **endocrine glands** are ductless and are composed of epithelial cells in which hormones are manufactured or stored. Because the hormone is secreted directly into the blood or lymph, the endocrine glands are referred to as *glands of internal secretion.*

As just mentioned, hormones cause a specific effect on the activities of target organs. This effect, which may require minutes or hours to occur, is brought about mainly by increasing or decreasing an ongoing cellular process rather than by initiating a new one. For example, hormones may[17]: (1) activate enzyme systems, (2) alter cell membrane permeability, (3) cause muscular contraction or relaxation, (4) stimu-late protein synthesis, or (5) cause cellular secretion.

Three general characteristics of hormone action that need to be discussed are (1) specificity of hormone action, (2) physiological mechanisms of hormone action and (3) control of hormone secretion.

Specificity of Hormone Action

Although some hormones have an effect on all tissues of the body, most have an effect only on a *specific* target organ. This specificity is accomplished by the presence of a specific **hormone receptor** located within the cell membrane of the target organ. As shown in Figure 22-1, the receptor is specific to and can react with only one hormone. It is analogous to a lock and key; only a specific key (hormone) will fit the lock (receptor), thus opening the way for a given action. Hormones may be so specific that they affect only a specific part of an organ or tissue. For example, antidi-

Figure 22-1. Specificity of hormone action is accomplished by the presence of a specific hormone receptor ("lock") located within the cell membrane of the target organ. The receptor is specific to and can react only with one hormone ("key").

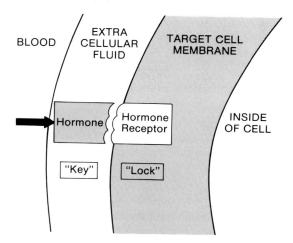

uretic hormone (ADH) affects cells of the collecting tubules in the kidney, but not those of the ascending limb of the loop of Henle.

It is thought that hormones that cause an effect on all the tissues of the body also work by the receptor mechanism. However, in this case, the receptor is more general and widespread so that all the cells have them. Examples are the receptors for thyroxin and growth hormone.

Mechanisms of Hormone Action

Physiologically, how does a hormone cause an effect on a cell? There are many different physiological mechanisms of hormonal action. However, the most common mechanism of action of the majority of hormones is the **cyclic AMP mechanism.** AMP is an abbreviation for adenosine monophosphate, a compound similar to ATP. Because it is involved in the mechanism of action of so many hormones, it is often referred to as a *messenger for hormone mediation.*

The cyclic AMP mechanism is shown schematically in Figure 22-2. A hormone, upon reaching the cell via the blood, interacts with its specific receptor located within the cell membrane. This interaction activates an enzyme called *adenyl cyclase,* which is also located within the cell membrane. In turn, the activated adenyl cyclase causes cyclic AMP to be formed from ATP, which is located inside the cell in the cytoplasm. Once cyclic AMP is formed, one or more of the physiological responses mentioned before can occur (Fig. 22-2). The response ceases when cyclic AMP is destroyed. The particular response that occurs depends on the type of cell itself. For example, thyroid cells stimulated by cyclic AMP form thyroid hormone, whereas epithelial cells of the renal tubules are affected by cyclic AMP by increasing their permeability to water. Also, several hormones may

Figure 22-2. The cyclic AMP mechanism of hormone action. A hormone, upon reaching the cell via the blood, interacts with its specific receptor located within the cell membrane. This interaction activates an enzyme called adenyl cyclase, which is also located with the membrane. The activated adenyl cyclase causes cyclic AMP to be formed from ATP, which is located inside the cell. Once cyclic AMP is formed, physiological responses can occur. (Modified and redrawn from Guyton.[17])

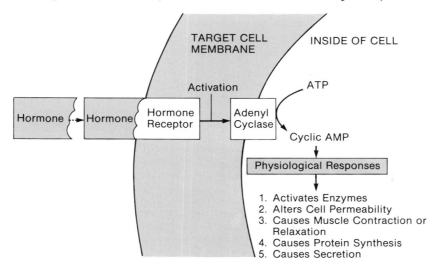

cause the same response in a given cell. Fat cells, for instance, can be stimulated through the cyclic AMP mechanism to break down triglycerides by the hormones epinephrine, norepinephrine, adrenocorticotropic hormone, and glucagon.

It is thought that cyclic AMP is not the only type of intracellular hormone mediator. Other such substances might include: (1) *prostaglandins,* a series of lipid compounds present in most cells throughout the body; and (2) a compound called *cyclic guanosine monophosphate,* which is similar to cyclic AMP. In addition, the intracellular hormone mediator mechanism is not the only mechanism whereby hormones can elicit a cellular effect. For example, insulin causes a direct effect on the permeability of cell membranes to glucose, whereas the catecholamine hormones cause a direct effect on membrane permeability to various ions.

Control of Hormone Secretion

Because hormones have a precise effect on cellular function, their secretion must also be precisely controlled. How is this accomplished? Again, several control systems exist. One of these is the nervous system. However, the predominant hormonal control system is the **negative feedback mechanism.** This mechanism was mentioned earlier in the control of the cardiorespiratory system (p. 274) and in body temperature regulation (p. 488). Basically, in this mechanism, the secretion of the hormone is turned off or decreased due to the end result of the response caused by that hormone.

An example of this is illustrated in Figure 22-3. An increase in blood glucose concentration stimulates the pancreas to secrete the hormone insulin. Insulin causes an increase in cellular glucose uptake, which decreases the blood glucose concentration. This decrease in blood glucose

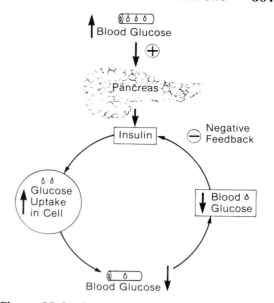

Figure 22-3. An example of negative feedback control of hormone secretion. An increase in blood glucose concentration stimulates the pancreas to secrete the hormone insulin. Insulin causes an increase in cellular glucose uptake which decreases the blood glucose concentration. This decrease in blood glucose "feeds back" to the pancreas, having a negative (decreased) effect on the secretion of insulin.

"feeds back" to the pancreas, having a "negative" (decreased) effect on the secretion of insulin (hence, the term "negative feedback"). In other words, the end result of the action of insulin (decreased blood glucose) causes its secretion to be turned off or reduced.

While this is a relatively simple example, some hormones are controlled by a more complex version of the negative feedback mechanism. The secretion of thyroxin from the thyroid gland, for instance, is stimulated by another hormone called thyroid-stimulating hormone or TSH from the anterior pituitary gland. The negative feedback in this case is provided by the level of thyroxin in the blood. When it is high, secretion of TSH is reduced; when it is low, TSH secretion is increased. In still other feedback systems, several endocrine glands and their hormones might be involved.

As mentioned previously, the nervous system is also involved in the control of hormone secretion. For example, epinephrine and norepinephrine from the adrenal medulla are secreted in direct response to stimulation by the sympathetic nervous system. The release of antidiuretic hormone (ADH) from the posterior pituitary gland is also under control from the brain. Actually, the control of hormone secretion by the nervous system is not surprising. These two systems must, and do, work together to bring about the precise regulation necessary for maintenance of homeostatic function.

The Hormones and Their Glands

Table 22-1 contains a list of hormones, their origin or endocrine gland, their stimulating factors, their target organs, and a brief description of their actions. The following features in the table should be noted.

The Pituitary Gland, or Hypophysis

The **pituitary gland,** also called the **hypophysis,** releases many hormones. The pituitary gland is an extremely small gland located at the base of the brain and is connected to the hypothalamus (Fig. 22-4). Physiologically, it has two distinctive lobes, each of which secretes specific hormones.

1. The **posterior lobe,** also referred to as the **neurohypophysis** (because of its direct connection with the hypothalamus of the brain), is responsible for the secretion of *antidiuretic hormone (ADH),* or *vasopressin,* that functions mainly to promote water reabsorption from the collecting tubules of the kidney. The other hormone se-

creted from the neurohypophysis is *oxytocin.* Its main functions are stimulation of milk ejection and contraction of the pregnant uterus.

2. The **anterior lobe,** also called the **adenohypophysis,** secretes the following hormones: (a) *growth hormone (GH),* or *somatotropin (STH),* which stimulates growth and development; (b) *thyroid-stimulating hormone (TSH),* which stimulates production and release of the thyroid hormones; (c) *adrenocorticotropic hormone (ACTH),* or *corticotropin,* which stimulates the production and release of the glucocorticoid hormones from the adrenal cortex; (d) *follicle-stimulating hormone (FSH),* which promotes growth of the ovarian follicle in the female and spermatogenesis in the male; (e) *luteinizing hormone (LH),* or *lutropin,* which stimulates ovulation, formation of the corpus luteum, and hormone secretion in the female, and stimulates secretion of interstitial cells in the male; (f) *prolactin (PRL),* which stimulates secretion of milk after pregnancy; and endorphins, which are related to relief of pain and production of euphoria.

As may be seen, the pituitary gland is a very important endocrine gland and because of its many hormones, it is sometimes referred to as the "master" gland. This title might be challenged from the perspective of the hypothalamus. After all, it produces releasing factors and "hormones" that stimulate or inhibit the release of all hormones produced by the adenohypophysis except for the endorphins. For the most part, tagging **releasing factor** or **releasing hormone** onto the hormone name or abbreviation describes these hypothalamic substances. For example, GH, TSH, ACTH, FSH, LH, and PRL releasing factors. Note, however, that growth hor-

TABLE 22–1

A Summary of Endocrine Systems and Their Functions*

Hormone	Origin or Endocrine Gland	Stimulating Factors	Target Organ	Action
Oxytocin	Neurohypophysis (posterior pituitary)	Neural influence ?	Mammary gland, uterus	Milk production, feeding young, contraction of pregnant uterus
Antidiuretic hormone (ADH) (also called vasopressin)	Neurohypophysis (hypothalamus)	↓ Blood volume, hypertonic plasma	Kidney, vascular smooth muscle	Water retention, possibly vasoconstriction during hemorrhage
Growth hormone (GH)	Adenohypophysis (anterior pituitary)	Neural influence: generalized stress	All cells	Growth and development, free fatty acid release
Thyroid-stimulating hormone (TSH)	Adenohypophysis	Neural influence: ↓ blood thyroxin	Thyroid gland	Production and release of the thyroid hormones
Thyroxin (T_4) Triiodothyronine (T_3)	Thyroid	TSH	All tissues	↑ Basal metabolic rate, necessary for normal growth and development, lipid metabolism
Adrenocorticotropic hormone (ACTH) (also called corticotropin)	Adenohypophysis	Neural influence: generalized stress	Adrenal cortex	Production and release of the glucocorticoids (e.g., cortisol)
Glucocorticoids (cortisol)	Adrenal cortex	ACTH, generalized stress	Liver, all tissues	Promotes gluconeogenesis, muscle protein breakdown, anti-inflammatory
Mineralocorticoids (aldosterone)	Adrenal cortex	↓ Blood Na^+	Kidney	Na^+ retention
Luteinizing hormone (LH)	Adenohypophysis	Neural influence: stimulated by estrogen, inhibited by progesterone	Male: testis Female: ovary	Androgen production Estrogen production, follicular development

TABLE 22-1

A Summary of Endocrine Systems and Their Functions* (*Continued*)

Hormone	Origin or Endocrine Gland	Stimulating Factors	Target Organ	Action
Prolactin [also called lactogenic or luteotropic hormone (LTH)]	Adenohypophysis	Neural influence: estrogen and progesterone stimulates	Mammary gland	Secretion of milk after pregnancy
Follicle-stimulating hormone (FSH)	Adenohypophysis	Neural influence: ↓ estrogen stimulates ↑ estrogen inhibits	Male: testis Female: ovary	Spermatogenesis, follicular development
Estrogens (estradiol)	Ovary, placenta	LH	Uterus, mammary gland, others	Uterine development, secondary sex characteristics, Ca^{++} and Na^+ retention
Progesterone	Ovary, placenta	Dependent on LH, FSH	Uterus, mammary gland	Uterine development, mammary gland growth
Androgens (testosterone)	Testes Adrenal cortex	LH —	Seminal vesicles, prostate, muscle, bone	Supports spermatogenesis, secondary sex characteristics, general anabolic function
Parathyroid hormone (PTH)	Parathyroid	↓ Blood Ca^{++}	Bone, kidney	Increases blood Ca^{++} level, enhances Ca^{++} reabsorption
Calcitonin	Thyroid C-cells	↑ Blood Ca^{++}	Bone	Decreases blood Ca^{++} level

Hormone	Source	Stimulus	Target tissue	Effect
Insulin	Pancreas β-cells	↑ Blood glucose	All tissues	Decreases blood glucose, increases fat deposition, is protein anabolic
Glucagon	Pancreas α-cells	↓ Blood glucose ↑ Blood amino acids	Liver, other tissue	Increases blood glucose, is gluconeogenic, glycogenolytic, lipolytic
Epinephrine Norepinephrine	Adrenal medulla Sympathetic nerve endings	Sympathetic activation	All tissues	Increase blood glucose, free fatty acid mobilization, enhanced cardiac performance, vasomotor control
Erythropoietin	Kidney, other tissues?	Hypoxia	Bone marrow	Promotes red blood cell production
Endorphins	Adenohypophysis	Neural influence(?)	Brain	Pain relief, euphoric state
Prostaglandins	Blood vessels, muscles, heart, other tissues	Metabolic influence(?)	Blood vessels, heart	Blood flow regulation, primarily via vasodilation
Somatomedins	Liver, other tissues	Growth hormone, other influence(?)	Muscles, cartilage	Growth of muscle and connective tissue

*Modified from Terjung.[53]

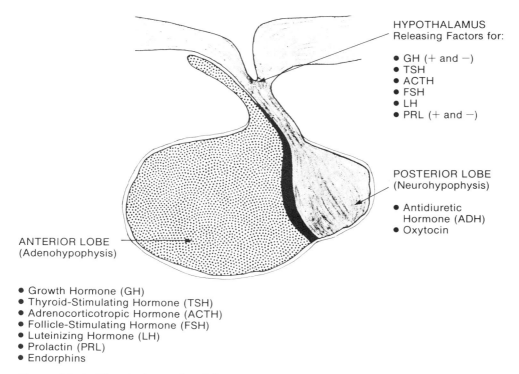

Figure 22-4. The pituitary gland (hypophysis) has two distinct lobes, each of which secretes specific hormones—the posterior lobe, also referred to as the neurohypophysis, and the anterior lobe, also called the adenohypophysis. Note the close proximity of the hypothalamus, which produces releasing factors and "hormones," which regulate the release of the majority of hormones from the adenohypophysis. The pituitary gland is sometimes called the "master gland" because of its control over the secretion of hormones by various endocrine glands located throughout the body.

mone and prolactin also have hypothalamic factors that inhibit their release. These are appropriately named growth hormone release inhibiting hormone (GHRIH) or **somatostatin** and prolactin inhibiting factor (PIF) or **prolactostatin.** The presence of hypothalamic releasing and inhibiting factors is shown with positive and negative signs in Figure 22-4. Once again, a perfect example of the tightly coupled workings of the neural and endocrine systems as they function jointly to regulate and control physiological functions throughout the organism.

The Adrenal Glands

The adrenal glands, as their name implies, sit on top of the kidneys. Physiologically, the adrenal gland is really two separate endocrine glands, the *adrenal medulla,* or inner portion of the gland; and the *adrenal cortex,* or outer portion.

1. The **adrenal medulla** is similar to and under the direct influence of the sympathetic nervous system. Its hormones are also similar to the nervous system in that they secrete *epineph-*

rine and *norepinephrine.* * These two hormones are referred to as *catecholamines*. The catecholamines are the type of hormones referred to earlier that have effects on all the tissues of the body. A comparison of the physiological effects of epinephrine and norepinephrine in the human is given in Table 22-2.

2. The **adrenal cortex** secretes some 40 hormones that belong to the class of compounds known as *steroids*. They are divided into the following three groups on the basis of their major actions.

(a) The **mineralocorticoids** primarily affect electrolyte metabolism. The most important mineralocorticoid is *aldosterone,* which functions to increase the reabsorption

of sodium from the distal tubules of the kidney. This, in turn, causes the reabsorption of chloride and water.

(b) The **glucocorticoids,** although named because of their effects on glucose metabolism, also have an effect on protein and fat metabolism. The most important glucocorticoid is *cortisol.* The glucocorticoids (principally cortisol) promote the increased synthesis of glucose (gluconeogenesis) from amino acids, depress liver lipogenesis, and mobilize fat in adipose tissues. Two other effects of cortisol are maintenance of vascular reactivity (without cortisol, the blood vessels are unable to respond to circulating catecholamines) and inhibition of the inflammatory reaction, the normal response of tissues to injury. Because of this latter action, glucocorticoids are

---

*Norepinephrine is the neurotransmitter substance released at the ends of the sympathetic postganglionic fibers of the autonomic nervous system.

TABLE 22-2

Comparison of Epinephrine and Norepinephrine in Humans*

Parameter	Epinephrine	Norepinephrine
Heart		
Heart rate	+	−
Force of contraction	+++	0,−
Cardiac output	+++	− −
Vascular effects		
Mean arterial pressure	+	+++
Systolic pressure	++	+++
Diastolic pressure	+,0,−	++
Total peripheral resistance	−	++
Metabolic effects		
Hyperglycemia	+++	0,+
Heat production	++	0,+
Blood lactic acid (result of glucose utilization)	+++	0,+
Free fatty acid mobilization	+++	0
Central nervous system stimulation	+++	+++

+ = increase; 0 = no change; − = decrease.

*Modified from Landau.[28]

often administered in massive pharmacological doses as anti-inflammatory steroids.

(c) The **androgens** cause development of male secondary sex characteristics. Androgens are also secreted by the testes. The most important androgen is *testosterone*. The female counterpart to the androgens are the **estrogens.** The effects of oral ingestion of androgens by some athletes for the sole purpose of improving athletic performance are discussed in the next chapter (p. 636).

The Pancreas

The two major hormones secreted by the **pancreas** are **insulin** and **glucagon.** Both of these hormones are secreted by the cells of the *islets of Langerhans,* insulin from the beta cells and glucagon from the alpha cells. Insulin is *hypoglycemic,* i.e., it lowers the blood glucose levels. It does this by increasing the rate of glucose transport through the membranes of most cells in the body. The mechanism of this process was discussed earlier in Chapter 16. Essentially, insulin stimulates the process of facilitated diffusion of glucose (see Fig. 16-3, p. 452). Aside from its effects on cellular glucose uptake, insulin increases fat deposition in the adipocytes (fat cells). A lack of insulin results in *diabetes mellitus.*

Glucagon has effects that are the opposite of insulin. Therefore, secretion of glucagon causes increased blood glucose levels. Glucagon has two major effects on carbohydrate or glucose metabolism; (1) *glycogenolysis,* or the breakdown of glycogen; and (2) increased *gluconeogenesis,* or the synthesis of glucose from molecules which are not themselves carbohydrates, such as protein or fat.

The Thyroid Gland

The **thyroid gland** is located on the upper part of the trachea just below the larynx (voice box). Its principal hormones are **thyroxin** and **triiodothyronine,** although it also secretes a hormone called **calcitonin.** Both thyroxin and triiodothyronine require small amounts of iodine (1 mg per week) for their formation. To prevent iodine deficiency, common table salt is iodized. The release of thyroxin and triiodothyronine is controlled by the thyroid-stimulating hormone (TSH) secreted from the adenohypophysis.

The major action of the thyroid hormones is a general increase in the metabolic rate. Some specific functions associated with this increased metabolism are (1) an increased protein synthesis making the thyroid hormones necessary for normal growth and development in the young; (2) an increased quantity of intracellular enzymes; (3) an increased size and number of mitochondria; (4) an increased cellular uptake of glucose, and enhanced glycolysis and gluconeogenesis; and (5) an increased mobilization and oxidation of free fatty acids.

Calcitonin causes a decrease in the blood calcium level. This hormone works in conjunction with the parathyroid hormone, which will be discussed next.

The Parathyroid Glands

The **parathyroid glands** are tiny glands embedded in the dorsal surface of the thyroid gland. **Parathyroid hormone (PTH)** is the hormone they secrete. This hormone, together with calcitonin, regulates the calcium equilibrium in the body. PTH causes more calcium to be absorbed from the digestive tract; therefore, less calcium is lost through the feces and urine. This, along with its action of removing calcium from the bone, causes an increase in the blood calcium level. Calcitonin acts in the opposite way from PTH, i.e., it causes a decrease in blood calcium levels by preventing the removal of calcium from the bone.

The Ovaries and the Testes

As endocrine glands, the **ovaries** (female), and the **testes** (male) produce the sex hormones, **androgens** in the male and **estrogens (estradiol)** and **progesterone** in the female. The most important androgen is **testosterone.** You may recall that the production and release of the sex hormones are under the control of luteinizing hormone (LH) from the adenohypophysis. The androgens promote secondary sex characteristics, and are recognized as promoting protein anabolism (synthesis) and reducing protein catabolism (breakdown). As will be pointed out in the next chapter, excessive dosages of anabolic steroids cause harmful side effects.

Estrogens from the ovaries have actions in the female comparable to those of androgens in the male. They are responsible for the development and function of the uterus, uterine tubes, and vagina and promote the secondary sex characteristics of the female. The estrogens and progesterone work, along with FSH and LH, to regulate the menstrual cycles of women. In addition, as mentioned in Chapter 15 (p. 423), estrogens are thought to provide protection against atherosclerosis and thus coronary heart disease.

Progesterone is secreted in large quantities only after ovulation. It promotes further development of the uterus and mammary glands.

Other Production Sites

A few substances with hormone-like qualities are produced by various tissues of the body other than the endocrine glands. For example, under hypoxic conditions, the kidney synthesizes **erythropoietin,** which in turn stimulates bone marrow to increase production of red blood cells. Since erythropoietin is produced at one location and is carried via the blood to a second location where it exerts its biological effect, it meets most of the definitional qualifications for a hormone. Likewise, **prostaglandins** are produced by a variety of body tissues including the blood vessels, skeletal muscles, and the heart. Prostaglandins vary in their makeup and actions but primarily influence blood flow regulation through their ability to produce vasodilation. Finally, the **somatomedins** are a class of substances produced by the liver and several other tissues. These substances stimulate the growth of muscle and cartilage through a turn on of various phases of protein synthesis. The somatomedins themselves are comprised of amino acid chains that are produced as a result of increased growth hormone release from the adenohypophysis. Consequently, they are often viewed as factors that support growth hormone action rather than as hormones in their own right.

Hormonal Responses to Exercise and Training

Exercise and training cause blood levels of some of the hormones previously mentioned to either increase or decrease in comparison to resting values. The increases or decreases often directly reflect adjustments in the rate of hormone secretion by an endocrine gland. You should be aware, however, that changes in blood levels also may reflect changes in metabolic turnover rates or clearance rates and hemoconcentration effects. For example, an increase in the circulating plasma concentration (level) of a given hormone during exercise might be due to an increased rate of secretion, a reduced turnover or clearance of the hormone, a reduction in plasma volume due to water losses in sweat, or a combination of one or more of these factors. Current research techniques allow rather precise explanations for observed changes in circulating hormone levels.

Although the physiological significance of many of these changes is not presently known, the fact that they even respond to exercise is in itself significant. The following is a brief review of the effects of exercise and training on hormonal responses. Excellent in-depth reviews of this topic have been written by Métivier[34] and by Terjung.[55]

Growth Hormone (GH)

Growth hormone (GH) secreted from the adenohypophysis, increases in the blood during exercise, being more pronounced the greater the exercise intensity.[16,20,21,30,48,51] There is some evidence that the increases may be due to increases in body temperature rather than the effects of the exercise per se.[5] An example of the response of growth hormone is shown in Figure 22-5. In this study,[51] exercise was performed for 20 minutes on a bicycle ergometer. Notice that with light exercise loads (e.g., 300 kg-m/min), there was no increase in the concentration of growth hormone in the blood. However, at a workload of 900 kg-m/min, the peak increase in growth hormone was about 35 times the resting value. Although not shown in the figure, growth hormone does not immediately increase during exercise, but rather gradually increases with time. This finding refutes the idea that an increased release of growth hormone during exercise plays a significant role in free fatty acid mobilization and metabolism.

The response of growth hormone to exercise appears to be related to the fitness level of the individual.[21,44,52] This is demonstrable in two ways: (1) there is a lesser increase in growth hormone during exercise of the same intensity in the trained

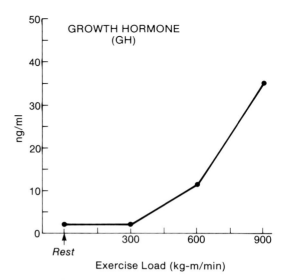

Figure 22-5. Response of growth hormone (GH) to bicycle exercise. Notice that with light loads, blood levels of GH do not increase. However, with higher loads, GH increases substantially. (Based on data from Sutton and Lazarus.[51])

individual than in the untrained and (2) the decrease in growth hormone following exhaustive exercise is faster in the trained than in the untrained individual. Although the significance of these differences between trained and untrained individuals is not known exactly, it has been suggested that chronic physical training establishes a difference in the control processes of growth hormone.[53]

An excellent review of the effects of exercise and training on the response of growth hormone has been written by Shephard and Sidney.[48]

Thyroid and Parathyroid Hormones

The intensity and duration of exercise apparently has considerable influence over whether circulating levels of thyroid hormones will be altered during activity. For example, swimming 0.18 to 0.9 kilometers or pedalling a bicycle ergometer for 90 minutes at a moderate intensity had no effect on thyroid hormone concentrations that could not be explained by hemoconcentration effects.[42] Likewise, neither prolonged submaximal or short-term maximal exercise produced any consistent pattern of change in circulating levels of thyroid hormones.[45] Serum concentrations of thyroid hormones also were unaffected by prolonged submaximal exercise in the form of a 9-hour, 37-kilometer march.[56]

The thyroid hormones, thyroxin and triiodothyronine, are increased during prolonged strenuous exercise,[43] as is shown in Figure 22-6. Blood levels of thyroid-stimulating hormone (TSH) are also shown in the figure. In this study, the exercise consisted of a 70-kilometer (43.4 miles) cross-country ski race, which required between 5 and 7½ hours to complete. The most interesting change is not the fact that both thyroxin and triiodothyronine increased during the race, but that they were actually below their prerace levels for several days after the race. This, coupled with postrace elevations of TSH, reflects obvious deviations in the ordinary balance between secretion, distribution, and removal of the individual hormones.

There is considerable conflict concerning TSH changes with exercise. There is evidence that at low submaximal workloads, TSH does not change either during exercise or within the subsequent 24

hours.[54] These findings have been confirmed for bicycle ergometry exercise at 15, 30, and 40% of maximal work capacity.[16] Other studies indicate a continuous rise in TSH levels during and up to 15 minutes after prolonged submaximal exercise but a decrease during maximal exercise.[45] Nevertheless, the most probable physiological explanation for observed changes in thyroid hormones with heavy exercise is as follows:[43]

1. The prolonged and marked rise in blood levels of TSH is most probably

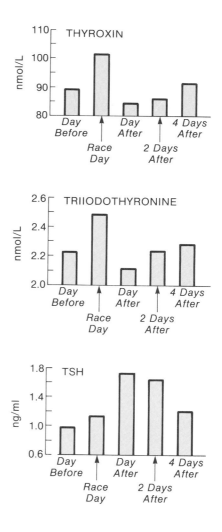

Figure 22-6. Thyroxin, triiodothyronine, and thyroid-stimulating hormone (TSH) before, during, and after a 70-kilometer (43.4 miles) cross-country ski race. The most interesting change is not the fact that both thyroxin and triiodothyronine increased during prolonged strenuous, exercise, but that they were actually below their pre-race levels for several days after the race. (Based on data from Refsum and Strömme.[43])

due to a persistent peripheral deficit in thyroid hormone caused by exercise. This stimulates TSH release from the adenohypophysis.

2. The increase in thyroxin and triiodothyronine at the end of exercise may be due to an early TSH-induced release of these hormones, whereas the subsequent decrease following exercise of thyroxin and triiodothyronine may be due to an inability of the thyroid gland to meet the enhanced cellular demands for these hormones. This results in the marked rise in TSH observed in the first few days following exercise (Fig. 22-6).

Incidentally, another interesting finding concerning the response of the thyroid hormones to exercise is that they are similar in magnitude to those found in many hyperthyroid patients.[53] However, the hormonal levels in response to exercise are not accompanied by any clinical signs of hyperthyroidism. Signs of hyperthyroidism include increased basal metabolic rate, intolerance to heat, increased sweating, weight loss, diarrhea, weakness, fatigue, nervousness, and insomnia.

Little is known concerning the responses of parathyroid hormone and calcitonin to exercise or physical training. One study of six normal men before, during, and after maximal treadmill exercise (Bruce protocol) indicated no change in PTH levels.[57]

Antidiuretic Hormone (ADH) and Aldosterone

It should be recalled that antidiuretic hormone (ADH) is a hormone released from the neurohypophysis and that aldosterone is a mineralocorticoid released from the adrenal cortex. Both of these hormones are involved in the regulation and control of electrolytes, water metabolism, and fluid volume. During exercise, considerable water and sodium can be lost, particularly during prolonged exercise in the heat. The hormonal control mechanism for maintenance of fluid (plasma) volume during exercise is as follows:

1. Exercise causes the release of antidiuretic hormone (ADH) from the posterior pituitary (neurohypophysis) and the release of renin, an enzyme that breaks down protein, from specialized cells located in the kidney. The stimuli for these changes are (a) an increased sympathetic nervous system activity, (b) sodium loss, (c) a decreased plasma volume, and (d) an increased plasma osmolarity.*

2. ADH causes water retention by acting on the collecting tubules of the kidney. Renin acts on a plasma protein called angiotensin I to form angiotensin II. Angiotensin II stimulates the adrenal cortex to release aldosterone. Aldosterone increases the reabsorption of sodium from the distal tubules of the kidney. This in turn causes the passive reabsorption of water. Thus both water and sodium are conserved.

Because of this mechanism, it is not surprising to find that aldosterone, renin, angiotensin II, and ADH all increase substantially during exercise.[6,9,10,26,29]

Insulin and Glucagon

As mentioned previously, insulin causes an increase in cellular uptake of glucose resulting in a lowered blood glucose level. In addition to this function, insulin also inhibits glucose release from the liver and free fatty acid release from adipose tissue. Glucagon, on the other hand, causes just the opposite effects, i.e., glucose mobiliza-

---

*Osmolarity refers to the number of osmotically active particles in a solution. Osmosis was defined in Chapter 16 (p. 000).

tion from the liver (through glycogenolysis and gluconeogenesis) and free fatty acid mobilization from the adipocytes (fat cells). During exercise, in which both glucose and free fatty acids are needed as metabolic fuels, glucagon has been shown to increase and insulin to decrease.[1,14,18,61]

An example of these changes before and after exercise training is presented in Figure 22-7. The exercise bout in this case consisted of 60 minutes of submaximal bicycle exercise at an intensity that required 60% of the subjects' max $\dot{V}O_2$. The training program consisted of running and cycling 40 minutes per day, 4 times per week for 10 weeks. As shown in the figure, blood insulin levels decreased whereas glucagon levels increased during the exercise. While this was generally true both before and after training, the most pronounced changes occurred before training. The lesser response of insulin and glucagon following the training program can be explained by a decreased catecholamine (epinephrine and norepinephrine) response to submaximal exercise that also results from physical training, as will be discussed next. Both the glucagon and insulin responses are thought to be mediated in large part by the release of the catecholamines.[18]

Before we leave this area, you should be aware of some special relationships that are known to exist between blood glucose levels during exercise and circulating levels of insulin and glucagon. These relationships have been summarized in detail by Terjung.[55] Decreased insulin levels during exercise do not mean that glucose uptake by muscle cells is reduced. In fact, it is enhanced. It appears that a small amount of insulin is adequate and necessary to "permit" this exercise-related increase in glucose uptake. The increased glucose clearance must be matched, however, by an equivalent or greater glucose supply in order to avoid the condition called **hypoglycemia**. This is where glucagon comes

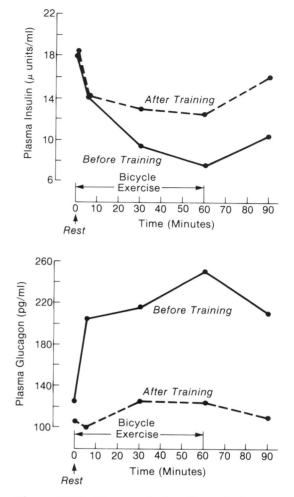

Figure 22-7. Changes in insulin and glucagon during and following 60 minutes of bicycle exercise before and after physical training. Blood insulin levels decreased whereas glucagon levels increased during the exercise. Both responses are blunted by physical training. (Based on data from Gyntelberg et al.[18])

into the picture. Glucose output by the liver is influenced by appropriate changes in both insulin and glucagon. The mechanism that controls glucagon release is not clearly known but appears to be related to glucose demand in a manner that is not necessarily reflected in changes in blood glucose levels. Once again, sympathetic neural influences have been implicated since it is known that the catecholamines stimulate glucagon release in rats and that running causes increases in glucagon, catecholamines, and cyclic AMP in human subjects.[36,37] Decreases in insulin levels during exercise, however, appear to be related directly to diminished insulin secretion rates.

The Catecholamines: Epinephrine and Norepinephrine

As pointed out earlier, the catecholamines secreted by the adrenal medulla are physiologically related closely to the actions of the sympathetic nervous system. Therefore, since the sympathetic system is activated under "fight or flight" conditions, an elevated blood concentration of catecholamines would be expected during bouts of exercise. This, in fact, is the case.[7,9,14,19,22,36,39,41,61] The increase in these hormones is related to the work intensity—the greater the intensity, the greater the increase. This rule holds true with some limitations, which will be described below. The increases are similar during submaximal exercise for both male and female subjects.[12] There does appear to be a lower limit of submaximal exercise that must be exceeded. For example, mild to moderate treadmill exercise did not produce any significant increase in venous plasma epinephrine levels in normal male subjects.[58] At the other end of the exercise intensity-duration continuum, incremental treadmill tests leading to exhaustion produced a cumulative effect that was reflected in an overproportional response increase in catecholamines.[31]

The increases in plasma epinephrine and norepinephrine during both progressive and continuous exercise are highly correlated with plasma cyclic AMP concentrations.[38] In these studies, plasma catecholamines were significantly elevated by the time subjects reached 80% of max $\dot{V}O_2$ in the progressive experiments and after exercising continuously for 10 minutes at 80% of max $\dot{V}O_2$. The fact that the increases in cyclic AMP levels always followed increases in catecholamine levels further implicates the central role of the sympathetic nervous system in mediating a variety of perceived and real stresses during exercise.[38] There is some evidence that, while exercise induces a response of the sympathetic nervous system, psychological stress induces primarily an adrenal response.[8]

In addition, as mentioned above, the increased blood levels of catecholamines during submaximal exercise are not as great following exercise training.[40,61] This is shown in Figure 22-8. Note the large magnitude of the drop (e.g., norepinephrine dropped 50% and epinephrine 70%) and the rapid onset of the response. After just 1 week of training, there was a 40% decrease in epinephrine and a 25% decrease in norepinephrine. Another reported effect of training is that plasma catecholamine

Figure 22-8. Blood levels of catecholamines (epinephrine and norepinephrine) decrease during submaximal exercise with exercise training. (Based on data from Winder et al.[61])

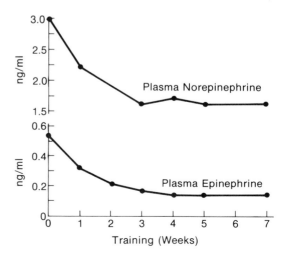

levels at the time of exhaustion are higher in trained athletes than they are in sedentary subjects.[25] These higher levels in athletes could not be explained by differences in catecholamine clearance and were assumed to be due to increased rates of secretion as the athletes endured the exercise tests for much longer periods of time.

The increased levels of catecholamines are obviously important contributors to exercise performance. For example, as pointed out in Table 22-2, epinephrine and norepinephrine have a variety of positive effects on the cardiovascular and metabolic systems with respect to aiding exercise performance. On the other hand, the decrease in catecholamine response seen during exercise following training also appears to be in the direction of "bettering" performance. Such lower levels of these hormones, for instance, would imply a lesser overall "stress" on all systems performing. Furthermore, the lower exercise heart rate that is also a result of physical training can be explained, at least in part, by this decreased catecholamine response (p. 340).

The Sex Hormones

Studies dealing with the responses of the sex hormones (androgens in the male and estrogens in the female) are not numerous. Nevertheless, it has been demonstrated that both androgens (testosterone) and estrogens (estradiol) are increased with exercise.[15,23,24,50] A recent review of gonadal secretory variations and control mechanisms during exercise has been written by Métivier.[35] He reports that blood testosterone levels increased in both young and old men following an acute work bout on a motor-driven treadmill. These findings are consistent with reports of increased androgen levels in highly trained athletes in response to maximal but not to submaximal exercise.[50] They also are consistent

with reports that plasma testosterone responses to bicycle ergometer tests are more closely related to work intensity than they are to work duration or total work output.[22] One report sounded a note of caution in that increases in peripheral venous plasma testosterone concentrations, which were proportional to exercise intensity, could nearly all be accounted for through decreases in plasma volume.[60]

All of the above studies were conducted using male subjects as might be expected. Women have approximately one-tenth to one-half as much circulating testosterone as males and it is therefore possible to study exercise-induced changes. For example, 30 minutes of running at each subject's own pace caused a significant elevation of plasma testosterone in six women recreational runners.[47] A comparison of serum testosterone and androstenedione responses to weight lifting in men and women also has been made.[59] The ovaries and adrenals are the main source of androstenedione and testosterone production in women while the testes and adrenals serve this function in men. At rest, testosterone levels were 10 times higher in men whereas androstenedione levels were 43% higher in women. Immediately after 30 minutes of weight lifting, testosterone levels increased in men but not women and were restored to resting levels within 30 minutes. On the other hand, androstenedione responses were similar in men and women in that levels decreased below pre-exercise levels at the 2-hour time point in recovery. Such studies ultimately should prove useful in better understanding gender-specific responses to different types of exercise and training.

An example of the responses to exercise of the blood levels of the ovarian hormones, estradiol (the most important estrogen), progesterone, follicle-stimulating hormone (FSH), and luteinizing hormone (LH) (the last two from the adenohypophysis), is shown in Figure 22-9. Both estradiol and progesterone increase more or less linearly with exercise (Fig. 22-9A). Follicle-stimulating hormone also increases with exercise, but the response is not large in magni-

Figure 22-9. Responses to exercise of the ovarian hormones during the luteal phase of the menstrual cycle (6 to 9 days after ovulation). As shown in *A*, both estradiol (estrogen) and progesterone increase linearly with exercise. In *B*, follicle-stimulating hormone (FSH) also increases with exercise, but the response is not large in magnitude nor does it appear to be related to the exercise intensity. The blood concentration of luteinizing hormone (LH) does not appear to be affected by exercise. (Based on data from Jurkowski et al.[23])

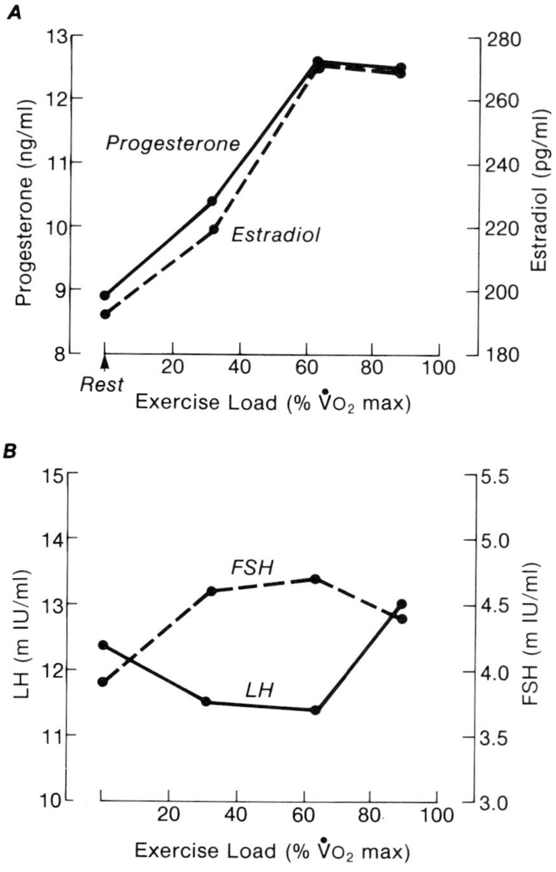

tude nor does it appear to be related to the exercise intensity. The blood concentration of LH does not appear to be affected by exercise (Fig. 22-9B). It should be mentioned that these responses were measured during the luteal phase of the menstrual cycle (6 to 9 days after ovulation). The hormonal responses during the follicular phase of the cycle (6 to 9 days after the beginning of menstruation) were somewhat different. Estradiol was the only hormone to increase with exercise during the follicular phase.

Additional studies have verified the findings shown in Figure 22-9 and have provided some new insights regarding the effects of exercise on the sex hormones. Many of these studies have been reviewed and summarized by Shangold.[47] In one of these studies, ten young women performed 30 minutes of intense bicycle ergometer exercise.[3] This resulted in a significant increase in progesterone and estradiol levels but produced no change in FSH or LH levels. It should be noted here that the same response patterns have been reported for testosterone, FSH, and LH for male subjects.[16] After 8 to 11 weeks of training the women in the first study[3] displayed marked irregularities in their menstrual cycles, which made it impossible to retest in the same cycle phase. Yet, when subjects were tested with the same absolute workloads used before training, no changes in serum progesterone, estradiol, or LH were observed. Training apparently suppressed the release of these sex hormones or altered some aspect of clearance so circulating levels remained unchanged.

LH also has been studied in young male sprinters and long-distance runners.[27] No changes in LH levels were found after maximal short-term running or after moderate (90 minutes, 4.3 min/km) or intense (45 minutes, 3.3 min/km) long-term running. One-half hour after the long-term runs, LH dropped to about half of the pre-run levels. Plasma testosterone was significantly decreased after the intense long-term run and remained depressed for up to 3 hours after the end of exercise. It was concluded that changes in testosterone and LH levels depend more on the intensity of exercise than on its duration. These findings also verify earlier reports[16] that some exercise-induced changes in sex hormone levels may not be apparent until after the cessation of activity.

It was mentioned above that the menstrual cycles of females became irregular with rigorous physical training. The irregular periods can, in fact, lead to a stoppage of menses altogether, which is called **amenorrhea.** This means that the ovaries would reduce their production of estrogenic steroids. Such reductions in female athletes have raised considerable concern because of known relationships between estrogen deficiency and **osteoporosis.** Osteoporosis is a condition of the bones where they become thin and brittle due to loss of mineral content and are therefore more susceptible to fractures. This condition is especially common in postmenopausal women.

Although there is evidence that amenorrhea may only predispose female athletes to a reduced bone mineral content when combined with excessive body thinness[32] and that female marathon runners maintain their bone mass longer than do sedentary women of similar age and body size,[4] the concerns persist with good reason. For example, a comparison of amenorrheic elite distance runners to those with regular menses (called **eumenorrheic**) disclosed a lesser mineral density in the lumbar spines of the amenorrheic group and a higher incidence of running-related fractures. It was concluded that, while intense exercise may reduce the impact of amenorrhea on bone mass (because amenorrheic runners who trained more intensely had denser bones than amenorrheic runners

who trained less intensely) amenorrheic runners as a group remain at elevated risk for exercise-related fractures. In terms of our discussion of exercise effects on sex hormones, the amenorrhea of women athletes has been related to a decrease in resting gonadotropin levels, namely LH and FSH. The decreases in LH and FSH are believed to be related to an alteration in hypothalamic control as a result of rigorous training.[13] Recall here that LH and FSH both are under regulatory control of hypothalamic releasing factors (see Fig. 22-4). The consequence of this is that resting estradiol levels of amenorrheic athletes are only one-fourth to one-third of eumenorrheic athletes.[13,33]

The changes in the blood concentration of the male and female sex hormones during exercise are not well understood with respect to their roles in performance. Aside from the relationship of testosterone to muscular strength (p. 167), little significance can be attached to these hormonal responses. Further research will be needed to clarify this problem.

The Glucocorticoids (Cortisol) and Adrenocorticotropic Hormone (ACTH)

The responses to exercise of the adrenal cortex hormone, cortisol, are inconsistent and varied.[48,49] For example, with light or moderate exercise, there may be no change or a small decrease in blood levels of cortisol. However if the exercise is prolonged to exhaustion, an increase in cortisol may be seen.[11,16,36] In addition, physical training does not appear to alter the responses of cortisol to exercise. The changes in cortisol secretion with exercise are presumably stimulated by an increased release of adrenocorticotropic hormone (ACTH) from the adenohypophysis. Venous plasma levels of ACTH have been reported to increase to 2 and 5 times above resting levels, respectively, following 20 minutes of running at

80% of max $\dot{V}O_2$ and a progressive run to exhaustion.[11]

An increased secretion of cortisol is a general response to stress. Therefore, in mild or light exercise where the stress may be low, no change in cortisol can be detected. On the other hand, during exhaustive exercise, stress is maximal, and cortisol would be expected to increase. One way in which cortisol might benefit exercise performance would be its gluconeogenic effect on the liver. Gluconeogenesis, you will recall, involves the formation of glucose from noncarbohydrate sources (e.g., fat and protein) and would, therefore, make more glucose available as a metabolic fuel.

Prostaglandins and Endorphins

Exercise and training research related to these hormonelike substances, which are produced by a variety of tissues in the body, is rather limited. Many of the experiments involve the electrical stimulation of muscles in anesthetized dogs and center on the role of prostaglandins in mediating blood flow changes. Although prostaglandins are released during direct muscle stimulation,[63] there is no clear evidence that these locally synthesized products are important to the maintenance of blood flow during exercise.[2] At this point, it is likely most appropriate to conclude that the prostaglandins may have some influence over resting blood flow because of their known ability to produce vasodilation.

Shangold's[47] review indicates that immunoreactive opoid peptides, which would include beta-endorphin, increase peripherally during exercise and that this response is facilitated by training. Interpretation of these observations are made difficult for two reasons. First, these substances are produced by so many different tissues in the body that it is impossible to know where the endorphins that are showing up in the blood are coming from, i.e., what is the source of production? If the source is uncertain, then it is difficult to place any physiological or functional significance on the increased levels that are induced by exercise. Second, many of the endorphins are produced in regions of the brain or central nervous system, e.g., hypothalamus, pituitary gland, spinal cord, etc., and may never leave these regions to show up in the peripheral circulation. There is recent evidence, however, that the exercise-induced activation of the endogenous opoid system may serve to regulate the secretion of several hormones during and after exercise (Farrell, et al., *J Appl Physiol.* 61:1051, 1986). Since the list of hormones that might be regulated includes epinephrine, the endorphins might eventually be implicated in a variety of exercise- and training-related matters.

A summary of the effects of exercise and training on hormonal changes is presented in Table 22-3.

Summary

The purpose of this chapter was to describe the hormonal or endocrine system with respect to maintenance of homeostasis during both resting and exercising conditions.

A hormone is a chemical substance secreted into the body fluids by an endocrine gland and has a specific effect on the activities of other organs (target organs). An endocrine gland is ductless and secretes a hormone directly into the blood or lymph. The actions of hormones on target organs include: (1) activation of enzyme systems, (2) alterations of cell membrane permeability, (3) muscular contraction or relaxation, (4) protein synthesis, or (5) cellular secretion. These actions are brought about through a mechanism referred to as the cyclic AMP mechanism.

Some hormones have an effect only on a specific target organ. This specificity is

TABLE 22-3

A Summary of Hormonal Changes During Exercise and Training*

Hormone	Exercise Response	Special Relationships	Probable Significance
Catecholamines	Increase	Greater increase with intense exercise, norepinephrine > epinephrine, increase less after training	Increased blood glucose, regulation of cardiovascular system
Growth hormone (GH)	Increase	Increases more in unfit person, declines faster in fit person	Uncertain, possibly delayed FFA release
ACTH-cortisol	Increase	Greater increase with intense exercise; increase less after training with submaximal exercise	Increased gluconeogenesis in liver (kidney)
TSH-thyroxine	Increase with prolonged high intensity	Increased thyroxin turnover with training but no toxic effects evident	Uncertain, may enhance FFA metabolism
LH-FSH	No change	Decrease with rigorous training	Amenorrhea
Testosterone	Increase	—	?
Estradiol-progesterone	Increase	Increase during luteal phase or cycle	?
Insulin	Decrease	Decreases less after training	Decreased stimulus to utilize blood glucose
Glucagon	Increase	Increases less after training	Increased blood glucose via glycogenolysis and gluconeogenesis
Renin-angiotensin-aldosterone	Increase	Same increase after training in rats	Sodium retention to maintain plasma volume
ADH	Increase	—	Water retention to maintain plasma volume
PTH-calcitonin	No change	—	Needed to establish proper bone development

TABLE 22-3

A Summary of Hormonal Changes During Exercise and Training* *(Continued)*

Hormone	Exercise Response	Special Relationships	Probable Significance
Erythropoietin	—	—	Would be important to increase erythropoiesis
Prostaglandins	May increase	May increase in response to sustained isometric contractions—may need ischemic stress	May be local vasodilators
Endorphins	Increase	Increases more after training	Regulation of other hormones

*From Terjung, R. L.: Endocrine systems. In Strauss, R. H. (ed.): *Sports Medicine and Physiology.* Philadelphia, W. B. Saunders, 1979, pp. 147–165.

accomplished by the presence of a specific hormone receptor located within the cell membrane of the target organ. The receptor is specific to and can only react with one hormone.

The predominant hormonal control system is the negative feedback mechanism. In this mechanism, the secretion of the hormone is turned off or decreased due to the end result of the response caused by that hormone. The nervous system is also involved in the control of hormone secretion, primarily through the functions of the hypothalamus and the sympathetic branch of the autonomic nervous system.

The hormones and their endocrine glands include the following:

1. *The Pituitary Gland.* Antidiuretic hormone (ADH) and oxytocin (from the posterior lobe), growth hormone (GH), thyroid-stimulating hormone (TSH), adrenocorticotropic hormone (ACTH), follicle-stimulating hormone (FSH), luteinizing hormone (LH), prolactin (PRL), and endorphins (from anterior lobe).

2. *The Adrenal Glands.* The catecholamines, epinephrine and norepinephrine (adrenal medulla), mineralocorticoids, glucocorticoids, and androgens (adrenal cortex).

3. *Pancreas.* Insulin and glucagon.

4. *The Thyroid Gland.* Thyroxin (T_4), triiodothyronine (T_3), and calcitonin.

5. *The Parathyroid Glands.* Parathyroid hormone (PTH).

6. *The Ovaries and Testes.* Estrogen and progesterone in females and testosterone in males.

Blood levels of hormones known to increase with exercise include: (1) growth hormone, (2) catecholamines, (3) ACTH, (4) glucocorticoids, (5) mineralocorticoids, (6) glucagon, (7) testosterone, (8) estrogen, (9) progesterone, (10) TSH, (11) thyroxin, and (12) triiodothyronine. Blood levels of LH and FSH do not change with exercise, whereas insulin decreases with exercise.

Questions

1. Define the terms "hormone" and "endocrine gland."
2. Explain the mechanism of specificity of hormone action.
3. Describe the mechanisms of hormone action.
4. How is hormone secretion controlled?
5. Construct a table listing the endocrine glands and their hormones.
6. Why is the pituitary gland called the "master" gland?
7. Construct a table listing the hormonal responses to exercise. Where possible, describe the significance of such changes.

References

1. Ahlborg, G., and Felig, P.: Influence of glucose ingestion on fuel-hormone response during prolonged exercise. *J Appl Physiol.* 41(5):683–688, 1976.
2. Beaty, O., III, and Donald, D. E.: Contribution of prostaglandins to muscle blood flow in anesthetized dogs at rest, during exercise, and following inflow occlusion. *Circ Res.* 44:67–75, 1979.
3. Bonen, A., Ling, W. Y., MacIntyre, K. P., Neil, R., McGrail, J. C., and Belcastro, A. N.: Effects of exercise on the serum concentrations of FSH, LH, progesterone, and Estradiol. *Europ J Appl Physiol.* 42:15–23, 1979.
4. Brewer, V., Meyer, B. M., Keele, M. S., Upton, S. J., and Hagan, R. D.: Role of exercise in prevention of involutional bone loss. *Med Sci Sports Exer.* 15(6):445–449, 1983.
5. Christensen, S. E., Jørgensen, O. L., Møller, N., and Ørskov, H.: Characterization of growth hormone release in response to external heating: comparison to exercise induced release. *Acta Endrocrinol.* 107:295–301, 1984.
6. Convertino, V. A., Brock, P. J., Keil, L. C., Bernauer, E. M., and Greenleaf, J. E.: Exercise training—induced hypervolemia: role of plasma albumin, renin, and vasopressin. *J Appl Physiol.* 48(4):665–669, 1980.
7. Cousineau, D., Ferguson, R. J., deChamplain, J., Gauthier, P., Côté, P., and Bourassa, M.: Catecholamines in coronary sinus during exercise in man before and after

8. training. *J Appl Physiol.* 43(5):801–806, 1977.
9. Dimsdale, J. E., and Moss, J.: Plasma catecholamines in stress and exercise. *JAMA.* 243(4):340–342, 1980.
9. Fagard, R., Amery, A., Reybrouck, T., Lijnen, P., Moerman, E., Bogaert, M., and De-Schaepdryver, A.: Effects of angiotensin antagonism on hemodynamics, renin, and catecholamines during exercise. *J Appl Physiol.* 43(3):440–444, 1977.
10. Fagard, R., Lijnen, P., and Amery, A.: Effects of angiotensin II on arterial pressure, renin and aldosterone during exercise. *Europ J Appl Physiol.* 54:254–261, 1985.
11. Farrell, P. A., Garthwaite, T. L., and Gustafson, A. B.: Plasma adrenocorticotropin and cortisol responses to submaximal and exhaustive exercise. *J Appl Physiol.* 55(5):1441–1444, 1983.
12. Favier, R., Pequignot, J. M., Desplanches, D., Mayet, M. H., Lacour, J. R., Peyrin, L., and Flandrois, R.: Catecholamines and metabolic responses to submaximal exercise in untrained men and women. *Europ J Appl Physiol.* 50:393–404, 1983.
13. Fisher, E. C., Nelson, M. E., Frontera, W. R., Turksoy, R. N., and Evans, W. J.: Bone mineral content and levels of gonadotropins and estrogens in amenorrheic running women. *J Clin Endocrinol Metab.* 62:1232–1236, 1986.
14. Galbo, H., Holst, J. J., Christensen, N. J., and Hilsted, J.: Glucagon and plasma catecholamines during beta-receptor blockade in exercising man. *J Appl Physiol.* 40(6):855–863, 1976.
15. Galbo, H., Hummer, L., Petersen, I. B., Christensen, N. J., and Bie, N.: Thyroid and testicular hormone responses to graded and prolonged exercise in man. *Europ J Appl Physiol.* 36:101–106, 1977.
16. Gawel, M. J., Park, D. M., Alaghband-Zadeh, J., and Rose, F. C.: Exercise and hormonal secretion: *Postgrad Med J.* 55:373–376, 1979.
17. Guyton, A. C.: *Textbook of Medical Physiology,* 5th ed. Philadelphia, W. B. Saunders, 1976.
18. Gyntelberg, F., Rennie, M. J., Hickson, R. C., and Holloszy, J. O.: Effect of training on the response of plasma glucagon to exercise. *J Appl Physiol.* 43(2):302–305, 1977.
19. Hagberg, J. M., Hickson, R. C., McLane, J. A., Ehsani, A. A., and Winder, W. W.:

Disappearance of norepinephrine from the circulation following strenuous exercise. *J Appl Physiol.* 47(6):1311–1314, 1979.

20. Hartley, L. H.: Growth hormone and catecholamine response to exercise in relation to physical training. *Med Sci Sports.* 7(1): 34–36, 1975.

21. Hartley, L. H., Mason, J. W., Hogan, R. P., Jones, L. G., Kotchen, T. A., Mongey, E. H., Wherry, F. E., Pennington, L. L., and Ricketts, P. T.: Multiple hormonal responses to graded exercise in relation to physical training. *J Appl Physiol.* 33(5):602–606, 1972.

22. Jezová, D., Vigaš, M., Tatár, P., Kvetňanský, R., Nazar, K., Kaciuba-Uścilko, H., and Kozlowski, S.: Plasma testosterone and catecholamine responses to physical exercise of different intensities in men. *Europ J Appl Physiol.* 54:62–66, 1985.

23. Jurkowski, J. E., Jones, N. L., Walker, W. C., Younglai, E. V., and Sutton, J. R.: Ovarian hormonal responses to exercise. *J Appl Physiol.* 44(1):109–114, 1978.

24. Keizer, H. A., Poortman, J., and Bunnik, G. S. J.: Influence of physical exercise on sex-hormone metabolism. *J Appl Physiol.* 48(5):765–769, 1980.

25. Kjaer, M., Christensen, N. J., Sonne, B., Richter, E. A., and Galbo, H.: Effect of exercise on epinephrine turnover in trained and untrained male subjects. *J Appl Physiol.* 59(4):1061–1067, 1985.

26. Kosunen, K. J., and Pakarinen, A. J.: Plasma renin, angiotensin II, and plasma and urinary aldosterone in running exercise. *J Appl Physiol.* 41(1):26–29, 1976.

27. Kuoppasalmi, K., Näveri, H., Härkönen, M., and Adlercreutz, H.: Plasma cortisol, androstenedione, testosterone and luteinizing hormone in running exercise of different intensities. *Scand J Clin Invest.* 40: 403–409, 1980.

28. Landau, B. R.: *Essential Human Anatomy and Physiology.* Glenview, Ill., Scott, Foresman, 1976.

29. Landgraf, R., Häcker, R., and Buhl, H.: Plasma vasopressin and oxytocin in response to exercise and during a day-night cycle in man. *Endokrinologie.* 79(2):281–291, 1982.

30. Lassarre, C., Girard, F., Durand, J., and Raynand, J.: Kinetics of human growth hormone during submaximal exercise. *J Appl Physiol.* 37(6):826–830, 1974.

31. Lehmann, M., Schmid, P., and Keul, J.: Plasma catecholamine and blood lactate cumulation during incremental exhaustive exercise. *Int J Sports Med.* 6:78–81, 1985.

32. Linnell, S. L., Stager, J. M., Blue, P. W., Oyster, N., and Robertshaw, D.: Bone mineral content and menstrual regularity in female runners. *Med Sci Sports Exer.* 16(4): 343–348, 1984.

33. Marcus, R., Cann, C., Madvig, P., Minkoff, J., Goddard, M., Bayer, M., Martin, M., Gaudiani, L., Haskell, W., and Genant, H.: Menstrual function and bone mass in elite women distance runners. *Anns Intern Med.* 102(2):158–163, 1985.

34. Métivier, G.: The effects of long lasting physical exercise and training on hormonal regulation. In Howald, H., and Poortmans, J. R. (eds.): *Metabolic Adaptation to Prolonged Physical Exercise.* Basel, Switzerland, Birkhäuser Verlag, 1975, pp. 276–292.

35. Métivier, G.: Pituitary and gonadal secretory variations and control mechanism during physical exercise. *J Sports Med.* 25: 18–26, 1985.

36. Näveri, H.: Blood hormone and metabolite levels during graded cycle ergometer exercise. *Scand J Clin Invest.* 45:599–603, 1985.

37. Näveri, H., Kuoppasalmi, K., and Härkönen, M.: Plasma glucagon and catecholamines during exhaustive short-term exercise. *Europ J Appl Physiol.* 53:308–311, 1985.

38. Painter, P. C., Howley, E. T., and Liles, J. N.: Change in plasma cAMP and catecholamines in men subjected to the same relative amount of physical work stress. *Aviat Space Environ Med.* 53(7):683–686, 1982.

39. Peguignot, J. M., Peyrin, L., and Pirès, G.: Catecholamine-fuel interrelationships during exercise in fasting men. *J Appl Physiol.* 48(1):109–113, 1980.

40. Péronnet, F., Cléroux, J., Perrault, H., Cousineau, D., deChamplain, J., and Nadeau, R.: Plasma norepinephrine response to exercise before and after training in humans. *J Appl Physiol.* 51(4):812–815, 1981.

41. Péronnet, F., Cleroux, J., Perrault, H., Thibault, G., Cousineau, D., deChamplain, J., Guilland, J. C., and Klepping, J.: Plasma norepinephrine, epinephrine and dopamine β-hydroxylase activity during exercise in man. *Med Sci Sports Exer.* 17(6): 683–688, 1985.

42. Premachandra, B. N., Winder, W. W., Hickson, R., Lang, S., and Holloszy, J. O.: Circulating reverse triiodothyronine in humans during exercise. *Europ J Appl Physiol.* 47:281–288, 1981.

43. Refsum, H. E., and Strömme, S. B.: Serum thyroxine, triiodothyronine, and thyroid-stimulating hormone after prolonged heavy exercise. *Scand J Clin Invest.* 39:455–459, 1979.

44. Rennie, M. J., and Johnson, R. H.: Alterations of metabolic and hormonal responses to exercise by physical training. *Europ J Appl Physiol.* 33:215–226, 1974.

45. Schmid, P., Wolf, W., Pilger, E., Schwaberger, G., Pessenhofer, H., Pristautz, H., and Leb, G.: TSH, T_3, rT_3 and fT_4 in maximal and submaximal physical exercise. *Europ J Appl Physiol.* 48:31–39, 1982.

46. Schürmeyer, T., Jung, K., and Nieschlag, E.: The effect of an 1100 km run on testicular, adrenal and thyroid hormones. Intern. *J Andro.* 7:276–282, 1984.

47. Shangold, M. M.: Exercise and the adult female: hormonal and endrocrine effects. *Exer Sports Sci Rev.* 12:53–79, 1984.

48. Shephard, R. J., and Sidney, K. H.: Effects of physical exercise on plasma growth hormone and cortisol levels in human subjects. In Wilmore, J. H., and Keogh, J. F. (eds.): *Exercise and Sport Sciences Reviews.* vol. 3. New York, Academic Press, 1975, pp. 1–30.

49. Sundsfjord, J. A., Stromme, S. B., and Aakvaag, A.: Plasma aldosterone, plasma renin activity and cortisol during exercise. In Howald, H., and Poortmans, J. R. (eds.): *Metabolic Adaptation to Prolonged Exercise.* Basel, Switzerland, Birkhäuser Verlag, 1975, pp. 308–314.

50. Sutton, J. R., Coleman, M. J., Casey, J., and Lazarus, L.: Androgen responses during physical exercise. *Br Med J.* 1:520–522, 1973.

51. Sutton, J., and Lazarus, L.: Growth hormone in exercise: comparison of physiological and pharmacological stimuli. *J Appl Physiol.* 41(4):523–527, 1976.

52. Sutton, J. R., Young, J. D., Lazarus, L., Hickie, J. B., and Maksvytis, J.: The hormonal response to physical exercise. *Aust Ann Med.* 18:84–90, 1969.

53. Terjung, R. L.: Endocrine systems. In Strauss, R. H. (ed.): *Sports Medicine and Physiology.* Philadelphia, W. B. Saunders, 1979, pp. 147–165.

54. Terjung, R. L., and Tipton, C. M.: Plasma thyroxine and thyroid-stimulating hormone level during submaximal exercise in humans. *Am J Physiol.* 220:1840–1845, 1971.

55. Terjung, R.: Endocrine response to exercise. *Exer Sports Sci Rev.* 7:153–180, 1979.

56. Theilade, P., Hansen, J. M., Skovsted, L., and Kampmann, J. P.: Effect of exercise on thyroid parameters and on metabolic clearance rate of antipyrine in man. *Acta Endocrinol.* 92:271–276, 1979.

57. Vora, Nila, M., Kukreja, S. C., York, P. A. J., Bowser, E. N., Hargis, G. K., and Williams, G. A.: Effect of exercise on serum calcium and parathyroid hormone. *J Clin Endocrinol Metab.* 57:1067–1069, 1983.

58. Warren, J. B., Dalton, N., Turner, C., Clark, T. J. H., and Toseland, P. A.: Adrenaline secretion during exercise. *Clin Sci.* 66:87–90, 1984.

59. Weiss, L. W., Cureton, K. J., and Thompson, F. N.: Comparison of serum testosterone and androstenedione responses to weight lifting in men and women. *Europ J Appl Physiol.* 50:413–419, 1983.

60. Wilkerson, J. E., Horvath, S. M., and Gutin, B.: Plasma testosterone during treadmill exercise. *J Appl Physiol.* 49(2):249–253, 1980.

61. Winder, W. W., Hagberg, J. M., Hickson, R. C., Ehsani, A. A., and McLane, J. A.: Time course of sympathoadrenal adaptation to endurance exercise training in man. *J Appl Physiol.* 45(3):370–374, 1978.

62. Winder, W. W., Hickson, R. C., Hagberg, J. M., Ehsani, A. A., and McLane, J. A.: Training-induced changes in hormonal and metabolic responses to submaximal exercise. *J Appl Physiol.* 46(4):766–771, 1979.

63. Young, E. W., and Sparks, H. V.: Prostaglandins and exercise hyperemia of dog skeletal muscle. *Am J Physiol.* 238:H190–H195, 1980.

SELECTED READINGS

American College of Sports Medicine: Symposium on hormonal responses in exercise. *Med Sci Sports.* 7(1):1–36, 1975.

Euler, U. S. von.: Sympatho-adrenal activity in physical exercise. *Med Sci Sports.* 6(3):165–173, 1974.

Nicholl, C. S. (ed.): Prolactin. *Fed Proc.* 39(8): 2561–2598, 1980.

Shephard, R. J., and Sidney, K. H.: Effects of physical exercise on plasma growth hormone and cortisol levels in human subjects. In Wilmore, J. H., and Keough, J. F. (eds.): *Exercise and Sport Sciences Reviews,* vol. 3. New York, Academic Press, 1975, pp. 1–30.

Terjung, R. L.: Endocrine Systems. In Strauss, R. H. (ed.): *Sports Medicine and Physiology.* Philadelphia, W. B. Saunders, 1979, pp. 147–165.

chapter 23

Drugs and Ergogenic Aids

Doping is the administration of or the use by a competing athlete of any substance foreign to the body or of any physiological substance taken in abnormal quantity or taken by an abnormal route of entry into the body, with the sole intention of increasing in an artificial and unfair manner his performance in competition. When necessity demands medical treatment with any substance which because of its nature, dosage, or application is able to boost the athlete's performance in competition in an artificial and unfair manner, this is to be regarded as doping.

U.S.O.C. Drug Control Program Protocol[81]

The major concepts to be learned from this chapter are as follows:

- An ergogenic aid is anything that improves or is thought to improve physical performance.
- The lack of objective and consistent information regarding effects of drugs and ergogenic aids is in part attributable to individual physiological and psychological variations among people.
- A placebo is an inert substance with the identical physical characteristics of a real drug.
- By far, the majority of studies dealing with the effects of drugs and other so-called ergogenic aids show little if any positive influence on exercise performance.

- The taking of drugs or other so-called ergogenic aids for the sole purpose of improving exercise performance may be dangerous to health and is not recommended.

Even though the International Olympic Committee (IOC) disallows drugs, several Olympic athletes have died during competition from the use of drugs. For example, two Danish cyclists died of heat stroke following the use of a vasodilator, and a French basketball player died during a game; he was using an amphetamine.

Dr. Robert Murphy, team physician at The Ohio State University, claims that there is no substitute for athletic ability, superb conditioning, and excellence in coaching to produce a great athletic performance.

Almost all athletic and medical associations, including the American College of Sports Medicine, the International Olympic Committee, the United States Olympic Committee (USOC), and the American Medical Association, are strongly against the use of drugs in sports. Athletes known to use them are banned from competition. Joining such organizations in raising their voices against drug use are coaches, trainers, team physicians, and physical educators. Unfortunately, there is also widespread clandestine support for the use of certain illegal pharmacologic agents among other coaches, trainers, physicians, and athletes. Not only is the practice contrary to the moral code underlying all athletics but also it is potentially injurious to the health of the athlete. The purpose of this chapter will be to discuss the effects of drugs and so-called ergogenic aids on physiological responses and on physical performance.

Ergogenic Aids Defined

An ergogenic aid, simply defined, is any substance, process, or procedure which may, or is perceived to, enhance performance through improved strength, speed, response time, or endurance of the athlete. Another area of interest in ergogenic aids is to hasten recovery (see Chapters 12 and 15). The nature of the action of any supposed ergogenic aid may be elicited through the following: (1) direct action on muscle fiber; (2) counteraction of fatigue products; (3) supply fuel needed for muscular contraction; (4) affect the heart and circulatory system; (5) affect the respiratory center; (6) delay the onset of fatigue or the perception of fatigue; and (7) counteract the inhibitory effects of the central nervous system upon muscular contraction and other functions.

Frequently, ergogenic aids are thought of only as pharmacologic agents that may be consumed in order to give the athlete an advantage. Pharmacological agents constitute only one of several classes of ergogenic aids. Others include nutritional (carbohydrates, proteins, vitamins, minerals, water, and electrolytes), physiological (oxygen, blood boosting, conditioning, and recovery procedures), psychological (hypnosis, suggestion, and rehearsal), and mechanical (improved body mechanics, clothing, equipment, and skill training) components.[77] In its broadest sense, one could call anything that can be related to an improvement in work or performance an ergogenic aid.

Obviously, some ergogenic aids are clearly acceptable as adjuncts to improved performance and safety. Such things as training and conditioning, use of water, improved equipment, carbohydrate-loading, vitamin (questionable effects) and iron supplements, warm-up techniques, rehearsal strategies, and cool-down techniques are within the spirit of competition.

The use of anabolic steroids, amphetamines, and other pharmacological agents are clearly outside the bounds of the spirit of competition and have been declared illegal by national and international sports-governing bodies and denounced by medical societies and sportsmedicine groups. In this chapter, we will present information on selected nutritional, physiological, and pharmacological agents. It is well recognized that psychological and mechanical components play a very important role in athletic performance. The reader is referred to Williams' *Ergogenic Aids in Sport* for information in these two areas.[77]

Ergogenic aids affect different people differently, as might be expected. For some, studies show a positive influence upon work performance and for others, no effect whatsoever. What might prove effective with the athlete may prove inconsequential to the nonathlete and vice versa. Certain ergogenic aids may influence a person's endurance performance but may have little or no effect upon activities requiring short bursts of strength and power.

Problems in Research Design

Unquestionably, the lack of objective and consistent information regarding effects of ergogenic aids is in part attributable to (1) considerable individual physiological and psychological variations among people; and (2) difficulties in developing foolproof research protocol.

For example, a company wished to learn the effects of lighting in an industrial plant on the performance of the workers. As the illumination increased, so did work production. However, as illumination decreased, production did not! Apparently, the results were a consequence of the workers' realizing that they were in an experiment and were not solely because of increased illumination.

Drug studies use **placebos** in order to deal with possible psychological contaminants. For example, if we tell you that a certain pill will help you to run faster (suggestion), you might run faster simply because of what we have said. Who knows whether it was the pill or the suggestion? A placebo is an inert substance with the identical physical characteristics of the real drug. Thus, in experiments the placebo is administered to half the subjects, while the actual drug is administered to the other half. Neither the investigator nor the subjects know which is which. Frequently, such a design is referred to as a double-blind study. Even though this design appears to be foolproof, some subjects will react to the placebo, confusing the final results of the study.

Some years ago, we were studying the effects of vitamin E on physical work. By coincidence, one subject in the experiment had been married for about a year. The couple had been attempting to have children, but without success. Halfway through the study, the subject's wife became pregnant. For the remainder of the experiment, this subject went about extolling the virtues of vitamin E, to which he attributed his apparent new-found virility. At the conclusion of this double-blind experiment, the investigator and subject learned that the latter had been taking the placebo! Perhaps the moral of this story for husband and athlete alike might be "It's all in your head"!

The ability to experimentally isolate the true effect of any drug or ergogenic aid is extremely difficult and in many cases nearly impossible. This has been scientifically demonstrated,[4] as shown in Figure 23-1. The amount of weight that could be lifted each week during a weight-training program is shown on the left. On the right is the amount of weight that could be lifted each week during a placebo period. The placebo period consisted also of a weight-

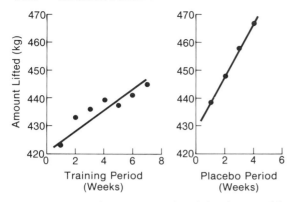

Figure 23-1. The amount of weight that could be lifted each week during a weight-training program is shown on the left. On the right is the amount of weight that could be lifted each week during a placebo period. The placebo period consisted also of a weight-training program, but in addition, the subjects were given placebo pills daily and told that the pills contained 10 mg of Dianabol, an oral anabolic steroid. Notice the greater increase in the amount of weight lifted weekly (indicated by the steepness of the line) when the subjects thought they were taking steroid pills. (Based on data from Ariel and Saville.[4])

training program, but in addition, the subjects were given placebo pills daily with the information that they contained 10 mg of Dianabol, an oral anabolic steroid. Notice the much greater gain in the amount of weight lifted weekly (as indicated by the steepness of the line) when the subjects thought they were taking steroid pills. This very nicely points out the psychological effects that some drugs have on physical performance.

We should be alerted to the fact that just because one study shows positive results, it might not necessarily be true or apply to all individuals. Early studies are often criticized because of research design weaknesses. However, they have served a very useful purpose, namely, in giving

other researchers a base upon which to design more "air-tight" studies.

Today, prime interest in ergogenic aids deals mostly with the effects of drugs on athletic performance and of steroids upon increasing muscle size and strength. Those interested in a review of the effects of drugs and ergogenic aids should consult the excellent books *Ergogenic Aids and Muscular Performance,* edited by William P. Morgan (Academic Press, 1972), *Ergogenic Aids in Sport,* by Melvin H. Williams (Human Kinetics Publishers, 1983), and the review article written by E. C. Percy.[55]

Nutrition Aids

There is a variety of nutrition supplements and manipulations that may or may not be beneficial to the athlete. Among these are manipulation of carbohydrate stores for endurance events, vitamin and mineral supplements, and water and electrolytes.

Carbohydrates

As discussed in Chapter 2, carbohydrate and fatty acids are the primary sources of fuel for muscular contraction. For activities where work intensity exceeds 70 to 90% of the aerobic capacity of the athlete, muscle glycogen stores and utilization are critical. Both absolute and relative muscle glycogen depletion are related to the intensity of the work (Chapter 2, Fig. 2-14).

A process called glycogen supercompensation (carbohydrate-loading) may be incorporated to elevate muscle glycogen stores above their normal resting levels prior to endurance competition. A recently described procedure involves several days of preparation including six days of tapering aerobic training while maintaining a normal carbohydrate intake (approximately 50% of total calories) for the first three days. During the last three days, the athlete increases carbohydrate intake to

70% of the total caloric intake.[65] This will result in significant increases in glycogen storage and is not as severe a regimen as has been described by others.[6]

Generally, glycogen supercompensation is applicable in athletic events where the athlete is continuously in motion for more than an hour at a time. Supercompensation may have applicability for events with an anaerobic component (400 m to 1500 m) to the extent that lowered levels of muscle glycogen can have adverse effects on lactate production (anaerobic power).[64] Under circumstances where multiple events are run or swum in a single day, supercompensation is appropriate.[64] For these purposes, simply increasing the dietary intake of carbohydrates for 48 to 72 hours prior to competition is adequate.

The practice of ingesting glucose 30 to 45 minutes before competition is not recommended. It can lead to a rapid fall in blood glucose levels with the onset of exercise and increase the rate of glycogen utilization.[10,17,30] Fructose ingestion appears to blunt the shift in blood glucose versus glucose ingestion.[41] One final point, with the storage of 1 gram of glucose about 2.7 grams of water will be taken into storage. Thus, with a storage of 700 gm of glucose an additional storage of about 1.9 kg (4 lb) of water will occur. So the athlete should not be surprised to have a precompetition weight gain. This can be an advantage or disadvantage depending on the event.

Water and Electrolytes

The importance of water ingestion and maintenance of electrolyte levels was discussed in Chapter 18. Water loss in amounts as low as 2 to 3% of body weight can impair performance through disruption of circulatory and thermoregulatory functions.[43]

The diet normally contains sufficient electrolyte to compensate for any acute losses experienced through activity. Exception is noted where very high sweat rates over a period of days may occur. A concerted effort will be needed to ensure added electrolyte intake, especially as it relates to potassium.

Vitamins and Minerals

In spite of widespread usage, there appears to be little compelling evidence for supplemental intake of various vitamins and minerals, with the exception of iron.[5,42] Most vitamins, when taken in excess, are merely excreted in the urine. The most "popular" of the supplemental vitamins include thiamine (B_1), ascorbic acid (C), and alpha-tocopherol (E).

Thiamine (B_1)

Thiamine is one of a series of B vitamins that plays a role in proper digestion, muscle contraction, and energy release. Thiamine is one of the water-soluble vitamins and therefore is not stored to any extent in the body. One might logically think that because thiamine is not stored in the body and is important in energy release that supplemental intake is beneficial. However, thiamine requirements can easily be met by the normal intake of carbohydrates since it is found in abundance in carbohydrates.[5]

Ascorbic Acid (C)

Ascorbic acid is found in many fresh fruits and vegetables. Anyone who is consuming a well-balanced diet is going to receive adequate vitamin C intake (50 to 60 mg/day). Almost any form of orange juice provides at least 100 mg of vitamin C in a 6-ounce serving. As vitamin B_1, Vitamin C is water soluble and is not stored in the body.

Vitamin E

Vitamin E appears to be important for normal creatine excretion and for prevention of certain blood disorders, including anemia. Salad oils and margarines, whole grains, liver, beans, fruits, and vegetables contain vitamin E. Wheat germ oil is an excellent natural source. Vitamin E deficiencies are extremely rare.

Even though some studies demonstrate that this vitamin is an ergogenic aid,[18] most research concludes that this is not true;[62,63] nor does vitamin E reduce heart disease, aid the sex drive, or increase longevity, as some people are inclined to claim.

In one study, Shephard et al.[63] studied 20 swimmers (mostly middle-distance competitors) in an attempt to determine whether athletes need vitamin E supplement. The 20 subjects were divided into two matched groups. The study lasted 85 days. Among the findings were the following:

1. No significant gains in maximum oxygen consumption in either test or control subjects.
2. Both groups showed a reduction in the lactacid component of the oxygen debt.
3. Both demonstrated a more rapid pulse recovery rate following maximal effort.

It was concluded that vitamin E supplement has no significant effect as an ergogenic aid.

Incidentally, as discussed in an earlier chapter (p. 534), none of the known vitamins, when taken in excess of their recommended daily allowance, produces an ergogenic effect.

Iron

In many instances there is a legitimate concern for iron deficiency among athletes and the general population. Iron is an important component in hemoglobin of the red blood cell. Although iron deficiency is more prevalent among women, it can also occur in men. Monitoring of iron intake along with clinical evaluation is recommended for those who may suspect an iron deficiency. Daily iron needs for men and women are about 10 mg and 18 mg, respectively.[5,42]

In summary, the need for any supplemental intake of vitamins and minerals, with the exception of iron, is minimal. If it gives the athlete peace of mind, then an over-the-counter multiple vitamin could be taken on a daily basis. The practice of taking megadoses of certain vitamins and minerals is a waste of time and money and, in some instances, will precipitate certain toxic responses.[5]

Pharmacological Agents

The practice of using various pharmacological agents and drugs has raised the most controversy and presents more ethical, legal, and clinical questions than any other area. The indiscriminate use of pharmacological agents also poses the greatest threat to the health and welfare of the athlete. Most of the contemporary controversy centers on the use of steroids. Other substances of concern include amphetamines and, to a lesser degree, aspartic acid salts, bicarbonates, caffeine, and pangamic acid. Appendix H contains a partial list of substances that are banned by the International Olympic Committee.

Steroids

Considerable interest has arisen, particularly among football players, weight lifters, wrestlers, and those athletes participating in the weight events, regarding the effects of anabolic-androgenic steroids on performance. The androgenic steroids are derivatives of the male sex hormone, testosterone, secreted by the testicles. Testosterone causes the particular physical characteristics of the male body. Being produced mostly between the ages of 11 and 13, testosterone quickens the onset of puberty and is continually produced throughout life.

Secretion of testosterone causes descent of the testes into the scrotum and enlargement of the testes, penis, and scrotum. It also affects the secondary male characteristics including (1) distribution of hair, (2) voice, (3) growth and development of bones, and (4) development of musculature following puberty. It is small wonder, therefore, that some drug companies have placed a number of these androgenic steroids on the market in hopes of capitalizing on the athletic market. As Guyton notes, "Testosterone has often been considered to be a 'youth hormone' because of its effect on the musculature, and it is occasionally used for treatment of persons who have poorly developed muscles."[39]

The drug trade names for some of the synthetic testosterone preparations include: Adroyd, Dianabol (no longer on the market), Deca-Durabolin, Maxibolin, Nilevar, and Winstrol. These drugs are chemically structured to emphasize the anabolic (protein-building) attributes of testosterone while minimizing the androgenic (producing masculine characteristics) properties.

Recognizing the problems we mentioned earlier in designing scientific studies to probe the effects of these drugs on performance and development of musculature, many have been completed with equivocal results.[12,28,31,35,46,59,67,71]

It appears that steroids may increase strength and muscle mass for some but not for others. Perhaps the real issue is that of side effects. Physicians are most concerned with the effects of these drugs on the liver. Under no circumstances should persons with histories of liver ailment involve themselves with steroid experimentation. Women taking steroids have developed acne and exhibited positive symptoms on liver function tests.

The American College of Sports Medicine conducted a comprehensive survey of the world literature and carefully analyzed the claims made for and against the efficacy of anabolic-androgenic steroids in improving human physical performance.[3] The following is their position statement:

1. Anabolic-androgenic steroids in the presence of an adequate diet can contribute to increases in body weight, often in the lean mass compartment.

2. The gains in muscular strength achieved through high-intensity exercise and proper diet can occur by the increased use of anabolic-androgenic steroids in some individuals.

3. Anabolic-androgenic steroids do not increase aerobic power or capacity for muscular exercise.

4. Anabolic-androgenic steroids have been associated with adverse effects on the liver, cardiovascular system, reproductive system, and psychological status in therapeutic trials and in limited research on athletes. Until further research is completed, the potential hazards of the use of the anabolic-androgenic steroids in athletes must include those found in therapeutic trials.

5. The use of anabolic-androgenic steroids by athletes is contrary to the rules and ethical principles of athletic competition as set forth by many of the sports governing bodies. The American College of Sports Medicine supports these ethical principles and deplores the use of anabolic-androgenic steroids by athletes.

There are recent reports where weight lifters, consuming a variety of steroids, showed a consistent pattern of low to very low blood levels of HDL-C (high-density lipoprotein).[15,18,50,56,59] HDL-C levels below about 38 mg/100 ml of blood are associated with high risk for premature coronary artery disease.[15] The mean value for

HDL-C for all of the studies was 20.5 mg/100 ml for the "users" and 48.9 for the non-users. A summary of the results of these studies appears in Table 23-1. In one study where both female and male steroid users were included, the patterns were similar, regardless of gender.[15] In another, weight-lifting users and nonusers were compared with non-weight-lifting nonuser controls.[69] In two of the studies where subjects stopped taking the steroids for a period of time, HDL-C levels rebounded to normal values within 3 to 6 weeks.[18,56] Thus, it is possible to reverse the low HDL-C levels but the ominous question remains: "What is the effect on the possible development of coronary artery disease while the HDL-C levels are depressed? This question is particularly pertinent for those athletes who continue usage over several years. There is anecdotal evidence that some athletes (professional football players and weight lifters) have developed coronary artery disease in their mid-30s.

The prolonged use of oral anabolic-androgenic steroids (C_{17}-alkylated derivatives of testosterone) has resulted in liver disorders in some persons. Some of these disorders are apparently reversible with the cessation of drug usage, but others are not.

The administration of anabolic-androgenic steroids to men may result in a decrease in testicular size and function and a decrease in sperm production. Although these effects appear to be reversible when small doses of steroids are used for short periods of time, the reversibility of the effects of large doses over extended periods of time is unclear.

Strauss et al. reported the results of a survey of ten female weight lifters who were using a variety of steroids, both injectable and oral, over a prolonged period of time.[68] Table 23-2 shows the responses by the participants to a questionnaire. Questions were asked to determine if the respon-

dents had noticed changes in any of the items included in the list in Table 23-2. It should be noted that the responses were subjective in nature and, as such, do not represent a scientifically controlled research design. Nonetheless, the results should be heeded.

Serious and continuing efforts should be made to educate male and female athletes, coaches, physical educators, physicians, trainers, and the general public regarding the inconsistent effects of anabolic-androgenic steroids on improvement of human physical performance and the potential dangers of taking certain forms of these substances, especially in large doses, for prolonged periods.

Growth Hormone

In recent years, athletes desiring weight gain have combined usages of illegal anabolic-androgenic steroids with growth hormones. Biosynthetic human growth hormone (HGH) can now be obtained relatively easily where formerly it could be obtained only from the pituitary glands of cadavers.[53] Although there are no laboratory-controlled studies available to examine the effects of HGH on athletes (and there likely will not be any), certain athletes are blindly using this substance hoping for short-term gains and ignoring possible long-term side effects. The potential side effects are as ominous as those for steroids.

Amphetamines

It generally is reported that **amphetamines** are the most popular drugs for increasing athletic performance among those inclined toward usage. Amphetamine (Benzedrine being a popular brand) is a synthetic structured drug closely related to epinephrine. Like epinephrine, it produces stimulation of the central nervous system, resulting in increased alertness in motor

TABLE 23–1

Summary of studies examining the effects of anabolic steroids on HDL-C levels in weight lifters. (Values are in mg/100 ml of blood).

Reference	Gender	Weight Lifter User		Weight Lifter Nonuser		Non-Weight-Lifter Nonuser	
		Cholesterol	HDL-C	Cholesterol	HDL-C	Cholesterol	HDL-C
15	M	291.1	23.5	182.9	52		
50	M	183	26	176	50		
69	M		34.7		53.8		53.7
18	M	218.1	17	203.7	44.6	209.6	46.1
(OFF)*			(43)				
56	M	223.4	15.6			209.5	49.5
(OFF)*		(199.8)	(51.6)				
Mean		228.9	20.6	187.5	48.9	209.6	47.8
15	F	216.4	30.6			182.7	52

*OFF following a reference means that the subjects in that study stopped consuming the anabolic steroid.

TABLE 23–2

Results of a survey of 10 female weight lifters who were users of both injectable and oral anabolic-androgenic steroids. The questions were designed to acquire respondents perceptions of the effects of the steroids on the following items.[68]

Question	Increased	Decreased	No Change
1. Increased facial hair	9		1
2. Clitoris enlargement	8		2
3. Libido	6	1	3
4. Breast size		5	5
5. Menstruation (2 hysterectomized)		7 (or stopped)	1
6. Aggressiveness	8		2
7. Acne	6		4
8. Body hair	5		5
9. Scalp hair loss	2		8
10. Appetite	8		2
11. Body fat	8		2

and physical activity, decrease in fatigue, and sometimes insomnia. Most often there is a rise in blood pressure with increased heart rate and perhaps some irregularities such as extrasystoles (extra beats) and paroxysmal tachycardia (attacks of excessively rapid heart action that occur abruptly and terminate with equal abruptness). Also, there is a moderate rise in metabolism, which may be accompanied by some loss in weight. Excessive dosages result in hyperexcitability and insomnia followed by depression. This may be accompanied by abdominal cramps, hematuria (discharge of blood into the urine), collapse, convulsions, and coma.

Characteristically, amphetamines affect different people differently. For this reason, small doses are administered initially to ascertain individual reactions. Certainly, amphetamines are contraindicated for easily excitable people and for those with high blood pressure.

Scientific investigations of the effects of amphetamines on endurance performance have not always produced consistent findings.[36,49,60,75] Most studies, though, have shown no significant influence of amphetamines on endurance performance. In one well-designed study,[75] it was shown that variant dosages of amphetamines do not affect heart rate or maximal endurance capacity during submaximal exercise. Although *maximal* heart rate was found to be significantly increased, such an effect does not appear to be related to endurance capacity. In another study,[66] it was shown that ephedrine, a medication similar in action to amphetamine, has no effect on several measures of physical work capacity. Incidentally, in the 1972 Olympic Games, an American swimmer, Rick DeMont, was denied an earned gold medal because he was taking ephedrine for his asthmatic condition. (It was prescribed).

Chandler and Blair examined several physiological components related to athletic success, including strength, power, speed, anaerobic and aerobic capacity, and heart rate.[13] The results were mixed with one of two strength components unaffected. Also, leg power, speed, and aerobic capacity were unaffected. Acceleration, anaerobic capacity, time to exhaustion on the treadmill, pre-exercise heart rate, and maximal heart rate all had higher values.

We remind the reader again that, regardless of any real or perceived benefits, amphetamines are banned substances for athletic competition, even when they are prescribed for clinically justifiable reasons.

Aspartic Acid Salts

Blood ammonia levels rise following physical activity. The excess ammonia, through a complex series of chemical reactions, is removed from the body by being converted to urea in the liver (urea cycle). It has been conjectured that the weakest part of the cycle is due to limited amounts of **aspartic acid** (an amino acid). If it were true that excessive amounts of ammonia in the blood cause fatigue, exogenously administered aspartates might clear the blood of ammonia more completely, delaying fatigue and acting as an ergogenic aid.

Studies on humans concerning the performance effects of oral ingestion of aspartic acid salts are rare and, as you might expect, somewhat conflicting in their results. One study[16] concluded that the onset of fatigue in an all-out run was *not* delayed; another[1] indicated that endurance capacity for prolonged exercise (1½ hours) was significantly increased; and a third[29] concluded that there was no difference in fatigue or endurance in weight-lifting activities. It should be noted that none of the studies used athletes as subjects. However, in the first study, where no effects on delaying fatigue were shown, a 7-week physical training program was involved.

In view of the limited research and conflicting results, it is difficult to make any definite judgment relative to the ergogenic merits of aspartic acid salts. However, since the above studies involved different activities performed over different time periods, it is possible that the effects of aspartates vary according to the type and duration of the performance.

An excellent review of the literature on the ergogenic effects of steroids, amphetamines, and aspartic acid can be found in the article by Golding.[34]

Alkaline (Bicarbonate) Ingestion

In Chapter 21, it was pointed out that during anaerobic exercise, blood and muscle pH decrease, whereas lactic acid concentrations increase. Both of these factors (decreased pH and increased lactic acid concentration) have been implicated in the muscular fatigue process (p. 124).

Working from these facts, early researchers reasoned that increasing the body's alkali reserve (buffering system) prior to heavy exercise might significantly retard the decrease in pH, thus delaying fatigue and increasing exercise performance. Their reasoning was correct in that Dr. D. B. Dill and colleagues of the Harvard Fatigue Laboratories showed that runners in an alkaline state could run 13% longer on a treadmill before fatiguing.[24]

The preceding results have been substantiated in two recent studies, both of which used the same dosage of sodium bicarbonate of 300 mg/kg of body weight as the alkalinizing agent.[47,72] In the first study, treadmill time to exhaustion was increased from 4.5 minutes to 7.3 minutes. When ammonium chloride was ingested (making the blood more acidic) endurance time deteriorated to 2.6 minutes.[47] In the second study, running time in an 800 m run was improved by almost 3 seconds (from 2:05.8 to 2:02.9). Because of high pH values and HCO_3^- in the urine, this form of doping would be relatively easy to detect.[72]

Caffeine

The many people who feel that a cup of coffee helps them "get going" in the morning may well have a scientifically valid point. Recently it has been shown that **caffeine** can have a substantial positive effect on endurance performance.[19,20,45] For example, in one study,[45] it was found that more work was produced and more oxygen consumed when caffeine was ingested before and during 2 hours of cycling than when this same endurance task was performed without caffeine. These "ergogenic" effects—literally "work-producing" effects—were in this case brought about by ingestion of 250 milligrams of caffeine 1 hour before the exercise and an additional 250 milligrams over the first 90 minutes of the exercise. Other research work[20] has suggested that runners who can complete the marathon in 2½ hours *without* caffeine can cut their times by 10 minutes *with* caffeine; if they ordinarily take 3½ hours to run the marathon, ingestion of caffeine can cut their time by as much as 15 minutes. Incidentally, a cup of coffee contains between 100 to 150 milligrams of caffeine; a cup of tea contains somewhat less.

The ergogenic effects of caffeine are probably related to caffeine's role in aiding the mobilization of free fatty acids. You will recall from Chapter 19 (p. 529) that free fatty acids are the usable form of fat as a fuel for the aerobic system. Thus caffeine has a glycogen-sparing effect in that it enables more fat to be used as a fuel, with *less* usage of glycogen. As previously mentioned, glycogen-sparing reduces muscular fatigue.

Pangamic Acid (Vitamin B-15)

Of considerable recent interest has been a chemical compound called *pangamic acid* or *vitamin B-15*. According to the Federal Drug Administration, there is no scientific evidence to suggest that pangamic acid is a vitamin. They further state that it is not only an illegal drug, but possibly dangerous. Nevertheless, coaches and athletes around the world have claimed that chronic ingestion of pangamic acid improves physical and athletic performance.

Two studies, utilizing treadmill performance, are cited.[33,37] In the first study, submaximal treadmill running at 70% of aerobic capacity showed no beneficial effects.[33] The second study, utilizing much more elaborate procedures, failed to show any significant effect of pangamic acid on maximal performance.[37] Much of the interest in pangamic acid has come from the Russian literature.

Physiological Agents

Of the physiological methods for improving performance the two most often cited are blood doping and use of supplemental oxygen. Blood doping is, again, an illegal procedure and supplemental oxygen has practical benefits only in helping an athlete in recovery.

Blood Doping

Before proceeding with a description of blood doping we will describe the position of the USOC relevant to this phenomenon.[81]

> "The practice of blood doping . . . is considered a form of doping by the United States Olympic Committee, and is therefore prohibited. Blood doping is the intravenous (I.V.) injection of blood (whole, packed red blood cells, or blood substitute) into an athlete's body, whether that blood be the athletes' own blood, or that of another person for the purpose of enhancing performance . . . Any evidence confirming . . . that the practice of blood doping . . . was administered to an athlete will be cause for punitive action, comparable to that for using a banned substance, relative to anyone implicated by that evidence . . ."[81]

In the 1976 Olympic Games, the Finnish long-distance runner Lasse Viren was said by the press to be "**blood doping,**" since he placed first both in the 5,000- and 10,000-meter races and fifth in the marathon. Such a performance was indeed spectacular; no wonder an "excuse" was sought! Blood doping, the removal and subsequent reinfusion of blood, is done to temporarily increase blood volume and, most importantly, raise the number of red blood cells. As was discussed in Chapter 9, red blood cells contain hemoglobin. Thus overloading the blood with hemoglobin would increase the oxygen-carrying capacity of the blood and, theoretically at least, lead to an increased endurance performance.

Scientific studies of blood doping and endurance performance have produced conflicting results.[8,11,21,25,26,32,54,57,58,70,73,74,76] Several studies have shown that blood doping increases endurance performance between 13 and 39% (measured by a treadmill run to exhaustion) and maximal oxygen consumption between 5 and 31% in both non-athletic subjects and highly trained endurance athletes.[11,25,26,32,57,58] An equal number of studies, however, have found no effects of blood doping on endurance performance, maximal oxygen consumption, heart rate responses during exercise, or perceived exertion.[21,54,70,73,74,76] (Perceived exertion is a measure of how difficult the subjects think the exercise is that they are performing.)

An examination of research design differences clarifies much of the conflicting evidence. Two critical factors become apparent: (1) when between 800 and 1200 ml of blood, or its equivalent, is reinfused (as opposed to 450 to 500 ml) aerobic capacity and endurance increase and (2) when 5 to 6 weeks elapse before reinfusion, "positive" results also are seen.[78]

In practice, two sources of blood are available, autologous (reinfusion of one's own blood) and homologous (infusion from a donor) sources. By law, blood that is refrigerated cannot be stored for more than 21 days before usage. On the other hand, frozen supplies may be used after much longer periods of time.

Blood doping should not be recommended at any level of endurance competition. However, perhaps even more convincingly, blood doping should not be attempted because of the methodology involved, i.e., blood withdrawal and reinfusion. Some possible complications resulting from blood doping are[23] (1) blood incompatibilities; (2) viral disease transmission; (3) septicemia (a morbid blood infection); (4) air embolism; and (5) thrombosis (blood clot).

Oxygen

Studies have been conducted regarding the ergogenic effects of breathing oxygen (1) prior to exercise, (2) during exercise, and (3) during recovery from exercise.

O$_2$ Breathing Prior to Exercise

There is some evidence that breathing oxygen immediately prior to exercise has some beneficial effects on performance, provided that the exercise is performed while holding the breath.[48,79] This effect might be related to the fact that breath-holding time is increased by "blowing off" or washing out carbon dioxide. It is common, for example, to see swimmers hyperventilate (blow off CO_2) immediately before the gun goes off. (It should be noted that while this technique may be effective in increasing performance, it is very dangerous in that the possibility of drowning is also increased.)

Studies in which oxygen was breathed prior to a non–breath-holding type of exercise show very little if any effect on performance.[27,51,61]

O$_2$ Breathing during Exercise

There is a rather large body of information indicating that breathing oxygen-enriched air (33 to 100% oxygen) has a beneficial effect upon exercise performance.[2,7,40,44,51,80] During maximal work, these benefits include a greater endurance capacity, and during submaximal work, lower heart rate, lower blood lactic acid accumulation, and lower minute ventilation have been observed. The mechanisms responsible for these changes are associated with the increased partial pressure of oxygen, which facilitates the transport of oxygen by hemoglobin and in physical solution and by increased diffusion across the alveolar-capillary and tissue-capillary membranes (p. 225). It must be emphasized here that as an ergogenic aid for the purpose of improving athletic performance, breathing oxygen during exercise is not useful simply because it is not practical.

O₂ Breathing during Recovery

We are sue that you have seen oxygen being administered to professional athletes during time-outs or rest breaks. Although there is not a great deal of research on this practice, any beneficial effects, either on the recovery process itself or on performance of a subsequent work bout, are inconsequential.[9,27,40,51] Although there may be a psychological effect, there is no physiological basis for use of oxygen during recovery.

Sports and Drug Testing

Prior to the 1984 Olympic Games in Los Angeles, the application of sanctions against athletes detected with various drugs in their systems was inconsistent and uneven. There are a variety of reasons for this. One such reason was that drug testing protocols were not reliable. With the development of newer methods of drug detection and equipment utilizing gas chromatography/mass spectrometry, the detection of minute levels of foreign substances in the bodies of athletes has been made possible.

The United States Olympic Committee formally established its own drug-testing program during a meeting at the 1983 Pan-American Games in Caracas.[14] The USOC utilizes a laboratory at the University of California at Los Angeles that is certified by the International Olympic Committee. The USOC Drug Control Program protocol defines the drug testing program and details of the procedures including human rights and "chain of custody" expectations.[81] All athletes who are selected for the U.S. Olympic Team at the olympic trials will be tested. If the olympic trials occurred more than 60 days prior to the Olympic Games, they will be re-tested prior to departing for the games. National governing bodies of the various sports may request formal testing during sanctioned competition.

The National Collegiate Athletic Association, in its 1986 annual meeting, approved a drug-testing program for athletes participating in its various championships, including football bowl games. With the USOC and the NCAA drug-testing programs, a new environment for the conduct of sporting events is evolving that should provide more fair competition for all athletes.

Summary

An ergogenic aid is anything that improves or is thought to improve physical performance. Ergogenic aids may be classified as nutritional, pharmacological, physiological, psychological, or mechanical.

The lack of objective and consistent information regarding effects of drugs and ergogenic aids is in part attributable to individual physiological and psychological variations among people. In order to deal with possible psychological effects, a placebo (an inert substance with the identical physical characteristics of a real drug) is used in the research design.

Nutrition aids in the form of glycogen supercompensation can enhance endurance performance by providing larger initial glycogen stores in muscle, thus delaying the onset of fatigue. The intake of supplemental vitamins generally has no benefit for the athlete and is harmless, except in some instances where megadoses of vitamins might be ingested. Maintaining water and electrolyte balance is essential to normal performance.

It is now evident that anabolic-androgenic steroids can be effective in increasing body mass and strength. However, the potential dangers and risks of taking steroids are well documented. There are inherent dangers for both male and female users of this class of drugs. Human growth hormone has been used alone and in combination with steroids. This represents a further heightening of risk to the health of an individual. The intake of steroids and growth hormone for the sole purpose of improving physique and athletic performance is ill-advised.

The American College of Sports Medicine, The United States Olympic Committee, the International Olympic Committee, and other sports-governing bodies have all taken strong stands against the use of the various pharmacological substances. Steroids, human growth hormone, and amphetamines represent the largest classes of banned substances.

Among physiological agents, blood doping represents a major concern. Because of both ethical and clinical reasons, blood doping is not recommended. The practice has been banned in national and international competition. Oxygen can have short-term benefits if breathed prior to breath-holding activities. Otherwise, supplemental oxygen is ineffective.

Oral ingestion of aspartic acid salts does not consistently result in increased exercise performance. However, the ingestion of alkaline salts (sodium bicarbonate) appears to increase endurance during heavy, short-term exercise. Caffeine has been shown to increase significantly the amount of work performance before fatiguing.

Drug testing in sports has become a highly sophisticated and reliable procedure. The use of gas chromotography/mass spectrometry has made the detection of doping substances, even in very minute levels, in urine samples "easily" detectable.

Questions

1. Define an ergogenic aid.
2. What are some of the problems associated with obtaining consistent and objective information on the effects of ergogenic aids?
3. How do anabolic-androgenic steroids affect performance?
4. What are the physiological effects of amphetamines?
5. What is blood doping, and does it improve athletic performance?
6. Explain the effects of aspartic acid salts, bicarbonate, oxygen, caffeine, and vitamin E on athletic performance.

References

1. Ahlborg, B., Ekelund, L. G., and Nilsson, C. G.: Effect of potassium-magnesium-asparate on the capacity for prolonged exercise in man. *Acta Physiol Scand.* 74:238–245, 1968.
2. Allen, P. D., and Pandolf, K. B.: Perceived exertion associated with breathing hyperoxic mixtures during submaximal work. *Med Sci Sports.* 9(2):122–127, 1977.
3. American College of Sports Medicine: *Position stand on the use of anabolic-androgenic steroids in sports.* Indianapolis, Ind., 1984.
4. Ariel, G., and Saville, W.: Anabolic steroids: the physiological effects of placebos. *Med Sci Sports.* 4(2):124–126, 1972.

5. Aronson, V.: Vitamins and minerals as ergogenic aids. *Physician Sportsmed.* 14(3):209–212, 1986.

6. Åstrand, P. O., and Rodahl, K.: *Textbook of Work Physiology*, 2nd ed. New York, McGraw-Hill, 1977.

7. Bannister, R., and Cunningham, D.: The effects on the respiration and performance during exercise of adding oxygen to the inspired air. *J Physiol Lond.* 125:118–137, 1954.

8. Bell, R. D., Card, R. T., Johnson, M. A., Cunningham, T. A., and Baker, F.: Blood doping and athletic performance. *Aust J Sports Med.* 8(2):133–139, 1977.

9. Bjorgum, R. K., and Sharkey, B. J.: Inhalation of oxygen as an aid to recovery after exertion. *Res Q.* 37:462–467, 1966.

10. Bonen, J., Malcolm, S. A., Kilgour, R. D., MacIntyre, K. P., and Belcastro, A. N.: Glucose ingestion before and during intense exercise. *J Appl Physiol.* 50:766–771, 1981.

11. Buick, F. J., Gledhill, N., Froese, A. B., Spriet, L., and Meyers, E. C.: Double blind study of blood boosting in highly trained runners. *Med Sci Sports.* 10(1):49, 1978.

12. Casner, S., Early, R., and Carlson, B.: Anabolic steroid effects on body composition in normal young men. *J Sports Med Phys Fit.* 11:98–103, 1971.

13. Chandler, J. V., and Blair, S. N.: The effect of amphetamine on selected physiological components related to athletic success. *Med Sci Sports Exer.* 12(1):65–69, 1980.

14. Clarke, K. S.: Sports medicine and drug control programs of the U.S. Olympic Committee. *J Allergy Clin Immunol.* 73:740–744, 1984.

15. Cohen, J. C., Faber, W. M., Spinnler, A. J., and Noakes, T. D.: Altered serum lipoprotein profiles in male and female power lifters ingesting anabolic steroids. *Physician Sportsmed.* 14(6):131–136, 1986.

16. Consolazio, C. F., Nelson, R. A., Matousch, L. O., and Isaac, G. J.: Effects of aspartic acid salts (Mg + K) on physical performance of men. *J Appl Physiol.* 19:257–261, 1964.

17. Costill, D. L., Coyle, E., Dalsky, G., Evans, W., Fink, W., and Hoopes, D.: Effects of elevated plasma FFA and insulin on muscle glycogen usage during exercise. *J Appl Physiol.* 43:695–699, 1977.

18. Costill, D. L., Pearson, D. R., and Fink, W. J.: Anabolic steroid use among athletes: changes in HDL-C levels. *Physician Sportsmed.* 12(6):112–117, 1984.

19. Costill, D. L., Dalsky, G. P., and Fink, W. J.: Effects of caffeine ingestion on metabolism and exercise performance. *Med Sci Sports.* 10(3):155–158, 1978.

20. Costill, D. L.: Performance secrets. *Runners World.* 13(7):50–55, July, 1978.

21. Cunningham, K. G.: The effect of transfusional polycythemia on aerobic work capacity. *J Sports Med.* 18:353–358, 1978.

22. Cureton, T. K.: Effects of wheat germ oil and vitamin E on normal human subjects in physical training programs. *Am J Physiol.* 179:628, 1954.

23. Desbleds, M., Rapp, J. P., Dumas, P., and Jolis, P.: Risk of blood transfusion doping in athletes. *Med Sport (Paris).* 53(4):191–194, 1979.

24. Dill, D. B., Edwards, H. T., and Talbott, J. H.: Alkalosis and the capacity for work. *J Biol Chem.* 97:58–59, 1932.

25. Ekblom, B., Goldbard, A., and Gullbring, B.: Response to exercise after blood loss and reinfusion. *J Appl Physiol.* 33(2):175–180, 1973.

26. Ekblom, B., Wilson, G., and Astrand, P. O.: Central circulation during exercise after venesection and reinfusion of red blood cells. *J Appl Physiol.* 40:379–383, 1976.

27. Elbel, E., Ormond, D., and Close, D.: Some effects of breathing O_2 before and after exercise. *J Appl Physiol.* 16:48–52, 1961.

28. Fahey, Thomas D., and Brown, C. Harmon: The effects of anabolic steroids on the strength, body composition and endurance of college males when accompanied by a weight training program. *Med Sci Sports.* 5(4):272–276, 1973.

29. Fallis, N., Wilson, W., Tetreault, L., and LaSagna, L.: Effect of potassium and magnesium aspartates on athletic performance. *JAMA.* 185(2):129, 1963.

30. Foster, C., Costill, D. L., and Fink, W. J.: Effects of pre-exercise feedings on endurance performance. *Med Sci Sports.* 11(1):1–5, 1979.

31. Fowler, W. H., Garner, G. W., and Egstrom, G. H.: Effect of an anabolic steroid on physical performance of young men. *J Appl Physiol.* 20:1038–1040, 1965.

32. Frye, A., and Ruhling, R.: RBC infusion, exercise, hemoconcentration and $\dot{V}O_2$. *Med Sci Sports.* 9(1):69, 1977.

33. Girandola, R. N., Wiswell, R. A., and Bulbulian, R.: Effects of pangamic acid (B-15)

ingestion on metabolic response to exercise. *Med Sci Sports Exer.* 12(2):98, 1980.

34. Golding, L.: Drugs and hormones. In Morgan, W. (ed.): *Ergogenic Aids and Muscular Performance.* New York, Academic Press, 1972, pp. 367–397.
35. Golding, L., Freydinger, J., and Fishel, S.: Weight, size and strength—unchanged with steroids. *Physician Sportsmed.* June, 1974, pp. 39–43.
36. Golding, L. A., and Barnard, R. J.: The effects of d-amphetamine sulfate on physical performance. *J Sports Med Phys Fit.* 3:221–224, 1963.
37. Gray, M. E., and Titlow, L. W.: Effect of pangamic acid on maximal treadmill performance. *Med Sci Sports Exer.* 14(6):277–280, 1983.
38. Guyton, A. C.: *Textbook of Medical Physiology,* 6th ed. Philadelphia, W. B. Saunders, 1981.
39. Guyton, Arthur: *Basic Human Physiology: Normal Function and Mechanisms of Disease.* Philadelphia, W. B. Saunders, 1971, p. 668.
40. Hagerman, F., Bowers, R., Fox, E., and Ersing, W.: The effects of breathing 100 per cent oxygen during rest, heavy work, and recovery. *Res Q.* 39(4):965–974, 1968.
41. Hargreaves, M. W., Costill, D. L., Katz, A., and Fink, W. J.: Effects of fructose on muscle glycogen usage during exercise. *Med Sci Sports Exer.* 17(3):360–363, 1985.
42. Haymes, E. M.: Proteins, vitamins, and iron. In Williams, M. H. (ed.): *Ergogenic Aids in Sports.* Champaign, Ill. Human Kinetics Publishers, 1983.
43. Herbert, W. G.: Water and electrolytes. In Williams, M. H. (ed.): *Ergogenic Aids in Sports.* Champaign, Ill., Human Kinetics Publishers, 1983.
44. Hughes, R., Clode, M., Edwards, R., Goodwin, T., and Jones, N.: Effect of inspired O_2 on cardiopulmonary and metabolic responses to exercise in man. *J Appl Physiol.* 24(3):336–347, 1968.
45. Ivy, J. L., Costill, D. L., Fink, W. J., and Lower, R. W.: Influence of caffeine and carbohydrate feedings on endurance performance. *Med Sci Sports.* 11(1):6–11, 1979.
46. Johnson, L., Fisher, G., Silvester, L., and Hofheins, C.: Anabolic steroid: effects on strength, body weight, oxygen uptake and spermatogenesis upon mature males. *Med Sci Sports.* 4(1):43–45, 1972.
47. Jones, N. L., Sutton, J. R., Taylor, R., and

Toews, C. J.: Effect of pH on cardiorespiratory and metabolic responses to exercise. *J Appl Physiol.* 43(6):959–964, 1977.
48. Karpovich, P.: The effect of oxygen inhalation on swimming performance. *Res Q.* 5(2):24, 1934.
49. Karpovich, P.: Effect of amphetamine sulphate on athletic performance. *JAMA.* 170:558–561, 1959.
50. Kantor, M. A., Bianchini, A., Bernier, D., Sady, S. P., and Thompson, P. D.: Androgens reduce HDL-cholesterol and increase hepatic triglyceride lipase activity. *Med Sci Sports Exer.* 17(4):462–465, 1985.
51. Miller, A.: Influence of oxygen administration on the cardiovascular function during exercise and recovery. *J Appl Physiol.* 5:165–168, 1952.
52. Murphy, R. J.: The problem of environmental heat in athletics. *Ohio State Med J.* 59:799, 1963.
53. Murray, T. H.: Human growth hormone in sports-no. *Physician Sportsmed.* 14(5):29, 1986.
54. Pate, R. R., McFarland, J., Van Wyk, J., and Okocha, A.: Effects of blood reinfusion on endurance exercise performance in female distance runners. *Med Sci Sports.* 11(1):97, 1979.
55. Percy, E. C.: Ergogenic aids in athletics. *Med Sci Sports.* 10(4):298–303, 1978.
56. Peterson, G. E., and Fahey, T. D.: HDL-C in five elite athletes using anabolic-androgenic steroids. *Physician Sportsmed.* 12(6):120–130, 1984.
57. Robertson, R., Gilcher, R., Metz, K., Bahnson, H., Allison, T., Skrinar, G., Abbott, A., and Becker, R.: Effect of red blood cell reinfusion on physical working capacity and perceived exertion at normal and reduced oxygen pressure. *Med Sci Sports.* 10(1):49, 1978.
58. Robertson, R., Gilcher, R., Metz, K., Casperson, C., Abbott, A., Allison, T., Skrinar, G., Werner, K., Zelicoff, S., and Drause, J.: Central circulation and work capacity after red blood cell reinfusion under normoxia and hypoxia in women. *Med Sci Sports.* 11(1):98, 1979.
59. Rogozkin, V.: Metabolic effects of anabolic steroids on skeletal muscle. *Med Sci Sports.* 11(2):160–163, 1979.
60. Ryan, A. J.: Use of amphetamines in athletics. *JAMA.* 170:562, 1959.
61. Sharkey, B.: *The Effect of Preliminary Oxygen Inhalation on Performance in Swim-*

ming. Master's Thesis, West Chester State College, West Chester, PA, 1961.

62. Sharman, I. M., Down, M. G., and Sen, R. N.: The effects of vitamin E on physiological function and athletic performance in adolescent swimmers. *Br J Nutr.* 26:265–276, 1971.

63. Shephard, R., Campbell, R., Pimm, P., Stuart, D., and Wright, G.: Do athletes need vitamin E? *Physician Sportsmed.* 2(9):57–60, 1974.

64. Sherman, W. M.: Carbohydrates, muscle glycogen, and muscle glycogen supercompensation. In Williams, M. H. (ed.): *Ergogenic Aids in Sports.* Champaign, Ill., Human Kinetics Publishers, 1983.

65. Sherman, W. M., Costill, D. L., Fink, W. J., and Miller, J. M.: The effect of exercise and diet manipulation on muscle glycogen and its subsequent utilization during performance. *Int J Sports Med.* 2:114–118, 1981.

66. Sidney, K. H., and Lefcoe, N. M.: The effect of ephedrine on the physiological and psychological responses to submaximal and maximal exercise in man. Med. Sci. Sports, 9(2):95–99, 1977.

67. Sone, M. H., and Lipner, H.: Responses to intensive training and methandrostenelone administration. I. Contractile and performance variables. Pflugers Arch., 375(2):141–146, 1978.

68. Strauss, R. H., Liggett, M. T., and Lanese, R. R.: Anabolic steroid use and perceived effects in ten weight trained women athletes. JAMA, 253:2871–2873. (May 17) 1985.

69. Strauss, R. H., Wright, J. E., Finerman, G. A. M., and Catlin, D. H.: Side effects of anabolic steroids in weight-trained men. Phys. Sportsmed., 11(12):87–95, 1983.

70. Videman, T., and Rytomaa, T.: Effect of blood removal and autoinfusion on heart rate response to a submaximal workload. J. Sports Med., 17:387–390, 1977.

71. Ward, P.: The effect of an anabolic steroid on strength and lean body mass. Med. Sci. Sports, 5(4):277–282, 1973.

72. Wilkes, D., Gledhill, N., and Smyth, R.: Effects of acute induced metabolic alkalosis on 800-m racing time. Med. Sci. Spt. Exer., 15(4):277–280, 1983.

73. Williams, M. H., Goodwin, H., Perkins, R., and Bocrie, J.: Effect of blood reinjection upon endurance capacity and heart rate. Med. Sci. Sports. 5(3):181–185, 1973.

74. Williams, M. H., Lindhiem M., and Schuster, R.: The effect of blood-infusion upon endurance capacity and ratings of perceived exertion. Med. Sci. Sports. 10(2):113–118, 1978.

75. Williams, M. H., and Thompson J.: Effect of varient dosages of amphetamine upon endurance. Res. Quart. 44(4):417–422, 1973.

76. Williams, M. H.: Blood doping—does it really help athletes? Physician Sportsmed., Jan., 1975, p. 52.

77. Williams, M. H., ed.: Ergogenic aids in sports. Champaign. Human Kinetics Publishers. 1983.

78. Williams, M. H.: Blood Doping. In M. H. Williams: Ergogenic aids in sports. Champaign. Human Kinetics Publishers. 1983.

79. Wilmore, J.: Oxygen In Morgan, W., (ed.): Ergogenic Aids and Muscular Performance. New York Academic Press. 1972, pp. 321–342.

80. Wilson, G. D., and Welch, H. G.: Effects of hyperoxic gas mixtures on exercise tolerance in man. Med. Sci. Sports 7(1):48–52, 1975.

81. United States Olympic Committee: Drug control program protocol. U.S. Olympic House. Colorado Springs, June 1986.

SELECTED READINGS

deMerode, A.: Doping tests at the Olympic Games in 1976. J. Sports Med., 19(1):91–96, 1979.

Lamb. D. R.: Androgens and exercise. Med. Sci. Sports. 7(1):1–5, 1975.

Morgan, W. (ed.): Ergogenic Aids and Muscular Performance, New York. Academic Press, 1972.

Williams, M. H.: Drugs and Athletic Performance. Springfield, Ill., Charles C. Thomas, 1974.

appendices

Symbols and Abbreviations

ADP adenosine diphosphate

ATP adenosine triphosphate

a-$\bar{v}O_2$diff arterial-mixed venous oxygen difference

°C. degrees Celsius (centigrade)

CA carbonic anhydrase

Ca^{++} calcium ion

CO_2 carbon dioxide

d distance

db dry bulb

e^- electron

F force

f frequency of breathing per minute

°F. degrees Fahrenheit

FFA free fatty acids

FFW fat-free weight

FT (or FG) fast-twitch muscle fibers or motor units (or fast, glycolytic fibers)

F_x fractional concentration of gas

g black globe temperature (radiant energy)

H hydrogen atom

H^+ hydrogen ion

Hb hemoglobin

HbO_2 oxyhemoglobin

HCO_3^- bicarbonate ion

Hg mercury

HR heart rate

H_2CO_3 carbonic acid

H_2O water

kcal kilocalorie

kcal/min kilocalories per minute

kg kilogram

LA lactic acid

LBW lean body weight

LBM lean body mass

m meter

max $\dot{V}O_2$ maximal volume of oxygen consumed per minute during exercise

meq milliequivalent

MET metabolic equivalent equal to 3.5 ml of O_2 consumed per kg and per minute

min minute

ml milliliter

mm millimeter

mmol millimole

Na^+ sodium ion

O_2 oxygen

P power

P_B barometric pressure

PC phosphocreatine

P_{CO_2} partial pressure of carbon dioxide

Pi inorganic phosphate

P_{N_2} partial pressure of nitrogen

P_{O_2} partial pressure of oxygen

P_x partial pressure of gas

$\dot{Q}$ cardiac output

RM repetition maximum

sec second

ST (or SO) slow-twitch muscle fibers or motor units (or slow, oxidative fibers)

SV stroke volume

t time

TV tidal volume

V volume

$\dot{V}_E$ minute ventilation, or amount of air expired in one minute

$\dot{V}O_2$ volume of oxygen consumed per minute

wb wet bulb

WBGT wet bulb globe temperature

WBT wet bulb temperature

Appendix B

Pulmonary Symbols and Norms*

Symbols and Abbreviations Used By Pulmonary Physiologists*

Before 1950, each pulmonary physiologist had developed a jargon of his or her own. In 1950 a group of American pulmonary physiologists, in order to lessen confusion, agreed to use a standard set of symbols and abbreviations. The symbols below are used in equations in this book and in most original articles published since 1950; they cannot be applied to earlier articles.

Special Symbols

- Dash above any symbol indicates a *mean value*.
· Dot above any symbol indicates a *time derivative*.

For Gases

PRIMARY SYMBOLS (LARGE CAPITAL LETTERS)

		EXAMPLES	
V	= gas volume	V_A	= volume of alveolar gas
$\dot{V}$	= gas volume per unit time	$\dot{V}_{O_2}$	= O_2 consumption per minute
P	= gas pressure	$P_{A_{O_2}}$	= alveolar O_2 pressure
$\bar{P}$	= mean gas pressure	$P_{C_{O_2}}$	= mean capillary O_2 pressure
F	= fractional concentration in dry gas phase	$F_{I_{O_2}}$	= fractional concentration of O_2 in inspired gas
f	= respiratory frequency (breaths per unit time)		
D	= diffusing capacity	D_{O_2}	= diffusing capacity for O_2 (ml O_2 per minute per mm Hg)
R	= respiratory exchange ratio	R	= $\dot{V}_{CO_2}/\dot{V}_{O_2}$

SECONDARY SYMBOLS (SMALL CAPITAL LETTERS)

		EXAMPLES	
I	= inspired gas	$F_{I_{CO_2}}$	= fractional concentration of CO_2 in inspired gas
E	= expired gas	V_E	= volume of expired gas
A	= alveolar gas	$\dot{V}_A$	= alveolar ventilation per minute
T	= tidal gas	V_T	= tidal volume

*Based on report in *Fed Proc* 9:602–605, 1950.
*From Comroe, J. H. et al: *The Lung,* 2nd ed. Chicago, Year Book Medical Publishers, Inc., 1962.

SECONDARY SYMBOLS
(SMALL CAPITAL LETTERS)

D   = dead space gas
B   = barometric
STPD = $0°$ C, 760 mm Hg, dry
BTPS = body temperature and pressure
        saturated with water vapor
ATPS = ambient temperature and pressure
        saturated with water vapor

EXAMPLES

VD   = volume of dead space gas
PB   = barometric pressure

For Blood

PRIMARY SYMBOLS
(LARGE CAPITAL LETTERS)

Q   = volume of blood

$\dot{Q}$ = volume flow of blood per unit time

C   = concentration of gas in blood phase
S   = per cent saturation of Hb with O_2
      or CO

EXAMPLES

QC   = volume of blood in pulmonary
        capillaries
$\dot{Q}C$ = blood flow through pulmonary
        capillaries per minute
Ca_{O_2} = ml O_2 in 100 ml arterial blood
$S\bar{v}_{O_2}$ = saturation of Hb with O_2 in
        mixed venous blood

SECONDARY SYMBOLS
(small letters)

a   = arterial blood

v   = venous blood

c   = capillary blood

EXAMPLES

Pa_{CO_2} = partial pressure of CO_2 in arte-
        rial blood
$P\bar{v}_{O_2}$ = partial pressure of O_2 in mixed
        venous blood
Pc_{CO} = partial pressure of CO in pulmo-
        nary capillary blood

For Lung Volumes

VC   = vital capacity

IC   = inspiratory capacity

IRV = inspiratory reserve volume

ERV = expiratory reserve volume

FRC = function residual capacity

RV   = residual volume

TLC = total lung capacity

= maximal volume that can be expired
  after maximal inspiration
= maximal volume that can be inspired
  from resting expiratory level
= maximal volume that can be inspired
  from end-tidal inspiration
= maximal volume that can be expired
  from resting expiratory level
= volume of gas in lungs at resting expiratory level
= volume of gas in lungs at end of maximal
  expiration
= volume of gas in lungs at end of maximal
  inspiration

Typical Values for Pulmonary Function Tests

These are values for a healthy, resting, recumbent young male (1.7 square meters of surface area), breathing air at sea level, unless other conditions are specified. They are presented merely to give approximate figures. These values may change with position, age, size, sex, and altitude; variability occurs among members of a homogeneous group under standard conditions.

Lung Volume (BTPS)

Inspiratory capacity, ml 3600
Expiratory reserve volume, ml 1200
Vital capacity, ml 4800
Residual volume (RV), ml 1200
Functional residual capacity, ml 2400
Thoracic gas volume, ml 2400
Total lung capacity (TLC), ml 6000
RV/TLC × 100, per cent 20

Ventilation (BTPS)

Tidal volume, ml 500
Frequency, respirations per minute 12
Minute volume, ml per minute 6000
Respiratory dead space, ml 150
Alveolar ventilation, ml per minute 4200

Distribution of Inspired Gas

Single-breath test (per cent increase N_2 for 500 ml expired alveolar gas),
    per cent N_2 .... <1.5
Pulmonary nitrogen emptying rate (7 minute test), per cent N_2 .... <2.5
Helium closed circuit (mixing efficiency related to perfect mixing) per cent 76

Alveolar Ventilation/Pulmonary Capillary Blood Flow

Alveolar ventilation (liters per minute)/blood flow (liters per minute) 0.8
Physiologic shunt/cardiac output × 100, per cent .... <7
Physiologic dead space/tidal volume × 100, per cent .... <30

Pulmonary Circulation

Pulmonary capillary blood flow, ml per minute 5400
Pulmonary artery pressure, mm Hg 25/8
Pulmonary capillary blood volume, ml 90
Pulmonary "capillary" blood pressure (wedge), mm Hg 8

Alveolar Gas

Oxygen partial pressure, mm Hg.. 104
CO_2 partial pressure, mm Hg 40

Diffusion and Gas Exchange

O_2 consumption (STPD), ml per minute.. 240
CO_2 output (STPD), ml per minute 192
Respiratory exchange ratio, R (CO_2 output/O_2 uptake)........................ 0.8
Diffusing capacity, O_2 (STPD) resting, ml O_2 per minute per mm Hg .... >15
Diffusing capacity, CO (steady state) (STPD) resting, ml CO per minute
  per mm Hg 17
Diffusing capacity, CO (single-breath) (STPD) resting, ml CO per minute
  per mm Hg 25
Diffusing capacity, CO (rebreathing) (STPD) resting, ml CO per minute
  per mm Hg 25
Fractional CO uptake, resting, per cent.. 53
Maximal diffusing capacity, O_2 (exercise) (STPD), ml O_2 per minute
  per mm Hg 60

Arterial Blood

O_2 saturation (per cent saturation of Hb with O_2) per cent 97.1
O_2 tension, mm Hg 95
CO_2 tension, mm Hg 40
Alveolar-arterial PO_2 difference, mm Hg.. 9
Alveolar-arterial PO_2 difference (12–14% O_2) mm Hg 10
Alveolar-arterial PO_2 difference (100% O_2), mm Hg........................... 35
O_2 saturation (100% O_2) per cent (+1.9 ml dissolved O_2 per 100 ml blood) 100
O_2 tension (100% O_2) mm Hg 640
pH 7.4

Mechanics of Breathing

Maximal voluntary ventilation (BTPS), liters per minute 170
Forced expiratory volume, per cent in 1 second 83
                 per cent in 3 seconds 97
Maximal expiratory flow rate (for 1 liter) (ATPS), liters per minute.............. >400
Maximal inspiratory flow rate (for 1 liter) (ATPS), liters per minute............. >300
Compliance of lungs and thoracic cage, liters per cm H_2O 0.1
Compliance of lungs, liters per cm H_2O... 0.2
Airway resistance, cm H_2O per liter per second................................. 1.6
Pulmonary resistance, cm H_2O per liter per second.............................. 1.9
Work of quiet breathing, kg-meter per minute...................................... 0.5
Maximal work of breathing, kg-meter per breath 10
Maximal inspiratory and expiratory pressures, mm Hg............................... 60–100

Appendix C

The Gas Laws

Gas volume is dependent on temperature and pressure. For example, a given number of gas molecules occupies a greater volume at a higher temperature and lower pressure than at a lower temperature and higher pressure. By the same token, an unequal number of gas molecules could occupy the same volume, but only at different temperatures or pressures. In other words, two gas volumes of one liter each could contain an unequal number of gas molecules only if the temperature or pressure of the two volumes were different. On the other hand, whenever the temperature and pressure of two equal volumes of gases are the same, the two volumes will always contain the same number of molecules. For these reasons, respiratory gas volumes *must* be corrected to a reference temperature and pressure so that valid comparisons can be made. Temperature and pressure vary from day to day and from one laboratory to another.

ATPS Conditions

The conditions of temperature and pressure at the time a respiratory gas volume is measured are abbreviated ATPS. This abbreviation means ambient temperature and pressure, saturated with water vapor. Since most respiratory volumes are measured with a wet spirometer, ambient temperature refers to the temperature of the gas in the spirometer (Ts) and ambient pressure refers to the environment or barometric pressure at the time of the measurement. The volume is also assumed to be saturated with water vapor at spirometer temperature because a wet spirometer is water sealed (p. 213). In other words the gas is collected over water and is assumed to be saturated with water vapor. It is this volume, under various ATPS conditions, which must be corrected to a reference temperature and pressure before any comparisons can be made.

STPD Conditions

There are two reference conditions of temperature and pressure with which you will be concerned. The first of these is standard temperature and pressure, dry, abbreviated STPD. Standard temperature is $0°$ C. and standard pressure is 760 mm Hg. "Dry" means that the volume occupied by molecules of water vapor has been accounted for, i.e., the gas volume at STPD is that volume occupied by all gas molecules except those of water vapor. The number of gas molecules and the volume they occupy under STPD conditions is constant and independent of the particular gas involved. In other words, one mole of any gas (e.g., 32 grams of oxygen) at STPD contains 6.02×10^{23} molecules and occupies 22.4 liters. Therefore, a volume of gas under STPD conditions represents qualitatively the number of gas molecules present. Corrections of gas volumes from ATPS to STPD are made whenever we need to know the *amount* or number of gas molecules, e.g., when calculating the amount of oxygen consumed and the amount of carbon dioxide produced. Such corrections always result in a reduction of volume for several reasons: (1) ambient (spirometer) temperature is higher than 0°C, e.g., from 20° to 25°C; (2) ambient pressure in most parts of the country is below 760 mm Hg; and (3) the gas is "dry."

BTPS Conditions

The other reference point for making gas volume corrections is body temperature and pressure, saturated with water vapor, abbreviated BTPS. Body temperature is 37° C and body pressure is the same as ambient pressure. Corrections of gas volumes from ATPS (or from STPD, for that matter) to BTPS are made when we are interested in knowing the volume of air that is ventilated by the lungs and not the number of gas molecules present. When air at room temperature (e.g., 22° C) is inspired, its volume will expand in the lungs as a result of: (1) the increase in temperature (from 22° to 37° C); and (2) the addition of water vapor molecules because of the increase in temperature. Corrections to BTPS are necessary, therefore, for all respiratory gas measurements dealing with volume only; e.g., vital capacity, tidal volume, minute volume, and maximal breathing capacity.

Calculation of Volume Corrections

Calculations of gas volume corrections for differences in temperature, pressure, and water vapor are based upon several gas laws irrespective of the specific correction to be made. Remember that correction from ATPS to STPD is made when we are concerned with the amount or number of gas molecules present, such as in calculating oxygen consumption and carbon dioxide production; correction to BTPS is made when we are concerned with the volume occupied by the gas molecules, such as in determining lung volumes.

Temperature Correction

Gas volume is directly related to temperature, so that increasing or decreasing the temperature of a gas (at constant pressure) causes a proportional increase or decrease, respectively, in volume. This is known as *Charles's Law*. It states that the change in temperature as determined by the ratio of the initial temperature (T_1) to that of the final corrected temperature (T_2) is equal to the change in volume or to the ratio of the initial volume (V_1) and the final or corrected volume (V_2). In mathematical form:

$$\frac{T_1}{T_2} = \frac{V_1}{V_2} \tag{1}$$

The units for temperature in this case are those of either the Absolute (A) or the Kelvin (K) scale, i.e., 273° K = 0°C; °K = 273° + °C (e.g., 22° C = 273° + 22° = 295°K).

Rearranging equation (1) to solve for V_2:

$$V_2 = \frac{V_1 \times T_2}{T_1} \tag{2}$$

In correcting a gas volume to standard temperature (0° C):

V_1 = volume ATPS (VATPS)
V_2 = volume corrected to standard temperature (VST)
T_1 = absolute spirometer temperature (273° K + Ts ° C)
T_2 = absolute standard temperature (273° K)

and

$$V\text{ST} = V\text{ATPS} \frac{273°}{273° + \text{Ts}}$$ (3)

In correcting to body temperature (BT) or 37° C, then:

V_2 = volume corrected to body temperature (VBT)
T_2 = absolute body temperature (273° K + 37° C = 310°)

and

$$V\text{BT} = V\text{ATPS} \frac{310°}{273° + \text{Ts}}$$ (4)

Pressure and Water Vapor Corrections

Gas volume is inversely related to pressure, so that increasing or decreasing the pressure of a gas (at constant temperature) causes a proportional decrease or increase, respectively, in volume. This is known as *Boyle's Law*. It states that the change in pressure as determined by the ratio of the initial pressure (P_1) to the final or corrected pressure (P_2) is equal to the volume change or the ratio of the final or corrected volume (V_2) and the initial volume (V_1). In other words:

$$\frac{P_1}{P_2} = \frac{V_2}{V_1}$$ (5)

Again, rearranging to solve for V_2:

$$V_2 = V_1 \left(\frac{P_1}{P_2} \right)$$ (6)

Pressure is measured in millimeters of mercury (mm Hg).

Correction for water vapor is made along with the correction for pressure even though water vapor pressure is dependent only on temperature. When the gas volume is to be "dried," as in STPD, the vapor pressure of water at ambient temperature T_1 (PH$_2$O) is subtracted from the ambient or initial pressure (P_2) as follows:

$$V_2 - V_1 \left(\frac{P_1 - P\text{H}_2\text{O}}{P_2} \right)$$ (7)

For example, correcting to standard pressure (760 mm Hg, dry or SPD), we would have:

$$\text{VSPD} = \text{VATPS} \left(\frac{P_1 - PH_2O}{760} \right) \tag{8}$$

When the gas volume is to be saturated, as in BTPS, PH_2O is subtracted from P_1 as previously, but in addition the vapor pressure of water at T_2 or body temperature (PH_2O') is subtracted from P_2 or body pressure. In other words:

$$V_2 = V_1 \left(\frac{P_1 - PH_2O}{P_2 - PH_2O'} \right) \tag{9}$$

The reason why this procedure accounts for the increase in volume due to the addition of water vapor molecules when the temperature is increased to body temperature is because body pressure (P_2) obviously must equal ambient pressure (P_1), therefore no correction for pressure per se is necessary in going from ATPS to BTPS; i.e., $\frac{P_1}{P_2} = 1$. When PH_2O and PH_2O' are subtracted from P_1 and P_2, respectively, the resulting ratio, which is greater than 1, is proportional to the increase in volume due to the addition of water vapor molecules.

When correcting to body pressure, saturated with water vapor (BPS):

$$\text{VBPS} = \text{VATPS} \left(\frac{P_1 - PH_2O}{P_2 - 47 \text{ mm Hg}} \right) \tag{10}$$

The 47 mm Hg pressure is the vapor pressure of water at body temperature.

Combined Correction Factors

We can now combine the temperature, pressure, and water vapor corrections into one equation for STPD and one equation for BTPS. Correcting from ATPS to STPD, we would combine equation (3) for temperature and equation (8) for pressure and water vapor as follows:

$$\text{VSTPD} = \text{VAPTS} \left(\frac{273°}{273° + Ts} \right) \left(\frac{P_1 - PH_2O}{760} \right) \tag{11}$$

Correcting from ATPS to BTPS we would combine equations (4) and (10) for temperature and water vapor pressure, respectively:

$$\text{VBTPS} = \text{VATPS} \left(\frac{310°}{273° + Ts} \right) \left(\frac{P_1 - PH_2O}{P_2 - 47} \right) \tag{12}$$

Problems

Suppose you have collected in a spirometer 100 liters of expired gas. At the time you measured the gas volume, ambient temperature in the spirometer was 22° C, ambient pressure was 747 mm Hg and PH_2O at 22° C is equal to 19.8 mm Hg.

1. Correct the volume from ATPS to STPD.
2. Correct the volume from ATPS to BTPS.
3. Correct the volume from STPD to BTPS.

Solutions

1. Using equation (11) and substituting, we have:

$$V_{STPD} = 100 \text{ liters} \left(\frac{273°}{295°}\right)\left(\frac{727.2 \text{ mm}}{760 \text{ mm}}\right)$$

$$= 100 \ (0.925) \ (0.957)$$

$$= 100 \ (0.885)$$

$$= \textbf{88.5 liters}$$

2. Using equation (12) and substituting, we have:

$$V_{BTPS} = 100 \text{ liters} \left(\frac{310°}{295°}\right)\left(\frac{727.2 \text{ mm}}{700 \text{ mm}}\right)$$

$$= 100 \ (1.051) \ (1.039)$$

$$= 100 \ (1.092)$$

$$= \textbf{109.2 liters}$$

3. You can also use equation (12) for this solution but remember that the gas volume to be corrected is under conditions of STPD and *not* ATPS. Therefore, in equation (12):
   a. V_{STPD} replaces V_{ATPS}.
   b. $273° + T_s$ now represents standard temperature, or $273° K + 0° C$.
   c. P_1 represents standard pressure, or 760 mm Hg, and P_{H_2O} at $0° C$ is negligible. Therefore,

$$V_{BTPS} = 88.5 \text{ liters} \left(\frac{310°}{273°}\right)\left(\frac{760 \text{ mm}}{700 \text{ mm}}\right)$$

$$= 88.5 \ (1.136) \ (1.086)$$

$$= 88.5 \ (1.233)$$

$$= \textbf{109.2 liters}$$

Calculation of Oxygen Consumption and Carbon Dioxide Production

Oxygen Consumption

The amount of oxygen consumed per minute ($\dot{V}O_2$) is equal to the difference between the amount of oxygen inspired ($\dot{V}I_{O_2}$) and the amount of oxygen expired ($\dot{V}E_{O_2}$) or:

$$\dot{V}O_{2_{STPD}} = \dot{V}I_{O_{2_{STPD}}} - \dot{V}E_{O_{2_{STPD}}} \tag{13}$$

In order to use equation (13), the following variables must be measured:

1. $\dot{V}E$ the volume of air exhaled per minute.
2. FE_{O_2} the fractional concentration of oxygen in exhaled air.
3. FI_{O_2} the fractional concentration of oxygen in inspired air.*
4. FE_{CO_2} the fractional concentration of carbon dioxide in expired air.
5. FI_{CO_2} the fractional concentration of carbon dioxide in inspired air.

An *amount* is defined as a volume times a concentration. The volume in this case, as you will recall, is a volume which has been corrected to STPD. All volumes referred to from here on are STPD. In a 100-liter volume of gas containing 20% oxygen ($FO_2 = 0.2$) and 80% nitrogen ($FN_2 = 0.8$), the *amount* of oxygen is equal to 20 liters (100 liters $\times$ 0.2) and the amount of nitrogen is equal to 80 liters (100 liters $\times$ 0.8). As a result, the amount of oxygen inspired per minute according to equation (13) is equal to:

$$\dot{V}I_{O_2} = (\dot{V}I) (FI_{O_2}) \tag{14}$$

The same is true for the amount of oxygen expired; that is:

$$\dot{V}E_{O_2} = (\dot{V}E) (FE_{O_2}) \tag{15}$$

Substituting equations (14) and (15) into equation (13), we have:

$$\dot{V}O_2 = (\dot{V}I) (FI_{O_2}) - (\dot{V}E) (FE_{O_2}) \tag{16}$$

---

*If fresh air (i.e., outside air) is inspired, then FI_{O_2}, and FI_{CO_2}, and FI_{N_2}, will be 0.2093, 0.0004, and 0.7903 respectively.

Since FI_{O_2}, $\dot{V}E$, and FE_{O_2} are either known or measured directly, only $\dot{V}I$ and $\dot{V}O_2$ are unknown. Therefore, we must measure or calculate $\dot{V}I$ in order to solve equation (16) for $\dot{V}O_2$.

You may first think that $\dot{V}I$ equals $\dot{V}E$, i.e., that the volume we inspire is the same as that which we expire. This is true if, and only if, the amount of CO_2 given off is equal to the amount of oxygen consumed. In other words, $\dot{V}I = \dot{V}E$ only when $\dot{V}CO_2 = \dot{V}O_2$ or when $R = 1$. When more O_2 is consumed than CO_2 given off, $\dot{V}E$ is less than $\dot{V}I$. The opposite is true, i.e., $\dot{V}E$ is greater than $\dot{V}I$, when $\dot{V}CO_2$ is greater than $\dot{V}O_2$.

Rather than measuring $\dot{V}I$ directly, there is a simple method by which we can calculate it accurately. The calculation, sometimes referred to as the Haldane transformation, is based on the fact that the *amount* of nitrogen we inspire is equal to that which we expire, or:

$$(\dot{V}I)\,(FI_{N_2}) = (\dot{V}E)\,(FE_{N_2}) \tag{17}$$

where

FI_{N_2} = fractional concentration of nitrogen in inspired air.
FE_{N_2} = fractional concentration of nitrogen in expired air.

This relationship holds true because nitrogen is neither consumed nor given off, i.e., it is physiologically inert, and therefore the amounts inspired and expired are essentially equal.*

The fractional concentration of inspired nitrogen is given by the following relationship:

$$FI_{N_2} = 1 - (FI_{O_2} + FI_{CO_2}) \tag{18}$$

and the fractional concentration of expired nitrogen by:

$$FE_{N_2} = 1 - (FE_{O_2} + FE_{CO_2}) \tag{19}$$

These relationships are based on the fact that oxygen, carbon dioxide, and nitrogen are the only gases present, for all practical purposes, in inspired and expired air. The small concentrations of rare gases, such as argon and helium, which are also physiologically inert, are included in the nitrogen fraction. Substituting equations (18) and (19) in equation (17) we have:

$$\dot{V}I\,[1 - (FI_{O_2} + FI_{CO_2})] = \dot{V}E\,[1 - (FE_{O_2} + FE_{CO_2})] \tag{20}$$

---

*Recently, the concept of equality of respiratory gaseous nitrogen in man has been challenged, mainly by one laboratory,[1,3,4,5] and with it the accuracy of calculating oxygen consumption by the Haldane transformation.[2] However, subsequent studies from a number of different laboratories,[6,7,8,9,10] have shown that nitrogen differences are small and inconsistent and do not significantly affect oxygen consumption values calculated by assuming nitrogen equality.

Rearranging to solve for $\dot{V}I$:

$$\dot{V}I = \dot{V}E \, [1 - (FE_{O_2} + FE_{CO_2})] \, / \, [1 - (FI_{O_2} + FI_{CO_2})] \qquad (21)$$

This latter equation (sometimes referred to as the *nitrogen factor*) gives us a simple yet accurate estimate of $\dot{V}I$.*

By substituting the right side of equation (21) for $\dot{V}I$ in equation (16) we have the final equation for the calculation of $\dot{V}O_2$:

$$\dot{V}O_2 = \dot{V}E \left[\frac{1 - (FE_{O_2} + FE_{CO_2})}{1 - (FI_{O_2} + FI_{CO_2})} \right] FI_{O_2} - \dot{V}E \, FE_{O_2} \qquad (22)$$

As mentioned earlier, if fresh air is inspired, then equation (22) will reduce to:

$$\dot{V}O_2 = \dot{V}E \left[\frac{1 - (FE_{O_2} + FE_{CO_2})}{0.7903} \right] 0.2093 - \dot{V}E \, FE_{O_2} \qquad (23)$$

In the case where $\dot{V}I = \dot{V}E$, equation (22) will reduce even further. Substituting $\dot{V}E$ for $\dot{V}I$ in equation (16) gives us:

$$\dot{V}O_2 = (\dot{V}E) \, (FI_{O_2}) - (\dot{V}E) \, (FE_{O_2}) \qquad (24)$$

Collecting terms, we have:

$$\dot{V}O_2 = \dot{V}E \, (FI_{O_2} - FE_{O_2}) \qquad (25)$$

when $\dot{V}I = \dot{V}E$.

Carbon Dioxide Production

Calculation of the amount of CO_2 produced per minute is based on the same principles as those used in computing $\dot{V}O_2$. The basic equation is:

$$\dot{V}CO_2 = \dot{V}E_{CO_2} - \dot{V}I_{CO_2} \qquad (26)$$

Applying the "amount rule" gives us:

$$\dot{V}CO_2 = (\dot{V}E) \, (FE_{CO_2}) = (\dot{V}I) \, (FI_{CO_2}) \qquad (27)$$

If $\dot{V}O_2$ is calculated first, which is usually the case, then all the factors to the right of equation (27) are known and $\dot{V}CO_2$ can be determined. However, since the amount of CO_2

---

*If $\dot{V}I$ is measured and $\dot{V}E$ is to be calculated, which is sometimes the case, then:

$$\dot{V}E = \dot{V}I \, [1 - (FI_{O_2} + FI_{CO_2})] \, / \, [1 - (FE_{O_2} + FE_{CO_2})]$$

inspired $[\dot{V}_{I}(F_{I_{CO_2}})]$ is usually negligible (because $F_{I_{CO_2}}$ in inspired air is only 0.0004), equation (27) reduces to:

$$\dot{V}_{CO_2} = (\dot{V}_E)\,(F_{E_{CO_2}}) \tag{28}$$

This latter equation is the one most frequently used to calculate $\dot{V}_{CO_2}$.

Problems

Suppose you have made a 5-minute collection of expired air from a resting subject breathing fresh air and the following results were obtained:

$\dot{V}_{E_{ATPS}}$ = 33.5 liters per 5 minutes
$F_{E_{O_2}}$ = 0.1593
$F_{I_{O_2}}$ = 0.2093
$F_{E_{CO_2}}$ = 0.0400
$F_{I_{CO_2}}$ = 0.0004

P_B = 745 mm Hg
T_s = 24° C
P_{H_2O} at 24° C = 22.4 mm Hg
P_{H_2O} at 37° C = 47 mm Hg

1. What is the subject's $\dot{V}_{O_2}$?
2. What is the subject's $\dot{V}_{CO_2}$?
3. What is the subject's R?
4. What is the subject's $\dot{V}_{E_{BTPS}}$?

Solutions

1. To calculate $\dot{V}_{O_2}$, the first thing we must do is to convert $\dot{V}_{E_{ATPS}}$ to $\dot{V}_{E_{STPD}}$. Therefore, from equation (11):

$$\dot{V}_{STPD} = 33.5 \text{ liters} \left(\frac{273°}{297°}\right)\left(\frac{722.6 \text{ mm}}{760 \text{ mm}}\right)$$

$$= 33.5\,(0.919)\,(0.951)$$

$$= 33.5\,(0.874)$$

$$= \textbf{29.27 liters per 5 minutes or 5.85 liters per minute}$$

Substituting in equation (23), we have:

$$\dot{V}_{O_2} = 29.27 \text{ liters} \left[\frac{1 - (0.1593 + 0.0400)}{0.7903}\right] \times 0.2093 - [(29.27)\,(.1593)]$$

$$= 29.27\,(1.0131)\,(0.2093) - 4.663$$

$$= 6.206 - 4.663$$

$$= \textbf{1.543 liters per 5 minutes, or 309 ml per minute}$$

2. For $\dot{V}CO_2$, substitution in equation (28) gives us:

$$\dot{V}CO_2 = 29.27 \text{ liters } (0.0400)$$

$$= \mathbf{1.171 \text{ liters per 5 minutes or 234 ml per minute}}$$

3. The respiratory exchange ratio (R) is defined as $\dot{V}CO_2/\dot{V}O_2$; therefore:

$$\frac{234 \text{ ml per minute}}{309 \text{ ml per minute}} = \mathbf{0.757}$$

4. To calculate $\dot{V}E_{BTPS}$ we would use equation (12):

$$\dot{V}E_{BTPS} = 33.5 \text{ liters } \left(\frac{310°}{297°}\right)\left(\frac{722.6 \text{ mm}}{698 \text{ mm}}\right)$$

$$= 33.5 \ (1.044) \ (1.035)$$

$$= 33.5 \ (1.0805)$$

$$= \mathbf{36.2 \text{ liters per 5 minutes or 7.24 liters per minute}}$$

References

1. Cissik, J., and Johnson, R.: Myth of nitrogen equality in respiration: its history and implications. *Aerospace Med.* 43:755–758, 1972.
2. Cissik, J., and Johnson, R.: Regression analysis for steady state N_2 inequality in O_2 consumption calculations. *Aerospace Med.* 43:589–591, 1972.
3. Cissik, J., Johnson, R., and Hertig, B.: Production of gaseous nitrogen during human steady state exercise. *Physiologist.* 15:108, 1972.
4. Cissik, J., Johnson, R., and Rokosch, D.: Production of gaseous nitrogen in human steady-state conditions. *J Appl Physiol.* 32:155–159, 1972.
5. Dudka, L., Inglis, H., Johnson, R., Pechinski, J., and Plowman, S.: Inequality of inspired and expired gaseous nitrogen in man. *Nature.* 232:265–267, 1971.
6. Fox, E. L., and Bowers, R.: Steady-state equality of respiratory gaseous N_2 in resting man. *J Appl Physiol.* 35(1):143–144, 1973.
7. Herron, J., Saltzman, H., Hills, B., and Kylstra, J.: Differences between inspired and expired volumes of nitrogen in man. *J Appl Physiol.* 35(4):546–551, 1973.
8. Luft, U., Myhre, L., and Loeppky, J.: Validity of Haldane calculation for estimating respiratory gas exchange. *J Appl Physiol.* 34(6):864–865, 1973.
9. Wagner, J., Horvath, S., Dahms, T., and Reed, S.: Validation of open-circuit method for the determination of oxygen consumption. *J Appl Physiol.* 34(6):859–863, 1973.
10. Wilmore, J., and Costill, D.: Adequacy of the Haldane transformation in the computation of exercise $\dot{V}O_2$ in man. *J Appl Physiol.* 35(1):85–89, 1973.

SELECTED READINGS

Consolazio, C., Johnson, R., and Pecora, L.: *Physiological Measurements of Metabolic Functions in Man.* New York. McGraw-Hill, 1963.

Nomogram for Calculating Body Surface Area and Body Weight in Kilograms from Pounds

Body Surface Area

The nomogram for calculating body surface area in square meters (m^2) from height, measured either in centimeters (cm) or feet (ft) and inches (in) and for calculating body weight, measured either in kilograms (kg) or pounds (lb), is given in Figure E-1. The nomogram is used by placing one end of a straightedge on the body height and the other end on the body weight. Where the straightedge intersects the middle scale is the body surface area.

As an example, consider the following:

Weight = 154 lb or 70 kg
Height = 5 ft, 9 in or 175 cm
Surface area = **1.84 m²**

Conversion of Body Weight From Pounds to Kilograms

The conversion of body weight from pounds to kilograms is presented in Table E-1. To use the table, find the appropriate body weight in pounds and read the equivalent body weight in kilograms from the table. For example, a body weight of 173 pounds is equal to **78.5 kg.**

TABLE E-1

Conversion of Pounds to Kilograms

Pounds*	0	1	2	3	4	5	6	7	8	9
100	45.4	45.9	46.3	46.8	47.2	47.7	48.1	48.6	49.0	49.5
110	49.9	50.4	50.8	51.3	51.7	52.2	52.7	53.1	53.6	54.0
120	54.5	54.9	55.4	55.8	56.3	56.7	57.2	57.6	58.1	58.6
130	59.0	59.5	59.9	60.4	60.8	61.3	61.7	62.2	62.6	63.1
140	63.6	64.0	64.5	64.9	65.4	65.8	66.3	66.7	67.2	67.6
150	68.1	68.6	69.0	69.5	69.9	70.4	70.8	71.3	71.7	72.2
160	72.6	73.1	73.5	74.0	74.4	74.9	75.4	75.8	76.3	76.7
170	77.2	77.6	78.1	**78.5**	79.0	79.4	79.9	80.3	80.8	81.3
180	81.7	82.2	82.6	83.1	83.5	84.0	84.4	84.9	85.3	85.8
190	86.3	86.7	87.2	87.6	88.1	88.5	89.0	89.4	89.9	90.3
200	90.8	91.2	91.7	92.2	92.6	93.1	93.5	94.0	94.4	94.9
210	95.3	95.8	96.2	96.7	97.1	97.6	98.1	98.5	99.0	99.4
220	99.9	100.3	100.8	101.2	101.7	102.1	102.6	103.0	103.5	104.0
230	104.4	104.9	105.3	105.8	106.2	106.7	107.1	107.6	108.0	108.5
240	109.0	109.4	109.9	110.3	110.8	111.2	111.7	112.1	112.6	113.0

*1 pound = 0.454 kilograms; 1 kilogram = 2.2 pounds

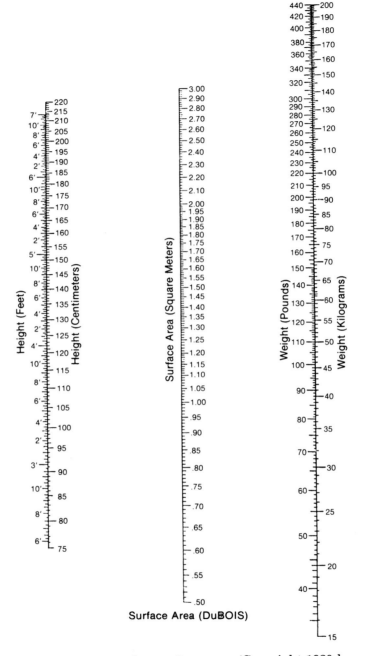

Figure E-1. Nomographic chart for computing surface area. (Copyright 1920 by W. M. Boothby and R. B. Sandiford.)

Group Interval Training Programs for Unconditioned College Men and Women

Training Prescriptions for Men and Women

The times given below are for unconditioned men and women between the ages of 18 to 21 years. Application of the program can be made to various age groups by following the principles as presented in Chapter 12. The programs are given in prescription form, for example:

$$6 \times 220 \text{ at } 0.33 \text{ } (1{:}39)$$

where

$$6 = \text{number of repetitions}$$
$$220 = \text{training distance in yards}$$
$$0{:}33 = \text{training time in minutes:seconds}$$
$$(1{:}39) = \text{time of relief interval in minutes:seconds}$$

Complete programs for running as well as for most other exercise modes are given in: Fox, E. L., and Mathews, D.: *Interval Training: Conditioning for Sports and General Fitness.* Philadelphia, W. B. Saunders, 1974.

MEN

Week 1

Day 1	Set 1	4 × 220 at Easy (1:3)*
	Set 2	8 × 110 at Easy (1:3)
Day 2	Set 1	2 × 440 at Easy (1:3)
	Set 2	8 × 110 at Easy (1:3)
Day 3	Set 1	2 × 440 at Easy (1:3)
	Set 2	6 × 220 at Easy (1:3)
Day 4	Set 1	1 × 880 at Easy
	Set 2	6 × 220 at Easy (1:3)

Week 2

Day 1	Set 1	2 × 880 at Easy (1:3)
	Set 2	2 × 440 at Easy (1:3)
Day 2	Set 1	6 × 440 at Easy (1:3)
Day 3	Set 1	3 × 880 at Easy (1:3)
Day 4	Set 1	1 × 2640 at Easy (1:3)

Week 3

Day 1	Set 1	2 × 660 at 2:15 (4:30)*
	Set 2	2 × 440 at 1:20 (2:40)
Day 2	Set 1	4 × 220 at 0:38 (1:54)
	Set 2	4 × 220 at 0:38 (1:54)
	Set 3	4 × 220 at 0:38 (1:54)
Day 3	Set 1	1 × 880 at 3:00 (3:00)

*Minutes: seconds
†Work-relief ratio

667

Week 4

Day 1	Set 1	3 × 660 at 2:10 (4:20)
	Set 2	3 × 440 at 1:20 (2:40)
Day 2	Set 1	4 × 220 at 0:38 (1:54)
	Set 2	4 × 220 at 0:38 (1:54)
	Set 3	4 × 220 at 0:38 (1:54)
	Set 4	4 × 220 at 0:38 (1:54)
Day 3	Set 1	2 × 880 at 2:55 (2:55)
	Set 2	2 × 440 at 1:20 (2:40)

Week 5

Day 1	Set 1	4 × 660 at 2:05 (4:10)
	Set 2	2 × 440 at 1:20 (2:40)
Day 2	Set 1	4 × 220 at 0:37 (1:51)
	Set 2	4 × 220 at 0:37 (1:51)
	Set 3	4 × 220 at 0:37 (1:51)
	Set 4	4 × 220 at 0:37 (1:51)
Day 3	Set 1	2 × 880 at 2:55 (2:55)
	Set 2	2 × 440 at 1:20 (2:40)

Week 6

Day 1	Set 1	4 × 660 at 2:00 (4:00)
	Set 2	2 × 440 at 1:18 (2:36)
Day 2	Set 1	4 × 220 at 0:36 (1:48)
	Set 2	4 × 220 at 0:36 (1:48)
	Set 3	4 × 220 at 0:36 (1:48)
	Set 4	4 × 220 at 0:36 (1:48)
Day 3	Set 1	2 × 880 at 2:50 (2:50)
	Set 2	2 × 440 at 1:18 (2:36)

Week 7

Day 1	Set 1	2 × 880 at 2:45 (2:45)
	Set 2	2 × 440 at 1:16 (2:32)
Day 2	Set 1	4 × 220 at 0:35 (1:45)
	Set 2	4 × 220 at 0:35 (1:45)
	Set 3	4 × 220 at 0:35 (1:45)
	Set 4	4 × 220 at 0:35 (1:45)
Day 3	Set 1	1 × 1320 at 4:30 (2:15)
	Set 2	2 × 1100 at 3:40 (1:50)

Week 8

Day 1	Set 1	2 × 880 at 2:40 (2:40)
	Set 2	2 × 440 at 1:16 (2:32)
Day 2	Set 1	4 × 220 at 0:34 (1:42)
	Set 2	4 × 220 at 0:34 (1:42)
	Set 3	4 × 220 at 0:34 (1:42)
	Set 4	4 × 220 at 0:34 (1:42)
Day 3	Set 1	1 × 1320 at 4:24 (2:12)
	Set 2	2 × 1100 at 3:34 (1:47)

WOMEN

Week 1

Day 1	Set 1	4 × 220 at easy (1:3)†
	Set 2	8 × 110 at easy (1:3)
Day 2	Set 1	2 × 440 at easy (1:3)
	Set 2	8 × 110 at easy (1:3)
Day 3	Set 1	2 × 440 at easy (1:3)
	Set 2	6 × 220 at easy (1:3)
Day 4	Set 1	1 × 880 at easy
	Set 2	6 × 220 at easy (1:3)

Week 2

Day 1	Set 1	2 × 880 at easy (1:3)
	Set 2	2 × 440 at easy (1:3)
Day 2	Set 1	6 × 440 at easy (1:3)
Day 3	Set 1	3 × 880 at easy (1:3)
Day 4	Set 1	3 × 880 at easy (1:3)

Week 3

Day 1	Set 1	2 × 660 at 2:45 (5:30)*
	Set 2	4 × 110 at 0:25 (1:15)
Day 2	Set 1	6 × 220 at 0:45 (2:15)
	Set 2	6 × 110 at 0:25 (1:15)

*Minutes:seconds
†Work-relief ratio

Day 3   Set 1   6 × 220 at 0:45 (2:15)
          Set 2   6 × 110 at 0:25 (1:15)

Week 4

Day 1   Set 1   4 × 220 at 0:45 (2:15)
          Set 2   8 × 110 at 0:25 (1:15)
          Set 3   10 × 55 at 0:10 (0:30)

Day 2   Set 1   2 × 660 at 2:45 (5:30)
          Set 2   3 × 220 at 0:45 (2:15)
          Set 3   3 × 220 at 0:45 (2:15)

Day 3   Set 1   4 × 220 at 0:45 (2:15)
          Set 2   4 × 220 at 0:45 (2:15)
          Set 3   8 × 110 at 0:25 (1:15)

Week 6

Day 1   Set 1   4 × 220 at 0:42 (2:06)
          Set 2   8 × 110 at 0:22 (1:06)
          Set 3   8 × 110 at 0:22 (1:06)

Day 2   Set 1   2 × 660 at 2:40 (5:20)
          Set 2   8 × 110 at 0:22 (1:06)
          Set 3   8 × 55 at 0:08 (0:24)

Day 3   Set 1   2 × 880 at 4:00 (4:00)
          Set 2   8 × 55 at 0:08 (0:24)
          Set 3   8 × 55 at 0:08 (0:24)

Week 5

Day 1   Set 1   4 × 220 at 0:45 (2:15)
          Set 2   8 × 110 at 0:25 (1:15)
          Set 3   10 × 55 at 0:10 (0:30)

Day 2   Set 1   2 × 660 at 2:45 (5:30)
          Set 2   3 × 220 at 0:45 (2:15)
          Set 3   3 × 220 at 0:45 (2:15)

Day 3   Set 1   4 × 220 at 0:45 (2:15)
          Set 2   4 × 220 at 0:45 (2:15)
          Set 3   8 × 110 at 0:25 (1:15)

Week 7

Day 1   Set 1   2 × 660 at 2:40 (5:20)
          Set 2   6 × 110 at 0:22 (1:06)
          Set 3   6 × 110 at 0:22 (1:06)

Day 2   Set 1   4 × 220 at 0:42 (2:06)
          Set 2   4 × 220 at 0:42 (2:06)
          Set 3   4 × 220 at 0:42 (2:06)

Day 3   Set 1   8 × 110 at 0:22 (1:06)
          Set 2   8 × 110 at 0:22 (1:06)
          Set 3   8 × 110 at 0:22 (1:06)

Week 8

Day 1   Set 1   2 × 660 at 2:35 (5:10)
          Set 2   6 × 110 at 0:20 (1:00)
          Set 3   6 × 110 at 0:20 (1:00)

Day 2   Set 1   4 × 220 at 0:40 (2:00)
          Set 2   4 × 220 at 0:40 (2:00)
          Set 3   4 × 220 at 0:40 (2:00)

Day 3   Set 1   8 × 110 at 0:20 (1:00)
          Set 2   8 × 110 at 0:20 (1:00)
          Set 3   8 × 110 at 0:20 (1:00)

Administering the Group Program

The first two weeks will perhaps be the most difficult. Unlike the trained athlete, the nonconditioned individual will be unaccustomed to running; and care must be executed to prevent severe muscle soreness and overindulgence. Your primary objective will be to condition the participants until they can run 1.5 to 2 miles without considerable stress. This should be accomplished in about two weeks with four workouts each week. Running should be easy, allowing the students to select their own paces. Such an approach should enable the participant to be active throughout the entire exercise period.

Body of the Training Program

After the first 2 weeks, which should have conditioned the legs sufficiently so that they can stand more strenuous training, sessions should be conducted three times each week, including at least 1.5 to 2.0 miles of running per session. Therefore, during the third week a typical workout prescription might be as follows:

Day 1	Set 1	2 × 660 at 2:15 (4:30)*
	Set 2	2 × 440 at 1:20 (2:40)
Day 2	Set 1	4 × 220 at 0:38 (1:54)
	Set 2	4 × 220 at 0:38 (1:54)
	Set 3	4 × 220 at 0:38 (1:54)
Day 3	Set 1	1 × 880 at 3:00 (3:00)

Observe that the total distance for the week is 3¼ miles, with 1¼ miles of longer runs (greater than 440 yd) and 2 miles of shorter, more intensive sprints (less than 440 yd).

In keeping with the overload principle, the training process should be accomplished on a progressive basis, with the average workout of each week being more difficult than that of the week before. The progression is accomplished by (1) establishing more intensive work intervals (e.g., running faster); (2) initiating shorter relief intervals (because of the more intensive work interval, and relief interval is necessarily shortened); (3) performing more sets; and (4) a combination of the first three factors. To illustrate, during the last week of an 8-week program, the prescriptions might read as follows:

Day 1	Set 1	2 × 880 at 2:40 (2:40)
	Set 2	2 × 440 at 1:16 (2:32)
Day 2	Set 1	4 × 220 at 0:34 (1:42)
	Set 2	4 × 220 at 0:34 (1:42)
	Set 3	4 × 220 at 0:34 (1:42)
	Set 4	4 × 220 at 0:34 (1:42)
Day 3	Set 1	1 × 1320 at 4:24 (2:12)
	Set 2	2 × 1100 at 3:34 (1:47)

Notice that the progression has been accomplished through a combination of the three factors mentioned previously. For instance, the intensity of the work interval was increased as reflected by faster running times; as a result the duration of the relief interval was reduced; and more sets were performed so that the total distance run per week was increased from 3¼ to 5½ miles.

The response of virtually every person undergoing such a training program is different, and the program frequently has to be adjusted to allow for these differences. However, nearly every person who trains in this fashion benefits from the program, provided that he or she adheres to the above outline.

---

*Work-relief time ratio in minutes:seconds.

Conducting the Program on an Open Field

Although the interval program may be conducted either on an open field or a track, it may be easier, in working with larger groups, to run in a field where a 440-yard straightaway can be marked out. All distances up to 440 yards may be performed by having the participants run first in one direction, then in the other, between two lines the desired distance apart. Distances greater than 440 yards may be run around pegs at either end of the 440-yard straightaway.

Conducting the Program on a 220-Yard Track

A 220-yard track may be laid out. It may be constructed of cinders or rubberized asphalt. The runs on such a track are laid out as follows:

55 Yards. Fifty-five-yard runs are performed on a marked straightaway on the track's infield. Runners go first in one direction, then return to the start on the next run.

110 Yards. Runs of 110 yards are executed around one curve of the track from a starting line to marked finish lines in each lane. Runners may then turn around to do the next run in the reverse direction, but each runner stays in his or her own lane.

220 Yards. This distance is run in lanes from staggered starting marks to a finish line. The runner in the inside lane runs exactly one lap of the track.

440 Yards and Up. All of these training runs are conducted in multiples of 220 yards. The participants start and finish at the same place. Runners are not required to run in lanes.

Administering the Running Program

Two persons are needed to conduct the training program, one person being stationed at the start and another at the finish. Each of these people should have a stop watch, preferably one with a split hand. At the beginning of each run, the runners are started with the commands: "Take your marks," "Get Set," "Go!" At the command, "Go!" both watches are started. The person at the start times the relief interval and the person at the finish calls off the time in seconds as the runners cross the finish line. The runners themselves are then able to estimate their running times to approximately a half-second.

Organizing the Workout

In general, it is easiest to have the runners run in three groups (group *A*, group *B*, and group *C*). Thus, group *A* runs first, then performs the relief interval while groups *B* and *C* are running, then runs again. The time of each group's relief interval is approximately twice the time it takes to complete the succeeding run. This work-to-relief ratio of 1:2 has been found to be satisfactory in that the heart rate of the majority of the group will be at or below the recommended 140 beats per minute before they begin their next work interval. By having four people run in each of the six running lanes in each group, 24 people may be included in each of the three groups, so that a total of 72 people may run at one workout. More may participate by increasing the number of people in each lane. The fastest person, however, must be first in each lane, with the slowest person going last. This is done to make certain that each person can run at his or her own pace.

Controlling Stress

It should be remembered that the times included for the various work intervals are only *target* times, and that people vary in their abilities to run. After the first 2 weeks of the program, the time of each work interval should be individually adjusted, and should be strenuous enough to raise the heart rate to the level recommended in Chapter 12 (p. 289). This may be checked on any individual during the few seconds *immediately* following the work interval by counting the pulse for 10 seconds and multiplying by six to yield a minute rate. If after the first couple of work intervals in a set, the heart rate does not approach the recommended level, the individual should be encouraged to run faster.

In running each set, the runners should be told to maintain an average time by running the first work intervals of a set slightly slower than the target time, and finishing the set with work intervals that are faster than the target times. Thus, a set of six 110-yard runs with a target time of 16 seconds might be run in the following manner:

1. 17.0 seconds
2. 16.5 seconds
3. 16.0 seconds
4. 16.0 seconds
5. 15.5 seconds
6. 15.0 seconds

Overstress

Occasionally, a runner will run too hard and will not recover between work intervals as he or she should. When this happens, the individual should wait until the heart rate drops to the level mentioned above. He or she may then run again, but if the heart rate does not recover within the relief interval, the runner should be dropped from the workout for the remainder of the day. Exhaustion is the enemy of training. If runners are allowed to exhaust themselves, it may be several days before they are capable of another good workout.

Another problem is soreness. Some fatigue is natural, of course, but exhaustion and soreness, particularly soreness of the hip, thigh, and front of the leg (shin splints) must be guarded against. Soreness is the signal for overstress. It may require medical attention, but whether or not it is treated medically, a person with acute or chronic soreness should not be allowed to run in an interval training program until completely recovered.

Tests of Anaerobic and Aerobic Power

Anaerobic Power Tests

The ability to jump, sprint, put the shot, throw the javelin, or perform fast starts as would be required of backs and linemen are a few examples of athlete's converting energy to power. The ability to develop considerable power is a prime factor in athletic success. Power is performance of work expressed per unit of time. The term *explosive power* has been associated with this anaerobic metabolism and the tests to measure it. However, "explosive" itself connotes power, leaving us to consider the term "explosive power" as redundant. Consequently, we will simply use the term *anaerobic power test* to reflect such measurement.

As you may recall from Chapter 2, the development of power is related to muscular strength and especially to the amount and rate of utilization of the ATP-PC system. Therefore, the tests that follow reflect primarily one's depth and ability to employ the ATP-PC system.

Sargent Jump

Measuring the difference between a person's standing reach and the height to which he or she can jump and touch (similar to basketball tipoff) has erroneously been used as a power test of the legs. If body weight and the speed in performing the jump are not a part of the measurement, one can't regard this test as a true measure of power. Certainly a 150-pound boy who jumps vertically 2 feet produces less power than the 160-pound boy who jumps 2 feet.

The Lewis Nomogram
In order to make the jump reach test more valid as a measure of leg power, the Lewis nomogram (Fig. G–1), can be used as follows:

Body weight = 180 pounds
Distance jumped = 24 inches

Lay a straightedge across the nomogram connecting 180 pounds (right column) and 24 inches (left column). Read, from the center column, foot-pounds per second (ft-lb/sec)* as the power output (1025 ft-lb/sec). Note also that the measurements may be either in English or in metric units. In the latter units the body weight in our example would be 82 kg (1 lb = 0.454 kg), the distance jumped would be equal to 0.61 meter (39.37 in = 1 m), and the power output would be 142 kilogram-meters/second (kg-m/sec).**

---

*1025 ft-lb/sec = 1.8 horsepower (HP). To convert ft-lb/sec to HP, multiply by 0.0018.
**To convert kg-m/sec to HP, multiply by 0.013. For more conversions see Table 4-2, page 65.

THE LEWIS NOMOGRAM FOR DETERMINING ANAEROBIC POWER FROM
JUMP-REACH SCORE AND BODY WEIGHT

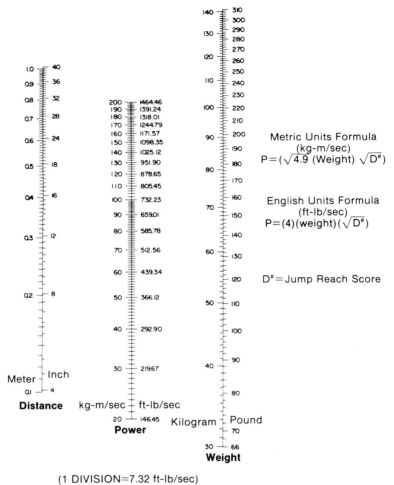

(1 DIVISION=7.32 ft-lb/sec)

Figure G-1. The Lewis Nomogram. A person's power output can be determined by knowing the score on the jump reach and the body weight. See text for example.

Margaria-Kalamen Power Test (Fig. G-2)

R. Margaria[11] suggested an excellent test of power, which has been modified by J. Kalamen.[9] The modification results in greater power output than in Margaria's original test. The subjects stand 6 meters in front of a staircase. At their pleasure they run up the stairs as rapidly as possible, taking three at a time. A switchmat is placed on the third and ninth stair. (An average stair is about 174 mm high). A clock starts as the person steps on the first switchmat (on the third step) and stops as he or she steps on the second (on the

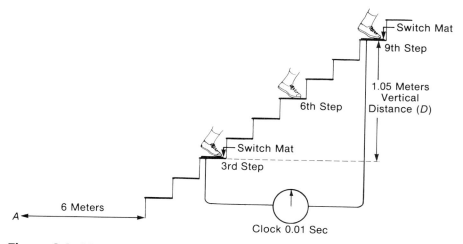

Figure G-2. Margaria-Kalamen power test. Subject starts at point A and runs as rapidly as possible up the flight of stairs, taking them three at a time. The time it takes to traverse the distance between stair 3 and stair 9 is recorded in 0.01 second. The power generated is a product of the subject's weight and the vertical distance (D), divided by the time. An example appears in the text.

ninth step). Time is recorded to a hundredth of a second. It is best to administer the test several times, recording the best score. Power output is computed using the formula:

$$P = \frac{W \times D}{t}$$

in which

P = Power
W = Weight of person
D = Vertical height between first and last test stairs
t = Time from first to last test stairs

The test is scored as follows:

W = 75 kg
D = 1.05 meters
t = 0.49 second
$P = \dfrac{75 \times 1.05}{0.49}$ = 161 kg-meters per sec
P = 161 kg-meters per sec

Kalamen,[9] using 23 nonathletic males, obtained a mean power output of 168.5 kg-meters per second. Some standards based on these data, plus those of Margaria et al.,[11] are listed in Table G-1. When evaluating seven sprinters from the Ohio State University track team he obtained a mean power outlet of 200 kg-meters per second. Furthermore, with this test, power outputs of professional football players (backs) ranging between 240 and 271 kg-m/sec have been recorded.[7] The greater power outputs of these trained athletes contribute evidence of the validity of this test.

50-Yard Dash Test

Kalamen[9] obtained a high coefficient of relationship between the time of running the 50-yard dash with a 15-yard running start and the Margaria-Kalamen Power test ($r = 0.974$). This indicates that one could probably substitute the 50-yard dash test and get more or less the same results, eliminating expensive equipment. However, Kalamen obtained an insignificant correlation between the power test and the Sargent Jump Test when merely height of jump was recorded. As mentioned earlier, it is doubtful whether one should use the Sargent Jump Test as a test of power unless speed and weight of the subject are part of the measurement (Lewis nomogram). If timing equipment is available, the Margaria-Kalamen test is superior; if not, the 50-yard dash from a running start may be used.

Tests of Maximal Aerobic Power

As was mentioned in Chapter 2, the maximal oxygen consumption test is perhaps the most valid means of determining a person's maximal aerobic power (max $\dot{V}O_2$). It is the first choice in measuring to assess a person's cardiorespiratory fitness.

Maximal oxygen consumption is dependent upon age, sex, and body size and/or composition. These relationships plus average values for different age groups of men and

TABLE G-1

Guidelines for the Margaria-Kalamen Test (ATP-PC System)*

| | **MEN** | | | | |
| | **Age Groups (years)** | | | | |
Classification	15–20	20–30	30–40	40–50	Over 50
Poor	Under 113**	Under 106**	Under 85**	Under 65**	Under 50**
Fair	113–149	106–139	85–111	65–84	50–65
Average	150–187	140–175	112–140	85–105	66–82
Good	188–224	176–210	141–168	106–125	83–98
Excellent	Over 224	Over 210	Over 168	Over 125	Over 98
	WOMEN				
	Age Groups (years)				
Classification	15–20	20–30	30–40	40–50	Over 50
Poor	Under 92**	Under 85**	Under 65**	Under 50**	Under 38**
Fair	92–120	85–111	65–84	50–65	38–48
Average	121–151	112–140	85–105	66–82	49–61
Good	152–182	141–168	106–125	83–98	62–75
Excellent	Over 182	Over 168	Over 125	Over 98	Over 75

*Based on data from Kalamen,[9] and Margaria.[11]
**kg-m/sec.

women were given in Chapter 14 (pp. 384–388). Most individuals will reach their maximal aerobic power as a result of growth around 15 to 17 years of age. For the majority of the population, a gradual decline begins around age 30. An average max $\dot{V}O_2$ as measured on the bicycle ergometer, for college men is between 3.0 and 3.5 liters per minute or 41 to 48 ml per kg per minute.[5] For college women it is between 2.0 and 2.5 liters per minute or 35 to 43 ml per kg per minute.[1]

Methods of Directly Assessing Aerobic Power

There are three general methods of appraising maximal oxygen consumption: (1) treadmill (running and walking); (2) cycling (bicycle ergometer); and (3) stepping (step bench). Values of max $\dot{V}O_2$ measured on an inclined treadmill are usually 5 to 15 per cent higher than those obtained on either the bicycle or the step bench.[8,13] The reason for this might be related to differences in the size of the active muscle mass, this being largest during uphill treadmill running. Another factor might be that cycling leads to localized fatigue, since it mainly involves only the large muscles of the thigh. Such fatigue would occur prior to maximally stressing the circulatory and respiratory systems, thus leading to a smaller max $\dot{V}O_2$.

Treadmill Methods

The following are several reliable test procedures that are known to measure a person's max $\dot{V}O_2$.

1. *Mitchell, Sproule, Chapman Method.*[14] In this test the subject walks for 10 minutes at 3 miles per hour (4.8 km per hour) on a 10% grade. This is a preliminary light exercise period (warm-up) and allows the individual to become adjusted to the equipment. Following a 10-minute rest period, the subject begins running at 6 miles per hour (9.7 km per hour) at a 0% grade for 2.5 minutes. The expired gas is collected for purposes of analysis from minute 1:30 to 2:30 of the run. Following the first bout, a 10-minute rest period is allowed. For the next run the speed remains constant, but the grade is elevated to 2.5%. The procedure is repeated until maximal values are obtained.

2. *Saltin-Åstrand Method.*[15] The subject first performs a 5-minute submaximal bicycle ergometer ride; heart rate and oxygen consumption are measured during the last minute. These data are then used to predict the subject's max $\dot{V}O_2$. This is done by use of a nomogram (Fig. G-4, p. 683). From Table G-2, the predicted max $\dot{V}O_2$ is used to determine the appropriate initial speed and inclination of the treadmill, so that the all-out run will last between 3 and 7 minutes. For example, suppose a subject's predicted max $\dot{V}O_2$ were 45 ml/kg-min. The starting speed and inclination of the treadmill would be 7.8 miles per hour (12.5 km per hour) and 5.2% grade, respectively (Table G-2). Prior to the run, each subject walks for 10 minutes at a workload approximately 50% of his or her predetermined starting load. During the all-out run, the treadmill is elevated 2.7% every 3 minutes until the subject is exhausted. Consecutive 1-minute gas collections are started when the heart rate reaches 175 beats per minute.

3. *The Ohio State Method.*[3,6] The OSU test is similar to the Saltin-Åstrand method. It includes a 5-minute warm-up walk at 3.5 miles per hour (5.6 km per hour) on a 10% grade followed by a 4 to 8 minute run to exhaustion. Running speeds usually vary between 6.0 and 9.3 miles per hour (9.6 and 15.0 km per hour) depending on the anticipated fitness level of the subject. Generally, for untrained college females, the speed is 6.0 miles per hour, for

TABLE G-2

Starting Workload Used for the Saltin-Åstrand Maximal Aerobic
Power Test*

Predicted Max V̇O₂, ml/kg-min	Men Speed mi/hr	km/hr	Grade per cent	Women Speed mi/hr	km/hr	Grade per cent
below 40	6.2	10.0	5.2	6.2	10.0	2.7
40–54	7.8	12.5	5.2	6.2	10.0	5.2
55–75	9.3	15.0	5.2	7.8	12.5	5.2
above 75	10.9	17.5	5.2			

*Modified from Saltin and Åstrand.[19]

untrained college males, 7.8 miles per hour, and for athletes, 9.3 to 10 miles per hour. In all cases, the treadmill inclination is set initially at a 2 per cent grade and elevated 2 per cent every 2 minutes thereafter. The subject runs to exhaustion. Consecutive 1-minute gas collections are started when the heart rate reaches 175 beats per minute.

It should be noted that the manner in which the workload can be increased in these tests is either discontinuous, as in the Mitchell, Sproule, Chapman test, or continuous as in the other two tests. Since there are no differences in the max V̇O₂ value obtained in the two types of loading,[10,12] either method can be used. However, the discontinuous method requires more time and in fact often requires several separate trips to the laboratory to complete. In this respect the continuous method is preferable.

Bicycle Methods

Although the treadmill test generally yields higher max V̇O₂ values, the bicycle has many advantages as an exercise ergometer: (1) it is relatively inexpensive; (2) it is, as of the last few years in this country, a familiar exercise for many people and thus less apt to cause apprehension; (3) like the treadmill, its results are reproducible; and (4) it is portable and therefore usable in field studies.

As with the treadmill test, the bicycle test can consist of either continuous or discontinuous loading; the results are the same.[12] Following are several protocols.

1. *Discontinuous Loading.* The pedal speed should be 60 revolutions per minute. This frequency elicits the highest max V̇O₂ compared with 50, 70, and 80 revolutions per minute.[8] In the Laboratory of Work Physiology at The Ohio State University,[4,5] the subjects perform a series of 5-minute rides with 10-minute rest periods between rides. The initial workload is light—for men, between 125 and 150 watts (750 and 900 kg-meters per min)* and for women, between 75 and 100 watts. The workloads in subsequent rides are made progressively heavier according to the subjects' heart rate response to the preceding ride; the lower the heart rate response, the higher the next load (e.g., 50 watts higher. Usually the load increments for both men and women are 20 to 30 watts). The subjects are considered exhausted (usually after 5 or 6 rides) when they can no longer ride for at least 3

---

*To convert watts to kg-meters per min, multiply by 6.

minutes at a workload 10 to 15 watts higher than their previous ride. Gas collections can be made during the last minute of each ride.

2. *Continuous Loading.*[12]   The subjects again pedal at 60 revolutions per minute. With a starting load of 150 to 180 watts, the load is increased by 30 watts every 2 minutes until the subject can no longer continue or until the pedal speed drops below 50 revolutions per minute. Gas collections can be made during the last minute of each work increment after the heart rate reaches 175 beats per minute.

In summary, the following can be said concerning direct measurement of maximal oxygen consumption:

1. The treadmill elicits higher max $\dot{V}O_2$ values than does the bicycle.
2. Loading can be either continuous or discontinuous, since both methods yield the same results.
3. The length of time for exhaustion should be between 3 and 10 minutes.
4. A warm-up bout of exercise is useful psychologically and physiologically and for adjustment to the equipment.

Criteria for Max $\dot{V}O_2$ Attainment

How does one know when a subject has reached his or her maximum aerobic power? Figure G-3 contains the plots for each of the increasing workloads in milliliters per kilogram of body weight per minute. Note that even though the workload was increased, $\dot{V}O_2$ remained constant. As a matter of fact, at the fourth and most severe workload, $\dot{V}O_2$ decreased slightly. The main criterion for determining that maximal aerobic power has been attained, therefore, is a leveling or decrease in $\dot{V}O_2$ with increasing workload. Other criteria are (1) volitional exhaustion; (2) heart rate in excess of 190 beats per minute; (3) a respiratory exchange ratio (R) greater than unity; and (4) a blood lactic acid level above 100 mg per cent.

Methods of Indirectly Assessing Aerobic Power

As you may have concluded from the preceding descriptions, direct assessment of max $\dot{V}O_2$ is limited in that the test is difficult, exhausting, and often hazardous to perform

Figure G-3. Determining the point at which maximal aerobic capacity has been reached. The primary criterion for such a determination depends upon the individual's inability to consume additional oxygen when the work load is increased.

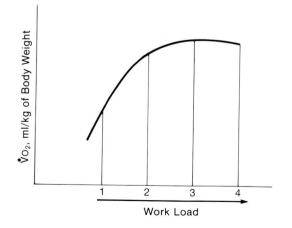

regardless of the type of ergometer used. For this reason, several methods for predicting max $\dot{V}O_2$ from submaximal exercise data have been developed. Following are two such methods.

Åstrand-Åstrand Nomogram[2]

This nomogram, shown in Figure G-4, was the first to be developed for prediction of max $\dot{V}O_2$ from submaximal data. It was originally constructed from data gathered on young (18 to 30), healthy, physical-education students, and it is based on the ideas that (1) heart rate during submaximal cycling and walking increases approximately linearly (in a straight line) with oxygen uptake and (2) the maximal heart rate of the subjects during this type of maximal work is about 195 beats per minute. Also, the nomogram was said to be more accurate if heart rates between 125 and 170 beats per minute were used to make the predictions of max $\dot{V}O_2$.

Later the nomogram was revised so that now it can be used for male and female subjects 15 years of age or older, and in addition to the treadmill and bicycle, predictions can be made from submaximal heart rate and oxygen consumption data obtained during bench stepping. For subjects older than 25 years, age correction factors must be used; these are given in Table G-3. The reason for this is that although heart rate and oxygen consumption during submaximal work do not vary greatly with age, max $\dot{V}O_2$ declines with age. Thus, max $\dot{V}O_2$ is overestimated in older subjects.

Here is how to use the nomogram:

1. A workload, either cycling, walking, or running, is selected that will elicit a heart rate of between 125 and 170 beats per minute. If bench stepping is preferred, the bench height should be 33 cm (13 inches) for females and 40 cm (16 inches) for males. The stepping frequency should be 30 steps per minute. In all cases, 1-minute determinations of heart rate and oxygen consumption are made at some time between minutes 5 and 10 of the work.
2. The heart rate and oxygen consumption data are then applied to the nomogram shown in Figure G-4 in order to predict the max $\dot{V}O_2$. This is done by connecting, with a straightedge, the point on the "$\dot{V}O_2$" scale with the corresponding point on the "pulse" (heart) rate scale and the predicted max $\dot{V}O_2$ is read from the middle scale. If it

TABLE G-3	
Age Correction Factors for Predicting Maximal Aerobic Power*	
Age, Years	**Age Correction Factor**
25	1.00
35	0.87
45	0.78
55	0.71
65	0.65

*From Åstrand.[1]

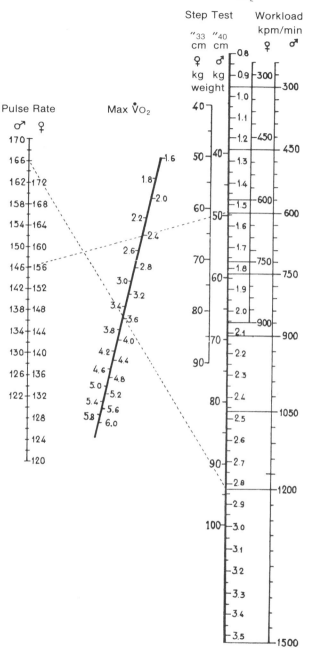

Figure G-4. The adjusted nomogram for calculation of aerobic work capacity from submaximal pulse rate and O_2 uptake values (cycling, running, or walking and step test). In tests without direct O_2 uptake measurement, it can be estimated by reading horizontally from the "body weight" scale (step test) or "work load" scale (cycle test) to the "O_2 uptake" scale. The point on the "O_2 uptake" scale ($\dot{V}O_2$) shall be connected with the corresponding point of the "pulse rate" scale and the predicted maximal O_2 uptake read on the middle scale. A female subject (61 kg) reaches a heart rate of 156 at step test; predicted max $\dot{V}O_2 = 2.4$ L. A male subject reaches a heart rate of 166 at cycling test on a work load of 1200 kpm/min; predicted max $\dot{V}O_2 = 3.6$L (exemplified by dotted lines). From Astrand.[1]

is not possible to directly measure the oxygen consumption during stepping or cycling, it can be estimated by reading horizontally from the "body weight" scale (stepping) or "workload" scale (cycling) to the "$\dot{V}O_2$" scale, and then the connections are made from there. Several examples are given in the legend to Figure G-4.

3. If the subject is older than 25 years, the appropriate age correction factor (given in Table G–3) must be applied to the predicted max $\dot{V}O_2$ value obtained in the above manner. For example, if the woman whose max $\dot{V}O_2$ was predicted to be 2.4 liters per minute (see legend of Fig. G–4), were 45 years old, her age-corrected max $\dot{V}O_2$ would be $2.4 \times 0.78 = 1.87$ liters per minute.

Whenever any variable is predicted rather than measured, the question most often asked is "How accurate is it?" In the case of the Åstrand-Åstrand nomogram, the standard deviation from the measured max $\dot{V}O_2$ is $\pm 15\%$. As an example of what this means, for every 1000 persons whose max $\dot{V}O_2$ is predicted to be 3.0 liters per minute, 25 of them will have actual max $\dot{V}O_2$ values less than 2.1 liters per minute and 25 will be greater than 3.9 liters per minute. This clearly points out that such predictions are at best only rough approximations of the true power. Precise values can be determined only by direct methods.

The Fox Equation[4]

More recently, a simple method for predicting max $\dot{V}O_2$ in males has been described. It is based on a linear equation relating the directly measured max $\dot{V}O_2$ to the submaximal heart rate (HR_{sub}) response recorded during the fifth minute of bicycle exercise at 150 watts (900 kg-meters per min). The equation is:

$$\text{predicted max } \dot{V}O_2 \text{ (liters per min)} = 6.3 - 0.0193 \times HR_{sub}$$

Consider the following example of how to use the equation:

Suppose the heart rate during the fifth minute of cycling at 150 watts is 160 beats per minute. The predicted max $\dot{V}O_2$ would be

$$
\begin{aligned}
\text{predicted max } \dot{V}O_2 &= 6.3 - (0.0193 \times 160) \\
&= 6.3 - 3.09 \\
&= \textbf{3.21 liters per minute}
\end{aligned}
$$

To facilitate use of the equation, we have solved the equation for submaximal heart rates between 100 and 200 beats per minute as given in Table G-4.

If the subject is older than 25 years, the Åstrand-Åstrand age correction factor (Table G–3) should be used. In the previous example, if the man were 50 years of age, the age-corrected max $\dot{V}O_2$ would be $3.21 \times 0.745 = 2.39$ liters per minute. Notice that the age correction factor of 0.745 was interpolated; this increases the accuracy of predictions.

Again, the question of accuracy comes up. Using 74 subjects, the Fox equation was shown to have a standard deviation of ± 0.24 liters per minute or ± 7.7 per cent. In this case, for every 1000 persons whose max $\dot{V}O_2$ is predicted to be 3.0 liters per minute, 25 will have actual values less than 2.54 liters per minute and 25 will have values greater than

TABLE G-4

Prediction of $\dot{V}O_2$ max (L/min.) from Heart Rate (beats/min.) at 150 Watts (900 kg-m/min.) on a Bicycle Ergometer (men only)*

HR Beats/ Min.	$\dot{V}O_2$ Max, Liters Per Min.									
	0	1	2	3	4	5	6	7	8	9
100	4.37	4.35	4.33	4.31	4.29	4.27	4.25	4.23	4.22	4.20
110	4.18	4.16	4.14	4.12	4.10	4.09	4.07	4.05	4.03	4.01
120	3.99	3.97	3.95	3.93	3.91	3.89	3.87	3.85	3.84	3.82
130	3.80	3.78	3.76	3.74	3.72	3.70	3.68	3.66	3.64	3.62
140	3.60	3.58	3.57	3.55	3.53	3.51	3.49	3.47	3.45	3.43
150	3.41	3.39	3.37	3.35	3.33	3.32	3.30	3.28	3.26	3.24
160	3.22	3.20	3.18	3.16	3.14	3.12	3.10	3.08	3.06	3.05
170	3.03	3.01	2.99	2.97	2.95	2.93	2.91	2.89	2.87	2.85
180	2.83	2.81	2.80	2.78	2.76	2.74	2.72	2.70	2.68	2.66
190	2.64	2.62	2.60	2.58	2.56	2.54	2.53	2.51	2.49	2.47
200	2.45									

*Based on the equation: max $\dot{V}O_2 = 6.3 - 0.0193 \times HR_{sub}$. From Fox.[4]

3.46 liters per minute. While this is more accurate than the Åstrand-Åstrand nomogram, it still should be remembered that it is only an approximation and that the most accurate max $\dot{V}O_2$ value will be the one that is directly measured.

References

1. Åstrand, I.: Aerobic work capacity in men and women with special reference to age. *Acta Physiol Scand* 49, Suppl. 169, 1-92, 1960.
2. Åstrand, P., and Ryhming, I.: A nomogram for calculation of aerobic capacity (physical fitness) from pulse rate during submaximal work. *J Appl Physiol* 7:218-221, 1954.
3. Camaione, D. N.: *A Comparison Among Three Tests for Measuring Maximal Oxygen Consumption.* Doctoral Dissertation. The Ohio State University, Columbus, Ohio, 1969.
4. Fox, E.: A simple, accurate technique for predicting maximal aerobic power. *J Appl Physiol.* 35(6):914-916, 1973.
5. Fox, E., Billings, C., Bartels, R., Bason, R., and Mathews, D.: Fitness standards for male college students. *Int Z Angew Physiol.* 31:231-236, 1973.
6. Fox, E.: Differences in metabolic alterations with sprint versus endurance interval training. In Howald, H., and Poortmans, J. (eds.): *Metabolic Adaptation to Prolonged Physical Exercise.* Basel, Switzerland, Birkhäuser Verlag, 1975, pp. 119-126.
7. Fox, E., and Mathews, D.: *Interval Training: Conditioning for Sports and General Fitness.* Philadelphia, W. B. Saunders, 1974.
8. Hermansen, L., and Saltin, B.: Oxygen uptake during maximal treadmill and bicycle exercise. *J Appl Physiol* 26(1):31-37, 1969.
9. Kalamen, J.: *Measurement of Maximum Muscular Power in Man.* Doctoral Dissertation, The Ohio State University, 1968.
10. Maksud, M., and Coutts, K.: Comparison of a continuous and discontinuous graded treadmill test for maximal oxygen uptake. *Med Sci Sports* 3(2):63-65, 1971.

11. Margaria, R., Aghemo, I., and Rovelli, E.: Measurement of muscular power (anaerobic) in man. *J Appl Physiol* 21:1662-1664, 1966.
12. McArdle, W., Katch, F., and Pechar, G.: Comparison of continuous and discontinuous treadmill and bicycle tests for max $\dot{V}O_2$. *Med Sci Sports* 5(3):156-160, 1973.
13. McArdle, W., and Magel, J.: Physical work capacity and maximum oxygen uptake in treadmill and bicycle exercise. *Med Sci Sports* 2(3):118-123, 1970.
14. Mitchell, J., Sproule, B., and Chapman, C.: The physiological meaning of the maximal oxygen intake test. *J Clin Invest* 37:538-547, 1957.
15. Saltin, B., and Åstrand, P.: Maximal oxygen uptake in athletes. *J Appl Physiol* 23:353-358, 1967.

Partial List of the International Olympic Committee Doping Substances

(As of July 8, 1986.)
It should be noted that new products are being introduced to the market on a regular basis and the list undergoes periodic updating.

Psychomotor Stimulant Drug

1. Amphetamine — Delcobese, Obetrol, Benzedrine, Dexedrine
2. Benzphetamine — Didrex
3. Cocaine — "Coke"
4. Diethylpropion — Tenuate, Tepanil
5. Dimethylamphetamine — Phenopane
6. Ethylamphetamine — Apetinil
7. Fencamfamine — Envitrol, Altimine, Phencamine
8. Meclofenoxate — Lucidril, Brenal
9. Methylamphetamine — Desoxyn, Met-Ampi
10. Methylphenidate — Ritalin
11. Norpseudoephedrine — Nabese, Cathine, Amorphan, Reduform
12. Pemoline — Cylert, Deltamin, Stimul
13. Phendimetrazine — Phenazine, Bontril, Plegine
14. Phenmetrazine — Preludin
15. Phentermine — Adipex, Fastin, Ionamin
16. Pipradol — Meratran, Constituent of Alertonic
17. Prolintane — Villescon, Promotil, Katovit
    And related compounds . . .

Miscellaneous Central Nervous System Stimulants

1. Amiphenazole — Daptizole, Amphisol
2. Bemigride — Megimide
3. Doxapram — Dopram
4. Ethamivan — Emivan, Vandid
5. Leptazol — Pentylententrazal, Cardiazol, Metrazol, Ventrasol
6. Nikethamide — Coramine
7. Picrotoxine — Cocculin
8. Strychnine
    And related compounds . . .

9. Caffeine

Greater than 12 mcg/ml in the urine.
(2 cups coffee = 3–6 mcg/ml)
2 colas = 1.5–3 mcg/ml
1 NO-DOZE = 3–6 mcg/ml
1 APC, Empirin, Anacin = 2–3 mcg/ml)

Sympathomimetic Amines

These drugs act as central nervous system stimulants and are used for asthma, allergy, colds, sinus infections, etc.

1. Chlorprenaline — Vortel, Asthone (Japanese)
2. Ephedrine — Amesec, Quibron, Lufyllin, Quadrinal, Tedral, Vereguad, Bronkotabs, Rynatuss, Marax, Primatene
3. Etafedrine — Mercodal, Decapryn, Netamine
4. Isoetharine — Bronkosol, Bronkometer, Numotac, Dilabron
5. Methoxyphenamine — Ritalin, Orthoxicol Cough Syrup
6. Methylephedrine — Tzbraine, Methep (German, GB)
7. Metaproterenol — Alupent, Metaprel
8. Isoproterenol — Isuprel, Norisodrine, Metihaler-ISO
   And related products . . .
9. Epinephrine — Primetene products, Vaponephrin

Narcotic Analgesics

1. Anileridine — Leritine, Apodol
2. Codeine — Present in many cough syrups
3. Dextromoramide — Palfium, Jetrium, D-Moramid, Dimorlin
4. Dihydrocodeine — Synalgos DC, Paracodin
5. Dipipanone — Pipadone
6. Ethylmorphine — Dionin
7. Heroin
8. Hydrocodone — Adatuss, Citra Forte, Dicodid, Enturss, Hycodan, Hycomine, Robidane, Tussionex, Tussend, Vicodin (commonly found in cough medicines)
9. Hydromorphone — Dilaudid
10. Levorphanol — Levo-Dromoran
11. Methadone — Dolophine, Amidon
12. Morphine
13. Oxocodone — Percocet, Percodan, Tylex, Supeudol
14. Oxomorphine — Narcan, Numorphan
15. Pentazocine — Talwin
16. Pethidine — Centralgin, Dolantin, Dolosol, Pethold
17. Phenazocine — Narphen, Prinadol
18. Piminodine — Alvodine, Cimadon

19. Thebacon   Adedicon, Thebacetyl
20. Trimerperidine   Demerol, Mepergan
21. And related compounds:
    A. Propoxyphene   Darvon
    B. Dextromethorphan   DM
    C. Diphenoxylate   Lomotil (without atropine sulfate—Lomotil with atropine sulfate is permissible)
    D. Camphorated tincture of opium   Paregoric

Anabolic Steroids

1. Clostebol   Steranobol
2. Dehydrochlor-methyltestosterone   Turinabol
3. Danazol   Danocrine
4. Fluoxymesterone   Android F, Halotestin, Ora-Testryl, Ultandren
5. Mesterolone   Androviron, Proviron
6. Methenolone   Primobolan, Primonabol-Depot
7. Methandienone   Dianabol, Danabol
8. Methyltestosterone   Android, Estratest, Methandren, Oreton, Testred, Vigorex, Virilon
9. Norethandrolone   Nilevar
10. Nandrolone (19-nortestosterone)   Durabolin, Deca-Durabolin, Kabolin, Nandrobolic, Anabol
11. Oxandrolone   Anavar
12. Oxymesterone   Oranabol, Theranabol
13. Oxymetholone   Anadrol, Nilevar, Anapolon 50, Adroyd
14. Stanozolol   Winstrol, Stromba
15. Testosterone   Malogen, Malogex, Delatestryl, Oreton
    A. If the ratio of the total concentration of testosterone to that of epitestosterone in the urine exceeds 6.
    And related compounds . . .

Over-the-Counter Drugs for Colds and Sinus

1. Pseudoephedrine   Actifed, Ambenyl, Anamine, Afrinol, Co-Tylenol, Deconamine, Dimacol, Emprazil, Fedahist, Fedrazil, Histalet, Historal, Isoclor, Lo-Tussin, Nasalspan, Novafed, Nucofed, Poly-Hisine, Pseudo-bid Pseudohist, Rhymosyn, Ryna, Sudafed, Triprolidine, Tussend, Afrinal, Chlorafed, Chlortrimeton-DC, Disophoral, Drixoral, Polaramine, Rondec

2. Phenylephrine   Coricidin, Dristan, NTZ, Neo-Synephrine, Sinex

3. Phenylpropanolamine   ARM, Allerest, Contac, Dexatrim, Dietac, 4 Way Formula 44, Naldecon, Novahistine, Arnex, Sine-Aid, Sine-Off, Sinutab, Triaminic, Triaminicin, Sucrets Cold Decongestant, and related "cold" products

4. Propylhexedrine   Benzedrex inhaler

5. Ephedrine   Bronkaid, Collyrium with Ephedrine, Pazo Suppository, Wyanoid Suppository, Vitronal Nose Drops, Nyquil Nighttime Cold Medicine, Vicks Nighttime Cold Medicine, herbal teas and medicines containing Ma Huang (Chinese ephedra)

Others

1. Alcohol
2. Beta-blockers
3. Blood doping
4. Growth hormone (human, synthetic, or animal)

Reference

United States Olympic Committee: Committee of Substance Abuse, Research and Education USOC/IOC Banned Drugs. Colorado Springs, July 8, 1986.

glossary

A Band That area located in the center of the sarcomere containing both actin and myosin.

Acceleration Sprint Sprint in which running speed is gradually increased from jogging to striding and finally to sprinting.

Acclimatization Pertaining to certain physiological adjustments brought about through continued exposure to a different climate, e.g., changes in altitude and heat.

Acetylcholine (ACh) A chemical substance involved in several important physiological functions such as transmission of an impulse from one nerve fiber to another across a synapse.

Acid A chemical compound that gives up hydrogen ions (H^+) in solution.

Actin A protein involved in muscular contraction.

Action Potential The electrical activity developed in a muscle or nerve cell during activity or depolarization.

Active Transport The movement of substances or materials against their concentration gradients by the expenditure of metabolic energy.

Adenosine Diphosphate (ADP) A complex chemical compound which, when combined with inorganic phosphate (P_i), forms ATP.

Adenosine Triphosphate (ATP) A complex chemical compound formed with the energy released from food and stored in all cells, particularly muscles.

Only from the energy released by the breakdown of this compound can the cell perform work.

Adipocyte A fat cell; a cell that stores fat.

Adipose Tissue Fat tissue.

Adrenocorticotropic Hormone (ACTH; or Corticotropin) A hormone secreted by the anterior lobe of the pituitary gland that stimulates the production and release of the glucocorticoid hormones from the adrenal cortex.

Aerobic In the presence of oxygen.

Aerobic Glycolysis See *Glycolysis*.

Aerotitis Inflammation or disease of the ear.

Afferent Nerve A neuron that conveys sensory impulses from a receptor to the central nervous system.

Alactacid Oxygen Debt That portion of the recovery oxygen used to resynthesize and restore ATP + PC in muscle following exercise. The rapid recovery phase.

Aldosterone A mineralocorticoid.

Alkaline Pertaining to a base.

Alkali Reserve The amount of bicarbonate (base) available in the body for buffering.

Alkalosis Excessive base (bicarbonate ions) in the extracellular fluids.

All-Or-None Law A stimulated muscle or nerve fiber contracts or propagates a nerve impulse either completely or not at all; in other words, a minimal stimulus causes a maximal response.

Alpha Motor Neuron A type of efferent nerve cell that innervates extrafusal muscle fibers.

Alveolar-Capillary Membrane The thin layer of tissue dividing the alveoli and the pulmonary capillaries where gaseous exchange occurs.

Alveolar Ventilation The portion of inspired air that reaches the alveoli.

Alveoli (plural); Alveolus (singular) Tiny terminal air sacs in the lungs where gaseous exchange with the blood in the pulmonary capillaries occurs.

Ambient Pertaining to the surrounding environment.

Amphetamine A synthetically structured drug closely related to epinephrine; it produces stimulation of the central nervous system.

Anabolic Protein building.

Anabolic Steroid A compound that promotes tissue-building, i.e., is conducive to the constructive process of metabolism (other processes of metabolism are called *catabolic,* meaning breaking down.

Anaerobic In the absence of oxygen.

Anaerobic Glycolysis The incomplete chemical breakdown of carbohydrate. The anaerobic reactions in this breakdown release energy for the manufacture of ATP as they produce lactic acid (anaerobic glycolysis is known as the lactic acid system).

Anaerobic Threshold That intensity of workload or oxygen consumption in which anaerobic metabolism is accelerated.

Anatomical Dead Space (DS) That volume of fresh air that remains in the respiratory passages (nose, mouth, pharynx, larynx, trachea, bronchi, and bronchioles) and does not participate in gaseous exchange.

Androgen Any substance that possesses masculinizing properties.

Anemia A lack of sufficient red blood cells or hemoglobin.

Aneurysm Blood-filled pouches that balloon out from a weak spot in the arterial wall.

Anthropometry The measurement of the size and proportions of the human body.

Antidiuretic Hormone (ADH; also called Vasopressin) A hormone secreted by the posterior lobe of the pituitary gland that functions mainly to promote water reabsorption from the collecting tubules of the kidney.

Apnea (Apneic) Cessation of breathing.

Aqueous Pertaining to water.

Arteriovenous Oxygen Difference (a-$\overline{v}O_2$ diff.) The difference between the oxygen content of arterial and mixed venous blood.

Artery A vessel carrying blood away from the heart.

Atherosclerosis A disease of the arteries in which lipid (fat) material and cholesterol accumulate on the inside walls of the arteries.

ATP See *Adenosine triphosphate.*

ATPase An enzyme that facilitates the breakdown of ATP.

ATP-PC System An anaerobic energy system in which ATP is manufactured when phosphocreatine (PC) is broken down. This system represents the most rapidly available source of ATP for use by muscle. Activities performed at maximum intensity in a period of 10 seconds or less derive energy (ATP) from this system.

ATPS Ambient temperature, pressure, saturated (see Appendix C, p. 655).

Atrioventricular Node (AV Node) A specialized area of tissue located in the right atrium of the heart from which the electrical impulse initiated by the sino-atrial node spreads throughout the heart.

Autonomic Nervous System A self-controlled system that helps to control activities such as those involving movement and secretion by the visceral organs, urinary output, body temperature, heart rate, adrenal secretion, and blood pressure.

Axon A nerve fiber.

Barometric (Atmospheric) Pressure (P_B) The force per unit area exerted by the earth's atmosphere. At sea level, it is 14.7 pounds per square inch or 760 millimeters of mercury (mm Hg).

Bends (Decompression Sickness) A condition induced by the evolution of nitrogen bubbles resulting from rapid decompression (gas emboli) and which may cause circulatory blockage and tissue damage.

Beta Oxidation The series of reactions by which fat is broken down from long carbon chains to two carbon units in preparation for entry into the Krebs Cycle.

Bicarbonate Ion (HCO_3^-) A by-product of the dissociation (ionizing) of carbonic acid.

Bioenergetics The study of energy transformations in living organisms.

Biopsy The removal and examination of tissue from the living body.

Black Bulb Thermometer An ordinary thermometer placed in a black globe. The black bulb temperature measures radiant energy or solar radiation and is one of three temperatures used to compute the WBGT index.

Blood Doping The removal and subsequent reinfusion of blood, undertaken for the purpose of temporarily increasing blood volume and the number of red blood cells.

Blood Pressure The driving force that moves blood through the circulatory system. Systolic pressure is obtained when blood is ejected into the arteries; diastolic pressure is obtained when the blood drains from the arteries.

Bradycardia A decreased or slowed heart rate.

BTPS Body temperature, pressure, saturated (see Appendix C, p. 655).

Buffer Any substance in a fluid that lessens the change in hydrogen ion (H^+) concentration which otherwise would occur, by adding acids or bases.

Calcitonin A hormone secreted by the thyroid gland that causes a decrease in the blood calcium level. It is thought that calcitonin may also be secreted from the parathyroid glands.

Calorie (cal) A unit of work or energy equal to the amount of heat required to raise the temperature of one gram of water 1°C.

Calorimeter Measures heat production in the human body.

Capillary A fine network of small vessels located between arteries and veins where exchanges between tissue and blood occur.

Carbamino Compounds The end product obtained from the chemical combination of plasma proteins and/or hemoglobin (Hb) and carbon dioxide (CO_2).

Carbaminohemoglobin A carbamino compound formed in the red blood cells when CO_2 reacts with Hb.

Carbohydrate Any of a group of chemical compounds, including sugars, starches, and cellulose, containing carbon, hydrogen, and oxygen only. One of the basic foodstuffs.

Carbonic Anhydrase An enzyme that speeds up the reaction of carbon dioxide (CO_2) with water (H_2O).

Cardiac Cycle Contraction (systole) and relaxation (diastole) of the heart.

Cardiac Output ($\dot{Q}$) The amount of blood pumped by the heart in one minute; the product of the stroke volume and the heart rate.

Cardiorespiratory Endurance The ability of the lungs and heart to take in and transport adequate amounts of oxygen to the working muscles, allowing activities that involve large muscle masses (e.g., running, swimming, bicycling) to be performed over long periods of time.

Catecholamines Epinephrine and norepinephrine.

Central Nervous System The spinal cord and brain.

Cerebellum That division or part of the brain concerned with coordination of movements.

Cerebral Cortex That portion of the brain responsible for mental functions, movement, visceral functions, perception, and behavioral reactions, and for the association and integration of these functions.

Cerebral Thrombosis A blood clot in the brain.

Cholesterol A fat-like compound found in animal tissues thought to cause atherosclerosis.

Cholinesterase A chemical that deactivates or breaks down acetylcholine.

Concentric Contraction The shortening of a muscle during contraction.

Conditioning Augmentation of the energy capacity of muscle through an exercise program. Conditioning is not primarily concerned with the skill of performance, as would be the case in training.

Conduction The transfer of heat between objects of different temperatures in direct contact with each other.

Continuous Work Exercises performed to completion without relief periods.

Convection The transfer of heat from one place to another by the motion of a heated substance.

Cortisol A glucocorticoid.

Coupled Reactions Two series of chemical reactions, one of which releases energy (heat) for use by the other.

Cross-Bridges Extensions of myosin.

Cryogenic Pertaining to the production of low temperatures.

Dehydration The condition that results from excessive loss of body water.

Dendrite A nerve fiber.

Density The mass per unit volume of an object.

Diaphragmatic Pleura See *Pleura*.

Diastole The resting phase of the cardiac cycle.

Diastolic Volume The amount of blood that fills the ventricle during diastole.

Diffusion The random movement of molecules due to their kinetic energy.

Dopamine An excitatory neurotransmitter chemical.

Double Blind Study An experimental protocol in which neither the investigators nor the subjects know which group is receiving a placebo and which group the real drug.

Douglas Bag A rubber-lined, canvas bag used for collection of expired gas. Rubber meterologic balloons now are used.

Drug A chemical substance given with the intention of preventing or curing disease or otherwise enhancing the physical or mental welfare of humans or animals.

Dry Bulb Thermometer A common thermometer used to record temperature of the air.

Dynamic Contraction See *Concentric contraction.*

Dysmenorrhea Painful menstruation.

Dyspnea Labored breathing.

Eccentric Contraction The muscle lengthens while contracting (developing tension).

Ectomorphy A body type component characterized by linearity, fragility, and delicacy of body.

Efferent Nerve A neuron that conveys motor impulses away from the central nervous system to an organ of response such as skeletal muscle.

Efficiency The ratio of work output to work input expressed as a percentage.

Electrical Potential The capacity for producing electrical effects, such as an electric current, between two bodies (e.g., between the inside and outside of a cell).

Electrocardiogram (EKG) A recording of the electrical activity of the heart.

Electrolyte A substance that ionizes in solution, such as salt ($NaCl$), and is capable of conducting an electrical current.

Electron A negatively charged particle.

Electron Transport System (ETS) A series of chemical reactions occurring in mitochondria, in which electrons and hydrogen ions combine with oxygen to form water, and ATP is resynthesized. Also referred to as the *respiratory chain.*

Embolus (singular); Emboli (plural) A clot or other plug transported by the blood from another vessel and forced into a smaller one, thus obstructing circulation.

Endocrine Gland An organ or gland that produces an internal secretion (hormone).

Endomorphy A body type component characterized by roundness and softness of the body.

Endomysium A connective tissue surrounding a muscle fiber or cell.

Energy The capacity or ability to perform work.

Energy System One of three metabolic systems involving a series of chemical reactions resulting in the formation of waste products and the manufacture of ATP.

Engram A memorized motor pattern stored in the brain; a permanent trace left by a stimulus in the tissue protoplasm.

Enzyme A protein compound that speeds up a chemical reaction.

Epimysium A connective tissue surrounding the entire muscle.

Epinephrine A hormone secreted by the medulla of the adrenal gland that has effects on the heart, the blood vessels, metabolism, and the central nervous system.

Ergogenic Aid Any factor that improves work performance.

Ergometer An apparatus or device, such as a treadmill or stationary bicycle, used for measuring the physiological effects of exercise.

Estrogen The female androgen.

Evaporation The loss of heat resulting from changing a liquid to a vapor.

Excitation A response to a stimulus.

Excitatory Postsynaptic Potential (EPSP) A transient increase in electrical potential (depolarization) in a postsynaptic neuron from its resting membrane potential.

Exercise-Recovery The performance of light exercise during recovery from exercise.

Expiratory Reserve Volume (ERV) Maximal volume of air expired from end-expiration.

Extracellular Outside the cell.

Extrafusal Fiber A typical or normal muscle cell or fiber.

Extrasystole An extra heartbeat.

Facilitated Diffusion Diffusion that takes place with the help of a carrier substance.

Fasciculus (singular); Fasciculi (plural) A group or bundle of skeletal muscle fibers held together by a connective tissue called the perimysium.

Fast-Twitch Fiber (FT) A muscle fiber characterized by fast contraction time, high anaerobic capacity, and low aerobic capacity, all making the fiber suited for high power output activities.

Fat A compound containing glycerol and fatty acids. One of the basic foodstuffs.

Fatigue A state of discomfort and decreased efficiency resulting from prolonged or excessive exertion.

Fatty Acid (Free Fatty Acid) The usable form of triglycerides.

Fibrillation Irregularity in force and rhythm of the heart, or quivering of the muscle fibers, causing inefficient emptying.

Fibrinolysis The dissolving of a blood clot.

Flaccid Lacking muscular tonus.

Flexibility The range of motion about a joint (static flexibility); opposition or resistance of a joint to motion (dynamic flexibility).

Flexometer An instrument used for measuring the range of motion about a joint (static flexibility).

Follicle-Stimulating Hormone (FSH) A hormone secreted by the anterior lobe of the pituitary gland that promotes growth of the ovarian follicle in the female, and spermatogenesis in the male.

Foot-Pound A work unit; that is, application of a one-pound force through a distance of one foot.

Fulcrum The axis of rotation for a lever.

Functional Residual Capacity (FRC) Volume of air in the lungs at resting expiratory level.

Gamma-Aminobutyric Acid (GABA) An inhibitory neurotransmitter substance.

Gamma Motor Neuron A type of efferent nerve cell that innervates the ends of an intrafusal muscle fiber.

Gamma System (Gamma Loop) The contraction of a muscle as a result of stretching the muscle spindle by way of stimulation of the gamma motor neurons.

Glucagon A hormone secreted by the alpha cells of the pancreas that causes increased blood glucose levels.

Glucocorticoids A class of hormones secreted by the cortex of the adrenal gland, that promote the increased synthesis of glucose from amino acids (gluconeogenesis), depress liver lipogenesis (formation of fat), mobilize fat in adipose tissues, maintain vascular reactivity, and inhibit the inflammatory reaction.

Glucose A sugar.

Glycine A simple amino acid, thought to be the main inhibitory transmitter in the spinal cord.

Glycogen A polymer of glucose; the form in which glucose (sugar) is stored in the body, mainly in muscles and the liver.

Glycogenesis The manufacture of glycogen from glucose.

Glycogen Loading (supercompensation) An exercise-diet procedure that elevates muscle glycogen stores to concentrations 2 to 3 times normal.

Glycogenolysis The breakdown of glycogen to glucose.

Glycogen Sparing The diminished utilization of glycogen that results when other fuels are available (and are used) for activity. If, for instance, fat is used to a greater extent than usual, glycogen is "spared"; glycogen will thus be available longer before ultimately being depleted.

Glycolysis The incomplete chemical breakdown of glycogen. In aerobic glycolysis, the end product is pyruvic acid; in anaerobic glycolysis (lactic acid system), the end product is lactic acid.

Gluconeogenesis The manufacturing of carbohydrates (glycogen) from non-carbohydrate sources such as fat and protein.

Golgi Tendon Organ A proprioceptor located within a muscular tendon.

Growth Hormone (GH; also called Somatotropin (STH) A hormone secreted by the anterior lobe of the pituitary gland that stimulates growth and development.

Heart Attack The blocking of blood flow to a portion of the heart muscle. Also myocardial infarction.

Heat A form of energy.

Heat Cramps Painful muscular contractions caused by prolonged exposure to environmental heat.

Heat Exhaustion A condition of fatigue caused by prolonged exposure to environmental heat.

Heat Stroke A disease caused by over-exposure to heat and characterized by high body (rectal) temperature, hot, dry skin (usually flushed), and unconsciousness. It can be fatal.

Hematuria Discharge of blood into the urine.

Hemoconcentration Concentration of the blood.

Hemodilution Dilution of the blood.

Hemodynamics The study of the physical laws governing blood flow.

Hemoglobin (Hb) A complex molecule found in red blood cells, which contains iron (heme) and protein (globin) and is capable of combining with oxygen.

Hemolysis The rupture of a cell, such as the red blood cell.

High Density Lipoproteins (HDL) A specific kind of cholesterol found in the blood, thought to be protective against coronary heart disease.

Hollow Sprints Two sprints interrupted by a (hollow) period involving either jogging or walking.

Hormone A discrete chemical substance secreted into the body fluids by an endocrine gland that has a specific effect on the activities of other cells, tissues, and organs.

Humidity Pertaining to the moisture in the air.

Hydraulic Pressure The force per unit area resulting from a vertical column of water of a certain height.

Hypernatremia Increased sodium concentration in the blood.

Hyperplasia An increase in the number of cells in a tissue or organ.

Hypertension High blood pressure.

Hyperthermia Increased body temperature.

Hypertonic Pertaining to a solution having a greater tension or osmotic pressure than one with which it is being compared.

Hypertrophy An increase in the size of a cell or organ.

Hyperventilation Excessive ventilation of the lungs caused by increased depth and frequency of breathing and usually resulting in elimination of carbon dioxide.

Hypervolemia An increased blood volume.

Hypotension Low blood pressure.

Hypothalamus That portion of the brain that exerts control over visceral activities, water balance, body temperature, and sleep.

Hypotonic Pertaining to a solution having a lesser tension or osmotic pressure than one with which it is being compared.

Hypoxia Lack of adequate oxygen due to a reduced oxygen partial pressure.

H Zone The area in the center of the A band where the cross-bridges are absent.

I Band That area of a myofibril containing actin and bisected by a Z line.

Inert Having no action.

Inhibitory Postsynaptic Potential (IPSP) A transient decrease in electrical potential (hyperpolarization) in a postsynaptic neuron from its resting membrane potential.

Inspiratory Capacity (IC) Maximal volume of air inspired from resting expiratory level.

Inspiratory Reserve Volume (IRV) Maximal volume of air inspired from end-inspiration.

Insulin A hormone secreted by the beta cells of the pancreas that causes increased cellular uptake of glucose.

Intermittent Work Exercises performed with alternate periods of relief, as opposed to continuous work.

Interneuron (Internuncial Neuron) A nerve cell located between afferent (sensory) and efferent (motor) nerve cells. It acts as a "middleman" between incoming and outgoing impulses.

Interstitial Pertaining to the area or space between cells.

Interstitial Fluid The fluid between the cells.

Interval Sprinting A method of training whereby an athlete alternately sprints 50 yards and jogs 60 yards for distances up to three miles.

Interval Training A system of physical conditioning in which the body is subjected to short but regularly repeated periods of work stress interspersed with adequate periods of relief.

Intrafusal Fiber A muscle cell (fiber) that houses the muscle spindle.

Ion An electrically charged particle.

Ischemia Local and temporary deficiency of blood, chiefly due to the contraction of a blood vessel.

Isokinetic Contraction Contraction in which the tension developed by the muscle while shortening at constant speed is maximal over the full range of motion.

Isometric (Static) Contraction Contraction in which tension is developed, but there is no change in the length of the muscle.

Isotonic Pertaining to solutions having the same tension or osmotic pressure.

Isotonic Contraction Contraction in which the muscle shortens with varying tension while lifting a constant load. Also referred to as a *dynamic* or *concentric contraction.*

Jogging Slow, continuous running. Also refers to all speeds of running.

Joint Receptors A group of sense organs located in joints concerned with kinesthesis.

Kilocalorie (kcal) A unit of work or energy equal to the amount of heat required to raise the temperature of one kilogram of water 1°C.

Kilogram-Meters (kg-m) A unit of work.

Kilojoules (kJ) Unit of energy.

Kinesthesis Awareness of body position.

Krebs Cycle A series of chemical reactions occurring in mitochondria, in which carbon dioxide is produced and hydrogen ions and electrons are removed from carbon atoms (oxidation). Also referred to as the *tricarboxcylic acid cycle (TCA),* or *citric acid cycle.*

Lactacid Oxygen Debt That portion of the recovery oxygen used to remove accumulated lactic acid from the blood following exercise. The slow recovery phase.

Lactic Acid (Lactate) A fatiguing metabolite of the lactic acid system resulting from the incomplete breakdown of glucose (sugar).

Lactic Acid System (LA System) An anaerobic energy system in which ATP is manufactured when glucose (sugar) is broken down to lactic acid. High intensity efforts requiring one to three minutes to perform draw energy (ATP) primarily from this system.

Lean Body Mass (Weight) The body weight minus the weight of the body fat.

Lever A rigid bar (such as a bone) that is free to rotate about a fixed point or axis called a fulcrum (such as a joint).

Linear Pertaining to a straight line.

Low Density Lipoproteins (LDL) A specific kind of cholesterol found in the blood, thought to cause atherosclerosis.

Luteinizing Hormone (LH) or Interstitial Cell-Stimulating Hormone (ICSH) A hormone secreted by the anterior lobe of the pituitary gland that stimulates ovulation, formation of the corpus luteum, and hormone secretion in the female; and stimulates secretion by interstitial cells in the male.

Maximal Aerobic Power See *Maximal oxygen consumption.*

Maximal Heart Rate Reserve (HRR) The difference between the resting heart rate and the maximal heart rate.

Maximal Oxygen Consumption (max $\dot{V}O_2$) The maximal rate at which oxygen can be consumed per minute; the power or capacity of the aerobic or oxygen system.

Medulla Oblongata That portion or area of the brain continuous above with the pons and below with the spinal cord and containing the cardiorespiratory control area.

Medullated Nerve Fiber A nerve fiber containing a myelin sheath.

Membrane A thin layer of tissue that covers a surface or divides a space or organ.

Menarche The onset of menstruation.

Menses The monthly flow of blood from the genital tract of women.

Menstruation The process or an instance of discharging the menses.

Mesomorphy A body type component characterized by a square body with hard, rugged, and prominent musculature.

MET (Metabolic Equivalent) The amount of oxygen required per minute under quiet resting conditions. It is equal to 3.5 ml of oxygen consumed per kilogram of body weight per minute (ml/kg-min).

Metabolic System A system of biochemical reactions that cause the formation of waste products (metabolites) and the manufacture of ATP; for example, the ATP-PC, lactic acid, and oxygen systems.

Metabolism The sum total of the chemical changes or reactions occurring in the body.

Metabolite Any substance produced by a metabolic reaction.

Millimole One thousandth of a mole.

Mineralocorticoids A class of hormones secreted by the cortex of the adrenal gland, that function to increase the reabsorption of sodium from the distal tubules of the kidney. The most important mineralocorticoid is aldosterone.

Minute Ventilation The amount of air inspired ($\dot{V}_I$) or expired ($\dot{V}_E$) in one minute; usually it refers to the expired amount.

Mitochondrion (singular); Mitochondria (plural) A subcellular structure found in all aerobic cells in which the reactions of the Krebs Cycle and electron transport system take place.

Mole The gram-molecular weight or gram-formula weight of a substance. For example, one mole of glucose. $C_6H_{12}O_6$ weighs $(6 \times 12) + (12 \times 1) + (16 \times 6) = 72 + 12 + 96 = 180$ grams, where the atomic weight of carbon (C) = 12; hydrogen (H) = 1; and oxygen (O) = 16.

Moment (Moment Arm) The perpendicular distance from the line of action of the force to the point of rotation.

Motoneuron (Motor Neuron) A nerve cell, which when stimulated, effects muscular contraction. Most motoneurons innervate skeletal muscle.

Motor End-Plate The neuromuscular or myoneural junction.

Motor Engrams Memorized motor patterns that are stored in the motor area of the brain.

Motor Fiber See *Efferent nerve.*

Motor Unit An individual motor nerve and all the muscle fibers it innervates.

Mountain (Altitude) Sickness A condition resulting from exposure to high altitude. Symptoms include nausea, vomiting, headache, rapid pulse, and loss of appetite.

Multiple Motor Unit Summation The varying of the number of motor units contracting within a muscle at any given time.

Muscle Bundle A fasciculus.

Muscle Spindle A proprioceptor surrounded by intrafusal muscle fibers.

Muscular Endurance The ability of a muscle or muscle group to perform repeated contractions against a light load for an extended period of time.

Myelin Sheath A structure composed mainly of lipid (fat) and protein that surrounds some nerve fibers (axons).

Myocardial Contractility The strength of ventricular contraction.

Myofibril That part of a muscle fiber containing two protein filaments, myosin and actin.

Myoglobin An oxygen-binding pigment similar to hemoglobin that gives the red muscle fiber its color. It acts as an oxygen store and aids in the diffusion of oxygen.

Myosin A protein involved in muscular contraction.

Necrosis Death of a cell or group of cells in contact with living tissue.

Negative Energy Balance A condition in which less energy (food) is taken in than is given off; body weight decreases as a result.

Nerve Cell See *Neuron.*

Nerve Impulse An electrical disturbance at the point of stimulation of a nerve that is self-propagated along the entire length of the axon.

Net Oxygen Cost The amount of oxygen, above resting values, required to perform a given amount of work. Also referred to as *net cost of exercise.*

Neuromuscular (Myoneural) Junction The union of a muscle and its nerve. Also referred to as the *motor endplate.*

Neuron A nerve cell consisting of a cell body (soma), with its nucleus and cytoplasm, dendrites and axons.

Nitrogen Narcosis (Raptures of The Deep) A condition affecting the central nervous system (much as does alcohol) due to the forcing (by pressure) of nitrogen into solution within the body; symptoms include dizziness, slowing of mental processes, euphoria, and fixation of ideas.

Nodes of Ranvier Those areas on a medullated nerve that are devoid of a myelin sheath.

Nomogram A graph enabling one to determine by aid of a straight-edge the value of a dependent variable when the values of two independent variables are known.

Nonmedullated Nerve Fiber A nerve fiber entirely devoid of a myelin sheath.

Norepinephrine A hormone secreted by the medulla of the adrenal gland that has effects on the heart, the blood vessels, metabolism, and the central nervous system. Also, the major neurotransmitter substance released at the ends of the sympathetic postganglionic fibers of the autonomic nervous system.

Obese (Obesity) Having excessive accumulation and storage of fatty tissue.

Osmosis The diffusion through a semipermeable membrane of a solvent such as water from a lower to a more concentrated solution.

Osmotic Pressure The force per unit area needed to stop osmosis.

Overload Principle Progressively increasing the intensity of the workouts over the course of the training program as fitness capacity improves.

Oxidation The removal of electrons.

Oxygen Debt The amount of oxygen consumed during recovery from exercise, above that ordinarily consumed at rest in the same time period. There is a rapid component (alactacid) and a slow component (lactacid).

Oxygen Deficit The time period during exercise in which the level of oxygen consumption is below that necessary to supply all the ATP required for the exercise; the time period during which an oxygen debt is contracted.

Oxygen Poisoning (Toxicity) A condition caused by breathing oxygen under high pressure. Symptoms include tingling of fingers and toes, visual disturbances, auditory hallucinations, confusion, muscle and lip twitching, nausea, vertigo, and convulsions.

Oxygen System An aerobic energy system in which ATP is manufactured when food (principally sugar and fat) is broken down. This system produces ATP most abundantly and is the prime energy source during long-lasting (endurance) activities.

Oxygen Transport System ($\dot{V}O_2$) Composed of the stroke volume (SV), the heart rate (HR), and the arterial-mixed venous oxygen difference (a-$\bar{v}O_2$ diff.). Mathematically, it is defined as $\dot{V}O_2 = SV \times HR \times$ a-$\bar{v}O_2$ diff.

Oxyhemoglobin (HbO_2) Hemoglobin chemically combined with oxygen.

Oxyhemoglobin (HbO_2) Dissociation Curve The graph of the relationship between the amount of oxygen combined with hemoglobin and the partial pressure of oxygen.

Oxytocin A hormone secreted by the posterior lobe of the pituitary gland that stimulates milk ejection and contraction of the pregnant uterus.

Parasympathetic Pertaining to the craniosacral portion of the autonomic nervous system.

Parathormone (PTH) A hormone secreted by the parathyroid gland that causes an increase in the blood calcium levels.

Partial Pressure The pressure exerted by a single gas in a gas mixture or in a liquid.

Parietal Pleura See *Pleura.*

PC See *Phosphocreatine.*

Perimysium A connective tissue surrounding a fasciculus or muscle bundle.

Periosteum A fibrous membrane surrounding bone.

Peritoneum The thin membrane that secretes serous fluid and lines the walls of the abdominal cavity and encloses the viscera.

Peritonitis Inflammation of the peritoneum.

pH The power of the hydrogen ion; the negative logarithm of the hydrogen ion concentration.

Phosphagen A group of compounds; collectively refers to ATP and PC.

Phosphagen System See *ATP-PC system.*

Phosphocreatine (PC) A chemical compound stored in muscle, which when broken down aids in manufacturing ATP.

Photosynthesis The process whereby green plants manufacture their own food from carbon dioxide, water, and energy from the sun.

Placebo An inert substance having the identical physical characteristics of a real drug.

Plasma The liquid portion of the blood.

Plasmolysis The shrinking of a cell such as the red blood cell.

Pleura (singular); Pleurae (plural) A thin membrane that secretes serous fluid and lines the thoracic wall (parietal pleura), the diaphragm (diaphragmatic pleura), and the lungs (visceral pleura).

Pleural Cavity The potential space between the parietal and visceral pleura.

Pneumothorax The entrance of air into the pleural cavity.

Polycythemia An increased production of red blood cells.

Ponderal Index Body height divided by the cube root of body weight.

Positive Energy Balance A condition in which more energy (food) is taken in than is given off; body weight increases as a result.

Postsynaptic Neuron A nerve cell located distal to a synapse.

Power Performance of work expressed per unit of time. For example, if one pound is raised one foot in one second, power is expressed as 1 foot-pound per second.

Premotor Area The area of the brain just forward of the primary motor cortex.

Pressure Force per unit area.

Primary Motor Cortex That area of the brain (cortex) containing groups of motor neurons other than Betz cells.

Progesterone A hormone secreted by the ovary that promotes further development of the uterus and mammary glands.

Prolactin or Lactogenic Hormone (LTH) A hormone secreted by the anterior lobe of the pituitary gland that stimulates secretion of milk after pregnancy.

Proprioceptor Sensory organs found in muscles, joints, and tendons, which give information concerning movement and position of the body (kinesthesis).

Protein A compound containing amino acids. One of the basic foodstuffs.

Proton A positively charged particle.

Psychrometer An instrument used for measuring the relative humidity.

Pulmonary Circuit The flow of arterial blood from the heart to the pulmonary (lung) capillaries and of venous blood from the pulmonary capillaries back to the heart.

Pyramidal (Corticospinal) Tract The area in which impulses from the motor area of the cortex are sent down to the anterior motoneurons of the spinal cord.

Pyruvic Acid (Pyruvate) The end product of aerobic glycolysis; the precursor of lactic acid (lactate).

Radiation The transfer of heat between objects through electromagnetic waves.

Receptor A sense organ that receives stimuli.

Reflex An automatic response induced by stimulation of a receptor.

Relative Humidity Ratio of water vapor in the atmosphere to the amount of water vapor required to saturate the atmosphere at the same temperature.

Relief Interval In an interval training program, the time between work intervals as well as between sets.

Repetition In an interval training program, the number of work intervals within one set. For example, six 220-yard runs would constitute one set of six repetitions.

Repetition Maximum (RM) The maximal load that a muscle group can lift over a given number of repetitions before fatiguing. For example, a 10 RM load is the maximal load that can be lifted over 10 repetitions.

Repetition Running Similar to interval training but differs in the length of the work interval and the degree of recovery between repetitions.

Residual Volume (RV) Volume of air remaining in the lungs at end of maximal expiration.

Respiratory Exchange Ratio (R) The ratio of the amount of carbon dioxide produced by the body to the amount of oxygen consumed ($\dot{V}CO_2/\dot{V}O_2$).

Resting Membrane Potential The electrical difference between the inside and outside of the cell (i.e., across the cell membrane) at rest.

Rest-Recovery Resting during recovery from exercise.

Rest-Relief In an interval training program, a type of relief interval involving moderate moving about, such as walking and flexing of arms and legs.

Saline A 0.9% salt solution that is isotonic to the blood.

Salpingitis Inflammation of a fallopian tube.

Saltatory Conduction The propagation of a nerve impulse from one node of Ranvier to another along a medullated fiber.

Sarcolemma The muscle cell membrane.

Sarcomere The distance between two Z lines; the smallest contractile unit of skeletal muscle.

Sarcoplasm Muscle protoplasm.

Sarcoplasmic Reticulum A network of tubules and vesicles surrounding the myofibril.

Second Wind A phenomenon characterized by a sudden transition from an ill-defined feeling of distress or fatigue during the early portion of prolonged exercise to a more comfortable, less stressful feeling later in the exercise.

Semipermeable Membrane A membrane permeable to some but not all particles or substances.

Sensory Fiber See *Afferent nerve.*

Sensory Neuron A nerve cell that conveys impulses from a receptor to the central nervous system. Examples of sensory neurons are those excited by sound, pain, light, and taste.

Serotonin An excitatory neurotransmitter chemical.

Serous Fluid A watery fluid secreted by the pleurae.

Set In an interval training program, a group of work and relief intervals.

Sinoatrial Node (S-A Node) A specialized area of tissue located in the right atrium of the heart, which originates the electrical impulse to initiate the heartbeat.

Slow-Twitch Fiber (ST) A muscle fiber characterized by slow contraction time, low anaerobic capacity, and high aerobic capacity, all making the fiber suited for low power output activities.

Soma The cell body of a neuron.

Somatic Pertaining to the body.

Somatotype The body type or physical classification of the human body.

Spatial Summation An increase in responsiveness of a nerve resulting from the additive effect of numerous stimuli.

Specific Gravity The ratio of the density of an object to the density of water.

Specific Heat The heat required to change the temperature of a unit mass of a substance by one degree.

Specificity of Training Principle underlying construction of a training program for a specific activity or skill and the primary energy system(s) involved during performance. For example, a training program for sprinters would consist of repeated bouts of sprints in order to develop both sprinting performance and the ATP-PC system.

Speed Play (Fartlek Training) Involves alternating fast and slow running over natural terrains. It is the forerunner of the interval training system.

Spirometer A steel container used to collect, store, and measure either inspired or expired gas volume.

Sprint Training A type of training system employing repeated sprints at maximal speed.

Starling's Law of the Heart An increase in stroke volume in response to an increase in the volume of blood filling the heart ventricle during diastole.

Static Contraction See *Isometric contraction.*

Steadystate Pertaining to the time period during which a physiological function (such as $\dot{V}O_2$) remains at a constant (steady) value.

Steroid A general class of hormones including derivatives of the male sex hormone, testosterone, which has masculinizing properties.

Stimulus (singular); Stimuli (plural) Any agent, act, or influence that modifies the activity of a receptor or irritable tissue.

STPD Standard temperature, pressure, dry (see Appendix C, p. 655).

Strength The force that a muscle or muscle group can exert against a resistance in one maximal effort.

Stroke Volume (SV) The amount of blood pumped by the left ventricle of the heart per beat.

Sudomotor Pertaining to activation of the sweat glands.

Sympathetic Pertaining to the thoraco-lumbar portion of the autonomic nervous system.

Synapse The connection or junction of one neuron to another.

Synaptic Cleft The gap or space between presynaptic and postsynaptic neurons.

Systemic Circuit The flow of arterial blood from the heart to the body tissues (such as the muscles) and of the venous blood from the tissues back to the heart.

Systole The contractile or emptying phase of the cardiac cycle.

Tachycardia An increased or rapid heart rate.

Target Heart Rate (THR) A predetermined heart rate to be obtained during exercise.

Target Organ The cell, tissue, or organ upon which a hormone has an effect.

Temperature The degree of sensible heat or cold.

Temporal Summation An increase in responsiveness of a nerve, resulting from the additive effect of frequently occurring stimuli.

Testosterone The male sex hormone secreted by the testicles; it possesses masculinizing properties.

Tetanus The maintenance of tension of a motor unit at a high level as long as the stimuli continue or until fatigue sets in.

Thermodynamics The science of the transformation of heat and energy.

Threshold for Excitation The minimal electrical level at which a neuron will transmit or conduct an impulse.

Thrombus A blood clot that remains at the point of its formation.

Thyroid-Stimulating Hormone (TSH) A hormone secreted from the anterior lobe of the pituitary gland that stimulates production and release of the thyroid hormones, thyroxin, and triiodithyronine.

Thyroxin A hormone secreted by the thyroid gland that causes an increase in metabolic rate.

Tidal Volume (TV) Volume of air inspired or expired per breath.

Tissue-Capillary Membrane The thin layer of tissue dividing the capillaries and an organ (such as skeletal muscle); site at which gaseous exchange occurs.

Tonus Resiliency and resistance to stretch in a relaxed, resting muscle.

Total Lung Capacity (TLC) Volume of air in the lungs at end of maximal inspiration.

Training An exercise program to develop an athlete for a particular event. Increasing skill of performance and energy capacities are of equal consideration.

Training Distance In an interval training program, the distance of the work interval; e.g., running 220 yards.

Training Duration The length of the training program.

Training Frequency The number of times per week for the training workout.

Training Time The rate at which the work is to be accomplished during a work interval in an interval training program.

Triglycerides The storage form of free fatty acids.

Triiodothyronine A hormone secreted by the thyroid gland that causes an increase in metabolic rate.

Trophic Pertaining to nutrition or nourishment.

Tropomyosin A protein involved in muscular contraction.

Troponin A protein involved in muscular contraction.

Twitch A brief period of contraction followed by relaxation in the response of a motor unit to a stimulus (nerve impulse).

Valsalva Maneuver Making an expiratory effort with the glottis closed.

Vasoconstriction A decrease in the diameter of a blood vessel (usually an arteriole) resulting in a reduction of blood flow to the area supplied by the vessel.

Vasodilation An increase in the diameter of a blood vessel (usually an arteriole) resulting in an increased blood flow to the area supplied by the vessel.

Vasomotor Pertaining to vasoconstriction and vasodilation.

Vein A vessel carrying blood toward the heart.

Venoconstriction A decrease in the diameter of a vein.

Ventilatory Efficiency The amount of ventilation required per liter of oxygen consumed; i.e., $\dot{V}E/\dot{V}O_2$.

Very Low Density Lipoproteins (VLDL) A specific kind of cholesterol found in the blood that is thought to cause atherosclerosis.

Viscera (plural); Viscus (singular) The internal organs of the body.

Visceral Pertaining to the viscera.

Visceral Pleura See *Pleura*.

Vital Capacity (VC) Maximal volume of air forcefully expired after maximal inspiration.

Vitamin An organic material in the presence of which important chemical (metabolic) reactions occur.

Watt A unit of power.

Wave Summation The varying of the frequency of contraction of individual motor units.

WBGT Index An index calculated from dry bulb, wet bulb, and black bulb temperatures. It indicates the severity of the environmental heat conditions.

Wet Bulb Thermometer An ordinary thermometer with a wetted wick wrapped around the bulb. The wet bulb's temperature is related to the amount of moisture in the air. When the wet bulb and dry bulb temperatures are equal, the air is completely saturated with water and the relative humidity is equal to 100 per cent.

Work Application of a force through a distance. For example, application of one pound through one foot equals one foot-pound of work.

Work Interval That portion of an interval training program consisting of the work effort.

Work-Relief In an interval training program, a type of relief interval involving light or mild exercise such as rapid walking or jogging.

Work:Relief Ratio In an interval training program, a ratio relating the duration of the work interval to the duration of the relief interval. As an example, a work:relief ratio of 1:1 means that the durations of the work and relief intervals are equal.

Z Line A protein band that defines the distance of one sarcomere in the myofibril.

AUTHOR INDEX

SUBJECT INDEX